D1685403

3 0116 00535 8492

This book is due for return not later than the last date stamped below, unless recalled sooner.

International and Global Strategy

Strategic Management

Series Editor: Stephen B. Tallman
E. Claiborne Robins Distinguished Professor, Robins School of Business, University of Richmond, USA

Wherever possible, the articles in these volumes have been reproduced as originally published using facsimile reproduction, inclusive of footnotes and pagination to facilitate ease of reference.

For a list of all Edward Elgar published titles visit our website at
www.e-elgar.com

International and Global Strategy

Edited by

Torben Pedersen

Professor in Global Strategy
Bocconi University, Italy

STRATEGIC MANAGEMENT

An Elgar Research Collection
Cheltenham, UK • Northampton, MA, USA

Published by
Edward Elgar Publishing Limited
The Lypiatts
15 Lansdown Road
Cheltenham
Glos GL50 2JA
UK

Edward Elgar Publishing, Inc.
William Pratt House
9 Dewey Court
Northampton
Massachusetts 01060
USA

A catalogue record for this book is available from the British Library

Library of Congress Control Number: 2014937089

ISBN 978 1 84844 234 4

Printed and bound in Great Britain by T.J. International Ltd, Padstow

Contents

Acknowledgements

The editor and publishers wish to thank the authors and the following publishers who have kindly given permission for the use of copyright material.

Academy of Management via the Copyright Clearance Center for articles: Sumantra Ghoshal and Christopher A. Bartlett (1990), 'The Multinational Corporation as an Interorganizational Network', *Academy of Management Review*, **15** (4), October, 603–25; Harry G. Barkema, Oded Shenkar, Freek Vermeulen and John H.J. Bell (1997), 'Working Abroad, Working with Others: How Firms Learn to Operate International Joint Ventures', *Academy of Management Journal*, **40** (2), April, 426–42; Julian Birkinshaw and Neil Hood (1998), 'Multinational Subsidiary Evolution: Capability and Charter Change in Foreign-Owned Subsidiary Companies', *Academy of Management Review*, **23** (4), October, 773–95; Tatiana Kostova and Srilata Zaheer (1999), 'Organizational Legitimacy under Conditions of Complexity: The Case of the Multinational Enterprise', *Academy of Management Review*, **24** (1), January, 64–81.

Blackwell Publishing Ltd for article: Gunnar Hedlund (1986), 'The Hypermodern MNC – A Heterarchy?', *Human Resource Management*, **25** (1), Spring, 9–35.

Elsevier for article: Anil K. Gupta and Vijay Govindarajan (2000), 'Managing Global Expansion: A Conceptual Framework', *Business Horizons*, **43** (2), March–April, 45–54.

Harvard University School Publishing for articles: Theodore Levitt (1983), 'The Globalization of Markets', *Harvard Business Review*, **61** (3), May–June, 92–102; Kenichi Ohmae (1989), 'Managing in a Borderless World', *Harvard Business Review*, **67** (3), May–June, 152–61; Tarun Khanna and Krishna Palepu (1997), 'Why Focused Strategies May Be Wrong for Emerging Markets', *Harvard Business Review*, **75** (4), July–August, 41–42, 44, 46, 48–51; C.K. Prahalad and Allen Hammond (2002), 'Serving the World's Poor, *Profitably*', *Harvard Business Review*, **80** (9), September, 48–57; Ravi Aron and Jitendra V. Singh (2005), 'Getting Offshoring Right', *Harvard Business Review*, **83** (12), December, 135–43.

Institute for Operations Research and the Management Sciences (INFORMS) for article: Timothy M. Devinney, David F. Midgley and Sunil Venaik (2000), 'The Optimal Performance of the Global Firm: Formalizing and Extending the Integration-Responsiveness Framework', *Organization Science*, **11** (6), November–December, 674–95.

John Wiley & Sons Ltd. for articles: Sumantra Ghoshal (1987), 'Global Strategy: An Organizing Framework', *Strategic Management Journal*, **8** (5), September–October, 425–40; Gunnar Hedlund (1994), 'A Model of Knowledge Management and the N-Form Corporation', *Strategic Management Journal – Special Issue: Strategy: Search for New Paradigms*, **15**, Summer, 73–90;

Anil K. Gupta and Vijay Govindarajan (2000), 'Knowledge Flows within Multinational Corporations', *Strategic Management Journal*, **21** (4), April, 473–96; Tony S. Frost (2001), 'The Geographic Sources of Foreign Subsidiaries' Innovations', *Strategic Management Journal*, **22** (2), February, 101–23; Morten T. Hansen and Bjørn Løvås (2004), 'How do Multinational Companies Leverage Technological Competencies? Moving from Single to Interdependent Explanations', *Strategic Management Journal*, **25** (8–9), August–September, 801–22; John Cantwell and Ram Mudambi (2005), 'MNE Competence-Creating Subsidiary Mandates', *Strategic Management Journal*, **26** (12), December, 1109–28.

Oxford University Press for article: Ram Mudambi (2008), 'Location, Control and Innovation in Knowledge-Intensive Industries', *Journal of Economic Geography*, **8** (5), September, 699–725.

Palgrave Macmillan for articles: W. Chan Kim and Renée A. Mauborgne (1993), 'Effectively Conceiving and Executing Multinationals' Worldwide Strategies', *Journal of International Business Studies*, **24** (3), Third Quarter, 419–48; Pankaj Ghemawat (2003), 'Semiglobalization and International Business Strategy', *Journal of International Business Studies*, **34** (2), March, 138–52; D. Minbaeva, T. Pedersen, I. Björkman, C.F. Fey and H.J. Park (2003), 'MNC Knowledge Transfer, Subsidiary Absorptive Capacity, and HRM', *Journal of International Business Studies*, **34** (6), November, 586–99; Alan M. Rugman and Alain Verbeke (2004), 'A Perspective on Regional and Global Strategies of Multinational Enterprises', *Journal of International Business Studies*, **35** (1), January, 3–18; Peter J. Buckley and Pervez N. Ghauri (2004), 'Globalisation, Economic Geography and the Strategy of Multinational Enterprises', *Journal of International Business Studies*, **35** (2), March, 81–98; Kwok Leung, Rabi S. Bhagat, Nancy R. Buchan, Miriam Erez and Cristina B. Gibson (2005), 'Culture and International Business: Recent Advances and their Implications for Future Research', *Journal of International Business Studies*, **36** (4), July, 357–78; Orly Levy, Schon Beechler, Sully Taylor and Nakiye A. Boyacigiller (2007), 'What We Talk About When We Talk About "Global Mindset": Managerial Cognition in Multinational Corporations', *Journal of International Business Studies*, **38** (2), March, 231–58; Alvaro Cuervo-Cazurra, Mary M. Maloney and Shalini Manrakhan (2007), 'Causes of the Difficulties in Internationalization', *Journal of International Business Studies*, **38** (5), September, 709–25; Christian Geisler Asmussen, Torben Pedersen and Charles Dhanaraj (2009), 'Host-Country Environment and Subsidiary Competence: Extending the Diamond Network Model', *Journal of International Business Studies*, **40** (1), January, 42–57.

Regents of the University of California for article: Christopher H. Lovelock and George S. Yip (1996), 'Developing Global Strategies for Service Businesses', *California Management Review*, **38** (2), Winter, 64–86.

Sage Publications via the Copyright Clearance Center for article: Stephen B. Tallman (1992), 'A Strategic Management Perspective on Host Country Structure of Multinational Enterprises', *Journal of Management*, **18** (3), September, 455–71.

Tribune Media Services for article: Yves L. Doz (1980), 'Strategic Management in Multinational Companies', *Sloan Management Review*, **21** (2), Winter, 27–46.

Every effort has been made to trace all the copyright holders but if any have been inadvertently overlooked the publishers will be pleased to make the necessary arrangement at the first opportunity.

In addition the publishers wish to thank the Library at the University of Warwick, UK for their assistance in obtaining these articles.

Introduction

Torben Pedersen

We are bombarded daily with terms like 'globalization', 'internationalization' and 'global strategy' in the media and in public debate. Globalization is one of the mega changes in today's world that affect individuals as well as firms. In fact, globalization and internationalization is blamed for much of the change in today's world. Firms are instrumental in the process of globalization as many cross-border activities are organized and conducted by firms – and those firms that conduct border-spanning activities are denoted Multinational Companies (MNCs). As such the global strategies of MNCs have extensive impact on how our lives are woven together across boundaries.

International or global strategy means matching a firm's internal strengths (in other words, its resources and organization) with the opportunities and challenges found in geographically dispersed environments. The reality is that geographically dispersed environments entail opportunities, like access to new markets, talented people, knowledge, low-cost resources, as well as challenges that follow from lack of knowledge on how things work in foreign environments (liability of foreignness). Firms form strategies in order to overcome challenges and get the most out of the opportunities in foreign environments. For example, they make strategic choices on the global configuration of their activities, which governance structure to apply when entering foreign markets, how to integrate subsidiaries, or from where to source different inputs, etc.

Global strategy addresses the question of why firms go international and, in particular, how they do it. The core of global strategy is to identify optimal strategies given the internal strengths of firms and the opportunities/challenges offered in foreign environments. As such, global strategies rest on the interplay of the competitive advantage of firms and the comparative advantage of countries. This interplay involves much more complexity and variation than conducting business in a single country, which is the domain of the general strategy. Firms operating with activities in different countries and selling products in different cultures will face more difficult and varied choices but will also have more options to choose from when deciding strategies on what to do – which markets to serve, in what form, with which products, and how to organize production.

The conditions for this interaction have changed dramatically in the last decades, where we have witnessed major changes in transportation technology, information technology, and the opening up of new markets that were previously more or less separated from the rest of the world. The Internet that we all take for granted today was only opened for commercial use two decades ago. Before then very few people had access to the Internet and the fast communication that comes with it. Containerization has made it much more efficient and cheaper to transport almost everything from one part of the world to other continents. Countries like China, India, Russia, and Vietnam were previously isolated from the world trading system. They have all opened up more and more and become part of the global value chain over the last two to three decades. These major changes have facilitated globalization and forced firms to re-think and sharpen their global strategies – since the development entails new opportunities as well as new challenges.

Global strategy is a relatively young field of study; however, it has grown in importance over the last couple of decades in pace with increased globalization and the surge in firms' global activities. This is best illustrated by the fact that the field of global strategy now has its own journal – *Global Strategy Journal* – that is a sister journal to both *Strategic Management Journal* and *Strategic Entrepreneurship Journal*, all of which are associated with the Strategic Management Society.

Themes of Research in Global Strategy

In this collection we will feature key articles in the field of global strategy and as such unfold its breadth in a form that can be used as a comprehensive introduction to the subject. As a first step we have divided the contributions in the field into three major themes: 1) The Emergence of a Global Village; 2) Advantages of a Global Strategy; and 3) Challenges in Implementing a Global Strategy.

These three themes reflect bigger issues that have dominated research on global strategy and the classic articles of the three themes roughly present a timeline on how research on global strategy has developed. The first topic (the emergence of a global village) is responding to the question *why* go international? The second (advantages of a global strategy) focuses on *what* and *where* to internationalize, while the third topic (challenges in implementing a global strategy) is occupied with the question *how* to do it? To a large extent this also reflects how the attention of research on global strategy has developed, where the focus in the early years was on justification of a global strategy in order to exploit home-based advantages, subsequently followed by research pointing out the additional advantages that might be gained in a global network and, finally, research on how to implement the many aspects of global strategy.

The articles in this collection are organized along the three themes, each of which includes some (2–3) classic articles that present the basic arguments and initial insights for the theme. Then a number of newer contributions are added. These newer contributions might argue with the classics, extend them, or fill some of the gaps. However, in all cases the newer contributions build on the classics, so the combination of reading the classics and the newer contributions provides an excellent introduction to the theme. A schematic listing of the articles in the collection is given in Table 1.

The Emergence of a Global Village

In the early days a lot of attention was put on explaining how firms would benefit from more global strategies. It was highlighted that the world was converging, which allowed for more standardized offerings across the world, with prominent examples as Coca-Cola, Levi's and McDonalds. The claim was that firms could reap substantial benefits in exploiting their home-based competencies if they adapted a geocentric mindset (Levitt, 1983, Chapter 1) or global mentality (Ohmae, 1989, Chapter 2) that allowed them to understand the new opportunities.

Table 1   Schematic listing of the articles

	The Emergence of a Global Village	Advantages of a Global Strategy	Challenges in Implementing a Global Strategy
The classics	*The world is flat:* – Levitt (1983) – Ohmae (1989)	*International arbitrage:* – Ghoshal (1987) – Tallman (1992) – Lovelock and Yip (1996)	*Creating a global organization:* – Doz (1980) – Hedlund (1986) – Levy et al. (2007)
Newer contributions	*The world is still spiky:* – Ghemawat (2003) – Rugman and Verbeke (2004) *Remaining barriers* – Leung et al. (2005) – Cuervo-Cazurra et al. (2007)	*Emerging markets:* – Khanna and Palepu (1997) – Prahalad and Hammond (2002) *Global sourcing strategies:* – Frost (2001) – Buckley and Ghauri (2004) – Aron and Singh (2005) – Mudambi (2008) – Asmussen et al. (2009)	*Balancing local and global:* – Kostova and Zaheer (1999) – Devinney et al. (2000) *Executing global strategies:* – Kim and Mauborgne (1993) – Gupta and Govindarajan (2000) *The role of subsidiaries:* – Ghoshal and Bartlett (1990) – Barkema et al. (1997) – Birkinshaw and Hood (1998) – Cantwell and Mudambi (2005) *Knowledge sharing across boundaries:* – Hedlund (1994) – Gupta and Govindarajan (2000) – Minbaeva et al. (2003) – Hansen and Løvås (2004)

Ohmae (1989) argues that most managers in the world are nearsighted, meaning that their field of vision is dominated by home-country customers, and that everything else is simply 'the rest of the world'. However, due to an increasing global flow of information, national borders are losing their significance and 'through this flow of information, we've become global citizens, and so must the companies that want to sell us things' (Ohmae, 1989, p. 154). Levitt (1983) proposes, along the same line, that companies can achieve sustainable competitive advantages in adapting and capitalizing on economic convergences: 'Only global companies will achieve long-term success by concentrating on what everyone wants rather than worrying about the details of what everyone thinks they might like' (Levitt, 1983, p. 92).

Newer contributions around this topic have questioned the extent to which the world is really that globalized. Much of this debate is captured under the headings of whether the world is flat (no significant barriers left) or spiky (still many barriers are left). It is proposed that the world might, in fact, be better characterized as semi-globalized (Ghemawat, 2003, Chapter 3) or regionalized (Rugman and Verbeke, 2004, Chapter 4). Ghemawat (2003) presents a large number of measures of globalization and concludes: 'Most measures of cross-border economic integration have increased significantly in the last few decades, but still fall far short of the theoretical extreme of total integration.' Rugman and Verbeke (2004) argue similarly that the world's largest companies are not global as such (even in terms of 'triad power'), but regionally based in terms of breadth and depth of market coverage. This debate on the state of globalization in the world is a key issue that runs through the field of global strategy, and it is not a trivial issue as it has significant implications for how much firms need to adapt their strategies to the local conditions versus applying similar strategies across borders.

The two papers by Leung et al. (2005, Chapter 5) and Cuervo-Cazurra et al. (2007, Chapter 6) both look into some of the remaining barriers in globalization. As such they examine the challenges rather than the opportunities. The paper by Leung et al. (2005) focuses on cultural differences and applies a more complex conceptualization of culture in order to understand how culture is changing and interacting with socio-economic development, while the paper by Cuervo-Cazurra et al. (2007) investigates the question: what causes the difficulties faced by firms when they internationalize in search of new markets? The authors employ a resource-based theory (RBT) to answer the question, by disaggregating the difficulties into their component pieces and identifying the root causes of distinct internationalization difficulties.

Advantages of a Global Strategy

Many of the early contributions sought to explain internationalization as if the firm were investing in a foreign country for the first time. Therefore, the main questions were more on why to internationalize in the first place and on how to exploit the home-based advantages of the firms. However, the number of firms with a global network of subsidiaries was increasing substantially and for them the issue was not how to go international in the first place, but rather how to make best use of the existing global network of subsidiaries, suppliers, and customers. Out of this recognition emerged a literature that focused more on the advantages of multinationality, in other words, that national diversity of its global operations has become a source of advantage beyond the access to local markets. The argument is that the global network of subsidiaries provides important advantages in terms of arbitrage opportunities in relation to operational flexibility (for example, ability to move production tasks among plants), tapping into talent and knowledge in different locations, etc. The point being that global networks of subsidiaries are not just seen as vehicles for exploiting home-based advantages, but also as units that contribute to the competitive advantage of the MNC in new ways.

Ghoshal (1987, Chapter 7) highlights the opportunities for arbitrage and suggests that an MNC has three sets of tools or means for developing competitive advantage: 'It can exploit the differences in input and output markets among the many countries in which it operates. It can benefit from scale economies in its different activities. It can also exploit synergies or economies of scope that may be available because of the diversity of its activities and organization ... the key to a successful global strategy is to manage the interactions between these different goals and means' (Ghoshal, 1987, p. 427). In their article, Lovelock and Yip (1996, Chapter 9) take these insights further and apply them to service businesses. They highlight how specific globalization drivers and distinctive characteristics of the service business affect the available strategic options. Tallman (1992, Chapter 8) takes a more theoretical perspective and shows how a resource-based model can be extended to capture the interplay between firm-specific resources and foreign activities.

The emerging markets have attracted large amounts of attention among the newer contributions, both as markets in their own rights and as locations with new features and other characteristics to those seen in developed countries, for example, institutional voids (Khanna and Palepu, 1997, Chapter 10) and bottom-of-the-pyramid strategies (Prahalad and Hammond, 2002, Chapter 12). Khanna and Palepu (1997) point out that emerging markets have institutional voids, which refers to the absence of intermediaries like market research firms and of credit card systems to efficiently connect buyers and sellers, and this creates significant obstacles for firms trying to operate in emerging markets. The main argument of the text by Khanna and Palepu (1997) is that while conglomerate strategies are increasingly being replaced by focused strategies in developed countries, the opposite might be true in emerging markets. Conglomerates, in contrast to focused businesses, stand in a better position to fill (and imitate) the institutional voids of emerging markets, and can hence create added value. The paper by Prahalad and Hammond (2002) argues that MNCs operating in emerging markets have mainly focused on the wealthy elite at the top of the economic pyramid and are only seeing the tip of the proverbial iceberg while almost ignoring the bottom/base of the economic pyramid, which clearly presents a vast potential untapped market opportunity. Therefore, firms operating in emerging markets should develop strategies for product targeting the bottom of the pyramid.

The listed contributions concerning global sourcing strategies are more looking into changes in the global architecture or configuration of the MNC. Based on a comprehensive study on subsidiary innovation and host-country resources, Frost (2001, Chapter 11) concludes that 'our results both support and extend a widely debated (but largely untested) conjecture in the multinational literature, namely that foreign direct investment may be driven, at least in part, by the desire to gain knowledge from the diverse institutional contexts in which multinational firms operate' (p. 120). Hence, what Frost (2001) proposes is a change in research focus from 'whether foreign subsidiaries "tap into" local sources of knowledge' to the more nuanced question of under what conditions they tap into local sources of knowledge. Along the same line, Asmussen et al. (2009, Chapter 16) examine the subsidiaries' sources of knowledge and argue 'that host-country diamond heterogeneity – the presence of unbalanced diamonds – may lead MNEs to locate specialized competences in host countries in order to access complementary knowledge' (p. 14). Buckley and Ghauri (2004, Chapter 13) link the literature on firms' strategies and economic geography and, as an illustrative model of the modern MNC that balances ownership and location strategies, propose 'the global factory'.

Mudambi (2008, Chapter 15) seeks to answer the following research question: to what extent should the firm implement vertical integration and geographical dispersion with respect to its value chain activities? In answering this question, the paper draws on literatures from the fields of both the organization of firms across national borders and the economic geography regarding the location of economic activity. Aron and Singh (2005, Chapter 14) takes its starting point as the observation that many companies obtain below-expected results with their offshoring strategies and, as a response, the paper outlines tools that will help firms choose the right processes to offshore and discusses the associated risks.

Challenges in Implementing a Global Strategy

The articles in this theme scrutinize how to realize the global strategies, so the focus here is much more on the organization design issues and mechanism for executing global strategies. One overriding issue in this theme is how to solve the tension between local adaptation and global efficiency. The article by Doz (1980, Chapter 17) takes its starting point as this dilemma and, in particular, focuses on the demands of the host government (the political imperative). It analyses strategies and administrative processes used by MNCs to reconcile the conflicting economic and political imperative. The notion of the heterarchical MNC is proposed by Hedlund (1986, Chapter 18) as a model for coping with conflicting demands. The heterachical MNC is characterized by the following: it has many centres; subsidiary managers are given a strategic role for the MNC as a whole; it is flexible in the selection of governance; integration is achieved through normative control; and radical problem-oriented orientation is used as guiding strategy formulation. The article by Levy et al. (2007, Chapter 31) is a review that synthesizes the current thinking about global mindset and as such build bridges to the early contributions, for example, by Levitt (1983, Chapter 1). The authors define global mindset as 'a highly complex cognitive structure characterized by an openness to and articulation of multiple cultural and strategic realities on both global and local levels, and the cognitive ability to mediate and integrate across this multiplicity' (p. 244).

Two newer contributions, by Devinney et al. (2000, Chapter 27) and Kostova and Zaheer (1999, Chapter 24), study strategies on how to balance local and global demands. While Devinney et al. (2000) formalize and extend the classic integration-responsiveness framework, Kostova and Zaheer (1999) apply the lens of organizational legitimacy and develop hypotheses on the tension between internal and external legitimacy for MNCs and MNC units.

Gupta and Govindarajan (2000, Chapter 26) present a framework and a set of conceptual ideas that can guide firms in approaching the strategic challenge of building global presence. In their article, Kim and Mauborgne (1993, Chapter 20) set to address how an MNC can simultaneously pursue the objective of effectively conceiving and executing a worldwide strategy, as well as the ways in which the dynamics of the strategy-making process between head office and subsidiary units influence the MNC's ability to achieve these two objectives.

Four articles investigate the different roles of subsidiaries and how they have changed over the years. Ghoshal and Bartlett (1990, Chapter 19) propose that the MNC should be conceptualized as an interorganizational network: 'We believe that the concept of a network, both as a metaphor and in terms of the tools and techniques of analysis it provides, reflects the nature and complexity of the multinational organization and can provide a useful lens through which to examine such an entity' (p. 604). The theoretical paper by Birkinshaw and Hood (1998, Chapter 23) identifies three factors that in combination determine subsidiary evolution: decisions made by head-office managers regarding the allocation of activities to the subsidiary (head-office assignment), decisions made by subsidiary managers regarding the activities undertaken by the subsidiary (subsidiary choice), and influence of environmental factors on these decisions (local environment determinism). Cantwell and Mudambi (2005, Chapter 30) conduct an empirical test of factors determining the R&D intensity of subsidiaries and in that sense pursue an empirical test of the factors identified by Birkinshaw and Hood (1998) as drivers for upgrading subsidiary mandates. The paper by Barkema et al. (1997, Chapter 22) explores the learning process and, in particular, to what extent firms learn from previous failures when going international.

The remaining four articles scrutinize the mechanism for knowledge sharing across borders in the MNC, as sharing of tacit knowledge is perceived as an area where the MNC might be more efficient than the external market. A model of knowledge management is developed by Hedlund (1994, Chapter 21), which distinguishes between tacit and articulated knowledge on the one hand, and between four different agents of knowledge (the individual, the team, the organization and interorganizational domain) on the other. Gupta and Govindarajan (2000, Chapter 25) take these ideas further in their study on determinants of knowledge inflow into and outflow from subsidiaries. Along the same line, Hansen and Løvås (2004, Chapter 29) explore the importance of formal organization structure, informal relations, geographical distance and relatedness of competencies for knowledge transfer among teams and subsidiaries in an MNC. Finally, Minbaeva et al. (2003, Chapter 28) focus on how HR mechanisms can be applied in order to facilitate subsidiary absorptive capacity and subsequently transfer knowledge among subsidiaries.

Taken together these articles provide an excellent entrance and overview of the breadth and depth of the field of global strategy. Each article can be read separately or as part of a theme/topic as indicated in the introduction above.

Part I
The Emergence of a Global Village

[1]

The globalization of markets

Companies must learn to operate as if the world were one large market – ignoring superficial regional and national differences

Theodore Levitt

Many companies have become disillusioned with sales in the international marketplace as old markets become saturated and new ones must be found. How can they customize products for the demands of new markets? Which items will consumers want? With wily international competitors breathing down their necks, many organizations think that the game just isn't worth the effort.

In this powerful essay, the author asserts that well-managed companies have moved from emphasis on customizing items to offering globally standardized products that are advanced, functional, reliable – and low priced. Multinational companies that concentrated on idiosyncratic consumer preferences have become befuddled and unable to take in the forest because of the trees. Only global companies will achieve long-term success by concentrating on what everyone wants rather than worrying about the details of what everyone thinks they might like.

Mr. Levitt is Edward W. Carter Professor of Business Administration and head of the marketing area at the Harvard Business School. This is Mr. Levitt's twenty-third article for HBR; his classic "Marketing Myopia," first published in 1960, was reprinted in September-October 1975, and his last article was "Marketing Intangible Products and Product Intangibles" (May-June 1981).

Illustration by Karen Watson.

A powerful force drives the world toward a converging commonality, and that force is technology. It has proletarianized communication, transport, and travel. It has made isolated places and impoverished peoples eager for modernity's allurements. Almost everyone everywhere wants all the things they have heard about, seen, or experienced via the new technologies.

The result is a new commercial reality – the emergence of global markets for standardized consumer products on a previously unimagined scale of magnitude. Corporations geared to this new reality benefit from enormous economies of scale in production, distribution, marketing, and management. By translating these benefits into reduced world prices, they can decimate competitors that still live in the disabling grip of old assumptions about how the world works.

Gone are accustomed differences in national or regional preference. Gone are the days when a company could sell last year's models – or lesser versions of advanced products – in the less-developed world. And gone are the days when prices, margins, and profits abroad were generally higher than at home.

The globalization of markets is at hand. With that, the multinational commercial world nears its end, and so does the multinational corporation.

The multinational and the global corporation are not the same thing. The multinational corporation operates in a number of countries, and adjusts its products and practices in each – at high relative costs. The global corporation operates with resolute constancy – at low relative cost – as if the entire world

1 In a landmark article, Robert D. Buzzell pointed out the rapidity with which barriers to standardization were falling. In all cases they succumbed to more and cheaper advanced ways of doing things. See "Can You Standardize Multinational Marketing?" HBR November-December 1968, p. 102.

(or major regions of it) were a single entity; it sells the same things in the same way everywhere.

Which strategy is better is not a matter of opinion but of necessity. Worldwide communications carry everywhere the constant drumbeat of modern possibilities to lighten and enhance work, raise living standards, divert, and entertain. The same countries that ask the world to recognize and respect the individuality of their cultures insist on the wholesale transfer to them of modern goods, services, and technologies. Modernity is not just a wish but also a widespread practice among those who cling, with unyielding passion or religious fervor, to ancient attitudes and heritages.

Who can forget the televised scenes during the 1979 Iranian uprisings of young men in fashionable French-cut trousers and silky body shirts thirsting with raised modern weapons for blood in the name of Islamic fundamentalism?

In Brazil, thousands swarm daily from pre-industrial Bahian darkness into exploding coastal cities, there quickly to install television sets in crowded corrugated huts and, next to battered Volkswagens, make sacrificial offerings of fruit and fresh-killed chickens to Macumban spirits by candlelight.

During Biafra's fratricidal war against the Ibos, daily televised reports showed soldiers carrying bloodstained swords and listening to transistor radios while drinking Coca-Cola.

In the isolated Siberian city of Krasnoyarsk, with no paved streets and censored news, occasional Western travelers are stealthily propositioned for cigarettes, digital watches, and even the clothes off their backs.

The organized smuggling of electronic equipment, used automobiles, western clothing, cosmetics, and pirated movies into primitive places exceeds even the thriving underground trade in modern weapons and their military mercenaries.

A thousand suggestive ways attest to the ubiquity of the desire for the most advanced things that the world makes and sells – goods of the best quality and reliability at the lowest price. The world's needs and desires have been irrevocably homogenized. This makes the multinational corporation obsolete and the global corporation absolute.

Living in the Republic of Technology

Daniel J. Boorstin, author of the monumental trilogy *The Americans*, characterized our age

as driven by "the Republic of Technology [whose] supreme law...is convergence, the tendency for everything to become more like everything else."

In business, this trend has pushed markets toward global commonality. Corporations sell standardized products in the same way everywhere – autos, steel, chemicals, petroleum, cement, agricultural commodities and equipment, industrial and commercial construction, banking and insurance services, computers, semiconductors, transport, electronic instruments, pharmaceuticals, and telecommunications, to mention some of the obvious.

Nor is the sweeping gale of globalization confined to these raw material or high-tech products, where the universal language of customers and users facilitates standardization. The transforming winds whipped up by the proletarianization of communication and travel enter every crevice of life.

Commercially, nothing confirms this as much as the success of McDonald's from the Champs Elysées to the Ginza, of Coca-Cola in Bahrain and Pepsi-Cola in Moscow, and of rock music, Greek salad, Hollywood movies, Revlon cosmetics, Sony televisions, and Levi jeans everywhere. "High-touch" products are as ubiquitous as high-tech.

Starting from opposing sides, the high-tech and the high-touch ends of the commercial spectrum gradually consume the undistributed middle in their cosmopolitan orbit. No one is exempt and nothing can stop the process. Everywhere everything gets more and more like everything else as the world's preference structure is relentlessly homogenized.

Consider the cases of Coca-Cola and Pepsi-Cola, which are globally standardized products sold everywhere and welcomed by everyone. Both successfully cross multitudes of national, regional, and ethnic taste buds trained to a variety of deeply ingrained local preferences of taste, flavor, consistency, effervescence, and aftertaste. Everywhere both sell well. Cigarettes, too, especially American-made, make year-to-year global inroads on territories previously held in the firm grip of other, mostly local, blends.

These are not exceptional examples. (Indeed their global reach would be even greater were it not for artificial trade barriers.) They exemplify a general drift toward the homogenization of the world and how companies distribute, finance, and price products.[1] Nothing is exempt. The products and methods of the industrialized world play a single tune for all the world, and all the world eagerly dances to it.

Ancient differences in national tastes or modes of doing business disappear. The commonality of preference leads inescapably to the standardization of products, manufacturing, and the institutions of trade and commerce. Small nation-based markets transmogrify and expand. Success in world competition turns on efficiency in production, distribution,

Harvard Business Review   May-June 1983

marketing, and management, and inevitably becomes focused on price.

The most effective world competitors incorporate superior quality and reliability into their cost structures. They sell in all national markets the same kind of products sold at home or in their largest export market. They compete on the basis of appropriate value – the best combinations of price, quality, reliability, and delivery for products that are globally identical with respect to design, function, and even fashion.

That, and little else, explains the surging success of Japanese companies dealing worldwide in a vast variety of products – both tangible products like steel, cars, motorcyles, hi-fi equipment, farm machinery, robots, microprocessors, carbon fibers, and now even textiles, and intangibles like banking, shipping, general contracting, and soon computer software. Nor are high-quality and low-cost operations incompatible, as a host of consulting organizations and data engineers argue with vigorous vacuity. The reported data are incomplete, wrongly analyzed, and contradictory. The truth is that low-cost operations are the hallmark of corporate cultures that require and produce quality in all that they do. High quality and low costs are not opposing postures. They are compatible, twin identities of superior practice.[2]

To say that Japan's companies are not global because they export cars with left-side drives to the United States and the European continent, while those in Japan have right-side drives, or because they sell office machines through distributors in the United States but directly at home, or speak Portuguese in Brazil is to mistake a difference for a distinction. The same is true of Safeway and Southland retail chains operating effectively in the Middle East, and to not only native but also imported populations from Korea, the Philippines, Pakistan, India, Thailand, Britain, and the United States. National rules of the road differ, and so do distribution channels and languages. Japan's distinction is its unrelenting push for economy and value enhancement. That translates into a drive for standardization at high quality levels.

Vindication of the Model T

If a company forces costs and prices down and pushes quality and reliability up – while maintaining reasonable concern for suitability – customers will prefer its world-standardized products. The theory holds, at this stage in the evolution of globalization, no matter what conventional market research and even common sense may suggest about different national and regional tastes, preferences, needs, and institutions. The Japanese have repeatedly

vindicated this theory, as did Henry Ford with the Model T. Most important, so have their imitators, including companies from South Korea (television sets and heavy construction), Malaysia (personal calculators and microcomputers), Brazil (auto parts and tools), Colombia (apparel), Singapore (optical equipment), and yes, even from the United States (office copiers, computers, bicycles, castings), Western Europe (automatic washing machines), Rumania (housewares), Hungary (apparel), Yugoslavia (furniture), and Israel (pagination equipment).

Of course, large companies operating in a single nation or even a single city don't standardize everything they make, sell, or do. They have product lines instead of a single product version, and multiple distribution channels. There are neighborhood, local, regional, ethnic, and institutional differences, even within metropolitan areas. But although companies customize products for particular market segments, they know that success in a world with homogenized demand requires a search for sales opportunities in similar segments across the globe in order to achieve the economies of scale necessary to compete.

Such a search works because a market segment in one country is seldom unique; it has close cousins everywhere precisely because technology has homogenized the globe. Even small local segments have their global equivalents everywhere and become subject to global competition, especially on price.

The global competitor will seek constantly to standardize his offering everywhere. He will digress from this standardization only after exhausting all possibilities to retain it, and he will push for reinstatement of standardization whenever digression and divergence have occurred. He will never assume that the customer is a king who knows his own wishes.

Trouble increasingly stalks companies that lack clarified global focus and remain inattentive to the economics of simplicity and standardization. The most endangered companies in the rapidly evolving world tend to be those that dominate rather small domestic markets with high value-added products for which there are smaller markets elsewhere. With transportation costs proportionately low, distant competitors will enter the now-sheltered markets of those companies with goods produced more cheaply under scale-efficient conditions. Global competition spells the end of domestic territoriality, no matter how diminutive the territory may be.

2. There is powerful new evidence for this, even though the opposite has been urged by analysts of PIMS data for nearly a decade. See "Product Quality: Cost Production and Business Performance – A Test of Some Key Hypotheses" by Lynn W. Phillips, Dae Chang, and Robert D. Buzzell, Harvard Business School Working Paper No. 83-13.

Economies of scope

One argument that opposes globalization says that flexible factory automation will enable plants of massive size to change products and product features quickly, without stopping the manufacturing process. These factories of the future could thus produce broad lines of customized products without sacrificing the scale economies that come from long production runs of standardized items. Computer-aided design and manufacturing (CAD/CAM), combined with robotics, will create a new equipment and process technology (EPT) that will make small plants located close to their markets as efficient as large ones located distantly. Economies of scale will not dominate, but rather economies of scope – the ability of either large or small plants to produce great varieties of relatively customized products at remarkably low costs. If that happens, customers will have no need to abandon special preferences.

I will not deny the power of these possibilities. But possibilities do not make probabilities. There is no conceivable way in which flexible factory automation can achieve the scale economies of a modernized plant dedicated to mass production of standardized lines. The new digitized equipment and process technologies are available to all. Manufacturers with minimal customization and narrow product-line breadth will have costs far below those with more customization and wider lines.

When the global producer offers his lower costs internationally, his patronage expands exponentially. He not only reaches into distant markets, but also attracts customers who previously held to local preferences and now capitulate to the attractions of lesser prices. The strategy of standardization not only responds to worldwide homogenized markets but also expands those markets with aggressive low pricing. The new technological juggernaut taps an ancient motivation – to make one's money go as far as possible. This is universal – not simply a motivation but actually a need.

The hedgehog knows

The difference between the hedgehog and the fox, wrote Sir Isaiah Berlin in distinguishing between Dostoevski and Tolstoy, is that the fox knows a lot about a great many things, but the hedgehog knows everything about one great thing. The multinational corporation knows a lot about a great many

countries and congenially adapts to supposed differences. It willingly accepts vestigial national differences, not questioning the possibility of their transformation, not recognizing how the world is ready and eager for the benefit of modernity, especially when the price is right. The multinational corporation's accommodating mode to visible national differences is medieval.

By contrast, the global corporation knows everything about one great thing. It knows about the absolute need to be competitive on a worldwide basis as well as nationally and seeks constantly to drive down prices by standardizing what it sells and how it operates. It treats the world as composed of few standardized markets rather than many customized markets. It actively seeks and vigorously works toward global convergence. Its mission is modernity and its mode, price competition, even when it sells top-of-the-line, high-end products. It knows about the one great thing all nations and people have in common: scarcity.

Nobody takes scarcity lying down; everyone wants more. This in part explains division of labor and specialization of production. They enable people and nations to optimize their conditions through trade. The median is usually money.

Experience teaches that money has three special qualities: scarcity, difficulty of acquisition, and transience. People understandably treat it with respect. Everyone in the increasingly homogenized world market wants products and features that everybody else wants. If the price is low enough, they will take highly standardized world products, even if these aren't exactly what mother said was suitable, what immemorial custom decreed was right, or what market-research fabulists asserted was preferred.

The implacable truth of all modern production – whether of tangible or intangible goods – is that large-scale production of standardized items is generally cheaper within a wide range of volume than small-scale production. Some argue that CAD/CAM will allow companies to manufacture customized products on a small scale – but cheaply. But the argument misses the point. (For a more detailed discussion, see the insert, "Economies of scope.") If a company treats the world as one or two distinctive product markets, it can serve the world more economically than if it treats it as three, four, or five product markets.

Why remaining differences?

Different cultural preferences, national tastes and standards, and business institutions are vestiges of the past. Some inheritances die gradually; others prosper and expand into mainstream global preferences. So-called ethnic markets are a good example. Chinese food, pita bread, country and western music, pizza, and jazz are everywhere. They are market segments that exist in worldwide proportions. They don't deny or contradict global homogenization but confirm it.

Many of today's differences among nations as to products and their features actually reflect the respectful accommodation of multinational corporations to what they believe are fixed local preferences. They *believe* preferences are fixed, not because they are but because of rigid habits of thinking about what actually is. Most executives in multinational corporations are thoughtlessly accommodating. They falsely presume that marketing means giving the customer what he says he wants rather than trying to understand exactly what he'd like. So they persist with high-cost, customized multinational products and practices instead of pressing hard and pressing properly for global standardization.

I do not advocate the systematic disregard of local or national differences. But a company's sensitivity to such differences does not require that it ignore the possibilities of doing things differently or better.

There are, for example, enormous differences among Middle Eastern countries. Some are socialist, some monarchies, some republics. Some take their legal heritage from the Napoleonic Code, some from the Ottoman Empire, and some from the British common law; except for Israel, all are influenced by Islam. Doing business means personalizing the business relationship in an obsessively intimate fashion. During the month of Ramadan, business discussions can start only after 10 o'clock at night, when people are tired and full of food after a day of fasting. A company must almost certainly have a local partner; a local lawyer is required (as, say, in New York), and irrevocable letters of credit are essential. Yet, as Coca-Cola's Senior Vice President Sam Ayoub noted, "Arabs are much more capable of making distinctions between cultural and religious purposes on the one hand and economic realities on the other than is generally assumed. Islam is compatible with science and modern times."

Barriers to globalization are not confined to the Middle East. The free transfer of technology and data across the boundaries of the European Common Market countries are hampered by legal and financial impediments. And there is resistence to radio and television interference ("pollution") among neighboring European countries.

But the past is a good guide to the future. With persistence and appropriate means, barriers against superior technologies and economics have always fallen. There is no recorded exception where reasonable effort has been made to overcome them. It is very much a matter of time and effort.

A failure in global imagination

Many companies have tried to standardize world practice by exporting domestic products and processes without accommodation or change – and have failed miserably. Their deficiencies have been seized on as evidence of bovine stupidity in the face of abject impossibility. Advocates of global standardization see them as examples of failures in execution.

In fact, poor execution is often an important cause. More important, however, is failure of nerve – failure of imagination.

Consider the case for the introduction of fully automatic home laundry equipment in Western Europe at a time when few homes had even semiautomatic machines. Hoover, Ltd., whose parent company was headquartered in North Canton, Ohio had a prominent presence in Britain as a producer of vacuum cleaners and washing machines. Due to insufficient demand in the home market and low exports to the European continent, the large washing machine plant in England operated far below capacity. The company needed to sell more of its semiautomatic or automatic machines.

Because it had a "proper" marketing orientation, Hoover conducted consumer preference studies in Britain and each major continental country. The results showed feature preferences clearly enough among several countries (see the *Exhibit*).

The incremental unit variable costs (in pounds sterling) of customizing to meet just a few of the national preferences were:

	£	s.	d.
Stainless steel vs. enamel drum	1	0	0
Porthole window		10	0
Spin speed of 800 rpm vs. 700 rpm		15	0
Water heater	2	15	0
6 vs. 5 kilos capacity	1	10	0
	£6	10 s	0 d

$18.20 at the exchange rate of that time.

Considerable plant investment was needed to meet other preferences.

The lowest retail prices (in pounds sterling) of leading locally produced brands in the various countries were approximately:

U.K.	£110
France	114
West Germany	113
Sweden	134
Italy	57

Product customization in each country would have put Hoover in a poor competitive position on the basis of price, mostly due to the higher manufacturing costs incurred by short production runs for separate features. Because Common Market tariff reduction programs were then incomplete, Hoover also paid tariff duties in each continental country.

How to make a creative analysis

In the Hoover case, an imaginative analysis of automatic washing machine sales in each country would have revealed that:

1   Italian automatics, small in capacity and size, low-powered, without built-in heaters, with porcelain enamel tubs, were priced aggressively low and were gaining large market shares in all countries, including West Germany.

2   The best-selling automatics in West Germany were heavily advertised (three times more than the next most promoted brand), were ideally suited to national tastes, and were also by far the highest priced machines available in that country.

3   Italy, with the lowest penetration of washing machines of any kind (manual, semiautomatic, or automatic) was rapidly going directly to automatics, skipping the pattern of first buying handwringer, manually assisted machines and then semiautomatics.

4   Detergent manufacturers were just beginning to promote the technique of cold-water and tepid-water laundering then used in the United States.

The growing success of small, low-powered, low-speed, low-capacity, low-priced Italian machines, even against the preferred but highly priced and highly promoted brand in West Germany, was significant. It contained a powerful message that was lost on managers confidently wedded to a distorted version of the marketing concept according to which you give the customer what he says he wants. In fact the customers *said* they wanted certain features, but their

behavior demonstrated they'd take other features provided the price and the promotion were right.

In this case it was obvious that, under prevailing conditions, people preferred a low-priced automatic over any kind of manual or semiautomatic machine and certainly over higher priced automatics, even though the low-priced automatics failed to fulfill all their expressed preferences. The supposedly meticulous and demanding German consumers violated all expectations by buying the simple, low-priced Italian machines.

It was equally clear that people were profoundly influenced by promotions of automatic washers; in West Germany, the most heavily promoted ideal machine also had the largest market share despite its high price. Two things clearly influenced customers to buy: low price regardless of feature preferences and heavy promotion regardless of price. Both factors helped homemakers get what they most wanted – the superior benefits bestowed by fully automatic machines.

Hoover should have aggressively sold a simple, standardized high-quality machine at a low price (afforded by the 17% variable cost reduction that the elimination of £6-10-0 worth of extra features made possible). The suggested retail prices could have been somewhat less than £100. The extra funds "saved" by avoiding unnecessary plant modifications would have supported an extended service network and aggressive media promotions.

Hoover's media message should have been: *this* is the machine that you, the homemaker, *deserve* to have to reduce the repetitive heavy daily household burdens, so that *you* may have more constructive time to spend with your children and your husband. The promotion should also have targeted the husband to give him, preferably in the presence of his wife, a sense of obligation to provide an automatic washer for her even before he bought an automobile for himself. An aggressively low price, combined with heavy promotion of this kind, would have overcome previously expressed preferences for particular features.

The Hoover case illustrates how the perverse practice of the marketing concept and the absence of any kind of marketing imagination let multinational attitudes survive when customers actually want the benefits of global standardization. The whole project got off on the wrong foot. It asked people what features they wanted in a washing machine rather than what they wanted out of life. Selling a line of products individually tailored to each nation is thoughtless. Managers who took pride in practicing the marketing concept to the fullest did not, in fact, practice it at all. Hoover asked the wrong questions, then applied neither thought nor imagination to the answers. Such companies are like the ethnocentricists

Exhibit	Consumer preferences as to automatic washing machine features in the 1960s					
Features		Great Britain	Italy	West Germany	France	Sweden
Shell dimensions*		34" and narrow	Low and narrow	34" and wide	34" and narrow	34" and wide
Drum material		Enamel	Enamel	Stainless steel	Enamel	Stainless steel
Loading		Top	Front	Front	Front	Front
Front porthole		Yes/no	Yes	Yes	Yes	Yes
Capacity		5 kilos	4 kilos	6 kilos	5 kilos	6 kilos
Spin speed		700 rpm	400 rpm	850 rpm	600 rpm	800 rpm
Water-heating system		No†	Yes	Yes††	Yes	No†
Washing action		Agitator	Tumble	Tumble	Agitator	Tumble
Styling features		Inconspicuous appearance	Brightly colored	Indestructible appearance	Elegant appearance	Strong appearance

*34" height was (in the process of being adopted as) a standard work-surface height in Europe.

†Most British and Swedish homes had centrally heated hot water.

††West Germans preferred to launder at temperatures higher than generally provided centrally.

in the Middle Ages who saw with everyday clarity the sun revolving around the earth and offered it as Truth. With no additional data but a more searching mind, Copernicus, like the hedgehog, interpreted a more compelling and accurate reality. Data do not yield information except with the intervention of the mind. Information does not yield meaning except with the intervention of imagination.

Accepting the inevitable

The global corporation accepts for better or for worse that technology drives consumers relentlessly toward the same common goals—alleviation of life's burdens and the expansion of discretionary time and spending power. Its role is profoundly different from what it has been for the ordinary corporation during its brief, turbulent, and remarkably protean history. It orchestrates the twin vectors of technology and globalization for the world's benefit. Neither fate, nor nature, nor God but rather the necessity of commerce created this role.

In the United States two industries became global long before they were consciously aware of it. After over a generation of persistent and acrimonious labor shutdowns, the United Steelworkers of America have not called an industrywide strike since 1959; the United Auto Workers have

not shut down General Motors since 1970. Both unions realize that they have become global—shutting down all or most of U.S. manufacturing would not shut out U.S. customers. Overseas suppliers are there to supply the market.

Cracking the code of Western markets

Since the theory of the marketing concept emerged a quarter of a century ago, the more managerially advanced corporations have been eager to offer what customers clearly wanted rather than what was merely convenient. They have created marketing departments supported by professional market researchers of awesome and often costly proportions. And they have proliferated extraordinary numbers of operations and product lines—highly tailored products and delivery systems for many different markets, market segments, and nations.

Significantly, Japanese companies operate almost entirely without marketing departments or market research of the kind so prevalent in the West. Yet, in the colorful words of General Electric's chairman John F. Welch, Jr., the Japanese, coming from a small cluster of resource-poor islands, with an entirely alien culture and an almost impenetrably complex language, have cracked the code of Western markets. They have done it not by looking with mechanistic thoroughness at the way markets are different but rather by searching for meaning with a deeper wisdom. They have discovered the one great thing all markets have in common – an overwhelming desire for dependable, world-standard modernity in all things, at aggressively low prices. In response, they deliver irresistible value everywhere, attracting people with products that market-research technocrats described with superficial certainty as being unsuitable and uncompetitive.

The wider a company's global reach, the greater the number of regional and national preferences it will encounter for certain product features, distribution systems, or promotional media. There will always need to be some accommodation to differences. But the widely prevailing and often unthinking belief in the immutability of these differences is generally mistaken. Evidence of business failure because of lack of accommodation is often evidence of other shortcomings.

Take the case of Revlon in Japan. The company unnecessarily alienated retailers and confused customers by selling world-standardized cosmetics only in elite outlets; then it tried to recover with low-priced world-standardized products in broader distribution, followed by a change in the company president and cutbacks in distribution as costs rose faster than sales. The problem was not that Revlon didn't understand the Japanese market; it didn't do the job right, wavered in its programs, and was impatient to boot.

By contrast, the Outboard Marine Corporation, with imagination, push, and persistence, collapsed long-established three-tiered distribution channels in Europe into a more focused and controllable two-step system – and did so despite the vociferous warnings of local trade groups. It also reduced the number and types of retail outlets. The result was greater improvement in credit and product-installation service to customers, major cost reductions, and sales advances.

In its highly successful introduction of Contac 600 (the timed-release decongestant) into Japan, SmithKline Corporation used 35 wholesalers instead of the 1,000-plus that established practice required. Daily contacts with the wholesalers and key retailers, also in violation of established practice, supplemented the plan, and it worked.

Denied access to established distribution institutions in the United States, Komatsu, the Japanese manufacturer of lightweight farm machinery, entered the market through over-the-road construction equipment dealers in rural areas of the Sunbelt, where farms are smaller, the soil sandier and easier to work. Here inexperienced distributors were able to attract customers on the basis of Komatsu's product and price appropriateness.

In cases of successful challenge to prevailing institutions and practices, a combination of product reliability and quality, strong and sustained support systems, aggressively low prices, and sales-compensation packages, as well as audacity and implacability, circumvented, shattered, and transformed very different distribution systems. Instead of resentment, there was admiration.

Still, some differences between nations are unyielding, even in a world of microprocessors. In the United States almost all manufacturers of microprocessors check them for reliability through a so-called parallel system of testing. Japan prefers the totally different sequential testing system. So Teradyne Corporation, the world's largest producer of microprocessor test equipment, makes one line for the United States and one for Japan. That's easy.

What's not so easy for Teradyne is to know how best to organize and manage, in this instance, its marketing effort. Companies can organize by product, region, function, or by using some combination of these. A company can have separate marketing organizations for Japan and for the United States, or it can have separate product groups, one working largely in Japan and the other in the United States. A single manufacturing facility or marketing operation might service both markets, or a company might use separate marketing operations for each.

Questions arise if the company organizes by product. In the case of Teradyne, should the group handling the parallel system, whose major market is the United States, sell in Japan and compete with the group focused on the Japanese market? If the company organizes regionally, how do regional groups divide their efforts between promoting the parallel vs. the sequential system? If the company organizes in terms of function, how does it get commitment in marketing, for example, for one line instead of the other?

There is no one reliably right answer – no one formula by which to get it. There isn't even a satisfactory contingent answer. What works well for one company or one place may fail for another in precisely the same place, depending on the capabilities, histories, reputations, resources, and even the cultures of both.

The earth is flat

The differences that persist throughout the world despite its globalization affirm an ancient dictum of economics – that things are driven by what happens at the margin, not at the core. Thus, in ordinary competitive analysis, what's important is not the average price but the marginal price; what happens not in the usual case but at the interface of newly erupting conditions. What counts in commercial affairs is what happens at the cutting edge. What is most striking today is the underlying similarities of what is happening now to national preferences at the margin. These similarities at the cutting edge cumulatively form an overwhelming, predominant commonality everywhere.

To refer to the persistence of economic nationalism (protective and subsidized trade practices, special tax aids, or restrictions for home market producers) as a barrier to the globalization of markets is to make a valid point. Economic nationalism does have a powerful persistence. But, as with the present almost totally smooth internationalization of investment capital, the past alone does not shape or predict the future. (For reflections on the internationalization of capital, see the insert, "The shortening of Japanese horizons.")

Reality is not a fixed paradigm, dominated by immemorial customs and derived attitudes, heedless of powerful and abundant new forces. The world is becoming increasingly informed about the liberating and enhancing possibilities of modernity. The persistence of the inherited varieties of national preferences rests uneasily on increasing evidence of, and restlessness regarding, their inefficiency, costliness, and confinement. The historic past, and the national differences respecting commerce and industry it spawned and fostered everywhere, is now subject to relatively easy transformation.

Cosmopolitanism is no longer the monopoly of the intellectual and leisure classes; it is becoming the established property and defining characteristic of all sectors everywhere in the world. Gradually and irresistibly it breaks down the walls of economic insularity, nationalism, and chauvinism. What we see today as escalating commercial nationalism is simply the last violent death rattle of an obsolete institution.

Companies that adapt to and capitalize on economic convergence can still make distinctions and adjustments in different markets. Persistent differences in the world are consistent with fundamental underlying commonalities; they often complement rather than oppose each other—in business as they do in physics. There is, in physics, simultaneously matter and anti-matter working in symbiotic harmony.

The earth is round, but for most purposes it's sensible to treat it as flat. Space is curved, but not much for everyday life here on earth.

Divergence from established practice happens all the time. But the multinational mind,

---

The shortening of Japanese horizons

One of the most powerful yet least celebrated forces driving commerce toward global standardization is the monetary system, along with the international investment process.

Today money is simply electronic impulses. With the speed of light it moves effortlessly between distant centers (and even lesser places). A change of ten basis points in the price of a bond causes an instant and massive shift of money from London to Tokyo. The system has profound impact on the way companies operate throughout the world.

Take Japan, where high debt-to-equity balance sheets are "guaranteed" by various societal presumptions about the virtue of "a long view," or by government policy in other ways. Even here, upward shifts in interest rates in other parts of the world attract capital out of the country in powerful proportions. In recent years more and more Japanese global corporations have gone to the world's equity markets for funds. Debt is too remunerative in high-yielding countries to keep capital at home to feed the Japanese need. As interest rates rise, equity becomes a more attractive option for the issuer.

The long-term impact on Japanese enterprise will be transforming. As the equity proportion of Japanese corporate capitalization rises, companies will respond to the shorter-term investment horizons of the equity markets. Thus the much-vaunted Japanese corporate practice to taking the long view will gradually disappear.

---

warped into circumspection and timidity by years of stumbles and transnational troubles, now rarely challenges existing overseas practices. More often it considers any departure from inherited domestic routines as mindless, disrespectful, or impossible. It is the mind of a bygone day.

The successful global corporation does not abjure customization or differentiation for the requirements of markets that differ in product preferences, spending patterns, shopping preferences, and institutional or legal arrangements. But the global corporation accepts and adjusts to these differences only reluctantly, only after relentlessly testing their immutability, after trying in various ways to circumvent and reshape them as we saw in the cases of Outboard Marine in Europe, SmithKline in Japan, and Komatsu in the United States.

There is only one significant respect in which a company's activities around the world are important, and this is in what it produces and how it sells. Everything else derives from, and is subsidiary to, these activities.

The purpose of business is to get and keep a customer. Or, to use Peter Drucker's more refined construction, to *create* and keep a customer. A

---

3 For a discussion of
multinational reorganization,
see Christopher A. Bartlett,

"MNCs: Get Off the Reorganization
Merry-Go-Round,"
HBR March-April 1983, p. 138.

company must be wedded to the ideal of innovation – offering better or more preferred products in such combinations of ways, means, places, and at such prices that prospects *prefer* doing business with the company rather than with others.

Preferences are constantly shaped and reshaped. Within our global commonality enormous variety constantly asserts itself and thrives, as can be seen within the world's single largest domestic market, the United States. But in the process of world homogenization, modern markets expand to reach cost-reducing global proportions. With better and cheaper communication and transport, even small local market segments hitherto protected from distant competitors now feel the pressure of their presence. Nobody is safe from global reach and the irresistible economies of scale.

Two vectors shape the world – technology and globalization. The first helps determine human preferences; the second, economic realities. Regardless of how much preferences evolve and diverge, they also gradually converge and form markets where economies of scale lead to reduction of costs and prices.

The modern global corporation contrasts powerfully with the aging multinational corporation. Instead of adapting to superficial and even entrenched differences within and between nations, it will seek sensibly to force suitably standardized products and practices on the entire globe. They are exactly what the world will take, if they come also with low prices, high quality, and blessed reliability. The global company will operate, in this regard, precisely as Henry Kissinger wrote in *Years of Upheaval* about the continuing Japanese economic success – "voracious in its collection of information, impervious to pressure, and implacable in execution."

Given what is everywhere the purpose of commerce, the global company will shape the vectors of technology and globalization into its great strategic fecundity. It will systematically push these vectors toward their own convergence, offering everyone simultaneously high-quality, more or less standardized products at optimally low prices, thereby achieving for itself vastly expanded markets and profits. Companies that do not adapt to the new global realities will become victims of those that do. ⊖

Turtles all the way down

There is an Indian story – at least I heard it as an Indian story – about an Englishman who, having been told that the world rested on a platform which rested on the back of an elephant which rested in turn on the back of a turtle, asked (perhaps he was an ethnographer; it is the way they behave), what did the turtle rest on? Another turtle. And that turtle? "Ah, Sahib, after that it is turtles all the way down."...

The danger that cultural analysis, in search of all-too-deep-lying turtles, will lose touch with the hard surfaces of life – with the political, economic, stratificatory realities within which men are everywhere contained – and with the biological and physical necessities on which those surfaces rest, is an ever-present one. The only defense against it, and against, thus, turning cultural analysis into a kind of sociological aestheticism, is to train such analysis on such realities and such necessities in the first place.

From
Clifford Geertz,
The Interpretation of Cultures
(New York: Basic Books 1973),
With permission of the publisher

[2]

The global manager operates as an "insider" in every market.

Managing in a Borderless World

by Kenichi Ohmae

Most managers are nearsighted. Even though to-day's competitive landscape often stretches to a global horizon, they see best what they know best: the customers geographically closest to home. These managers may have factories or laboratories in a dozen countries. They may have joint ventures in a dozen more. They may source materials and sell in markets all over the world. But when push comes to shove, their field of vision is dominated by home-country customers and the organizational units that serve them. Everyone—and everything—else is simply part of "the rest of the world."

This nearsightedness is not intentional. No responsible manager purposefully devises or imple-ments an astigmatic strategy. But by the same token, too few managers consciously try to set plans and build organizations as if they saw all key customers equidistant from the corporate center. Whatever the trade figures show, home markets are usually in fo-cus; overseas markets are not.

Effective global operations require a genuine equidistance of perspective. But even with the best will in the world, managers find that kind of vision hard to develop—and harder to maintain. Not long ago, the CEO of a major Japanese capital-goods pro-ducer canceled several important meetings to attend the funeral of one of his company's local dealers. When I asked him if he would have done the same for a Belgian dealer, one who did a larger volume of business each year than his late counterpart in Japan, the unequivocal answer was no. Perhaps headquarters would have had the relevant European manager send a letter of condolence. No more than that. In Japan, however, tradition dictated the CEO's presence. But Japanese tradition isn't everything, I reminded him. After all, he was the head of a global, not just a Japanese organization. By violating the principle of equidistance, his attendance underscored distinctions among dealers. He was sending the wrong signals and reinforcing the wrong values. Poor vision has consequences.

It may be unfamiliar and awkward, but the primary rule of equidistance is to see – and to think – global first. Honda, for example, has manufacturing divisions in Japan, North America, and Europe – all three legs of the Triad – but its managers do not think or act as if the company were divided between Japanese and overseas operations. Indeed, the very word "overseas" has no place in Honda's vocabulary because the corporation sees itself as equidistant from all its key customers. At Casio, the top managers gather information directly from each of their primary markets and then sit down together once a month to lay out revised plans for global product development.

There is no single best way to avoid or overcome nearsightedness. An equidistant perspective can take many forms. However managers do it, however they get there, building a value system that emphasizes seeing and thinking globally is the bottom-line price of admission to today's borderless economy.

A Geography Without Borders

On a political map, the boundaries between countries are as clear as ever. But on a competitive map, a map showing the real flows of financial and industrial activity, those boundaries have largely disappeared. What has eaten them away is the persistent, ever speedier flow of information – information that governments previously monopolized, cooking it up as they saw fit and redistributing in forms of their own devising. Their monopoly of knowledge about things happening around the world enabled them to fool, mislead, or control the people because

Kenichi Ohmae heads McKinsey's office in Tokyo. He is the author of The Mind of the Strategist: The Art of Japanese Business *(McGraw-Hill, 1982),* Triad Power: The Coming Shape of Global Competition *(Free Press, 1985), and* Beyond National Borders *(Dow Jones-Irwin, 1987). Mr. Ohmae's articles for HBR will be part of a book on global strategy to be published by Doubleday in 1990.*

only the governments possessed real facts in anything like real time.

Today, of course, people everywhere are more and more able to get the information they want directly from all corners of the world. They can see for themselves what the tastes and preferences are in other countries, the styles of clothing now in fashion, the sports, the lifestyles. In Japan, for example, our leaders can no longer keep the people in substandard housing because we now know – directly – how people elsewhere live. We now travel abroad. In fact, ten million Japanese travel abroad annually these days.

Information has made us all into global citizens.

Or we can sit in our living rooms at home, watch CNN, and know instantaneously what is happening in the United States. During 1988, nearly 90% of all Japanese honeymooners went abroad. This kind of fact is hard to ignore. The government now seriously recognizes that it has built plants and offices but has failed to meet the needs of its young people for relaxation and recreation. So, for the first time in 2,000 years, our people are revolting against their government and telling it what it must do for them. This would have been unthinkable when only a small, official elite controlled access to all information.

In the past, there were gross inefficiencies – some purposeful, some not – in the flow of information around the world. New technologies are eliminating those inefficiencies, and, with them, the opportunity for a kind of top-down information arbitrage – that is, the ability of a government to benefit itself or powerful special interests at the expense of its people by following policies that would never win their support if they had unfettered access to all relevant information. A government could, for example, protect weak industries for fear of provoking social unrest over unemployment. That is less easy to do now, for more of its people have become cosmopolitan and have their own sources of information. They know what such a policy would cost them.

In Korea, students demonstrate in front of the American embassy because the government allows the United States to export cigarettes to Korea and thus threaten local farmers. That's what happens when per capita GNP runs in the neighborhood of $5,000 a year and governments can still control the flow of information and mislead their people. When GNP gets up to around $10,000 a year, religion becomes a declining industry. So does government.

At $26,000 a year, where Japan is now, things are really different. People want to buy the best and the

BORDERLESS WORLD

cheapest products – no matter where in the world they are produced. People become genuinely global consumers. We import beef and oranges from the United States, and everyone thinks it's great. Ten years ago, however, our students would have been the ones throwing stones at the American embassy. Our leaders used to tell us American and Australian beef was too lean and too tough to chew. But we've been there and tasted it and know for ourselves that it is cheap and good.

Through this flow of information, we've become global citizens, and so must the companies that want to sell us things. Black-and-white television sets extensively penetrated households in the United States nearly a dozen years before they reached comparable numbers of viewers in Europe and Japan. With color television, the time lag fell to about five or six years for Japan and a few more for Europe. With videocassette recorders, the difference was only three or four years – but this time, Europe and Japan led the way; the United States, with its focus on cable TV, followed. With the compact disc, household penetration rates evened up after only one year. Now, with MTV available by satellite across Europe, there is no lag at all. New music, styles, and fashion reach all European youngsters almost at the same time they are reaching their counterparts in America. We all share the same information.

More than that, we are all coming to share it in a common language. Ten years ago when I would speak in English to students at Bocconi, an Italian university, most of them would listen to me through a translator. Last year, they listened to me directly in English and asked me questions in English. (They even laughed when they should at what I said, although my jokes have not improved.) This is a momentous change. The preparation for 1992 has taken place in language much sooner than it has in politics. We can all talk to each other now, understand each other, and governments cannot stop us. "Global citizenship" is no longer just a nice phrase in the lexicon of rosy futurologists. It is every bit as real and concrete as measurable changes in GNP or trade flows. It is actually coming to pass.

The same is true for corporations. In the pharmaceutical industry, for example, the critical activities of drug discovery, screening, and testing are now virtually the same among the best companies everywhere in the world. Scientists can move from one laboratory to another and start working the next day with few hesitations or problems. They will find equipment with which they are familiar, equipment they have used before, equipment that comes from the same manufacturers.

The drug companies are not alone in this. Most people, for example, believed that it would be a very long time before Korean companies could produce state-of-the-art semiconductor chips – things like 256K NMOS DRAMs. Not so. They caught up with the rest of the Triad in only a few short years. In Japan, not that long ago, a common joke among the chip-making fraternity had to do with the "Friday Express." The Japanese engineers working for different companies on Kyūshū, Japan's southwestern "Silicon Island" only 100 km or so away from Korea, would catch a late flight to Korea on Friday evenings. During the weekend, they would work privately for Korean semiconductor companies. This was illegal, of course, and violated the engineers' employment agreements in Japan. Nonetheless, so many took the flight that they had a tacit gentleman's agreement not to greet or openly recognize each other on the

Have your vision checked for a nearsighted strategy.

plane. Their trip would have made no sense, however, if semiconductor-related machines, methods, software, and workstations had not already become quite similar throughout the developed world.

Walk into a capital-goods factory anywhere in the developed world, and you will find the same welding machines, the same robots, the same machine tools. When information flows with relative freedom, the old geographic barriers become irrelevant. Global needs lead to global products. For managers, this universal flow of information puts a high premium on learning how to build the strategies and the organizations capable of meeting the requirements of a borderless world.

What Is a Universal Product?

Imagine that you are the CEO of a major automobile company reviewing your product plans for the years ahead. Your market data tell you that you will have to develop four dozen different models if you want to design separate cars for each distinct segment of the Triad market. But you don't have enough world-class engineers to design so many models. You don't have enough managerial talent or enough money. No one does. Worse, there is no single "global" car that will solve your problems for you. America, Europe, and Japan are quite different markets with quite different mixes of needs and preferences. Worse still, as head of a worldwide company, you cannot write off any of these Triad markets. You simply have to be in each of them – and with first-rate successful products. What do you do?

If you are the CEO of Nissan, you first look at the Triad region by region and identify each market's dominant requirements. In the United Kingdom, for example, tax policies make it essential that you develop a car suitable for corporate fleet sales. In the United States, you need a sporty "Z" model as well as a four-wheel drive family vehicle. Each of these categories is what Nissan's president, Yutaka Kume, calls a "lead country" model – a product carefully tailored to the dominant and distinct needs of individual national markets. Once you have your short list of "lead-country" models in hand, you can ask your top managers in other parts of the Triad whether minor changes can make any of them suitable for local sales. But you start with the lead-country models.

"With this kind of thinking," says Mr. Kume, "we have been able to halve the number of basic models needed to cover the global markets and, at the same time, to cover 80% of our sales with cars designed for specific national markets. Not to miss the remaining 20%, however, we also provided each country manager with a range of additional model types that could be adapted to the needs of local segments. This approach," Mr. Kume reports, "allowed us to focus our resources on each of our largest core markets and, at the same time, provide a pool of supplemental designs that could be adapted to local preferences. We told our engineers to 'be American,' 'be European,' or 'be Japanese.' If the Japanese happened to like something we tailored for the American market, so much the better. Low-cost, incremental sales never hurt. Our main challenge, however, was to avoid the trap of pleasing no one well by trying to please everyone halfway."

Imagine, instead, if Nissan had taken its core team of engineers and designers in Japan and asked them to design only global cars, cars that would sell all over the world. Their only possible response would have been to add up all the various national preferences and divide by the number of countries. They would have had to optimize across markets by a kind of rough averaging. But when it comes to questions of taste and, especially, aesthetic preference, consumers do not like averages. They like what they like, not some mathematical compromise. Kume is emphatic about this particular point. "Our success in the U.S. with Maxima, 240 SX, and Pathfinder – all designed for the American market – shows our approach to be right."

In high school physics, I remember learning about a phenomenon called diminishing primaries. If you mix together the primary colors of red, blue, and yel-

> ## Nissan's "lead country" model is tailored to the dominant needs of each market.

low, what you get is black. If Europe says its consumers want a product in green, let them have it. If Japan says red, let them have red. No one wants the average. No one wants the colors all mixed together. Of course it makes sense to take advantage of, say, any technological commonalities in creating the paint. But local managers close to local customers have to be able to pick the color.

When it comes to product strategy, managing in a borderless world doesn't mean managing by averages. It doesn't mean that all tastes run together into one amorphous mass of universal appeal. And it doesn't mean that the appeal of operating globally removes the obligation to localize products. The lure of a universal product is a false allure. The truth is a bit more subtle.

Although the needs and tastes of the Triad markets vary considerably, there may well be market segments of different sizes in each part of the Triad that share many of the same preferences. In the hair-care market, for instance, Japanese companies know a lot more about certain kinds of black hair, which is hard and thick, than about blond or brown hair, which is often soft and thin. As a result, they have been able to capture a few segments of the U.S. market in, say, shampoos. That makes a nice addition to their sales, of course. But it does not position them to make inroads into the mainstream segments of that market.

Back to the automobile example: there is a small but identifiable group of Japanese consumers who want a "Z" model car like the one much in demand in the United States. Fair enough. During the peak season, Nissan sells about 5,000 "Z" cars a month in the United States and only 500 in Japan. Those 500 cars make a nice addition, of course, generating additional revenue and expanding the perceived richness of a local dealer's portfolio. But they are not – and cannot be – the mainstay of such portfolios.

> ## Nissan reduced the number of basic models it needed from 48 to 18.

There is no universal "montage" car – a rear axle from Japan, a braking system from Italy, a drive train from the United States – that will quicken pulses on all continents. Remember the way the tabloids used to cover major beauty contests? They would create a composite picture using the best features from all of the most beautiful entrants – this one's nose, that one's mouth, the other one's forehead. Ironically, the portrait that emerged was never very appealing. It always seemed odd, a bit off, lacking in distinctive character. But there will always be beauty judges – and car buyers – in, say, Europe, who, though more used to continental standards, find a special attractiveness in the features of a Japanese or a Latin American. Again, so much the better.

For some kinds of products, however, the kind of globalization that Ted Levitt talks about makes excellent sense. One of the most obvious is, oddly enough, battery-powered products like cameras, watches, and pocket calculators. These are all part of the "Japan game" – that is, they come from industries dominated by Japanese electronics companies. What makes these products successful across the Triad? Popular prices, for one thing, based on aggressive cost reduction and global economies of scale. Also important, however, is the fact that many general design

choices reflect an in-depth understanding of the preferences of leading consumer segments in key markets throughout the Triad. Rigid model changes during the past decade have helped educate consumers about the "fashion" aspects of these products and have led them to base their buying decisions in large measure on such fashion-related criteria.

With other products, the same electronics companies use quite different approaches. Those that make stereophonic equipment, for example, offer products based on aesthetics and product concepts that vary by region. Europeans tend to want physically small, high-performance equipment that can be hidden in a closet; Americans prefer large speakers that rise from the floor of living rooms and dens like the structural columns of ancient temples. Companies that have been globally successful in white goods like kitchen appliances focus on close interaction with individual users; those that have prospered with equipment that requires installation (air conditioners, say, or elevators) focus on interactions with designers, engineers, and trade unions. To repeat: approaches to global products vary.

Another important cluster of these global products is made up of fashion-oriented, premium-priced branded goods. Gucci bags are sold around the world, unchanged from one place to another. They are marketed in virtually the same way. They appeal to an upper bracket market segment that shares a consistent set of tastes and preferences. By definition, not everyone in the United States or Europe or Japan belongs to that segment. But for those who do, the growing commonality of their tastes qualifies them as members of a genuinely cross-Triad, global segment. There is even such a segment for top-of-the-line automobiles like the Rolls-Royce and the Mercedes-Benz. You can – in fact, should – design such cars for select buyers around the globe. But you cannot do that with Nissans or Toyotas or Hondas. Truly universal products are few and far between.

Insiderization

Some may argue that my definition of universal products is unnecessarily narrow, that many such products exist that do not fit neatly into top-bracket segments: Coca-Cola, Levi's, things like that. On closer examination, however, these turn out to be very different sorts of things. Think about Coca-Cola for a moment. Before it got established in each of its markets, the company had to build up a fairly complete local infrastructure and do the groundwork to establish local demand.

Access to markets was by no means assured from day one; consumer preference was not assured from day one. In Japan, the long-established preference was for carbonated lemon drinks known as saida. Unlike Gucci bags, consumer demand did not "pull" Coke into these markets; the company had to establish the infrastructure to "push" it. Today, because the company has done its homework and done it well, Coke is a universally desired brand. But it got there by a different route: local replication of an entire business system in every important market over a long period of time.

For Gucci-like products, the ready flow of information around the world stimulates consistent primary demand in top-bracket segments. For relatively undifferentiated, commodity-like products, demand expands only when corporate muscle pushes hard. If Coke is to establish a preference, it has to build it, piece by piece.

Perhaps the best way to distinguish these two kinds of global products is to think of yourself browsing in a duty-free shop. Here you are in something of an oasis. National barriers to entry do not apply. Products from all over the world lie available to you on the shelves. What do you reach for? Do you think

about climbing on board your jetliner with a newly purchased six-pack of Coke? Hardly. But what about a Gucci bag? Yes, of course. In a sense, duty-free shops are the precursor to what life will be like in a genuinely borderless environment. Customer pull, shaped

If you were in a duty-free shop, which would you choose: a six-pack of Coke or a Gucci bag?

by images and information from around the world, determine your product choices. You want the designer handbag or the sneakers by Reebok, which are made in Korea and sold at three times the price of equivalent no-brand sneakers. And there are others like you in every corner of the Triad.

At bottom, the choice to buy Gucci or Reebok is a choice about fashion. And the information that shapes fashion-driven choices is different in kind from the information that shapes choices about commodity products. When you walk into the 7-Elevens of the world and look for a bottle of cola, the one you

Think of the world as a giant duty-free shop.

BORDERLESS WORLD

pick depends on its location on the shelf, its price, or perhaps the special in-store promotion going on at the moment. In other words, your preference is shaped by the effects of the cola company's complete business system in that country.

Now, to be sure, the quality of that business system will depend to some extent on the company's ability to leverage skills developed elsewhere or to exploit synergies with other parts of its operations — marketing competence, for example, or economies of scale in the production of concentrates. Even so, your choice as a consumer rests on the power with which all such functional strengths have been brought to bear in your particular local market – that is, on the company's ability to become a full-fledged insider in that local market.

With fashion-based items, where the price is relatively high and the purchase frequency low, insiderization does not matter all that much. With commodity items, however, where the price is low and the frequency of purchase high, the insiderization of functional skills is all-important. There is simply no way to be successful around the world with this latter category of products without replicating your business system in each key market.

Coke has 70% of the Japanese market for soft drinks. The reason is that Coke took the time and made the investments to build up a full range of local functional strengths, particularly in its route sales force and franchised vending machines. It is, after all, the Coke van or truck that replaces empty bottles with new ones, not the trucks of independent wholesalers or distributors. When Coke first moved into Japan, it did not understand the complex, many-layered distribution system for such products. So it used the capital of local bottlers to re-create the kind of sales force it has used so well in the United States. This represented a heavy, front-end, fixed investment, but it has paid off handsomely. Coke redefined the domestic game in Japan – and it did so, not from a distance, but with a deliberate "insiderization" of functional strengths. Once this sales force is in place, for example, once the company has become a full-fledged insider, it can move not only soft drinks but also fruit juice, sport drinks, vitamin drinks, and canned coffee through the same sales network. It can sell pretty much whatever it wants to. For Coke's competitors, foreign and domestic, the millions of dollars they are spending on advertising are like little droplets of water sprinkled over a desert. Nothing is going to bloom – at least, not if that is all they do. Not if they fail to build up their own distinctive "insider" strengths.

When global success rests on market-by-market functional strength, you have to play a series of domestic games against well-defined competitors. If the market requires a first-class sales force, you simply have to have one. If competition turns on dealer support programs, that's where you have to excel. Some occasions *do* exist when doing more better is the right, the necessary, course to follow. Still, there are usually opportunities to redefine these domestic games to your own advantage. Companies that fail to establish a strong insider position tend to mix up the strategies followed by the Cokes and the Guccis. The managers of many leading branded-goods companies are often loud in their complaints about how the Japanese market is closed to their products. Or, more mysteriously, about the inexplicable refusal of Japanese consumers to buy their products when they are obviously better than those of any competitor anywhere in the world. Instead of making the effort to understand Japanese distribution and Japanese consumers, they assume that something is wrong with the Japanese market. Instead of spending time in their plants and offices or on the ground in Japan, they spend time in Washington.

Not everyone, of course. There are plenty of branded-goods companies that *are* very well represented on the Japanese retailing scene – Coke, to be sure, but also Nestlé, Schick, Wella, Vicks, Scott, Del Monte, Kraft, Campbell, Unilever (its Timotei shampoo is number one in Japan), Twinings, Kellogg, Borden, Ragu', Oscar Mayer, Hershey, and a host of others. These have all become household names in Japan. They have all become insiders.

> ▌ When things go really well – or very badly – misplaced home-country reflexes start to intervene.

For industrial products companies, becoming an insider often poses a different set of challenges. Because these products are chosen largely on the basis of their performance characteristics, if they cut costs or boost productivity, they stand a fair chance of being accepted anywhere in the world. Even so, however, these machines do not operate in a vacuum. Their success may have to wait until the companies that make them have developed a full range of insider functions – engineering, sales, installation, finance, service, and so on. So, as these factors become more critical, it often makes sense for the companies to link up with local operations that already have these functions in place.

Financial services have their own special characteristics. Product globalization already takes place at the institutional investor level but much less so at the retail level. Still, many retail products now originate overseas, and the money collected from them is often invested across national borders. Indeed, foreign exchange, stock markets, and other trading facilities have already made money a legitimately global product.

In all these categories, then, as distinct from premium fashion-driven products like Gucci bags, insiderization in key markets is the route to global success. Yes, some top-of-the-line tastes and preferences have become common across the Triad. In many other cases, however, creating a global product means building the capability to understand and respond to customer needs and business system requirements in each critical market.

The Headquarters Mentality

By all reasonable measures, Coke's experience in Japan has been a happy one. More often than not, however, the path it took to insiderization – replicating a home-country business system in a new national market – creates many more problems than it solves. Managers back at headquarters, who have had experience with only one way to succeed, are commonly inclined to force that model on each new opportunity that arises. Of course, sometimes it will work. Sometimes it will be exactly the right answer. But chances are that the home-country reflex, the impulse to generalize globally from a sample of one, will lead efforts astray.

In the pharmaceutical industry, for example, Coke's approach would not work. Foreign entrants simply have to find ways to adapt to the Japanese distribution system. Local doctors will not accept or respond favorably to an American-style sales force. When the doctor asks a local detail man to take a moment and photocopy some articles for him, he has to be willing to run the errands. No ifs, ands, or buts.

One common problem with insiderization, then, is a misplaced home-country reflex. Another, perhaps more subtle, problem is what happens back at headquarters after initial operations in another market really start paying off. When this happens, in most companies everyone at home starts to pay close attention. Without really understanding why things have turned out as well as they have, managers at headquarters take an increasing interest in what is going on in Japan or wherever it happens to be.

Functionaries of all stripes itch to intervene. Corporate heavyweights decide they had better get into the act, monitor key decisions, ask for timely reports, take extensive tours of local activities. Every power-that-be wants a say in what has become a critical portion of the overall company's operations. When minor difficulties arise, no one is willing to let local managers continue to handle things themselves. Corporate jets fill the skies with impatient satraps eager to set things right.

We know perfectly well where all this is likely to lead. A cosmetics company, with a once enviable position in Japan, went through a series of management shake-ups at home. As a result, the Japanese operation, which had grown progressively more important, was no longer able to enjoy the rough autonomy that made its success possible. Several times, eager U.S. hands reached in to change the head of activities in Japan, and crisp memos and phone calls kept up a steady barrage of challenges to the unlucky soul who happened to be in the hot seat at the moment. Relations became antagonistic, profits fell, the intervention grew worse, and the whole thing just fell apart. Overeager and overanxious managers back at headquarters did not have the patience to learn what really worked in the Japanese market. By trying to supervise things in the regular "corporate" fashion, they destroyed a very profitable business.

This is an all-too-familiar pattern. With dizzying regularity, the local top manager changes from a Japanese national to a foreigner, to a Japanese, to a foreigner. Impatient, headquarters keeps fitfully searching for a never-never ideal "person on the spot." Persistence and perseverance are the keys to long-term survival and success. Everyone knows it. But headquarters is just not able to wait for a few years until local managers – of whatever nationality – build up the needed rapport with vendors, employees, distributors, and customers. And if, by a miracle, they do, then headquarters is likely to see them as having become too "Japanized" to represent

> **Most global companies expect comparable levels of return from every market.**

their interests abroad. They are no longer "one of us." If they do not, then obviously they have failed to win local acceptance.

This headquarters mentality is not just a problem of bad attitude or misguided enthusiasm. Too bad, because these would be relatively easy to fix. Instead, it rests on – and is reinforced by – a company's entrenched systems, structures, and behaviors. Dividend payout ratios, for example, vary from country to country. But most global companies find it hard to ac-

BORDERLESS WORLD

cept low or no payout from investment in Japan, medium returns from Germany, and larger returns from the United States. The usual wish is to get comparable levels of return from all activities, and internal benchmarks of performance reflect that wish. This is trouble waiting to happen. Looking for 15% ROI a year from new commitments in Japan is going to sour a company on Japan very quickly. The companies that have done the best there – the Coca-Colas and the IBMs – were willing to adjust their conventional expectations and settle in for the long term.

Or, for example, when top managers rely heavily on financial statements, they can easily lose sight of the value of operating globally – because these statements usually mask the performance of activities outside the home country. Accounting and reporting systems that are parent-company dominated – and remember, genuinely consolidated statements are still the exception, not the rule – merely confirm the lukewarm commitment of many managers to global competition. They may talk a lot about doing business globally, but it is just lip service. It sounds nice, and it may convince the business press to write glowing stories, but when things get tough, most of the talk turns out to be only talk.

Take a closer look at what actually happens. If a divisionalized Japanese company like Matsushita or Toshiba wants to build a plant to make widgets in Tennessee, the home-country division manager responsible for widgets often finds himself in a tough position. No doubt, the CEO will tell him to get that Tennessee facility up and running as soon as possible. But the division manager knows that, when the plant does come on-stream, his own operations are going to look worse on paper. At a minimum, his division is not going to get credit for American sales that he used to make by export from Japan. Those are now going to come out of Tennessee. The CEO tells him to collaborate, to help out, but he is afraid that the better the job he does, the worse it will be for him – and with good reason!

This is crazy. Why not change company systems? Have the Tennessee plant report directly to him, and consolidate all widget-making activities at the divisional level. Easier said than done. Most companies use accounting systems that consolidate at the corporate, not the divisional, level. That's traditional corporate practice. And every staff person since the time of Homer comes fully equipped with a thousand reasons not to make exceptions to time-honored institutional procedures. As a result, the division manager is going to drag his feet. The moment Tennessee comes on-line, he sees his numbers go down, he has to lay off people, and he has to worry about excess capacity. Who is going to remember his fine efforts in getting

Tennessee started up? More to the point, who is going to care – when his Japanese numbers look so bad?

If you want to operate globally, you have to think and act globally, and that means challenging entrenched systems that work against collaborative efforts. Say our widget maker has a change of heart and goes to a division-level consolidation of accounts. This helps, but the problems are just beginning. The American managers of a sister division that uses these widgets look at the Tennessee plant as just another vendor, perhaps even a troublesome one because it is new and not entirely reliable. Their inclination is to treat the new plant as a problem, ignore it if possible, and to continue to buy from Japan where quality is high and delivery guaranteed. They are not going to do anything to help the new plant come on-stream or to plan for long-term capital investment. They are not going to supply technical assistance or design help or anything. All it represents is fairly unattractive marginal capacity.

If we solve this problem by having the plant head report to the division manager, then we are back where we started. If we do nothing, then this new plant is just going to struggle along. Clearly, what we need is to move toward a system of double counting of credits – so that both the American manager *and* the division head in Japan have strong reasons to make the new facility work. But this runs afoul of our entrenched systems, and they are very hard to change. If our commitment to acting globally is not terribly strong, we are not going to be inclined to make the painful efforts needed to make it work.

Under normal circumstances, these kinds of entrepreneurial decisions are hard enough to reach anyway. It is no surprise that many of the most globally

---

▌ Too many entrenched systems work against collaborative efforts.

---

successful Japanese companies – Honda, Sony, Matsushita, Canon, and the like – have been led by a strong owner-founder for at least a decade. They can override bureaucratic inertia; they can tear down institutional barriers. In practice, the managerial decision to tackle wrenching organizational and systems changes is made even more difficult by the way in which problems become visible. Usually, a global systems problem first comes into view in the form of explicitly local symptoms. Rarely do global problems show up where the real underlying causes are.

Troubled CEOs may say that their Japanese operations are not doing well, that the money being spent on advertising is just not paying off as expected. They will not say that their problems are really back at headquarters with its superficial understanding of what it takes to market effectively in Japan. They will not say that it lies in the design of their financial reporting systems. They will not say that it is part and parcel of their own reluctance to make long-term, front-end capital investments in new markets. They will not say that it lies in their failure to do well the central job of any headquarters operation: the development of good people at the local level. Or at least they are not likely to. They will diagnose the problems as local problems and try to fix them.

Thinking Global

Top managers are always slow to point the finger of responsibility at headquarters or at themselves. When global faults have local symptoms, they will be slower still. When taking corrective action means a full, zero-based review of all systems, skills, and structures, their speed will decrease even further. And when their commitment to acting globally is itself far from complete, it is a wonder there is any motion at all. Headquarters mentality is the prime expression of managerial nearsightedness, the sworn enemy of a genuinely equidistant perspective on global markets.

In the early days of global business, experts like Raymond Vernon of the Harvard Business School proposed, in effect, a United Nations model of globalization. Companies with aspirations to diversify and expand throughout the Triad were to do so by cloning the parent company in each new country of operation. If successful, they would create a mini-U.N. of clonelike subsidiaries repatriating profits to the parent company, which remained the dominant force at the center. We know that successful companies enter fewer countries but penetrate each of them more

> Customer needs have globalized, and we must globalize to meet them.

deeply. That is why this model gave way by the early 1980s to a competitor-focused approach to globalization. By this logic, if we were a European producer of medical electronics equipment, we had to take on General Electric in the United States so that it would not come over here and attack us on our home ground. Today, however, the pressure for globalization is driven not so much by diversification or competition as by the needs and preferences of customers. Their needs have globalized, and the fixed costs of meeting them have soared. That is why we must globalize.

Managing effectively in this new borderless environment does not mean building pyramids of cash flow by focusing on the discovery of new places to invest. Nor does it mean tracking your competitors to their lair and preemptively undercutting them in their own home market. Nor does it mean blindly trying to replicate home-country business systems in new colonial territories. Instead, it means paying central attention to delivering value to customers – and to developing an equidistant view of who they are and what they want. Before everything else comes the need to see your customers clearly. They – and only they – can provide legitimate reasons for thinking global. ☡

Reprint 89312

[3]

Journal of International Business Studies (2003) 34, 138–152
© 2003 Palgrave Macmillan Ltd. All rights reserved 0047-2506 $25.00
www.jibs.net

Semiglobalization and international business strategy

Pankaj Ghemawat

Harvard Business School, Boston, MA, USA

Correspondence:
Dr P Ghemawat, Harvard Business School,
Soldiers Field Road, Morgan Hall 227,
Boston, MA 02163, USA.
Tel: +1-617-495-6275;
Fax: +1-617-495-0355;
E-mail: pghemawat@hbs.edu

Abstract
If markets were either completely isolated by or integrated across borders, there would be little room for international business strategy to have content distinctive from 'mainstream' strategy. But a review of the economic evidence about the international integration of markets indicates that we fall in between these extremes, into a state of incomplete cross-border integration that I refer to as semiglobalization. More specifically, most measures of market integration have scaled new heights in the last few decades, but still fall far short of economic theory's ideal of perfect integration. The diagnosis of semiglobalization does more than just supply a relatively stable frame of reference for thinking about the environment of cross-border operations. It also calls attention to the critical role of location-specificity in the prospects of distinctive content for international business strategy relative to mainstream business and corporate strategy. In addition, it flags factors/products subject to location-specificity as being salient from the perspective of international business. Finally, it highlights the scope for strategies that strive to capitalize on the (large) residual barriers to cross-border integration, as well as those that simply try to cope with them.
Journal of International Business Studies (2003) 34, 138–152. doi:10.1057/palgrave.jibs.8400013

Keywords: semiglobalization; globalization market integrations; market inperfections; location/location-specificity; firm strategy

Introduction

The first of the three postulates on which Buckley and Casson (1976, 32) based their theory of the multinational enterprise was that 'firms maximize profit in a world of imperfect markets.' This structural insight has proved as fruitful in international business strategy as it has in 'mainstream' (single-country) business strategy, where it has been in circulation for even longer. What is somewhat odd, however, is that work in this vein in international business strategy has tended to focus on the same sources of market imperfections as mainstream business strategy: small numbers and, often related, the *business/usage-specificity* of key activities, resources, competencies, capabilities, knowledge, etc., or their *firm-specificity* in the sense of being collectively held by the firm's managerial hierarchy or employee pool and inalienable from it. However, the obvious potential source of market imperfections added by the international dimension – the possibly limited cross-border integration of markets or, more generally, the possible *location-specificity* of key activities, resources, etc. – has received less attention. Location-specificity of the specific sort wrought by

Received: September 2001
Revised: June 2002
Accepted: August 2002
Online publication date: 27 March 2003

market segmentation at national boundaries is at the core of this paper.[1]

This paper consists of two halves. The first half contains a broad – and therefore inevitably compressed – review of the empirical evidence on the cross-border integration of markets of different types: for products (via both trade and FDI), capital, labor, and knowledge. The review points to the conclusions that, on the one hand, the observed levels of cross-border integration of these types of markets are significant and in many cases have recently reached highs without historical precedent, but that, on the other hand, the observed levels of cross-border integration are also very far from complete and, extrapolating from historical rates of increase (not to mention recent setbacks), are likely to remain that way for a long time. This condition of incomplete cross-border integration, referred to here as *semiglobalization*, is more complex than the extremes of total insulation and total integration because it involves situations in which the barriers to market integration at borders are high, but not high enough to insulate countries completely from each other. Another way of putting this is that semiglobalization covers the range – apparently broad as well as complex – of situations in which neither the barriers nor the links among markets in different countries can be neglected.

The second half of this paper can be read as a short essay on the implications of the empirical finding of semi-globalization for international business strategy. It begins by noting that semigloblization is a sufficient condition for location-specificity to matter. Although complete market insulation also suffices, it is a less challenging condition since, under it, international business strategy could simply be chunked up into applications of mainstream (that is, single-location) strategy, performed location by location – although some problems of coordination would still remain. Thus semi-globlalization is the underlying structural condition most conducive to thinking in careful ways about competing across multiple locations and how that might differ from competing at a single location. The essay elaborates on this and other, more specific, implications of the general diagnosis of semi-globalization. It discusses the balance to be struck in international business strategy between attention to location-specificity and other types of-specificity, and examines the conditions under which imperfections in particular types of market (especially knowledge, which was emphasized by Buckley and Casson, 1976) should

be granted elevated status. Finally, the essay highlights the scope for strategies that strive to capitalize on the (large) residual barriers to cross-border integration, as well as those that simply try to cope with such barriers. The treatment is meant as much to stimulate and direct further research as to summarize research efforts to date.

It is worth adding that the first half of this paper – the next two sections – focuses on reviewing the economic evidence about the cross-border integration of markets of different types. The economic perspective is adopted because economics offers both a relatively well-developed conceptual framework for the analysis of market integration and some empirical basis for making judgments about levels of and changes in cross-border integration of the kinds that occupy its attention. Thus the next section of this paper looks at the cross-border integration of product markets, and the section that follows at markets for various types of resource or factor – capital, labor, and knowledge. The questions asked about each type of market concern changes in its level of international integration, measured in terms of quantity and price outcomes, over recent decades or the course of the 20th century, as well as its absolute level of international integration at the millennium. For a more specific delineation of what is included in and excluded from the review, see Table 1. While there is arguably a logic to the pattern of inclusions and exclusions, the more fundamental point is simply that one cannot talk about everything in Table 1 in a paper of this scope.

Product market integration

This section begins by looking at the most obvious quantity measure of the cross-border integration of

Table I Dimensions of integration

Dimension	Possible emphases		
Criteria for evaluating integration	Economic	Non-economic	
Key boundaries	Countries	Others Continents/regions Localities	
Locus of integration	Markets	Others Firms Networks	
Type of markets	Products	Factors	
Input/output emphasis	Outcomes	Drivers	
Outcome variables	Quantities	Prices	

Dark shading = primary emphasis. Gray shading = secondary emphasis.

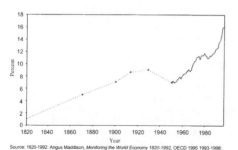

Source: 1820-1992: Angus Maddison, *Monitoring the World Economy 1820-1992*, OECD 1995 1993-1998: World Trade Organization and International Monetary Fund data.

Figure 1 Exports divided by GDP. *Source*: 1820–1992, Maddison (1995); 1993–1998, World Trade Organization and International Monetary Fund data.

product markets: trade flows. It then looks at foreign direct investment (FDI) stocks and, finally and very briefly, at cross-border price integration.

Trade flows

To begin with a very long-run perspective, consider data on world exports divided by world GDP (the usual normalization) over the last two centuries based on and updated from data in Maddison (1995). As Figure 1 indicates, this ratio increased from about 1% at the beginning of the 19th century to nearly 10% towards the beginning of the 20th century, and, despite a period of stagnation and decline bounded by the two World Wars, has since managed to edge up towards 20%. Trade intensity has clearly reached new heights in the last quarter of the 20th century.

The increase in trade intensity over the course of the 20th century looks all the more remarkable when one accounts for the increasing share of GDP contributed, especially in developed countries, by two sectors that account for relatively little trade – services and government. One way of stripping out the effects of these 'non-traded' sectors is to remove them from the calculations and focus on the ratio of merchandise trade to merchandise value added. This leads to striking increases in measured trade exposure, as illustrated by Feenstra's (1998) sample of 11 relatively developed countries between 1913 and 1990. Over this period, the ratio of merchandise trade to merchandise value added increased for nine of these countries; the median change was +22 percentage points, compared with an initial median value of 36%, and total unweighted increases were close to 20 times as large as total unweighted decreases. The corresponding statistics

for the ratio of merchandise trade to *total* GDP are increases for only six of the 11 countries, a median change of +2 percentage points from an initial median value of 20%, and total unweighted increases less than one-half as large as total unweighted decreases.

One interpretation of the historical patterns is that:

(1) trade had taken off in many commodities by the beginning of the 20th century;
(2) there were substantial increases in the trade of manufactures over the course of the 20th century, particularly its second half; and
(3) the service sector continues to be a very large bottleneck for trade-related flows even though it is growing.

Irwin's (1996) comparison of the composition of US merchandise trade over a century is suggestive in this regard: see Table 2. While this neat ordering of the globalization of commodities, manufactures and services is obviously an oversimplification, it is nevertheless useful.

So trade has clearly increased over the last 50, 100 and 200 years. But it is useful to supplement this observation with some data about the absolute level of integration of product markets through trade. Economists who study international trade generally do not regard trade intensity as very high in absolute terms. In fact, they tend to find the issue of why there is not much more trade more interesting than the new records being set. To see the room for increase, consider a hypothetical benchmark, suggested by Frankel (2001), in which national borders did not affect buying patterns at all. In such a situation, buyers in a particular nation

Table 2 Commodity composition of US merchandise trade

Year	Percentage distribution	
	Exports	Imports
Agricultural goods		
1890	42.2	33.1
1990	11.5	5.6
Raw materials		
1890	36.6	22.8
1990	11.6	14.8
Manufactures		
1890	21.2	44.1
1990	77.0	79.6

Figures may not total to 100 due to rounding. Agricultural goods includes processed foods. *Source*: Irwin (1996).

Semiglobalization and international business strategy   Pankaj Ghemawat

141

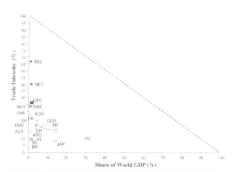

Sources: GNP Rankings based World Development Bank's World Development Indicators. 2000.Import/Export Data from WTO.

Figure 2   Actual *vs* perfect product market integration through trade.

would be as prone to obtain goods and services from foreign producers as from domestic ones, and the share of imports in total domestic consumption would equal 1 minus the nation's share of world product. For example, as the US economy accounts for about one-quarter of gross world product, the US import/GDP ratio would, at this benchmark, equal 1 minus the US share of world production, or 0.75, as would, under the first-order assumption of balanced trade, the US export/GDP ratio. However, the actual ratios are only about one-sixth as large as these hypothetical levels![2]

The line with slope −1 in Figure 2 traces out this hypothetical benchmark of perfect product market integration as national shares of world product vary. It also plots the position of the 20 largest nations in these terms. Notice that most of the nations cluster close to the origin, and all fall well below the hypothetical maximum – including the two high-fliers, Belgium and the Netherlands.

While the hypothetical benchmark suggests significant barriers to cross-border product flows, it also embodies a number of extreme assumptions. A real example that points in the same direction is provided by Canadian provinces' patterns of trade with each other compared with their trade with the USA. In addition to the fact that data for these patterns are available, they have the added advantage of involving (international) trading partners that are close to each other along a number of dimensions. As of 1988, trade linkages between Canadian provinces were 20 times as large as their linkages with the 30 US states that traded the most intensively with Canada. This was true despite the fact that Canada and the USA share a common land

border and language (mostly) and have friendly relations with each other, making theirs the largest bilateral trading relationship in the world (McCallum, 1995). The free trade agreement signed in 1988 between the two countries did reduce this domestic multiple by the mid-1990s, but only to 12 (and with the multiple remaining stuck at 30–40 in the case of services) (Helliwell, 1998, Chapter 2). Cruder data suggest a multiple of about six for trade within as opposed to between the member states of the European Union (Helliwell, 1998, Chapter 3). Given the regionalization of world trade that has been under way, the multiples of domestic-to-international economic exchange would obviously be higher if one were comparing trade within countries with trade outside the regional blocs to which they belong.

To sum up, trade intensity has clearly reached unprecedented levels, but still reveals significant impediments to the cross-border integration of product markets.

Foreign direct investment

Trade is not the only way in which the cross-border integration of product markets might be accomplished: FDI, which involves product-specific investment across borders, is an obvious alternative. To start with a long-run perspective, consider data on FDI stocks divided by GDP over the last century based on calculations in *World Investment Reports* issued by the UN Center on Transnational Corporations. As Table 3 indicates, FDI survived the interwar years better than trade (it even came to substitute for the latter as tariff barriers rose), but did not take off again quite as rapidly in the immediate postwar years. FDI has surged, however, since 1980 and, by 1997, had come to exceed the previous (prewar) peak in its share of gross world GDP by a significant margin: 12% to 9%. Despite the declines in the ratio of outward FDI stock to GDP exhibited by the UK and France, the largest foreign investors prior to World War I, the aggregate comparison is suggestive of an increase to unprecedented levels. In sectoral terms, FDI has mirrored trade over this time period by shifting away from natural resources and raw materials (the 'primary' sector) towards manufacturing and, more recently, services.

Obviously, such historical comparisons come with some caveats. For one thing, they are affected in important ways by fundamental shifts in relative exchange rates (and purchasing power). For another, they are based on book values rather than

Table 3 Outward FDI stock as a percentage of GDP

	1914	1938	1960	1980	1985	1990	1995	1997
France	21.1	27.8	6.8	2.7	6.0	9.2	12.0	13.6
Germany	11.1	0.8	1.1	5.3	9.7	9.2	11.1	14.4
Japan	0.8	9.9	1.2	1.9	3.3	6.9	4.7	6.5
UK	52.3	38.5	15.0	15.0	21.9	23.8	28.3	29.1
USA	7.2	8.5	6.2	8.1	6.2	7.9	10.0	10.6
World	9.0[a]	—	4.4	4.8	6.4	8.5[b]	—	11.8

[a]1913 data. [b]1991 data.
Figure for 1913 is an estimate. *Sources*: 1913–1991, World Investment Report 1994; 1997, World Investment Report 1999.

on market values of FDI. The magnitude of this omission seems to be large: data compiled by the US Commerce Department suggest that measurement on the basis of market values rather than book values doubles the estimated values of both US FDI abroad and FDI in the USA. One could argue that this omission leads to greater underestimation of the true values of FDI stocks towards the end of the 20th century than towards its beginning, because of higher inflation rates (until relatively recently) in the modern period and the increased importance of intangible assets that are more prone to slip through accountants' nets.

Once again, it is useful to look at the current level of integration of product markets through this channel in absolute terms, not just in relation to the levels experienced earlier. Assume, as in the analogous calculation undertaken earlier for trade, that inflows/outflows are, to a first approximation, balanced, and consider a country that accounts for $x\%$ of world investment. Then, if national borders did not affect investment patterns at all, foreign capital would account for $(100-x)\%$ of total investment in that country. The line with slope -1 in Figure 3 traces out this hypothetical benchmark of perfect integration as a function of national shares of gross fixed investment (x). It also plots the position of the 20 largest nations in these terms, based on their recorded FDI inflows. As in the case of trade, most of the nations cluster close to the origin, and all fall well below the hypothetical maximum. Also note that this broad conclusion would not be affected by looking at FDI outflows, although the positions of individual countries would shift substantially. China, for instance, would be less of a high-flier.

Overall, FDI intensity has, like trade intensity, reached unprecedented levels while continuing to fall far short of the levels that would be implied by

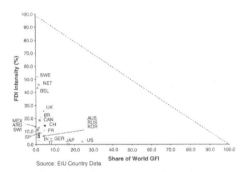

Figure 3 Actual *vs* perfect product market integration through FDI. *Source*: EIU country data.

perfect cross-border integration of product markets through this channel.

Price integration
Viewed in terms of prices rather than quantities, the ultimate in market integration is achieved when two (or more) markets are yoked together by the so-called *law of one price* (LOP) – that is, prices equalize across them. Implicit in LOP is a (strong) zero-arbitrage-profits principle. Note that the degree of price integration of product markets can be high even when the quantity flows across them are limited – for example, for some commodities whose local prices are pegged to world benchmark prices, including ones with high value-to-weight ratios. As a result, economists often treat tests of market integration based on prices as being more definitive than tests based on quantities.

Quantity-based tests of cross-border market integration predominate, nonetheless, because, except for (nearly) perfect commodities, tests of price integration are generally hampered by the lack of data on local currency prices of identical products across countries. The relatively few studies of products and services that meet these objections generally indicate substantial, sustained departures from LOP. Cross-country price dispersions tend to be large and to die down at a slow pace, and there is little evidence of recent movement toward smaller dispersions or speedier dampening (Rogoff, 1996). In conjunction with the data presented earlier concerning integration through trade and FDI flows, an overall inference that product market integration has increased significantly in recent decades, while continuing to fall far short of perfection, seems most plausible.

Factor market integration
Product markets are not the only type of market whose cross-border integration one might find interesting; factor markets of various types are also candidates for attention. This section presents and discusses evidence on the extent of cross-border integration of markets for capital, labor, and knowledge, in that order. Both quantity-based and price-based measures of integration are looked at wherever possible.

Capital
The previous section's discussion of FDI can be broadened to look at international capital flows over the last 100 years.[3] Because of identities in national income accounting, countries' net capital flows can be measured as the reverse of their current account balances. Data assembled by Obstfeld and Taylor (1997) on absolute net capital flows divided by GDPs for 12 countries suggest that this index of capital mobility has increased in

recent decades, but was higher still around the beginning of the 20th century (see Table 4). Note that the impressive performance 100 years ago was accomplished in spite of informational and contracting problems. Such problems were, most likely, much more severe given the lack of generally accepted accounting principles and commensurately weak reporting requirements.

Of course, not all capital flows are equally important from the perspective of economic globalization. In particular, the recent period has seen a surge in short-run flows, or at least transactions, that is most strikingly evident in the volume of foreign exchange transactions, which exceeds $1 trillion *daily*. Foreign exchange trading can, however, be regarded as a response to a source of volatility – exchange rate risk – that was mitigated significantly in the earlier period by the prevalence of the gold standard. For this reason, and because most trades of this sort seem to be purely speculative, it is problematic to use the size of foreign exchange markets today to infer a much greater level of cross-border integration of capital markets than at the beginning of the century.

This suggests focusing attention on long-run capital flows, which include portfolio investment as well as FDI. Portfolio investment has increased significantly in absolute terms in recent decades, but seems to have failed to keep pace with FDI, with its share slipping from about two-thirds of total long-run cross-border investment in the early 20th century to about one-half today (Bloomfield, 1968). Nevertheless, the range of securities traded today across borders is much broader, in type as well as in number – a shift that, some argue, has contributed to increased cross-border integration along this dimension.

Table 4 Size of net capital flows since 1870 (mean absolute value of current account as percentage of GDP, annual data)

Period	Arg	Aus	Can	Den	Fra	Ger	Ita	Jap	Nor	Swe	UK	USA	All
1870–1889	18.7	8.2	7.0	1.9	2.4	1.7	1.2	0.6	1.6	3.2	4.6	0.7	3.7
1890–1913	6.2	4.1	7.0	2.9	1.3	1.5	1.8	2.4	4.2	2.3	4.6	1.0	3.3
1914–1918	2.7	3.4	3.6	5.1	—	—	11.6	6.8	3.8	6.5	3.1	4.1	5.1[a]
1919–1926	4.9	4.2	2.5	1.2	2.8	2.4	4.2	2.1	4.9	2.0	2.7	1.7	3.1
1927–1931	3.7	5.9	2.7	0.7	1.4	2.0	1.5	0.6	2.0	1.8	1.9	0.7	2.1
1932–1939	1.6	1.7	2.6	0.8	1.0	0.6	0.7	1.0	1.1	1.5	1.1	0.4	1.2
1940–1946	4.8	3.5	3.3	2.3	—	—	3.4	1.0	4.9	2.0	7.2	1.1	3.2[a]
1947–1959	2.3	3.4	2.3	1.4	1.5	2.0	1.4	1.3	3.1	1.1	1.2	0.6	1.8
1960–1973	1.0	2.3	1.2	1.9	0.6	1.0	2.1	1.0	2.4	0.7	0.8	0.5	1.3
1974–1989	1.9	3.6	1.7	3.2	0.8	2.1	1.3	1.8	5.2	1.5	1.5	1.4	2.2
1989–1996	2.0	4.5	4.0	1.8	0.7	2.7	1.6	2.1	2.9	2.0	2.6	1.2	2.3

Source: Obstfeld and Taylor (1997).
a: Average with some countries missing.

International financial crises represent the flip side of international capital mobility. Once again, historical comparisons suggest that international financial crises, particularly in emerging markets, are not without precedent. Thus data on the currency and banking crises experienced by 21 countries between 1880 and 1998 indicate that the most severe crises, on average, were in the interwar period, followed by the prewar period; postwar crises, in contrast, have been milder in terms of the drops in output experienced, and shorter-lived (Bordo *et al.*, 1999). And even when the sample is restricted to emerging countries, recent levels of instability do no worse than 'match' prewar levels, in which the gold standard acted as a crisis transmission belt, and emerging countries, at least, tended to lack lenders of last resort.[4]

In addition to these historical comparisons, quantity-based measures also permit some inferences about the absolute level of cross-border integration of capital markets. As in the case of trade, the professional curiosity of economists has focused on smaller-than-expected flows (or stocks). Probably the most famous 'anomaly' of this sort is the one uncovered by Feldstein and Horioka (1980), who calculated a 90% correlation between domestic savings and domestic investment across a panel of countries. Their estimate is much higher than benchmark models that assume perfect capital mobility would lead us to expect. Another anomaly that points in the same direction concerns what is called home-country bias: investors in each country hold much larger proportions of their wealth in the form of domestic securities than they would with internationally well-diversified portfolios. Thus, by one estimate, US investors should have held more than half their wealth in foreign equities in the 1980s, instead of the less than 10% that they actually held (Lewis, 1995).

Price-based measures of capital market integration – with price integration reinterpreted in terms of the equalization of rates of return on common or comparable securities across national boundaries – supply additional evidence about the continued segmentation of capital markets. One benchmark example is provided by Obstfeld and Taylor's (1997) comparison of 1-year interest rates on sterling-denominated assets sold in London and in New York over the last 100-plus years. Figure 4 tracks the standard deviation of differences in returns in the two cities as an inverse measure of capital market integration. The data indicate significant cross-border integration of capital markets

prior to 1914, the breakdown of that integration in the interwar period, and its slow restoration in the postwar period. Qualitatively similar conclusions are suggested by comparing real rather than nominal returns, although that does increase the standard deviation of the dispersion of returns, presumably reflecting the effects of currency risk, both nominal and real.[5] At a more macro level, studies of returns, such as Bekaert and Harvey (1995), indicate that the cointegration of capital markets varies greatly in its level and extent over time.

Overall, like product market integration, capital market integration has increased significantly in recent decades, but seems to continue to fall far short of perfection.

Labor

Data on the cross-border integration of labor markets are sparser than for product or capital markets. However, they generally suggest that the number of international migrants (defined as people residing in foreign countries for more than 1 year) has grown with world population in recent decades, but represents a smaller share of world population than 100 years ago. With regard to the first point, there were, according to the World Migration Report, an estimated 150 million long-term international migrants in 2000, or 2.5% of world population (Martin, 2000). The comparable numbers for 1965 were 75 million migrants and 2.2% of world population.

Over a longer time frame, the period between 1880 and 1915/1920 stands out as the heyday of international migration. During these years, 32 million people migrated from Europe, most of them to the USA (Kenwood and Lougheed, 1989). In addition, there were 6–8 million net migrants – mostly 'coolie' or indentured labor – from India,

Source: Maurice Obstfeld and Alan Taylor, "The Great Depression As A Watershed: International Capital Mobility Over the Long Run," NBER Working Paper 5960, March 1997.

Figure 4 Standard deviation of nominal return differentials. *Source*: Obstfeld and Taylor (1997).

Semiglobalization and international business strategy   Pankaj Ghemawat

145

China, and other Asian countries to the rest of the world (Held *et al.*, 1999, 293–295, 311). Adding in other cross-border movements could push the total past 45 million, or 3% of world population in 1900. Higher migration rates 100 years ago are also evident in country-level data – for example, for the largest receiver, the USA. Thus census data indicate that 14% of the US population was foreign-born at the turn of the century, compared with 10% today (Dune, 2001). Note that, through a substantial part of the earlier period, a number of large receivers, including the USA, placed no restrictions on immigration.

Turning from quantity-based to price-based measures, the most obvious indicator of cross-border integration of labor markets would be the cross-border convergence of wages. Data on the evolution of average per capita incomes (a rough and ready proxy for average wages) indicate that, while incomes in industrialized countries have tended to converge over the last few decades, a few Asian 'tigers' have been the only countries able to break away from the rest of the developing world and catch up with the industrialized world (see Figure 5).[6] More sophisticated tests confirm this conclusion, and indicate that the failure of most developing countries to catch up can be reconciled only with a weaker notion of convergence – *conditional convergence* (Barro and Sala-i-Martin, 1995). Conditional convergence allows for differences in the steady-state incomes toward which different economies are trending, based on differences along dimensions such as investment, education, and population growth. Human capital turns out, in attempts to fit conditional convergence models to the data, to have a particularly marked effect on the predicted extent of convergence.

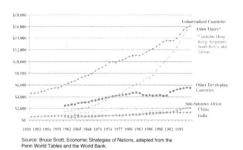

Source: Bruce Scott, Economic Strategies of Nations, adapted from the Penn World Tables and the World Bank.

Figure 5 Convergence? GDP per capita across economic groups, 1950–1997 (PPP-adjusted). *Source*: Scott (2000), adapted from the *Penn World Tables* and the World Bank).

Taking a somewhat longer view, it is worth emphasizing that the 19th century apparently saw a divergence, rather than a convergence, of incomes across countries that has been only partially reversed in the 20th century (Baldwin and Martin, 1999). So, over that kind of time frame, the dispersion of incomes across countries increased, in net terms, instead of decreasing. This, along with the other data presented in this subsection, would seem to imply skepticism about the extent to which labor markets have integrated across national boundaries.

Knowledge
The other types of cross-border flows that have been discussed already can carry knowledge across national borders as well, since it can be congealed in products, embedded in capital equipment, vested in skilled personnel, etc. Given the topics already covered in this paper, this subsection will focus on cross-border flows of knowledge in pure, disembodied form. In addition to rounding out the coverage, this focus has the advantage of offering a relatively simple benchmark: as disembodied knowledge has a 'non-rival' character – that is, as its use in one market, whether defined in geographic or product-related terms, should not preclude its application to others – perfect cross-border integration in this context should imply that knowledge, once developed anywhere in the world, is available everywhere else as well.

The conceptual simplicity of focusing on disembodied knowledge flows does, however, exact an empirical toll: because of their intrinsic intangibility, such flows are particularly hard to measure. The evidence presented in this subsection is correspondingly sketchy. It tentatively suggests, however, that there have been substantial increases in cross-border knowledge flows over time and, a bit more definitely, that cross-border integration in this regard nevertheless remains very incomplete. Consider these inferences in turn.

With regard to technological knowledge, cross-border licensing provides one indicator that supports the inference of increased cross-border knowledge flows over time. Such licensing is not new – international royalties accounted for a significant component of James Watt's receipts from his steam engine patents in the early nineteenth century, for example. However, the available data, along with informational and contracting problems that were even more acute early on than they are now, suggest that the voluntary transfer of knowledge across national borders is far more common than it used to be. Concerning more general managerial knowledge, the post-World War II period, in particular, has seen the development of new types of organizations and organizational forms that have also facilitated knowledge transfer. Franchising, which really emerged in its modern form in the USA in the 1950s, is one example. And management consulting firms, which began their international expansion at roughly the same time, are regarded as having evolved into major channels for the international diffusion of new managerial techniques (Micklethwait and Wooldridge, 2000). Of course, the spread of multinational enterprises, intent on applying the same technological and managerial knowledge to more and more markets, points in the same direction. So, arguably, does the explosion in cross-border information transmission capacity since the early 1980s.

These increases in cross-border knowledge flows notwithstanding, there are also numerous indications of the continued geographical localization of knowledge. The survey evidence on the size of knowledge transfer costs, although not altogether satisfying, is suggestive. An influential study by Teece (1977) concluded that transfer costs accounted for an average of 19% of total project costs – and ranged from 2 to 59% – in a sample of technology transfers in the chemicals, petroleum refining, and machinery sectors. Outcome-based perspectives that point in the same direction are numerous. Through the 1980s, nearly 90% of the US patents taken out by the world's 600 largest corporations listed the inventor as a resident of the corporation's 'home base' (Patel and Pavitt, 1994). Patents whose inventors reside in the same country are typically 30–80% more likely to cite each other than inventors from other countries, and, on average, these citations come 1 year sooner (Jaffe and Trajtenberg, 1999). A recent study of R&D and productivity spillovers across large OECD economies estimated the average elasticity of such spillovers with respect to distance as -1 to -2.4%

(Keller, 2000). The importance of locally dense information flows is also evident in internationally successful geographic clusters.[7] Such perspectives remind us that, although the availability of information transmission capacity may help knowledge to travel across national borders, it is far from sufficient to make knowledge perfectly portable.

Semiglobalization as a research program

In summary, most measures of cross-border economic integration have increased significantly in the last few decades, but still fall far short of the theoretical extreme of total integration. This empirical conclusion of semiglobalization is valuable in and of itself given the ongoing debate between two polar perspectives: one maintaining that we have achieved a state of (near) globality, in which there is so much integration across national borders that the latter can, for many practical purposes, be ignored, and the other professing skepticism that there is anything fundamentally new about the levels of cross-border integration that have been achieved to date (Giddens, 1996; Held *et al.*, 1999). It seems possible to achieve some closure to this debate, at least in the economic arena.

As a bonus, semiglobalization affords – unlike alternate possibilities – room for international business strategy to have content that is distinctive from 'mainstream' (single country or location) business strategy or, for that matter, corporate strategy. To make this point as precisely as possible, it is useful to classify the field of strategy into the domains depicted in Table 5. Note the somewhat paradoxical character of domain 1, mainstream business strategy: by assuming total specificity, it allots the least attention to understanding either business/usage-specificity or location-specificity. As a result, we have to look to domain 2, that of mainstream corporate strategy, for interesting analyses of variations in the extent to which key firm activities, resources or knowledge are business-

Table 5 Strategy domains

		Increasing attention to business-specificity/non-specificity	
Focus		*Single business*	*Multiple businesses*
Increasing attention to location-specificity/non-specificity	Single country/location	1. (Mainstream) business strategy	2. (Mainstream) corporate strategy
	Multiple countries/locations	3. International business strategy	4. International corporate strategy

specific as opposed to generic (fungible across businesses). And we must also look to domain 3, that of international business strategy, for analyses of variations in the extent to which activities, resources or knowledge are location-specific as opposed to free-flowing (fungible across locations). Domain 4, featuring international corporate strategy, purports to combine both business/usage-specificity and domain-specificity, but it is the one about which we currently know the least.

The key point to be made here is that semiglobalization and the location-specificity or geographic segmentation of markets implicit in it is critical to the possibility of domain 3 having content qualitatively distinct from domains 1 and 2. Begin by comparing domains 3 and 1. The critical role of semiglobalization can be illustrated by contrasting it with the extreme alternatives of markets totally insulated from each other by national boundaries or, at the opposite extreme, perfectly integrated with each other across them. Obviously, with complete market insulation, firms could simply decompose their choice problems into country-sized chunks. And if markets were completely integrated with each other, the analysis of multiple countries could, once again, be folded back to the single-country base case that is the staple of mainstream business strategy (domain 1), as there would effectively be a single large country. Situations with intermediate levels of cross-border integration cannot be dealt with in the same way, however, in that they do not lend themselves to purely country-level analysis.[8]

Next, compare domain 3 with domain 2. The role of semiglobalization or, more precisely, location-specificity in affording scope for international business strategy to have content distinctive from mainstream corporate strategy is, perhaps, subtler but no less important than in the previous case. Specifically, note that the insights into firm boundaries and expansion derived, respectively, from Coase (1937) and Penrose (1959), were not only worked into international business strategy by Buckley and Casson (1976), among others, but also into mainstream corporate strategy by, in particular, a large body of work on corporate diversification. So, although such insights have been very valuable, they do not by themselves imply content for domain 3 that is conceptually or otherwise qualitatively distinct from that of domain 2; they are a common element of both. For that, what is needed is attention to operations across multiple locations that are distinct from, but not entirely independent of, each other.

Looking more broadly across domains 1–3, Table 5 indicates that location-specificity must be invoked to distinguish domain 3 from mainstream strategy of the business and corporate varieties (domains 1 and 2). Semiglobalization ensures such location-specificity, and therefore supplies a conceptually coherent foundation for further analyses at the market and firm levels.

Market/factor-level issues

The preceding argument is equivalent, in some respects, to saying that international business strategy should pay more attention to market imperfections involving location-specificity rather than business/usage-specificity. Those who work primarily on the latter are likely to be somewhat skeptical. One frequently cited concern in this context is the argument that business/usage-specificity affords more room for firm-specific advantages (and disadvantages) than location-specificity. But given complementarities among activities, resources, etc., this argument is a bit of a red herring.

To see why, consider a stylized example in which there are two factors – knowledge, denoted by N (to avoid confusion with K for capital), and labor, denoted by L, with N entirely business/usage-specific and subject to internalization pressures as a result, and L entirely location-specific. Given complementarities between L and N, profit-maximizing firms cannot afford to ignore the labor cost differences across their various cross-border options even if their management of L itself does not offer the prospect for sustainable firm-specific advantages. In particular, if cross-border differences in the cost of L loom sufficiently large, economic viability will require either that they be capitalized on or that some powerful way of countering them be found. It is hard to see how creative thinking along either of these lines is fostered by suppressing consideration of location-specificity, even if it applies only to a 'generic' factor, L. And even if labor-cost variations cannot underpin sustained competitive advantages for the firms that exploit them because all competitors tap into them, exploitation of them may be necessary to avoid unsustainable disadvantages. The whole point of incomplete integration, after all, is that such factor price equalization will occur, if at all, only in the very long run and cannot, therefore, be assumed in decisions being made in the short-to-medium run.

Analogous points can be made in the context of K as opposed to L. Note that if capital markets were perfectly integrated, there would be one global pool of capital available to fund ventures, and decisions on whether to proceed with investments could be separated from decisions about how to finance them. Such separation of investment and financing decisions, while often assumed domestically, does not fare well in an international context. Foreign investment is, to a significant extent, financed locally in the host country. Thus Feldstein (1995) concluded that only 20% of the value of assets owned by US affiliates abroad was financed by cross-border flows of capital from the USA, with an additional 18% accounted for by retained earnings and the rest representing financing with foreign debt and equity. In such a context, it is hard to believe that MNEs allocate capital globally to equalize marginal returns on investment projects wherever they are undertaken. Instead, firms' investments in real assets seem to be affected by local financing possibilities – or wealth effects. And the impact of financial variables on real ones may be more than marginal: some major merger and acquisition waves, for example, seem to have been driven, in large part, by changes in exchange rates (e.g. Blonigen, 1997). This is just one of many areas for additional research related to semiglobalization – in this case, concerning segmented international markets for capital and how they interact with real (non-financial) variables.[9]

The broader point that emerges from this discussion is that semiglobalization or incomplete integration is often underplayed because of inadequate attention to the location-specificity of L and K on the grounds that they are generic factors of production incapable of sustaining firm-specific advantages. Capital also seems to get pulled down, as markets for it are supposed to be subject to a high degree of cross-border integration[10] and labor because it is seen to represent a 'low' basis for cross-border competition. In any case, whatever the precise reasoning, the effect is to devalue capital and labor for being relatively non-specialized factors and to focus attention on knowledge. This may seem a reasonable approach. However, recall that it is controverted by the evidence, summarized in the previous section, that markets for capital and labor, just like markets for knowledge, exhibit significant barriers to cross-border integration. As a result, even the apparently unspecialized factors of capital and labor are specialized at the level of location, if in no other sense. Thus they can assume strategic importance in an international context and should be attended to.

Having said that K and L merit more attention than they have historically attracted, it must be added that this is not necessarily inconsistent with the focus of much of the relevant literature, including Buckley and Casson (1976) early on, on knowledge, or as the key factor underlying the market imperfections that are most critical for international business. Instead, what the discussion implies in this regard is that claims of special status for N as a factor in international business strategy (domain 3 in Table 5) have to be based on the location-specificity of N. Otherwise, international business strategy and multimarket corporate strategy will be difficult to differentiate. Also note that in some cross-border contexts, at least, considerations of location-specificity do seem to dominate in knowledge-related decision making (e.g. Alcacer and Chung, 2001). Nevertheless, there would seem to be great demand for additional research on this much-discussed topic.

Firm-level issues
In addition to flagging factors/products subject to location-specificity as being salient from the perspective of international business strategy, the diagnosis of semiglobalization sheds some light on the content of such strategy at the firm (as opposed to market) level. Most broadly, semiglobalization significantly enriches the strategy space open to firms relative to the straitjacketing structural extremes of (1) complete isolation at the borders, which would dictate localization, and (2) complete integration, which would dictate standardization. Cases intermediate to 'one country' and 'one world' present decision-makers with more than one obvious strategy option. Therefore these cases require some higher-level decisions about how their firms are going to compete to add value.

There are many specific ways in which firms might try to add value through cross-border operations under conditions of incomplete integration, but they can be grouped in terms of two fundamental economic functions – in the sense of mechanisms for adding value, as opposed to marketing, production, etc. – that organizations try to fulfill by crossing borders. The first function, *aggregation*, involves exploiting the similarities across countries, while somehow side-stepping the differences among them, so as to tap increasing returns to scale. The second, *arbitrage*, involves exploiting differences among countries by taking advantage of variations in absolute costs or willingness-to-pay. The prototypical aggregator is a firm that takes advantage of (partly) locationally mobile resources subject to increasing returns to perform roughly the same activities in different countries (a 'horizontal' MNE). The prototypical arbitrageur takes advantage of international differences by geographically separating activities in an integrated vertical chain (the vertical MNE).

Arbitrage was the function that dominated early international economic activity, as evident in the operations of the trading companies chartered in the 16th and 17th centuries, the whaling fleets of the 18th century, and the vertically integrated agricultural and extractive (mining) companies that emerged in the 19th century (Ghemawat, 2000). In contrast, aggregation first came to the fore – with the possible exception of a few international banking chains that emerged earlier in the 19th century – with the manufacturing multinationals that began to appear in the second half of the 19th century. Despite this late start, however, casual evidence suggests that aggregation has commandeered researchers' attention to the point where the arbitrage function is often ignored. The long-running discussion of the tensions between integration and responsiveness and their resolution is a good example (Prahalad and Doz, 1987). These issues are salient in the context of aggregation, but not in the context of arbitrage, which is often passed over in silence as a result. Note that such a bias towards aggregation would lead to suboptimal responses to conditions of incomplete integration because of an undue emphasis on treating important differences across countries as sources of difficulty to be ignored or minimized (as part of an aggregation approach) rather than as possible sources of value (as part of an arbitrage approach). To consider all possible levers of value, it is important to supplement horizontal approaches that emphasize aggregation with vertical approaches that seek to capitalize on (as opposed to merely cope with) differences – that is, that emphasize arbitrage.

Unbundling the two functions should help in this regard. To start with the one that tends to get overlooked more, arbitrage, the schema used earlier in this paper to distinguish among markets for products, capital, labor, and knowledge also suggests a correspondingly broad array of arbitrage-based mechanisms for (potentially) adding value. Firms can arbitrage the incomplete integration of product markets across borders by becoming traders. Capital market differences provide them with a strong incentive to account for international differences in the cost of capital. They can arbitrage labor cost differences by relocating labor-intensive activities to countries with low labor costs. And they can try to harness knowledge differences and, more broadly, geographically dispersed knowledge by making asset-seeking (rather than asset-exploiting) investments in critical locations – a task that involves detailed coordination across multiple locations rather than, as some would have it, the death of geography.

The aggregation function also lends itself to unbundling. Here, there are continua of possibilities ranging, as noted above, from the complete localization of a business by country at one extreme to complete standardization across countries at the other. Interestingly distinct – and progressively less researched – intermediate possibilities include:

(1) adaptation, in which the business model originated in the 'home base' becomes the basis for local modification;
(2) platform or front-to-back approaches, in which certain core features of a business model (the 'platform') are preset globally, while others can be altered in light of local conditions; and
(3) clustering, which emphasizes grouping countries – regionalization is a subcase – in order to pursue commonalities more aggressively than would be possible with pure country-by-country adaptation.

Developing a contingency theory of choice that operates this level of disaggregation would seem to be a high priority.

An additional assumption that is worth discussing in this context is the textbook distinction between horizontal MNEs that emphasize aggregation and vertical MNEs that emphasize arbitrage. This dichotomy assumes that it is often possible – and useful – to distinguish firms in terms of the one function that is economically central, over long periods of time, to their strategies for adding value by competing around the world.[11] If one accepts this, then it is clear that there are two mutually exclusive approaches to achieving geographic coherence or fit – the international business analogue of mainstream business strategy's focus on internal and external fit at the level of the individual business, and corporate strategy's focus on fit or coherence across businesses. But there also seem to be indications that large multinationals engage, at least to some extent, in both aggregation and arbitrage. This naturally raises the question of the extent to which it is possible to mix and match across aggregation-oriented and arbitrage-oriented activities. Or to put matters more starkly, how feasible are transformation strategies that extensively exploit both aggregation opportunities and arbitrage possibilities?

A final question concerns whether intra-firm cross-border economic activity should be seen as a substitute for or driver of market integration. It is customary to think of (cross-border) firms as remedies for the infirmities of (cross-border) markets. However, the importance of intra-firm trade and FDI, in particular, hints that it might make sense to shift towards seeing firms as global connectors or conduits responsible, to a significant extent, for cross-border integration rather than as islands embedded in seas of market relationships. Of course, whether firms' cross-border activities substitute for or complement the cross-border integration of markets is yet another open and obviously important agenda item for future research.

Conclusions

Accounts of the cross-border integration of markets have tended to get very wrapped up in the times in which they were written – perhaps too much so. Thus Deutsch and Eckstein (1961) emphasized that, by the 1950s, the internationalization of transactions had declined significantly since the beginning of the 20th century, and averred that this trend was unlikely to be reversed any time soon. Contrary to their predictions, cross-border economic activity surged in the 1960s onward and, as it breached prewar records, inspired forked responses. Globalists stressed that international economic integration had reached new heights, while skeptics insisted that it had barely returned to levels experienced nearly a century earlier. Globalists gained confidence with the fall of the Berlin Wall in 1989 and the rapid growth in much of Asia through much of the 1990s. But then came the Asian financial crisis, episodes of instability in Russia and Latin America, a perceived 'globalization backlash,' a global economic slowdown, and the war on global terrorism. By mid-2002, the mood, at least among practitioners, seemed to be one of skepticism rather than optimism about globalization.

The empirical evidence reviewed in this article suggests that it might be preferable to take a more measured, historically self-conscious perspective on cross-border integration instead of frequently announcing changes in its direction or speed. Specifically, the empirical review indicated that most measures of market integration have scaled new heights in the last few decades, but still fall far short of economic theory's ideal of perfect integration. Looking forward, levels of cross-border integration may increase, stagnate or even suffer a sharp reversal if the experience between and during the two World Wars is any indication of the possibilities: while technological changes may be irreversible, political changes need not be. But given the parameters of the current situation, it seems unlikely that increases will any time soon yield a state in which the differences among countries can be ignored, multinationals' best efforts to connect markets across borders notwithstanding. Or that decreases could soon lead to a state in which cross-border linkages can be forgotten about. So, one does not have to make a precise forecast to diagnose that semiglobalization as a condition is sufficiently broad to persist for some time to come. Achieving similar stability in attitudes toward cross-border operations would seem preferable to manic-depressive swings in attitudes about the outlook, if only for purely pragmatic reasons.

The diagnosis of semiglobalization does more than just supply a relatively stable frame of reference for thinking about the environment of cross-border operations. Semiglobalization also calls attention to the critical role that location-specificity plays in the prospects of distinctive content for international business strategy relative to mainstream business and corporate strategy. In addition, it flags factors/products subject to location-specificity as being salient from the perspective of international business. And, finally, it highlights the scope for strategies that strive to capitalize on the (large) residual barriers to cross-border integration, as well as those that simply try to cope with them.

Such considerations motivate the modest proposal that semiglobalization or location-specificity merits the status of a major research program in international business. In other words, that a significant volume of research activity should be redirected along lines that take explicit account of both the importance and the incompleteness of the integration of markets across borders. In addition to reflecting empirical reality, a research program of this sort would directly address the apparent dearth of 'big research questions' in international business. As Buckley (2002, 370) recently put it:

> International business has succeeded because it has focused on, in sequence, a number of big questions, which arise from empirical developments in the world economy. The agenda is stalled because no such big question has currently been identified. This calls into question the separate existence of the subject area. It raises the old problem of the relationship between international business and other functional areas of management and social science.

From this perspective, the issue is not whether a big research question is needed at this juncture in the development of international business, but, instead, what it should be about: semiglobalization / location-specificity or something else?

Acknowledgements

This paper has benefited from research assistance by Jamie Matthews and Raluca Lupu, helpful comments by David Collis, Beulah D'Souza, Vijay Govindarajan, Mauro Guillen, Tarun Khanna, Walter Kuemmerle, Christos Pitelis, Ravi Ramamurti, Louis T. Wells Jr., George S. Yip and, especially, Bernard Y. Yeung, as well as from presentation of material at the AIB Panel Session, in summer 2002, celebrating Buckley and Casson (1976). The Division of Research at the Harvard Business School provided financial support.

Notes

[1] While location-specificity can also operate at the local or (intranational) regional level, a full treatment of it at all these levels of analyses is beyond the scope of this paper, even though many of the analytical issues that arise are similar.

[2] The disparity is even greater if one recognizes that the denominator of the ratio should really be a measure of gross sales rather than a value-added measure like GDP.

[3] Foreign direct investment currently accounts for roughly one-half of total foreign investment, but its share was significantly smaller at the start of the 20th century. See Bloomfield (1968, 3–4), cited in Bordo et al. (1999).

[4] Note that the spread of domestic safety nets does increase the likelihood that banking crises will turn into currency crises.

[5] For further discussion of currency risk, see Frankel (1992).

[6] Note the caveat that the extent of catch-up by the Asian tigers would look somewhat less remarkable if the data in Figure 5 were updated to take account of the Asian currency crisis.

[7] The other (overlapping) reasons for the localization of international competitiveness identified by Porter (1990) are sophisticated local demand and the local availability of specialized inputs and complements as well as basic factors of production.

[8] This point can be demonstrated formally in the context of standard supply–demand analysis. To start at one extreme, with complete insulation between two country markets, the price and quantity outcomes can be pinned down (under the assumption of atomistic competition) at the intersection of supply and demand curves in each market. At the other extreme, with complete integration – that is, zero extra costs of trading, transporting, transacting and so on across national boundaries – one could still add up the supply curves for the two markets on the one hand and their demand curves on the other and use the point of intersection of the two aggregate curves to determine the (common) prices and the quantities in the unified market. But the continuum of situations between zero and complete economic integration that I refer to as semi-globalization creates additional challenges. Given semi-globalization, the analysis of prices and quantities in the two markets cannot be reduced to supply–demand analysis of an individual market. Instead, attention has to be paid to distinct markets that are neither totally segmented nor totally integrated – an intrinsically more complex, and interesting, setup.

[9] For further discussion along these lines, see Caves (1998).

[10] Such integration would make access to a global pool of capital a 'given' for any worthy enterprise and thereby limit the scope for purely financial sources of advantage or disadvantage.

[11] Caves (1996) also identifies a third, residual category of multinational enterprise: international diversifiers whose operations in different countries are neither horizontally nor vertically related to each other. These can be thought of as falling in domain 4 of Table 5 rather than domain 3.

References

Alcacer, J. and Chung, W. (2001) 'Knowledge seeking, human capital and location choice of foreign entrants in the United States', Working Paper, Stern School of Business, New York University.

Baldwin, R.E. and Martin, P. (1999) *Two Waves of Globalization: Superficial Similarities, Fundamental Differences*, National Bureau of Economic Research: Cambridge, MA, NBER Working Paper No. 6904.

Barro, R.J. and Sala-i-Martin, X. (1995) *Economic Growth*, McGraw-Hill: New York.

Bekaert, G. and Harvey, C.R. (1995) 'Time-varying world market integration', *Journal of Finance* **50**(2): 403–444.

Blonigen, B.A. (1997) 'Firm-specific assets and the link between exchange rates and foreign direct investment', *American Economic Review* **87**(3): 447–465.

Bloomfield, A.I. (1968) *Patterns of Fluctuation in International Finance Before 1914*, Princeton Studies in International Finance No. 21, International Finance Section, Department of Economics, Princeton University.

Bordo, M.D., Eichengreen, B. and Irwin, D.A. (1999) *Is Globalization Today Really Different than Globalization a Hundred Years Ago?*, National Bureau of Economic Research: Cambridge, MA, NBER Working Paper 7195 (Prepared for the Brookings Trade Policy Forum on Governing in a Global Economy, Washington, DC, 15–16 April 1999. Published: shorter version in Austrian Economic Papers, Vols. 1 and 2, 2000).

Buckley, P.J. (2002) 'Is the international business agenda running out of steam', *Journal of International Business Studies* **33**(2): 365–373.

Buckley, P.J. and Casson, M. (1976) *The Future of the Multinational Enterprise*, Macmillan: London.

Caves, R.E. (1996) *Multinational Enterprise and Economic Analysis*, Cambridge University Press: Cambridge.

Caves, R.E. (1998) 'Research on international business: problems and prospects', *Journal of International Business Studies* **29**(1): 5–19.

Coase, R.H. (1937) 'The nature of the firm', *Economica* **4**(16): 396–405.

Deutsch, K.W. and Eckstein, A. (1961) 'National industrialization and the declining share of the international economic sector, 1890–1959', *World Politics* **13**(2): 267–272.

Dune, N. (2001) 'US population is now more than 10% foreign-born', *Financial Times*, 4 January 2001, The Americas, p. 4.

Feenstra, RC (1998) 'Integration of trade and disintegration of production in the global economy', *Journal of Economic Perspectives* **12**(4): 31–50.

Feldstein, M (1995) 'The Effects of Outbound Foreign Direct Investment on the Domestic Capital Stock', in M. Feldstein, J. Hines and R.G. Hubbard (eds.) *The Effects of Taxation on Multinational Corporations*, University of Chicago Press: Chicago, pp: 43–63.

Feldstein, M. and Horioka, C. (1980) 'Domestic savings and international capital flows', *Economic Journal* **90**(358): 314–329.

Frankel, J.A. (1992) 'Measuring international capital mobility: a review', *American Economic Review* **82**(2): 197–202.

Frankel, Jeffrey, A. (2001) 'Assessing the Efficiency Gain from Further Liberalization', in Porter, Roger B., Pierre Sauvé, Arvind Subramanian & Americo Beviglia Zampetti, (eds.) *Efficiency, equity, and legitimacy: the multilateral trading system at the millennium*, Brookings Institution Press: Washington, D.C.

Ghemawat, P. (2000) 'Global advantage: arbitrage, replication, and transformation', unpublished note, Harvard Business School, December.

Giddens, A. (1996) 'Keynote address at the United Nations Research Institute for Social Development, as excerpted in 'Essential matter'', *UNRISD News*, No. 15.

Held, D., McGrew, A.G., Goldblatt, D. and Perraton, J. (1999) *Global Transformations: Politics, Economics, and Culture*, Stanford University Press: Stanford.

Helliwell, J.F. (1998) *How Much Do National Borders Matter?*, Brookings Institution Press: Washington, DC.

Irwin, D.A. (1996) 'The United States in a new global economy? A century's perspective', *American Economic Review* **86**(2): 41–46.

Jaffe, A.B. and Trajtenberg, M. (1999) 'International knowledge flows: evidence from patent citations', *Economics of Innovation and New Technology* **8**(1–2): 105–136.

Keller, W. (2000) *Geographic Localization of International Technology Diffusion*, National Bureau of Economic Research: Cambridge, MA, NBER Working Paper No. 7509.

Kenwood, A.G. and Lougheed, A.L. (1989) *The Growth of the International Economy, 1920–1960*, Allen & Unwin: London.

Lewis, K.K. (1995) 'Puzzles in International Financial Markets', in G. Grossman and K. Rogoff (eds.) *Handbook of International Economics*, Vol. III, Elsevier Science: Amsterdam. pp: 1913–1971.

Maddison, A. (1995) *Monitoring the World Economy: 1820–1992*, Development Centre of the Organization for Economic Cooperation and Development: Paris.

Martin, S.F. (ed.) (2000) *World Migration Report: 2000*, Copublished by the International Organization for Migration and the United Nations.

McCallum, J. (1995) 'National borders matter: Canada–US regional trade patterns', *American Economic Review* **85**(3): 615–623.

Micklethwait, J. and Wooldridge, A. (2000) *A Future Perfect: The Challenge and Hidden Promise of Globalization*, Crown Business: New York.

Obstfeld, M. and Taylor, A. (1997) *The Great Depression as a Watershed: International Capital Mobility over the Long Run*, National Bureau of Economic Research: Cambridge, MA, NBER Working Paper 5960.

Patel, P. and Pavitt, K. (1994) *National Innovation Systems: Why they are Important and How they Might be Measured and Compared*, Mimeo, Science Policy Research Unit, University of Sussex.

Penrose, E.T. (1959) *The Theory of the Growth of the Firm*, Basil Blackwell, Wiley: Oxford, New York.

Porter, M.E. (1990) *The Competitive Advantage of Nations*, Free Press: New York.

Prahalad, C.K. and Doz, Y. (1987) *The Multinational Mission: Balancing Local Demands and Global Vision*, Free Press: New York.

Rogoff, K. (1996) 'The purchasing power parity puzzle', *Journal of Economic Literature* **34**(2): 647–668.

Scott, B. (2000) *Economic Strategies of Nations*, Mimeo, Harvard Business School.

Teece, D.J. (1977) 'Technology transfer by multinational firms: the resource cost of transferring technological know-how', *The Economic Journal* **87**(346): 242–261.

UN Center on Transnational Corporations, World Investment Report (various issues).

World Economic Forum, Global Competitiveness Report (various issues).

Accepted by Tom Brewer; outgoing Editor, August 2002.

[4]

Journal of International Business Studies (2004) 35, 3–18
© 2004 Palgrave Macmillan Ltd. All rights reserved 0047-2506 $25.00
www.jibs.net

PERSPECTIVE

A perspective on regional and global strategies of multinational enterprises

Alan M Rugman[1]
and Alain Verbeke[2]

[1]Kelley School of Business, Indiana University, Bloomington, USA, [2]Haskayne School of Business, University of Calgary, Canada

Correspondence:
Professor AM Rugman, L Leslie Waters Chair in International Business, Kelley School of Business, Indiana University, 1309 E. Tenth Street, Bloomington, IN 47401-1701, USA.
Tel: +1 812 855 5415
Fax: +1 812 856 4971
E-mail: rugman@indiana.edu

Abstract
Multinational enterprises (MNEs) are the key drivers of globalization, as they foster increased economic interdependence among national markets. The ultimate test to assess whether these MNEs are global themselves is their actual penetration level of markets across the globe, especially in the broad 'triad' markets of NAFTA, the European Union and Asia. Yet, data on the activities of the 500 largest MNEs reveal that very few are successful globally. For 320 of the 380 firms for which geographic sales data are available, an average of 80.3% of total sales are in their home region of the triad. This means that many of the world's largest firms are not global but regionally based, in terms of breadth and depth of market coverage. Globalization, in terms of a balanced geographic distribution of sales across the triad, thus reflects a special, and rather unusual, outcome of doing international business (IB). The regional concentration of sales has important implications for various strands of mainstream IB research, as well as for the broader managerial debate on the design of optimal strategies and governance structures for MNEs.
Journal of International Business Studies (2004) **35**, 3–18. doi:10.1057/palgrave. jibs.8400073

Keywords: firm-specific advantages; global strategy; localization; regional strategy; semi-globalization; triad; value chain

Introduction
Globalization, in the sense of increased economic interdependence among nations, is a poorly understood phenomenon. In this paper, we focus on the key actors in the globalization process, namely the firms that drive this process. A relatively small set of multinational enterprises (MNEs) accounts for most of the world's trade and investment. Indeed, the largest 500 MNEs account for over 90% of the world's stock of foreign direct investment (FDI) and they, themselves, conduct about half the world's trade (Rugman, 2000). Yet, this paper demonstrates that most of these firms are not 'global' companies, in the sense of having a broad and deep penetration of foreign markets across the world. Instead, most of them have the vast majority of their sales within their home leg of the 'triad', namely in North America, the European Union (EU) or Asia. This new view on 'globalization' is very different from the conventional, mainstream perspective. The latter perspective focuses primarily on macro-level growth patterns in trade and FDI, and compares these data with national GDP growth rates, but without ever analyzing the equivalent micro-level growth data for the MNEs responsible for the trade and FDI flows (United Nations, 2002).

Received: 21 April 2003
Revised: 14 October 2003
Accepted: 26 November 2003
Online publication date: 8 January 2004

The triad power concept

American economic hegemony, characteristic of the post-World War II era, ended in the early 1970s. The closing of the gold window and the floating of the dollar in 1971 can be considered an early indicator of the new world order, with economic power more dispersed across the triad of North America, the EU and Asia. The evolution of the world stock of FDI is indicative of the relative decline in US economic power: in 1967 the United States still represented the majority (50.4%) of the total stock of outward FDI; by 1990 this share had declined to only one-quarter (25.4%) (Dunning, 2001). Van Den Bulcke (1995) provides an insightful account of the evolution toward a triadic world economy.

In 1985 Kenichi Ohmae, at that stage a leading McKinsey consultant in Japan, published his landmark study *Triad Power*, arguably one of the most insightful, international management books of the last two decades. The triad, in Ohmae's work, was a geographic space consisting of the United States, the EU and Japan. This geographic space, according to Ohmae, shares a number of commonalities: low macroeconomic growth; a similar technological infrastructure; the presence of large, both capital- and knowledge-intensive, firms in most industries; a relative homogenization of demand (with a convergence of required key product attributes); and protectionist pressures. The triad is home to most innovations in industry, and includes the three largest markets in the world for most new products.

A useful indicator of this 'core' triad's enduring importance is the concentration of the world's largest MNEs in the United States, the EU and Japan, as reported in Rugman (2000). In 2000, of the world's largest 500 MNEs, 430 had their corporate headquarters in these core triad regions. In 1996 it was 443, in 1991 it was 410, and back in 1981 it was 445. The problem faced by many of these MNEs, according to Ohmae, is that they sell *engineered commodities*: that is, innovative and differentiated products, resulting from high investments in capital-intensive production processes and knowledge development. Unfortunately, these products rapidly lose their *monopoly status*. In spite of patents and brand names, technology often diffuses more rapidly to rivals than the required distribution capabilities can be built in foreign markets, thereby making it difficult to recoup innovation costs. The dilemma for any company that has developed a new 'superproduct' with large

expected demand throughout the triad is thus as follows: setting up an extensive distribution capability for the product *ex ante*, throughout the triad, may entail high, irreversible, fixed costs, and therefore high risks, if the superproduct somehow does not deliver on its sales expectations. Conversely, if the superproduct is first marketed at home, rival companies in other legs of the triad are expected to rapidly create an equivalent product, capture their home triad region market, and dominate distribution in that market.

In this context, Ohmae introduces the concept of *global impasse* to describe the problems faced by even the largest companies to repeat their home triad base market share performance in the two other triad markets. Only a limited number of firms, such as Coca-Cola and IBM, have, according to Ohmae, succeeded in becoming a *triad power*. A triad power is defined as a company that has ' (1) equal penetration and exploitation capabilities, and (2) no blind spots, in each of the triad regions' (Ohmae, 1985: 165). In Ohmae's view the deep penetration into each triad market is critical to the recovery of innovation costs. The absence of blind spots is important in order to 'avoid surprises': that is, unexpected strategic moves by foreign rivals or home country competitors setting up alliances with foreign firms. A triad power is thus an MNE that has been successful in 'insiderization'. The importance of the absence of blind spots was also emphasized by Hamel and Prahalad (1985), who defined a global company as a firm with distribution systems in key foreign markets that permit cross-subsidization, international retaliation, and world-scale volume. These authors focused especially on the importance of strong, worldwide brand positions and distribution channels, and highlighted the limited value to large firms of mere cost advantages through offshore sourcing and rationalized manufacturing.

Given the global impasse challenge described above, Ohmae (1985: Chapter 12) suggests the use of consortia and joint ventures to capture the non-home triad markets. In case the MNE wishes to become a triad power on its own, through wholly owned operations, Ohmae prescribes an 'Anchorage' perspective: that is, a corporate center that is mentally located in Anchorage (Alaska), equidistant from the economic and political power bases in the United States, the EU and Japan. This is in line with Perlmutter's (1969) prescription of developing a geocentric mentality in MNEs. In practice, such a firm should operate with regional headquarters in each leg of the triad in order to capitalize on commonalities within each region, at a lower cost and with more market knowledge than if corporate headquarters performed those activities.

Finally, Ohmae (1985) contains one last important insight, namely that MNEs from each triad region should identify a *fourth region*, where it should be easy, relative to the rest of the world, to earn an important market share. This fourth region will depend on the industry and firm involved, but for Japan it would typically include Asian markets, for the United States its neighboring trading partners, and for Europe those countries with which much trade or trade potential exists.

However, Ohmae (1985) did not actually anticipate the extension of the core triad to the 'broad' triad of today. The broad triad consists of NAFTA, the expanded EU and Asia. In parallel with the introduction of the Canada US Free Trade Agreement in 1989, NAFTA in 1994 and its expansion to the Free Trade Area of the Americas by 2005, the EU will further expand to 25 countries in 2004 (and perhaps more in the future). In Asia, in November 2002, China agreed to a free trade agreement with the 10 members of the Association of South East Asian Nations (ASEAN), signaling a wide trade and investment agreement for Asia. In September 2003, India and the ASEAN members agreed to forge a free trade area by 2012, while Japan and ASEAN agreed to begin negotiations on far-reaching trade and investment liberalization by 2005. Such institutional arrangements represent the agglomeration of attractive, proximate foreign markets (from a geographical, cultural, economic, and administrative perspective) into a 'broad' triad region. This will facilitate even deeper intra-regional market penetration. In contrast, little progress has been achieved in recent years in the realm of more global integration among nations through multilateral negotiations, especially at the level of the World Trade Organization (WTO). This situation is not expected to improve in the near future (for a discussion, see Rugman and Verbeke (2003)). At present, a majority of trade is intra-regional, and conducted in each part of the broad triad of NAFTA, the EU and Asia (Rugman, 2000).

The present paper tests whether the world's largest firms have been capable of implementing Kenichi Ohmae's visionary strategy and becoming (broad) triad powers during the two decades after his path-breaking book. Our work has three caveats. First, our paper presents data on the distribution of

sales across the broad triad regions. This should be considered as a starting point for introducing systematically a regional component in international business (IB) research. Individual MNEs may be faced with specific environmental requirements/ opportunities, as well as internal company ones that suggest a different regional delineation, consistent with Ghemawat's (2001) framework on the 'distance' between countries. In a similar vein, the subnational level (i.e. regions within a single country) may also be important in the IB context, both for manufacturing location decisions and for the targeting of specific subnational areas for sales and distribution. Second, a balanced distribution of sales across the triad, although likely beneficial to an MNE's sustained performance, is not necessarily critical to all MNEs. For example, firms may attempt to establish a dominant position in their home market, and may have little interest in pursuing a balanced, triad-based distribution of sales. Third, different activities in the value chain may be associated with varying levels of globalization. In this paper we focus primarily on sales, simply because these constitute the ultimate reflection of market success, but we also discuss the issue of downstream *vs* upstream globalization.

Empirical evidence of triad power
The 500 largest companies in the world accounted for over $14 trillion of total sales (revenues) in fiscal year 2001. The average revenues for a firm in the top 500 were $28 billion, ranging from Wal-Mart at $220 billion to Takenaka at $10 billion. In this study of the intra-regional sales of these 500 firms, a total of 380 were included with available geographic segment data. These 380 firms account for 79.2% of the total revenues of all the 500 firms. The average sales volume of a firm in the set of 380 is $29.2 billion. Across these 380 large firms the average intra-regional sales represent 71.9%.

A relative sales dominance in a specific regional market, rather than a very wide and evenly distributed spread of sales, reflects five underlying issues critical to the MNE's functioning. First, if most MNEs' sales are unevenly distributed across the globe, and usually concentrated in just one geographic market, this means that the firms' products are not really equally accessible and/or attractive to consumers all around the world, in spite of many MNEs attempting to adapt their products to local demand.

Second, the lack of global market success, although based on aggregate company-level data, could be interpreted as a reflection of the limits to the non-location-bound nature of the MNEs' knowledge base – that is, their firm-specific advantages (FSAs). Firms may have sophisticated and proprietary technological knowledge, brand names, etc., but there may be severe limits to the joint international transferability of this knowledge, and its acceptance by customers across regions. These limits may exist irrespective of whether the knowledge is embodied in final products and then exported, transferred as an intermediate product through licensing, or utilized in foreign affiliates through FDI. It should be recognized that some examples exist of rapid cross-border integration of sales, as exemplified by the success of Airbus aircraft in the United States, Japanese cars in Europe, and a variety of American consumer goods in Japan and China, but the magnitude of this trend, as compared with overall sales volumes, remains small across the 500 largest companies.

Third, the observed lack of market performance across regions may also point to a relative inability to access and deploy the required location-bound FSAs, which would lead to benefits of regional and national responsiveness.

Fourth, if the MNE's market position is very different in the various regions of the world this indicates the need for very different competitive strategies: a leadership role in one market may require different patterns of decisions and actions than the role of a (perhaps ambitious) junior player in another market. These differential roles should then be reflected in the deployment of specific combinations of non-location-bound and location-bound FSAs in each region. Unfortunately, in spite of much 'think global, act local' rhetoric in both the academic and popular business press, there appears to be little empirical evidence that this approach has permitted host region market penetration levels similar to those obtained in the home region.

Fifth, the four elements above have important implications for MNE governance. It might be incorrect to attribute the present relative lack of overseas market success of many firms to an inappropriate governance structure. The presence of multiple environmental circumstances may also be critical here (powerful foreign rivals in other triad regions; government shelter of domestic industries; buyer preferences for local products; cultural and administrative differences as compared to the home region; etc.). However, the need for regional strategies does suggest the parallel intro-

duction of a regional component in the MNEs' governance structure to deal appropriately with the distinctive characteristics of each leg of the triad, and with the regions outside it, much in line with Ohmae's (1985) prescriptions. This perspective is developed further in the later sections of the paper.

This need for distinct regional strategies should be viewed as a complement to the well-known normative models that advocate simple globalization strategies as a set of purposive decisions and actions instrumental to a broad and deep penetration of foreign markets (Govindarajan and Gupta, 2001; Jeannet, 2000; Yip, 2002). Regionalization should be viewed as an expression of semi-globalization (Ghemawat, 2003). Semi-globalization implies that we observe neither extreme geographical fragmentation of the world in national markets nor complete integration. Incomplete integration means that location specificity, in this case regional specificity, matters. Only in the context of incomplete integration is there scope for international MNE strategy that is conceptually distinct from conventional domestic strategy.

Empirical evidence and meaning of regional strategies

The majority of the world's largest 500 companies (the *Fortune 500*) are MNEs: that is, they produce and/or distribute products and/or services across national borders. Yet, very few MNEs have the ability to sell standardized products and services around the world, a type of globalization originally advocated by Levitt (1983). In the mainstream IB literature it is now widely recognized that benefits of integration resulting from global-scale economies can be reaped only if accompanied by strategies of national responsiveness, guided by both external pressures for local adaptation and internal pressures for requisite variation. What is unfortunately often neglected is that, irrespective of MNEs' efforts to augment their alleged non-location-bound FSAs with a location-bound component, no *balanced* geographical dispersion of sales is achieved in most cases.

For 365 of the 380 firms included in our study, data were available that permitted a further decomposition of their foreign sales. It should be noted that many of the remaining 135 *Fortune 500* companies are actually operating solely in their home region, with no sales elsewhere, and for others there are insufficient data. Of the 365 with data, only nine MNEs are unambiguously 'global', with at least 20% of their sales in all three regions of the triad, but less than 50% in any one region. This picture of regionalization, rather than globalization, is shown in Table 1.

The definitions adopted in Table 1 are as follows:

(1) *Home region oriented*: In all, 320 firms have at least 50% of their sales in their home region of the triad. The threshold of 50% was chosen as we assume that a region representing more than 50% of total sales will systematically both shape and constrain most important decisions and actions taken by the MNE. It also implies a concentration of the MNE's downstream FSAs in that region, as explained in the next section.

(2) *Bi-regional*: In all, 25 MNEs are bi-regional, defined as firms with at least 20% of their sales in each of two regions, but less than 50% in any one region. This set includes 25 firms with sales ranging between 20 and 50% in the home region and 20% or over in a second region. The threshold of 20% was chosen because we assume that having two regional markets, each representing at least one fifth of a large firm's sales, reflects impressive market success resulting from extensive downstream FSAs in those two markets.

(3) *Host region oriented*: In all, 11 firms have more than 50% of their sales in a triad market other than their home region.

(4) *Global*: Only nine of the MNEs included are global, defined as having sales of 20% or more in each of the three parts of the triad, but less than 50% in any one region of the triad. The

20% figure is less than the one-third required for an equal triad distribution, and so is biased downwards in favor of finding global MNEs. Conceptually, it implies the successful deployment of downstream FSAs in three distinct markets. The North American and European region of the broad triad are of approximate equal size, as measured by GDP. Asia is smaller than either as measured by GDP, but is nearly equal when taking into account purchasing power parity (PPP). Weighing the three legs of the broad triad by GDP, and even correcting for PPP, will not generate a larger number of global firms.

Within each of the groups above, the home triad region sales weighted averages are as follows:

(1) home region oriented (320 firms): 80.3%;
(2) bi-regional (25 firms): 42%;
(3) host region oriented (11 firms): 30.9%; and
(4) global (nine firms): 38.3%.

The above data also confirm the study of the 49 retail MNEs in the 500, by Rugman and Girod (2003). In that study, only one retail MNE was found to be global, namely LVMH (Moët Hennessy Louis Vuitton SA). While it could be argued that there is much more to globalization than sales dispersion – for example, foreign assets and foreign employment have sometimes been used together with foreign sales to compose a *transnationality index* – it should be recognized that only sales dispersion constitutes a true performance measure at the output level. In this context, Rugman and Brain (2003) report an analysis of the regional sales of the world's 20 most transnational firms as defined by the United Nations' *World Investment Report 2002*. Of these 20 firms with the highest transnationality index, only one was global, namely Philips. Another five were bi-regional. Two were host region oriented. Of the 20 most transnational firms, 12 were home region oriented.

Given the above classification of MNEs, we should note five limitations of the data for purposes of strategy prescription. First, most large MNEs consist of several strategic business units (SBUs); the geographical sales distribution may vary for each SBU, even within a single MNE. Second, although the percentage thresholds adopted (50%; 20%) are to permit a coherent analysis across the sample of companies, the actual sales percentages perceived by management as a reflection of successful

Table 1   Classification of the top 500 MNEs

Type of MNE	No. of MNEs	Percentage of 500	Percentage of 380	Percentage intra-regional sales
Global	9	1.8	2.4	38.3
Bi-regional	25	5.0	6.6	42.0
Host region oriented	11	2.2	2.9	30.9
Home region oriented (1)	320	64.0	84.2	80.3
Insufficient data	15	3.0	3.9	40.9
No data	120	24.0		NA
Total	500	100.0	100.0	71.9

Data are for 2001.
Source: Braintrust Research Group, The Regional Nature of Global Multinational Activity, 2003 (www.braintrustresearch.com).
NA—not available.

presence in host triad regions may differ from firm to firm. Owing to data limitations it may be difficult to attribute particular sales to a specific region. For example, Asian tourists may purchase a substantial part of the total sales of a European luxury goods manufacturer duty-free in the United States, and those sales would be registered as US based. Similarly, industrial goods may be sold to global accounts located in another leg of the triad, but the sales might still be registered in the home region. Third, the implications of particular sales percentages for differential corporate strategy and structure across the triad may also be firm specific. Fourth, large home region sales percentages do not imply the absence of vulnerability to outsiders. The case of the US automobile industry suggests that even large market shares in the home region may be eroded over time by dynamic rivals from other legs of the triad. Fifth, the minimum market share (and therefore firm-level sales volume) required in host regions to permit effective rivalry, and even retaliation against domestic incumbents, is largely industry specific, and not captured by the data.

The nine triad-based global MNEs are identified in Table 2. Most of these MNEs are in the computer, telecom, and hi-tech sectors. These global firms are spread across the triad, with three in each region of North America, Europe, and Asia-Pacific.

The bi-regional MNEs are listed in Table 3. This table includes MNEs such as Unilever and McDonald's, which are nearly global (in both cases they have under 20% of their sales in Asia). These bi-regional MNEs may be well positioned to extend their market reach further, across all three triad markets. Most bi-regionals are European or Asian firms with successful access to the US market. There are only six North American bi-regionals.

The 11 host region MNEs are reported in Table 4. These include DaimlerChrysler as one of eight MNEs with head offices in Europe, but with more than half of their sales in North America. There are also two Asian businesses, Honda and the Australian-based News Corporation, which have most of their sales in North America. Only one US MNE, Manpower, has more sales in Europe than in its home market. Most of these MNEs have been attracted by the size of the US economy. Their geographical expansion strategies have been driven by market access considerations and, in several cases, as with DaimlerChrysler, have been largely implemented through mergers and acquisitions, reflecting to some extent the inability to

Table 2   Global MNEs

	500 rank	Company	Region	Revenues (US$bn)	F/T sales	Percentage intra-regional	North America percentage of total sales	Europe percentage of total sales	Asia-Pacific percentage of total sales
1	19	Intl. Business Machines	North America	85.9	64.8	43.5	43.5[a]	28.0[b]	20.0
2	37	Sony	Asia-Pacific	60.6	67.2	32.8	29.8[c]	20.2	32.8[d]
3	143	Royal Philips Electronics	Europe	29.0	NA	43.0	28.7[e]	43.0	21.5
4	147	Nokia	Europe	27.9	98.5	49.0	25.0[a]	49.0	26.0
5	162	Intel	North America	26.5	64.6	35.4	35.4[c]	24.5	40.2
6	190	Canon	Asia-Pacific	23.9	71.5	28.5	33.8[a]	20.8	28.5[d]
7	239	Coca-Cola	North America	20.1	NA	38.4	38.4	22.4[b]	24.9
8	388	Flextronics International	Asia-Pacific	13.1	NA	22.4	46.3[c]	30.9	22.4
9	459	LVMH	Europe	11.0	83.4	36.0	26.0[c]	36.0	32.0
		Weighted average		33.1		38.3			
		Total		298.0					

Data are for 2001.
Source: Braintrust Research Group, The Regional Nature of Global Multinational Activity, 2003 (www.braintrustresearch.com).
Notes: [a]Refers to Americas; [b]Refers to EMEA: Europe Middle East and Africa; [c]Refers only to the US; [d]Refers only to Japan; [e]Includes only the US and Canada.
NA=not available.

Table 3 Bi-regional MNEs

500 rank		Company	Region	Revenues (US$bn)	F/T sales	Percentage intra-regional	North America percentage of total sales	Europe percentage of total sales	Asia-Pacific percentage of total sales
1	4	BP	Europe	174.2	80.4	36.3	48.1[a]	36.3	NA
2	10	Toyota Motor	Asia-Pacific	120.8	50.8	49.2	36.6	7.7	49.2[b]
3	58	Nissan Motor	Asia-Pacific	49.6	50.3	49.7	34.6	11.0	49.7[b]
4	68	Unilever	Europe	46.1	NA	38.7	26.6	38.7	15.4
5	138	Motorola	North America	30.0	56.0	44.0	44.0[a]	14.0	26.0
6	140	GlaxoSmithKline	Europe	29.5	50.8	28.6	49.2[a]	28.6	NA
7	153	EADS	Europe	27.6	NA	44.9	33.7	44.9	10.2
8	158	Bayer	Europe	27.1	NA	40.3	32.7	40.3	16.1
9	210	LM Ericsson	Europe	22.4	97.0	46.0	13.2	46.0[c]	25.9
10	228	Alstom	Europe	20.7	88.0	45.1	28.0	45.1	16.1
11	230	Aventis	Europe	20.5	87.2	32.1	38.8[d]	32.1	6.4[b]
12	262	Diageo	Europe	18.6	NA	31.8	49.9	31.8	7.7
13	268	Sun Microsystems	North America	18.3	52.6	47.4	47.4[a]	30.2[c]	17.2
14	285	Bridgestone	Asia-Pacific	17.6	61.2	38.8	43.0[e]	10.1	38.8[b]
15	288	Roche Group	Europe	17.3	98.2	36.8	38.6	36.8	11.7
16	316	3M	North America	16.1	53.1	46.9	46.9[a]	24.6	18.9
17	317	Skanska	Europe	15.9	83.0	40.0	41.0	40.0	NA
18	340	McDonald's	North America	14.9	62.4	40.4	40.4[d]	31.9	14.8
19	342	Michelin	Europe	14.6	NA	47.0	40.0	47.0	NA
20	383	Eastman Kodak	North America	13.2	NA	48.5	48.5[a]	24.7[c]	17.2
21	386	Electrolux	Europe	13.1	NA	47.0	39.0	47.0	9.0
22	390	BAE Systems	Europe	13.0	82.7	38.1	32.3[d]	38.1	2.7
23	408	Alcan	North America	12.6	95.4	41.1	41.1[d]	39.6	13.9
24	415	L'Oréal	Europe	12.3	NA	48.5	32.4	48.5	NA
25	416	Lafarge	Europe	12.3	NA	40.0	32.0	40.0	8.0
		Weighted average		31.1		42.0			
		Total		778.3					

Data are for 2001.
Source: Braintrust Research Group, The Regional Nature of Global Multinational Activity, 2003 (www.braintrustresearch.com).
Notes: [a]Refers only to the US; [b]Refers only to Japan; [c]Refers to EMEA: Europe Middle East and Africa; [d]Includes only the US and Canada; [e]Refers to Americas.
NA=not available.

achieve a similar penetration through internal, organic growth.

Table 5 lists the 25 largest home region oriented MNEs. As noted above, there are 320 of these. They pursue essentially an intra-regional strategy.

A small set of firms are 'near miss' global MNEs, as they approximate the percentages required to be considered global. One subset includes ExxonMobil, Royal Dutch/Shell and Nestlé, which are probably global in terms of geographic spread of their sales, but cannot be so classified due to absent data. Several firms, such as Aventis, are bi-regional and probably would be classified as global if the missing data for Asia were available. Four other MNEs, namely McDonald's, Eastman Kodak, Anglo-American, and 3M, just miss the 'global firm' status. For example, McDonald's has only 14.8% of sales in

Asia, Eastman Kodak has only 17.2%, Anglo American has 17.8%, and 3M has 18.9%.

Some special cases

The two MNEs conventionally regarded as 'global', indeed as primary agents of globalization, are Coca-Cola and McDonald's. Yet, only Coca-Cola is truly a global MNE. Ranking as 129th in the *Fortune 500* list, it has over 20% of its sales across all three parts of the triad: 38.4% in North America, 22.4% in Europe, and 24.9% in Asia. Of Coca-Cola's sales in Asia, 74% are in Japan, but the company is attempting to increase its market in China. In contrast, McDonald's, ranked as 340th in the *Fortune 500* list, is a bi-regional MNE. It has 36.6% of its sales in North America, 37.1% in Europe, but only 13.8% in Asia.

Table 4 Host region-based MNEs

500 rank	Company	Region	Revenues (US$bn)	F/T sales	Percentage intra-regional	North America percentage of total sales	Europe percentage of total sales	Asia-Pacific percentage of total sales
1	7	DaimlerChrysler	Europe	136.9	NA	29.9	60.1	29.9	NA
2	20	ING Group	Europe	83.0	77.3	35.1	51.4	35.1	3.4
3	38	Royal Ahold	Europe	59.6	85.0	32.8	59.2	32.8	0.6
4	41	Honda Motor	Asia-Pacific	58.9	73.1	26.9	53.9	8.1	26.9[a]
5	136	Santander Central Hispano Group	Europe	30.4	66.1	44.3	55.7[b]	44.3	NA
6	245	Delhaize 'Le Lion'	Europe	19.6	84.0	22.0	75.9	22.0	1.0
7	301	AstraZeneca	Europe	16.5	NA	32.0	52.8[c]	32.0	5.2[a]
8	364	News Corp.	Asia-Pacific	13.8	NA	9.0	75.0[c]	16.0[d]	9.0
9	476	Sodexho Alliance	Europe	10.6	NA	42.0	50.0	42.0	NA
10	482	Manpower	North America	10.5	80.9	19.1	19.1[c]	68.6	NA
11	487	Wolseley	Europe	10.4	79.1	28.7	66.3	28.7	NA
		Weighted average		40.9		30.9			
		Total		450.1					

Data are for 2001.
Source: Braintrust Research Group, The Regional Nature of Global Multinational Activity, 2003 (www.braintrustresearch.com).
Notes: [a]Refers only to Japan; [b]Refers to Americas; [c]Refers only to the US; [d]Refers only to the UK.
NA—not available.

Nike is another interesting case. It is not one of the largest 500 firms, as its sales are under $10 billion. It sources 99% of its products offshore, primarily in China (38%) and South East Asia (61%), and much of its apparel (86%) is produced outside the United States. Yet, Nike is a company with the majority of its sales in the Americas (58.2%). Indeed, it has 52.1% of sales in its home market of the United States. Nike also competes in Europe with 29% of its sales there, but not much in Asia with only 12.9% of sales there.

In terms of employment, of the 22,000 Nike employees, over half are located in the United States (54.7%). If we include other countries in the Americas, this number rises to 60.2%. Europe, the Middle East and Africa account for another 24.9%. Asia and the Pacific account for about 14.9% (or 3000 employees), but this region is also home to about 660,000 employees of independent contract companies that supply Nike products. These independent contractors are not owned by Nike, but are part of its supply network. Nike is only indirectly responsible for the working conditions of the employees working for these independent firms. Yet, owing to the adverse perceived impact on its brand image of 'sweatshop' conditions in these factories, Nike is now assuming some responsibility for the labor conditions in the factories of its independent suppliers.

The Nike case indicates the importance of understanding the precise FSAs of an MNE. Nike is not successful because it outsources most of its production in Asia. Instead, it outperforms other competitors because of its business model, in which its brand name is the dominant FSA. This brand name signifies high-quality, stylish, 'cool' sports shoes and sports apparel. All its competitors also outsource in South East Asia significant portions of production. This access to cheap labor represents a country factor condition, not an FSA by itself. In a similar vein, Wal-Mart outperforms other firms owing to its unique business model, not primarily by outsourcing to China. These firms' outsourcing strategies reflect internalization arbitrage – more specifically the ability to link attractive (but generally available), host country production factors, used at the upstream end of the value chain with upstream FSAs. However, only in the presence of downstream FSAs (especially branding) do such strategies lead to market success, and this is often restricted to the home triad region. The Nike and Wal-Mart cases illustrate the crucial importance of the sales data used in this paper to assess market success.

Implications for emerging research themes
In this section, some of the implications of the lack of empirical evidence for globalization are considered

Table 5 The Top 25 home region-based companies

500 rank	Company	Region	Revenues (US$bn)	F/T sales	Percentage intra-regional	North America percentage of total sales	Europe percentage of total sales	Asia-Pacific percentage of total sales
1	1	Wal-Mart Stores (q)	North America	219.8	16.3	94.1	94.1	4.8	0.4
2	3	General Motors	North America	177.3	25.5	81.1	81.1	14.6	NA
3	5	Ford Motor	North America	162.4	33.3	66.7	66.7[a]	21.9	NA
4	9	General Electric	North America	125.9	40.9	59.1	59.1[a]	19.0	9.1
5	12	Mitsubishi	Asia-Pacific	105.8	13.2	86.8	5.4[a]	1.7[b]	86.8[c]
6	13	Mitsui	Asia-Pacific	101.2	34.0	78.9	7.4	11.1	78.9
7	15	Total Fina Elf	Europe	94.3	NA	55.6	8.4	55.6	NA
8	17	Itochu	Asia-Pacific	91.2	19.1	91.2	5.5	1.7	91.2
9	18	Allianz	Europe	85.9	69.4	78.0	17.6[d]	78.0	4.4[e]
10	21	Volkswagen	Europe	79.3	72.3	68.2	20.1	68.2	5.3
11	22	Siemens	Europe	77.4	78.0	52.0	30.0[d]	52.0	13.0
12	23	Sumitomo	Asia-Pacific	77.1	12.7	87.3	4.8[a]	NA	87.3[c]
13	24	Philip Morris	North America	72.9	42.1	57.9	57.9[a]	25.8	NA
14	25	Marubeni (q)	Asia-Pacific	71.8	28.2	74.5	11.6[a]	NA	74.5
15	26	Verizon Communications	North America	67.2	3.8	96.2	96.2[a]	NA	NA
16	27	Deutsche Bank	Europe	66.8	69.0	63.1	29.3	63.1	6.5
17	28	E.ON	Europe	66.5	43.4	80.1	9.4[a]	80.1	NA
18	29	US Postal Service (q)	North America	65.8	3.0	97.0	97.0[a]	NA	NA
19	30	AXA (q)	Europe	65.6	77.3	51.2	24.1[a]	51.2	19.9
20	31	Credit Suisse	Europe	64.2	73.3	60.9	34.9[d]	60.9	4.1[e]
21	32	Hitachi	Asia-Pacific	63.9	31.0	80.0	11.0	7.0	80.0
22	34	American International Group	North America	62.4	NA	59.0	59.0[f]	NA	NA
23	35	Carrefour	Europe	62.2	50.8	81.3	NA	81.3	6.6
24	36	American Electric Power	North America	61.3	12.3	87.7	87.7[a]	11.8[b]	NA
25	39	Duke Energy	North America	59.5	13.1	96.5	96.5	NA	NA

Data are for 2001.
Source: Braintrust Research Group, The Regional Nature of Global Multinational Activity, 2003 (www.braintrustresearch.com).
Notes: [a]Refers only to the US; [b]Refers only to the UK; [c]Refers only to Japan; [d]Refers to Americas; [e]Includes Africa; [f]Includes only the US and Canada; NA—not available.

across the field of IB research. Five research areas of particular relevance are selected. The first two areas deal with the foundations of MNE competitive advantage, namely FSAs and location advantages, respectively. The next three areas are related to MNE strategy, structure and performance.

Implications for the relevance of the internalization and internationalization models of international expansion

The internalization model of foreign expansion (Buckley and Casson, 1976; Rugman, 1981), and especially its *eclectic paradigm* version, has been the dominant conceptual model in IB research during the past two decades. It suggests that firms will establish foreign affiliates in the case of strong ownership advantages, location advantages, and internalization advantages (Dunning, 1981). The model assumes that MNEs systematically engage in

a cost–benefit calculus of all possible entry modes, namely exports, licensing, and FDI (including, more recently, hybrid modes). Here, FDI may be the preferred mode from the outset if government-imposed and natural market imperfections make exports and licensing impossible or comparatively more expensive, and if the firm has already been operating abroad (Buckley and Casson, 1981).

In contrast, the internationalization model of the Scandinavian school argues that firms will incrementally build foreign operations, starting with low resource commitments in culturally proximate countries, and then expanding these commitments and geographic scope. Here experiential learning is critical, and path dependencies can be observed in the growth of the MNE's experiential knowledge base, especially as regards knowledge of the markets involved (Barkema *et al.*, 1996; Johansson and Vahlne, 1977, 1990). Little integration has occurred between the two schools, which have largely flourished on their own without much cross-fertilization, and each has a loyal following of researchers. The internalization school focuses at the outset on market imperfections involving *business/usage specificity*, whereas the internationalization school starts from imperfections arising from *location specificity*, in the spirit of Ghemawat (2003). The data presented in this paper suggest that the two approaches may actually be closer to each other than usually thought.

The relative lack of market success in host triad regions can be interpreted, at least partly, as a reflection of the limited customer value attributed to home triad region FSAs, whether transferred through exports (FSAs embodied in final products), through licensing (FSAs transferred to foreign licensees), or through FDI (FSAs transferred to foreign affiliates, whether subsidiaries or hybrid units). In such cases the internalization question of optimal entry mode choice becomes redundant. In other words, it is only in locations where the MNE's home region FSAs are valued by customers, as compared with relevant rivals, and for which minimum sales volumes can be expected (at least as far as market-seeking FDI is concerned), that conventional internalization theory is fully relevant. In such case of easy market penetration there is no need for a lengthy learning process, in the sense of an incremental accumulation of host region experience, to compensate for the liability of foreignness. The case of easy market penetration is consistent with Vernon's (1966) product life cycle (whereby all innovations with global market potential originate in one country), but with the choice of entry mode contingent upon transaction cost considerations. Paradoxically, internationalization theory identifies the locations where MNEs have the luxury of such an extensive, transaction-cost-driven entry mode selection and where they do not, namely in the case of high location-driven learning requirements. The data suggest that extensive choice options occur mainly in the home triad region, for most companies. Future research should therefore explore in more depth the complementarities, rather than the differences, between the internalization and internationalization perspectives on international expansion.

Implications for research on the diamond of international competitiveness

Porter (1990) has suggested that international competitiveness at the level of specific industries depends critically on a favorable configuration of home country diamond conditions. Here, four determinants have been viewed as critical: factor conditions (with a focus on created and advanced production factors); demand conditions (with a focus on total demand and sophistication of demand, based on precursor status); related and supporting industries (with a focus on the presence of world-class firms with which cluster type linkages exist); and strategy, structure and rivalry (whereby strong rivalry and benchmarking against the toughest competitors are critical to innovation). Porter's perspective has led to several follow-up studies, providing extensions and suggestions to augment his path-breaking model (Cartwright, 1993; Dunning, 1996; Moon *et al.*, 1998; Rugman and D'Cruz, 1993; Rugman and Verbeke, 1993; Rugman *et al.*, 1995).

The data in this paper suggest two important extensions of research building upon the diamond concept. First, the diamond may be useful primarily to expand internationally in the home triad region, meaning that 'favorable diamond conditions' in the home country may be insufficient in most cases to permit a truly global expansion. IB research should focus on the reasons for this lack of relevance of the home country diamond in host triad regions.

Second, a limited geographic scope of the national diamond's significance for international competitiveness has asymmetric implications for large economies such as the United States, Japan, and Germany, and small open economies such as Canada, Belgium, and Singapore. For MNEs originating in large countries, it means reassessing the market attractiveness of the so-called small markets in the home triad region. The presence of FSAs instrumental to achieving a high market share in geographically proximate markets, but that are region bound, should refocus these MNEs' efforts from assessing foreign market attractiveness through using macroeconomic data toward developing and using data that better indicate the firm's real market penetration potential, as illustrated by the Tricon case discussed in Ghemawat (2001). As regards MNEs from small open economies, the data suggest that it makes sense to focus on demand in adjacent, large economies that are part of the home region. This is consistent with the double diamond thinking in IB research that focuses on MNEs in these small open economies, much in line with Moon *et al.* (1998), Rugman and Verbeke (1993), and Rugman *et al.* (1995). Here it should be emphasized that regional integration not only benefits MNEs in the form of creating supply side efficiencies, but also improves market integration on the demand side, for example in terms of positively influencing buyers' confidence, attitudes and purchase intentions *vis-à-vis* products from foreign countries inside the triad region (Agarwal *et al.*, 2002). Here it would appear that, within one triad region, country of origin effects in purchasing decisions are complemented by 'region of origin' preferences.

Implications for research adopting a resource-based perspective on the integration/national responsiveness framework

Perhaps the most important implications of the empirical data on triad-based MNE activities are for research adopting a resource-based approach to MNE functioning. The integration/national responsiveness framework, an application to the IB context of the differentiation–integration approach in organization theory (Lawrence and Lorsch, 1967), was developed by Prahalad (1975), and further extended by Doz (1979), Bartlett (1979), and Bartlett and Ghoshal (1989). The integration–national responsiveness framework was given a TCE and resource-based interpretation by Rugman and Verbeke (1992, 2001). The latter authors have argued that benefits of integration, in the form of scale economies, scope economies, and benefits of exploiting national differences, require non-location-bound FSAs. In contrast, benefits of national responsiveness require location-bound FSAs. In this revised model Bartlett and Ghoshal's (1989) *transnational solution* could be interpreted as a firm that can effectively access and deploy the required dual knowledge bundles (of NLB and LB FSAs) for each activity to be performed, for each product, within each SBU. The data presented in this paper, however, suggest the need for an extension of the framework.

The conventional framework needs to be augmented, as operating in the *home* triad region may be associated with new needs for the development of *region-bound* FSAs, imposed by regional integration: see for example the nine cases discussed by Rugman and Verbeke (1991), especially the Volvo Trucks case. Hence regional integration creates both a threat and an opportunity for MNEs as they need to complement the conventional bundles of non-location-bound FSAs and location-bound FSAs with a set of region-bound FSAs. The data in this paper suggest that many of the world's largest and

most international MNEs have been quite successful in doing so.

In contrast, few of these firms appear capable of developing and deploying the required set of region-bound FSAs in *host* regions. The few cases where MNEs have been exceptionally successful in a host region (see Table 4) merit further attention. Here the focus should not be on those firms that acquired a position merely because of a merger (as in the Daimler–Chrysler case), but on those where FSAs have really been built over time, for example by finding ways to access or 'plug in' to pockets of new knowledge (Doz *et al.*, 2001).

Many large MNEs do have a strong geographical dispersion of their sourcing and production, both in resource industries and in manufacturing, but appear incapable (or unwilling) of capitalizing on this position to achieve global sales penetration. The observed asymmetry between sourcing/manufacturing and sales has two critical implications. First, it means that the concept of location-bound *vs* non-location-bound FSAs needs to be extended. The former concept usually implies that profitable deployment is possible only in the home country. The latter concept assumes global transferability. The data suggest that many MNEs have FSAs that are region bound: that is, they can be deployed across national borders, but only in a limited geographic region. Here, value added through aggregation, in the sense of exploiting similarities across countries (Ghemawat, 2003), can be achieved in the home region but appears difficult across regions. Second, the required MNEs' FSAs in upstream activities to achieve global sourcing (of R&D outputs, raw materials, intermediate inputs, labor and capital) and production, may be very different from the FSAs required in downstream activities to achieve a global distribution of sales. Here, value added through arbitrage (Ghemawat, 2003) – that is, exploiting differences between countries – appears to be achievable more often across regions.

In this context, Figure 1 shows two hypothetical accumulation patterns over time, of the MNE's FSAs at the upstream end (sourcing/production) and the downstream end (sales). At either end of the value chain these resource bundles consist of non-location-bound FSAs, location (read country)-bound FSAs and region-bound FSAs. The limited market performance achieved in host triad regions suggests that most firms are not capable of accessing and deploying the required knowledge bundles at the downstream end, because these bundles are likely to be quite different from the knowledge combinations effective in the home triad region, whereas this does not necessarily hold for more upstream activities. In broader terms, national and home region organizing principles adopted by MNEs, and engrained in their FSAs, appear to limit most MNEs' repertoire of downstream strategies required to be effective in the host region market. This is particularly interesting given that many markets, especially for commodity products, are characterized by 'global' (uniform) prices, driven by 'global' competition. In contrast, it appears much easier to adopt effective sourcing (and manufacturing) strategies associated with a broad geographical coverage. The liability of foreignness faced by the MNE (Hymer, 1976; Zaheer, 1995) thus needs to be unbundled into downstream and upstream components.

The diagonal arrow in Figure 1 shows a hypothetical expansion path over time, whereby the FSAs available for effective global sourcing/production (here in the sense of broad geographical coverage, but not necessarily limited to a triad context, as the optimal geographical configuration of sourcing and production is firm and industry specific) and those for global market penetration grow in very similar ways.

In contrast, the arrow on the left-hand side of the diagonal in Figure 1 reflects a new perspective on the typical large top-500 MNE, which is trapped in its home triad region as far as market penetration is concerned. Here the development of downstream FSAs seriously lags behind the growth in upstream FSAs. It may thus be potentially easy to achieve a global distribution of sourcing/production, whereas a global distribution of sales may be more difficult to accomplish.

To a large extent, much of the recent work on the globalization of particular value chain functions, such as finance, R&D, purchasing and logistics, and

production, has focused solely on the upstream portion of the MNE's FSA bundles. This largely reflects an arbitration issue, with the MNE taking advantage of the incomplete integration of factor markets (Ghemawat, 2003). This may reflect a 'global logic' in the minds of managers, but is distinct from a strong global market performance.

Implications for research on MNE structure

A large body of work has been written on the need for a fit between strategy and structure in MNEs, as a precondition for survival, profitability and growth, much in line with mainstream work in strategy and industrial organization on domestic firms. In this particular case the strategic importance of each triad region, combined with the different market characteristics faced by MNEs in each of these regions, would suggest the introduction of geographic components in the MNEs' structure.

The data in this paper, suggesting a strong discrepancy between intra-regional and inter-regional sales, may have important implications for MNE structure. In addition, the differentiation between downstream and upstream activities, building upon different sets of FSAs, should be reflected in the MNE's organizational structure, systems and perhaps even culture.

Several papers have been written on regional components in MNE organizational structure, such as regional headquarters (Daniels, 1987; D'Cruz, 1986; Dunning and Norman, 1987; Grosse, 1981; Heenan, 1979; Lasserre, 1996; Morrison *et al.*, 1991). Yeung *et al.*'s (2001) analysis of such regional headquarters in Singapore argues that their roles will depend on a number of parameters, which include geographical distance, familiarity with the host region, commitment to the host region, and regional integration, thus implicitly suggesting the importance of using the regional headquarters to complement in an idiosyncratic way each MNE's existing FSA bundles.

More research is needed that links the required knowledge bundles for each critical value-added activity in host triad regions with specific structural elements, which may also include elements of organizational physiology and psychology (Yeung *et al.*, 2001). Here it should be recognized that such regional elements may increase the difficulty of managing multidivisional (M-form) companies, as performance evaluation should be differentiated for units operating in the various regions, even within similar businesses, given the enormous differences

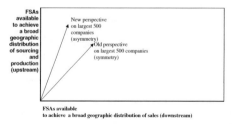

Figure 1 Old and new perspectives on the largest 500 companies.

Regional and global strategies of MNEs   Alan M Rugman and Alain Verbeke

15

in environmental circumstances faced by the affiliates in each region. In other words, even at a single point in time, MNEs may adopt both participative decentralization and administrative centralization simultaneously.

These two approaches have traditionally been viewed as inefficient corruptions of the M-form (Freeland, 1996; Williamson, 1975), but may in reality constitute a precondition for the effective governance of MNEs with regional strategies. Here participative decentralization reflects the involvement of regional divisions in corporate strategic planning, and this may be critical for successfully conducting downstream activities in host regions, given both the relative lack of appropriate information at the corporate headquarters' level on host regions, and the need to preserve subsidiary commitment and initiative in those host regions. In contrast, administrative centralization may be more appropriate for the management of upstream activities across regions, given the relative availability of information at corporate headquarters on these activities and the possibility of reducing both production and coordination costs through optimally exploiting imperfections in national and regional factor markets.

Implications for research on the performance effects of geographical diversification

Much of the literature on geographical diversification has attempted to evaluate the impact of diversification on profit performance (Buckley *et al.*, 1977, 1984; Geringer *et al.*, 1989; Hitt *et al.*, 1997; Morck and Yeung, 1991; Rugman, 1976). Usually some proxy is adopted for the share of foreign sales in total sales (or in some cases a more upstream end related measure, such as the number of subsidiaries abroad) to assess the degree of geographical diversification. Recent research has established the importance of the home country environment – that is, the *locus of origin* of geographic diversification efforts – for the scope and financial performance effects of geographic diversification (Wan and Hoskisson, 2003).

In this paper, however, we emphasize the importance of the *locus of destination*. The relative sales in host triad regions, *vis-à-vis* the home triad region, are themselves a critical performance parameter. Perhaps the mixed results in past research on the profit impact of geographical diversification, may be partly explained by (1) a lack of investigation of the *locus of destination* of the diversification efforts (intra-regional *vs* inter-regional), and (2) the fact

that market share success in non-home triad markets may be at the expense of profit performance. Thus future research on the impacts of geographic diversification should study explicitly the regional patterns and scope of MNE sales growth. In addition, it could include relative sales in host region markets as a performance parameter (dependent variable), rather than as a mere independent variable affecting financial profitability. Recent work by Vermeulen and Barkema (2002) correctly points out that some benefits of international expansion (such as tax benefits, common purchasing, and improved access to inexpensive labor) are easier to realize than other benefits, which require learning. Although these authors do not view host region market penetration performance relative to home region performance as a proxy for international success, their work does suggest that a broader geographic scope of the expansion process negatively moderates the impact of a firm's foreign subsidiaries on its profitability. More specifically, they demonstrate that a broader geographic scope strains the MNE's absorptive capacity (Cohen and Levinthal, 1990), particularly in the short run, leading to time compression diseconomies. They also show that foreign expansion is easier to absorb for MNEs if it occurs in 'related' countries, following the classification of countries into clusters developed by Ronen and Shenkar (1985).

Another recent paper by Ruigrok and Warner with a focus on upstream FSAs confirms this perspective. Ruigrok and Wagner (2003) suggest that US firms are usually characterized by an inverted J-curve, in terms of internationalization impact on performance (measured by return on assets). Internationalization is associated with performance improvements, until a threshold is reached, when performance starts to decline. The reason is that US firms usually expand in a first stage to culturally proximate countries such as Canada, the United Kingdom and Australia. In contrast, German firms face a U-curve in terms of performance effects of internationalization. A low psychic distance is found in only two small economies, namely Austria and Switzerland, which implies that German firms are required to target a much wider and more varied market (the EU) from the outset, thereby incurring higher learning costs. Ruigrok and Wagner's (2003) perspective on upstream internationalization suggests that, even there, the linkages between country of origin and country of destination are critical in determining the optimal route of internationalization and organizational learning.

This is an important observation, as influential work in IB has argued that the operational flexibility of MNEs, resulting from their internationally dispersed network of affiliates, confers arbitraging advantages, information-related network externalities, etc. (Kogut, 1983; Kogut and Kulatilaka, 1994). However, the analysis above suggests that the locus of destination determines the extent to which such benefits can be earned. More specifically, a lower (cultural, administrative, geographic and economic) distance, although reducing the hypothetical, maximum arbitraging and network externality benefits, will facilitate earning such benefits in practice.

Future research should investigate whether the prior existence of a strong internal network in the home region (and the related proven ability to learn and to manage risks) is critical for subsequent positive performance effects of inter-regional expansion. The creation of a strong competitive position in the home region may reflect one step in an evolutionary strategy of resource recombinations, which follows a clear sequential pattern and creates platforms for future investments (Kogut and Zander, 1993). However, it is unclear whether such platforms are themselves truly non-location-bound, or can only be applied in a limited geographic space.

Conclusions

Most large MNEs have an average of 80% of total sales in their home triad region. Only nine firms among the largest 500 companies are unambiguously global. What are the normative implications of this observation? It could be argued that these few examples of global corporate success should be viewed as best practices and benchmarks, to be carefully studied, and emulated by other large MNEs, most of which are characterized by a much more narrow and shallow penetration of host region markets. However, the observed weak market position in host regions, as compared with the home triad market, may also be interpreted as the outcome of a rational preference for regionally based activities, resulting from a careful cost–benefit calculation. Here, strategic interactions among large players, taking the form of 'inter-regional chess', may influence international sales patterns and the selection of target markets.

More generally, it could be argued, from a co-evolutionary perspective, that regional strategies of MNEs are embedded in – and co-evolve with – the broader competitive, organizational and institutional contexts at the regional level, in the spirit of Koza and Lewin (1998). In this situation, MNE regional strategy choices evolve interdependently with changes in prevailing industry practices, legitimate organizational forms, government regulations, etc. It should be recognized that regions themselves may change over time (as with the inclusion of all the Americas in NAFTA and further EU expansion), and therefore provide new opportunities for MNE growth. The triad perspective developed in this paper should therefore be viewed as a starting point for future empirical analyses, recognizing that regionalization is open-ended over time.

When globalization does occur, it is restricted to the upstream end of the value chain. Some of the world's largest MNEs master the art of connecting globally dispersed inputs. These can be in the form of financial capital, human capital, R&D knowledge, components, etc., and can be integrated to better serve home region clients. Hence it appears possible to be global at the upstream end of the value chain, and much can undoubtedly be learned from observing and imitating the routines of global leaders in this portion of the value chain.

Does this imply that large MNEs should be complacent as far as the downstream end is concerned and focus solely on their home region of the triad? Probably not, but senior MNE management should understand that widespread geographic diversification may well have managerial pitfalls similar to the conventional drawbacks of product diversification. A clear focus is required in terms of scope of geographic expansion, and the economic evaluation of international growth plans must take into account the costs of inter-regional 'distance' and the liability of inter-regional foreignness.

Finally, this paper has uncovered two fundamental paradoxes of IB that so far have eluded most, if not all, scholars in the field. First, at the downstream end, national responsiveness and localized adaptation are almost universally advocated as a panacea for penetrating international markets, but in reality most MNEs attempt to add value primarily by capitalizing on similarities across markets. This is an aggregation strategy often met with success in the home region. Second, at the upstream end (including FDI-driven foreign manufacturing), opportunities for scale and scope are usually considered abundant. Yet, in reality, MNEs add value primarily through arbitrage – that is, exploiting differences across nations and regions. Successful integration thus reflects locational specificities, and entails a process of *internalization arbitrage*: it refers essentially to the combination of the MNE's upstream FSAs, deployed in host countries, with these countries' location advantages.

We live in a world of semi-globalization, where IB research needs to rethink fundamentally the substance of aggregation and arbitrage opportunities. A renewed focus on MNE strategies, distinguishing between home and host triad regions, and between upstream and downstream activities, may be a good starting point for such an endeavor.

Acknowledgements

An earlier version of this paper was presented at the Duke University JIBS and CIBER Conference on 'Emerging Frontiers in International Business Research', 6–9 March 2003. We are pleased to acknowledge the help of Arie Lewin in stimulating this article. Helpful comments on earlier drafts have been provided by Vern Bachor, Paul Beamish, Peter Buckley, Yves Doz, John Dunning, Michael Enright, Stephane Girod, Robert Grosse, Mike Kotabe, Mitchell Koza, Klaus Meyer, John Mezias, Karl Moore, Mona Sellers, Lorn Sheehan, and two anonymous *JIBS* referees. We also acknowledge the excellent research assistance of Cecilia Brain.

References

Agarwal, J., Malhotra, N. and Wu, T. (2002) 'Does NAFTA influence Mexico's product image? A theoretical framework and an empirical investigation in two countries', *Management International Review* 42(4): 441–471.

Barkema, H., Bell, J. and Pennings, J. (1996) 'Foreign entry, cultural barriers and learning', *Strategic Management Journal* 17(2): 151–166.

Bartlett, C. (1979) 'Multinational structural evolution: the changing decision environment in international divisions', Doctoral dissertation Harvard Graduate School of Business Administration.

Bartlett, C. and Ghoshal, S. (1989) *Managing Across Borders: The Transnational Solution*, Harvard Business School Press: Boston, MA.

Buckley, P.J. and Casson, M.C. (1976) *The Future of the Multinational Enterprise*, Macmillan: London.

Buckley, P.J. and Casson, M.C. (1981) 'The optimal timing of a foreign direct investment', *Economic Journal* 91(361): 75–87.

Buckley, P.J., Dunning, J.H. and Pearce, R.B. (1977) 'The influence of firm size, sector, nationality, and degree of multinationality in the growth and profitability of the world's largest firms', *Weltwirtschaftliches Archiv* 114: 243–257.

Buckley, P.J., Dunning, J.H. and Pearce, R.B. (1984) 'An analysis of the growth and profitability of the world's largest firms 1972 to 1977', *Kyklos* 37(1): 3–27.

Cartwright, W.R. (1993) 'Multiple linked diamonds and the international competitiveness of export-dependent industries: the New Zealand experience', *Management International Review* 33(2): 55–70.

Cohen, W. and Levinthal, D. (1990) 'Absorptive capacity: a new perspective on learning and innovation', *Administrative Science Quarterly* 35: 128–152.

Daniels, J. (1987) 'Bridging national and global marketing strategies through regional operations', *International Marketing Review* 4(3): 29–44.

D'Cruz, J. (1986) 'Strategic Management of Subsidiaries', in H. Etemad and L.S. Dulude (eds.) *Managing the Multinational Subsidiary*, Croom Helm: London, pp. 75–80.

Doz, Y. (1979) *Government Control and Multinational Strategic Management: Power Systems and Telecommunications Equipment*, Praeger: New York.

Doz, Y., Santos, J. and Williamson, P. (2001) *From Global to Metanational*, Harvard Business School Press: Boston, MA.

Dunning, J.H. (1981) *International Production and the Multinational Enterprise*, George Allen & Unwin: London.

Dunning, J.H. (1996) 'The geographic sources of competitiveness of firms: some results of a new survey', *Transnational Corporations* 5(3): 1–30.

Dunning, J.H. (2001) 'The Key Literature on IB Activities: 1960–2000', in A.M. Rugman and T.L. Brewer (eds.) *The Oxford*

Handbook of International Business, Oxford University Press: Oxford, pp. 36–68.

Dunning, J. and Norman, G. (1987) 'The location choice of offices of international companies', *Environmental Planning A* 19: 613–631.

Freeland, R.F. (1996) 'The myth of the M-Form? Governance, consent, and organizational change', *American Journal of Sociology* 102(2): 483–526.

Geringer, J.M., Beamish, P. and daCosta, R.C. (1989) 'Diversification strategy and internationalization: implications for MNE performance', *Strategic Management Journal* 10(2): 109–119.

Ghemawat, P. (2001) 'Distance still matters: the hard reality of global expansion', *Harvard Business Review* 79(8): 137–147.

Ghemawat, P. (2003Q5) 'Semiglobalization and international business strategy', *Journal of International Business Studies* 34(2): 138–152.

Govindarajan, V. and Gupta, A. (2001) *The Quest for Global Dominance*, Jossey-Bass/Wiley: San Francisco.

Grosse, R. (1981) 'Regional offices of MNCs', *Management International Review* 21: 48–55.

Hamel, G. and Prahalad, C.K. (1985) 'Do you really have a global strategy?', *Harvard Business Review* 63(4): 139–148.

Heenan, D.A. (1979) 'The regional headquarters division: a comparative analysis', *Academy of Management Journal* 22(2): 410–415.

Hitt, M.A., Hoskisson, R.E. and Kim, H. (1997) 'International diversification: effects on innovation and firm performance in product-diversified firms', *Academy of Management Journal* 40: 767–798.

Hymer, S. (1976) *The International Operations of National Firms*, MIT Press: Cambridge, MA.

Jeannet, J.P. (2000) *Managing with a Global Mindset*, Financial Times/Prentice Hall, Pearson: London.

Johansson, J. and Vahlne, J.E. (1977) 'The internationalization process of the firm: a model of knowledge development and increasing foreign market commitments', *Journal of International Business Studies* 8(1): 23–32.

Johansson, J. and Vahlne, J.E. (1990) 'The mechanism of internationalization', *International Marketing Review* 7(4): 1–24.

Kogut, B. (1983) 'Foreign Direct Investment as a Sequential Process', in: C.P. Kindleberger and D.B. Audretsch (eds.) *The Multinational Corporation in the 1980s*, MIT Press: Cambridge, MA, pp. 38–56.

Kogut, B. and Kulatilaka, N. (1994) 'Operating flexibility, global manufacturing, and the option value of a multinational network', *Management Science* 40(1): 123–139.

Kogut, B. and Zander, U. (1993) 'Knowledge of the firm and the evolutionary theory of the multinational enterprise', *Journal of International Business Studies* 24(4): 625–645.

Koza, M.P. and Lewin, A.Y. (1998) 'The co-evolution of strategic alliances', *Organization Science* **9**(3): 255–264.

Lasserre, P. (1996) 'Regional headquarters: the spearhead for Asia Pacific markets', *Long Range Planning* **29**: 30–37.

Lawrence, P. and Lorsch, J. (1967) *Organization and Environment*, Harvard Business School, Division of Research: Boston, MA.

Levitt, T. (1983) 'The globalization of markets', *Harvard Business Review*, May–June(3): 92–102.

Moon, C., Rugman, A.M. and Verbeke, A. (1998) 'A generalized double diamond approach to the global competitiveness of Korea and Singapore', *International Business Review* **7**(2): 135–150.

Morck, R. and Yeung, B. (1991) 'Why investors value multi-nationality', *Journal of Business* **64**(2): 165–187.

Morrison, A.J., Ricks, D.A. and Roth, K. (1991) 'Globalization versus regionalization: which way for the multinational?', *Organizational Dynamics* **19**(3): 17–29.

Ohmae, K. (1985) *Triad Power: The Coming Shape of Global Competition*, The Free Press: New York.

Perlmutter, H. (1969) 'The tortuous evolution of the multinational enterprise', *The Columbia Journal of World Business* **4**(1): 9–18.

Porter, M.E. (1990) *The Competitive Advantage of Nations*, The Free Press: New York.

Prahalad, C.K. (1975) 'The strategic process in a multinational corporation', Doctoral dissertation Harvard Graduate School of Business Administration.

Ronen, S. and Shenkar, O. (1985) 'Clustering countries on attitudinal dimensions: a review and syntheses', *Academy of Management Review* **10**: 435–454.

Rugman, A.M. (1976Q10) 'Risk reduction by international diversification', *Journal of International Business Studies* **7**(2): 80–85.

Rugman, A.M. (1981) *Inside the MultinationalsThe Economics of Internal Markets*, Columbia University Press: New York.

Rugman, A.M. (2000) *The End of Globalization*, Random House: London/Amacom–McGraw-Hill: New York.

Rugman, A.M. and Brain, C. (2003) 'Multinational enterprises are regional, not global', *Multinational Business Review* **11**(1): 3–12.

Rugman, A.M. and D'Cruz, J.R. (1993) 'The 'double diamond' model of international competitiveness: the Canadian experience', *Management International Review* **33**(Special Issue 1993/2): 17–40.

Rugman, A.M. and Girod, S. (2003) 'Retail multinationals and globalization: the evidence is regional', *European Management Review* **21**(1): 24–37.

Rugman, A.M., Van den Broeck, J. and Verbeke, A.J. (eds.) (1995) *Global Strategic Management: Beyond the Diamond*, JAI Press: Greenwich, CN.

Rugman, A.M. and Verbeke, A. (1991) 'Environmental Change and Global Competitive Strategy in Europe', in A. Rugman and A. Verbeke (eds.) *Global Competition and the European Community*, JAI Press: Greenwich, CN, pp. 3–28.

Rugman, A.M. and Verbeke, A. (1992) 'A note on the transnational solution and the transaction cost theory of multinational strategic management', *Journal of International Business Studies* **23**(4): 761–771.

Rugman, A.M. and Verbeke, A. (1993) 'Foreign subsidiaries and multinational strategic management: an extension of Porter's single diamond framework', *Management International Review* **33**(2): 71–84.

Rugman, A.M. and Verbeke, A. (2001) 'Subsidiary-specific advantages in multinational enterprises', *Strategic Management Journal* **22**(3): 237–250.

Rugman, A.M. and Verbeke, A. (2003) 'The World Trade Organization, Multinational Enterprises, and the Civil Society', in M. Fratianni, P. Savona and J. Kirton (eds.) *Sustaining Global Growth and Development*, Ashgate: Aldershot, pp. 81–97.

Ruigrok, W. and Wagner, H. (2003) 'Internationalization and performance: an organizational learning perspective', *Management International Review* **43**(1): 63–83.

United Nations (2002) *World Investment Report 2002*, UN Conference on Trade and Development: New York and Geneva.

Van den Bulcke, D. (1995) 'The Strategic Management of Multinationals in a Triad-based World economy', in A.M. Rugman, J. Van den Broeck and A. Verbeke (eds.) *Global Strategic Management: Beyond the Diamond*, JAI Press: Greenwich, CN, pp. 25–63.

Vermeulen, F. and Barkema, H. (2002) 'Pace, rhythm, and scope: process dependence in building a profitable multinational corporation', *Strategic Management Journal* **23**: 637–653.

Vernon, R. (1966) 'International investment and international trade in the product cycle', *Quarterly Journal of Economics* **80**: 190–207.

Wan, W.P. and Hoskisson, R.E. (2003) 'Home country environments, corporate diversification strategies and firm performance', *Academy of Management Journal* **46**(1): 27–45.

Williamson, O.E. (1975) *Markets and Hierarchies: Analysis and Antitrust Implications.*, Free Press: New York.

Yeung, H., Wai-chung, P., Martin, J. and Martin, P. (2001) 'Towards a regional strategy: the role of regional headquarters of foreign firms in Singapore', *Urban Studies* **38**(1): 157–183.

Yip, G. (2002) *Total Global Strategy II*, Prentice Hall: Upper Saddle River, NJ.

Zaheer, S. (1995) 'Overcoming the liability of foreignness', *Academy of Management Journal* **38**(2): 341–363.

About the authors

Alan M Rugman is L Leslie Waters Chair of International Business and a professor at the Kelley School of Business, Indiana University, Bloomington, USA. He is also Director of the IU CIBER. He is also an Associate Fellow of Templeton College, University of Oxford. Previously, he was a professor at the University of Toronto in Canada. He has published numerous books and articles dealing with the strategic management of multinational enterprises and trade and investment policy. His recent books include: the Oxford Handbook of International Business (2001), Multinationals as Flagship Firms (2000), and Environmental Regulations and Corporate Strategy (1999), all published by Oxford University Press.

Alain Verbeke holds the McCaig Chair in Management at the Haskayne School of Business, University of Calgary (Canada), and is an Associate Fellow of Templeton College, University of Oxford (UK). He was previously the Director of the MBA programme, Solvay Business School, Free University of Brussels (VUB) (Belgium), and has extensive practical experience in multinational strategic planning and complex project evaluation. This is his seventh article in *JIBS*.

Accepted by Arie Lewin, Editor in Chief, 26 November 2003. This paper has been with the author for two revisions.

[5]

Journal of International Business Studies (2005) 36, 357–378
© 2005 Academy of International Business   All rights reserved 0047-2506 $30.00
www.jibs.net

PERSPECTIVE

Culture and international business: recent advances and their implications for future research

Kwok Leung[1], Rabi S Bhagat[2], Nancy R Buchan[3], Miriam Erez[4] and Cristina B Gibson[5]

[1]Department of Management, City University of Hong Kong, Kowloon, Hong Kong; [2]University of Memphis, Memphis, TN, USA; [3]University of Wisconsin, Madison, WI, USA; [4]Technion-Israel Institute of Technology, Haifa, Israel; [5]University of California, Irvine, CA, USA

Correspondence:
Dr K Leung, Department of Management, City University of Hong Kong, Tat Chee Avenue, Kowloon, Hong Kong.
Tel: +852 2788 9592;
Fax: +852 2788 9085;
E-mail: mkkleung@cityu.edu.hk

Authors' note: This paper is based on a symposium organized by Kwok Leung with the co-authors as participants in the First Annual Conference on Emerging Research Frontiers in International Business at Duke University in March 2003. The co-authors have contributed equally to the development of this paper.

Received: 13 August 2003
Revised: 20 December 2004
Accepted: 25 February 2005
Online publication date: 2 June 2005

Abstract
The paper provides a state-of-the-art review of several innovative advances in culture and international business (IB) to stimulate new avenues for future research. We first review the issues surrounding cultural convergence and divergence, and the processes underlying cultural changes. We then examine novel constructs for characterizing cultures, and how to enhance the precision of cultural models by pinpointing when cultural effects are important. Finally, we examine the usefulness of experimental methods, which are rarely used by IB researchers. Implications of these path-breaking approaches for future research on culture and IB are discussed.
Journal of International Business Studies (2005) 36, 357–378.
doi:10.1057/palgrave.jibs.8400150

Keywords: culture and international business; convergence and divergence of cultures; cultural change; cultural dimensions; cross-cultural experiments

Introduction

In this new millennium, few executives can afford to turn a blind eye to global business opportunities. Japanese auto-executives monitor carefully what their European and Korean competitors are up to in getting a bigger slice of the Chinese auto-market. Executives of Hollywood movie studios need to weigh the appeal of an expensive movie in Europe and Asia as much as in the US before a firm commitment. The globalizing wind has broadened the mindsets of executives, extended the geographical reach of firms, and nudged international business (IB) research into some new trajectories.

One such new trajectory is the concern with national culture. Whereas traditional IB research has been concerned with economic/legal issues and organizational forms and structures, the importance of national culture – broadly defined as values, beliefs, norms, and behavioral patterns of a national group – has become increasingly important in the last two decades, largely as a result of the classic work of Hofstede (1980). National culture has been shown to impact on major business activities, from capital structure (Chui *et al.*, 2002) to group performance (Gibson, 1999). For reviews, see Boyacigiller and Adler (1991) and Earley and Gibson (2002).

The purpose of this paper is to provide a state-of-the-art review of several recent advances in culture and IB research, with an eye

Table 1 A schematic summary of the paper

Section focus	Key conceptual question	Key implication for IB research
Cultural convergence and divergence	Are cultures becoming more similar under the force of globalization?	Whether standard business practices will emerge
Cultural change	What are the dynamics of cultural change?	How will business practices change over time?
Novel constructs of culture	What is new about culture?	New concepts for understanding cultural differences in business practices
Moderating effects of culture	When is culture important?	When to adopt standard business practices
Experimental approaches	How to test the effects of culture experimentally	Causal inferences about the effects of culture on standard business practices

toward productive avenues for future research. It is not our purpose to be comprehensive; our goal is to spotlight a few highly promising areas for leapfrogging the field in an increasingly boundaryless business world. We first review the issues surrounding cultural convergence and divergence, and the processes underlying cultural changes. We then examine novel constructs for characterizing cultures, and how to enhance the precision of cultural models by pinpointing when the effects of culture are important. Finally, we examine the usefulness of experimental methods, which are rarely employed in the field of culture and IB. A schematic summary of our coverage is given in Table 1, which suggests that the topics reviewed are loosely related, and that their juxtaposition in the present paper represents our attempt to highlight their importance rather than their coherence as elements of an integrative framework.

Cultural change, convergence and divergence in an era of partial globalization

An issue of considerable theoretical significance is concerned with cultural changes and transformations taking place in different parts of the world. In fact, since the landmark study of Haire *et al.* (1966) and the publication of *Industrialism and Industrial Man* by Kerr *et al.* (1960), researchers have continued to search for similarities in culture-specific beliefs and attitudes in various aspects of work-related attitudes and behaviors, consumption patterns, and the like. If cultures of the various locales of the world are indeed converging (e.g., Heuer *et al.*, 1999), IB-related practices would indeed become increasingly similar. Standard, culture-free business practices would eventually emerge, and inefficiencies and complexities associated with divergent beliefs and practices in the past era would disappear. In the following section, we review the

evidence on the issue and conclude that such an outlook pertaining to the convergence of various IB practices is overly optimistic.

Evolution of partial globalization

Globalization refers to a 'growing economic interdependence among countries, as reflected in the increased cross-border flow of three types of entities: goods and services, capital, and know-how' (Govindarajan and Gupta, 2001, 4). Few spoke of 'world economy' 25 years ago, and the prevalent term was 'international trade' (Drucker, 1995). However today, international trade has culminated in the emergence of a global economy, consisting of flows of information, technology, money, and people, and is conducted via government international organizations such as the North American Free Trade Agreement (NAFTA) and the European Community; global organizations such as the International Organization for Standardization (ISO); multinational companies (MNCs); and cross-border alliances in the form of joint ventures, international mergers, and acquisitions. These inter-relationships have enhanced participation in the world economy, and have become a key to domestic economic growth and prosperity (Drucker, 1995, 153).

Yet, globalization is not without its misgivings and discontents (Sassan, 1998). A vivid image associated with the G8 summits is the fervent protests against globalization in many parts of the world, as shown in television and reported in the popular media. Strong opposition to globalization usually originates from developing countries that have been hurt by the destabilizing effects of globalization, but in recent times we have also seen heated debates in Western economies triggered by significant loss of professional jobs as a result of offshoring to low-wage countries. Indeed, workers in manufacturing and farming in advanced economies are becoming increasingly wary of globalization, as their income continues to decline significantly. In parallel to the angry protests against globalization, the flow of goods, services, and investments across national borders has continued to fall after the rapid gains of the 1990s. Furthermore, the creation of regional trade blocs, such as NAFTA, the European Union, and the Association of Southeast Asian Nations, have stimulated discussions about creating other trade zones involving countries in South Asia, Africa, and other parts of the world. Although it is often assumed that countries belonging to the World Trade Organization (WTO) have embraced globalization, the fact is that the world is only partially globalized, at best (Schaeffer, 2003). Many parts of Central Asia and Eastern Europe, including the former republics of the Soviet Union, parts of Latin America, Africa, and parts of South Asia, have been skeptical of globalization (Greider, 1997). In fact, less than 10% of the world's population are fully globalized (i.e., being active participants in the consumption of global products and services) (Schaeffer, 2003). Therefore, it is imperative that we analyze the issues of cultural convergence and divergence in this partially globalized world.

'Universal culture' often refers to the assumptions, values, and practices of people in the West and some elites in non-Western cultures. Huntington (1996) suggested that it originates from the intellectual elites from a selected group of countries who meet annually in the World Economic Forum in Davos, Switzerland. These individuals are highly educated, work with symbols and numbers, are fluent in English, are extensively involved with international commitments, and travel frequently outside their country. They share the cultural value of individualism, and believe strongly in market economics and political democracy. Although those belonging to the Davos group control virtually all of the world's important international institutions, many of the world's governments, and a great majority of the world's economic and military capabilities, the cultural values of the Davos group are probably embraced by only a small fraction of the six billion people of the world.

Popular culture, again mostly Western European and American in origin, also contributes to a convergence of consumption patterns and leisure activities around the world. However, the convergence may be superficial, and have only a small influence on fundamental issues such as beliefs, norms, and ideas about how individuals, groups, institutions, and other important social agencies ought to function. In fact, Huntington (1996, 58) noted that 'The essence of Western civilization is the Magna Carta, not the Magna Mac. The fact that non-Westerners may bite into the latter has no implications for their accepting the former'. This argument is obvious if we reverse the typical situation and put Western Europeans and Americans in the shoes of recipients of cultural influence. For instance, while Chinese Kung Fu dominates fight scenes in Hollywood movies such as *Matrix Reloaded*, and Chinese restaurants abound in the West, it seems implausible that Americans and Europeans have espoused more Chinese values because of their fondness of Chinese Kung Fu and food.

A major argument against cultural convergence is that traditionalism and modernity may be unrelated (Smith and Bond, 1998). Strong traditional values, such as group solidarity, interpersonal harmony, paternalism, and familism, can co-exist with modern values of individual achievement and competition. A case in point is the findings that Chinese in Singapore and China indeed endorsed both traditional and modern values (Chang *et al.*, 2003; Zhang *et al.*, 2003). It is also conceivable that, just as we talk about Westernization of cultural values around the world, we may also talk about Easternization of values in response to forces of modernity and consumption values imposed by globalization (Marsella and Choi, 1993).

Although the argument that the world is becoming one culture seems untenable, there are some areas that do show signs of convergence. We explore in the following the role of several factors that simultaneously cause cultures of the world to either converge or diverge, in an attempt to identify several productive avenues for future research.

Role of international trade
Clyde V Prestowitz Jr., President of the Economic Strategy Institute, Washington, DC, observed that most international trade negotiations are in trouble (Leonhardt, 2003). These negotiations were successful in the last decade, but complex issues have emerged that have the potential to derail the growth of international trade in the future. For instance, many representatives of large agricultural countries, such as Brazil and Argentina, notice little significant progress in the area of trade in international exports. Similarly, countries in East and Southeast Asia specializing in exporting complex

technological products to the West have undergone significant declines in international trade as a result of fiscal crises. They are beginning to question whether globalization will bring benefits greater than regionalization of trade. In recent years, Japan, for example, has expanded trade activities with China and other East Asian countries rather than with the West. Our review and analysis of the literature suggests that because globalization tends to redistribute economic rewards in a non-uniform manner, a backlash against globalization may occur in countries often confronted with unpredictable and adverse consequences of globalization, causing them to revert to their own cultural-specific patterns of economic growth and development (Guillén, 2001). These trends might indicate that globalization is being impeded by tendencies towards country-specific modes of economic development, making the convergence of IB-related values and practices difficult to achieve. We do not know much about these dynamics, which definitely need to be explored in future research.

Role of computer-mediated communication
Technology, particularly computer-mediated communication, has been hailed as a major force in creating cultural convergence around the world and facilitating the spread of IB. Autonomous business units of global corporations are continuously connected, not necessarily in large physical structures, but in global electronic networks functioning interdependently. Some authors even claim that physical distance is no longer a major factor in the spread of global business (Cairncross, 2001; Govindarajan and Gupta, 2001). Computer-mediated communication enables users to access a huge amount of factual information globally; however, it does not necessarily increase their capacity to absorb the information at the same rate as the information is disseminated or diffused. In addition, information and knowledge are interpreted through cultural lenses, and the transfer or diffusion of organizational knowledge is not easy to accomplish across cultural boundaries (Bhagat *et al.*, 2002).

Hofstede (2001) observed that not only will cultural diversity among countries persist but also new technologies might even intensify the cultural differences between and within countries. As was noted earlier, the spread of information about people's lives in different parts of the world has affected some minorities who compare their fate in life with that of others with a higher standard of living. Ethnic groups around the world observe the lifestyles and cultural values of other countries, and some are interested in adopting part of the lifestyle and values, but others reject it completely. The effects of new technologies on improving efficiencies of multinational and global corporations are well known, but it is not known how these new technologies, especially computer-mediated communication and the Internet, might create significant shifts in the cultural patterns of different ethnic groups.

To summarize, computer-mediated communication has the simultaneous effects of increasing both cultural convergence and divergence. We need to explore how its spread is affecting the progress of globalization in different parts of the world by incorporating the role of cultural syndromes, organizational cultures, and other processes, which has recently been attempted by scholars such as Bhagat *et al.* (2003) and Gibson and Cohen (2003). Unfortunately, empirical work on these processes is scanty, and more research is needed before comprehensive theoretical statements can be formulated.

Role of multiculturalism and cultural identity
The broad ideological framework of a country, corporation, or situation is the most important determinant of the cultural identity that people develop in a given locale (Triandis, 1994). The 'melting pot' ideology suggests that each cultural group loses some of its dominant characteristics in order to become mainstream: this is *assimilation*, or what Triandis (1994) calls *subtractive multiculturalism*. In contrast, when people from a cultural group add appropriate skills and characteristics of other groups, it may be called *integration*, or *additive multiculturalism*.

Both of these processes are essential for cultural convergence to proceed. However, if there is a significant history of conflict between the cultural groups, it is hard to initiate these processes, as in the case of Israelis and Palestinians. In general, although there has been some research on the typology of animosity against other nations (e.g., Jung *et al.*, 2002), we do not know much about how emotional antagonism against other cultural groups affects trade patterns and intercultural cooperation in a business context. The issues of cultural identity and emotional reactions to other cultural groups in an IB context constitute a significant gap in our research effort in this area.

Implications of convergence and divergence issues

One message is clear: while convergence in some domains of IB activity is easily noticeable, especially in consumer values and lifestyles, significant divergence of cultures persists. In fact, Hofstede (2001) asserts that mental programs of people around the world do not change rapidly, but remain rather consistent over time. His findings indicate that cultural shifts are relative as opposed to absolute. Although clusters of some countries in given geographical locales (e.g., Argentina, Brazil, Chile) might indicate significant culture shifts towards embracing Anglo values, the changes do not diminish the absolute differences between such countries and those of the Anglo countries (i.e., US, Canada, UK). Huntington, in his *The Clash of Civilizations* (1996), presents the view that there is indeed a resurgence of non-Western cultures around the world, which could result in the redistribution of national power in the conduct of international affairs. The attempt by the Davos group to bring about uniform practices in various aspects of IB and work culture, thereby sustaining the forces of globalization, is certainly worthwhile. However, our analysis suggests that there is no guarantee that such convergence will come about easily, or without long periods of resistance.

IB scholars need to understand that although some countries might exhibit strong tendencies toward cultural convergence, as is found in Western countries, there are countries that will reject globalization, not only because of its adverse economic impacts (Greider, 1997) but also because globalization tends to introduce distortions (in their view) in profound cultural syndromes that characterize their national character. Furthermore, reactions to globalization may take other forms. Bhagat *et al.* (2003) have recently argued that *adaptation* is another approach that could characterize the tendencies of some cultures in the face of mounting pressures to globalize. Other approaches are *rejection, creative synthesis*, and *innovation* (Bhagat *et al.*, 2003). These different approaches highlight once again the complex dynamics that underlie cultural convergence and divergence in a partially globalized world. Also, in discussing issues of convergence and divergence, it is necessary to recognize that the shift in values is not always *from* Western society to others, but can result in the change of Western cultural values as well. For example, the emphasis on quality and teamwork in the West is partly a result of the popularity of Japanese management two decades ago.

Scholars of IB should recognize that the issue of convergence and divergence in this era of partial globalization will remain as a persistent and complex issue whose direction might only be assessed on a region-by-region basis. It is also wise to adopt an interdisciplinary perspective in understanding the forces that create both convergence and divergence of cultures in different parts of the world. For instance, in *Understanding Globalization*, Schaeffer (2003) has provided an insightful discussion of the social consequences of political, economic and other changes, which have significant implications for IB. The cause–effect relationships of globalization and its various outcomes, especially the cultural outcomes, are not only characterized by bi-directional arrows, but are embedded in a complex web of relationships. How these complex relationships and processes play out on the stage of IB remains to be uncovered by IB researchers.

Processes of cultural changes

In the previous section, we make the point that, through the process of globalization, cultures influence each other and change, but whether or not these changes will bring about cultural convergence is yet to be seen. In this section, we delineate a general model that describes and explains the complex processes underlying cultural changes. As explained before, IB is both an agent and a recipient of cultural change, and for international business to flourish it is important to understand its complex, reciprocal relationships with cultural change.

In line with the view of Hofstede (2001) that culture changes very slowly, culture has been treated as a relatively stable characteristic, reflecting a shared knowledge structure that attenuates variability in values, behavioral norms, and patterns of behaviors (Erez and Earley, 1993).

Cultural stability helps to reduce ambiguity, and leads to more control over expected behavioral outcomes (Weick and Quinn, 1999; Leana and Barry, 2000). For instance, most existing models of culture and work behavior assume cultural stability and emphasize the fit between a given culture and certain managerial and motivational practices (Erez and Earley, 1993). High fit means high adaptation of managerial practices to a given culture and, therefore, high effectiveness. The assumption of cultural stability is valid as long as there are no environmental changes that precipitate adaptation and cultural change. Yet, the end of the 20th century and the beginning of the new millennium have been characterized by turbulent political and economical changes, which instigate cultural changes. In line with this argument, Lewin and Kim (2004), in their comprehensive chapter on adaptation and selection in strategy and change, distinguished between theories driven by the underlying assumption that adaptation is the mechanism to cope with change, and theories driven by the underlying assumption of selection and the survival of the fittest, suggesting that ineffective forms of organization disappear, and new forms emerge. However, although organizational changes as a reaction to environmental changes have been subjected to considerable conceptual analyses, the issue of cultural change at the national level has rarely been addressed.

There are relatively few theories of culture that pertain to the dynamic aspect of culture. One exception is the ecocultural model by Berry *et al.* (2002), which views culture as evolving adaptations to ecological and socio-political influences, and views individual psychological characteristics in a population as adaptive to their cultural context, as well as to the broader ecological and socio-political influences. Similarly, Kitayama (2002) proposes a *system view* to understanding the dynamic nature of culture, as opposed to the *entity view* that sees culture as a static entity. This *system view* suggests that each person's psychological processes are organized through the active effort to coordinate one's behaviors with the pertinent cultural systems of practices and public meanings. Yet, concurrently, many aspects of the psychological systems develop rather flexibly as they are attuned to the surrounding socio-cultural environment, and are likely to be configured in different ways across different socio-cultural groups.

These adaptive views of culture are supported by empirical evidence. For example, Van de Vliert *et al.* (1999) identified curvilinear relationships between temperature, masculinity and domestic political violence across 53 countries. Their findings showed that masculinity and domestic violence are higher in moderately warm countries than in countries with extreme temperatures. Inglehart and Baker (2000) examined cultural change as reflected by changes in basic values in three waves of the World Values Surveys, which included 65 societies and 75% of the world's population. Their analysis showed that economic development was associated with shifts away from traditional norms and values toward values that are increasingly rational, tolerant, trusting, and participatory. However, the data also showed that the broad cultural heritage of a society, whether it is Protestant, Roman Catholic, Orthodox, Confucian, or Communist, leaves an enduring imprint on traditional values despite the forces of modernization.

The process of globalization described before has introduced the most significant change in IB, with its effects filtering down to the national, organizational, group and individual levels. Reciprocally, changes at micro-levels of culture, when shared by the members of the society, culminate into macro-level phenomena and change the macro-levels of culture. In the absence of research models that can shed light on this complex process of cultural change, Erez and Gati (2004) proposed that the general model of multi-level analysis (Klein and Kozlowski, 2000) could be adopted for understanding the dynamics of culture and cultural change.

The dynamics of culture as a multi-level, multi-layer construct

The proposed model consists of two building blocks. One is a multi-level approach, viewing culture as a multi-level construct that consists of various levels nested within each other from the most macro-level of a global culture, through national cultures, organizational cultures, group cultures, and cultural values that are represented in the self at the individual level, as portrayed in Figure 1. The second is based on Schein's (1992) model viewing culture as a multi-layer construct consisting of the most external layer of observed artifacts and behaviors, the deeper level of values, which is testable by social consensus, and the deepest level of basic assumption, which is invisible and taken for granted. The present model proposes that culture as a multi-layer construct exists at all levels – from the global to the individual – and that at each level change first occurs at the most external layer of behavior, and then, when shared by individuals who belong to the same cultural context, it becomes a shared value that characterizes the aggregated unit (group, organizations, or nations).

In the model, the most macro-level is that of a global culture being created by global networks and global institutions that cross national and cultural borders. As exemplified by the effort of the Davos group discussed earlier, global organizational structures need to adopt common rules and procedures in order to have a common 'language' for communicating across cultural borders (Kostova, 1999; Kostova and Roth, 2003; Gupta and Govindarajan,

Advances in culture and international business   Kwok Leung *et al*

363

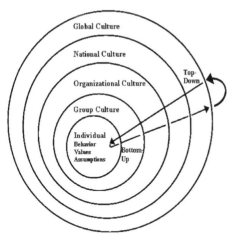

Figure 1 The dynamic of top-down–bottom-up processes across levels of culture.

2000). Given the dominance of Western MNCs, the values that dominate the global context are often based on a free market economy, democracy, acceptance and tolerance of diversity, respect of freedom of choice, individual rights, and openness to change (Gupta and Govindarajan, 2000).

Below the global level are nested organizations and networks at the national level with their local cultures varying from one nation, or network to another. Further down are local organizations, and although all of them share some common values of their national culture, they vary in their local organizational cultures, which are also shaped by the type of industry that they represent, the type of ownership, the values of the founders, etc. Within each organization are sub-units and groups that share the common national and organizational culture, but that differ from each other in their unit culture on the basis of the differences in their functions (e.g., R&D *vs* manufacturing), their leaders' values, and the professional and educational level of their members. At the bottom of this structure are individuals who through the process of socialization acquire the cultural values transmitted to them from higher levels of culture. Individuals who belong to the same group share the same values that differentiate them from other groups and create a group-level culture through a bottom-up process of aggregation of shared values. For example, employees of an R&D unit are selected

into the unit because of their creative cognitive style and professional expertise. Their leader also typically facilitates the display of these personal characteristics because they are crucial for developing innovative products. Thus, all members of this unit share similar core values, which differentiate them from other organizational units. Groups that share similar values create the organizational culture through a process of aggregation, and local organizations that share similar values create the national culture that is different from other national cultures.

Both top-down and bottom-up processes reflect the dynamic nature of culture, and explain how culture at different levels is being shaped and reshaped by changes that occur at other levels, either above it through top-down processes or below it through bottom-up processes. Similarly, changes at each level affect lower levels through a top-down process, and upper levels through a bottom-up process of aggregation. The changes in national cultures observed by Inglehart and Baker (2000) could serve as an example for top-down effects of economic growth, enhanced by globalization, on a cultural shift from traditional values to modernization. However, in line with Schein (1992), the deep basic assumptions still reflect the traditional values shaped by the broad cultural heritage of a society.

Global organizations and networks are being formed by having local-level organizations join the global arena. That means that there is a continuous reciprocal process of shaping and reshaping organizations at both levels. For example, multinational companies that operate in the global market develop common rules and cultural values that enable them to create a synergy between the various regions, and different parts of the multinational company. These global rules and values filter down to the local organizations that constitute the global company, and, over time, they shape the local organizations. Reciprocally, having local organizations join a global company may introduce changes into the global company because of its need to function effectively across different cultural boarders.

A study by Erez-Rein *et al.* (2004) demonstrated how a multinational company that acquired an Israeli company that develops and produces medical instruments changed the organizational culture of the acquired company. The study identified a cultural gap between the two companies, with the Israeli company being higher on the cultural dimension of innovation and lower on the cultural dimension of attention to detail and conformity to rules and standards as compared with the acquiring company. The latter insisted on sending the Israeli managers to intensive courses in Six-Sigma, which is an advanced method of quality improvement, and a managerial philosophy that encompasses all organizational functions. Upon returning to their company, these managers introduced quality improvement work methods and procedures to the local company, and caused behavioral changes, followed by the internalization of quality-oriented values. Thus, a top-down process of training and education led to changes in work behavior and work values. Sharing common behaviors and values by all employees of the local company then shaped the organizational culture through bottom-up processes. The case of cultural change via international acquisitions demonstrated the two building blocks of our dynamic model of culture: the multi-level structure explains how a lower-level culture is being shaped by top-down effects, and that the cultural layer that changes first is the most external layer of behavior. In the long run, bottom-up processes of shared behaviors and norms shape the local organizational culture.

Globalization and self-identity

Top-down processes from the global culture to the individual level may lead to changes in the self as cultural values are represented in the self. The self is a multi-facet construct that consists of self- and social identities. Self-identity differentiates one person from another, whereas social identity is based on the groups in which one participates (Tajfel and Turner, 1979). Social identity theory has commonly been examined in relation to membership in social groups and national cultures. However, the global environment creates a new collective and impersonal entity that affects people's identity. Global identity means that people develop a sense of belongingness to a worldwide culture, by adopting practices, styles, and information that are part of the global culture (Arnett, 2002). However, in parallel, people continue to hold their local identity as well, based on their socialization to their local culture. Arnett (2002) defines these two facets of self-identity as a bi-cultural identity, in which part of the self-identity is rooted in the local culture, while another part develops in relation to the global culture. Thus, people all over the world wear jeans, enjoy fried rice, eat at McDonald's, listen to Discmans, and surf

on the Internet; yet, at the same time, they keep their own cultural values, their social group, and their national identity, drawing on each identity according to what they deem necessary in a given context. Through a top-down process, the global environment – a macro-level construct – affects the development of a bi-cultural identity at the individual level, by shaping the individual's global identity, and thus facilitating adaptation to the global world. As discussed before, however, the extent to which a bi-cultural identity develops depends on whether subtractive or additive multiculturalism is encouraged. This dual nature of identity presents a challenge to the operation of multinational firms, as we know little about how complex self-identity processes are related to behavior and performance in an IB setting.

Factors that facilitate cultural change

Culture itself influences the level of resistance or acceptance of change. Harzing and Hofstede (1996) proposed that certain cultural values facilitate change, whereas others hinder it. The values of low power distance, low uncertainty avoidance, and individualism facilitate change. Change threatens stability, and introduces uncertainty, and resistance to change will therefore be higher in cultures of high rather than low uncertainty avoidance (Steensma *et al.*, 2000). Change also threatens the power structure, and therefore will be avoided in high power distance cultures. Finally, change breaks the existing harmony, which is highly valued in collectivistic cultures, and therefore will not be easily accepted by collectivists (Levine and Norenzayan, 1999).

A recent study by Erez and Gati (2004) examined the effects of three factors on the change process and its outcomes:

(1) the cultural value of individualism–collectivism;

(2) the reward structure and its congruence with the underlying cultural values; and

(3) the degree of ambiguity in the reward structure.

The change process examined was a shift from choosing to work *alone* to a behavioral choice of working as part of a *team,* and *vice versa.* Working alone is more prevalent in individualistic cultures, whereas working in teams dominates the collectivistic ones. Two sub-cultures from Israel participated in the study: Arab Israeli citizens, who scored high on collectivism; and Jewish citizens, who grew up in big cities and scored significantly lower on collectivism than did the Arab participants. Results showed that the behavioral choices of the Arab participants remained more or less unchanged despite different manipulations of reward congruence and ambiguity, suggesting that collectivism was related to resistance to change. In addition, resistance to change was higher when the rewarded alternative was incongruent with their underlying cultural values, and when the level of ambiguity was high rather than low.

This study demonstrated that the top-down effects on cultural change are moderated by culture itself, and by the reward system. Changes are more likely to occur in individualistic cultures when the reward structure is clear, and when the rewarded behavior does not conflict with the dominant value system. Change is first observed in people's behavior, as shown in Erez and Gati's (2004) study. In the long run, when the new behavioral norms are being shared by all group members, they filter down to the deeper level of cultural values as they are represented in the self. The representation of new values in the self may subsequently shape a more collectivistic (or individualistic) society. To sum up, this study tested the dynamic nature of culture by integrating two constructs, multi-level and multi-layer views of culture, into one dynamic model. The multi-level construct helps us understand how culture is being shaped and reshaped by the dynamic top-down, bottom-up processes, which transmit the effect of one cultural level to another. The multi-layer construct provides a framework to describe the nature of the cultural changes.

In summary, the proposed multi-level, multi-layer model is useful to IB researchers who are interested in modeling and studying the process of cultural change along two continua: from the global to the individual level, and from the external layer of behavior to the internal layer of basic assumptions and axioms. Understanding these processes is obviously crucial to the effective operation of multinational business operations.

Novel cultural constructs
In addition to rethinking our general conceptualization of culture and cultural processes, we encourage researchers to re-examine the specific cultural constructs utilized in theory and research. A major approach in the literature has been to relate IB phenomena to special cultural characteristics, and to improve upon this approach it is important to expand our conceptualization of culture. In this section, we focus on novel conceptualizations of culture that are emerging in the literature.

There are two interesting directions for identifying novel cultural constructs in the literature, which are almost diametric in their orientation. The first development follows in the footsteps of Hofstede in the search of novel trait-like, static cultural dimensions, whereas the second development is inspired by breakthroughs in cognitive psychology, which increasingly portray the human mind as dynamic, elastic, and situated.

Novel cultural dimensions
The classic work of Hofstede (1980) has revolutionized the research on culture and IB. Subsequent to his original work, Hofstede (2001) has added one more dimension to his framework: Confucian Work Dynamism or short- vs long-term orientation, based on the work of the Chinese Culture Connection (1987). The validity of the cultural dimensions identified by Hofstede has been controversial (for a recent debate surrounding individualism–collectivism, see Oyserman *et al.*, 2002a), but they have provided a broad framework that has inspired much IB research.

Subsequent to the work of Hofstede, a few global projects have attempted to search for new cultural dimensions. Schwartz (1994) has identified seven culture-level dimensions of values: Conservatism, Intellectual Autonomy, Affective Autonomy, Hierarchy, Egalitarian Commitment, Mastery, and Harmony. These dimensions have been used to predict cultural differences, including locus of control (Smith *et al.*, 1995) and work-related issues, such as the sources of guidance that managers relied on (Smith *et al.*, 2002), and capital structure (Chui *et al.*, 2002). Smith *et al.* (1996) have identified two culture-level dimensions from an analysis of managerial values: Egalitarian Commitment *vs* Conservatism, and Utilitarian Involvement *vs* Loyal Involvement. Smith and Bond (1998, Chapter 3) have concluded that these different value surveys have produced convergent results, lending support to the validity of the cultural dimensions originally identified by Hofstede (1980).

Recently, in an attempt to understand leadership behavior around the world, House and his associates have identified nine culture-level dimensions: Performance Orientation, Assertiveness Orientation, Future Orientation, Humane Orientation, Institutional Collectivism, Family Collectivism, Gender Egalitarianism, Power Distance, and Uncertainty Avoidance (Gupta and House, 2004;

House *et al.*, 2004). The GLOBE project adopted a theory-based approach, and *a priori* dimensions were formulated based primarily on Hofstede's dimensions, values described by Kluckhohn and Strodtbeck (1961) and McClelland (1961), and the interpersonal communication literature (Sarros and Woodman, 1993). Thus, despite the use of different items to identify cultural dimensions, the results are consistent with previous results, and most of the cultural dimensions identified are related conceptually and correlated empirically with Hofstede's dimensions. Assertiveness Orientation and Gender Egalitarianism are related to Hofstede's construct of Masculinity–Femininity, Institutional Collectivism and Family Collectivism to Individualism–Collectivism, Power Distance and Uncertainty Avoidance to the two Hofstede dimensions with the same labels, and Future Orientation to Long-term Orientation. The usefulness of a more refined typology of the Hofstede dimensions remains to be demonstrated. Two dimensions are independent of the Hofstede dimensions. Performance Orientation seems conceptually related to McClelland's (1961) concept of need for achievement, and Humane Orientation seems conceptually related to the Human Nature is Good *vs* Bad dimension of Kluckhohn and Strodtbeck (1961). Although these dimensions are not new, they may prove useful for understanding some IB phenomena. Take leadership as an example: we know that leaders vary in their task orientation, and Performance Orientation may be related to a general emphasis on task orientation. Leaders also vary in their supervisory style, and Humane Orientation may be negatively related to close supervision. Obviously, relationships with other variables are also possible, and hopefully future research will yield theoretically interesting correlates of these two dimensions.

The most recent large-scale attempt to expand the dimensional map of culture is the global study on social axioms orchestrated by Leung and Bond. Social axioms are general beliefs that may be conceptualized as *generalized expectancies*, a concept introduced by Rotter (1966) to characterize locus of control. Leung *et al.* (2002) have created a social axiom survey based on items culled from the psychological literature as well as from qualitative research conducted in Hong Kong and Venezuela. Factor analysis of these items has unearthed a five-factor structure within each of five cultures: Hong Kong, Venezuela, the USA, Japan, and Germany. A subsequent round-the-world study has confirmed

the robustness of this structure in over 40 cultural groups (Leung and Bond, 2004), and this five-dimensional structure at the individual level has already been applied to the investigation of influence tactics in an IB context (Fu *et al.*, 2004). A culture-level factor analysis based on 41 cultural groups has yielded only two factors (Bond *et al.*, 2004). *Dynamic Externality* refers to beliefs in fate, the existence of a supreme being, positive functions of religion practice, which give rise to the label 'externality'. However, the content also suggests beliefs in effort and knowledge, as well complexity in the social world, which gives a dynamic slant to this construct. *Societal Cynicism* reflects a negative view of human nature and a mistrust in social institutions. Correlations with a wide range of country-level indexes support the interpretation of these two dimensions given before. Furthermore, dynamic externality is related to collectivism and high power distance, but Societal Cynicism is relatively distinct from previous cultural dimensions. These two dimensions may have significant implications for IB research. For instance, across a wide variety of cultures, dynamic externality is related to the reliance on superiors as a source of guidance, and Societal Cynicism to job dissatisfaction. Future research may reveal interesting relationships between these two cultural dimensions and other IB phenomena.

The global projects reviewed above suggest that the Hofstede dimensions are robust, although subsequent work has led to some important refinement and clarification. More importantly, at least three novel dimensions have been identified: Performance Orientation, Humane Orientation, and Societal Cynicism. We do not know much about these cultural dimensions, and their importance for IB research is obviously an important area for future exploration.

A dynamic view of culture

Current research in cognitive psychology shows that the human mind is fluid and adaptive, and is engaged in active, dynamic interaction with the environment. This conception of the human mind gives rises to a dynamic view of culture, which contrasts sharply with traditional views that regard culture as more or less stable and static. This dynamic view of culture argues that culture is represented by cognitive structures and processes that are sensitive to environmental influences. For instance, Tinsley and Brodt (2004) have provided a cognitive analysis of cultural differences in conflict behaviors. *Frames* direct attention to certain aspects of the environment; *schemas* are knowledge structures that give meaning to encoded information; and *scripts* are a special type of schema that involve a temporal sequence and are most relevant for events and actions. These constructs are dynamic in the sense that their content and salience are sensitive to environmental influences. Tinsley and Brodt suggest that these cognitive constructs are useful in understanding cross-cultural differences in conflict behaviors. As an example, whereas conflict frames that emphasize self-interest and mutual interest are appropriate for Americans, a different conflict frame that emphasizes a collective or community orientation is more useful in describing the conflict behaviors of Asians. Another example comes from a connectionist approach to leadership and culture proposed by Hanges *et al.* (2000). In this framework, leadership behaviors are interpreted with schemas, which involve components such as scripts and beliefs. These components are under the influence of higher-order components such as values, affect, and self-image. Hanges *et al.* proposed that this complex, distributed view of schemas captures the essence of cultural meaning systems. Given that the components of a schema and their associations can change over time as a function of experience and situational influence, this model does not assume static effects of culture, and is well suited for the analysis of its dynamic effects.

An important implication of this dynamic view of culture is that cultural changes are more frequent than previously assumed. A good example is provided by the research of Hong *et al.* (2000). It is well known that, compared with people from individualist cultures, people from collectivist cultures are more likely to attribute the cause of other people's behaviors to external causes such as situational demands (as opposed to internal causes such as personality traits) (e.g., Morris and Peng, 1994). Hong *et al.* (2000) argued that a dynamic view of culture is indeed valid: a priming technique should be able to alter the mindset of people and as a result change their attributional style. To test this notion, Hong Kong Chinese, who were collectivists and inclined to make external attributions for others' behavior, were randomly exposed to one of two sets of experimental stimuli: one set included American icons such as Superman, and the other set contained Chinese icons such as the Monkey King (Hong *et al.*, 1997). Consistent with the dynamic view of culture, compared with the

Chinese primes, the American primes were able to shift the attribution of the Chinese participants in the internal direction. In other words, the American primes caused the Chinese participants to act more like Americans in their attributional style. Peng and Knowles (2003) replicated these findings with Asian Americans. When they were asked to recall an experience that highlighted their American identity, their attributional style was more in the internal direction than when they were asked to recall an experience that made their Asian identity more salient. In fact, Oyserman *et al.* (2002a) concluded after their meta-analysis of the individualism–collectivism literature that priming experiments such as those described above provide a promising tool to examine the dynamics of cultural influence. However, future research needs to explore whether priming results are too transient to be robust in the real world, and what the processes are that underlie these priming effects.

The implications of a dynamic view of culture for IB have not been explored. One intriguing possibility is that cultural differences may be easier to overcome than previously assumed, if mental processes associated with national culture are relatively fluid, and can be changed and sustained by appropriate situational influences. For instance, Leung and his associates (Leung *et al.*, 1996, 2001b) have found that local employees in international joint ventures in China reported more positive job attitudes working with Western expatriate managers than with overseas Chinese and Japanese expatriate managers. These findings contradict the cultural distance argument, which suggests that people from very different cultures have more problems working together than people from similar cultures. Undoubtedly, this new perspective will provide the basis for some exciting work on culture and IB in the future.

Understanding when culture matters: increasing the precision of cultural models
Beyond exploring new cultural constructs and the dynamic nature of culture, we also argue for the importance of examining contingency factors that enhance or mitigate the effect of national culture. Consider the following scenario. A senior human resource manager in a multinational firm is charged with implementing an integrative training program in several of the firm's subsidiaries around the globe. Over the term of her career, the manager has been educated about differences in national culture and is sensitive to intercultural opportunities and

challenges. At the same time, she understands the strategic need to create a unified global program that serves to further integrate the firm's basic processes, creating efficiencies and synergies across the remote sites. She approaches the implementation with trepidation. A key challenge is to determine whether the program should be implemented in the same manner in each subsidiary or modified according to the local culture at each site. Put another way, in this complex circumstance, does culture matter?

The dilemma
A review of the IB literature, as well as our experience in working with managers in multinational organizations, suggests that there are very few instances where culture does not matter at all. Likewise, few people would argue to ignore national culture. Research has demonstrated that national culture impacts on many different individual-level outcomes such as perceptions, beliefs, and behavior (Harrison and Huntington, 2000; Hofstede, 2001; Kirkman *et al.*, in press). For example, in their comprehensive review of 181 articles published in top-tier journals between 1980 and 2002 that empirically assessed the five dimensions of cultural values identified by Hofstede (1980), Kirkman *et al.* (in press) documented 61 studies that demonstrated a direct effect of culture on individual outcomes. The authors reviewed relationships between cultural values and 10 categories of individual outcomes: change management behavior, conflict management, negotiation behavior, reward allocation, decision-making, human resource management, leadership, individual behavior in groups, personality, and work attitudes/emotion.

Yet, research and practice provide numerous examples of instances in which the impact of culture was overshadowed by unique personalities, strong leadership, or uniformity of practices (e.g., Wetlaufer, 1999; Maznevski and Chudoba, 2000; Earley and Gibson, 2002). Furthermore, in many studies culture demonstrates a statistically significant relationship with individual outcomes, but the strength of the relationship (i.e., the size of the coefficient) is relatively weak in practical terms, indicating that culture does not explain a large amount of variance in those outcomes, and that, in fact, other variables must be considered as important predictors alongside culture (e.g., Peterson *et al.*, 1995; Brett and Okumura, 1998; Gibson, 1999; Clugston *et al.*, 2000; Mitchell *et al.*, 2000; Kirkman and Shapiro, 2001). While researchers are

able to draw implications for managers, they cannot reach a high level of precision regarding the specific impacts and the circumstances in which culture should be a central focus, or when it might be less critical (Gibson *et al.*, forthcoming). For example, several studies have found relationships between collectivism and individual attitudes toward teamwork (e.g., Bochner and Hesketh, 1994; Casimir and Keats, 1996; Eby and Dobbins, 1997; Earley *et al.*, 1999; Kirkman and Shapiro, 2000; Gibson and Zellmer-Bruhn, 2001). However, do these cultural proclivities come into play in every circumstance? Might there be situations, such as in times of crisis, when members of organizations have fairly universally positive attitudes toward teamwork?

The field of international management, therefore, is faced with a dilemma. On the one hand, researchers and managers need to understand patterns of individual-level outcomes associated with different national cultures in the world. On the other hand, research examining relationships between culture and individual outcomes has not captured enough variance to make the specific recommendations that managers need with confidence (Gibson *et al.*, forthcoming). Thus, recently, scholars have argued that, instead of addressing whether or not national culture makes a difference, it is more useful to address the issue of *how* and *when* it makes a difference (Leung *et al.*, 2001a; Earley and Gibson, 2002; Oyserman *et al.*, 2002b; Gibson *et al.*, forthcoming; Kirkman *et al.*, in press).

Determining when cultural effects occur
Suppose for the moment that our focus is on assisting the multinational human resource manager (mentioned earlier) in terms of understanding how certain individual-level outcomes change as a function of cultures. An important question then becomes, 'What are the conditions that increase an individual's propensity to think, feel, or behave in accordance with cultural prescriptions?' Answering this question requires identifying possible moderating conditions. This in itself is a critical task for future theory and research, because the stronger the impact of the moderating conditions, the less predictive culture will be of individual outcomes. Gibson *et al.* (forthcoming) identified a set of moderating conditions operating across three different categories – individual, group, and situational characteristics – that serve to moderate the impact of national culture on individual perceptions, beliefs, and behavior. Understanding the extent to

which the factors are present in any given circumstance thus provides clues as to whether (or not) national culture will matter in those circumstances. So, although by no means exhaustive, their framework is a useful foundation in the quest for greater precision in cultural theoretical models.

For example, an important individual amplifier of the impact of national culture on beliefs is the degree to which an individual identifies with the culture (Gibson *et al.*, forthcoming). Based on social identity theory (Turner, 1987) and theories of the self-concept (Markus and Kitayama, 1991), it seems likely that, when a person views him or herself as a member of the national culture, and the culture is a large component of his or her self-concept, culture will have a strong and pervasive impact on his or her beliefs. In every culture, there are people who hold beliefs different from those typical. Instead, other sources of self-identity such as educational or professional affiliation may play a much stronger role in defining who they are, what motivates them personally, and which values they hold. So, culture matters more when a person identifies with the culture; for those who do not, culture is a less potent predictor of their values. Along these same lines, researchers such as Van Dyne *et al.* (2000) have uncovered evidence that collectivism is positively related to organizational citizenship behavior, but certain individual-level factors such as self-esteem moderate this relationship. Thus, self-esteem is an element that moderates the impact of culture on an important set of individual behaviors.

Beyond individual-level factors, an example of a group-level moderator is the stage of group development that a group is at, powerfully amplifying or mitigating the impact of national culture on group member behavior (Gibson *et al.*, forthcoming). National culture is often a more readily detectable attribute, and therefore is a potent influence early on when the group is just beginning to take shape (Watson *et al.*, 1993; Chatman and Flynn, 2001). Once group members understand the contribution of other attributes, culture may play less of a role. For example, national culture is likely a stronger predictor of group member communication behavior during the early stages of a group's tenure, before members come to understand how deep attributes such as expertise will impact on the group. Indeed, research conducted by Zellmer-Bruhn *et al.* (2002) provides some evidence of this phenomenon. Information exchange between group members was more strongly related to national cultural heterogeneity in young, rather

than old, teams in their large sample across five multinational firms. Likewise, Eby and Dobbins (1997) found that, although collectivism relates to performance in teams, the level of team cooperation – an important group-level factor – moderates this relationship. Thus, culture matters for team performance, but certain group-level characteristics can increase or decrease the impact of culture.

Finally, in addition to individual and group characteristics, Gibson *et al.* (forthcoming) identified several situational characteristics that moderate the impact of culture. An example in the situational category is the impact of the technological environment – specifically, technological uncertainty. Research has demonstrated that people tend to respond in accordance with cultural prescriptions under conditions of uncertainty and ambiguity (Meglino *et al.*, 1989; Ravlin *et al.*, 2000), and, more generally, that uncertainty provokes rigidity (Staw *et al.*, 1981). Thus, technological uncertainty likely amplifies the impact of culture on individual perceptions. When there are very specific rules, procedures or equipment for completing a task (such as tools for manufacturing and assembly or rules for quality assessment), national culture will have less impact. When the task technology is ambiguous, culture is more likely to be the default. This occurred in an aerospace product development team that Gibson and Cohen (2003) worked with. The team was multicultural, and the most substantial cultural clashes occurred when the team confronted implementation of new technology. Members retreated to culturally prescribed scripts and preferences, and these were at odds. Once the technology had been adopted, and through trial and error the clashes were resolved, cultural proclivities were less of a factor in provoking conflict.

Implications

Admittedly, individuals' perceptions, beliefs, and behavior are influenced by more than one aspect of culture at any given time, and the moderators (or amplifiers) likely work in concert rather than isolation. For example, three of the moderators of cultural impacts described above – social identification, stage of group development, and technological uncertainty – can all simultaneously characterize a given cause–effect relationship between culture and individual outcomes. Consider again the scenario that opened this section – the senior human resource manager challenged with implementing the global training program. If aware of potential conditions that amplify the impact of culture, she might then be able to conduct a more precise diagnosis of the circumstances in each subsidiary. For example, in the North American subsidiary, teams may comprise many expatriates who do not identify as much with the local national culture, the team may have been in existence for several years and thus be very well developed, and the team may have familiarity with the program. Based on the prior research reviewed here, these factors would imply that culture will have less impact in this subsidiary. In the Indian subsidiary, the human resource manager may find a very different set of circumstances, in which all team members identify with the Indian national cultural characteristics, the team is early in its stage of development, and the technology is ambiguous (i.e., they have no familiarity with the program). In these circumstances, culture will likely matter a great deal, and the manager would do well to implement the program in a manner sensitive to the local culture. In our experience, most managers are entirely unaware of the impact of culture. The general models developed by Adler (1997) and Earley and Erez (1997) are extremely helpful in alerting us to the important role that culture plays. However, examination of the contingencies mentioned here can add much more precision to those recommendations.

Along these same lines, Leung *et al*. (2001a, b), for example, caution against two types of attribution error that managers can make: universal attributions and cultural attributions. The universal attribution error assumes that all workers share the same orientations, and will respond similarly to managerial practices. The cultural attribution error involves establishment of stereotypes based on nationality, and the assumption that all members of a particular nation will behave in accordance with that stereotype. Leung *et al*. argue that neither extreme is productive, and instead suggest that mangers need to be aware of the dangers associated with each type of error. Although it is important to be aware that a misunderstanding may be explicated by bicultural experience, at the same time it is always advisable to obtain input from others who share the same culture as each party, in order to untangle cultural effects from other factors such as personality, group-level phenomena or situational elements.

To help increase the precision of our cultural models, then, future research must identify the most critical set of moderators, together with cultural orientations and outcomes, for particular focus in managerial diagnosis, implementation,

and change programs. The scenario above implies that future research must, whenever possible, include multiple potential moderators at various levels of analysis. We are aware of very few past research efforts that have done so, although it seems clear that moderators may interact in interesting ways. For example, a situational moderator – technological uncertainty – may interact with personality characteristics, such that it drives only certain individuals to behave in ways more consistent with cultural proclivities; other individuals (with a different configuration of personality characteristics) may behave in ways less consistent with culture under conditions of technological uncertainty. Future research should address this issue to provide more precise guidance for theory development and practice. Equally important, a single cultural characteristic does not influence individuals in isolation from other characteristics (e.g., both universalism and collectivism likely work simultaneously to influence a given behavior or reaction). Thus, it is also critical that future research include configurations of cultural characteristics, rather than a single predictor. Practically speaking, these suggestions must of course be balanced with constraints around sample size, survey length, and analytical techniques for complex models.

Still, the point remains that we are in dire need of more comprehensive specification in our models of cultural impacts. Yes, culture does matter. However, there will be certain circumstances when it matters more, and others when it matters less. Including moderators of the impact, such as those highlighted here, helps us become much more precise in our theories. Investigation of these models, some of which is already under way, will help us understand and advise when culture must be considered in managerial initiatives.

Experimental approaches to the study of culture

The previous sections are concerned with conceptual and substantive issues of culture and IB, but the focus of this final section is methodological. Specifically, we discuss experimental methodology, which is sorely underrepresented in IB research, but which has a unique capacity to provide the comprehensive specification in models of culture called for above. As evidence of the scarcity of experimental research in our field, an analysis of the research methodologies used in manuscripts published in the *Journal of International Business Studies* shows that the ratio of survey- or case-study-based research to experimentally based research is greater than 10 to 1.[1] Certainly every research methodology has its weaknesses and strengths, but the narrow focus on survey, ethnography or case studies to understand cultural phenomena to the exclusion of experiments is denying our field the balance inherent in a multi-method approach, one in which the strengths and weaknesses of one method are compensated for by another (Leung and Su, 2004). The unique contribution that experimentation provides comes from its superior ability to demonstrate causality: that is, whereas other methodologies may infer covariation or even spurious correlation between variables, experimentation provides for the controlled manipulation of a hypothesized variable, protecting results from such interpretations (Leung and Su, 2004).[2] The goal of this section is to discuss the contribution that experimental research can make to more clearly define the individual, group, and situational factors that moderate the influence of culture on thoughts, feelings, and behaviors, and to more precisely pinpoint the boundary conditions where culture (or culture alone) is not likely to have an effect.

Investigating the moderating influence of individual, group, and situational characteristics

The essence of experimentation is the ability to control and manipulate variables in a systematic manner. Furthermore, the analysis and manipulation may be of a single variable, or of multiple variables in conjunction: that is, the experiments may be univariate or multivariate in either the dependent or independent variables (Winer, 1991). This quality makes experimentation particularly suited to deepen understanding of the individual, group, and situational characteristics (singly or in conjunction) that moderate culture's influence.

The moderating influence of individual characteristics

Cross-cultural experimental literature examining the influence of individual characteristics has evolved, yielding greater sophistication and specification to our understanding of culture's influence. Much early cross-cultural work tested only for the main effects of culture – often using national culture as a proxy variable for a given cultural orientation. That work, exploring the influence of the *presence* (a main effect) of a given cultural orientation, laid the groundwork for more complex experiments to follow, which test how differences

in the *levels* (a moderating influence) of a cultural orientation (even a primed, temporary one) influence behaviors or perceptions.

The research of Gelfand *et al.* (2002) examined both the main effects and the moderating effects of individual characteristics on the presence of egocentric perceptions of fairness in negotiations within Japan and the US. Using national culture as proxy for cultural orientation, their results support robust findings of self-serving biases in individualist cultures (Thompson and Loewenstein, 1992), where 'the self is served by enhancing one's positive attributes to stand out and be better than others', but find relatively less bias in a collectivistic culture, in which 'the self is served by focusing on one's weaknesses to blend in and maintain interdependence with others' (p 847). However, they also measured individual self-construals (Markus and Kitayama, 1991), and demonstrate that independent self-construals are higher in the United States and are positively related to self-serving biases. Thus, not only is a main effect of national culture on egocentric biases demonstrated, but the examination of individual self-construals helps to explain why such an effect exists.

Research of this type is especially valuable given that much of the theory underlying business research has been developed and tested exclusively in Western contexts. Experimental research focusing on the moderating influence of individual characteristics contributes to this literature because it directly tests whether these processes, biases, and behaviors are indeed universal phenomena, or whether they are specific to Western populations.

As Oyserman *et al.* (2002b) point out in their meta-analysis of research on collectivism/individualism, cultural priming is one of the most promising areas of cross-cultural research. The theoretical underpinnings of priming stem from social cognition research, which shows that accessible knowledge influences behavior, and that temporarily accessible and chronically salient knowledge produce equivalent effects in the laboratory. Thus, priming techniques 'create an experimental analogue of chronic differences between cultural groups by temporarily focusing participants' attention on different cultural content or values' (p 7). Examples of this research would be the Hong *et al.* (2000) study mentioned in an earlier section, as well as Kuhnen and Oyserman (2002) and Aaker (2000), which primed participants with cues that were or were not congruent with their cultural orientation (e.g., using pronouns such as 'I' and 'me' for an independence priming or 'we' and 'our' for an interdependent priming) and examined the influence on factors such as cognitive speed and accuracy, memory, and attitudes. Results across all the experiments indicate the existence of a chronic cultural orientation, and one that is more malleable in the face of a primed orientation.

The moderating influence of group characteristics

Previously in this paper the importance of understanding group characteristics, such as the level of group development, was discussed. Furthermore, it was suggested that, to the extent possible, research that can simultaneously examine the moderating influence of both individual and group characteristics should be encouraged. The following is an example of such research.

Buchan *et al*. (2002) demonstrated that differences in the definition and method of group formation prompt variance across cultural orientations in terms of response to ingroup/outgroup manipulations. In support of research using the minimal group paradigm (Tajfel and Turner, 1979), participants with an individualist orientation were expectedly biased toward the experimentally manipulated ingroup in terms of trust and reciprocity; however, collectively oriented participants were not (thus a statistically significant interaction between cultural orientation and group manipulation emerged). For individualists, groups are seen as temporary and flexible to allow entry and exit in the pursuit of self-interest; for collectivists, groups are permanent, based on personal characteristics, and preservation of the group takes priority over individual goals (Triandis, 1995). These results deepen understanding of the complex relationship between culture and group relationships, and indicate when culturally influenced group biases are likely to be present.

The moderating influence of situational characteristics

Experimental research examining the influence of situational characteristics proves especially valuable in clarifying the influence of the 'other' on one's thoughts, feelings, and behavior, thus promoting understanding of the interaction between individual and situational characteristics. For example, Adair *et al*. (2001) examined intra- and intercultural negotiations among Japanese and American managers. They demonstrate behavioral differences across cultures in negotiation (main effects), and, perhaps more significantly, support the conjecture

that intercultural negotiations are more difficult and less successful than intracultural negotiations (Graham, 1985; Brett and Okumura, 1998) owing to the interaction of individual cultural characteristics and the bi-cultural context of the negotiation.

An interesting twist on priming research is presented by Chatman and Barsade (1995). They measured participants' levels of cooperativeness and agreeableness, and manipulated a business environment to reflect goals typically associated with collectivism or individualism. Results demonstrate that highly cooperative individuals were more responsive to the norms characterizing their organization's culture, such that they exhibited greater differences in behavior across the two cultural environments. Like research priming individual characteristics, this research demonstrates that people may behave or think differently when faced with situations exhibiting differing cultural values – and indeed, may modify their own values – thus rendering a whole new set of complex, but theoretically rich, issues to be studied through intercultural experiments.

Experimentation as a tool to understand the limits of culture's influence

Experimentation provides a powerful tool for identifying the limits of the influence of culture – that is, understanding when cultural values will have an influence, and when they will not, a topic that we have already discussed in a previous section. Currently, much of the experimental research in this direction is couched in the context of economic games in which the pull of self-interest is pitted against the interest of the collective. For instance, Roth *et al*. (1991) conducted two different economic games in four countries, and highlighted the importance of situational characteristics in making salient the influence of cultural values. They demonstrate that behavior in all countries converged to the equilibrium in a four-person market game (a situation similar to an auction), while behavior in a two-person ultimatum game (a resource allocation problem) deviated from equilibrium and, furthermore, differed across the countries. This pattern of results suggests the influence of differing culturally influenced values regarding what is fair in allocation: because of the structure of the economic interactions, fairness concerns were not salient in the four-person market game, but were quite salient when bargaining with a partner in the ultimatum game.

Advances in culture and international business   Kwok Leung *et al*

373

Similarly, Buchan *et al.* (2004) actually demonstrate divergent perceptions of fairness in a repeated ultimatum game in Japan and the US and differing behavior across the two countries, but show that culturally influenced perceptions of fairness (such as those that may dictate more generosity to the partner) do not influence behavior once the pull of self-interest in the game becomes too strong.

Kachelmeier and Shehata (1997) investigated the influence of individual cultural orientation on the effectiveness and demand for auditing. Their results show that collective cultural values are most likely to challenge self-interest in conditions of low anonymity. That is, only when a reporting system could identify the actions of group members were participants from Hong Kong and China more willing than participants from Canada to forgo self-interest. When anonymity was high, participants from all countries pursued self-interest with equal intensity.

In sum, these experimental studies echo our earlier conclusion that there are times when cultural orientation does not matter. The question of the limits of cultural influence represents a challenge to cross-cultural research, and experimentation can play a major role in resolving many of the complex issues involved.

Broadening our understanding of culture

Recent research highlights the need to broaden our analysis of culture – to perhaps take a closer look at manifestations of culture such as folklore, the manner in which we are educated, political systems, and methods of economic exchange – in order to fully assess the influence of culture on an individual. Examples of experimental studies that play a role in this broadening are given below.

Weber and Hsee (1998) demonstrated that respondents from China are significantly less risk averse than those in the US in financial decisions but more risk averse in social decisions. To determine whether these differences were truly cultural, or instead resulted from current economic or political circumstances, Weber *et al.* (1998) undertook a study in which participants from China, Germany and the US rated the risk-taking advice imparted in Chinese and American proverbs. Their results support earlier findings, and suggest that the interpretation of proverbs revealed 'longstanding cultural differences in social cohesion and cooperation' that contributed to the explanation of these differences in risky behavior (p 183).

Yates *et al.* (Yates *et al.*, 1989, 1998) have shown that Chinese respondents exhibit extreme overconfidence in probability judgments as well as in general knowledge, as compared with those in the US and Japan. They suggest that there may be important differences in culturally influenced 'cognitive customs' that account for the cross-cultural variations such as 'rules' (such as memorization) that Chinese children are taught for approaching cognitive tasks (Liu, 1986), the rareness with which Chinese culture demands that people generate multiple arguments on both sides of an issue, and the typical characterization of decision problems based on the logic of historical precedence rather than on the logic of the decision tree. These cognitive customs, born out of cultural values and reinforced throughout education, may be at the core of cross-national variations in overconfidence.

An anthropologist-led study in economics examined bargaining behavior in 12 small-scale cultures (e.g., Peru's Machiguenga farmers and Paraguay's Ache headhunters). This study reveals stark differences in behavior across cultures, and addresses the influence of market development on cooperative behavior (Henrich *et al.*, 2001). Two variables account for 68% of the variance in offers across cultures; cultures with more cooperative activity (e.g., collective hunting of whales) and market integration (an index combining the existence of a national language, of a labor market for cash wages, and farming of crops for cash) have sharing norms closer to equal splits. These results are startling to some theorists in that they suggest that real-world, 'enculturated' market experience tempers rather than amplifies the pursuit of self-interest. As researchers are interested in understanding the full influence of culture, this work indicates that we need to take into account the interplay of more traditional measures of culture such as collectivism–individualism with those that measure market development and level of integration.

As shown by this research, broadening our analysis of culture has enormous potential for increasing understanding of the manner, and the multiplicity of ways, in which individuals are influenced by their environment. An appropriate summary of this section may be to discuss the public goods research of Yamagishi and colleagues (see, Yamagishi, 2003, for a summary), which presents a perfect and pressing example of the need to gain a broader understanding of the influences and implications of culture and the potential that experimental research has to do so. Yamagishi's research consistently demonstrates that Americans are more cooperative than Japanese in public good situations, and that Japanese are only more cooperative when a system of sanctions and monitoring is in place to assure the cooperation of the other members of the group. On the one hand, Yamagishi (2003, 367) suggests that 'the commonly held notion of cross-cultural differences between Japanese and Americans – the former being collectivists and the latter individualists – cease to exist once all theoretically relevant factors are experimentally controlled'. On the other hand, he also suggests that the system of social sanction and monitoring may be a particularly collectivist solution to the problem of fostering cooperation among a group (Yamagishi *et al.*, 1998). Thus this issue is multifaceted. Not only are there likely influences of individual, group, and situational characteristics that moderate cultures' impact on thoughts and behavior in this context. There likely are factors such as economic and legal constraints, and embedded social networks in each society, that themselves are influenced by cultural norms and in turn are directly or indirectly influencing the individual.

Through careful construction of experiments, through precise manipulation of each of the suspected influences, and by drawing on fields such as economics, sociology, and anthropology to broaden our understanding of culture, we can begin to tease out the multiplicity of effects in this problem, and others. Essentially, we shall be refining our knowledge of the dynamics of the top-down–bottom-up processes involved in culture shown in Figure 1. In doing so, we shall be gaining a deeper and richer understanding of the nature of cultural differences, why and when they occur.

Conclusion

Research on culture and IB is definitely a 'growth' area, because the business world is in many ways becoming one. At least four themes are apparent in our state-of-the-art review of current research trends in this area. First, much of previous research on culture and IB has adopted what we view as a simplistic view of culture, which tends to examine the static influence of a few cultural elements in isolation from other cultural elements and contextual variables. For instance, much of the research inspired by the Hofstede dimensions falls into this category, which, in our view, was instrumental in kickstarting the field. However, the advances

reviewed here are able to provide the conceptual and empirical basis for moving into more complex conceptualizations of culture. The several new perspectives on culture reviewed in this paper all point to multi-layer, multi-facet, contextual, and systems views of culture. These views converge to suggest that culture entails much more than cultural dimensions, and culture manifests itself in many levels and domains. Some cultural elements are stable, whereas others are dynamic and changing. Sweeping statements about cultures are useful to the extent that they provide an abstract framework for organizing more situated description of the effects of cultures. A major challenge for the field is to develop mid-range, dynamic frameworks of culture that are sensitive to their nuances in different contexts.

Second, a more complex conceptualization of culture will necessarily give rise to a more complex view of its effects. Culture can be an antecedent, a moderator or a mediator, and a consequence, and its effects may be domain-specific and are subjected to boundary conditions. Much of the research on culture and IB tends to focus on main effects of culture. The immediate challenge for the field is to map out other more complex effects of culture systematically and integrate these effects routinely into substantive theories, so that cultural elements constitute a major type of building block for theoretical models in IB. A recent, highly visible attempt in this direction is the GLOBE project discussed before, which attempts to build a model of leadership with cultural elements as integral elements of the model.

Third, the plea for studying the effects of culture in conjunction with socio-economic-political variables is not new, but our review has provided specific theoretical rationale and concrete directions for such research efforts. We have shown that cultural change is intertwined with socio-economic-political variables, and that these contextual variables may also add to, moderate, and/or mediate the effects of culture. Fortunately, there is a long tradition in IB research to take the effects of such variables into account, and future research needs to evaluate the effects of culture in conjunction with the impact of socio-economic-political conditions. Culture may relate to socio-economic-political variables in complex ways, and a simple consideration of their joint effects is inadequate. A more complete picture of the forces impinging upon IB calls for a precise description of these complex relationships.

Finally, a multi-method approach to research has been advocated for decades, and for research on culture and IB, its importance cannot be exaggerated. Most research in IB research is correlational in nature, and we are more or less ignorant when it comes to the causal processes involved. Experimentation provides a powerful tool for probing causal relationships, and we need both correlational and experimental approaches to enrich our understanding of IB phenomena, and to develop effective practical advice for international managers. Culture is such a fuzzy concept that we need to probe it with all the tools we have at our disposal, and we look forward to the bloom of multi-method approaches for moving the field of international business research forward by leaps and bounds.

Notes

[1] Evidence from three databases supports this argument. A search of the methodologies as they are described in the full citation of *JIBS* articles (1987–present) as listed in ABI/INFORM results in the ratio of 13.62:1. A search of *JIBS* abstracts (1970–2000) appearing in JSTORE provides the ratio of 11.5:1. Finally, a search within the *JIBS* website gives the ratio of 12.66:1.

[2] See Leung and Su (2004) and Buchan (2003) for comprehensive discussions comparing cross-cultural experimentation with other research methodologies, and concerning the specific controls employed in experimental research to strengthen causal inferences.

References

Aaker, J.L. (2000) 'Accessibility or diagnosticity? Disentangling the influence of culture on persuasion processes and attitudes', *Journal of Consumer Research* **26**(3): 340–357.

Adair, W.L., Okumura, T. and Brett, J.M. (2001) 'Negotiation behavior when cultures collide: The United States and Japan', *Journal of Applied Psychology* **86**(3): 371–385.

Adler, N.J. (1997) *International Dimensions of Organizational Behavior* (3rd edn), South-Western College Publishing: Cincinnati, OH.

Arnett, J.J. (2002) 'The psychology of globalization', *American Psychologist* **57**(10): 774–783.

Berry, J.W., Poortinga, Y.H., Segall, M.H. and Dasen, P.R. (2002) *Cross-Cultural Psychology: Research and Application* (2nd edn), Cambridge University Press: New York.

Bhagat, R.S., Baliga, B.R., Moustafa, K.S. and Krishnan, B. (2003) 'Knowledge in Cross-Cultural Management in Era of Globalization: Where Do we Go from Here?', in D. Tjosvold and K. Leung (eds.) *Cross-Cultural Management: Foundations and Future*, Ashgate: England, pp: 155–176.

Bhagat, R.S., Kedia, B.L., Harveston, P. and Triandis, H.C. (2002) 'Cultural variations in the cross-border transfer of organizational knowledge: an integrative framework', *Academy of Management Review* **27**(2): 204–221.

Bochner, S. and Hesketh, B. (1994) 'Power distance, individualism/collectivism, and job-related attitudes in a culturally diverse work group', *Journal of Cross-Cultural Psychology* **25**: 233–257.

Bond, M.H., Leung, K., Au, A., Tong, K.K., Reimel de Carrasquel, S., Murakami, F., Yamaguchi, S., Bierbrauer, G., Singelis, T.M., Broer, M., Boen, F., Lambert, S.M., Ferreira, M.C., Noels, K.A., van Bavel, J., Safdar, S., Zhang, J., Chen, L., Solcova, I., Stetovska, I., Niit, T., Niit, K.K., Hurme, H., Böling, M., Franchi, V., Magradze, G., Javakhishvili, N., Boehnke, K., Klinger, E., Huang, X., Fulop, M., Berkics, M., Panagiotopoulou, P., Sriram, S., Chaudhary, N., Ghosh, A., Vohra, N., Iqbal, D.F., Kurman, J., Thein, R.D., Comunian, A.L., Son, K.A., Austers, I., Harb, C., Odusanya, J.O.T., Ahmed, Z.A., Ismail, R., van de Vijver, F., Ward, C., Mogaji, A., Sam, D.L., Khan, M.J.Z., Cabanillas, W.E., Sycip, L., Neto, F., Cabecinhas, R., Xavier, P., Dinca, M., Lebedeva, N., Viskochil, A., Ponomareva, O., Burgess, S.M., Oceja, L., Campo, S., Hwang, K.K., D'souza, J.B., Ataca, B., Furnham, A. and Lewis, J.R. (2004) 'Culture-level dimensions of social axioms and their correlates across 41 cultures', *Journal of Cross-Cultural Psychology* **35**(5): 548–570.

Boyacigiller, N.A. and Adler, N.J. (1991) 'The parochial dinosaur: organizational science in a global context', *Academy of Management Review* **16**(2): 262–290.

Brett, J.M. and Okumura, T. (1998) 'Inter- and intracultural negotiation: US and Japanese negotiators', *Academy of Management Journal* **41**: 495–510.

Buchan, N.R. (2003) 'Experimental Economic Approaches to International Marketing Research', in S. Jain (ed.) *Handbook of Research in International Education*, Kluwer Publishing: Boston, MA, pp: 190–208.

Buchan, N.R., Croson, R.T.A. and Dawes, R. (2002) 'Swift neighbors and persistent strangers: a cross-cultural investigation of trust and reciprocity in social exchange', *American Journal of Sociology* **108**: 168–206.

Buchan, N.R., Croson, R.T.A. and Johnson, E.J. (2004) 'When do fair beliefs influence bargaining behavior? Experimental bargaining in Japan and The United States', *Journal of Consumer Research* **31**: 181–191.

Cairncross, F. (2001) *The Death of Distance*, Harvard Business School Press: Boston, MA.

Casimir, G. and Keats, D. (1996) 'The effects of work environment and in-group membership on the leadership preferences of Anglo-Australians and Chinese Australians', *Journal of Cross-Cultural Psychology* **27**: 357–436.

Chang, W.C., Wong, W.K. and Koh, J.B.K. (2003) 'Chinese values in Singapore: traditional and modern', *Asian Journal of Social Psychology* **6**: 5–29.

Chatman, J.A. and Barsade, S.G. (1995) 'Personality, organizational culture, and cooperation: evidence from a business simulation', *Administrative Science Quarterly* **40**(3): 423–443.

Chatman, J.A. and Flynn, F.J. (2001) 'The influence of demographic heterogeneity on the emergence and consequences of cooperative norms in work teams', *Academy of Management Journal* **44**(5): 956–974.

Chinese Culture Connection (1987) 'Chinese values and the search for culture-free dimensions of culture', *Journal of Cross-Cultural Psychology* **18**: 143–164.

Chui, A.C.W., Lloyd, A.E. and Kwok, C.C.Y. (2002) 'The determination of capital structure: is national culture a missing piece to the puzzle?' *Journal of International Business Studies* **33**(1): 99–127.

Clugston, M., Howell, J.P. and Dorfman, P.W. (2000) 'Does cultural socialization predict multiple bases and foci of commitment?' *Journal of Management* **26**: 5–30.

Drucker, P.F. (1995) *Managing in a Time of Great Change*, Truman Talley Books/Dutton: New York.

Earley, P.C. and Erez, M. (1997) *The Transplanted Executive: Why You Need to Understand How Workers in Other Countries See the World Differently*, Oxford University Press: New York.

Earley, P.C. and Gibson, C.B. (2002) *Multinational Teams: A New Perspective*, Lawrence Earlbaum and Associates: Mahwah, NJ.

Earley, P.C., Gibson, C.B. and Chen, C.C. (1999) '"How did I do?" versus "How did we do?" cultural contrasts of performance feedback use and self-efficacy', *Journal of Cross-Cultural Psychology* 30(5): 594–619.

Eby, L.T. and Dobbins, G.H. (1997) 'Collectivistic orientation in teams: an individual and group-level analysis', *Journal of Organizational Behavior* 18: 275–295.

Erez, M. and Earley, P.C. (1993) *Culture, Self-Identity, and Work*, Oxford University Press: Oxford.

Erez, M. and Gati, E. (2004) 'A dynamic, multi-level model of culture: from the micro level of the individual to the macro level of a global culture', *Applied Psychology: An International Review* 53(4): 583–598.

Erez-Rein, N., Erez, M. and Maital, S. (2004) 'Mind the Gap: Key Success Factors in Cross-Border Acquisitions', in A.L. Pablo and M. Javidan (eds.) *Mergers and Acquisitions: Creating Integrative Knowledge*, Blackwell Publishing: Malden, MA, pp: 20–44.

Fu, P.P., Kennedy, J., Tata, J., Yukl, G., Bond, M.H., Peng, T.K., Srinivas, E.S., Howell, J.P., Prieto, L., Koopman, P., Boonstra, J.J., Pasa, S., Lacassagne, M.F., Higashide, H. and Cheosakul, A. (2004) 'The impact of societal cultural values and individual social beliefs on the perceived effectiveness of managerial influence strategies: a meso approach', *Journal of International Business Studies* 35(4): 284–305.

Gelfand, M.J., Higgins, M., Nishii, L.H., Raver, J.L., Dominguez, A., Murakami, F., Yamaguchi, S. and Toyama, M. (2002) 'Culture and egocentric perceptions of fairness in conflict and negotiation', *Journal of Applied Psychology* 87(5): 833–845.

Gibson, C.B. (1999) 'Do they do what they believe they can? Group-efficacy beliefs and group performance across tasks and cultures', *Academy of Management Journal* 42(2): 138–152.

Gibson, C.B. and Cohen, S.G. (2003) *Virtual Teams that Work: Creating Conditions for Virtual Team Effectiveness*, Jossey-Bass: San Francisco.

Gibson, C.B. and Zellmer-Bruhn, M. (2001) 'Metaphor and meaning: an intercultural analysis of the concept of team-work', *Administrative Science Quarterly* 46: 274–303.

Gibson, C.B., Maznevski, M. and Kirkman, B.L. (forthcoming),' When Does Culture Matter?', in A.Y. Lewin (ed.) *Emerging Research in International Business*, MacMillan Press: New York.

Govindarajan, V. and Gupta, A.K. (2001) *The Quest for Global Dominance: Transforming Global Presence into Global Competitive Advantage*, Jossey-Bass: San Francisco.

Graham, J.L. (1985) 'Cross-cultural marketing negotiations: a laboratory experiment', *Marketing Science* 4(2): 130–146.

Greider, W. (1997) *One World: Ready or Not*, Crown Business: New York.

Guillén, M. (2001) 'Is globalization civilizing, destructive, or feeble? A critique of five key debates in the social science literature', *Annual Review of Sociology* 27: 235–260.

Gupta, A.K. and Govindarajan, V. (2000) 'Knowledge flows within multinational corporations', *Strategic Management Journal* 21(4): 473–496.

Gupta, V. and House, R. (2004) 'Understanding Leadership in Diverse Cultures: Implications of Project GLOBE for Leading International Ventures', in D. Tjosvold and K. Leung (eds.) *Leading in High Growth Asia: Managing Relationship for Teamwork and Change*, World Scientific Publishing: Singapore, pp: 13–54.

Haire, M., Ghiselli, E.E. and Porter, L.W. (1966) *Managerial Thinking: An International Study*, Wiley: New York.

Hanges, P.J., Lord, R.G. and Dickson, M.W. (2000) 'An information processing perspective on leadership and culture: a case for connectionist architecture', *Applied Psychology: An International Review* 49(1): 133–161.

Harrison, L.E. and Huntington, S.P. (2000) *Culture Matters: How Values Shaped Human Progress*, Basic Books: New York.

Harzing, A.W. and Hofstede, G. (1996) 'Planned change in organizations: the influence of national culture', *Research in the Sociology of Organizations* 14: 297–340.

Henrich, J., Boyd, R., Bowles, S., Camerer, C., Fehr, E., Gintis, H. and McElreath, R. (2001) 'In search of homo economicus: behavioral experiments in 15 small-scale societies', *The American Economic Review* 91(2): 73–78.

Heuer, M., Cummings, J.L. and Hutabarat, W. (1999) 'Cultural stability or change among managers in Indonesia', *Journal of International Business Studies* 30(3): 599–610.

Hofstede, G. (1980) *Culture's Consequences: International Differences in Work-Related Values*, Sage: Newbury Park, CA.

Hofstede, G. (2001) *Culture's Consequences* (2nd edn), Sage: Thousand Oaks, CA.

Hong, Y.Y., Chiu, C.Y. and Kung, T.M. (1997) 'Bringing Culture Out in Front: Effects of Cultural Meaning System Activation on Social Cognition', in K. Leung, Y. Kashima, U. Kim and S. Yamaguchi (eds.) *Progress in Asian Social Psychology*, Vol. 1. Wiley: Singapore, pp: 135–146.

Hong, Y.Y., Morris, M.W., Chiu, C.Y. and Benet-Martínez, V. (2000) 'Multicultural minds: a dynamic constructivist approach to culture and cognition', *American Psychologist* 55: 709–720.

House, R.J., Hanges, P.J., Javidan, M., Dorfman, P. and Gupta, V. (eds.) (2004) *GLOBE, Cultures, Leadership, and Organizations: GLOBE Study of 62 Societies*, Sage Publications: Newbury Park, CA.

Huntington, S.P. (1996) *The Clash of Civilizations and the Remaking of World Order*, New York: Simon & Schuster.

Inglehart, R. and Baker, W.E. (2000) 'Modernization, cultural change, and the persistence of traditional values', *American Sociological Review* 61(1): 19–51.

Jung, K., Ang, S.H., Leong, S.M., Tan, S.J., Pompitakpan, C. and Kau, A.K. (2002) 'A typology of animosity and its cross-national validation', *Journal of Cross-Cultural Psychology* 33(6): 525–539.

Kachelmeier, S.J. and Shehata, M. (1997) 'Internal auditing and voluntary cooperation in firms: a cross-cultural experiment', *The Accounting Review* 72(3): 407–431.

Kerr, C., Dunlop, J.T., Harbison, F.H. and Myers, C.A. (1960) *Industrialism and Industrial Man*, Harvard University Press: Cambridge, MA.

Kirkman, B.L. and Shapiro, D.L. (2000) 'Understanding why team members won't share: an examination of factors related to employee receptivity to team-based rewards', *Small Group Research* 31(2): 175–209.

Kirkman, B.L. and Shapiro, D.L. (2001) 'The impact of team members' cultural values on productivity, cooperation, and empowerment in self-managing work teams', *Journal of Cross-Cultural Psychology* 32: 597–617.

Kirkman, B.L., Lowe, K. and Gibson, C.B. (in press) Two decades of culture's consequences: a review of empirical research incorporating Hofstede's cultural values framework', *Journal of International Business Studies*.

Kitayama, S. (2002) 'Cultural Psychology of the Self: A Renewed Look at Independence and Interdependence', in C. von Hofsten and L. Bäckman (eds.) *Psychology at the Turn of the Millennium, Vol. 2: Social, Developmental, and Clinical Perspectives*, Taylor & Francis/Routledge: Florence, KY, pp: 305–322.

Klein, K. and Kozlowski, S.W. (2000) *Multilevel Theory, Research and Methods in Organizations*, Jossey-Bass: San Francisco.

Kluckhohn, F.R. and Strodtbeck, F.L. (1961) *Variations in Value Orientations*, Row, Peterson: Evanston, IL.

Kostova, T. (1999) 'Transnational transfer of strategic organizational practices: a contextual perspective', *Academy of Management Review* 24(2): 308–324.

Kostova, T. and Roth, K. (2003) 'Social capital in multinational corporations and a micro-macro model of its formation', *Academy of Management Review* 28(2): 297–317.

Kuhnen, U. and Oyserman, D. (2002) 'Thinking about the self influences thinking in general: cognitive consequences of salient self-concept', *Journal of Experimental Social Psychology* **38**: 492–499.

Leana, C.R. and Barry, B. (2000) 'Stability and change as simultaneous experiences in organizational life', *Academy of Management Review* **25**(4): 753–759.

Leonhardt, D. (2003) 'Globalization hits a political speed bump', *New York Times*, 1 June 2003.

Leung, K. and Bond, M.H. (2004) 'Social Axioms: A Model for Social Beliefs in Multicultural Perspective ', in M.P. Zanna (ed.) *Advances in Experimental Social Psychology, Vol. 36*, Elsevier Academic Press: San Diego, CA, pp: 119–197.

Leung, K., Bond, M.H., Reimel de Carrasquel, S., Muñoz, C., Hernández, M., Murakami, F., Yamaguchi, S., Bierbrauer, G. and Singelis, T.M. (2002) 'Social axioms: the search for universal dimensions of general beliefs about how the world functions', *Journal of Cross-Cultural Psychology* **33**(3): 286–302.

Leung, K., Smith, P.B., Wang, Z.M. and Sun, H.F. (1996) 'Job satisfaction in joint venture hotels in China: an organizational justice analysis', *Journal of International Business Studies* **27**: 947–962.

Leung, K. and Su, S.K. (2004) 'Experimental Methods for Research on Culture and Management', in B.J. Punnett and O. Shenkar (eds.) *Handbook for International Management Research* (2nd edn.), Blackwell: Cambridge, MA, pp: 68–97.

Leung, K., Su, S.K. and Morris, M. (2001a) 'Justice in the Culturally Diverse Workplace: The Problems of Over and Under Emphasis of Culture', in S. Gilliland, D. Steiner and D. Skarlicki (eds.) *Theoretical and Cultural Perspectives on Organizational Justice*, Information Age Publishing: Greenwich, CT, pp: 161–186.

Leung, K., Wang, Z.M. and Smith, P.B. (2001b) 'Job attitudes and organizational justice in joint venture hotels in China: the role of expatriate managers', *International Journal of Human Resource Management* **12**: 926–945.

Levine, R.V. and Norenzayan, A. (1999) 'The pace of life in 31 countries', *Journal of Cross Cultural Psychology* **30**(2): 178–205.

Lewin, A.Y. and Kim, J. (2004) 'The National-State and Culture as Influences on Organizational Change and Innovation', in M.S. Poole and A.H. van de Ven (eds.) *Handbook of Organizational Change and Innovation*, Oxford University Press: New York, pp: 324–353.

Liu, I.M. (1986) 'Chinese Cognition', in M.H. Bond (ed.) *The Psychology of the Chinese People*, Oxford University Press: Hong Kong, pp: 73–105.

Markus, H. and Kitayama, S. (1991) 'Culture and self: implications for cognition, emotion, and motivation', *Psychological Review* **98**: 224–253.

Marsella, A.J. and Choi, S.C. (1993) 'Psychological aspects of modernization and economic development in East Asian nations', *Psychologia* **36**: 201–213.

Maznevski, M.L. and Chudoba, K. (2000) 'Bridging space over time: global virtual team dynamics and effectiveness', *Organization Science* **11**(5): 473–492.

McClelland, D.C. (1961) *The Achieving Society*, Van Nostrand Reinhold: Princeton, NJ.

Meglino, B.M., Ravlin, E.C. and Adkins, C.L. (1989) 'A work values approach to corporate culture: a field test of the value congruence process and its relationship to individual outcomes', *Journal of Applied Psychology* **74**: 424–432.

Mitchell, R.K., Smith, B., Seawright, K.W. and Morse, E.A. (2000) 'Cross-cultural cognitions and the venture creation decision', *Academy of Management Journal* **43**: 974–993.

Morris, M.W. and Peng, K.P. (1994) 'Culture and cause: American and Chinese attributions for social and physical events', *Journal of Personality and Social Psychology* **67**: 949–971.

Oyserman, D., Coon, H.M. and Kemmelmeier, M. (2002a) 'Rethinking individualism and collectivism: evaluation of theoretical assumptions and meta-analyses', *Psychological Bulletin* **128**(1): 3–72.

Oyserman, D., Kemmelmeier, M. and Coon, H.M. (2002b) 'Cultural psychology, a new look: reply to Bond (2002), Fiske (2002), Kitayama (2002), and Miller (2002)', *Psychological Bulletin* **128**(1): 110–117.

Peng, K.P. and Knowles, E.D. (2003) 'Culture, education, and the attribution of physical causality', *Personality and Social Psychology Bulletin* **29**(10): 1272–1284.

Peterson, M.F., Smith, P.B., Akande, A., Ayestaran, S., Bochner, S., Callan, V., Cho, N.G., Jesuino, J.C., D'Amorim, M., Francois, P.H., Hofmann, K., Koopman, P.L., Leung, K., Lim, T.K., Mortazavi, S., Munene, J., Radford, M., Ropo, A., Savage, G., Setiadi, B., Sinha, T.N., Sorenson, R. and Viedge, C. (1995) 'Role conflict, ambiguity, and overload: a 21-nation study', *Academy of Management Journal* **38**(2): 429–452.

Ravlin, E.C., Thomas, D.C. and Ilsev, A. (2000) 'Beliefs about Values, Status, and Legitimacy in Multicultural Groups', in P.C. Earley and H. Singh (eds.) *Innovations in International and Cross-Cultural Management*, Sage: Thousands Oaks, CA, pp: 17–51.

Roth, A.E., Prasnikar, V., Okuno-Fujiwara, M. and Zamir, S. (1991) 'Bargaining and market behavior in Jerusalem, Ljubljana, Pittsburgh, and Tokyo: an experimental study', *The American Economic Review* **81**(5): 1068–1096.

Rotter, J.B. (1966) 'Generalized expectancies for internal versus external control of reinforcement', *Psychological Monographs* **80**: 1–28.

Sarros, J.C. and Woodman, D.S. (1993) 'Leadership in Australia and its organizational outcomes', *Leadership and Organization Development Journal* **14**: 3–9.

Sassan, S. (1998) *Globalization and its Discontent*, Free Press: New York.

Schaeffer, R.K. (2003) *Understanding Globalization: The Social Consequences of Political, Economic, and Environmental Change*, Rowman & Littlefield: Lanham, MD.

Schein, E.H. (1992) *Organizational Culture and Leadership*, Jossey-Bass: San Francisco.

Schwartz, S.H. (1994) 'Beyond Individualism/Collectivism: New Dimensions of Values', in U. Kim, H.C. Triandis, C. Kagitcibasi, S.C. Choi and G. Yoon (eds.) *Individualism and Collectivism: Theory, Method, and Applications*, Sage: Newbury Park, CA, pp: 85–119.

Smith, P.B. and Bond, M.H. (1998) *Social Psychology across Cultures* (2nd edn), Allyn & Bacon: Boston, MA.

Smith, P.B., Dugan, S. and Trompenaars, F. (1996) 'National culture and managerial values: a dimensional analysis across 43 nations', *Journal of Cross-Cultural Psychology* **27**: 231–264.

Smith, P.B., Peterson, M.F. and Schwartz, S.H. (2002) 'Cultural values, source of guidance, and their relevance to managerial behavior: a 47-nation study', *Journal of Cross-Cultural Psychology* **33**(2): 188–208.

Smith, P.B., Trompenaars, F. and Dungan, S. (1995) 'The Rotter locus of control scale in 43 countries: a test of cultural relativity', *International Journal of Psychology* **30**(3): 377–400.

Staw, B.M., Sandelands, L.E. and Dutton, J.E. (1981) 'Threat-rigidity effects in organizational behavior: a multi-level analysis', *Administrative Science Quarterly* **26**: 501–524.

Steensma, H.K., Marino, L. and Dickson, P.H. (2000) 'The influence of national culture on the formation of technology alliances by entrepreneurial firms', *Academy of Management Journal* **43**(5): 951–973.

Tajfel, H. and Turner, J.C. (1979) 'An Integrative Theory of Intergroup Conflict', in W.G. Austin and S. Worchel (eds.) *The Social Psychology of Group Relations*, Brooks-Cole: Monterey, CA, pp: 33–47.

Thompson, L. and Loewenstein, G. (1992) 'Egocentric interpretations of fairness and interpersonal conflict', *Organizational Behavior and Human Decision Processes* **51**(2): 176–198.

Tinsley, C.H. and Brodt, S.E. (2004) 'Conflict Management in Asia: A Dynamic Framework and Future Directions', in K. Leung and S. White (eds.) *Handbook of Asian Management*, Kluwer: New York, pp: 439–458.

Triandis, H.C. (1994) *Culture and Social Behavior*, McGraw-Hill: New York.

Triandis, H.C. (1995) *Individualism and Collectivism*, Westview Press: Boulder, CO.

Turner, J.C. (1987) *Rediscovering the Social Group*, Basil Blackwell: Oxford.

Van de Vliert, E., Schwartz, S.H., Huismans, S.E., Hofstede, G. and Daan, S. (1999) 'Temperature, cultural masculinity, and domestic political violence: a cross-national study', *Journal of Cross-Cultural Psychology* **30**(3): 291–314.

Van Dyne, L., Vandewalle, D., Kostova, T., Latham, M.E. and Cummings, L.L. (2000) 'Collectivism, propensity to trust and self-esteem as predictors of organizational citizenship in a nonwork setting', *Journal of Organizational Behavior* **21**: 3–23.

Watson, E.W., Kumar, K. and Michaelson, L.K. (1993) 'Cultural diversity impact on interaction process and performance: comparing homogeneous and diverse task groups', *Academy of Management Journal* **36**: 590–606.

Weber, E.U. and Hsee, C.K. (1998) 'Cross-cultural differences in risk perception, but cross-cultural similarities in attitudes towards perceived risk', *Management Science* **44**(9): 1205–1217.

Weber, E.U., Hsee, C.K. and Sokolowska, J. (1998) 'What folklore tells us about risk and risk taking: cross-cultural comparisons of American, German, and Chinese proverbs', *Organizational Behavior and Human Decision Processes* **75**(2): 170–186.

Weick, K.E. and Quinn, R.E. (1999) 'Organizational change and development', *Annual Review of Psychology* **50**: 361–386.

Wetlaufer, S. (1999) 'Organizing for empowerment: an interview with AES's Roger Sant and Dennis Bakke', *Harvard Business Review* **77**(1): 110–123.

Winer, B.J. (1991) *Statistical Principles in Experimental Design* (3rd edn), McGraw-Hill: New York.

Yamagishi, T. (2003) 'Cross-Societal Experimentation on Trust: A Comparison of the United States and Japan', in E. Ostrom and J. Walker (eds.) *Trust and Reciprocity*, Russell Sage Foundation: New York, pp: 352–370.

Yamagishi, T., Cook, K.S. and Watabe, M. (1998) 'Uncertainty, trust, and commitment formation in the United States and Japan', *American Journal of Sociology* **104**: 165–194.

Yates, J.F., Lee, J.W., Shinotsuka, H., Patalano, A.L. and Sieck, W.R. (1998) 'Crosscultural variations in probability judgment accuracy: beyond general knowledge overconfidence?,', *Organizational Behavior and Human Decision Processes* **74**(2): 89–118.

Yates, J.F., Zhu, Y., Ronis, D.L., Wang, D.F., Shinotsuka, H. and Toda, M. (1989) 'Probability judgment accuracy: China, Japan, and the United States', *Organizational Behavior and Human Decision Processes* **43**: 145–171.

Zellmer-Bruhn, M., Gibson, C.B. and Earley, P.C. (2002) 'Some of these things are not like the others: an exploration of heterogeneity in work', Paper Presented at the National Academy of Management Meetings, Denver, CO.

Zhang, X., Zheng, X. and Wang, L. (2003) 'Comparative research on individual modernity of adolescents between town and countryside in China', *Asian Journal of Social Psychology* **6**: 61–73.

About the authors

Kwok Leung is Professor of Management at City University of Hong Kong. His research areas include justice and conflict, international business, and cross-cultural psychology. He is a departmental editor of *Journal of International Business Studies*, and a consulting editor for several journals, including *Journal of Applied Psychology, Organizational Research Methods*, and *Journal of Management*. He is the Chair-Elect of the Research Methods Division of the Academy of Management.

Rabi S Bhagat (Ph.D. University of Illinois at Urbana-Champaign) is Professor of Organizational Behavior and International Management at the Fogelman College of Business at the University of Memphis. His research interests include international and cross-cultural variations in the creation, diffusion, and transmission of organizational knowledge, human stress and cognition in organizations, and developing global mindset.

Nancy Buchan is an Assistant Professor of Marketing at the University of Wisconsin, Madison. Her research focuses on the influence of national, cultural, and gender differences on trust and reciprocity, and has appeared in the *American Journal of Sociology*, the *American Economic Review*, the *Journal of Consumer Research*, and the *Journal of Economic Behavior and Organization*.

Miriam Erez is the Mendes France Professor of Management and Economics, the Faculty of Industrial Engineering and Management, Technion, Israel. Her research focuses on cross-cultural management, work motivation, and innovation. She studies the moderating effect of culture on the relationship between managerial practices and performance, and the interplay between the global and local cultures in global companies.

Cristina B Gibson, Ph.D., is currently Associate Professor at the Graduate School of Management, University of California, Irvine. Her research interests include collective cognition, interaction, and effectiveness in teams; the impact of culture on work behavior; and international management. Her research has appeared in journals such as *Administrative Science Quarterly, Academy of Management Journal, Academy of Management Review, Journal of Management, Journal of International Business Studies*, and *Journal of Cross-Cultural Psychology*. She is co-author with P Christopher Earley of *New Perspectives on Multinational Teams* (Lawrence Erlbaum Associates, 2002) and co-editor with Susan G Cohen of *Virtual Teams That Work: Creating Conditions For Virtual Team Effectiveness* (Jossey-Bass, 2002).

Accepted by Arie Y Lewin, Editor-in-Chief, 25 February 2005. This paper has been with the author for one revision.

[6]

Journal of International Business Studies (2007) 38, 709–725
© 2007 Academy of International Business   All rights reserved 0047-2506 $30.00
www.jibs.net

Causes of the difficulties in internationalization

Alvaro Cuervo-Cazurra[1],
Mary M Maloney[2] and
Shalini Manrakhan[3]

[1]Moore School of Business, University of South Carolina, Columbia, SC, USA; [2]Department of Management, Opus College of Business, University of St Thomas, Minneapolis, MN, USA; [3]Faculty of Engineering, University of Mauritius, Reduit, Mauritius

Correspondence:
A Cuervo-Cazurra, Sonoco International Business Department, Moore School of Business, University of South Carolina, 1705 College Street, Columbia, SC 29208, USA.
Tel: +1 803 777 0314;
Fax: +1 803 777 3609;
E-mail: acuervo@moore.sc.edu

Abstract
We study the causes of the difficulties faced by firms when they internationalize in search of new markets. We build on the resource-based theory to argue that the difficulties in internationalization can be separated into three main sets based on their relationship to advantage: loss of advantage provided by resources transferred abroad; creation of a disadvantage by resources transferred abroad; and lack of complementary resources required to operate abroad. In each set, we further distinguish difficulties that are specific to a firm from those that are common to a set of firms. We argue that only a few of the resulting types of difficulties of internationalization are exclusive to the cross-border expansion, and propose solutions that address the root cause of each type.
Journal of International Business Studies (2007) 38, 709–725.
doi:10.1057/palgrave.jibs.8400295

Keywords: cost of doing business abroad; liability of foreignness; internationalization; multinational enterprises; resource-based theory

Introduction
In 1986, Lincoln Electric Company, a US arc-welding firm, started internationalizing aggressively and ran into difficulties despite the firm's distinctive manufacturing capabilities and incentive system, which had made it the leader in its field in the US. When Donald Hastings was appointed CEO he realized that, despite having superior operations and products, the firm faced multiple challenges that limited its ability to succeed abroad: its effective incentive system was often unsuited to foreign operations; managers at headquarters lacked experience in international markets and knowledge in running a complex, dispersed firm; managers of foreign operations convinced managers at headquarters that products made in the US would be rejected in Europe; and Lincoln lacked adequate distribution, relationships in the marketplace, and a sales force that could understand and help customers abroad (Hastings, 1999).

The problems that Lincoln experienced in its internationalization illustrate the numerous difficulties firms face when expanding abroad in search of new markets. These difficulties in internationalization – the problems that a firm encounters as it expands across borders – have traditionally been discussed in aggregate form as the cost of doing business abroad (Hymer, 1976) or the liability of foreignness (Zaheer, 1995). Existing literature on these difficulties has developed into three streams. Studies based in economics label the concept 'the cost of doing business abroad' and discuss its consequences in terms of the additional costs undertaken by the firm operating under uncertainty in foreign markets (Buckley and

Received: 20 February 2004
Revised: 23 October 2006
Accepted: 20 April 2007
Online publication date: 5 July 2007

Casson, 1976; Hymer, 1976). Organizational studies label the concept 'the liability of foreignness' and suggest that its consequences are lower performance and increased failure rates (Zaheer, 1995; Zaheer and Mosakowski, 1997). Strategic management analyses highlight the difficulties of managing dispersed operations in multiple countries, rather than the costs of expanding to a specific country as in the other two research streams, and argue that these difficulties lead to lower performance (Tallman and Li, 1996; Hitt *et al.*, 1997). These studies have focused mainly on analyzing the *consequences* of difficulties in internationalization;[1] we know less about what *causes* them.

Therefore, in this paper, we answer the question: *What causes the difficulties faced by firms when they internationalize in search of new markets?* We answer this question by building on the resource-based theory (RBT) (Penrose, 1959) to disaggregate the difficulties into their component pieces and identify the root causes of distinct internationalization difficulties. Understanding the root causes of these difficulties is important both for researchers studying internationalization and for managers leading the expansion of their firms. For researchers, we separate the different causes of difficulties into related but theoretically distinct types. We thereby provide a richer understanding of the sources of internationalizing difficulties, which will enable more focused empirical analysis in the future. For managers, our identification of the root causes of existing or potential difficulties will enable them to find better targeted and more effective solutions.

Before proceeding further, we detail the boundary conditions of our conceptual framework. First, we focus on firms with market-seeking motivations for internationalization. Unlike firms that expand in search of resources (natural, efficiency, or strategic) to transfer back to existing operations, market-seeking firms must face new competitors and new customers. As we describe in detail below, this affects both the relative advantage of resources when they are transferred and the need for complementary resources. Of course, resource-seeking firms also face difficulties; in the concluding section of this paper we suggest which parts of our typology may also be relevant to resource-seeking firms. Second, for parsimony, we limit our analysis to the difficulties associated with internationalization to one country. This condition provides a basis from which to differentiate the difficulties associated with international expansion from the difficulties associated with more general expansion

across regions, markets and industries. Third, we exclude from our discussion firm advantages. Advantages have been widely analyzed in existing research (see Tallman and Yip, 2001, for a summary), and some authors argue that advantages compensate for difficulties. In our analysis, we choose to find specific solutions to address each difficulty instead of relying on compensating advantages. Fourth, for the purposes of this analysis we assume the firm is able to transfer some resources. In order to internationalize, the firm must be able to transfer some resources across national borders, either indirectly through their embodiment in products (Penrose, 1959), or directly as foreign direct investment (Dunning, 1993).[2] Cross-border transfer of resources is not always simple, since resources may be location-bound (Rugman and Verbeke, 1992; Hu, 1995), have tacit components (Kogut and Zander, 1993), or be subject to legal restrictions (Zaheer, 1995). However, if the firm is completely unable to transfer resources across borders, it would be unable to internationalize.

In the first section of the paper we provide the building blocks for understanding the relationship between resources and difficulties in internationalization. Following arguments from RBT, we develop conceptual categories to distinguish difficulties, and devote a section of the paper to each category. In addition, we discuss how resources the firm possesses prior to its entry in the new country help it avoid specific difficulties; we suggest actions managers can take to overcome each difficulty by targeting its root cause; and we identify which difficulties are exclusive to internationalization and which are not. We conclude the paper with a review of the contributions to existing knowledge, the limitations of the study, and avenues for future research.

Resources and difficulties in internationalization

RBT describes a firm as a bundle of resources that are used to generate products or services that provide value for customers in competition with the offers of other firms (Penrose, 1959). Firm resources are the tangible and intangible assets that are tied semi-permanently to a firm (Wernerfelt, 1984).

RBT offers two important theoretical dimensions by which to classify resources and, therefore, better understand difficulties in internationalization: (1) the relationship between a resource and advantage;

and (2) the specificity of a resource to the firm. The first dimension ties directly to a core idea of RBT: resources are the basis of the firm's advantage (Barney, 1991; Peteraf, 1993), but not all resources provide an advantage to the firm (Montgomery, 1995; Ray *et al*., 2004). The second dimension is based on the idea that, while some resources are the firm's alone, other resources are available widely (Penrose, 1959). Whether a resource is advantageous or firm-specific depends on the competitors against which the firm is compared (Tallman, 1992; Amit and Schoemaker, 1993; Brush and Artz, 1999). Since competitors vary across locations, these two dimensions help identify the type of difficulties the firm faces when it internationalizes. We describe each of these dimensions in more detail in the paragraphs below.

Relationship to advantage
In any particular environment, and at any given time, a resource can be advantageous, disadvantageous, or complementary (Montgomery, 1995). First, a resource is considered advantageous or strategic (Amit and Schoemaker, 1993) when it provides the firm with an advantage in comparison with a determined set of competitors, thus supporting the generation of rents (Peteraf, 1993). To sustain advantage, a resource has to be valuable, rare, difficult to imitate, and difficult to substitute (VRIS) (Barney, 1991). Typically, only a few resources in the firm are the basis of the firm's advantage (Ray *et al*., 2004). Second, a resource is considered disadvantageous when it detracts from the firm's advantage and reduces value creation. Core rigidities (Leonard-Barton, 1992) are an example of disadvantageous resources. Third, a resource is considered complementary when it provides neither advantage nor disadvantage to the firm. Nevertheless, complementary resources are still important since they are necessary for the firm to operate even if they are not the basis of an advantage on their own (Teece, 1986; Montgomery, 1995).

The type of advantage a resource provides is an important dimension to understand when considering difficulties in internationalization because this relationship may change when the firm moves to another country. A resource transferred to another country may unexpectedly lose its ability to provide an advantage to the firm there, or may even become a source of disadvantage (Tallman, 1992; Hu, 1995). In addition, when internationalizing, the firm may suffer from a lack of some

complementary resources that limits the effectiveness of its new foreign operation (Eriksson *et al*., 1997).

Specificity
Resources can also be classified into those that are: (1) specific to a particular firm, or (2) common to a set of firms. Resources are firm-specific when only the focal firm has access to them. These are the resources traditionally discussed in resource-based analyses (e.g., Teece *et al*., 1997). Resources are common to a set of firms when several companies have access to them. As such, they are inputs in the production process (Penrose, 1959). For example, an efficient transportation system is a common resource available to all firms requiring its use in a location. Although these resources are common to a set of firms, and therefore are unlikely to provide advantage to one firm over the others, they are still important. Access to some common resources can be restricted to firms from or in a particular location (Dunning, 1977; Rugman and Verbeke, 1992). In this case, they become a location advantage that is common across a set of firms in one location in comparison with firms in other locations (Dunning, 1977; Fladmoe-Lindquist and Tallman, 1994).

Just as resources can be classified as firm-specific or common to a set of companies, difficulties can also be classified as firm-specific or common to a set of firms. Some difficulties affect a particular firm, and other difficulties affect all firms operating in a particular location. If difficulties are firm-specific, the firm must look to itself to overcome them. If difficulties are common to a set of firms, then the firm may find allies to help confront the problems.

Difficulties in internationalization
The two dimensions described above (relationship to advantage and specificity) allow us to develop six theoretically distinct categories of difficulties in internationalization. The first dimension – relationship to advantage – generates three categories of difficulties:

(1) *loss of an advantage*, which occurs when resources lose their advantageous nature when transferred to a new country;
(2) *creation of a disadvantage*, which occurs when resources generate a disadvantage when transferred to a new country; and
(3) *lack of the complementary resources*, which occurs when the firms lack complementary resources required to operate in the new country.

The second dimension – specificity – results in a further separation of each of the above categories into two subgroups based on whether the difficulties are firm-specific or common to a set of firms. Table 1 summarizes the resulting categorization scheme.

In the following sections, we discuss in detail each category of difficulties. In each section we first describe the cause of the difficulty, then discuss how resources the firm possesses prior to its expansion to the new country may reduce that difficulty, and then suggest actions managers can take to surmount that difficulty. We conclude by explaining whether the difficulty is specific to internationalization or not.

Loss of an advantage

The advantage provided by resources is relative to the competitive environment in which the firm operates (Tallman, 1992; Amit and Schoemaker, 1993; Brush and Artz, 1999). The environment in a new country will differ from a firm's home country owing to variations in physical characteristics, such as geography and climate, or in the characteristics of its people and institutions, such as government, businesses, religion, language, wealth, or culture (Bartlett and Ghoshal, 1989; Tallman, 1992; Praha-lad and Lieberthal, 1998; Ghemawat, 2001). When competitors and customers differ across countries, a resource that supported a firm's advantage in one country may lose its ability to support that advantage in a new country (Tallman, 1992; Hu, 1995). The loss of advantage may be firm-specific or common to a set of firms.

Firm-specific loss of an advantage: inability to transfer advantage

A firm will face a firm-specific loss of advantage when a resource that is advantageous in existing operations is transferred to a new country, but the advantage provided by that resource does not transfer. We refer to this as *the inability to transfer advantage*. Causal ambiguity (Lippman and Rumelt, 1982) limits the ability of not only competitors, but also the firm, to correctly identify the source of the advantage provided by a resource. Understanding the source of advantage is even more difficult when the firm expands abroad. A resource that is rare (i.e., few competitors have it) in one country may not be rare in another country because of differences in the countries' endowments (Kogut, 1985a). Thus a resource that supported advantage in one country may not support advantage in another. Alternatively, domestic competitors may

already have the resource, have imitated it, or have substituted it with another that provides a similar or improved benefit. For example, although the US retailer Wal-Mart achieved an advantage based on a low-cost strategy in the US, this was not a source of advantage in Germany. There, Wal-Mart faced well-established rivals, such as Metro, and hard dis-counters, such as Aldi and Lidl, that already used a low-cost strategy (*Economist*, 2004; *Business Week*, 2004). Similarly, some local firms in developing countries have managed to compete against large foreign multinational enterprises (MNEs) despite their smaller resource bundle (Wells, 1983; Dawar and Frost, 1999).

Not all firms, of course, face this difficulty when they enter a new country. In many cases the impetus for entry into a new country is precisely the fact that local competitors are weak or non-existent. For example, in contrast to the expansion in Germany, Wal-Mart's expansion in Mexico was very successful because there were few national chains or 'category killers' that could match its low-cost strategy (Neuborne, 1991). In some cases a domestic competitor does not exist: for example, when a firm is an innovator and its advantageous resource is a product in the introduction stage of the product life cycle. In this stage, the innovator has an advantage both in its domestic market and also in foreign countries (Vernon, 1966).

There is little the firm can do to overcome the inability to transfer advantage. The firm can invest in the development of other advantageous resources locally, or allow the subsidiary to create its own strategy and advantage (Bartlett and Ghoshal, 1986; Birkinshaw *et al.*, 1998). However, such solutions defeat the purpose of entering a new country to leverage resources already developed, and open the firm up to additional difficulties. Although managers may not be able to overcome the inability to transfer advantage, they can reduce the potential cost by following a gradual inter-nationalization process, for example, by exporting before investing in a wholly owned subsidiary (Johanson and Vahlne, 1977). If the firm has already invested, and still faces an inability to transfer advantage it can de-internationalize and exit to reduce the losses (Benito and Welch, 1997).

The inability to transfer advantage is not exclu-sive to the firm's internationalization. The advan-tage provided by an advantageous resource in any location is limited to a period of time (Miller and Shamsie, 1996), and changes in customers' prefer-ences or among competitors within the industry

Table 1 Causes of the difficulties in internationalization and their solutions

Causes		Difficulties	Solutions	
Relationship to advantage:	Specificity:	Type:	Reduced when:	To solve it:
Loss of an advantage	Specific to a firm	*Inability to transfer advantage*: A resource that was the source of advantage in existing operations loses its advantageous characteristic when transferred to the new country	Competitors in the new country are not up to par, or do not exist, particularly in the introduction stage of an innovation	Develop advantageous resources locally, allowing the subsidiary to create its own strategy and advantage
	Common to a set of firms	*Inability to create value*: A set of firms in an industry do not obtain value from the transferred resources that were a source of advantage in existing operations because their products are not useful in the new country	Not reduced	Avoid entering the new country, or exit it if already entered
Creation of a disadvantage	Specific to a firm	*Disadvantage of transfer*: A resource becomes disadvantageous when transferred to the new country	Firm internationalizes through trade or reduces the value-added activities undertaken abroad	Evaluate the appropriateness of the resources to the new host country, modify the resource transferred if it creates a disadvantage
	Common to a set of firms	*Government-based disadvantage of foreignness*: A set of firms from the same country are discriminated against by the host government because it dislikes their country of origin	Political relations between the home- and host-country governments are good	Obtain support from government, directly by negotiating or lobbying the government; indirectly by linking with prominent local actors who obtain support
		Consumer-based disadvantage of foreignness: A set of firms from the same country are discriminated against by consumers because they dislike their country of origin	Firm or its products lack association with the discriminated country of origin	Avoid connection between firm and country of origin, directly by hiding country of origin, indirectly by using country of origin that is different from true one
Lack of complementary resources	Specific to a firm	*Liability of expansion*: The firm lacks complementary resources needed to operate at the larger scale required by the expansion in the new country	Firm already developed resources to manage the additional scale and complexity before expanding in the new country because it is a large, diversified, or multinational firm	Develop management and information systems in existing operations; alter the organizational structure
		Liability of newness: The firm lacks complementary resources required to compete in the industry of the new country	Firm operates in a global industry with similar competitors and customers across different countries	Invest to develop the complementary resource needed to compete in the industry of the new country; purchase the resource; access the resource of a local firm through an acquisition or alliance
		Liability of foreignness: The firm lacks complementary resources required to operate in the institutional environment of the new country	Firm has operations in countries with institutional environments similar to the new country	Invest to develop the complementary resource needed to operate in the new institutional environment; purchase the resource; access the resource of a local firm through an alliance
	Common to a set of firms	*Liability of infrastructure*: A set of firms do not obtain value from transferred resources because customers in the new country lack complementary assets to use their products	Products are simple to use or standalone	Provide customers with the complementary tangible or intangible asset necessary to use the product

can lead to the obsolescence of the advantage provided by a resource (Teece *et al.*, 1997). The likelihood of facing this difficulty, however, is greater when crossing national borders, since managers are unlikely to have as much knowledge about the new market as they do about their home market, and therefore misjudge the transfer of advantage abroad.

These ideas can be summarized in the following proposition:

> **Proposition 1a**: A firm entering a country in search of new markets is more likely to face difficulties when the advantageous nature of resources disappears upon transfer to a new country – specifically, when a resource is not rare in the new country or when local competitors have imitated or substituted the resource.

Non-firm-specific loss of an advantage: inability to create value

In some extreme cases the environment in the new country is so different that an entire set of companies, or all the companies in an industry, are unable to transfer their advantage to the new country. We refer to this as *the inability to create value*. In such cases the industry is not viable in the new country, as customers cannot use, do not need, or do not pay for the products or services of the firms. There are several causes of this. In countries where labor costs are low, products or services that are specifically designed to provide labor savings may not create value. For example, remote security monitoring is less necessary when guards are inexpensive. Cultural norms may also preclude the viability of certain products or services. For example, firms producing alcoholic beverages are limited in their ability to create value in countries where alcohol consumption is banned by religious precept. Geographic characteristics may also determine the viability of an industry. For example, firms producing mining equipment will not have a market in countries without valuable minerals. Institutional characteristics can also limit the ability of firms in an industry to appropriate rents. For example, in countries with weak protection of property rights, software or music firms are unable to benefit from their innovations because customers copy programs or songs and piracy is not prosecuted. These differences across countries affect all firms in their respective industries, so it is not a firm-specific difficulty. It is unlikely that firms would choose to enter a country when such

conditions exist, but there are many cases of firms doing inadequate up-front planning and overestimating the value they can potentially create in a new country (Ricks, 2000).

Managers can avoid the inability to create value by collectively working to alter the environment and make their industry viable, for example lobbying the government to enforce property rights or changing cultural norms to make the product acceptable to customers.

The inability to create value is not necessarily exclusive to internationalization. Again, in an extreme case, a firm could theoretically diversify into an unrelated industry that is not viable in its home country.

In sum, in some instances a whole industry is not viable in a foreign country and, as a result, a set of firms will not be able to transfer their advantages there. Hence we argue that:

> **Proposition 1b**: A set of firms entering a country in search of new markets are more likely to face difficulties when the advantageous nature of resources disappears when transferred to a new country because the industry is not viable – specifically, where resources of a set of firms that supported the creation of value in existing locations do not create value for clients in the new country because clients there cannot use, do not need, or do not pay for the products generated with the resources.

Creation of a disadvantage

In the previous section, resources simply ceased providing an advantage in the new country. In this section, we discuss resources that actually become liabilities, or disadvantageous, when transferred. In some cases this affects one specific firm only, and in other cases it affects a set of firms.

Firm-specific creation of a disadvantage: disadvantage of transfer

Some of the firm resources transferred to the new country may create a disadvantage in relationship to other firms, resulting in the destruction of value created by other resources. We refer to this as the *disadvantage of transfer*. The firm develops resources adapted to the characteristics of the environment in which it operates (Penrose, 1959; Porter, 1985, 1990). This resource accumulation is path-dependent, resulting in firms with distinct resource bundles (Dierickx and Cool, 1989). Such resources and the knowledge associated with their use are then codified into routines to facilitate the retrieval and replication of resources over time and across locations (Nelson and Winter, 1982; Kogut and Zander, 1993; Winter and Szulanski, 2001). As the company transfers them to another country, however, routines that were embedded in technical and managerial systems and supported by values and norms prevailing in the original context may be incompatible with the characteristics of new host-country environment, and create a disadvantage. For example, Lincoln Electric had a unique and highly successful incentive system based on piece-work and bonuses, which worked very well in the US. However, this incentive system engendered conflicts and discontent among the employees of its European operations because the prevailing culture of labor was hostile to such systems (Hastings, 1999). A resource that in the US created an advantage against its competitors became a source of disadvantage in Europe.

Some firms may be less susceptible to the disadvantage of transfer. The fewer the resources transferred to a new country, the lower the problems generated if the resource is disadvantageous in the new country. Thus firms adopting a gradual internationalization process (Johanson and Vahlne, 1977) will be more likely to avoid unexpected costs associated with the disadvantage of transfer. A firm that internationalizes by exporting, transferring its resources indirectly through their embodiment in products created with those resources (Penrose, 1959; Tallman, 1992), reduces the resources transferred and therefore the costs incurred if resources become disadvantageous abroad.

Managers can actively overcome this difficulty by being selective in choosing which resources are appropriate in the new host country, and which require modification (Prahalad and Doz, 1987; Bartlett and Ghoshal, 1989). However, the literature on causal ambiguity suggests that this assessment is not always simple (Lippman and Rumelt, 1982; Szulanski, 1996). Managers who are able to move from blind to conscious replication through deliberate learning (Zollo and Winter, 2002) may more successfully judge which resources are inappropriate in the new host country. Alternatively, the firm can transfer the resource at an intermediate stage, where the resource is not as fully embedded within the original context, and the accumulation trajectory can occur within the new context.

Even firms that are not internationalizing can face a disadvantage of transfer – resources that were

a source of advantage can also become a source of disadvantage in the same country, For example, a firm may diversify into an industry where the resources transferred create a disadvantage. Alternatively, conditions can change such that what used to be an advantage becomes a disadvantage. For example, core capabilities can become core rigidities even in a strictly domestic context, as Leonard-Barton (1992) describes. Nevertheless, internationalizing firms are far more susceptible to this type of difficulty owing to their unfamiliarity with the new host country's market.

We summarize these arguments in the following proposition:

Proposition 2a: A firm entering a country in search of new markets is more likely to face difficulties when some of its resources become disadvantageous when transferred to a new country – specifically, when a firm-specific resource developed in one context conflicts with a characteristic of the new context.

Non-firm-specific creation of a disadvantage: disadvantage of foreignness

Disadvantages may result from causes that affect more than one firm, and are therefore not firm-specific. When conducting business in other countries, the government or consumers in a country may discriminate against a certain nationality. Nationality is something that is common to multiple firms, and therefore non-firm-specific. When a firm's nationality puts it at a disadvantage relative to domestic firms, we call it *the disadvantage of foreignness*. A resource in the firms' bundle, their country of origin, becomes a source of disadvantage in the new country when it was not necessarily so in other operations. Unlike the other difficulties discussed thus far (the inability to transfer advantage, the inability to transfer value, and the disadvantage of transfer), the disadvantage of foreignness is specific to internationalization because it is linked to national origin, and a firm faces it when it crosses national boundaries.

The disadvantage of foreignness can occur when either the government or consumers discriminate against the firm's country of origin. These two groups differ in terms of awareness of the true country of origin of the company and in the impact on the firm. The government is in a position to know the country of origin of the firm and limit or block a firm's operations. In contrast, consumers in the host country are less likely to be aware of the true country of origin, and may react more to the perceived country of origin than to the real one. Consumers cannot block the operations of the firm, but they can negatively affect the sale of products. Hence we discuss government-based and consumer-based disadvantage of foreignness separately.

Government-based disadvantage of foreignness

Some host-country governments discriminate against foreign firms in general, or firms from one country in particular, because these companies pose a threat to their sovereignty (Hymer, 1976; Stopford and Strange, 1992; Kobrin, 2001). To reduce such threat, the government in the host country establishes limitations to the activities of foreign firms there (Buckley and Casson, 1976; Stopford and Strange, 1992; Kobrin, 2001; Spar, 2001), increasing the risk of operating in the host country (Kobrin, 1979; Fitzpatrick, 1983). The local government can go to the extreme of reneging on previous contracts or nationalizing investments, particularly when there are weak protections against this (Henisz and Williamson, 1999). Discrimination can also occur in countries considered to have low political risk. For example, in early 2006 the US Congress interfered in the acquisition by Dubai Ports World of the British company P&O, which managed terminals in six US ports. Alternatively, governments may discriminate against foreign firms indirectly by making only domestic companies eligible for benefits, such as subsidies or preferential purchase contracts (Zaheer, 1995; Mezias, 2002b). In other cases, discrimination can be subtle. In the late 1990s, for example, Coca-Cola in Brazil claimed that local soft drink manufacturers were able to sustain much lower prices because local firms were engaging in tax evasion that was overlooked by the government (Gertner *et al.*, 2005). The disadvantage of foreignness can lead to lower revenues when foreign firms are constrained in their operations, to higher costs of operation when foreign firms are excluded from subsidies, and to outright losses when foreign firms have investments expropriated.

This risk of facing government-based disadvantage is very low when political relations between the home- and host-country governments are good, since the treatment of foreign firms by the host country becomes intermingled with the relationships between the home- and host-country governments (Stopford and Strange, 1992). Unlike other difficulties that tend to decrease over time and with experience, however, the disadvantage of foreignness can increase, sometimes quite abruptly, as the political environment changes; conversely, it can also cease rapidly. For example, as a result of the lack of support by the French, German, and Russian governments for the US-led war in Iraq, the US government excluded companies from those countries from bidding for reconstruction contracts (*Economist*, 2003). The ban was later lifted as the countries pardoned part of Iraq's foreign debt. Additionally, a government disadvantage of foreignness may not be consistently applied. For example, in late 2004 the US Congress allowed the acquisition of the personal computer division of the US firm IBM by the state-controlled Chinese firm Lenovo, but in 2005 the US Congress blocked the acquisition of the US oil firm Unocal by the also state-owned Chinese firm CNOOC.

Managers of a firm that face government-based discrimination can attempt to overcome it directly, by negotiating with the government, highlighting the benefits the firm brings to the country, while emphasizing its flexibility in moving to another country if the unfavorable treatment by the government continues (Kogut, 1985b; Stopford and Strange, 1992). Coca-Cola lobbied tax agencies and lawmakers in Brazil to make a case for stronger government control over local beverage producers, for example (Gertner *et al.*, 2005). Alternatively, managers can overcome this disadvantage indirectly by establishing links with prominent local actors who can obtain the support of the government (Luo *et al.*, 2002).

Consumer-based disadvantage of foreignness

Consumers, acting independently of their government, may discriminate against the foreignness or the specific country of origin of the firm. Consumers may dislike the country of origin for nationalistic reasons, or may have a negative perception of the quality of products generated in the foreign country. As a result, firms experience reduced revenues independent of product or service quality (Bilkey and Nes, 1982; Peterson and Jolibert, 1995). For example, Sarik Tara, chairman of Enka Holding, Turkey's biggest construction company, indicated that its company had to look for contracts in Russia rather than in France because in France 'I am stamped "Made in Turkey", not "Made in Germany"' (Munir, 2002: 2). Like government-based discrimination, this difficulty can vary with current events. For example, when France opposed the US invasion of Iraq, some consumers in the US boycotted French wine, independently of the brand (Debord, 2003). Although this form of the disadvantage of foreignness tends, primarily, to affect the marketing of products, it may take other forms such as labor lawsuits, which target foreign firms more often than local ones (Mezias, 2002a). The disadvantage of foreignness can lead to lower revenues when firms sell less than they would otherwise, or to higher costs in the case of lawsuits.

A firm reduces its risk of encountering consumer-based disadvantage of foreignness when it does not have a country of origin clearly associated with it or with its products. In contrast to the government, consumers do not always know the true country of origin of products, but rather act on their perceptions. Thus, when the product has multiple countries of origin for its parts, assembly, and design, there is less association with a single country of origin (Chao, 2001). Alternatively, when the firm produces for original equipment manufacturers (OEMs) who, in turn, stamp the product with the OEM's brand name and the image of their own country of origin, there is a reduced association with the actual country of origin.

Managers of firms that face the consumer-based disadvantage of foreignness can overcome it by actively avoiding the connection between the firm and its country of origin. They can do this directly by not indicating where the firm is headquartered or where the product is manufactured, or by using a regional label, such as 'Made in the European Union', to mask the country of origin (Schweiger *et al.*, 1995). Managers can go even further and disguise the country of origin under a local image by using a local-sounding brand, acquiring a local brand, or allying with a local partner who provides the interface with local customers.

In sum, we argue that:

Proposition 2b: A set of firms entering a country in search of new markets are more likely to face difficulties when a common resource becomes disadvantageous when transferred to a new country – specifically, when the government or consumers in the new country have an aversion to the specific country of origin or to the foreign nature of firms.

Lack of complementary resources
A company may also face difficulties because of a lack of complementary resources. Owing to differences across countries, some resources cannot be transferred to the new country (Rugman and Verbeke, 1992; Hu, 1995). Alternatively, additional

resources may be necessary in the new country that are not necessary in the home country. The lack of such resources can negatively affect the operations in the new country *vis-à-vis* local competitors, since the internationalizing firm will need to incur expenses that local competitors do not. To obtain these complementary resources, the firm may have to purchase, or establish an alliance with, a domestic firm (Anand and Delios, 1997, 2002).

In resource-based thinking, complementary resources (those that are necessary to operate but do not provide advantage) do not receive the same attention as advantageous resources (those that are valuable, rare, difficult to imitate, and difficult to substitute). Nonetheless, complementary resources are recognized to be critical to the functioning of the firm (Montgomery, 1995). They are especially noteworthy in the context of internationalization, where determining which resources are necessary may not be obvious.

We distinguish two types of difficulties that arise from the lack of complementary resources. The first type is encountered by a firm when it needs additional resources to complement its existing resource bundle in order to operate at a larger scale, under different industry conditions, and within a context of different institutions. The second type of difficulty is common to a set of foreign firms in an industry entering the new country where the potential customers, not the firms, lack the complementary resources needed to use the firms' products.

Firm-specific lack of complementary resources: liabilities of expansion, newness and foreignness
Among the firm-specific difficulties that arise from the lack of complementary resources we separate three types based on the nature of the complementary resources the firm lacks:

(1) the liability of expansion, or the lack of complementary resources needed to operate at a larger scale;
(2) the liability of newness or the lack of complementary resources needed to compete in a new competitive environment; and
(3) the liability of foreignness[3] or the lack of complementary resources needed to operate in a new institutional environment.

These three types correspond to the types of experiential knowledge required for successful internationalization proposed by Eriksson *et al.* (1997): internationalization knowledge about how to be an international firm; business knowledge about the new country's competitive environment; and institutional knowledge of the new country's institutional environment. We build on their conceptualization to include the lack of *tangible* complementary resources.

Liability of expansion

Internationalization is often accompanied by an increase in the scale of a firm's activities. Adding new operations, especially when they are geographically distant, requires the firm to deal with additional transportation, communication, and coordination (Vernon, 1977), and complexity (Tallman and Li, 1996; Hitt *et al.*, 1997). To manage this, the firm needs spare resource capacity. If it does not have this capacity, the firm may have to stretch its existing resources so thinly that they become ineffective (Penrose, 1959). We call this the *liability of expansion*. This may affect the overall operations, not just those in the new location. For example, when Lincoln Electric rapidly internationalized in the late 1980s, it had few managers and no members of the board with international experience, and the negative impact of this extended to the entire company (Hastings, 1999).

A firm has a reduced risk of facing the liability of expansion when it has already developed experience and resources from operating on a large scale and coordinating dispersed operations before entering the new country. Firms that are already MNEs have usually developed the necessary resources to manage operations across many countries. Such firms can more easily manage the expansion into a new country. Additionally, a firm that is not yet international, but is product-diversified or manages businesses across several geographic locations in its domestic market, will also be less likely to suffer this difficulty. It will already have many of the complementary resources needed to operate on a larger scale, such as an efficient structure, better governance, and enhanced managerial capabilities (Hitt *et al.*, 1997: 776).

Managers of a firm suffering from a liability of expansion can overcome it through changes to information systems (Hagstrom, 1991), human resources (Hedlund, 1986), organizational culture and managerial expertise (Bartlett and Ghoshal, 1989) or structure (Chandler, 1962; Stopford and Wells, 1972; Galbraith, 2000). These changes positively affect not only the current foreign expansion, but also future expansion.

The liability of expansion is not exclusive to internationalization. A firm faces similar difficulties when it grows from being a local competitor to being a regional or national competitor (Welch and Wiedersheim-Paul, 1980), or when it diversifies into multiple industries (e.g., Hoskisson and Hitt, 1990). The coordination costs involved with internationalization, however, are usually higher than in a domestic context (Hitt *et al.*, 1997; Vernon, 1977).

Liability of newness

A firm's existing competitive environment induces it to develop certain strategies and resources to compete against other firms within a particular industry structure (Porter, 1985). When the firm moves to another country, the competitive environment often differs, requiring some additional resources that the firm does not have there, either because it cannot transfer them across countries or because it has not developed them. For example, Lincoln Electric found that, in its international expansion in Europe, it lacked several resources, such as proper distribution, relationships in the marketplace, and people who could understand and help customers, which limited its success (Hastings, 1999). We call this the *liability of newness*.

Some internationalizing firms face a reduced liability of newness owing to similarities in industry conditions across countries. In so-called 'global' industries the firm faces similar competitors, customers and suppliers in multiple countries (Levitt, 1983; Prahalad and Doz, 1987). As a result, the same set of resources developed to meet the needs in existing markets helps the firm meet the needs in a new country.

Managers can overcome the liability of newness by actively developing or acquiring the complementary resource needed to compete in the new country. The firm can invest to internally develop the resource it needs: for example, if it needs a sales force, it can hire, train, and deploy one. Alternatively, the firm may acquire the resource in the host market: for example, if it lacks an office building, it can buy one. Acquiring a complementary resource in the market may be quicker than internally developing it. If there is no market for the individual resource, the firm may consider obtaining it by acquiring or allying with a domestic firm that has the resource (Anand and Delios, 1997, 2002). In this case the firm needs to take into account the cost of acquiring additional resources it does not need and the challenge of integrating them within the firm's operations (Hennart and Park, 1993; Hennart and Reddy, 1997), later disposing of excess resources that it did not desire (Capron *et al.*, 1998).

The liability of newness is also not exclusive to the internationalization of the firm. New entrants even in domestic situations lack some complementary resources to compete in a new industry environment – resources that established competitors already have – and therefore suffer disadvantages relative to established firms (Lieberman, 1989). Although a domestic situation may also require new complementary resources, in an international situation the need for new complementary resources may not be as obvious or understandable, and the resources may not be as simple to obtain.

Liability of foreignness
The institutional environment, the set of norms and rules that constrain human behavior, such as culture, language, religion, and the political, legal, and economic systems (North, 1990), affects all firms operating in the country. A firm's home-country institutional environment induces it to develop certain resources to operate effectively in that environment and interact with other social actors (Tallman, 1992; Oliver, 1997). However, when the firm moves into a new country with a different institutional environment, it may lack the complementary resources, such as understanding, relationships, and social capital needed for dealing with other entities and prevailing rules of behavior (Calhoun, 2002; Zaheer, 2002). We call this the *liability of foreignness*. This lack of complementary resources needed for understanding the new institutions creates difficulties. For example, when Jollibee, a fast food company from the Philippines, expanded to Hong Kong it had trouble interacting with clients. Jollibee lacked the complementary resources in the form of local Chinese staff who could understand Cantonese. Chinese customers needed to speak English to Filipino and Nepalese staff, and this kept some customers away (Bartlett and O'Connell, 1998).

A firm may suffer little or no liability of foreignness when its existing operations, either in the home country or in other countries, are in institutional environments that are similar to the one in the new host country (Johanson and Wiedersheim-Paul, 1975; Barkema *et al.*, 1996; Barkema and Vermeulen, 1998). In this case, the firm can use the resources developed in existing operations to deal with institutions in the new country.

Managers can overcome the liability of foreignness by developing the complementary resources internally. Overcoming the liability of foreignness is more challenging than solving other liabilities because it involves the transformation of deep-seated assumptions about the appropriate rules of behavior (Prahalad and Bettis, 1986; Prahalad and Lieberthal, 1998), the development of tacit knowledge of how to operate in the new institutional environment (Johanson and Wiedersheim-Paul, 1975; Eriksson *et al.*, 1997), and the creation of new information networks (Zaheer, 2002). The firm can do so through internal learning-by-doing, gradually increasing the commitment to the new country (Johanson and Wiedersheim-Paul, 1975; Johanson and Vahlne, 1977; Petersen and Pedersen, 2002). Although the firm can use external methods such as acquisitions and alliance, these are less adequate in dealing with the tacit dimensions of the institutional environment (Johanson and Vahlne, 1977, 1990).

Similar to the disadvantage of foreignness, the liability of foreignness affects only firms that internationalize, since it originates in the differences in social and institutional contexts that exist across countries. A firm that expands nationally in countries with several religious, language, and ethnic groups, such as India or China, faces aspects of this difficulty, but these countries still have common legal, political and economic systems.

This discussion of the three liabilities that the firm suffers when it lacks necessary resources to successfully operate in a new host country can be summarized in this proposition:

Proposition 3a: A firm entering a country in search of new markets is more likely to face difficulties when it lacks complementary resources required to (1) manage an increase in scale, (2) compete against established local players, or (3) operate in the institutional context of the new host country.

Non-firm-specific lack of complementary resources: liability of infrastructure
Occasionally, difficulties arise not from the firm's lack of complementary resources, but from the host country customers' lack of complementary resources needed to use the firm's products or services. We refer to this as the *liability of infrastructure*. This difficulty creates problems for all firms seeking to market a similar product or service. For example, when Star TV moved to launch

satellite television in Asia, it found that both a retail network for satellite dishes, and a way to track viewers (which is critical to attract advertisers), simply did not exist in many of the countries it was targeting (Laurence *et al.*, 1994). Any satellite firm would have faced such difficulty. The complementary resources necessary may be tangible (e.g., the availability of refrigeration for products that need to be kept cold), or intangible (e.g., knowledge about how to use an innovative product). Firms that attempt to internationalize to countries where customers lack necessary complementary resources are unable to market their goods as they are, and therefore face difficulties.

A firm will be less likely to face the liability of infrastructure if its products are standalone or simple to use. When products are standalone, even if they are complex and have several high-tech subsystems (Dyerson and Pilkington, 2000), customers can use the products without additional investments in complementary assets. For example, hand-crank-powered radios are appropriate in countries where the electric supply is sporadic and it is difficult to find batteries. When products are simple to use, customers utilize them without the need to invest in developing the complementary knowledge. In both cases, early investment in design reduces the likelihood of facing the liability of infrastructure later.

Managers can overcome this difficulty by providing customers with the tangible complementary assets needed to use the firm's products, or the knowledge necessary to use the products. For example, the cereal firm Kellogg developed a marketing campaign to train Indian consumers to eat cereals for breakfast, a new eating habit for many of them (Prahalad and Lieberthal, 1998). Providing customers with complementary assets is expensive, however, and does not ensure the firm will reap the benefits because competitors can free-ride (Heil *et al.*, 1991). Indeed, Kellogg found that local Indian competitors benefited from its consumer education efforts and introduced their own cereals with local flavors. To avoid this, firms can use bundling strategies, providing complementary assets that are compatible only with the firm's offer (Burstein, 1984; Tirole, 1988). Alternatively, the firm can redesign the product to the conditions of the existing infrastructure of the new country. For example, a Western frozen dessert firm redesigned its products to withstand higher temperatures for the Indian market because in most retail outlets refrigerators were not cold enough (Prahalad and Lieberthal, 1998).

The liability of infrastructure is not exclusive to the firm's internationalization. Firms may face similar problems when they move across market segments in their home country. Alternatively, firms may face this difficulty when they introduce an innovative product and customers lack the knowledge to use it or fully understand its benefits. However, the problems caused by the liability of infrastructure are much more likely to appear in situations where firms are operating in countries with large differences in terms of infrastructure development, for example between developed and emerging markets, which occurs in an international situation (Khanna *et al.*, 2005).

We summarize these arguments in the following proposition:

Proposition 3b: A set of firms entering a country in search of new markets are more likely to face difficulties when the customers in the new country lack complementary resources needed to use the firms' products or services.

Conclusions
In this paper we analyzed the causes of the difficulties associated with seeking new markets across national borders. Using the theoretical lens of RBT, we classified these difficulties into six types by their relationship to advantage and by their specificity. We discussed how each type requires different solutions, and argued that only a few of them are exclusive to the internationalization of the firm.

The resulting classification and discussion contributes to theory in five ways. First, we extend the study of the liability of foreignness beyond an understanding of its *consequences* to an understanding of the underlying *causes* of the difficulties firms face when they internationalize in search of new markets. This is an area that has received remarkably little in-depth attention, despite its importance for understanding the challenges that firms encounter when they internationalize.

Second, by using one theoretical approach our study clarifies in a systematic manner the relationship among the diverse list of potential causes that have been mentioned in the literature. Previous studies have indicated a variety of factors that cause the difficulties and lead to higher costs (for a recent review of the costs, see Eden and Miller, 2001), such as unfamiliarity with the foreign market (Hymer, 1976), discrimination by the host government (Buckley and Casson, 1976; Hymer, 1976), additional coordination and communication needed to manage spatial distance (Vernon, 1977), lack of legitimacy (Kostova and Zaheer, 1999), lack of membership in information networks (Zaheer, 2002), or additional complexity (Tallman and Li, 1996; Hitt *et al.*, 1997). By using a single theoretical lens we organized these causes in a coherent framework, and are able to show that few of the causes are exclusive to international expansion. The two that are exclusive – the disadvantage of foreignness and the liability of foreignness – are intimately related to the social and institutional dimensions of a foreign country. The other difficulties in our typology can be suffered by firms expanding within a single country, across industries, or across market segments. However, firms that expand across borders are more likely to suffer several of them at the same time. The framework outlined in this paper enables future empirical analyses to move toward more fine-grained tests that separate different types of difficulties in internationalization by their cause. This will expand our understanding and help explain conflicting findings.

Third, by adopting a RBT stance, we move away from analyzing difficulties in internationalization as the additional costs foreign firms incur, and toward a discussion that also includes reduced revenues. In fact, an increase in costs is commonly the consequence of solving a difficulty in internationalization rather than its cause.

Fourth, our analysis extends current work in RBT by redirecting attention toward the resources a firm *lacks*, not just the resources a firm already has. RBT has increasingly been used in the field of international management (e.g., Collis, 1991; Tallman, 1991, 1992; Madhok, 1997; Peng, 2001), but has focused primarily on the advantages that MNEs draw from existing resources (see Tallman and Yip, 2001, for a recent review), not the additional resources required.

Fifth, and finally, we contribute to RBT by expanding the discussion of how the advantage provided by a resource can vary across locations. Other research has identified that the advantageous nature of resources can change over time (Miller and Shamsie, 1996) and with a changing competitive environment (Teece *et al.*, 1997). Our work adds considerable depth to work that initially recognized that the advantageous nature of resources can change in new host country environ-

ments (Tallman, 1992; Hu, 1995), and that resources can also become disadvantageous abroad, even when they were the source of advantage at home.

Our analysis also has practical implications. As the opening example illustrated, despite the apparent advantages that a firm may have at home, internationalizing is difficult. The framework and solutions discussed in this paper will help managers target solutions to the root causes of the difficulties encountered, or avoid them altogether by doing thorough analysis up-front. Unlike other RBT analyses, the solutions we present go beyond the simplistic argument of using advantages to compensate for difficulties.

Our paper has some limitations that suggest additional avenues for future research. First, we centered our attention on firms internationalizing in search of new markets. Future research can adapt the typology presented here to study the difficulties in internationalization suffered by firms that expand abroad to obtain resources (natural, strategic, or knowledge). Firms will suffer difficulties in internationalization regardless of the motivation for foreign expansion, but the importance and specifics of the difficulty will vary. For example, when firms internationalize in search of new markets, the primary motivation is to transfer the advantage provided by existing resources to a new country. In such case, a lack of complementary resources may not be as salient a concern, at least not initially. In contrast, when internationalizing to obtain resources, the primary motivation is to access better or different resources in the new country. In this case, the lack of such resources may be more salient than the loss of advantage or the creation of a disadvantage, since this was the primary motivation for the expansion. Moreover, there are other aspects of the difficulties that differ, depending on the motive. For example, the inability to create value, the liability of newness, and the liability of infrastructure are all associated with the firm's relationship with customers in the new host country. Firms that internationalize to access resources are less likely to be concerned about the customers in the new country and more likely to be concerned about their relationship with the government (which may control access to natural resources through a license system) and with individual employees (who may control the knowledge sought, or are the resource that helps improve efficiency). Future research can build and extend the framework outlined here to analyze these subtleties in the difficulties in internationalization when the company expands abroad in search of resources.

A second limitation of our analysis that can be the basis of future research is that we chose to explore the difficulties faced by firms in a single country in order to develop a parsimonious framework. However, the difficulties faced by a firm may vary when it expands into multiple foreign countries at the same time, and when it is present in several countries. When the firm enters or operates in multiple countries, the relationship between resources and the context will vary by country, and difficulties may interact to produce situations that may be detrimental in one country and beneficial in another. For example, facing a variety of difficulties simultaneously may put a strain on a firm that is greater than the 'sum' of those difficulties. Alternatively, facing similar types of difficulties in various contexts may provide experiential learning that helps firms overcome difficulties sooner than they would have otherwise. Future studies can consider configuration patterns across various difficulties, and can address the heterogeneity of difficulties suffered not only across firms, but also across host countries.

A third limitation that can serve as a building block for future studies is the focus on difficulties to the exclusion of advantages. The firm can use its advantages to compensate for some of its difficulties. It can also find that some of the resources that it transferred and that did not provide an advantage in existing operations become a source of advantage in the new country. Future studies can analyze the interactions between advantages and disadvantages on the competitive behavior and performance of the operation in the new country.

Fourth, and finally, in this paper we implicitly discuss the difficulties faced at the point of initial international expansion. Over time the firm may overcome the difficulties in internationalization and achieve parity with local companies in terms of likelihood of survival (Zaheer and Mosakowski, 1997). This alone does not ensure that it will achieve a competitive advantage and the associated superior profitability in that foreign operation, but only that the foreign operation and the incumbent local firm will be equally likely to perform well or poorly. The foreign operation may achieve a competitive advantage if resources it transfers from other operations or develops in the host country provide it with an advantage over local competitors. Future research can explore the interaction

between the difficulties and the advantages of the firm in determining the success of the internationalization effort over time.

In summary, we adopted the perspective of RBT to disaggregate difficulties associated with internationalization into their respective root causes. We encourage future research that embraces the multidimensional nature, and therefore a deeper understanding, of these difficulties.

Acknowledgements
The paper was created when the first author was Assistant Professor and the second and third authors were PhD students at the University of Minnesota. The financial support of the University of Minnesota is gratefully acknowledged. The comments of Scott Johnson, Miguel Ramos, Kendall Roth, Annique Un, Sri Zaheer, anonymous reviewers, the associate editor Nicolai Foss, and participants at the Research Seminar at the University of Minnesota, Academy of Management annual meeting, European International Business Academy annual meeting, and Academy of International Business annual meeting, helped improve previous versions of the paper. All errors remain ours.

Notes
[1] Empirical studies have analyzed the consequences of these difficulties, finding that subsidiaries of foreign firms have lower performance (Zaheer, 1995), are more likely to exit markets (Zaheer and Mosakowski, 1997), face more lawsuits (Mezias, 2002a), and are less efficient (Miller and Parkhe, 2002) than domestic firms. However, foreign firms are not always at a disadvantage; some studies find that domestic and foreign firms have similar chances for survival (Mata and Portugal, 2002), and that foreign firms acquire better-performing companies than do their domestic counterparts (Goethals and Ooghe, 1997).

[2] Another form of international expansion is licensing (Buckley and Casson, 1976). Licensing is typically initiated by the licensee in the foreign market, who bears the costs of the various liabilities if the licensed technology or brand fails to deliver. The licensor is generally paid up-front and therefore avoids difficulties in internationalization. We thank an anonymous reviewer for this suggestion.

[3] Although the term 'liability of foreignness' was initially introduced as a synonym for the costs of doing business abroad or overall difficulties (Zaheer, 1995), in later studies it was narrowed to represent difficulties that arise from the lack of social relationships abroad (Zaheer, 2002). Here we adopt the narrower definition of the term.

References

Amit, R. and Schoemaker, P.J.H. (1993) 'Strategic assets and organizational rent', *Strategic Management Journal* **14**(1): 33–46.

Anand, J. and Delios, A. (1997) 'Location specificity and the transferability of downstream assets to foreign subsidiaries', *Journal of International Business Studies* **28**(3): 579–603.

Anand, J. and Delios, A. (2002) 'Absolute and relative resources as determinants of international acquisitions', *Strategic Management Journal* **23**(2): 119–134.

Barkema, H.G. and Vermeulen, F. (1998) 'International expansion through start-up or acquisition: a learning perspective', *Academy of Management Journal* **41**(1): 7–27.

Barkema, H.G., Bell, J. and Pennings, J.M. (1996) 'Foreign entry, cultural barriers, and learning', *Strategic Management Journal* **17**(2): 151–166.

Barney, J. (1991) 'Firm resources and sustained competitive advantage', *Journal of Management* **17**(1): 99–120.

Bartlett, C.A. and Ghoshal, S. (1986) 'Tap your subsidiaries for global reach', *Harvard Business Review* **64**(6): 87–94.

Bartlett, C.A. and Ghoshal, S. (1989) *Managing Across Borders: The Transnational Solution*, Harvard Business School Press: Boston, MA.

Bartlett, C.A. and O'Connell, J. (1998) *Jollibee Foods Corp. (A): International Expansion*, Harvard Business School Case 9-399-007, Boston, Harvard Business School, pp: 1–22.

Benito, G.R.G. and Welch, L.S. (1997) 'De-internationalization', *Management International Review* **37**(2): 7–25.

Bilkey, W.J. and Nes, E. (1982) 'Country-of-origin effects on product evaluations', *Journal of International Business Studies* **13**(1): 89–99.

Birkinshaw, J., Hood, N. and Jonsson, S. (1998) 'Building firm-specific advantages in multinational corporations: the role of subsidiary initiative', *Strategic Management Journal* **19**(3): 221–241.

Brush, T. and Artz, K. (1999) 'Toward a contingent resource-based theory: the impact of information asymmetry on the value of capabilities in veterinary medicine', *Strategic Management Journal* **20**(3): 223–250.

Buckley, P. and Casson, M. (1976) *The Future of the Multinational Corporation*, Macmillan: London.

Burstein, M.L. (1984) 'Diffusion of knowledge-based products: applications to developing economies', *Economic Inquiry* **22**(4): 612–633.

Business Week (2004) 'The next Wal-Mart?' *Business Week* **3880**: 60–62.

Calhoun, M.A. (2002) 'Unpacking liability of foreignness: identifying culturally driven external and internal sources of liability for the foreign subsidiary', *Journal of International Management* **8**(3): 301–321.

Capron, L., Dussauge, P. and Mitchell, W. (1998) 'Resource redeployment following horizontal acquisitions in Europe and North America, 1988–1992', *Strategic Management Journal* **19**(7): 631–661.

Chandler, A.D. (1962) *Strategy and Structure*, MIT Press: Cambridge, MA.

Chao, P. (2001) 'The moderating effects of country of assembly, country of parts, and country of design on hybrid product evaluations', *Journal of Advertising* **30**(4): 67–81.

Collis, D.J. (1991) 'A resource-based analysis of global competition: the case of the bearings industry', *Strategic Management Journal* **12**(Special Issue): 49–68.

Dawar, N. and Frost, T. (1999) 'Competing with giants', *Harvard Business Review* **77**(2): 119–129.

Debord, M. (2003) 'Just say "non!" to French wine', *Wine Spectator* **28**(3): 152.

Dierickx, I. and Cool, K. (1989) 'Asset stock accumulation and sustainability of competitive advantage', *Management Science* **35**(12): 1504–1511.

Dunning, J.H. (1977) 'Trade, Location of Economic Activity and the MNE: A Search for an Eclectic Approach', in B. Ohlin,

P.O. Hesselborn and P.M. Wijkman (eds.) *The International Allocation of Economic Activity*, Macmillan: London, pp: 395–419.

Dunning, J.H. (1993) *Multinational Enterprises and the Global Economy*, Addison-Wesley: New York.

Dyerson, R. and Pilkington, A. (2000) 'Innovation in complex systems: regulation and technology towards the electric vehicle', *International Journal of Innovation Management* **4**(1): 33–49.

Economist (2003) 'You're not all right, Jacques', *The Economist* **369**(8354): 30–31.

Economist (2004) 'How big can it grow? – Wal-Mart', *The Economist* **371**(8371): 67–70.

Eden, L. and Miller, S. (2001) 'Opening the black box: multinationals and the cost of doing business abroad', *Academy of Management Proceedings*, **IM**: C1–C6.

Eriksson, K., Johanson, J., Majkgard, A. and Sharma, D.D. (1997) 'Experimental knowledge and costs in the internationalization process', *Journal of International Business Studies* **28**(2): 337–360.

Fitzpatrick, M. (1983) 'The definition and assessment of political risk in international business: a review of the literature', *Academy of Management Review* **8**(2): 249–255.

Fladmoe-Lindquist, K. and Tallman, S. (1994) 'Resource-Based Strategy and Competitive Advantage Among Multinationals', in P. Shrivastava, A.S. Huff and J.E. Dutton (eds.) *Advances in Strategic Management*, Vol. **10**, Greenwich: CTL JAI Press, pp: 45–72.

Galbraith, J.R. (2000) *Designing the Global Corporation*, Jossey-Bass: San Francisco, CA.

Gertner, D., Gertner, R. and Guthery, D. (2005) 'Coca-Cola's marketing challenges in Brazil: the *tubaínas* war', *Thunderbird International Business Review* **47**(2): 231–254.

Ghemawat, P. (2001) 'Distance still matters', *Harvard Business Review* **79**(8): 137–145.

Goethals, J. and Ooghe, H. (1997) 'The performance of foreign and national take-overs in Belgium', *European Business Review* **97**(1): 24–37.

Hagstrom, P. (1991) *The 'Wired MNC': The Role of Information Systems for Structural Change in Complex Organizations*, Stockholm School of Economics: Stockholm.

Hastings, D.F. (1999) 'Lincoln Electric's harsh lessons from international expansion', *Harvard Business Review* **77**(3): 162–178.

Heil, O., Geroski, P. and Vlassopoulos, T. (1991) 'The rise and fall of a market leader: frozen foods in the UK', *Strategic Management Journal* **12**(6): 467–478.

Hedlund, G. (1986) 'The hypermodern MNC: a heterarchy?' *Human Resource Management* **25**(1): 9–35.

Henisz, W.J. and Williamson, O.E. (1999) 'Comparative economic organization within and between countries', *Business and Politics* **1**(3): 261–277.

Hennart, J.-F. and Park, Y.-R. (1993) 'Greenfield vs. acquisition: the strategy of Japanese investors in the United States', *Management Science* **39**(9): 1054–1070.

Hennart, J.-F. and Reddy, S. (1997) 'The choice between mergers/acquisitions and joint ventures: the case of Japanese investors in the United States', *Strategic Management Journal* **18**(1): 1–12.

Hitt, M.A., Hoskisson, R.E. and Kim, H. (1997) 'International diversification: effects on innovation and firm performance in product-diversified firms', *Academy of Management Journal* **40**(4): 767–798.

Hoskisson, R.E. and Hitt, M.A. (1990) 'Antecedents and performance outcomes of diversification: a review and critique of theoretical perspectives', *Journal of Management* **16**(2): 461–510.

Hu, Y.S. (1995) 'The international transferability of the firm's advantages', *California Management Review* **37**(4): 73–88.

Hymer, S. (1976) *The International Operations of National Firms: A Study of Direct Investment*, MIT Press: Cambridge, MA.

Johanson, J. and Vahlne, J.-E. (1977) 'The internationalization process of the firm: a model of knowledge development and increasing foreign market commitments', *Journal of International Business Studies* **8**(1): 23–32.

Johanson, J. and Vahlne, J.-E. (1990) 'The mechanism of internationalisation', *International Marketing Review* **7**(4): 11–24.

Johanson, J. and Wiedersheim-Paul, F. (1975) 'The internationalization of the firm: four Swedish case studies', *Journal of Management Studies* **12**(3): 305–322.

Khanna, T., Palepu, K.G. and Sinha, J. (2005) 'Strategies that fit emerging markets', *Harvard Business Review* **83**(6): 63–76.

Kobrin, S.J. (1979) 'Political risk: a review and reconsideration', *Journal of International Business Studies* **10**(1): 67–80.

Kobrin, S.J. (2001) 'Sovereignty@bay: Globalization, Multinational Enterprise, and the International Political System', in A.M. Rugman and T.L. Brewer (eds.) *The Oxford Handbook of International Business*, Oxford University Press: New York, pp: 181–205.

Kogut, B. (1985a) 'Designing global strategies: comparative and competitive value-added chain', *Sloan Management Review* **26**(4): 15–28.

Kogut, B. (1985b) 'Designing global strategies: profiting from operational flexibility', *Sloan Management Review* **27**(1): 27–38.

Kogut, B. and Zander, U. (1993) 'Knowledge of the firm and the evolutionary theory of the multinational corporation', *Journal of International Business Studies* **24**(4): 625–645.

Kostova, T. and Zaheer, S. (1999) 'Organizational legitimacy under conditions of complexity: the case of the multinational enterprise', *Academy of Management Review* **24**(1): 64–81.

Laurence, H., Yoshino, M. and Williamson, P.J. (1994) 'Star TV', in C.A. Bartlett and S. Ghoshal (eds.) *Transnational Management: Text, Cases and Readings in Cross-Border Management*, 3rd edn, Irwin McGraw-Hill: Boston, MA, pp. 464–482.

Leonard-Barton, D. (1992) 'Core capabilities and core rigidities: a paradox in managing new product development', *Strategic Management Journal* **13**(Summer special issue): 111–126.

Levitt, T. (1983) 'The globalization of markets', *Harvard Business Review* **61**(3): 92–102.

Lieberman, M.B. (1989) 'The learning curve, technology barriers to entry, and competitive survival in the chemical processing industries', *Strategic Management Journal* **10**(5): 431–447.

Lippman, S.A. and Rumelt, R.P. (1982) 'Uncertain imitability: an analysis of interfirm differences in efficiency under competition', *Bell Journal of Economics* **13**(2): 418–439.

Luo, Y., Shenkar, O. and Nyaw, M.K. (2002) 'Mitigating liabilities of foreignness: defensive versus offensive approaches', *Journal of International Management* **8**(3): 283–300.

Madhok, A. (1997) 'Cost, value and foreign market entry mode: the transaction and the firm', *Strategic Management Journal* **18**(1): 39–61.

Mata, J. and Portugal, P. (2002) 'The survival of new domestic and foreign-owned firms', *Strategic Management Journal* **23**(4): 323–343.

Mezias, J.M. (2002a) 'Identifying liabilities of foreignness and strategies to minimize their effects: the case of labor lawsuit judgments in the United States', *Strategic Management Journal* **23**(3): 229–244.

Mezias, J.M. (2002b) 'How to identify liabilities of foreignness and assess their effects on multinational corporations', *Journal of International Management* **8**: 265–282.

Miller, D. and Shamsie, J. (1996) 'The resource-based view of the firm in two environments: the Hollywood film studios from 1936 to 1965', *Academy of Management Journal* **39**(3): 519–543.

Miller, S.R. and Parkhe, A. (2002) 'Is there a liability of foreignness in global banking? An empirical test of banks' x-efficiency', *Strategic Management Journal* **23**(1): 55–75.

Montgomery, C.A. (1995) 'Of Diamonds and Rust: A New Look at Resources', in C.A. Montgomery (ed.) *Resource-Based and*

Evolutionary Theories of the Firm: Towards a Synthesis, Kluwer Academic Publishers: Boston, MA, pp: 251–268.

Munir, M. (2002) 'Builder of troublesome projects in difficult places. Survey – Turkey: Infrastructure and investment', *Financial Times*, 26 March, p: 2.

Nelson, R.R. and Winter, S.G. (1982) *An Evolutionary Theory of Economic Change*, Belknap Harvard: Cambridge, MA.

Neuborne, E. (1991) 'Wal-Mart: Mexico offers rich retail market', *USA Today*, 12 July, p: 03.B.

North, D.C. (1990) *Institutions, Institutional Change, and Economic Performance*, Cambridge University Press: New York.

Oliver, C. (1997) 'Sustainable competitive advantage: combining institutional and resource-based views', *Strategic Management Journal* **18**(9): 697–6713.

Peng, M.W. (2001) 'The resource-based view and international business', *Journal of Management* **27**(6): 803–829.

Penrose, E. (1959) *The Theory of the Growth of the Firm*, Oxford University Press: Oxford.

Peteraf, M.A. (1993) 'The cornerstones of competitive advantage: a resource-based view', *Strategic Management Journal* **14**(3): 179–191.

Petersen, B. and Pedersen, T. (2002) 'Coping with liability of foreignness: different learning engagements of entrant firms', *Journal of International Management* **8**(3): 339–350.

Peterson, R.A. and Jolibert, A.J.P. (1995) 'A meta-analysis of country-of-origin effects', *Journal of International Business Studies* **26**(4): 883–900.

Porter, M.E. (1985) *Competitive Advantage*, The Free Press: New York.

Porter, M.E. (1990) *The Competitive Advantage of Nations*, The Free Press: New York.

Prahalad, C.K. and Bettis, R.A. (1986) 'The dominant logic: a new linkage between diversity and performance', *Strategic Management Journal* **7**(6): 485–502.

Prahalad, C.K. and Doz, Y.L. (1987) *The Multinational Mission*, The Free Press: New York.

Prahalad, C.K. and Lieberthal, K. (1998) 'The end of corporate imperialism', *Harvard Business Review* **76**(4): 69–79.

Ray, G., Barney, J.B. and Muhanna, W.A. (2004) 'Capabilities, business processes, and competitive advantage: choosing the dependent variable in empirical tests of the resource-based view', *Strategic Management Journal* **25**(1): 23–37.

Ricks, D.A. (2000) *Blunders in International Business*, 3rd edn, Blackwell Publishers: Malden, MA.

Rugman, A.M. and Verbeke, A. (1992) 'A note on the transnational solution and the transaction cost theory of multinational strategic management', *Journal of International Business Studies* **23**(4): 761–771.

Schweiger, G., Haubl, G. and Friederes, G. (1995) 'Consumers' evaluations of products labeled "Made in Europe"', *Marketing and Research Today* **23**(1): 25–34.

Spar, D.L. (2001) 'National Policies and Domestic Politics', in A.M. Rugman and T.L. Brewer (eds.) *The Oxford Handbook of International Business*, Oxford University Press: New York, pp: 206–231.

Stopford, J.M. and Strange, S. (1992) *Rival States, Rival Firms: Competition for World Market Shares*, Cambridge University Press: New York.

Stopford, J.M. and Wells, L.T. (1972) *Managing the Multinational Enterprise: Organization of the Firm and Ownership of the Subsidiaries*, Basic Books: New York.

Szulanski, G. (1996) 'Exploring internal stickiness: impediments to the transfer of best practice within the firm', *Strategic Management Journal* **17**(Winter special issue): 27–43.

Tallman, S.B. (1991) 'Strategic management models and resource-based strategies among MNEs in a host market', *Strategic Management Journal* **12**(Summer special issue): 69–82.

Tallman, S.B. (1992) 'A strategic management perspective on host country structure of multinational enterprises', *Journal of Management* **18**(3): 455–471.

Tallman, S.B. and Li, J. (1996) 'Effects of international diversity and product diversity on the performance of multinational firms', *Academy of Management Journal* **39**(1): 179–197.

Tallman, S.B. and Yip, G.S. (2001) 'Strategy and the Multinational Enterprise', in A.M. Rugman and T.L. Brewer (eds.) *The Oxford Handbook of International Business*, Oxford University Press: New York, pp: 317–348.

Teece, D.J. (1986) 'Profiting from technological innovation: implications for integration, collaboration, licensing and public policy', *Research Policy* **15**(6): 285–305.

Teece, D.J., Pisano, G. and Shuen, A. (1997) 'Dynamic capabilities and strategic management', *Strategic Management Journal* **18**(7): 509–533.

Tirole, J. (1988) *The Theory of Industrial Organization*, MIT Press: Cambridge, MA.

Vernon, R. (1966) 'International investment and international trade in the product cycle', *Quarterly Journal of Economics* **80**(2): 190–207.

Vernon, R. (1977) *Storm Over the Multinationals: The Real Issues*, Harvard University Press: Boston, MA.

Welch, L. and Wiedersheim-Paul, F. (1980) 'Internationalization at home', *Essays in International Business* **2**: 1–31.

Wells, L.T. (1983) *Third World Multinationals*, MIT Press: Cambridge, MA.

Wernerfelt, B. (1984) 'A resource-based view of the firm', *Strategic Management Journal* **5**(2): 171–180.

Winter, S.G. and Szulanski, G. (2001) 'Replication as strategy', *Organization Science* **12**(6): 730–743.

Zaheer, S. (1995) 'Overcoming the liability of foreignness', *Academy of Management Journal* **38**(2): 341–363.

Zaheer, S. (2002) 'The liability of foreignness, redux: a commentary', *Journal of International Management* **8**(3): 351–358.

Zaheer, S. and Mosakowski, E. (1997) 'The dynamics of the liability of foreignness: a global study of survival in financial services', *Strategic Management Journal* **18**(6): 439–464.

Zollo, M. and Winter, S.G. (2002) 'Deliberate learning and the evolution of dynamic capabilities', *Organization Science* **13**(3): 339–351.

About the authors

Alvaro Cuervo-Cazurra (PhD Massachusetts Institute of Technology) is an assistant professor of International Business at the Moore School of Business, University of South Carolina. His primary research interest is understanding how firms become competitive and then international. He is also interested in governance issues, corruption in particular. He has started a long-term project to analyze the emergence and success of developing-country multinational firms. Before joining the University of South Carolina he was an assistant professor at the University of Minnesota and a Visiting Assistant Professor at Cornell University.

Mary M Maloney (PhD University of Minnesota) is an assistant professor at the Opus College of Business, University of St Thomas. Her research focuses on the challenges of coordinating activities across borders within MNEs, global teams, and cross-border social capital. She has previously published in *Management International Review*.

Shalini N Manrakhan (PhD University of Minnesota) is a lecturer at the University of Mauritius, Mauritius. Her research interests include knowledge creation in strategic alliance portfolios, and renewable energy management. She has previously published in the *Journal of International Business Studies*.

Accepted by Arie Y Lewin, Editor-in-Chief, and Nicolai Juul Foss, Departmental Editor, 20 April 2007. This paper has been with the authors for two revisions.

Part II
Advantages of a Global Strategy

[7]

Strategic Management Journal, Vol. 8, 425–440 (1987)

GLOBAL STRATEGY: AN ORGANIZING FRAMEWORK

SUMANTRA GHOSHAL
INSEAD, Fontainebleau, France

Global strategy has recently emerged as a popular concept among managers of multinational corporations as well as among researchers and students in the field of international management. This paper presents a conceptual framework encompassing a range of different issues relevant to global strategies. The framework provides a basis for organizing existing literature on the topic and for creating a map of the field. Such a map can be useful for teaching and also for guiding future research in this area. The article, however, is primarily directed at managers of multinational corporations, and is aimed at providing them with a basis for relating and synthesizing the different perspectives and prescriptions that are currently available for global strategic management.

Over the past few years the concept of global strategy has taken the world of multinational corporations (MNCs) by storm. Scores of articles in the *Harvard Business Review, Fortune, The Economist* and other popular journals have urged multinationals to 'go global' in their strategies. The topic has clearly captured the attention of MNC managers. Conferences on global strategy, whether organized by the Conference Board in New York, *The Financial Times* in London, or Nomura Securities in Tokoyo, have invariably attracted enthusiastic corporate support and sizeable audiences. Even in the relatively slow-moving world of academe the issue of globalization of industries and companies has emerged as a new bandwagon, as manifest in the large number of papers on the topic presented at recent meetings of the Academy of Management, the Academy of International Business and the Strategic Management Society. 'Manage globally' appears to be the latest battlecry in the world of international business.

MULTIPLE PERSPECTIVES, MANY PRESCRIPTIONS

This enthusiasm notwithstanding, there is a great deal of conceptual ambiguity about what a 'global' strategy really means. As pointed out by Hamel and Prahalad (1985), the distinction among a global industry, a global firm, and a global strategy is somewhat blurred in the literature. According to Hout, Porter and Rudden (1982), a global strategy is appropriate for global industries which are defined as those in which a firm's competitive position in one national market is significantly affected by its competitive position in other national markets. Such interactions between a firm's positions in different markets may arise from scale benefits or from the potential of synergies or sharing of costs and resources across markets. However, as argued by Bartlett (1985), Kogut (1984) and many others, those scale and synergy benefits may often be created by strategic actions of individual firms and may

0143–2095/87/050425–16$08.00
© 1987 by John Wiley & Sons, Ltd.

Received 6 January 1986
Revised 3 October 1986

426   *S. Ghoshal*

not be 'given' in any *a priori* sense. For some industries, such as aeroframes or aeroengines, the economies of scale may be large enough to make the need for global integration of activities obvious. However, in a large number of cases industries may not be born global but may have globalness thrust upon them by the entrepreneurship of a company such as Yoshida Kagyo KK (YKK) or Procter and Gamble. In such cases the global industry–global strategy link may be more useful for ex-post explanation of outcomes than for ex-ante predictions or strategizing.

Further, the concept of a global strategy is not as new as some of the recent authors on the topic have assumed it to be. It was stated quite explicitly about 20 years ago by Perlmutter (1969) when he distinguished between the geocentric, polycentric, and ethnocentric approaches to multinational management. The starting point for Perlmutter's categorization scheme was the worldview of a firm, which was seen as the driving force behind its management processes and the way it structured its world-wide activities (see Robinson, 1978 and Rutenberg, 1982 for detailed reviews and expositions). In much of the current literature, in contrast, the focus has been narrowed and the concept of global strategy has been linked almost exclusively with how the firm structures the flow of tasks within its world-wide value-adding system. The more integrated and rationalized the flow of tasks appears to be, the more global the firm's strategy is assumed to be (e.g. Leontiades, 1984). On the one hand, this focus has led to improved understanding of the fact that different tasks offer different degrees of advantages from global integration and national differentiation and that, optimally, a firm must configure its value chain to obtain the best possible advantages from both (Porter, 1984). But, on the other hand, it has also led to certain dysfunctional simplifications. The complexities of managing large, world-wide organizations have been obscured by creating polar alternatives between centralization and decentralization, or between global and multidomestic strategies (e.g. Hout *et al.*, 1982). Complex management tasks have been seen as composites of simple global and local components. By emphasizing the importance of rationalizing the flow of components and final products within a multinational system, the importance of internal flows of

people, technology, information, and values has been de-emphasized.

Differences among authors writing on the topic of global strategy are not limited to concepts and perspectives. Their prescriptions on how to manage globally have also been very different, and often contradictory.

1. Levitt (1983) has argued that effective global strategy is not a bag of many tricks but the successful practice of just one: product standardization. According to him, the core of a global strategy lies in developing a standardized product to be produced and sold the same way throughout the world.

2. According to Hout, *et al.* (1982), on the other hand, effective global strategy requires the approach not of a hedgehog, who knows only one trick, but that of a fox, who knows many. Exploiting economies of scale through global volume, taking pre-emptive positions through quick and large investments, and managing interdependently to achieve synergies across different activities are, according to these authors, some of the more important moves that a winning global strategist must muster.

3. Hamel and Prahalad's (1985) prescription for a global strategy contradicts that of Levitt (1983) even more sharply. Instead of a single standardized product, they recommend a broad product portfolio, with many product varieties, so that investments on technologies and distribution channels can be shared. Cross-subsidization across products and markets, and the development of a strong world-wide distribution system, are the two moves that find the pride of place in these authors' views on how to succeed in the game of global chess.

4. If Hout, *et al.*'s (1982) global strategist is the heavyweight champion who knocks out opponents with scale and pre-emptive investments, Kogut's (1985b) global strategist is the nimble-footed athlete who wins through flexibility and arbitrage. He creates options so as to turn the uncertainties of an increasingly volatile global economy to his own advantage. Multiple sourcing, production shifting to benefit from changing factor costs and exchange rates, and arbitrage to exploit imperfections in financial and information markets are,

according to Kogut, some of the hallmarks of a superior global strategy.

These are only a few of the many prescriptions available to MNC managers about how to build a global strategy for their firms. All these suggestions have been derived from rich and insightful analyses of real-life situations. They are all reasonable and intuitively appealing, but their managerial implications are not easy to reconcile.

THE NEED FOR AN ORGANIZING FRAMEWORK

The difficulty for both practitioners and researchers in dealing with the small but rich literature on global strategies is that there is no organizing framework within which the different perspectives and prescriptions can be assimilated. An unfortunate fact of corporate life is that any particular strategic action is rarely an unmixed blessing. Corporate objectives are multidimensional, and often mutually contradictory. Contrary to received wisdom, it is also usually difficult to prioritize them. Actions to achieve a particular objective often impede another equally important objective. Each of these prescriptions is aimed at achieving certain objectives of a global strategy. An overall framework can be particularly useful in identifying the trade-offs between those objectives and therefore in understanding not only the benefits but also the potential costs associated with the different strategic alternatives.

The objective of this paper is to suggest such an organizing framework which may help managers and academics in formulating the various issues that arise in global strategic management. The underlying premise is that simple categorization schemes such as the distinction between global and multidomestic strategies are not very helpful in understanding the complexities of corporate-level strategy in large multinational corporations. Instead, what may be more useful is to understand what the key strategic objectives of an MNC are, and the tools that it possesses for achieving them. An integrated analysis of the different means and the different ends can help both managers and researchers in formulating, describing, classifying and analyzing

the content of global strategies. Besides, such a framework can relate academic research, that is often partial, to the totality of real life that managers must deal with.

THE FRAMEWORK: MAPPING MEANS AND ENDS

The proposed framework is shown in Table 1. While the specific construct may be new, the conceptual foundation on which it is built is derived from a synthesis of existing literature.

The basic argument is simple. The goals of a multinational—as indeed of any organization—can be classified into three broad categories. The firm must achieve efficiency in its current activities; it must manage the risks that it assumes in carrying out those activities; and it must develop internal learning capabilities so as to be able to innovate and adapt to future changes. Competitive advantage is developed by taking strategic actions that optimize the firm's achievement of these different and, at times, conflicting goals.

A multinational has three sets of tools for developing such competitive advantage. It can exploit the differences in input and output markets among the many countries in which it operates. It can benefit from scale economies in its different activities. It can also exploit synergies or economies of scope that may be available because of the diversity of its activities and organization.

The strategic task of managing globally is to use all three sources of competitive advantage to optimize efficiency, risk and learning simultaneously in a world-wide business. The key to a successful global strategy is to manage the interactions between these different goals and means. That, in essence, is the organizing framework. Viewing the tasks of global strategy this way can be helpful to both managers and academics in a number of ways. For example, it can help managers in generating a comprehensive checklist of factors and issues that must be considered in reviewing different strategic alternatives. Such a checklist can serve as a basis for mapping the overall strategies of their own companies and those of their competitors so as to understand the comparative strengths and

428   S. *Ghoshal*

Table 1. Global strategy: an organizing framework

Strategic objectives	Sources of competitive advantage		
	National differences	Scale economies	Scope economies
Achieving efficiency in current operations	Benefiting from differences in factor costs—wages and cost of capital	Expanding and exploiting potential scale economies in each activity	Sharing of investments and costs across products, markets and businesses
Managing risks	Managing different kinds of risks arising from market or policy-induced changes in comparative advantages of different countries	Balancing scale with strategic and operational flexibility	Portfolio diversification of risks and creation of options and side-bets
Innovation learning and adaptation	Learning from societal differences in organizational and managerial processes and systems	Benefiting from experience—cost reduction and innovation	Shared learning across organizational components in different products, markets or businesses

vulnerabilities of both. Table 1 shows some illustrative examples of factors that must be considered while carrying out such comprehensive strategic audits. Another practical utility of the framework is that it can highlight the contradictions between the different goals and between the different means, and thereby make salient the strategic dilemmas that may otherwise get resolved through omission.

In the next two sections the framework is explained more fully by describing the two dimensions of its construct, viz. the strategic objectives of the firm and the sources of competitive advantage available to a multinational corporation. Subsequent sections show how selected articles contribute to the literature and fit within the overall framework. The paper concludes with a brief discussion of the trade-offs that are implicit in some of the more recent prescriptions on global strategic management.

THE GOALS: STRATEGIC OBJECTIVES

Achieving efficiency

A general premise in the literature on strategic management is that the concept of strategy is

relevant only when the actions of one firm can affect the actions or performance of another. Firms competing in imperfect markets earn different 'efficiency rents' from the use of their resources (Caves, 1980). The objective of strategy, given this perspective, is to enhance such efficiency rents.

Viewing a firm broadly as an input–output system, the overall efficiency of the firm can be defined as the ratio of the value of its outputs to the costs of all its inputs. It is by maximizing this ratio that the firm obtains the surplus resources required to secure its own future. Thus it differentiates its products to enhance the exchange value of its outputs, and seeks low cost factors to minimize the costs of its inputs. It also tries to enhance the efficiency of its throughput processes by achieving higher scale economies or by finding more efficient production processes.

The field of strategic management is currently dominated by this efficiency perspective. The generic strategies of Porter (1980), different versions of the portfolio model, as well as overall strategic management frameworks such as those proposed by Hofer and Schendel (1978) and Hax and Majluf (1984) are all based on the underlying notion of maximizing efficiency rents of the different resources available to the firm.

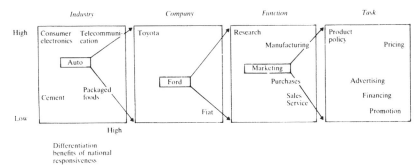

Figure 1. The integration–responsiveness framework (reproduced from Bartlett, 1985)

In the field of global strategy this efficiency perspective has been reflected in the widespread use of the integration–responsiveness framework originally proposed by Prahalad (1975) and subsequently developed and applied by a number of authors including Doz, Bartlett and Prahalad (1981) and Porter (1984). In essence, the framework is a conceptual lens for visualizing the cost advantages of global integration of certain tasks *vis-à-vis* the differentiation benefits of responding to national differences in tastes, industry structures, distribution systems, and government regulations. As suggested by Bartlett (1985), the same framework can be used to understand differences in the benefits of integration and responsiveness at the aggregate level of industries, at the level of individual companies within an industry, or even at the level of different functions within a company (see Figure 1, reproduced from Bartlett, 1985). Thus the consumer electronics industry may be characterized by low differentiation benefits and high integration advantages, while the position of the packaged foods industry may be quite the opposite. In the telecommunications switching industry, in contrast, both local and global forces may be strong, while in the automobile industry both may be of moderate and comparable importance.

Within an industry (say, automobile), the strategy of one firm (such as Toyota) may be based on exploiting the advantages of global integration through centralized production and decision-making, while that of another (such as Fiat) may aim at exploiting the benefits of national differentiation by creating integrated

and autonomous subsidiaries which can exploit strong links with local stakeholders to defend themselves against more efficient global competitors. Within a firm, research may offer greater efficiency benefits of integration, while sales and service may provide greater differentiation advantages. One can, as illustrated in Figure 1, apply the framework to even lower levels of analysis, right down to the level of individual tasks. Based on such analysis, a multinational firm can determine the optimum way to configure its value chain so as to achieve the highest overall efficiency in the use of its resources (Porter, 1984).

However, while efficiency is clearly an important strategic objective, it is not the only one. As argued recently by a number of authors, the broader objective of strategic management is to create value which is determined not only by the returns that specific assets are expected to generate, but also by the risks that are assumed in the process (see Woo and Cool (1985) for a review). This leads to the second strategic objective of firms—that of managing risks.[1]

Managing risks

A multinational corporation faces many different kinds of risks, some of which are endemic to all firms and some others are unique to organizations

---

[1] In the interest of simplicity the distinction between risk and uncertainty is ignored, as is the distinction between systematic and unsystematic risks.

430   *S. Ghoshal*

operating across national boundaries. For analytical simplicity these different kinds of risks may be collapsed into four broad categories.

First, an MNC faces certain *macroeconomic risks* which are completely outside its control. These include cataclysmic events such as wars and natural calamities, and also equilibrium-seeking or even random movements in wage rates, interest rates, exchange rates, commodity prices, and so on.

Second, the MNC faces what is usually referred to in the literature as political risks but may be more appropriately called *policy risks* to emphasize that they arise from policy actions of national governments and not from either long-term equilibrium-seeking forces of global markets, nor from short-term random fluctuations in economic variables arising out of stickiness or unpredictability of market mechanisms. The net effect of such policy actions may often be indistinguishable from the effect of macroeconomic forces; for example, both may lead to changes in the exchange rate of a particular currency. But from a management perspective the two must be distinguished, since the former is uncontrollable but the latter is at least partially controllable.

Third, a firm also faces certain *competitive risks* arising from the uncertainties of competitors' responses to its own strategies (including the strategy of doing nothing and trying to maintain the status quo). While all companies face such risks to varying extents (since both monopolies and perfect competition are rare), their implications are particularly complex in the context of global strategies since the responses of competitors may take place in many different forms and in many different markets. Further, technological risk can also be considered as a part of competitive risk since a new technology can adversely affect a firm only when it is adopted by a competitor, and not otherwise.[2]

Finally, a firm also faces what may be called *resource risks*. This is the risk that the adopted strategy will require resources that the firm does not have, cannot acquire, or cannot spare. A key scarce resource for most firms is managerial

talent. But resource risks can also arise from lack of appropriate technology, or even capital (if managers, for reasons of control, do not want to use capital markets, or if the market is less efficient than finance theorists would have us believe).

One important issue with regard to risks is that they change over time. Vernon (1977) has highlighted this issue in the context of policy risks, but the same is true of the others. Consider resource risks as an example. Often the strategy of a multinational will assume that appropriate resources will be acquired as the strategy unfolds. Yet the initial conditions on which the plans for on-going resource acquisition and development have been based may change over time. Nissan, for instance, based its aggressive internationalization strategy on the expectation of developing technological, financial, and managerial resources out of its home base. Changing competitive positions among local car manufacturers in Japan have affected these resource development plans of the company, and its internationalizing strategy has been threatened significantly. A more careful analysis of alternative competitive scenarios, and of their effects on the resource allocation plans of the company, may have led Nissan to either a slower pace of internationalization, or to a more aggressive process of resource acquisition at an earlier stage of implementing its strategy.

The strategic task, with regard to management of risks, is to consider these different kinds of risks *jointly* in the context of particular strategic decisions. However, not all forms of risk are strategic since some risks can be easily diversified, shifted, or shared through routine market transactions. It is only those risks which cannot be diversified through a readily available external market that are of concern at the strategic level.

As an example, consider the case of currency risks. These can be classified as contractual, semi-contractual and operating risks (Lessard and Lightstone, 1983). Contractual risks arise when a firm enters into a contract for which costs and revenues are expected to be generated in different currencies: for example a Japanese firm entering into a contract for supplying an item to be made in Japan to an American customer at a price fixed in dollars. Semi-contractual risks are assumed when a firm offers an option denominated in foreign currencies, such as a British

---

[2] This assumes that the firm has defined its business correctly and has identified as competitors all the firms whose offerings are aimed at meeting the same set of market needs that the firm meets.

company quoting a firm rate in guilders. Operating risks, on the other hand, refer to exchange rate-related changes in the firm's competitiveness arising out of long-term commitments of revenues or costs in different currencies. For example, to compete with a Korean firm, an American firm may set up production facilities in Singapore for supplying its customers in the United States and Europe. A gradual strengthening of the Singapore dollar, in comparison with the Korean won, can erode the overall competitiveness of the Singapore plant.

Both contractual and semi-contractual currency risks can be easily shifted or diversified, at relatively low cost, through various hedging mechanisms. If a firm does not so hedge these risks, it is essentially operating as a currency speculator and the risks must be associated with the speculation business and not to its product-market operations. Operating risks, on the other hand, cannot be hedged so easily, [3] and must be considered at the strategic rather than the operational level.

Analysis of strategic risks will have significant implications for a firm's decisions regarding the structures and locations of its cost and revenue streams. It will lead to more explicit analysis of the effects of environmental uncertainties on the configuration of its value chain. There may be a shift from ownership to rental of resources; from fixed to variable costs. Output and activity distributions may be broadened to achieve the benefits of diversification. Incrementalism and opportunism may be given greater emphasis in its strategy in comparison to pre-emptive resource commitments and long-term planning. Overall strategies may be formulated in more general and flexible terms, so as to be robust to different environmental scenarios. In addition, side-bets may be laid to cover contingencies and to create strategic options which may or may not be exercised in the future (see Kogut, 1985b; Aaker and Mascarenhas, 1984; and Mascarenhas, 1982).

Innovation, learning and adaptation

Most existing theories of the multinational corpor-

ation view it as an instrument to extract additional rents from capabilities internalized by the firm (see Calvet, 1981, for a review). A firm goes abroad to make more profits by exploiting its technology, or brand name, or management capabilities in different countries around the world. It is assumed that the key competencies of the multinational always reside at the center.

While the search for additional profits or the desire to protect existing revenues may explain why multinationals come to exist, they may not provide an equally complete explanation of why some of them continue to grow and flourish. An alternative view may well be that a key asset of the multinational is the diversity of environments in which it operates. This diversity exposes it to multiple stimuli, allows it to develop diverse capabilities, and provides it with a broader learning opportunity than is available to a purely domestic firm. The enhanced organizational learning that results from the diversity internalized by the multinational may be a key explanator of its ongoing success, while its initial stock of knowledge may well be the strength that allows it to create such organizational diversity in the first place (Bartlett and Ghoshal, 1985).

Internal diversity may lead to strategic advantages for a firm in many different ways. In an unpredictable environment it may not be possible, ex ante, to predict the competencies that will be required in the future. Diversity of internal capabilities, following the logic of population ecologists (e.g. Hannan and Freeman, 1977; Aldrich, 1979), will enhance the probability of the firm's survival by enhancing the chances that it will be in possession of the capabilities required to cope with an uncertain future state. Similarly, diversity of resources and competencies may also enhance the firm's ability to create joint innovations, and to exploit them in multiple locations. One example of such benefits of diversity was recently described in the *Wall Street Journal* (April 29, 1985):

> P&G [Procter and Gamble Co.] recently introduced its new Liquid Tide, but the product has a distinctly international heritage. A new ingredient that helps suspend dirt in wash water came from the company's research center near P&G's Cincinnati headquarters. But the formula for Liquid Tide's surfactants, or cleaning agents, was developed by P&G technicians in Japan.

---

[3] Some market mechanisms such as long-term currency swaps are now available which can allow at least partial hedging of operating risks.

432   *S. Ghoshal*

The ingredients that fight mineral salts present in hard water came from P&G's scientists in Brussels.

As discussed in the same *WSJ* article, P&G's research center in Brussels has developed a special capability in water softening technology due, in part, to the fact that water in Europe contains more than twice the level of mineral content compared to wash water available in the United States. Similarly, surfactant technology is particularly advanced in Japan because Japanese consumers wash their clothes in colder waters compared to consumers in the US or Europe, and this makes greater demands on the cleaning ability of the surfactants. The advantage of P&G as a multinational is that it is exposed to these different operating environments and has learned, in each environment, the skills and knowledge that coping with that environment specially requires. Liquid Tide is an example of the strategic advantages that accrue from such diverse learning.

The mere existence of diversity, however, does not enhance learning. It only creates the potential for learning. To exploit this potential, the organization must consider learning as an explicit objective, and must create mechanisms and systems for such learning to take place. In the absence of explicit intention and appropriate mechanisms, the learning potential may be lost. In some companies, where all organizational resources are centralized and where the national subsidiaries are seen as mere delivery pipelines to supply the organization's value-added to different countries, diverse learning may not take place either because the subsidiaries may not possess appropriate sensing, analyzing, and responding capabilities to learn from their local environments, or because the centralized decision processes may be insensitive to knowledge accumulated outside the corporate headquarters. Other companies, in which the subsidiaries may enjoy very high levels of local resources and autonomy, may similarly fail to exploit global learning benefits because of their inability to transfer and synthesize knowledge and expertise developed in different organizational components. Local loyalties, turf protection, and the 'not invented here' (NIH) syndrome—the three handmaidens of decentralization—may restrict internal flow of information across national

boundaries which is essential for global learning to occur. In other words, both centralization and decentralization may impede learning.

THE MEANS: SOURCES OF COMPETITIVE ADVANTAGE

Most recent articles on global strategy have been aimed at identifying generic strategies (such as global cost leadership, focus or niche) and advocating particular strategic moves (such as cross-subsidy or pre-emptive investments). Underlying these concepts, however, are three fundamental tools for building global competitive advantage: exploiting differences in input and output markets in different countries, exploiting economies of scale, and exploiting economies of scope (Porter, 1985).

National differences

The comparative advantage of locations in terms of differences in factor costs is perhaps the most discussed, and also the best understood, source of competitive advantage in international business.

Different nations have different factor endowments, and in the absence of efficient markets this leads to inter-country differences in factor costs. Different activities of the firm, such as R&D, production, marketing, etc., have different factor intensities. A firm can therefore gain cost advantages by configuring its value-chain so that each activity is located in the country which has the least cost for the factor that the activity uses most intensely. This is the core concept of comparative advantage-based competitive advantage—a concept for which highly developed analytical tools are available from the discipline of international economics. Kogut (1985a) provides an excellent managerial overview of this concept.

National differences may also exist in output markets. Customer tastes and preferences may be different in different countries, as may be distribution systems, government regulations applicable to the concerned product-markets, or the effectiveness of different promotion strategies and other marketing techniques. A firm can augment the exchange value of its ouput by tailoring its offerings to fit the unique requirements in each national market. This, in essence, is the strategy of national differentiation, and it lies at the core of what has come to be referred to as the multidomestic approach in multinational management (Hout *et al.*, 1982).

From a strategic perspective, however, this static and purely economic view of national differences may not be adequate. What may be more useful is to take a dynamic view of comparative advantage and to broaden the concept to include both societal and economic factors.

In the traditional economics view, comparative advantages of countries are determined by their relative factor endowments and they do not change. However, in reality one lesson of the past four decades is that comparative advantages change and a prime objective of the industrial policies of many nations is to effect such changes. Thus, for any nation, the availability and cost of capital change, as do the availability of technical manpower and the wages of skilled and unskilled labor. Such changes take place, in the long run, to accommodate different levels of economic and social performance of nations, and in the short run they occur in response to specific policies and regulations of governments.

This dynamic aspect of comparative advantages adds considerable complexity to the strategic considerations of the firm. There is a first-order effect of such changes—such as possible increases in wage rates, interest rates or currency exchange rates for particular countries that can affect future viability of a strategy that has been based on the current levels of these economic variables. There can also be a more intriguing second-order effect. If an activity is located in an economically inefficient environment, and if the firm is able to achieve a higher level of efficiency in its own operations compared to the rest of the local economy, its competitive advantage may actually increase as the local economy slips lower and lower. This is because the macroeconomic variables such as wage or exchange rates may change to reflect the overall performance of the economy relative to the rest of the world and, to the extent that the firm's performance is better than this national aggregate, it may benefit from these macro-level changes (Kiechel, 1981).

Consistent with the discipline that gave birth to the concept, the usual view of comparative advantage is limited to factors that an economist

admits into the production function, such as the costs of labor and capital. However, from a managerial perspective it may be more appropriate to take a broader view of societal comparative advantages to include 'all the relative advantages conferred on a society by the quality, quantity and configuration of its material, human and institutional resources, including "soft" resources such as inter-organizational linkages, the nature of its educational system, and organizational and managerial know-how' (Westney, 1985: 4). As argued by Westney, these 'soft' societal factors, if absorbed in the overall organizational system, can provide benefits as real to a multinational as those provided by such economic factors as cheap labor or low-cost capital.

While the concept of comparative advantage is quite clear, available evidence on its actual effect on the overall competitiveness of firms is weak and conflicting. For example, it has often been claimed that one source of competitive advantage for Japanese firms is the lower cost of capital in Japan (Hatsopoulos, 1983). However, more systematic studies have shown that there is practically no difference in the risk-adjusted cost of capital in the United States and Japan, and that capital cost advantages of Japanese firms, if any, arise from complex interactions between government subsidies and corporate ownership structures (Flaherty and Itami, 1984). Similarly, relatively low wage rates in Japan have been suggested by some authors as the primary reason for the success of Japanese companies in the US market (Itami, 1978). However, recently, companies such as Honda and Nissan have commissioned plants in the USA and have been able to retain practically the same levels of cost advantages over US manufacturers as they had for their production in Japan (Allen, 1985). Overall, there is increasing evidence that while comparative advantages of countries can provide competitive advantages to firms, the realization of such benefits is not automatic but depends on complex organizational factors and processes.

Scale economies

Scale economies, again, is a fairly well established concept, and its implications for competitive advantage are quite well understood. Microeconomic theory provides a strong theoretical and empirical basis for evaluating the effect of scale on cost reduction, and the use of scale as a competitive tool is common in practice. Its primary implication for strategy is that a firm must expand the volume of its output so as to achieve available scale benefits. Otherwise a competitor who can achieve such volume can build cost advantages, and this can lead to a vicious cycle in which the low-volume firm can progressively lose its competitive viability.

While scale, by itself, is a static concept, there may be dynamic benefits of scale through what has been variously described as the experience or learning effect. The higher volume that helps a firm to exploit scale benefits also allows it to accumulate learning, and this leads to progressive cost reduction as the firm moves down its learning curve.

The concept of the value-added chain recently popularized by Porter (1985) adds considerable richness to the analysis of scale as a source of competitive advantage. This conceptual apparatus allows a disaggregated analysis of scale benefits in different value-creating activities of the firm. The efficient scale may vary widely by activity—being higher for component production, say, than for assembly. In contrast to a unitary view of scale, this disaggregated view permits the firm to configure different elements of its value chain to attain optimum scale economies in each.

Traditionally, scale has been seen as an unmixed blessing—something that always helps and never hurts. Recently, however, many researchers have argued otherwise (e.g. Evans, 1982). It has been suggested that scale efficiencies are obtained through increased specialization and through creation of dedicated assets and systems. The same processes cause inflexibilities and limit the firm's ability to cope with change. As environmental turbulence has increased, so has the need for strategic and operational flexibility (Mascarenhas, 1982). At the extreme, this line of argument has led to predictions of a re-emergence of the craft form of production to replace the scale-dominated assembly form (Piore and Sabel, 1984). A more typical argument has been to emphasize the need to balance scale and flexibility, through the use of modern technologies such as CAD/CAM and flexible manufacturing systems (Gold, 1982).

Scope economies

Relatively speaking, the concept of scope economies is both new and not very well understood. It is based on the notion that certain economies arise from the fact that the cost of the joint production of two or more products can be less than the cost of producing them separately. Such cost reductions can take place due to many reasons—for example resources such as information or technologies, once acquired for use in producing one item, may be available costlessly for production of other items (Baumol, Panzer and Willig, 1982).

The strategic importance of scope economies arise from a diversified firm's ability to share investments and costs across the same or different value chains that competitors, not possessing such internal and external diversity, cannot. Such sharing can take place across segments, products, or markets (Porter, 1985) and may involve joint use of different kinds of assets (see Table 2).

A diversified firm may share physical assets such as production equipment, cash, or brand names across different businesses and markets. Flexible manufacturing systems using robots, which can be used for production of different items, is one example of how a firm can exploit such scope benefits. Cross-subsidization of markets and exploitation of a global brand name are other examples of sharing a tangible asset across different components of a firm's product and market portfolios.

A second important source of scope economies is shared external relations: with customers, suppliers, distributors, governments, and other institutions. A multinational bank like Citibank can provide relatively more effective service to a multinational customer than can a bank that operates in a single country (see Terpstra, 1982). Similarly, as argued by Hamel and Prahalad (1985), companies such as Matsushita have benefited considerably from their ability to market a diverse range of products through the same distribution channel. In another variation, Japanese trading companies have expanded into new businesses to meet different requirements of their existing customers.

Finally, shared knowledge is the third important component of scope economies. The fundamental thrust of NEC's global strategy is 'C&C'—

Table 2. Scope economies in product and market diversification

| | Sources of scope economies | |
	Product diversification	Market diversification
Shared physical assets	Factory automation with flexibility to produce multiple products	Global brand name
	(Ford)	(Coca-Cola)
Shared external relations	Using common distribution channel for multiple products	Servicing multi-national customers world-wide
	(Matsushita)	(Citibank)
Shared learning	Sharing R&D in computer and communications businesses	Pooling knowledge developed in different markets
	(NEC)	(Procter and Gamble)

computers and communication. The company firmly believes that its even strengths in the two technologies and resulting capabilities of merging them in-house to create new products gives it a competitive edge over global giants such as IBM and AT&T, who have technological strength in only one of these two areas. Another example of the scope advantages of shared learning is the case of Liquid Tide described earlier in this paper.

Even scope economies, however, may not be costless. Different segments, products or markets of a diversified company face different environmental demands. To succeed, a firm needs to differentiate its management systems and processes so that each of its activities can develop *external consistency* with the requirments of its own environment. The search for scope economies, on the other hand, is a search for *internal consistencies* within the firm and across its different activities. The effort to create such synergies may invariably result in some compromise with the objective of external consistency in each activity.

Further, the search for internal synergies also enhances the complexities in a firm's management processes. In the extreme, such complexities can overwhelm the organization, as it did in the case of EMI, the UK-based music, electronics, and leisure products company which attempted to manage its new CT scanner business within the framework of its existing organizational structure and processes (see EMI and the CT scanner,

ICCH case 9–383–194). Certain parts of a company's portfolio of businesses or markets may be inherently very different from some others, and it may be best not to look for economies of scope across them. For example, in the soft drinks industry, bottling and distribution are intensely local in scope, while the tasks of creating and maintaining a brand image, or that of designing efficient bottling plants, may offer significant benefits from global integration. Carrying out both these sets of functions in-house would clearly lead to internalizing enormous differences within the company with regard to the organizing, coordinating, and controlling tasks. Instead of trying to cope with these complexities, Coca-Cola has externalized those functions which are purely local in scope (in all but some key strategic markets). In a variation of the same theme, IBM has 'externalized' the PC business by setting up an almost stand-alone organization, instead of trying to exploit scope benefits by integrating this business within the structure of its existing organization (for a more detailed discussion on multinational scope economies and on the conflicts between internal and external consistencies, see Lorange, Scott Morton and Ghoshal, 1986).

PRESCRIPTIONS IN PERSPECTIVE

Existing literature on global strategy offers analytical insights and helpful prescriptions for

436   *S. Ghoshal*

Table 3.   Selected references for further reading

Strategic objectives	Sources of competitive advantage		
	National differences	Scale economies	Scope economies
Achieving efficiency in current operations	Kogut (1985a); Itami (1978); Okimoto, Sugano and Weinstein (1984)	Hout, Porter and Rudden (1982); Levitt (1983); Doz (1978); Leontiades (1984); Gluck (1983)	Hamel and Prahalad (1985); Hout, Porter and Rudden (1982); Porter (1985); Ohmae (1985)
Managing risks	Kiechel (1981); Kobrin (1982); Poynter (1985); Lessard and Lightstone (1983); Srinivasulu (1981); Herring (1983)	Evans (1982); Piore and Sabel (1984); Gold (1982); Aaker and Mascarenhas (1984)	Kogut (1985b); Lorange, Scott Morton and Ghoshal (1986)
Innovation, learning and adaptation	Westney (1985); Terpstra (1977); Ronstadt and Krammer (1982)	BCG (1982); Rapp (1973)	Bartlett and Ghoshal (1985)

almost all the different issues indicated in Table 1. Table 3 shows a selective list of relevant publications, categorized on the basis of issues that, according to this author's interpretations, the pieces primarily focus on.[4]

Pigeon-holing academic contributions into different parts of a conceptual framework tends to be unfair to their authors. In highlighting what the authors focus on, such categorization often amounts to an implicit criticism for what they did not write. Besides, most publications cover a broader range of issues and ideas than can be reflected in any such categorization scheme. Table 3 suffers from all these deficiencies. At the same time, however, it suggests how the proposed framework can be helpful in integrating the literature and in relating the individual pieces to each other.

---

[4] From an academic point of view, strategy of the multinational corporation is a specialized and highly applied field of study. It is built on the broader field of business policy and strategy which, in turn, rests on the foundation of a number of academic disciplines such as economics, organization theory, finance theory, operations research, etc. A number of publications in those underlying disciplines, and a significant body of research carried out in the field of strategy, in general, provide interesting insights on the different issues highlighted in Table 1. However, given the objective of suggesting a limited list of further readings that *managers* may find useful, such publications have not been included in Table 3. Further, even for the more applied and prescriptive literature on global strategy, the list is only illustrative and not exhaustive.

From parts to the whole

For managers, the advantage of such synthesis is that it allows them to combine a set of insightful but often partial analyses to address the totality of a multidimensional and complex phenomenon. Consider, for example, a topic that has been the staple for academics interested in international management: explaining and drawing normative conclusions from the global successes of many Japanese companies. Based on detailed comparisons across a set of matched pairs of US and Japanese firms, Itami concludes that the relative successes of the Japanese firms can be wholly explained as due to the advantages of lower wage rates and higher labor productivity. In the context of a specific industry, on the other hand, Toder (1978) shows that manufacturing scale is the single most important source of the Japanese competitive advantage. In the small car business, for example, the minimum efficient scale requires an annual production level of about 400,000 units. In the late 1970s no US auto manufacturer produced even 200,000 units of any subcompact configuration vehicle, while Toyota produced around 500,000 Corollas and Nissan produced between 300,000 and 400,000 B210s per year. Toder estimates that US manufacturers suffered a cost disadvantage of between 9 and 17 percent on account of inefficient scale alone. Add to it the effects of wage rate differentials and exchange rate movements, and Japanese success in the

US auto market may not require any further explanation. Yet process-orientated scholars such as Hamel and Prahalad suggest a much more complex explanation of the Japanese tidal wave. They see it as arising out of a dynamic process of strategic evolution that exploits scope economies as a crucial weapon in the final stages. All these authors provide compelling arguments to support their own explanations, but do not consider or refute each other's hypotheses.

This multiplicity of explanations only shows the complexity of global strategic management. However, though different, these explanations and prescriptions are not always mutually exclusive. The manager's task is to find how these insights can be combined to build a multidimensional and flexible strategy that is robust to the different assumptions and explanations.

The strategic trade-offs

This, however, is not always possible because there are certain inherent contradictions between the different strategic objectives and between the different sources of competitive advantage. Consider, for instance, the popular distinction between a global and a multidomestic strategy described by Hout *et al.* (1982). A global strategy requires that the firm should carefully separate different value elements, and should locate each activity at the most efficient level of scale in the location where the activity can be carried out at the cheapest cost. Each activity should then be integrated and managed interdependently so as to exploit available scope economies. In essence, it is a strategy to maximize efficiency of current operations.

Such a strategy may, however, increase both endogenous and exogenous risks for the firm. Global scale of certain activities such as R&D and manufacturing may result in the firm's costs being concentrated in a few countries, while its revenues accrue globally, from sales in many different countries. This increases the operating exposure of the firm to the vicissitudes of exchange rate movements because of the mismatch between the currencies in which revenues are obtained and those in which costs are incurred. Similarly, the search for efficiency in a global business may lead to greater amounts of intra-company, but inter-country, flows of goods, capital, information and other resources. These

flows are visible, salient and tend to attract policy interventions from different host governments. Organizationally, such an integrated system requires a high degree of coordination, which enhances the risks of management failures. These are lessons that many Japanese companies have learned well recently.

Similarly, consideration of the learning objective will again contradict some of the proclaimed benefits of a global strategy. The implementation of a global strategy tends to enhance the forces of centralization and to shift organizational power from the subsidiaries to the headquarters. This may result in demotivation of subsidiary managers and may erode one key asset of the MNC—the potential for learning from its many environments. The experiences of Caterpillar is a case in point. An exemplary practioner of global strategy, Cat has recently spilled a lot of red ink on its balance sheet and has lost ground steadily to its archrival, Komatsu. Many factors contributed to Caterpillar's woes, not the least of which was the inability of its centralized management processes to benefit from the experiences of its foreign subsidiaries.

On the flipside of the coin, strategies aimed at optimizing risk or learning may compromise current efficiency. Poynter (1985) has recommended 'upgrade', i.e. increasing commitment of technology and resources in subsidiaries, as a way to overcome risk of policy interventions by host governments. Kogut (1985b), Mascarenhas (1982) and many others have suggested creating strategic and operational flexibility as a mechanism for coping with macroenvironmental risks. Bartlett and Ghoshal (1985) have proposed the differentiated network model of multinational organizations as a way to operationalize the benefits of global learning. All these recommendations carry certain efficiency penalties, which the authors have ignored.

Similar trade-offs exist between the different sources of competitive advantages. Trying to make the most of factor cost economies may prevent scale efficiency, and may impede benefiting from synergies across products or functions. Trying to benefit from scope through product diversification may affect scale, and so on. In effect these contradictions between the different strategic objectives, and between the different means for achieving them, lead to trade-offs between each cell in the framework and practically all others.

438   *S. Ghoshal*

These trade-offs imply that to formulate and implement a global strategy, MNC managers must consider all the issues suggested in Table 1, and must evaluate the implications of different strategic alternatives on each of these issues. Under a particular set of circumstances a particular strategic objective may dominate and a particular source of competitive advantage may play a more important role than the others (Fayerweather, 1981). The complexity of global strategic management arises from the need to understand those situational contingencies, and to adopt a strategy after evaluating the trade-offs it implies. Existing prescriptions can sensitize MNC managers to the different factors they must consider, but cannot provide ready-made and standardized solutions for them to adopt.

CONCLUSION

This paper has proposed a framework that can help MNC managers in reviewing and analyzing the strategies of their firms. It is not a blueprint for formulating strategies; it is a road map for reviewing them. Irrespective of whether strategies are analytically formulated or organizationally formed (Mintzberg, 1978), every firm has a realized strategy. To the extent that the realized strategy may differ from the intended one, managers need to review what the strategies of their firms really are. The paper suggests a scheme for such a review which can be an effective instrument for exercising strategic control.

Three arguments underlie the construct of the framework. First, in the global strategy literature, a kind of industry determinism has come to prevail not unlike the technological determinism that dominated management literature in the 1960s. The structures of industries may often have important influences on the appropriateness of corporate strategy, but they are only one of many such influences. Besides, corporate strategy may influence industry structure just as much as be influenced by it.

Second, simple schemes for categorizing strategies of firms under different labels tend to hide more than they reveal. A map for more detailed comparison of the content of strategies can be more helpful to managers in understanding and improving the competitive positions of their companies.

Third, the issues of risk and learning have not been given adequate importance in the strategy literature in general, and in the area of global strategies in particular. Both these are important strategic objectives and must be explicitly considered while evaluating or reviewing the strategic positions of companies.

The proposed framework is not a replacement of existing analytical tools but an enhancement that incorporates these beliefs. It does not present any new concepts or solutions, but only a synthesis of existing ideas and techniques. The benefit of such synthesis is that it can help managers in integrating an array of strategic moves into an overall strategic thrust by revealing the consistencies and contradictions among those moves.

For academics this brief view of the existing literature on global strategy will clearly reveal the need for more empirically grounded and systematic research to test and validate the hypotheses which currently appear in the literature as prescriptions and research conclusions. For partial analyses to lead to valid conclusions, excluded variables must be controlled for, and rival hypotheses must be considered and eliminated. The existing body of descriptive and normative research is rich enough to allow future researchers to adopt a more rigorous and systematic approach to enhance the reliability and validity of their findings and suggestions. The proposed framework, it is hoped, may be of value to some researchers in thinking about appropriate research issues and designs for furthering the field of global strategic management.

ACKNOWLEDGEMENTS

The ideas presented in this paper emerged in the course of discussions with many friends and colleagues. Don Lessard, Eleanor Westney, Bruce Kogut, Chris Bartlett and Nitin Nohria were particularly helpful. I also benefited greatly from the comments and suggestions of the two anonymous referees from the *Strategic Management Journal*.

REFERENCES

Aaker, D. A. and B. Mascarenhas. 'The need for strategic flexibility', *Journal of Business Strategy*, 5(2), Fall 1984, pp. 74–82.

Aldrich, H. E. *Organizations and Environments*, Prentice-Hall, Englewood Cliffs, NJ, 1979.

Allen, M. K. 'Japanese companies in the United States: the success of Nissan and Honda'. Unpublished manuscript, Sloan School of Management, MIT, November 1985.

Bartlett, C. A. 'Global competition and MNC managers', ICCH Note No. 0–385–287, Harvard Business School, Boston. 1985.

Bartlett, C. A. and S. Ghoshal. 'The new global organization: differentiated roles and dispersed responsibilities', Working Paper No. 9–786–013, Harvard Business School, Boston, October 1985.

Baumol, W. J., J. C. Panzer and R. D. Willig. *Contestable Markets and the Theory of Industry Structure*, Harcourt, Brace, Jovanovich, New York, 1982.

Boston Consulting Group, *Perspectives on Experience*, BCG, Boston, MA, 1982.

Calvet, A. L. 'A synthesis of foreign direct investment theories and theories of the multinational firm', *Journal of International Business Studies*, Spring–Summer 1981, pp. 43–60.

Caves, R. E. 'Industrial organization, corporate strategy and structure', *Journal of Economic Literature*, **XVIII**, March 1980, pp. 64–92.

Doz, Y. L. 'Managing manufacturing rationalization within multinational companies', *Columbia Journal of World Business*, Fall 1978, pp. 82–94.

Doz, Y. L., C. A. Bartlett and C. K. Prahalad. 'Global competitive pressures and host country demands: managing tensions in MNC's, *California Management Review*, Spring 1981, pp. 63–74.

Evans, J. S. *Strategic Flexibility in Business*, Report No. 678, SRI International, December 1982.

Fayerweather, J. 'Four winning strategies for the international corporation', *Journal of Business Strategy*, Fall 1981, pp. 25–36.

Flaherty, M. T. and H. Itami. 'Finance', in Okimoto, D.I., T. Sugano and F. B. Weinstein (Eds), *Competitive Edge*, Stanford University Press, Stanford, CA, 1984.

Gluck, F. 'Global competition in the 1980's', *Journal of Business Strategy*, Spring 1983, pp. 22–27.

Gold, B. 'Robotics, programmable automation, and international competitiveness', *IEEE Transactions on Engineering Management*, November 1982.

Hamel, G. and C. K. Prahalad. 'Do you really have a global strategy?', *Harvard Business Review*, July–August 1985, pp. 139–148.

Hannan, M. T. and J. Freeman. 'The population ecology of organizations', *American Journal of Sociology*, **82**, 1977, pp. 929–964.

Hatsopoulos, G. N. 'High cost of capital: handicap of American industry', Report Sponsored by the American Business Conference and Thermo-Electron Corporation, April 1983.

Hax, A. C. and N. S. Majluf. *Strategic Management: An Integrative Perspective*, Prentice-Hall, Englewood Cliffs, NJ, 1984.

Herring, R. J. (ed.), *Managing International Risk*, Cambridge University Press, Cambridge, 1983.

Hofer, C. W. and D. Schendel. *Strategy Formulation: Analytical Concepts*, West Publishing Co., St Paul, MN, 1978.

Hout, T., M. E. Porter and E. Rudden. 'How global companies win out', *Harvard Business Review*, September–October 1982, pp. 98–108.

Itami, H. 'Japanese–U.S. comparison of managerial productivity', *Japanese Economic Studies*, Fall 1978.

Kiechel, W. 'Playing the global game', *Fortune*, November 16, 1981, pp. 111–126.

Kobrin, S. J. *Managing Political Risk Assessment*, University of California Press, Los Angeles, CA, 1982.

Kogut, B. 'Normative observations on the international value-added chain and strategic groups', *Journal of International Business Studies*, Fall 1984, pp. 151–167.

Kogut, B. 'Designing global strategies: comparative and competitive value added chains', *Sloan Management Review*, **26**(4), Summer 1985a, pp. 15–28.

Kogut, B. 'Designing global strategies: profiting from operational flexibility', *Sloan Management Review*, Fall 1985b, pp. 27–38.

Leontiades, J. 'Market share and corporate strategy in international industries', *Journal of Business Strategy*, 5(1), Summer 1984, pp. 30–37.

Lessard, D. and J. Lightstone. 'The impact of exchange rates on operating profits: new business and financial responses', mimeo, Lightstone-Lessard Associates, 1983.

Levitt, T. 'The globalization of markets', *Harvard Business Review*, May–June 1983, pp. 92–102.

Lorange, P., M. S. Scott Morton and S. Ghoshal. *Strategic Control*, West Publishing Co., St Paul, MN, 1986.

Mascarenhas, B. 'Coping with uncertainty in international business', *Journal of International Business Studies*, Fall 1982, pp. 87–98.

Mintzberg, H. 'Patterns in strategic formation', *Management Science*, **24**, 1978, pp. 934–948.

Ohmae, K. *Triad Power: The Coming Shape of Global Competition*, Free Press, New York, 1985.

Okimoto, D. I., T. Sugano and F. B. Weinstein (eds). *Competitive Edge*, Stanford University Press, Stanford, CA, 1984.

Perlmutter, H. V. 'The tortuous evolution of the multinational corporation', *Columbia Journal of World Business*, January–February 1969, pp. 9–18.

Piore, M. J. and C. Sabel. *The Second Industrial Divide: Possibilities and Prospects*, Basic Books, New York, 1984.

Porter, M. E. *Competitive Strategy*, Basic Books, New York, 1980.

Porter, M. E. 'Competition in global industries: a conceptual framework', paper presented to the Colloquium on Competition in Global Industries, Harvard Business School, 1984.

440   *S. Ghoshal*

Porter, M. E. *Competitive Advantage*, Free Press, New York, 1985.

Poynter, T. A. *International Enterprises and Government Intervention*, Croom Helm, London, 1985.

Prahalad, C. K. 'The strategic process in a multinational corporation'. Unpublished doctoral dissertation, Graduate School of Business Administration, Harvard University, 1975.

Rapp, W. V. 'Strategy formulation and international competition', *Columbia Journal of World Business*, Summer 1983, pp. 98–112.

Robinson, R. D. *International Business Management: A Guide to Decision Making*, Dryden Press, Illinois, 1978.

Ronstadt, R. and R. J. Krammer. 'Getting the most out of innovations abroad', *Harvard Business Review*, March–April 1982, pp. 94–99.

Rutenberg, D. P. *Multinational Management*, Little, Brown, Boston, MA, 1982.

Srinivasula, S. 'Strategic response to foreign exchange risks', *Columbia Journal of World Business*, Spring 1981, pp. 13–23.

Terpstra, V. 'International product policy: the role of foreign R&D', *Columbia Journal of World Business*, Winter 1977, pp. 24–32.

Terpstra, V. *International Dimensions of Marketing*, Kent, Boston, MA, 1982.

Toder, E. J. *Trade Policy and the U.S. Automobile Industry*, Praeger Special Studies, New York, 1978.

Vernon, R. *Storm Over the Multinationals*, Harvard University Press, Cambridge, MA, 1977.

The Wall Street Journal, April 29, 1985, p. 1.

Westney, D. E. 'International dimensions of information and communications technology'. Unpublished manuscript, Sloan School of Management, MIT, 1985.

Woo, C. Y. and K. O. Cool. 'The impact of strategic management of systematic risk', Mimeo, Krannert Graduate School of Management, Purdue University, 1985.

[8]

Journal of Management
1992, Vol. 18, No. 3, 455-471

A Strategic Management Perspective on Host Country Structure of Multinational Enterprises

Stephen B. Tallman
University of Utah

This article proposes that the oligopoly power and internalization models of the multinational enterprise should be reviewed in light of the newly developing resource-based model of strategy and managerial decision-making models of strategic management. The perspective described here suggests that strategy-making under conditions of uncertainty and the drive to gain competitive advantage from deployment of firm-specific resources are important issues in the internalization decision of the MNE in a host market. The role of transaction cost efficiency in generating subsidiary governance structures is redefined to be compatible with the demands of these additional considerations of the multinational strategic manager.

Two broad perspectives dominate the theoretical literature concerning the development and operations of multinational enterprises (MNEs). Kogut (1988) describes these viewpoints as the strategic behavior explanation and the transaction cost explanation for multinational activity. Each of these explanations suggests certain factors that determine the choice of entry form in host markets. However, neither of these two views has been able to displace the other [See, for example, Calvet (1981) and Porter (1986)], implying that each has an underlying intuition that is correct but incomplete. This article proposes that integrating a managerial behavior perspective and certain concepts from resource-based strategy with existing models of MNE structure can provide an improved explanation for MNE activity in host countries.

The traditional definitions of the MNE have been based on comparative usage of exports, licensing, and foreign direct investment as governance structures for operations in foreign markets. These definitions have decreasing relevance in a globalizing marketplace in which firms are defined more by their terms of competition, or strategy, than by their mode of operation, or structure. This article integrates concepts of business strategy with the established maxims of multinational firm structure. Strategic management models incorporate behavioral and organizational concepts that provide an essential role for the manager in creating strat-

---

Address all correspondence to Stephen B. Tallman, David Eccles School of Business, University of Utah, Salt Lake City, UT 84112.

egy and structure. This role is missing from current economics-based theories of the MNE. The model of MNE strategy and structure proposed here treats managerial decision making as the central issue in selecting a strategy and a governance structure for a foreign market. Resource-based models propose that possession by a firm of unique or improperly valued firm-specific resources, which are matched to the local environment by firm strategy and structure, provides the opportunity for above-normal performance. Governance cost efficiencies, central to transaction cost models, are viewed here as having limited importance to the initial entry decision, due to their uncertain nature. However, transaction cost efficiencies are vital to the process of review and restructuring that reconciles strategic intentions with efficient economics.

The first part of the article reviews two current sets of theory about the MNE and foreign direct investment (FDI). This is followed by a discussion of the resource-based model and managerial decision models. A detailed model of MNE host market entry is developed that emphasizes firm-specific resources as the bases for superior performance and managerial discretion as an explanatory framework for choosing a particular entry mode or structure. The model suggests a narrowly defined role for transaction costs. The article closes by outlining the potential for conceptual and empirical symbiosis between the managerial and resource-based models of strategy and the study of MNEs.

The Theoretical Models of the MNE

The Oligopoly Power Models

Kogut's "strategic behavior" explanation of the MNE is an extension of the industrial organization (IO) model of competition, in which strategy and performance are related to market power in oligopolistic industries. Oligopoly models focus on the market structure of an industry as the primary determinant of firm performance (Cool & Schendel, 1987). Certain industries (Bain, 1956) or, in more recent forms, industry groups (Caves & Porter, 1977) provide the opportunity for firms to acquire excess profits. Firm strategy (conduct) consists of identifying and occupying favored positions in the industry structure. Sustained supernormal performance is attained through collective action by groups of firms that hold such favored positions. These strategic groups are found to establish mobility barriers to exclude new entry and to collude within their protected strategic position (Porter, 1979). Market efficiencies and cost controls are not central to oligopoly models because profits are based on the natural defensibility of industry segments and on firm conduct in exercising market power. Porter's discussion of generic strategies and competitive advantage is typical of this approach to strategy (Porter, 1980) and reflects the importance of size and share to this paradigm. These models focus on static profit maximization through exploiting industry structural barriers as the primary goal of the firm.

This model of the firm is the basis for the Hymer (1960) and Kindleberger (1969) models of the large MNE and of FDI. It is quite evident in the oligopolistic activities tested by Knickerbocker's (1973) "follow the leader" concept of FDI and Graham's (1974) "exchange of hostages" model. IO assumptions are also behind the International Life Cycle of Vernon (1971), Caves' proposal that MNE product differentiation skills explain FDI (1971), and Porter's Configuration/Co-ordination model of global competition (1986).

Oligopoly models suggest that MNEs will select host country entry modes to deter other entry or to block competitors' positions (Kogut, 1988). Large firms with market power could be expected to use FDI to project their market power into foreign host markets. Direct investment on a large scale preempts the development of local competitors and provides market access and tariff relief not available to importers. FDI thereby permits international extension of the oligopolistic practices used in home markets. These models predict greater use of FDI among large MNEs and higher levels of performance among these same firms.

Oligopoly power models of the MNE have received much criticism for their reliance on oligopolistic ownership advantages to explain FDI. Buckley & Casson (1976) reject Hymer's and Kindleberger's models due to their focus on initial firm endowments without consideration of costs. Teece (1986) finds that a focus on market power rather than efficiency limits applicability of oligopoly models to non-competitive industries. Calvet (1981) rejects the market power approach for its reliance on static, technologically determined market structure imperfections. Casson (1987) provides a detailed rebuttal of what he refers to as the "collusion" model of the MNE and finds that transaction cost efficiencies fully explain FDI. Empirical studies of FDI into the United States (Lall & Siddharthan, 1982; McClain, 1982) generally do not support the assumptions of the oligopoly power model, suggesting that the empirical support for this perspective is situational, limited to certain MNEs in specific contexts.

Internalization Models

Models of the MNE in the second theoretical group use transaction cost economics as their primary explanation for the existence of MNEs and direct investment. In the international literature, this perspective dates from Buckley & Casson's (1976) Internalization Model of the MNE, so this term will be retained. *Internalization* refers to the decision to internalize across borders intermediate good transactions that are inefficient or subject to failure when left to international market forces. Although transaction costs were not specifically described in the original internalization model, this perspective is closely related to the transaction cost economics of Coase (1937) and Williamson (1975), as discussed by Casson (1987). Williamson explains that firms develop from markets and expand into large multidivisional forms due to excessive transaction costs in external markets. When market transaction costs exceed the governance costs of a hierarchical structure, the firm will expand to absorb the transaction. In this perspective, above average performance results from minimizing the sum of transaction and governance costs of the firm in a competitive end market.

The internalization models (Buckley, 1988; Buckley & Casson, 1976; Casson, 1987; Rugman, 1979) apply the same logic to international markets. They propose that MNEs are created when international market transactions for intermediate goods are brought inside the firm, or internalized, via FDI in order to reduce the cost of organizing or controlling the transactions. In foreign host markets, internalization of markets will take place until the increased governance costs of internalization equal the economic benefits of reduced transaction costs (Buckley, 1988; Hill & Kim, 1988). In the international context, the structural decision involves selecting a control structure for foreign activities, such as licensing, exporting, or direct investing, either wholly-owned or joint venture.

The choice of market entry form is recognized as a firm-level decision, but most internalization models define the transaction costs of a firm from the characteristics of its industry. Firms in information or technology intensive industries face flawed or non-existent markets for their critical knowledge assets and are expected to use horizontal internalization through extensive FDI in host market nations. Firms in natural resource-based industries are expected to use vertical FDI to secure limited sources of specific input resources. Both conditions are due to the impossibility of pricing, monitoring, and enforcing a contract for a transaction-specific asset under conditions of small-numbers bargaining where opportunism risk is high (Gatignon & Anderson, 1988). These often-used examples of the internalization model imply a continued reliance on technological determinism to explain uniform behavior among similar firms in a given industry, with little provision for firm-specific managerial choices.

More recent versions of internalization theory focus on the transaction rather than the firm and leave room for alternative ways of exploiting a given technology under different conditions (Calvet, 1981; Casson, 1987; Gatignon & Anderson, 1988; Hennart, 1982; Teece, 1981, 1983, 1986). However, these versions still suffer from a condition that we might call economic determinism. As Buckley (1988) puts it: "(1) Firms choose the least cost location for each activity they perform, and (2) firms grow by internalizing markets up to the point where the benefits of further internalization are outweighed by the costs" (181-182). The requirement for minimization of combined market transaction and hierarchical governance costs is taken to provide a complete explanation for why firms have attained a particular structural equilibrium. Under given conditions and for a group of similar firms, only those that install the minimum cost transaction management structure are expected to survive.

Dunning's Eclectic Model (1981, 1988) combines the effects of *ownership factors* (i.e., rent-producing firm skills), *location factors* (i.e., environmental differences), and *internalization factors* (i.e., transaction-related concerns), to explain the structural choice of export, license, or investment to enter a foreign host market. Dunning proposes that ownership factors (firm-level competitive advantages) provide unique products for which a foreign market can be developed; that location factors (country-level factor price advantages) dictate the choice of production site; and that internalization (transaction cost) factors determine whether overseas production will be organized through markets (licensing) or hierarchies (FDI). Although Dunning does include certain aspects of the oligopoly power model and of location economics, he relies on internalization arguments to justify the use of one entry mode or another after the product and market are selected. He also continues to define multinationality by the use of FDI.

Teece (1986) develops a model similar to that of Dunning, but with explicit transaction level cost analysis. Strategic advantage factors replace ownership factors, and transaction cost factors are used instead of internalization. Teece is somewhat more specific than Dunning and better reflects the business strategy literature. However, he assumes that strategic advantage, or rent-yielding assets, must exist for virtually any MNE, and that location characteristics have only to do with placement of operations, not governance method. Transaction costs are the only basis he provides for choice of organizational form.

Even proponents of internalization models admit to limitations for this structural model. Models based on transaction cost economics tend toward the assumption that because cost structures must be efficient, then existing structures are the efficient optimum. Calvet (1981) shows that transaction cost models are essentially static, capable of determining the optimum structure for an MNE in a particular set of circumstances but not designed to respond to changing circumstances. Buckley (1988) discusses the need for empirical tests in which transaction costs are actually estimated *a priori*. However, Nelson & Winter (1982) show that, even when dynamic adjustment is permitted, simple economic efficiency will not drive real firms to consistently optimized structural choices. Borys & Jemison state that "transaction cost analysis offers a rigorous post hoc discussion of the criteria for boundary definition, yet it has little to say about how to identify important factors ex ante" (1989: 240). Transaction cost determinism does not show why a particular factor organization is needed in the first place and focuses tightly on avoiding the costs of opportunism in describing how to organize. Strategic management, particularly from the resource-based perspective, provides a conceptual motive for deploying resources in new markets in search of competitive advantage (Conner, 1991). Organizational efficiency is but one side of the strategy-structure-environment construct.

Empirical studies, other than those that focus on American MNEs (such as Buckley & Casson's original, 1976, study), provide mixed support for transaction cost models. Clegg (1987), in testing Dunning's model, found that high R&D levels (a common proxy for high transaction costs) lead generally to more export activity in most cases, rather than more FDI. Only for U.S. industry did FDI increase with R&D ratios. Swedenborg (1979) tested firm-level data for a number of Swedish firms and found that neither size (key to oligopoly power models) nor firm R&D intensity (often used as a key input variable in transaction cost models) accounted for higher levels of FDI activity. She proposes that firm-specific skills (resources) and idiosyncratic choices (managerial decisions) determine the likelihood of foreign manufacture. More recently, Collis (1991) shows the value of organizational resource analysis in understanding the strategies of MNEs in the bearings industry.

Resource-Based Strategy and a Managerial Perspective

Swedenborg's and Clegg's findings, plus the partial support found for both oligopoly power and internalization models in other studies, indicate the need for a perspective that truly differentiates firm-specific characteristics, if we are to explain the activities of MNEs. The resource-based strategy concept (Wernerfelt, 1984; Rumelt, 1984; Barney, 1986, 1991; Dierickx & Cool, 1989; Conner, 1991) provides a firm-specific explanation of strategy and structure. Resource-based strategy suggests that sustained competitive superiority is based on possession of rent-yielding, non-imitable and non-substitutable resources (Barney, 1991), and is specifically related to the entrepreneurial model of Schumpeter (1934). Specialized resources are of two types, industry-specific and firm-specific. The resource-based strategy model of the MNE presented here locates competitive advantage with the firm-specific resources (FSRs). These may be tangible, such as proprietary knowledge, or intangible, such as reputation or brand name, and are based on the firm's history and other complex social interactions (Collis, 1991). These FSRs are the bases for any economic rents that may accrue to the firm and are approximately what Dunning (1981) means by ownership factors of the MNE. FSRs have also been described as strategic advantage factors (Teece, 1986), distinctive competencies (Hannan & Freeman, 1976), or intangible assets (Itami, 1987). The transaction-specific assets that are key to transaction cost models (Teece, 1986) may be considered a subset of FSRs, with the potential to yield rents only in specific transactions. Conner (1991) shows that asset specificity is part of both transaction cost theory and resource-based models, but that the resource-based models focus on deployment of specialized assets in search of sustained competitive advantage rather than on avoidance of opportunism costs when such resources are exposed.

In resource-based models, the focus of strategic success is placed on the resources accessible to the firm, either internally or through external factor markets. Super-normal profits are considered to be economic quasi-rents to unique or unequally available FSRs (Dierickx & Cool, 1989). Such profits result from combinations of strategy and structure that efficiently exploit these FSRs within a particular environment. Profits are protected from imitators by means of isolating mechanisms (Lippman & Rumelt, 1982) or resource-position barriers (Wernerfelt, 1984) that make imitative strategies inherently uncertain of success, rather than by deliberately constructed mobility barriers (Rumelt 1984). Because the resource base is specific to the firm, the strategy and structure by which these resources are exploited must also be specific to the firm, not the industry or group. Firm-level managerial decisions become significant to strategy and performance when these idiosyncratic elements are introduced. Managerial limitations are critical to sustained competitive advantage because the isolating mechanisms protecting any firm are the result of uncertain information and limited rationality. A resource such as tacit, organizationally bound knowledge is a source of advantage only so long as it remains poorly defined.

Acceptance of managerialism means that the economic determinism that is key to the oligopoly power and internalization perspectives on the MNE must be replaced by concepts from more recent behavioral (Romanelli & Tushman, 1986) and economic (Nelson & Winter, 1982) models. Managerial theory (Cyert & March, 1963; Simon, 1945) suggests that managerial predispositions and uncertainty of information and outcomes result in "satisficing" behavior. Nelson & Winter (1982) replace static profit maximization as the prime motive of the firm with a more dynamic model of a firm that uses "routines" while searching for marginally improved performance. They postulate that combining a limited set of perceived alternatives with environmental selection will result in diversity and pluralism in outcomes. Managerial process models (Bower & Doz, 1979) perceive strategy in even more behavioralistic terms as the outcome of managed negotiations among various internal political power coalitions. From a managerialist perspective, economic factors such as transaction costs do not automatically and instantaneously determine firm actions, but are filtered through managerial decision processes. For the MNE, our model of managerial strategy and resource-based competitive advantage suggests that strategic and structural decisions are more subject to managerial processes than in the two currently popular models, and that managers deal primarily with concerns about resource positions in making strategic decisions. Key points of the three theoretical perspectives are summarized in Table 1.

A Strategic Management Perspective on the MNE in a Host Market

Collis (1991) addresses overall global strategies from a resource-based perspective. Resource-based and managerial concepts of strategic management are used here to develop a model of the organizational structure of the MNE in a single foreign host country that provides a complementary association of strategy and efficiency as part of a global strategy. Oligopoly power models focus on market power and entry barriers to explain the use of FDI in a host market. Resource-based strategies recognize that sustained superior performance is based on applying unique FSRs in a market rather than on the use of market power in an inefficiently structured industry.

Table 1
Theoretical Perspectives on the MNE

Model	Perspectives
IO-based Oligopoly Power	Strategy consists of identifying and exploiting profitable industry segments
	Firms in profitable segments use market power in inefficient final goods markets and collusion to attain above normal returns
	MNEs use FDI to propagate oligopolistic industry structures in foreign host markets
Transaction Cost based Internalization	Firms internalize market transactions until the sum of transaction and governance costs is minimized. "Strategy" is irrelevant.
	Supernormal performance results from optimal combinations of transaction and governance costs to control specialized assets, given efficient final goods markets.
	MNEs use FDI when internal cross-border transactions are more efficient than external market transactions.
Resourced-based Strategy	Strategy is the effort to identify, exploit, and protect rent-yielding firm specific resources.
	Supernormal returns result when firm strategy and structure best match the rent-yielding FSRs to the environment.
	*MNEs use FDI when a structure providing more managerial control is required to better extract rents from the FSRs in a host market.

*Contention of this paper

Internalization models of the MNE describe *strategies* of licensing, exporting, or FDI. However, the focus of these models on structural cost efficiencies clearly shows that these alternatives are what business strategy and organization theory would consider *structural* variants. A managerial perspective differentiates strategic plans (highly subject to managerial limitations but providing motivation for actions) from structures (institutionalizing these plans in the economic environment). From such a perspective, we cannot predict governance structure preferences without understanding the MNE's strategy and knowing the characteristics of its underlying resources. The discretionary aspect of strategy, unavoidable due to the uncertain identity of FSRs and the bounded rationality of managers, explains why MNEs in a single industry may enter the same host market using different structures, rather than responding uniformly to the same set of industry and location conditions (Ghoshal & Nohria, 1989).

Overview of the Model—The Basic Argument

The decision to enter a particular host market, from resource-based and managerial decision-making perspectives on strategic management, results from analysis of the worldwide strategy of the MNE and of its available FSRs to determine its apparent sources of competitive advantage in a particular host country context. The managers of the MNE must select FSRs that seem most likely to generate sustained competitive advantage in the context of the local market's unique demands, generate a local market strategy, and choose the best apparent resource governance structure or level of internalization (see Figure 1).

Both the host market strategy and governance structure of the MNE result directly from discretionary managerial decisions and only indirectly from the pressures of the host country economic environment (see Romanelli & Tushman, 1986). The managers make decisions with incomplete information under condi-

Figure 1
The Internalization Decision

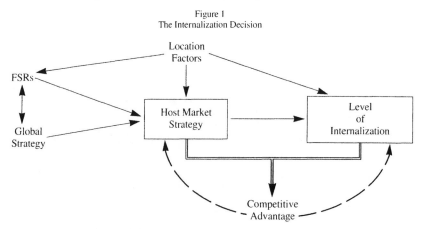

Solid lines indicate interactive inputs to the strategy/structure decision.
Double lines indicate direct output of competitive advantage.
Dashed lines indicate feedback effects.

tions of uncertainty. The MNE may reduce its uncertainty in a given situation by attempting to imitate either its own previously successful strategies and structures or those of its competitors in the new market. (See Nelson & Winter, 1982; Rumelt, 1984) In this way, experiences with effective strategies and efficient transaction structures from previous situations enter the structuring decision.

Once a strategy and structure are in place, performance levels can be observed, providing feedback on the relative competitive advantage of the local subsidiary. The managers can be expected to adapt to unforeseen pressures and circumstances that generate poor performance. Comparatively good performance, indicating that competitive advantage has been secured, will result in stable strategies and structures. Subsidiaries that perform relatively poorly will change strategy, structure, or both; often they will try to imitate high performers. Incremental modifications to the resource strategy and structure in response to various competitive pressures, to include transaction cost efficiency, will improve the performance of some subsidiaries. If change is not effective in fitting the FSRs to the environment more effectively, firms eventually may fail (Hannan & Freeman, 1976).

With this overview in mind, let us attempt a deliberate, detailed development of our model of host market entry from a strategic management perspective.

Goals of the MNE under Conditions of Uncertainty

A key component of any strategy is the purpose or goal of the strategy. The MNE selects its goals and plans its strategy within the constraints of its environment. In this analysis, a key aspect of the environment is its uncertainty. The parent MNE can diversify away many of the risks of incomplete information by entering many host countries. To the managers of a single host country operation, without diversification options, incomplete information must have a significant impact on strategic decisions.

Nelson & Winter (1982) suggest that in an uncertain environment, firms seek comparative goals: success compared to their competitors and to their previous experience. Managers with limited foresight and incomplete information are incapable of identifying truly optimal performance, much less attaining it, except through luck. One long-term goal of an MNE in a host market, therefore, is to improve its overall performance relative to its historic and competitive levels, thus at least improving shareholder value. The internalization model of the MNE addresses only one side of the cost-revenue issue by focusing on governance cost minimization (Hill & Kim, 1988). Oligopoly power models address the revenue maximizing side of profit-making (Cool & Schendel, 1987). The resource-based model provides for conditions under which firms can accrue higher profits if they have a resource advantage, but where close potential substitutes make cost efficiency vital to sustainable advantage, sharing some characteristics of both models (Conner, 1991). In such a situation, net economic benefits, neither costs *nor* revenues alone, must be the major financial focus of the firm (Jones & Hill, 1988). Non-economic goals are essentially incompatible with purely economic models, but can be adopted directly within a strategic management model.

Uncertainty reduction is a second, and equally relevant, goal of risk-averse managers (DiMaggio & Powell, 1983). Uncertainty can be reduced by increased

464   STEPHEN B. TALLMAN

information gathering, which increases transaction costs, or by internalizing control, which increases governance costs. The MNE can also reduce its uncertainty by limiting its strategic options in a host country. Therefore, we can expect to encounter often a condition of inertia (the retention of a tried strategy for the sake of lowered uncertainty) in pursuing goals (Romanelli & Tushman, 1986). The host market manager, without market diversification options, will attempt simultaneously to increase performance levels and to reduce uncertainty levels through strategic and structural limitations.

Internalization and Resource Structure

In pursuing goals of sustained superior performance and reduced uncertainty, the managers of the MNE must identify their sources of potential advantage (FSRs), decide how to apply them in the local market context, and organize a governance or control structure for their efforts. Traditional economic models of the MNE focus on the governance structure chosen for host countries. Therefore, the choice of structure or level of internalization will also be the focus of this discussion (See Fig. 1). The following sections use arguments from managerial and resource-based strategy models to explain why MNEs might select and maintain certain structures under differing conditions. This explanation incorporates strategic behavior and transaction costs, but transcends the economic determinism of current explanations for the MNE.

As the MNE expands into the international marketplace, it selects structural forms to support its new strategic scope, in much the same way that a product-diversifying firm selects a multi-divisional structure to support its new product scope. These structural forms then become part of the MNE's resource structure and influence future strategic decisions. A firm using a market type structure may trade in products, via imports and exports, or in ideas, via licensing. An internalized structure uses some form of FDI to increase the MNE's ability to control the execution of strategy and the application of the critical resources in a foreign host country.

Structural choices influence performance levels by determining how the market strategy will be applied and controlled, and by determining the balance of resource and transaction costs in the country market. For instance, maximum revenues from a consumer product strategy based on brand image may require close central control of advertising and therefore some form of FDI. However, if the MNE does not have the capital resources to set up or buy a local advertising firm, it may be forced to save on resource costs by accepting a joint venture deal. The net returns to operations are affected on both revenue and cost sides by the MNE's resource governance structure in the host country.

Structural choice also affects uncertainty levels. The uncertainty of that portion of the environment with which the firm interacts regularly is lessened through experience. Therefore, one way of reducing the information costs of resource control is to extend the governance structure of the firm (see McManus, 1972). When the firm extends its structure, it both internalizes some previously external transactions and expands its region of reduced uncertainty. In the international realm, the MNE can reduce its uncertainty about a market through FDI, but must accept increased governance costs for its increased assets and increased opportunity costs from reduced flexibility for future strategic moves.

Traditional models of the MNE suggest similar structures for all markets (Dunning, 1981), but real MNEs have different structures in different markets (Bartlett & Ghoshal, 1989). The level of internalization of international transactions can only be chosen in relation to a particular part of the environment, as each national market has location factors and competitive conditions that will influence the choice of resources, strategy, and structure in that market. Location, or context, provides influences on the strategic and structuring decisions other than simple comparative factor prices (Porter, 1990), contrary to Dunning (1988) and Teece (1986). Structural choice in strategic management models is not based purely on industry characteristics, collusive strategies, or rational economic consideration of transaction costs. Rather, structure is chosen in tandem with a particular strategy by all-too-human managers to fit certain FSRs to a perceived market. Interactions among resource, strategic, and location considerations in choosing a host country governance structure are described in the next sections.

Strategy and FSR Selection for the Host Country

The national firm about to enter an international market is made up of resources from its home country environment, structured in a fashion developed in the home country industry of which it is a part. Entry strategies at this point will be largely based on home market experiences. As the MNE gains international experience, it acquires resources and develops interaction modes (routines) in the larger environment. Strategic options will expand to reflect this broadened resource structure.

Resources and interactions can be positively identified as sources of competitive advantage and economic rents only after they have generated rents; until then, managers must make imperfect judgements as to resource values. Therefore, the set of identified rent-yielding FSRs that belong to an MNE at any given time is a function of the strategies that the MNE has used before that time. Dependence on past performance encourages the natural conservatism, or risk-aversion, of strategic managers entering a new host country. If resources with profit potential are identified through certain strategies in the past, uncertainty about the future will be allayed by reference to past policies.

FSRs and Business Strategy in the Host Country

We have said that strategy from one time period plays a key role in identifying the unique FSRs of the firm for subsequent time periods. We must also recognize that for an MNE contemplating a new market, its existing FSR structure will limit the range of strategic possibilities considered for that country. Thus, the two-way interaction of strategy and FSRs shown in Figure 1 is suggested. The FSRs identified from previous strategic successes will suggest the most likely entry strategy for the new market. Under conditions of uncertainty, high at initial entry, inertia is likely to result in deploying these resources in the same manner used before. Although the decision to enter a new market is entrepreneurial at its heart, we would most often expect to find essential strategic boldness tempered with some imitative caution.

The entire inventory of FSRs may not be available to an MNE in a particular host location. Even to the incompletely knowledgeable manager, some resources will not fit in a new environment. For instance, skills developed in industrialized nations are often inappropriate or impossible to apply in less developed locations. Market strategies oriented toward only part of a market, such as an intent to skim a consumer product market by focusing on the local elite, will provide little opportunity to exploit resources related to size or capital availability. In other cases, local government requirements for licensing or cooperative ventures may limit the ability of the firm to apply resources relating to internal organizational systems. Only those FSRs that are compatible with the characteristics of the market are likely to generate economic rents.

Strategies and FSRs interact with each other and with location effects to generate competitive advantage for the MNE in a particular market through the structural form chosen for that market (Fig. 1). The distinctive impact of location effects on the firm's strategic and structural decisions for the home market, international market, and specific host country is unique to MNEs. This contextual sequence provides a way to identify the development of certain FSRs and to trace their strategic application under specific conditions.

Measuring Performance: Returns and Costs as Feedback

After entry and a period of operation in any market, new FSRs may develop in the host market that were not among the original set of parent resources and that may not be available outside of that market. Such assets as a host country dealer network may fit in this set. These new market-specific FSRs, plus the experience of competition in the host market will force changes over time in the strategy and structure chosen at entry. Guided change requires feedback by which managers can monitor performance. Observation of market returns and associated costs can provide this feedback.

Revenues and returns. In resource-based models, the firm judges its performance based on rents it receives from its FSRs. In a host market model the MNE therefore would be concerned with returns on investment in a market, not just with costs. In strategic modelling, Jones & Hill (1988) compare the net results of economic benefits and bureaucratic costs for various product diversification strategies. This article proposes a similar decision rule: firms will try to generate relative improvements in net returns on investment (Nelson & Winter, 1982) while reducing uncertainty about future outcomes.

Imitative strategies and inherent uncertainties imply that goal success will be judged in comparison to competitors because "real" potential maximum returns are unknowable. The strategy and the combination of FSRs and location factors determine the revenue potential for the product/market choice over any period. The internalization, or governance structure, decision determines how the unique firm resources will interact with environmental factors to determine the cost structure over the same time span. Success, or the generation of positive economic rents, indicates that the combination of strategy and structure has generated a competitive advantage for the firm in a specific host market.

The costs of structural variations. Among the host country structural options for the MNE, licensing can be described as entailing the lowest additional resource costs for the firm, but as adding to its expected *ex post* transaction costs (Hill & Kim, 1988) by exposing technology assets to competitors. Licensing may therefore be considered to have potentially high total transaction costs, though it internalizes the fewest new resources and has low governance costs. Exporting increases resource costs moderately to provide added home country production capacity, but it also has high immediate transactions costs (*ex ante* in Hill & Kim) due to the need for continually making a market for its products. FDI is the extension of firm ownership to internal assets in a host country. As such, it has the highest additional resource costs and the greatest internal governance costs, but it reduces external uncertainty in the host country and therefore reduces overall transaction costs. Higher information costs make FDI more likely when critical resources are intangible than when host market FSRs are tangible assets, as commonly asserted by transaction cost analysts (Hennart, 1988).

Internalization models of the MNE emphasize the importance of transactions costs to the exclusion of the other aspects of the cost/revenue function in selecting a control structure. In a managerial strategy model, transactions costs are limited to a role as part of the structural decision, "Should we use licensing, exports, or a form of FDI?" Although managers can use experience to estimate them in the initial structuring decision, transaction costs are defined fully only after an activity takes place. As a result, they can cause unforeseeable reductions in returns and therefore are important to the stochastic nature of the strategic feedback loop and to changes in structural form. This important part of the nature of transactions costs has resulted in their dominance of internalization models of the MNE, which focus on structural efficiency after equilibrium conditions are established.

Cost control does provide pressure toward structural efficiency. However, a high revenue strategy may support a high cost structure in a national market, if net benefits are higher than for alternative low-cost structural forms. Uncertainty about sources of competitive advantage and the limited rationality of managerial decision makers also obstruct the instantaneous adjustment of firms toward an optimal structure. In addition, competitive conditions may move firms to accept cost inefficiencies or risks in exchange for increased revenues.

Expected Outcomes from the Strategic Management Perspective

In order to be of any practical use, or to be testable as a theory, a concept such as the resource-based strategy model of MNE market entry must be usable in predicting the actions of relevant firms. If the new concept is to be compared to older models, at least some of these expected actions must be different from those predicted by the other models. In this section, certain expected patterns of MNE behavior will be discussed. For a compatible set of empirical tests in a single-industry context, see Collis (1991).

The most comprehensive prediction is that MNEs will use very different structural arrangements in different markets, depending on specific strategic commitments and locational conditions. This broad argument is in agreement with the empirical work and modelling in Hedlund (1986), Bartlett & Ghoshal (1989),

Ghoshal & Nohria (1989), and Sundaram (1990). Idiosyncratic strategy and locational differences make the implied homogeneity of structure in the oligopoly or internalization models unlikely. However, the impact of uncertainty considerations suggests that initial structures of a firm will reflect inertia by imitating previous strategic success of that firm. The model presented here suggests that firms will most often imitate their own previous actions when entering a new country. Over time, though, firms will tend to imitate more successful competitors. However, differences in available resources and the effects of "isolating mechanisms" will result in differential levels of performance, even among host country organizations with closely imitative strategic purposes and homogeneous governance structures.

Specific suggestions could concern the activities of large firms. The oligopoly model suggests that larger firms should use much more FDI. The resource-based model suggests that large MNEs can afford to use FDI more often, but that this structure will only be used under some conditions. Large firms with resources that require close management control and that must fit into a worldwide network will emphasize FDI, such as we might expect from IBM. Other firms, with more definable resource systems and less global interaction, such as McDonald's or Coca-Cola, might focus on franchising or supplier agreements in foreign markets.

High technology industries have been the focus of internalization models, with more FDI expected in high tech industries. The resource-based model suggests that researchers must look at the FSRs of individual MNEs to predict the relative usage of the various structural modes. Small, cutting-edge technology firms often use cooperative ventures, with a mixture of licensing and joint ownership, to exploit their knowledge resources in foreign markets in the absence of capital resources. In other cases, very high tech products can often be exported because host markets have no access to alternatives and because they often require the application of human capital (high skill workers) in the home market for adequate quality control. From this perspective, we might expect that FDI would be used more by large firms that require market position or service arrangements to offset relatively lower technology. For instance, we might expect IBM to use more FDI to extend its sales and service network, whereas smaller Cray, with its supercomputers, can access foreign markets with exports.

Recent empirical studies of foreign direct investment have tested new directions of investment flow against established concepts, and have found only limited support for hypotheses based on traditional internalization models (Caves & Mehra, 1986; Clegg, 1987; Lall & Siddharthan, 1982). The model presented here indicates that firm level resource bases and managerial decision processes must be studied if we are to understand the structural activities of MNEs. This provides a new direction for empirical investigation in international business studies using concepts and techniques from the strategic management field.

Conclusion: Strategic Management as an Inclusive Model

The extensive development of a strategic management perspective on how the MNE might make and evaluate its structural decision for one host market is intended to demonstrate a model that includes both strategic motivations and cost efficiency with a strong reliance on resource-based concepts. This model provides the complementarity of strategy and transaction costs that Kogut (1988) suggests. The common basic focus on specialized assets of the resource-based model of strategy and internalization models of the MNE indicates that an inclusive model is possible. The realities of idiosyncratic skills and differential worldwide structures among MNEs indicate that an inclusive model is essential.

Internalization models of the MNE have had success in supplanting oligopoly power models of FDI because they are more generally applicable. However, they have retained their reputation as tautological concepts (Buckley, 1988) because they have not provided a convincing motivation for the initial choice of entry and for changes in strategy. In addition, the reality of strategic motivations is too well established to ignore. The resource-based strategic management model provides a firm-specific model of strategy that is consistent with efficiency objectives, but is not dominated by cost concerns alone.

A resource-based strategy model of the MNE suggests that studies of international business operations may also have value for analyzing general resource-based models of strategy. These models have had difficulty in identifying the firm-specific sources of FSRs in a domestic market. A group of closely related firms that have interacted and imitated each other over a long period of time does not provide clearly delineated resource advantages to operationalize the reality of 'causal ambiguity' (Rumelt, 1984) on the firm level. Tests of these models on MNEs from different home countries as they interact in a host market, or as they begin to compete in global markets, may help to clarify sources of FSRs. If firms can be found to possess different FSRs due to unique home country experiences, the bases for strategic differences are easily identified. In addition, MNEs provide the opportunity to observe structural forms across geographical markets, in contrast to most strategy-structure studies that focus on product line strategies and strategic business unit structure. A new dimension of structural variation would add depth to studies of strategic fit. Finally, the 'chicken and egg' question of whether structure follows strategy or vice versa is uniquely addressed when host country entry is examined. Although under most circumstances, strategy and structure interact inextricably, the strategic decision to enter a particular host country must precede any structural form in that market. Although the initial strategy is derived from the larger parent firm resource structure, we can identify a specific start point for the strategy-structure circle in the narrow context of the host country market.

References

Bain, J.S. 1956. *Barriers to new competition.* Cambridge, MA: Harvard University Press.
Barney, J. 1986. Strategic factor markets: Expectations, luck, and business strategy. *Management Science*, October: 1231-1241.
Barney, J. 1991. Firm resources and sustained competitive advantage. *Journal of Management*, 17(1): 99-120.
Bartlett, C.A. & Ghoshal, S. 1989. *Managing across borders: the transnational solution.* Boston: Harvard Business School Press.
Borys, B., & Jemison, D.B. 1989. Hybrid arrangements as strategic alliances: theoretical issues in organizational combinations. *Academy of Management Review*, 14: 234-249.
Bower, J.L., & Doz, Y. 1979. Strategy formulation: A social and political process. In D. Schendel &

C.W. Hofer (Eds.) *Strategic management*: 152-166. Boston: Little, Brown.

Buckley, P.J. 1988. The limits of explanation: Testing the internalization theory of the multinational enterprise. *Journal of International Business Studies*, 19(2): 181-194.

Buckley, P.J., & Casson, M. 1976. *The future of the multinational enterprise*. London: Macmillan.

Calvet, A.L. 1981. A synthesis of foreign direct investment theories and theories of the multinational firm. *Journal of International Business Studies*. Spring/Summer: 43-59.

Casson, M. 1987. *The firm and the market*. Oxford: Basil Blackwell.

Caves, R.E. 1971. International corporations: The industrial economics of foreign investment. *Economica*, 38: 1-27.

Caves, R.E. & Mehra, S.K. 1986. Entry of foreign multinationals into U.S. manufacturing industries. In Michael E. Porter (Ed.), *Competition in global industries*: 449-482. Boston: Harvard Business School Press.

Caves, R.E., & Porter, M.E. 1977. From entry barriers to mobility barriers: conjectural decisions and contrived deterrence to new competition. *Quarterly Journal of Economics*: 241-261.

Chamberlin, E. 1933. *The theory of monopolistic competition*. Cambridge, MA: Harvard University Press.

Clegg, J. 1987. *Multinational enterprise and world competition*. New York: St. Martin's Press.

Coase, R.H. 1937. The nature of the firm. *Economica*, 4: 386-405.

Collis, D.J. 1991. A resource-based analysis of global competition: the case of the bearings industry. *Strategic Management Journal*, 12(SI): 49-68.

Conner, K.R. 1991 A historical comparison of resource-based theory and five schools of thought within industrial organization economics: do we have a new theory of the firm. *Journal of Management*, 17(1): 121-154.

Cool, K., & Schendel, D. 1987. Strategic group formation and performance: U.S. pharmaceutical industry, 1963-82. *Management Science*, 33: 1102-1124.

Cyert, R.M., & March, J.G. 1963. *A behavioral theory of the firm*. Englewood Cliffs, NJ: Prentice-Hall.

Dierickx, I., & Cool, K. 1989. Asset stock accumulation and sustainability of competitive advantage. *Management Science*, 35(12): 1504-1511.

DiMaggio, P.J., & Powell, W.W. 1983. The iron cage revisited: institutional isomorphism and collective rationality in organizational fields. *American Sociological Review*, 48(2): 147-160.

Dunning, J.H. 1981. *International production and the multinational enterprise*. London: George Allen and Unwin.

Dunning, J.H. 1988. The eclectic paradigm of international production: a restatement and some possible extensions. *Journal of International Business Studies*, 19(1): 1-32.

Gatignon, H., & Anderson, E. 1988. The multinational corporation's degree of control over foreign subsidiaries: an empirical test of a transaction cost explanation. *Journal of Law, Economics, and Organization*, 4(2): 305-336.

Ghoshal, S., & Nohria, N. 1989. Internal differentiation within multinational corporations. *Strategic Management Journal*, 10: 323-337.

Graham, E.M. 1974. *Oligopolistic imitation and european direct investment in the United States*. Unpublished Ph.D. dissertation, Harvard University.

Hannan, M.T., & Freeman, J. 1976. The population ecology of organizations. *American Sociological Review*, 49: 149-164.

Hedlund, G. 1986. The hypermodern MNC: A heterarchy? *Human Resource Management*, Spring: 9-35.

Hennart, J.F. 1982. *A theory of the multinational enterprise*. Ann Arbor: The University of Michigan Press.

Hennart, J.F. 1988. A transaction costs theory of equity joint ventures. *Strategic Management Journal*, 9: 361-374.

Hill, C.W., & Kim, W.C. 1988. Searching for a dynamic theory of the multinational enterprise: A transaction cost model. *Strategic Management Journal*, 9: 93-104.

Hymer, S.H. 1960. *The international operations of national firms: A study of direct foreign investment*. Unpublished Ph.D. dissertation, Massachusetts Institute of Technology.

Itami, H. 1987. *Mobilizing invisible assets*. Cambridge, MA: Harvard University Press.

Jones, G.R., & Hill, C.W.L. 1988. Transaction cost analysis of strategy-structure choice. *Strategic Management Journal*, 9: 159-172.

Kindleberger, C.P. 1969. *American business abroad: six lectures on direct investment.* New Haven: Yale University Press.

Knickerbocker, F.T. 1973. *Oligopolistic reaction and multinational enterprise.* Cambridge: Harvard Business School Division of Research.

Kogut, B. 1988. Joint ventures: theoretical and empirical perspectives. *Strategic Management Journal*, 9: 319-332.

Lall, S., & Siddharthan, N.S. 1982. The monopolistic advantages of multinationals: Lessons from foreign investment in the U. S. *The Economic Journal*, 92: 668-683.

Lippman, S.A., & Rumelt, R.P. 1982. Uncertain imitability: An analysis of interfirm differences in efficiency under competition. *The Bell Journal of Economics*: 418-438.

McClain, D. 1982. FDI in the U.S.: Old currents, "new waves," and the theory of direct investment. In C.P. Kindleberger & D.B. Andretsch (Eds.) *The multinational corporation in the 1980s*: 278-333. Cambridge, MA: MIT Press.

McManus, J. 1972. The theory of the international firm. In G. Paquet (Ed.) *The multinational firm and the nation state*: 66-93. Ontario, Canada: Collier-MacMillan.

Nelson, R.R., & Winter, S.G. 1982. *An evolutionary theory of economic change.* Cambridge, MA: Belknap Press of Harvard University Press.

Porter, M.E. 1979. The structure within industries and companies' performance. *Review of Economics and Statistics*, 61: 214-219.

Porter, M.E. 1980. *Competitive strategy.* New York: Free Press.

Porter, M.E. 1986. *Competition in global industries.* Boston: Harvard Business School Press.

Porter, M.E. 1990. *The competitive advantage of nations.* New York: Free Press.

Romanelli, E., & Tushman, M.L. 1986. Inertia, environments, and strategic choice: A quasi-experimental design for comparative-longitudinal research. *Management Science*, 32(5): 608-621.

Rugman, A. M. 1979. *International diversification and the multinational enterprise.* Lexington, MA: Lexington Books.

Rumelt, R.P. 1984. Towards a strategic theory of the firm. In R. B. Lamb (Ed.), *Competitive strategic management*: 556-570. Englewood Cliffs, NJ: Prentice-Hall.

Schumpeter, J.A. 1934. *The theory of economic development.* Cambridge, MA: Harvard University Press.

Simon, H. 1945. *Administrative behavior.* New York: The Free Press.

Sundaram, A.K. 1990. *Unique attributes of multinational enterprises: A top-down approach for research and pedagogy.* Paper presented at the Academy of International Business Conference.

Swedenborg, B. 1979. *The multinational operations of Swedish firms.* Stockholm: Almqvist and Wicksell.

Teece, D.J. 1981. The market for know-how and the efficient international transfer of technology. *The Annals of the American Academy of Political and Social Science*, 458 (November): 81-96.

Teece, D.J. 1983. Multinational enterprise, internal governance, and industrial organization. *American Economic Review*, 75: 233-238.

Teece, D.J. 1986. Transactions cost economics and the multinational enterprise. *Journal of Economic Behavior and Organization*, 7: 21-45.

Vernon, R. 1971. *Storm over the multinationals.* New York: Basic Books.

Wernerfelt, B. 1984. A resource-based view of the firm. *Strategic Management Journal*, 5: 171-180.

Williamson, O.E. 1975. *Markets and hierarchies.* New York: Free Press.

[9]

Developing Global Strategies for Service Businesses

Christopher H. Lovelock
George S. Yip

H ow do the distinctive characteristics of service businesses affect globalization and the use of global strategy? This is a crucial question for managers in numerous industries. Not only are services continuing to grow rapidly in domestic economies, but international trade in services is increasing, too. The United States, like some other developed countries, has a trade surplus in services that helps offset the deficit in merchandise trade. In contrast, Japan has been much less successful in internationalizing its service businesses.[1] So it is essential to national competitiveness that governments, as well as companies, achieve a better understanding of how to develop effective global strategies for different types of service businesses.

Most research to date has focused either on why and how service firms internationalize or on different modes of internationalization.[2] In contrast, we examine how globalization drivers and the use of global strategy might apply to various types of services, and what differences might exist relative to manufacturing businesses. In doing so, we combine two different frameworks, one developed to analyze global strategy[3] and one for service businesses.[4]

Overview

A major theme in international business is the increasing use of global strategies. These involve the worldwide integration of strategy formulation and implementation, in contrast to a multidomestic (or multilocal) approach that provides for independent development and implementation of strategies by country or regional units.[5] One key theme is that globalization potential depends on industry characteristics,[6] and on specific industry globalization drivers—

Developing Global Strategies for Service Businesses

market, cost, government, and competitive.[7] A second key theme is that the use of global strategy should differ by dimension of strategy and for different elements of the value-adding chain.[8] The linkage between industry globalization drivers and global strategy—as well as the relationship of these drivers to organization structure and management processes and to consequent effects on performance—have been empirically tested for manufacturing businesses in major American and Japanese multinational corporations (MNCs).[9] But research into global strategy for service businesses is still in an evolutionary stage.[10]

Defining Globalization

The terms "global" and "globalization" are often used rather loosely. Many writers use them interchangeably with words such as international (and internationalization), transnational,[11] and multinational. We believe that some clarification is in order. Strictly speaking, any service firm doing business across national frontiers can claim to be international. When passengers ride a scheduled bus line from Buffalo, New York, to Toronto, Ontario, they are using an international transportation service. A retail chain that operates in both the United Kingdom and Ireland can claim to be an international business. Moving up a notch, a bank with offices in several European countries could even claim to be multinational. None of these services, however, is global in scope. Nor, for that matter, is an insurance company doing business throughout Europe and North America.

In our view, a truly global company is one that not only does business in both the eastern and western hemispheres, but also in both the northern and southern ones. In the process, geographic distances and time zone variations are maximized. With the rise of non-Japan Asia, Latin America, and Eastern Europe, operating in just the 'Triad' of North America, Western Europe and Japan is no longer sufficient. Other differences also tend to be sharpened, such as the variety of languages, currencies, cultures, legal and political systems, government policies and regulations, educational backgrounds of managers and employees, levels of national economic development, and climates. In this article, we will emphasize companies that meet our criterion of being truly global, although not all our examples will do so. Furthermore, we shall stress that simply operating globally does not mean that a company possesses a global strategy.

Defining Service Businesses

We will examine the ways in which global strategy for service businesses, given their distinctive characteristics, should be significantly different from manufacturing businesses. Furthermore, a fundamental premise underlying our analysis is that not all services are the same. So we will use three "lenses" with which to examine the global strategies of service-based businesses:

- A set of characteristics by which service-based businesses differ from goods-based businesses.

- A categorization of three fundamental types of service businesses.
- A set of eight supplementary services surrounding the core product or offering.

An Overall Global Strategy Framework for Service Businesses

Our overall global strategy framework is illustrated in Figure 1. In this framework, industry globalization drivers give rise to industry globalization potential, but this effect is filtered by the special characteristics of service businesses. In turn, industry globalization potential should result in four types of global strategy response: in terms of market participation, the service offering, the location and configuration of the value-adding chain, and in the nature of the marketing strategy. Here, the global strategy response is filtered by the three distinct types of service businesses. Lastly, supplementary services, which augment the core product like petals around the center of a flower, play a direct role in the make up of each aspect of global strategy.

Understanding the Nature of Services

"Services versus Goods" Distinctions

Early research into services sought to differentiate them from goods, focusing particularly on four generic differences—intangibility, heterogeneity (variability), perishability of output, and simultaneity of production and consumption.[12] Although these characteristics are still commonly cited, they have been criticized as too generic,[13] and there is growing recognition that they are not universally applicable to all services. A better sense of the processes underlying service delivery is provided in an alternative set of eight characteristics.[14] These characteristics begin with the nature of the output—a performance rather than an object—and also include customer involvement in production, people as part of the service experience, greater likelihood of quality control problems, harder for customers to evaluate, lack of inventories for services, greater importance of the time factor, and availability of electronic channels of distribution. Although these characteristics provide a useful starting point for thinking about the distinctive aspects of service management, not every service is equally affected by all of them.

Three Categories of Services

The previous list helps distinguish service-based businesses from goods-based ones. But service businesses also differ from each other. All products—both goods and services—consist of a core element that is surrounded by a variety of sometimes optional supplementary elements. Whether one is looking at service strategy locally or globally, it is unwise to talk in broad brush terms about the service sector or service industries as though all organizations faced more or less the same strategic problems. At the same time, it is also a mistake

Developing Global Strategies for Service Businesses

FIGURE I. Globalization Framework for Service Businesses

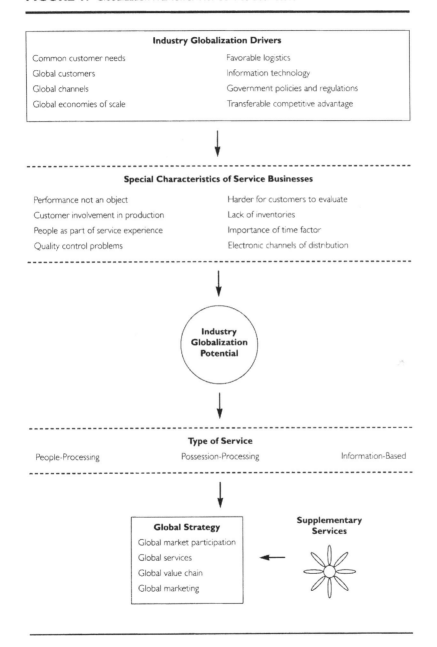

CALIFORNIA MANAGEMENT REVIEW   VOL. 38, NO. 2   WINTER 1996   67

to fall into the trap of examining services only on an industry-by-industry basis. Probably the most useful and relevant classification concerns differences and commonalities in operational processes, since the way in which inputs are transformed into outputs has a significant effect on strategy.[15]

By looking at core services from an operational perspective, we can assign them to one of three broad categories, depending on the nature of the process (whether it is primarily tangible or intangible) and the extent to which customers need to be physically present during service production.

People-processing services involve tangible actions to customers in person. These services require that customers themselves become part of the production process, which tends to be simultaneous with consumption. In businesses such as passenger transportation, health care, food service, and lodging services, the customer needs to enter the "service factory" (although we know it by such names as an airliner and air terminal, a hospital, a restaurant, or a hotel) and remain there during service delivery. Either customers must travel to the factory or service providers and equipment must come to the customer. In both instances, the firm needs to maintain a local geographic presence, stationing the necessary personnel, buildings, equipment, vehicles, and supplies within reach of target customers. If the customers are themselves mobile—as in the case of business travelers and tourists—then they may patronize a company's offerings in many different locations and make comparisons between them.

Possession-processing services involve tangible actions to physical objects to improve their value to customers. Examples include freight transport, warehousing, equipment installation and maintenance, car repair, laundry, and disposal. The object needs to be involved in the production process, but the customer does not, since consumption of the output tends to follow production. Again, the service "factory" may be fixed or mobile. A local geographic presence is required when the supplier needs to provide service to physical objects in a specific location on a repeated basis. In the case of smaller, transportable items, the vendor can provide remote service centers for servicing—although transportation costs, customs duties, and government regulations may constrain shipment across large distances or national frontiers. Modern technology now allows a few service processes to be administered from a distance, using electronic diagnostics to pinpoint the problem.

Information-based services are, perhaps, the most interesting category from the standpoint of global strategy development because they depend on collecting, manipulating, interpreting, and transmitting data to create value. Examples include accounting, banking, consulting, education, insurance, legal services, and news. Customer involvement in production of such services is often minimal. The advent of modern global telecommunications, linking intelligent machines to powerful databases, makes it possible to use electronic channels to deliver information-based services from a single "hub" to almost any location. Local presence requirements may be limited to a terminal—ranging from a telephone or fax machine to a computer or more specialized equipment like a bank

Developing Global Strategies for Service Businesses

ATM—connected to a reliable telecommunications infrastructure. If the latter is inadequate, then use of mobile or satellite communications may solve the problem in some instances.

Service production and delivery systems can be divided into "back office" and "front office," the latter being the portion of the "service factory" encountered by customers.[16] People-processing services necessarily involve a high degree of contact with service personnel and facilities; possession-processing and information-based services, by contrast, have the potential to be much lower contact in nature. Retail banking, for instance, can take place either through traditional branch banks or through such channels as mail, telephone, and Internet.

The Role of Supplementary Services

The core service product—a bed for the night, restoring a defective computer to good working order, or a bank account—is typically accompanied by a variety of supplementary elements. Most businesses, whether they are classified in government statistics as manufacturing or service, offer their customers a package that includes a variety of service-related activities, too. Increasingly, these supplementary elements not only add value, but also provide the differentiation that separates successful firms from the also-rans; they also offer opportunities for firms to develop effective globalization strategies. Writers and managers alike often use the terms "augmented product,"[17] "extended product," or "product package" to describe the supplementary elements that add value to the core product.[18]

There are potentially dozens of different supplementary services, although they can be grouped into eight categories (information, consultation, order-taking, hospitality, caretaking, exceptions, billing, and payment) encircling the core product like a corona of petals: collectively, they comprise "the flower of service" (Figure 2 and Table 1).[19] Many of these petals are based on informational processes that can be located in one part of the world and delivered electronically to another. Not every core product—whether a good or a service—is surrounded by supplementary elements from all eight clusters. In practice, the nature of the product, customer requirements, and competitive practices help managers to determine which supplementary service must be offered and which might usefully be added to enhance value and make it easy to do business with the organization.

One determinant of what supplementary services to include is the market positioning strategy that management has selected. A strategy of adding benefits to gain a competitive edge will probably require more supplementary services (and also a higher level of performance on all such elements). In developing a global strategy, management must decide which, if any, supplementary elements should be consistent across all markets and which might be tailored to meet local needs, expectations, and competitive dynamics. This is the essence of standardization and customization, but services offer much more flexibility in this respect

Developing Global Strategies for Service Businesses

FIGURE 2. Supplementary Services Surrounding the Core Product

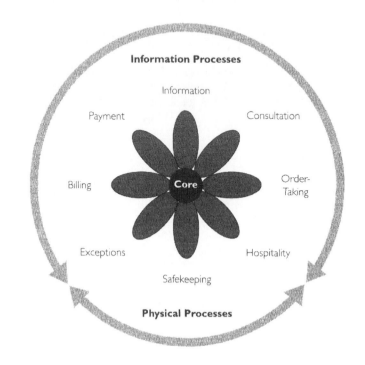

than do physical goods, lending themselves in many contexts to what is known as "mass customization."[20]

Industry Globalization Drivers

What drives globalization of service businesses? Many types of drivers have been suggested for the analysis of manufacturing firms.[21] We identify here the eight most relevant ones (listed in Figure 1) for service businesses, then systematically evaluate how the characteristics of different types of services might strengthen or weaken the effects of these drivers. We will also examine how these effects differ among the three categories of service business—people-processing, possession-processing, and information-based services.

Developing Global Strategies for Service Businesses

TABLE I. Eight Categories of Supplementary Services

Information

To obtain full value from any good or service, customers need relevant information about it, ranging from schedules to operating instructions, and from user warnings to prices. Globalization affects the nature of that information (including the languages and format in which it is provided). New customers and prospects are especially information hungry and may need training in how to use an unfamiliar service.

Consultation and Advice

Consultation and advice involve a dialogue to probe customer requirements and then develop a tailored solution. Customers' need for advice may vary widely around the world, reflecting such factors as level of economic development, nature of the local infrastructure, topography and climate, technical standards, and educational levels.

Order-Taking

Once customers are ready to buy, suppliers need to make it easy for them to place orders or reservations in the language of their choice, through telecommunications and other channels, at times and in locations that are convenient to them.

Hospitality: Taking Care of the Customer

Well-managed businesses try, at least in small ways, to treat customers as guests when they have to visit the supplier's facilities (especially when, as is true for many people-processing operations, the period extends over several hours or more). Cultural definitions of appropriate hospitality may differ widely from one country to another, such as the tolerable length of waiting time (much longer in Brazil than in Germany) and the degree of personal service expected (not much in Scandinavia but lavish in Indonesia).

Safekeeping: Looking After the Customer's Possessions

When visiting a service site, customers often want assistance with their personal possessions, ranging form car parking to packaging and delivery of new purchases. Expectations may vary by country, reflecting culture and levels of affluence.

Exceptions

Exceptions fall outside the routine of normal service delivery. They include special requests, problem solving, handling of complaints/suggestions/ compliments, and restitution (compensating customers for performance failures). Special requests are particularly common in people-processing services, as in the travel and lodging industries and may be complicated by differing cultural norms. International airlines, for example, find it necessary to respond to an array of medical and dietary needs, sometimes reflecting religious and cultural values. Problem solving is often more difficult for people who are traveling overseas than it would be in the familiar environment of their native country.

Billing

Customers need clear, timely bills that explain how charges are computed. With abolition of currency exchange restrictions in many countries, bills can be converted to the customer's home currency. Hence, currencies and conversion rates need to be clarified on billing statements. In some instances, prices may be displayed in several currencies, even though this policy may require frequent adjustments in the light of currency fluctuations.

Payment

Ease and convenience of payment (including credit) are increasingly expected by customers when purchasing a broad array of services. Major credit cards and travelers' checks solve the problem of paying in foreign funds for many retail purchases, but corporate purchasers may prefer to use electronic fund transfers in the currency of their choice.

Developing Global Strategies for Service Businesses

Common Customer Needs

Industries with customer needs and tastes that are common across countries offer more potential for globalization. Product categories such as consumer electronic devices, cigarettes, soft drinks, and computer hardware provide many instances of successful global standardization. (The simultaneous presence of successful local strategies in these categories in no way undermines the global opportunity for multinational companies. Similarly, less than total standardization, as in Coca-Cola's local adaptation of its syrup, does not void the benefits of pursuing global standardization as much possible in the appropriate industries and categories.) The service characteristic of "customer involvement in production" reduces the degree to which many services can be standardized and still meet the needs of a broad cross section of customers around the world. In general, the less the involvement, whether physical or psychological, the better the opportunity for a global approach. So we are more likely to see global standardization in fast food and airlines, where customer involvement is tightly controlled, than in medical care or education, where customer involvement is both stronger and more prolonged. Note that our observations apply to the broad "middle market" rather than to the relatively small market segment composed of affluent, highly educated, cosmopolitan customers.

The service characteristic of "people as part of the service experience" also limits the potential commonality of customer needs and tastes. Differences can arise even within the same industry. In banking, the service provided by human tellers is far less standardized and standardizable than that provided by automated teller machines. Accounting services depend heavily on people. The higher status of accountants in Britain than in the United States means that British accountants provide more general business advice than do their American counterparts. And U.S.-style psychotherapy is unlikely to yield a global "McShrink" franchise.

One of the greatest dilemmas in global strategy for manufacturing businesses is the need to balance global standardization with local customization. Designing, then manufacturing, a global product with a degree of local customization requires major tradeoffs. In contrast, the nature of service delivery—at the point of consumption in many cases—makes both standardization and customization equally feasible. Local elements (e.g., Balinese dancing in Indonesia) can be easily added to a global formula (Club Med vacations); using local nationals as service providers may overcome the foreignness of a standardized service (e.g., use of local cabin crews by international airlines). The practice of augmenting a core service with many supplementary elements makes it relatively easy to provide a globally standardized core service augmented (and differentiated) by nationally customized supplementary service elements. This tends to be easier than for manufacturing businesses.[22]

Developing Global Strategies for Service Businesses

Global Customers

As large corporate customers become global, they often seek to standard-ize and simplify the array of services they consume. For instance, firms may seek to minimize the number of auditors they use around the world, using "Big Six" accounting firms that can apply a consistent worldwide approach (within the context of national rules within each country of operation). Global management of telecommunications is provided by the "Concert" service offered by British Telecom and its American partner MCI, allowing a multinational company to outsource all responsibility for management of its purchase and use of telecom-munications. Corporate banking, insurance, business logistics, and management consulting are further examples. Individuals act as global customers when they purchase goods and services on their travels. The service characteristics of "a performance rather than an object" and "greater importance of the time factor" create special opportunities for travel-related services, a very large and growing segment that starts with transportation but extends to credit, communication, and emergency support.

Global customers for possession-processing services prefer common pro-cedures and standards. For example, airlines absolutely depend on their aircraft being maintained in the same way everywhere—and, increasingly, so do cus-tomers of factory and machinery maintenance services. Global customers for people-processing services may care particularly about ubiquity, especially when traveling. The New Zealander who breaks her leg in Pamplona needs medical treatment on the spot. Global customers for information-based services may have a more diffuse set of needs, but these certainly include comprehensiveness, accuracy, and accessibility. The American executive who has lost his traveler's checks in Shanghai needs reimbursement there, now, not back home in Indiana, later.

Global Channels

Distributors of physical goods have globalized relatively slowly. Few dis-tributors in any category have adequate worldwide coverage. National giants like Wal-Mart and Toys R Us from the United States, Carrefour and IKEA from Europe, and Watson's and Dairy Farm from Asia, are beginning to establish regional networks, but all are far from being able to distribute worldwide. In contrast, the "availability of electronic channels of distribution" for services pro-vides nearly total global coverage for more and more service offerings—notably travel services, banking, customer support services, entertainment, and most forms of information products themselves. Furthermore, these electronic global channels support not just information-based services but augment people-pro-cessing (e.g., health care) and possession-processing (e.g., delivery of time-sensi-tive materials) services. The latest electronic channel, the World Wide Web, now offers global outreach to even the smallest of companies. The Web can help sell any type of core product through information-based supplementary services and can actually deliver many information-based services directly to customers.

Developing Global Strategies for Service Businesses

Global Economies of Scale

Global scale economies apply when single-country markets are not large enough to allow competitors to achieve optimum scale. Scale can then be increased through participation in multiple markets, combined with product standardization and/or concentration of selected value activities. But "lack of inventories," "customer involvement in production," and "people as part of the service experience" all work against being able to concentrate production to achieve scale. So service companies typically have to find global scale economies by standardizing production processes rather than through physical concentration, as well as by concentrating the upstream, rather than the downstream, stages of the value chain.

The effect of cost globalization drivers, like global scale economies, varies sharply according to the level of fixed costs required to enter an industry (although equipment leasing schemes, or awarding franchises to local investors, provide a way to minimize such entry barriers). So cost globalization drivers may be less favorable for services that are primarily people-based and face lesser scale economies and flatter experience curves. One common solution for the would-be global company is to do as McDonald's does—substitute equipment for labor in order to achieve lower costs and better performance than local companies using traditional business systems.

Favorable Logistics

Low transportation costs allow concentration of production for physical goods. For services, "customer involvement in production" raises the logistical stakes in globalization. In most people-processing services, the need for convenience prevents concentration. But in some possession-processing services, customers are willing to transport their possessions to another location for better service. Thus, many airlines bring their aircraft to Singapore. Some people-processing services have achieved similar success in having customers come to them. London hospitals maintain a flourishing business among wealthy Middle Eastern patients, as do Miami hospitals for patients from Latin America.

Companies have to balance the tradeoffs between logistics and appeal. Disney favored logistics over appeal in selecting northern France rather than southern Spain for the location of Euro Disney. More people can get more easily to the Euro Disney site outside Paris, but once there they often face cold weather and colder service. Service businesses can also create their own favorable logistics. Club Med organizes charter flights from urban centers to its off-the-beaten-path locations. British Airways and Air France provide limousine ground transport to and from their Concorde flights.

Lastly, logistics is seldom a barrier to globalization for information-based services. Using electronic channels to deliver such services allows providers to concentrate production in locations that have specific expertise and to offer cost savings or other meaningful advantages. For instance, banks in the Cayman

Developing Global Strategies for Service Businesses

Islands are not conveniently located from a purely geographic standpoint, but money can be shipped there electronically to take advantage of the tax benefits conferred by offshore funds status.

Information Technology

For information-based services, the growing availability of broad-band telecommunication channels, capable of moving vast amounts of data at great speed, is playing a major role in opening up new markets. Access to the Internet or World Wide Web is accelerating around the world. But there may be no need to duplicate all informational elements in each new location. Significant economies may be gained by centralizing "information hubs" on a global basis, as Federal Express does in Memphis. For all three types of services, the use of information technology may allow companies to benefit from favorable labor costs or exchange rates by consolidating operations of supplementary services (such as reservations) or back office functions (such as accounting) in just one or a few countries. While a globalization driver in its own right, information technology also interacts with all of the other drivers.

Government Policies and Regulations

Host governments affect globalization potential through import tariffs and quotas, non-tariff barriers, export subsidies, local content requirements, currency and capital flow restrictions, technical and other standards, ownership restrictions and requirements on technology transfer. Governments' exercise of these policies and regulations can make it difficult for companies to globalize. For services, "customer involvement in production" may mitigate many government barriers to global strategy. Government drivers are often favorable for people-processing and possession-processing services that require a significant local presence, since they create local employment opportunities. On the other hand, governments often impose regulations to protect home carriers in the case of mobile services, such as passenger and freight transportation. For instance, restricting foreign airlines' landing rights or ability to pick up passengers at an intermediate stop ("third freedom" rights) provides a way to protect home-based airlines on international routes.

Nations may perceive both an economic and a cultural threat in unrestricted imports of information-based services through electronic channels. Government regulations range from controls on international banking to bans on private ownership of satellite dishes (as in countries such as China, Singapore, and Saudi Arabia). Some nations are now trying to manage citizen access to the Worldwide Web.

For people-processing services, government barriers to global strategy include country differences in social policies (e.g., health) affecting labor costs, the role of women in front line jobs, and the hours or days on which work can be performed. For possession-processing services, tax laws, environmental regulations, and technical standards may decrease/increase costs and encourage/discourage certain types of activity. For information-based services, special policies on education, censorship, public ownership of communications, and infrastructure quality may apply; technical standards may vary; and government policies may distort pricing.

Transferable Competitive Advantage

The single most important competitive globalization driver arises from transferability of competitive advantage. If one industry participant can leverage its competitive position in one country to build an advantage in other countries, all its competitors need to develop a global strategy too.[23] For services, "customer involvement in production," and "lack of inventories" limit the leverage of competitive advantage based on foreign factors of production such as labor productivity (e.g., no "Toyota" exports), although advantage in management systems can be a basis for globalization (e.g., Hilton). So Hong Kong hotel chains, such as Mandarin, Peninsula and Regent, that have set world class standards for service, find such excellence far harder to reproduce as they expand overseas. Similarly, Disney has suffered from not been able to transfer to Paris Disneyland the highly motivated and pliant staff of its U.S. parks.

Overall Assessment of Drivers

As we look at the three categories of services identified earlier, it seems that most industry globalization drivers do apply to services, but their impact varies by service type and even by industry. For example, government drivers (expressed in terms of economic policy, regulation, and protectionism) are often industry specific (as evidenced by the recent Uruguay Round of negotiations on GATT and bilateral British-American negotiations on commercial air travel). This conclusion highlights the importance of conducting a systematic evaluation of globalization drivers for individual industries, rather than taking generalized views that service businesses can be more (or less) easily globalized than can manufacturing businesses.

Service Effects In Global Strategy

To complete our analysis, we now present a more detailed view of how each dimension of global strategy might differ for service businesses. We use four dimensions ("global strategy levers") that determine whether international strategy is more multilocal or more global.[24] The global end of each dimension consists of the following:

- *Global Market Participation*—countries are selected not just on the basis of stand-alone attractiveness, but also in terms of their potential contribution to globalization benefits.

- *Global Products and Services*—a standardized core product or service that requires a minimum of local adaptation.

Developing Global Strategies for Service Businesses

- *Global Location of Value-Adding Activities*—the value chain is broken up; each activity may be conducted in a different country, rather than many activities being duplicated around the world.
- *Global Marketing*—a uniform marketing approach is applied around the world, although not all elements of the marketing mix need be identical.

Services and Global Market Participation

A global strategy approach to market participation involves building significant share in globally strategic markets. Such countries are important beyond their stand-alone attractiveness and may be a source of volume to meet economies of scale, the home or significant market of global customers or global competitors, or a major source of industry innovation. Failure to participate in strategic markets can undermine global competitiveness. Many American and European manufacturing companies have suffered from not building significant positions in Japan, thereby limiting their potential economies of scale in manufacturing, lacking exposure to the innovation and high customer standards in Japan, and being unable to create a hostage for good behavior on the part of Japanese rivals.

A few Western service companies have built successful businesses in Japan, either because their Western orientation (such as American-style fast food) appealed to Japanese consumers or because they were creating an international network that could not afford to be absent from such a major market. For network firms, such as airlines, financial services, and logistics firms, highly specific geographic locations may be seen as essential. No financial service firm with global ambitions, for instance, can afford not to have a presence in New York, London, and Tokyo. With the exception of such network organizations, it is hard to see how presence or absence in Japan (or any other individual country) significantly affects a service firm's global strategic position, other than contributing revenues and profits.

Travel-related services pose an exception. Inherently, wider global market participation makes a brand of service more valuable to a customer. Thus, American Express traveler's checks and credit cards are useful precisely because they are widely accepted in most countries. Similarly, international airlines enhance their appeal as they fly to more destinations.

Designing and Delivering Globally Standardized Services

Globally standardized products or "global products" are, perhaps, the one feature most commonly identified with global strategy. As mentioned earlier, the fact that services comprise a bundle of core and supplementary services makes them particularly easy to both globalize and localize. In perhaps the most extreme example, McDonald's now plans to open restaurants in India that, in deference to Hindu reverence for cows, will not serve hamburgers at all. Were McDonald's a goods-based business, that would be equivalent to selling a car

without an engine. But as a service-based business, the other core and supplementary elements can make up for the lack of beef. McDonald's also adds items,
such as Veggie Burgers, to menus to meet local tastes. In Britain, McDonald's
includes both tea and coffee in its menus, while in France and Germany it also
serves beer. Interestingly, these local variations are in the food itself, the product
element, rather than in the service elements.

Hewlett-Packard is a global leader in computer-based customer support
services for its customers. It maintains a globally standardized set of services that
range from site design to systems integration and remote diagnostics. This global
standardization includes seamless service at any hour of the day or night from
anywhere in the world.

Professional service firms vary in their ability to provide a globally
standardized service. Some firms, such as those in the accounting industry, face
significant international differences in technical standards, making uniformity
more difficult. But it is also a matter of strategy. Arthur Andersen has chosen to
lead in offering globally standardized services. Its competitors now have to play
catch-up. Similarly, advertising agencies face international differences in culture
and consumer behavior, but some have chosen to overcome these differences.

Global Location of Value-Adding Service Activities

Where to locate a business's activities and how to coordinate them constitute critical choices in global strategy. Every functional or value-adding activity—from research to manufacturing to customer service—is a candidate for
globalization.[25] Traditionally, multinational companies (MNCs) have faced two
choices in activity location. The classic MNC strategy has been to reproduce
activities in many countries. Alternatively, an MNC can concentrate activities
in its home country.

The trend in global strategy is to concentrate each activity as much
as possible, although not necessarily all activities in the same country.[26] As discussed earlier, many service businesses need local presence for their downstream
activities. But at the same time, they can take advantage of differences in
national comparative advantage to build more efficient and effective value
chains. Some service-based businesses conduct key activities that can be conducted in a different country from their customers. For example, some U.S.
banks and insurance companies now send checks and claims to be processed in
East Asia or in Ireland. McKinsey & Company, the management consulting firm,
now sends some of its work for clients from high-cost countries to its offices in
low-cost countries like India.

To provide its global customer support service, Hewlett-Packard maintains
a global chain of activity locations—its more than 30 Response Centers around
the world are integrated into a global network headed by four major centers:
Bracknell (United Kingdom), Atlanta (Georgia) and Mountain View (California)
in the United States, and Melbourne (Australia). Each center is staffed during

extended daytime hours, seven days a week, by between 12 and 200 engineers. Problems that cannot be resolved in a smaller center may be transferred to one of the major centers. Because of time-zone differentials, at least one of the major centers is always in full operation at any time.

Citibank, one of the world's largest banks, has positioned itself as a "uniquely global consumer bank."[27] The company's objective is to allow its customers to do their banking "any way, any where, any time." To provide this service it has expanded its Citicard Banking Centers with their automated teller machines to 28 countries. These centers are globally linked, allowing 24 hour, seven days a week access. And, of course, non-cash transactions can be conducted by phone.

Global Marketing of Services

A worldwide business uses global marketing when it takes the same or similar approach or content for one or more elements of the marketing mix, i.e., the same or similar brand names, advertising, and other marketing elements in different countries. The uncertainty engendered by intangibility requires strong branding to offset it. So the primary task of the brand name or trademark for a service is to offer recognition and reassurance, rather than performing other functions such as positioning or local adaptation. McDonald's, for instance, has to be the same name around the world, so that both locals and travelers know that they will get the genuine McDonald's experience. (We doubt, however, that the Spago and Planet Saigon restaurants in Ho Chi Minh City will provide the same experiences as the Hollywood originals after which they are named.) Travel-related services virtually require the same brand name globally. What use would an American Express card be if the brand were Russian Express in Moscow? One solution is to be both global and local. Federal Express combines global and local brand names. In France the company uses partly localized names like FedEx Priorité, FedEx Rapide, and FedEx Fret.

Global positioning is also important. McDonald's has a globally consistent positioning and image, but this is not a globally neutral image. It is clearly American, so it stands for "us" in the United States, and "them" elsewhere. Similarly, Chili's, a U.S.-based restaurant chain offering Mexican food, has its largest store in Monterrey, Mexico. But customers there go for an "American experience," not a Mexican one. In contrast, Benetton, both a goods-based (clothes) and a service-based (stores) company, strives for a universalistic, non-national image.

Global advertising works equally for goods-based and service-based businesses. Whether to use it depends on such industry globalization drivers as common customer needs and the salience of global customers or global channels. Travel-related services can obviously benefit from global advertising, although the communications task may vary by country. A solution is the dual campaign, one for global themes and one for local messages. For many years, British Airways has used a succession of dramatic global advertising campaigns to establish its position as "The World's Favourite Airline" (backed up by significant improvements in service quality since privatization). At the same time, British Airways provides a smaller budget for local campaigns that focus on schedules, prices, and promotion of special tour packages. Singapore Airlines has achieved significant advertising impact with its temporally and globally consistent theme of the "Singapore Girl," a highly successful way of personalizing and differentiating a commodity service.

While most services are not physically packaged, staff uniforms and the layout and decor of facilities can be considered part of the package. Global consistency can bring significant benefits. Singapore Airlines has maintained the same uniform for its stewardesses for over 25 years. The "sarong kebaya," designed by Paris couturier, Pierre Balmain, makes the Singapore Airlines stewardess globally recognizable, unlike those of most other airlines. And like McDonald's, Citibank designs its new retail branches to look and operate in the same way around the world.

In contrast, "lack of inventories" in many service businesses means that such firms need worry less about using global pricing. Manufacturing businesses increasingly need to charge globally uniform prices to provide consistency with global customers and distribution channels, and to avoid "gray market" parallel importation or "trans-shipment." It is relatively difficult to buy a service in one country and to re-sell it in another.

McDonald's prices certainly vary, so much so that *The Economist* magazine uses a "McDonald's Big Mac Price Index" to compare the cost of living in major business cities around the world. In the case of multinational customers as opposed to individuals, however, even service businesses need to avoid charging different prices in different countries to the same customer without good justification. Increasingly, multinational companies are beginning to behave as global rather than multilocal customers. Hewlett-Packard, for example, now provides worldwide contracts to its major global accounts for both products and services.

Implications for Types of Service Businesses

While there are always exceptions, some overall conclusions can be made about the three types of service business and how easily they can use each of the four dimensions of global strategy.

Global Market Participation

Some types of service business seem very easy to spread around the world, and others very difficult. In the easy category fall simple service concepts that are easily replicable (and therefore franchisable). All three types of services have such simple examples (e.g., fast food in the people processing category, package delivery in the possession-processing category, and English-language news in the information-based category). In contrast, some "essential" services—such as banking, telecommunications, hospitals, and airlines—operate in heavily regulated environments, making it difficult to get rapid penetration of foreign markets.

Historically, businesses that rely on trust and the reputation of their personnel—such as law firms and other professional service providers—have found it difficult to demonstrate quality to potential foreign customers and to adopt a professional style that fits the local culture. Ways to overcome such hurdles include extensive advertising and public relations as well as hiring host country nationals who have obtained education and work experience in other countries.

Globally Standardized Service

Possession-processing businesses can probably provide the most globally standardized offerings. These services need not cope with cultural and taste differences, only with those technical specifications that vary geographically, such as differences in electrical voltages or measurement systems . For people-processing services some deviation from standardization is almost always needed. For information-based services, such deviation will vary widely, from none at all (e.g., information on international flight schedules) to near total (e.g., local weather forecasts or tax advice).

Global Location of Value Chain

By their "virtual" nature, most information-based services should find it the easiest to locate globally. In many cases, such as pure information services, no local physical presence may be needed at all. In other cases, information services that also have a physical component (e.g., the provision of currency or traveler's checks) or require specialized delivery equipment (e.g., pay-per-view entertainment) will need some local physical presence, provided by the company itself or by local partners. The ease of global value chain location for people-processing and possession-processing services will depend on the extent of local presence needed. In general, more local sites will be needed for people-processing, making that type of service probably the most difficult to operate globally.

Globally Uniform Marketing

All three types of services should be able to make use of globally uniform marketing, although the extent will differ for each element of the marketing mix. Uniform pricing will be least possible for people-processing services, given the wide international variations in both costs and per capita income. Conversely, people-processing services probably have the most to gain from uniform branding as a way to build recognition with both local and foreign (visiting) customers. Possession-processing services often attract multinational customers (e.g., aircraft maintenance and package delivery), making it necessary to coordinate global marketing strategy and offer uniform terms of service.

Discussion: Implications for Theory and Practice

What are the implications of our framework for both theory building and management practice? A key point is that making broad generalizations about "services" cannot be expected to provide useful insights into opportunities for globalization. Instead, researchers and managers alike have to understand the components of a service and the processes by which its different elements are created and delivered. First, they need to distinguish between the core product (which may be either a service or a physical object) and supplementary service elements. Second, they must recognize that there are three broad categories of core product, reflecting differences in the underlying processes, degree of customer involvement, and potential for delivery through electronic channels. Third, the Flower of Service model offers both researchers and practitioners a means of understanding and disaggregating the package of "supplementary services" that augments and adds value to the core product.

Locating the Service Facility

In the future, we shall see a greater distinction between services that require an on-site "factory" in each country and those that require only a delivery system. By definition, all people-processing services that do not require customers to travel outside their home country for service delivery will require on-site operations in each country. The same will be true of any possession-processing service that cannot readily transport the object in question to another location for servicing. In these instances, managers may find that the best way to achieve global consistency in the core product is to create easily replicable service concepts, backed by clear standards, that allow for either franchises or country managers to clone the original core product in a new setting.

Information-based services offer management greater flexibility to split the back office and front office, with opportunities to centralize the former on a global or regional basis. Production can thus take place in one location (or just a few), yielding economies of scale and access to global expertise, while delivery remains local. Banking, insurance, and other financial service products lend themselves well to delivery through electronic channels. Many forms of news, information, and entertainment can also be delivered worldwide through public or private networks. Key issues in globalization include the constraints imposed by language, culture, and government regulations.

Customizing Global Services through Supplementary Service Elements

Increasingly, core service products that are sold globally are more likely to be standardized than customized (McDonald's Veggie Burgers should be seen as an exception rather than a trend). Managers should, however, be looking for supplementary service elements that can be customized in ways that tailor the overall service package to meet local requirements. Each of the eight petals in the Flower of Service lends itself to adaptation on three dimensions: the level of service provided can be adapted to reflect local preferences and ability to pay; the style of delivery can be adapted to cultural norms; and information transfers can be adapted to local idioms and offered in local languages.

Global Location of Value Chain

Different service elements can be sourced from different locations. The physical supplies needed for certain types of service delivery (such as food for hotels, fuel for transport vehicles, or spare parts for repair jobs) are often shipped from one country for consumption in another. The same is sometimes true for imported labor. But some companies, like McDonald's, are choosing to build up a network of local suppliers and to train host country nationals for local jobs as quickly as possible.[28]

As noted earlier, information-based services can be produced in one part of the world and delivered through electronic channels for consumption elsewhere. Indeed, information technology is emerging as a key globalization driver for such services. In mutual funds, for instance, offerings are now being pieced together from elements created in many different countries. Unlike physical goods, the logistics of service "assembly" and delivery tend to be much simpler once the necessary infrastructure and network are in place. Further, as shown in Table 1 earlier, a majority of the petals of the Flower of Service are information-dependent and can potentially be delivered from remote locations. In theory, a global company could centralize its billing on a global basis, using postal or telecommunication distribution channels to deliver the bills to customers, suitably converted to the relevant currency.

Similarly, information, consultation, order-taking/reservations, and many aspects of problem solving and payment could all be handled through telecommunications channels, ranging from voice telephone to the World Wide Web. So long as service personnel speaking the appropriate languages are available, many such service elements could be delivered from almost anywhere. Recent patterns of immigration in a country may create a comparative advantage in multilingual capabilities. By contrast, hospitality and safekeeping will always have to be provided locally because they are responsive to the physical presence of customers and their possessions.

Like manufacturers, service firms should be looking for opportunities to exploit differences in national comparative advantages as they seek to build more efficient value chains. Significant economies may be gained by centralizing "information hubs" on a global basis, as Federal Express does in Memphis. Through outsourcing, firms can also reduce the need for large fixed cost investments. Taking advantage of favorable labor costs and exchange rates, a growing number of service-based businesses have identified key back-office activities that can be conducted more cheaply but without loss of quality in a different country from where their customers are located. This is happening with front-office elements, too, as companies build global reservation and customer service systems that are networked around the world.

Global Marketing of Services

Difficulties in evaluating services lead to uncertainty, but this problem can be offset by strong branding and a globally consistent use of corporate design elements. Hence, the primary task of the brand name or trademark for a service may be to offer recognition and reassurance, rather than performing other functions such as positioning or local adaptation. Global branding should be supported by global advertising and globally-consistent corporate design, featuring recognizable color schemes (yellow for Hertz, bright green for BP service stations), an easily identified logo and trademark, and even consistency in retail office design. One of the challenges when creating global campaigns is to create visual themes that will travel well across different cultures (it is relatively simple to add voice-overs in the local language). This requirement may pose a need to retain a global advertising agency.

In contrast, simultaneity of production and consumption in many service businesses means that firms have less need to worry about globally consistent pricing. Except for those information-based services that can be captured in printed or electronic hard copies, it is still relatively difficult to buy a service created in one country for resale in another. On the other hand, there are sometimes wide disparities between prices for international telephone calls, depending on the country in which it originates. For instance, a call from Rome to New York is far more expensive than from New York to Rome. (This anomaly has been exploited by companies such as AT&T, which offers customers traveling abroad the opportunity to dial a local number to place the call and charge it at American rates to the customer's home account.) In the case of multinational customers, service businesses need to consider the use of global account management as a means of achieving coordination and consistency.[29]

Conclusion

More and more service businesses are now operating across national borders. Globalization and global strategy concepts developed for manufacturing businesses can also be applied to service businesses. Some significant differences may exist, particularly among people-processing, possession-processing and information-based services. Companies can develop effective global strategies by systematically analyzing the specific globalization drivers affecting their industries and the distinctive characteristics of their service businesses.

Notes

1. Johny K. Johansson, "Japanese Service Industries and their Overseas Potential," *The Service Industries Journal*, 10/1 (January 1990): 85-109.
2. See John H. Dunning, "Transnational Corporations and the Growth of Services: Some Conceptual and Theoretical Issues," *United Nations Centre on Transnational Corporations*, Series A, No. 9 (March 1989); Hervé Mathe and Cynthia Perras, "Successful Global Strategies for Service Companies," *Long Range Planning*, 7/1

Developing Global Strategies for Service Businesses

(1994): 36-49; Sandra Vandermerwe and Michael Chadwick, "The International-ization of Services," *The Services Industry Journal* (January 1989), pp. 79-93.

3. George S. Yip, *Total Global Strategy: Managing for Worldwide Competitive Advantage* (Englewood Cliffs, NJ: Prentice Hall, 1992).

4. Christopher H. Lovelock, *Services Marketing* (Englewood Cliffs, NJ: Prentice Hall, 1991); Christopher H. Lovelock, *Product Plus: How Product + Service = Competitive Advantage* (New York, NY: McGraw-Hill, 1994).

5. See Thomas Hout, Michael E. Porter, and Eileen Rudden, "How global companies win out," *Harvard Business Review* (September/October 1982), pp. 98-108; C. K. Prahalad and Yves L. Doz, *The Multinational Mission: Balancing Local Demands and Global Vision* (New York, NY: Free Press, 1987); George S. Yip, "Global Strategy . . . In a World of Nations?" *Sloan Management Review*, 31/1 (Fall 1989): 29-41.

6. Michael E. Porter, "Changing Patterns of International Competition," *California Management Review*, 28/2 (Winter 1986): 9-40.

7. Yip (1989), op. cit.; Yip (1992), op. cit.

8. See, for example, Bruce Kogut, "Designing Global Strategies: Comparative and Competitive Value-Added Chains," *Sloan Management Review* (Summer 1985), pp. 27-38; Prahalad and Doz, op. cit.

9. Johny K. Johansson and George S. Yip, "Exploiting Globalization Potential: U.S. and Japanese Strategies," *Strategic Management Journal* (October 1994), pp. 579-601.

10. See Susan Segal-Horn, "Strategic Issues in the Globalization of Service Industries: A discussion paper," in P. Jones, ed., *The Management of Service Industries* (London: Pittman, 1988/89); Ram Kesavan and Eric Panitz, "Standardizing Services for Global Competitiveness: Literature Review and Hypotheses Generation," in Ben L. Kedia and Lars Larson, eds., *U.S. Competitiveness in the Global Marketplace: A Special Focus on the Service Sector*, Conference Proceedings, CIBER, Memphis State University, Memphis, TN, 1991; Alexandra Campbell and Alain Verbeke, "The Globaliza-tion of Service Multinationals," *Long Range Planning*, 2 (1994): 95-102; and Mathe and Perras, op. cit.

11. Christopher A. Bartlett and Sumantra Ghoshal, *Managing Across Borders: The Transnational Solution* (Boston, MA: Harvard Business School Press, 1989).

12. W. Earl Sasser, R. Paul Olsen, and D. Daryl Wyckoff, *Management of Service Opera-tions: Text, Cases, and Readings* (Boston, MA: Allyn & Bacon, 1978).

13. Christopher H. Lovelock, "Think Before You Leap in Services Marketing," in L.L. Berry, G. Lynn Shostack, and G. D. Upah, Proceedings of Conference on *Emerging Perspectives in Services Marketing*, American Marketing Association, Chicago, 1983, pp. 115-119.

14. Lovelock (1991), op. cit.

15. Christopher J. Lovelock, "Classifying Services to Gain Strategic Marketing Insights, " *Journal of Marketing*, 47 (Summer 1983): 9-20; Lovelock (1991), op. cit.; Lovelock (1994), op. cit.

16. Richard B. Chase, "Where Does the Customer Fit in a Service Operation?" *Harvard Business Review* (November/December 1978), pp. 137-142.

17. See Theodore Levitt, *Marketing for Business Growth* (New York, NY: McGraw-Hill, 1974), p. 47.

18. Several theorists have attempted to develop frameworks for understanding the structure of service products. G. Lynn Shostack, "Breaking Free from Product Marketing" *Journal of Marketing*, 41 (April 1977): 73-80, developed a molecular model, applicable to either goods or services, to help marketers visualize and manage what she termed a "total market entity." At the centre is the core benefit, addressing the basic customer need, which is then linked to a series of other service elements. She argues that, as in chemical formulations, a change in one

element may completely alter the nature of the entity. Surrounding the molecules
are a series of bands representing price, distribution, and market positioning
(communication messages).

19. Lovelock (1994), op. cit.
20. B. Joseph Pine, *Mass Customization: a New Frontier in Business Competition* (Boston, MA: ABS Press, 1993).
21. See review in Yip (1989), op. cit.; Yip (1992), op. cit.
22. Kesavan and Panitz (1991), op. cit.
23. Gary Hamel and C.K. Prahalad. "Do you really have a global strategy?" *Harvard Business Review* (July/August 1985), pp. 139-148.
24. Yip (1992), op. cit.
25. For an in-depth discussion of the role of value-adding activities in competitive strategy, see Michael E. Porter, *Competitive Advantage* (New York, NY: The Free Press, 1985).
26. Johansson and Yip (1994), op. cit.
27. Pei-yuan Chia, "Citibanking the World," *Bank Management* (July/August 1995).
28. Andrew E. Serwer, "McDonald's Conquers the World," *Fortune*, October 17, 1994, pp. 103-116.
29. See George S. Yip and Tammy L. Madsen, "Global Account Management: The New Frontier in Relationship Marketing, " *International Marketing Review* (Forthcoming 1996).

[10]

Seen as dinosaurs in the West, conglomerates can still add value in other contexts.

Why Focused Strategies May Be Wrong for Emerging Markets

by Tarun Khanna and Krishna Palepu

Core competencies and focus are now the mantras of corporate strategists in Western economies. But while managers in the West have dismantled many conglomerates assembled in the 1960s and 1970s, the large, diversified business group remains the dominant form of enterprise throughout most emerging markets. Some groups operate as holding companies with full ownership in many enterprises, others are collections of publicly traded companies, but all have some degree of central control.

As emerging markets open up to global competition, consultants and foreign investors are increasingly pressuring these groups to conform to Western practice by scaling back the scope of their business activities. The conglomerate is the dinosaur of organizational design, they argue, too unwieldy and slow to compete in today's fast-paced markets. Already a number of executives have decided to break up their groups in order to show that they are focusing on only a few core businesses.

There are reasons to worry about this trend. Focus is good advice in New York or London, but something important gets lost in translation when that advice is given to groups in emerging markets. Western companies take for granted a range of

institutions that support their business activities, but many of these institutions are absent in other regions of the world. (See the insert "What Is an Emerging Market?") Without effective securities regulation and venture capital firms, for example, focused companies may be unable to raise adequate financing; and without strong educational institutions, they will struggle to hire skilled employees. Communicating with customers is difficult when the local infrastructure is poor, and unpredictable government behavior can stymie any operation. Although a focused strategy may enable a company to perform a few activities well, companies in emerging markets must take responsibility for a wide range of functions in order to do business effectively.

As a result, companies must adapt their strategies to fit their *institutional context* – a country's product, capital, and labor markets; its regulatory system; and its mechanisms for enforcing contracts. Unlike advanced economies, emerging markets suffer from weak institutions in all or most of these areas. (See the table "How Institutional Context Drives Strategy.") It is this difference in institutional context that explains the success of large, diversified corporations in developing

economies such as Indonesia and India and their failure in advanced economies such as the United States and the United Kingdom.

In our research, we have found that highly diversified business groups can be particularly well suited to the institutional context in most developing countries. From the *chaebols* of Korea to the *business houses* of India to the *grupos* of Latin America, conglomerates can add value by imitating the functions of several institutions that are present only in advanced economies. Successful groups effectively mediate between their member companies and the rest of the economy.

Filling the Institutional Voids

Emerging markets are hardly uniform. Nevertheless, they all fall short to varying degrees in providing the institutions necessary to support basic business operations.

Product Markets. In the case of product markets, buyers and sellers usually suffer from a severe dearth of

Tarun Khanna is an assistant professor and Krishna Palepu a professor at the Harvard Business School in Boston, Massachusetts. This article is part of a major project the authors are conducting that investigates corporate strategy in emerging markets.

information for three reasons. First, the communications infrastructure in emerging markets is often underdeveloped. Even as wireless communication spreads throughout the West, vast stretches in countries such as China and India remain without telephones. Power shortages often render the modes of communication that do exist ineffective. The postal service is typically inefficient, slow, or unreliable; and the private sector rarely provides efficient courier services. High rates of illiteracy make it difficult for marketers to communicate effectively with customers.

Second, even when information about products does get around, there are no mechanisms to corroborate the claims made by sellers. Independent consumer-information organizations are rare, and government watchdog agencies are of little

use. The few analysts who rate products are generally less sophisticated than their counterparts in advanced economies.

Third, consumers have no redress mechanisms if a product does not deliver on its promise. Law enforcement is often capricious and so slow that few who assign any value to time would resort to it. Unlike in advanced markets, there are few extrajudicial arbitration mechanisms to which one can appeal.

As a result of this lack of information, companies in emerging markets face much higher costs in building credible brands than their counterparts in advanced economies. In turn, established brands wield tremendous power. A conglomerate with a reputation for quality products and services can use its group name to enter new businesses, even if those businesses are com-

pletely unrelated to its current lines. Groups also have an advantage when they do try to build up a brand because they can spread the cost of maintaining it across multiple lines of business. Such groups then have a greater incentive not to damage brand quality in any one business because they will pay the price in their other businesses as well.

The Korean chaebols are famous throughout the world for extending their group identity over multiple product categories. Samsung, for example, has used its name for a range of goods from televisions to microwave ovens. Groups in India and Malaysia are beginning to follow suit. The business media in India, for example, abound with advertisements that promote group identity rather than emphasize the products or services of individual companies within a group.

What Is an Emerging Market?

Most analysts define an emerging market according to such characteristics as size, growth rate, or how recently it has opened up to the global economy. In our view, the most important criterion is how well an economy helps buyers and sellers come together. Ideally, every economy would provide a range of institutions in order to facilitate the functioning of markets, but developing countries fall short in a number of ways.

For the purposes of our argument, there are three main sources of market failure:
☐ **Information Problems.** Buyers – broadly defined not only as consumers in product markets but also as employers in labor markets and investors in financial markets – need reliable information to assess the goods and services that they purchase and the investments that they make. Without adequate information, they are reluctant to do business.

☐ **Misguided Regulations.** When regulators place political goals over economic efficiency, they can distort the functioning of markets. Many emerging markets, for example, restrict the ability of companies to lay off workers. These rules do add some stability to society – and in some cases, they may even be intended to overcome market failures from other sources. However, the result is that companies are less able to take advantage of opportunities than they are in advanced economies.

☐ **Inefficient Judicial Systems.** Companies are reluctant to do business without ways of ensuring that their partners will hold up their end of the bargain. Contracts can facilitate cooperation by aligning the incentives of the different parties. Markets therefore depend on judicial systems that are strong enough to enforce contracts in a reliable and predictable way.

In advanced economies, companies can rely on a variety of outside institutions that minimize these sources of market failure. In such a context, companies create value primarily by focusing on a narrow set of activities. At the opposite extreme, stagnant or declining economies usually suffer from near-complete market failure because of the utter absence of basic institutions.

Emerging markets, in the middle of this continuum, offer the prospect of substantial growth because they have developed at least some of the institutions necessary to encourage commerce. But institutional voids are still common enough to cause market failures; as a result, companies in emerging markets often have to perform these basic functions themselves. In our view, that is the crucial distinction between doing business in an emerging market and operating in an advanced economy.

How Institutional Context Drives Strategy

Institutional Dimension	United States	Japan	India
Capital market	equity-focused; monitoring by disclosure rules and the market for corporate control	bank-focused; monitoring by interlocking investments and directors	underdeveloped, illiquid equity markets and nationalized banks; weak monitoring by bureaucrats
Labor market	many business schools and consulting firms offering talent; certified skills enhance mobility	few business schools; training internal to companies; company-specific development of talent	few business schools and little training; management talent scarce
Product market	reliable enforcement of liability laws; efficient dissemination of information; many activist consumers	reliable enforcement of liability laws; efficient dissemination of information; some activist consumers	limited enforcement of liability laws; little dissemination of information; few activist consumers
Government regulation	low; relatively free of corruption	moderate; relatively free of corruption	high; corruption common
Contract enforcement	predictable	predictable	unpredictable
Result	**diversified groups have many disadvantages**	**diversified groups have some advantages**	**diversified groups have many advantages**

Capital Markets. Similar problems occur in capital markets because, without access to information, investors refrain from putting money into unfamiliar ventures. The U.S. capital markets minimize these problems through institutional mechanisms such as reliable financial reporting, a dynamic community of analysts, and an aggressive, independent financial press. Venture capital firms and other intermediaries specialize in investigating and assessing new opportunities. The Securities and Exchange Commission and other watchdog bodies make it difficult for unscrupulous entrepreneurs to mislead unsophisticated investors. As a result, investors have a free flow of largely accurate information about companies. And they can hold corporate managers and directors accountable through the threat of securities litigation, proxy fights, and hostile takeovers. By reducing risks to investors, these institutions make it possible for new enterprises to raise capital on approximately equal terms as big, established companies.

Almost all the institutional mechanisms that make advanced capital markets work so well are either absent or ineffective in emerging markets. Having little information and few safeguards, investors are reluctant to put money into new enterprises. In such a context, diversified groups can point to their track record of returns to investors. As a result, large and well-established companies have superior access to capital markets. This advantage is so pronounced that governments in India and South Korea, for example, have attempted to restrict the amount of credit exposure that banks are permitted to have in large companies.

Conglomerates also can use their internally generated capital to grow existing businesses or to enter new ones. In fact, their superior ability to raise capital makes groups a prime source of capital for new enterprises and gives them a great advantage over small companies seeking funding. Besides acting as venture capitalists, groups also act as lending institutions to existing member enterprises that are otherwise too small to obtain capital from financial institutions. And some Indian groups, especially those in the automobile sector, have set up subsidiaries whose primary purpose is to provide financing to important suppliers and customers.

At the same time, conglomerates are attractive to foreign investors eager to put money into these often fast-growing markets. With so few financial analysts and knowledgeable mutual-fund managers available to guide them, outsiders instead turn to diversified groups and invest in a wide range of industries. Investors trust groups to evaluate new opportunities and to exercise an auditing and supervisory function. The groups thus become the conduit for large amounts of investment in their capital-starved countries.

Labor Markets. Most emerging markets suffer from a scarcity of well-trained people. While the United States has more than 600 business schools training thousands of future managers every year, Thailand has a handful of high-quality business schools that produce far fewer entry-level managers than the economy needs. Vocational training facilities are also scarce in emerging markets.

Groups can create value by developing promising managers, and they can spread the fixed costs of professional development over the businesses in the group. Many of the large groups in India, for example, have internal management-development programs – often with dedicated facilities. These programs typically are geared toward developing the skills of experienced managers; but some groups, such as the Malaysian conglomerate Sime Darby, have instituted training programs for all levels of employees in an attempt to develop their human capital. And some of the Korean chaebols have set up special programs in collaboration with top U.S. business schools in order to train their own people.

Groups also can provide much needed flexibility for labor markets in general. Governments in emerging markets usually make it difficult for companies to adjust their workforces to changing economic conditions. Rigid laws often prevent companies from laying off their employees, and labor unions insist on job security in the absence of government-provided unemployment benefits. To counteract the rigidities of the overall labor market, groups can develop extensive internal labor markets of their own. When one company in a group faces declining prospects, its employees can be transferred to other group companies that are on the rise – even to companies in otherwise undesirable locations. India's Aditya Birla group, for example, has acquired a reputation for building communities around its manufacturing plants in the remotest parts of the country. Because the group provides services such as schools, hospitals, and places of worship, managers and other trained employees are more willing to relocate. The growing companies benefit by receiving a ready source of reliable employees.

Groups are also able to put new talent to good use. By allocating talent to where it is most needed, conglomerates have a head start in beginning new activities. The Wipro Group in India successfully moved beyond computers into financial services by relocating skilled engineers first to computer-leasing services that would make use of their technical know-how and then to a broad range of financial services. In contrast, unaffiliated companies usually

have to recruit publicly in order to build their operations – a difficult proposition in countries where labor varies widely in quality and lacks certification from respected educational institutions.

Regulation. As multinational companies know all too well, governments in most emerging markets operate very differently from those in the West. Not only does the state intervene much more extensively in business operations, but companies also have a hard time predicting the actions of regulatory bodies.

Governments in emerging markets are heavily involved in an intricate array of business decisions. Despite the elimination of the old "license raj," for example, Indian law still requires that companies get permission for a range of decisions, such as exiting businesses, changing prices on commodities, and importing raw materials. The law establishes subjective criteria for many of these decisions, so Indian bureaucrats have a great deal of discretion in how they apply the rules.

Diversified groups can add value by acting as intermediaries when their individual companies or foreign partners need to deal with the regulatory bureaucracy. Experience and connections give conglomerates an advantage. The larger the company, the easier it is to carry the cost of maintaining government relationships. Indeed, political economist Dennis Encarnation found that India's large groups maintain "industrial embassies" in New Delhi to facilitate interaction with bureaucrats. Several groups in India also are known for their ability to manage bureaucratic relations at levels all the way down to the village council.

India and other countries may be bearing costs for the uncertainty of their regulatory systems. But as long as government officials have so much discretion, companies often end up working with them. Intricate relations between business and government actually appear to be the norm throughout the developing

world. The major Malaysian political parties, for example, all have affiliated conglomerates. Until recently, the ties between government and industry in South Korea have been a centerpiece of that country's economic program. Even today in Indonesia, there are groups whose greatest assets appear to include access to high government officials. Because political leaders are so eager to work with companies, managers must be prepared to deal with the government and the bureaucracy.

Bribes and other corrupt practices may be part of working with the bureaucracy. But that's not the whole story. In many cases, educating officials is more important than exchanging favors. The Enron Corporation, a large U.S.-based multinational, discovered just that when it entered the power generation sector in India. Prepared to invest \$2.8 billion, the single largest foreign venture in Indian history, the company had to spend four years and about \$20 million educating regulators on the ways international power projects are financed and regulated. Along the way, Enron learned its own lessons about dealing with the Indian bureaucracy and government; the project was almost canceled when Enron's aggressive deal-making style put off newly elected offi-

> **Not every group adds value in the same way, and no group can hope to fill every institutional void.**

cials in the state where the power plant was to be built. As Enron's executives now acknowledge, experience with Indian politics and bureaucracy might have saved the company a great deal of trouble.

Contract Enforcement. Despite the extensive involvement of government in emerging markets, these economies lack effective mechanisms to enforce contracts. In advanced economies, companies can work together under arm's-length contractual arrangements because

How Groups Can Add Value

Institutional Dimension	Institutions That Groups Imitate
Capital market	venture capital firm, private equity provider, mutual fund, bank, auditor
Labor market	management institute/business school, certification agency, head-hunting firm, relocation service
Product market	certification agency, regulatory authority, extrajudicial arbitration service
Government regulation	lobbyist
Contract enforcement	courts, extrajudicial arbitration service

they know the courts will protect them if their partners break their contracts. Confidence in the judicial system makes it easier for everyone to do business. But courts in emerging markets often enforce contracts capriciously or inefficiently; as a result, companies are less likely to be able to resolve disputes through judicial channels.

In such situations, conglomerates can leverage reputations established by honest dealings in the past. Because the misdeeds of one company in a group will damage the prospects of the others, all the group companies have credibility when they promise to honor their agreements with any single partner. They provide a haven where property rights are respected. As a result, suppliers and customers are more willing to work with them.

This credibility pays off the most in relationships with companies seeking to enter emerging markets. Foreign providers of technology or finance need local partners to carry out their strategies, but they worry about being cheated. A reputation for honesty and reliability thus can be a source of enormous competitive advantage. As Alice Amsden and Takashi Hikino have argued, conglomerates in several emerging markets have based much of their success on their ability to access foreign technology. And in India, the largest and most diversified business groups receive a disproportionate share of

technology and financial support from advanced economies around the world. The head of RPG Enterprises, India's third largest conglomerate, considers his group's relations with foreign providers – including 16 of the 500 largest U.S. companies – to be among its greatest assets.

Managing the House of Tata

India's largest conglomerate in sales and assets exemplifies how well-run groups can add value in emerging markets. Spanning most sectors of the Indian economy, the Tata companies employ close to 300,000 people and had sales of Rupees 289 billion (U.S. $8.6 billion) in the fiscal year 1995 to 1996. Of the group's 90 companies, more than 40 are publicly traded, and these account for approximately 8% of the total capitalization of the country's publicly traded companies. The companies are all held together by the internationally recognized Tata name and by interlocking investments and directorates.

The Tatas began as a textile mill in 1874, but Indian independence in 1947 brought antimonopoly legislation and high taxes on dividends that encouraged the group to diversify into a variety of unrelated areas. When India began liberalizing its economy in 1991, removing the barriers to growth within any given sector, the group had a stark choice to make. Outside experts advised executives to concentrate on a few strong

sectors of economic activity instead of continuing as an extensively diversified entity. But the executives decided to remain in most of their existing businesses.

One reason for staying diversified was the difficulty of exiting businesses because of some remaining legal restrictions in India as well as the Tatas' reputation as a benevolent employer. But the Tatas also believed that they could leverage their size and wide scope to help their constituent companies in a variety of ways. So they decided to diversify even further.

Historically, the Tata companies have always come together to finance the launch of new enterprises. But initially there was no formal structure for doing so. Then in 1982, the group created Tata Industries, a venture capital vehicle funded with a special pool of investment money drawn from the member companies. Since then, Tata Industries has sought to lead the Tata group into information technology, process control, advanced materials, oil-field services, and other areas. It has provided seed money for several successful ventures, including two computer-manufacturing enterprises – one cosponsored by Honeywell and another cosponsored by IBM. Today the Tatas are leading the way in building an information-technology industrial park in cooperation with the state of Karnataka and with money and expertise from a consortium that includes the government of Singapore.

The Tatas were so active in new ventures that by 1995 they needed additional capital. They decided to sell a stake in Tata Industries at a substantial premium to Jardine Matheson, itself a diversified company based in Hong Kong. As a result of the sale, Jardine Matheson ended up owning 20% of the equity in Tata Industries. The sale gave the Tatas (and the Indian economy) $200 million in "patient" capital from a conglomerate that shared their long-term approach to investment. Jardine Matheson, in turn, gained exposure to sectors across the Indian economy without having to supervise individual companies.

Many of the group's new ventures benefited from being able to borrow skilled managers from the Tatas' existing businesses. Since 1956, Tata Administrative Services (TAS) – an in-house training program with a national reputation for excellence – has aimed to create a cadre of general managers. Entry into TAS is extremely selective and primarily restricted to graduates of Indian management institutes. Recruits spend their first year on courses, interactive sessions with Tata executives, and visits to major Tata plants around the country. Mentoring and career direction continue for at least five years, as candidates are exposed to three different line functions in three industries to gain a general management perspective.

Fully half of these trainees remain with the Tatas over the long term, in contrast to some other large Indian groups that have to reinvent themselves every few years because of high turnover. For those who do leave, the exit options are attractive, increasing the appeal of joining the Tatas in the first place. In effect, the group provides both management education and a certification service in a country where both are scarce.

TAS consciously organizes its recruits into cohorts according to the year they entered. As recruits spread out to the different companies within the group, they maintain lasting ties with their cohort group, and these networks improve information flows across the group. The head office, mindful of the resources invested in these graduates, encourages group companies to "sacrifice" a talented employee to another company if it is in the interest of both the managers' career development and the group. Cross-company teams of "stars" are assembled to resolve knotty problems that individual companies are having. The group now plans a new initiative, the Tata Group Mobility Plan, to improve the mobility of all skilled managers, including non-TAS graduates, across group companies – and without any loss of benefits.

The Tatas are a favorite of foreign technology providers that are comfortable entering India only with a reputable party. Tata executives consider their reputation for honesty and integrity to be among their greatest assets, and that reputation has led to joint ventures with Daimler Benz and AT&T, as well as a number of computer companies. Understanding the value of its reputation, the group is developing an internal code of conduct and other elaborate standards regarding the use of the group name. Special fees from the member companies will pay for an internal auditing function to enforce those standards. To foster an orientation toward quality among its companies, Tata also has set up an internal system of awards akin to the United States' Baldrige awards.

By keeping and extending their diversified holdings, the Tatas have maintained a scale and scope that gives them a host of advantages within India's specific institutional context. And these advantage are mutually reinforcing. The more access Tata or any group has to financial capital, the more business opportunities it can offer to talented employees – which in turn helps the group improve quality and enhance its reputation with consumers. Continued success in existing lines of business has made it all the easier for the Tatas to enter new lines of business. The Tatas today have the largest market shares in many sectors of the Indian economy, from steel to computers to hotels.

The Tatas, in turn, benefit the Indian economy. When management consultants told a Tata executive that diversification into unrelated activities did not create value, he replied, "Don't enunciate a theory that will bring everything to a dead halt. If we don't start these businesses, no one else will either, and society will be worse off."

Ensuring That Diversification Adds Value

Once one understands the institutional context of any given emerging market, it is clear why diversified business groups have the potential to add value. (See the table "How Groups Can Add Value.") Nevertheless, groups do not automatically realize that potential. They must be actively managed to capture the advantages offered by scale and scope. Our statistical analysis comparing groups and independent companies in India – and a similar analysis on South Korean companies that Tarun Khanna conducted with Yishay Yafeh – suggests that many groups add little or no value to their operations. The largest and most diversified groups, however, do add a good deal of value – perhaps because only these groups have the scale and scope to perform the kind of functions we have described.

Indeed, many groups have actually diminished the value of their member companies through poor management. Conglomerates in emerging markets, after all, suffer from the

same problems that plague those in the West: the more activities a business engages in, the harder it is for the head office to coordinate, control, and invest properly in them. Unless a group is ready to offer concrete benefits to its affiliates, companies are better off independent.

Group executives should ask in a systematic way whether they are adding enough value to overcome the costs of complexity and coordination. They should start by assessing their conglomerate's strengths. A group that enjoys brand name recognition in rural markets might think of leveraging its name in unrelated products targeted to the same markets. Or a group that enjoys preferential access to large amounts of

capital might consider ventures that require substantial investment.

Of course, not every group will be able to add value in the same way, and no group can hope to fill every institutional void. Decisions to diversify should be based on the group's strengths, not just on growth prospects. Today a number of groups are rushing willy-nilly into power plants and other infrastructure projects all over Asia, and their total-capacity plans already appear to outstrip the likely demand. But there are a few exceptions, such as India's Satyam Group. This group has tried to leverage its reputation for honest and efficient partnerships with foreign companies in order to win the better contracts.

What Is the Best Institutional Context?

Even if they admit to the advantages of diversification in emerging markets, some investors or partners may still urge companies to concentrate on a few core activities on the grounds that all markets will eventually develop the West's set of institutions. But their advice assumes that there is one single set of institutions toward which all countries should move. It is unclear, however, whether any one institutional context is obviously superior to others.

Consider the financial system in the United States. That system, based on atomistic shareholders, ensures great liquidity, which generally reduces the cost of funds. Because shareholders can "vote with their feet" if they do not like what management is doing, however, they are less inclined to expend the effort needed to discipline management. As a result, corporate governance may suffer. Similarly, a labor market in which employees freely move from one company to another increases the likelihood that, at any given time, there will be an efficient match between workers'

skills and the opportunities to which those skills can be applied. But it reduces the likelihood that workers will invest in anything but the most general skills; as a result, society does not reap the benefits of the long-term, company-specific training of workers.

Japan's institutional context reveals a different resolution to these trade-offs. Japan's capital market is bank centered, not equity centered. Banks monitor managers through equity cross-holdings between companies and board directorships, and the difficulty financial institutions have in unloading their shares encourages them to keep management in line. (Banks, in fact, are at the center of Japan's major *keiretsu*, and these groups offer some of the same advantages of conglomeration that are present in emerging markets.) Japanese managers and workers get their training largely within companies. Managers rarely move around because their expertise is geared toward the specific needs of their company and because they lack credentials from such external institutions as business schools.

Institutional context also takes a long time to evolve. Because different aspects of the institutional environment have often co-evolved into a well-functioning system, changes along any one dimension of an institutional environment can have unanticipated, adverse effects along other dimensions. Economies around the world today are experimenting with moving from one system to another using either "shock therapy" or gradual adjustment – there is much debate about which is the better approach. Deep-seated institutional voids might take decades to be filled. The United States is an extreme example of a country where there are relatively few such voids.

Even if the institutional context of emerging markets evolves to the point that there are no advantages to diversification, executives there should realize that their current opportunities will persist for some time. They are much better served by developing corporate strategies that match their particular contexts instead of blindly applying the management mantra of the day.

Once a group identifies its opportunities, its executives need to install systems to ensure consistent execution. For example, they must impose discipline over field managers, who will be tempted to take advantage of ready financing to try to build empires. The most successful groups usually have a strong internal auditing system. Sime Darby, the Malaysian conglomerate, benefits from a tradition of strict financial controls and planning that began under its original British managers. Its recent entry into financial services by acquiring UMBC bank was welcomed by the Southeast Asian stock markets, which saw the conglomerate adding value through its management discipline to a large but underperforming company in a rapidly growing sector.

Another strategic imperative for groups is to manage their corporate identities. Given that much of their success depends on the trust of their customers and partners, diversified groups must enforce standards of reliability and quality. The head of Mahindra & Mahindra, a group operating in automobiles and infrastructure in India, grabs every symbolic opportunity he gets to dramatize the importance of never compromising on the product and after-sales service offered to customers.

When a group's strategy depends on supplying functions that are absent in the institutional context, it is important to move with deliberation. Mimicking institutions that are undeveloped in the economy at large requires time and effort. A group that acts as a venture capital firm, for example, needs to develop a track record for nurturing businesses in order to become a magnet for risk capital. It needs to train and retain individuals who are skilled at identifying deals and who can bring their start-up expertise to bear on a variety of situations; it also needs to have disciplined managers to run its high-risk ventures.

Communicating the Strategy to Investors

Even successful conglomerates still face resistance from Western investors and partners who believe that focus is always best. Although many executives may well be tempted to concentrate their operations in order to win favor with outside analysts, a better solution for well-managed groups is to educate investors about the logic underpinning the group's corporate strategy. (See the insert "What Is the Best Institutional Context?")

Institutional investors are often most worried not about diversification per se but about the lack of openness in internal group operations. Under the current structure of many conglomerates, investment analysts find it difficult to tell which business segments are creating value within a conglomerate. They fear that a group executive will shuffle funds from one company to another. Faced with these concerns, managers of conglomerates should increase the transparency of their operations, communicate this change to investors, and develop a reputation for doing so.

The Indian group Mahindra & Mahindra is doing just that. While it focuses on automobiles and closely related businesses, the group has set up a holding company to invest in a range of other projects. The automobile company has made a onetime, fully documented infusion of capital to start the holding company so that the group will not have to make repeated transfers of funds for ad-hoc line extensions. If and when the holding company's ventures take off and require new capital, the group will take the company public rather than draw on funds from the automobile company.

If groups are not adding value, they should consider focusing. But they should not break up simply because their competitors are focused foreign companies from advanced economies. Western companies have access to advanced technology, cheap financing, and sophisticated managerial know-how. In the absence of institutions providing these and other functions in emerging markets, diversification may be the best way to match up against the competition.

Reprint 97404

To order reprints, see the last page of this issue.

[11]

Strategic Management Journal
Strat. Mgmt. J., **22**: 101–123 (2001)

THE GEOGRAPHIC SOURCES OF FOREIGN SUBSIDIARIES' INNOVATIONS

TONY S. FROST*
Richard Ivey School of Business, University of Western Ontario, London, Ontario, Canada

This study contributes to the literature on the nature and evolution of the multinational enterprise by exploring the geographic origins of the knowledge sources utilized by foreign subsidiaries during the process of technological innovation. Through a synthesis of the multinational literature and the broader literature on external sources of innovation, I develop and test a set of hypotheses that explain the conditions under which innovating subsidiaries are likely to draw upon sources of knowledge located in the home base of the firm and/or the subsidiary's host country environment. The hypotheses are tested through an analysis of the citations listed on over 10,000 patents issued to U.S. greenfield subsidiaries between 1980 and 1990. Copyright © 2001 John Wiley & Sons, Ltd.

Innovation has long played a central role in theories of foreign direct investment and the multinational enterprise. Beginning with Vernon's (1966) product life cycle model, scholars have viewed the multinational principally in terms of its ability to exploit proprietary advantages (knowledge, innovations) generated in the home base by the parent firm. However, in recent years this view has been challenged by a number of scholars focusing on the knowledge-creating potential of firms with value chain activities that span borders (Bartlett and Ghoshal, 1989; Cantwell, 1992, 1993; Dunning, 1998; Nobel and Birkinshaw, 1998). According to this alternative perspective, a potentially important source of competitive advantage for multinational firms is the capacity of their foreign subsidiaries to generate innovations based on stimuli and resources resident in the heterogeneous host country

environments in which they operate. In this sense, foreign direct investment may also be interpreted as a mechanism through which firms seek to develop new resources and capabilities on a global basis (Kogut and Chang, 1991; Teece, 1992; Westney, 1990).

Despite widespread interest in this debate among academics, practitioners, and policy-makers, empirical research on subsidiary innovation and knowledge-seeking FDI has been slow to progress, in large part because of the difficulty of obtaining subsidiary-level innovation data from a representative sample of multinational firms (Kogut and Chang, 1991). As a result, our understanding of the phenomenon has tended to proceed more through the accumulation of anecdotes than through systematic empirical examination. In addition, research on overseas innovation has thus far missed the opportunity for theoretical advancement that might arise from drawing upon more general theories of innovation and technological progress in organizations (Cohen and Levinthal, 1990; Dosi, 1988; Freeman, 1991; Nelson, 1993; Powell, Koput, and Smith-Doerr, 1996; von Hippel, 1988).

Key words: multinational; innovation; geography; foreign subsidiary
*Correspondence to: Tony S. Frost, Richard Ivey School of Business, University of Western Ontario, London, Ontario, Canada N6G 2L1

Received 28 July 1998
Final revision received 3 October 2000

102   *T. S. Frost*

This study contributes to the literature on the nature and evolution of the multinational enterprise by exploring the origins of the knowledge sources utilized by foreign subsidiaries during the process of technological innovation. I focus specifically on geographic aspects of the phenomenon—where subsidiaries' knowledge sources originate in territorial space. In the remainder of the paper, I develop and test a set of hypotheses that, taken together, constitutes an explanation of the conditions under which innovating subsidiaries are likely to draw upon sources of knowledge located in the home base of the firm and/or the subsidiary's host country environment. The argument is based upon a synthesis of the literature on knowledge creation in multinational firms and the broader innovation literature, particularly recent work looking at the importance of external actors and institutions to the development of knowledge in organizations (e.g., Bierly and Chakrabarti, 1996; Cohen and Levinthal, 1990; Freeman, 1991; Powell *et al.*, 1996; von Hippel, 1988).

To break the logjam in the current empirical literature, this study draws upon recent advances in the use of U.S. patent data, in particular upon the methodology of patent citation analysis pioneered by Jaffe, Trajtenberg, and Henderson (1993). For every patent issued between 1980 and 1990 to U.S.-based greenfield subsidiaries (over 10,000 patents) I have assembled a detailed set of geographic, organizational, and technological indicators, which I believe is the most comprehensive data base on subsidiary innovations yet developed. Critical to the objectives of the study, each subsidiary patent is also cross-referenced with each of the prior patents it cites as a reference. These patent citations represent the technological building blocks of the current invention. Using the Jaffe *et al.* (1993) methodology, the detailed information contained in these citations is used to draw inferences about the geographic origin of the technical ideas embodied in U.S. subsidiaries' innovations.

The decision to focus the study on U.S.-based subsidiaries established through greenfield foreign investment was made for several reasons. A single host country design controls for major variations in institutional setting. As Nelson (1993) and others have pointed out, national institutions such as labor markets and university–firm linkages are likely to have an important effect on the process and mechanisms through which knowledge travels within technical communities. A single host country design also facilitates the testing of my hypotheses at more finely grained geographic levels, i.e., below the country level. This is an important advantage of this study over much of the previous literature on innovation in multinational firms and brings this research into closer alignment with research on innovation and economic geography, which has consistently highlighted the importance of the subnational level in delimiting the boundaries of technological capabilities and expertise (Krugman, 1990; Porter, 1990; Storper, 1992).

The United States is an interesting and particularly important setting for this research because of the excellence and permeability of its national innovation system, which many commentators have argued are major attractions for foreign multinationals seeking new sources of science and technology (Herbert, 1989; Dalton and Serapio, 1993; Teece, 1992). The decision to limit the scope of the study to greenfield subsidiaries was driven by theoretical considerations and by the desire to maximize the interpretability of the results. In particular, it seems plausible that acquired U.S. firms (or international joint ventures) may have systematically different external innovation networks than subsidiaries established through greenfield investment for a variety of historical, strategic, and organizational reasons. Including acquisitions and joint ventures in the current study risked a major decrease in the transparency and interpretability of the results for a marginal gain in generalizability.

The paper is structured as follows. First, I provide a brief overview of the subsidiary innovation literature before developing my theoretical argument and hypotheses. Data and research methods follow in the next section. I then present the results and conclude with a discussion of the implications of my findings as well as directions for future research.

SUBSIDIARY INNOVATION AND HOST COUNTRY RESOURCES

Conventionally, innovation in multinational firms has been understood as the domain of the parent organization located in the home base of the firm. This was Vernon's (1966) view, at least as the product life cycle hypothesis was initially formulated, and this is also the predominant view found in Porter's (1990) most recent book.[1] Beginning in the mid-1980s, however, changes in the structure of the global economy as well as an apparent trend toward internationalization of the R&D function within major multinational firms motivated researchers to treat more seriously the possibility that foreign subsidiaries could play an important role as sources of new ideas and capabilities (Bartlett and Ghoshal, 1989; Hedlund, 1986; Hakanson and Nobel, 1993).

Increasingly, the debate among researchers has centered around the idea that what makes the multinational unique as a knowledge-creating organization is its structural position spanning diverse institutional contexts. As Cantwell (1992, 1993) has argued, firms with research facilities in foreign locations may be able to transcend limitations in the technological specializations of their home country and take advantage of different specializations abroad. This claim has been bolstered by the growing number of countries with advanced capabilities in science and technology (Lee and Proctor, 1991), and by evidence that industrialized countries are also becoming more technologically specialized and differentiated from each other over time (Archibugi and Pianta, 1992), leading to the emergence of 'pockets' of expertise and advanced technology in regions around the world (Cantwell, 1993; Porter, 1990; Storper, 1992).[2]

---

[1] In later work, Vernon (1979) substantially revised his views on the life cycle hypothesis. Of most relevance here is Vernon's vision that foreign subsidiaries could play an important role in the creation of new products and ideas, primarily through a scanning capability. The later work does not necessarily contradict his earlier views. Rather, Vernon was commenting on changes in the nature of the global economy and the resulting co-evolution of organizational forms in the multinational enterprise.

[2] The trend towards scientific and technological parity across nations is something the economic development literature has long argued ought to result from flows of technology from the developed countries to the developing world. This is the so-called 'catch-up' effect that is an especially important part of the literature on 'late development' (cf. Dore, 1990; Gerschenkron, 1962). In addition to this argument, I am also arguing that the world's most technologically advanced nations are becoming more technologically specialized and differentiated from each other. This is especially likely in global high-tech industries such as biotechnology and medical instruments where companies draw heavily upon local constellations of actors and institutions in the course of developing differentiated products for sale in global markets (see Storper, 1992, for an extended discussion). I thank an anonymous reviewer for pointing out these connections.

Notwithstanding the intuitive appeal of the argument, evidence that multinationals actually utilize this technological and institutional diversity to generate innovations is fragmented and contradictory. Most of the positive findings with respect to the 'technology-seeking' hypothesis are based upon case studies of particular R&D units, with the attendant problems of generalizability and sample selection bias. For example, Herbert (1989) documents examples of Japanese multinationals that have situated R&D facilities in U.S. science valleys and established relationships with nearby universities and other centers of science and technology. Other studies of Japanese multinationals by Florida and Kenney (1994), Westney (1992), and Dalton and Serapio (1993) have also produced evidence that an important subset of Japanese R&D facilities in the United States is 'located near major U.S. research centers to secure access to new sources of scientific and technical talent' (Florida and Kenney, 1994: 344). Kim's (1997) historical analysis of Korea's technological development highlights the importance of Samsung's Silicon Valley research site in the company's drive to reach a leading position in DRAM technology. His finding is extended by Almeida's (1996) study of semiconductor innovation by U.S.-based foreign subsidiaries. Using the Jaffe *et al.* (1993) patent citation methodology that is also used in this paper, Almeida finds that subsidiaries located in Silicon Valley draw upon local knowledge sources even more than comparable U.S. firms located in the same region.

Hakanson and Nobel (1993) extend these results in their study of Swedish multinationals. They argue that the character of foreign R&D has shifted over time toward objectives emphasizing the monitoring and assimilation of foreign technology. This may explain the results contained in Ronstadt's (1977) early study of overseas R&D in seven U.S. multinationals, in which he explicitly rejected the proposition that 'monitoring foreign R&D activities' was an important objective in any of the 42 R&D units he studied. Rather, the majority of these sites were initially geared to adapting headquarters-generated technology to local market conditions, although some later developed a more autonomous set of technological capabilities and objectives. Wortmann (1990) notes a similar evolution in the overseas R&D activities of German multinationals toward local knowledge assimilation and development.

Strat. Mgmt. J., **22**: 101–123 (2001)

These results are consistent with Bartlett and Ghoshal's (1989) more general arguments about the evolution of distributed capabilities in multinational firms.

Larger sample studies are generally much less supportive of the proposition that multinationals 'tap into' sources of knowledge and technology in foreign locations. Cantwell (1992), for example, finds that patents belonging to foreign subsidiaries tend to be concentrated in technical fields of *host* country specialization, suggesting that innovating subsidiaries build upon local technological trajectories, but this result holds only for some host countries, and not in all time periods studied. A similar study by Zander (1994) covering nearly 100 years of patenting activities by Swedish multinationals also found mixed support over time for the hypothesis that foreign subsidiaries innovate in fields of host country expertise. Dunning and Narula's (1995) analysis of R&D expenditures by foreign multinationals in the United States found no support for the hypothesis that foreign R&D is concentrated in sectors and technologies of host country comparative advantage. A similar 'not proven' verdict is turned in by more general work on foreign entry into the United States by Kogut and Chang (1991) and Anand and Kogut (1997). Using industry-level count data, these studies suggest that sourcing of host country technology is not a major motivation for foreign direct investment into the United States.

THEORY AND HYPOTHESES

Existing research on the subsidiary–host country interface provides many clues and suggestions about the importance of the host country as a source of innovation to foreign subsidiaries, although data and methodological shortcomings have greatly hampered the progress of this line of inquiry. More fundamentally, in the rush to find evidence that innovating subsidiaries are assimilating host country knowledge, researchers have tended to ignore important underlying conceptual issues, such as how this phenomenon fits into a more general explanation of the conditions under which innovating subsidiaries are likely to utilize home (including headquarters) and/or host country sources of knowledge. In short, what is missing from the multinational literature is an understanding of the innovation process in foreign subsidiaries that can be used to generate predictions about the location of the knowledge sources they utilize. In the remainder of this section, I attempt to remedy this shortcoming in the literature by developing a set of hypotheses that predict the geographic sources of foreign subsidiaries' innovations. In short, the goal of the paper is to offer an explanation of where (home or host) the technical ideas that underpin and inform foreign subsidiaries' innovations are likely to originate. For theoretical guidance, I turn to the broader literature on innovation and technological progress, especially the rapidly developing literature on external sources of innovation.

The geographic sources of subsidiaries' innovations: the strategic perspective

A centerpiece of the innovation literature is the proposition that technological progress involves the combination of proprietary and public sources of knowledge (Cohen and Levinthal, 1990; Dosi, 1988). The locus of technological innovation resides not only within the boundaries of the innovating organization, but also outside it, in the 'interstices between firms, universities, research laboratories, suppliers, and customers' (Powell *et al.*, 1996: 118). Many studies have established the importance of external sources of knowledge to the progress and commercial success of technological innovation (Allen, 1984; Czepiel, 1974; DeBresson and Amesse, 1991; von Hippel, 1988).

The balance between internal and external sources of innovation varies not only across innovating organizations, but also within them over time. In technical fields that are nascent or changing rapidly, the innovation process is informed to a large degree by new developments occurring outside the firm. In such cases, learning and technical progress are facilitated by active participation in the 'technological community' that defines the individual and organizational structure of the field (Powell *et al.*, 1996). The location of innovative search needs, therefore, to be understood as a dynamic process, evolving over time depending upon the type of innovative activity (e.g., the distinction between 'R' and 'D'), the stage of the technology development cycle (design vs. pilot manufacturing), and the organization's capabilities and experience in a particular technological trajectory (Dosi, 1988).

March's (1991) distinction between exploitation and exploration offers a useful encapsulation of this view. Exploitation, he argues, is characterized by 'the refinement and extension of existing competencies, technologies and paradigms' (March, 1991: 85). The scope of innovative search may be reduced, and is more likely to reside in the routines and problem-solving heuristics that constitute the organization's established knowledge base. Emphasis is placed on the appropriation of profits from current knowledge. Exploration, on the other hand, is characterized by 'experimentation with new alternatives' (March, 1991: 85), the returns from which are 'systematically less certain, more remote in time, and organizationally more distant from the locus of action and adaptation' (March, 1991: 73). The scope of innovative search may be broadened, and is more likely to incorporate resources that lie outside of the organization's existing external network since the breadth and content of the required skills may be new.

Processes of exploitation and exploration also have many referents in the multinational literature. Many of the studies cited previously suggest that the most frequent motivation for overseas technical activity is the customization of existing products and technologies to local market needs. Indeed, the classical theory of the multinational firm holds that international expansion tends to be based upon the firm's technical core—i.e., products and technologies with which the firm has achieved competitive advantage in its home market (Dunning, 1988; Porter, 1990; Vernon, 1966). In March's terms, adaptive technical activities performed by foreign subsidiaries are exploitation oriented in the sense that they are directed at capitalizing upon the firm's existing knowledge base. Although the adaptive process may be motivated by host country stimuli (e.g., from customers, regulatory agencies, or competitors), the technology embodied in the products and processes being adapted is likely to have its intellectual roots elsewhere, most immediately in the parent organization itself, but also in the parent's own innovation network in the home base of the firm. In short, I am arguing that the nature of the subsidiary's innovation will be one of the factors that determines where, geographically, the subsidiary's sources of innovation are likely to originate. Specifically:

Hypothesis 1a: If a foreign subsidiary's innovation is adaptive in nature, it will be more likely to draw upon technical ideas originating in the home country.

Hypothesis 1b: If a foreign subsidiary's innovation is adaptive in nature, it will be less likely to draw upon technical ideas originating in the host country.

The multinational literature further suggests that exploration—the search for and development of new technical ideas, products, and processes—is also an important dimension of at least some overseas technical activity. Firms may have explicit technology-seeking objectives in mind when establishing a particular facility, or, as suggested by Ronstadt (1977), Hakanson and Nobel (1993) and others, the technological orientation of the subsidiary may evolve over time toward a more autonomous set of activities that are less closely aligned to the existing knowledge base of the firm. The subsidiary itself may emerge as the center of excellence (i.e., of technical know-how and expertise) within the firm for particular products and technologies (Birkinshaw, 1997). In such cases, the locus of innovative search is more likely to reside within external networks that are distinct from those of the parent firm. Host country signals—commercial and technical—are likely to predominate because of their salience and immediacy, and the clearer prospect they offer of returns to innovative effort. In addition, on the resource side, specialized competence—and the technical autonomy that often goes with it—allows scientists and engineers the opportunity to pursue technical paths that are more compatible with their own education, training, and experience than would otherwise be the case. In such cases, the subsidiary's knowledge-sharing network is likely to have its geographic locus in the host country environment. In extreme cases, where the subsidiary is the only competence center within the firm for a particular technology, there may exist few ties with the traditional networks of the parent firm in the home base, and local search seems likely to predominate. In essence, I am arguing that one of the factors that will predict whether a subsidiary innovation builds upon home or host country ideas is the strength of the sub-

106   *T. S. Frost*

sidiary's technical capabilities (relative to the other units in the firm) within a particular field of technology. Specifically:

> *Hypothesis 2a: The greater the leadership position of the subsidiary in a particular technical field, the greater the likelihood that a subsidiary innovation in that field will draw upon technical ideas originating in the host country.*

> *Hypothesis 2b: The greater the leadership position of the subsidiary in a particular technical field, the lower the likelihood that a subsidiary innovation in that field will draw upon technical ideas originating in the home country.*

March's distinction between exploitation and exploration suggests, then, a basic association between the nature of the innovative activities performed by foreign subsidiaries and the location of the knowledge sources that underpin those activities. In the modal case, subsidiary innovation reinforces the existing knowledge base of the firm through reproduction and incremental extension. The focus on refinement and adaptation is more likely to preserve the existing search routines of the organization, which are weighted toward internal knowledge flows (i.e., parent–subsidiary) and the parent firm's existing external network in the home base. In such cases, the technological advantages of the home base—which manifest themselves in the technological foci and capabilities of the parent—become a focal point for innovative search by foreign subsidiaries. Therefore:

> *Hypothesis 3a: Innovations in technical fields of home country technological advantage will be more likely to draw upon technical ideas originating in the home country.*

In other cases, subsidiaries are directed toward, or evolve toward, the development of new technical capabilities and knowledge. Here, market signals from important local customers as well as the availability of distinctive technical skills and resources are more likely to drive the pattern of innovative search, which naturally pulls toward the path of least resistance or, equivalently, the

path of greatest potential reward. These demand and supply side forces reflect and reinforce locational advantages of the host country and its regions (Cantwell, 1992; Florida and Kenney, 1994; Krugman, 1990; Porter, 1990; Saxenian, 1994; Storper, 1992). Regardless of whether firms consciously seek to match the technological foci of foreign units to the technological specializations and market opportunities of particular locations, or, as seems just as likely, evolutionary processes push subsidiaries in such a direction, it follows that subsidiaries innovating in fields of local technological advantage are more likely to draw upon market and technological signals originating in the host country since this, by definition, is the where the geographic locus of advanced capabilities resides. Thus:

> *Hypothesis 3b: Innovations in technical fields of host country technological advantage will be more likely to draw upon technical ideas originating in the host country.*

Further, as Cantwell (1992) has argued, multinationals may seek new technological capabilities in institutional environments that are qualitatively different from the home base of the firm. In extreme cases, as in the Samsung example cited earlier (Kim, 1997), firms may establish foreign R&D facilities to overcome locational disadvantages of the home base by tapping into locational advantages abroad. In the opposite case—the purest form of exploitation-oriented innovation—the local (host country) environment is barren of relevant or important technological resources, and innovative search is directed toward the interrelated capabilities of the parent firm and the home base. In short, the argument is that there is likely to be a home–host interaction effect that influences the geographic sources of foreign subsidiaries' innovations. Specifically:

> *Hypothesis 3c: Innovations in technical fields characterized by home advantaged–host disadvantaged will be more likely to draw upon technical ideas originating in the home country.*

> *Hypothesis 3d: Innovations in technical fields characterized by home disadvantaged–host advantaged will be more likely to draw upon technical ideas originating in the host country.*

                    Strat. Mgmt. J., **22**: 101–123 (2001)

The geographic sources of subsidiaries' innovations: the embeddedness perspective

The linkage between exploitation/exploration on the one hand, and the location of the subsidiary's external knowledge sources on the other, fits into what may be described as the strategic perspective on external sources of innovation (Powell *et al.*, 1996). The basic assumption of this perspective is that participation in external technical communities (whether and in which communities to participate) is a strategic choice of the firm (Bierly and Chakrabarti, 1996). A second, rather different strand of thinking emphasizes the emergent properties of such networks and their 'embeddedness' (Granovetter, 1985) in the social relations of technological innovation. Allen (1984) and Saxenian (1994), for example, note that school, career, and friendship ties are important mechanisms through which external technical knowledge is located, accessed, and assimilated. Bianchi and Bellini (1991: 488) argue that innovation networks are underpinned importantly by 'social solidarity ... best sustained through constant interaction and geographic proximity.' Schrader (1991) and von Hippel (1988) suggest that the norm of reciprocity is a governing feature of knowledge-sharing activity between actors in technological communities.

At the most general level, the embeddedness perspective points to the possibility that overseas subsidiaries may experience a 'liability of foreignness' (Hymer, 1976) that may impede their ability to participate in local innovation networks. This basic proposition is supported by Zaheer and Mosakowski's (1997) study of currency trading rooms, in which it was found that foreign subsidiaries face formidable social and cultural barriers that impede their effective participation in local knowledge-sharing communities.

A more specific formulation of the argument points to several factors that may influence a subsidiary's capacity to engage in reciprocal knowledge sharing within local technical communities. In particular, the norm of reciprocity implies that the innovating organization needs to have the capacity to provide potentially valuable knowledge as well as to receive it. Schrader (1991: 166), for example, finds that 'the probability of information exchange increases significantly if the inquiring party is known to control considerable technical knowledge.' This suggests

that the scale of a subsidiary's innovative activities may influence perceptions of its worthiness and credibility as an exchange partner within local knowledge-sharing networks. Specifically subsidiaries with greater innovation scale may be more likely to access and utilize local sources of knowledge during the innovation process. Subsidiaries with only limited innovation scale, on the other hand, may not have the resources to credibly offer would-be exchange partners with knowledge about important technical developments, and hence may be precluded from meaningful participation in local networks. Lacking visibility, stature, and legitimacy in the host country, these subsidiaries are more likely to be dependent upon ideas and know-how originating in the headquarters organization and in the parent firm's external network in the home base of the firm. In this spirit I propose:

Hypothesis 4a: The greater the innovation scale of the subsidiary, the greater the likelihood that its innovations will draw upon technical ideas originating in the host country.

Hypothesis 4b: The lesser the innovation scale of the subsidiary, the greater the likelihood that its innovations will draw upon technical ideas originating in the home country.

Although a narrow interpretation of reciprocity suggests that exchange is conditioned upon the strict equivalence of benefits, social exchange theorists (e.g., Gouldner, 1960) point out that exchange is often governed by notions of diffuse reciprocity—a rough equivalence of exchange benefits within a group over some period of time. Diffuse reciprocity tends to be established through repeat experience and the observation of cooperative behavior (Axelrod, 1984), or, in Sabel's (1994) terminology, through simultaneous 'learning by monitoring.' Zaheer and Mosakowski (1997) adopt a similar line of reasoning in hypothesizing that the degree of legitimacy of foreign subsidiaries in a particular host country environment is likely to increase with the tenure of the subsidiary in that environment. Thus, all else equal, it seems apparent that older, more established subsidiaries—i.e., those with time to have gained a reputation for cooperative behavior—are more likely to have access to local

108   *T. S. Frost*

sources of knowledge than their younger, less well-established counterparts. As a result, young subsidiaries, who may be said to experience a 'liability of newness' (Stinchcombe, 1965; Venkataraman and Van de Ven, 1998) in the host country environment, are more likely to draw upon ideas originating at home, in the existing technical network of the parent firm. Therefore:

Hypothesis 5a: The older the subsidiary, the greater the likelihood that its innovations will draw upon technical ideas originating in the host country.

Hypothesis 5b: The younger the subsidiary, the greater the likelihood that its innovations will draw upon technical ideas originating in the home country.

It is also clear that a subsidiary's reputation for cooperation, as well as its capacity to exchange leading-edge technical developments, do not operate in isolation from the larger organization of which it is part. Some multinational firms have multiple technical facilities in a particular host country, some with long experience and considerable technical resources. In the United States, for example, several foreign multinationals with sizeable local R&D organizations have gained membership in the Industrial Research Institute, an influential trade association of U.S.-based technology companies. In addition to providing valuable connections to technical elites in the host country, this kind of participation in local institutional arrangements provides symbolic evidence of the corporation's legitimacy and membership in the host technical community. In other words, the reputation of the parent firm as an 'insider' in local technical circles may be an important determinant of a subsidiary's capacity to gain access to local knowledge-sharing networks. Following the same logic, subsidiaries that are not able to leverage the reputation-based advantages of being part of a large host country network are likely to be more dependent on knowledge sources at home, where the parent firm's stature and legitimacy are typically well established. This implies:

Hypothesis 6a: The greater the parent firm's technical presence in the host country, the

greater the likelihood that a subsidiary's innovations will draw upon technical ideas originating in the host country.

Hypothesis 6b: The smaller the parent firm's technical presence in the host country, the greater the likelihood that a subsidiary's innovations will draw upon technical ideas originating in the home country.

To recap, the overarching argument is that the orientation of a subsidiary's technical activities toward the exploitation of existing capabilities or the exploration for new ones is the primary driver of the geography of its external sources of innovation. Factors indicating a logic of exploitation are hypothesized to predict a greater propensity by the subsidiary to draw upon sources of innovation originating in the home country. Factors indicating a logic of exploration, on the other hand, are hypothesized to predict a greater propensity to draw upon technical ideas originating in the host country. Moderating this argument, however, I also posited that a subsidiary's ability to gain access to local knowledge sources is likely to be dependent upon its embeddedness in the host country context and the social relations of technological innovation. Factors indicating a greater level of embeddedness in the local milieu are hypothesized to predict a greater propensity by the subsidiary to draw upon local knowledge, i.e., technical ideas originating in the host country environment. Conversely, subsidiaries lacking local stature and legitimacy will necessarily be more dependent on sources of innovation in the home base, where the parent firm's reputation is established and secure. Thus, factors associated with lower levels of local embeddedness on the part of foreign subsidiaries are hypothesized to predict a greater propensity to build upon technical ideas originating at home.

METHOD

Patents and patent citation analysis

This study seeks to explain the geographic origin of the technical ideas embodied in U.S. subsidiaries' innovations. As an indicator of a subsidiary innovation, I used the granting of a patent by the U.S. Patent Office. For a patent to be issued, an invention must meet three basic criteria: (1) it must be novel; (2) it must be neither trivial nor obvious to an informed practitioner in the relevant technical field; and (3) it must have commercial potential. U.S. patent data have an extensive history in studies of technological innovation, including several prior studies of innovation in multinational firms (Cantwell, 1993; Patel and Pavitt, 1991; Zander, 1994). For a more general discussion of the advantages, limitations, and interpretation of U.S. patent data the reader is referred to this earlier work, especially Griliches (1992).

Because every U.S. patent lists the address of the inventor as well as her organizational affiliation (the 'assignee'), it is possible to identify the location of the technical unit responsible for a particular patented invention. For multinational firms, this means it is possible to classify a patent as stemming from technical activity performed by inventors located in the home base of the firm, or abroad—i.e., by the parent organization or by a foreign subsidiary. Using this information, I was able to identify a total of 16,210 patents as originating in technical work performed by U.S.-based subsidiaries of foreign multinationals during the 1980–90 time period of my study. A significant proportion of these patents belonged to U.S. firms that were acquired by foreign firms before or during this time period.[3] For reasons discussed earlier, these patents were eliminated from the sample, leaving a total of 10,589 patents.

For the purposes of this study, the key feature of U.S. patent data is that each patent record includes a list of references or 'citations' to earlier patents. These citations indicate a link between the technical ideas embodied in the current and prior inventions. In Jaffe *et al.*'s (1993: 580) words, 'a citation of Patent X by Patent Y means that X represents a piece of previously existing knowledge upon which Y builds.' Because each citation is also itself a patent, it is

possible to develop measures of association—technological, organizational, geographic, temporal—between citing and cited patents. In this paper, I focus on geographic aspects, specifically on the conditions under which subsidiary inventions cite prior patents originating in the home base of the firm and/or in the subsidiary's local (host country) environment. In recent years, a number of scholars have used a similar methodology to draw inferences about technological trajectories (e.g., Stuart and Podolny, 1996), the localization of technological spillovers (e.g., Jaffe *et al.*, 1993), and interorganizational learning among alliance partners (Mowery, Oxley, and Silverman, 1996). Almeida's (1996) study of multinationals' patent citations in the semiconductor industry is a close methodological analogue to the current study. For a more detailed discussion of patent citation analysis, readers are referred to these earlier articles, especially Jaffe *et al.* (1993).

Measures

Table 1 provides names and operational definitions of dependent and independent variables.

Geographic dependent variables

The dependent variables used in this study are derived from the geographic information contained on each of the citations listed by a U.S. subsidiary's patent. Thus the fundamental unit of analysis in the regressions presented below is a patent citation. For each citation, I developed a set of dichotomous measures that capture whether or not the cited invention was developed by inventors in (1) the home base of the firm; (2) the host country (i.e., the United States); and (3) the U.S. state in which the subsidiary is based ('host state').[4] I test my hypotheses by running separate regressions for each of the three locations, giving the study three geographic

---

[3] To classify a patent as originating in a greenfield subsidiary, an acquired U.S. firm, or a joint venture, I used a variety of print and electronic references on foreign direct investment in the United States, as well as listings of M&A activity contained in Moody's and various electronic data bases. Using these sources, I traced the timing of mergers, acquisitions, and dispositions for over 400 non-American industrial firms from the mid-1960s to the early 1990s. Acquired U.S. firms were classified as a subsidiary of a foreign parent when the parent had obtained a controlling interest (i.e., greater than 50% equity ownership).

[4] The debate about the correct subnational geographic unit of analysis is relevant here (cf. Dicken, 1994; Krugman, 1990; Porter, 1990; Storper, 1992). Economic geographers have long pointed out that political boundaries do not necessarily correspond to boundaries of economic regions. In addition to U.S. states, I also experimented with measures constructed at the level of the 'economic area' as defined by the U.S. Bureau of Economic Analysis. However, the results presented below were highly robust to this alternative approach, which for space reasons I do not present.

Strat. Mgmt. J., **22**: 101–123 (2001)

110   *T. S. Frost*

Table 1. Names and definitions of variables and expected signs

Variable	Operational definition	Expected Sign	
Dependent variables			
Home country citation	1 if the citation originates in the subsidiary's home country; 0 otherwise		
Host country citation	1 if the citation originates anywhere in the U.S.; 0 otherwise.		
Host state citation	1 if the citation originates in the subsidiary's host state; 0 otherwise.		
Independent variables		Home	Host
H1 Adaptation of HQ technology	1 if the subsidiary patent cites a prior headquarters patent[a]; 0 otherwise.	+	−
H2 Technical leadership	Share of total company patents attributable to the subsidiary, by technical field[b] and application year of the citing patent.	−	+
H3a Home country advantage	1 if the citing subsidiary patent is in a technical field in which the subsidiary's home country has an RTA greater than 1 in the application year; 0 otherwise.	+	
H3b Host country advantage	1 if the citing subsidiary patent is in a technical field in which the U.S. has an RTA greater than 1 in the application year; 0 otherwise.		+
H3b Host state advantage	1 if the citing subsidiary patent is in a technical field in which the host state has an RTA greater than 1 in the application year; 0 otherwise.		+
H4 Innovation scale	Log of the total number of patents issued to the subsidiary in the application year.	−	+
H5 Subsidiary age	Log of the number of days between the application date of the citing subsidiary patent and the subsidiary's first patent application.	−	+
H6 Parent presence in host	Log of the number of patents issued to all U.S.-based subsidiaries of the parent firm minus the number of patents issued to the subsidiary responsible for the citing patent in the application year.	−	+

[a]Headquarters patents are operationalized as patents assigned to the parent firm that are issued to inventors in the home country of the firm. For example, a patent assigned to the Swiss firm Roche that was issued to an inventor residing in Switzerland is considered a headquarters patent. As in the rest of the study, where multiple inventors are listed on a particular patent, the address of the first inventor is used to determine the originating location of the patent.
[b]Technical field is defined at the level of 33 broad fields of technology.

dependent variables: *Home Country Citation*, *Host Country Citation*, and *Host State Citation*.

Independent variables

The hypotheses relate the geographic sources of foreign subsidiaries' innovations to (1) characteristics of the subsidiary's innovation, (2) characteristics of the subsidiary, and (3) characteristics of the parent firm. Measures to operationalize these hypotheses were constructed from the patent data base.

As a measure of whether the subsidiary innovation is adaptive in nature, i.e., builds directly upon the existing knowledge base of the parent firm (Hypothesis 1), I created a dichotomous variable, *Adaptation of HQ Technology*, that takes on the value of unity if *any* of the citations referenced by a particular subsidiary patent are to prior patents generated by the headquarters organization. Following the same methodology used to identify U.S. subsidiary patents, a headquarters' patent was defined as a patent that is (1) assigned to the parent firm, and (2) whose first inventor is located in the home base of the firm. Note that this measure does not merely capture a process of *adoption* of the headquarters technology by the subsidiary, but rather a process

Strat. Mgmt. J., **22**: 101–123 (2001)

of *adaptation*—as indicated by the issuance of a patent to the subsidiary for its work.[5] Thus a citation to a prior headquarters' patent indicates that the subsidiary's invention builds directly upon headquarters' technology while at the same time making a nontrivial advancement over that technology (and, indeed, over *all* prior art in the particular technical area).

The capability of a subsidiary in a particular technical field, and in particular its position as a center of technical expertise within the firm (Hypothesis 2), was measured by calculating the subsidiary's share of total company patents in the particular technical field of the citing patent. Our assumption is that the larger the share of corporate patents accounted for by a subsidiary in a particular technical field, the greater its capability in that field relative to other units in the company.[6] *Technical Leadership* was calculated based on the company's patenting profile in the same year as the subsidiary's patent application. The definition of a technical field was based on a concordance (listed in Zander, 1994) between the approximately 400 patent classes in the U.S. patent classification system and 33 broad fields of technology. Examples of these broad fields include pharmaceuticals, semiconductors, and photographic instruments.

Measures of locational technological advantage (Hypothesis 3) were derived from indexes of 'revealed technological advantage' (RTA), a measure which has been widely adopted in prior research on innovation using patent data (Cantwell, 1993; Zander, 1994). The RTA of a particular location technology captures the extent to which that location specializes in a particular technical field. It is analogous to measures of export specialization used in the trade literature. Scores greater than unity indicate that the location has a disproportionate position (relative to its position in other technical fields) of the world's patents in a particular technical field.[7] The measure is independent of the overall size of the location. For example, Switzerland, a small country, has an RTA of well over 1 in fields such as pharmaceuticals and dyes. The raw RTA scores, which were calculated in the same year as the subsidiary patent and were based on the full set of 400 patent classes, were then converted to dummy variables, which take on the value of 1 if the RTA is greater than 1, and 0 otherwise. In addition to measures at the country level (*Home Country Advantage* and *Host Country Advantage*), RTA indexes were also calculated for the subsidiary's host state in the application year of the subsidiary patent. *Host State Advantage* is a proxy for patterns of *local* technological specialization (i.e., within the subsidiary's immediate geographic locale), which it was argued earlier may be more relevant in terms of knowledge generation and assimilation than aggregate country-level indicators.

To capture the interaction between home and host locational characteristics (Hypotheses 3c, 3d), I created a set of dummy variables reflecting the four possible combinations derived from interacting home/host and advantaged–disadvantaged. 'Advantaged' is measured by RTA scores greater than unity; 'disadvantaged' by scores less than unity. Following the argument laid out earlier, I hypothesize that the strongest effects will be in the off-diagonals: *Home Advantaged–Host Disadvantaged* (indicating a logic of exploitation) will be most strongly associated with innovations that build upon home country sources of knowledge; *Home Disadvantaged–Host Advantaged* (logic of exploration) will be most strongly associated with subsidiaries drawing upon host country (and host state) sources of innovation.

To capture the innovation scale of the subsidiary (Hypothesis 4) I constructed a count-based measure of the total number of patents issued to the focal subsidiary across all technical fields. *Innovation Scale* is the log of this number, measured in the application year of the citing subsidi-

---

[5] This follows directly from the criteria, discussed earlier, for the issuance of a patent by the U.S. Patent and Trademark Office, which states that the inventor must establish, to the satisfaction of an expert in the field (the patent examiner), that its invention is novel and 'nontrivial'—i.e., a significant improvement over prior work.

[6] Note that this variable is distinct, both conceptually and operationally, from *Innovation Scale* (Hypothesis 4). *Technical Leadership* is intended to capture the subsidiary's technical position in a particular technical domain relative to the rest of the firm. In contrast, *Innovation Scale* is a measure of the subsidiary's total technical resources across all fields. The two measures are also different in the sense that *Innovation Scale* is an absolute measure (count of total patents) whereas *Technical Leadership* is a proportional measure. The fairly low correlation between the two variables ($r = 0.12$) supports the claim that the variables are operationally distinct.

[7] Denoting P_{ij} as the number of patents issued in technical field j to inventors in location i, the RTA index is calculated as: $RTA_{ij} = (P_{ij} / \Sigma_i P_{ij}) / (\Sigma_j P_{ij} / \Sigma_{ij} P_{ij})$.

112   *T. S. Frost*

ary patent. The use of this measure as a proxy for the scale of the unit's technical effort is supported by Griliches (1992), who notes that patents have been used in many studies as a measure of *inputs* into the innovation process (other input measures being R&D expenditures and number of scientists and engineers).[8] One drawback of this measure is the implicit (and empirically incorrect) assumption of equality in the 'propensity to patent' across technical fields. I considered an alternative approach, which would have weighted patents in different technical classes by a factor reflecting the technological opportunity (Jaffe, 1986) in that class. However, the absence of a well-established basis in the patent literature for such a measure persuaded me to adopt the more straightforward and transparent count measure used here.[9]

The subsidiary's tenure in the host country (Hypothesis 5) was measured by the log of the number of days between the application date of the citing subsidiary patent and the application date of the subsidiary's first patent. Although I believe the measure, *Subsidiary Age*, captures the essence of the construct, it suffers from the problem of left censoring of the first patent application date. The earliest patent application in the data base was filed in the early 1970s, whereas it is well known that some U.S. subsidiaries, especially those belonging to large European chemical firms, have been conducting research in the United States since before World War II. Data on establishment dates were not readily available for the large number of subsidiaries in the sample, hence the use of this proxy. Fortunately, the impact of this measurement error is likely to bias the results in a conservative direc-

tion. That is, precisely because there will be less of an age difference between the youngest and oldest subsidiaries in the sample than is actually the case, the measure used is likely to capture less variation in the dependent variable. However, given the limitations of the measure, I experimented with several alternatives, the results of which are discussed below.

Finally, the overall size of the parent company's technical presence in the host country (Hypothesis 6) is operationalized using a count-based measure of the total number of patents issued to all U.S.-based units (including acquisitions and joint ventures) belonging to the company. *Parent Presence in Host* is given by the log of that total, measured in the application year of the citing subsidiary patent. To capture the effect of the parent's network independent of the focal subsidiary's own technical scale, the number of patents issued to the focal subsidiary was subtracted out of the company's U.S. total before taking the log. I also experimented with an alternative measure based on the total number of patenting subsidiaries in the United States belonging to the parent firm, and with an index of number of subsidiaries multiplied by number of patents, but the results described below proved insensitive to these alternative measures.

Control variables

One of the main difficulties with using patent citations to draw inferences about geographic aspects of the innovation process arises from the high degree of spatial clustering of patenting activity in the real world. An example best illustrates the problem. It is well known that New Jersey is a center of pharmaceutical research in the United States, a fact that can be easily verified by reference to the large number of pharmaceutical patents granted to New Jersey inventors each year. Although it may be tempting to infer a pattern of local knowledge sourcing from the observation that foreign subsidiaries based in New Jersey and patenting in pharmaceuticals cite a large number of New Jersey pharmaceutical patents, such an inference runs into the problem that such a pattern is exactly what would be predicted from the patent records of *any* organization innovating in pharmaceuticals—wherever located. Put differently, such a pattern is consistent with a random or 'dartboard' model (Ellison

---

[8] Supporting this claim, Griliches (1992) points out that the cross-sectional correlation between R&D expenditures and patents is about 0.9.
[9] The use of 'nonweighted' patent counts as a measure of innovation scale raises the question of how differences across technical fields in the propensity to patent are likely to impact the empirical results. I believe that any measurement error from this operationalization is likely to bias the results *against* a finding in support of this hypothesis. That is, if the hypothesis is correct, then the failure to measure the innovation scale of the subsidiary correctly should cause an attenuation of the results with respect to this variable. In addition, to the extent that the measure is capturing systematic industry or technical field effects (e.g., subsidiaries in the chemical industry—a high-propensity-to patent industry—tend to be large by my measure), these effects will be captured by the geographic and technical field control variables.

and Glaeser, 1994) of innovative search in which the citation pattern simply reflects the underlying geography of patenting activity for a particular technology–location–time period. A similar problem exists with respect to home country citation patterns: subsidiaries of Japanese electronics firms, for example, can be expected to cite their home base more often than subsidiaries of Italian electronics firms because of the differing levels of innovative activity in electronics in those two countries.

Following Jaffe *et al.* (1993) and Almeida (1996), I control for the underlying geography of patenting by matching each citation listed on a subsidiary's patent with a 'control citation'—a patent that has the same technological and temporal (application year) characteristics as the cited patent but which itself is not cited by the subsidiary patent. In the regressions that follow, *Geographic Controls* accounts for both the geographic distribution of patenting activity in a particular technical field as well as secular changes in that distribution over time. As demonstrated in the Jaffe *et al.* (1993) paper, this control variable will, by construction, capture a large proportion of the variation in the dependent variable, thus creating a high hurdle for the independent variables to reach significance—and a conservative test of my hypotheses.

Finally, I also included a set of dummy variables to control for unobserved differences in patterns of knowledge sourcing across technical fields. Although it is possible to develop many conjectures about industry/technical field effects, there is very little in the way of theoretical guidance—or prior empirical research—that allows for a meaningful set of hypotheses to be derived *a priori*. However, the *suggestion* that there may be differences across these categories motivates the inclusion of dummy variables that control for their effects on the hypothesized relationships. Using a concordance obtained from Adam Jaffe, patent classes were broken down into five broad areas of technology (Chemicals, excluding Drugs; Drugs and Medical Technology; Electronic Arts; Mechanical Arts; and Other) and the resulting dummy variables included in the models.

Specification issues

The data are organized as a panel of citations indexed by year (1980 to 1990), subsidiary, parent

firm, and technical field. Ideally it would have been possible to use panel regression techniques to investigate dynamic aspects of the phenomenon, especially with respect to the hypotheses about subsidiary age and resources and the evolution of the parent firm's technical network in the United States. Unfortunately, this approach runs into the problem that the patent data base is severely unbalanced: many subsidiaries are not issued patents each year. Moreover, of those subsidiaries that are issued patents in a given year, many are issued very small numbers—one or two is not uncommon. In practice, these features of the data set mean that in a fixed-effects specification it would have been impossible to distinguish unobserved 'subsidiary effects' (i.e., idiosyncratic behavior of a particular subsidiary) from effects due to the independent variables. The solution to this problem was twofold. First, I ran the main set of regression equations using the full 1980 to 1990 series. To control for unobserved year effects, i.e., effects that vary over time but are constant across subsidiaries such as changes in patent filing procedures, I included a set of dummy variables for each year in the model. Second, I ran the same models in cross-section (i.e., using a single year of data) as a way of controlling for fixed subsidiary effects. Results are discussed below after the main findings are presented.

Finally, because of my interest in the geography of *external* sources of innovation, I excluded from the statistical analysis all self-citations, i.e., all citations to prior patents generated by any unit of the firm: headquarters, other subsidiaries, or the patenting subsidiary itself. This approach accords with both the theoretical literature on technological spillovers, which typically defines a spillover as an *inter*-organizational knowledge flow, and with previous practice in the empirical literature (e.g., Jaffe *et al.*, 1993). In future work I plan to examine directly patterns of *intra*-organizational patent citations as a way of studying internal transfers of knowledge within multinational firms.

RESULTS

Table 2 provides descriptive statistics and a correlation matrix. Table 2 shows that several of the independent variables are significantly correlated

114   T. S. Frost

Table 2. Descriptive statistics and Pearson correlations

Variable	Mean	S.D.	1	2	3	4	5	6	7	8	9	10
1. Home country citation	0.05	0.23										
2. Host country citation	0.65	0.48	-0.33***									
3. Host state citation	0.10	0.31	-0.08***	0.25***								
4. Adaptation of HQ technology	0.14	0.35	0.05***	-0.02***	0.00							
5. Technical leadership	0.39	0.35	-0.02**	0.01*	0.03***	-0.14***						
6. Home country advantage	0.59	0.49	0.06***	-0.04***	-0.01	0.09***	-0.11***					
7. Host country advantage	0.51	0.50	-0.05***	0.11***	0.02**	-0.06***	0.09***	-0.17***				
8. Host state advantage	0.74	0.44	-0.04***	0.01**	0.05***	0.02***	0.04***	0.06***	0.15***			
9. Innovation scale	2.06	1.58	-0.09***	0.05***	0.04***	0.07***	0.12***	0.11***	0.02***	0.15***		
10. Subsidiary age	7.15	2.64	-0.05***	0.01**	0.02**	0.08***	-0.04***	0.09***	0.01*	0.11***	0.53***	
11. Parent presence in host	2.08	1.88	-0.13***	0.06***	0.00	0.08***	-0.43***	0.04***	0.02***	0.07***	0.39***	0.40***

$N = 40,808$
$*p < 0.10$; $**p < 0.01$; $***p < 0.001$

with each other, suggesting that multicollinearity may be a problem in the regression analysis. Although the large sample size mitigates the impact of this problem to some extent, I ran several checks, including joint tests for significance for highly correlated variables and dropping and/or creating indexes out of collinear variables to address this issue. Although the results of these checks are generally not shown, I include a discussion of the problem and my treatment of it wherever multicollinearity is a plausible explanation for a particular result.

Because the dependent variables used in this study are binary (geographic match/no match), I used logistic regression techniques. Results are reported in Table 3. The table is divided into three sections by geographic dependent variable. Numbers in parentheses represent standard errors. Interpretation of the logistic regression coefficients follows the normal pattern: positive, significant values indicate that an increase in that variable (or a movement from 0 to 1 for indicator variables) increases the odds that a citation will have originated in the particular location modeled, *ceteris paribus*. Negative values indicate the reverse. The magnitude of the logistic regression coefficients is more difficult to interpret and is discussed for selected variables below.[10]

Overall, the data provide strong support for most of my hypotheses and suggest that the geographic sources of foreign subsidiaries' innovations are influenced by characteristics of the subsidiary's innovation, the subsidiary itself, and the parent firm. For each of the three geographic dependent variables, the inclusion of the independent variables in addition to the control variables adds significantly to the overall explanatory power of the models, as evidenced by the significant change in the chi-square statistic as these variables are added to the baseline models (i.e., Models 1, 4 and 7).

Hypothesis 1 predicted that 'adaptive' kinds of subsidiary innovations would be more (less) likely to draw upon technical ideas originating in the home (host) country. Consistent with the prediction of Hypothesis 1a, the positive, significant coefficient on *Adaptation of HQ Technology* in Models 2 and 3 indicates that subsidiary innovations that build directly on prior parent tech-

nology have a significantly higher likelihood of citing patents originating in the home base of the parent firm. Note that this result is not driven by direct citations to headquarters' patents, since all intrafirm citations are excluded from the analysis.[11] Rather, the interpretation of this finding is that when a subsidiary patent cites an earlier patent belonging to the parent firm, the odds that the *remaining* citations listed on that patent will reference a home country source (other than the parent firm) increase. The coefficient on *Adaptation of HQ Technology* implies that these remaining citations are about 1.6 times as likely to originate in the home base as citations listed on patents that do not build directly upon technology developed by the parent firm. In the host country models (Models 5 and 6), *Adaptation of HQ Technology* is negative and significant, consistent with Hypothesis 1b. However, in the host state models it is statistically insignificant.

Hypothesis 2 posited that the leadership position of a subsidiary in a particular technical field would be a predictor of the location of its external innovation network. The host country and host state results on *Technical Leadership* provide strong support for Hypothesis 2a: the larger the share of company patents generated by the subsidiary in a particular technical field, the greater the likelihood that these patents build upon prior inventions originating in the subsidiary's local (host country) environment. Interestingly, the magnitude and significance of the coefficient on *Technical Leadership* increase as the analysis moves from the host country level to the host state level, suggesting that subnational sources of innovation act as particularly important basis for subsidiary technical capabilities. Consistent with Hypothesis 2b, the negative sign on *Technical Leadership* in the home country models suggests that as the subsidiary's share of total company patents in a particular technical field increases, citations listed on those patents are less likely to originate in the home base of the firm.

---

[10] The coefficients in logistic regression analysis, **B**, represent the natural logs of the odds ratios, e^B.

[11] Note that the exclusion of all internal (same-firm) citations from the analysis implies a more difficult (but also more meaningful) test of this hypothesis. Not surprisingly, including citations to prior headquarters' patents, which by definition originate in the home base of the firm, greatly increases the significance and effect size of *Adaptation of HQ Technology* in the home country models below. The more stringent test of my hypothesis—and the one investigated here—is whether citations to *external* patents are systematically associated with technology originating in the home base.

International and Global Strategy

Table 3. Results of logistic regressions on geographic match/no match, 1980–90 citing U.S. subsidiary patents

Variable	Home country citation			Host country (U.S.) citation				Host state citation	
	1	2	3	4	5	6	7	8	9
Adaptation of HQ technology		0.484*** (0.057)	0.474*** (0.057)		-0.120*** (0.031)	-0.113*** (0.031)		0.022 (0.048)	0.029 (0.048)
Technical leadership		-0.643*** (0.078)	-0.571*** (0.078)		0.096* (0.038)	0.079* (0.038)		0.211*** (0.058)	0.197*** (0.058)
Home country advantage		0.568*** (0.050)							
Host country advantage					0.434*** (0.022)				
Host state advantage								0.355*** (0.042)	
Home advantaged–host disadvantaged			0.367*** (0.058)			-0.377*** (0.028)			-0.327*** (0.056)
Home disadvantaged–host advantaged			-0.304*** (0.070)			0.155*** (0.031)			0.079* (0.039)
Home disadvantaged–host disadvantaged			-0.410*** (0.083)			-0.324*** (0.034)			-0.316*** (0.060)
Innovation scale		-0.115*** (0.021)	-0.122*** (0.021)		0.046*** (0.009)	0.050*** (0.009)		0.075*** (0.014)	0.079*** (0.014)
Subsidiary age		0.023* (0.009)	0.023* (0.009)		-0.020*** (0.005)	-0.020*** (0.005)		-0.004 (0.008)	-0.004 (0.008)
Parent presence in host		-0.296*** (0.015)	-0.287*** (0.015)		0.071*** (0.007)	0.069*** (0.007)		0.003 (0.012)	0.001 (0.012)
Geographic controls	1.441*** (0.062) ***	1.092*** (0.065) ***	1.063*** (0.065) ***	0.385*** (0.021)	0.349*** (0.021)	0.347*** (0.021)	1.239*** (0.051) ***	1.176*** (0.052) ***	1.173*** (0.052) ***
Technical field dummies (group sig.):									
Chemicals	-0.192*** (0.043)	-0.080* (0.045)	-0.055 (0.045)	0.000 (0.019)	-0.027 (0.020)	-0.019 (0.020)	-0.044 (0.031)	-0.058* (0.032)	-0.053* (0.032)
Drugs and medical	0.210*** (0.054)	0.271*** (0.055)	0.244*** (0.056)	-0.105*** (0.026)	-0.139*** (0.027)	-0.152*** (0.028)	-0.133*** (0.045)	-0.138*** (0.046)	-0.141*** (0.046)
Electronic arts	0.282*** (0.038)	0.157*** (0.040)	0.145*** (0.040)	0.033* (0.019)	0.071*** (0.019)	0.068*** (0.019)	0.246*** (0.029)	0.308*** (0.030)	0.306*** (0.030)
Mechanical arts	0.202*** (0.047)	0.005 (0.050)	-0.005 (0.050)	-0.070*** (0.023)	-0.046* (0.024)	-0.036 (0.024)	0.272*** (0.035)	0.247*** (0.036)	0.250*** (0.036)
Year dummies	***	***	***	***	***	***	**	***	***
Constant	-3.042*** (0.031)	-2.683*** (0.076)	-2.368*** (0.082)	0.434*** (0.018)	0.134*** (0.027)	0.488*** (0.440)	-2.33*** (0.023)	-2.833*** (0.066)	-2.511*** (0.063)
Model chi-square	635.08***	1541.18***	1584.04***	447.39***	1099.48***	1126.62***	685.77***	852.63***	856.85***
Significance of change in model chi-square	***	***	***	***	***	***	***	***	***
N	40,760	40,621	40,621	40,760	40,621	40,621	40,760	40,621	40,621

$^*p < 0.10$; $^{**}p < 0.01$; $^{***}p < 0.001$

Hypothesis 3 linked the geographic sources of foreign subsidiaries' innovations to a further characteristic of the actual innovation, namely whether it is in a field of home and/or host country technical advantage. The RTA measures used to operationalize this hypothesis are consistently significant with signs in the expected directions. The positive, significant coefficient on *Home Country Advantage* in Models 2 and 3 supports Hypothesis 3a and indicates that subsidiary patents in technical fields in which the home country is comparatively advantaged (RTA > 1) are significantly more likely to cite the home base than are innovations in technical fields of home country disadvantage. The coefficient implies a near doubling in the likelihood of a home country citation. Recall that the significance of the locational advantage variables exists even after controlling for the geographic distribution of patenting activities in the real world. In other words, the results are not consistent with a random or 'dartboard' model of innovative search; rather, the significance of these variables represents a *disproportionate* level of citing to the particular location. Host country and host state results also work well (Models 5 and 8): coefficients on the host country and host state technical advantage variables are in all cases positive and significant, supporting Hypothesis 3b.

When the single-location RTA measures are replaced with dummy variables capturing home–host interaction effects (Hypotheses 3c, 3d), the signs on the three included variables (*Home Advantaged–Host Advantaged* is the dropped category) are in all cases significant and in the expected direction. As predicted, the highest likelihood of a home country citation arises in the case of subsidiary patents in technical fields characterized by home country advantage *and* host (country or state, depending on the model) disadvantage—the case that was argued to be most representative of exploitation-oriented innovation. Conversely, the highest likelihood of a host citation (again host country or host state, depending on the model) is associated with *Home Disadvantaged–Host Advantaged*—the purest exploration case. These results support Hypotheses 3c and 3d.

The remaining hypotheses were based on the argument that the location of innovative search would be influenced by factors that facilitate or impede a subsidiary's ability to embed itself in the local (host) technical milieu. These explanatory factors were hypothesized to operate at both the subsidiary and parent firm levels.

Hypothesis 4a posited that larger subsidiaries would be more likely to draw upon local sources of knowledge due to their greater stature and legitimacy in the host context. This hypothesis is supported at both the host country and host state levels, as indicated by the positive significant sign on *Innovation Scale* in Models 5–6 and 8–9. The likelihood of a subsidiary patent citing a host country or host state patent rises as the total number of patents (across all fields) issued to the subsidiary increases. Supporting Hypothesis 4b, the negative sign on *Innovation Scale* in the home country models implies that smaller subsidiaries are more likely to draw upon technology originating in the home base of the firm.[12]

Hypothesis 5a predicted that older subsidiaries would be more embedded in the local context and thus be more likely to utilize knowledge originating there. This hypothesis is not supported: the sign on *Subsidiary Age* is in the wrong direction in the host country models (Models 5 and 6) and fails to reach significance at the host state level (Models 8 and 9). In addition, *Subsidiary Age* turns out to be *positively* related to home country sources (Models 2 and 3), contrary to Hypothesis 5b. This implies that older subsidiaries are apparently more likely to draw upon home country sources of innovation, not less likely as was hypothesized. Several explanations for the result are possible, including measurement errors (discussed earlier) and multicollinearity, as well as substantive reasons. I explore these issues further below.

Hypothesis 6a predicted that a subsidiary's propensity to draw upon knowledge sources in the host country environment would be conditioned not only on its own structural attributes (innovation scale, age) but also on the overall presence of the parent firm in the host country. This hypothesis receives support at the host coun-

---

[12] As a further test of this claim, I also reran the models replacing *Subsidiary Age* with separate categorical variables for small and large subsidiaries. Consistent with the above results, small subsidiaries—those in the bottom quartile of all subsidiaries in terms of total patent counts in the application year—were more likely to cite home country patents than those not in the bottom quartile. Similarly, subsidiaries in the top quartile in overall patenting for the year were more likely to cite host country and host state patents than subsidiaries not in the top quartile.

118   *T. S. Frost*

try level, as indicated by the positive sign on *Parent Presence in Host* in Models 5 and 6. However, at the host state level (Models 8 and 9), this variable fails to reach significance. This raises the intriguing possibility that the benefit of a large host country organization is that it connects the subsidiary to a broader technical network—i.e., a *national* network—than would otherwise be the case. Hypothesis 6b receives support in Models 2 and 3: the larger the parent's host country network, the less likely is the focal subsidiary to cite patents originating in the home base of the firm.

Robustness checks and additional tests

Although the results presented above generally support the hypothesized relationships, I conducted a further set of tests, primarily as a check on the robustness of the main results. These are presented in Table 4. First, I ran the models in cross-section using a single year of citing subsidiary patent to control for 'fixed effects' (i.e., unobserved subsidiary effects that might be driving the results).[13] The results were generally robust, although not all variables were significant in all models due likely to the combined effects of a dramatic drop in sample size and the inherent noisiness of patent data (Griliches, 1992). None of the earlier results was directly contradicted.

Second, I ran a set of models with home base dummy variables included as an additional set of controls. Here, the results did not work as well, with general home base effects attenuating the effects of *Technical Leadership* in the host models (Models 14 and 15), although this variable still reaches significance at the host state level (Model 15). However, in the home country model (Model 13), *Technical Leadership* switches sign, becoming positive. The most likely interpretation of this result is that the home base dummies are picking up systematic differences across firms from different home countries in the technical autonomy of their foreign subsidiaries and the size of their total U.S. network. Japanese subsidi-

aries, for example, rarely seem to account for a significant proportion of company patents in a particular technical field. For Swiss, Swedish, and British firms, foreign subsidiaries with distinctive technical specializations are more common. Results with respect to the other hypotheses were generally unaffected by the inclusion of the home base controls.

Third, I tested for joint significance of the variables that were used to test the two main perspectives on external innovation networks discussed in the theory section, namely the strategic perspective and the embeddedness perspective. Both blocks of variables were found to add significantly to the explanatory power of the models (results not shown).

Fourth, I checked for methodological problems that may be driving the anomalous results with respect to the subsidiary age hypothesis. Multicollinearity, in particular, is a plausible explanation given the fairly high correlation between *Subsidiary Age* and *Innovation Scale* ($r = 0.53$; $p < 0.01$). Another possible explanation stems from the inclusion of year dummies in the models, which might be controlling for the effects of *Subsidiary Age*. I checked both possibilities by rerunning the models omitting each and then both of the possible confounding variables. The initial anomalous results proved robust to either intervention. As a way of addressing potential problems with my measure of the subsidiary's age, I tried substituting a categorical variable (old/young) for the continuous measure. Again, the original results were supported. Finally, I tried utilizing a cohort approach, testing the hypotheses on a subgroup of patenting subsidiaries with similar entry dates. By choosing an old enough cohort (I focused on 1979–81 entries), I was able to eliminate to a large extent the problem that the age of the oldest group of subsidiaries in the complete sample is left censored. In fact, the cohort analysis (also presented in Table 4) produced a positive relationship between the age of the subsidiary and the propensity to cite local (host state) patents (Model 18), contradicting the earlier results, but supporting the initial hypothesized relationship.

Given the considerable robustness of the main findings with respect to *Subsidiary Age*, it is worthwhile considering possible substantive reasons for rejecting this hypothesis. One possibility is that a significant proportion of older

---

[13] I experimented with several different years of data, all from the latest point in the series (1988, 1989, 1990), as well as pooled 1988–90 results. The results were not particularly sensitive to the choice of year, although the models worked noticeably better for the 3 years of pooled data, confirming the oft-noted sensitivity of patent data to sample size (Griliches, 1992).

Table 4. Robustness checks

Variable	1990 Citing patents			1980–90 citing patents (with home base dummies)			1980–90 citing patents (1979–81 entering cohort)		
	10 Home	11 U.S.	12 Host state	13 Home	14 U.S.	15 Host state	16 Home	17 U.S.	18 Host state
Adaptation of HQ technology	0.475** (0.145)	0.021 (0.081)	-0.084 (0.132)	0.313*** (0.059)	-0.095** (0.031)	0.044 (0.049)	-0.134 (0.169)	-0.137 (0.096)	0.094 (0.170)
Technical leadership	-0.871*** (0.208)	-0.023 (0.097)	0.327* (0.151)	0.245** (0.081)	0.054 (0.041)	0.121* (0.062)	-0.376* (0.209)	-0.023 (0.108)	-0.090 (0.177)
Home advantaged–host disadvantaged	1.017*** (0.161)	-0.454*** (0.071)	-0.197 (0.137)	0.096 (0.060)	-0.346*** (0.029)	-0.323*** (0.057)	0.094 (0.191)	-0.387*** (0.094)	-0.574*** (0.171)
Home disadvantaged–host advantaged	0.320 (0.196)	0.070 (0.083)	-0.001 (0.107)	-0.625*** (0.074)	0.157*** (0.032)	0.063 (0.039)	-0.026 (0.204)	-0.003 (0.100)	-0.106 (0.125)
Home disadvantaged–host disadvantaged	-0.374 (0.275)	-0.260** (0.088)	-0.160 (0.154)	-0.515*** (0.085)	-0.332*** (0.034)	-0.309*** (0.060)	-0.197 (0.266)	-0.477*** (0.114)	-0.422 (0.195)
Innovation scale	-0.068 (0.053)	0.052* (0.021)	0.072* (0.035)	-0.007 (0.024)	0.050*** (0.009)(	0.116*** (0.016)	0.176* (0.073)	-0.004 (0.034)	-0.048 (0.058)
Subsidiary age	0.004 (0.023)	0.010 (0.013)	0.000 (0.023)	0.019* (0.010)	-0.020*** (0.005)	-0.007 (0.008)	-0.047 (0.056)	0.033 (0.030)	0.157*** (0.047)
Parent presence in host	-0.222*** (0.035)	0.050** (0.018)	0.012 (0.030)	-0.066*** (0.018)	0.056*** (0.009)	0.007 (0.014)	-0.166*** (0.045)	0.025 (0.024)	-0.053 (0.041)
Geographic controls	1.163*** (0.149)	0.511*** (0.054)	1.281*** (0.130)	0.547*** (0.067)	0.342*** (0.022)	0.347*** (0.021)	0.470*** (0.159)	0.367*** (0.060)	1.114*** (0.171)
Technical field dummies (group sig.):	***		**		***	***			
Chemicals	-0.356** (0.137)	0.019 (0.051)	-0.060 (0.084)	-0.063 (0.047)	-0.017 (0.020)	-0.073* (0.033)	0.002 (0.162)	0.067 (0.072)	0.120 (0.115)
Drugs and medical	0.303* (0.144)	-0.106 (0.068)	-0.242* (0.116)	0.270*** (0.060)	-0.086*** (0.029)	-0.108* (0.049)	-0.030 (0.170)	0.016 (0.091)	-0.159 (0.163)
Electronic arts	0.065 (0.116)	0.069 (0.052)	0.182* (0.084)	-0.060 (0.045)	0.022 (0.021)	0.211*** (0.032)	-0.055 (0.119)	-0.063 (0.057)	0.139 (0.100)
Mechanical arts	0.593*** (0.118)	-0.056 (0.057)	0.250** (0.088)	0.142* (0.052)	-0.061* (0.025)	0.254*** (0.037)	0.286* (0.128)	-0.084 (0.072)	-0.182 (0.129)
Year dummies (group sig.)				***	***	***	***	***	***
Home base dummies (group sig.)				***	***	***	***	***	***
Constant	-2.671*** (0.240)	0.234* (0.118)	-2.622*** (0.181)	-4.956*** (1.221)	0.438*** (0.088)	-3.025*** (0.424)	-4.642 (3.449)	0.576 (0.448)	-4.959* (2.154)
Model chi-square	399.69***	200.81***	128.78***	2933.42***	1301.74***	1080.82***	457.34***	276.73***	322.49***
N	6,083	6,083	6,083	40,621	40,621	40,621	5,145	5,145	5,145

*p < 0.10; **p < 0.01; ***p < 0.001

120   *T. S. Frost*

subsidiaries never evolve their technological orientations toward local stimuli and resources, perhaps as a result of being locked into older technological trajectories where the product life cycle places less of a premium on innovation. Ronstadt's (1977) case studies of overseas R&D labs support this possibility: the majority of the units he studies did not, in fact, evolve their mandates and orientations over time. In future research I plan to explore more fully how subsidiaries' external innovation networks evolve over time in the host country. Another possibility is that younger subsidiaries do not experience a liability of newness in the host country, as was hypothesized. Perhaps in the realm of technology and innovation, the scale and competence of the facility play more of a role than the length of time the subsidiary has been in existence. Such an explanation is, in fact, supported by the results on *Innovation Scale* and *Technical Leadership*.

DISCUSSION AND CONCLUSION

Where foreign subsidiaries draw their ideas from during the process of technological innovation is a central question in current debates about the nature and evolution of the multinational enterprise. This study has sought to advance this debate by developing and testing a set of hypotheses about the geographic location of the knowledge sources that underpin foreign subsidiaries' innovations. Our results both support and extend a widely debated (but largely untested) conjecture in the multinational literature, namely that foreign direct investment may be driven, at least in part, by the desire to gain knowledge from the diverse institutional contexts in which multinational firms operate. The results of this study support this conjecture by linking distinctive technical capabilities of foreign subsidiaries to local sources of knowledge and locational technological advantage. At the same time, the results also highlight the role played by the home country as a source of knowledge for innovating subsidiaries. One of the key contributions of this study, then, is to underscore the need to recast the literature in terms of a more nuanced question than has preoccupied researchers to date: not *whether* foreign subsidiaries 'tap into' local sources of knowledge (e.g., Almeida, 1996), but *under what conditions* do they? This question leads naturally to this

paper's focus on developing and exploring a broader construct—the geographic sources of innovation—than has preoccupied much of the existing research in this area.

In addition to addressing a previously unexplored question, this paper makes several specific contributions that distinguish it from prior research on the topic. Theoretically, this work reconciles two rather autonomous and at times divergent strands of literature on multinational firms, one emphasizing the exploitation of existing assets and capabilities in foreign markets, the other emphasizing the exploration for new ones. Drawing on research originating outside the mainstream international business literature, I argued that insights into the subsidiary innovation process could be gained from drawing on more general theories of innovation in organizations, especially theories of the structure and governance of external innovation networks. Our results generally support both perspectives on external innovation networks—the strategic perspective and the embeddedness perspective—that were used to generate specific hypotheses about the geographic sources of foreign subsidiaries' innovations. Future work would benefit from more finely grained research that would shed light on the mechanisms of interorganizational knowledge flows and perhaps uncover how foreign subsidiaries and other organizations strategize around the assimilation and utilization of such knowledge.

This paper also breaks new ground empirically. Here, the key contribution of the study is the illumination of systematic patterns linking the characteristics of foreign subsidiaries' innovations to sources of knowledge originating in different geographic locations. Key factors that emerged from the analysis include (1) characteristics of the subsidiary's innovation that suggested a logic of exploitation (positively linked to home country sources) or a logic of exploration (positive to host); (2) characteristics of the subsidiary itself, in particular the overall technical scale of the unit (larger subsidiaries linked to host country sources; smaller to home); and (3) the technical presence of the parent firm in the host country (larger presence linked to host; smaller to home). At a higher level of abstraction, these results suggest that innovative search in foreign subsidiaries is driven by the interplay between the subsidiary's innovation strategy, its evolving technical capabilities, and its 'membership' in the local knowledge sharing community. Future research should focus on exploring these dimensions in more detail and on the relationships between them. Exploring the dynamics of the subsidiary innovation process—how strategy, capabilities, and embeddedness evolve over time—holds particular promise as a future research direction.

Because of the richness of the data set used to conduct the analysis, this paper is able to overcome many of the limitations of previous research on subsidiary innovation. Whereas earlier work has been conducted mostly at the national level of analysis, the empirical analysis here spanned levels down to the subsidiary's host state, showing, in particular, that areas of technological expertise within foreign subsidiaries are underpinned by sources of knowledge that originate in the subsidiary's immediate geographic locale. In addition, the broad industry and technical field coverage of my data set means that the study is not limited to a small number of firms, industries or home countries—improving the generalizability of the results. Previous work has tended to focus on what may be described as 'least conservative' cases for finding evidence of asset-seeking FDI, e.g., foreign subsidiaries in high-tech industries such as biotechnology and semiconductors, often located in dynamic regional settings such as Silicon Valley (e.g., Almeida, 1996; Herbert, 1989; Kim, 1997; Shan and Song, 1997; Westney, 1992).

The results of this study also have potentially important implications for issues and debates in strategic management that do not directly involve a multinational context. Consider the literature on corporate diversification. The mainstream explanation of diversification in the strategy literature is roughly analogous to the argument developed in this paper on the exploitation of existing assets and capabilities. Indeed this argument is central to the 'relatedness' hypothesis that has driven much of the research agenda concerning the relationship between diversification and performance (Chaterjee and Wernerfelt, 1991; Rumelt, 1974). Less discussed in the literature is how firms might use diversification to acquire new resources and capabilities, i.e., the exploration model (although see Anand and Singh, 1997; and Mitchell, Capron, and Swaminathan, 1998). Interpreted this way, a promising area of research may be to view strategic decisions about the scope of the firm—vertical, horizontal, geographic—through the lens of dynamic capability accumulation rather than (or in addition to) more traditional approaches emphasizing static efficiency, transactional hazards, and/or agency problems.

Finally, this study also contributes to the old and once again vital stream of research looking at the relationship between 'location' (and all that term implies) and firm-level competitive advantage (Nelson, 1993; Porter, 1990; Storper, 1992). How the strategies, capabilities and behaviors of firms are shaped by the institutional contexts in which they operate remains an important frontier for strategy research, one with important implications for both practicing managers and public policy-makers. The results of this study contribute to our knowledge in this area by highlighting the locational underpinnings of technical competencies within organizational subunits. Particularly important is the finding that an organization's technological capabilities tend to build to an important degree upon ideas originating in its immediate geographic locale. This result supports a longstanding proposition in the economic geography literature (Marshall, 1920) that is now also being treated seriously by a growing number of researchers in strategy. Interestingly, the multinational firm may offer an ideal context for advancing our understanding of the firm–location nexus precisely because of the ability to study a single corporate entity in multiple institutional contexts. How firms with border-spanning operations identify, assimilate, and integrate external sources of knowledge is a critical question for researchers operating at the intersection of strategic management and international business. Whether firms differ systematically in this regard in terms of strategy or the execution of strategy are important and largely unexplored questions. Of even more concern is the relationship to performance, i.e., how firms turn external sources of knowledge—by definition nonproprietary—into proprietary and *differential* sources of competitive advantage. The results of this study suggests that further research in this area is warranted.

ACKNOWLEDGEMENTS

The author would like to thank his thesis committee—Rebecca Henderson, Don Lessard, Eleanor Westney and Nicholas Ziegler. Also thanks to

122   *T. S. Frost*

Jay Anand, Ann Frost and Amy Hillman for helpful comments. This research was supported by the Industrial Performance Center at MIT.

REFERENCES

Allen T. 1984. *Managing the Flow of Technology: Technology Transfer and the Dissemination of Technological Information Within the R&D Organization.* MIT Press: Cambridge, MA.

Almeida P. 1996. Knowledge sourcing by foreign multinationals: patent citation analysis in the U.S. semiconductor industry. *Strategic Management Journal*, Winter Special Issue **17**: 155–165.

Anand J, Kogut B. 1997. Technological capabilities of countries, firm rivalry and direct investment in the United States. *Journal of International Business Studies* **28**(3): 445–466.

Anand J, Singh H. 1997. Asset redeployment, acquisitions and corporate strategy in declining industries. *Strategic Management Journal*, Summer Special Issue **18**: 99–118.

Archibugi D, Pianta M. 1992. Specialization and size of technological activities in industrial countries: the analysis of patent data. *Research Policy* **21**(1): 79–93.

Axelrod R. 1984. *The Evolution of Cooperation.* Basic Books: New York.

Bartlett CA, Ghoshal S. 1989. *Managing Across Borders: The Transnational Solution.* Harvard Business School Press: Boston, MA.

Bianchi P, Bellini N. 1991. Public policies for local networks of innovators. *Research Policy* **20**(5): 487–497.

Bierly P, Chakrabarti A. 1996. Generic knowledge strategies in the U.S. pharmaceutical industry. *Strategic Management Journal*, Winter Special Issue **17**: 123–137.

Birkinshaw J. 1997. Entrepreneurship in multinational corporations: the characteristics of subsidiary initiatives. *Strategic Management Journal* **18**(3): 207–229.

Cantwell J. 1992. The theory of technological competence and its application to international production. In *Foreign Investment, Technology and Economic Growth*, McFeteridge DG (ed.). University of Calgary Press: Calgary; 33–67.

Cantwell J. 1993. The internationalization of technological activity and its implications for competitiveness. In *Technology Management and International Business*, Granstrand O, Hakanson H, Sjolander S (eds.). Wiley: Chichester; 137–162.

Chaterjee S, Wernerfelt B. 1991. The link between resources and type of diversification: theory and evidence. *Strategic Management Journal* **12**(1): 33–49.

Cohen W, Levinthal D. 1990. Absorptive capacity: a new perspective on learning and innovation. *Administrative Science Quarterly* **35**(1): 128–152.

Czepiel JA. 1974. Word of mouth processes in the diffusion of a major technological innovation. *Journal of Marketing Research* **11**: 172–180.

Dalton D, Serapio M. 1993. *U.S. Research Facilities of Foreign Companies.* U.S. Department of Commerce: Washington, DC.

DeBresson C, Amesse F. 1991. Networks of innovators: a review and introduction to the issues. *Research Policy* **20**(5): 363–379.

Dicken P. 1994. Global–local tensions: firms and states in the global space-economy. *Economic Geography* **70**(2): 101–128.

Dore R. 1990. *British Factory–Japanese Factory.* California University Press: Berkeley, CA.

Dosi G. 1988. Sources, procedures and microeconomic effects of innovation. *Journal of Economic Literature* **26**(3): 1120–1171.

Dunning JH. 1988. The eclectic paradigm of multinational production: a restatement and some possible extensions. *Journal of International Business Studies* **19**(1): 1–31.

Dunning JH. 1998. Globalization, technological change and the spatial organization of economic activity. In *The Dynamic Firm: The Role of Technology, Strategy, Organization and Regions*, Chandler A Jr, Hagstrom P, Solvell O (eds.). Oxford University Press: Oxford; 289–314.

Dunning J, Narula R. 1995. The R&D activities of foreign firms in the United States. *International Studies of Management and Organization* **25**(1–2): 39–73.

Ellison R, Glaeser E. 1994. The geographic concentration in U.S. manufacturing industries: a dartboard approach. NBER Working Paper, Cambridge, MA.

Florida R, Kenney M. 1994. The globalization of Japanese R&D: the economic geography of Japanese R&D investment in the United States. *Economic Geography* **70**(4): 305–323.

Freeman C. 1991. Networks of innovators: a synthesis of research issues. *Research Policy* **20**(5): 499–514.

Gerschenkron A. 1962. *Economic Backwardness in Historical Perspective.* Belknap Press: Cambridge, MA.

Gouldner A. 1960. The norm of reciprocity: a preliminary statement. *American Sociological Review* **25**: 161–185.

Granovetter M. 1985. Economic action and social structure: the problem of embeddedness. *American Journal of Sociology* **91**(3): 481–510.

Griliches Z. 1992. Patent statistics as economic indicators: a survey. *Journal of Economic Literature* **28**: 1661–1707.

Hakanson L, Nobel R. 1993. Foreign research and development in Swedish multinationals. *Research Policy* **22**(5,6): 373–396.

Hedlund G. 1986. The hypermodern MNC—a heterarchy? *Human Resource Management* **25**(1): 9–35.

Herbert E. 1989. Japanese R&D in the United States. *Research Technology Management* **32**(6): 11–20.

Hymer SH. 1976. *The International Operations of National Firms: A Study of Direct Investment.* MIT Press: Cambridge, MA.

Jaffe A. 1986. Technological opportunity and spillovers of R&D: evidence from firms' patents, profits and market value. *American Economic Review* **76**(5): 984–1001.

Jaffe A, Trajtenberg M, Henderson R. 1993. Geographic localization of knowledge spillovers as evidenced by patent citations. *Quarterly Journal of Economics* **108**(3): 577–598.

Kim L. 1997. *Imitation to Innovation: The Dynamics of Korea's Technological Learning.* Harvard Business School Press: Boston, MA.

Kogut B, Chang S. 1991. Technological capabilities and Japanese foreign direct investment in the United States. *Review of Economics and Statistics* **73**(3): 401–413.

Krugman P. 1990. *Geography and Trade.* MIT Press: Cambridge, MA.

Lee T, Proctor P. (eds). 1991. *The Emerging Global Technical Enterprise.* National Academy of Sciences: Washington, DC.

March JG. 1991. Exploration and exploitation in organizational learning. *Organization Science* **2**: 71–87.

Marshall A. 1920. *Principles of Economics.* Macmillan: London.

Mitchell W, Capron L, Swaminathan A. 1998. Asset divestiture after post-acquisition resource redeployment. Mitsubishi International Conference, Transformation of Organizations and Strategies in the 21st Century, 27–29 August 1998, Yokohama, Japan.

Mowery DC, Oxley JE, Silverman BS. 1996. Strategic alliances and interfirm knowledge transfer. *Strategic Management Journal*, Winter Special Issue **17**: 77–91.

Nelson R. 1993. *National Innovation Systems.* Oxford University Press: Oxford.

Nobel R, Birkinshaw J. 1998. Innovation in multinational corporations: control and communication patterns in international R&D operations. *Strategic Management Journal* **19**(5): 479–496.

Patel P, Pavitt K. 1991. Large firms in the production of the world's technology: an important case of non-globalization. *Journal of International Business Studies* **22**(1): 1–21.

Porter M. 1990. *The Competitive Advantage of Nations.* Free Press: New York.

Powell WW, Koput K, Smith-Doerr L. 1996. Interorganizational collaboration and the locus of innovation: networks of learning in biotechnology. *Administrative Science Quarterly* **41**(1): 116–145.

Ronstadt R. 1977. *Research and Development Abroad by U.S. Multinationals.* Praeger: New York.

Rumelt R. 1974. *Strategy, Structure, and Economic Performance.* Division of Research. Harvard Business School: Boston, MA.

Sabel C. 1994. Learning and monitoring. The institutions of economic development. In *Handbook of*

Economic Sociology, Smelser N, Swedberg R (eds.). Princeton University Press: Princeton, NJ; 136–165.

Saxenian A. 1994. *Regional Advantage: Culture and Competition in Silicon Valley and Route 128.* Harvard University Press: Cambridge, MA.

Schrader S. 1991. Informal technology transfer between firms: cooperation through information trading. *Research Policy* **20**(2): 153–170.

Shan W, Song J. 1997. Foreign direct investment and the sourcing of technological advantage: evidence from the biotechnology industry. *Journal of International Business Studies* **28**(2): 267–284.

Stinchcombe AL. 1965. Social structure and organizations. In *Handbook of Organizations.* March JG (ed.). Rand-McNally: Chicago, IL; 142–193.

Storper M. 1992. The limits to globalization: technology districts and international trade. *Economic Geography* **68**(1): 60–93.

Stuart T, Podolny J. 1996. Local search and the evolution of technological capabilities. *Strategic Management Journal*, Summer Special Issue **17**: 21–38.

Teece D. 1992. Foreign investment and technological development in Silicon Valley. *California Management Review* **34**(2): 88–107.

Venkataraman S, Van de Ven A. 1998. Hostile environmental jolts, transaction set, and new business. *Journal of Business Venturing* **13**(3): 231–255.

Vernon R. 1966. International investment and international trade in the product cycle. *Quarterly Journal of Economics* **80**: 190–207.

Vernon R. 1979. The product cycle hypothesis in a new international environment. *Oxford Bulletin of Economics and Statistics* **41**: 255–2670.

von Hippel E. 1988. *Sources of Innovation.* Oxford University Press: New York.

Westney DE. 1990. The globalization of technology and the internationalization of R&D. MIT–Japan Program Working Paper, MIT, Cambridge, MA.

Westney DE. 1992. Cross-pacific internationalisation of R&D by U.S. and Japanese firms. Paper presented at the conference Managing R&D Internationally, Manchester Business School, 6–8 July.

Wortmann M. 1990. Multinationals and the internationalization of R&D: new developments in German companies. *Research Policy* **19**(2): 175–183.

Zaheer S, Mosakowski E. 1997. The dynamics of the liability of foreignness: a global study of survival in financial services. *Strategic Management Journal* **18**(6): 439–464.

Zander I. 1994. *The Tortoise Evolution of the Multinational Corporation: Foreign Technological Activity in Swedish Multinational Firms 1890–1990.* Institute of International Business: Stockholm.

[12]

*Improving the lives of the billions of people at the bottom
of the economic pyramid is a noble endeavor.
It can also be a lucrative one.*

Serving the World's Poor,
Profitably

by C.K. Prahalad and Allen Hammond

ONSIDER THIS BLEAK VISION of the world 15 years from now: The global economy recovers from its current stagnation but growth remains anemic. Deflation continues to threaten, the gap between rich and poor keeps widening, and incidents of economic chaos, governmental collapse, and civil war plague developing regions. Terrorism remains a constant threat, diverting significant public and private resources to security concerns. Opposition to the global market system intensifies. Multinational companies find it difficult to expand, and many become risk averse, slowing investment and pulling back from emerging markets.

Now consider this much brighter scenario: Driven by private investment and widespread entrepreneurial activity, the economies of developing regions grow vigorously, creating jobs and wealth and bringing hundreds of millions of new consumers into the global marketplace every year. China, India, Brazil, and, gradually, South Africa become new engines of global economic growth, promoting prosperity around the world. The resulting decrease in poverty produces a range of social benefits, helping to stabilize many developing regions and reduce civil and cross-border conflicts. The threat of terrorism and war recedes. Multinational companies expand rapidly in an era of intense innovation and competition.

Both of these scenarios are possible. Which one comes to pass will be determined primarily by one factor: the willingness of big, multinational companies to enter and invest in the world's poorest markets. By stimulating commerce and development at the bottom of the economic pyramid, MNCs could radically improve the lives of billions of people and help bring into being a more stable, less dangerous world. Achieving this goal does not require multinationals to spearhead global social development initiatives for charitable purposes. They need only act in their own self-interest, for there are enormous business benefits to be gained by entering developing markets. In fact, many innovative companies – entrepreneurial outfits and large, established enterprises alike – are already serving the world's poor in ways that generate strong revenues, lead to greater operating efficiencies, and uncover new sources of innovation. For these companies–and those that follow their lead – building businesses aimed at the bottom of the pyramid promises to provide important competitive advantages as the twenty-first century unfolds.

Big companies are not going to solve the economic ills of developing countries by themselves, of course. It will also

48

CHRISTOPHER CORR

take targeted financial aid from the developed world and improvements in the governance of the developing nations themselves. But it's clear to us that prosperity can come to the poorest regions only through the direct and sustained involvement of multinational companies. And it's equally clear that the multinationals can enhance their own prosperity in the process.

Untapped Potential

Everyone knows that the world's poor are distressingly plentiful. Fully 65% of the world's population earns less than $2,000 each per year – that's 4 billion people. But despite the vastness of this market, it remains largely untapped by multinational companies. The reluctance to invest is easy to understand. Companies assume that people with such low incomes have little to spend on goods and services and that what they do spend goes to basic needs like food and shelter. They also assume that various barriers to commerce – corruption, illiteracy, inadequate infrastructure, currency fluctuations, bureaucratic red tape – make it impossible to do business profitably in these regions.

But such assumptions reflect a narrow and largely outdated view of the developing world. The fact is, many multinationals already successfully do business in developing countries (although most currently focus on selling to the small upper-middle-class segments of these markets), and their experience shows that the barriers to commerce – although real – are much lower than is typically thought. Moreover, several positive trends in developing countries – from political reform, to a growing openness to investment, to the development of low-cost wireless communication networks – are reducing the barriers further while also providing businesses with greater access to even the poorest city slums and rural areas. Indeed, once the misperceptions are wiped away, the enormous economic potential that lies at the bottom of the pyramid becomes clear.

Take the assumption that the poor have no money. It sounds obvious on the surface, but it's wrong. While individual incomes may be low, the aggregate buying power of poor communities is actually quite large. The average per capita income of villagers in rural Bangladesh, for instance, is less than $200 per year, but as a group they are avid consumers of telecommunications services. Grameen Telecom's village phones, which are owned by a single entrepreneur but used by the entire community, generate an average revenue of roughly $90 a month – and as much as $1,000 a month in some large villages.

Customers of these village phones, who pay cash for each use, spend an average of 7% of their income on phone services–a far higher percentage than consumers in traditional markets do.

It's also incorrect to assume that the poor are too concerned with fulfilling their basic needs to "waste" money on nonessential goods. In fact, the poor often do buy "luxury" items. In the Mumbai shantytown of Dharavi, for example, 85% of households own a television set, 75% own a pressure cooker and a mixer, 56% own a gas stove, and 21% have telephones. That's because buying a house in Mumbai, for most people at the bottom of the pyramid, is not a realistic option. Neither is getting access to running water. They accept that reality, and rather than saving for a rainy day, they spend their income on things they can get now that improve the quality of their lives.

Another big misperception about developing markets is that the goods sold there are incredibly cheap and, hence, there's no room for a new competitor to come in and turn a profit. In reality, consumers at the bottom of the pyramid pay much higher prices for most things than middle-class consumers do, which means that there's a real opportunity for companies, particularly big corporations with economies of scale and efficient supply chains, to capture market share by offering higher quality goods at lower prices while maintaining attractive margins. In fact, throughout the developing world, urban slum dwellers pay, for instance, between four and 100 times as much for drinking water as middle- and upper-class families. Food also costs 20% to 30% more in the poorest communities since there is no access to bulk discount stores. On the service side of the economy, local moneylenders charge interest of 10% to 15% *per day*, with annual rates running as high as 2,000%. Even the lucky small-scale entrepreneurs who

get loans from nonprofit microfinance institutions pay between 40% and 70% interest per year–rates that are illegal in most developed countries. (For a closer look at how the prices of goods compare in rich and poor areas, see the exhibit "The High-Cost Economy of the Poor.")

It can also be surprisingly cheap to market and deliver products and services to the world's poor. That's because many of them live in cities that are densely populated today and will be

> Markets at the bottom of the economic pyramid are fundamentally new sources of growth for multinationals. And because these markets are in the earliest stages, growth can be extremely rapid.

even more so in the years to come. Figures from the UN and the World Resources Institute indicate that by 2015, in Africa, 225 cities will each have populations of more than 1 million; in Latin America, another 225; and in Asia, 903. The population of at least 27 cities will reach or exceed 8 million. Collectively, the 1,300 largest cities will account for some 1.5 billion to 2 billion people, roughly half of whom will be bottom-of-the-pyramid (BOP) consumers now served primarily by informal economies. Companies that operate in these areas will have access to millions of potential new customers, who together have billions of dollars to spend. The poor in Rio de Janeiro, for instance, have a total purchasing power of $1.2 billion ($600 per person). Shantytowns in Johannesburg or Mumbai are no different.

The slums of these cities already have distinct ecosystems, with retail shops,

small businesses, schools, clinics, and moneylenders. Although there are few reliable estimates of the value of commercial transactions in slums, business activity appears to be thriving. Dharavi–covering an area of just 435 acres–boasts scores of businesses ranging from leather, textiles, plastic recycling, and surgical sutures to gold jewelry, illicit liquor, detergents, and groceries. The scale of the businesses varies from one-person operations to bigger, well-recognized producers of brand-name products. Dharavi generates an estimated $450 million in manufacturing revenues, or about $1 million per acre of land. Established shantytowns in São Paulo, Rio, and Mexico City are equally productive. The seeds of a vibrant commercial sector have been sown.

While the rural poor are naturally harder to reach than the urban poor, they also represent a large untapped opportunity for companies. Indeed, 60% of India's GDP is generated in rural areas. The critical barrier to doing business in rural regions is distribution access, not a lack of buying power. But new information technology and communications infrastructures – especially wireless–promise to become an inexpensive way to establish marketing and distribution channels in these communities.

Conventional wisdom says that people in BOP markets cannot use such advanced technologies, but that's just another misconception. Poor rural women in Bangladesh have had no difficulty using GSM cell phones, despite never before using phones of any type. In Kenya, teenagers from slums are being successfully trained as Web page designers. Poor farmers in El Salvador use telecenters to negotiate the sale of their crops over the Internet. And women in Indian coastal villages have in less than a week learned to use PCs to interpret real-time satellite images showing concentrations of schools of fish in the Arabian Sea so they can direct their husbands to the best fishing areas. Clearly, poor communities are ready to adopt new technologies that improve their economic opportunities or their quality of life. The lesson for multinationals:

C.K. Prahalad is the Harvey C. Fruehauf Professor of Business Administration at the University of Michigan Business School in Ann Arbor and the chairman of Praja, a software company in San Diego. Allen Hammond is the CIO, senior scientist, and director of the Digital Dividend project at the World Resources Institute in Washington, DC.

Don't hesitate to deploy advanced technologies at the bottom of the pyramid while, or even before, deploying them in advanced countries.

A final misperception concerns the highly charged issue of exploitation of the poor by MNCs. The informal economies that now serve poor communities are full of inefficiencies and exploitive intermediaries. So if a microfinance institution charges 50% annual interest when the alternative is either 1,000% interest or no loan at all, is that exploiting or helping the poor? If a large financial company such as Citigroup were to use its scale to offer microloans at 20%, is that exploiting or helping the poor? The issue is not just cost but also quality – quality in the range and fairness of financial services, quality of food, quality of water. We argue that when MNCs provide basic goods and services that reduce costs to the poor and help improve their standard of living – while generating an acceptable return on investment – the results benefit everyone.

The Business Case

The business opportunities at the bottom of the pyramid have not gone unnoticed. Over the last five years, we have seen nongovernmental organizations (NGOs), entrepreneurial start-ups, and a handful of forward-thinking multinationals conduct vigorous commercial experiments in poor communities. Their experience is a proof of concept: Businesses can gain three important advantages by serving the poor – a new source of revenue growth, greater efficiency, and access to innovation. Let's look at examples of each.

Top-Line Growth. Growth is an important challenge for every company, but today it is especially critical for very large companies, many of which appear to have nearly saturated their existing markets. That's why BOP markets represent such an opportunity for MNCs: They are fundamentally new sources of growth. And because these markets are in the earliest stages of economic development, growth can be extremely rapid.

Latent demand for low-priced, high-quality goods is enormous. Consider

the reaction when Hindustan Lever, the Indian subsidiary of Unilever, recently introduced what was for it a new product category – candy – aimed at the bottom of the pyramid. A high-quality confection made with real sugar and fruit, the candy sells for only about a penny a serving. At such a price, it may seem like a marginal business opportunity, but in just six months it became the fastest-growing category in the company's portfolio. Not only is it profitable, but the company estimates it has the potential to generate revenues of $200 million

per year in India and comparable markets in five years. Hindustan Lever has had similar successes in India with low-priced detergent and iodized salt. Beyond generating new sales, the company is establishing its business and its brand in a vast new market.

There is equally strong demand for affordable services. TARAhaat, a start-up focused on rural India, has introduced a range of computer-enabled education services ranging from basic IT training

to English proficiency to vocational skills. The products are expected to be the largest single revenue generator for the company and its franchisees over the next several years.[1] Credit and financial services are also in high demand among the poor. Citibank's ATM-based banking experiment in India, called Suvidha, for instance, which requires a minimum deposit of just $25, enlisted 150,000 customers in one year in the city of Bangalore alone.

Small-business services are also popular in BOP markets. Centers run in

Uganda by the Women's Information Resource Electronic Service (WIRES) provide female entrepreneurs with information on markets and prices, as well as credit and trade support services, packaged in simple, ready-to-use formats in local languages. The centers are planning to offer other small-business services such as printing, faxing, and copying, along with access to accounting, spreadsheet, and other software. In Bolivia, a start-up has partnered with

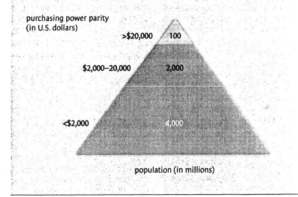

The World Pyramid

Most companies target consumers at the upper tiers of the economic pyramid, completely overlooking the business potential at its base. But though they may each be earning the equivalent of less than $2,000 a year, the people at the bottom of the pyramid make up a colossal market – 4 billion strong – the vast majority of the world's population.

purchasing power parity (in U.S. dollars)

>$20,000   100

$2,000–20,000   2,000

<$2,000   4,000

population (in millions)

the Bolivian Association of Ecological Producers Organizations to offer business information and communications services to more than 25,000 small producers of ecoagricultural products.

It's true that some services simply cannot be offered at a low-enough cost to be profitable, at least not with traditional technologies or business models. Most mobile telecommunications providers, for example, cannot yet profitably operate their networks at affordable prices in the developing world. One answer is to find alternative technology. A microfinance organization in Bolivia named PRODEM, for example, uses multilingual smart-card ATMs to substantially reduce its marginal cost per customer. Smart cards store a customer's personal details, account numbers, transaction records, and a fingerprint, allowing cash dispensers to operate without permanent network connections – which is key in remote areas. What's more, the machines offer voice commands in Spanish and several local dialects and are equipped with touch screens so that PRODEM's customer base can be extended to illiterate and semiliterate people.

Another answer is to aggregate demand, making the community – not the individual – the network customer. Gyandoot, a start-up in the Dhar district of central India, where 60% of the population falls below the poverty level, illustrates the benefits of a shared access model. The company has a network of 39 Internet-enabled kiosks that provide local entrepreneurs with Internet and telecommunications access, as well as with governmental, educational, and other services. Each kiosk serves 25 to 30 surrounding villages; the entire network reaches more than 600 villages and over half a million people.

Networks like these can be useful channels for marketing and distributing many kinds of low-cost products and services. Aptech's Computer Education division, for example, has built its own network of 1,000 learning centers in India to market and distribute Vidya, a computer-training course specially designed for BOP consumers and available

in seven Indian languages. Pioneer Hi-Bred, a DuPont company, uses Internet kiosks in Latin America to deliver agricultural information and to interact with customers. Farmers can report different crop diseases or weather conditions, receive advice over the wire, and order seeds, fertilizers, and pesticides. This network strategy increases both sales and customer loyalty.

Reduced Costs. No less important than top-line growth are cost-saving opportunities. Outsourcing operations to low-cost labor markets has, of course, long been a popular way to contain costs, and it has led to the increasing prominence of China in manufacturing and India in software. Now, thanks to the rapid expansion of high-speed digital networks, companies are realizing even greater savings by locating such labor-intensive service functions as call centers, marketing services, and back-office transaction processing in developing areas. For example, the nearly 20 companies that use OrphanIT.com's affiliate-marketing services, provided via its telecenters in India and the Philippines, pay one-tenth the going rate

for similar services in the United States or Australia. Venture capitalist Vinod Khosla describes the remote-services opportunity this way: "I suspect that by 2010, we will be talking about [remote services] as the fastest-growing part of the world economy, with many trillions of dollars of new markets created." Besides keeping costs down, outsourcing jobs to BOP markets can enhance growth, since job creation ultimately increases local consumers' purchasing power.

But tapping into cheap labor pools is not the only way MNCs can enhance their efficiency by operating in developing regions. The competitive necessity of maintaining a low cost structure in these areas can push companies to discover creative ways to configure their products, finances, and supply chains to enhance productivity. And these discoveries can often be incorporated back into their existing operations in developed markets.

For instance, companies targeting the BOP market are finding that the shared access model, which disaggregates access from ownership, not only widens their

The High-Cost Economy of the Poor

When we compare the costs of essentials in Dharavi, a shantytown of more than 1 million people in the heart of Mumbai, India, with those of Warden Road, an upper-class community in a nice Mumbai suburb, a disturbing picture emerges. Clearly, costs could be dramatically reduced if the poor could benefit from the scope, scale, and supply-chain efficiencies of large enterprises, as their middle-class counterparts do. This pattern is common around the world, even in developed countries. For instance, a similar, if less exaggerated, disparity exists between the inner-city poor and the suburban rich in the United States.

Cost	Dharavi	Warden Road	Poverty premium
credit (annual interest)	600%–1,000%	12%–18%	53X
municipal-grade water (per cubic meter)	$1.12	$0.03	37X
phone call (per minute)	$0.04–$0.05	$0.025	1.8X
diarrhea medication	$20	$2	10X
rice (per kilogram)	$0.28	$0.24	1.2X

customer base but increases asset productivity as well. Poor people, rather than buying their own computers, Internet connections, cell phones, refrigerators, and even cars, can use such equipment on a pay-per-use basis. Typically, the providers of such services get considerably more revenue per dollar of investment in the underlying assets. One shared Internet line, for example, can serve as many as 50 people, generating more revenue per day than if it were dedicated to a single customer at a flat fee. Shared access creates the opportunity to gain far greater returns from all sorts of infrastructure investments.

In terms of finances, to operate successfully in BOP markets, managers must also rethink their business metrics – specifically, the traditional focus on high gross margins. In developing markets, the profit margin on individual units will always be low. What really counts is capital efficiency – getting the highest possible returns on capital employed (ROCE). Hindustan Lever, for instance, operates a \$2.6 billion business portfolio with zero working capital. The key is constant efforts to reduce capital investments by extensively outsourcing manufacturing, streamlining supply chains, actively managing receivables, and paying close attention to distributors' performance. Very low capital needs, focused distribution and technology investments, and very large volumes at low margins lead to very high ROCE businesses, creating great economic value for shareholders. It's a model that can be equally attractive in developed and developing markets.

Streamlining supply chains often involves replacing assets with information. Consider, for example, the experience of ITC, one of India's largest companies. Its agribusiness division has deployed a total of 970 kiosks serving 600,000 farmers who supply it with soy, coffee, shrimp, and wheat from 5,000 villages spread across India. This kiosk program, called e-Choupal, helps increase the farmers' productivity by disseminating the latest information on weather and best practices in farming, and by supporting other services like soil and water testing, thus facilitating the supply of quality inputs to both the farmers and ITC. The kiosks also serve as an e-procurement system, helping farmers earn higher prices by minimizing transaction costs involved in marketing farm produce. The head of ITC's agribusiness reports that the company's procurement costs have fallen since e-Choupal was implemented. And that's despite paying higher prices to its farmers: The program has enabled the company to eliminate multiple transportation, bagging, and handling steps – from farm to local market, from market to broker, from broker to processor – that did not add value in the chain.

Innovation. BOP markets are hotbeds of commercial and technological experimentation. The Swedish wireless company Ericsson, for instance, has developed a small cellular telephone system, called a MiniGSM, that local operators in BOP markets can use to offer cell phone service to a small area at a radically lower cost than conventional equipment entails. Packaged for easy shipment and deployment, it provides stand-alone or networked voice and data communications for up to 5,000 users within a 35-kilometer radius. Capital costs to the operator can be as low as \$4 per user, assuming a shared-use model with individual phones operated by local entrepreneurs. The MIT Media Lab, in collaboration with the Indian government, is developing low-cost devices that allow people to use voice commands to communicate – without keyboards – with various Internet sites in multiple languages. These new access devices promise to be far less complex than traditional computers but would perform many of the same basic functions.[2]

As we have seen, connectivity is a big issue for BOP consumers. Companies that can find ways to dramatically lower connection costs, therefore, will have a very strong market position. And that is exactly what the Indian company n-Logue is trying to do. It connects hundreds of franchised village kiosks containing both a computer and a phone with centralized nodes that are, in turn, connected to the national phone network and the Internet. Each node, also a franchise, can serve between 30,000 and 50,000 customers, providing phone, e-mail, Internet services, and relevant local information at affordable prices to villagers in rural India. Capital costs for the n-Logue system are now about $400 per wireless "line" and are projected to decline to $100 – at least ten times lower than conventional telecom costs. On a per-customer basis, the cost may amount to as little as $1.[3] This appears to be a powerful model for ending rural isolation and linking untapped rural markets to the global economy.

New wireless technologies are likely to spur further business model innovations and lower costs even more. Ultrawideband, for example, is currently licensed in the United States only for limited, very low-power applications, in part because it spreads a signal across already-crowded portions of the broadcast spectrum. In many developing countries, however, the spectrum is less congested. In fact, the U.S.-based Dandin Group is already building an ultrawideband communications system for the Kingdom of Tonga, whose population of about 100,000 is spread over dozens of islands, making it a test bed for a next-generation technology that could transform the economics of Internet access.

E-commerce systems that run over the phone or the Internet are enormously important in BOP markets because they eliminate the need for layers of intermediaries. Consider how the U.S. start-up Voxiva has changed the way information is shared and business is transacted in Peru. The company partners with Telefónica, the dominant local carrier, to offer automated business applications over the phone. The inexpensive services include voice mail, data entry, and order placement; customers can check account balances, monitor delivery status, and access prerecorded information directories. According to the Boston Consulting Group, the Peruvian

Ministry of Health uses Voxiva to disseminate information, take pharmaceutical orders, and link health care workers spread across 6,000 offices and clinics. Microfinance institutions use Voxiva to process loan applications and communicate with borrowers. Voxiva offers Web-based services, too, but far more of its potential customers in Latin America have access to a phone.

E-commerce companies are not the only ones turning the limitations of BOP markets to strategic advantage. A lack of dependable electric power stimulated the UK-based start-up Free-

play Group to introduce hand-cranked radios in South Africa that subsequently became popular with hikers in the United States. Similar breakthroughs are being pioneered in the use of solar-powered devices such as battery chargers and water pumps. In China, where pesticide costs have often limited the use of modern agricultural techniques, there are now 13,000 small farmers – more than in the rest of the world combined – growing cotton that has been genetically engineered to be pest resistant.

Strategies for Serving BOP Markets

Certainly, succeeding in BOP markets requires multinationals to think creatively. The biggest change, though, has to come in the attitudes and practices of executives. Unless CEOs and other business leaders confront their own preconceptions, companies are unlikely to master the challenges of BOP markets. The traditional workforce is so rigidly conditioned to operate in higher-margin markets that, without formal training, it is unlikely to see the vast potential of the BOP market. The most pressing need, then, is education. Perhaps MNCs should create the equivalent of the Peace Corps: Having young managers spend a couple of formative years in BOP markets would open their eyes to

the promise and the realities of doing business there.

To date, few multinationals have developed a cadre of people who are comfortable with these markets. Hindustan Lever is one of the exceptions. The company expects executive recruits to spend at least eight weeks in the villages of India to get a gut-level experience of Indian BOP markets. The new executives must become involved in some community project – building a road, cleaning up a water catchment area, teaching in a school, improving a health clinic. The goal is to engage with the local population. To buttress this effort, Hindustan Lever is initiating a massive program for managers at all levels – from the CEO down – to reconnect with their poorest customers. They'll talk with the poor in both rural and urban areas, visit the shops these customers frequent, and ask them about their experience with the company's products and those of its competitors.

In addition to expanding managers' understanding of BOP markets, companies will need to make structural changes. To capitalize on the innovation potential of these markets, for example, they might set up R&D units in developing countries that are specifically focused on local opportunities. When Hewlett-Packard launched its e-Inclusion division, which concentrates on rural markets, it established a branch of its famed HP Labs in India charged with developing products and services explicitly for this market. Hindustan Lever maintains a significant R&D effort in India, as well.

Companies might also create venture groups and internal investment funds aimed at seeding entrepreneurial efforts in BOP markets. Such investments reap direct benefits in terms of business experience and market development. They can also play an indirect but vital role in growing the overall BOP market in sectors that will ultimately benefit the multinational. At least one major U.S. corporation is planning to launch such a fund, and the G8's Digital Opportunity Task Force is proposing a similar one focused on digital ventures.

MNCs should also consider creating a business development task force aimed at these markets. Assembling a diverse group of people from across the corporation and empowering it to function as a skunk works team that ignores conventional dogma will likely lead to

should look beyond businesses to NGOs and community groups. They are key sources of knowledge about customers' behavior, and they often experiment the most with new services and new delivery models. In fact, of the social enterprises experimenting with creative uses

> To operate successfully in developing markets, managers
> must rethink their business metrics – specifically,
> the traditional focus on high gross margins.

greater innovation. Companies that have tried this approach have been surprised by the amount of interest such a task force generates. Many employees want to work on projects that have the potential to make a real difference in improving the lives of the poor. When Hewlett-Packard announced its e-Inclusion division, for example, it was overwhelmed by far more volunteers than it could accommodate.

Making internal changes is important, but so is reaching out to external partners. Joining with businesses that are already established in these markets can be an effective entry strategy, since these companies will naturally understand the market dynamics better. In addition to limiting the risks for each player, partnerships also maximize the existing infrastructure – both physical and social. MNCs seeking partners

of digital technology that the Digital Dividend Project Clearinghouse tracked, nearly 80% are NGOs. In Namibia, for instance, an organization called School-Net is providing low-cost, alternative technology solutions – such as solar power and wireless approaches – to schools and community-based groups throughout the country. SchoolNet is currently linking as many as 35 new schools every month.

Entrepreneurs also will be critical partners. According to an analysis by McKinsey & Company, the rapid growth of cable TV in India – there are 50 million connections a decade after introduction – is largely due to small entrepreneurs. These individuals have been building the last mile of the network, typically by putting a satellite dish on their own houses and laying cable to connect their neighbors. A note of caution,

---

Sharing Intelligence

What creative new approaches to serving the bottom-of-the-pyramid markets have digital technologies made possible? Which sectors or countries show the most economic activity or the fastest growth? What new business models show promise? What kinds of partnerships – for funding, distribution, public relations – have been most successful?

The Digital Dividend Project Clearinghouse (digitaldividend.org) helps answer those types of questions. The Web site tracks the activities of organizations that use digital tools to provide connectivity and deliver services to underserved populations in developing countries. Currently, it contains information on 700 active projects around the world. Maintained under the auspices of the nonprofit World Resources Institute, the site lets participants in different projects share experiences and swap knowledge with one another. Moreover, the site provides data for trend analyses and other specialized studies that facilitate market analyses, local partnerships, and rapid, low-cost learning.

---

however. Entrepreneurs in BOP markets lack access to the advice, technical help, seed funding, and business support services available in the industrial world. So MNCs may need to take on mentoring roles or partner with local business development organizations that can help entrepreneurs create investment and partnering opportunities.

It's worth noting that, contrary to popular opinion, women play a significant role in the economic development of these regions. MNCs, therefore, should pay particular attention to women entrepreneurs. Women are also likely to play the most critical role in product acceptance not only because of their childcare and household management activities but also because of the social capital that they have built up in their communities. Listening to and educating such customers is essential for success.

Regardless of the opportunities, many companies will consider the bottom of the pyramid to be too risky. We've shown how partnerships can limit risk; another option is to enter into consortia. Imagine sharing the costs of building a rural network with the communications company that would operate it, a consumer goods company seeking channels to expand its sales, and a bank that is financing the construction and wants to make loans to and collect deposits from rural customers.

Investing where powerful synergies exist will also mitigate risk. The Global Digital Opportunity Initiative, a partnership of the Markle Foundation and the UN Development Programme, will help a small number of countries implement a strategy to harness the power of information and communications technologies to increase development. The countries will be chosen in part based on their interest and their willingness to make supportive regulatory and market reforms. To concentrate resources and create reinforcing effects, the initiative will encourage international aid agencies and global companies to assist with implementation.

All of the strategies we've outlined here will be of little use, however, unless the external barriers we've touched on – poor infrastructure, inadequate connectivity, corrupt intermediaries, and the like – are removed. Here's where technology holds the most promise. Information and communications technologies can grant access to otherwise isolated communities, provide marketing and distribution channels, bypass intermediaries, drive down transaction costs, and help aggregate demand and

buying power. Smart cards and other emerging technologies are inexpensive ways to give poor customers a secure identity, a transaction or credit history, and even a virtual address – prerequisites for interacting with the formal economy. That's why high-tech companies aren't the only ones that should be interested in closing the global digital divide; encouraging the spread of low-cost digital networks at the bottom of the pyramid is a priority for virtually all companies that want to enter and engage with these markets. Improved connectivity is an important catalyst for more effective markets, which are critical to boosting income levels and accelerating economic growth.

Moreover, global companies stand to gain from the effects of network expansion in these markets. According to Metcalfe's Law, the usefulness of a network equals the square of the number of users. By the same logic, the value and vigor of the economic activity that will be generated when hundreds of thousands of previously isolated rural communities can buy and sell from one another and from urban markets will increase dramatically – to the benefit of all participants.

• • •

Since BOP markets require significant rethinking of managerial practices, it is legitimate for managers to ask: Is it worth the effort?

We think the answer is yes. For one thing, big corporations should solve big problems – and what is a more pressing concern than alleviating the poverty that 4 billion people are currently mired in? It is hard to argue that the wealth of technology and talent within leading multinationals is better allocated to producing incremental variations of existing products than to addressing the real needs – and real opportunities – at the bottom of the pyramid. Moreover, through competition, multinationals are likely to bring to BOP markets a level of accountability for performance and resources that neither international development agencies nor national governments have demonstrated during the last 50 years. Participation by MNCs could set a new standard, as well as a new market-driven paradigm, for addressing poverty.

But ethical concerns aside, we've shown that the potential for expanding the bottom of the market is just too great to ignore. Big companies need to focus on big market opportunities if they want to generate real growth. It is simply good business strategy to be involved in large, untapped markets that offer new customers, cost-saving opportunities, and access to radical innovation. The business opportunities at the bottom of the pyramid are real, and they are open to any MNC willing to engage and learn.

1. Andrew Lawlor, Caitlin Peterson, and Vivek Sandell, "Catalyzing Rural Development: TARAhaat.com" (World Resources Institute, July 2001).

2. Michael Best and Colin M. Maclay, "Community Internet Access in Rural Areas: Solving the Economic Sustainability Puzzle," *The Global Information Technology Report 2001–2002: Readiness for the Networked World*, ed., Geoffrey Kirkman (Oxford University Press, 2002), available on-line at http://www.cid.harvard.edu/cr/gitrr_030202.html.

3. Joy Howard, Erik Simanis, and Charis Simms, "Sustainable Deployment for Rural Connectivity: The n-Logue Model" (World Resources Institute, July 2001).

Reprint R0209C
To order reprints, see the last page of Executive Summaries.

[13]

Journal of International Business Studies (2004) 35, 81–98
© 2004 Palgrave Macmillan Ltd.   All rights reserved 0047-2506 $25.00
www.jibs.net

PERSPECTIVE

Globalisation, economic geography and the strategy of multinational enterprises

Peter J Buckley[1] and
Pervez N Ghauri[2]

[1]Centre for International Business, University of
Leeds, Maurice Keyworth Building, Leeds, UK;
[2]Manchester School of Management, UMIST,
Manchester, UK

Correspondence:
Peter J Buckley, Centre for International
Business, University of Leeds, Maurice
Keyworth Building, Leeds LS2 9JT, UK
Tel: + 44 113 343 4646;
Fax: + 44 133 343 4754;
E-mail: pjb@lubs.leeds.ac.uk

Abstract
The intention of this paper is to review the literature linking ownership and
location strategies to economic geography and theories of globalisation and to
explore new areas of research. This paper examines globalisation in terms of
conflicts between markets and economic management, and suggests that the
differential pace of globalisation across markets presents a number of
challenges to policy makers in local, national and regional governments, and
in international institutions. In examining the changing location and ownership
strategies of MNEs, it shows that the increasingly sophisticated decision making
of managers in MNEs is slicing the activities of firms more finely and in finding
optimum locations for each closely defined activity, they are deepening the
international division of labour. Ownership strategies, too, are becoming
increasingly complex, leading to a control matrix that runs from wholly owned
units via FDI through market relationships such as subcontracting, including
joint ventures as options on subsequent decisions in a dynamic pattern. The
input of lessons from economic geography is thus becoming more important in
understanding the key developments in international business. The consequences of the globalisation of production and consumption represent political
challenges, and reaction against these changes has led to a questioning of the
effects of global capitalism as well as to its moral basis. These four issues are
closely intertwined and present a formidable research agenda to which the
international business research community is uniquely fitted to respond.
Journal of International Business Studies (2004) **35,** 81–98.
doi:10.1057/palgrave.jibs.8400076

Keywords: globalisation; economic geography; strategy; multinational enterprises;
location strategy

Introduction
The analysis in Buckley (2002) suggested that international
business research succeeded when it focused on, in sequence, a
number of big questions which arise from empirical developments
in the world economy. The agenda is stalled because no such big
question has currently been identified. This calls into question the
separate existence of the subject area. This paper suggests that the
analysis of globalisation, with a focus on economic geography,
arising from the changing strategy and the external impact of
multinational enterprises (MNEs) on the world economy can be
that 'big question'. Researchers also need to take on board
challenges to global capitalism and to understand the roots of
current discontent.

The intention of this paper is to review the literature linking
ownership and location strategies to economic geography and

Received: 21 July 2003
Revised: 1 December 2003
Accepted: 1 December 2003
Online publication date: 4 March 2004

theories of globalisation and to explore new areas of research. Thus, the paper focuses on the relationship between the evolving strategies of MNEs, the changing economic geography of the world economy and globalisation. The first section charts the conflicts between markets and government policies as markets integrate across national borders. Markets are globalised by the actions of MNEs. This is a deliberate process, but it is proceeding at a differential pace in different types of market. The drivers of this process – the location and ownership strategies of MNEs – are examined in the second section. These strategies revolve around the ability of MNEs to subdivide their activities more precisely and to place them in the optimal location. At the same time, more sophisticated and wider control strategies ranging from full ownership to market relationships are used to coordinate global activities. This, it is argued in the third section, makes economic geography more important than ever. Where an activity is placed it interacts with its immediate hinterland and this has profound consequences for changing economic power and development. Finally, the article examines protests against globalisation that leads to the concluding research agenda.

Conflict of markets with national policies in the global economy

As Sideri (1997, 38) says 'globalisation is essentially a process driven by economic forces. Its immediate causes are: the spatial reorganisation of production, international trade and the integration of financial markets'. It is not therefore uniform across economic space – 'the segmentation of the manufacturing process into multiple partial operations

which combined with the development of cheap transportation and communication networks, has brought the increasing division of production into separate stages carried out in different locations'. The strategies of multinational firms are therefore crucial to the causes and consequences of globalisation.

We can examine globalisation as a conflict between markets and management (policies). Figure 1 identifies three levels of markets – financial markets, markets in goods and services and labour markets. Each of these is moving at a different speed towards global integration. Financial markets are already very closely integrated internationally, so that no individual 'national capital markets' can have a sustainable independent existence. However, attempts at national regulation do persist (Laulajainen, 2000) and the role of localities in the financial markets still provides differentiation (Berg and Guisinger, 2001; Tickell, 2000). Despite this, it is legitimate for analytical purposes to hypothesise a single integrated global capital market. Regional economic integration (REI) is becoming increasingly effective in integrating goods and services markets at the regional level. The relationship between company strategy and policy-making within regional blocs such as the EU is a fascinating area for the development of new research streams (Chapman, 1999; Raines and Wishlade, 1999; see also, Wood, 2003 on the Industrial Midwest of America). Labour markets, however, are functionally separate at the national level and here integration is largely resisted by national governments (Buckley *et al.*, 2001).

While the largest MNEs are already perfectly placed to exploit these differences in the interna-

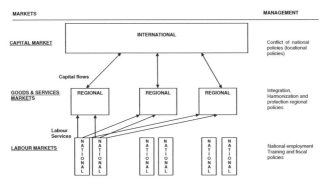

Figure 1 Internationalisation of firms – conflict of markets.

tional integration of markets (Buckley, 1997), REI offers both large and small firms the opportunity to enjoy the advantages of a large 'home' market, whether it is their native home or their adoptive home. The operation of international capital markets (which allow firms to drive their capital costs down to a minimum) has largely transcended policy on regional integration, although each region would hope to retain its own regional financial centre. It is primarily in the arena of the creation and fostering of regional goods and services markets that firms are enabled to exploit economies of scale across several countries, and that REI offers the most substantial size-of-country benefits. However, regional integration that encompasses countries with differential labour markets is becoming increasingly beneficial. This regional integration enables costs to be reduced by locating the labour-intensive stages of production in the cheaper labour economies within the integrated area. Firms that serve just one regional market, as well as those that serve several of the regional goods and services markets of the world through horizontally integrated foreign direct investment (FDI), are able to complement this with vertically integrated FDI in quality-differentiated labour markets. Vertical integration also reflects the spatial distribution of supplies of key inputs and raw materials. The MNE achieves advantages through both vertical and horizontal integration. Each strategy is promoted by the 'size-of-country benefits' of REI in goods and services markets, which reduce or eliminate artificial barriers to trade between the members. This maximises the ability of firms to exploit intra-regional differences in factor abundance, including differentiated human capital.

At industry level, globalisation can be shown to have an increasing impact. Gersbach (2002) defines globalisation at the micro-level as 'the exposure of a productivity follower industry in one country to the productivity leader in another country' (p. 209). The transmission mechanisms of change across country borders are trade and FDI. Gersbach found a strong relationship between globalisation and productivity differences with the most efficient producers. He concludes that globalisation matters and that its influence spreads beyond a single region (e.g., Europe, North America).

More attention has been paid to vertical relationships (the supply chain). The differentiation of labour markets is most acute between advanced and less-developed countries that are typically not part

of the same regional bloc. The managers of MNEs are increasingly able to segment their activities and to seek the optimal location for increasingly specialised slivers of activity. This ability to separate and relocate stages of production has led to a boom in manufacturing in China and service activities (e.g., call centres) in India. MNEs are also increasingly able to coordinate these activities by means of a wide variety of mechanisms from wholly owned FDI through licensing and subcontracting to market relationships. The more precise use of location and ownership strategies by MNEs is the very essence of increasing globalisation.

In parallel with the growth of the globalisation of production, globalisation of consumption has accelerated and it is perhaps this which has excited most opposition. The alleged globalisation of tastes provokes nationalistic protectionist sentiments and is here analysed in terms of the balance of strategies within MNEs between 'local' and 'global' pressures on the firm.

The process of globalisation is thus not only reorganising power at world level but also at national and subnational levels (Alden, 1999; Dunning and Wallace, 1999; Graham, 2003; Mirza, 1998; Oxelheim et al., 2001; Peck and Durnin, 1999; Pike, 1999; Yeung, 2003). As domestic firms move part of their production to other countries, technology, knowledge and capital become more important than land, the traditional source of state power, and this redefines the function of the state (Rosecrance, 1996; Sideri, 1997). The loss of sovereignty to supra-national regional institutions is more acceptable than to international institutions that are more remote. The EU is an example of such regional integration and governance (Bressand, 1990). Social programmes within the EU are enforcing major redistributions of revenue between the individual nations. The nation state as the possessor of the sense of identity is being replaced by subnations and internal regions as government is devolved.

A recent study by Subramanian and Lawrence (1999) found that national locations remained distinctive. Policy barriers at the borders, differences in local cultures in their widest sense and nature and geography contribute to distinctiveness. This, together with the ability of incumbents to keep outsiders at a disadvantage (Buckley et al., 2001) and the first entrant benefits of local firms, reinforces the differentiation of national economies. International competition remains imperfect and international price differences persist because arbitrage is costly. Domestic market conditions largely determine prices and wages. Multinational company affiliates remain firmly embedded in their local economy and such local firms identify closely with the national government. Subramanian and Lawrence (1999) conclude that national borders still matter. Borders continue to engender and to coincide with important discontinuities stemming from government policies, geography and societal differences. The authors stress information discontinuities that coincide with national boundaries and so create search and deliberation problems for trading and manufacturing firms. These issues also account for the alleged 'home bias' of multinational firms. FDI is the key tool by which multinationals bridge cross-border discontinuities.

The two contrasting paradigms of a world made up of self-contained national economies and a 'borderless world' are incomplete and capture only part of a complex and subtle story. Lenway and Murtha (1994) examine the role of the state as a strategist along four dimensions: authority *vs* markets, communitarianism *vs* individualism, political *vs* economic objectives and equity *vs* efficiency. They state that international business scholarship 'places a benchmark value on efficient international markets and tends to regard states as causes of deviation from this ideal' (p. 530).

Globalisation and corporate governance

Two key issues interact to provide governance issues arising from the globalisation of business. The first is the existence of unpriced externalities. These impose costs (e.g., pollution) on the local economy and environment. The second is the remoteness of production and service activities from their ultimate owners or controllers (e.g., the shareholders). These two factors interact because the mechanism for correcting negative externalities becomes difficult to implement because of remoteness and lack of immediate responsibility.

Perceived difficulties of global governance in multinational firms are exacerbated by the current crises in governance of firms in the West. The shareholder return-driven environment which prevails today is very much the creature of the merger wave of the 1980s (Buckley and Ghauri, 2002). The feeling that corporations are outside social controls and that current forms of governance benefit only executives (and owners) rather than other stakeholders contribute to the concerns outlined in the previous section.

MNE – host country relations in middle-income countries have fully emerged onto the world stage, leaving behind a group of largely inert less developed countries that have so far been bypassed by globalisation. Large, emerging countries, which contain significant middle class markets, cheaper and well-educated labour and stabilising political regimes (India, China, Brazil) are no longer seen just as new markets for old products (Prahalad and Lieberthal, 1998) but as significant locations requiring reconfigurations of the economic geography of MNE's operations. Not only do MNEs adapt products to local markets – but local markets also provide ideas for new global products (Murtha *et al.*, 2001). Increasing location 'tournaments' to attract FDI (Oxelheim and Ghauri, 2003), may have reduced the benefits to the host countries as have the increasing skill of the managers of MNEs in making their investments more 'footloose'. Corresponding skills on the part of host countries to make FDI 'sticky' are not developing at the same rate. Differences within developing countries may lead to divergence between those which can develop the velocity to catch up and those which will fall behind as the world economy becomes more interdependent.

Location and ownership strategies of multinational firms

The traditional MNE was a vertically, as well as horizontally, integrated firm. In consequence, each division of the firm was locked into linkages with other divisions of the same firm. As global competition intensified, there was growing recognition of the costs of integration of this kind. Commitment to a particular source of supply or demand of any product, intermediate good or service is relatively low cost in a high-growth scenario, since it is unlikely that any investment will need to be reversed. It is much more costly in a low-growth scenario, where production may need to be switched to a cheaper source of supply or sales diverted away from a depressed market. The desire for flexibility therefore discourages vertical integration – whether it is backward integration into production or forward integration into distribution. It is better to subcontract production and to franchise sales instead. The subcontracting of production is similar in principle to a 'putting out' arrangement, but differs in the sense that the subcontractor is now a firm rather than just a single worker.

Disintermediation and reintermediation

Disintegration was further encouraged by a low-trust atmosphere that developed in many firms. Fear of internal monopoly became rife as explained above. Production managers faced with falling demand wished that they did not have to sell all their output through a single sales manager. Sales managers resented the fact that they had to obtain all their supplies from the same small set of plants. Each manager doubted the competence of the others and ascribed loss of corporate competitiveness to selfishness and inefficiency elsewhere in the firm. Divisions aspired to be spun off so that they could deal with other business units instead. On the other hand, managers were wary of the risks that would be involved if they severed their links with other divisions altogether. The result is that a much more complex strategy set faces decision-makers in multinational firms.

Strategy, e-commerce and networks

These changes are challenges for 'old economy' companies including the integration of on-line functions with existing brand and back office infrastructure. Business-to-business and building online links with suppliers and customers imply the redesign of business process networks. Smaller companies may find it easier to operate internationally because it is easier to reach customers, but there are still information problems, logistics and management control. Products still have to be delivered to customers. This is not just a matter of transport costs, but also regulatory differences between countries, cultural distance and other factors.

A natural way to cope with these pressures is to allow each division to deal with external business units, as well as internal ones. In terms of internalisation theory, internal markets become 'open' rather than 'closed'. This provides divisional managers with an opportunity to bypass weak or incompetent sections of the company. It also provides a competitive discipline on internal transfer prices, preventing their manipulation for internal political ends and bringing them more into line with external prices. There are other advantages too. Opening up internal markets severs the link between the capacities operated at adjacent stages of production. The resulting opportunity to supply other firms facilitates the exploitation of scale economies because it permits the capacity of any individual plant to exceed internal demand. Conversely, it encourages the firm to buy in

supplies from other firms that have installed capacity in excess of their own needs.

The alignment of internal prices with external prices increases the objectivity of profit measurement at the divisional level. This allows divisional managers to be rewarded by profit-related pay based on divisional profit rather than firm-wide profit. Management may even buy out part of the company. Alternatively, the firm may restructure by buying in a part on an independent firm. The net effect is the same in both cases. The firm becomes the hub of a network of inter-locking joint ventures (Buckley and Casson, 1996; Buckley and Casson, 1988). Each joint venture partner is responsible for the day-to-day management of the venture. The headquarters of the firm coordinates the links between the ventures. Internal trade is diverted away from the weaker ventures towards the stronger ones, thereby providing price and profit signals to which the weaker partners need to respond. Unlike a pure external market situation, the partners are able to draw upon expertise at headquarters, which can in turn tap into expertise in other parts of the group.

A network does not have to be built around a single firm, of course. A network may consist of a group of independent firms instead (Ghauri, 1999). Sometimes these firms are neighbours, as in the regional industrial clusters described by Best (1990), Porter (1990) and Rugman *et al.* (1995). Industrial districts, such as 'Toyota city,' have been hailed as an Asian innovation in flexible management, although the practice has been common in Europe for centuries (Marshall, 1919). As tariffs and transport costs have fallen, networks have become more international and 'virtual'. This is demonstrated by the dramatic growth in intermediate product trade under long-term contracts. For example, an international trading company may operate a network of independent suppliers in different countries, substituting different sources of supply in response to both short-term exchange rate movements and long-term shifts in comparative advantage.

By establishing a network of joint ventures covering alternative technological trajectories, the firm can spread its costs while retaining a measure of proprietary control over new technologies. The advantage of joint ventures is further reinforced by technological convergence, for example, the integration of computers, telecommunications and photography. This favours the creation of networks of joint ventures based on complementary technologies, rather than on the substitute technologies described above (Cantwell, 1995). Joint ventures are important because they afford a number of real options (Trigeorgis, 1996) which can be taken up or dropped depending upon how the project turns out. The early phase of a joint venture provides important information that could not be obtained through investigation before the venture began. It affords an opportunity later on to buy more fully into a successful venture – an opportunity that is not available to those who have not taken any stake. It therefore provides greater flexibility than does either outright ownership or an alternative involving no equity stake (Buckley *et al.*, 2002).

Global knowledge diffusion

As Buckley and Carter (2002) point out, problems in the global organisation of MNEs are frequently presented as oppositions. Typical are global *vs* local, centralise *vs* decentralise, standardisation *vs* adaptation and efficiency *vs* responsiveness. These issues are not independent of knowledge management. Global/local issues centre on the costs of managing knowledge flows and the combination of general 'company-wide' knowledge and separable, spatially fixed local-specific knowledge. Spatial questions are one part of dealing with knowledge-intensive organisations, but spatial issues are bound up with a whole set of temporal, organisational, strategic and process issues (Buckley and Carter, 2002, 46). As Murtha *et al.* (1998) show, strategy emerges from mind-sets which are changing over time – global and local issues are capable of synthesis. The role of management knowledge is a crucial and under-researched phenomenon of globalisation. Global management of knowledge does enable the separation of key activities that can therefore be managed in different ways. This has led to strategies of outsourcing, mass customisation and deduplication of functions, which can be spatially separated, bundled and differentiated and consolidated, respectively. Murtha *et al.* (2001) examine the process of global knowledge creation and dissemination in a fascinating, detailed industry case study of the type that can be replicated and extended.

The goal of a modern sourcing strategy is to obtain the optimum combination of inputs from the variety of opportunities open in the global market. Normally, this will be geographically diverse and the means of procurement will be varied. Thus, both the location factor (where the inputs are acquired) and the internalisation/externalisation choice of means of procurement will vary with circumstances and will change over time.

The ability of firms to 'mix and match' their sourcing strategy has been greatly enhanced by the use of the internet for procurement and the increasing use of 'outsourcing', whereby external offers can be compared to internal courses of supply, and the scope of the firm's internal activity adjusted accordingly. These strategies enable increased specialisation and localisation to enhance the division of labour globally and for individual firms to benefit from this by creating a global business network, which encompasses many locations for activities with mixed ownership/contracting modes of procurement. The reduced need for colocation locationally diversifies the firm's production base.

Similarly, the market servicing strategy comprises a mix of exporting, licensing/contracting and investment activities, again suggesting a mix of ownership and location strategies in different spatial and temporal circumstances. Here, too, different functions (more housing, distribution and advertising) can be either centrally and globally organised or differentially localised. Ownership too may be fully internal, joint venture/alliance or outsourced.

The interaction of the supply and demand side is yet to be fully studied, but it is safe to assume that large markets exercise a locational pull on inputs, and key input sources encourage local marketing. MNEs thus seek optimal locations for raw materials, intermediate goods, services 'brain arbitrage' and assembly plants. They also seek entry and exit strategies for markets as they wax and wane over time. This is a suitably complex subject for detailed analysis.

Global/local operations

In the strategic decisions of multinational firms, there has always been a tension between the pressures to globalise and the need to stay local and to serve individual customers (Ghauri, 1992). The advantages of global operations are cost-based, maximising economies of scale and reducing duplication, thus achieving efficiency. The advantages of localisation are revenue based, allowing differentiation to reach all customer niches and achieving responsiveness. The tension can be summed up in the phrase 'the cost advantages of standardisation *vs* the revenue advantages of adaptation' (Table 1).

Much of the strategy of the multinational firm can be explained by the attempts of management to reconcile these pressures (Devinney *et al.*, 2000).

Table 1   Global and local operation

Global	Local
Cost	Revenue
Efficiency	Responsiveness
Centralisation	Decentralisation
Standardisation	Adaptation
GLOCAL?	

Over time, firms have (been advised to) switch their organisation so as to balance these pressures – one example is the 'transnational' type of organisation advocated by Bartlett and Ghoshal (1989). However, pressures in different industries push firms towards a strategic imperative (scale in electronics, local demand differences in consumer goods) and different functions require different balances of global/local orientation (finance, production, sales functions). The 'hub and spoke' model below is a key method of attempting to reconcile these conflicts. Global and Local oppositions are shown in Table 1. Cultural differences are of great importance in determining the extent of this balance.

The globalisation of markets has been a major factor in the growth of volatility (Buckley and Casson, 1998). A feature of many global markets is the use of regional production and distribution hubs, where several neighbouring countries are serviced from the same location. The regional hub, like the IJV, can be understood as a strategy that offers superior flexibility. Just as an IJV offers a compromise ownership strategy, a regional hub offers a compromise location strategy. As the hub is nearer to each market that is the home location, it reduces transport costs, and offers better information capture too. Yet, because it is close to several markets, it avoids exclusive commitment to any one. If one market declines, production can be switched to other markets instead, provided the shocks affecting the national markets are independent (or less than perfectly correlated, at any rate) and the hub provide gains from diversification. These are real gains that only the firm can achieve, as opposed to the financial gains from unrelated product diversification, which have proved disappointing in the past because they are best exploited through the diversification of individual share portfolios instead.

Location and ownership strategies revisited: 'hub and spoke strategies'

The two strategies of IJV and hub can be combined (Figure 2). Since one (the IJV) is an ownership strategy and the other a location strategy, they can, if desired, be combined directly in an IJV production hub. Closer examination of the issues suggests that this is not normally the best approach, however. The model suggests that a combination of a wholly owned production hub supplying IJV distribution facilities in each national market is a better solution. A hub facility is too critical to global strategy to allow a partner to become involved, because the damage they could do is far too great. Even with a wholly owned hub facility,

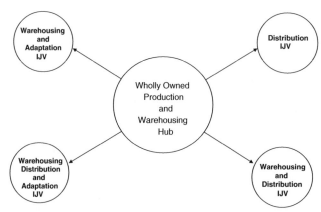

Figure 2   'Hub and spoke' strategies: an example.

the combination still affords considerable flexibility to divest or withdraw from any single market. The advantage of the combination is that when divesting, the distribution facility can be sold to the partner, while the production capacity can be diverted to markets elsewhere. These options for divestment are combined with useful options for expansion too. This example illustrates the crucial role that the concepts of flexibility and volatility play in analysing foreign market entry in the modern global economy. Without these concepts it is impossible to fully understand the rationale for IJVs and production hubs. It is also impossible to understand why these strategies have emerged at this particular historical juncture and not before.

Outsourcing and logistics
Many input functions are now viably outsourced – even human resource departments and procurement (The Economist, 2001a, b). Digital delivery of product is analogous on the output side. The danger is the loss of core competencies (outsourcing IT 'loses part of company's brain'). This development contributes to volatility and increases the mobility of activities internationally, as a great deal of outsourcing functions are competed for on a global basis. The policy of promoting linkages (forward as well as backward) followed by many agencies of national and local government needs to account for these changing decision-making parameters.

As is always the case, disintegration of established supply chains is followed by reintegration and consolidation. The trend to outsource (disinternalise) manufacturing by major multinationals led initially to subcontracting to independents – many of them located in South East Asia (and Mexico). Contract manufacturing (The Economist, 2000) has been growing by 20% per year in the late 1990s and early part of this century. However, contract manufacturers are rapidly consolidating, through mergers and are expected to reach an oligopolistic equilibrium, with around six firms dominating the global market. These firms are becoming supply chain managers, sometimes even organising distribution and repair. These links between customers and suppliers are, of course, facilitated by the use of the internet. Contract manufacturers, ensured of future contracts are thus able to achieve economies of scale and to become more capital intensive, replacing unskilled labour by high-tech capital equipment. This trend is accelerated by the

competitive imperative becoming speed-to-market, rather than cost. A linked supply of available factories in different national locations mean that the contract manufacturers can switch production lines between these units. Flexibility is achieved by moving these 'shell' factories between principals – entire production lines can be flown in from another location.

Vertical disintegration is thus accompanied by specialisation. The principal concentrates on R&D, design and marketing, while the contract manufacturer provides a service to the global supplier. Companies with a strong manufacturing culture, and a commitment to a fixed location, may be outcompeted by more agile 'virtual' firms owning no manufacturing facilities at all.

Mass customisation is an important method of reconciling scale and differentiation (efficiency and responsiveness). An example is the textile industry where bespoke garments are ordered *en masse* from offshore sites with rapid delivery. This is associated with 'lean retailing' where distribution and design centres are linked to production centres by electronic means. Electronic ordering and automated distribution centres and inventory management systems linked to customers enable rapid response to customer needs. This combines information technology, speed and flexibility with low labour costs. So the custom-made *vs* bulk manufacture divide becomes fine. ('Cyber consumers expect to be able to customise everything'.)

Deduplication of function becomes possible where electronic links allow single locations to service the whole firm's needs. Rather than a call centre for each division or country, a single one can serve all. There is also a tendency for reintegration of the supply chain from independents back to the major manufactures or in specialist subcontracting firms as e-commerce matures.

The global factory
The above review suggests that the manufacturing system of the future will use 'distributed manufacturing' (The Economist, 2002) where products are more responsive to customer needs through flexible factories. In flexible factories, all plants within the system can make all the firms' product models and can switch between models very quickly by a combination of software and robots. The global factory will be the very antithesis of 'any colour as long as it's black'. It will have a single factory design for its distributed global plants and attention to staff training so that replication and perfect

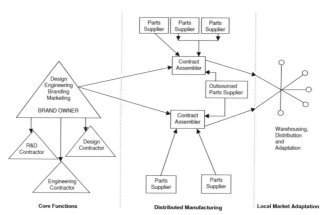

Figure 3   The global factory.

substitutability between plants is achieved. Customers will be able to dictate which parts, subassemblies or 'add-ons', they require in the final assembly and the distributed manufacturing function will reassemble (Figure 3), where production is pushed from the hub into the spoke. Brand owners will control design, engineering and marketing while outsourcing large areas of production to parts suppliers, and they may well contract out final assembly. Thus 'built to order' products will be produced close to the final customer. Globalisation implies location near the customer, not a single large-scale plant. It is the high fixed costs of existing factories which compel manufacturers to achieve large-scale production, and a reduction of fixed costs means that production can be more easily tailored to final demand.

Geography of globalisation

Much has been made of the 'death of distance' (Cairncross, 1997) and 'the end of geography' by authors trumpeting the importance of the internet and the ascendancy of virtual space over physical distance. Recent evidence, however, suggests that geography still matters. As Castells (2001, 209) says '...the internet backbone is global in its reach, but territorially uneven in its layout in terms of capacity'. The internet is built on top of existing infrastructure and relies on fibre optic cables. The creation of data centres, 'web hotels' and 'server farms' has become conglomerated in key urban centres. Indeed, 49 of the servers for the top 100

web sites are colocated in Exodus Communications, Santa Clara, Cal, USA (The Economist, 2001a, b). The storage of information has become more physically concentrated, not less, and economies of agglomeration, including the need for a reliable power source, are creating these server farms, some of which come with their own power stations (iXguardian is building the biggest one in Europe just outside London, *Economist*, op. cit.). Sellers have a vested interest in determining the location of users of the internet. The difference in laws and taxes governing these consumers is determined by geography, not network topography, and firms delivering goods ordered over the internet stick with the old geographical (i.e., national) approach but are taking it online with 'geolocational services', largely using local postcodes. Web content can then be matched to the user's location. As national regulations still apply, particularly to goods such or pharmaceuticals and services, especially financial services, it is essential that companies stay within the law. So borders (national borders) are returning to the net.

Location thus becomes a search parameter for services. Filtering via precise targeting of customers (e.g., through mobile phones) is possible through satellite-based global positioning systems. The Economist concludes: 'The internet means that the distance between two points on the network is no longer terribly important. However, where those points are still matters very much. Distance is dying, but geography it seems is still alive and kicking' (p. 20).

Recently, technological advances have made it easier to argue for the link between geography and growth. Innovation has surged in developing links between places on the Internet and real-world locations – stitching together the virtual and physical worlds (The Economist, 2003). Geolocational services are being developed both to locate end-users and to find the internet access point nearest to a particular location. Thus, suitably equipped laptops can access wireless internet services close to a small base station (or 'hotspot'). Anyone in the locality can then avail themselves of these services. Mapping of base stations confirms that these are located in areas of highest economic activity. Again, virtual space reinforces existing spatial dispersion of activity, it does not substitute for them. Internet pages are becoming 'goecoded' or 'geotagged' to make geographical location explicit.

Deepening spatial division of labour

The evolving locational policies of MNEs have led to a deepening of the spatial division of labour. This interacts with changing ownership policies to produce radically new outcomes for the world economy (Ruigrok and Van Tulder, 1995). This section goes on to review three extant approaches to the deepening spatial division of labour (Dicken, 2003; Yeung, 2001) and then suggests future research developments.

Approach 1: The New International Division of Labour (NIDL).

The NIDL is not particularly new. It was foreshadowed by the analysis of Hymer (1972) who developed 'the law of uneven development'. Hymer envisaged a strict hierarchy in the world economy with 'higher order functions' (finance, design) being carried out in the advanced countries, with less-developed countries being relegated to the role of 'hewers of wood and drawers of water'. Frobel *et al*. (1980) foresaw the increasingly disaggregated spatial nature of production under the control of MNEs. The increasing intensity of intra-firm trade, (priced at internally determined transfer prices; Emmanuel and Mehafdi, 1994; Hirshleifer, 1986; Rugman and Eden, 1985; UNCTAD, 1999), which accounts for over half of world trade, is a concomitant of this fine spatial division. The ability of MNEs to create new specialised roles – largely corporate services – and to relocate them in

favourable locations is a further innovation tracked by the NIDL approach.

Approach 2: Global commodity Chains (GCCs).

Gereffi *et al*. (1994, 2) define GCCs as 'sets of inter-organisational networks clustered round one commodity of product, linking households, enterprises and states to one another within the world economy. These networks are situationally specific, socially constructed and locally integrated, underscoring the social embeddedness of economic organisation'. Buyer-driven chains are distinguished from producer-driven chains. Buyer-driven GCCs are dominated by large retailers and brand-name manufacturers or trading companies that organise decentralised production networks in developing countries for export. Typical industry settings include labour-intensive consumer goods industries organised by OEM (original equipment manufacturing) arrangements. Producer-driven GCCs are controlled by global oligopolies where TNCs control capital and knowledge-intensive production (Yeung, 2001). Empirical work on GCCs includes Dicken and Hassler (2000) and Gereffi (1999), while Jenkins (1987) applies this to development issues.

Approach 3: Regional Networks.

The role of regions and regional integration in the spatial organisation of the world economy is clearly critical as was shown above. Considerable work has been undertaken on Asian production networks which unfortunately took a wrong turn with the 'flying geese model' where it was alleged that the leading goose (Japan) would pull others in the flock (the smaller economies of Asia) along in its slipstream. Not only is this an inaccurate description of the way geese fly (different geese assume the leadership for different periods), it ignores vertical linkages across and between those economies and those of the rest of the world, it also overplays the benign effects of leadership and underplays power relationships (see Bernard and Ravenhill, 1995; Edgington and Hayet, 2000; Hart-Landsberg and Burkett, 1998; Hatch and Yamamura, 1996; Hill and Fujita, 1996; Tsui-Auch, 1999). There is a parallel here with the French 'filière' approach which has not permeated and influenced mainstream English language literature (Raikes *et al*., 2000).

However, regional networks in Asia are important both theoretically (Markusen and Venables, 2000) and empirically as well (for instance, Yeung (2001) on Singapore firms in South East Asia and Ghauri and Prasad (1995) on Asian networks).

Geographical analyses of globalisation

The NIDL, global commodity chains and (regional) production networks all fit well with the international business research agenda. The progress of research in this area depends on inter-disciplinarity and connectivity.

Economic geography has a long history (Clark *et al.*, 2000; Krugman, 1991, 2000) and is currently enjoying a renaissance (Scott, 2000). The importance of the new geography is attested to by the concern for 'the new geography of competition' for mobile investment (Raines, 2003) and the increasingly complex interplay between states, economic regional blocs such as the EU and subnational regions such as states in the USA and semi-autonomous regions such as Catalonia or Scotland (Oxelheim and Ghauri, 2003; Phelps and Alden, 1999; Phelps and Rains, 2003).

Economic geographers have made many significant contributions to the analysis of globalisation that can, with profit, be noted by international business scholars. Regional integration and the division of world markets into trade and investment blocs have been extensively analysed by geographers (for summaries on Asia, North America and Europe see Abo, 2000; Holmes, 2000; and Amin, 2000). However, the incorporation of real geographical features such as climate, coastline, river transport, soil quality and terrain has perhaps been underplayed and this represents a real opportunity for future development. This links physical geography and economic development. A research agenda of this kind is proposed by Mellinger *et al.* (2000) and Buckley and Casson (1991) included 'geographical factors that influence entrepôt potential' in their analysis of factors in the long-run economic success of a nation (p. 33). The links between economic geography and development are also worthy of attention in the literature on 'spillovers' from MNEs to the local economy. Many of these spillovers are enhanced by geographical proximity (in the formation of clusters of supporting industries, for instance) and this factor is not often explicitly included in the examination of spillovers.

Aspects of the strategy of MNEs can also be enhanced by a deeper understanding of spatial issues. Geographical models can illuminate strategic decisions both through the use of models (Storper, 2000) and empirically as well (Wrigley, 2000). Local labour markets, which are a key attraction for efficiency-seeking FDI, are also geographically configured and analysis here also

benefits from the insights of economic geography (Hanson, 2000). As we have seen above, the strategy of MNEs cannot be fully comprehended without an understanding of the role of knowledge management including both its spatial and temporal aspects (Auderetsh, 2000; Schoenberger, 2000). One of the most brilliant analyses of the management of knowledge across time and space was, of course, made by Raymond Vernon (1966) in his analysis of the product cycle. There is much here for international business researchers to build on.

One of the most celebrated analyses combining economics and geography in the analysis of national economic strategies is that of Michael Porter (1990, 2000) building on a previous synthesis of work with a strong spatial element in the analysis of competitive advantage (Porter, 1985). The essence of concentrations of mutually supportive industries – clusters or industrial districts – goes back to the work of Alfred Marshall (1919, 1930) who seized on the ability of firms in close proximity to capture the external economies which might otherwise not be appropriated (Asheim, 2000). There are close connections here with mainstream work in international business notably John Dunning's OLI paradigm, with a focus on the L for location (Dunning, 2000, 1995, 1977). The ability of foreign MNEs to tap into local clusters and to create their own spatially distinct growth poles have long been a major features of international business analyses of the dynamics of growth. Perhaps the most developed of this stream of analysis is its links with 'clusters of innovation' and 'national systems of innovation' (Cantwell, 1989). The geography of innovation is an area of great potential and one to which international business scholars will continue to contribute (Antonelli, 2000; Feldman, 2000; Lundvall and Maskell, 2000; Maskell, 2000).

The geographic sources of competitiveness of international firms have attracted sporadic attention (Birkenshaw and Hood, 2000; Dunning, 1996; Frost, 2001), particularly as regards creative subsidiaries, but have not, as yet, become a mainstream preoccupation of international business theory. However, attention to foreign (decentralised) R&D and patenting activity has been studied (Almeida, 1996; Belderbos, 2001; Cantwell, 1993; Cantwell and Janne, 2000; Dalton and Serapio, 1999; Jones and Davies., 2000; Pearce, 1999) as has the internationalisation, geographic locational advantages and competitiveness of service firms (Dunning and McKaig-Berliner, 2002; Nachum, 1999).

Despite this considerable research progress in the economic geography of globalisation, there are still areas of great opportunity for further development and innovation. One of these is the geography of culture (Thrift, 2000) where international business scholars drawing on their long tradition of work in this area (Hofstede, 1997, 1980; Ronen and Shenkar, 1985) have an unrivalled ability to contribute. The spatial boundaries of 'a culture' are of enormous practical and theoretical interest, particularly with regard to their alignment or non-alignment with national, linguistic and other frontiers (Braudel, 1995; Shenkar, 2001).

A second key area of potential development is the furtherance of the research agenda of the 'Janus face of globalisation' and in particular its geographical aspects. Spatially, do the benefits of globalisation accrue to the rich (capital exporting) countries or to the poor (host) countries? (Eden and Lenway, 2001). As MNEs became more sophisticated in exploiting the spatial division of labour by slicing their activities even more finely, the question of who benefits becomes more pressing and the answer more sophisticated. The countervailing power of NGOs also requires further analysis (Doh and Teegan, 2003).

Demographic changes and migration are two of the other under-researched phenomena in examining the deepening spatial division of labour. The comparative advantage of international business scholars has always been their ability to combine different approaches and to see the big picture. This type of creative connectivity is needed in pushing forward the frontiers of research on the geography of globalisation and the role of MNEs.

Challenges to globalisation

Market capitalism, as described above, has inherent global tendencies. These stem directly from the central role of trade in a market system. The tendency of trade to promote globalisation can be seen in the empires of classical antiquity, as well as in the globalisation that occurred in the Age of High Imperialism before World War I (Prior, 2000). This age was the culmination of almost a millennium of incremental development, in which local markets became integrated into regional trading systems, and these trading systems were in turn integrated across continents as a consequence of trans-oceanic voyages of discovery. This integration of markets is a defining characteristic of globalisation.

Market capitalism also encourages the globalisation of finance and promotes the mobility of labour. Large financial markets offer investors greater liquidity, and more competitive pricing of stocks and shares, combined with greater legal security. This leads to the agglomeration of economic power in major metropolitan centres where financial dealings predominate. Peripheral regions of the integrated economy are plundered for their raw materials, or farmed intensively to feed the urban areas, or relegated to unskilled labour-intensive work. This is simply the imperative of efficiency seeking in a world of constant change.

This discussion provides a suitable framework for examining some of the major complaints levelled at the World Trade Organisation at their 1999 Seattle meeting. The substance of the complaints appears to be that:

- the progressive reduction of trade and investment barriers leads to loss of jobs;
- an accelerating pace of technological change leads to greater insecurity of jobs and to the end of the lifetime employment system;
- inadequate environmental standards lead to increases in pollution which are incompatible with sustainable development;
- greater income inequality emerges, both within countries and between them, creating new social and political divisions;
- destruction of local communities is caused by an extension of global linkages;
- cultural diversity is reduced, because culture is homogenised by standardisation on modern Western values;
- national sovereignty is threatened, and the power of the state is undermined; and
- deregulation of industry and services leads to increased uncertainty, and to greater opportunities for stock-market speculation.

Little can be done to address some of these objections because they hit directly at the logic of the capitalist process (Rugman, 2000). For example, the dynamics of the market system mean that old jobs are destroyed at the same time that new jobs are created, and as this process accelerates, jobs become progressively more insecure. Many of these objections can be addressed fully only by changes which would dramatically reduce the long-run efficiency of the capitalist system. It is perfectly possible, for example, to insist that the metropolitan trading centres be deglomerated, thereby redistributing entrepreneurial profits to more peripheral

Table 2 Winners and losers from the globalisation of capitalism

	Winners	Losers	Factor
Labour	Labour in newly industrialising countries	Labour in mature industrial countries	Reductions in transport costs and tariffs for manufactured goods
Profit earners	Owners of successful globalised firms or of the firms that supply them	Owners of firms that fail to globalise or of firms that are dependent on them	Reduced communication costs facilitate international transfer of proprietary knowledge
Government	Non-interventionist governments with strong respect for property rights	Interventionist governments with weak respect for property rights	Reduced transport and communication costs give increased scope for international specialisation and exploitation of agglomeration economies, providing firms with a wider choice of political regimes from which to operate

Source: Buckley and Casson (2001, p. 320).

regions. However, the costs of transporting and distributing commodities would increase, and consumers as a whole would be worse off. Similar measures could be applied to deglomerate R&D from major clusters like Silicon Valley to a host of minor ones, but again there would be efficiency losses in terms of innovations foregone. Moreover, it is likely that plans for enforced deglomeration would quickly become distorted by local politics, so that any redistribution of income would mainly favour corrupt officials.

Indeed, contrary to the claims of the Seattle protestors, globalisation confers important benefits. As Table 2 indicates, the opening up of trade frees domestic workers from the need to produce for subsistence and allows them to specialise, if they wish, on export production. Provided they work in a free society, they will switch to export production only if they perceive a benefit from doing so. There is little direct evidence that local producers are systematically duped into producing for export markets through selfish manipulation, although it is often alleged by critics of free trade that this is what local money lenders and export merchants do.

While some of the objections are invalid, however, others have substance to them. The moral ambiguities of the capitalist system generate a range of problems connected with negative externalities of one sort or another. No set of market contracts can cover all of the issues involved in coordinating a complex global economic system – except at prohibitive transaction cost. It is wrong to suggest that nothing can or should be done about

these problems. Consider, for example, the issue of financing mineral industries in developing countries. In a world where entrepreneurial greed was constrained by Protestant guilt, profits in resource-based industries would be voluntarily sacrificed to render development more sustainable. Bankers would think twice before lending large sums of money to inexperienced borrowers, such as the governments of less-developed countries. In a more secular society, issues of sustainability and manipulative lending practices can be addressed through statutory regulation, but this requires a high level of inter-governmental cooperation. The institutions of inter-governmental cooperation are often slow and bureaucratic, creating considerable impatience among activists awaiting a policy response. It is inherently wasteful to operate a capitalist system that encourages selfish profit-seeking behaviour, and to then establish a cumbersome inter-governmental bureaucracy to restrict it. Regulating profit seeking through self-restraint is, in principle, a much cheaper option, provided that the moral infrastructure is in place.

Secular ideologies provided an outlet for creative talents throughout much of the 20th century, and their demise leaves a serious vacuum. The protesters at Seattle were struggling to find a relevant language in which to express their discontent. Their demonstrations showed that they did not trust existing international institutions to make the changes that they believe are required. They sensed intuitively that there is a lack of restraint by those who hold economic power – namely by those who influence key decisions about future policy regimes in the global economy. In this sense their attitudes simply reflect the low-trust culture that modern capitalism has created.

Admittedly, many of their criticisms are not new – they echo the criticisms of international capitalism advanced by socialists in the past. Some of their claims may also be misguided. It was shown above, for example, that low-wage workers in developing countries can benefit substantially from global capitalism. However, there is always a tendency for people who are making a point to support their position with as many arguments as they can find – good as well as bad. Groups that wish to engage in collective action often have to promote an eclectic position in order to mobilise support as widely as possible.

The analysis in Buckley and Casson (2001a, b) suggests that the protesters' accusations of bad faith against modern capitalist enterprises may have substance. Some marketing techniques systematically probe for ignorance and lack of self-awareness among the consuming public. Popular brands are targeted at poor consumers, offering them subjective rewards, such as higher status, at a price they cannot afford to pay. Children and young people make easy targets, especially when advertisements can be skilfully designed to undermine parental veto power. When people find the time to relax, and reflect on their experience as consumers, their higher nature intuitively alerts them to the problem. However, they cannot easily articulate their feelings because they have been brought up to believe that they are rational all of the time. Even if the products they buy seem useless in retrospect, it has to be admitted that shopping for them seemed like fun at the time (see Frank, 1999). Shopping becomes an end in itself – exercising the impulse to buy being the immediate source of pleasure – and the product is just the excuse. Products have to be thrown away because otherwise storage space would limit indulgence in the shopping experience. On this view, it is when shopping palls, and the meaninglessness of the impulse to buy becomes obvious, that protests become attractive instead. People become angry when they finally have to face the fact that they have been systematically manipulated by the producers of the branded trivia of the modern capitalist system.

Moral arguments are rarely clearcut, however. Here is Lord Desai, no lover of capitalism: 'globalisation is nothing but the resurgence of capitalism in the late 20th century. As FDI spreads to the poor countries of Asia, many of the people living there decide to quit their life of rural idiocy and join sweat shops in town. This may seem horrible to moralists of non-governmental organisations, but it is betterment for those making the decision to move. No doubt a concern for their rights in developed countries will price them out of their jobs. Thus does altruism of the rich often kill the poor by kindness' (Desai, 2003, 23).

However, it is not the poor who protest (in Seattle or elsewhere). The worry is that it is the beneficiaries of global capitalism who are its fiercest critics.

Conclusion – a research agenda

There are serious issues surrounding the notion of globalisation. There are also some myths. Empirical evidence is often disassociated from polemical writings on the subject. There is a great opportunity in front of international business scholars to confront assertions about globalisation with facts (or stylised facts).

This paper has examined globalisation in terms of conflicts between markets and economic management and suggested that the differential pace of globalisation across markets presents a number of challenges to policy makers in local, national and regional governments and in international institutions. In examining the changing location and ownership strategies of MNEs, it has shown that the increasingly sophisticated decision making of managers in MNEs is slicing the activities of firms more finely and in finding optimum locations for each closely defined activity, they are deepening the international division of labour. Ownership strategies, too, are becoming increasingly complex, leading to a control matrix that runs from wholly owned units via FDI through market relationships such as subcontracting, including joint ventures, as options on subsequent decisions in a dynamic pattern. The input of lessons from economic geography is thus becoming more important in understanding the key developments in international business. The consequences of the globalisation of production and consumption represent political challenges and reaction against these changes has led to a questioning of the effects of global capitalism as well as to its moral basis.

These four issues are closely intertwined and present a formidable research agenda to which the international business research community is uniquely fitted to respond. This agenda can encompass work from the empirical to the theoretical. Empirical issues include: the careful mapping and spatial analysis of FDI flows, the spatial and temporal spread of MNEs, and the geographical determinants of strategy. The underplaying of physical geography (rivers, coastlines, climate, soil types) from explanations of FDI and MNE strategies needs to be corrected. The external effects of MNEs (linkages, spillovers) need to be more closely related to the analysis of strategy so that IB researchers can contribute more to the literature on development and underdevelopment.

Theoretical avenues include the full incorporation of spatial issues in the strategy of MNEs, the integration of the role of new institutions such as NGOs and fuller attention to the political implica-

tions of the activities and changing organisation of MNEs. The management of space and time by MNEs should be in the forefront of the analysis of globalisation.

Acknowledgements
The analysis in this paper draws on three earlier pieces – Buckley and Casson (1998, 2001a, b) and Ghauri and Buckley (2002). We are grateful for comments on an earlier version at the JIBS Conference, Duke University, NC, USA, 6–8 March 2003, from Stefanie Lenway, and from three anonymous referees and the editor of *JIBS*, Arie Lewin.

References
Abo, T. (2000) 'Spontaneous Integration in Japan and East Asia: Development, Crises and Beyond', in G.L. Clark, M.P. Feldman and M.S. Gertler (eds.) *The Oxford Handbook of Economic Geography*, Oxford University Press: Oxford, pp: 625–648.

Alden, J (1999) 'The Impact of Foreign Direct Investment on Job Creation: The Experience of Wales', in N.A. Phelps and J. Alden (eds.) *Foreign Direct Investment and the Global Economy*, The Stationery Office: London, pp: 269–280.

Almeida, P. (1996) 'Knowledge sourcing by foreign multi-nationals: patent citation analysis in the US semi-conductor industry', *Strategic Management Journal* **17**(winter): 155–165.

Amin, A. (2000) 'The European Union as more than a Triad Market for National Economic Spaces', in G.L. Clark, M.P. Feldman and M.S. Gertler (eds.) *The Oxford Handbook of Economic Geography*, Oxford University Press: Oxford, pp: 671–687.

Antonelli, C. (2000) 'Restructuring and Innovation in Long-Term Regional Change', in G.L. Clark, M.P. Feldman and M.S. Gertler (eds.) *The Oxford Handbook of Economic Geography*, Oxford University Press: Oxford, pp: 395–412.

Asheim, B.T. (2000) 'Industrial Districts; The Contributions of Marshall and Beyond', in G.L. Clark, M.P. Feldman and M.S. Gertler (eds.) *The Oxford Handbook of Economic Geography*, Oxford University Press: Oxford, pp: 413–431.

Auderetsh, D.B. (2000) 'Corporate Form and Spatial Form', in G.L. Clark, M.P. Feldman and M.S. Gertler (eds.) *The Oxford Handbook of Economic Geography*, Oxford University Press: Oxford, pp: 333–351.

Bartlett, C.A. and Ghoshal, S. (1989) *Managing Across Borders: The Transnational Solution*, Hutchinson Business Books: Boston.

Belderbos, R.A. (2001) 'Overseas innovations by Japanese firms: an analysis of patent and subsidiary data', *Research Policy* **30**(2): 313–332.

Berg, D.M. and Guisinger, S.E. (2001) 'Capital flows, capital controls and international business risk', in A.M. Rugman and T.L. Brewer (eds.) *The Oxford Handbook of International Business*, Oxford University Press: Oxford, pp: 259–281.

Bernard, M. and Ravenhill, J. (1995) 'Beyond product cycles and flying geese: regionalisation, hierarchy and industrialisation in East Asia', *World Politics* **47**(1): 171–209.

Best, M.H. (1990) *The New Competition: Institutions of Industrial Restructuring*, Polity Press: Oxford.

Birkenshaw, J. and Hood, N. (2000) 'Characteristics of foreign subsidiaries in industry clusters', *Journal of International Business Studies* **31**(1): 141–154.

Braudel, F. (1995) *A History of Civilizations*, Penguin Books: Harmondsworth.

Bressand, A. (1990) 'Beyond interdependence: 1992 as a global challenge', *International Affairs* **66**(1): 47–65.

Buckley, P.J. (1997) 'Cooperative Form of Transnational Corporation Activity', in J.H. Dunning and K.P. Sauvant (eds.) *Transnational Corporations and World Development*, Thomson: London, pp: 473–493.

Buckley, P.J. (2002) 'Is the international business research agenda running out of steam?', *Journal of International Business Studies* **33**(2): 365–373.

Buckley, P.J. and Carter, M.J. (2002) 'Process and structure in knowledge management practices of British and US multinational enterprises', *Journal of International Management* **8**(1): 29–48.

Buckley, P.J. and Casson, M. (1988) 'A Theory of Cooperation in International Business', in F. Contractor and P. Lorange (eds.) *Cooperative Strategies in International Business*, New Lexington Press: Lexington MA, pp: 31–53.

Buckley, P.J. and Casson, M. (1996) 'An economic model of international joint ventures', *Journal of International Business Studies* **27**(5): 849–876.

Buckley, P.J. and Casson, M. (1998) 'Analysing foreign market entry strategies: extending the internalisation approach', *Journal of International Business Studies* **29**(3): 539–561.

Buckley, P.J. and Casson, M. (2001a) 'The moral basis of global capitalism: beyond the eclectic theory', *International Journal of the Economics of Business* **8**(2): 303–327.

Buckley, P.J. and Casson, M.C. (1991) 'Multinational Enterprises in less Developed Countries: Cultural and Economic Interaction', in P.J. Buckley and J. Clegg (eds.) *Multinational Enterprises in Less Developed Countries*, Macmillan: London.

Buckley, P.J. and Casson, M.C. (2001b) 'Strategic Complexity and International Business', in A.M. Rugman and T.L. Brewer (eds.) *The Oxford Handbook of International Business*, Oxford University Press: Oxford, pp: 88–126.

Buckley, P.J., Casson, M.C. and Gulamhussen, M.A. (2002) 'Internationalisation – Real Options, Knowledge Management and the Uppsala Approach', in V. Havila, M. Forsgren and H. Håkansson (eds.) *Critical Perspectives on Internationalisation*, Isevier: Oxford, pp: 229–262.

Buckley, P.J., Clegg, J., Forsans, N. and Reilly, K.T. (2001) 'Increasing the size of the 'country': regional economic integration and foreign direct investment in a globalised world economy'', *Management International Review* **41**(3): 251–274.

Buckley, P.J. and Ghauri, P.N. (2002) *International Mergers and Acquisitions*, International Thomson Business Press: London.

Cairncross, F. (1997) *The Death of Distance: How the Communications Revolution Will Change our Lives*, Harvard Business School Press: Boston, MA.

Cantwell, J. (1995) 'The globalisation of technology: what remains of the product cycle model', *Cambridge Journal of Economics* 19(1): 155–174.

Cantwell, J.A. (1989) *Technological Innovation and the Multinational Enterprise*, Basil Blackwell: Oxford.

Cantwell, J.A. (1993) 'The internationalisation of technological activity and its implication for competitiveness', in O. Grandstand, H. Håkanson and S. Sjölander (eds.) *Technological Management and International Business*, John Wiley: Chichester, pp: 137–162.

Cantwell, J.A. and Janne, O. (2000) 'Technological globalisation and innovative centres: the role of corporate technological leadership and locational hierarchy', *Research Policy* 28(2–3): 119–144.

Castells, M. (2001) *The Internet Galaxy*, Oxford University Press: Oxford.

Chapman, K. (1999) 'Merger/Acquisition Activity and Regional Cohesion in the EU', in N.A. Phelps and J. Alden (eds.) *Foreign Direct Investment and the Global Economy*, The Stationery Office: London, pp: 121–138.

Clark, G.L., Feldman, M.P. and Gerther, M.S. (2000) 'Economic Geography: Transition and Growth', in G.L. Clark, M.P. Feldman and M.S. Gertler (eds.) *The Oxford Handbook of Economic Geography*, Oxford University Press: Oxford, pp: 3–17.

Dalton, D.H. and Serapio, M.G. (1999) *Globalising Industrial Research and Development*, US Department of Commerce, Office of Technology Policy: Washington, DC.

Desai, M (2003) *With the Best Will in the World: Review of One World: The Ethics of Globalisation*, Times Higher Education Supplement (21.02.03). London, pp: 23.

Devinney, T., Midgley, D. and Venaik, S. (2000) 'The optimal performance of the global firm: formalising and extending the integration: responsiveness framework', *Organization Science* 11(6): 674–695.

Dicken, P. (2003) *Global Shift*, 4th edn. Sage: London.

Dicken, P. and Hassler, M. (2000) 'Organizing the Indonesian clothing industry in the global economy: the role of business networks', *Environment and Planning A* 32(2): 263–280.

Doh, J.P. and Teegan, H. (2003) *Globalization and NGOs*, Praeger: Westport, CT.

Dunning, J.H. (1977) 'Trade, Location of Economic Activity and the MNE: A Search for an Eclectic Approach', in B. Ohlin, P.O. Hesselborn and P.M. Wijkmon (eds.) *The International Allocation of Economic Activity*, Macmillan: London, pp: 395–418.

Dunning, J.H. (1995) 'Reappraising the eclectic paradigm in the age of alliance capitalism', *Journal of International Business Studies* 26(3): 461–491.

Dunning, J.H. (1996) 'The geographical sources of the competitiveness of firms: some results of a new survey', *Transnational Corporations* 5(3): 1–30.

Dunning, J.H. (2000) 'The eclectic paradigm as an envelope for economic and business theories of MNE activity', *International Business Review* 9(2): 163–190.

Dunning, J.H. and McKaig-Berliner, A. (2002) 'The geographical sources of competitiveness: the professional business services industry', *Transnational Corporations* 11(3): 1–38.

Dunning, J.H. and Wallace, L. (1999) 'New Jersey in a Globalising Economy', in N.A. Phelps and J. Alden (eds.) *Foreign Direct Investment and the Global Economy*, The Stationery Office: London, pp: 253–269.

Eden, L. and Lenway, S. (2001) 'Introduction to the symposium, multinationals: the Janus face of globalisation', *Journal of International Business Studies* 32(3): 383–400.

Edgington, D.W. and Hayet, R. (2000) 'Foreign direct investment and the flying geese model: Japanese electronics firms in the Asia Pacific', *Environment and Planning A* 32(2): 281–304.

Emmanuel, C. and Mehafdi, M. (1994) *Transfer Pricing*, Academic Press: London.

Feldman, M.P. (2000) 'Location and Innovation: The New Economic Geography of Innovation, Spillovers and Agglomeration', in G.L. Clark, M.P. Feldman and M.S. Gertler (eds.) *The Oxford Handbook of Economic Geography*, Oxford University Press: Oxford, pp: 373–395.

Frank, R.H. (1999) *Luxury Fever: Why Money Fails to Satisfy in an Era of Excess*, Free Press: New York.

Frobel, F., Heinrichs, J. and Kreye, O. (1980) *The New International Division of Labour*, Cambridge University Press: Cambridge, MA.

Frost, T.S. (2001) 'The geographical source of foreign subsidiaries' innovation', *Strategic Management Journal* 22(2): 101–123.

Gereffi, G. (1999) 'International trade and industrial upgrading in the apparel commodity chain', *Journal of International Economics* 48(1): 37–70.

Gereffi, G., Korzeniewics, M. and Korzeniewics, R.P. (1994) 'Introduction: Global Commodity Chains', in G. Gereffi and M. Korzeniewics (eds.) *Commodity Chains and Global Capitalism*, Praeger: Westport, CT, pp: 1–14.

Gersbach, H. (2002) 'Does and how does globalisation matter at industry level?', *World Economy* 25(2): 209–229.

Ghauri, P.N. (1992) 'New structures in MNCs based in small countries: a network approach', *European Management Journal* 10(3): 357–364.

Ghauri, P.N. (1999) *Advances in International Marketing: International Marketing Purchasing*, JAI Press: Conneticut.

Ghauri, P.N. and Buckley, P.J. (2002) 'Globalization and the End of Competition: A Critical Review of Rent-Seeking Multinationals', in V. Havila, M. Forsgren and H. Håkansson (eds.) *Critical Research on Multinational Corporations*, Pergamon Press: Oxford, pp: 7–28.

Ghauri, P.N. and Prasad, S.B. (1995) 'A network approach to probing Asia's interfirm linkages', *Advances in International Comparative Management* 10: 63–77.

Graham, E.M. (2003) 'Attracting Foreign Direct Investment to the United States: The Joust between the Federal Government and the States', in N.A. Phelps and P. Rains (eds.) *The New Competition for Inward Investment*, Edward Elgar: Cheltenham, pp: 61–78.

Hanson, G.H. (2000) 'Firms, Workers and the Geographic Concentration of Economic Activity', in G.L. Clark, M.P. Feldman and M.S. Gertler (eds.) *The Oxford Handbook of Economic Geography*, Oxford University Press: Oxford, pp: 477–497.

Hart-Landsberg, M. and Burkett, P. (1998) 'Contradictions of capitalist industrialization in East Asia: a critique of 'flying geese' theories of development', *Economic Geography* 74(2): 87–110.

Hatch, W. and Yamamura, K. (1996) *Asia in Japan's Embrace: Building a Regional Production Alliance*, Cambridge University Press: Cambridge, MA.

Hill, R.C. and Fujita, K. (1996) 'Flying geese, swarming sparrows or preying hawks? Perspectives on East Asian industrialization', *Competition and Change* 1(3): 285–298.

Hirshleifer, J. (1986) 'Internal Pricing and Decentralised Decisions', in C.P. Bonini, R.K. Jaedicke and H.M. Wagner (eds.) *Management Controls: New Directions in Basic Research*, Gartland: London, pp: 27–37.

Hofstede, G. (1997) *Cultures and Organizations: Software of The Mind*, McGraw-Hill: New York.

Hofstede, G. (1980) *Culture's Consequences: International Differences in Work Related Values*, Sage: Beverly Hills, CA.

Holmes, J. (2000) 'Regional Integration in North America', in G.L. Clark, M.P. Feldman and M.S. Gertler (eds.) *The Oxford Handbook of Economic Geography*, Oxford University Press: Oxford, pp: 649–671.

Hymer, S. (1972) 'The Multinational Corporation and The Law of Uneven Development', in J. Bhagwati (ed.) *Economics and World Order from The 1970s to the 1990s*, Collier-MacMillan: New York, pp: 113–140.

Jenkins, R. (1987) *Transnational Corporations and Uneven Development: The Internationalisation of Capital in the Third World*, Methuen: London.

Jones, G.K. and Davies, H.J. (2000) 'National culture and innovation: implications for locating global R&D operations', *Management International Review* **40**(1): 11–39.

Krugman, P. (1991) *Geography and Trade*, MIT Press: Cambridge MA.

Krugman, P. (2000) 'Where in the World is the 'New Economic Geography?', in G.L. Clark, M.P. Feldman and M.S. Gertler (eds.) *The Oxford Handbook of Economic Geography*, Oxford University Press: Oxford, pp: 49–60.

Laulajainen, R.I. (2000) 'The Regulation of International Finance', in G.L. Clark, M.P. Feldman and M.S. Gertler (eds.) *The Oxford Handbook of Economic Geography*, Oxford University Press: Oxford, pp: 215–229.

Lenway, S.A. and Murtha, T.P. (1994) 'The State as strategist in international business research', *Journal of International Business Studies* **25**(3): 513–535.

Lundvall, B.-A. and Maskell, P. (2000) 'Nation States and Economic Development: From National Systems of Production to National Systems of Knowledge Creation and Learning', in G.L. Clark, M.P. Feldman and M.S. Gertler (eds.) *The Oxford Handbook of Economic Geography*, Oxford University Press: Oxford, pp: 535–573.

Markusen, J.R. and Venables, A.J. (2000) 'The theory of endowment, intra-industry and multi-national trade', *Journal of International Economics* **52**(2): 209–234.

Marshall, A. (1919) *Industry and Trade*, Macmillan: London.

Marshall, A. (1930) *Principles of Economics*, 8th edn. Macmillan: London.

Maskell, P. (2000) 'Future Challenges and Institutional Preconditions for Regional Development Policy of Economic Globalisation', in I. Karppi (ed.) *Future Challenges and Institutional Preconditions for Regional Development Policy*, Nordregio: Stockholm, pp: 27–88.

Mellinger, A.D., Sachs, J.D. and Gallup, J.L. (2000) 'Climate, Coastal Proximity and Development', in G.L. Clark, M.P. Feldman and M.S. Gertler (eds.) *The Oxford Handbook of Economic Geography*, Oxford University Press: Oxford, pp: 169–195.

Mirza, H. (ed.) (1998) *Global Competitive Strategies in the New World Economy: Multilateralism, Regionalization and the Transnational Firm*, Edward Elgar: Cheltenham.

Murtha, T.P., Lenway, S.A. and Bagazzi, R.P. (1998) 'Global mind-sets and cognitive shift in a complex multinational corporation', *Strategic Management Journal* **19**(2): 97–114.

Murtha, T.P., Lenway, S.A. and Hart, J.A. (2001) *Managing New Industry Creation*, Stanford University Press: Stanford.

Nachum, L. (1999) *The Origins of the International Competitiveness of Firms: The Impact of Location and Ownership in Professional Service firms*, Edward Elgar: Cheltenham.

Oxelheim, L. and Ghauri, P.N. (eds.) (2003) *European Union and the Race for Inward FDI in Europe*, Elsevier: Oxford.

Oxelheim, L., Randoy, T. and Stonehill, A. (2001) 'On the treatment of finance-specific factors within the OLI paradigm', *International Business Review* **10**(4): 381–398.

Pearce, R.D. (1999) 'The evolution of technology in multinational enterprises: the role of creative subsidiaries', *International Business Review* **8**(2): 125–148.

Peck, F. and Durnin, J. (1999) 'Institutional Marginalisation and Inward Investment Strategies in the North of England: The Case of Cumbria', in N.A. Phelps and J. Alden (eds.) *Foreign Direct Investment and the Global Economy*, The Stationery Office: London, pp: 237–253.

Phelps, N.A. and Alden, J. (eds.) (1999) *Foreign Direct Investment and the Global Economy*, The Stationery Office: London.

Phelps, N.A. and Rains, P. (2003) *The New Competition for Inward Investment*, Edward Elgar: Cheltenham.

Pike, A. (1999) '*In situ* Restructuring in Branch Plants and their Local Economic Development Implications', in N.A. Phelps and J. Alden (eds.) *Foreign Direct Investment and the Global Economy*, The Stationery Office: London, pp: 221–237.

Porter, M.E. (1985) *Competitive Advantage: Creating and Sustaining Superior Performance*, Free Press: New York.

Porter, M.E. (1990) *The Competitive Advantage of Nationals*, Free Press: New York.

Porter, M.E. (2000) 'Locations, Clusters and Company Strategy', in G.L. Clark, M.P. Feldman and M.S. Gertler (eds.) *The Oxford Handbook of Economic Geography*, Oxford University Press: Oxford, pp: 253–275.

Prahalad, C.K. and Lieberthal, K. (1998) 'The end of corporate imperialism', *Harvard Business Review*, Vol 76, July–August 69–79.

Prior, F.L. (2000) 'Internationalisation and Globalisation of the American Economy', in T.L. Brewer and G. Boyd (eds.) *Globalising America: The USA in World Integration*, Edward Elgar: Cheltenham, pp: 1–39.

Raikes, P., Jensen, M.F. and Ponte, S. (2000) 'Global commodity chain analysis and the French filiere approach: comparison and critique', *Economy and Society* **29**(3): 390–417.

Raines, P. (2003) 'Flows and Territories: the New Geography of Competition for Mobile Investment in Europe', in N.A. Phelps and P. Rains (eds.) *The New Competition for Inward Investment*, Edward Elgar: Cheltenham, pp. 119–135.

Raines, P. and Wishlade, F. (1999) 'E.C. Policy-Making and the Challenges of Foreign Investment', in N.A. Phelps and J. Alden (eds.) *Foreign Direct Investment and the Global Economy*, The Stationery Office: London, pp: 71–87.

Ronen, S. and Shenkar, O. (1985) 'Clustering countries in altitudinal dimensions: a review and synthesis', *Academy of Management Review* **10**(3): 435–454.

Rosecrance, R. (1996) 'The rise of virtual state', *Foreign Affairs* **47**(1): 45–61.

Rugman, A.M. (2000) *The End of Globalisation*, Random House: London.

Rugman, A.M., D'Cruz, J.R. and Verbeke, A. (1995) 'Internalisation and De-Internalisation: Will Business Networks Replace Multinationals?', in G. Boyd (ed.) *Competitive and Cooperative Macromanagement*, Edward Elgar: Aldershot, pp: 107–129.

Rugman, A.M. and Eden, L. (eds.) (1985) *Multinationals and Transfer Pricing*, Croom Helm: Beckenham.

Ruigrok, W. and Van Tulder, R. (1995) *The Logic of International Restructuring*, Routledge: London.

Schoenberger, E. (2000) 'The Management of Time and Space', in G.L. Clark, M.P. Feldman and M.S. Gertler (eds.) *The Oxford Handbook of Economic Geography*, Oxford University Press: Oxford, pp: 317–333.

Scott, A.J. (2000) 'Economic Geography: The Great Half Century', in G.L. Clark, M.P. Feldman and M.S. Gertler (eds.) *The Oxford Handbook of Economic Geography*, Oxford University Press: Oxford, pp: 483–504.

Shenkar, O. (2001) 'Cultural distance revisited: towards a more rigorous conceptualisation and measurement of cultural distance', *Journal of International Business Studies* **32**(3): 519–535.

Sideri, S. (1997) 'Globalisation and regional integration', *European Journal of Development Research* **9**(1): 38–81.

Storper, M. (2000) 'Globalization, Localization and Trade', in G.L. Clark, M.P. Feldman and M.S. Gertler (eds.) *The Oxford Handbook of Economic Geography*, Oxford University Press: Oxford, pp: 146–169.

Subramanian, R. and Lawrence, R.Z. (1999) *A Prism on Globalization: Corporate Responses to the Dollar*, Brookings Institution Press: Washington, DC.

The Economist (2000) *Factories for Hire*, London, 12 February. pp: 8.

The Economist (2002) *Incredible Shrinking Plants*, London, 23 February. pp: 71–73.

The Economist (2001a) *Out of the Back Room*, London, 1 December, pp: 75–76.

The Economist (2001b) *Putting it in its Place – Geography and The Net*, London, 11 August. pp: 18.

The Economist (2003) *The Revenge of Geography – Technology Quarterly*, London, 15 March, pp: 22–27.

Thrift, N. (2000) 'Pandora's Box? Cultural Geographies of Economies', in G.L. Clark, M.P. Feldman and M.S. Gertler (eds.) *The Oxford Handbook of Economic Geography*, Oxford University Press: Oxford, pp: 689–704.

Tickell, A. (2000) 'Finance and Localities', in G.L. Clark, M.P. Feldman and M.S. Gertler (eds.) *The Oxford Handbook of Economic Geography*, Oxford University Press: Oxford, pp: 230–251.

Trigeorgis, L. (1996) *Real Options*, MIT Press: Cambridge, MA.

Tsui-Auch, L.S. (1999) 'Regional production relationship and developmental impacts: a comparative study of three regional networks', *International Journal of Urban and Regional Research* **23**(2): 345–360.

UNCTAD (1999) *Transfer Pricing. UNCTAD Series on Issues in International Investment Agreements*, UNCTAD: Geneva and New York.

Vernon, R. (1966) 'International investment and international trade in the product cycle', *The Quarterly Journal of Economics* **80**(2): 190–207.

Wood, A. (2003) 'The Politics of Orchestrating Inward Investment: Institutions, Policy and Practice in the Industrial Midwest', in N.A. Phelps and P. Rains (eds.) *The New ompetition for Inward Investment*, Edward Elgar: Cheltenham, pp: 79–98.

Wrigley, N. (2000) 'The Globalization of Retail Capital: Themes for Economic Geography', in G.L. Clark, M.P. Feldman and M.S. Gertler (eds.) *The Oxford Handbook of Economic Geography*, Oxford University Press: Oxford, pp: 292–317.

Yeung, G. (2003) 'Scramble for FDI: The Experience of Guangdong Province in Southern China', in N.A. Phelps and P. Rains (eds.) *The New Competition for Inward Investment*, Edward Elgar: Cheltenham, pp. 193–212.

Yeung, H.W. (2001) *Entrepreneurship and the Internationalisation of Asian Firms: An Institutional Perspective*, Edward Elgar: Cheltenham.

About the author

Peter J Buckley is Professor of International Business and Director of the Centre for International Business University of Leeds (CIBUL), UK. Professor Buckley has published extensively on the theory of the MNE, methods of foreign market entry and development, the management of cooperative strategies and on theoretical and empirical aspects of joint ventures and alliances. He currently serves as the President of the Academy of International Business (AIB).

Pervez Ghauri completed his Ph.D. at Uppsala University in Sweden. Where he also taught for several years. At present he is Professor of International Business at Manchester School of Management, UMIST, UK. Pervez Ghauri has published more than 15 books and numerous articles on international business topics. He is also Editor of International Business Review, the official journal of European International Buisness Academy (EIBA).

Accepted by Arie Lewin, Editor in Chief, 1 December 2003. This paper has been with the author for one revision.

[14]

It's not easy to make money by offshoring business processes, many CEOs are discovering. Companies benefit only when they pick the right processes, calculate both the operational and structural risks, and match organizational forms to needs.

Getting Offshoring Right

by Ravi Aron and Jitendra V. Singh

IN 2003, ALPHA CORP., a well-known U.S.-based organization, offshored and outsourced several customer-retention processes. When the company found that some of its customers seemed likely to switch to rivals, it provided data on them to an outsourcing firm in India. The service provider called those customers and, on Alpha Corp.'s behalf, offered them fee waivers, upgrades, and free financial products as incentives to remain with Alpha Corp.

A common, but rarely discussed, offshoring scenario then played out.

The vendor's employees were enthusiastic, but they didn't have much experience selling sophisticated financial products such as disability and loss-of-income insurance. As a result, they didn't know how to interpret customers' responses to the incentives they were offering and found it difficult to decide what to do when customers asked them for other incentives. In fact, the provider's employees often placed people on hold in order to contact Alpha Corp.'s supervisors and ask whether to give customers what they wanted.[1] As the demands on Alpha Corp.'s marketing managers rose and the vendor was unable to retain as many customers as it had hoped, Alpha Corp.'s executives began to wonder, "What have we done?"

They aren't the only executives asking that question today. Cut through the hype, and you'll find that, like Alpha Corp., many companies are waking up and smelling the harsh realities of offshoring. Sure, the prospect of offshoring and outsourcing business processes has captured the imagination of CEOs everywhere. In the last five years, many companies in North America and Europe have experimented with this strategy, hoping to reduce costs, become more efficient, and gain a little strategic advantage. However, contrary to popular perception, many businesses have had, at best, mixed results. According to several studies, half the organizations that shifted processes offshore failed to generate the financial benefits they expected to. Many also faced resistance from employees as well as consumer dissatisfaction. In early 2005, both the Boston Consulting Group and Gartner predicted that 50% of the offshoring contracts that companies in North America had signed between 2001 and 2004 would fail to meet expectations. No wonder the "I" words, inshoring and insourcing, have become almost as popular in business circles as the two "O" words.

As academics who have studied the subject in several countries, industries, and companies for more than four years, we can't say we're shocked. Most companies believe it's easy to offshore business processes – easier than it was in the 1980s to procure components from global suppliers or to set up manufacturing plants overseas. Businesses therefore don't make decisions about offshoring systematically enough. As a result, they commit at least one of three fundamental mistakes.

First, most companies focus their efforts on choosing countries, cities, and vendors, as well as on negotiating prices, but they don't spend time evaluating which processes they should offshore and which they shouldn't. Without a standard methodology for differentiating processes, most executives find it tough to distinguish among *core* processes that they must control, *critical* processes that they might buy from best-in-class vendors, and *commodity* processes that they can outsource. They endlessly debate the differences between the core and critical ones, and after political tussles break out, diktats

Ravi Aron (raviaron@wharton.upenn.edu) is an assistant professor of operations and information management, and Jitendra V. Singh (singhj@wharton.upenn.edu) is the Saul P. Steinberg Professor of Management, at the University of Pennsylvania's Wharton School in Philadelphia.

from the top mandate that some processes be sent offshore. Companies inevitably make the wrong choices and, after offshoring or outsourcing processes that they think aren't strategic, have to bring some back in-house.

Second, most organizations don't take into account all the risks that accompany offshoring. Executives use simple cost/benefit analyses to make decisions without realizing, for instance, that after they transfer processes, their vendors will gain the upper hand. Providers can hold companies to ransom; it's almost impossible for organizations to reabsorb business processes on short notice. Most organizations naively ignore these latent risks and are shocked when vendors demand price hikes that erode the savings from outsourcing.

Finally, most companies don't realize that outsourcing is no longer an all-or-nothing choice—that they have a continuum of options. At one end, there's executing processes in-house; at the other, there's outsourcing them to service

providers. Along that continuum, companies can buy services from local providers (a lot of outsourcing is local), enter into joint ventures, or set up captive centers overseas. Most businesses don't consider all the available options and end up using organizational forms that are inappropriate for their purposes. They also analyze processes too narrowly, looking only at direct costs and failing to examine interdependencies that might tip the cost/benefit analysis in favor of keeping services in-house. Making the right governance choices is critical; our research shows that both location and organizational form decide the fate of offshoring strategies.

Clearly, companies have to rethink the manner in which they formulate their offshoring strategies if they wish to succeed. In the following pages, we'll

outline tools that will help companies choose the right processes to offshore, and discuss the associated risks. We will also describe a new kind of organizational structure and show how companies can use it to benefit from offshoring. Don't misunderstand; smart companies have gained strategic advantage by offshoring processes. Your company can also harness the power of the services revolution by taking three steps, one at a time.

Rank Processes by Value

Executives can distinguish, at the outset, between business processes they should and shouldn't offshore by figuring out how each process helps them to create value for customers and to capture some of that value. The relative importance of a process along those two dimensions indicates the risks and rewards associated with moving its execution outside the organization or country. Executives instinctively know the importance of these criteria but usually

According to several studies, half the organizations that shift processes offshore fail to generate the expected financial benefits.

don't know how to factor them into decisions about offshoring.

There's a simple way executives can do that. They should answer the question, How crucial is each process (or subprocess) compared with others in creating value for my company's customers? The answers will differ from business to business and, often, by industry. In the consumer goods industry, for instance, executives usually rate product-development processes higher than customer-service processes, while in the hotel industry, the opposite is true. Next, managers must ask, In relative terms, to what degree does each process enable my company to capture some of the value that it has created for customers? They must rank each process along these two dimensions, then add the two rankings together to arrive at a total ranking for each process. Sometimes, executives may feel that one of the two dimensions is more important in the industry or for their company. In that case, they must calculate the total rankings after assigning greater weight to the more important aspect. For instance, retail banks believe that making money is tougher than developing new consumer finance products. They tend to rate the value-capture aspect of their processes higher than they do the value-creation dimension.

By ranking all the company's processes, executives can create a value hierarchy. The higher a process's rank in the hierarchy, the more crucial it is to the company's strategy, and the less the organization should think about moving it offshore or outsourcing it. The hierarchy tells companies where the fault lines between processes are and lays out an offshore migration path. For exam-

ple, at one U.S.-based computer and communications equipment manufacturer we worked with, senior executives unanimously agreed that of six processes in the finance function, managing the float for suppliers and dealers had the highest relative importance (see the exhibit "Creating a Value Hierarchy of Processes"). That alerted managers that it would be risky to offshore or outsource the process; even if the service provider made only a few errors, it would hurt the firm's dealers and suppliers financially and tarnish the company's reputation. The executives also felt that managing the company's working capital was too important to offshore. At the same time, the group decided that three other processes – invoice verification, payment authorization, and revenue and expense reporting – were less valuable and that the company could think about off-

shoring or even outsourcing them. Some of the executives also believed that at a later date, the business could offshore the cash-flow forecasting operation. This analysis became the basis of the company's offshoring strategy, which so far has been successful.

When executives, usually from the same department, sit around a table and draw up a value hierarchy, it serves several purposes. The ranking provides a standard basis for comparing processes across the company, which makes discussions about offshoring more constructive. Executives often rank the same business process differently; drawing up the hierarchy highlights these differences. That helps surface tensions around offshoring decisions. Above all, the value hierarchy allows managers to think systematically about the importance of processes without getting into interminable debates about what the company's core processes are or how critical its critical processes are.

Creating a Value Hierarchy of Processes

Executives in a company's finance department, charged with identifying business processes to offshore, ranked six processes on their ability to create value for customers and on their ability to capture value for the business. They then added the value-creation ranking and the value-capture ranking together to arrive at a total for each process. When they studied the final rankings, or hierarchy, the executives agreed that they could offshore the three lowest-ranking processes; the two highest-ranking processes, they decided, were too strategically valuable to offshore.

Process	Value-creation ranking*	Value-capture ranking*	Total ranking	
Float management for suppliers and dealers	1	1	2	Processes the company shouldn't offshore
Working capital management	2	3	5	
Cash-flow forecasting	4	2	6	
Revenue and expense reporting	3	4	7	Processes the company might offshore
Payment authorization	5	5	10	
Invoice verification	6	6	12	

*Determined by executive consensus

Identify and Manage Risk

Once a company has established that some of its processes can be offshored or outsourced, it must tackle all the risks that could affect their migration. Companies face two very different kinds of risk: operational and structural. The former may be more critical in the initial stages of offshoring and outsourcing, but over time, the latter swells in importance.

Operational Risk. Smart companies start off assuming that service providers won't be able to execute business processes as well as their employees perform them in-house – at least, not for a long time. Unlike the manufacture of components, firms can't provide vendors with specifications and expect them to carry out tasks perfectly. Until service providers move up the learning curve, they will make more errors and execute tasks more slowly than companies' employees do. That often results in lower customer satisfaction.

Businesses can try to lower operational risk by tackling its twin causes, the first of which is an organization's ability to codify work. When companies document the work that employees

TOOL KIT • Getting Offshoring Right

Evaluating Operational Risk

To evaluate operational risk (the risk that processes won't operate smoothly after being offshored), companies should classify processes by how precise their metrics for quality are, as well as the extent to which work can be codified. We've listed some processes that, our research shows, fall into each category.

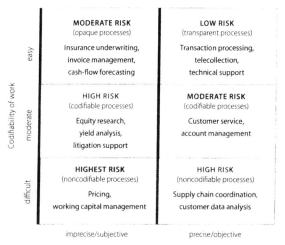

	MODERATE RISK (opaque processes) Insurance underwriting, invoice management, cash-flow forecasting	LOW RISK (transparent processes) Transaction processing, telecollection, technical support
	HIGH RISK (codifiable processes) Equity research, yield analysis, litigation support	MODERATE RISK (codifiable processes) Customer service, account management
	HIGHEST RISK (noncodifiable processes) Pricing, working capital management	HIGH RISK (noncodifiable processes) Supply chain coordination, customer data analysis

Codifiability of work: easy / moderate / difficult

imprecise/subjective — precise/objective

Precision of metrics used to measure process quality

Evaluating Structural Risk

To ascertain structural risk (the risk that relationships with service providers may not work as expected), companies should look at how precise their quality metrics are, as well as the extent to which the execution of processes can be monitered. Most processes fall into one of four categories.

	HIGH RISK Equity research, litigation support, R&D support	LOW RISK Transaction processing, insurance claims processing, customer service
	HIGHEST RISK Pricing, product design	MODERATE RISK Supply chain coordination, customer data analysis

Ability to monitor work: easy / difficult

imprecise/subjective — precise/objective

Precision of metrics used to measure process quality

do, describe the different situations they face, and stipulate what employees' responses should be in each scenario, people anywhere in the world can do the job for them. For instance, if a European retail bank has drawn up rules about when it will give customers loans, has stipulated the procedures for resolving exceptions to accounting norms, and has laid down when it will hold financial instruments in suspense accounts, managers on any continent can perform those tasks for the bank with minimal supervision. Investment banks can outsource even complex tasks like equity research as long as they codify the tasks involved. However, if a service provider's employees require a great deal of domain experience – information about the client's customers, a deep understanding of how its product and geographic markets function, and knowledge that the client's managers carry in their heads – to execute processes, they are unlikely to get those processes right for a long time. (For more on codifying knowledge in the workplace, see Dorothy Leonard and Walter Swap's article "Deep Smarts," HBR September 2004.)

The second cause of operational risk is a company's use of metrics to measure the quality of processes. Many businesses, we find, haven't developed effective metrics, or they formulate metrics for the first time when they outsource processes. Both increase operational risk because, when such companies offshore or outsource processes, they have no way of knowing if providers have executed those processes better or worse than their employees did. Businesses would do better to create metrics, measure the quality of processes for a while, and improve their quality in-house before deciding to offshore or outsource them.

We cannot stress enough the importance of drawing up metrics; what a firm doesn't measure, it can't offshore well. According to our research, companies that define metrics subjectively usually end up with costly errors and long gestation periods before their providers execute processes effectively. Only firms that set tolerance limits for errors, draw up completion times and productivity norms, and continuously measure employees' performance are able to move processes offshore. In 2002, when Lehman Brothers decided to offshore the development of some information technology–related processes, it identified lower costs, higher quality, and faster deployment of new systems as its goals. The investment bank drew up several metrics that allowed it to measure its service providers' performance along each of those dimensions. Lehman Brothers measured vendors' performance every month and, after a year, found that its providers had exceeded the cost-savings targets while delivering the same quality of execution as the bank's in-house operations. However, the time the vendors took to develop new systems was below expectations. Not only was Lehman Brothers able to take corrective action, but its focus on continuous measurement also allowed it to quickly ramp up its offshore operations, both in terms of volume and complexity.

Interestingly, the belief that offshoring linear processes – where one person hands off work to another person – poses less operational risk than offshoring processes where work flows back and forth between people is dead wrong. Just because a process is linear doesn't mean that it's easy to outsource. We've seen several linear processes, such as inventory control in consumer goods industries and wealth management–related processes in financial services, that businesses couldn't offshore because they didn't have good metrics to measure process quality. Moreover, our studies show that the nature of information flows doesn't affect the quality of execution. If companies codify work and develop metrics to evaluate quality, they can contain operational risk even if work constantly moves between companies' employees and vendors' agents.

When companies look at the extent to which they codify work and use metrics to measure process quality, they'll see that their processes fall into four distinct categories (see the exhibit "Evaluating Operational Risk").

Transparent Processes. Companies have metrics to measure the quality of processes, and they can codify the work. The operational risk of offshoring and outsourcing these processes is very low.

Codifiable Processes. Companies have some ability to measure the quality of execution and can codify most of the work. Still, only people who have formally mastered a body of knowledge, such as accountants and lawyers, can execute these tasks. It's also inherently difficult to manage the quality of the work in real time. If firms can measure the quality of the end result, the risk of offshoring or outsourcing the processes becomes manageable. However, if measuring the results is difficult, the risk of offshoring becomes very high.

Opaque Processes. Companies can codify the work, but they cannot measure the quality of process outputs. When firms underwrite insurance policies, for instance, it's difficult for them to measure how well their employees have executed the task since the events that

policy buyers are protecting themselves from may never occur. Although the risks of offshoring these processes are moderate, companies have to inspect samples to ensure that the output meets their quality standards. That's often cumbersome and expensive. If companies specify how the outsourcer's agents should do their work and offer them performance-based rewards and penalties, they can lower the risk of offshoring these processes.

Noncodifiable Processes. Companies cannot easily codify the work because the variation in business events and employees' responses are too great to permit standard responses. Although it's often tough, companies may be able to evaluate the quality of execution. For instance, if employees don't fulfill orders correctly, customers will cancel those orders or return products. These processes are prone to a high degree of operational risk. If organizations do outsource them, they should closely supervise the service provider's agents.

For example, in 2003, Ford Motor Company outsourced the task of handling supplier inquiries to India-based Allsec Technologies. Ford insisted that the Indian employees who handle those calls work under the supervision of Ford managers on the company's premises in Chennai. That allows the American giant to monitor the agents' work closely and to provide decision-making input in real time. Ford has compensated for the difficulty in codifying work by getting its managers to help the vendor's agents do that work.

Structural Risk. Most companies don't worry about the behavior of service providers when they enter into contracts with them. They assume vendors will always act in ways that maximize both groups' interests. That isn't a wise assumption to make, even when

had reduced their own capabilities to a bare minimum. They had no choice but to bear the costs of training and upgrading the provider's agents until they came up to speed. Another problem is that service providers sometimes put in less effort than they initially agreed to. For instance, an offshore transactions processor hired by a large American bank agreed to check at random 12% of all the transactions it would process. The bank later found that, once its representatives stopped monitoring the provider, the provider checked only 5% of transactions. That reduced the provider's costs, but the bank had to absorb larger costs because of a rise in the number of undetected errors.

When companies supervise providers' work, structural risk falls. Thanks to advances in information technology,

eliminated its processing capacity. It reluctantly paid the vendor the new price for a year and later shifted all its business to another provider.

Two factors amplify these latent risks. First, when firms outsource processes that require the transfer of a large amount of tacit knowledge, they have to invest time and effort in training providers' employees. Second, some processes take a long time to stabilize when companies offshore them. In both cases, the cost of switching from existing providers is very high. That accentuates the risk that over time, vendors will dictate terms to buyers.

Buyers are never powerless, and they can hedge structural risks in several ways. When a firm negotiates a contract with a provider, it should specify a period after the contract's expiry during which the provider must continue to offer the service at a certain price. As a rule of thumb, the buffer should specify 150% of the time that it took the provider to deliver output that matched the company's quality standards. If it took 12 months for the vendor to come up to speed, the vendor must continue to provide the service for 18 months after the contract has expired. Lehman Brothers, for instance, has insisted on adding this clause to all its contracts with providers.

Although it may be difficult, companies should also split business between two providers. In the event a company wants to discontinue doing business with one of them, it can then transfer a process to the other vendor that is already executing the same process, however small the volumes may be. It will take the company less time to do that than to train a new provider from scratch. Having a second provider may also lower costs since the junior provider will bid low for contracts in exchange for greater volumes. That will put pressure on the senior provider. For example, Bank of America has developed relationships with two offshore providers of IT services. The vendors are comparable in many ways, and both realize that the bank can transfer work from one to the other if it wants to. When companies transfer complex

What a firm doesn't measure, it can't offshore well.

companies are buying services from captive centers that they have set up. Like all supply chain partners, service providers can, and do, have incentives to behave in ways that reduce buyers' financial benefits from outsourcing. (For more on the role of incentives in supply chains, see V.G. Narayanan and Ananth Raman's article "Aligning Incentives in Supply Chains," HBR November 2004.)

Some structural risk arises because vendors can stop investing in training or employ people who aren't as qualified as the agents they presented during negotiations. Take the case of one Asian vendor that designs surveys, analyzes data, and develops customer profiles to help clients segment their markets better. When it signed contracts, the firm said that it would hire people only with postgraduate degrees in statistics or marketing and with four to six years of experience. However, as the firm's business grew, it began staffing projects with managers who had master's degrees, but not necessarily in statistics or marketing, and with less than two years of relevant experience. The quality of its services fell, but clients couldn't stop using the provider because they

businesses can track providers' efforts in real time. In fact, most successful outsourcers monitor their agents as they're working, and the best service providers encourage this practice. Structural risk also falls when companies have metrics to gauge the quality of providers' work (see the exhibit "Evaluating Structural Risk").

Companies face another kind of structural risk when service providers alter the terms of contracts after clients have turned over processes to them. That happens because, as outsourcing contracts mature, the power in relationships shifts from the buyers to the sellers. Once companies have transferred processes to providers and terminated the services of employees who performed the tasks, they cannot bring those processes back into the organization on short notice. Knowing that, providers can demand exorbitant price increases when contracts come up for renewal. For instance, one vendor that archives, documents, and analyzes insurance claims raised its price by 65% when a contract came up for renewal. The client couldn't cancel the contract with the vendor because it had virtually processes, like equity research, cash-flow management, and forecasting, they should also retain some residual capacity so that they can bring processes back into the company if they have to. In the case of relatively vital processes, firms must retain enough in-house expertise to train new providers. Otherwise, businesses will have to ask incumbent providers to train potential rivals, which, in our experience, never works well.

Finally, companies face the risk that rivals may steal their intellectual property and proprietary processes if they transfer processes offshore, especially to emerging markets. There's no sure-fire way organizations can protect themselves against this risk unless they set up dedicated facilities offshore. Companies should decide they want to do that only after evaluating all their organizational options, and in the next section of this article, we will explore that process of evaluation.

Choose the Right Organizational Form

Most companies believe that they must either perform processes in-house or outsource them. That was true in the 1990s; today, however, companies can enter into joint ventures with other companies in the same industry or in other industries to generate services or, like GE, use the build-operate-transfer mechanism to create ventures that evolve from being part of the company into independent service providers.

Companies should match organizational structures to needs by considering both the structural and operational risks of offshoring processes. In general, they can use location – onshore, nearshore, or offshore – to combat operational risk, and organizational structures – such as captive centers and joint ventures – to respond to structural risk (see the exhibit "Choosing the Right Location and Organizational Form"). When both the operational and structural risks of offshoring processes are low, companies can outsource them to overseas service providers. As the operational risk of offshoring processes rises, locating them offshore becomes more dangerous. Companies should transfer processes that possess high levels of operational risk to nearby countries rather than to distant overseas locations. When the operational risk is very high, setting up captive centers locally is often the best solution. Outsourcing is less attractive in the case of processes with moderate or high structural risk; here, other forms of governance, such as joint ventures and captive centers, become better options. In the case of processes that have very high levels of structural risk, outsourcing isn't feasible. Companies must set up captive centers to execute those processes. Finally, when both operational and structural risks are very high,

Choosing the Right Location and Organizational Form

Once a company has determined the operational and structural risks of outsourcing its processes, it can use this grid to choose the best locations and organizational forms for those tasks. The nine cells in this table show the optimal offshoring responses to different levels of risk.

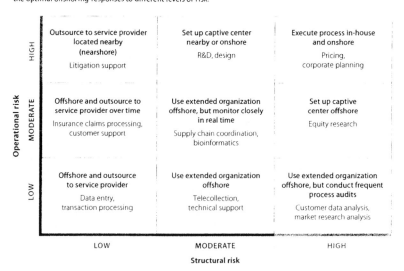

		LOW	MODERATE	HIGH
Operational risk	HIGH	Outsource to service provider located nearby (nearshore) — Litigation support	Set up captive center nearby or onshore — R&D, design	Execute process in-house and onshore — Pricing, corporate planning
	MODERATE	Offshore and outsource to service provider over time — Insurance claims processing, customer support	Use extended organization offshore, but monitor closely in real time — Supply chain coordination, bioinformatics	Set up captive center offshore — Equity research
	LOW	Offshore and outsource to service provider — Data entry, transaction processing	Use extended organization offshore — Telecollection, technical support	Use extended organization offshore, but conduct frequent process audits — Customer data analysis, market research analysis

Structural risk

offshoring and outsourcing are out of the question. Companies must execute those processes onshore and in-house.

When choosing organizational forms, companies have to trade off the control and quality they bring to the table with the scale economies and gains from the specialization that providers offer. Interestingly, offshoring has led to a hybrid form of organization that allows companies to, in a sense, have their cake and eat it, too. We call this structure the *extended organization*. In this hybrid organizational form, companies specify the quality of services they want and work closely alongside providers to get that quality. They manage providers carefully and monitor the agents' work to ensure that things are done properly. Technology enables buyers and sellers of services to exchange information in real time and to embed themselves deeply in each other's companies. Firms can thus move away from command-and-control structures to sense-and-respond forms of collaboration.

Consider, by way of illustration, Chennai-based Office Tiger, which offers research support and real-time scenario analysis, and builds investment

and to alter project priorities. Crucially, Office Tiger's agents and the investment bankers they support work in tandem. Both can see, in real time, the models and scenarios their counterparts are creating. They work off the same files, the same spreadsheets and data feeds, and, when necessary, they work iteratively. Buyer and seller are separated by boundaries that are porous and constantly shifting; it's impossible to tell where one boundary ends and the other begins. Walk through Office Tiger's offices, and you will see how closely its agents work with clients. The provider has created different premises for each client, and agents working for one investment bank cannot enter the offices of agents working for another bank.

Similarly, Gecis – GE's erstwhile captive center and, in 2004, an independent $426 million service provider based in India – has created a version of the extended organization. Gecis (recently renamed Genpact) always configures project teams with two leaders, one of whom is an employee of the buyer's company. He or she, along with a Gecis manager, sets priorities, tracks progress, helps define quality standards, and mon-

Service providers can, and do, have incentives to behave in ways that reduce companies' financial benefits from outsourcing.

models for some leading investment banks in the United States and UK. The banks tolerate very few mistakes, so Office Tiger's employees can't learn through trial and error. Moreover, nearly a third of the company's deadlines must be met within an hour. To make the tie-ups work, the investment banks' managers and Office Tiger's executives jointly manage both long-term goals and day-to-day operations. Office Tiger has developed an information system, T-Track, to monitor the productivity and quality of groups of employees and, if required, the performance of each agent. Its clients use the system to ask for changes in agent assignments, to modify quality control mechanisms,

itors the team. Every year, the two leaders jointly decide team members' pay, bonuses, and promotions. Gecis encourages its employees to see themselves as extensions of their clients. In fact, if you visit the floor in the Gecis center that executes several processes for a leading U.S. retail chain, you'll think you're in the retailer's own offices because of the decor and the vision statements on the walls.

Our studies suggest that the extended organization is the most effective way to manage offshoring. In a two-year study, we compared how a captive center, a provider, and an extended organization executed several moderately complex processes in the financial services sector. While the captive center produced the highest quality throughout the period of our study, the extended organization showed the greatest improvement and, over time, produced almost the same quality as the captive center. Moreover, the extended organization delivered that level of quality more cheaply than the captive center did. When we studied processes that were more complex, the same results held: The extended organization started out relatively poorly but, after it reached a stable state, was the most cost-effective way to execute processes. Clearly, offshoring isn't just about companies moving across geographical boundaries; it's also about companies redrawing organizational boundaries to achieve collaborative supply chains of information, expertise, and knowledge.

•••

It may sound like a cliché, but companies must treat offshoring as a strategic imperative if they wish to capture all its benefits. Offshoring initiatives that have cost savings as their raison d'être, our studies show, don't allow companies to capture greater revenues from the market. That's because such companies don't commit themselves to the organizational changes that are necessary for offshoring to help them, say, customize products or services, lock in buyers, compress new product-development cycles, or enhance profit margins. Besides, when offshoring is only about cutting costs, businesses are reluctant to outsource complex processes, even though doing so will have a bigger impact on their bottom lines. However, when corporations begin with the desire to create strategic advantage through offshoring, they commit themselves to transferring complex processes relatively early. Companies would do well to remember that the manner in which they start their offshoring initiatives often determines how they will end. ⊟

1. "Alpha Corp." is a pseudonym. For more details on the offshoring problems faced by this company, see Ravi Aron, Eric K. Clemons, and Sashi Reddi, "Just Right Outsourcing: Understanding and Managing Risk," *Journal of Management Information Systems,* Fall 2005.

Reprint R0512J
To order, see page 155.

[15]

Journal of Economic Geography **8** (2008) pp. 699–725
Advance Access Published on 24 July 2008

doi:10.1093/jeg/lbn024

Location, control and innovation in knowledge-intensive industries

*Ram Mudambi**

Abstract

The rising share of intangibles in economies worldwide highlights the crucial role of knowledge-intensive and creative industries in current and future wealth generation. The recognition of this trend has led to intense competition in these industries. At the micro-level, firms from both advanced and emerging economies are globally dispersing their value chains to control costs and leverage capabilities. The geography of innovation is the outcome of a dynamic process whereby firms from emerging economies strive to catch-up with advanced economy competitors, creating strong pressures for continued innovation. However, two distinct strategies can be discerned with regard to the control of the value chain. A vertical integration strategy emphasizes taking advantage of 'linkage economies' whereby controlling multiple value chain activities enhances the efficiency and effectiveness of each one of them. In contrast, a specialization strategy focuses on identifying and controlling the creative heart of the value chain, while outsourcing all other activities. The global mobile handset industry is used as the template to illustrate the theory.

Keywords: innovation, value chains, intangibles, vertical integration, specialization, knowledge-intensive industries
JEL classifications: F23, O33, O32, F02
Date submitted: 15 September 2007   **Date accepted:** 28 May 2008

1. Introduction

The first industrial revolution of the 18th and 19th century moved value creation from the direct application of human labor to tangible assets like industrial plants and machinery. Countries that grew wealthy in this revolution transferred their productive resources out of agriculture and craft manufacture into large-scale manufacturing industry. Over the last several decades, the world economy has been witnessing what can only be described as another revolution in terms of the nature of value creation. The source of value has been shifting from tangible assets to intangible assets at an accelerating pace. For all the G-7 economies put together, intangible assets have been estimated to constitute about 30% of the stock of all long-term assets (IMF, 2006).[1] Intangible assets are the lifeblood

---

*Department of Strategic Management, Fox School of Business, Speakman Hall, Temple University, Philadelphia PA 19122, USA.
email <ram.mudambi@temple.edu>

1   The percentage of market valuation of the S&P 500 US firms related to intangible assets increased from 38% in 1982 to 62% in 1991 (Blair and Wallman, 2001) and to about 85% by 2001 (Nakamura, 2003). By 2004, annual investment in intangibles in the US economy was conservatively estimated at over 8% of GDP or about $1 trillion [Hofmann (2005), citing unpublished data from Nakamura]. In these estimates, about a third of the $1 trillion in intangibles is software; one-third is intellectual property, such as patents and copyrights and one-third is advertising and marketing.

of creative and knowledge-intensive industries, which may be defined as those where value creation is disproportionately based on specialized, nonrepetitious activities (Malecki, 1984). These data indicate that such industries will be fundamental to the creation of wealth in the future.

The returns to intangible assets can appear in the form of legally defensible rents as in the case of patents, copyrights and brands (Lev, 2001).[2] However, they can also appear in the form of superior returns generated by inimitable organizational structures and inter-organizational relationships (Kogut and Zander, 1993; Grant, 1996; Augier and Teece, 2006). A key aspect of intangible assets is the overwhelming importance of human creativity (Florida, 2002; Howkins, 2001). In all cases, the firm controlling an intangible asset is able to generate higher returns, *ceteris paribus*, than a competing firm that does not control the asset.

Intangible assets have also been called 'intellectual assets' (Lev, 2001), a terminology that is more helpful since it makes clear that all these assets are based on various forms of commercial knowledge. The role of commercial knowledge in value generation has long been recognized (Hayek, 1945), especially in creative industries. Value creation in these industries is almost entirely based on intellectual content in the form of texts, music, media, etc. (Caves, 2000; Scott, 2000). Traditionally, creative industries have also been characterized by very strong cluster effects (Florida, 2002; Maskell and Lorenzen, 2004). 'Creative centers' like Hollywood, Hong Kong and Mumbai (movies), Nashville (country music), New York and London (media) have occupied dominant global positions (Malone, 1993; Martin and Sunley, 2003; Scott, 2004, 2005). The economic geography literature has developed fine-grained analyses of location, regional specialization and clustering in knowledge-intensive industries, focusing especially on urbanization, the power of cities and the consequent rise of regional disparities (Scott and Storper, 2003; Lorenzen, 2004; Amin and Thrift, 2005).

However, the geographical dispersion of value creation has recently begun to play an increasingly important role in the analysis of creative industries (Cantwell and Santangelo, 1999; Iammarino and McCann, 2008). National systems of innovation (NSIs) provide 'the location-specific supply base of technological and knowledge externalities that firms draw upon for their competitiveness' (Amin and Cohendet, 2004) and NSIs vary dramatically in terms of their comparative strengths and weaknesses (Lundvall, 2007). Thus, firms can enhance their competitive advantage by dispersing their creative endeavors, tapping into multiple centers of excellence and coordinating knowledge across geographic space (Lorenzen, 2004). For example, Canon U.S. Life Sciences Inc. is networked into the U.S. NSI, specifically into the life sciences cluster along the eastern seaboard, thousands of miles away from its home-based R&D headquarters in Japan (Uchida, 2008).

This example illustrates that understanding the effects of this dispersion on the creation and use of intellectual assets requires relating them to the optimizing decisions made by the individual business firm. The relevant decisions focus on the firm's value chain that is composed of the 'technologically and economically distinct activities that it

---

2   Intangible assets are intangible in the sense that they cannot be valued with certainty or precision. However, they are assets in that they generate a stream of future returns. Lev (2001) defines an intangible asset as 'a claim to future benefits that does not have a physical or financial (a stock or a bond) embodiment'.

Table 1. Strategic choice: location and control

		Geographical location strategy	
		Concentrated	Dispersed
Control strategy	Vertical integration	1. Onshore in-house	3. Captive Offshore
	Specialization	2. Onshore outsourced	4. Offshore outsource

performs to do business' (Porter and Millar, 1985). Addressing these questions requires analyzing the value chain along two dimensions: control and location.

Activities within the firm's value chain can be broadly grouped into three categories: the upstream (input) end, the downstream (output or market) end and the middle. Activities at the upstream end generally comprise design, basic and applied research and the commercialization of creative endeavors. Activities at the downstream end typically comprise marketing, advertising and brand management and after-sales services. Activities in the middle comprise manufacturing, standardized service delivery and other repetitious processes in which commercialized prototypes are implemented on a mass scale.

How should the firm control the various parts of the value chain and where should it locate them? More specifically, the research questions addressed in this article are: to what extent should the firm implement vertical integration and geographical dispersion with respect to its value chain activities? These location and control choices are presented in a simplified manner in Table 1. The answers to these fundamental questions with regard to firm organization and activity location are crucial: they will determine the global geography of economic activity in general and creative activity in particular during the coming decades.

There is a voluminous literature in international business examining the organization of the firm across national borders (Buckley and Casson, 1976; Dunning, 1993). The economic geography literature has dealt exhaustively with questions regarding the location of economic activity, both in the regional and international context (Fujita et al., 1999; Dicken, 2003). However, the interface between these two literatures is surprisingly thin (McCann and Mudambi, 2005). This article draws on both literatures in an attempt to incorporate both the firm and the location perspectives on value creation in creative industries. This analysis enables us to highlight both macro (country level) and micro (firm level) implications for creative industries of the ongoing process of globalization.[3]

At the macro-level, the value chains of individual firms inter-weave through complex relationships and complementarities to form the 'value constellations' of creative industries (Normann and Ramirez, 1993). These are becoming locationally

---

3 For the purposes of this article, we adopt the relatively narrow definition of globalization as 'the shift towards a more integrated and interdependent world economy ... including the globalization of markets and the globalization of production' (Hill, 2008). This is in contrast to those who define globalization as a broader phenomenon that transcends economic development and includes political, technological and cultural dimensions, owing in large part to the rise of 'instantaneous electronic communication' (Giddens, 2003).

disaggregated as discrete parts of firm value chains are coalescing in different country locations. Under the current location pattern, high value-added activities are largely performed in advanced market economies, with low value-added activities performed in emerging market economies.[4] However, this pattern is under pressure from three separate processes. Firms from emerging market economies are striving to develop competencies in high value-added activities ('catch-up'). Firms from advanced market economies are stripping out standardized parts of their high value-added activities and cutting costs by relocating these in emerging market economies ('spillover'). This spillover process is reinforced by obsolescence that is creating pressures for the relocation of 'sunset' industries to emerging market economies. Rapid innovation, so far largely in advanced market economies, is spawning entirely new value constellations ('industry creation').

Examining global creative industries at the firm level, distinct trends are emerging. Two divergent strategies can be discerned with regard to the control of the value chain. A vertical integration strategy emphasizes taking advantage of 'linkage economies' whereby controlling multiple value chain activities enhances the efficiency and effectiveness of each one of them. In contrast, a specialization strategy focuses on identifying and controlling the creative heart of the value chain, while outsourcing all other activities. However, along the location dimension, a common pattern of geographical dispersion appears to be developing. Firms are increasingly implementing strategies to take advantage of the comparative advantages of locations. This results in a wider geographic dispersion of firms' activities, with direct implications for the future of creative industries' global value constellations.

The article is organized as follows. A theoretical framework for the analysis of the economic organization of creative and knowledge-intensive industries is developed in Section 2. The theory is illustrated within the context of a case study of the global mobile handset industry in Section 3. Implications of the theory and research propositions are presented in Section 4.

2. Control, location and economic organization in creative industries

In his seminal work, Caves (2000) indicated that 'arts and entertainment' are exemplars of creative industries. Several attempts have been made at more specific definitions. For example, in 2001 the UK government specified the creative industries sector to include advertising, architecture, arts and antique markets, crafts, design, designer fashion, film, interactive leisure software, music, television and radio, performing arts, publishing and software (Creative Industries Task Force, 2001; quoted in Cunningham, 2002). This specification includes an eclectic mix of commercial and noncommercial activities. A broader definition is provided by Howkins (2001), who includes all sectors covered with significant copyright, patent, trademark and design activity. This is a

---

4   For the purposes of this article, the advanced market economies may be taken to be the Triad economies of North America, Western Europe and Japan, also including Oceania. Emerging market economies range from the large BRIC economies (Brazil, Russia, India and China) to many smaller economies in Asia, transition economies of Central and Eastern Europe and some economies in South America (BIS, 2007).

dramatic expansion of the UK government definition since it includes all patent-based R&D in all science-engineering-technology sectors. It is not the purpose of this article to offer a resolution of this debate. Rather, the article draws from this discussion the core idea that creative industries are those where the production and control of knowledge-based assets have crucial roles in value creation and appropriation (Kogut and Zander, 1993; Grant, 1996; Augier and Teece, 2006).

Further, there is no well accepted definition of knowledge-intensive industries (Malecki, 1984). The OECD definition of 'high technology' industries is limited to manufacturing (OECD, 1996). More importantly, for the purposes of the article, we are interested in knowledge-intensive activities, not knowledge intensive firms. We specify that high knowledge activities are creative and specialized, whereas low knowledge activities are repetitious and standardized (Nelson and Winter, 1982). In other words, the difference between high knowledge and low knowledge activities is based on a 'fundamental difference between a focus on new products and a primary concern with low-cost, standardized production' (Malecki, 1984). This definition underpins the conceptualization of knowledge used in the article as related to 'new concept development' and 'marketing': the two ends of the firm's value chain. Thus, the R&D activities of a textile manufacturer are included, while the repetitious printing and binding activities of a book publisher are not.

The macro data indicating the rapidly rising share of intangible assets in major economies implies that creative and knowledge-intensive industries account for an increasing share of value created. Creating and capturing value from knowledge assets is becoming a cornerstone of firm strategy (Teece, 1998). We argue that our understanding of the strategic aspects of creating and capturing value from knowledge can be enhanced by placing them within the context of the firm's value chain (Porter and Millar, 1985, p. 150), i.e. a conceptualization of value creation, identifying the value-added by each activity. The value chain should *not* be read as an intertemporal sequence going from inputs to outputs. It is quite possible that sources of value at the 'market' or right end may be created before sources of value at the 'input' or left end. For instance, market research efforts may occur first or jointly with product or service design, with prototyping and production occurring later.

Successfully extracting and capturing value in creative industries depends on two crucial strategic nexuses: the control and location of value chain activities. In other words, for a firm to be successful in creating and capturing value from knowledge it is essential that it makes optimal decisions within these two domains.

2.1. Organization and control: Coasian approaches to the firm

Optimal decisions regarding the governance of the firm's value chain emerge from the application of transaction cost analysis. Traditionally, transaction costs have been defined as the costs of using the market mechanism (Coase, 1937; Williamson, 1975). Since this definition means that almost anything can be explained as a suitably defined transaction cost (Williamson, 1979), subsequent literature has specified transaction costs to be those associated with coordinating and policing market transactions (Ricketts, 2002). It readily follows that whenever firms obtain significant benefits from vertical integration, the costs of using market transactions to perform these activities is relatively high and outsourcing is unattractive.

The firm simultaneously disaggregates the value chain and selects the activities over which to maintain control. Coasian analysis implies that the firm should retain control over the activities or operations where it can create and appropriate the most value. Conversely, operations where it can create and appropriate less value should be implemented through market transactions. In their seminal work, Buckley and Casson (1976) applied this reasoning to the geographical context, providing a theoretical rationale for the existence and organization of multinational enterprises (MNEs).

Technological advances, especially in the areas of information and communication have made it possible to disaggregate the firm's business processes into progressively finer slices. Firms are able to specialize in increasingly narrow niches, which need not even be contiguous in the value chain. This makes it crucial for the firm to identify the process activities over which it has competitive advantage, since these are the basis of the firm's core competencies (Hamel and Prahalad, 1990) and enable it to generate rents.

For example, the US motion picture industry has moved from the vertically integrated studio system to what has been called 'flexible specialization', where much of the actual production work is carried out by crews that are employed on a film by film basis (Christopherson and Storper, 1989). Flexible specialization increases the importance of external linkages (Storper, 1997), since film companies undertake market transactions with producers who assemble appropriate crews for each film project. The firms retain tight internal control only of global distribution and marketing—the downstream end of the value chain (Scott, 2005).

For some firms, the logic of transaction cost analysis pushes them towards exercising high control over and concentrating resources on specific activities while having a strong tendency to outsource others (Calantone and Stanko, 2007). Other firms tend to exercise greater control over the entire value chain, with much less outsourcing, though bounded rationality arguments—decreasing returns to management in the words of Coase (1937)—imply that such control cannot be extended indefinitely. In the terminology of industrial organization, these strategies correspond to greater and lesser degrees of vertical integration and focus on the strategic choice between cells 1 and 2 in Table 1.[5]

A critical research question that arises in this context pertains to the observation that competing firms within the same industry often implement widely differing levels of vertical integration. For example, in the US auto industry GM typically implemented the highest degree of vertical integration followed by Ford and Chrysler (including its successor, DaimlerChrysler).[6] Through its ownership of Denso, Toyota has maintained an even higher level of vertical integration than GM (Conybeare, 2003). These differences have been observed over long periods of time and have not historically been related to differences in firm performance (Mudambi and Helper, 1998; Rubenstein, 2001). The persistence of these differences along with the lack of a systematic link to firm performance suggests that they are not disequilibrium phenomena.

---

5   Attempts at developing internal hybrids by introducing market forces within the firm have been dogged by severe problems. It is very difficult for managers to make credible commitments to workers that they will consistently allow internal market forces to work. Hence the motivational benefits of internal markets are seldom realized and almost never sustained. See for example, Foss (2003).

6   In the 1990s, GM controlled the production of about two-thirds of the parts that went into its cars, while Ford controlled about half and Chrysler a third (Rubenstein, 2001).

A direct implication of these observations is that transaction costs have significant firm-level components in addition to industry-level components. The study of technology in neoclassical economics has tended to focus on the industry level of analysis. The industrial organization literature has developed sophisticated analyses explaining why and how industries to differ from each other in terms of the extent of vertical integration. However, it is the firm-level components cause firms within a single industry to differ from each other in terms of the control of their value chain activities. We argue that these firm-level transaction costs are not easily captured using standard tools of neoclassical economics.

Technologies largely determine economies of scale, scope and experience and these are generally common across leading edge firms in most industries (Mansfield 1985; Pavitt 1998). This implies that these economies cannot be the source of firm-level transaction costs; they cannot be used to explain systematic and persistent differences in the extent of vertical integration amongst these leading firms (Appendix A).

A particularly important aspect of value chain organization concerns not its constituent activities *per se*, but the linkage between them. Economies of scale, scope and experience relate to the technologies associated with individual activities, i.e. they are properties of individual production functions and are directly determined by technology. However, firms may also realize economies simply because they control multiple activities in the value chain. Design activities may become more efficient due to control of manufacturing, since information may flow more readily between units within a single firm. These economies may be defined as linkage economies. Linkage economies arise from linkages between the production functions associated with *different* activities. An illustrative theoretical model demonstrating the nature of linkage economies and distinguishing them from economies of scale, scope and experience is presented in Appendix A.

Hirschman (1968, 1977) was one of the first to note that linkages in the value chain of inputs and outputs create benefits beyond the direct gains from trade. Within his generalized analysis of linkages, his conceptualization of 'technological linkages' is the most relevant for purposes of this article. Technological 'linkages can be expected to be rather weak if the required input comes from an industry whose process and technique is totally unfamiliar ... The linkage dynamic may thus be held back by the difficulties of making a technological leap' (Hirschman, 1977, p. 77). This idea translates quite readily to an input–output interface at the level of the individual firm. Some firms will have the competencies to devise better routines to stimulate cross-activity coordination, learning and innovation. Such firms enjoy high levels of linkage economies. Vertical integration is attractive for such firms since it results in falling costs and improved quality for both inputs and outputs. Other firms will find that controlling a wide range of activities detracts from their focus on each one. Such firms have low linkage economies or may even suffer from linkage diseconomies. Specialization is attractive for such firms and they have lower costs and superior quality by focusing on a narrow spectrum of activities while buying inputs from market.

High linkage economies mean that controlling multiple activities in the value chain improves the efficiency and effectiveness of each one of them. Linkage economies are likely to be based on firm-specific routines and procedures (Zollo and Winter, 2002). These routines often vary across firms even when the underlying technologies being implemented are common (Rosenberg, 1982, p. 257). Linkage economies are likely to arise from the transfer of knowledge from one activity to another within the firm; the intra-firm context is expected to be particularly efficient when transfers involve highly tacit knowledge and skills (Nelson and Winter, 1982; Cantwell and Santangelo, 1999; Maskell and Malmberg, 1999). Further, different firms within the same industry have been shown to implement different knowledge management strategies (McMillan et al., 2000). Thus, linkage economies are an important knowledge-based means of explaining different levels of vertical integration within an industry.[7]

It is beyond the scope of the present article to explore the sources of linkage economies in detail. However, a few conjectures may be offered. A firm that is able to minimize knowledge 'stickiness' (Szulanski, 1996) may enjoy high levels of linkage economies, since it is able to stimulate intra-firm knowledge transfer. Such transfers are likely to occur over activity boundaries, e.g. between production engineering and marketing, suggesting that an effective boundary spanning function may be a key resource in this context (Marrone et al., 2007).

2.2. Location: value-added and the value chain

Mechanization and standardization have reduced the costs of manufacturing and logistics processes. Processes supporting mass customization (Kotha, 1995) have become widely available and subject to rapid imitation. This in turn has reduced the scope for the use of such processes to generate the differentiation required to support value creation. It is difficult for firms to extract high value-added from either tangible products or standardized services (Maskell and Malmberg, 1999). Firms are finding that value-added is becoming increasingly concentrated at the upstream and downstream ends of the value chain (Mudambi, 2007). Activities at both ends of the value chain are intensive in their application of knowledge and creativity.

Activities at the left or 'input' end are supported by R&D knowledge (basic and applied research and design), while activities at the right or 'output' end are supported by marketing knowledge (marketing, advertising and brand management, sales and after-sales service). The pattern of value-added along the value chain may, therefore, be represented by the 'smiling curve' (Everatt et al., 1999) or the 'smile of value creation' as depicted in Figure 1 (Mudambi, 2007). Firms combine the comparative advantages of geographic locations with their own resources and competencies to maximize their competitive advantage (McCann and Mudambi, 2005). The classic international diversification question focuses on evaluating the comparative advantage of different geographic locations against the costs of geographically dispersed operations, i.e. the strategic choices between cells 1 and 3 or between cells 2 and 4 in Table 1.

The geographic realities associated with the smile of value creation are that the activities at the ends of the overall value constellation are largely located in advanced market economies, while those in the middle of the value chain are moving (or have moved) to emerging market economies (Gereffi, 1999; Smakman, 2003; Pyndt and

---

7   Spulber (1989) defines economies of sequence, a concept that is related to linkage economies. Economies of sequence arise when 'cost gains (are) achieved by combining a sequence of production stages.' (Spulber, 1989, p. 113). These economies arise from the firm's technology, as defined within the neoclassical paradigm; a logical implication is that if two firms have access to the same technology, they are able to enjoy the same economies of sequence. In other words, they are not meant to explain firm-level differences.

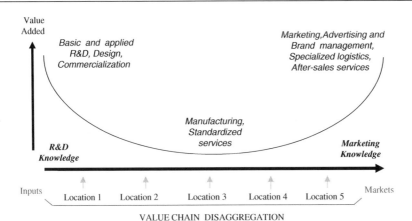

Figure 1. The smile of value creation (Mudambi, 2007).

Pedersen, 2006).[8] Trade across national borders is increasingly in terms of value chain activities (so-called 'tasks') rather than complete goods or services (see for example, Pyndt and Pedersen, 2006, p. 14; Smakman, 2003, p. 17). These realities emerge naturally from the application of the classic product cycle model (Vernon, 1966), at a point in time, to industry value constellations.

Examples of the 'smile of value creation' are ubiquitous. In the athletic shoe industry, the locational disaggregation of Nike's value chain has been in place for decades. Research, design and marketing are located in advanced market economies, intermediate manufacture and assembly in emerging market economies and basic component manufacture in low cost locations (Yoffie, 1991). Nike concentrates on design and marketing, while outsourcing and closely coordinating production through a hierarchical offshore network of low cost suppliers. Nike controls and owns the core intangible asset, the brand. The value of this intangible asset is crucially dependent on the highly creative design and marketing activities that Nike controls at the two ends of the value chain. Nike has been particularly successful at decoupling the tangible from the intangible aspects of its business, both in space and in time. However, a similar pattern of locational disaggregation may be seen in the operations of firms in many other industries. In the auto industry, the value chains underlying GM's Pontiac Le Mans and Ford's Fiesta incorporate design and marketing in advanced market economies and assembly in emerging market economies (Cao, 2002). In the pop music industry, 'artistic' and 'humdrum' activities are often locationally disaggregated with the former driven by creativity and the latter by cost (Maskell and Lorenzen, 2004). In the film industry, Vang and Chaminade (2007) report that the Toronto cluster services the creative center in Hollywood by specializing in 'humdrum' activities.

---

8   Pyndt and Pedersen (2006) present compelling and in-depth evidence of this trend for Denmark at both the firm and industry levels. Smakman (2003) presents consistent evidence for the Singapore garment industry.

This analysis provides the rationale for the enormous efforts by some technologically leading firms to break their final products or services into separable self-contained elements or modules (Kotabe et al., 2007). Increasing modularization allows the firm to amplify its focus on narrower activities within the value chain associated with the highest value-added, an approach which may be called 'fine slicing'. In tandem, it allows the firm to outsource other activities (associated with lower value-added) more cheaply and efficiently (Ernst and Lim, 2002).

The firms to which these lower value-added activities are outsourced view them as stepping stones in the course of moving into higher value-added activities. This is what underlies the enormous efforts of firms from emerging markets to develop R&D and marketing capabilities (Everatt et al., 1999; Smakman, 2003). These efforts often generate negative cashflow in the short run as resources are withdrawn from low margin contract manufacturing and assembly or standardized service delivery and transferred to R&D and marketing where the firm has little experience. However, many emerging market firms view these short run losses as investments in developing crucial competencies.

2.3. Location: dynamic analysis of the value constellation

2.3.1. Firm strategy

Over time, a firm's dynamic competencies are based on linking the two ends of the 'smile' so that marketing knowledge is used to calibrate and focus R&D-based knowledge creation (Leenders and Wierenga, 2002; Winter, 2003). At the firm level, such an integration of marketing with design and R&D underpins the ability to sustain competitive advantage by a constant process of market led innovation.

Improving process technology depresses the middle of the smile and pulls up the ends, making the smile more intense. The middle of the smile is driven down by increased efficiency in the operation of standardized processes that are not however, rare, inimitable or organizationally embedded (Maskell and Malmberg, 1999). The ends of the smile are pulled upwards by increased personalization and customization in design and delivery. These competencies are based on R&D and market knowledge and skills that are rare, highly tacit, inimitable and unique to each organization (Wernerfelt, 1984). Such resources often reside within the firm's human capital that then becomes a crucial source of value creation (Amit and Schoemaker, 1993).

2.3.2. Economy-wide processes

As noted above, firms controlling various activities within the value chain have differing incentives. Their responses to these incentives generate processes that change economy-wide patterns of economic activity. These processes can be broadly grouped into three categories that may be labeled 'catch-up', 'spillover' and 'industry creation' (Figure 2).

Firms controlling activities in the middle of the value chain have strong incentives to acquire the resources and competencies that will enable them to control higher value-added activities. Thus, firms from emerging market economies like China, India, Brazil and Mexico are moving to develop their own brands and marketing expertise in advanced economies to increase their control over the downstream end of the value chain. Locating their R&D and marketing operations in advanced market economies also enables them to increase their absorptive capacity (Zahra and George, 2002;

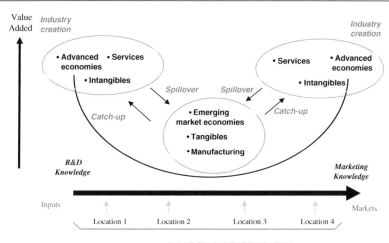

Figure 2. The smile—dynamic analysis.

Phelps, 2008). They are attempting to develop capabilities to 'catch-up' with rivals based in advanced market economies.

Firms that control the ends of the value chain, mostly from advanced market economies, are faced with an increasingly competitive landscape, including aggressive new entrants from emerging market economies intent on catching up. They have strong incentives to increase the efficiency and effectiveness of the high value-added activities that they control. Modularization enables these firms to strip out standardized activities from both the upstream R&D and downstream marketing activities that can then be relocated to emerging market economies. Thus, as firms like Microsoft and IBM locate R&D sites in India they improve the cost efficiency of their overall R&D operations. The high value-added local activities of such MNEs create knowledge 'spillover' into emerging market economies.

The two processes can act in concert when MNE subsidiaries established with the objective of controlling cost through implementing low level tasks, evolve over time to compete for more advanced mandates within the firm. This process of subsidiary evolution is well documented (Cantwell and Mudambi, 2005). Motorola's Singapore subsidiary may be considered a case in point (Natarajan and Tan, 1992).

Finally, the ends of the 'smile' are not static. Innovation at these two ends is the essence of Schumpeterian entrepreneurship (Schumpeter, 1934). New industries emerge from basic and applied R&D at the upstream end (e.g. biotech, nanotech) and through marketing and distribution innovations at the downstream end (e.g. e-tailing, online auctions). At the moment, this process is overwhelmingly concentrated in advanced market economies. The process of 'industry creation' is the manifestation of Schumpeter's gale of creative destruction. It accelerates obsolescence in advanced market economies and pressures some sunset industries to relocate to emerging market economies.

3. An illustration: the mobile handset industry

The mobile handset industry provides a particularly useful setting to illustrate both the micro and macro aspects of the theory developed in this article.[9] Mobile handsets are the product of the successful convergence of technology and design aimed at fitting into cultural and lifestyle niches. They are rapidly morphing from 'technological objects' into key 'social objects'. Firms in the industry strive to provide mobility to a range of desired functionalities, ranging from simple internet access through audio and video entertainment to social networking. As with personal computers, consumers want mobile devices to serve as platforms to run a wide range of work and leisure applications supplied by creative industries. In this role, the mobile handset industry provides the consumer interface that creative industries use to deliver content like text, audio, video and application services.

Perhaps more importantly, mobile devices are argued to be the linchpin of the next technocultural shift, following personal computing in the 1980s and the Internet in the 1990s (Rheingold, 2002). Super efficient mobile communications (cellular phones, personal digital assistants, wireless paging and Internet-access devices) allow people to connect with anyone, anywhere, anytime. Mobile devices make possible the new convergence of pop culture, cutting-edge technology and social activism. The cultural impact of these devices comes not from the technology itself, but from how people adapt to it and ultimately use it to transform themselves, their communities and their institutions.

Examples abound of new social and cultural activities made possible by mobile devices. 'Lovegetty' devices in Japan light up when a person with the right date potential characteristics appears in the vicinity (Iwatani, 1998). Social networking applications allow users to instantly share experiences using voice, data and video (Donath and Boyd, 2004). Video sharing services like YouTube are increasingly dependent on mobile devices for uploads and viewers. Political activists have used mobile devices to galvanize support and organize demonstrations (Pertierra, 2005) while on the dark side, terrorists have used them to coordinate strikes (van Meter, 2002).

The industry has global importance with sales exceeding $100 billion and volume growth of 29% in 2004 (Maheshwari, 2005). However, revenue growth in 2004 was more modest at 18%, reflecting the increasing intensity of competition along the lines discussed above. Markets in emerging economies like India and China are expanding rapidly as the penetration rate of mobile devices rises, while markets in most advanced market economies have matured. In all markets, consumers are becoming more design conscious and resistant to standardized offerings. Over the period 1991–2003, the industry has coalesced around a core set of product features in both voice and data communications, reflecting the emergence a dominant design (Koski and Kretschmer, 2007).

Analyzing the industry's value chain reveals the 'smile of value creation'. As illustrated in Figure 3, high value-added activities appear at the ends of the value chain. Firms from emerging market economies like Huawei of China that began as electronics manufacturing service companies, supplying private label products to firms from advanced market economies, are building marketing competencies to develop and

---

9   This case was developed using secondary sources. Industry studies, consulting reports, company annual reports and web sources were used.

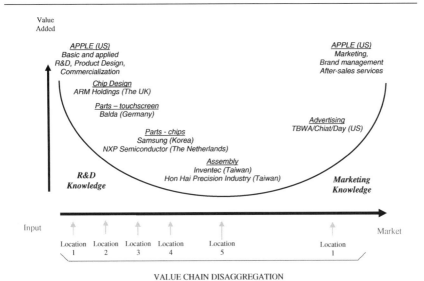

Figure 3. Value creation in the iPhone.

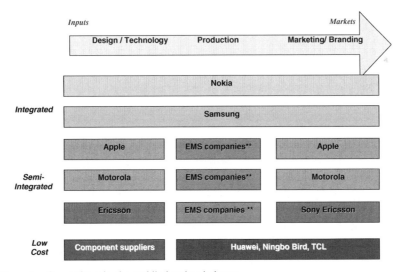

Figure 4. Competitors in the mobile handset industry.
Sources: Gartner Dataquest, HSBC, BCG (**Electronics Manufacturing Service Companies).

support their own brands (Figure 4). At the moment such firms compete on the basis of low cost. However, it is likely that over time their brands will become more valuable. This puts pressure on manufacturers in advanced market economies like Nokia, Motorola, Apple and Ericsson to continually innovate to maintain their high levels of value-added. These established players' innovations are increasingly design driven, recognizing the highly variegated needs of individual markets. All these firms' design strategies are aimed at buttressing and enhancing the value of their brands.

Firms from recently developed countries like Samsung of Korea find themselves pushed to differentiate themselves from their competitors from emerging market economies. This poses a significant challenge since they often remain dependent on suppliers from advanced market economies for their core technologies. For example, in common with Chinese manufacturers, Samsung depends on Qualcomm for its CDMA base-band chips.[10] It has accelerated its R&D efforts to minimize this dependency by attempting to develop its own chipsets. In addition to efforts in manufacturing, it is implementing a design driven strategy with design centers in London and Milan in Europe, Tokyo in Japan and Silicon Valley in the US. However, it faces a creativity challenge, since at the moment it excels 'only in technologies such as … mobile phones for which there are industry standards with clear trajectories' (Chang, 2008, p. 58).

Thus, we observe a convergence in the location strategies of all firms in the industry. Firms from advanced market economies, those from emerging market economies and those from recently developed countries are all conforming to the 'smile of value creation'. In the short run, these strategies increase the concentration of high value-added activities in advanced market economies. However, local demands in emerging market economies are already imposing demands on the design capabilities of firms from advanced market economies. Nokia Design, a unit comprising 250 people worldwide has implemented design projects in locations as diverse as Uganda and India. The unit involves psychologists, industrial designers, materials experts and anthropologists. It leverages human behavioral research to deliver location-focused product design.

3.1. Differences in firm strategy and organization

Along with the convergence in location strategies, we observe a divergence in control strategies. Nokia at the high value end and Samsung at the low cost end of the industry, remain highly vertically integrated, while Apple, Motorola and Ericsson have largely outsourced the middle of the value chain. Both strategies are responses to the same pressures being exerted by mobile service providers like Vodafone and AT&T. As service providers face tougher market competition, they are increasingly using the unique software and features (different menus, features, branding, languages, etc.) built into the devices they offer to generate competitive advantage. They want that software to be installed by manufacturers before the handsets leave the factory. Further, they

---

10 As recently as the end of 2004 no domestic firm in China or Korea had yet grasped the core technology of GSM and CDMA mobile phones. In fact, as of 2004, this was true also for many companies from advanced economies like Japan. The core technologies of chip design were controlled by Texas Instruments, Qualcomm and a few other companies (Ding and Haynes, 2006). This underlines the importance of controlling knowledge assets in this industry.

want the handsets to be capable of supporting an increasingly wide range of application software.

Mobile handset manufacturers have responded and oriented production into two distinct processes. In the first, they build the internal components of the handset, the so-called 'engine'. These are generic devices that can be customized to take on different jobs. In the second process, the raw engines are customized to the requirements of different service providers and markets. Vertically integrated manufacturers retain control over both processes, while so-called 'semi-integrated' players retain design and customization while outsourcing actual manufacture. This organizational divergence may be explored by comparing Nokia on the one hand with Apple on the other.

Nokia is an engineering driven company with a focus on manufacturing excellence. In 2006, it shipped more than 300 million units: twice as many handsets as it did just 4 years earlier. To do so, it handled more than 100 billion parts in its 10 factories scattered around the world.[11] These plants are in located advanced market economies as well as in emerging market economies. The challenges of handling such huge volumes are enormous, but over the past 15 years Nokia has turned high tech manufacturing and logistics into one of its core competencies.

Nokia's control of manufacturing enables it to execute the second process of customization extremely rapidly, transforming raw engines into hundreds of thousands of built-to-order phones in a matter of days. The need to control this complex process with the highest precision and quality is the reason Nokia has never chosen to outsource its manufacturing.[12] Indeed, Nokia sees its manufacturing expertise as a key means of enhancing its design skills. Reciprocally, its huge volume and customization requirements put pressure on its design capabilities. In short, Nokia is a firm with high levels of linkage economies.

Apple, on the other hand is a company that focuses on the intangible aspects of its product offering. From its earliest days, it recognized that style and ease of use are as important as substance in terms of developing a brand. This strategic approach implies that it is crucial to control the fundamental building blocks that support the brand, i.e. design and marketing. On the other hand, manufacturing is less important for such a firm.

In the mobile handset industry, Apple's well-known iPhone provides an apt illustration of the implementation of its strategy (Figure 3). Apple controls R&D intensive activities at the upstream end of the value chain and marketing intensive activities associated with brand management at the downstream end. However, the more manufacturing and applications oriented activities in the middle of the value chain are outsourced. These activities are more strongly connected to the tangible aspects of the iPhone and less linked to the intangible aspects. Like Nike, Apple has decoupled the tangible and intangible aspects of its business.

Reinforcing its strategy to appropriate value from intangibles, Apple runs the iTunes, an online service that delivers audio, video and gaming content. While the iTunes service is only marginally profitable in its own right, it is a powerful complementary asset that supports Apple's iPod and iPhone sales (Carr, 2004). The ability of Apple's

---

11 Source: Nokia annual reports.
12 It does use contractors for a small number of handsets, mainly older models that do not require customization or rapid delivery.

products to run device neutral content like MP3 audio and Mpg video, along with the incompatibility of iTunes with competitors' hardware products establishes a powerful competitive advantage in the crucial link between the device and creative content. Users of Apple's devices face large switching costs since their portfolio of music from iTunes will not work on a rival device.

Apple's focus on the core intangibles within the value proposition has enabled it to take advantage of huge network externalities. It has carved out its own iPod- and iPhone-related community, which has been buttressed by the general acceptance of 'podcasts' (a technology that aggregates audio content into easily downloadable files) by a wide variety of content producers (McFedries, 2005). As complementary products compatible with iPods and iPhones appear in cars, clubs, airlines and commercial establishments to service this community, the so-called iWorld subculture expands and Apple benefits.

Apple's outsourcing pattern conforms to the 'smile of value creation', whereby higher value-added activities are located in the UK and Germany and controlled by firms like ARM Holdings (chip design) and Balda AG (touchscreens). Marketing support activities at the downstream end are located in the US and controlled by firms like TBWA/Chiat/Day. Repetitious manufacturing and assembly is undertaken in Taiwan by firms like Inventec and Hon Hai Precision Industry. Relatively complex items like chips are manufactured to design specifications by Samsung in Korea and NXP Semiconductor in The Netherlands. The subassemblies subsumed within the iPhone may be subjected to similar analysis. Thus, there may be a 'smile' underlying the value chain of Balda's touchscreens. 'Smiles of value creation' may be nested one inside the other, like Russian dolls.

The differences between the vertical integration strategy of Nokia and the special-ization strategy of Apple illustrate some fundamental differences in the approaches to generating knowledge, innovation and value in creative industries. The stark differences between the two appear in their approaches to the nexus of control. Apple implements a very high degree of outsourcing, while Nokia is highly vertically integrated. We have argued that one of the key drivers of this difference is the extent of linkage economies. Linkage economies may, therefore, be seen as an aspect of 'organizational architecture' on the basis of which firms to differ in terms of their ability to replicate the intimacy of local networks over long distances (Amin and Cohendet, 2005).

Nokia's manufacturing generates significant economies in its (upstream) design and (downstream) marketing activities and vice versa. This creates strong incentives to choose a hierarchical approach to firm organization, since the marginal value product of investments in manufacturing are relatively high. Apple, on the other hand, has rela-tively strong brand intangibles. These provide strong incentives to outsource manu-facturing, since the marginal value product of investments in manufacturing are relatively low. Conversely, Apple has strong incentives to reinforce its brand as the center of a loyal community by investing in complementary corporate assets like iTunes.

While both Nokia and Apple have geographically dispersed value chain activities, their strategic decisions regarding control affect their location patterns. Nokia maintains manufacturing facilities in Salo, Finland as well as Germany and the UK, in addition to facilities in emerging market economies like China, India, Brazil and Mexico. The location of Apple's outsourced manufacturing is determined more flexibly, since it can simply choose the best partner or supplier for the components that it designs.

Finally, Apple's R&D is focused on specific activities in the value chain. It does not need to spend its R&D budget on activities that are outsourced. Thus, it is able to piggy back and profit from the R&D expenditures of its suppliers. Nokia is obliged to spread its R&D budget over the entire value chain. The two different control strategies, therefore, have direct implications with regard to innovation performance. Apple's focused R&D has produced significantly better financial performance in recent years. Apple's R&D/sales ratio was 3.8% in 2005, compared with Nokia's 11%. However, Apple outperformed Nokia on a wide range of measures of financial performance over the 2001–2005 period, reflecting greater leverage of its R&D spending.[13]

4. Discussion and concluding remarks

The large and growing share of intangibles in wealthy economies underscores the importance of knowledge-intensive and creative industries as the engines of wealth generation, now and into the future. Definitions of what does and what does not constitute a creative industry vary widely and are rapidly overtaken by events. What is clear is that technology and culture are increasingly interlinked and difficult to disconnect. Technology and the resulting tools and devices strongly influence the nature, form and social context of popular culture. In turn devices like the iPod have become inseparable parts of popular culture (McFedries, 2005).

It is also clear that knowledge-based assets are becoming the most important source of value. Strategies to control these assets and their output of content, whether in the form of a design, a video or a software application, are now the key to firm-level value appropriation. The success or failure of such strategies depends crucially on the firm's ability to span the technocultural divide. Apple's relatively successful use of iTunes (Carr, 2004) stands in contrast with the attempts of Hollywood studios to resist technology and create a '"closed" sphere of innovation on a global scale' (Currah, 2007). The results of resistance to technological advances can also be seen in the recorded music industry, where record labels continue to push digital music CDs despite plummeting sales (Bockstedt et al., 2006).

4.1. Implications

The current study presents a theoretical analysis of the future of creative processes over geographical space. The evidence presented is based on a case study: it is illustrative and suggestive, but does not provide any conclusive results. Its objective is to highlight and delineate the research questions that should be addressed in more in-depth empirical research.

The implications of this analysis for businesses appear along the two basic nexuses of location and control. There appears to be strong evidence that strategies along the location nexus will lead firms in creative industries to geographically disperse their value chain activities. The evidence here is impossible to ignore (Smakman, 2003; Pyndt and

---

13 These data were drawn from Apple and Nokia annual reports and other public sources. Financial performance was measured in terms of sales growth, gross margin percentage, gross profit growth, operating margin percentage, operating income growth, total shareholder returns and market capitalization growth. However, using Nokia's larger total sales, its brand was judged to be considerably more valuable than Apple's in 2005 and 2006 by the marketing consulting company, Interbrand.

Pedersen, 2006). The continual dispersion of design, R&D and other creative activities by even smaller firms is moving hand in hand with the emergence of increasingly specialized niche business activities, many of which are strongly anchored in geographic space (Calderini and Scellato, 2005).

However, it appears that two fundamentally different strategies are emerging in terms of how the value chain is controlled. One strategy is based on maintaining high control over both tangible and intangible aspects of the firm's value proposition. Such a strategy is likely to appeal to firms that have relatively strong competencies in repetitive or 'humdrum' activities (Caves, 2000) as well as the ability to link these competencies to the high value-added upstream and downstream activities within the value chain. In other words, such firms have strong linkage economies whereby their repetitive activities become more efficient and their creative activities become more effective through common ownership. The successful value propositions that emerge from such firms are likely to deliver excellence based on a deep understanding of current market expectations. The implication of the above argument is that the vertical integration strategy involves being attuned to and closely following current market demands. It follows that this strategy requires the firm to continually improve the quality and lower the cost of individual activities, while 'the underlying core design concepts, and the links between them, remain the same' (Henderson and Clark, 1990, p. 12), i.e. to excel at incremental innovation.

An alternative strategy is based on focusing on the activities in the value chain that require the highest levels of commercial creativity and generate the highest levels of value-added. Such a strategy is likely to appeal to firms that have relatively stronger competencies at the ends of the value chain in design and marketing. Specialized firms that outsource their repetitive activities to focused suppliers (that therefore do not enjoy linkage economies) may not be able to match the costs of their vertically integrated rivals. This disadvantage implies that for specialized firms to survive and excel, they must look beyond the expectations of the existing market by developing entirely new value propositions. The specialization strategy involves predicting where the market is going and leading it.

Firms that implement specialized strategies often create and maintain competitive advantage by reconfiguring existing core technologies in novel ways i.e. through 'architectural innovation' (Henderson and Clark, 1990). Architectural innovation falls between incremental innovation, where vertically integrated firms are likely to have an edge and radical innovation where considerations of uncertainty are so acute that it is difficult to fund within the firm. Firms with specialized strategies implementing successful architectural innovation make 'modest changes to the existing technology ... that have quite dramatic competitive consequences' (Henderson and Clark, 1990, p. 10).[14] In short, successful architectural innovation requires developing and controlling system design by, for example, black-boxing proprietary intellectual assets.

A successful specialized strategy also requires the implementation of modularization. For instance, in the case of manufacturing, individual technologies must be compartmentalized, developed as modular subassemblies and contracted to specialist suppliers

---

14 In the formative years of the personal computer industry in the late 1970s and early 1980s, Apple implemented a specialized strategy, focusing on a novel system architecture made up of relatively modest (and outsourced) component technologies (Christensen, 1997). This control of system design and outsourcing of modular components persists in the iPhone as seen in Figure 3.

as illustrated by the example of the iPhone (Figure 3). Activities in the value chain must be decoupled from each other. Coordination across organizational boundaries and orchestration of the entire network is particularly important to the success of modularization (Dhanaraj and Parkhe, 2006).

4.2. Propositions for future research

A number of testable propositions emerge from the above analysis. Greater vertical integration based on linkage economies should enhance a firm's advantage in delivering excellence to an existing customer base. Further, a greater extent of vertical integration is likely to be associated with a tendency to favor incremental innovation. Vertical integration also implies that intra-firm coordination of value chain activities is a crucial source of competitive advantage, while modularization is relatively less important. The firm tends to be better at in-house cross-functional innovation.

By the same token, specialized firms are likely to counter these advantages by developing new value propositions, aimed at extending the existing customer base or developing a new one. This strategy is more likely to be associated with architectural innovation. Firms implementing a specialized strategy are likely to use modularization as a crucial basis of competitive advantage and to develop more sophisticated external networks as noted in the example of the US motion picture industry (Scott, 2005).

The high linkage economies that increase the attractions of vertical integration are likely to lead to continually falling costs in repetitive activities and improved quality in knowledge-intensive activities. Low linkage economies that predispose the firm towards a specialization strategy also increase the appeal of technology black boxing and modularization. Both strategies of vertical integration and specialization become self-reinforcing, so that firms are unlikely to switch between the two. It is unclear that either strategy dominates the other. Both are knowledge-based strategies that generate value on the basis of creative endeavors.

In terms of economic geography, the specialization strategy is based on the cost-driven outsourcing of standardized activities to local firms in emerging market economies. It is likely that the strategy of specialization will generate greater flexibility, at the firm and geographic levels (Doh, 2005; Graf and Mudambi, 2005). Outsourced activities can be rapidly transferred to competing vendors in alternative locations. Through the industry life cycle, more and more complex activities become commodified and require greater technical and managerial sophistication in the emerging economy supplier network (Ernst and Lim, 2002). This process supports capability formation in the emerging economy and provides the basis for local firms to begin the process of 'catch-up'. As the catch-up process gathers steam, emerging economy firms, often from these supplier networks, begin making competency-seeking R&D investments in advanced market economies. Thus, a critical research question concerns whether firms implementing a specialized strategy will lose the key complementary knowledge assets associated with standardized activities and become technologically hollow over time.[15]

---

15 Examples abound of firms that transferred technology to outsourcers in emerging market economies only to be eventually surpassed and supplanted by their former suppliers. In 1981, Schwinn Bicycle Company of Chicago transferred equipment and technology to Giant Bicycles of Taiwan and outsourced millions of bicycles for the US market. Over time Giant drove its former mentor into bankruptcy and today is the dominant firm in the industry (Witte, 2004).

The strategy of vertical integration is also driven by cost considerations. However, since the need for modularization and black boxing is considerably lower and firm-specific knowledge tends to be geographically bounded (Pinch et al., 2003; Henderson et al., 2005), the firm retains a wider repository of activities and competencies in advanced market economies. It also has a lower risk of finding itself without key competencies as technology trajectories change. It is more resilient in institutional contexts with weak intellectual property rights, since it transfers less knowledge to its supplier network (Gertler, 2003).

The local activities of the firm in an emerging market economy are nonetheless likely to create opportunities for 'spillover' as cost pressures drive it to locate increasingly creative and knowledge-intensive activities there. Local wholly owned units of MNEs function as hubs of local networks within which there are inevitable intentional and unintentional knowledge flows (Carlsson and Mudambi, 2003). Over time, local firms in the network arise as competitors to their MNE partners (Ding and Haynes, 2006).

Finally, the entire dynamic system is driven by the entrepreneurial process of 'industry creation' at the two ends of the value chain. This process has a strong cultural component as the boundary between arts and commerce is becoming increasingly blurred (Caves, 2000). More and more creative firms are recognizing that technology platforms can enrich their interface with their customers or audiences. Conversely, business firms are recognizing that their brands, suitably managed, can be leveraged to become the hubs of virtual communities, enhancing their presence in the popular culture. Ironically, the extent to which firms and locations can benefit from the entrepreneurial value propositions that they create depends on the extent to which the key creative and knowledge assets are embedded within organizational and geographical boundaries, and, therefore, resistant to imitation by rivals in competing locations (Maskell and Malmberg, 1999). Success in this dynamic environment depends on not only creating value, but also appropriating it.

Acknowledgements

I would like to thank Tina Ambos, Simona Iammarino, Mark Lorenzen and three anonymous reviewers for comments that substantially improved the article. The usual disclaimer applies.

References

Amin, A. and Cohendet, P. (2004) *Architectures of Knowledge: Firms, Capabilities and Communities*. Oxford: Oxford University Press.

Amin, A. and Cohendet, P. (2005) Geographies of knowledge formation in firms. *Industry and Innovation*, 12(4): 465–486.

Amin, A. and Thrift, N. (2005) Citizens of the world. *Harvard International Review*, 27(3): 14–17.

Amit, R. and Schoemaker, P. J. H. (1993) Strategic assets and organizational rent. *Strategic Management Journal*, 14(1): 33–46.

Augier, M. and Teece, D. J. (2006) Understanding complex organization: the role of know-how, internal structure and human behavior in the evolution of capabilities. *Industrial and Corporate Change*, 15(2): 395–416.

BIS (2007) *Bank for International Settlements 77th Annual Report*. Basel, Switzerland: BIS.

Blair, M. M. and Wallman, S. M. H. (2001) *Unseen Wealth: The Value of Corporate Intangible Assets*. Washington, DC: Brookings Institution Press.

Bockstedt, J. C., Kauffman, R. J., Riggins, F. J. (2006) The move to artist-led on-line music distribution: a theory-based assessment and prospects for structural changes in the digital music market. *International Journal of Electronic Commerce*, 10(3): 7–38.

Buckley, P. J. and Casson, M. C. (1976) *The Future of Multinational Enterprise*. London: Macmillan.

Calantone, R. J. and Stanko, M. A. (2007) Drivers of outsourced innovation: an exploratory study. *Journal of Product Innovation Management*, 24(3): 230–241.

Calderini, M. and Scellato, G. (2005) Academic research, technological specialization and the innovation performance in European regions: an empirical analysis in the wireless sector. *Industrial & Corporate Change*, 14(2): 279–305.

Cantwell, J. A. and Mudambi, R. (2005) MNE competence-creating subsidiary mandates. *Strategic Management Journal*, 26(12): 1109–1128.

Cantwell, J. A. and Santangelo, G. D. (1999) The frontier of international technology networks: sourcing abroad the most highly tacit capabilities. *Information Economics & Policy*, 11(1): 101–123.

Cao, L. (2002) Corporate and product identity in the postnational economy: rethinking U.S. trade laws. *California Law Review*, 90(2): 401–484.

Carlsson, B. and Mudambi, R. (2003) Globalization, entrepreneurship and public policy: a systems view. *Industry and Innovation*, 10(1): 103–116.

Carr, N. (2004) The corrosion of IT advantage: strategy makes a comeback. *Journal of Business Strategy*, 25(5): 10–15.

Caves, R. (2000) *Creative Industries: Contracts between Art and Commerce*. Cambridge: Harvard University Press.

Chang, S. (2008) *Sony vs. Samsung: The Inside Story of the Electronics Giants' Battle for Global Supremacy*. Singapore: John Wiley & Sons.

Christensen, C. (1997) *The Innovator's Dilemma: When New Technologies Cause Great Firms to Fail*. Boston: Harvard Business School Press.

Christopherson, S. and Storper, M. (1989) The effects of flexible specialization on industrial politics and the labor market: the motion picture industry. *Industrial & Labor Relations Review*, 42(3): 331–347.

Coase, R. H. (1937) The nature of the firm. *Economica New Series*, 4(16): 386–405.

Conybeare, J. A. C. (2003) *Merging Traffic: The Consolidation of the International Automotive Industry*. Oxford: Rowman and Littlefield.

Cunningham, S. (2002) From cultural to creative industries: theory, industry and policy implications. *Media International Australia*, 102: 54–65.

Currah, A. (2007) Hollywood, the Internet and the world: a geography of disruptive innovation. *Industry and Innovation*, 14(4): 359–384.

Dhanaraj, C. and Parkhe, A. (2006) Orchestrating innovation networks. *Academy of Management Review*, 31(3): 659–669.

Dicken, P. (2003) *Global Shift: Reshaping the Global Economic Map in the 21st Century*. Thousand Oaks, CA: Sage.

Ding, L. and Haynes, K. E. (2006) Technology, innovation and latecomer strategies: evidence from the mobile handset manufacturing sector in China. Paper presented at the ERSA Conference, Athens, Greece.

Doh, J. P. (2005) Offshore outsourcing: implications for international business and strategic management theory and practice. *Journal of Management Studies*, 42(3): 695–704.

Donath, J. and Boyd, D. (2004) Public displays of connection. *BT Technology Journal*, 22(4): 71–82.

Dunning, J. H. (1993) *Multinational Enterprises and the Global Economy*. Reading, MA: Addison-Wesley.

Ernst, D. and Lim, L. (2002) Global production networks, knowledge diffusion and local capability formation. *Research Policy*, 31: 1417–1429.

Everatt, D., Tsai, T., Cheng, B. (1999) The Acer Group's China manufacturing decision, Version A. Ivey Case Series #9A99M009, Richard Ivey School of Business, University of Western Ontario.

Florida, R. (2002) *The Rise of the Creative Class: And How it's Transforming Work, Leisure, Community and Everyday Life*. New York: Basic Books.

Foss, N. J. (2003) Selective intervention and internal hybrids: interpreting and learning from the rise and decline of the Oticon spaghetti organization. *Organization Science*, 14(3): 331–349.

Fujita, M., Krugman, P. R., Venables, A. J. (1999) *The Spatial Economy: Cities, Regions and International Trade*. Boston: The MIT Press.

Gereffi, G. (1999) International trade and industrial upgrading in the apparel commodity chain. *Journal of International Economics*, 48(1): 37–70.

Gertler, M. (2003) Tacit knowledge and the economic geography of context, or the undefinable tacitness of being (there). *Journal of Economic Geography*, 3(1): 75–99.

Giddens, A. (2003) *Runaway World: How Globalization is Re-shaping Our Lives*. London: Taylor & Francis.

Graf, M. and Mudambi, S. (2005) The outsourcing of IT-enabled business processes: a conceptual model of the location decision. *Journal of International Management*, 11(2): 253–268.

Grant, R. M. (1996) Towards a knowledge-based theory of the firm. *Strategic Management Journal*, 17: 109–122.

Hamel, G. and Prahalad, C. K. (1990) The core competence of the corporation. *Harvard Business Review*, 68(3): 79–93.

Hayek, F. A. (1945) The use of knowledge in society. *American Economic Review*, 35(4): 519–530.

Henderson, R. M. and Clark, K. B. (1990) Architectural innovation: the reconfiguration of existing product technologies and the failure of established firms. *Administrative Science Quarterly*, 35(1): 9–30.

Henderson, R. M., Jaffe, A., Trajtenbeg, M. (2005) Patent citations and the geography of knowledge spillovers: a reassessment. *American Economic Review*, 95(1): 461–464.

Hill, C. W. L. (2008) *International Business*, 7th revised edition. New York: McGraw-Hill.

Hirschman, A. O. (1968) The political economy of import-substituting industrialization in Latin America. *Quarterly Journal of Economics*, 82(1): 1–32.

Hirschman, A. O. (1977) A generalized linkage approach to economic development with special reference to staples. *Economic Development and Cultural Change*, 25: 67–97.

Hofmann, J. (2005) Value intangibles. *Current Issues*, Deutsche Bank Research, 19 October.

Howkins, J. (2001) *The Creative Economy: How People Make Money from Ideas*. Allen Lane: The Penguin Press.

Iammarino, S. and McCann, P. (2008) *Multinationals and Economic Geography: Location, Technology and Innovation*. Princeton: Princeton University Press.

IMF (2006) *World Economic Outlook: Globalization and Inflation, April*. Washington, DC: The International Monetary Fund.

Iwatani, Y. (1998) Love: Japanese style. *Wired*, 6 November.

Kogut, B. and Zander, U. (1993) Knowledge of the firm and the evolutionary theory of the multinational corporation. *Journal of International Business Studies*, 24(4): 625–645.

Koski, H. and Kretschmer, T. (2007) Innovation and dominant design in mobile telephony. *Industry & Innovation*, 14(3): 305–324.

Kotabe, M., Parente, R., Murray, J. (2007) Antecedents and outcomes of modular production in the Brazilian automobile industry: a grounded theory approach. *Journal of International Business Studies*, 38(1): 84–106.

Kotha, S. (1995) Mass customization: implementing the emerging paradigm for competitive advantage. *Strategic Management Journal*, 16(5): 21–42.

Leenders, M. and Wierenga, B. (2002) The effectiveness of different mechanisms for integrating marketing and R&D. *Journal of Product Innovation Management*, 19(4): 305–317.

Lev, B. (2001) *Intangibles: Management, Measurement and Reporting*. Washington, DC: Brookings Institution Press.

Lorenzen, M. (2004) Knowledge and geography. *Industry and Innovation*, 12(4): 399–407.

Lundvall, B.-Å. (2007) National Innovation Systems: analytical concept and development tool. *Industry & Innovation*, 14(1): 95–119.

Maheshwari, S. (2005) *The Mobile Handset Industry Asia, 2004–2009*. Washington, DC: Research Connect Inc.

Malecki, E. J. (1984) High technology and local economic development. *Journal of the American Planning Association,* 50(3): 262–269.

Malone, B. C. (1993) *Singing Cowboys and Musical Mountaineers: Southern Culture and the Roots of Country Music.* Athens, GA: University of Georgia Press.

Mansfield, E. (1985) How rapidly does new industrial technology leak out? *Journal of Industrial Economics,* 34(2): 217–223.

Marrone, J. A., Tesluk, P. E., Carson, J. B. (2007) A multilevel investigation of antecedents and consequences of team member boundary-spanning behavior. *Academy of Management Journal,* 50(6): 1423–1439.

Martin, R. and Sunley, P. (2003) Deconstructing clusters: chaotic concept or policy panacea? *Journal of Economic Geography,* 3: 5–35.

Maskell, P. and Malmberg, A. (1999) Localised learning and industrial competitiveness. *Cambridge Journal of Economics,* 23: 167–186.

Maskell, P. and Lorenzen, M. (2004) The cluster as market organization. *Urban Studies,* 41(5–6): 991–1009.

McCann, P. and Mudambi, R. (2005) Analytical differences in the economics of geography: the case of the multinational firm. *Environment and Planning A,* 37(10): 1857–1876.

McFedries, P. (2005) The iPod people. *IEEE Spectrum,* 42(2): 76.

McMillan, G. S., Hamilton, R. D.III, Deeds, D. L. (2000) Firm management of scientific information: an empirical update. *R&D Management,* 30(2): 177–182.

Mudambi, R. (2007) Offshoring: economic geography and the multinational firm. *Journal of International Business Studies,* 38(1): 206.

Mudambi, R. and Helper, S. (1998) The 'close but adversarial' model of supplier relations in the U.S. auto industry. *Strategic Management Journal,* 19(8): 775–792.

Nakamura, L. (2003) A trillion dollars a year in intangible investment and the new economy. In J. R. M. Hand and B. Lev (eds) *Intangible Assets: Values, Measures and Risks.* Oxford: Oxford University Press, 19–47.

Natarajan, S. and Tan, J. M. (1992) *The Impact of MNC Investments in Malaysia, Singapore and Thailand.* Singapore: Institute of Southeast Asian Studies.

Nelson, R. R. and Winter, S. G. (1982) *An Evolutionary Theory of Economic Change.* Boston: Belknap Press of Harvard University Press.

Normann, R. and Ramírez, R. (1993) From value chain to value constellation: designing interactive strategy. *Harvard Business Review,* 71(4): 65–77.

OECD (1996) *Technology, Productivity and Job Creation.* Paris: OECD.

Pavitt, K. (1998) Technologies, products and organization in the innovating firm: what Adam Smith tells us and Joseph Schumpeter doesn't. *Industrial & Corporate Change,* 7(3): 433–452.

Pertierra, R. (2005) Mobile phones, identity and discursive intimacy. *Human Technology,* 1(1): 23–44.

Phelps, N. A. (2008) Cluster or capture? Manufacturing foreign direct investment, external economies and agglomeration. *Regional Studies,* 42(4): 457–473.

Pinch, S., Henry, N., Jenkins, M., Tallman, S. (2003) From industrial districts to knowledge clusters: a model of knowledge dissemination and competitive advantage in industrial agglomerations. *Journal of Economic Geography,* 3(4): 373–388.

Porter, M. and Millar, V. E. (1985) How information gives you competitive advantage. *Harvard Business Review,* 63(4): 149–160.

Pyndt, J. and Pedersen, T. (2006) *Managing Global Offshoring Strategies: A Case Approach.* Copenhagen: Copenhagen Business School Press.

Rheingold, H. (2002) *Smart Mobs, the Next Social Revolution: Transforming Cultures and Communities in the Age of Instant Access.* New York: Basic Books.

Ricketts, M. J. (2002) *The Economics of Business Enterprise.* Cheltenham: Edward Elgar.

Rosenberg, R. (1982) *Inside the Black Box: Technology and Economics.* Cambridge: Cambridge University Press.

Rubenstein, J. M. (2001) *Making and Selling Cars: Innovation and Change in the U.S. Automotive Industry.* Baltimore: Johns Hopkins University Press.

Schumpeter, J. A. (1934) *The Theory of Economic Development.* Cambridge, MA: Harvard University Press (originally published in German in 1911; reprinted by Transaction Publishers, New Brunswick, New Jersey in 1997).

Scott, A. J. (2000) *The Cultural Economy of Cities*. London: Sage.

Scott, A. J. (2004) Cultural-products industries and urban economic development. *Urban Affairs Review*, 39(4): 461–490.

Scott, A. J. (2005) *On Hollywood: The Place, the Industry*. Princeton: Princeton University Press.

Scott, A. J. and Storper, M. (2003) Regions, globalization, development. *Regional Studies*, 37(6–7): 579–593.

Smakman, F. (2003) Local Industry in Global Networks: Changing Competiveness, Corporate Strategies and Pathways of Development in Singapore and Malaysia's Garment Industry. PhD. dissertation, Utrecht University. Rozenberg Publishers: The Netherlands.

Spulber, D. F. (1989) *Regulation and Markets*. Boston: The MIT Press.

Storper, M. (1997) Regional economies as relational assets. In R. Lee and J. Willis (eds) *Society, Place, Economy: States of the Art in Economic Geography*. London: Edward Arnold.

Szulanski, G. (1996) Exploring internal stickiness: impediments to the transfer of best practices within the firm. *Strategic Management Journal*, 17: 27–43.

Teece, D. J. (1998) Capturing value from knowledge assets: the new economy, markets for know-how and intangible assets. *California Management Review*, 40(3): 55–79.

Uchida, T. (2008) Presentation to the Canon Strategy Conference, Tokyo, 8 March.

Vang, J. and Chaminade, C. (2007) Global-local linkages, spillovers and cultural clusters: theoretical and empirical insights from an exploratory study of Toronto's film cluster. *Industry and Innovation*, 14(4): 401–420.

Van Meter, K. (2002) Terrorists/liberators: researching and dealing with adversary social networks. *Connections*, 24(3): 66–78.

Vernon, R. (1966) International investment and international trade in the product cycle. *Quarterly Journal of Economics*, 80(2): 190–207.

Wernerfelt, B. (1984) A resource-based view of the firm. *Strategic Management Journal*, 5(2): 171–180.

Williamson, O. E. (1975) *Markets and Hierarchies: Analysis and Antitrust Implications, a Study in the Economics of Internal Organization*. New York: The Free Press.

Williamson, O. E. (1979) Transaction-cost economics: the governance of contractual relations. *Journal of Law & Economics*, 22(2): 233–261.

Winter, S. (2003) Understanding dynamic capabilities. *Strategic Management Journal*, 24(10): 991–995.

Witte, G. (2004) A rough ride for Schwinn Bicycle. *The Washington Post*, 3 December, A01.

Yoffie, D. (1991) Case #391238, Boston: Harvard Business School Press.

Zahra, S. A. and George, G. (2002) Absorptive capacity: a review, reconceptualization and extension. *Academy of Management Review*, 27(2): 185–203.

Zollo, M. and Winter, S. G. (2002) Deliberate learning and the evolution of dynamic capabilities. *Organization Science*, 13(3): 339–351.

Appendix A

Consider a value chain composed of two processes—downstream and upstream. Define the downstream firm to be the focal firm that uses an input k. The quantity of the input used by the downstream firm is denoted by k_i. The downstream firm's production function is denoted by

$$q(k_i), q' > 0, q'' < 0.$$

The production function $q(.)$ can be generalized to include multiple inputs without affecting any of the analysis presented here.

The upstream production function may be written as

$$k_T = g(z_T), g' > 0, g'' < 0.$$

where z is the upstream input. For simplicity, it is assumed that the upstream input 'z' produced using a constant returns technology in a competitive market. Therefore, it is available at the competitive price (equal to marginal cost) and this is denoted by 'c'.

The downstream producer can produce the input in-house at an average cost of $\rho(k_i)$ per unit. There are economies of scale in the production of k so that $\rho' < 0$.

Alternatively, the downstream firm can purchase the input k in the market from an upstream firm at a price of 'r' per unit. The upstream producer sells the input to 'n' downstream firms and its optimal price may be written as:

$$r^* = r(k_T), \quad \text{where } k_T = \Sigma k_j, j = 1, 2, \dots, n$$

Normalizing the downstream price to unity, the downstream profit may be written as:

$$\Pi^d(k_i) = q(k_i) - (1 - \theta)r(k_T)k_i - \theta \rho(k_i)k_i \tag{1}$$

A fraction θ of the input k is produced in-house while a fraction $(1-\theta)$ is outsourced to the external upstream producer.

The corresponding upstream profit may be written as:

$$\Pi^u(k_T) = (1 - \theta)[r(k_T)g(z_T) - cz_T]$$

With total vertical integration, $\theta = 1$ and the downstream profit function reduces to

$$\Pi^d(k) = q(k_i) - \rho(k_i)k_i \tag{2}$$

At the other extreme of complete outsourcing, $\theta = 0$ so that

$$\Pi^d(k) = q(k_i) - r(k_T)k_i \tag{3}$$

Within this simple model, firm optimization leads to a corner solution where the downstream firm chooses total vertical integration ($\theta = 1$) or complete outsourcing ($\theta = 0$) of the input. The crucial determinants of organizational choice are (i) the extent of economies of scale in the production of the input k and (ii) the extent of the upstream price markup. The extent of the price markup depends mainly on the market structure of the input good. For a given market structure, the economies of scale in production become the determining factor. (In general, the more competitive the market for the input good, the smaller the price markup.) We will assume a given market structure throughout the analysis, so that we can focus on the production technology.

If economies of scale are strong, the unit cost of internally producing the relatively small requirement of the input is very high. The external firm's large production volume ensures that even with the price markup, $r(k_T) < \rho(k_i)$. The firm's optimal organization involves complete outsourcing.

On the other hand, if economies of scale are weak, the relatively small volume of internal production is not such a disadvantage and the associated unit cost of is not very high. Corresponding, the external firm's large volume is not such an advantage, so that $r(k_T) > \rho(k_i)$. The firm's optimal organization involves total vertical integration.

The model may be generalized to introduce economies of scope by setting up either the downstream production function $q(.)$ or the upstream production function $g(.)$ (or both) to include multiple outputs (as vector-valued functions). Economies of scope are measured in terms of the effect of the level of one output on the marginal product of another output. The basic insights from the simple model carry over to this more general model. (The details are not presented in interests of brevity.) For a given level of economies of scale, stronger economies of scope make vertical integration more attractive as they reduce the burden of small internal production volume. Weaker economies of scope raise the unit costs of internal production and make outsourcing more attractive.

Economies of experience may also be included at the expense of some cumbersome notation. The average cost function of in-house production of the upstream input is time variant and includes cumulative production as a second argument. At time 't' this specification is written as:

$$\rho_t\left(k_{it}, \sum_{s=1}^{t-1} k_{is}\right), \rho_{t1}<0, \rho_{t2}<0.$$

This specification incorporates both economies of scale ($\rho_{t1}<0$) and experience ($\rho_{t2}<0$). Greater economies of experience, *ceteris paribus*, lower average costs and make outsourcing less attractive.

Finally, economies of sequence arise when quantity of downstream production appears as an argument reducing the average cost function of in-house production of the upstream input (Spulber, 1989). The general Coasian insight remains appears intact all these situations—the firm makes its optimal organizational choice by comparing internal production with outsourcing.

Economies of scale, scope and experience relate separately to the production functions at each stage of the value chain. Thus, the production functions $q(.)$ and $g(.)$ independently display economies of scale and generate the relevant cost functions. Similarly, when $q(.)$ and $g(.)$ are set up to include multiple outputs, economies of scope measured in terms of the effect of the level of one output on the marginal cost of another output. Economies of experience are measured in terms of the effect of cumulative past output on current costs. None of these economies relate the two functions $q(.)$ and $g(.)$.

However, there is considerable empirical evidence that suggests that joint control of the production functions $q(.)$ and $g(.)$ can affect the efficiencies of each. In other words, this is the extent to which the control of upstream production improves the efficiency of the downstream production process and vice versa. Since these economies arise from linking different production processes we define these to be 'linkage economies'. We may rewrite Equation (1) to include linkage economies in the following form:

$$\Pi^d(k) = q\left[(1+\theta)^{\alpha(i)}k_i\right] - (1-\theta)r(k_T)k_i - \theta\,\rho(k_i)k_i \tag{4}$$

In other words, the productivity of the input k depends on the extent of vertical integration. The parameter $\alpha(i)$ is a measure of the extent of linkage economies. In this specification, $\alpha(i)=0$ is a situation of no linkage economies so that Equation (4) collapses to Equation (1). Whenever $\alpha(i)>0$, we have positive linkage economies, i.e. increasing vertical integration increases the efficiency of the input k in the downstream production process. This can occur either through innovation or improved quality (which increases effective output by reducing the rejection rate). If $\alpha(i)<0$, we have linkage diseconomies, so that increasing vertical integration actually reduces the efficiency of the input k. The existence of coordination and scheduling costs would suggest that in most cases, $\alpha(i) \geq 0$.

The indicator 'i' in the measure $\alpha(i)$ is a specification that implies that linkage economies are firm-specific. In other words, two firms in the same industry may have different levels of linkage economies. This perspective strongly differentiates linkage economies from economies of scale, scope, experience and sequence.

Economies of scale, scope and experience are largely based on technology and are generally common across leading edge firms in an industry (Mansfield, 1985; Pavitt 1998). Economies of sequence also have in-built performance implications, so that for firms with access to a common technology, *ceteris paribus*, the optimum extent of vertical integration is the same (Spulber, 1989). Therefore, none of these theoretical concepts can be used to explain the observed intra-industry diversity in firm organization. On the other hand, linkage economies are explicitly firm specific and vary across firms even when the underlying technologies being implemented are common (Rosenberg, 1982, p. 257).

Thus, a firm with strong linkage economies (say, firm A) and a firm with weak linkage economies (say, firm B) may coexist within the same industry. Firm A is likely to be more vertically integrated while firm B is likely to undertake more outsourcing. However, the concept of linkage economies has further implications regarding the processes implemented in the two firms. Since firm A has a higher level of linkage economies, it is likely to have superior internal production processes as these get progressively enhanced. Since firm B has a higher level of outsourcing, it is likely be more reliant on economies of scale at its supplier firms. Over time, it likely that firm A will be more focused on production excellence within the entire vertically integrated value chain. Firm B is more likely to be focused on excellence in the specific niches of the value chain over which it retains control.

[16]

Journal of International Business Studies (2009) 40, 42–57
www.jibs.net

Host-country environment and subsidiary competence: Extending the diamond network model

Christian Geisler Asmussen[1], Torben Pedersen[1] and Charles Dhanaraj[2]

[1]Center for Strategic Management and Globalization, Copenhagen Business School, Frederiksberg, Denmark; [2]Kelley School of Business, Indiana University, Indianapolis, USA

Correspondence:
CG Asmussen, Center for Strategic Management and Globalization, Copenhagen Business School, Porcelænshaven 24, 2000 Frederiksberg, Denmark.
Tel: +45 3815 3034;
Fax: +45 3815 3035;
E-mail: cga.smg@cbs.dk

Abstract
We extend the "centers of excellence" concept to address the diversity and multidimensionality of subsidiary competence. Using Rugman and Verbeke's diamond network model, we hypothesize the contingencies influencing the links between host-country environments and subsidiary competence configuration, and provide evidence from more than 2000 subsidiaries in seven European countries. Our results provide new insights into how multinational enterprises can overcome "unbalanced" national diamonds by acquiring complementary capabilities across borders.
Journal of International Business Studies (2009) **40,** 42–57.
doi:10.1057/palgrave.jibs.8400420

Keywords: MNE environment; subsidiary competence configuration; industrial clusters; differentiated networks; subsidiary embeddedness

INTRODUCTION

The roles played by national subsidiaries have become pivotal to the discussion of the strategy and structure of multinational enterprises (MNEs). In the global firm subsidiaries are passive recipients of both resources and strategic imperatives from the parent firm, whereas in the multinational firm subsidiaries are self-sufficient entities with considerable autonomy. However, in recent decades a growing body of research has been building on the idea of the MNE as a network of specialized, interdependent units (Bartlett & Ghoshal, 1989; Ghoshal & Nohria, 1997; Hedlund, 1986; Westney, 1990). In the networked MNE the role of the subsidiaries is much more complex than in the global or multinational firm, since each subsidiary can be simultaneously a recipient and a contributor of knowledge, products, and services (Gupta & Govindarajan, 1991). By building dispersed and specialized competences in its subsidiaries the MNE can ideally arbitrage national differences in comparative and competitive advantage, and generate superior returns compared with its domestic and non-specialized international competitors.

A powerful and well-known model of environmentally determined competitive advantage is Porter's (1990) diamond model, which states that firms derive competitive advantage from the presence of local industrial clusters. However, surprisingly few

Received: 29 December 2006
Revised: 8 March 2007
Accepted: 23 August 2007
Online publication date: 10 July 2008

studies have applied this framework to the study of *subsidiary* competences. Some researchers have touched upon aspects of the diamond framework by relating the characteristics of the subsidiary's environment to its competences (e.g., Almeida & Phene, 2004; Cantwell & Mudambi, 2005; Mariotti & Piscitello, 1995). Frost, Birkinshaw, and Ensign (2002) use Porter's framework more explicitly to relate aggregated perceptual measures of "diamond strength" to the emergence of subsidiary centers of excellence, but they found no significant relationship between the two phenomena.

Other authors have evoked the diamond model in a more indirect way, by using industrial cluster membership rather than host-country diamond components to predict subsidiary strength. For example, Birkinshaw and Hood (2000) found that membership in local cluster industries led to higher subsidiary embeddedness, autonomy, and international sales. However, Benito (2000) examined whether subsidiary centers of excellence emerge in Norway's cluster industries, and found mixed support for this proposition. As pointed out by Birkinshaw and Hood (2000: 151), "it is not just cluster membership but the specific characteristics of the cluster in question that impacts the likely subsidiary role." At present we have very little knowledge about the mechanisms by which and dimensions along which these cluster characteristics work.

This paper attempts to fill this research gap by moving away from the concepts of environment and subsidiary *strength* and toward the concept of *configuration*, which captures both the strength and the diversity of the combinations of strength across value chain activities. Thus, while an industrial cluster is characterized by a well-balanced configuration of diamond conditions – a self-reinforcing system of factor conditions, demand conditions, local competitive rivalry, and related and supporting industries – we ask the question of how firms respond to configurations of *unbalanced diamonds*, that is, local country environments where some of these conditions are present but others are missing. We build on the logic that such a heterogeneous diamond configuration at the host-country level should lead to a heterogeneous and diverse competence configuration at the subsidiary level, by drawing on insights from the diamond network model propounded by Rugman and Verbeke (1993). A diamond network refers to an MNE combining the distinct strengths of various unbalanced, national diamonds that have been tapped by its subsidiaries, without any individual national

diamond possessing all the strengths necessary for overall competitiveness. By empirically testing this idea on a large sample of subsidiaries in western Europe we make two important contributions: we incorporate a value chain distinction into the diamond framework; and we extend the scope of the diamond network model by explicitly relating it to the geographical competence distribution of the MNE.

The remainder of this paper is structured as follows. The next section develops the conceptual framework by revisiting Porter's (1990) diamond framework and Rugman and Verbeke's (1993) diamond network model. Then we develop a set of four hypotheses, which together present a multidimensional perspective of subsidiary competence and their antecedents. Subsequently we present the research design and our results. Finally, we discuss the implications of our research for MNE theory and practice.

HOST-COUNTRY ENVIRONMENT AND SUBSIDIARY COMPETENCE

How do local environments influence the competitive advantage of local firms? Consistent with observations made by Marshall (1920), Porter proposed the simple and powerful notion that firms based in "industrial clusters"[1] could appropriate location-specific competitive advantages. A cluster's strength is determined by a system of reinforcing environmental elements – the national "diamond" – consisting of factor conditions, demand conditions, local competitive rivalry, and related and supporting industries. Porter (1990) hypothesized that MNEs based in industrial clusters in their home countries would be highly competitive in the global marketplace, resulting, for instance, in an increased export propensity from those clusters. Porter's contribution was positioned firmly in the traditional foreign direct investment (FDI) literature, in which the MNE is seen to exploit its firm-specific advantages – developed at home – to overcome the inherent disadvantage of foreign operations (Hennart, 1982; Hymer, 1976; Vernon, 1966).

The need for a strong home country diamond seems to be consistent with the broadly accepted premise that the transfer of tacit knowledge between firms occurs more effectively in cases of geographical proximity and cultural similarity (Almeida & Kogut, 1999; Porter, 1990). Indeed, this would be the case if the MNE's competitive advantage could only emerge from its home base.

However, as Rugman and Verbeke (2001) suggest, a cluster-based competitive advantage may be just one of many patterns of capability generation that can potentially take place in the home country, or in host countries, or within a multinational network. This theory implies that the absorption of non-location-bound knowledge may occur through foreign subsidiaries' external networks, and that this knowledge can subsequently be filtered, codified, and transferred *internally* to other subsidiaries through the knowledge-sharing routines and infrastructure that constitute the internal network of the MNE (Kogut & Zander, 1993). Thus MNEs can potentially use FDI to access and combine dispersed and complementary sources of competitive advantage by selectively sourcing components of diamonds abroad, leading some scholars to suggest that MNEs' approach resembles a "multi-home-base" structure (Dunning, 1996; Sölvell & Zander, 1995) involving several distinct bases for competence building, often referred to as "centers of excellence". This line of thinking is also prevalent in the model of the metanational MNE proposed by Doz, Santos, and Williamson (2001) in which the process of searching for pockets of knowledge and then mobilizing this knowledge in the global MNE network is the key to competitiveness.

When the network view is integrated with the diamond model of competitive advantage, a unique capacity of the MNE emerges. By virtue of its multinationality, an MNE can synthesize the different factors of the diamond by building on advantages not only at the national level but also at regional and even global levels. Scholars have characterized this as the "double diamond" or "diamond network" model of competitive advantage (Rugman & D'Cruz, 1993; Rugman & Verbeke, 1993). For example, Sölvell, Zander, and Porter (1991) describe how Swedish MNEs benefited from combining the advanced technical and supply resources in their home country – the factor conditions of the diamond – with their exposure to demanding customers in other countries. Almeida (1996) shows that European and Korean firms invest in the US to extract local knowledge in areas in which their home countries are relatively weak. In a survey based on the diamond model, Dunning (1996) estimates that between 40 and 50% of MNEs' competitive advantage is derived from FDI and international alliances, and, in particular, from tapping into natural resources and inter-firm rivalry in other countries. In the words of Dunning (1993: 12), "The *principle* of the

diamond may still hold good – but its geographical constituency has to be established on very different criteria." If MNEs can co-specialize and create complementarities across borders – using foreign subsidiaries to interact *locally* with complementary firms in other countries – individual specialized diamond elements may develop in different locations, and reinforcing cluster dynamics may take place across borders.

The diamond network suggested by Rugman and Verbeke (1993) is, in fact, a natural extension of the network-based MNE structure (Bartlett & Ghoshal, 1989; Ghoshal & Nohria, 1997; Hedlund, 1986; Westney, 1990), which presents the MNE as an organization that combines diamond components from different countries through a high degree of external embeddedness in each local environment and a high degree of integration between these dispersed units. Furthermore, external embeddedness is not a general property of each subsidiary but is often particular to certain value chain activities (Rugman & Verbeke, 2001). Thus it is the role of the individual subsidiary in the diamond network to *specialize* in the type of knowledge or resource that the MNE wishes to source in the host country. Although specialization is often asserted as a stylized fact, or described as a key property of the network-based MNE, we have very little knowledge of the antecedents of subsidiary specialization. We deal with this subject in the next section.

A MULTIDIMENSIONAL VIEW OF SUBSIDIARY COMPETENCE

Although the MNE literature acknowledges that subsidiaries can specialize in a limited range of activities in the value chain (Birkinshaw & Hood, 1998), most studies have taken a one-dimensional view of subsidiary competence by looking at individual activities in isolation (e.g., Frost et al., 2002), or by averaging the competence of the subsidiary in different parts of the value chain (Benito, Grøgaard, & Narula, 2003). Such an approach effectively conceals the degree of specialization. Just as the firm can be seen as a collection of activities (Porter, 1985), a subsidiary contains a *subset* of those activities and the capabilities that reside within them.

The term *subsidiary competence* captures both the existence of the activity in the value chain and proficiency in that activity – the former being a prerequisite for the latter. A subsidiary's competence within a part of the value chain ranges from the example where the relevant activities are not performed at all in the host country over a minimal activity volume, to the example where the subsidiary conducts the activities with high skill and expertise. Some of the subsidiary's activities may cluster into natural groups based on co-location advantages, similar skill requirements, and shared links with the environment. International business scholars have suggested several such groupings. In a factor analysis of subsidiary capabilities, Forsgren, Pedersen, and Foss (1999) identified one factor consisting of product development expertise, technological expertise, and knowledge among professional staff, and another factor comprising supplier relationships, advanced user contact, and insight into competitors. The former was called the "internal" factor and the latter the "business network" factor. However, in a similar distinction, Andersson, Forsgren, and Holm (2002) measured the embeddedness of subsidiaries along both a "business" dimension and a "technical" dimension, reflecting that both types of competence may actually be linked to the environment.

Building on these two studies, we propose a three-way segmentation of subsidiary competences into supply, market, and technical competences. *Supply* competences describe the firm's skill and expertise in handling its production inputs, and include such activities as procurement and distribution of intermediary products. *Market* competences, on the other hand, are concerned with production outputs, and include sales, marketing, and service activities. Finally, *technical* competences are needed to transform inputs to outputs, and reside in the research, development, and production departments. The combination of supply and market competences corresponds to the business or business network factors described in the above studies; however, we separate the two because they deal with different parts (upstream and downstream) of the subsidiary's external network. Together, the supply, technical, and market aspects constitute the "competence configuration" of the subsidiary – a multidimensional construct capturing both the depth and the breadth of the firm's capabilities.

When we look at the diamond elements described by Porter (1990), a similar distinction can be made concerning the subsidiary's supply, technical, and market environments. Broadly speaking, the supply environment consists of upstream business partners and raw material suppliers. The technical environment consists of labor with industry-specific skills, local research institutions, and related industries using similar technol-

ogies, thereby providing synergies and technology spillovers. The market environment consists of demanding customers and competitive rivalry, providing market inputs to the firm and pressuring it to position its product offering. The combination of supply, technical, and market environments can be called the "diamond configuration" of a given country. By recognizing distinct groupings of competences and environmental resources we implicitly open up the possibility of "unbalanced diamonds" and specialized subsidiaries. The diamond can be said to be unbalanced if one element is much weaker or much stronger than the others. Indeed, we suggest that MNEs can respond to unbalanced diamonds by linking specialized subsidiaries together in a diamond network. This scenario is illustrated in Figure 1.

HYPOTHESES DEVELOPMENT
In the diamond network, the MNE generates its competitive advantage by using dispersed competences to access complementary diamond elements in different countries. The means of achieving this advantage is subsidiary specialization: one subsidiary has local supply competences that enable it to tap into the local supply environment, another has the technical competences to assimilate local technical resources, and the third subsidiary has market competences to enhance learning from the market environment. Such a competence distribution is crucial in the diamond network, because host-country knowledge absorption requires both localized *and* specialized competences.

Localized competences are required because positive knowledge externalities are geographically bounded, and proximity is conducive to knowledge sourcing and technological spillovers between firms (Almeida & Kogut, 1999; Almeida & Phene, 2004; Jaffe, Trajtenberg, & Henderson, 1993; Porter, 1990, 1998). Hence the local external network of the firm and the embeddedness in this network are facilitators of knowledge acquisition, which has been shown to be true for both the business (supply and market) network and the technical network of MNE subsidiaries (Andersson et al., 2002).

Specialized competences, on the other hand, are necessary because absorptive capacity – the ability to assimilate knowledge from the environment – is a function of existing knowledge within a particular field (Cohen & Levinthal, 1990). In other words, host market embeddedness must be specialized to certain value chain activities (Rugman & Verbeke, 2001), which, in our framework, implies that the

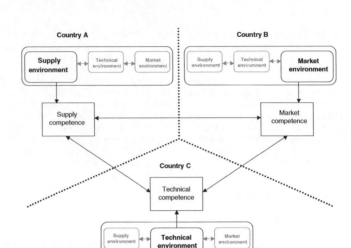

Figure 1 The MNE as a diamond network.

competences of a local MNE unit should be embedded in the local environment along each of our three dimensions. For example, local market competence is clearly necessary to access the market components of the national diamond: in order to benefit from demanding consumers in a certain area, the firm would need competent sales-people who can interact closely with these custo-mers and convey market information and pressures up the value chain. Similarly, technical competence is necessary to access the technical diamond components: if the firm wants to tap into research synergies with universities, it would need engineers with the skills required to assimilate this research. Finally, to take full advantage of world-class suppliers in a certain location, skilled procurement specialists must work with these suppliers to enable tight integration and knowledge-sharing in the supply chain.

Host-Country Diamond Configuration
It is instructive to compare the diamond network model with the industrial cluster view, since the two scenarios paint very different pictures of how the environment affects subsidiary competences. The subsidiaries of Porter's (1990) globally compe-titive firm have competence profiles inherited from their parent – if they have any significant compe-tences at all – since they are merely implementers

of the corporate competitive advantage generated in the home base. Because this type of MNE can access all diamond components in the home country industrial cluster, it has little incentive to facilitate learning abroad by locating specialized competences in its subsidiaries. Hence the relation-ship between the diamond configuration of the host country and the competence configuration of the subsidiary is conceptually weak.

In contrast, the MNE diamond network locates specialized competences where needed in order to access idiosyncratic environmental resources. This behavior implies that the supply competences of a given subsidiary should be highly correlated with the strength of the supply environment in the host country, its technical competences with the technical environment, and its market compe-tences with the market environment. These rela-tionships are the "direct paths" in the causal model presented in Figure 2. Owing to the necessity of localized and specialized competences, these direct paths should be significant, as opposed to the "cross-paths", which leads us to the following hypotheses:

Hypothesis 1: The strengths of the supply envir-onment, the technical environment, and the market environment positively affect their directly corresponding subsidiary competence type.

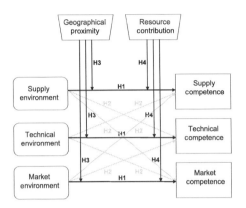

H1=hypothesis 1; H2=hypothesis 2; H3=hypothesis 3; H4=hypothesis 4

Figure 2 Causal model and hypotheses.

Hypothesis 2: The strengths of the supply environment, the technical environment, and the market environment have no effect on the subsidiary's competences other than on their directly corresponding competence type.

Geographical Proximity

It is necessary to draw certain contingencies that can significantly influence the relationships hypothesized above. In particular, two contingencies determine whether a given subsidiary is likely to be a node in a diamond network: the proximity of the host country to the location of the MNE headquarters, and the degree to which the host-country environment can contribute with complementary resources to other MNE units.

The value of gaining access to specialized resources is contingent upon the ability to combine these specialized resources with complementary resources through the MNE's international network (Malnight, 1996). The cross-fertilization obtained by combining different types of knowledge is generally believed to be conducive to innovation (Zander & Sölvell, 2000), which is consistent with the view that a firm needs to access *all* elements of the diamond in order to innovate and create competitive advantage – a key insight of Porter's (1990) model. For instance, accessing a pool of technical skills is not enough if a strong market environment does not exist to create the pressures and the market knowledge necessary to put these skills to their best use, or if a supply environment is

not present to provide the component technology on which to apply the skills. Thus a firm tapping into the supply environment in one country, the technical environment in another, and the market environment in a third country (as does the firm in Figure 1) must bring these crucial inputs together by transferring knowledge across borders. This poses a challenge, since knowledge is "sticky", and may flow only imperfectly between different units of a firm (Szulanski, 1996), and since the barriers to knowledge diffusion may be aggravated by geographic dispersion and national boundaries. Hence the need for international knowledge transfer in the diamond network may create both direct and indirect costs. The direct costs are related to travel, communication, meeting expenses, administrative wages, investments in technology, codification of knowledge, the opportunity cost of employee time, etc. The indirect costs reflect the knowledge that is lost or distorted in the process, or the knowledge that is not conveyed because it would be too costly. Greater geographical distances between the different units in the network are likely to aggravate these costs, making the specialized resources in an individual host-country environment less valuable to the MNE.

In other words, geographical proximity is an important contingency affecting the feasibility of sourcing diamond components abroad. In markets close to the rest of the organization, and particularly to the MNE headquarters, such sourcing could be feasible, and the MNE would have a strong incentive to locate the necessary competences there in order to facilitate learning. These markets effectively constitute the MNE's enlarged diamond from which to derive competitive advantage, and here we expect to observe a strong relationship between particular environmental strengths and the competences needed to access them. In more distant markets, conversely, selective sourcing may be prohibitively costly, and the incentives for investing in specialized local competence consequently weaker. These effects are expressed in Hypothesis 3:

Hypothesis 3: Geographical proximity to headquarters positively moderates the relationship between the environment and the subsidiary competences.

Resource Contribution

There are contexts when even geographically proximate subsidiaries with access to valuable resources may not be tightly integrated with the rest of the organization. One such context could occur when the resources in the subsidiary's local environment are location-bound, and hence difficult to exploit in the global market (Rugman & Verbeke, 2001). Another example is an MNE that is already tapping similar resources in other locations, or an MNE that is based in an industrial cluster in its home country, making an otherwise valuable host-country environment redundant. In all of these cases the host country is likely to be most valuable as an output market, and hence we expect the subsidiary's perceived resource contribution – the degree to which the rest of the organization depends on the subsidiary's competences – to be low.

A subsidiary with low resource contribution is essentially a market-seeking unit: it contributes to the rest of the MNE with revenue, rather than with competences. In this type of subsidiary there is little incentive to invest in specialized competence acquisition, and the link between environment and competence configuration is therefore expected to be weak. In contrast, subsidiaries with high resource contribution could be described as resource-seeking units. In fact, the variable of subsidiary contribution has been used to identify centers of excellence in previous empirical studies (e.g., Frost et al., 2002), and Andersson and Forsgren (2000) show that such centers of excellence have higher degrees of external embeddedness than do other subsidiaries. In the diamond network this result should be valid for each of the three competence dimensions, as we can see from Figure 1; and a strong relationship between environment and competence configuration is therefore to be expected. In short, the integration of the subsidiary with the rest of the MNE correlates with its learning from the local environment, as reflected by Hypothesis 4.

Hypothesis 4: The contribution of the subsidiary to the rest of the MNE positively moderates the relationship between the environment and the subsidiary competences.

RESEARCH DESIGN

Data
The data were collected as part of the Centers of Excellence project that surveyed the Nordic countries, the United Kingdom, Germany, Austria, Italy, Portugal, and Canada (Holm & Pedersen, 2000). We

believe survey data are the most reliable way to capture our constructs, owing to the tacit and industry- and firm-specific nature of location advantages and organizational competences.

The project was launched in May 1996, with the purpose of investigating headquarter–subsidiary relationships and the internal flow of knowledge in MNEs. In order to collect comparable quantitative data on acquisition of subsidiary knowledge it was decided to construct a questionnaire that could be applied in all the involved countries. This inclusive design was accomplished after several project meetings and extensive reliability tests of the questionnaire on both academics and business managers.

For practical reasons, project members were responsible for gathering data on foreign-owned subsidiaries within their own countries: thus all subsidiaries in the database belong to MNEs. One advantage in choosing subsidiary respondents rather than headquarters respondents is that the subsidiaries are directly engaged in the local environment, and are therefore more acquainted with its characteristics. Although we may expect any subsidiary to have a reliable awareness and understanding of its own knowledge elements, it would be an advantage to gather information on intra-MNE knowledge flows from other corporate units as well. However, the identification of the subsidiaries in each country and the subsequent identification of the relevant management units in the foreign MNEs would be an unmanageable task.

This paper is based on data from seven countries: Austria, Denmark, Finland, Germany, Norway, Sweden, and the UK. All countries are located in the northern part of Europe. The four Nordic countries and Austria are relatively small, whereas Germany and the UK are among the largest countries in Europe. Approximately 80% of the questionnaires were answered by subsidiary executive officers, and the remaining 20% were answered by the subsidiary's financial managers, marketing managers, or controllers. The overall response rate was 30%, and the quality of the data was quite high: a general level of missing values was not greater than 5%. The total sample covers information on 2107 subsidiaries, comprising all types of subsidiary in all fields of business. Because of missing data, this number was subsequently reduced to 1936. The average number of employees in the subsidiaries was 742, with a median of 102. Average annual subsidiary sales were US$42 million. The average subsidiary age at the time of

Table 1 Sample overview

Host country	Response rate (%)	N	Average subsidiary age	Share of greenfield investments (%)	Average no. of employees	Average sales (million US$)
Austria	28	313	18	61	318	61
Denmark	41	308	17	29	284	57
Finland	24	238	13	44	200	50
Germany	21	254	20	30	1574	465
Norway	22	262	15	52	130	63
Sweden	55	530	16	39	244	74
UK	20	202	18	42	3787	377
Total sample	30	2107	17	42	742	142

the survey was 17 years, and 42% of all the subsidiaries were established as greenfield investments; the remaining 58% were acquisitions. Table 1 shows these sample properties segmented by country. Country variations emerge in the response rates, which range from 20% (in the UK) to 55% (in Sweden), and in the sizes of the subsidiaries, which tend to correlate with the sizes of the host countries and with subsidiary age. In general, the Nordic subsidiaries were younger and smaller than those in other countries.

Measures

The configuration of the environment was measured by several items, reflecting the subsidiary manager's perception of the strength of the host-country diamond. The competence configuration of the subsidiary consists of perceptual measures of the subsidiary's competence in different value chain activities. Both sets of items were collected using seven-point Likert scales,[2] and each item was then assigned to one of the six theoretical constructs (the proposed three dimensions of both environment and competence). Table 2 lists the two sets of items and inter-item correlations.

Geographical proximity is a dichotomous variable, taking the value of 1 if the MNE was headquartered in Europe and the value of 0 if it was headquartered outside Europe. Since we cannot observe the overall location pattern of each MNE, we take the location of headquarters as a proxy for the geographical "center of gravity" of the firm. Of the subsidiaries in the sample, 27% had headquarters outside Europe. Finally, resource contribution is operationalized as the degree to which the subsidiary manager perceives the rest of the MNE to be dependent on the competences of the subsidiary.

Resource contribution was originally measured on a seven-point Likert scale and subsequently collapsed into a dichotomous variable, where "low contribution" reflects values of 1 to 3[3] and "high contribution" reflects values of 4 to 7.

Structural Equation Models

The hypotheses were tested in LISREL models that allow for simultaneous formation of underlying constructs (the measurement model) and also test structural relationships among these constructs (the structural model). First, we performed four different analyses with the same measurement model but with different structural models. These four models were *nested*, allowing an increasing number of relationships among the latent constructs, the validity of which could then be evaluated by comparative χ^2 tests.

Model 1 was the measurement model, where no relationships between the latent constructs are allowed. Model 2 was a highly restricted model, with only the three direct paths linking the three diamond components with their respective competence types. A comparison of these two models would be able to reveal information about the hypothesized embeddedness of the subsidiaries. In Model 3 we allowed correlations among the environment factors as well as among the competence factors. There were specific theoretical reasons for this structure: different diamond components were likely to be correlated because of their reinforcing nature (Porter, 1990), and different competences were likely to be correlated because co-location economizes on international transfer costs. Comparing Models 2 and 3 enabled us to evaluate the validity of these theoretical expectations. Finally, Model 4 added the

Table 2 Measured items and correlations

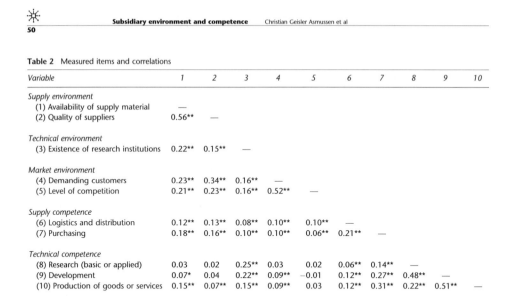

Variable	1	2	3	4	5	6	7	8	9	10
Supply environment										
(1) Availability of supply material	—									
(2) Quality of suppliers	0.56**	—								
Technical environment										
(3) Existence of research institutions	0.22**	0.15**	—							
Market environment										
(4) Demanding customers	0.23**	0.34**	0.16**	—						
(5) Level of competition	0.21**	0.23**	0.16**	0.52**	—					
Supply competence										
(6) Logistics and distribution	0.12**	0.13**	0.08**	0.10**	0.10**	—				
(7) Purchasing	0.18**	0.16**	0.10**	0.10**	0.06**	0.21**	—			
Technical competence										
(8) Research (basic or applied)	0.03	0.02	0.25**	0.03	0.02	0.06**	0.14**	—		
(9) Development	0.07*	0.04	0.22**	0.09**	−0.01	0.12**	0.27**	0.48**	—	
(10) Production of goods or services	0.15**	0.07**	0.15**	0.09**	0.03	0.12**	0.31**	0.22**	0.51**	—
Market competence										
(11) Marketing and sales	0.04	0.04	0.01	0.08**	0.11**	0.30**	0.48**	0.01	0.03	−0.05*

$*p<0.05; **p<0.01.$

cross-paths and showed whether these were significant both individually and as a group. In combination, these models and the estimated relationships would enable us to evaluate Hypotheses 1 and 2. Since we hypothesized a weak impact of the cross-paths, Model 3 was the causal model that corresponded most closely to our theoretical framework.

Subsequently, we tested the moderating effects of geographical proximity and resource contribution by two group analyses. First, the sample was split into low-proximity and high-proximity subsidiaries, and the model was estimated for both subsamples. Comparing the strength of the direct paths across the two groups allowed us to test Hypothesis 3. The same procedure was then applied to compare low-contribution and high-contribution subsidiaries, allowing us to test Hypothesis 4.

Validity and Reliability of Measures
The validity of LISREL models is estimated by the validity of the measurement and the structural model combined: that is, by the nomological validity. Before estimating the nomological validity of the model with the causal relations specified, it is important to judge the hypothesized relationships between constructs and items, as well as the

convergent validity (homogeneity) and the discriminant validity (distinctness) of the constructs. In Table 3 the constructs are judged by the factor loading for each indicator, measuring the strength of the linear relationships, and the *t*-values, a significance test of each relationship in the model (Jöreskog & Sörbom, 1993). For each construct, one item was set to have an unstandardized loading of 1. Therefore *t*-values are not reported for that item, and the loadings of the other items are measured *relative* to that item.

As can be seen in Table 3, the strength of the linearity in the relationship between constructs and items is relatively strong in most cases, with standardized factor loadings all at or above 0.53. We can also conclude that the *t*-values are highly significant, as they are all above 13 (compared with the critical *t*-value of 3.29 at p=0.001).

To determine whether the constructs were internally coherent, we report several tests of convergent validity in Table 3. First, after the reliability of each construct was calculated, we observed that some of the constructs fell slightly below the recommended threshold of 0.70 (Gerbing & Anderson, 1988). This result could indicate that these constructs are too heterogeneous, in the sense that they contain subdimensions not recognized by our theoretical

Table 3 Factor loadings in measurement model

Constructs and items	Loading[a]	t-value[b]	Construct reliability	Variance extracted	(Highest C/p)^2
Supply environment			0.71	0.55	0.25
Availability of supply material	0.70	16.7			
Quality of supply material	0.78	—			
Technical environment			0.67	0.67	0.10
Existence of research institutions	0.82	—			
Market environment			0.67	0.51	0.25
Demanding customers	0.78	—			
Level of competition	0.64	13.7			
Supply competence			0.64	0.47	0.14
Logistics and distribution	0.58	13.3			
Purchasing	0.78	—			
Technical competence			0.71	0.47	0.14
Research (basic or applied)	0.53	17.3			
Development	0.88	—			
Production of goods or services	0.59	18.3			
Market competence			1.00	1.00	0.03
Marketing and sales	1.00	—			

[a]Standardized factor loadings.
[b]All t-values are highly significant at p<0.001 (requires t-values above 3.29).

model. However, we could not decompose the constructs further, owing to our relatively small number of measured items: therefore we leave this challenge for future research. Also, when we looked at the variance extracted, the picture is better: all constructs are very close to or above the recommended threshold of 0.50. Since the overall fit of the model was acceptable and the sample size was large, we can accept a marginal lack of convergent validity.

From a theoretical point of view it is particularly important to assess discriminant validity, since the multidimensionality of the constructs is a central proposition in this paper. Our theoretical model breaks both the national diamond and the subsidiary competence into dimensions that are hypothesized to be conceptually distinct, and discriminant validity is the empirical means of assessing this distinctness. Several measures of discriminant validity were obtained from the data. First, we compared Model 3 with a one-dimensional model in which only one broadly defined environment factor was set to influence one competence factor. Model 3 was better (based on a χ^2-difference of 1202 with 12 degrees of freedom, significant at

p<0.001), leading us to reject the one-dimensional model. To determine whether this result was due to the sample size, we also checked the normalized residuals. The one-dimensional model had 36% of its normalized residuals above 2.58, indicating a very bad fit to the data, whereas Model 3 was at 13%, which is closer to the statistical threshold of 5%.

Another indication of discriminant validity is to test whether the correlations and causal paths between the latent constructs are significantly different from 1 (e.g., Burnkrant & Page, 1982). Constructing 99.9% confidence intervals around the correlations and causal paths in Model 2, we confirmed that none of them is close to including 1. Finally, Fornell and Larcker (1981) suggest comparing the variance extracted for each construct with the squared correlations or paths between the constructs. Both are given in Table 3, and the variance extracted is clearly the higher of the two values for all constructs. In combination, these tests indicate that the discriminant validity of the six constructs is good.

Since both the dependent and independent variables were drawn from the same survey, we conducted Harman's single-factor test to ensure that there was no common method bias. We also used confirmatory factor analysis, which is considered a more sophisticated method to conduct such a test (Podsakoff, MacKenzie, Lee, & Podsakoff, 2003), and could clearly reject models where either one or three (market, supply and technical) factors were set to account for all of the variance in the data. The strong discriminant validity of our constructs, as described above, further confirmed their distinctiveness.

Model Fit

We assessed the entire model by different goodness-of-fit measures, including the χ^2-value, the goodness-of-fit index (GFI), and the normed fit index (NFI), all of which are measures of the distance between data and model, that is, nomological validity (Jöreskog & Sörbom, 1993). Since the nested models have different degrees of freedom, we also looked at the parsimonious normed fit index (PNFI), which takes these differences into account. Table 4 presents goodness-of-fit statistics for all eight estimated structural equation models.

Of the first four models, Model 3 fits the data best and is highly significant, with a GFI of 0.97 and a NFI of 0.92. The χ^2-value is still both high and significant, which may indicate a problem but is more likely a result of the large sample size (Rigdon, 1998: 269). Instead, we can use root mean square error of approximation (RMSEA), which controls for sample size. At 0.0635 the RMSEA is within the acceptable range (between 0.05 and 0.08) with a 90% confidence interval. The PNFI is also higher for Model 3 than for the other models, indicating good explanatory power per estimated relationship. As mentioned above, an inspection of the normalized residuals in Model 3 showed that 13% of normalized residuals were above 2.58, compared with

the 5% that is statistically justifiable. The item "Production of Goods and Services" applied to approximately half of the high residuals, which could indicate that production may not, as hypothesized in our model, always be co-located with research and development – a proposition supported by anecdotal evidence of current offshoring trends. Future studies should look more closely into this factor and its potential subdimensions.

Because Model 3 is superior to the other models, and because it is theoretically grounded, it forms the basis of the two group analyses. The goodness-of-fit statistics for these analyses correspond approximately to those of the main model.

RESULTS

We can test individual relationships between the constructs in the model with t-values, and groups of relationships with χ^2-comparisons of the nested models. Figure 3 shows Model 3 with standardized factor loadings, causal paths, and correlations.

A comparison between the χ^2-values of the nested models (cf. Table 4) indicates that the direct paths added in Model 2 are highly significant as a group ($\chi^2=2951$, $p<0.001$). From Figure 3 we can see that they are highly significant individually as well, which lends support to Hypothesis 1.

The correlations added in Model 3 are also collectively significant ($\chi^2=597$, $p<0.001$). Hence the fit of the model to the data improves significantly by allowing these correlations, indicating that both the environment and the competence components are internally reinforcing, as expected.[4] This relationship is also indicated by the fact that most of the correlations estimated in Models 3 and 4 are significant individually. However, the correlations among the competence factors are clearly weaker than those among the environment factors, indicat-

Table 4 Goodness-of-fit statistics

Model	Description	N	χ^2	d.f.	GFI	NFI	RMSEA	PNFI
1	Measurement model	1936	3,848*	50	0.70	—	0.2009	—
2	With direct paths	1936	897*	41	0.92	0.77	0.1054	0.57
3	With direct paths, correlations	1936	300*	35	0.97	0.92	0.0635	0.59
4	With direct paths, correlations, cross-paths	1936	293*	29	0.97	0.92	0.0696	0.49
5a[a]	Low-proximity subsidiaries	514	98*	35	0.97	0.91	0.0603	0.58
5b[a]	High-proximity subsidiaries	1421	261*	35	0.97	0.91	0.0684	0.58
6a[a]	Low-contribution subsidiaries	820	155*	35	0.97	0.90	0.0653	0.57
6b[a]	High-contribution subsidiaries	1106	171*	35	0.97	0.92	0.0605	0.59

*All χ^2 values are significant at $p<0.001$.
[a]Models 5 and 6 resemble Model 3L that is, they include direct paths and correlations.
N=number; d.f.=degrees of freedom; GFI=goodness-of-fit index; NFI=normed fit index; RMSEA=root mean square error of approximation; PNFI=parsimonious normed fit index.

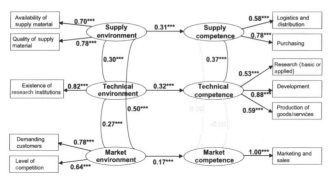

Figure 3 Structural equation model (Model 3). *$p<0.05$; **$p<0.01$; ***$p<0.001$.

Table 5 Moderating effects of proximity and contribution

Model	Description	Direct supply path		Direct technical path		Direct market path	
		β	t	β	t	β	t
5a	Low-proximity subsidiaries	0.26	4.39***	0.25	2.02*	0.05	1.13
5b	High-proximity subsidiaries	0.33	8.03***	0.36	3.15***	0.15	4.78***
6a	Low-contribution subsidiaries	0.27	5.14***	0.13	1.30***	0.09	2.19*
6b	High-contribution subsidiaries	0.35	7.56***	0.34	3.23***	0.15	4.30***

Note: All betas are standardized path coefficients.
*$p<0.05$; **$p<0.01$; ***$p<0.001$.

ing that co-location advantages may be less important *within* the individual MNE than they are *between* co-specialized firms.

Finally, the χ^2-values show that the system of cross-paths added in Model 4 is insignificant ($\chi^2=6$), which indicates that restricting the cross-paths to 0 is valid at $p=0.05$ and lower. The GFI and RMSEA statistics also suggested that Model 4 is inferior to Model 3, and the PNFI drops rapidly as well when we add the cross-paths. If we look at the cross-paths individually we find a similar result, as only one – the path from technical environment to supply competence – is significant, and only at $p<0.05$. On the one hand this result could suggest that supply competences are more broadly embedded than are technical or market competences. On the other hand the cross-path from the technical environment is weaker than the direct path from the supply environment. All in all, this evidence is in favor of Hypothesis 2: the data generally support the idea that subsidiary learning occurs primarily along the three proposed dimensions and not across them.

Table 5 lists the standardized path coefficients for the two group analyses. A comparison of the low-proximity and high-proximity subsamples shows a clear pattern: all direct path coefficients are stronger and much more significant for the high-proximity subsidiaries, supporting Hypothesis 3 – proximity does matter as determinant of local resource acquisition. In fact, for low-proximity subsidiaries the relationship between environment and competence is very weak, valid only on the supply dimension. Similarly, the degree of resource contribution reinforces the direct paths in Model 6, in support of Hypothesis 4. Still, even for low-contribution subsidiaries, the technical and supply paths are quite strong. This relationship could indicate that also some market-seeking units embed those two types of competence, for example to exploit location-bound resources by providing locally engineered products based on local components for increased national responsiveness (Rugman & Verbeke, 2001). However, these types of subsidiary are likely to be more interested in market *attractiveness* (revenue growth and income) than in market environment *strength* (demanding customers and competition).

DISCUSSION AND CONCLUSIONS

In particular, three significant implications can be drawn from this study. First, our results indicate that the strength of the host-country environment should be conceptualized and operationalized in a multidimensional way. Environment strength seems to vary along (at least) three distinct dimensions – the supply, technical, and market environments – and perhaps even further decomposition is warranted. The industrial cluster view may overestimate the reinforcing nature of the different diamond elements: the data show a correlation, but nowhere near equifinality, between the three environmental dimensions, and the discriminant validity of the three environment factors is high. This tells us clearly that "unbalanced diamonds" do exist, as individual host-country environments may be strong in some dimensions and weak in others. However, as demonstrated by case studies of successful firms emerging from such environments (e.g., the success of Korean firms in the consumer electronics industry or that of Indian firms in the software services industry), this need not prevent MNEs from obtaining competitive advantage if they can operate across countries that are strong in different dimensions. Indeed, it is possible that the multidimensional nature of host environment resources may explain why some previous studies that rely on one-dimensional constructs – for example, industrial cluster membership (Benito, 2000; Benito et al., 2003) or host-country diamond strength (Frost et al., 2002) – could not identify a clear relationship between host-country environment and subsidiary competences.

The second important implication of this paper is that subsidiary competences, like the environment, should be seen as multidimensional. This is not a new idea in the literature, and the center-of-excellence line of research has brought significant advances in that direction. However, our typology suggests that the dichotomous center-of-excellence distinction may be too coarse, in part because it can be difficult to draw the line between what is a center of excellence and what is not – significant competences may also exist in subsidiaries that are not denoted centers of excellence – but most importantly because it does not capture the actual variety of subsidiary competence configurations. The idea of subsidiary competence configuration captures both the overall competence and the

diversity of this competence along three dimensions that are empirically distinct, providing a more complete picture of subsidiary specialization.

Finally, and tying together the two previous points, the results suggest a link between the configuration of the environment and that of the subsidiary's competences. We have shown empirically that a strong supply environment leads to strong supply competences, a strong market environment leads to strong market competences, and a strong technical environment leads to strong technical competences – with very weak, if any, interaction between the three dimensions. This result challenges the industrial cluster view of the evolution of subsidiary competences. We acknowledge that the presence of an industrial cluster (with strong supply, technical, *and* market environment) may be a sufficient condition for subsidiary competences to arise. We know such clusters exist, and we have some tentative evidence of their impact on subsidiary competence. However, industrial clusters need not be a *necessary* condition for subsidiary competence; environments with specialized resources may also be valuable to MNEs, presumably because they can be matched with complementary resources derived from other nodes in the internal network. As noted by Rugman and Verbeke (2001: 240), such environments may exert a "pull" on MNEs' resource-seeking activities. Our study shows that the gravity of this "pull", in turn, is moderated by the proximity and the integration of the subsidiary. For example, if the subsidiary's technical environment is advanced *and* located close to the rest of the MNE, it will be attractive to have technical competences in place in order to tap into this knowledge and transmit it to other parts of the organization. On the other hand, if these technical resources are located in a distant market, it may not be worthwhile to source them, since the costs of combining this knowledge with that of the rest of the firm would be too high. In a similar argument, if the subsidiary is not integrated with the rest of the MNE, knowledge transfer is difficult (Gupta & Govindarajan, 1991, 2000; Szulanski, 1996), and the value of specialized resources is accordingly lower. Some degree of reverse causality could also exist: the MNE has a strong incentive to integrate specialized subsidiaries with non-location-bound advantages in order to leverage these advantages. In any case, the explanation of competences provided here differs from a direct knowledge spillover explanation, in the sense that it emphasizes the role of MNE and subsidiary *incentives* in the subsidiary competence acquisition process. Learning from the environment requires an effort, and such an effort is more likely to take place if this knowledge is easily integrated into the differentiated network of the MNE.

An alternative justification for the proximity effect is that the resource-seeking efforts of the firm are constrained by a liability of foreignness (Hymer, 1976; Zaheer, 1995), which gives outsiders a disadvantage relative to incumbent firms in tapping into local knowledge. This liability of foreignness thus seems to be exacerbated by geographic distance, as also posited by Zaheer (1995). In our data the significance of the regional dummy variable suggests a liability of regional foreignness (Rugman & Verbeke, 2007), as non-European firms apparently have more difficulties translating specialized environment resources into subsidiary competences than do European firms. This liability of regional foreignness may be caused by several factors: regulations pertaining to the local resources, unwillingness of local firms to share knowledge, or lack of absorptive capacity in the subsidiary due to unfamiliarity with the market, making it difficult for regional outsiders to identify, understand, absorb, and subsequently transfer the local knowledge.

Including proximity and resource contribution as a contingency makes our model sufficiently general to include both Porter (1990) and Ghoshal and Nohria (1997) as special cases. In distant host countries, and in units that are loosely linked to the MNE network structure – perhaps because their resources are either redundant or location-bound – specialization is not attractive. The firm is likely to leave such local units to pursue their revenue markets and generate MNE-wide competitive advantage elsewhere, for instance in the home base. In contrast, tightly integrated subsidiaries sufficiently close to one another and each with access to complementary non-location-bound resources can effectively constitute an enlarged diamond network from which it is feasible to source selective environmental resources. Hence this paper mediates in the highly polarized debate between the two "extreme views" – the industrial cluster school of thought, arguing that competitive advantage should be developed in one location, and the differentiated network view, arguing for competitive advantage generated by combining resources from a geographically dispersed network. These views rely on different assumptions, and hence each may be valid in its own right *given* the

appropriate context. Geographic proximity and resource contribution are two contextual variables that apparently have a strong influence on the relative predictive power of the two theories.

Although the complex relationship between host-country environments and subsidiary competences is still an area of uncharted territories, this study highlights some directions for further investigation. Most importantly, our findings point to the need for further efforts to explore the multidimensional nature of Porter's (1990) diamond model. The relatively weak convergent validity of our constructs indicates that future studies could theorize toward an even more fine-grained and multidimensional model of environment strength and subsidiary competence, and that a more comprehensive set of measurement items could be obtained. Also, whereas Porter's industrial clusters are defined by their export propensity, this study has used perceptual measures of individual diamond elements to predict subsidiary competences. A more direct approach that combines the benefits of these two approaches would derive objective measures of the individual diamond components, for instance using well-established measures of competitive intensity or local research activity.

As a contribution to the literature on subsidiary-specific advantages, the prime focus of this paper is the determination of subsidiary competences. An equally important question, however, is how these competences influence the role played by the subsidiary in the larger context of the MNE. In particular, the model presented here strongly implies that the configuration of subsidiary competence is related to the knowledge flows within the MNE network, and that specialized subsidiaries should be both recipients and senders of such knowledge. We touched upon this aspect with our group analysis on resource contribution. However, further testing of the diamond network model with an emphasis on the flows rather than the stocks of resources could be useful in this respect.

"Modern" MNEs are often asserted to be transforming themselves into networks of specialized, interdependent units operating across borders. Yet we still have few means of measuring this specialization, and little knowledge about what drives it. This paper has attempted, based on the diamond network model of Rugman and Verbeke (1993), to fill this research gap. In particular, we posit that host-country diamond heterogeneity – the presence of unbalanced diamonds – may lead MNEs to locate specialized competences in host countries in order to access complementary knowledge. A multidimensional specification of both environment strength and subsidiary competences may enable us to capture the richness of these links more profoundly than can be achieved through a single-dimensional specification.

ACKNOWLEDGEMENTS
We thank Professors Bent Petersen, Alan M Rugman, Nicolai J Foss, and Dan Li. We are also grateful to the Copenhagen Business School for sponsoring the empirical part of this study, and to the Indiana University Center for International Business Education and Research (IU CIBER). We are grateful to Departmental Editor Professor Alain Verbeke and the anonymous reviewers whose comments and suggestions were helpful in developing this final version.

NOTES

[1] An industrial cluster consists of a proximate group of "interconnected companies and associated institutions linked by commonalities and complementarities" (Martin & Sunley, 2003: 10).

[2] The competence scales were coded to include 0, which indicates that a given activity is not performed at all in the host country.

[3] Other cut-off points were tried, but this segmentation had the highest discriminating power when used as a grouping variable in the structural equation models. Incidentally, previous studies have used the same cut-off point as a way of operationalizing the "center of excellence" construct (e.g., Frost et al., 2002). Although the use of cut-off points is always quite arbitrary, it was necessary to create a categorical variable, since LISREL models cannot accept interval-scaled variables as moderators.

[4] To see this effect more clearly, Model 4 can be compared with a similar model without correlations (not presented here). Such a comparison reveals that allowing correlations weakens all the cross-paths, and thus the indirect causality indicated in such a restricted model is largely spurious. For example, if the market environment reinforces the supply environment, and the supply environment determines the subsidiary's supply competences, the model without correlations would capture this indirect effect and falsely indicate that the market environment actually affects the supply competences.

REFERENCES

Almeida, P. 1996. Knowledge sourcing by foreign multinationals: Patent citation analysis in the US semiconductor industry. *Strategic Management Journal*, 17(Winter Special Issue): 155–165.

Almeida, P., & Kogut, B. 1999. Localization of knowledge and the mobility of engineers in regional networks. *Management Science*, 45(7): 905–917.

Almeida, P., & Phene, A. 2004. Subsidiaries and knowledge creation: The influence of the MNC and host country on innovation. *Strategic Management Journal*, 25(8/9): 847–864.

Andersson, U., & Forsgren, M. 2000. In search of centre of excellence: Network embeddedness and subsidiary roles in multinational corporations. *Management International Review*, 40(4): 329–350.

Andersson, U., Forsgren, M., & Holm, U. 2002. The strategic impact of external networks: Subsidiary performance and competence development in the multinational corporation. *Strategic Management Journal*, 23(11): 979–996.

Bartlett, C. A., & Ghoshal, S. 1989. *Managing across borders: The transnational solution.* Boston, MA: Harvard Business School Press.

Benito, G. R. G. 2000. Industrial clusters and foreign companies: Centres of excellence in Norway. In U. Holm & T. Pedersen (Eds) *The emergence and impact of MNC centers of excellence: A subsidiary perspective*: 97–110. London: Macmillan.

Benito, G. R. G., Grøgaard, B., & Narula, R. 2003. Environmental influences on MNE subsidiary roles: Economic integration and the Nordic countries. *Journal of International Business Studies*, 34(5): 443–456.

Birkinshaw, J., & Hood, N. 1998. Multinational subsidiary evolution: Capability and charter change in foreign-owned subsidiary companies. *Academy of Management Review*, 23(4): 773–795.

Birkinshaw, J., & Hood, N. 2000. Characteristics of foreign subsidiaries in industry clusters. *Journal of International Business Studies*, 31(1): 141–154.

Burnkrant, R. E., & Page Jr., T. J. 1982. An examination of the convergent, discriminant, and predictive validity of Fishbein's behavioral intention model. *Journal of Marketing Research*, 19(4): 550–561.

Cantwell, J., & Mudambi, R. 2005. MNE competence-creating subsidiary mandates. *Strategic Management Journal*, 26(12): 1109–1128.

Cohen, W. M., & Levinthal, D. A. 1990. Absorptive capacity: A new perspective on learning and innovation. *Administrative Science Quarterly*, 35(1): 128–152.

Doz, Y. L., Santos, J., & Williamson, P. 2001. *From global to metanational: How companies win in the knowledge economy.* Boston, MA: Harvard Business School Press.

Dunning, J. H. 1993. Internationalizing Porter's diamond. *Management International Review*, 33(2): 7–15.

Dunning, J. H. 1996. The geographical sources of the competitiveness of firms: Some results of a new survey. *Transnational Corporations*, 5(3): 1–29.

Fornell, C., & Larcker, D. F. 1981. Evaluating structural equation models with unobservable variables and measurement error. *Journal of Marketing Research*, 18(1): 39–50.

Forsgren, M., Pedersen, T., & Foss, N. J. 1999. Accounting for the strengths of MNC subsidiaries: The case of foreign-owned firms in Denmark. *International Business Review*, 8(2): 181–196.

Frost, T. M., Birkinshaw, J. M., & Ensign, P. C. 2002. Centers of excellence in multinational corporations. *Strategic Management Journal*, 23(11): 997–1018.

Gerbing, D. W., & Anderson, J. C. 1988. An updated paradigm for scale development incorporating unidimensionality and its assessment. *Journal of Marketing Research*, 25(2): 186–192.

Ghoshal, S., & Nohria, N. 1997. *The differentiated network: Organizing multinational corporations for value creation.* San Francisco: Jossey-Bass.

Gupta, A. K., & Govindarajan, V. 1991. Knowledge flows and the structure of control within multinational corporations. *Academy of Management Review,* 16(4): 768–792.

Gupta, A. K., & Govindarajan, V. 2000. Knowledge flows within multinational corporations. *Strategic Management Journal,* 21(4): 473–496.

Hedlund, G. 1986. The hypermodern MNC: A heterarchy? *Human Resource Management,* 2(1): 9–36.

Hennart, J.-F. 1982. *A theory of multinational enterprise.* Ann Arbor, MI: University of Michigan Press.

Holm, U., & Pedersen, T. (Eds) 2000. *The emergence and impact of MNC centers of excellence: A subsidiary perspective.* London: Macmillan.

Hymer, S. H. 1976. *The international operations of national firms: A study of direct foreign investment.* Cambridge, MA: MIT Press.

Jaffe, A., Trajtenberg, M., & Henderson, R. 1993. Geographic localization of knowledge spillovers as evidenced by patent citations. *Quarterly Journal of Economics,* 108(3): 577–598.

Jöreskog, K. O., & Sörbom, D. 1993. *LISREL 8: Structural equation modeling with the SIMPLIS command language.* Chicago: Scientific Software International, Inc.

Kogut, B., & Zander, U. 1993. Knowledge of the firm and the evolutionary theory of the multinational corporation. *Journal of International Business Studies,* 25(4): 625–646.

Malnight, T. 1996. The transition from decentralized to network-based MNC structures: An evolutionary perspective. *Journal of International Business Studies,* 27(1): 43–66.

Mariotti, S., & Piscitello, L. 1995. Information costs and location of FDIs within the host country: Empirical evidence from Italy. *Journal of International Business Studies,* 26(4): 815–841.

Marshall, A. 1920. *Principles of economics.* London: Macmillan.

Martin, R., & Sunley, P. 2003. Deconstructing clusters: Chaotic concept or policy panacea? *Journal of Economic Geography,* 3(1): 5–35.

Podsakoff, P. M., MacKenzie, S. B., Lee, J.-Y., & Podsakoff, N. P. 2003. Common method biases in behavioral research: A critical review of the literature and recommended remedies. *Journal of Applied Psychology,* 88(5): 879–903.

Porter, M. E. 1985. *Competitive advantage.* New York: Free Press.

Porter, M. E. 1990. *The competitive advantage of nations.* New York: Free Press.

Porter, M. E. 1998. *On competition.* Boston, MA: Harvard Business School Press.

Rigdon, E. E. 1998. Structural equation modeling. In G. Marcoulides (Ed.) *Modern methods for business research:* 251–294. Mahwah, NJ: Lawrence Erlbaum.

Rugman, A. M., & D'Cruz, J. R. 1993. The "double diamond" model of international competitiveness: The Canadian experience. *Management International Review,* 33(special issue 2): 17–39.

Rugman, A. M., & Verbeke, A. 1993. Foreign subsidiaries and multinational strategic management: An extension and correction of Porter's single diamond framework. *Management International Review,* 33(2): 71–84.

Rugman, A. M., & Verbeke, A. 2001. Subsidiary-specific advantages in multinational enterprises. *Strategic Management Journal,* 22(3): 237–250.

Rugman, A. M., & Verbeke, A. 2007. Liabilities of regional foreignness and the use of firm-level versus country-level data: A response to Dunning et al. (2007). *Journal of International Business Studies,* 38(1): 200–205.

Sölvell, Ö., & Zander, I. 1995. Organization of the dynamic multinational enterprise: The home based and heterarchical

MNE. *International Studies of Management and Organization,* 25(1–2): 17–38.

Sölvell, Ö., Zander, I., & Porter, M. E. 1991. *Advantage Sweden.* Stockholm: Norstedts.

Szulanski, G. 1996. Exploring internal stickiness: Impediments to the transfer of best practice within the firm. *Strategic Management Journal,* 17(Winter Special Issue): 27–43.

Vernon, R. 1966. International investment and international trade in the product cycle. *Quarterly Journal of Economics,* 80(2): 190–207.

Westney, D. E. 1990. Internal and external linkages in the MNC: The case of R&D subsidiaries in Japan. In C. Bartlett, Y. Doz, & G. Hedlund (Eds) *Managing the global firm:* 279–300. London: Routledge.

Zaheer, S. 1995. Overcoming the liability of foreignness. *Academy of Management Journal,* 38(2): 341–363.

Zander, I., & Sölvell, Ö. 2000. Cross-border innovation in the multinational corporation: A research agenda. *International Studies of Management and Organization,* 30(2): 44–67.

ABOUT THE AUTHORS

Christian Geisler Asmussen (cga.smg@cbs.dk) is an assistant professor of international business and strategic management at Copenhagen Business School's Center for Strategic Management and Globalization. He is a Danish citizen and was born in Copenhagen, Denmark, where he also earned his PhD from CBS in 2007. His research is about the globalization of multinational enterprises, focusing on the interaction of geographic scope and competitive advantage.

Torben Pedersen (tp.smg@cbs.dk) is a professor of international business at Copenhagen Business School's Center for Strategic Management and Globalization. He is a native of Denmark and earned his PhD at Copenhagen Business School. He has published over 50 books and articles in prominent journals about the strategic aspects of globalization. His latest book, entitled *Managing Global Offshoring Strategies – A Case Approach,* has been well received among academics, students, and practitioners.

Charles Dhanaraj (dhanaraj@iupui.edu) is an associate professor of management at Kelley School of Business, Indiana University. His research interests are in global strategy, international alliances and joint ventures, learning in organizational networks and innovation in emerging markets. Born in India, he is an Indian citizen and a US permanent resident. He earned his PhD in international strategy from Ivey Business School, the University of Western Ontario.

Accepted by Alain Verbeke, Departmental Editor, 23 August 2007. This paper has been with the authors for two revisions.

Part III
Challenges in Implementing a Global Strategy

[17]

Sloan Management Review   Winter 1980   27

Strategic Management in Multinational Companies

Yves L. Doz   **Harvard University**

The evolution of multinational companies (MNCs) over the last decade has been characterized by a growing conflict between the requirements for economic survival and success (the *economic* imperative) and the adjustments made necessary by the demands of host governments (the *political* imperative). Faced with the conflict between the economic and political imperatives within a business, MNCs can respond in several ways. This article, based on intensive field research of the management processes in about a dozen MNCs, analyzes *strategies and administrative processes* used by MNCs to reconcile the conflicting economic and political imperatives. *Ed.*

The evolution of multinational companies (MNCs) over the last decade has been characterized by a growing conflict between the requirements for economic survival and success (the *economic* imperative) and the adjustments made necessary by the demands of host governments (the *political* imperative). The lowering of trade barriers and the substantial economies of scale still available in many industries combined with vigorous competition from low cost exporters push the MNCs toward the integration and rationalization of their activities among various countries.[1] Yet, the very international interdependence created by freer trade and MNC rationalization make individual countries more vulnerable to external factors and their traditional domestic economic policies less effective.[2] As a result, most governments turn more and more to specific sectorial policies implemented through direct negotiations with the companies involved and through incentives tailored to them.[3] Both the economic and political imperatives thus take on increasing importance in the management of the multinationals.

This article, based on intensive field research of the management processes in about a dozen MNCs, analyzes *strategies and administrative processes* used by MNCs to reconcile the conflicting economic and political imperatives. Findings are presented in four sections. First, MNC strategies to respond to the dual imperatives are described and contrasted. Second, conditions under which MNCs are likely to find one or another strategy most suitable for individual businesses are reviewed. Third, the interaction between strategies and the nature of internal management processes is analyzed. Fourth, implications for the management of interdependencies between businesses in diversified multinationals are outlined. In the

conclusion, means to increase the overall managerial capability of the company are explored.

Multinational Strategies

Faced with the conflict between the economic and political imperatives within a business, MNCs can respond in several ways. Some companies clearly respond first to the economic imperatives, and follow a worldwide (or regional)[4] business strategy where the activities in various countries are integrated and centrally managed. Other companies forgo the economic benefits of integration and let their subsidiaries adjust to the demands of their host government (as if they were national companies), thus clearly giving the upper hand to the political imperative. Finally, some companies try to leave their strategy unclear and reap benefits from economic integration and political responsiveness, in turn, or find compromises between the two. These three strategies are described in this section.

Worldwide Integration Strategy
Some companies choose to respond to the economic imperative and improve their international competitiveness. For companies that already have extensive manufacturing operations in several countries, the most attractive solution is to integrate and rationalize their activities among these countries. Individual plants are to provide only part of the product range (but for sales in all subsidiaries), thereby achieving greater economies of scale.[5] Plants can also be specialized by stages in the production process, and can be located in various countries according to the cost and availability of production factors for each stage (energy, labor,

Yves L. Doz is Assistant Professor in the General Management Area at the Harvard Graduate School of Business Administration. Dr. Doz did graduate work at the Ecole des Hautes Etudes Commerciales, and he received the Ph.D. degree from the Harvard Graduate School of Business Administration. He is the author of *Government Control and Multinational Strategic Management: Power Systems and Telecommunication Equipment.*

raw materials, skills).[6] Texas Instruments's location of labor-intensive semiconductor finishing activities in Southeast Asia, or Ford's and GM's Europe-wide manufacturing rationalization, as well as their investments in Spain, illustrate this integration strategy.

Extensive transshipments of components and finished products between subsidiaries located in different countries result from such a strategy. Integration also involves the development of products acceptable on a worldwide basis. The "world car" concept pushed by GM, Ford, and Japanese exporters is an example of this approach. The driving principle of this integration strategy is the reduction of unit costs and the capture of large sales volumes; in industries where economies of scale are significant and not fully exploited within the size of national markets, it can bring sizable productivity advantages. For instance, Ford's unit direct manufacturing costs in Europe were estimated to be well below those of national competitors supplying a comparable car range. In industries where dynamic economies of scale are very strong (such as semiconductors), the cost level differences between such leaders as Texas Instruments and smaller national firms were significant. Similarly, IBM was believed to have costs significantly lower than its competitors.[7]

Where integration brought substantial cost advantages over competitors, the integrated firms could allocate part of the benefits from their higher internal efficiency to incur "good citizenship" costs in the host countries, and still remain competitive with non-integrated firms. Some companies had a policy of full employment, balanced internal trade among countries, and performance of R&D in various countries. Such a policy may lead to less than optimal decisions, in a short-term financial sense, as it has some opportunity costs (for instance, the location of new plants and research centers in countries where a company sells more than it buys, instead of in low wage or low manufacturing cost countries). However, such a policy may also be the key to host countries' long-term

acceptance of companies as leading worldwide corporations.

The benefits of integration not only enable the MNC to be better tolerated thanks to its ability to incur higher good citizenship costs, but integration itself can be seen as making expropriation less likely in developing countries.[8] Integration provides more bargaining power to MNCs for ongoing operations and also makes extreme solutions to conflicts with host governments (such as expropriation) into outcomes where both the host country and the MNC stand to lose.

A well-articulated, worldwide integration strategy also simplifies the management of international operations by providing a point of view on the environment, a framework to identify key sources of uncertainties, and a purpose in dealing with them. The worldwide integration strategy can guide managers in adopting a *proactive* stance. The simplicity of the driving principle of the integration strategy also makes a consistent, detailed strategic planning process possible, as it provides a unifying focus to the various parts of the organization. This process both guides the implementation of strategy and provides for its refinement and evolution over time.

National Responsiveness Strategy

Some companies forgo the potential benefits of integration and give much more leeway to their subsidiaries to respond to the political imperative by having them behave almost as if they were national companies. Yet, the affiliation of subsidiaries to a multinational company can bring them four distinct advantages over purely national competitors. These advantages are:

1. The pooling of financial risks;

2. The spreading of research and development costs over a larger sales volume (than that of local competitors) without the difficulties involved in licensing transactions;

3. The coordination of export marketing to increase overall success in export markets;

Sloan Management Review   Winter 1980   29

4. The transfer of specific skills between subsidiaries (e.g., process technology or merchandising methods).

In this approach, each subsidiary remains free to pursue an autonomous economic or political strategy nationally as its management sees fit, given the situation of the national industry. In industries where the government plays a key role (nuclear engineering and electrical power, for instance), national strategies are primarily political; in industries where other local factors are important sources of differentiation (e.g., food processing), but where government plays a less prominent role, strategies are economic.[9]

In a nationally responsive MNC, the resources, know-how, or services of the headquarters (or of other subsidiaries) are called upon only when the subsidiary management finds them helpful. Little central influence is exercised on the subsidiaries. The nationally responsive MNC, as a whole, has no strategy, except in a limited sense (Brown Boveri's technical excellence, for instance), and the strategy is usually not binding: subsidiaries follow it only when they see it in their own interest. Manufacturing is usually done on a local-for-local basis, with few intersubsidiary transfers. Coordination of R&D and avoidance of duplications are often difficult, particularly when host governments insist upon R&D being carried on locally on specific projects for which government support is available (new telecommunication technologies or microelectronics, for instance).

Administrative Coordination Strategy
Rejecting both clear-cut strategic solutions to the conflict between the economic and political imperatives offered by worldwide integration and national responsiveness, MNCs can choose to live with the conflict and look for structural and administrative adjustments instead of strategic solutions. Such adjustments are aimed at providing some of the benefits of both worldwide (or regional) integration and national responsiveness.

The strategy (literally) is to have no set strategy, but to let each strategic decision be made on its own merits and to challenge prior commitments. Individual decisions thus do not fit into the logic of clear goals, the reasonableness of which is tested against a comprehensive analysis of the environment and an assessment of the organization's capabilities. Strategy is not the search for an overall optimal fit, but a series of limited adjustments made in response to specific developments, without an attempt to integrate these adjustments into a consistent comprehensive strategy.[10]

The need for such adjustments emerges when new uncertainties are identified. These uncertainties can offer opportunities (e.g., the possibility to invest in a new country) or threats (e.g., the development of new technologies by competitors), or lend themselves to conflicting interpretation (the willingness of a government to grant R&D subsidies, but with some local production requirements). Instead of taking a stable proactive stance vis-à-vis the environment and relying on the chosen strategy to provide a framework within which to deal with sources of uncertainties and to make specific decisions as the need arises, companies using administrative coordination absorb uncertainties and try to resolve conflicts internally each time new uncertainties question prior allocations of strategic resources. In short, strategy becomes unclear, shifting with the perceived importance of changes in the economic or political environment, and it may become dissolved into a set of incremental decisions with a pattern which may make sense only ex *post*. Administrative coordination does not allow strategic planning: we are farther from the "timed sequence of conditional moves" representing the usual goal of strategic planning and much closer to public administration where issues get shaped, defined, attended to, and resolved one at a time in a "muddling through" process that never gives analytical consideration to the full implications of a step.[11]

By adopting such an internally flexible

and negotiable posture, administratively coordinated companies make themselves more accessible to government influence, and become Janus-faced. On certain issues and at certain points in time, a view consistent with worldwide rationalization will prevail, in other cases national responsiveness will prevail, and in many cases some uneasy blend of the two will result. Some of the central control of the subsidiaries so critical in multinational integration is abandoned, making it easier for subsidiaries to cooperate with powerful partners such as government agencies or national companies on specific projects. Because commitments of resources are not all made consistently over time, and as the company is not likely to be very rationalized (given the role accorded to host governments' demands), excess resources are not likely to allow for large costs of good citizenship. In short, compared with multinational integration, *administrative coordination trades off internal efficiency for external flexibility.* Whereas multinational integration seeks to provide the organization with enough economic power for success, administrative coordination seeks to provide the flexibility needed for a constantly adjusted coalignment of the firm with the more powerful factors in the environment and with the most critical sources of uncertainty.[12] Acceptability to host governments derives from flexibility.

The Three Strategies Compared

Both the worldwide (or regional) integration strategy and the national responsiveness strategy correspond to clear tradeoffs between the economic and the political imperatives. Integration demonstrates a clear preference for the economic imperative; the MNC attempts to fully exploit integration's potential for economic performance and shows willingness to incur large citizenship costs in exchange for being allowed to be very different from national companies. Conversely, national responsiveness minimizes the difference between the MNC and national companies, and thus minimizes the acceptability problems. It expresses a clear

sensitivity to the political imperative, at the expense of economic performance. The economic advantages of multinationality are confined to a few domains: financial risks, amortization of R&D costs, export marketing, and skill transfers among the subsidiaries.

Administrative coordination, because it aims at a constantly fluctuating balance between the imperatives, is an ambiguous form of management. There is a constant tension within the organization between the drive for economic success based on clear economic strategy, and the need to consider major uncertainties springing from the political imperative. The following comment, made by a senior manager in an administratively coordinated MNC, illustrates the tension:

> In the long run we risk becoming a collection of inefficient, government-subsidized national companies unable to compete on the world market. Yet, if we rationalize our operations, we lose our preferential access to government R&D contracts and subsidies. So we try to develop an overall strategic plan that makes some competitive sense, and then bargain for each part of it with individual governments, trying to sell them on particular programs that contribute to the plan as a whole. Often we have to revise or abandon parts of our plan for lack of government support.

Markets, Competition, Technology, and Strategy

In thinking about which type of strategy may suit a particular MNC or an individual business within a diversified MNC, it is important to consider the markets being served, the competition being faced, and the technology being used by the firm. The argument will focus on products and industries for which multinational integration pressures are significant, leaving aside products for which national taste differences (food), high bulk to value added ratio (furniture), dependence on perishable products (food), small optimal size (garments and leather goods), or other such factors usually make rationalization unattractive or unfeasible.

Sloan Management Review   Winter 1980   **31**

Market Structure and Competition

The range of possible multinational strategies depends upon the structure of the world market in terms of customers and barriers to trade. First, for some products (such as electrical power systems or telecommunications equipment), the technology and economies of production would very strongly suggest global rationalization, but political imperatives are so strong as to prevent it. The international trade volumes, either captive within MNCs or in toto, for telecommunications equipment or power systems are extremely low.[13] In developed countries theoretically committed to free trade, restrictions come through monopoly market power of government-controlled entities — Post, Telegraph, Telephone (PTT), for instance — or through complex legislation and regulation that create artificial market differentiation. EEC regulations on trucks, officially designed for safety and road degradation reasons, effectively create barriers to entry for importers. In a similar way, inspection regulations for equipment (including the parts and components) purchased by state agencies in many European countries, effectively make it difficult to incorporate imported components into end products sold to the state.

In developing countries, market access restrictions are more straightforward. Under such conditions of restricted trade and controlled market access, worldwide strategic integration is obviously difficult. Often, the very nature of the goods, their strategic importance, as well as characteristics such as bulky, massive equipment produced in small volumes for a few large customers, reinforce the desire on the part of governments to control suppliers closely.[14]

Second, at another extreme, there are some goods that are traded quite freely, whose sales do not depend on location of manufacture or nationality of the manufacturer, and for which economies of scale beyond the size of national markets are significant. In such industries the only viable strategy is worldwide (or regional) integration. This is the strategy followed by all volume car man-

ufacturers in Europe, led by Ford and General Motors but also including such national champions as Fiat, Renault, or Volkswagen. Smaller companies are adopting a specialization strategy by moving out of the price-sensitive volume market and serving the world market from a single location (BMW, Daimler Benz).

Third, and most interesting, are businesses (such as computers or semiconductors) whose markets are partly government-controlled and partly internationally competitive. In such businesses the market is split between customers who select their suppliers on economic grounds and customers that are state-owned or state-influenced and evidence strong preference for some control over their suppliers. Products, such as computers or integrated circuits, are of sufficient strategic and economic importance for host governments to try to have some control over their technology and their production.[15] In such industries governments try to restrict the strategic freedom of all multinationals and show great willingness to reward flexibility. Honeywell, for instance, was liberally rewarded for agreeing to create a joint venture between its French subsidiary and Compagnie Internationale pour l'Informatique, the ailing leader of the French computer industry. In addition to favored access to the French state-controlled markets, the joint venture received substantial grants and research contracts.

In these industries where both the economic and political imperatives are critical, multinationals face the most difficult choice between various possible strategies. Some companies may choose to integrate their operations multinationally, and some may choose to decentralize their operations to better match the demands of individual governments and benefit from their support and assistance. Still others may not make a clear strategic commitment and may instead resort to administrative coordination.

Yet, this choice is likely to look significantly different to various MNCs according to their competitive posture within their industry. In broad terms, firms *with the largest overall shares of the world market are likely to find integration more desirable.* There are several reasons for this choice.

Benefits of Integration. First, still assuming that there are unexploited economies of scale, large firms can achieve lower costs through integration than can smaller firms. The company with the largest overall share of the world market can become the low cost producer in an industry by integrating its operations, thus making life difficult for smaller competitors. Conversely, smaller firms (with significant market shares in only a few countries) can remain cost competitive so long as larger competitors do not move to regional or worldwide integration. Firms that integrate across boundaries in a market that is partly price competitive and partly government-controlled, can expect to gain a larger share of the price competitive market and confine smaller competitors to segments protected by governments that value flexibility and control more than lower prices.[16]

Influence. Second, one can hypothesize that larger firms can have more influence on their environment than smaller ones, and thus find it more suitable to centralize strategic decision making and ignore some of the uncertainty and variety in the environment.[17] In particular, larger firms can take a tougher stance vis-à-vis individual governments when needed, and woo them with higher costs of good citizenship. How much integrated firms may be willing to give to host governments as costs of citizenship to maintain strategic integration may vary substantially. One can argue that a leading integrated firm in a partly government-controlled market with no comparable direct competitor (IBM, for instance), may be willing to provide a lot to host countries in order to maintain its integration. Conversely, when keen worldwide competition takes place among integrated companies of comparable strength (e.g., Texas Instruments, Motorola, and Fairchild), the economic imperative becomes much more demanding for each of them, and none may be willing to be

accommodating for fear that the others would not match such behavior. In short, the following proposition can be made: *the more one integrated firm is submitted to direct competition from other integrated companies, the less it will be willing to provide host governments, except in exchange for profitable nonmatchable moves.*

The implications of this proposition in terms of public policy toward industry structure are significant. At the regional or worldwide level it raises the issue of whether to encourage competition, or to favor the emergence of a single integrated leading MNC and then bargain with that company on the sharing of revenues. Similarly, a significant industrial policy issue at the national level is whether to encourage competition, or to provide a single multinational with the opportunity for a profitable nonmatchable move.[18]

Conversely, smaller firms (such as Honeywell in comparison with IBM) could draw only lesser benefits from rationalization and had to be extremely flexible in dealing with the uncertainties represented by host governments. Thus, *smaller firms are likely to find administrative coordination more suitable and will enlist host governments' support and subsidies to compete against leading MNCs.* Market access protection, financial assistance, or both can be the only way for these smaller firms — multinational or not — to keep a semblance of competitiveness. In the same way that firms in competitive markets can differentiate their products (or even their strategy) to avoid competing head on against larger firms, firms in these markets under partial government control differentiate their strategy by trading off central control over their strategy for government protection. The willingness of governments to trade off economic efficiency for some amount of political control, as well as the importance of short-term social issues (chiefly employment protection) make such strategic differentiation possible.[19]

For smaller MNCs such differentiation usually involves forgoing integration and letting host governments gain a say in strategic decisions affecting the various subsidiaries. Yet, because the MNC still attempts to maintain some competitiveness in market segments not protected by governments, it is likely to find administrative coordination — despite the ambiguity and managerial difficulty it involves — the least evil.

Finally, national companies can attempt to achieve some economies of scale through interfirm agreements for the joint manufacture of particular components (car engines) or product lines (Airbus A300). Over time, national companies can move to develop a globally integrated system. A case in point is Volkswagen, whose U.S.-assembled "Rabbits" incorporate parts from Brazil, Germany, and Mexico. Where free trade prevails among developed countries, as in the automobile industry, this may be the only suitable strategy for national companies.

In summary, one can hypothesize a relationship between the extent of government control over (and limits to) international trade in an industry, the relative international market share of a firm active in that industry, and the type of strategy it adopts. In industries where free trade prevails, all competitors are expected to have to follow a worldwide (or regional) integration strategy. In industries in which governments take a keen interest, but where they control the markets only partly, and where formal free trade prevails (computers, for instance), all three strategies are likely to coexist within an industry. Finally, in industries where the political imperatives prevail and whose markets are mostly state-controlled, all competitors can be expected to adopt a national responsiveness strategy.

Data supporting the relationship summarized above are presented graphically in Figure 1. It shows the results of the in-depth study of six industries where the economic and the political imperatives strongly conflict. However, one word of caution is necessary here: the patterns shown can only represent the *preferred* strategy of a company. Most companies will have deviant subsidiaries, because within a given indus-

try trade restrictions vary among countries. The figure was built from data in Western Europe, and assumes that in a given industry, trade restrictions are about the same for all countries. That may be approximately true within Western Europe, but is obviously false in other regions. For instance, Ford's European operations achieve integration at the regional level; Ford's other international subsidiaries are much more nationally responsive and often isolated by tough local content restrictions (for instance, in Latin America). In passing, it may be hypothesized that companies with substantial operations in numerous countries (within the same industry) break them up into regional management units when they face wide differences in the conditions of trade among the regions. Obviously, the value added of products with respect to their weight or bulk also plays a role in limiting worldwide integration in a few industries where the value added per unit of weight is very high, and economies of scale and/or factor cost differences among regions are substantial (e.g., microelectronics).

Technology

Technology is usually seen as an important variable in the interface between MNCs and host governments. The introduction by MNCs of many innovative high technology products and the high market shares they still enjoy in their sales create much tension with host governments. Major industries, such as computers, microelectronics, or aerospace, remain dominated by U.S. multinationals. In tensions between economic and political imperatives within an industry, technology then plays a key role. MNCs that control the technology of specific industries have more power in bargaining with governments and also create technology barriers to competition from national firms. Often the minimal scale requirements increase so rapidly in high technology industries as to make it almost impossible for national firms to catch up.[20]

Figure 1 Customers, Market Shares, and Multinational Strategies

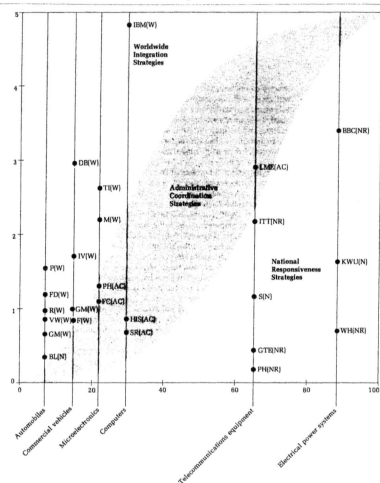

Relative market share (8 firms included) of MNCs in Western Europe

Worldwide Integration Strategies

Administrative Coordination Strategies

National Responsiveness Strategies

IBM(W)
BBC(NR)
DB(W)
LME(AC)
TI(W)
M(W)
ITT(NR)
IV(W)
KWU(N)
P(W)
PH(AC)
FD(W)
FC(AC)
S(N)
R(W) GM(W)
VW(W) F(W)
HIS(AC)
GM(W)
SR(AC)
WH(NR)
BL(N)
GTE(NR)
PH(NR)

Industries ranked by percentage of sales to government-controlled customers

Automobiles
Commercial vehicles
Microelectronics
Computers
Telecommunications equipment
Electrical power systems

Legend:

1. Types of Strategies are indicated next to company initials:

W: Worldwide (or regional) integration
AC: Administrative coordination
NR: National responsiveness
N: National company

2. Company Names are represented by initials:

P	= Peugeot S.A.	M	= Motorola	ITT = International
FD	= Ford of Europe	PH	= Philips	Telegraph &
R	= Renault	FC	= Fairchild	Telephone
VW	= Volkswagen	IBM	= International	S = Siemens
GM	= General Motors		Business	GTE = General
BL	= British Leyland		Machines	Telephone &
DB	= Daimler Benz	HIS	= Honeywell	Electronics
IV	= IVECO		Information	BBC = Brown Boveri
F	= Ford		Systems	KWU = Kraftwerk Union
TI	= Texas	SR	= Sperry Rand	WH = Westinghouse
	Instruments	LME	= LM Ericsson	

Sloan Management Review   Winter 1980   35

Technology, Trade, and Strategic Integration. Higher technology products are likely to correspond to freer trade. First, there is ample evidence that MNCs most often introduce their innovations in their home markets first.[21] So long as the new technology is not adopted by many countries, freer trade is likely to prevail for newer products than for older ones. Second, during the technology diffusion process within the MNC, the need to transfer the new technology quickly to subsidiaries creates pressures to increase coordination among them. Companies thus find it more desirable and easier to integrate regionally or to tilt their administrative coordination toward more integration. In terms of the graphics of Figure 1, a new higher technology can be represented by a move to the left. The move can affect a given industry as a whole if the technology is available to all MNCs but not to any national company, or more likely the move can be firm-specific.

In the study of the telecommunications industry, both moves were found. First, the shift to electronic switching and digital coding led the industry as a whole to be characterized by freer trade and by the opening of markets to new suppliers, as the various national PTTs were deciding upon their first orders for new equipment in the 1970s. Second, within the industry, LM Ericsson has always tried to be "one step ahead" of its competitors in technology, and to run its operations in a more integrated way than its competition. Conversely, ITT has most often been a technology follower, but let its subsidiaries be quite responsive to the demands of their host governments. It can be hypothesized that, *within an industry where the political imperatives are significant, higher technology firms (relative to their competitors) strive for integration, and can achieve some measure of it, and lower technology firms (relative to their competitors) strive for national responsiveness.*

Technology, Scale, and Government Intervention. It is also important to recognize that technological evolution can increase the minimal efficient scale of an industry and call to question the viability of national responsiveness. Even where restricted trade prevails, as the efficient scale increases in a high technology industry, pressures grow for domestic mergers and rationalization. Where multinational and national firms compete, the multinationals are unlikely to be the winners in a merger drive. Government interest is likely to prompt mergers into the "national champion" rather than to let the national industry be entirely controlled from outside. A national responsiveness strategy, i.e., a rather autonomous national subsidiary, makes such mergers into a national champion easier for the government to implement.

The examples of the French electrical power industry and telecommunications equipment in France and Great Britain tend to confirm the above analysis. In the case of electrical power systems, the transition from fossil fuel boilers to nuclear steam supply not only led to higher minimal efficient scale in the manufacture of turbogenerators, but also increased the interests of host governments in the industry. Two distinct effects were thus combined: minimal size increase and governments' greater interest in the technology itself.[22]

The Influence of Technology. This leaves us with less than a full understanding of the role of technology in the interface between MNCs and host governments in developed countries. On the one hand, for a given industry, a move to higher technology and new products can permit a firm (or all firms in an industry if they have access to the new technology) to be more multinationally integrated and centrally managed than it would otherwise be. There is some unclear causal relationship here, as integration is made possible by higher technology but is also required to facilitate technology transfer within the MNC.[23] On the other hand, it seems that very high technologies become extremely important in developed countries and prompt governments to try to narrowly control their development and use. Also, the move to higher technology often results in larger minimal efficient scale. This scale can be used by integrated multinationals to defend their market shares and attack smaller or less integrated firms, e.g., in microelectronics. In industries where trade is restricted, the government's usual responses are mergers into an emerging "national champion" first, and development of multinational government-sponsored programs second.

In both cases multinationals do not stand to benefit. This was clearly the case in electrical power systems. Telecommunications equipment was more ambiguous. Some countries were moving toward national consolidation (Brazil, France, the UK), and in others new electronic technology resulted in more open markets (Australia, South Africa, Spain, and several small European countries). Electronic technologies obviously increased the importance of the industry, yet provided opportunities to more integrated firms (e.g., LM Ericsson) or national firms with a distinctive technology (e.g., CIT Alcatel). When technology increases both the pressures to integrate within the industry and the interest governments take in the industry, either integration within MNCs across boundaries or integration within a country through government-directed mergers can prevail.

Managerial Implications

In practice, it is important to an MNC, or to executives running individual businesses in diversified multinationals, to recognize those changes in market openness, industry structure, and technology of an industry that foreshadow a need to change the overall strategy. Two simple examples are illuminating. Until the mid-1970s, General Motors ran its international operations as a collection of nationally responsive autonomous subsidiaries. With the globalization of the industry and the rationalization and integration of key competitors (mainly Ford), this posture became untenable. The strongest of the subsidiaries, Adam Opel in Germany, was able to hold its own in

Europe, competing as a national company. But other subsidiaries, particularly Vauxhall in the U.K., were severely hurt. In 1975, General Motors started to bring the various subsidiaries together more closely through a series of administrative changes. By 1978, these moves resulted in an administrative coordination approach where numerous contradictions and ambiguities emerged. GM Overseas Operations' top management considered such administrative coordination as a transitional stage toward global integration. Many GMOO managers, however, felt that contradictions between the lingering desire for national subsidiaries' responsiveness and the emerging worldwide integration needs would not be easily resolved. In any case, the company had missed several precious years and had to struggle hard to remain competitive in Europe.

Conversely, in the late 1960s, Westinghouse was looking for acquisitions in the European electrical power system industry. It hoped to expand its business in Europe quickly, thanks to its light water nuclear reactor technology that was emerging as a clear technological winner over indigenous European technologies. To "better" manage its European operations, Westinghouse moved to a worldwide product group structure, aiming at multinational integration. At the same time, as we have seen, the increased minimal scale of the industry, the strategic importance of nuclear-related technologies, and the failure of Europe's own efforts in commercial reactors all combined to increase government sensitiveness about the industry. The discrepancy between the national responsiveness demanded by governments and what Westinghouse appeared willing to provide resulted in tensions in Belgium, France, and Germany, a substantial scale-down of Westinghouse's European expansion plans, and a shift in its strategy. In 1975, a former president of Westinghouse's Power Group commented to the author: "Our basic policy (for nuclear engineering and power plants sales) is to do it in whatever way a country would require." Yet, Westinghouse had probably lost the one

Sloan Management Review   Winter 1980   37

opportunity to become a lasting factor in the European power system industry.

Choice of Strategy and Management Process

We have seen that both worldwide (or regional) integration and national responsiveness lead to relatively straightforward management processes that are grounded in a clear strategy and a clear-cut delineation of headquarters' and subsidiaries' roles and responsibilities. Yet, the relative managerial simplicity both these strategies offer has an opportunity cost: it makes specific adjustment to the varying demands of governments difficult, and may prevent the company from entering certain businesses or certain countries. Such limitations make administrative coordination attractive as a way to increase the MNC's flexibility in finding balances between the economic and the political imperatives that match more closely the specific conditions of a given business in a given country. It is important to recognize that both worldwide integration and national responsiveness almost represent ideal polar opposites. Some MNCs are likely not to wish (or be able) to exercise a clear choice, and thus find themselves improvising compromises through some process of administrative coordination.

In particular, when the political imperative is significant, its very nature makes clear-cut analytical choices impossible. Contrary to the economic imperative, information on the political imperative is most often indirect and not controllable centrally. When a subsidiary manager claims that his plans rest on the word of local intermediaries or on his relationships with national government officials, it is difficult, at best, for managers at headquarters to determine the soundness of his assumptions. The fact that the government's public logic is often quite different from the reality of the situation and from actual policy-making processes, makes it even more difficult for corporate or regional managers to under-

stand the situation. As a result, top management's inability to reach an analytical choice on decisions involving the political imperative leads to adaptive coalitional decision making in which the firm internalizes tensions and uncertainties and tries to incorporate them into its decision-making process.

Decision Processes and Administrative Coordination

On any particular strategic decision, the company is trying to reach a satisfactory compromise given past decisions and past commitments of resources. Decisions cannot be left to either the subsidiary or the regional (or global) headquarters levels. They have to be reached by some group that collectively captures contradictions in the environment, internalizes them, and resolves them through contention, coalition, and consensus. Individual managers, representing different interests within the company and approaching questions from different points of view, are left to take sides on decisions according to how they perceive problems and how they prefer to deal with sources of uncertainty. In short, the question of deciding "what is right" becomes linked to that of "who is right" and "whose views are favored." Top management, instead of providing the inspiration for a strategic design and managing its implementation, shifts to a new role of deciding how to make decisions: who should be represented, with which voice, on which decisions. Top management can also provide some limits: would such decisions represent too wide a departure from the usual to be accepted? Choices on how to reach decisions can still be guided by a sense of which decisions, or which classes of decisions, should be made with integration as a priority, and which should be made with responsiveness as a priority. The way to convey such sense of priority is not to decide in substance on specific decisions (except when irreconcilable conflicts occur) but to act on the way in which decisions are made, to influence the making and undoing of specific coalitions or to help the shift of coalitions among decisions.

Managing Dependencies

How can top management achieve such influence? Primarily by keeping control of dependencies between subunits competing for power and by regulating the game they pursue. Strategic and operational dependencies can be used to determine who, in the long run, has power over which class of decisions or what functions. For instance, the subsidiaries can be made dependent on the corporate headquarters or on domestic product divisions for key components or for process technology. Conversely, the domestic divisions can be dependent on subsidiaries for export sales. A central difficulty of this approach is the divisiveness introduced within the company by managing dependencies through arm's-length power relationships. Top management also has to develop some integrative forces (for instance, through training, career paths, and compensation) to balance these divisive forces and preserve some sense of corporate identity and loyalty.

Over the long run, successful administrative coordination thus hinges on the maintenance of a balance between divisive and integrative forces that reflects a structure of dependencies among subunits. Careful control of the dependencies between national subsidiary managers, and product unit managers through the use of functional managers and administrative managers, was found to provide top management tools for maintaining such a balance.

Functional Managers. The substantive expertise of functional managers is needed by supporters of multinational integration as well as by supporters of national responsiveness. Managers preferring multinational integration still depend upon functional managers and "the field" (in various countries) to achieve such integration. Conversely, national managers depend on support from functional and administrative headquarters staff and product divisions

even though they try to pursue national responsiveness strategies. Because the power of functional managers is based on needed expertise, they may preserve a relatively uncommitted posture between multinational integration and national responsiveness.

Yet functional managers, over time, can develop a functional logic that is aligned to either national responsiveness or worldwide integration. Manufacturing staffs, for instance, can develop a logic that calls for integration and rationalization or for flexible local plants serving separate national markets. Within each function, of course, further distinctions can develop. For instance, rationalized component plants and local-for-local end-product plants can be favored, or distribution channels can be perceived as very different, whereas similar advertising can be used. By influencing corporate functional managers directly in the development of their preference for integration or responsiveness, and by then bringing them to throw their weight to particular issues and not to others, top management can develop a repertoire of intervention methods on the making of particular decisions.

Administrative Managers. Administrative procedures and the managers in charge of them can also be used by top management to maintain the tension between integration and responsiveness. To begin with, the formal structure usually provides a dominant orientation. Even when this structure is a matrix, it is usually complemented by fairly elaborate administrative procedures and guidelines that provide a dominant orientation by defining who is responsible for what and whether it is a primary or a secondary responsibility. Various devices, such as committees and task forces that cut across the formal structure, can be used to bring about changes in perception or to reach actual decisions. Planning processes can also be designed so that integration and responsiveness are considered. For instance, a contention process can exist between subsidiaries and product divisions (e.g., LM Ericsson). Interestingly, IBM had such a sys-

Sloan Management Review   Winter 1980   39

tem very formalized and well developed among its regions and product groups, and between them and corporate functional staffs. Measurement systems can be set so that managers will see it as their duty to call to top management's attention "excessive" integration, autonomy, or responsiveness (e.g., GTE[24] or GM). Personal reward and punishment systems may be designed to reinforce tensions or ease them according to the measurement criteria and yardsticks used. Management of career paths can also be used to provide multiple views and facilitate coordination.

Administrative staff managers, and the way they design and run their administrative systems, provide top management with the same type of leverage as functional managers. One can expect the controller to strive for uniformity of accounting practices and comparability of results worldwide, opposing differentiation between subsidiaries. Personnel management, on the other hand, can either favor uniformity of pay scales and benefits worldwide, or leave this decision to subsidiaries. The way in which the administrative function develops its own operating paradigm[25] can be managed so that its specific procedures support responsiveness or integration.

Dangers of Administrative Coordination

Even with the potential offered by functional and administrative managers for managing administrative coordination effectively, certain drawbacks are inescapable. In particular, administrative coordination may lead to strategic paralysis, fragmentation, or bureaucratization.

Strategic Paralysis. The willingness to respond to environmental changes when the environment is intrinsically ambiguous and contradictory is likely to lead to strategic paralysis. Students of ambiguous situations where several environments are relevant to decisions have stressed the danger of paralysis created by giving relatively equal power to managers most sensitive to different aspects of the environment.[26] Not using a

stable pattern of resource commitment over time, according to spelled out goals, may lead to considerable waste and overall failure. It is fascinating to see that, in an environment where IBM is a strong leader, the agreements on the merger between C2I and Honeywell Bull in France spelled out a substantive strategy to avoid the risk of strategic paralysis. On the other hand, one could draw numerous examples of strategic paralysis from very refined, stable administrative coordination processes.[27]

Strategic Fragmentation. Administrative coordination involves the use of dependencies and the management of power, which create divisive forces. In the absence of a strategic design, the management groups' loyalty must be maintained lest managers' frustrations lead to increasingly disjointed and partial decisions and to fragmentation. Cultural identity is often a means to circumvent these divisive forces. For instance, all top managers at LM Ericsson come from the same Stockholm telecommunications engineering school; the whole top management of Philips remains Dutch and has gone through the same formative experiences. Similarly, strong cultural identity facilitates the foreign expansion of Japanese companies.

Bureaucratization. Managers faced with very uncertain situations and power relationships may be tempted to reduce their perceived uncertainties. By developing bureaucratic procedure to cope with uncertainties, managers will gain power for themselves. Bureaucratic procedure also creates uncertainties for other members of the organization.[28] This leads to bureaucratization and lack of sensitivity to the outside environment. More time is spent on infighting than on external action.

Even assuming that administrative coordination does not lead to strategic paralysis, fragmentation, or bureaucracy, it remains an expensive way to run a business. The internal management process, with its multiple negotiations and complex coalitional processes, consumes much managerial energy and time, and can slow down decision processes considerably. It can also lead to "horse trading" and more suboptimal decisions than would be warranted by the situation at hand.

Should administrative coordination be avoided wherever possible, then? The answer is probably yes, but with the qualifications developed in the first part of this article. When free trade prevails and competitors follow a worldwide integration strategy, a clear choice should be made between committing enough resources to a business and divestment. In industries where governments evince interest, administrative coordination seems, at best, to be a way for the weaker, smaller international companies to stay in certain industries (Honeywell in data processing, Philips in integrated circuits). In industries where trade is restricted, the alternative is between national responsiveness and administrative coordination. For technology leaders within their industry, administrative coordination makes sense, as it can possibly provide for easier technology transfer, and host governments can accept such coordination as a price for receiving the technology.

Strategy in the Diversified Multinational[29]

So long as the several businesses of the multinational rely on the same strategy, the overall corporate management task is not greatly complicated by business diversity. Texas Instruments uses one extreme posture which applies the same semiconductor business logic and global integration framework across the board to all of its businesses.

Another extreme would be a multinational conglomerate adopting a purely financial approach and letting each business develop its own business logic independently. Yet, in most cases, such simple solutions as that of Texas Instruments or the multinational conglomerate are not applicable: the various

businesses of the diversified multinational straddle several adaptation patterns and are interdependent. This raises the issues of strategic and administrative differentiation among the businesses, and of managing the interdependencies among differentiated businesses.

Differentiation and Interdependencies

Difficulties develop when the various businesses of a multinational straddle several adaptation patterns; some are most suitably managed through global strategic integration, others through administrative coordination, and still others through national responsiveness. It usually happens that, because of a history of dominance in one business, one pattern is preferred and applied across the board. For instance, Brown Boveri was slow to recognize that its industrial businesses, particularly small motors and breakers, would be faced with worldwide competition following the EEC trade liberalization. When competition came, Brown Boveri was even slower to react, because the logic of the whole organization and the energy of top management were geared to success in the government-controlled, restricted trade power system and heavy electrical equipment businesses.

In a similar vein, after World War II, Philips had strong national organizations and weak worldwide product groups coordinating its activities. With freer trade (following the development of the EEC), moves were made to increase the power of product divisions and to foster integration in similar businesses between national organizations. This led to a balanced product-geography-function matrix that faced great difficulties in businesses where administrative coordination did not fit well. Businesses, such as TV picture tubes or standard semiconductors, did not achieve full integration at a regional (color TV) or global (semiconductors) level, and telecommunications equipment did not enjoy sufficient national autonomy to achieve responsiveness comparable to that of competitors.

An obvious response to the difficulties

Sloan Management Review   Winter 1980   **41**

faced by Brown Boveri or Philips is to differentiate the management among product lines, letting each find the appropriate balance between the economic and the political imperatives.

Yet, extensive interdependencies among businesses would usually make this management differentiation difficult. Interdependencies are of several types. They can involve common technologies among several businesses. For instance, magnetic tape technology at Philips served several product groups: data systems, instrumentation, medical products, professional recording, and audio consumer products. Interdependencies can also derive from vertical integration. The bulk of Philips's electronic component production was transferred internally to be incorporated into Philips's end products; still Philips also wanted to compete on the open market for semiconductors. Interdependencies are also market related, with different products sold to the same customers. IBM's Data Processing Complex's and General Business Group's system offerings overlap at the lower end of medium systems and compete against each other for the same orders. Finally, when products are sold to government-controlled customers, interdependencies may become political. Brown Boveri was commonly told: "We are willing to import your power stations, but what about you creating an export-oriented motor plant in one of our depressed areas to generate employment and offset the trade deficit that importing your power stations would create?"

It is important to recognize the difference in nature between internal interdependencies (common technology, joint production, vertical integration) and external ones (same customers, host governments, and so forth). When interdependencies are internal, the choice of how to relate businesses (from pure arm's length to joint administration) can be made by management. When interdependencies are external, such choice is usually imposed by external agents. The terms under which to coordinate component and TV set production could be decided internally in

Philips. However, the Belgian Government's orders for Philips's computers were conditional upon the maintenance of Philips's employment levels in Belgium. The consumer product groups, whose internal interdependencies with the computer group were negligible, but who had high cost factories they wanted to close down in Belgium, suffered from the deal. Allegedly, this problem played some role in Philips's decision to withdraw from the mainframe computer business entirely.

Managing Interdependencies

The central tradeoff in the examples presented above is that between strategic and administrative clarity for individual businesses (i.e., enabling clear choices to be made between worldwide integration and national responsiveness), and the complexity of managing interdependencies.

Developing some clarity usually involves selectivity in the management of interdependencies. It is important to recognize that, within a diversified multinational, the relative importance of various interdependencies may change over time as the "critical factors"[30] in the strategy of a business evolve. ITT was able to revise frequently the formal structure of its European operations to respond to changes in the relative importance of interdependencies. The basic method used by ITT was to organize itself into several product groups worldwide. Each of these was managed somewhat differently: the Automotive Group (auto parts and accessories) and the Microelectronics Group, for instance, were pursuing worldwide integration strongly, whereas the Telecommunications Equipment Group stuck to its national responsiveness strategy. The Business Systems Group pursued regional integration in Europe. Individual businesses could be moved among these groups as warranted by competitive, technological, and government intervention changes. In the mid-1970s, ITT moved the private telephone exchange switching product line from the Telecommunications Equipment Group to the Business Systems Group, where it joined other office equipment. The successful adaptation of electronic switching technology to private exchange and the penetration of the private exchange market by such aggressive, integrated firms as IBM had shifted the key dependency from technology (Telecommunications Equipment Group) to marketing (Business Systems Group). In a similar vein, when ITT adopted worldwide strategic integration for its microelectronics business, it spun off the telecommunication-related components to the Telecommunications Equipment Group. Also ITT decreased the interdependencies between microelectronics and telecommunications in order to achieve a clear strategy for each business.

The development of clarity for Brown Boveri and Philips was more difficult than for ITT. Because they were less widely diversified (most of their products were related), they could not reduce any interdependencies easily. Yet some of their businesses were subject to worldwide product standardization and price competition (for instance, radios at Philips and motors at BBC), and others were more affected by regional or national differences (power systems at BBC, hi-fi at Philips). These different competitive conditions led to divergent strategic directions among businesses.

An approach to interbusiness coordination, under such circumstances, that is being tried by several companies, is the use of corporate functional staff in conjunction with planning committees. At Brown Boveri, corporate marketing staffs coordinated the activities of the various national subsidiaries product line by product line. It was between various members of the corporate marketing staffs that tradeoffs between businesses could be made and the interdependencies could be managed. Assisting the corporate marketing staff in the strategic coordination of each business were several levels of committees. Some of these committees were functional and others were product-oriented. Functional committees could coordinate certain types of interdependencies among technologies and markets of several product

groups. Other committees regrouped product division managers of the different subsidiaries and were in charge of managing the regional integration/national responsiveness tradeoffs. Unfortunately, the committees often lacked the consensus necessary for action, as each member adopted a parochial view.

Faced with similar problems, IBM gave operating units the right to formally take issue with the plans of other operating units ("nonconcurrence" in IBM's internal language) that would impact their activities adversely. Through this approach IBM was able to force subunits to consider interdependencies in their planning and budgeting process and to reach a joint solution before their plans could be approved. Top management could also take the initiative of presenting key strategic issues that would require coordination between subunits as "focus issues" to be dealt with explicitly in the planning process.[31] Other companies also sometimes pulled key interdependencies of great strategic importance out of the regular structure: Brown Boveri, for instance, established a separate nuclear policy committee with the task of managing all interdependencies relating to nuclear energy.

Despite the efforts described above, the management of interdependencies raises difficult issues. Because costs and benefits of interdependencies lend themselves to ambiguous conflicting interpretations, interdependencies provide a rich arena for power plays and coalition bargaining. While particular coalition configurations seem endless in their variety, they add to the task of strategic management. Furthermore, coalitions often involve external agents. For instance, individual managers can rely on their government to establish linkages among product groups. It is not uncommon for alliances to develop, at least tacitly, between host governments and subsidiaries to decrease the dependence of the subsidiary on headquarters and to develop "binding" commitments with the government.

Faced with such difficulties, the MNC corporate management level is likely to strive

Sloan Management Review   Winter 1980   43

for administrative uniformity across businesses. Yet, unless all businesses can be successful with the same strategic logic, some degree of differentiation between businesses remains necessary. In short, uniformity is impossible when businesses straddle several adaptation patterns. Uniformity is possible on some aspects (financial reporting and measurement at ITT, for instance), provided that great leeway for differentiation is left to other aspects. Yet, to avoid cognitive overload at the corporate management level, there are strong pressures toward administrative uniformity, thus making the substance of decisions at the business unit level accessible to the corporate level in a common format. Such administrative pressure for uniformity may prevent the appropriate strategic differentiation among businesses and the development of strategic clarity. These necessary strategic and administrative differentiations suggest that it is usually not possible to maintain unitary corporate office dealing with the substance of decisions. Similarly, a diversified multinational needs (beyond the divisionalized form) a corporate office that only manages selected aspects of the operations and influences decision processes while leaving room for differentiation among businesses — unless all follow the same worldwide integration strategy.

As a concluding note for this section, it may be hypothesized that the complex multinational structures, usually called matrix (or grid) and mixed types, represent an attempt by diversified MNCs to respond to the problems of combining the development of a strategy for each business with the need to manage interdependencies between businesses. Thus, they are not aberrant or transitory structural stages only. Matrix structures correspond to the corporate desire to manage interdependencies among businesses while allowing strategic integration to develop. Mixed structures correspond to a clear differentiation and separation between businesses that follow different adaptation patterns.

Conclusion — Combining Strategic Clarity and Administrative Coordination?

The most difficult tradeoff for the diversified MNC is the one between clarity at the business level (multicountry integration or national responsiveness) and the benefits derived from operating and strategic interdependencies between businesses. The added complexity, compared to domestic diversified companies, of coping with broader environmental variety, makes the management of interdependencies less straightforward and more difficult.

Some simplification can be obtained by limiting and buffering interdependencies. For instance, at LM Ericsson, the national subsidiaries were dependent upon the center for components and technology, but the center could be severed from any subsidiary without great difficulty. Interdependencies between subsidiaries were negligible. Japanese companies usually adopted similar approaches to manage their joint ventures abroad. Philips was treating its semiconductor acquisition in the U.S., Signetics, differently from its European operations, leaving much strategic freedom to the company. So both operating and strategic interdependencies can be structured in such a way as to minimize the need for managing them. There is a tradeoff between the complexity of managing many interdependencies and the joint benefits they bring.

One way companies have tried to order the above tradeoff is to manage simultaneously along several dimensions. For instance, as the Dow Chemical matrix was becoming unbalanced, the operating responsibilities moved toward area executives, thus providing regional integration across vertically interdependent businesses at the area level (Europe, Far East, etc.). Yet, a Corporate Product Department was created with veto power over strategic resource allocation and control over interdependencies between areas.[32] Administrative systems were used by Dow to provide autonomy for regional strategic integration, except for the planning and resource allocation process that was used to check strategic integration and keep the autonomy of areas within bounds.

In an even more discriminating way, IBM's strategic planning process provided for functions, product lines, and areas (or countries) to be managed jointly in a cohesive process. At various stages during the process, inputs and control points were set up so that both the need for integration in relevant units (that differed between functions, businesses, and areas of the world) and the administrative coordination needed between interdependent businesses were recognized, in turn, and conflicts were resolved through a contention process.

ITT was not only letting different businesses develop their own strategies, but also used the various management levels differently. Regional headquarters controlled product and business strategies, but their weight, compared to that of national subsidiary managers, varied considerably from one business to another. The overall planning process was managed from worldwide product group headquarters in New York. Finally, measurement, control, and evaluation were corporate level responsibilities.

More research is needed to conceptualize adequately the responses of these companies. However, these companies illustrate very sophisticated methods for providing both strategic integration and administrative coordination according to the needs for strategic focus and operating or strategic interdependencies between subunits.

References

1
See, for instance, L. G. Franko, *The European Multinationals* (Stamford, CT: Greylock, Inc., 1976).

2
See, for instance:
J. Dunning and M. Gilman, "Alternative Policy Prescriptions," in *The Multinational Enterprise in a Hostile World*, ed. Curzon and Curzon (London: Macmillan & Co., 1977);

R. Vernon, *Storm over the Multinationals* (Cambridge, MA: Harvard University Press, 1977);
R. Vernon, *Sovereignty at Bay* (New York: Basic Books, 1971).

3
See, for instance, C. Stoffaes, *La Grande Menace Industrielle* (Paris: Calmann-Levy, 1977).

4
Some authors have opposed worldwide and regional management within MNCs. See J. M. Stopford and L. T. Wells, Jr., *Managing the Multinational Enterprise* (New York: Basic Books, 1972).
The evidence in the companies studied suggests that in either case a business strategy responding to the economic imperative underlies regional or worldwide management. Which strategy is preferred in a particular company depends upon cost analysis based primarily on difference in factor costs, freight rates, and barriers to trade between various countries and regions of the world. In terms of responsiveness to individual country policies, there is little difference between regional and worldwide management. See L. G. Franko, *Joint Venture Survival in Multinational Corporations* (New York: Praeger, 1972).

5
See Y. Doz, "Managing Manufacturing Rationalization within Multinational Companies," *Columbia Journal of World Business*, Fall 1978.

6
See R. Vernon, "The Location of Economic Activity," in *Economic Analysis and the Multinational Corporation*, ed. Dunning (London: Allen and Unwin, 1974).

7
Ford's costs are estimated by the author from various industry interviews. For many product families, experience curve models suggested unit cost levels in smaller European firms equal to several times the costs in such firms as Texas Instruments for integrated circuits or Motorola for discrete semiconductors. Exact figures are not public, but their significance can be deduced from the Boston Consulting Group and Mackintosh publications. Large losses among European national semiconductor companies and private communications about losses in Philips's or Siemens's semiconductor businesses support the same point. See P. Gadonneix, "Le Plan Calcul" (DBA diss., Harvard Business School, 1974).

8
See:
D. G. Bradley, "Managing against Expropriation," *Harvard Business Review*, July-August 1977, pp. 75–83;
B. D. Wilson, "The Disinvestment of Foreign Subsidiaries by U.S. Multinational Companies" (DBA diss., Harvard Business School, 1979).

9

For political strategies, see:
J. Zysman, *Political Strategies for Industrial Order*
(Berkeley, CA: University of California Press, 1976);
Y. Doz, *Government Control and Multinational*
Strategic Management (New York: Praeger, 1979).
For economic strategies, see U. Wiechmann,
"Integrating Multinational Marketing Activities,"
Columbia Journal of World Business, Winter 1974.
Wiechmann studied intensively the food and beverage
industries.

10

For a comprehensive treatment of strategy as an optimal
fit between environmental opportunities and threats
and the organizational strengths and weaknesses
(consistent with the personal values of top management
and the social responsibilities of the corporation), see:
K. R. Andrews, *The Concept of Corporate Strategy*
(Homewood, IL: Dow Jones Irwin, 1971);
D. Braybrooke and C. E. Lindblom, *A Strategy of*
Decision (New York: The Free Press, 1963).

11

On strategic planning, see, for example:
G. A. Steiner, *Top Management Planning* (New York:
Macmillan, 1966);
H. I. Ansoff, *Corporate Strategy* (New York:
McGraw-Hill, 1965);
P. Lorange and R. F. Vancil, eds., *Strategic Planning*
Systems (Englewood Cliffs, NJ: Prentice-Hall, 1977).
On "muddling through," see:
Braybrooke and Lindblom (1963);
R. Cyert and J. March, *A Behavioral Theory of the Firm*
(Englewood Cliffs, NJ: Prentice-Hall, 1963);
J. D. Steinbruner, *The Cybernetic Theory of Decision*
(Princeton: Princeton University Press, 1974).

12

For instance, see S. M. Davis and P. R. Lawrence, *Matrix*
(Reading, MA: Addison-Wesley, 1977).

13

See:
N. Jéquier, *Les Télécommunications et l'Europe*
(Geneva: Centre d'Etudes Industrielles, 1976);
J. Surrey, *World Market for Electric Power Equipment*
(Brighton, England: SPRI, University of Sussex, 1972).

14

See O. Williamson, *Markets and Hierarchies: Analysis*
and Antitrust Implications (New York: The Free Press,
1975).

15

See:
Y. S. Hu, *The Impact of U.S. Investment in Europe* (New
York: Praeger, 1973);
N. Jéquier, "Computers," in *Big Business and the State*,
ed. R. Vernon (Cambridge, MA: Harvard University
Press, 1974).

16

There is ample evidence of this phenomenon in the
computer and microelectronics industries. See:
E. Sciberras, *Multinational Electronic Companies and*
National Economic Policies (Greenwich, CT: JAI Press,
1977);
"International Business Machines: Can the Europeans
Ever Compete?" *Multinational Business*, 1973, pp.
37–46.

17

For a discussion of strategic decision making and
environmental uncertainty, see E. Rhenman,
Organization Theory for Long-Range Planning (New
York: John Wiley & Sons, 1973).

18

See F. T. Knickerbocker, *Oligopolistic Reaction and*
Multinational Enterprise (Boston: Harvard Business
School Division of Research, 1973).

19

For a discussion of strategic differentiation and
competition in a domestic oligopoly, see R. Caves and
M. Porter, "From Barrier to Entry to Barrier to Mobility,"
Quarterly Journal of Economics, May 1977.

20

For instance, see Vernon (1977), chap. 3.
The evolution of industries such as nuclear power or
aerospace is revealing. As the technology for a given
product (e.g., light water nuclear reactors or bypass
turbofan jet engines) becomes more widespread, the
bargaining power of MNCs is eroded. See H. R. Nau,
National Politics and International Technology
(Baltimore, MD: Johns Hopkins University Press, 1974);
For lesser developed countries, see N. Fagre and L. T.
Wells, "Bargaining Power of Multinationals and Host
Governments" (Mimeo, 14 July 1978);
On increasing economies of scale, for instance, see M. S.
Hochmuth, "Aerospace," in *Big Business and the State*,
ed. R. Vernon (Cambridge, MA: Harvard University
Press, 1974).

21

Innovations in mature products are an occasional
exception. They are sometimes introduced in the most
competitive market. For instance, Sony introduced
several innovations in the U.S. before introducing them
in Japan. Yet many other Sony innovations were first
introduced in Japan. For a summary, see Vernon (1977),
chap. 3.

22

See Doz (1979).
For recent evidence, see "ITT Fights U.K. Bid for
Plessey Control of STC," *Electronic News*, 23 October
1978, p. 4.
On electrical power, see:
B. Epstein, *The Politics of Trade in Power Plants*
(London: The Atlantic Trade Center, 1972);

The author is indebted to
the Associates and the
Division of Research of
the Harvard Business
School for providing
support for the research
on which this article is
based. The author is most
grateful to Joseph L.
Bower and C. K. Prahalad
for their encouragement,
insights, and suggestions.
The ideas presented in
this article are drawn from
a book in preparation,
*Multinational Strategic
Management: Economic
and Political Imperatives.*

Central Policy Review Staff, *The Future of the United
Kingdom Power Plant Manufacturing Industry* (London:
Her Majesty's Stationery Office, 1976);
Commission des Communautés Européenes, *Situation
et Perspective des Industries des Gros Equipements
Electromécaniques et Nucléaires liés à la Production
d'Energie de la Communauté* (Brussels: CEE, 1976).
For related data on the U.S., see I. Bupp, Jr. and J. C.
Derian, *Light Water: How the Nuclear Dream Dissolved*
(New York: Basic Books, 1978).

23
See J. Behrman and H. Wallender, *Transfers of
Manufacturing Technology within Multinational
Enterprises* (Cambridge, MA: Ballinger, 1976).

24
For a detailed analysis of GTE and LM Ericsson's
administrative mechanisms, see Doz (1979).

25
Used here in the sense given by Steinbruner (1974), as
the simplifying logic used by a particular function to
reduce complexity in its environment by focusing on a
few key parameters and taking cybernetic decisions
based on them.

26
See:
Davis and Lawrence (1977);
C. K. Prahalad, "The Strategic Process in a
Multinational Company" (D.B.A. diss., Harvard
Business School, 1975).

27
See C. K. Prahalad and Y. Doz. "Strategic Change in the
Multidimensional Organization" (Harvard Business

School-University of Michigan Working Paper, October
1979).

28
See:
M. Crozier, *The Bureaucratic Phenomenon* (Chicago:
University of Chicago Press, 1964);
D. J. Hickson et al., "A Strategic Contingencies' Theory of
Intraorganizational Power," *Administrative Science
Quarterly* 2 (1971): 216–229.

29
This section draws upon Y. Doz and C. K. Prahalad,
"Strategic Management in Diversified Multinationals,"
in *Functioning of the Multinational Corporation in the
Global Context*, ed. A. Negandhi (New York: Pergamon
Press, forthcoming).

30
Taken here in the sense of Barnard's "strategic factors"
or Selznick's "critical factor."
See:
C. L. Barnard, *The Functions of the Executive*
(Cambridge, MA: Harvard University Press, 1938);
P. Selznick, *Leadership in Administration* (New York:
Harper & Row, 1957).

31
See A. Katz, "Planning in the IBM Corporation" (Paper
submitted to the TIMS-ORSA Strategic Planning
Conference, New Orleans, February 16–17, 1977).

32
See S. M. Davis, "Trends in the Organization of
Multinational Corporations," *Columbia Journal of
World Business*, Summer 1976, pp. 59–71.
Information on Dow Chemical came from the *1976
Annual Report* and the author's interviews.

[18]

The Hypermodern MNC—A Heterarchy?

——— Gunnar Hedlund ———

Commenting upon an early b7-b6 (or, in an alternative notation, PQKn2-Kn3 as black), Aron Nimzowitsch advertised his move as one of "hypermodern daring." The exaggeration contained in the expression served two purposes. It helped selling Nimzowitsch's pathbreaking books on chess strategy. It focused attention on the novelty of his ideas and thus inspired attempts to refute his conclusions.

The present paper is restricted to the second goal. The term "hypermodern MNC" is meant to convey the suspicion that some crucial aspects of developments of and in multinational corporations (MNCs) cannot be grasped by notions in the merely "modern" schools of thought. Even more than in the case of the grandmaster's rallying calls for the "hypermodern school," "my system," etc., the departure from supposedly conventional views is bound to be exaggerated. However, some polarization of issues is desirable in order to arrive at greater conceptual clarity. In addition, it seems that concepts and theories older than present variations on the theme of "global strategy," and sometimes not used by protagonists of the said theme, can usefully be applied.

The other word in the title—heterarchy—is no less problematical. It was used in a recent study by the Stanford Research Institute to describe a shift of perspective in a wide range of sciences. (See also Ogilvy, 1977.) A key idea is that of reality being organized non-hierarchically. A special case is holographic coding where entire systems are represented and, as it were, "known" at each component of the system. (As in a hologram, each part contains information sufficient to reproduce the whole original image, albeit somewhat blurred.)

The concept of heterarchy does not seem to have been used much, if at all, in discussing MNCs. Nor has it inspired more than passing allusions in organization studies in general. Sjöstrand (1985) uses the concept in contrast to hierarchy, but he does not give any definition, nor does the notion figure much in his discussion. The holographic paradigm is encountered more frequently (Mitroff, 1983; El Sawy, 1985). The discussion in Faucheux and Laurent (1980) about integrating others'

Human Resource Management, Spring 1986, Vol. 25, Number 1, Pp. 9–35
CCC 0090-4848/86/010009-27$04.00

roles and vantage point, and about "internalizing the environment" in decision-making in a more indirect way touches on many of the issues brought up below concerning heterarchy. So do contributions on self-referential systems, such as Varela (1975). Also Laurent (1978) discusses the concept of hierarchy.

As the previous discussion indicates, there are no strict definitions to hold on to. As always, consultation of the Oxford English Dictionary gives food for thought. The only direct reference to "heterarchy" gives the meaning "the rule of an alien." This is exactly what heterarchy in the present use of the term is not. This use, as well as SRI's and Ogilvy's, builds on putting "homo," rather than "auto," as the opposite of "hetero." It is not easy to arrive at a simple definition, for example by contradistinction in relation to "hierarchy." The apparent superiority of this latter term as to clarity of meaning derives mostly from the dulling effects of old habits. We have become so accustomed to the concept of hierarchy that we forget exactly what it is that we want to conceive of with it. For example, the etymological meaning of "ruling through the sacred" or "rule of the episcopate" is rather alien to transaction cost analyses of markets and "hierarchies." Certainly it would not make much sense to define heterarchy as non-hierarchy, meaning ruling through the profane. The abstruseness of novelty in "heterarchy" thus partly derives from the abstruseness of convention in "hierarchy." Many authors hail hierarchy as the dominant or even only stable form of organization of human as well as other systems. Space limitations do not permit a thorough discussion of this strain of thought. One contribution will, however, be briefly mentioned. Koestler (1978, p. 290) puts the argument for hierarchy very strongly:

> All complex structures and processes of a relatively stable character dispaly hierarchic organization, and this applies regardless whether we are considering inanimate systems, living organisms, social organizations, or patterns of behaviour.

Koestler himself mentions the suspicion that the hierarchic model's universal applicability may originate in the model being logically empty, or merely a reflection of the way in which a perceiver approaches an object or situation. He rejects these possibilities but does not discuss them at length. The pervasiveness of hierarchical thinking models is treated by Ogilvy (1977) and Bouvier (1984), who support the view that hierarchy to a large extent is in the eye of the beholder. Some other comments should also be made in relation to Koestler's arguments.

A key idea with Koestler is the existence of parts which are self-regulating, relatively autonomous, and which exhibit properties not deducible from lower units. At the same time, they are parts of larger wholes. Koestler calls these units "holons." This is not inconsistent with the hierarchy notion. However, he also discusses more complex networks, where "vertical" and "horizontal" connections intertwine. We are warned, however, not to forget the primacy of the vertical, hierarchical, dimension (ibid., p. 298):

> It is as if the sight of the foliage of the entwined branches in a forest made us forget that the branches originate in separate trees. The trees are vertical structures. The meeting points of branches from neighbouring trees form horizontal networks at several levels. Without the trees there could be no entwining, and no network. Without the networks, each tree would be isolated, and there would be no integration of functions. Arborization and reticulation seem to be complementary principles in the architecture of organisms. In symbolic universes of discourse arborization is reflected in the 'vertical' denotation (definition) of concepts, reticulation in their 'horizontal' connotations in associative networks.

The last paragraph indicates a tendency to define whatever cannot be captured in a hierarchical order as only a looser kind of "association." Another example is the discussion of "abstract" and "spotlight" memory. The latter—very vivid, almost photographic images resembling total recall of past situations—seems not to fit the hypothesis of hierarchic storing of information. Koestler (ibid., p. 48 ff, 296–297) "solves" this problem by assuming that there is something he calls "emotional relevance," which leads to lack of schematization in hierarchies. He also regards spotlight memory as more "primitive" (ibid., p. 53), and possibly phylogenetically older than abstractive memory.

Koestler even regards the supposedly older principles of storing and managing information in the human brain as harmful. He suggests to initiate (ibid., p. 103):

> Not an amputation, but a process of harmonization which assigns each level of the mind, from visceral impulses to abstract thought, its appropriate place in the hierarchy. This implies reinforcing the new brain's power of veto against that type of emotive behavior—and that type only—which cannot be reconciled with reason, such as the 'blind' passions of the group-mind.

The "process of harmonization" cannot be achieved by education: "It can be done only by 'tempering' with human nature itself to correct its endemic schizopsychological disposition" (p. 104). He expects "the laboratories to succeed in producing an immunizing substance conferring mental stability" (p. 105).

To the present author, this line of reasoning seems like trying to expurge and, if possible, eradicate thought patterns which do not fit a hierarchical model. The tree metaphor also hides an important aspect of much social organization. Any given unit may be a member of *several* systems, which each may be conceived of as a hierarchy. In a tree, every branch obviously primarily "belongs" to one tree. However, is it equally clear to what "arborizing structure" a U.S. citizen, born by Jewish parents, working for a French company in Spain belongs? Koestler quotes Hyden (1961), who suggests that the same neuron may be a member of several functional "clubs," as support for the distinction between arborizing and reticulating structures. However, it seems that this could rather be taken as an example of non-hierarchy. (Below, a heterarchy will be endowed with the attributes of having many centers of different kinds. This seems to fit the neuronal clubs better.)

Also on the empirical level, some of Koestler's examples of hierarchic organization may be questioned. Later research on memory, and on the entire functioning of the brain, does not appear to fit the hierarchic model (McCulloch, 1965; Pribram, 1971). Organizations, in their actual functioning, are far less hierarchic than their organization charts would imply. Action systems do not always work as a hierarchy of strategies transformed into action programs and simple final acts (Allison, 1971; Mintzberg, 1978).

The "holon property" of Koestler is fully consistent with the heterarchy model outlined below. The supposed inevitability of hierarchy, however, seems to be a Procrustean bed in describing life in real organizations. Therefore, rather than continuing the conceptual discussion, I will try to sketch some developments in MNCs, illustrating the need for a concept covering these developments. Thereafter, a tentative delimination of the concept of a heterarchical MNC will be provided.

A pioneer in reviewing the development of different kinds of MNCs was Howard V. Perlmutter (1965). His original scheme of an evolution of, or at least a distinction between, ethnocentric, polycentric, and geocentric MNCs has hardly been improved upon. Therefore, this is a natural starting point to discuss tendencies of change in the nature of multinational business.

ETHNOCENTRISM

Almost all now existing firms have started on a national basis and only gradually developed international ties. Foreign business was initially only marginal, more so for companies from large nations than for those with small "home markets." Internationalization was often based on monopolistic advantages which could be exploited by internalizing transactions within the firm. (See Hymer, 1976; and Dunning, 1977 for early and representative statements of theories of foreign direct investment based on "firm-specific advantages.") These advantages, in terms of, for example, proprietary technology were exploited in a slow, gradual process, by moving concentrically to markets further away from the home country, and by investing in increasingly committing forms. From sales outlets in the neighboring country, the firm cautiously moved towards manufacturing plants on alien continents. (Vernon, 1966; Stopford and Wells, 1972; and Johanson & Vahlne, 1977 are good examples of gradual learning theories of foreign direct investment.)

Ethnocentric companies are managed by home country people, and with time there is a lot of rotation between HQ and subsidiaries. The control style will vary in accordance with practice in the parent company and parent country. For example, Swedish firms transferred a reliance on normative control (Etzioni, 1961) to their international operations. U.S. companies used relatively more of calculative and coercive control, with less autonomy for the subsidiaries (Hedlund, 1980, 1984; Hedlund and Åman, 1983).

The role of a foreign subsidiary in such a company is operational rather than strategic. Strategies are derived from the prospects of extending the geographical scope of firm-specific advantages and formulated at the center. The subsidiaries implement, but there is also an entrepreneurial element to early stages of internationalization, which is lost as the firm gets used to going to foreign lands.

The environment of the MNC—as far as aspects of internationalization are concerned—could be characterized as Type 1 (placid random) or Type 2 (placid clustered) in the Emery and Trist (1965) classification. That is, opportunities and problems are either randomly distributed (Type 1) or clustered (Type 2), but competitive relations are not primary as in Type 3, nor is drastic environmental turbulence the main issue (Type 4). The absence of strategy in a Type 1 situation is particularly apparent in the subsidiary. The best strategy is to do as well as possible on a purely local and perhaps also short-term basis.

Interdependencies between the center and the subsidiaries in the enterprise are primarily sequential (Thompson, 1967). Products, know-how, and money for investment are sent from the center to the periphery. There is a vertical division of labor, so that activities up-stream the value-added chain are conducted at the center and down-stream operations at the periphery. (This, of course, does not hold for raw materials-based MNCs.) The novelty and uncertainty of foreign operations favor hierarchy rather than market or federation solutions (Williamson, 1975; Daems, 1980). That is, subsidiaries are controlled rather tightly, either through orders or shared outlooks; for example, by transferring people between units in the firm (Edström & Galbraith, 1977).

POLYCENTRISM

As time goes by, foreign business may become dominant rather than marginal, the subsidiaries get more activities and become more self-sufficient, management becomes more host-country oriented and consisting of host-country nationals. The MNC becomes an assemblage of semi-independent units. There is less rotation of personnel, and in a way, the polycentric MNC is less trans- or international than the ethno-centric version. Indeed, the term *multinational* fits better for the polycen-tric firm than for the other archetypes.

The competitive strengths move from proprietary technology to ac-cess to distribution channels, brand name, international experience, and finance. Economies of scale and scope become important. New invest-ments are sought worldwide, almost as in a portfolio placement strat-egy. As long as the firm stays in the original line of business, the size of the host market will be an important criterion for the decision on where to invest. The ethnocentric stage of confinement to near and familiar abodes looses in significance. (See Vernon, 1979; and Hedlund and Kverneland, 1984 for a discussion and some empirical support. Some of the results reported have to do with changes in the environment of MNCs, allowing "instant polycentrism," rather than with firm-specific developments.)

Subsidiaries are operationally independent and increasingly forced to take strategic decisions with respect to their operations in their market ("Disturbed reactive" local environment for the subsidiary). HQ control moves towards calculative, based on financial results rather than on influencing the substance of decisions. The extreme is reached when the parent company acts only as a holding company, buying and selling assets internationally, with no view to anything but the financial out-comes of its dispositions.

Interdependence between subsidiaries and center is *pooled*. Financial resources and some specialist competence are kept at the center, whereas product and technology flows are less pronounced. Activities are duplicated internationally, so that manufacturing, for example, is undertaken in most subsidiaries.

The tendency in terms of control mode is to move toward looser coupling between units and from the hierarchy (in this case also some-what in the etymological sense) of ethnocentrism to market solutions. Transfer pricing based on market prices rather than internal costs, free-dom to choose external suppliers, rewards and punishment in monetary terms, and elaborate bonus payment systems accompany greater turn-over rates of personnel and organizational units being sold off and bought. Internationalization is more and more conducted through ac-quisitions rather than green-field ventures. The tendency to market so-lutions could be interpreted in terms of increased routinization of inter-national transactions, with consequent reduction of uncertainty. Also, the idiosyncrasy of assets (technology, people, etc.) is not as pro-nounced as in the initial stages. According to Williamson (1975), this should lead to markets rather than hierarchies.

GEOCENTRISM

Perlmutter's (1965) original classification defines the various "centrisms" primarily according to the attitudes of management. Above, such aspects have been linked to strategic situations, stages in the "life cycle of internationalization," types of interdependence between parts of the firm, types of environment facing the company, etc. It becomes even more necessary to discuss these other aspects when describing a geocentric firm. One reason for this is that "geocentric strategies" may be accompanied by ethnocentric attitudes. Indeed, the shift from poly- to geocentric strategic focus is often perceived by host country management as a shift back to HQ and home country attitudes.

Writers on "global strategy" mostly mention interdependence between units in the firm as a distinguishing characteristic. (See, for example, Porter, 1980 and 1984.) The actions of a subsidiary in country A influence prospects for the subsidiary in country B, perhaps because they face the same competitor, who has to divide his resources between the two markets. Thus, competition is not confined within each national market, but system-wide. The MNC exploits systems advantages, subsidiaries, and country-specific advantages being considered the parts of the system. Thus, at the extreme, subsidiaries specialize and operate globally in limited fields. The MNC in this way *internalizes the exploitation of (country) comparative advantages.* This is very important from the point of view of theories of international trade and investment. Ricardo never thought that the same agent would produce both wine and cloth. Assumptions that the MNC is a reflection of firm-specific advantages à la Hymer must confront a very peculiar type of advantage, that is *multinationality in itself.* To say that the MNC exists because it exploits the advantages of being an MNC is tautological, so the convenient theoretical starting point in monopolistic advantages dissolves when applied to the geocentric firm. As Vernon (1979) himself has noted, the product life cycle theory of international trade and investment become less useful as the international spread of companies is extended.

Global competition, where a firm faces the same rivals on most markets, means that gradual internationalization strategies pose problems. Hedlund and Kverneland (1984) and Lundgren and Hedlund (1983) show how market entry by Swedish firms into Japan and South-East Asia respectively is faster and more committing than theories of gradualism would lead one to expect. Firms do not follow a neat sequence from agent over sales subsidiary and some local manufacturing to large-scale local production. Instead, the pattern is one of jumping steps in the chain and building up positions very rapidly. International strategy is increasingly driven by considerations of rivals', and sometimes actual or potential cooperators', behavior, rather than by the exploitation of FSAs (firm-specific advantages) as in the ethnocentric firm, or by the attractiveness of markets one by one as in the polycentric firm. Oligopolistic reaction, in terms of *imitating* competitors' moves (Knickerbocker, 1973) as well as *avoiding* competitors and building up *mutual hostage positions,* becomes common.

Perlmutter saw the use of third country nationals (TCNs) in management as a sign of geocentricity. Other aspects concerning the management process are reliance on global profitability goals and increased rotation of personnel. Probably a shift back to less calculative and more normative and coercive control is required in order for global strategies to work. The subsidiaries have to implement strategies formulated according to a global logic, they have to be able to act quickly in response to competitive conditions, they must be encouraged to look at a wider picture. Most writings on global strategy give the subsidiaries a less independent role than that implied in a polycentric MNC. A recentralization of authority to HQ often follows, and is recommended to follow, a globalization of competition. (See, for example, Channon and Jalland, 1979; Hedlund and Åman, 1983.) Often, global divisions structured around products, technologies, or customer types are created to coordinate activities in specific competitive niches. The business environment can be characterized as a global disturbed reactive one in the terms of Emery and Trist (1965).

Interdependence between parts of the firm moves from the polycentric pooling of resources at the center to sequential and *reciprocal.* Products, know-how, money, and people flow in increasingly complex patterns, and not as in the ethnocentric firm from one core to the periphery. (See also Bartlett, 1984 and his discussion of the "integrated network model" of an MNC. His other concepts of "centralized hub" and "decentralized federation" can be compared with ethnocentrism and polycentrism, respectively.) Particularly reciprocal interdependence is expected to lead to internalization in a hierarchy (cf Thompson, 1967), so the trend towards markets in the polycentric MNC is reversed. Also reversed is the tendency to duplicate activities in various subsidiaries.

The discussion so far is summarized in Table I. Obviously, it ignores many complexities and gives a very simple picture of the range of possibilities. For example, there certainly exist geocentric MNCs which build primarily upon sequential interdependencies between center and periphery. A clear example would be mining companies in highly concentrated industries. Nevertheless, one can better understand the character of most geocentricity and globality of competition if several strains of— in this context—often forgotten theoretical heritage are applied:

- Thompson's (1967) classification of various types of interdependence, and his hypotheses of mechanisms of integration related to those types.
- Transaction cost theorists' (Coase, 1937; Williamson, 1975) notions of alternative governance modes and the determinants of effective solutions to the governance problem.

Table I.

	Ethnocentrism	Polycentrism	Geocentrism
Importance of foreign business	Marginal	Substantial/dominant	Dominant
Basis for international strategy	Exploit firm-specific advantages	Market size, scale and scope economies, finance	Competition, multinationality as such
Expansion mode	Gradual, concentric, green-field	Market-driven, acquisitions, cash-constrained	Quick, direct, competition-driven
Organization structure	Mother/daughter international division	Mother/daughter, international division, holding company	Global divisions or matrix organization
Type of interdependence	Sequential center–subsidiary	Pooled center–subsidiary	System of sequential and reciprocal
Governance mode	Hierarchy	Market	Hierarchy, "hierarchy"
Specialization in value-added chain	Specialization up–downstream HQ-subsidiaries	Duplication	Specialization up–downstream, between subsidiaries
Control style	HQ-derived, coercive, normative	Calculative	Normative, coercive
MNC Internationalization environment	Placid–random Type I	Placid–clustered Type II	Disturbed–reactive, turbulent Type III→IV
Subsidiary environment	Type I, II	Type I, II, III	Type III→IV
Autonomy of subsidiary	Low–Medium	High	Low–Medium
Strategic role of subsidiary	Implement local strategy	Formulate + implement local strategy	Implement + adapt to global strategy
Recruitment and rotation	Home-country managers, much rotation	Local managers, little rotation	Mixed, TCNs, much rotation

- Classification of mechanisms of social integration such as Etzioni's (1961).
- Typologies of organizational environments (Emery and Trist, 1965) and hypotheses about behavioral implications of those environments.

Three entries in Table I have not been adequately foreshadowed in the discussion above. Organization structure has been added, using the results of Stopford and Wells (1972), Franko (1976) and others linking strategy to the structure of the international organization. "Hierarchy" as one governance mode in geocentric firms will be explained in the next section. I believe that pure hierarchy will be detrimental to many global strategies, and that there nevertheless is a strong possibility that this is what will happen in many firms. Emery and Trist's type 4 environment—the turbulent one—has been introduced as a likely development for both the entire geocentric MNC and its subsidiaries. This will also be discussed in the next section.

STRAINS ON THE GEOCENTRIC MNC

A radical view concerning geocentrism and globality is that we are witnessing the disappearance of the international dimension of business. For commercial and practical purposes, the nations do not exist, and the relevant business arena becomes something like a big unified "home market." Business action as well as concepts to describe firms and the situations they face will be similar to the case of a company working in one national market.

However, there are a number of difficulties facing the MNC, which wants to act as if the world was one big market and competitive arena, to be adapted to in a scaled-up version of "ordinary," national strategy.

- In spite of proclaimed increased homogenization of demand (Vernon, 1979), there are still strong differences between nations and regions. Protectionism is furthermore on the increase rather than the other way around. The loyalty of many employees is still primarily with their home country. (See Doz, 1979, and Doz and Prahalad, 1980.)

- The need for cooperation, in joint ventures or in other forms, characteristic of many branches of industry, makes unilateral strategy making problematical.

- Cultural differences in management style makes one at least question the viability of uniform, worldwide control systems and other management practices.

- Economizing by sharing resources between different lines of business, with different customers and competitors, mitigates against totally subduing the local country dimension in organization and strategy.

- Size itself may be a severe problem in coordinating operations globally in the same way as one would coordinate national business. The complexity and variability of environmental circumstances compound the size of problems. Response times may be too long to keep up with changes in markets. The cognitive limitations of integrating information are very real. Particularly at the strategic level, advances in information technology may not be sufficient, although no doubt be of value.

- The supply of managers able to carry out ambitious global strategies already is a bottleneck today for most firms. If strategy making is recentralized to the HQ "brain," it will become even more difficult to fill positions, since this requires more transfer of personnel.

- With the development of specialization between subsidiaries, these will become so large and important that it will be detrimental to assign narrow strategic roles to them. For example, a research center in India serving the whole network of an MNC would probably, with time, develop ideas and products which do not fit the prevailing strategies of the group, but which could well be a basis for a new line of business. It would be wasteful not to entertain a capacity to utilize the creativity and entrepreneurship of people at all nodes of the network. Besides, those people would probably resign if they did not get such opportunities.

- Finally, centrally guided global strategies for given products aimed at beating given competitors, looking at the world as one market, may lead to neglect of opportunities to exploit existing differences between nations. If the global thrust is combined with a reemphasis on HQ and home-country guidance, the company may return to ethnocentrism, only being able to exploit ideas originating at home. Advantage seeking and advantage development will not be main concerns, but only the exploitation of existing advantages. In the long run, such a firm may become sterile. The results in Davidson & Haspeslagh (1982) indicate that the global product division as an organizational solution may indeed entail such risks.

Most of the points illustrate the danger of seeing geocentricity just as the scaling up of the national corporation, thereby getting rid of the international dimension of business and reestablishing central strategic direction from a center, which is at the apex of one, big global hierarchy. Even if this characterization of global strategy is a charicature and may seem to be set up as a straw-man, I believe that both academic discussion and—but less so—practice in large MNCs are affected by outlooks, philosophies, strategies, and management practices similar to the ones described.

Perlmutter's original conception of geocentricity was not as restricted as the "mononational" version sketched above. He sketched a situation where subsidiaries were "parts of a whole whose focus is on worldwide objectives as well as local objectives, each part making its unique contribution with its unique competence." These lines do not clearly denote the attributes of geocentricity, but their connotative meaning is very rich. I believe one can usefully single out some of those connotations and specify a special case of geocentricity, an option which is still not fully developed in actuality but towards which many companies probably will, and should, move. This is the hypermodern MNC, and one of its distinguishing marks is its heterarchical nature.

THE HETERARCHICAL MNC

The heterarchical MNC differs from the standard geocentric one both in terms of strategy and in terms of structure. *Strategically*, the main dividing line is between exploiting competitive advantages derived from a home country base on the one hand, and actively seeking advantages originating in the global spread of the firm on the other. In its most extreme form, this would mean that one could not assign the company to any particular industry. Any opportunity which activates the potential inherent in broad geographical coverage would be a candidate for inclusion in the company's repertoire of products and services. Obviously, no MNC would like to go to this extreme. Specialization benefits apply also to information search, and in many contexts existing barriers to entry into a global industry would be prohibitively restrictive.

However, the concept of exploiting the advantage of multinationality as such also applies within a rather limited field of business. Information on competition, technological trends, developments in related fields, aspects of national environments, etc. lead to opportunities not easily identified by purely local firms, or by polycentric MNCs, or even by ethnocentrically tainted global MNCs. The difference between the latter and the heterarchy is most pronounced when it comes to the *structure* of the enterprise and the processes of managing it. Indeed, it may be that the idea of structure determining strategy (see Hall and Saias, 1980) is a fundamental one for the heterarchical MNC. Rather than identifying properties of the industry in which it competes and then adapting its structure to the demands thus established, the hypermodern MNC first defines its structural properties and then looks for strategic options following from these properties. In actual life, of course, every candidate for heterarchy will have come from a history in a given set of industries, regions, etc. The MNCs most likely to face the indeterminacy of strategically relatively open vistas are probably those described by Bartlett

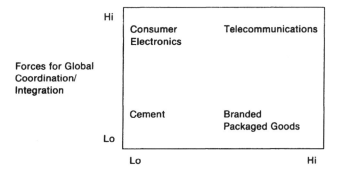

Industry Characteristics
Global Integration/National Responsiveness Grid

Hi

Consumer   Telecommunications
Electronics

Forces for Global
Coordination/
Integration

Cement   Branded
                  Packaged Goods

Lo

Lo   Hi

Forces for National Responsiveness/Differentiation

Figure 1   (Source: Bartlett, 1984).

(1984) as "transnational." Such firms are active in industries where it is important both to achieve global integration and local differentiation, for example, adaptation to host government demands (see Figure 1).

Thus, strategic imperatives of dual focus force some MNCs to adopt structural solutions and management practices in consonance with these task demands. These adaptations then constitute an opportunity for sometimes much wider and diverse strategic options, or at least more intensive utilizations of the global spread of the company. In order to achieve this, further development of structural traits are desirable. Their archetypical expressions will be ennumerated below.

1. First, the heterarchical MNC has *many centers*. One could speak of a polyarchical rather than monarchical MNC, were it not for the lack of integration implied in the former term. The main idea is that the foundations of competitive advantage no longer reside in any one country, but in many. New ideas and products may come up in many different countries and later be exploited on a global scale. A geographically diffused pattern of expertise is built up, corresponding to unique abilities in each node of the network. These abilities may be a reflection of dissimilarities between countries as in "demand theories" of international trade (Burenstam-Linder, 1961) or simply expressions of spatially distributed talents for technological development within the firm. At the extreme, each "subsidiary" is at the same time a center for and perhaps a global coordinator of activities within one field (such as for one product), and a more peripheral agent for local distribution in another.

   In diversified firms it is obviously easier to find examples of such international specialization. For example, the Swedish company

Atlas Copco has the headquarters for its Air Power division located in Belgium, whereas the other divisions are headquartered in Sweden. Esselte (office equipment) has put the center of its largest division in London.

However, even within one product division there is scope for multi-centeredness. The dangers of the global product division undiluted by geographical considerations have been discussed by Davidson and Haspeslagh (1982). Relations are restricted to those between one center and units in the periphery. Relations within the supposed periphery are not exploited, and information overload on the center and lack of motivation in subsidiaries create grave problems. Hedlund (1980) documents the strategic alienation of subsidiary managers in Swedish MNCs, and gives some suggestions of how to involve the subsidiaries more in strategy formulation. In this case, the mother—daughter structure, rather than global product divisions, is the organizational background. This seems to support the views of Bartlett (1981, 1984) that the importance of the formal organization structure is easily exaggerated. Simmonds (1985), reviewing the literature and discussing various ways to "achieve the geocentric ideal," concludes that other management systems, such as the planning, accounting, and reporting systems, are important obstacles.

2. A key idea in the conception of a heterarchical MNC is that *subsidiary managers are also given a strategic role, not only for their "own" company, but for the MNC as a whole*. The notions of "headquarters," "center," "home country," and "corporate level" dissolve and are not synonymous. Corporate level strategy has to be implemented *and* formulated in a geographically scattered network.

3. Heterarchy implies *different kinds of centers*. There is not only a set of global divisions and subdivisions, or only a set of geographical divisions further split up in national and regional subunits. A heterarchy consists of a mix of organizing principles. There may be an R&D center in Holland with global responsibilities for coordinating product development, product division headquarters in Germany responsible for the main product, a marketing center for Asia in Singapore, and a center for dealing with global purchases in London. The multidimensionality of organizing principles (functions, products, geography, customer type, etc.) reflects the need to coordinate activities along each and all of those dimensions. In a heterarchy, *there is not one overriding dimension superordinate to the rest*.

All this may seem an unduly complicated way of describing a matrix organization. Recognizing the probability of muddled thinking and expression, I still believe that there are important differences between what I call a heterarchy and a matrix structure, for example:

(I) In a matrix, all units are coordinated along all the dimensions of the matrix. In a heterarchy, the pattern is more mixed and flexible. The R&D center in the example above may not have all other R&D departments reporting to it or have the right to give them orders. Rather, it may have a "softer" coordinating role. Furthermore, not all units in the firm would fall within its direct sphere of interest.

(II) A matrix implies stability in the criticality of the dimensions included in the matrix. Mostly, not more than two dimensions can be formally included; for example, products and geography. If functional coordination, such as for the global logistical system, is suddenly required, the matrix is ill-equipped to handle the problem.

(III) The matrix ends in an apex, so that conflicts between, for example, product and country perspectives, are resolved by a corporate officer. The heterarchy would not rely much on this mechanism, but more on conflict resolution through negotiations based on shared perspectives and sometimes arms-length bargaining.

Admittedly, most writers on matrix organization would stress that the formal matrix is only a small part of the "matrix way of life." They stress the need for shift of focus over time, flexibility in applying dual reporting relationships, and care in not overloading the arbiter role of top management.

4. A further characteristic of a heterarchy concerns the degree of coupling between organizational units. In many cases, there would be a deintegration of relationships. A subsidiary will be given increased freedom to purchase components externally, and to sell to customers outside the corporation. Joint ventures and other types of cooperation with other firms will be more prevalent than in the tightly controlled global firm. If such freedom is not given, there will be little chance of really profiting from the opportunities provided by global reach.

Of course, negative effects on the rest of the operations of the MNC must be considered also. An important subset of global opportunities consist exactly in *internalizing* flows of information, products, and money within the bounds of the firm, saving on transaction costs associated with market solutions. Perhaps it is more appropriate to speak of *flexibility in the selection of governance mode*, rather than reintegration. A heterarchical MNC will have no problem in entering joint ventures, externalizing production and handling internal transactions according to arms-length principles in one business area, and insisting on unitary control, internalization, and governance by management fiat in another context. Full exploitation of global scanning and information processing capabilities will lead to a range of opportunities, some best handled in hierarchies, others rather suited to market-like governance. The heterarchical MNC could be seen as a *meta-institution*, which continuously creates new institutional arrangements, in the light of expertise concerning what works best for each specific purpose. This, assuming that choices are rational, speeds up the process of institutional evolution in comparison with a "Darwinian" process of selection. A "Lamarckian" development, where experience is accumulated, experiments fully exploited and memory over "generations" kept intact, guides the choice of governance forms.

Thus, it may be correct to speak of deintegration for firms coming from a tradition of strict global control from one center. For firms with a polycentric past, the tendency may be the opposite. Common to both is that the range of types of relationships between units in the company, as well as in relation to outside actors, will increase.

5. Another attribute of heterarchy is that *integration is achieved primarily through normative control*, and only secondarily through calculative and coercive/bureaucratic regulations. "Corporate culture," "management ethos" (Bartlett, 1984), "management style," "cultural control" (Jaeger and Baliga, 1985), etc. become critical. This is the only way to assure coordination in the diverse, extended, and fluctuating environment and activities of a heterarchical MNC. Pure bureaucratic control breaks down because of cognitive overload and motivational problems. Pure calculative control, which may serve well in the polycentric MNC, will not establish the mutual trust, the ability to "sacrifice" the local for the global and the short term for the long term, and the shared code of communication necessary for rapid action in a coordinated fashion. Thus, and paradoxically so, a heterarchy may contain more of hierarchy, in its etymological sense, than does bureaucratic hierarchy itself. This is the reason for "hierarchy" in Table I.

6. It was mentioned above that the hologram is a special type of heterarchy, where *information about the whole is contained in each part*. This is a critical characteristic of the heterarchical MNC. Every member of the company will in the extreme case be aware of all aspects of the firm's operations. Obviously, this is only a theoretical ideal. However, widely shared awareness of central goals and strategies, and of critical interdependencies between units in the firm, is not an impossibility. Some remarkable corporate turnarounds recently are no doubt partly attributable to initiatives in this direction. In Sweden, the cases of SAS and ASEA are particularly striking.

The distribution of information in every part of a hologram is possible because of laser technology. One could say that the corporate ethos is the analogue of the laser light. By sharing certain conceptions about the firm, and certain ways of acting in relation to other members of the firm, it becomes possible to rapidly share information, interpret the meaning of events in and outside the organization in similar ways, and see opportunities for local action in the interest of the global good. The laser beam effect of corporate culture is the unifying element of a heterarchical organization. It is crucial to support the formation of such a culture, since the risks of anarchy are otherwise very great.

Pessimism regarding the efficiency and integrity of non-hierarchical and unified control is less warranted on empirical than on "theoretical" grounds. Ogilvy (1977) discusses how ambitions to organize societies and polities hierarchically are influenced by and influence modes of thought and even the structure of the personality. The fact that a phenomenon may be hard to grasp and explain in terms familiar to the grasper does not mean, however, that the phenomenon does not exist. Ogilvy quotes McCulloch (1965) on heterarchical patterns of preference in neural networks.

> Circularities in preference instead of indicating inconsistencies, actually demonstrate consistency of a higher order than had been dreamed of in our philosophy. An organism possessed of this nervous system—six neurons—is sufficiently endowed to be unpredictable from any theory founded on a scale of values. It has a heterarchy of values, and is thus internectively too rich to submit to a summum bonum. (McCulloch, 1965, p. 43)

Yet, although we cannot explain how we are able to walk, for example, we still do. It is worth quoting McCullogh again, for some clues about the properties of heterarchies and possible analogies (no more but also no less) with a discussion on organization and control in human institutions. (Emphases added by the present author.)

> The details of its (the brain) neurons and their specific connections need not concern us here. In general, you may think of it as a computer *to any part* of which come signals from many parts of the body and from other parts of the brain and spinal cord. It is *only one cell deep* on the path from input to output, but it can set the filters on all of its inputs and can control the behavior of the programmed activity, the half-centers, and the reflexes. It gets a *substitute for depth by its intrinsic fore-and-aft connections*. Its business, given its *knowledge of the state* of the whole organism and the world impingent upon it, is to decide whether the rule is one requiring fighting, fleeing, eating, sleeping, etc. It must do it with millisecond component action and conduction velocities of usually less than 100 meters per second, and *do it in real time*, say, in a third of a second. That it has worked so well throughout evolution, without itself evolving, points to

its structure as the natural solution of the organization
of appropriate behavior. We know much experimentally
of the behavior of the components, but still have no
theory worthy of the name to explain its circuit actions.
(McCulloch, 1965, p. 397.)

7. The foregoing discussion on the heterarchical nature of the nervous system leads to another, perhaps hair-raising, analogy. The
metaphor underlying much thought on corporate strategy is one of
the firm consisting of a brain and a body. The strategy makers in
the center are the brain, and the implementors in the periphery are
the body. Thinking and acting take place at different locations.
Books like *The brain of the firm* (Beer, 1972) testify to the forcefulness
of the metaphor. However, the dangers of separating thinking and
acting too much in an organization have been well illustrated by
the decline and often fall of formal long-range planning departments in companies. One way of describing the heterarchical MNC
is to say that *thinking is not only restricted to one exclusive center, but
goes on in the whole enterprise.* Thus, an appropriate metaphor for
discussing a heterarchical firm would be a *"firm as a brain"* model
rather than a "brain of the firm" model.

A weakness of the metaphor is that it may lead one to see the
firm as only a cognitive entity. However, the core of the idea is that
not only does thinking take place also in the periphery, but *it goes
together with and directly informs action.*

8. *Coalitions with other companies and also other types of actors* are frequent in the heterarchical MNC. Exploiting global reach will often
mean to serve as a catalyst, bringing together elements with syner-
gistic potential, perhaps firms from different continents previously
not known to one another. It may be of interest to note that Emery
and Trist (1965) saw as two primary ways of coping with turbulence:

   (I) The creation of common values, binding people and organizations
   together and enabling them to respond quickly to environmental
   change. This corresponds to the emergence of corporate culture as a
   binding element discussed above.
   (II) Cooperation between heterogenous elements rather than competition
   between homogenous elements (as in "Type 3") as the primary occupation of top leaders.

The latter point includes things such as joint ventures and cooperation between firms and governments. A heterarchical MNC will
share and pool its power with other actors in order to benefit maximally from its global capabilities. This does not mean that it will do
so in all fields of business. Again, it is the *multitude* of governance
forms and degrees of internalization which characterizes a heterarchy.

9. Finally, and returning to the strategic ambitions rather than the structural properties of heterarchy, this type of MNC would be fit to attack the most difficult global problems of today. This may seem naive and even ridiculous to managers busy surviving producing and selling a narrow line of products or services. However, assuming a type of company that sees the exploitation of globality as such as its main source of strength, it does not seem that far-fetched to consider *radical problem-orientation* as guiding strategy formulation. (Rather than starting from existing physical or human resources, or from competitive positions in narrow fields of business.)

HUMAN RESOURCE MANAGEMENT IN A HETERARCHICAL MNC

No full discussion of human resource management in the context of a heterarchy will be attempted here. Instead, a few important points will be brought up, without pretense of exhaustive treatment.

1. Concerning *organization structure,* many models will be simultaneously used in a heterarchical MNC. The flexibility and multidimensionality of the structure defy easy categorization. Change of the formal organization will not give rise to heterarchy. Subtler changes in management processes are required. However, the formal organization may stop a movement towards heterarchy.

   One consequence of breaking down (up?) a large hierarchy is that it is *no longer possible to promote people mainly by giving them jobs "higher up."* Movement between centers will be more common, and movement from periphery towards center in the same unit will be less common. Also, the need to build up the "nervous system" of the heterarchy is of importance here, as is the need to use personal competence wherever it pays off best.

2. The core of a heterarchical enterprise will consist of *people with a long experience in it.* A firm invests considerably in the employee, and vice versa. The latter is a part of the communication system of the firm, and the history of the human system in the company may be its most strategic resource. This is often said and may sound like a platitude. However, it is less so in an organization which builds its strategy on advantage seeking and using its global coverage, rather than on advantage exploitation on the basis of known and stable assets.

   This communication network is not easily imitable by other firms. Much less so can a small part of it be used by others. In a limited sense, the employee is of value to competitors as a source of information, since he has a lot of it, also of a strategic nature. After having interrogated and "emptied" the unfaithful soul, however, it is of little use. Thus, from the point of view of the employee, the idiosyncracy of his relation with the firm is very great. This is also true the other way around, since it takes a long time to find and train a replacement. However, the "hologram quality" makes the firm *more* robust than in a hierarchy. Many employees will share the same information and be able to support or replace each other. This does not mean that the firm can easily fire the employee, since such behavior would undermine the mutual trust necessary to encourage investment in the long-term future of the MNC. Idiosyncratic assets should lead to internalization, according to Williamson (1975), so one can expect *more encompassing and long-term contracts* with employees. Another possibility is participation in the ownership of the company.

One can exaggerate the need for permanence, however. There is considerable flux in the activities of the heterarchical MNC, and this requires flexibility also concerning personnel. Joint ventures and other forms of cooperation, sometimes on a project basis, by definition mean that new members continuously enter and leave the system. Perhaps one can speak of a *dual career system*, just as one speaks of dual labor markets in some countries. There will be a limited but still numerous core of almost life-time employees, and a much larger number of people with more fleeting association with the firm. In the debate on the Japanese labor system, it is often pointed out that the core enjoying life-time employment and other marvels of the Japanese employment system is rather small. What has surprised most analysts is that the duality of the labor market has not disappeared with modernization. Perhaps the solution with an integrated core surrounded by quasi-integrated satellites (which themselves might constitute cores in other systems) is a good combination of stability and flexibility?

The core provides the memory and the information infrastructure necessary to grasp opportunities on a global scale. The looser links to the outside help against rigidification of response by establishing channels for the communication of new ideas. In this context, the *balance between young and old members* of the organization is probably critical. (See the discussion by Lorenz, 1971, on the balance between processes of acquiring, retaining, and dismantling cultural knowledge, and the importance of age in this respect.) Company demography needs to be planned more systematically than when the firm is a system of roles which can be easily communicated and learnt. Not allowing steady recruitment of "new blood," or dismantling of knowledge by early retirement, are traps in this area. However, much more research is needed on company demography before any strong statements can be made.

3. In order for internalization of norms to take place, *a lot of rotation of personnel* and international travel and postings are necessary. The tendency to man purportedly global firms with home country managers—and more so than in polycentric firms—will not work in a heterarchical MNC. Advances in information technology may help the formation of the nervous system of the firm, but this will not be enough for building strong internal cultures.

   The problems on the practical level of international transfers of people are well known. The solutions are less well known, apart from obvious hints such as paying well, giving spouses jobs, and being aware of re-entry problems. Perhaps recruitment of candidates for the core should be very selective, with a strong emphasis on willingness to travel and change function in the company. Sending people abroad very early is probably a good idea, possibly even before they have formed families. (Would the best be to have the new employee swear to chastity and keep unmarried, like in the very successful international operations of some ecclestiastical organizations such as the Jesuit Order?)

4. A much *broader range of people in the firm must develop capacity for strategic thinking and action.* This implies open communication of strategies and plans, decentralization of strategic tasks, using task forces on strategic issues actively, and providing early opportunities for development of "top management capabilities" also for "subsidiary" employees. (The words "subsidiary" and even "manager" sound a bit funny in the context of a heterarchical MNC. There is less obvious subordination, and the clear distinction between managing and operational functions is less relevant than in a clear hierarchy. Heterarchy may mean the beginning of the decline of the professional manager as a species within the organizational zoo.)

   Control systems which measure performance along many dimensions (products, regions, short and long term, etc.) are necessary. This is also almost a platitude, but in actual practice many companies who claim they do this really do not. Even if the systems are there, they are not used for more than very limited purposes. (Hedlund and Zander, 1985, report on the economic control systems of Swedish MNCs. See also Business International, 1982.)

5. *Reward and punishment systems are critical.* Carriers of bad news must not be killed. Kobrin (1984) shows how MNCs neglect to use the expertise of host country managers for the assessment of political risk. The long term must not be sacrificed. Perhaps a bonus should be given on the basis of profitability in the unit where the employee served five years ago? Particularly at very high levels, an effective career strategy is to turn "star" and "question mark" jobs into

"cash cow" jobs, and leave just before they start looking like "dogs." Top managers are rather adept at taking credit for other people's work and avoiding criticism for their own, and temporal extension of the review period may counter the tendency to misuse such talents.

Similarly, the global aspects may be supported by rewarding people for global rather than local profits, or whatever the objective is. The difficulty lies in matching responsibility with authority. Probably, a heterarchical MNC has to refrain from mechanical compensation formulae to a large extent. It is not possible to construct perfect equations for the distribution of bonuses, for example, particularly when circumstances change often and drastically. Paying employees partly on the basis of the performance of the entire firm is one possibility. SAB-Nife, a small Swedish MNC, has a large bonus element in its system for paying subsidiary managers. Half of the bonus is based on the performance of the entire company (90 percent of sales are abroad), and half depends on the results of the individual subsidiary.

Shareholding by employees may be a very potent instrument to stimulate action in the interest of the total company, and to encourage normative integration. Would it not be better to have the employees in, say, the Indian subsidiary own shares in the parent company than the Indian government forcing the subsidiary to joint ventures with local partners, some more sleeping than others? Not that the former would stop the latter, but in the long run this would constitute an important change in the identity of the MNC.

Global mentality may be required far "down" in the organization. Starting up new and closing down old activities is helped by understanding of the reasons for change. Technological developments are turning many workers into technicians, and to technicians needing to know a lot about customers. Global competition is changing the rules of the game for all employees. Some examples of action in Swedish firms in the direction indicated is given by:

- Volvo's gigantic program for improving substantially the technical know-how at all levels in the company.

- SAS' focus on foreign competition in mobilizing for turnaround, and the very public nature of its corporate strategy.

- SKF Steel's program to import steel technology from Japan and teach its employees about competitive facts (and, of course, technical matters) by sending workers on assignments with the Japanese licensor. (An informal race on productivity ensued, and the Swedes caught up with their teachers in Japan.)

6. It is hard to tell what the *personality type best suited to heterarchy* is.

Ogilvy (1977) argues that a sort of "polytheistic" personality, and acceptance of such Protean prospects, go together with more decentralized organizations and societies. Speculating on this, one could argue that people from polytheistic or atheistic cultures would be most comfortable in such situations. Old Greeks, Vikings, Hindus, and Japanese would do well. Christians (particularly protestants), Moslems, Jews, communists, and people affected by "scientism" would do worse. The respresentatives of western culture included in the former list are all dead, so many firms would do well to look around a bit for new managers.

Such speculation aside, it seems clear that a heterarchical MNC would require many employees with the following qualities:

- Aptitude for *searching for and combining elements* in new ways. Probably good knowledge in several fields of science and technology is one precondition for this.

- Skill in *communicating ideas* and rapidly *turning them into action.*

- Very good *command of several languages* and knowledge of and sympathy for several cultures. (Steiner, 1975, argues that bilingualism is *qualitatively* different from monolingualism, in that it gives a "stereo quality" to perception and interpretation. See also Maruyama, 1978.)

- *Honesty and personal integrity*. These old fashioned ideals are critical for heterarchy not to turn into chaos.

- *Willingness to take risks and to experiment*. Advantage seeking is much more risky than advantage exploitation. The organization must support such learning from failures. The heterarchical MNC would mean an attempt to innovate from the basis of a large firm, working across national boundaries at very early stages in the innovation process. As in all entrepreneurial activity, a high failure rate is to be expected. Therefore, in practice, every company needs *also* a part which makes money in more stable and predictable ways. The theoretical alternative of a perfect external capital market can be ignored for the moment, because of agency cost considerations (Jensen and Meckling, 1976). It would be very difficult for anonymous shareholders, as well as for lenders, to assess ex ante, monitor constantly, and even evaluate ex post, the activities of a genuinely and entirely heterarchical MNC. This also means that the financial strength of a well-run, fairly large traditional MNC makes it the *only* realistic candidate for heterarchy on an international level. Neither small firms on their own or together through market relationships nor governments, for various reasons but in both cases having to do with agency cost problems, are likely to succeed.

- *"Faith"* in the company and its activities. Enthusiasm for the company need not go to the etymological limits of the word, but genuine appreciation of the company and its culture is valuable. Perhaps this means that the widely admired sceptical thinking type of person is of less interest than the person able to form strong attachments?

7. *Management development activities* (in the more restricted sense) *should be seen as a primary instrument to build a corporate culture,* formulate and disseminate strategies, and establish links in the communication system of the firm. Its role for acquiring skills and for learning facts and methods is perhaps only subsidiary.

CONCLUSION

The heterarchical MNC is a so far loosely defined concept. It covers a particular brand of geocentric company, which differs significantly from a version that is likely to develop more rapidly in the immediate future. The importance in bringing up and further outlining the demands of and possibilities inherent in heterarchy lies in the risk of the purely global company regressing into a sized-up model of the large national firm. An ethnocentric backlash is a clear possibility, but mostly unnecessarily so. Therefore, firms should actively explore the dangers of recentralization, even if and when such moves are desirable, and find ways of compensating for those dangers. Only the broad outlines of response can be drawn without much experimentation and accumulation of experience. The MNC is a crucial arena for such institutional innovation, since it is uniquely powered to address some of the most urgent problems of a global scale.

Where should one look for signs of heterarchy? In terms of industries, probable fields are those characterized by the use of many different technologies, high but not maximum global homogeneity of demand, fast rate of technical and market change, non-trivial scale economies (but not necessarily in manufacturing), and absence of strong local barriers to entry. This means that information technology and biotechnology come to mind, which should make the reader (and writer) suspicious, since this seems too obvious (and boring). However, also the automobile industry, building and construction, and many services fit many, but not all, of the criteria.

In terms of geographical and corporate origins, heterarchical MNCs are more likely to evolve from less than gigantic firms, and from contexts with a history of rather autonomous and entrepreneurial subsidiaries. This may give European firms an advantage over U.S. ones. In a larger picture, MNCs from newly modernizing nations may stand an even better chance. Chandler and Daems (1980) show how institutional inertia and established forms of corporate organization in Europe delayed the formation of the large, managerially run firm as compared to in the USA. Olsen (1982) has discussed how the same mechanisms may make whole nations rise and fall. The heterarchical prospect may seem too remote, or even silly, to people in successful hierarchies likely to enjoy still some time of harvesting the fruits of investments in a powerful organization for the maximum utilization of existing physical assets and know-how. It may seem less remote for people who have little alternative but to directly exploit the amazing global fluidity of capital, technology, and people to develop *new* products, markets, and competences.

Gunnar Hedlund is affiliated with the Institute of International Business at the Stockholm School of Economics in Stockholm, Sweden.

REFERENCES

Allison, G. T. *Essence of decision: Explaining the Cuban missile crisis.* Little Brown, 1971.

Bartlett, C. A. "Multinational Structural Change: Evolution Versus Reorganization." In L. Otterbeck, (Ed.), *The Management of Headquarters-Subsidiary Relationships in Multinational Corporations,* Gower Publishing Company Limited, 1981.

Bartlett, C. A. "Organization and Control of Global Enterprises: Influences, Characteristics and Guidelines." Boston: Harvard Business School, 1984.

Beer, S. *The brain of the firm.* Allen Lane, 1972.

Bouvier, P. L. "Subjectivity and the concept of hierarchy: the dominant paradigm and the prevailing work system." In *Proceedings from the International Conference of Society for General Systems Research,* New York, June 1984.

Burenstam-Linder, S. *Essays on Trade and Transportation.* New York: Wiley, 1961.

Business International Corporation, *Assessing foreign subsidiary performance.* (By Czechowics, I. J., Choi, F. D. S., and Bashivi, V. B.), 1982.

Chandler, A. D. Jr., and Daems, H. (Eds.), Managerial Hierarchies. Cambridge, MA and London, England: Harvard University Press, 1980.

Channon, D. F., and Jalland, M. *Multinational Planning.* London: Basingstoke, 1979.

Coase, R. H. "The Nature of the Firm." *Economica N.S.,* 1937, **4**, 386–405.

Daems, H. "The rise of the modern industrial enterprise: A new perspective." In A. D. Chandler and H. Daems (Eds.), *Managerial Hierarchies.* Cambridge, MA and London: Harvard University Press, 1980.

Davidson, W. H., and Haspeslagh, P. "Shaping a Global Product Organization.", *Harvard Business Review,* July–August, 1982.

Doz, Y. L. *Government Control and Multinational Strategic Management: Power Systems and Telecommunications Equipment.* Praeger, 1979.

Doz, Y. L., and Prahalad, C. K. "How MNCs Cope with Host Government Intervention." *Harvard Business Review,* March–April 1980.

Dunning, J. H. "Trade, location of economic activity and the multinational enterprise. A search for an eclectic approach." In B. Ohlin, P. O. Hesselbom, and P. J. Wiskman, (Eds.), *The international allocation of economic activity.* London: Macmillan, 1977.

Edström, A., and Galbraith, J. R. "Transfers of Managers as a Coordination and Control Strategy in Multinational Organizations." *Administrative Science Quarterly,* June 1977, 248–263.

El Sawy, O. A. "From separation to holographic enfolding." Paper presented to TIMS meeting, Boston, May 1985.

Emery, F. E., and Trist, E. L. "The Causal Texture of Organizational Environments." *Human Relations*, 1965 **18**, pp. 21–32.

Etzioni, A. *A Comparative Analysis of Complex Organizations*. New York: Free Press, 1961.

Faucheux, C., and Laurent, A. "Significance of the epistemological revolution for a management science." In *Proceedings from the workshop on the epistemology of management*, EIASM, 1980.

Franko, L. G. *The European Multinationals*. Greenwich, CT: Greylock Press, 1976.

Hall, D., and Saias, M. "Strategy Follows Structure." *Strategic Management Journal*, 1980 **1**(2).

Hedlund, G. "The Role of Foreign Subsidiaries in Strategic Decision-Making in Swedish Multinational Corporations." *Strategic Management Journal*, 1980 **9**, 23–26.

Hedlund, G. "Organization In-Between: The Evolution of the Mother–Daughter Structure of Managing Foreign Subsidiaries in Swedish MNCs." *Journal of International Business Studies*, Fall, 1984.

Hedlund, G., and Kverneland, Å. *Investing in Japan—the experience of Swedish firms*. Stockholm: Institute of International Business, Stockholm School of Economics, 1984.

Hedlund, G., and Åman, P. *Managing Relationships with Foreign Subsidiaries— Organization and Control in Swedish MNCs*. Stockholm: Sveriges Mekanförbund, 1983.

Hedlund, G., and Zander, U. *Formulation of Goals and Follow-up of Performance for Foreign Subsidiaries in Swedish MNCs*. Working Paper 85/4, Institute of International Business, Stockholm School of Economics, 1985.

Hyden, H. "Control of the Mind." In Farber, S. M., and Wilson, R. H. L., (Eds.), *Control of the Mind*. New York, 1961.

Hymer, S. *The International Operations of National Firms: A Study of Direct Foreign Investment*. M.I.T. Press. (Originally published as doctoral dissertation in 1960.), 1976.

Jaeger, A. M., and Baliga, B. R. "Control Systems and Strategic Adaptation: Lessons from the Japanese Experience." *Strategic Management Journal*, 1985, **6**(2).

Jensen, M. C., and Meckling, W. H. "Theory of the firm: managerial behavior, agency costs and ownership structure." *Journal of Financial Economics*, October 1976, 305–360.

Johanson, J., and Vahlne, J-E. "The Internationalization Process of the Firm—A Model of Knowledge Development and Increasing Foreign Market Commitment." *Journal of Management Studies*, 1977, **12**(3).

Knickerbocker, F. T. *Oligopolistic Reaction and Multinational Enterprise*. Boston: Harvard Business School, 1973.

Kobrin, S. J. *Managing political risk assessment*. University of California Press, 1984.

Koestler, A. *Janus—a summing up*. New York: Random House, 1978.

Laurent, A. "Managerial subordinacy." *Academy of Management Review*, 1978, 220–230.

Lorenz, K. "Knowledge, belief and freedom." In P. H. Weiss, (Ed.), *Hierarchically organized systems in theory and practice*. Hafner Publishing Company, 1971.

Lundgren, S., and Hedlund, G. *Svenska företag i Sydostasien*. Stockholm: Institute of International Business, Stockholm School of Economics, 1983.

Maruyama, M. "The epistemological revolution." *Futures*, June 1978, 240–242.

McCulloch, W. *Embodiments of mind*. Cambridge, MA, 1965.

Mintzberg, H. "Patterns in Strategy Formation.", *Management Science*, 1978, 934–948.

Mitroff, I. *Why Our Old Pictures of the World Don't Work Anymore*. Research Paper, University of Southern California, 1983.

Ogilvy, J. *Multidimensional man*. Oxford University Press, 1977.

Ohlin, B., Hesselbom, P. O., and Wiskman, P. J. (Eds.) *The international allocation of economic activity*. London: Macmillan, 1977.

Olsen, M. *The rise and decline of nations*. New Haven and London: Yale University Press, 1982.

Perlmutter, H. V. "L'enterprise internationale—trois conceptions.". *Revue Economique et Sociale*, 1965, **23.**

Porter, M. E. *Competitive Strategy*. New York: Free Press, 1980.

Porter, M. E. *Competition in global industries—a conceptual framework*. Boston: Harvard Business School, 1984.

Pribram, K. *Languages of the brain*. Englewood Cliffs, NJ: Prentice-Hall, 1971.

Simmonds, K. "Global Strategy: Achieving the Geocentric Ideal." *International Marketing Review*, Spring 1985.

Sjöstrand, S-E. *Samhällsorganisation*. Stockholm: Doxa, 1985.

Steiner, G. *After Babel*. Oxford University Press, 1975.

Stopford, J. M., and Wells, L. T. *Managing the Multinational Enterprise*. New York: Basic Books, 1972.

Thompson, J. D. *Organizations in Action*. New York: McGraw-Hill, 1967.

Varela, F., "A Calculus for Self-Reference.", *Int. J. Gen. Systems*, 1975, **2,** 5–24.

Vernon, R. "International Investment and International Trade in the Product Cycle.", *Quarterly Journal of Economics*, May 1966.

Vernon, R. "The Product Cycle Hypothesis in a New International Environment." *Oxford Bulletin of Economics and Statistics*, 1979, **41.**

Williamson, O. E. *Markets and Hierarchies: Analysis and Antitrust Implications*. New York: Free Press, 1975.

[19]

© *Academy of Management Review*, 1990, Vol. 15, No. 4, 603–625.

The Multinational Corporation as an Interorganizational Network

SUMANTRA GHOSHAL
INSEAD
CHRISTOPHER A. BARTLETT
Harvard University

A multinational corporation consists of a group of geographically dispersed and goal-disparate organizations that include its head-quarters and the different national subsidiaries. Such an entity can be conceptualized as an interorganizational network that is embed-ded in an external network consisting of all other organizations such as customers, suppliers, regulators, and so on, with which the dif-ferent units of the multinational must interact. Based on such a con-ceptualization, the present authors draw on interorganization theory to develop a model of the multinational corporation as an internally differentiated interorganizational network. They propose hypotheses that relate certain attributes of the multinational, such as resource configuration and internal distribution of power, to certain structural properties of its external network.

As pointed out recently by Kogut (1989), the late 1980s have witnessed a significant evolution of academic interest in the multinational corpo-ration (MNC). An important element of this shift has been a change in the focus of research away from the dyadic headquarters-subsidiary relationship in MNCs, or the specific decision of a company to invest in a foreign location, to the coordination tasks of managing a network of es-tablished foreign subsidiaries and analysis of the competitive advantages that arise from the potential scope economies of such a network.

This new research focus demands new theo-retical, conceptual, and methodological an-chors. Analysis of international competition, for example, has already embraced a range of new theories such as those of multiplant production, multipoint competition, and valuation of options

to explore the costs and benefits of the MNC's geographic scope of activities (e.g., Kogut, 1983; Ghemawat & Spence, 1986; Teece, 1980). The present authors advocate a similar adoption of interorganizational theory for future MNC-related research, albeit with some modifications to reflect the ownership-based intraorganiza-tional ties that exist between the MNC head-quarters and its different foreign subsidiaries. We believe that interorganizational theory, properly adapted, can provide new insights about a complex and geographically dispersed organizational system like the MNC, and our main objective here is to propose an initial for-mulation regarding how the concepts and tools of interorganizational analysis can be applied to fit this slightly different but analogous case.

To frame the context of our discussions, it may

be useful to begin with an illustration. Figure 1 shows the simplest possible representation of N. V. Philips, a multinational company headquartered in the Netherlands. The company has its own operating units in 60 countries as diverse as the United States, France, Japan, South Korea, Nigeria, Uruguay, and Bangladesh. Some of these units are large, fully integrated companies developing, manufacturing, and marketing a diverse range of products from light bulbs to defense systems. Such subsidiaries might have 5,000 or more employees and might be among the largest companies in their host countries. Others are small, single-function operations responsible for only R & D, or manufacturing, or marketing for only one or a few of these different businesses. Some such units might employ 50 or fewer people. In some cases, the units have been in operation for more than 50 years; a few began their organizational lives less than 10 years ago. Some of these units are tightly controlled from the headquarters; others enjoy relationships with the headquarters more akin to those between equal partners than those between parent and subsidiary.

With only minor alterations, Figure 1 could also be a representation of an American multinational such as Procter & Gamble, or another European company such as Unilever, or a Japanese company such as Matsushita Electric (see descriptions of these companies in Bartlett & Ghoshal, 1986 and 1987). In many ways our description of Philips is a generic account that characterizes many large MNCs. As suggested by a number of authors, MNCs are physically dispersed in environmental settings that represent very different economic, social, and cultural milieus (Fayerweather, 1978; Hofstede, 1980; Robock, Simmons, & Zwick, 1977); are internally differentiated in complex ways to respond to both environmental and organizational differences in different businesses, functions, and geographic locations (Bartlett & Ghoshal, 1986; Prahalad & Doz, 1987); and, as a result of such dispersal and differentiation, possess internal linkages and coordination mechanisms that

represent and respond to many different kinds and extents of dependency and interdependency in interunit exchange relationships (Ghoshal & Nohria, 1989).

We believe that an entity such as any of these large multinational corporations can be more appropriately conceptualized as an interorganizational grouping rather than as a unitary *organization;* also, valuable insights can be gained on the internal structures and operations of such entities from the concepts of organization sets and networks that are more commonly used for exploring interorganizational phenomena (Aldrich & Whetten, 1981; Evan, 1967). In particular, we believe that the concept of a network, both as a metaphor and in terms of the tools and techniques of analysis it provides, reflects the nature and complexity of the multinational organization and can provide a useful lens through which to examine such an entity. We propose here a framework that conceptualizes the multinational as a network of exchange relationships among different organizational units, including the headquarters and the different national subsidiaries that are collectively embedded in what Homans (1974) described as a structured context. Further, continuing the thinking of Tichy, Tushman, and Fombrun (1979), we visualize this context as an *external network* consisting of all the organizations such as customers, suppliers, regulators, and competitors with which the different units of the MNC must interact. Our main proposal is that different attributes of a multinational such as the configuration of its organizational resources and the nature of interunit exchange relations that lead to such a configuration can be explained by selected attributes of the external network within which it is embedded and on which it depends for its survival.

A note of caution must, however, be sounded at this stage. Because network analysis is a rapidly emerging and highly complex field of study and because of the considerable divergence on definitions and approaches that exists within this field, it is unlikely that this initial attempt to apply network concepts to the study of MNCs

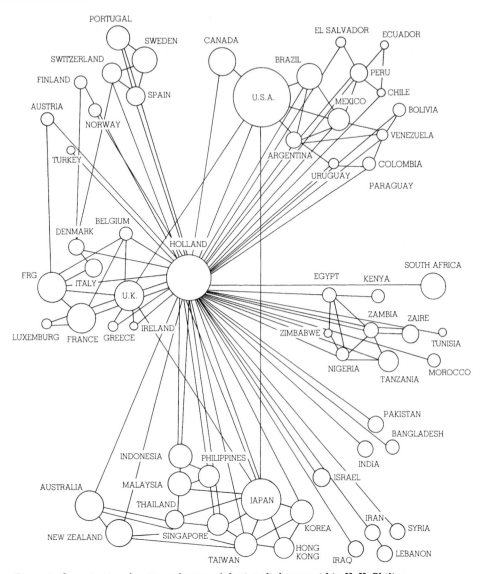

Figure 1. **Organizational units and some of the interlinkages within N. V. Philips.**

will be either complete or above reproach. In the concluding section of our article, we discuss some of the limitations of the present effort and suggest how these might be overcome through future conceptual and empirical research. This article must be viewed, therefore, as an initial attempt to identify the possibility of developing a *network theory of the MNC*, rather than as a rigorous presentation of such a theory.

Although the attempt to formally apply the interorganizational network perspective to the study of MNCs is relatively new, it should also be noted that the conceptual foundation for such an approach already exists in the international management literature. For example, Perlmutter's (1969) scheme for categorizing MNCs as ethnocentric, polycentric, and geocentric organizations is clearly consistent with a network theoretic view. Similarly, the stylized models of MNC organizations developed by Bartlett (1986) and Hedlund (1986), the concept of a *coordinated multinational system* proposed by Kogut (1983), and the application of the resource dependency model by Herbert (1984) for explicating strategy-structure configurations in MNCs have all been implicitly or explicitly grounded in the conceptualization of MNCs as interorganizational systems. Although it builds on this foundation, the article also differs from these earlier pieces in two important ways.

First, in most of these proposals, the structure and attributes of the MNC were explained as arising from the technical and economic rationality and constraints in resource allocation (Kogut, 1983) or from the administrative heritage (Bartlett, 1986) and cognitive orientation (Perlmutter, 1969) of its managers. Our explanation focuses instead on the social and institutional structure of the environments in which the MNC operates. As institutional theorists have argued, the relational networks in the institutional environment play an important role in influencing the structure and behavior of organizations (Meyer & Scott, 1983; Zucker, 1988). The uniqueness of the MNC as an organizational form arises from the fact that its different constituent units are embedded in different national environments in which the structures of these relational networks can be and often are very different (Westney, 1989). Further, in an era of expanding transnational linkages among individuals and organizations, these relational networks in the different countries are also increasingly interconnected among themselves in complex ways. These differences in national industry systems and the interconnections among them are central to our explanation of both economic action and administrative coordination within the dispersed system of the MNC.

Second, the concept of a network has so far been used in this literature mostly as a metaphor to describe and categorize MNC structures and to support normative arguments on the importance of lateral relationships, shared values, and reciprocal task interdependencies for effective management of MNCs. Even though we believe that such a metaphorical use of the term has been useful for descriptive and normative purposes, this paper represents an effort to move to the next step of theory building by using network concepts to explain specific structural attributes of multinational organizations.

Interorganizational Theories Applied to the Multinational Corporation

Much of the existing theory and almost all empirical analyses of interorganizational networks have focused on interorganizational groupings that are not connected by ownership ties (e.g., Pfeffer & Salancik, 1974; Bacharach & Aiken, 1976; Van de Ven & Walker, 1984). Before applying any of the concepts or empirical findings from such studies to the analysis of MNCs, it is first necessary to make a prima facie case that the ownership ties that exist within the multinational do not necessarily preclude the entire range of discretionary behaviors that are possible among interacting organizations that are not so connected.

A number of authors have argued that the

linkage between ownership and hierarchical power ("fiat") in complex organizations is much weaker than is often assumed (e.g., Granovetter, 1985, p. 499). We believe that this link is particularly weak in the case of MNCs because of the large physical and cultural distances between the owned and the owning units. Case histories of extreme subsidiary autonomy have been well documented in the literature on multinationals: the refusal of North American Philips to sell the V2000 video cassette recorder developed by its Dutch parent, preferring instead to purchase from a Japanese archrival, is a good example. Even more dramatic, however, is the case of the British and German subsidiaries of Ruberoid that unilaterally severed all ties with the parent and, with the support of local financial institutions, ultimately secured complete legal independence. Such situations are relatively more common for MNCs headquartered in small countries, many foreign subsidiaries of which often control more resources and contribute more revenues than the parent company. However, many such cases also have been observed in companies such as ITT and Unilever, even though the parents were headquartered in large countries such as the United States and the United Kingdom (Bartlett & Ghoshal, 1989).

The efficacy of fiat is particularly limited in the case of multinationals not only because some of the subsidiaries happen to be very distant and resource-rich but, more so, because they control critical linkages with key actors in their local environments, particularly the host government. To cite but one illustration, the Australian subsidiary of Ericsson, the Swedish telecommunications company, accumulated a very high level of R & D resources primarily because of a coalition between the local management and the Australian Post and Telegraph authorities that had as its principal goal the creation of a major R & D center in Australia. Subsidiary company links with local customers, suppliers, and investors also contribute to the local management's autonomy. For example, following deregulation of the U.S. telecommunications industry, the influence of the American subsidiary of NEC expanded significantly within the company, despite its relatively small size and short organizational life. This was so because of its role in building the company's relationships with the Bell operating companies, which came to be viewed by NEC not only as major potential customers but also as its main contacts for joint development of new products.

We do not claim that the relationships among the parent company and the national subsidiaries in an MNC are identical to those among an interacting group of universities, or social service organizations, or regulatory agencies. Some anecdotal evidence of extreme subsidiary autonomy notwithstanding, the parent company of a multinational typically enjoys considerable hierarchical authority. However, we suggest that the existence of such hierarchical authority does not necessarily lead to fiat as the dominant or even the "last resort" mechanism of control. Typically, in such large, dispersed, and interdependent organizations, hierarchical authority coexists with significant local autonomy and such a situation, we believe, is not inappropriate for the application of interorganizational theories.

For example, in one of the seminal articles on the topic, Warren (1967) developed a typology of interorganizational relationships that distinguished four ways in which members of an organizational field could interact: unitary, federative, coalitional, and social choice. Table 1 summarizes the different attributes of each of these different contexts of interorganizational interactions. In our view, the multinational organization lies somewhere between Warren's unitary and federative structures, both of which admit some level of hierarchical decision making at the top of the inclusive structure. Further, even though the formal structure of MNCs may often resemble the unitary form or what has been described in the literature as *mandated networks* (Aldrich, 1976; Hall, Clark, Giordano, Johnson, & Roekel, 1977), the actual relationships between the headquarters and the subsid-

Table 1
Different Contexts of Interorganizational Interactions

	Type of Context			
Dimension	Unitary	Federative	Coalitional	Social Choice
Relation of units to an inclusive goal	Units organized for achievement of inclusive goals	Units with disparate goals, but some formal organization for inclusive goals	Units with disparate goals, but informal collaboration for inclusive goals	No inclusive goals
Locus of inclusive decision making	At top of inclusive structure	At top of inclusive structure, subject to unit ratification	In interaction of units without a formal inclusive structure	Within units
Locus of authority	At top of hierarchy of inclusive structure	Primarily at unit level	Exclusively at unit level	Exclusively at unit level
Structural provision for division of labor	Units structured for division of labor within inclusive organization	Units structured autonomously; may agree to a division of labor, which may affect their structure	Units structured autonomously, may agree to ad hoc division of labor, without restructuring	No formally structured division of labor within an inclusive context
Commitment of a leadership subsystem	Norms of high commitment	Norms of moderate commitment	Commitment only to unit leaders	Commitment only to unit leaders
Prescribed collectivity-orientation of units	High	Moderate	Minimal	Little or none

iaries and among the subsidiaries themselves tend to be more federative because, contrary to the case of both unitary and mandated networks, issues of competency and power tend to be contested within the MNC and interdependencies among the units tend to be reciprocal as well as sequential (Ghoshal & Nohria, 1989). This claim is consistent with Provan's analysis of different kinds of federations and his observation that the network characteristics of divisionalized firms generally are similar to those of independent federations (see Table 1, p. 83 in Provan, 1983). As demonstrated by Provan, Beyer, and Kruytbosch, (1980), the interorganizational approach can be particularly useful for analyzing such federated relationships among units when the participants have only limited option for discretionary behavior and no opportunity to terminate the relationship.

Despite the broad theoretical scope of the interorganizational perspective as shown in Warren's classification of the field, empirical applications of this perspective have so far been limited to contexts that range from federative to social choice and interaction contexts that range from unitary to federative have been excluded from the domain of interorganizational inquiry and placed in the domain of intraorganizational analysis (Cook, 1977). As such, the relationships between the diverse units of a multidivisional or a multinational corporation have rarely been examined from an interorganizational perspective.

Meanwhile, the limitations of applying traditional intraorganizational theory to the analysis of such complex and dispersed business organizations have become increasingly clear. As summarized by Nohria and Venkatraman (1987), the most critical of these limitations stem from the need in such analysis to provide a relatively clear separation between the "organization" and its relevant "environment." As a result, "the environment is typically viewed as an exogenous entity and is reified as a source of undefined uncertainties (e.g., volatility, resource scarcity, etc.) as opposed to being seen as a field of specific interacting organizations which locate the source of those contingencies" (Nohria & Venkatraman, 1987, p. 2). The organization is seen as a well-defined collective and is assumed to be internally homogeneous, coherent, and consistent. "Therefore, it is typically described in distributional (e.g., organization chart, division of responsibility, authority, etc.) and categorical (e.g., centralized versus decentralized, mechanistic versus organic, differentiated versus integrated, etc.) terms as opposed to relational terms that focus on the actual interaction patterns based on both internal and external flows of products, information, and authority" (Nohria & Venkatraman, 1987, p. 2).

In contrast to these limitations of traditional intraorganizational analysis, a dominant construct in most interorganizational theories is an exchange relation (e.g., A_x and B_y) that is defined as consisting of "transactions involving the transfer of resources (x, y) between two or more actors (A, B) for mutual benefit" (Cook, 1977, p. 64). The term *resources* as used in this context includes "any *valued* activity, service or commodity" (Cook, 1977, p. 64, emphasis added) and therefore includes not only the flows of finances and products but also the flows of technology, people, and information. Furthermore, as Cook observed, "the term actor in the theory refers not only to individuals but also to

collective actors or corporate groups [thus making] it uniquely appropriate when organizations or subunits of organizations are used as the primary unit of analysis" (1977, p. 63). It is this suggestion of Cook that we adopt and develop in this article.

The Multinational as a Network: Constructs and Terminology

Let us consider a multinational corporation M with operating units in countries A, B, C, D, E, and F and a focal organization in the corporate headquarters H. For the purpose of analytical simplicity, let us assume that all the units of M are engaged in a single and common business (i.e., M is a single-industry company). Note that H serves as a coordinating agency and plays the role that Provan (1983) described as belonging to the Federation Management Organization (FMO) and, therefore, must be distinguished from the organizational unit, say A, that is responsible for operations in the home country of M, even though the two may be located in the same premises. By the term **multinational network** we shall refer to all the relationships and linkages that exist among the different units of M (i.e., among A, B, C, D, E, F, and H).

Each of the national operating units of M is embedded in a unique context and, for any specific type of exchange relationship, has its unique organization set (Aldrich & Whetten, 1981). For example, the unit A can have existing or potential exchange relationships with a specific set of suppliers $[s_A]$, buyers $[b_A]$, regulatory agencies $[r_A]$, and it competes for resources with an identifiable set of competitors $[c_A]$. Collectively, the group consisting of $[s_A, b_A, r_A, c_A,$ etc.] constitutes what we call the organization set of A and denote by the symbol $[OS_A]$.

Different members of the organization set $[OS_A]$ can be internally connected by exchange ties. In keeping with Aldrich and Whetten's thinking (1981) we can define the density of $[OS_A]$ as the extensiveness of exchange ties within the elements of the organization set of A. Density measures the extent to which actors within the set are connected, on average, to one another (i.e., the mean relation from any one actor to any other actor). As suggested by Aldrich and Whetten, such a construct of density can be operationalized in different ways. For present purposes, we can choose the simplest of these ways and define it as the percentage of actual to potential ties among members of $[OS_A]$. The concluding section of this article includes a more detailed discussion on identification of boundaries and measurement of densities for the different local organizations sets.

The density of such connections within the different local organization sets of A, B, C, and so on may vary. For example, it has been noted by many authors that the level of connectedness among different members of an industry group is significantly higher in Japan in comparison to some Western countries (e.g., see discussions and the quotation from Lohr cited in Granovetter, 1985, p. 497). Similarly, it has been shown in the management literature that within the same national environment, the level of cohesiveness among customers, suppliers, competitors, and so forth may be higher in certain businesses such as construction (Eccles, 1981), publishing (Powell, 1985), textiles (Sabel, Herrigel, Kazis, & Deeg, 1987), and investment banking (Eccles & Crane, 1987), compared to others.

The different organization sets of the different units of M may themselves be interconnected through exchange ties. For example, one of the supplying organizations in the local environment of A may be an affiliated unit of another multinational company, and it may have exchange linkages with its counterpart in the local environment of B. Similarly, the actions of regulatory agencies in one location (say, r_C) may influence the actions of their counterparts in other locations (say, r_D). Such influence may be manifest in actions such as retaliation by r_C to what is seen as protectionist action of r_D, or deregulation by r_D to reciprocate or just emulate similar action by r_C (Mahini & Wells, 1986). Such linkages also may exist among suppliers and competitors. In fact, much of the current literature on global strategy considers such cross-border linkages among customers, competitors, and other relevant organizations as a key factor that does or should influence the behaviors of MNCs (e.g., this is a focal issue for a number of essays in Porter, 1986).

Because of such linkages among the different local organization sets, all members of all the organization sets of the different units of M collectively constitute what we shall call the **external network** (Tichy, Tushman, & Fombrun, 1979) within which the multinational network is embedded. In the same manner as we defined the construct of density for each of the different organization sets of the different units of M, we can also describe the density of this external network as the ratio of actual to potential ties among all its constituents. To differentiate between these two densities, we shall refer to the density of ties within each of the local organization sets as **within density** and the density of ties within the total external network, that is, across the different organization sets, as **across density.**

The main thesis in this article is that different attributes of the MNC can be explained in terms of selected attributes of the external network within which it is embedded. Following the arguments of Benson (1975), the interactions within the different organizational units of the MNC are best explained at the level of resource exchange. This suggests two attributes of the MNC as particularly relevant to our analysis: (a) the distribution of resources among its different affiliated units and (b) the structural characteristics that mediate internal exchange relationships within the MNC and continually restructure the resource configuration (Zeitz, 1980). These two characteristics of the MNC and how they relate to within and across densities will provide the focus of our attention for the remaining part of this article.

Resource Configuration in MNCs

Resources such as production equipments, finance, technology, marketing skills, and management capabilities may be located in any one or more of the different units of M. By the term resource configuration we refer to the way in which the resources of *M* are distributed among *A, B, C, D, E, F*, and *H*. (We use the word *resource* in the sense of Cook [1977, p. 64] to refer to "any valuable activity, service, or commodity".) In some companies that Bartlett (1986) described as "centralized hubs," most of such resources may be concentrated in any one location, typically the parent company. For example, 90 percent of the manufacturing investments of Matsushita, the Japanese consumer electronics company, and 100 percent of its research facilities are located in Japan. In contrast, in companies such as Philips, Matsushita's European competitor and one that Bartlett categorized as a "decentralized federation," over 77 percent of total assets are located outside the company's home, which is in the Netherlands, and no single national subsidiary has more than 15 percent of the company's worldwide assets. This difference illustrates one aspect of resource configuration in MNCs that is of analytical interest, namely, **dispersal,** by which term we refer to the extent to which the company's resources are concentrated in one unit versus dispersed among the different units.

However, although both Philips and Electrolux (the Swedish home appliances company) have a relatively high level of dispersal in the sense that both companies have significant parts of their total assets distributed in a number of countries, the pattern of distribution of such assets is very different in the two cases. Let us consider their resources within Europe. For Electrolux, even though the resources are dispersed, they also are very specialized, that is, the resources and associated activities located in any one country are of sufficient scale to meet the company's worldwide or, at least, regional requirements for that activity, thereby avoiding the need for carrying out the same activity or task in multiple locations. For example, Electrolux's washing machine factory in France produces top-loading washing machines only and it meets the company's requirements in that product category for all of Europe. Similarly, the washing machine factory in Italy produces only

front-loading models to meet Europe-wide demand. Its research centers, product development laboratories, and component-producing units are all similarly differentiated and specialized. By contrast, despite considerable recent efforts to increase such specialization, Philips owns five factories in Europe that produce identical or near-identical models of television sets, each basically for a local market. In other words, the resources of Philips are dispersed on a local-for-local basis (Ghoshal, 1986)—they are dispersed but undifferentiated, with identical resources being used by each unit to carry out essentially similar tasks in and for its own local environment. We refer to this dimension of resource configuration as *specialization*, and it represents the extent to which the resources located in each unit are differentiated from those in others.

Resource configuration in MNCs traditionally has been analyzed from an economic perspective, typically under the assumption that resource location decisions are based on rational, self-interested considerations such as needing increasing profitability, gaining access to new markets or desired factors of production, protecting competitive position, and minimizing costs and risks (for reviews, see Buckley & Casson, 1985; Caves, 1982; Dunning, 1981; Hennart, 1982). Explanations of both dispersal and specialization have therefore focused on factors such as differences in costs of inputs (e.g., Stevens, 1974), potential scale economies in different activities (e.g., Porter, 1986), impacts of transportation and other "friction" costs (e.g., Hirsch, 1976), imperfections in information and other intermediate product markets (e.g., Magee, 1977; Rugman, 1980), defense against opportunism (e.g., Teece, 1986), and potential benefits of risk diversification (e.g., Lessard & Lightstone, 1986).

Following from Granovetter's (1985) ideas, much of this analysis can be criticized as *undersocialized* or *oversocialized* conceptualizations that ignore the important and ongoing effects that surrounding social structures have on economic behaviors of organizations. We present here an alternative framework that relates dispersal and specialization to the densities of interactions both within and across the different local organization sets of the company. As suggested in the introductory section, our conceptualization is strongly influenced by the work of institutional theorists who have argued that the structure and behavior of organizations are influenced by both technical and institutional factors (Meyer & Scott, 1983) and that "organizations compete not just for resources and customers, but for political power and institutional legitimacy, for social as well as economic fitness" (DiMaggio & Powell, 1983, p. 150). Although Meyer and Scott have been cautious in suggesting that business organizations belong to "technical sectors" in which the economic need for efficiency and effectiveness in controlling work processes dominates institutional need for legitimacy, they also have contended that "while the two dimensions (technical and institutional) tend to be negatively correlated, they are apparently not strongly so" (1983, p. 140). As suggested by Westney (1989), we believe that for MNCs, strong needs for legitimacy and local isomorphism in each host country environment coexist with strong demand for efficiency within its worldwide system and, therefore, the institutional structure of the environment (i.e., the attributes of the local organization sets and the external network) plays an important role in moderating the influence of technical and economic considerations. Even though they are different from traditional economic analysis, our arguments are much more consistent with recent work of economists such as Porter (in press) and Kogut (1988), both of whom have shown the importance of interinstitutional structure in determining the competitiveness of different countries and companies in different businesses.

Effects of Within Density in National Organization Sets

As Bower (1987) has shown through his indepth study of American, European, and Japanese companies in the petrochemical industry, the density of linkages among key players in a national industrial context greatly influences industry performance and company strategy. For a variety of economic, legal, sociological, cultural, and historical reasons, some countries such as Japan are characterized by dense linkages among the suppliers, producers, regulators, customers, and others involved in a particular field of industrial activity (Westney & Sakakibara, 1985). Such linkages among the different actors may involve different kinds of exchanges such as those involving funds, people, or information, and they may be established and maintained through many different mechanisms such as integrating governmental agencies, interlocking boards of directors, cross-holding of equity, institutionalizing systems of personnel flows, using long-term contracts and trust-based relationships, and mediating roles of organizations such as trade associations, banks, and consultants (e.g., the collected essays in Evan, 1976). Bower's study shows how Japanese petrochemical companies were able to capitalize on such linkages, not only to build entry barriers in the local market, but also as a means of restructuring and rationalizing the industry.

In locations in which the local organization sets are densely connected, the implications for local units of MNCs are clear. As argued by Granovetter (1973), strong and multiplexed ties among the existing members of the national organization sets will lead to exclusion from the sets of those who cannot establish equally strong and multiplexed ties with each member. Westney and Sakakibara's (1985) study on the R & D activities of Japanese and American computer companies illustrates this effect of within density in the local organization sets. According to these authors, the Japanese R & D centers of some of the American computer companies could not tap into local skills and technologies because the absence of associated manufacturing and marketing activities prevented the isolated research establishments from building linkages with the local "knowledge networks" that were embedded in the dense interactions among different members of the organization set for the computer industry in Japan.

Where the linkages within the local organization sets are sparse, no such barriers are created, as shown in the U.S. Department of Commerce's account of the television industry in the United States in the early 1970s (Paul, 1984). Absence of ties among producers because of rivalry and antitrust laws, and their arm's-length relationships with suppliers, labor, and government, created an environment that made it easy for Japanese producers to enter the U.S. market with local sales offices importing finished products from the parent companies. However, when the American companies responded in a unified manner through the Electronics Industry Association, with the support of labor unions and suppliers, they were able to obtain government support on antidumping suits, and the resulting politically negotiated import quotas forced the Japanese companies to establish local manufacturing facilities.

We can, therefore, make the following propositions about the effects of within density on dispersal and specialization in the configuration of resources in a multinational. When interaction densities within the different national organization sets are low, the social context exerts limited influence and intended economic rationality becomes dominant in resource configuration decisions. In this situation, therefore, the MNC will concentrate research, production, assembly, and other similar activities based on consideration of potential scale and scope economies and locate them on the basis of resource niches (Aldrich, 1979) that may exist in different countries as a result of their comparative advantages (e.g., R & D in the United States or Japan, manufacturing in Singapore or Brazil). As a result, its overall resource configuration will show relatively low dispersal and high specialization. When within densities are high, however, the company will be forced to fragment its activities and locate more of the different kinds of resources in each market so as to provide the va-

riety that is necessary to match the structures of the local organization sets. Consequently, in this case, dispersal will increase while specialization will decrease.

Effects of Across Density in the External Network

When the linkages across the different national organization sets are sparse, the MNC's resource configuration follows the pattern we have described previously based on consideration of the within densities alone. If there are high interactions across members of the different national organization sets, this situation changes significantly.

Consider first the case of low within density and high across density. We have argued that low within density will lead to low dispersal and high specialization, and the company will locate its resources according to the resource niches in different countries. But, with high across densities, many of these national resource niches are eliminated because of freer flows. If technologies developing in one location can be accessed instantaneously from another, or if excess capital available in one environment can be borrowed in markets located elsewhere, there is no longer any need to locate specific activities in specific locations to benefit from access to local resources. Therefore, with high across density, resource-seeking concentration will decline (though not necessarily be eliminated because regulatory and other barriers may selectively prohibit certain flows of people and products).

Consider now the case of high within densities coupled with high across densities. We have suggested that high within density will lead to high dispersal and low specialization because of the need for matching the structures of the local environments. However, when across densities are high, it is no longer necessary to establish a comprehensive range of resources in each market because exchange linkages can now be established across borders, without the need for complementary facilities on a location-by-location basis. In other words, if there is high across density, the logic of resource allocation for both high and low within densities becomes inappropriate. Instead, a completely different set of criteria emerges: In this situation, resource configuration is greatly influenced by the nodal characteristics of the complex external network.

Consider, for example, the situation in which customers in locations *A*, *B*, *D*, and *E* are strongly influenced by the standards and preferences of customers in location *C*. Bartlett and Ghoshal (1986) and Prahalad and Doz (1987) have described the existence of such *lead markets* in many businesses, and this existence is predicted by the *normative systems* that Laumann, Glaskiewicz, and Marsden (1978) proposed as one of the modalities that influence the behaviors of members in a network. In such a situation, the MNC will tend to locate a significant amount of resources in *C* so as to be able to sense the demands of local customers and respond to them in a fashion that attracts their patronage. The level of resources in *C* will exceed what is required to match the needs for membership of the local organization set (OS$_C$) and will, instead, be targeted to benefit from the greater role of *C* as a central node in the larger external network that is created by the linkages among (OS$_A$), (OS$_B$), (OS$_C$), and so on. Given that for different activities of the MNC, different locations might emerge as the nodes in the relevant external networks, and given that even for the same activity there might be multiple nodes instead of a single node, the consequence of increasing across density for the resource configuration of the company will be one of moderate dispersal (i.e., not as high as in the case of local-for-local distribution but higher than concentration only in countries offering specific resource niches) coupled with increasing specialization. Tasks will be divided into finer and finer segments so that each could be located at the appropriate nodal locations which, however, might well be different from those that would be predicted by the traditional considerations of

comparative advantages or resource niches as applicable to those tasks.

Chandler (1986), among others, has documented that because of improvements in communication and transportation infrastructures around the world, increasing across densities has been a dominant trend that has affected a wide range of industries in the recent past. The observed consequences of this trend are entirely consistent with our arguments. For example, until the late 1970s, the telecommunications switching industry was characterized by high within and low across densities. Interactions among members of the industry were high within each country because of its status as a *strategic industry* and the resulting coordinating role of the national governments. However, until the advent of digital technology, the industry was highly regulated in most countries, and the need to synchronize the switching equipment with the ideosyncrasies of local terminal equipments constrained opportunities for cross-border linkages. As a result, the resources of most multinational companies were highly dispersed, and they had low levels of specialization. ITT provides a good illustration: Each of its national subsidiaries in Europe had its own local facilities for product development, manufacturing, and marketing, and the corporate staff including the top management of the company consisted of fewer than 100 employees.

The context of this industry has changed significantly in the 1980s: Although within densities have remained high, across density has increased substantially due to the emergence of digital technology and the growing trends of standardization and deregulation, all of which have facilitated cross-border integration among suppliers, customers, and other industry participants. As a result, resource configurations of the producers have also changed. Even though the overall level of dispersal has been reduced to a limited extent, the level of specialization has increased drastically. Ericsson, for example, has closed only a few of its factories around the world, but it has converted many of them into focused manufacturing centers that produce a narrow range of components. Similarly, each of the laboratories of Alcatel, the company created by merging ITT and CIT-Alcatel, has now been given the mandate and resources to pursue a specific and well-defined technology or development task in contrast to the earlier situation when most of them operated quite independently, developing the entire range of products for their local markets.

Centrality and Power Within the Multinational Network

Our preceding arguments on resource configuration in MNCs were based on a notion of isomorphic fit with the characteristics of the external network; we did not address the question of how such a fit is achieved. An MNC's configuration of resources at any point in time is the outcome of previous resource flows and, as argued by Benson (1975), the flow of resources within an interorganizational network is influenced by the distribution of power within the network. In this section, we will suggest that within and across densities in the different national organization sets of an MNC predicate the relative power of the headquarters and the national units, and that the nature of resource flows generated by the resulting distribution of power leads to the pattern of isomorphic fit we have described.

Effects of Within Density in National Organization Sets

Applying Zald's (1970) political economy approach to the analysis of interorganizational relations, Benson (1975) suggested that an actor in such a network can enhance its power in dyadic relationships with other actors on the strength of its relationships with other organizational or social networks. Subsequently, Provan et al. (1980) provided empirical support to this proposal when they demonstrated that power relations

within the network of United Way organizations were significantly modified by the linkages between the individual agencies and other elements in their local communities upon which the United Way depended for its survival. The dependence of the United Way on the local communities of its different organizations is in some ways akin to the dependence of the multinational on the local organization sets of its different national units: Just as dense linkages with the key elements of their communities enhanced the power of the United Way organizations, dense exchange relationships with the members of their local organization sets can be expected to enhance the powers of the national units of the multinational.

It is inappropriate, however, to draw a direct correspondence between the United Way and an MNC because the central management organization of the United Way lacks the hierarchical power of the headquarters of the MNC. To incorporate this difference in our analysis, it is necessary to consider how hierarchical power might modify the interunit exchange patterns proposed by Benson.

We suggest that the efficacy of the hierarchical power of the headquarters to counteract the linkage-based power of the subsidiary is contingent on the density of interactions among members of the subsidiary's organization set. When this within density is low, the potential power of the subsidiary is derived from its individual dyadic relationships. In this situation, the headquarters is more effective in counteracting the power of the subsidiary because it is potentially easier to have "direct control" over such relationships through mechanisms such as periodic visits by the headquarters staff. However, such direct control becomes more difficult in this case, when the subsidiary's power is not derived from an individual dyadic relationship, but from the web of exchange relations in the local organization set of which it is a part. Remote control loses efficacy when "localness," by itself, is the key requirement for maintaining the relationships. For example, in the case of the Australian subsidiary of Ericsson that we referred to earlier, extensive cross-licensing arrangements among all the producers, and the resulting close relationships among equipment suppliers, customers, and regulators, was a main reason (other than distance) that impeded closer control of the local subsidiary from Stockholm and allowed the subsidiary to build up the high level of research and other resources.

Therefore, the positive relationship between environmental linkages and power of the local unit of an interorganizational network proposed by Benson (1975) will remain operational in the context of an MNC under the condition of high within density. Following the arguments of Emerson (1962) and Cook (1977), the local unit will use this power to reduce its dependence on the other units of the network. Therefore, it will bargain for and obtain a full range of resources so that it will be able to autonomously carry out as many of its functions as possible. If all or most of the units of the MNC are located in environments of high within density, the consequence of this process will be a high level of dispersal of its resources on a local-for-local basis.

Effects of Across Density in the External Network

Existing literature on the distribution of power in social networks reveals two main sources of power in such collectivities (Fombrun, 1983). First, power is an antipode of dependency in exchange relations (Emerson, 1962), and it accrues to members of the network who control critical resources required by others but do not depend on others for resources (Aldrich, 1979; Pfeffer & Salancik, 1978). In keeping with Cook (1977), this might be called *exchange power* to distinguish it from the second source of power that arises from structural rather than exchange dependencies. *Structural power* emanates from the position of a member within the network, as shown by Lazarsfeld and Menzel (1961); it is an attribute that is induced by a member's context.

Our preceding discussions on power-de-

pendency relationships within an MNC were based only on consideration of dyadic exchange between the headquarters and the national units. The situation changes when consideration of structural power is brought into the analysis. Structure of the external network now enters the calculation as an important variable because different members of the multinational network can potentially develop different levels of structural power based on their positions within the larger network of interactions among customers, suppliers, and so forth across different countries.

Ignoring for present purposes the exceptions to the rule pointed out by Cook, Emerson, Gilmore, and Yamagishi (1983), the structural power of actors in a network can be assumed to arise from their centrality within the network (Laumann & Pappi, 1976; Lehman, 1975). As pointed out by Freeman (1979), the term centrality has been defined and used in the literature in many different ways. For this article, we can limit our attention to what Freeman describes as point centrality of the different actors within the multinational network, and we can also define the point centrality of each actor as a function of its degree (i.e., the number of other actors within the multinational network with which it has direct exchange relations). Following the arguments of Freeman, the headquarters enjoys the highest levels of point centrality when linkages among the subsidiaries are minimal. In a situation of extensive interactions among the subsidiaries, the centrality of the headquarters declines relative to those of the subsidiaries, and the centrality of the different members of the network becomes dependent on the actual structure of such linkages. This explanation becomes clear from a comparison of the three network structures shown in Figure 2 (each of which is reproduced from Freeman, 1979).

High across density typically implies a high level of interactions among the subsidiaries of a multinational. As an illustration, consider the case of a manufacturer of automotive tires such as Italy's Pirelli and Company. The company produces and markets car and truck tires in a

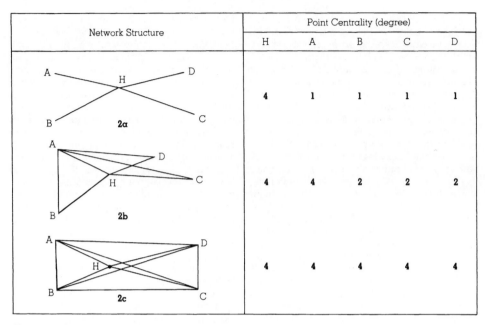

Network Structure	Point Centrality (degree)				
	H	A	B	C	D
2a	4	1	1	1	1
2b	4	4	2	2	2
2c	4	4	4	4	4

Figure 2. **Centrality measures for three different network structures.**

number of countries including the United States, Italy, and Germany. It also supplies tires to the Ford Motor Company in each of these countries.

Until such time that Ford's local units in these countries operated relatively autonomously, with minimal coordination, there was little need for Pirelli's local units to coordinate their own activities with regard to their supply to Ford. But as the interactions and coordination among Ford's operations in these countries increased, leading to internal comparisons of the prices, quality, and support provided by common vendors (thereby enhancing across density, as relevant to Pirelli), Pirelli's subsidiaries also needed to enhance their internal coordination and communication on issues of quality levels, pricing, service, and so on to prevent customer dissatisfaction (see Terpstra, 1982). In other words, as a general principle, it can be stated

that as across density increases, intersubsidiary linkages become more extensive, and the centrality of the headquarters declines, relative to other units.

It is more interesting to note, however, under this condition, multiple points can emerge within the MNC with the same or similar degree of point centrality. Note that for the star-shaped structure (Figure 2c), the headquarters and all the subsidiaries have the same point centrality, whereas in the hub-shaped structure (Figure 2a), the headquarters has a very high level of point centrality compared to the subsidiaries. In Figure 2b, however, whereas one subsidiary has the same point centrality as the headquarters, other subsidiaries have less.

An outcome such as the network structure shown in Figures 2b or 2c will follow from the existence of nodes in the external network. For example, for Pirelli, the United States, Italy, and Germany may emerge as external nodes because the headquarters for its major worldwide customers may be located in these markets. Further, only one of these external nodes (Italy) may coincide with the location of the company's own headquarters. Normative hierarchy in customer tastes and preferences (e.g., adoption by customers in other countries of a perfume or wine that is popular in France) and the advanced states of certain technologies in certain countries (e.g., ceramic technology in Japan, computer software technology in the United States and the United Kingdom) are some other examples of such external nodes that can affect the point centralities of different units within the MNC. For the different activities of the MNC, different locations can emerge as the nodes of the external network; for any particular activity, a number of different locations can possess such nodal characteristics. Consequently, following the arguments of Burt (1978), the multinational network typically will develop multiple centers that have different internal coalitions and nodes corresponding to the different coalitions and nodes that may exist in the external network.

Therefore, in such a situation, the nodal units of the multinational will develop structural power and use this power to attract resources from within the MNC network. As a result, the level of dispersal in the MNC's resources will be moderate—lower than local-for-local dispersal (because not all units will emerge as nodes) but higher than in the case of concentration in locations of specific resource niches (except for businesses where a specific country enjoys a dominant position in all activities). Further, a high level of specialization also will develop in the resource configuration because nodal positions within the MNC network can be expected to vary by activities and tasks as a reflection of similar variance in the external network. Note that both the process and the outcome aspects of this conclusion resonate with some recent empirical findings such as those of subsidiaries being given *world product mandates* (Poynter & Rug-

man, 1982) and *global leader* or *contributor* roles (Bartlett & Ghoshal, 1986) for specific activities and tasks.

Large MNCs as Differentiated Networks

Several highly simplifying assumptions were made in the foregoing discussions on resource configuration in MNCs under different conditions of local and global interlinkages. The enormous complexity of several disparate country-level organization sets and the diversity of the heterogeneous international business environment were dichotomized into high-low categories of within and across densities. In reality, the levels of connectedness within and across the national organization sets can be expected to vary across countries and groups of countries. Density of interactions across the national organization sets may be high for the developed countries, or among regional groupings, but low in developing countries, particularly the more regulated and autarchic. Similarly, interactions among members within the national organization sets may be high in homogeneous societies that have a tradition of strong interinstitutional linkages, and it may be low in countries where such linkages are discouraged through legislation, impeded because of societal heterogeneity, or rendered ineffective because of poor communication infrastructures or the absence of linking institutions.

Therefore, the configuration of resources in multinationals engaged in such businesses will be influenced by multiple criteria. In some locations internal interactions within the local organization sets may be high, but external linkages with other organization sets may be low. In such locations, the MNC may provide all the required resources in appropriate measures so that its local unit can build and maintain linkages with key members of its own community. The organization sets in some other countries may be sparsely connected internally, but different elements of the local environment may be strongly connected with their counterparts in other countries. For these locations, the MNC may create a resource structure that is concentrated and specialized, and in some cases the location of the specialized resources may reflect the desire to access special resource niches, whereas in other cases the location choice may be motivated by the modalities in the external network. Finally, the organization sets in a third group of countries may be characterized by high within and across linkages: In these locations, the MNC may establish all the complementary resources for integrated operations, but it may link these locations with others so as to leverage the resources and achieve economies of concentration and specialization.

The overall resource configuration for a company like Philips, then, will reflect a mix of some resources that are dispersed among some units on a purely local-for-local basis (e.g., product development, manufacturing, marketing, and other resources for the lighting business in India); some that are concentrated in different countries to access specialized local resource pools (e.g., the global scale audio factory in Singapore); and others that are concentrated in lead markets (e.g., development and manufacturing facilities for teletext television sets in the United Kingdom). Elsewhere we have described such a structure as the *differentiated network* and have shown that a number of large multinational companies such as Procter & Gamble, Unilever, Ericsson, NEC, and Matsushita are increasingly converging to this structural form despite the differences in their businesses and parent company nationalities (Bartlett & Ghoshal, 1989).

Such a convergence is consistent with the theoretical arguments we have presented here. Following the arguments of Chandler (1986), one effect of worldwide improvements in communication and transportation infrastructures is the increasing interlinkages among actors, both within and across national boundaries. When such linkages are low, the influence of structural embeddedness is low, and MNCs have a greater degree of freedom to locate their activities and resources to benefit from local resource niches and are in line with the economic and technological characteristics of their businesses. Thus, in such situations, the resource configurations of different MNCs can be expected to differ as a reflection of those differences in their businesses and as a result of their freedom to exercise strategic choices. However, in the context of high within and across densities, such freedom is reduced because of the network influences: Both dispersal and specialization now become essential, at least for the very large companies that have been the focus of our attention in this article. If within density is a country trait and across density is a world-system trait, the pattern of linkages in the overall structure of the external network is going to be increasingly similar for large multinational companies, irrespective of their businesses. In other words, mimetic and normative forces of isomorphism (DiMaggio & Powell, 1983) may be getting stronger as the world jolts along to Levitt's (1983) *global village*, and the observed trend of convergence to the differentiated network structure may be an outcome of these broader societal changes.

Implications for Research

We have proposed a reconceptualization of the MNC as an interorganizational system rather than as an organization. This reconceptualization creates the possibility of applying exchange theory and network methodologies to the study of MNCs and has some important implications for future research on MNC-related issues.

First, at the aggregate level of macrostructural differences among MNCs, traditional analysis has tended to assume internal homogeneity within such companies. This has resulted in generalized conclusions at the level of the overall company based on empirical studies that have focused on individual actors or specific dyadic links. For example, a sampled group of American MNCs have been inferred to be more centralized than their Japanese and European counterparts based on analysis of the parent companies' relationships with their subsidiaries located in one region (e.g., Hulbert & Brandt, 1980). However, as we have argued, headquarters-subsidiary relations within an MNC can vary widely from subsidiary to subsidiary. The interorganizational network conceptualization can provide new concepts such as graph centrality (Freeman, 1979) or hierarchy (Coleman, 1966), which appear to be theoretically more appropriate for such macrostructural comparisons among internally differentiated and heterogeneous organizational systems like MNCs.

Second, given such heterogeneity, macrostructural analysis alone may not be enough and may need to be complemented with microstructural analyses of these internal differences so as to build a more nearly complete theoretical understanding of the ways in which an MNC functions. For example, in the differentiated network MNC, there is no formal macrostructure that "fits" all parts of the company's heterogeneous environments. Yet, it has to choose a formal departmental structure and might, quite arbitrarily, choose one that appears to be simple and consistent with its own administrative heritage (Bartlett, 1983, 1986). Therefore, not only might macrostructure have become more difficult to predict theoretically—as seems true, given the significant empirically induced modifications to the Stopford and Wells (1972) contingency model proposed by subsequent studies of MNC macrostructures, such as those by Daniels, Pitts, and Tretter (1985) and Egelhoff (1988)—but it might also have become a less interesting attribute to study precisely because of such indeterminateness. For example, contrary to the predictions of structural contingency, NEC, Procter & Gamble, and Unilever have not changed their macrostructures in over two decades despite some very significant changes in their business conditions. What have changed in these companies are the internal management processes; subsidiaries have assumed new and specific roles to respond to changing local conditions, and the headquarters' control mechanisms

have evolved from ubiquitous "company ways" to multidimensional gestalts that are applied differently to different parts of the organization so as to respond to shifting global contexts (Bartlett & Ghoshal, 1989). The network perspective is particularly suited for investigation of such differences in internal roles, relations, and tasks of different affiliated units (e.g., through block modeling and analysis of functional equivalence) and of how internal coordination mechanisms might be differentiated to match the variety of subunit contexts (e.g., the papers by Burt on "distinguishing relational contents" (pp. 35–74) and "studying status/role-sets using mass surveys" (pp. 100–118) in Burt, Minor, & Associates, 1983).

The same argument we made for structure can also be made for strategy. Discussions on company- or even business-level generic strategies and how they "fit" generic types of competitive structures are too far removed from the reality of highly differentiated strategic approaches that can be expected in different parts of the differentiated network organization. Instead, it may be more useful to explore the actual content of strategy in such complex organizational systems: Network theoretic analysis of internal flows of resources, products, people, and information might be more relevant for developing middle-range theories on resource commitment, decision making, strategic control, normative integration, and creation and diffusion of innovations in such companies (e.g., the application of network analysis in Carley, 1986; Burt, 1987; and Walker, 1985). In this article we have focused primarily on the hierarchical network relationships between the headquarters and the national subsidiaries of an MNC. Investigation of the lateral network relations among the different subsidiaries can open up avenues for similar fine-grained analysis of both the causes and consequences of horizontal interdependencies and synergy.

Finally, as has been shown in some recent contributions, the interorganizational approach can be particularly useful for the study of another MNC-related phenomenon that is assuming increasing importance (viz., their forming complex webs of alliances and joint ventures with customers, suppliers, and competitors [Ohmae, 1989; Harrigan, 1985]). By focusing on relations among actors, the network analysis approach can provide both appropriate concepts and methodological tools for rigorous and theory-grounded investigation of the strategic and organizational aspects of such alliances (see, for example, the contributions by Walker [pp. 227–240], Westney [pp. 339–346], and Hakausson & Johanson [pp. 369–379] cited in Contractor & Lorange, 1988).

Building a Network Theory of the MNC

The concepts and arguments presented here suffer from a number of shortcomings that should be overcome before the network conceptualization can yield a useful and testable theory of the MNC. The necessary improvement and extension of these preliminary ideas will require both deductive theory building with more sophisticated use of network theory than has been achieved here; empirical studies are also needed to induce and test more fine-grained propositions and hypotheses.

First, our definitions of constructs such as within and across densities are too coarse because, as we point out in the concluding section, these densities cannot but differ for different parts of the total external network of any company. Such differences can be expected along both geographic and functional dimensions. For example, the external organizations relevant for the R & D department of a company may be far more interconnected across national borders compared to those that are relevant for the service department. Similarly, while within density, on average, may be higher in Japan than in the United States, there may be significant differences between the two contexts for different parts of the local organization sets. One of the main attractions of the network perspective is that the implications of such differences can be

explicitly included in both theoretical and empirical analyses, and elaboration of these distinctions must be a priority for future research on this topic.

Second, we have considered exchange very broadly to include many different kinds of transactions involving products, information, affect, and so on, without distinguishing among these different flows. As follows from the general arguments of Mitchell (1973) and Kadushin (1978), each of these different kinds of exchanges can have some very different implications for the strategy, organization, and management of an MNC; further, those effects are also likely to be interactive. Therefore, the next phase of theory development must explicate the separate and joint effects of these different kinds of exchanges.

Third, we have focused on density as the key parameter of the external network because density appeared to relate most closely to the implications of social embeddedness described by Granovetter (1985). Further, it is also a relatively simple construct that is easy to conceptualize and to measure once the relevant organization sets and external network are identified (see below). But density is not a complete description of a network, and it is possible that some other characteristics of the external network can significantly influence specific attributes of the MNC. Therefore, for more nearly complete development of theory, it would be desirable to identify a set of parameters that completely and unambiguously define the external network and then to explore the impact of each of these parameters on selected attributes of the multinational. Krackhardt (1989) has proposed four parameters (connectedness, hierarchy, least-upperboundedness, and graph efficiency) as necessary and sufficient descriptors of a network, and his work provides some interesting opportunities for modifying and extending our theoretical arguments.

Finally, besides (indeed, before) such extension and refinement of the concepts, it might also be necessary to improve the specificity and precision in our definition of some of the constructs so as to facilitate their operationalization in empirical research. One key issue concerns delineation of the boundaries of the different national organization sets, which is a general and widespread problem in network research (Laumann, Marsden, & Prensky, 1983). As suggested by Aldrich and Whetten (1981), the relevant organization sets may well differ according to different kinds of exchange, and the definition of the boundaries may, therefore, depend on the kind of exchange that is the focus of inquiry. In presenting our ideas here, we have been guided by the belief that these boundaries can be identified either through the naturalistic approach of an a priori commonsense definition, or empirically, through measurement of structural cohesion (DiMaggio, 1986). In the former approach, for example, all relevant suppliers, customers, regulators, and competitors in any country can be prespecified based on expert knowledge of the local structure of the business. In the latter approach, a broader population of potentially relevant members of the local organization set may be identified through a repeated process of snowball sampling until sufficient convergence is achieved, and the organization set can then be identified empirically from this population as the group of organizations that interact maximally with one another and minimally with other members of the population. Once the relevant local organization sets are identified by one or the other method, the external network can be defined as the collectivity of all these local organization sets.

Clearly, the former method for identifying the national organization sets is the more convenient, and it is our belief that experienced researchers should usually be able to prespecify most of the relevant actors with sufficient accuracy. Some researchers, however, may prefer the latter approach for it avoids the arbitrariness of an a priori selection. However, as Laumann et al. (1983) have argued, neither approach is fully satisfactory, and some better way for delineation of the boundaries remains as another important topic for further reflection.

References

Aldrich, H. E. (1976) Resource dependence and interorganizational relations: Relations between local employment service offices and social service sector organizations. *Administration and Society*, 7, 419–454.

Aldrich, H. E. (1979) *Organizations and environments*. Englewood Cliffs, NJ: Prentice-Hall.

Aldrich, H. E., & Whetten, D. A. (1981) Organization-sets, action-sets, and networks: Making the most of simplicity. In P. C. Nystrom & W. H. Starbuck (Eds.), *Handbook of organizational design* (pp. 385–408). London: Oxford University Press.

Bacharach, S. B., & Aiken, M. (1976) Structural and process constraints on influence in organizations: A level specific analysis. *Administrative Science Quarterly*, 21, 623–642.

Bartlett, C. A. (1983) MNCs: Get off the reorganization merry-go-round. *Harvard Business Review*, 6(2), 138–146.

Bartlett, C. A. (1986) Building and managing the transnational: The new organizational challenge. In M. E. Porter (Ed.), *Competition in global industries*. Boston: Harvard Business School Press.

Bartlett, C. A., & Ghoshal, S. (1986) Tap your subsidiaries for global reach. *Harvard Business Review*, 4(6), 87–94.

Bartlett, C. A., & Ghoshal, S. (1987) Managing across borders: New organizational responses. *Sloan Management Review*, 29(1), 43–53.

Bartlett, C. A., & Ghoshal, S. (1989) *Managing across borders: The transnational solution*. Boston: Harvard Business School Press.

Benson, J. K. (1975) The interorganizational network as a political economy. *Administrative Science Quarterly*, 20, 229–249.

Bower, J. L. (1987) *When markets quake*. Boston: Harvard Business School Press.

Buckley, P. J., & Casson, M. C. (1985) *The economic theory of the multinational enterprise*. London: Macmillan.

Burt, R. S. (1978) Stratification and prestige among elite experts in mathematical sociology circa 1975. *Social Networks*, 1, 105–158.

Burt, R. S. (1987) Social contagion and innovation: Cohesion versus structural equivalence. *American Journal of Sociology*, 92, 1287–1335.

Burt, R. S., Minor, M. J., & Associates (Eds.) (1983) *Applied network analysis: A methodological introduction.* Beverley Hills, CA: Sage.

Carley, K. (1986) An approach for relating social structure to cognitive structure. *Journal of Mathematical Sociology,* 12(2), 137–189.

Caves, R. E. (1982) *Multinational enterprise and economic analysis.* Cambridge: Cambridge University Press.

Chandler, A. D. (1986) The evolution of modern global competition. In M. E. Porter (Ed.), *Competition in global industries* (pp. 405–448). Boston: Harvard Business School Press.

Coleman, J. S. (1966) Foundations for a theory of collective decisions. *American Journal of Sociology,* 71, 615–627.

Contractor, F. J., & Lorange, P. (Eds.) (1988) *Cooperative strategies in international business.* Lexington, MA: Lexington Books.

Cook, K. S. (1977) Exchange and power in networks of interorganizational relations. *Sociological Quarterly,* 18, 62–82.

Cook, K. S., Emerson, R. M., Gilmore, M. R., & Yamagishi, T. (1983) The distribution of power in exchange networks: Theory and experimental results. *American Journal of Sociology,* 89, 275–305.

Daniels, J. D., Pitts, R. A., & Tretter, M. J. (1985) Organizing for dual strategies of product diversity and international expansion. *Strategic Management Journal,* 6, 223–237.

DiMaggio, P. (1986) Structural analysis of organizational fields: A blockmodel approach. In B. M. Staw & L. L. Cummings (Eds.), *Research in organizational behavior* (Vol. 8, pp. 335–370). Greenwich, CT: JAI Press.

DiMaggio, P. J., & Powell, W. W. (1983) The iron cage revisited: Institutional isomorphism and collective rationality in organizational fields. *American Sociological Review,* 48, 147–160.

Dunning, J. H. (1981) *International production and the multinational enterprise.* London: Allen and Unwin.

Eccles, R. G. (1981) The quasi firm in the construction industry. *Journal of Economic Behavior and Organization,* 2, 335–357.

Eccles, R. G., & Crane, D. B. (1987) Managing through networks in investment banking. *California Management Review,* 30(1), 176–195.

Egelhoff, W. G. (1988) Strategy and structure in multinational corporations: A revision of the Stopford and Wells model. *Strategic Management Journal,* 1–14.

Emerson, R. M. (1962) Power-dependence relations. *American Sociological Review,* 27, 31–41.

Evan, W. M. (1967) The organization-set: Toward a theory of interorganizational relations. In J. D. Thompson (Ed.), *Approaches to organizational design* (pp. 173–191). Pittsburgh: University of Pittsburgh Press.

Evan, W. M. (Ed.) (1976) *Interorganizational relations.* Harmondsworth, England: Penguin Books.

Fayerweather, J. (1978) *International business strategy and administration.* Cambridge, MA: Ballinger.

Fombrun, C. J. (1983) Attributions of power across a social network. *Human Relations,* 36, 493–508.

Freeman, L. C. (1979) Centrality in social networks: Conceptual clarification. *Social Networks,* 1(3), 215–239.

Ghemawat, P., & Spence, A. M. (1986) Modeling global competition. In M. E. Porter (Ed.), *Competition in global industries* (pp. 61–79). Boston: Harvard Business School Press.

Ghoshal, S. (1986) *The innovative multinational: A differentiated network of organizational roles and management processes.* Unpublished doctoral dissertation, Harvard University, Graduate School of Business Administration, Boston.

Ghoshal, S., & Nohria, N. (1989) Internal differentiation within the multinational corporation. *Strategic Management Journal,* 10, 323–337.

Granovetter, M. (1973) The strength of weak ties. *American Journal of Sociology,* 81, 1287–1303.

Granovetter, M. (1985) Economic action and social structure: The problem of embeddedness. *American Journal of Sociology,* 91, 481–510.

Hall, R. H., Clark, J. P., Giordano, P. C., Johnson, P. V., & Roekel, M. V. (1977) Patterns of interorganizational relationships. *Administrative Science Quarterly,* 22, 457–471.

Hakansson, H., & Johanson, J. (1988) Formal and informal cooperation strategies in international industrial networks. In F. J. Contractor & P. Lorange (Eds.), *Cooperative strategies in international business* (pp. 369–379). Lexington, MA: Lexington Books.

Harrigan, K. R. (1985) *Strategies for joint ventures.* Lexington, MA: Lexington Books.

Hedlund, G. (1986) The Hypermodern MNC—a heterarchy? *Human Resource Management,* 25, 9–36.

Hennart, J. F. (1982) *A theory of multinational enterprise.* Ann Arbor: University of Michigan Press.

Herbert, T. T. (1984) Strategy and multinational structure: An interorganizational relations perspective. *Academy of Management Review,* 9, 259–271.

Hirsch, S. (1976) An international trade and investment theory of the firm. *Oxford Economic Papers,* 28 (July), 258–270.

Hofstede, G. (1980) *Culture's consequences: International*

differences in work-related values. Beverly Hills, CA: Sage.

Homans, G. (1974) *Social behavior: Its elementary forms* (2nd ed.). New York: Harcourt Brace Jovanovich.

Hulbert, J. M., & Brandt, W. K. (1980) *Managing the multinational subsidiary*. New York: Holt, Rinehart & Winston.

Kadushin, C. (1978) *Introduction to macro-network analysis*. Unpublished manuscript, Columbia University Teachers College.

Kogut, B. (1983) Foreign direct investment as a sequential process. In C. P. Kindleberger & D. Andretsch (Eds.), *The multinational corporation in the 1980s*. Cambridge, MA: MIT Press.

Kogut, B. (1988) Country patterns in international competition: appropriability and oligopolistic agreement. In N. Hood & Vahlne. (Eds.), *Strategies in global competition*. London: Croom-Helm.

Kogut, B. (1989) A note on global strategies. *Strategic Management Journal*, 10, 383–389.

Krackhardt, D. (1989) *Graphing theoretical dimensions of the informal organization*. Presentation at the European Institute of Business Administration (INSEAD), Fontainebleau, France.

Laumann, E. O., & Pappi, F. (1976) *Networks of collective action: A perspective on community influence systems*. New York: Academic Press.

Laumann, E. O., Glaskiewicz, J., & Marsden, P. V. (1978) Community structure as interorganizational linkages. *Annual Review of Sociology*, 4, 455–484.

Laumann, E. O., Marsden, P. V., & Prensky, D. (1983) The boundary specification problem in network analysis. In R. S. Burt, M. J. Minor, and Associates (Eds.), *Applied network analysis: A methodological introduction* (pp. 18–34). Beverly Hills, CA: Sage.

Lazarsfeld, P. F., & Menzel, H. (1961) On the relation between individual and collective properties. In A. Etzioni (Ed.), *Complex organizations: A sociological reader* (pp. 422–440). New York: Holt, Rinehart & Winston.

Lehman, E. W. (1975) *Coordinating health care: Explorations in interorganizational relations*. Beverly Hills, CA: Sage.

Lessard, D., & Lightstone, J. B. (1986) Volatile exchange rates can put operations at risk. *Harvard Business Review*, 64(4), 107–114.

Levitt, T. (1983) The globalization of markets. *Harvard Business Review*, 61(3), 92–102.

Magee, S. P. (1977) Information and the multinational corporation: An appropriability theory of direct foreign investment. In J. N. Bhagwati (Ed.), *The new international economic order* (pp. 317–340). Cambridge, MA: MIT Press.

Mahini, A., & Wells, L. T. (1986) Government relations in the global firm. In M. E. Porter (Ed.), *Competition in global industries*. Boston: Harvard Business School Press.

Meyer, J. W., & Scott, W. R. (1983) *Organizational environments*. Beverly Hills, CA: Sage.

Mitchell, J. C. (1973) Networks, norms and institutions. In J. Boissevain & J. C. Mitchell (Eds.), *Network analysis* (pp. 15–35). The Hague: Mouton.

Nohria, N., & Venkatraman, N. (1987) *Interorganizational information systems via information technology: A network analytic perspective*. Working paper No. 1909–87, Massachusetts Institute of Technology, Sloan School of Management, Cambridge.

Ohmae, K. (1989) The global logic of strategic alliances. *Harvard Business Review*, 67(2), 143–154.

Paul, J. K. (Ed.) (1984) *High technology international trade and competition*. Park Ridge, NJ: Noyes Publications.

Perlmutter, H. V. (1969) The tortuous evolution of the multinational corporation. *Columbia Journal of World Business*, 4(4), 9–18.

Pfeffer, J., & Salancik, G. R. (1974) The bases and use of power in organizational decision making: The case of a university. *Administrative Science Quarterly*, 19, 453–473.

Pfeffer, J., & Salancik, G. R. (1978) *The external control of organizations: A resource dependency perspective*. New York: Harper and Row.

Porter, M. E. (in press) *The competitive advantage of nations and their firms*. New York: Free Press.

Porter, M. E. (Ed.) (1986) Competition in global industries: A conceptual framework. In M. E. Porter (Ed.), *Competition in global industries* (pp. 15–60). Boston: Harvard Business School Press.

Powell, W. W. (1985) *Getting into print: The decision-making process in scholarly publishing*. Chicago: University of Chicago Press.

Poynter, T. A., & Rugman, A. M. (1982) World product mandates: How will multinationals respond? *Business Quarterly*, 47(3), 54–61.

Prahalad, C. K., & Doz, Y. L. (1987) *The multinational mission: Balancing local demands and global vision*. New York: Free Press.

Provan, K. G. (1983) The federation as an interorganizational linkage network. *Academy of Management Review*, 8, 79–89.

Provan, K. G., Beyer, J. M., & Kruytbosch, C. (1980) Environmental linkages and power in resource dependence relations between organizations. *Administrative Science Quarterly*, 25, 200–225.

Robock, S. H., Simmons, K., & Zwick, J. (1977) *International business and multinational enterprise.* Homewood, IL: Irwin.

Rugman, A. M. (1980) A new theory of the multinational enterprise: Internationalization versus internalization. *Columbia Journal of World Business,* 15(1), 23–29.

Sabel, C., Herrigel, G., Kazis, R., & Deeg, R. (1987) How to keep mature industries innovative. *Technology Review,* 90(3), 26–35.

Stevens, G. V. G. (1974) The determinants of investment. In J. H. Dunning (Ed.), *Economic analysis and the multinational enterprise* (pp. 47–88). London: Allen & Unwin.

Stopford, J. M., & Wells, L. T. (1972) *Managing the multinational enterprise.* New York: Basic Books.

Teece, D. J. (1980) Economies of scale and the scope of the enterprise. *Journal of Economic Behavior and Organization,* 1, 223–247.

Teece, D. J. (1986) Transaction cost economies and the multinational enterprise. *Journal of Economic Behavior and Organization,* 7, 21–45.

Terpstra, V. (1982) *International dimensions of marketing.* Boston: Kent.

Tichy, N. M., Tushman, M. L., & Fombrun, C. (1979) Social network analysis for organizations. *Academy of Management Review,* 4, 507–519.

Van de Ven, A. H., & Walker, G. (1984) The dynamics of interorganizational coordination. *Administrative Science Quarterly,* 29, 598–621.

Walker, G. (1985) Network position and cognition in a computer software firm. *Administrative Science Quarterly,* 30, 103–130.

Walker, G. (1988) Network analysis for cooperative interfirm relationships. In F. J. Contractor & P. Lorange (Eds.), *Cooperative strategies in international business* (pp. 227–240). Lexington, MA: Lexington Books.

Warren, R. L. (1967) The interorganizational field as a focus for investigation. *Administrative Science Quarterly,* 12, 396–419.

Westney, D. E. (1988) Domestic and foreign learning curves in managing international cooperative strategies. In F. J. Contractor & P. Lorange (Eds.), *Cooperative strategies in international business* (pp. 339–346). Lexington, MA: Lexington Books.

Westney, D. E. (1989) *Institutionalization theory: The study of the multinational enterprise.* Paper presented at the conference on organization theory and the multinational enterprise, INSEAD, September 1–2, 1989.

Westney, D. E., & Sakakibara, D. (1985) *Comparative study of the training, careers, and organization of engineers on the computer industry in Japan and the United States.* MIT-Japan Science and Technology Program, MIT (mimeo).

Zald, M. N. (1970) Political economy: A framework for comparative analysis. In M. N. Zald (Ed.), *Power in organizations* (pp. 221–261). Nashville, TN: Vanderbilt University Press.

Zeitz, G. (1980) Interorganizational dialectics. *Administrative Science Quarterly,* 25, 72–88.

Zucker, L. G. (1988) *Institutional patterns and organizations.* Cambridge, MA: Ballinger.

Sumantra Ghoshal (PhD, MIT and DBA, Harvard) is Associate Professor of Management at the European Institute of Business Administration (INSEAD), Fontainebleau, France.

Christopher A. Bartlett (DBA, Harvard) is Professor at the Harvard Business School.

Nitin Nohria was an active and equal partner in the idea development phase and would have been a co-author of the paper but for the temporary distraction of having to write a doctoral dissertation. The paper benefitted from the comments of Martin Kilduff and Eleanor Westney.

[20]

EFFECTIVELY CONCEIVING AND EXECUTING MULTINATIONALS' WORLDWIDE STRATEGIES

W. Chan Kim* and Renée A. Mauborgne*
The European Institute of Business Administration

Abstract. This study addresses one of the most compelling questions in the field of international management: How can a multinational *simultaneously* pursue the double-ended objective of effectively conceiving and executing its worldwide strategy? Here we examine the ways in which the dynamics of the strategy-making process between head office and subsidiary units influence the multinational's ability to achieve these two objectives. Specifically, we introduce the concept of procedural justice, the intellectual root of which is grounded in social psychology and law, into international management and explore the impact of process fairness on multinationals' ability to conceive and execute effective worldwide strategies. The results of this research are based on a two-phase longitudinal study of the decisionmaking dynamics of nineteen multinationals. They provide support that the exercise of procedural justice is indeed a powerful way to organize the multinationals' strategy-making process. Procedural justice was found to significantly augment multinationals' ability to achieve this double-ended objective.

"In the next ten years . . . managers will have to increasingly shift the debate from resource-based advantages to advantages derived from the strategic capability of an organization—*its ability to conceive and execute complex strategies* . . . . [Multinationals] that develop this strategic capability are the ones with the best chance of winning" (Prahalad and Doz [1987, 258-59]). While this quote is taken from a discussion of the key challenges facing the modern multinational, the view that it contains is not an isolated one. Numerous other recent studies in international management have also proclaimed the growing indispensability of conceiving and implementing effective worldwide strategies (e.g., Hamel and Prahalad [1985]; Hedlund

---

*W. Chan Kim is professor of strategy and international management and Renée A. Mauborgne is research associate of management and international business, both at The European Institute of Business Administration (INSEAD), Fontainebleau, France.

Thanks are due to the five distinguished judges of the Eldridge Haynes Prize, John Dunning, Jean Boddewyn, David Rutenberg, an anonymous officer of Business International, and an anonymous trustee of the Eldridge Haynes Memorial Trust. The valuable time and effort they invested in judging this award is greatly appreciated. Special thanks are also due to INSEAD, especially Associate Dean Yves Doz, for the generous financial support of this research.

Received: November 1992; Revised: December 1992; Accepted: December 1992.

420   JOURNAL OF INTERNATIONAL BUSINESS STUDIES, THIRD QUARTER 1993

[1986]; Kogut [1989]; Porter [1986]; Bartlett and Ghoshal [1989]; Kim and Mauborgne [1991, 1993b, 1993c, 1993d]).

Yet, for all of the importance attached to multinationals building this strategic capability, virtually no systematic research effort exists on this issue. True, international management research is rich in studies dedicated to identifying the content of effective worldwide strategies (e.g., Hout, Porter and Rudden [1982]; Levitt [1983]; Kogut [1985a, 1985b]; Kim and Mauborgne [1988]; Yip [1989]). These studies provide valuable insight into *what* the dimensions of an effective worldwide strategy are. However, they do not directly address the question of *how* multinationals can actually both conceive and execute these strategic decisions.

The answer to this question is particularly challenging as the modern multinational needs to *simultaneously* pursue this double-ended objective. The traditional approach of sequentially treating the formulation and then the implementation of a multinational's strategy will no longer suffice. This is because worldwide strategies increasingly demand that subsidiaries trade off short term for long term, and subsystem for system priorities and considerations. This enhances subsidiary managers' reticence to accept and execute corporate strategic decisions. At the same time, however, the distinctive powers of hierarchy traditionally used to motivate subsidiary compliance—fiat and refined monitoring and appraisal capability [Williamson 1975]—have declined in effectiveness in the multinational [Hedlund 1986; Kim and Mauborgne 1993a, 1993b]. This creates room for managerial discretion at the national unit level. Taken together, the above two conditions suggest that, all else being equal, subsidiary top managers increasingly have not only a heightened desire but a heightened ability to subvert multinationals' strategic decisions. As Guth and MacMillan [1986] and Hedlund [1980] pointed out, under such conditions it is vital that multinationals secure subsidiary top managers' motivation to implement strategic decisions at the start of the decisionmaking process. Otherwise, subsidiary top managers are likely to delay and reduce the quality of strategy implementation.

This paper sets out to address how a multinational can *simultaneously* conceive and implement an effective worldwide strategy. During the course of the last five years we have engaged in a longitudinal two-phase study of the decisionmaking dynamics between the head offices and subsidiary units of nineteen multinationals. The particular decision dynamics studied were those occuring during the annual strategic planning process between head office and subsidiary executives. This strategic interaction represents one of the most critical in the generation and, we argue here, in the execution of multinationals' worldwide strategies. The particular theoretical lens applied in our analyses was that of procedural justice, the intellectual root of which is grounded in the two academic disciplines of social psychology and law. As depicted by the numbered arrows in Figure 1, there are three major reasons for applying procedural justice. The first is that, in line with the rich

FIGURE 1
Predicted Relations between Procedural Justice and the Formulation and Implementation of Multinationals' Strategies and Subsidiary Performance: Moderated by the Nature of a Subsidiary's Industry[a]

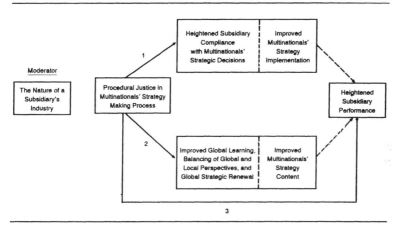

[a]the number for each relation corresponds with its specific hypothesis in the text; the arrows with broken lines indicate that no hypothesis is proposed.

body of procedural justice research (see Lind and Tyler [1988] for a review), the exercise of procedural justice is predicted to enhance subsidiaries' compliance with resulting strategic decisions, thereby resulting in the improved implementation of multinationals' worldwide strategies. The second is that the very underlying dimensions that lead to judgments of process fairness enhance the multinational's ability to gather, interpret, and synthesize the types of strategic information that are critical to achieve the multinational's three strategic missions of global learning, balancing global efficiency and local responsiveness, and global strategic renewal. This suggests that the exercise of procedural justice promotes the formation of superior worldwide strategy content as well. Third, to the extent that improved strategy implementation and better strategy content positively enhance organizational performance as indicated by the broken line arrows in Figure 1, procedural justice is also predicted to have a positive influence on the performance of subsidiary units.

First we define the meaning of procedural justice in multinationals' strategic planning process between head office and subsidiary executives. Next we develop the theoretical arguments and subsequently present hypotheses on the effects of procedural justice on improved strategy implementation, better worldwide strategy content, and on the enhanced performance of subsidiary

422   JOURNAL OF INTERNATIONAL BUSINESS STUDIES, THIRD QUARTER 1993

units in the multinational. After detailing the methods of our two-phase, longitudinal research design, we discuss the analyses, results, and conclusions of our study.

THE MEANING OF PROCEDURAL JUSTICE IN MULTINATIONALS' STRATEGY-MAKING PROCESS

Procedural justice is defined here as the extent to which the dynamics of the multinational's strategy-making process for its subsidiary units are judged to be fair by subsidiary top management. This conceptualization of procedural justice stands in accord with the general definition of procedural justice in the literature (see Lind and Tyler [1988]). Subsidiary top managers have translated procedural justice into five distinct characteristics (see Kim and Mauborgne [1991]). These are: (1) that two-way communication exists in the multinational's strategy-making process; (2) that subsidiary units can legitimately challenge the strategic views of the head office; (3) that the head office is knowledgeable of the local situation of subsidiary units; (4) that subsidiary units are provided an account of the multinational's final strategic decisions; and (5) that the head office is fairly consistent in making decisions across subsidiary units. Taken together, these five characteristics lead subsidiary top management to judge the multinational's strategy-making process for its subsidiary units to be procedurally just.

THEORY AND HYPOTHESES

Procedural Justice and Improved Implementation of Multinationals' Strategy

There are two conceptual bases for expecting the exercise of process fairness to exert a direct effect on subsidiary compliance with multinationals' strategic decisions. One is traceable to what Lind and Tyler [1988] refer to as a long-term, self-interest theory. Lind and Tyler assert that in deciding upon the extent of one's compliance with organizational decisions, organizational members implicitly adopt a *long-term* perspective of informed self-interest. This is because they recognize that their own unit's priorities and considerations cannot always be accorded and may even have to be occasionally traded off in an organization. This is based on the understanding that the diverse units of an organization have competing interests. As a result, all units of an organization will at times be required to sacrifice their own unit's priorities for those of other organizational units. Given the acknowledgement that short-term gains may not always be forthcoming, individuals look for organizational practices that will provide reasonable assurance that over the long term the interests of their unit will be adequately served by their organization. This is what procedural justice can provide.

When subsidiary top managers believe that the head office exercises procedural justice in strategic decisionmaking, they are sent an unambiguous signal that the opinions, priorities and concerns of their subsidiary unit are given due consideration in the making of strategic decisions. This provides subsidiary managers with a convincing form of assurance that merit and not politics or favoritism guides the determination of ultimate strategic decisions. These convictions build a feeling of confidence that in the long term the interests of not only the head office but also subsidiary units will be reasonably protected and advanced through the multinational's decisionmaking process. As a result, subsidiary top managers tend to develop a strong feeling of support for the strategic decisionmaking process and for the decisions resulting from that process. This heightens their motivation to comply with these strategic decisions.

The other conceptual base is traceable to norms of reciprocation [Thibaut and Walker 1975, 1978] or social exchange theory (e.g., Blau [1964]). According to this theory, when subsidiary top managers believe that their multinational's strategy-making process is governed by principles of procedural justice, they develop a feeling that their unit was fairly treated in the decision process. This feeling of having received fair treatment tends to create a corresponding obligation in subsidiary top managers to reciprocate that fairness and act fairly themselves by adhering to the strategic decisions resulting from the multinational's strategy-making process.

Four studies offer support that procedural justice may well exercise a direct effect on subsidiary compliance [Thibaut and Walker 1975, 1978; Friedland, Thibaut and Walker 1973; Thibaut, Friedland and Walker 1974]. The most classic of these is the seminal work of Thibaut and Walker [1975]. Thibaut and Walker advanced the theory that people's attitudes and behavior would be strongly influenced by the fairness of the procedures by which outcomes were determined. Specifically, they predicted that increases in procedural justice judgments would result in better acceptance of and compliance with the decision outcomes of those processes. This prediction was unambiguously supported in their research.

Taken together, the above theory and empirical studies lead to our first hypothesis,

> Hypothesis 1a: The exercise of procedural justice in a multinational's strategy-making process for its subsidiary units will have an overall positive effect on these units' compliance with resulting strategic decisions.

A review of the international management literature suggests that the nature of a multinational's subsidiary's industry may moderate the strength of the above predicted relation. Multinationals' subsidiaries operate in two extreme types of industries: multidomestic and global (e.g., Hout, Porter and Rudden [1982]; Hamel and Prahalad [1985]; Porter [1986]; Prahalad and Doz [1987]; Yip [1989]). These two types of industries differ in their economics and requirements for success.

424   JOURNAL OF INTERNATIONAL BUSINESS STUDIES, THIRD QUARTER 1993

In multidomestic industries, the competitive challenge tends to be more on a market-by-market basis than in global industries. This is because in such industries differences across national markets tend to be more pronounced in terms of customer tastes and preferences, competitive environments, and political, legal, and social structures. To exploit these differences effectively, the strategic mission assigned to subsidiary units is to be locally responsive to national market demands. Hence, the pursuit of local level efficiency maximization tends to be consistent rather than inconsistent with the corporate-level strategic goals of the multinational. This suggests that strategic decisions will be relatively in line with the individual self-interests of subsidiary units. As individual self-interest is a powerful motivator of behavior, it follows that subsidiary top managers may be naturally inclined to exercise a relatively high level of compliance with their multinational's strategic decisions. As a result, the incremental value of the exercise of procedural justice as an extra cushion of support for subsidiary compliance may not be that high in multidomestic industries.

In contrast, in global industries the strategic mission is to exploit the homogeneous market conditions that exist across national markets. This includes implementing universal products, rationalizing manufacturing, centralizing R&D, and transfering standardized marketing practices. It also entails implementing competitive moves based more on global-level concerns than on the dynamics of any one particular national market. As a result, in global industries, the final strategic decisions made for national units may often not be parallel with the individual self-interests of subsidiary units. This suggests that in the absence of any countervailing mechanisms, the level of subsidiary compliance that can naturally be expected is likely to be relatively low. As a result, the exercise of procedural justice may well act as a strong cushion of support which has the power to contribute substantially to subsidiary compliance in global industries.

Taken together, the above reasoning leads to the following hypothesis,

> Hypothesis 1b: The exercise of procedural justice in a multinational's strategy-making process for its subsidiary units will have a stronger positive effect on these units' compliance with resulting strategic decisions at the global end of these units' industry spectrum than at the multidomestic end.

Procedural Justice and the Formation of Superior Worldwide Strategy Content

There is strong theoretical ground to also expect that the exercise of procedural justice will lead to the formation of superior worldwide strategy content (Kim and Mauborgne [1993d]). The basis of this contention is grounded in information processing theory [Egelhoff 1991; Galbraith 1973, 1977;

Thompson 1967; Tushman and Nadler 1978]. Information processing theory states that for an organization to be effective, a match must exist between its information processing capacity and the information processing requirements imposed by its environmental and strategic conditions. An organization is considered to be effective if it is able to meet its formally defined goals and objectives.

Here the dimensions of procedural justice are conceptualized as the critical variables determining the information processing capability of a multinational's strategy-making process. If a close look is taken at the five dimensions of procedural justice, each can be seen to have important implications for the multinational's ability to gather, interpret, and synthesize strategic information. On the other hand, the overarching strategic objectives of multinationals' worldwide strategies can be seen as posing diverse information processing requirements in order to be able to design worldwide strategies that can effectively meet these strategic objectives. In line with information processing theory, the central contention here is that if procedural justice enhances multinationals' ability to gather, interpret, and synthesize the kinds of strategic information necessary to achieve the strategic objectives of multinationals, the exercise of procedural justice may well bear a positive influence on the design of effective worldwide strategies.

Although the strategic objectives of multinationals are diverse, here we focus on three that are frequently tied to the design of effective worldwide strategies in the international management literature (e.g., Bartlett and Ghoshal [1987a, 1989]; Ghoshal [1987]; Prahalad and Doz [1987]). These are: (1) global learning—the extent to which the creation, adoption, and diffusion of knowledge and expertise occurs within and across the nodes of the multinational's network of international operations; (2) the balancing of global efficiency and local responsiveness—the extent to which both efforts to exploit global economies of scale and scope and to respond to differences across national markets are effectively fostered; and (3) global strategic renewal—the extent to which multinationals unceasingly question the continuing merit of past successful strategic moves and avoid strategic complacency.

We are now ready to assess whether the five dimensions of procedural justice foster the types of strategic information necessary to achieve each of these strategic objectives. Let us start with the first dimension, the extent to which bilateral communication exists between managers of head offices and subsidiary units involved in the multinational's strategy-making process. When extensive two-way communication exists between head office and subsidiary executives, both parties not only transfer their distinctive points of view, knowledge, and expertise but are also required to hear the opposite party out. This diffusion and sharing of perceptions, knowledge and ideas should promote a higher rate of global learning [Ghoshal and Bartlett 1988]. At the same time, given that the head office's natural inclination is to argue for and defend the benefits of a global perspective while the subsidiary unit's natural inclination is to argue for the benefits of local adaptation [Perlmutter 1969; Prahalad 1976; Doz 1980], extensive two-way communication should likewise foster a better balancing of global efficiency and local responsiveness. Taking this logic one step further, we find that the different backgrounds and orientations brought to bear by head office and subsidiary managers should also result in a more creative and thorough testing of the appropriateness of past successful strategic moves, which is to say, two-way communication should heighten multinationals' ability to achieve global strategic renewal [Prahalad and Doz 1987]. In a different context, the recent work of Beamish [1988] is relevant here. He found that when multinationals and their joint venture partners hold regular meetings together—another measure of two-way communication, the performance of the joint venture is high.

The second dimension of procedural justice is the ability of subsidiary units to legitimately challenge and refute the strategic views of the head office. When subsidiary top managers are granted the right to challenge the head office's strategic views, the head office becomes limited in its ability to overdominate the decision process and crowd out the strategic views of subsidiary units. As a result, a better balance between the global and local perspectives may well be struck. Beyond this, the ability to refute creates a restless, self-questioning atmosphere in the multinational. This serves to break the multinational's inclination to maintain the status quo and simply assume the continuing merit of past strategic responses [Prahalad and Doz 1987]. Consequently, a higher rate of global strategic renewal should also result.

The third dimension of procedural justice is the extent to which head office managers are well informed and familiar with the local conditions of subsidiary units. When head office managers have a high degree of local familiarity, they expand their thinking and perceiving beyond issues of global efficiency alone. In essence, they cultivate a multidimensional vision that allows them to appreciate the subsidiary unit perspective. This should foster a greater awareness of the need to achieve local responsiveness in the making of strategic decisions [Bartlett and Ghoshal 1987b]. As a result, the local familiarity of head office managers should give rise to a better balance between global and local perspectives in multinationals' strategic decisions [Bartlett and Ghoshal 1990]. The recent work of Beamish [1988] is again relevant here. His research revealed that when multinationals have local familiarity with, and willingly visit and offer assistance to, their joint venture partners, the performance of the joint venture is high.

The fourth dimension of procedural justice is the extent to which subsidiary units are provided a full account for the final strategic decisions of the head office. When subsidiary managers receive a comprehensive explanation for why strategic decisions are made as they are, subsidiary managers are granted two things. One is a more comprehensive understanding of the cognitive maps of head office managers and the other is a sound rationale for why their subsidiary perspective may have been accepted or rejected in the making of ultimate strategic decisions. In this way, the provision of an account serves as a feedback loop that perpetually informs and educates subsidiary managers and gradually alters their conceptual lens for subsequent interpretations of the environment. Hence, the provision of an account should work to promote a greater rate of ongoing global learning [Daft and Weick 1984]. At the same time, by requiring the head office to provide an account of final strategic decisions, organizational members are insured that not only the head office but also the subsidiary perspective was given due consideration in the making of strategic decisions. This should, in turn, prompt head office managers to promote a higher level of balancing between these two perspectives in the making of ultimate strategic decisions.

The last dimension of procedural justice is the extent to which head offices do not discriminate but apply consistent decisionmaking procedures across subsidiary units. When head offices exercise consistent decisionmaking procedures, subsidiary top managers are sent a signal that a level playing field exists across subsidiary units and that political favoritism does not dominate the dynamics of the decision process. This fosters a feeling of trust and a cooperative atmosphere between head office and subsidiary executives that inspires both parties to work together to achieve joint success. As a result, both head office and subsidiary executives are motivated to actively share their distinctive knowledge and expertise and to maximize the quality and comprehensiveness of information used in reaching strategic decisions [Ghoshal and Bartlett 1988], which is to say that the application of consistent decisionmaking procedures is likely to induce a higher rate of global learning.

The above discussions suggest that each of the five dimensions of procedural justice has important implications for the multinational's ability to gather, interpret, and synthesize the types of strategic information that are necessary to achieve the multinational's three strategic objectives. Given that these five dimensions lead subsidiary top management to judge the multinational's strategy-making process to be procedurally just [Kim and Mauborgne 1991], we propose the following hypotheses:

Hypothesis 2a: The exercise of procedural justice in a multinational's strategy-making process for its subsidiary units will have an overall positive effect on these units' ability to promote global learning.

Hypothesis 2b: The exercise of procedural justice in a multinational's strategy-making process for its subsidiary units will have an overall positive effect on these units' ability to balance global efficiency and local responsiveness.

Hypothesis 2c: The exercise of procedural justice in a multinational's strategy-making process for its subsidiary units will

428   JOURNAL OF INTERNATIONAL BUSINESS STUDIES, THIRD QUARTER 1993

have an overall positive effect on these units' ability
to promote global strategic renewal.

Procedural Justice and Enhanced Subsidiary Performance

As just discussed, superior worldwide strategy content here is tied to the
effective attainment of what Prahalad and Doz [1987] call the three overriding multinational missions: global learning, balancing global efficiency
and local responsiveness, and global strategic renewal. The effective attainment of these multinational missions is a gateway to superior performance
(e.g., Prahalad and Doz [1987]; Bartlett and Ghoshal [1989]). Hence, if the
exercise of procedural justice indeed facilitates the generation and implementation of worldwide strategies that effectively achieve these objectives,
procedural justice can be predicted to bear a positive consequence for the
performance of multinationals' subsidiaries.

Given that various subsidiary units hold diverse resources and capabilities
and that the strategic importance of subsidiaries' local markets differs, it
follows that the roles and strategic missions of subsidiary units will vary in
achieving superior corporate-level performance [Bartlett and Ghoshal
1986]. Hence, subsidiaries' performance here needs to be viewed not only
from their 'stand alone' performance but also from their contribution to
overall corporate level missions and performance. Assessing subsidiary performance in this way takes into account subsidiary units' diverse roles and
tasks within a multinational network. While no theory exists to argue a
direct link between the exercise of procedural justice and subsidiary performance, the above arguments suggest the following hypothesis:

> Hypothesis 3a: The exercise of procedural justice in a multinational's
> strategy-making process for its subsidiary units will
> have an overall positive effect on these units' per-
> formance.

Recall, however, that Hypothesis 1b predicted that the effect of procedural
justice on strategy implementation would be stronger for subsidiaries operating in more global as opposed to more multidomestic industries. Given
that the impact of procedural justice on subsidiary performance is grounded
upon not only its strategy content but also its implementation consequences,
the positive influence of procedural justice over subsidiary performance is
likely to be stronger for subsidiary units operating in a more highly global
industry. Hence, we offer our last hypothesis:

> Hypothesis 3b: The exercise of procedural justice in a multinational's
> strategy-making process for its subsidiary units will
> have a stronger positive effect on these units' per-
> formance at the global end of these units' industry
> spectrum than at the multidomestic end.

METHODS

Survey Instrument

The data for this study were gathered via a longitudinal two-phase research design. This entailed having two questionnaires distributed at two different times to head office and subsidiary top managers directly participating in their multinationals' strategic decisionmaking process for their subsidiary units. Given that these managers hold high positions in their multinationals' strategic apex as well as directly participate in their multinationals' strategy generation process, this choice of respondents is well suited to provide meaningful responses to our survey questionnaires.

The first questionnaire was composed of three parts. In the first part, head office and subsidiary top managers were asked to reflect back upon the last annual strategic planning/strategy-making process between the head office and a given national unit. For subsidiary top managers this national unit referred to their national unit. For head office managers who were directly involved in multiple national units, they were asked to evaluate each unit separately, identifying the units under evaluation. Based on the dynamics of the decision process under evaluation, participants assessed the extent to which procedural justice was exercised. In the second part, participants evaluated the extent to which the strategic decisions resulting from the same decisionmaking process successfully met the multinational's three strategic objectives: global learning, the balancing of global efficiency and local responsiveness, and global strategic renewal. In the third part, participants evaluated the globalization level of subsidiaries' industries. This first questionnaire was distributed within six weeks after the completion of participating multinationals' annual strategic planning process between head office and subsidiary units. As all of our participating multinationals were on roughly the same planning cycle, all questionnaires were distributed at roughly the same point in time.

The second questionnaire distributed was composed of two parts. In the first part, head office and subsidiary top managers evaluated the extent of subsidiary compliance with the strategic decisions resulting from the preceding annual strategic planning process. In the second part, participants assessed the performance of those same subsidiary units. This second questionnaire was distributed approximately ten months after those distributed in step one. This was just before the beginning of another annual strategic planning process.

Sample

Nineteen multinationals participated in this study. The participation of these nineteen multinationals was solicited by means of direct and indirect personal contacts. Four reasons led us to choose this sampling methodology

430 JOURNAL OF INTERNATIONAL BUSINESS STUDIES, THIRD QUARTER 1993

over a random sampling approach. First, to receive meaningful and informed responses to our survey questionnaires, it was necessary to identify precisely those head office and subsidiary top managers directly participating in their multinationals' strategy-making process and to insure that these managers themselves directly answered the survey questionnaires. The use of personal contacts allowed us to identify such a well-defined target list of individuals and personally solicit their participation. Second, given the extensiveness of the information required from each participant, a high level of commitment was clearly required to encourage participants to complete our survey questionnaires. The use of personal contacts, which allowed us to gain head offices' strong endorsement of our study, was believed to increase this commitment level. Third, the use of personal contacts allowed us to carefully track the respondents to our two survey questionnaires. This ensured that the same individuals received and answered the questionnaires in both steps of our data collection and allowed us to make well-targeted follow-up reminders to these individuals to encourage them to send in their completed responses. Finally, the use of personal contacts allowed us to accurately establish the point in time of each participating multinational's annual strategic planning process so that questionnaires could be distributed in a timely manner to enhance the accuracy of respondent recall.

The dominant industries of these nineteen multinationals were: computers (five firms), packaged foods (four firms), electrical products (four firms), pharmaceuticals (three firms), automobiles (one firm), paper and wood products (one firm), and textiles (one firm). Fifteen of these multinationals were based in North America and four were based in Europe. One had annual sales below U.S. $1 billion and four had annual sales above U.S. $10 billion; the remaining firms had sales within this range.

The head offices of our nineteen participating multinationals provided a list of their ten largest subsidiaries in terms of annual sales and the names and addresses of both the subsidiary presidents heading those operations and the head office managers playing a central role in the strategy generation process for each of the identified subsidiary units. Altogether the names and addresses of 190 subsidiary presidents and 103 head office managers were supplied to the researchers.

We then sent a letter directly to each of the named individuals asking for commitment and outlining the nature and the demands of the study. Individuals were assured that all survey responses would be kept strictly confidential. In addition, all of the 190 subsidiary presidents were notified that the researchers would contact them within a few weeks time to ascertain the names of any other subsidiary managers playing a direct role in their last annual strategic planning process. This was necessary because while the nineteen participating multinationals found it easy to identify a list of the head office managers directly involved in the strategic decisionmaking process for each of their ten largest subsidiary units, they were not as confident in their ability to do the same at the subsidiary unit level. This meant that the researchers had to directly contact subsidiary presidents to get the equivalent list at the national unit level.

In total, of the 190 subsidiary presidents identified, the researchers were able to successfully contact 141 via telephone calls. Of these, 63 expressed a willingness to partake in the study. These 63 subsidiary presidents identified an additional 132 subsidiary top managers directly involved in the last annual strategic planning process. These 132 subsidiary top managers, along with the 63 subsidiary presidents, supplied the researchers with a well-defined target list of 195 subsidiary executives. The titles of these managers ranged from subsidiary president to director and each was typically responsible for at least one major functional activity of the subsidiary's operation. Hence, a total of 298 questionnaires were distributed, 103 to head office managers and 195 to subsidiary top managers.

Four weeks after all questionnaires were sent out, two follow-up efforts were made to all managers; one a telephone call, the other a formal letter. Altogether a total of 249 of the 298 distributed questionnaires were received by the researchers (161 at the subsidiary unit level, 88 at the head office level). Of these, 221 were complete in all respects (142 at the subsidiary unit level, 79 at the head office level).

In the second step of our data collection, the second questionnaire was distributed to the 221 managers who provided responses in step one that could be analyzed. Step two questionnaires were distributed approximately ten months after those distributed in step one; this was just before the beginning of another annual strategic planning process. Again two follow-up efforts were made in an attempt to improve respondent participation. As is typically the case with a longitudinal design, attrition of responses generally occurs with each successive step in data collection. In total, of the 221 questionnaires distributed in step two, 196 were received (129 at the subsidiary unit level, 67 at the head office level) of which only 180 were complete in all respects (119 at the subsidiary unit level, 61 at the head office level). The step one and step two responses of these 180 managers were then used in our analyses. These 180 managers participated in the strategic decisionmaking processes of sixty different subsidiary units.

Twenty-nine of these sixty subsidiary units were located in North America (Canada and the United States), twenty-four were located in Europe, and seven were located in Asia (Japan and Korea). Regarding the cultural background of our respondent pool, the great majority were North American (79%), with 17% being European and only 4% being Asian. Given the overwhelming percentage of respondents who identified English as their first language (84%) as well as the high percentage of other non-native English-speaking respondents who judged their English capability to be at level IV (level V=mother tongue) (96%) or at least fluent (4%), all questionnaires were presented in English.

432   JOURNAL OF INTERNATIONAL BUSINESS STUDIES, THIRD QUARTER 1993

We checked for the possibility of a response bias at both ends of step one and step two of our data collection. However, no evidence for such a bias was found. The specific characteristics compared to check for the possibility of a response bias were: (1) whether the head office or subsidiary top managers of any particular multinational, any particular subsidiary decision unit as defined below, or any particular geographic location systematically dropped out at a greater rate than in other multinationals, other subsidiary decision units, or other geographic locations, respectively; and (2) whether the head office or subsidiary top managers with any particular procedural justice profile systematically dropped out at a greater rate than did the head office or subsidiary top managers with other procedural justice profiles.

Unit of Analysis

The unit of analysis for this study is the subsidiary decision unit because our theoretical relationships focus on how the exercise of procedural justice in this unit's decisionmaking process influences the generation of superior worldwide strategy, its better implementation and hence enhanced subsidiary performance. A subsidiary decision unit is defined as the group of head office and subsidiary executives who work together to formulate the annual strategy of a given subsidiary unit. This includes determining the strategic role a subsidiary unit is to play in the multinational's overarching worldwide strategy and the attendant resources and responsibilities of that given subsidiary unit. Since the unit of analysis is the subsidiary decision unit, individual responses obtained from decision unit members had to be pooled to get the aggregated decision unit scores. Given the nature of our study variables, subsidiary top managers as opposed to head office managers are likely to have first-hand experience and more accurate knowledge needed to assess these variables. Hence, while subsidiary member responses were used to obtain subsidiary decision unit scores, head office responses were used to check these scores for the possibility of common methods and/or social desirability bias.

Before pooling, the homogeneity of subsidiary members' perceptions of each study variable was tested. One-way analysis of variance (ANOVA) and Bartlett's M-test were run across members in a given subsidiary decision unit to determine if there were any significant differences across subsidiary member perceptions [Dixon and Massey 1969]. While these tests eliminated between one and two decision units per study variable, the overall results suggested that pooling was appropriate for each of the study variables. For those units that passed the above tests, unit scores were then calculated for each study variable by averaging the scores of subsidiary member respondents from each decision unit. Equal weight was given to each unit member. We then checked these unit scores against member head office managers' assessment of our study variables through their correlations. In total, fifty-six subsidiary decision units offered an acceptable and complete data set across all study variables and were used in the final analyses.

Measurements: Independent and Dependent Variables

Procedural Justice. The independent variable of central interest in this study is the procedural justice of multinationals' strategic decisionmaking process. To measure this construct the five-item procedural justice measure developed by Kim and Mauborgne [1991] was employed. The items assessed were: the extent to which bilateral communication exists between managers of head offices and subsidiary units involved in multinationals' strategic decision-making; the extent to which subsidiary units can challenge and refute the strategic views of head office managers; the degree to which head office managers involved in strategic decisionmaking are well informed and familiar with the local situations of subsidiary units; the extent to which subsidiary units are provided a full account for the final strategic decisions of the head office; and the extent to which head offices do not discriminate but apply consistent decisionmaking procedures across subsidiary units. It is worth noting that the term 'head office' was defined as the center of authority with which the last annual strategic planning/strategy making of a national unit was settled; hence it could mean either the corporate or the divisional center depending on the administrative structure of the multinational in question.

Participants were asked to base their assessment of procedural justice upon the dynamics of the last annual strategic planning process between the head office and a given national unit. All five of the dimensions were measured upon a 7-point Likert-type scale with scale anchors labeled: (1) not at all; (7) great. The Cronbach's coefficient *alpha* for this five-item measure was .85. The correlation between subsidiary unit scores and the procedural justice scores of member head office managers was positive and significant ($r=.74$, $p<.01$). This indicates that our unit procedural justice scores were not seriously contaminated by common methods or social desirability bias.

Although participants were asked to assess procedural justice based solely on the interaction dynamics of the most recent annual strategic planning process, participants revealed that the dynamics of this process were not idiosyncratic. Rather, they were reflective of the overall approach to strategic decisionmaking they usually experience within their organization. This would suggest that the procedural justice practices in the last annual strategy-making process studied herein are typical of those applied on a regular basis in their formal and informal strategic decisionmaking interactions. These findings are in line with previous research indicating that both firms and subunits within firms tend to make decisions in a consistent pattern [Fredrickson and Iaquinto 1987; Miles and Snow 1978; Nystrom and Starbuck 1984].

Multinationals' Strategic Objectives. Multi-item scales with 7-point Likert response formats were used to measure the extent to which multinationals effectively met each of the three strategic objectives discussed in this paper. Because no established scales exist to measure these strategic objectives, it was necessary to review the literature and draw items that, taken together, could, in our judgment, capture the domain of each of these constructs. Except where otherwise indicated, in all instances question items were coded so that high scores indicated the effective achievement of each of these strategic objectives. Participants were asked to base their assessments solely on the strategic decisions resulting from their last annual strategic planning process between the head office and a given national unit. The correlations between subsidiary unit scores and member head office managers' assessment of each of these strategic objective scores were in all cases positive and significant: global learning ($r=.66$, $p<.01$); balancing global and local perspectives ($r=.68$, $p<.01$); global strategic renewal ($r=.63$, $p<.01$). The specific question items used to measure each of the three strategic objectives follows.

Global Learning. Three items measured this construct: (1) the extent to which the distinctive knowledge and insight of the head office and the national unit were effectively transfered to and shared with the opposite party; (2) the extent to which new ideas and joint innovations were successfully created through the exchange of the unique expertise residing in the head office and the subsidiary unit; and (3) the extent to which both head office and subsidiary executives gained new knowledge, an increased appreciation and awareness of the opposite party's distinctive expertise, and/or an expanded view of how the organization can compete successfully in the international arena. The Cronbach's coefficient *alpha* for this three-item measure was .81.

Balancing Global Efficiency and Local Responsiveness. Three items measured this construct: (1) the extent to which the concern for global economies of scale and scope as well as the concern for adaptation to national markets were well represented and given due consideration in the decision process; (2) the extent to which the strategic decisions resulting from this process effectively balanced the need for global efficiency and local responsiveness across all major activities; and (3) the extent to which neither concerns for global efficiency nor concerns for local responsiveness over-dominated all critical aspects of resulting strategic decisions to the virtual exclusion of the other. The Cronbach's coefficient *alpha* for this three-item measure was .89.

Global Strategic Renewal. Three items measured this construct: (1) the extent to which the organization's existing global strategic logic was carefully scrutinized and reexamined in the decision process; (2) the extent to which the assumptions underlying the viewpoints of decision participants were rigorously evaluated in the decision process; and (3) the extent to which the strategic decisions resulting from that process were not mere replications of past successful strategic moves but reflected instead new and updated thinking that was finely attuned to recent changes in the international business environment. The Cronbach's coefficient *alpha* for this three-item measure was .86.

Subsidiary Compliance. To measure subsidiary compliance with strategic decisions, two different measures were used: one for subsidiary top managers, another for head office managers. With respect to subsidiary top managers, a four-item measure was used. In responding to the question items, subsidiary top managers were asked to reflect back on their actions taken since the preceding annual planning process. The items assessed were: (1) I followed the final strategic decisions made by the head office with extreme care; (2) I accepted and fully implemented the head office's final strategic decisions even if they were not parallel with the strategic interests of my individual subsidiary unit; (3) When presented the opportunity, that is, room for managerial discretion, I tended to disregard and even subvert the multinational's strategic decisions in the interests of my national unit (reversely scored); and (4) Overall, my actions taken since the last annual planning process have been fully consonant with executing the strategic decisions to the letter and spirit with which they were set forth. All four items were measured on a 7-point Likert-type scale (1=strongly disagree; 7=strongly agree). The Cronbach's coefficient *alpha* for this four-item scale was .91.

We then checked this measure of subsidiary compliance against head office managers' assessment of the overall compliance of each subsidiary unit. Head office managers assessed subsidiary compliance using a three-item measure. The items assessed were the extent to which a given subsidiary unit: (1) adhered to the strategic decisions resulting from the last annual strategic planning/strategy-making process between the head office and that given subsidiary unit; (2) implemented the strategic decisions made for its national unit; and (3) failed to carry out those same strategic decisions (reversely scored). The Cronbach's coefficient *alpha* for this three-item measure was .88. The correlation between the pooled compliance scores of subsidiary top managers and the compliance scores of their member head office managers was positive and significant ($r=.72$, $p<.01$).

Subsidiary Performance. Recently, international management literature has placed great emphasis on the need for multinationals to differentiate the strategic missions of subsidiary units [Bartlett and Ghoshal 1986; Prahalad and Doz 1987]. For instance, Bartlett and Ghoshal [1986] have identified four distinct strategic missions of subsidiary units ranging from a 'contributor'— a subsidiary unit whose strategic mission is to build a distinctive capability, to a 'black hole'—a subsidiary unit whose strategic mission is to sense and analyze the international environment, to an 'implementer'—a subsidiary unit whose strategic mission is to build economies of scale and scope and to fund the international expansion of its multinationals, to a 'strategic leader'—a subsidiary unit whose strategic mission is to test and develop new and daring strategic moves. Also discussed by Prahalad and Doz [1987], the diversity of these strategic missions means that subsidiary units' performance cannot be assessed along uniform performance criteria such as 'stand alone' or objective financial performance. Rather, the performance of subsidiary units might be more meaningfully assessed based on the strategic contribution subsidiary units make to the competitive advantage of their overall organizations.

436   JOURNAL OF INTERNATIONAL BUSINESS STUDIES, THIRD QUARTER 1993

Accordingly, we did not use the 'stand alone' financial performance of subsidiary units to assess subsidiary performance. Rather we opted to use a more comprehensive performance measure that could take into account the diversity and the complexity of subsidiary units' strategic missions. Specifically, participants assessed the performance of a given subsidiary unit over the preceding year along seven dimensions: competitive position achieved in the national market; strategic contribution to the overall organization; cash flows generated from operations; efficiency of operations; distinctive competencies built (e.g., new product development, R&D activities); growth rate; and overall financial performance.

Each of these seven dimensions was rated on a 5-point Likert-type scale with scale anchors labeled: 1=much worse than expected; 5=much better than expected. Next participants assessed the importance of each of these dimensions in view of the strategic mission assigned in the last annual strategy-making process to the subsidiary unit under evaluation. The importance of each performance dimension was assessed on a 5-point scale with scale anchors labeled: 1=not at all important; 5=extremely important. Using the dimensional importance ratings as weights, a weighted average performance index was calculated for each subsidiary unit. Such a multivariate approach with criterion weights is consistent with Steer's [1975] advice and seemed particularly appropriate for taking into account the diverse and complex strategic missions assigned to subsidiary units in the multinational. The correlation between subsidiary unit performance scores and the unit performance scores of member head office managers was positive and significant ($r=.70$, $p<.01$).

Measurement: Moderating Variable

The Nature of a Multinational's Subsidiary's Industry. To measure the nature of a subsidiary unit's industry, we first defined multidomestic and global industries. Global industries were defined as industries where the principal strategic requirements for success are maximizing global economies of scale and scope, standardizing the majority of a business's value-added activities around the globe (e.g., transfering standardized marketing practices and developing and implementing universal products), and deploying its worldwide network of resources against its global competitors. In contrast, multidomestic industries were defined as industries where the principal strategic requirements for success are substantially customizing product offerings to local customer needs, adapting the marketing approach to the local market, and instituting competitive moves based essentially on the competitive dynamics in the local market.

We then asked subsidiary top managers to indicate the proportion of their unit's total sales accounted for by their industry segments that fell into each of the three following industry spectrums: (1) toward the multidomestic nature; (2) a balance between global and multidomestic; and (3) toward the global nature. These three industry spectrums were coded as 1, 2, and 3, respectively. The proportion breakdown of a subsidiary's industry segment sales across these three industry spectrums was then multiplied by each industry spectrum's code to derive a weighted average measure of the nature of each subsidiary unit's industry. Higher values indicated a more global industry while lower values indicated a more multidomestic industry.

The meaningfulness of subsidiary top managers' industry scores was then assessed by having their head office top managers evaluate the nature of given subsidiary units' industries. This was done by first defining the two polar extremes of global and multidomestic industries and then having head office top management assess which of the above three industry spectrums best reflected each subsidiary unit's overall industry. Hence, while subsidiary top managers' industry scores were derived using a weighted average, head office managers' industry scores were based on a one-item measure of their overall assessment of each subsidiary's industry. The correlation between these two scores was positive and significant ($r=.79$, $p<.01$).

Measurement: Control Variables

Decision Outcome Variables. Two of the three control variables included in this study are decision outcome variables: the perceived fairness or distributive justice of multinationals' strategic decision outcomes and the perceived favorability of multinationals' strategic decision outcomes. However, as the strategic decisions of multinationals are driven chiefly by economic and competitive concerns and not by concerns of decision outcome fairness and favorability at the subsidiary unit level (e.g., Hout, Porter and Rudden [1982]; Hamel and Prahalad [1985]; Kim and Mauborgne [1988]), these two variables cannot be treated as design criteria and hence are not focal variables in our study. Rather, these two variables are included as control variables.

Decision Outcome Fairness. A two-item measure, included in our step one questionnaire, was used to assess the perceived fairness of strategic decision outcomes. First, subsidiary top managers were asked to assess the extent to which the strategic roles, responsibilities, and resources allocated to their unit as a result of their last annual strategic planning process reflected their unit's individual performance achieved. Second, subsidiary top managers were asked to assess the extent to which the receipt of these strategic roles, responsibilities, and resources reflected their unit's relative contribution to the overall organization. Both of the items were measured on 7-point Likert-type scales. The Cronbach's coefficient *alpha* for this scale was .92.

Head office top management was also asked to assess the fairness of subsidiary units' strategic decision outcomes received in the last annual strategic planning process. This was done by having head office management assess the overall fairness or distributive justice of the strategic decisions received by the subsidiary unit under evaluation on a 7-point Likert-type scale. The correlation between these head office and subsidiary top management scores was positive and significant (r=.59, $p<.01$).

Decision Outcome Favorability. Two question items, included in our step one questionnaire, were used to assess the favorability of strategic decision outcomes received by subsidiary units. The first item asked subsidiary top managers to assess the extent to which the strategic roles, responsibilities, and resources received by their unit exceeded their unit's expectations. The second item asked subsidiary top managers to evaluate the absolute favorability of the strategic roles, responsibilities, and resources received by their unit, irrespective of whether they were perceived as deserved, i.e., fair or not. These two items were measured on 7-point Likert-type scales. The Cronbach's coefficient *alpha* for this scale was .88.

Head office top management was also asked to assess the favorability of subsidiary units' strategic decision outcomes received in the last annual strategic planning process. This was done by having head office management assess the overall favorability of the strategic decisions received by the subsidiary unit under evaluation on a 7-point Likert-type scale. The correlation between these head office and subsidiary top management scores was positive and significant (r=.61, $p<.01$).

Reward System. Given the potential of the reward system of multinationals to influence compliant behavior, organizational members' motivation to work together to achieve the strategic objectives of their multinational, and hence subsidiary performance as well, it seemed important to control for its possible effect. For instance, whether subsidiary top managers are more inclined to have compliant behavior toward corporate goal-driven strategic decisions may well be influenced by the extent to which rewards are based on subsidiary top managers' contribution to the overall organization. To assess this construct, head office managers were asked to identify the extent to which the total rewards (salary plus bonuses) of each of the subsidiary top management members participating in this study were based on their contribution to the overall organization. Without exception, the subsidiary top management members heading the same subsidiary unit were found to be subject to the same reward system. Hence, while at one extreme 100% meant that a given subsidiary unit's top management team was rewarded based completely on its contribution to overall corporate goals, at the other extreme 0% meant that a given subsidiary top management team was not at all rewarded based on its contribution to the overall organization.

ANALYSES AND RESULTS

Hypotheses 1a, 2a, 2b, 2c, and 3a are about the main effects of procedural justice on subsidiary compliance, the three strategic objectives of the multinational, and subsidiary performance, respectively. On the other hand, Hypotheses 1b and 3b are about the interaction effects of procedural justice and the nature of a subsidiary's industry on subsidiary compliance and subsidiary performance, respectively. The significance of the interaction term (procedural justice × the nature of a subsidiary's industry) would indicate if the effect of procedural justice (X) on each dependent variable (Y) is contingent upon the nature of a subsidiary's industry (Z). Mathematically, we can express this interaction relation as follows:

$$\frac{\partial Y}{\partial X} = a + bZ.$$

Here, b is predicted to be positive in Hypotheses 1b and 3b.

Our analytic strategy was, therefore, to regress each dependent variable on procedural justice and its associated control variables including the moderator in step one, and then to add the interaction term to the equation predicting each dependent variable in step two. To test our hypotheses, we estimated the equations in both steps. The main effects of procedural justice on our dependent variables were assessed based on the significance of the procedural justice coefficients in their corresponding equations. The significance of the effect of the interaction term on each dependent variable was tested based on the increase in R^2 that is due to the additional entry of the interaction term into the equation in the second step [Cohen and Cohen 1983]. ΔR^2 here indexes the unique contribution of the interaction term under test to the total variance of each dependent variable.

Before conducting multiple regression analyses to test our hypotheses, we checked a couple of critical conditions that must be met to ensure proper analyses. First, the internal consistency of our multi-item measures was checked through their Cronbach's coefficient *alphas*. The *alpha* coefficients for all of our multi-item scales exceeded the 0.70 value and hence their consistency reliabilities were judged to be acceptable [Nunnally 1978]. Second, the possibility of a multicollinearity condition was checked through the bivariate correlations among the independent variables of our study. The inter-correlations ranged from $-.12$ to $.68$ among which the higher values (i.e., around and above .50) were of particular concern. The highest intercorrelation was .68 between decision outcome fairness and favorability. Hence, we further assessed the possibility of multicollinearity by regressing each independent variable on all the others [Lewis-Beck 1980]. Except for the variable of decision outcome fairness and favorability, this multicollinearity assessment produced all R^2 far from unity, ranging from .09 to .17. Hence, our conclusion here was that multicollinearity is not a concern except for the variables of decision outcome fairness and favorability. To treat these two highly intercorrelated variables, which might well constitute a source of multicollinearity, we opted to combine them into a single construct called decision outcome concerns ($r=.68$, the Cronbach's $\alpha=.80$); the conceptual sense of this combined construct can be found in Kim and Mauborgne [1991].

TABLE 1
Means, Standard Deviations, and
Pearson Product-Moment Correlations[a]

Variables	Means	s.d.	1	2	3	4	5	6	7	8
1. Procedural justice	4.19	1.83								
2. Decision outcome concerns	3.31	1.91	.15							
3. Reward system	24.87	17.98	-.02	.10						
4. Industry globalization	2.36	0.48	.06	-.12	.30*					
5. Subsidiary compliance	4.60	1.73	.41**	.33*	.32*	.11				
6. Global learning	4.25	1.50	.35**	.23	.14	.03	.29*			
7. Balancing global and local	5.01	1.58	.37**	.16	.29*	.18	.31*	.07		
8. Global strategic renewal	4.13	1.29	.33*	.20	.18	.09	.17	.13	.21	
9. Subsidiary performance	3.22	0.97	.28*	.09	.39**	.13	.40**	.20	.31*	.16

[a]$N=56$
*$p<.05$
**$p<.01$

Table 1 presents means, standard deviations and Pearson product-moment correlations for the nine variables used in our final analyses. As can be seen in Table 1, the intercorrelations, which used the combined variable of decision outcome concerns for decision outcome fairness and favorability, were not of a magnitude warranting serious concern for multicollinearity (i.e., below .50; see Lewis-Beck [1980]). The data in Table 1 also show that each dependent variable does not have a bivariate correlation with the industry moderator, suggesting that the research design appears to have adequately controlled for the effects of industry context on each dependent variable.

Table 2 presents the results of the multiple regression analyses undertaken to test our hypotheses. Note that in Table 2, the unstandardized regression coefficients are reported. Given that the points of origin of our study variables are arbitrary, as is the case for most interval-scale variables, our regression coefficients need to be independent of these points of origin to be meaningful. In the presence of interaction or cross-product terms, the unstandardized, but not the standardized, regression coefficients are independent of these points of origin [Southwood 1978] and hence are used in Table 2.

Subsidiary Compliance. For Hypothesis 1a, dealing with the main effect of procedural justice on subsidiary compliance, the results are supportive. As equations 1 and 2 in Table 2 indicate, the coefficient of procedural justice, X_1, is positive and significant both before ($p<.01$) and after ($p<.01$) adding the interaction term, procedural justice × nature of a subsidiary's industry

TABLE 2
Results of Multiple Regression Analyses Assessing the Effects of Procedural Justice and Its Interaction Term[a]

Results of Equations[b]	Equation	R^2	F value[c]	ΔR^2 [d]	F value
Hypotheses 1a and 1b					
$Y_1 = 1.40 + 0.36X_1{}^{**} + 0.22X_2{}^* + 0.03X_3 + 0.09X_4$	1	.33	6.29** (4,51)		
$Y_1 = 0.52 + 0.39X_1{}^{**} + 0.17X_2{}^\dagger + 0.02X_3$ $+ 0.06X_4 + 0.11X_1X_4{}^{**}$	2			.09	7.68** (1,50)
Hypothesis 2a					
$Y_2 = 2.51 + 0.27X_1{}^* + 0.13X_2 + 0.01X_3 - 0.03X_4$	3	.18	2.80** (4,51)		
$Y_2 = 2.60 + 0.33X_1{}^{**} + 0.09X_2 - 0.01X_3$ $- 0.05X_4 - 0.02X_1X_4$	4			.01	0.52 (1,50)
Hypothesis 2b					
$Y_3 = 2.24 + 0.31X_1{}^{**} + 0.08X_2 + 0.02X_3 + 0.30X_4{}^*$	5	.24	4.04** (4,51)		
$Y_3 = 1.58 + 0.26X_1{}^* + 0.10X_2 + 0.01X_3{}^\dagger$ $+ 0.25X_4{}^* + 0.08X_1X_4{}^\dagger$	6			.05	2.85† (1,50)
Hypothesis 2c					
$Y_4 = 2.33 + 0.23X_1{}^* + 0.10X_2 + 0.01X_3 + 0.11X_4$	7	.17	2.65* (4,51)		
$Y_4 = 2.42 + 0.28X_1{}^* + 0.21X_2{}^* - 0.01X_3$ $+ 0.06X_4 - 0.01X_1X_4$	8			.00	0.15 (1,50)
Hypotheses 3a and 3b					
$Y_5 = 1.53 + 0.15X_1{}^\dagger + 0.01X_2 + 0.03X_3{}^* - 0.01X_4$	9	.24	4.03** (4,51)		
$Y_5 = 0.47 + 0.06X_1 - 0.02X_2 + 0.04X_3{}^*$ $+ 0.03X_4 + 0.12X_1X_4{}^{**}$	10			.13	9.82** (1,50)

[a]$N = 56$. Unstandardized regression coefficients are reported.
[b]Y_1 = subsidiary compliance, Y_2 = global learning, Y_3 = balancing global and local perspectives, Y_4 = global strategic revewal, Y_5 = subsidiary performance, X_1 = procedural justice, X_2 = decision outcome concerns, X_3 = reward system, and X_4 = the nature of a subsidiary's industry.
[c]Figures in parentheses represent degrees of freedom.
[d]the increment in R^2 over the preceding equation due to the additional entry of the interaction term of X_1X_4
$^\dagger p<.10$; $^*p<.05$; $^{**}p<.01$

(X_1X_4), to the equation. For Hypothesis 1b, dealing with the effect of the interaction term (X_1X_4) on subsidiary compliance, the results are also supportive. As shown in equation 2, the coefficient of the interaction term is positive and significant $(p<.01)$. To gain further insight into exactly how this effect varies across the nature of a subsidiary's industry, we derived the partial derivative of equation 2 as follows:

442   JOURNAL OF INTERNATIONAL BUSINESS STUDIES, THIRD QUARTER 1993

$$\frac{\partial Y_1}{\partial X_1} = .39 + .11X_4 \; .$$

Over the observed range of the industry variable ($1 \leq X_4 \leq 3$), we can see that $\partial Y_1 / \partial X_1$ is always positive. However, the effect is stronger for subsidiaries at the global end of the industry spectrum than at the multidomestic end. These results suggest that while the exercise of procedural justice in a multinational's strategy-making process has an overall positive effect on subsidiary compliance, the strength of this effect varies contingent upon the nature of a subsidiary's industry.

Global Learning. For Hypothesis 2a, dealing with the main effect of procedural justice on global learning, the results are supportive. As equations 3 and 4 indicate, the coefficient of procedural justice is positive and significant both before ($p < .05$) and after ($p < .01$) adding the interaction term ($X_1 X_4$) into the equation. Note, however, that in equation 4 the coefficient of the interaction term proves to be statistically insignificant. These results suggest that the exercise of procedural justice in the multinational's strategy-making process has a positive effect on the ability to promote global learning. But, no evidence was found to support that this effect varies contingent upon the nature of a subsidiary's industry.

Balancing Global and Local Perspectives. For Hypothesis 2b, dealing with the main effect of procedural justice on balancing global and local perspectives, the results are supportive. As equations 5 and 6 indicate, the coefficient of procedural justice is positive and significant both before ($p < .01$) and after ($p < .05$) introducing the interaction term ($X_1 X_4$) into the equation. Note, however, that in equation 6 the coefficient of the interaction term proves to be statistically insignificant. These results suggest that the exercise of procedural justice in the multinational's strategy-making process has a positive effect on the ability to balance global and local perspectives. But, no evidence was found to support that this effect varies contingent upon the nature of a subsidiary's industry.

Global Strategic Renewal. For Hypothesis 2c, dealing with the main effect of procedural justice on global strategic renewal, the results are supportive. As equations 7 and 8 indicate, the coefficient of procedural justice is positive and significant both before ($p < .05$) and after ($p < .05$) adding the interaction term ($X_1 X_4$) to the equation. In addition, the coefficient of the interaction term shown in equation 8 proves to be not statistically different from zero. These results suggest that the exercise of procedural justice in the multinational's strategy-making process has a positive effect on the ability to promote global strategic renewal. But, no evidence was found to support that this effect varies contingent upon the nature of a subsidiary's industry.

Subsidiary Performance. For Hypothesis 3a, dealing with the main effect of procedural justice on subsidiary performance, the results are not supportive.

As equations 9 and 10 indicate, the coefficient of procedural justice is not statistically significant either before or after introducing the interaction term into the equation. However, for Hypothesis 3b, dealing with the effect of the interaction term on subsidiary performance, the results are supportive. As shown in equation 10, the coefficient of the interaction term is positive and significant ($p < .01$). To gain further insight into exactly how this effect varies across the nature of a subsidiary's industry, we derived the partial derivative of equation 10 as follows:

$$\frac{\partial Y_5}{\partial X_1} = .06 + .12X_4 .$$

As can be calculated, over the observed range of the industry variable ($1 \leq X_4 \leq X_3$), the value of $\partial Y_5 / \partial X_1$, ranging from 0.18 to 0.42, reaches a significant magnitude at the global end of a subsidiary's industry spectrum. These results suggest that while the exercise of procedural justice in a multinational's strategy-making process does not generate an across-the-board salutary effect on subsidiary performance, its utility in enhancing subsidiary performance becomes distinctive at the global end of its industry spectrum.

We checked the stability of the main effect of procedural justice on each dependent variable by comparing the procedural justice coefficients across the two equations predicting the same dependent variable, one with the interaction-term and one without. This examination revealed marginal change in the statistical significance of these coefficients. In addition, the direction and the significance of the coefficients of the control variables appeared to be in reasonably good agreement with the arguments of the literature. To illustrate, subsidiary compliance and performance were found to be positively influenced by decision outcome fairness and favorability concerns and the reward system, respectively. Given the logical consistency and stability of the results, our findings can be said to be relatively robust.

DISCUSSION AND CONCLUSIONS

The results of our research provided strong support that the exercise of procedural justice presents a powerful way to organize the multinational's strategy-making process. The exercise of procedural justice was found to significantly augment subsidiary compliance with multinationals' strategic decisions, thereby bringing about the improved implementation of world-wide strategies. At the same time, the dimensions of process fairness were found to enhance a subsidiary unit's ability to gather, interpret, and synthe-size the types of strategic information that are critical to achieve global learning, the balancing of global and local perspectives, and global strategic renewal. To the extent that these three strategic missions are driving forces for the design of effective worldwide strategies, the exercise of procedural justice can be said to facilitate the formation of superior worldwide strategy

444 JOURNAL OF INTERNATIONAL BUSINESS STUDIES, THIRD QUARTER 1993

content as well. Taken together, these results suggest that the exercise of procedural justice presents a so far unexplored though powerful way to *simultaneously* pursue the double-ended objective of effectively conceiving and implementing multinationals' worldwide strategies.

At a more conceptual level, these results can be interpreted as indicating that the interaction relations between head office and subsidiary top managers should not be viewed as a governing mode but more as a coopting mode based on mutually shared and acceptable principles. Here we call these coopting principles procedural justice. To the extent that multinationals reinforce this coopting view of interaction relations they may well be better able to tap the distinctive knowledge, skills, and competencies of subsidiary units. They may also be better able to gain subsidiary managers' willing commitment to, and compliance with, the worldwide strategic objectives of their organizations.

While the exercise of procedural justice was not found to generate an across-the-board effect on subsidiary performance, its utility in enhancing subsidiary performance did become distinctive at the global end of a subsidiary's industry spectrum. Along with this evidence we also found that the utility of procedural justice in inducing subsidiary compliance is higher at the global end of a subsidiary's industry spectrum than at the multidomestic end. However, the effect of procedural justice on the multinational's three strategic missions was not contingent upon the nature of a subsidiary's industry. Overall, the above findings generally indicate that the *power* of procedural justice is contingent upon the nature of a multinational's subsidiary's industry. In net, the exercise of procedural justice appears to gain distinctive power when it deals with subsidiary units operating in a global industry.

This study used a set of two-stage longitudinal data in an attempt to strengthen the causal inference from procedural justice to strategy implementation and subsidiary performance. This was done via an assessment of procedural justice at time T_1 and assessment of subsidiary compliance and subsidiary performance at time T_2. Although the time period chosen for our sequential measurement conforms reasonably to the speed of the causal effects examined—a ten-month time lag was imposed between time T_1 and time T_2—ideally, to establish the causal relation among our study variables, each of the constructs should have been measured at two (or more) points in time (e.g., Billings and Wroten [1978]). This would have allowed us to eliminate the possibility, or to partial out the effect, of prior practices on the observed relations. However, time and funding constraints prevented the pursuit of this alternative. As 96% of our sample participants deemed their annual strategic planning process to be reflective of that held in the prior two years, the incremental value of having each variable measured at two points in time was also not convincingly clear. Nonetheless the fact that each of our variables was only measured at one point in time is clearly a weakness of this research. Evidently, the relations between procedural justice and subsidiary compliance and subsidiary performance must be interpreted with the potential limitation attached to one-time sequential measurement in mind.

In the absence of any objective measures of procedural justice, multinationals' strategic objectives, subsidiary compliance and subsidiary performance, we were required to use perceptual assessments of each of these constructs. Generally, the use of such perceptual measures may introduce common methods and/or social desirability bias. We would argue, however, that this is not a serious concern in the present research. Our reasoning is two-fold. First, although subsidiary top managers provided perceptual assessments of each of the focal variables, the fact that subsidiary top managers' scores were highly consistent not only among themselves within the same unit but also with the scores of their head office counterparts, suggests that the results of this study are not likely to be subject to the problem of such biases. Second, this study strictly followed the approach Heneman [1974] found to enhance the accuracy and validity of self-ratings: that confidentiality of responses be guaranteed and that respondents be assured that all responses will be used only for the purposes of scientific research and not for personal evaluation from the organization's perspective. It is worth noting that Heneman found a very high correlation between superior and self-ratings of managerial performance when these two conditions were met in full, as in this research.

An extension of this research would be to assess to what extent our procedural justice model of multinationals' strategy making is universal or culture bound. Although no prior procedural justice study has found the cultural background of study participants to influence the effects of procedural justice (see Lind and Tyler [1988]), we were unable to establish the universality of the effects found in the current study due to the over-dominance of North American participants. To address this question in a meaningful and conclusive manner, later studies should try to expand their base of subjects to include an even balance of participants from different cultural backgrounds such as German, French, and Japanese cultural orientations.

In examining the factors influencing our dependent variables, this study limited its attention to the effects of procedural and distributive justice concerns, the structure of a multinational's reward system, and the nature of a subsidiary's industry. It did not examine the effects of other possible variables that may also affect our dependent variables such as the type of organizational structure, the organizational culture, and other socialization systems on the managers involved. Hence, a second potentially interesting extension might be to assess the contribution of these other variables relative to those examined in this study to our dependent variables.

Overall, the results of this research demonstrate the value of introducing the concept of procedural justice, theoretically grounded in the two academic disciplines of social psychology and law, into the field of international business. To date, we have seen abundant applications of various streams

446 JOURNAL OF INTERNATIONAL BUSINESS STUDIES, THIRD QUARTER 1993

of economic and organization theory to the analyses of the issues of international business or specifically multinational organizations. Yet theories of social psychology and law, despite their powerful contribution potential as shown here, have scarcely been interplayed with the field of international business. The importance of, and the need for, building this line of work is clear when we consider that such an interdisciplinary approach can shed new light on the internal motive systems and processes of multinational organizations. These are understudied yet critical issues for understanding the effective functioning of the modern multinational (e.g., Hedlund [1986]; Prahalad and Doz [1987]). We hope that this paper provides a strong impetus for building this line of work.

REFERENCES

Bartlett, Christopher A. & Sumantra Ghoshal. 1986. Tap your subsidiaries for global reach. *Harvard Business Review*, November-December: 87-94.

_____. 1987a. Managing across borders: New strategic requirements. *Sloan Management Review*, Summer: 7-17.

_____. 1987b. Managing across borders: New organizational responses. *Sloan Management Review*, Fall : 43-53.

_____. 1989. *Managing across borders*. Boston, MA: Harvard Business School Press.

_____. 1990. Matrix management: Not a structure, a frame of mind. *Harvard Business Review*, July-August: 138-45.

Beamish, Paul W. 1988. *Multinational joint ventures in developing countries*. London and New York: Routledge.

Billings, Robert S. & Steve P. Wroten. 1978. Use of path analysis in industrial/organizational psychology: Criticisms and suggestions. *Journal of Applied Psychology*, 63: 677-88.

Blau, Peter. 1964. *Exchange and power in social life*. New York: Wiley, Inc.

Cohen, Jacob & Patricia Cohen. 1983 (second edition). *Applied multiple regression/correlation analyses for the behavioral sciences*. Hillsdale, NJ: Erlbaum.

Cyert, Richard M. & James G. March. 1963. *A behavioral theory of the firm*. Englewood Cliffs, NJ: Prentice-Hall.

Daft, Richard L. & Karl E. Weick. 1984. Toward a model of organizations as interpretation systems. *Academy of Management Review*, 9: 284-95.

Dixon, Wilfred & Frank Massey. 1969. *Statistical analyses*. New York: McGraw-Hill.

Doz, Yves L. 1980. Strategic management in multinational companies. *Sloan Management Review*, Winter: 27-46.

Egelhoff, William G. 1991. Information-processing theory and the multinational enterprise. *The Journal of International Business Studies*, 22(3): 341-68.

Fredrickson, James W. & Anthony L. Iaquinto. 1987. Incremental change, its correlates, and the comprehensiveness of strategic decision processes. *Academy of Management Proceedings*: 26-30.

Friedland, Nehemia, John Thibaut & Laurens Walker. 1973. Some determinants of the violation of rules. *Journal of Applied Social Psychology*, 3: 103-18.

Galbraith, Jay R. 1973. *Designing complex organizations*. Reading, MA: Addison-Wesley.

_____. 1977. *Organization design*. Reading, MA: Addison-Wesley.

Ghoshal, Sumantra. 1987. Global strategy: An organizing framework. *Strategic Management Journal*, 8(5): 425-40.

_____ & Christopher A. Bartlett. 1988. Creation, adoption, and diffusion of innovations by subsidiaries of MNCs. *Journal of International Business Studies*, 19(3): 365-88.

Ghoshal, Sumantra & Nitin Nohria. 1989. Internal differentiation within multinational corporations. *Strategic Management Journal*, 10: 323-37.

Greenberg, Jerald. 1986. Determinants of perceived fairness of performance evaluations. *Journal of Applied Psychology*, 71: 340-42.

Guth, William D. & Ian C. MacMillan. 1986. Strategy implementation versus middle management self-interest. *Strategic Management Journal*, 7: 313-27.

Hamel, Gary & C.K. Prahalad. 1985. Do you really have a global strategy? *Harvard Business Review*, July-August: 139-48.

Hedlund, Gunnar. 1980. The role of foreign subsidiaries in strategic decision making in Swedish multinationals. *Strategic Management Journal*, 9: 23-36.

_____. 1986. The hypermodern MNC—A heterarchy? *Human Resource Management*, 25: 9-25.

Heneman, Herbert G. 1974. Comparisons of self- and superior ratings of managerial performance. *Journal of Applied Psychology*, 59: 638-42.

Hout, Thomas, Michael E. Porter & Eileen Rudden. 1982. How global companies win out. *Harvard Business Review*, September-October: 98-108.

Kim, W. Chan & Renée A. Mauborgne. 1988. Becoming an effective global competitor. *The Journal of Business Strategy*, January-February: 33-37.

_____. 1993a. Procedural justice theory and the multinational enterprise. In Sumantra Ghoshal & D. Eleanor Westney, editors, *Organization theory and the multinational corporation*. London: Macmillan.

_____. 1993b. Making global strategies work. *Sloan Management Review*, Spring: 11-27.

_____. 1993c. Procedural justice, attitudes, and subsidiary top management compliance with multinationals' corporate strategic decisions. *Academy of Management Journal*, June: 502-26.

_____. 1993d. A procedural justice model of strategic decision making: Strategy content implications in the multinational. *Organization Science*, forthcoming.

_____. 1991. Implementing global strategies: The role of procedural justice. *Strategic Management Journal*, 12: 125-43.

Kogut, Bruce. 1985a. Designing global strategies: Comparative and competitive value added chains. *Sloan Management Review*, Summer: 15-28.

_____. 1985b. Designing global strategies: Profiting from operational flexibility. *Sloan Management Review*, Fall: 27-38.

_____. 1989. A note on global strategies. *Strategic Management Journal*, 10: 383-89.

Levitt, Theodore. 1983. The globalization of markets. *Harvard Business Review*, May-June: 92-102.

Lewis-Beck, Michael S. 1980. *Applied regression*. Beverly Hills, CA: Sage.

Lind, E. Allan. & Tom R. Tyler. 1988. *The social psychology of procedural justice*. New York: Plenum Press.

Miles, Raymond E. & Charles C. Snow. 1978. *Organizational strategy, structure, and processes*. New York: McGraw-Hill Press.

Nunnally, Jum C. 1978 (second edition). *Psychometric theory*. New York: McGraw-Hill.

Nystrom, Paul & William Starbuck. 1984. To avoid organizational crises, unlearn. *Organizational Dynamics*, 12: 53-65.

Perlmutter, Howard V. 1969. The tortuous evolution of the multinational corporation. *Columbia Journal of World Business*, January-February: 9-18.

Porter, Michael E. 1986. Competition in global industries: A conceptual framework. In M.E. Porter, editor, *Competition in global industries*, 15-60. Boston: Harvard Business School Press.

Prahalad, C.K. 1976. The strategic process in a multinational corporation. D.B.A. thesis, Graduate School of Business Administration, Harvard University.

_____ & Yves L. Doz. 1987. *The multinational mission*. New York: Free Press.

Southwood, Kenneth E. 1978. Substantive theory and statistical interaction: Five models. *American Journal of Sociology*, 83: 1154-1203.

Steers, Richard M. 1975. Problems in the measurement of organizational effectiveness. *Administrative Science Quarterly*, 20: 546-53.

Stephenson, W. 1953. *The study of behavior.* Chicago: University of Chicago Press.

Thibaut, John, Nehemia Friedland & Laurens Walker. 1974. Compliance with rules: Some social determinants. *Journal of Personality and Social Psychology,* 30: 792-801.

Thibaut, John & Laurens Walker. 1975. *Procedural justice: A psychological analysis.* Hillsdale, NJ: Erlbaum.

_____. 1978. A theory of procedure. *California Law Review,* 66: 541-66.

Thompson, James D. 1967. *Organizations in action.* New York: McGraw-Hill.

Tushman, Michael L. & David A. Nadler. 1978. Information processing as an integrating concept in organizational design. *Academy of Management Review,* 3: 613-24.

Williamson, Oliver E. 1975. *Markets and hierarchies: Analysis and antitrust implications.* New York: Free Press.

Yip, George S. 1989. Global strategy . . . in a world of nations? *Sloan Management Review,* Fall: 29-41.

[21]

Strategic Management Journal, Vol. 15, 73–90 (1994)

A MODEL OF KNOWLEDGE MANAGEMENT AND THE N-FORM CORPORATION

GUNNAR HEDLUND
Institute of International Business, Stockholm School of Economics, Stockholm, Sweden

A model of knowledge management is developed. It builds on the interplay between articulated and tacit knowledge at four different levels: the individual, the small group, the organization, and the interorganizational domain. The model is applied on differences between Western and Japanese patterns of knowledge management. These are related to organizational characteristics, such as employment systems, career patterns, and organization structure. Effective knowledge management is argued to require departures from the logic of hierarchical organization and the M-form structure. The alternative N-form is characterized and suggested as more appropriate. It entails combination of knowledge rather than its division, which is the basic principle in the M-form. Other attributes of the N-form are: temporary constellations of people, the importance of personnel at 'lower levels', lateral communication, a catalytic and architectural role for top management, strategies aimed at focusing and economies of depth, and heterarchical structures.

In recent discussions of needed foci for the analysis of corporate strategy and theories of the firm, two types of calls for a shift of emphasis are increasingly heard. First, the *internal organization and management of firms* are emphasized. Rumelt, Schendel and Teece (1991: 22) stress '— organizational capabilities, rather than product-market positions or tactics, as the enduring source of advantage.' Nelson and Winter (1982: 135) posed the challenge of developing the subject of 'organizational genetics,' indicating that 'the real work remains to be done.' Almost a decade later, Nelson (1991) insists even more strongly that differences between individual firms constitute a core problem, and that analyses have to consider firm strategies, structures and core capabilities in greater depth. The emerging ideas are claimed to serve as a basis 'not only as a guide to management, but also as a basis for a

serious theory of the firm in economics' (1991: 72). The resource based approach to strategy (Wernerfelt, 1984) similarly stresses internal capabilities, as does analyses in terms of core competences (Prahalad and Hamel, 1990).

Second, notions of change, dynamism and innovation become more prominent. The firm-specific capabilities that really make a difference are 'dynamic capabilities.' (For a review of work in this vein, see Teece, Pisano and Shuen, 1990). The Summer 1992 Special Issue of the *Strategic Management Journal* is devoted to 'Strategy Process: Managing Corporate Self-Renewal,' in which most papers deal with the dialectic of stability and change, identifying obstacles for renewal and their organizational implications. Relatedly, notions of knowledge and knowledge management are introduced into the strategy and economics discourse, sometimes clothed in the garb of 'organizational learning.' The special issue of *Organization Science* (February 1991) contains several examples. Dougherty (1992),

Key words: Knowledge, M-form, hierarchy, heterarchy

CCC 0143–2095/94/090073–18
© 1994 by John Wiley & Sons, Ltd.

74   *G. Hedlund*

Kogut and Zander (1992), and Nonaka (1987) constitute other recent efforts.

The often eloquent calls to arms notwithstanding, in my view there is much silence on what more precisely should be meant by knowledge and its management, or by dynamic capabilities. (Exceptions have been and will be referred to.) One reason is, I believe, that some dominant theoretical paradigms are inherently ill-suited to the particular task. For example, transaction cost approaches are hampered by taking transactions as given (rather than something to be created), adopting an atomistic view of the basic unit of analysis (rather than considering systemic aspects of transaction or action packages, cf. Winter, 1991: 191), not paying much attention to historical heritage and consequent inertia and path dependency, and by not considering what happens inside the firm in great detail. 'Hierarchy' denotes all forms of internal organization, and distinctions usually refer only to crude structural categories (M-form, U-form, etc).

Evolutionary theories do address questions of change, but often the focus is on selection mechanisms too crude to allow for internal adaptation in firms. 'Population ecology' approaches to organizational issues mostly see adaptation as less important than inertia, and renewal therefore as a 'Darwinian' process of selection of appropriate, inertial forms of organization. Nelson and Winter (1982) are refreshingly (and in my view appropriately) open about their theory being 'unabashedly Lamarckian' (1982: 11). Still, their analysis focuses on the inertia and permanence of 'routines,' and they admit that their discussion of routines as 'targets' and 'components' is only a preliminary effort to 'dynamize' the analysis. Later discussions from scholars in business strategy and organization theory take the analysis further by studying the 'intraorganizational ecology' (Burgelman, 1991) of selection and adaptation in greater detail. However, the starting point in the tacit nature of knowledge and skills adopted by Nelson and Winter (1982) is largely absent in the more 'micro-ecological' contributions.

The large literature on the management of technology and R&D, and on product development more specifically, of course provides many valuable insights concerning the nature of knowledge and its management. (See Tushman and Moore, 1988, and Van de Ven, Angle and Poole, 1989, for state-of-the-art selections and summaries.) However, if theories from economics and inspired by biological analogies are too crude to capture the intricacies of internal organization and how it relates to knowledge management, the literature on product development is too specific and theoretically eclectic to generate more comprehensive models, that constitute alternatives or at least complements to the dominant overarching theories of the firm.

This paper is an effort to contribute to the development of such models in the grey zone between economics, organization theory and strategic management. The specific framework proposed builds on Hedlund and Nonaka (1993) and on earlier work on knowledge creation (Nonaka, 1987), exploitation and experimentation strategies (Hedlund and Rolander, 1987, 1990), and heterarchical structures (Hedlund, 1986, 1993). First, a typology of knowledge types and of knowledge transfer and transformation processes is presented. The usefulness of the model is tested by trying to explain some apparent peculiarities of Japanese[1] industrial strengths and weaknesses. Organizational requirements for effective knowledge management are posited, partly based on the analysis of differences between Japanese and other approaches. The paper concludes by proposing the *N-form corporation* as a likely and desirable development. More ambitious knowledge management is argued to require departures from the logic of hierarchical organization in general, and the M-form in particular. The N-form logic is one of multiplication and combination rather than of division. It also implies role assignments differing from those inherent in the M-form, at all levels of the firm.

A MODEL OF KNOWLEDGE TYPES, AND TRANSFER AND TRANSFORMATION PROCESSES

The model builds on two primary distinctions, often made but rarely put together and, as far as I know, not previously analyzed systematically

---

[1] 'Japanese' and 'Western' of course hide significant differences between firms and environments. Still, as a first approximation it is useful to contrast a Western archetype with the Japanese one, also obviously simplified.

	INDIVIDUAL	GROUP	ORGANIZATION	INTERORGANIZATONAL DOMAIN
ARTICULATED KNOWLEDGE/ INFORMATION Cognitive Skills Embodied	Knowing calculus	Quality circle's documented analysis of its performance	Organization chart	Suppliers' patents and documented practices
TACIT KNOWLEDGE/ INFORMATION Cognitive Skills Embodied	Cross-cultural negotiation skills	Team coordination in complex work	Corporate culture	Customers' attitudes to products and expectations

Figure 1. A model of knowledge categories and transformation processes: Types of knowledge. Adapted from Hedlund and Nonaka, 1993.

in conjunction. First, we distinguish between *tacit* and *articulated* knowledge.[2] Tacit knowledge (TK) is defined as in Polanyi (1962), indicating knowledge which is nonverbalized or even non-verbalizable, intuitive, unarticulated. Articulated knowledge (AK) is specified either verbally or in writing, computer programs, patents, drawings or the like.

Second, we distinguish between four different levels of carriers, or agents, of knowledge: the *individual*, the small *group*, the *organization*, and the *interorganizational domain* (important customers, suppliers, competitors, etc). AK and TK exist at all levels. Figure 1 provides examples of the eight types of knowledge so defined. The notion that knowledge resides not only at the individual level is of course not new. Cyert and March (1963) and Nelson and Winter (1982) explicitly talk about organizational routines. Pavitt (1980) stresses the firm's knowledge and capabilities, and as in Nelson and Winter, the tacit nature of the firm's skills is given prominence. From a different angle, Itami (1987) stresses 'invisible assets,' similarly combining the ideas of organizational capabilities and tacitness.

Without pretensions of a full review, some other recent examples of analyses of organizational knowledge and related matters are: Stubbart (1989) and other students of managerial and organizational cognition, Porac, Thomas and Baden-Fuller (1988) on 'cognitive groups/oligopo-

lies,' Wolfe (1991) on mind as a social category, March (1991) on the balance between exploitation and exploration and between individual and organizational learning, Seely-Brown and Duguid (1991) on the 'communal context of learning,' Stiglitz (1987) on 'localized knowledge,' Kogut and Zander (1992).

The basic structure of our model is an effort to synthesize and clarify insights in these and other contributions. We differ from Nelson and Winter (1982) in that we focus on the *interaction* between, for example, individual and organizational knowledge, rather than only using the former as an analogy of the latter. Posing the group as an intermediate level allows a more fine-grained look at what goes on within the organization. The prominence of small groups, often temporary, in innovation and product development indicates that this is the level at which much of knowledge transfer and learning take place. The level superordinate to the organization, the interorganizational domain of units interacting with the focal one, is also critical to knowledge development, as evidenced by von Hippel (1976) with regard to customers and by many recent analysts with regard to suppliers. Analyses of national systems of innovation (Freeman, 1982; Nelson, 1993) also show that the texture of social ecology matters a great deal.

The model distinguishes between three forms— or, perhaps better—aspects of knowledge: *cognitive knowledge* in the form of mental constructs and precepts, *skills*, and knowledge *embodied* in

---

[2] I will use 'knowledge' and 'information' interchangeably although they should be distinguished in a fuller treatment.

76   *G. Hedlund*

products, well-defined services or artifacts. To include skills is consistent with Polany (1962), whose discussion is mostly about individual skills. In my view, adopters and adapters of Polanyi's ideas have perhaps been too enamoured by the focus on skills. (Competences, capabilities, resources—conceived broadly (too broadly?) as also encompassing propensities for certain action—are examples in later vocabulary.) Cognitive knowledge is *also* important, particularly since its development and management is likely to differ substantially from that of skills. For example, cognitive knowledge is usually easier to articulate and transfer and not as sensitive to problems of team embeddedness (Winter, 1987; Zander, 1991).

Introducing embodiment in products as a category of knowledge is more problematical. Starbuck (1984) would rather see products as one of many forms of embodiment of knowledge. (Others being, for example, in individuals, in computer programs, in production equipment, etc.) Our wide definition of knowledge is influenced by the fact that transfer of knowledge between but also within organizations to such a large extent takes place through product flows. An advantage is that the three forms correspond to three recognized primary modes of corporate expansion: through increased sales (embodied in products), by licensing (selling cognitive blueprints or recipes), or by capacity-increasing investment (transferring a whole set of skills). The parallelism is most apparent in the context of multinational corporations (MNCs). A large literature discusses the relative merits of exports, licensing, and foreign direct investment (FDI). The three modes imply our three categories of knowledge.

Further distinctions between types of knowledge can fruitfully be made, but more important for the purposes of this paper is to 'dynamize' the model by introducing processes of *transfer* and *transformation* of knowledge. Much of the literature referred to earlier speaks primarily in terms of *storage* of information, and only secondarily about its transfer, whereas its transformation is left outside most analyses. For example, Nelson and Winter (1982: 134) talk about coordinating information being '... stored in the routine functioning of the organization and 'remembered by doing'.' Their first concern is storage, and the second transfer, developing

models of imitation and emphasizing the differential abilities of social mechanisms (markets, firms) to 'actively *transmit* information' (1982: 403, my emphasis). Kogut and Zander (1992), as many others, rely on the concept of the organization as a 'repository of knowledge.' Their prime concern is the analysis of imitation and replication of knowledge, i.e., its transfer rather than its transformation.

Our model allows explicit distinctions between storage, transfer and transformation. I will discuss three basic sets of concepts (see Figure 2):

—*Articulation* and *internalization*, the interaction of which is termed *reflection*. (The processes are illustrated through vertical arrows in Figure 2).

—*Extension* and *appropriation*, together constituting *dialogue*. (Horizontal arrows in Figure 2.)

—*Assimilation* and *dissemination*, referring to knowledge imports from and exports to the environment.

Articulation refers to tacit knowledge being made explicit, articulated. This can take place at all four levels in the model. Articulation is essential in facilitating transfer of information, but also for its expansion and improvement, since it allows open scrutiny and critical testing. In international technology transfer, it is a crucial element both in the case of licensing and of FDI. Ledin (1990) contains an account of Ericsson's concerted and successful campaigns to articulate and transfer telecommunications know-how. This process of articulation is crucial in the growth of the firm. Without such articulation, it is difficult to involve new employees and to divide up and specialize work. The current, and justified, fascination with the tacit component of knowledge in much of the literature must not cloud the fact that organizations to a large extent are 'articulation machines,' built around codified practices and deriving some of their competitive advantages from clever, unique articulation. In fact, much of industrialization seems to have entailed exactly the progresssive articulation of craftsmanlike skills, difficult but not impossible to codify. (*And*, possible to appropriate within the firm in spite of being codified. The empirical results from Zander (1991) show that codifiability does not necessarily lead to quicker competitor imitation.)

Internalization is when articulated knowledge

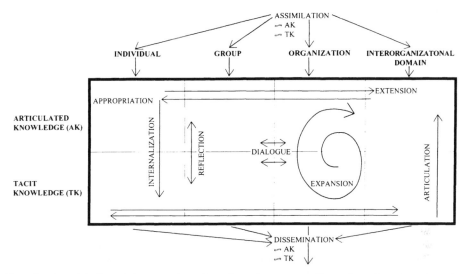

Figure 2.   A model of knowledge categories and transformation processes: Types of transfer and transformation. Adapted from Hedlund and Nonaka, 1993

becomes tacit. It is important in that internalization economizes on limited cognitive, perceptual and coordinative resources. The whole literature on and building on bounded rationality (Simon, 1955) shows how individual and organizational routines are paramount in understanding how human systems assemble and use information. It also provides many examples of the negative sides of internalization in withdrawing knowledge into the unreflective unconscious and packaging it in conservative and conserving ways.

The interplay of tacit and articulated knowledge is termed *reflection*. Genuine knowledge creation (see Nonaka, 1987) usually requires such interplay. Writing a scientific paper is a good example of such a process; moving between hunches and expositions, loose analogies and structural similarities, unreflective impressions from chance encounters with reality and systematic search for evidence, etc.

Extension is transfer of knowledge (possibly resulting in its transformation) from lower to higher agency levels in the model, in articulated or tacit form. An example of the former would be when a company sends drawings of its planned future products to its subcontractors. The latter, tacit mode of transfer is usually entailed in the teaching of complex, practical skills, as when an experienced management consultant coaches a group of younger colleagues through working together with them on a project. *Appropriation* is the reverse process, as when the organization teaches new employees about its products (mostly the articulate route) or indoctrinates them into the corporate culture (mostly through tacit transfer). *Dialogue* is the interaction of extension and appropriation. It also includes dialogue at a given agency level, for example within a working group. Dialogue takes place also at the tacit level. Craftsmanlike skills as well as corporate cultures probably develop and transfer largely through tacit communication.

The quantity and quality of dialogue and reflection are hypothesized to be important determinants of the type and effectiveness of knowledge management. It is significant that pedagogical practices usually involve the two basic processes in our model: dialogue between teachers and students in the classroom, and reflection in solitude in the library or at home. Great teachers have always known to inspire dialogue, and also to draw tacit knowledge out of the student. (Plato's dialogues (sic!) are prime examples, where Socrates always insists that the student really already knows the answer. The master's job (which Socrates compares to a

78　　G. Hedlund

midwife's) is to pull it from the depths of muddled tacitness, or forgetfullness, to clear articulation.)

Assimilation and *dissemination* are conceptually straight-forward concepts covering the input and output, respectively, of knowledge (in cognitive, product or skill form).[3] Also here, there are both articulated and tacit components. For example, complex packages of tacit knowledge are assimilated through selective recruiting of key individuals. Or, clearly articulated bits of information are accessed through data links to patent banks. Dissemination similarly can involve articulated as well as tacit elements. If knowledge is easily codifiable, selling patents is a feasible strategy, provided the 'appropriability régime' is benign (cf. Teece, 1977 and later work). Large doses of tacitness means that 'internalization' makes more sense, for example by investing in own manufacturing capability. (Teece interprets these maters in terms of transaction cost. I believe the original insight into the importance of the type of knowledge being transferred is somewhat lost and left unexplored in the reliance on assumptions of opportunism in most transaction cost literature.)

Hedlund and Nonaka (1993) argue for the descriptive incisiveness of the model in capturing essential differences between the Japanese and Western archetypical systems of knowledge management. Tacitness and tacit transfer of knowledge seem to be more important in large Japanese corporations, at the individual as well as at the group and organizational levels. The group and interorganizational levels, furthermore, appear to be most critical in the Japanese model, whereas the individual and organizational ones take precedence in the Western one.

Here, I will concentrate on the explanatory and potential predictive value of the model, also focusing on the Japanese case. This is not because of a taste for exoticism, but since the undeniable differences between large firms from Japan and the West pose a most serious challenge to all theories of the firm. Any model which can make sense of these differences is a stronger candidate for a more general theory than those limited by

---

[3] Note that input from and output to immediately related organizations are considered as appropriation and extension, respectively. We want to distinguish between the 'dense' transactional environment and the contextual, diffuse one.

behavioral and other assumptions peculiar to one or the other nation, tribe, etc. I will briefly discuss: the incrementalism of Japanese innovation strategies versus the 'large step' innovation in the West; the Japanese strength in fields relying on prespecified critical components or patents; the propensity to export products rather than sell know-how; the strength in fields requiring much intra- and interorganizational coordination; the weakness in large systems design; and, the special Japanese style of diversification.

INCREMENTALISM VS. LARGE-STEP INNOVATION

The Western system specializes in radical innovation, and large firms are the instruments more of exploiting such innovations than of generating them. At least, the large firm appears to have a *comparative* (in relation to smaller firms) disadvantage in the creation of novelty, particularly regarding the productivity of R&D, measured for example in terms of output per dollar spent on R&D. The review by Scherer (1984: 222–237) provides empirical evidence. Explanations of the difference usually center on problems of bureaucracy in the large complex organization. However, this does not explain why in Japan exactly the large firms contribute crucially to innovation. (See Taylor and Yamamura, 1990, and Caldwell-Harris, 1985, for empirical support both for the prevalence of incrementalism and for the seemingly less constraining effects of size.)

Not disputing the general effects of bureaucracy, I suggest that one reason for the innovation problems of the large, Western firm is the inflexibility of tightly specified and articulated systems of knowledge. This makes it difficult to be 'inconsistent,' to engage in projects not perceived to fit what the company is all about. In the extreme, the entire organization becomes a plan, where nothing can be changed without disturbing everything else. The root cause of these inflexibilities is in the design of the firm as essentially an instrument (cf. the etymology— organization = tool - and Morgan, 1986) to exploit given resources and knowledge (or administer transactions) efficiently. The fluid markets for human resources at all levels force articulation and formalization, constraining units and individuals to stick to current notions of strategies, products, communication routes, etc. It also inhibits the transfer of tacit knowledge, which requires greater intimacy and permanence than the combination of fluidity and formalism allow. The strength of the system is in the allowance of radical novelty through the importation of highly specialized human resources, and through links to strong universities and scientific knowledge bases. Also the possibility to utilize, and expertise in handling, mergers and acquisitions allow quantum jumps in the reservoir of capabilities.

The Japanese corporation and overall system is the mirror image of the Western one; namely, a myriad of small improvements and rapid incremental development of knowledge. The major factor is the permanence of staff and interorganizational relations, and the intensive dialogue following from this. Dore (1987, Ch. 7) provides theoretical as well as empirical support both for the posited differences and the explanation suggested. Reliance on tacit rather than articulate, explicit structuring of knowledge[4] leads to developments which would seem 'inconsistent' to a more 'rational' mind. Intensive dialogue and reflection at the group level is not inhibited by segmenting knowledge into functions, professional specializations, or hardware categories. Therefore, to exaggerate, the Japanese firm combines anything with anything else, as long as there is a market for the combination. This leads to frequent, small 'mutations' in offerings to the market. (Cf. Maruyama, 1978, on the differences between Japan and the West in terms of constraints through highly articulated, hierarchical classification systems. See also Baba and Imai, 1991, concerning Japanese company networks' competence in technology combinations.)

The crucial distinctions in analyzing incrementalism versus saltationism may have to do with organizational matters directly, rather than with knowledge categories in terms of the model, although of course the two are connected. Some of the argument above furthermore is really about different *types of articulated knowledge*,

rather than about tacit vs. articulated knowledge. The Japanes bias is to work with induction, lists, and eclectic combination. The Western one is for deduction, hierarchical classification, and division. The former is more likely to lead to many small steps, the latter to single large reconceptualizations or inventions. (See Hedlund and Zander, 1993.)

ASSIMILATION THROUGH PRE-EXISTING COMPONENTS, DISSEMINATION THROUGH PRODUCTS, AND TACIT THROUGHPUT

It is curious how Japanese strength resides in areas which build on clearly defined, crucial components, such as a transistor, an integrated circuit, automobile components, etc. In order to make sense of this, I first want to argue that the Japanese corporation is *biased in favor of articulated assimilation*. A patent or, even better, a tangible product is knowledge in a highly articulated form. The reason for this bias lies in the idiosyncracies of the internal company 'codes' (cf. Arrow, 1974) following from internalized labor markets and refusal to recruit senior and specialized personnel externally. Tacit knowledge probably comes packaged most efficiently in the form of individuals. (Or, on a larger scale, through the integration of whole organizations through acquisitions.) The Japanese willingness to buy technology in the form of patent rights or licenses is well documented, as is the resistance to acquisitions and recruitment at senior levels. (For technology trade, see Keizai Koho Center 1993: 25. For acquisitions and recruitment, see Abegglen and Stalk, 1985, and Dore, 1987, particularly pp. 33 and 141.)

Thus, and almost paradoxically, the internal tacitness and closure require external articulation. It is difficult for a Japanese firm to learn the tacit skills of their Western competitors, for example in the field of running an international organization. Bartlett and Ghosal (1989) contains many examples of the difficulties in Japanese firms of moving to more advanced, 'transnational' structures, where tacit elements encoded in corporate cultures have to be assimilated across borders. Imports or imitation of products is another matter. It is interesting to note that the colossal assimilation of knowledge since

---

[4] Hedlund and Nonaka (1993) pursue the logic only hinted at here. Tacit syntax is argued to be less constraining and allows more experimentation than articulated syntax.

80   *G. Hedlund*

the Meiji restoration has been a project of people in firms (and government) learning the Western tricks themselves, not one of having knowledge walk in by recruiting top scientists or buying expertise packaged in companies. In the process of tapping the world for knowledge, bits are sometimes quite picked up and used in ways and contexts quite surprising to the 'exporters,' since the purchase of the part does not necessarily imply buying in to the tacitly assumed totality. The use of the transistor in consumer products is one example.

The logic of dissemination is a similar one. The Japanese exhibit a bias for exports in product form, and against, particularly, export of skills. Japanese MNCs typically resort to skill transfer through FDI only when forced to do so. The big expansion of outward FDI from the mid-1980s was motivated to a large extent by political pressure and trade barriers. The idiosyncracy, tacitness and high involvement aspects of internal codes, I would argue, make adoption by external agents difficult. (Unless they are 'quasi-integrated,' as actors in the local interorganizational domain.) Better to sell products or, if that is not possible, licenses. *If* skills have to be transferred, the preference is for tightly controlled FDI (rather than, for example, management contracts and consulting services), where the tacit elements can be protected and transferred through sending along Japanese personnel and, as best one can, replicating the Japanese management systems in the alien environment. It is interesting that the concept of 'transplant' factories was used only when Japanese FDI became a significant reality in the Western countries. The word connotes a full-scale transfer of an identical copy from the Japanese to a foreign environment. There is little evocation of the adaptation to local circumstances that characterizes much of Western FDI.

Support for the contention that Japanese internal company codes are indeed very specific to the company, contain important tacit elements, and require and entail a high degree of employee commitment and active participation can be found in the popular literature on Japanese management as well as in academic writing. For the latter, see for example Kagono *et al.* (1985), Dore (1987), Aoki (1990), and Fruin (1992). Putting the pieces together, we get a picture of the Japanese model as one of importing articulated knowledge, transforming it through largely tacit

processes, and again exporting something articulate. Or, schematically:

$$AK \rightarrow TK \rightarrow AK$$

The Western typical case, analogously, exhibits a (relative) bias to import complex packages of both tacit and articulated input,[5] transform it in a machine-like fashion through articulated means (clear organization and division of labor, replaceable parts and people, etc.) and export in forms less restricted than in the Japanese case. Again, schematically:

$$AK + TK \rightarrow AK \rightarrow AK + TK$$

The middle category stands for what goes on in the firm and its immediate environment. By implication, the boundaries of the Japanese corporation are set largely through the demands for communication of tacit knowledge. For the Western firm, other considerations are more important. At least, this is so for the large, bureaucratic corporation, divided into parts where interunit dependencies are minimized. The difference with the Japanese case may be larger for some theoretical views of the firm than in reality. Some Western economists and organization theorists go to great length to formulate theories of the firm in terms of opportunism, moral hazard, incentive compatibility, and monitoring. Work in the transaction cost tradition following Coase (1937) and Williamson (1975), agency theory (for example Jensen and Meckling, 1976), and property rights (for example Alchian and Demsetz, 1972) all share the preoccupation with opportunism obstructing the achievement of efficiency in given, specified tasks or transactions.[6] Aoki (1990) stresses the shortcomings of such models for understanding the Japanese firm, arguing that aspects of information processing and decision making need to be given a greater place in the analysis.

The ideal Japanese 'industry', in our analysis, would be one with *readily existing and articulated input (components and technologies), entailing a through-put process with strong tacit elements,*

----

[5] There is no reason to suspect an inferiority in assimilating articulated elements in the West, other than because of 'too logical' and 'not invented here' syndromes.
[6] However, in many cases also properties of information processing and bounded rationality figure prominently. Also, of course, evolutionary economists take the notion of tacit routines as central.

requiring much intra- and interorganizational dialogue, and allowing the exports of articulated output (products or patents). The prediction seems to fit the real world well. However, stricter tests of the hypotheses require much new empiricial research. Many of the concepts proposed, furthermore, imply the development of measures hardly to be found in official statistics. Therefore, the empirical support claimed above has to be regarded as only tentative and illustrative.

An implication of the argument is success in relatively 'mature' technological fields, in the sense that inputs have 'materialized' into components, formulae, etc. Conversely, we arrive at a hypothesis of difficulties in fields where still much interpretation and prototyping remains to be done, and where different elements are not easily combinable. The electronics, computer, and mechanical engineering industries are characterized by rich possibilities of combination of elements. 'New products' are mostly 'simply' combinations of only marginally adapted components. The key to competitive advantage is in the speedy exploitation of opportunities for recombination, which in its turn requires flexible coordination and synchronized execution. Fields such as chemistry and biology differ in this regard, since they require more of new fundamental search, research and synthesis for each new product. The possible future decoding of the genetic language at the molecular level *may* make biology and biochemistry more like electronics, providing more scope for purposive combinatorial experiments.

WEAKNESS IN LARGE SYSTEMS DESIGN

Another interesting fact, and somewhat of an anomaly in other explanations of Japanese strengths, is the difficulties in integration of very large systems. For example, in telecommunications the Japanese suppliers have, so far, not made much progress in the West. According to the Western competitors, an important reason is weakness in complex systems design. In computers, software production is also lagging. In spite of a gigantic local market, leadership in autos and engine technology, and significant efforts, Japan has not yet given birth to a

significant passenger aircraft industry. This weakness in complex systems management is hard to explain in traditional frameworks of analysis. A 'Porterian' view would probably identify the existence of well developed 'diamonds' in all these fields (Porter, 1990). Likewise, those arguing that the Japanese take existing things, improve them and put them in new systems would rather assume that, for example, telecommunications systems design should be a strength of Japan. And, the defenders of strong customer orientation as a key determinant of Japanese success would say that these fields are exactly those where an ear close to the market and final customer is particularly crucial.

In our interpretation, a reason for the weakness in this area is instead that the reliance on internal dialogue, largely at the tacit level, is less effective when very complex tasks have to be coordinated. Articulation, systematization, written information, impersonal control become necessary, although not sufficient. The Japanese model of throughput is simply too time-consuming in these fields.

JAPANESE DIVERSIFICATION

Japanese industrial firms are generally smaller and less diversified than their Western counterparts (See Imai, 1980; Caves and Uekusa, 1976.) This in itself testifies to the requirements of close-knit, intensive communication with large doses of tacitness. Furthermore—although precise information, to my knowledge, does not exist on these matters—Japanese diversification seems to follow a logic of knowledge and competence development rather than of financial synergies or managerial expansionism. Empirical indications can be found in Taylor and Yamamura (1990: 38 ff.) and in examples provided by Prahalad and Hamel (1990). There seems to be a curious mixture of staying close to the knitting and trying anything. Japanese steel makers' ventures into electronics appear to be an example of the latter.[7] Less spectacular, but still daring,

---

[7] Many analysts attribute such moves to an urge to uphold an image of hi-tech and modernism, luring young talent into the firm. In this interpretation 'diversification' is one of the many indices of a strong commitment in Japan to continuous investment in upgrading human resources.

examples show that Japanese firms are willing to stray rather far from home. We do *not* observe Western-style conglomerate diversification, where the *objective* is to move into areas away from the core business. Thus, Japanese diversification is 'related,' but 'relation' is defined generously, and can only be understood in a company-specific, experimental framework, where the limits are set by the potential synergies given by intensive dialogue and combinatorial possibilities. (Cf. the notion of 'corporate coherence' in Dosi, Teece and Winter, 1990.) The *necessity* of finding new arenas for the exercise of basic company competences following from internalized labor markets is emphasized by Dore (1987, Ch. 7). Also Fruin (1992: 44 ff.) emphasizes the 'economies of learning' inherent in the organizational characteristics of the large, Japanese firm (low personnel turnover, in-company training, and egalitarian rewards coupled with opportunities for individual participation and meaningful contribution). Thus, there are both pressures to develop new, related products *and* the conditions to do it. It is interesting that the prevalence of vertical integration in many large Japanese corporations (see Taylor and Yamamura, 1990) can be understood as a consequence of such internal competence development. 'Diversification' in these firms is the unintended consequence of organic extension of internal skills, rather than the deliberate creation of semiautonomous units.

One example of the power of creative application of a key capability in a seemingly totally unrelated area is Kao's 'diversification' into floppy disc manufacturing from a base in chemicals and household cosmetics and detergents. The central idea here was to utilize a competence in surface chemistry. Such ideas are standard fare in Western marketing textbooks, but mostly the common thread is seen as residing in the market rather than in the competence of the firm. ('We are not in the railway business, but in transportation ...') The difference may be in at least some Japanese companies' ability to actually exploit such opportunities. This, in turn, we would hypothesize has to do with the focus on organizational and group level processes aiming at knowledge creation, albeit incremental and 'merely' combinatorial, rather than just the exploitation of existing knowledge.

MANAGING KNOWLEDGE—FROM M-FORM TO N-FORM?

The analysis above has attempted to show that our model captures important differences between Western and Japanese approaches to knowledge management in large firms. I have also related these differences to organizational practices such as employment systems, rotation schemes, and the reliance on groups. Taking the analysis a step further, I will argue that effective knowledge management (again, in large firms) requires a view of the firm that differs significantly from that of theorists of the 'M-form (multidivisional form). The latter is understood in the senses given by Williamson (1991) and Chandler (1991), to take two recent statements. 'M-form' here also implies a logic of hierarchical organization, built on assumptions and hypotheses like those articulated, for example, by Simon (1962) and Galbraith (1973). As an alternative, I suggest the '*N-form*.' 'N' stands for 'new,' and 'novelty,' and comes after M. It is too bad for the mnemonics that 'multiplication' does not begin with 'N,' since of the four basic arithmetic operations multiplication best represents the creation oriented, recombining and experimenting corporation. Addition corresponds to simple volume growth and acquisition, division to the necessary splitting of the unrelated assemblage of units following, and subtraction to the equally necessary and mostly painful pruning of excesses.

The differences between the two firms are summarized in Table 1. Six main themes defining the N-form corporation will be briefly discussed below.

1. Putting things together, *combining* rather than *dividing* them.
2. *Temporary constellations* of people and units rather than *permanent structures*.
3. The importance of *personnel* at '*lower*' levels in interfunctional, interdivisional, and international dialogue, rather than handling coordination through '*managers*' and only at the top.
4. *Lateral* communication and dialogue rather than *vertical*.
5. Top management as *catalyst*, *architect* of communications (technical and human) infrastructure and *protector* of knowledge invest-

Table 1. N-form vs. M-form

	N-form	M-form
Technological interdependence	Combination	Division
People interdependence	Temporary constellations, given pool of people	Permanent structures, changing pool of people
Critical organizational level	Middle	Top
Communication network	Lateral	Vertical
Top management role	Catalyst, architect, protector	Monitor, allocator
Competitive scope	Focus, economies of depth, combinable parts	Diversification, economies of scale and scope, semi-independent parts
Basic organizational form	Heterarchy	Hierarchy

ment rather than *monitor* and *resource allocator*.

6. *Focusing* the corporation on fields with rich potential for combining knowledge elements rather than *diversifying* to create semi-independent parts.

7. *Heterarchy* as the basic structure rather than *hierarchy*.

The conclusions form an integrated set. If the aim is combination (1), a certain focus is necessary (6). It also requires experiments with varying constellations of actors (2). In order to achieve some consistency of effort, investments in communications and coaching and catalyzing top management are necessary (5). The global dispersion of knowledge allowing combination (1) also requires involvement by many individuals at different levels (3), and lateral communication between them (4).

Combination vs. division

Dialogue in particular, but also assimilation, are processes aiming at the combination of pieces of knowledge. As such, they do not comfortably fit the logic of the M-form corporation. It arose essentially to *divide* complexity into units as independent of each other as possible. Apologizing for the glibness of the analogy, it is perhaps not surprising that the large M-form Western corporation faces difficulties of renewal. Only the most primitive organisms reproduce by division, whereas more innovative genetics require combination. Dividing something given

does not produce much novelty, whereas combination might.

Insisting on combination has important organizational implications. Integrating mechanisms become more important than differentiating ones. We know that the combination of different functional sets of expertise is critical for effective product development. (See, for example, Clark and Fujimoto, 1991). There are also indications that the trend towards ever finer division into independent business areas or divisions (sic!) has gone too far in some corporations and may be turning. Ericsson has recently reorganized to allow for more integration in technology, and on the market, between its radio systems and digital telecommunications exchange divisions. The analysis by Prahalad and Hamel (1990) points in the same direction, stressing the complementarity of corporate assets rather than their exclusivity to one part of the organization.

Temporary constellations from given people pool vs. permanent structures with changing pool

Multifaceted dialogue requires shifting groupings of individuals. The permanent hierarchical structure assumed in M-form reasoning provides for dialogue only along prespecified channels. Also assimilation benefits from a capacity to mobilize human resources flexibly. The 'scanner' in the environment running into something potentially interesting must be able to link up and work with people and units outside the normal structure. The temporary project—multifunctional, multi-

84   G. Hedlund

national, multidivisional—becomes the natural mechanism, and the quality of project management and project/organization interface critical for success.

In order for this type of combination and recombination of people to function, one needs, almost paradoxically, permanence in the personnel pool. Otherwise, the necessary commonality of communicative codes (cf. Arrow, 1974) is not achieved, particularly as regards tacit communication. Kogut and Zander (1992) distinguish between the 'know-what' and 'know-how' of an organization. Effective dialogue in shifting constellations also requires *know-who*. This is also necessary for deeper *reflection*, the interplay of articulated and tacit knowledge. To draw on tacit reservoirs of expertise, a certain permanence of employment and relations is desirable. This is obvious at the individual level. Reflection at supra-individual levels demands physical proximity and intensive interaction. Group or organizational level reflection also require great *trust* between agents, since much uncertainty is involved in, for example, a process of articulating tacit knowledge. In order to develop the smoothness of perfected routines, practice and continuity are also required. Long-term tenure within firms, development of interunit networks through personnel transfer and rotation, reward schemes that encourage long-term collaboration and sharing of knowledge, and investment in internal training contribute to reflection within the large corporation.

The M-form builds on the reverse principle of achieving robustness through a clear structure of specialized roles, where the individual parts can be changed through recruitment and interfirm mobility. Ideally, there should not be any necessity of moving competences or people between 'divisions'. *If* the logic is extended to apply within the divisions, in the many 'U-forms,' the limiting case is one where every individual is a semiindependent profit center, free from systemic interdependence with other individuals. In all fairness, this is not, as far as I know, a solution recommended by any proponent of the M-form. Still, there are two main problems. First, the appropriate organization of the corporation as a whole at the highest level is regarded to be the division into independent parts, excluding the possibility of building the firm on the basis of shared and synergetically linked competences.

Second, in the literature on the theory of the firm, there is great silence on how those units that do contain interdependences should be managed. In practice, we have indeed often seen 'a cascading M-form,' where managers at lower levels imitate the 'govern by division' principle of their superiors. (Organization theorists do, of course, discuss these matters in greater depth. See, for example, Galbraith, 1973.)

Middle vs. top levels

Insisting on intensive dialogue across all levels from the individual to the surrounding network of related organizations automatically implies a focus on less than the most senior personnel in the corporation. Such reemphasis is motivated also by the fact that knowledge is increasingly dispersed, due to rapid technological change, education, and global macroeconomic power shifts. Any good knowledge management system must elicit knowledge from many nodes, often distant from each other. The primary focus is on the middle levels, senior enough to be competent and trusted, but not so senior as to be out of touch, and perhaps energy. The arguments apply also to assimilation from the environment. It is interesting to note that Nonaka (1988), in arguing for a genuine knowledge creating company, emphasizes 'middle management.' I would agree, except that the middle may not be managing as much as exercising more specific competences. The M-form, in contrast, gives great importance to the top of the organization, and to general management capabilities rather than more specific ones.

Lateral vs. vertical communication

It is significant, I believe, that Galbraith (1973) stresses 'vertical information systems' as one of many organizational design devices. The M-form logic is a top-down, or bottom-up, one, rather than one of horizontal coordination. The N-form's reliance on the latter follows almost by definition from the focus on dialogue, temporary teams and middle-level initiative. To what has already been suggested, it may be worth noting that openness towards the environment (implied by the processes of assimilation, dissemination and interaction with the interorganizational domain) necessitates much communication at similar 'hierarchical' or status levels.

Top management: Catalyst vs. monitor

The problem with the N-form as described so far is that it may look like a totally 'emergent' entity—a kaleidoscope of shifting coalitions, chaotic communication patterns, random combinations, and general information overload. The advantage of the M-form and hierarchical ordering in general is the sealing off of complexity in units within a 'nearly decomposable system' (Simon, 1962). Therefore, there is a need for integration, to give direction and consistency to the knowledge development activities. In the N-form, this is top management's primary role. However, it must be exercised in a rather indirect way, lest the effectiveness of the intensive and diffused processes at 'lower' levels is compromised.

A clear vision of broad long term developments regarding both final products and internal competences is perhaps the most important integrative tool. This means that top management must know the substance of the business, and not only its results in financial or other equally abstract terms. Another main task is to build the infrastructure for interpersonal as well as more technical communication. (Recruitment policies, rotation schemes, assigning project teams, nurturing a shared corporate 'language' and culture, investing in computer networks: these are some of the practical dimensions of action. For the last point, see Hagström, 1991). A third function is 'simply' to promote and guard the investment in new knowledge, since this does not automatically occur in the decentralized structure suggested.

The roles differ from those implied in the M-form. Less substantive knowledge of the individual parts is required in the M-form, with consequent dangers of superficiality. Division into subunits is motivated by a need to reduce complexity for coordinating top management. Its role becomes one of monitor and resource allocator from 'the corporate office,' and it is argued that these roles are served more efficiently than by a noninternalized capital market. As corporations have grown more diversified, this argument becomes more important and its validity essential for an assessment of the *raison d'etre* of the M-form. I have emphasized quite different

roles for 'headquarters,' if that is an appropriate term.[8] In fact, these roles are more akin to those served within the 'U-form,' but instilling direct cross-unit interaction is even more important.

Focusing vs. diversifying

In order to be able to have a dialogue aiming at combination of different pieces of knowledge, a shared focus is necessary. This applies also for assimilation and, less obviously, reflection. A very diversified firm cannot internalize, at the corporate level, processes into a tacit organizational reservoir of routines. Extreme diversity does not permit the progressive 'automatizing' of skills and cognitive knowledge packages. In practice, everything has to be explicitly recognized to be noticed and effectuated. Also the reverse process—of articulation from the tacit domain—is compromised, since 'recipes' (cf. Spender, 1989) will differ too much between contexts to be generalized and articulated.

Although some proponents of the M-form have been critical of the conglomerate, others are not. At least, the logic of the argument (monitoring, allocating) is consistent with widely diversified forms.[9] Economies of scale and scope are emphasized (Chandler, 1990). My argument would recognize particularly arguments of scope, but emphasize the knowledge combination aspects of scope rather than monitoring economies, risk sharing, and financial synergies. In addition, I would suggest that *economies of depth* are heavily involved in knowledge transformation processes. 'Depth' refers to the experience and involvement in an area necessary to be able to generate new knowledge, and, increasingly importantly, to benefit from knowledge in related fields. Fertile combination requires intimate knowledge of both one's own and the other's capabilities. 'Depth' also refers to the virtues of experience in a specific company and industrial field. Sometimes, we notice efforts to integrate super-

---

[8] 'Headquarters' implies that the head *and brain* (presumably not only the spatial location in up-right, nonsleeping condition is referred to) reside at this place. Dispersed knowledge suggests that the concept is inappropriate. Cf. the discussion of brain-of-the-firm *vs.* firm-as-brain (Hedlund, 1986; Morgan, 1986).

[9] Cf. the argument that the M-form, although perhaps originally well-intentioned, spawned the 'monster of the conglomerate' in Shleifer and Vishny (1991).

ficially (or substantially, but without knowledge of more exactly how) related fields failing because of too shallow understanding of particularly the technological issues involved on the part of initiating top managers. Often these are presiding over very diversified firms. Semi-independent units harnessed in M-form are anathema to depth. Before turning to the last contrast between M- and N-form knowledge management—structuring in hierarchical and heterarchical form, respectively—I want to redress the balance of the discussion so far by briefly mentioning some of the weaknesses of the N-form and strengths of the M-form.

WHERE THE N-FORM FAILS

I have concentrated on the virtues of the N-form, as defined in Table 1 above, for effective knowledge management. However, the discussion of the relative merits of Japanese and Western models suggests that different organizational models are required for different types of innovation and knowledge processing generally. (It should be emphasized that the M/N distinction is *not* the same as the Japan/West one, although many of the attributes of the N-form are found in the product development organization of large, Japanese firms, but by no means only there.) Therefore, we should expect the M-form to hold

advantages over the N-form in some distinct areas. Table 2 summarizes some hypotheses (cf. also Nonaka, 1989).

Most points in Table 2 are self-explanatory. It is important to note that perhaps the most apparent strength of the M-form is not included. Since the discussion is focused on knowledge transfer and transformation, the possible (but not obvious) superiority of the M-form in more operational and unchanging matters is not recognized. A case could be made for the comparative effectiveness of M-form for exploitation, and of N-form for exploration (cf. March, 1991; Hedlund and Rolander, 1987, 1990).

The various trade-offs between M- and N-form show that the choice between them depends on the nature of the field in which the company operates and that the optimum probably is some mixture of the two. However, it seems that for most fields of international competition, the N-form has much to offer. Therefore, it is of interest to compare the N-form's structural archetype, emerging from the first six characteristics in Table 1, with some recent notions in the analysis of the modern multinational corporation.

Heterarchy vs. hierarchy

Williamson (1975: 149) argues that the M-form obviously is not the final word in governance

Table 2. Where the M-form is superior

N-form weaknesses	M-form strengths
Fundamental, radical innovation not achieved by (re)combination and experimentation only	Radical innovation through specialization, abstract articulation, and investment outside present competences
Long time to acquire fundamental new knowledge because of restrictions on senior recruitment and acquisitions	Rapid infusion and diffusion of drastically new perspectives through people, acquistions, and spin-offs
Difficulty in coordinating very large projects because of reliance on small groups	Large systems design capability through complex articulation and tightly controlled complexity
'Competence traps' through too constrained development path	Risk management through 'competence portfolio'
Bias for internal exploitation of ideas	Freedom to use most efective mode, internal or external
Difficult to change overall vision because of internal management promotion	Change of basic direction and culture through external recruitment of top management
Strategic vulnerability through strong focus and inter-relationships	Strategic robustness through quasi-independent parts

form, but that future ones (at least of a nonmarket, internalized, 'corporate') will be essentially hierarchical. It is not possible to discuss this contention in depth here. Suffice it to note that the six characteristics discussed above connote significant departures from what is ordinarily meant by hierarchy. The dispersal of knowledge and strategic action initiative to 'lower levels;' shifting bases of leadership and composition of teams; importance of internal, lateral communication and integration through shared culture; and, change or roles at all levels of the corporation: these all suggest that the basic structure of the N-form corporation is not a hierarchy. Instead, more 'network-like' conceptions of the firm seem appropriate. In the recent discussions of the modern MNC, there is a broad convergence of views among analysts such as Bartlett and Ghoshal (1989), Doz and Prahalad (1987), White and Poynter (1990), and Hedlund (1986, 1993). They all emphasize: geographical dispersion of strategic assets and leadership roles; upgrading of the role of 'foreign subsidiaries;' horizontal communication across borders; utilization of knowledge from several organizational bases; the impotence of solely formal methods of coordination; new roles for management at headquarters as well as other levels. It is significant that the arguments for the 'transnational' (Bartlett and Ghoshal) as well as the 'heterarchy' (Hedlund) rely to a large extent on an assumption that a significant role of the MNC is one of knowledge creation and transfer.

At least since the pioneering experiments on the optimal configuration of problem solving groups (Leavitt, 1951), organization theorists have claimed that the characteristics of the task, in terms of its knowledge requirements and knowledge distribution, should influence the design of the organization. The broad consensus has been that more 'organic' solutions have to be adapted when uncertainty is high, the environment unstable, and internal differentiation far-reaching (Burns and Stalker, 1961; Lawrence and Lorsch, 1967).[10] This undermining of the

idea of hierarchical and formal control has generally not been appreciated among economists. Arrow (1974) sees hierarchy as indeed the natural response to complex information processing. All the relevant knowledge is brought to a central decision point, thereby economizing on communication costs. The design of the hierarchy reflects an optimal break-down of knowledge and consequent specialization. Thus, the organization's structure and its strategy are mirror images of its information base.

What happens in today's leading companies, in fast-moving technological fields at least, is that the dispersal and rapid change of knowledge make such a match problematical. The challenge is not to divide a given task in a way ensuring maximally efficient performance. Rather, it is to position the company so that *new* tasks can be initiated, often on the basis of a combination of separate knowledge pieces from different organizational units. Instead of bringing the *information to the given decision point*, it becomes a matter of bringing the *decision to the knowledge bases*. Thereby, the center of initiative and action continuously shifts with consequent changes of roles at all 'levels' of the firm.

The characteristics of a corporation evolving according to a logic of knowledge management, rather than to a logic of exploitation of given resources or advantages, depart sufficiently from the common understanding of hierarchical structure in general and the multidivisional structure in particular to deserve new conceptions and names. I have suggested *heterarchy* as an ideal type in contradistinction to hierarchy (Hedlund, 1986, 1993). Some basic points are that *several strategic apexes* emerge, that these *shift over time*, and that there are *several ordering principles* at work. Knowledge is structured in one way, the formal organization—which will always have to be simpler and clearer than the processes of work it undertakes—in another, and action initiatives in yet a third. The unification of these three aspects in one clear structure underlies the conception of hierarchy and the M-form. In the N-form, they interweave in a dynamic process, where the requirements posed by the two types of interaction in our model are central. The interplay of tacit and articulated knowledge and the dialogue at and between individual and organizational levels suggest a partly new perspective on the sources of dynamic competitiveness and the heterogeneity of firms.

---

[10] However, recent work on the management of innovation suggests that the free-floating structure is not the whole truth. Strict discipline and formalization seem to characterize some 'high-tech' firms. The important point here is that this still does not connote a hierarchy in the classical sense, since the *tight structures are typically temporary* and disbanded after completing one task.

88   *G. Hedlund*

ACKNOWLEDGEMENTS

The author wishes to thank Ikujiro Nonaka for the collaboration on the model of knowledge management, Jerker Denrell, Peter Hagström, Jonas Ridderstråle, Udo Zander and two anonymous referees for helpful comments, the Japan Foundation and the Swedish Council for Research in the Humanities and Social Sciences for financial support for the research, and Blackwell Publishers for permission to reprint Figures 1 and 2.

REFERENCES

Abegglen, J. and G. Stalk (1985). *Kaisha: The Japanese Corporation: The New Competitors in World Business*. Basic Books, New York.

Alchian, A. and H. Demsetz (1972). 'Production, information costs, and economic organization', *American Economic Review*, **62**, pp. 777–795.

Aoki, M. (March 1990). 'Toward an economic model of the Japanese firm', *Journal of Economic Literature*, XXVIII, pp. 1–27.

Arrow, K. (1974). *The Limits of Organization*. W. W. Norton, New York.

Baba, Y. and K. Imai (September 5–6, 1991). 'Globalization and cross border networks of Japanese firms'. Paper presented at the conference: Japan in a Global Economy—A European Perspective. Stockholm.

Bartlett, C. A. and S. Ghoshal (1989). *Managing across Borders: The Transnational Solution*. Harvard Business School Press, Cambridge, MA.

Burgelman, R. A. (1991). 'Intraorganizational ecology of strategy making and organizational adaptation: Theory and field research', *Organization Science*, 2(3), pp. 239–262.

Burns, T. and G. M. Stalker (1961). *The Management of Innovation*. Tavistock, London.

Caldwell-Harris, M (1985). 'Japan's international technology transfers'. In the report to the Joint Economic Committee, Congress of the United States, *Japan's Economy and Trade with the United States*. U. S. Government Printing Office, Washington, DC. pp. 120 ff.

Caves, R. and M. Uekusa (1976). *Industrial Organization in Japan*. Brookings Institution, Washington, DC.

Chandler, A. D., Jr. (1990). *Scale and Scope: The Dynamics of Industrial Capitalism*. Belknap/ Harvard Press, Cambridge, MA.

Chandler, A. D., Jr. (1991). 'The functions of the HQ unit in the multibusiness firm', *Strategic Management Journal*, Winter Special Issue, **12**, pp. 31–50.

Clark, K. B. and T. Fujimoto (1991). *Product Development Performance*. Harvard Business School Press, Boston, MA.

Coase, R. H. (1937). 'The nature of the firm', *Economica* (new series), 4, pp. 386–405.

Cyert, R. M. and J. G. March (1963). *A Behavioral Theory of the Firm*. Prentice Hall, Englewood Cliffs, NJ.

Dore, R. (1987). *Taking Japan Seriously*. Athlone Press, London.

Dosi, G., D.J. Teece, and S. Winter. (March, 1990). 'Toward a theory of corporate coherence: Preliminary remarks'. Unpublished working paper.

Dougherty, D. (1992). 'A practice-centered model of organizational renewal through product innovation,' *Strategic Management Journal*, Summer Special Issue, **13**, pp. 77–92.

Doz, Y. L. and C. K. Prahalad (1987). 'A process model of strategic redirection in large complex firms: The case of multinational corporations'. In A. Petttigrew, (ed.), *The Management of Strategic Change*. Basil Blackwell Ltd., Oxford, pp. 63–83.

Freeman, C. (1982). *The Economics of Industrial Innovation* (2nd ed.). Pinter Publishers, London.

Fruin, W. M. (1992). *The Japanese Enterprise System*. Clarendon Press, Oxford.

Galbraith, J. R. (1973). *Designing Complex Organizations*. Addison-Wesley, Reading, MA.

Hagström, P. (1991). 'The 'Wired' MNC. The role of information systems for structural change in complex organizations'. (Doctoral dissertation), IIB, Stockholm.

Hedlund, G. (1986). 'The hypermodern MNC—a heterarchy?' *Human Resource Management*, **25**, pp. 9–25.

Hedlund, G. (1993). 'Assumptions of hierarchy and heterarchy: An application to the multinational corporation'. In S. Ghoshal and E. Westney (eds.), *Organization Theory and the Multinational Corporation*. Macmillan, London, pp. 211–236.

Hedlund, G. and I. Nonaka (1993). 'Models of knowledge management in the West and Japan'. In P. Lorange, B. G. Chakravarthy, J Roos and H. Van de Ven, (eds.). *Implementing Strategic Processes, Change, Learning, and Cooperation*. Basil Blackwell, London, pp. 117–144.

Hedlund, G. and J. Ridderstråle (May 21–24, 1992). 'Toward the N-form Corporation: Exploitation and creation in the MNC'. Paper presented at the conference 'Perspectives on International Business: Theory, Research and Institutional Arrangements', Columbia, SC.

Hedlund, G. and D. Rolander (1987). 'The strategy-structure paradigm in international business research and practice'. Research paper 87/4, Institute of International Business at the Stockholm School of Economics, Stockholm.

Hedlund, G. and D. Rolander (1990). 'Action in heterarchies: New approaches to managing the MNC'. In C. A. Bartlett, Y. L. Doz and G. Hedlund (eds.), *Managing the Global Firm*. Routledge, London and New York, pp. 15–46.

Hedlund, G. and U. Zander (1993). 'Architectonic and list-like knowledge structuring: A critique of modern concepts of knowledge management'. Research paper 93/2, Institute of International

Business at the Stockholm School of Economics, Stockholm.

Hippel, E. von (1976). 'The dominant role of users in the scientific instrument innovation process', *Research Policy*, 5(3), pp. 212–239.

Imai, K. (1980). *Japan's Industrial Organization and Its Vertical Structure*. Institute of Business Research, Hitotsubashi University, Tokyo.

Itami, H. (with T. Roehl) (1987). *Mobilizing Invisible Assets*. Harvard University Press, Cambridge, MA.

Jensen, M. and W. Meckling (1976). 'Theory of the firm: Managerial behavior, agency costs, and capital structure', *Journal of Financial Economics*, 3, pp. 305–360.

Kagono, T., I. Nonaka, K. Sakakibara, and A. Okumura (1985). *Strategic vs. Evolutionary Management*. Advanced Series in Management, Vol. 10. Elsevier Science Publishers B.V., Amsterdam.

Keizai Koho Center: Japan Institute for Social and Economic Affairs (1993). *Japan 1993. An International Comparison*. Tokyo.

Kogut, B. and U. Zander (1992). 'Knowledge of the firm and the replication of technology', *Organization Science*, 3(3), pp. 383–397.

Lawrence, P. R. and J. W. Lorsch (1967). *Organization and Environment: Managing Differentiation and Integration*. Harvard University Press, Cambridge, MA.

Leavitt, H. J. (1951). 'Some effects of certain communication patterns on group performance', *Journal of Abnormal and Social Psychology*, 46, pp. 38–50.

Ledin, H. (1990). 'Building a dynamic intelligent network: Lessons from the telecommunications revolution for the MNC organization of the future'. In C. A. Bartlett, Y. L. Doz and G. Hedlund, (eds.), *Managing the Global Firm*. Routledge, London and New York, pp. 326–353.

March, J. G. (1991). 'Exploitation and exploration in organizational learning', *Organization Science*, 2(1), pp. 71–87.

Maruyama, M. (June, 1978). 'The epistemological revolution', *Futures*, pp. 240–242.

Morgan, G. (1986). *Images of Organization*. Sage, Beverly Hills, CA.

Nelson, R. (ed.) (1993). *National Innovation Systems. A Comparative Analysis*. Oxford University Press, Inc., Oxford.

Nelson, R. (1991). 'Why do firms differ, and how does it matter?', *Strategic Management Journal*, Winter Special Issue, 12, pp. 61–74.

Nelson, R. and S. Winter, (1982). *An Evolutionary Theory of Economic Change*. Harvard University Press, Cambridge, MA.

Nonaka, I. (1987). 'Managing the firm as an information creation process'. Working paper, Institute of Business Research, Hitotsubashi University.

Nonaka, I. (Spring 1988). 'Toward middle-up-down management: Accelerating information creation', *Sloan Management Review*, pp. 9–18.

Nonaka, I. (1989). 'Organizing innovation as a knowledge-creation process: A suggested paradigm for self-renewing organizations'. Mimeo, Walter A.

Haas School of Business, University of California at Berkeley.

Pavitt, K. L. R. (1980). *Technical Innovation and British Economic Performance*. Macmillan, London.

Polanyi, M. (1962). *Personal Knowledge: Towards a Post-Critical Philosophy*. Harper Torchbooks, New York.

Porac, J. F., H. Thomas and C. Baden-Fuller (November 28, 1988). 'Competitive groups as cognitive communities: The case of Scottish knitwear manufacturers'. Paper presented at the Workshop on Competitive Strategy, EIASM, Brussels.

Porter, M. E. (1990). *The Competitive Advantage of Nations*. Free Press, New York.

Prahalad, C. K. and G. Hamel (1990). 'The core competence of the corporation', *Harvard Business Review*, 68(3), pp. 79–91.

Rumelt, R., D. Schendel and D. J. Teece (1991). 'Strategic management and economics', *Strategic Management Journal*, Winter Special Issue, 12, pp. 5–29.

Scherer, F. M. (1984). *Innovation and Growth*. The MIT Press, Cambridge, MA.

Seely-Brown, J. and P. Duguid (1991). 'Organizational learning and communities of practice: Toward a unified view of working, learning and innovation', *Organization Science*, 2(1), pp. 40–57.

Shleifer A. and R. W. Vishny (1991). 'Takeovers in the '60s and the '80s: Evidence and implications', *Strategic Management Journal*, Winter Special Issue, 12, pp. 51–59.

Simon, H. A. (1955). 'A behavioral model of rational choice', *Quarterly Journal of Economics*, 69, pp. 99–118.

Simon, H. A. (1962). 'The architecture of complexity'. Proceedings of the American Philosophical Society, No. 106, pp. 467–482.

Spender, J. C. (1989). *Industry Recipes: The Nature and Sources of Management Judgement*. Blackwell, Oxford.

Starbuck, W. H. (1984). 'Organizations as action generators', *American Sociological Review*, 48, pp. 91–102.

Stiglitz, J. E. (1987). 'Learning to learn, localized learning and technological progress'. In P. Dasgupta and P. Stoneman, (eds.), *Economic Policy and Technological Performance*. Cambridge University Press, Cambridge, pp. 123–153.

Stubbart, C. I. (1989). 'Managerial cognition: A missing link in strategic management research', *Journal of Management Studies*, 26(4), pp. 325–347.

Taylor, S. and K. Yamamura (1990). 'Japan's technological capabilities and its future: Overview and assessments'. In G. Heiduk and K. Yamamura, (eds.), *Technological Competition and Interdependence*. University of Washington Press, Seattle, WA, pp. 25–63.

Teece, D. (June 1977). 'Technological transfer by multinational firms: The resource cost of international technological transfer', *Economic Journal*, 87, pp. 242–261.

Teece, D. (1990). G. Pisano and A. Shuen (1990).

90   *G. Hedlund*

'Firm capabilities, resources, and the concept of strategy'. CCC Working Paper 90-8, Center for Research on Management, University of California, Berkeley, CA.

Tushman, M. L. and W. L. Moore (eds.) (1988). *Readings in the Management of Innovation*, 2nd ed. Ballinger, Cambridge, MA.

Van de Ven, A. H., H. L. Angle and M. S. Poole (1989). *Research on the Management of Innovation: The Minnesota Studies*. Harper & Row, New York.

Wernerfelt, B. (1984). 'A resource-based view of the firm'. *Strategic Management Journal*, **5**(2), pp. 171-181.

White, R. E. and T. A. Poynter (1990). 'Organizing for world-wide advantage'. In C. A. Bartlett, Y. Doz and G. Hedlund (eds.), *Managing the Global Firm*. Routledge, London, pp. 95-113.

Williamson, O. E. (1975). *Markets and Hierarchies: Analysis and Antitrust Implications*. Free Press, New York.

Williamson, O. E. (1991). 'Strategizing, economizing, and economic organization', *Strategic Management Journal*, **12**, Winter Special Issue, pp. 75-94.

Winter, S. G. (1987). 'Knowledge and competence as strategic assets'. In D. Teece (ed.), *The Competitive Challenge—Strategies for Industrial Innovation and Renewal*. Ballinger, Cambridge, MA, pp. 159-184.

Winter, S. G. (1991). 'On Coase, competence, and the corporation'. In O. E. Williamson and S. G. Winter (eds.), *The Nature of the Firm*. Oxford University Press, Oxford, pp. 179-195.

Wolfe, A. (1991). 'Mind, self, society, and computer: Artificial intelligence and the sociology of mind', *American Journal of Sociology*, **96**(5), pp. 1073-1096.

Zander, U. (1991). Exploiting a technological edge - Voluntary and involuntary dissemination of technology. Doctoral dissertation, IIB, Stockholm.

[22]

© *Academy of Management Journal*
1997, Vol. 40, No. 2, 426–442.

WORKING ABROAD, WORKING WITH OTHERS: HOW FIRMS LEARN TO OPERATE INTERNATIONAL JOINT VENTURES

HARRY G. BARKEMA
Tilburg University
ODED SHENKAR
Tel Aviv University, University of Hawaii
FREEK VERMEULEN
JOHN H. J. BELL
Tilburg University

Successful international joint ventures entail both learning to operate across national boundaries and learning to cooperate. Hypotheses grounded in organizational learning theory were tested with event-history analysis and data on 1,493 expansions of 25 large Dutch firms between 1966 and 1994. Experience with domestic joint ventures and with international wholly owned subsidiaries contributed to the longevity of international joint ventures, but prior experience with international joint ventures did not.

International joint ventures have become a prevalent mode of entry into global markets (Berg, Duncan, & Friedman, 1982; Harrigan, 1985; Hergert & Morris, 1988; Wysocki, 1990). Publications on the topic mostly focus on the motivations behind international joint venture formation (Buckley & Casson, 1988; Contractor & Lorange, 1988; Harrigan, 1985; Hennart, 1988; Hergert & Morris, 1988; Kogut, 1988) and the conditions encouraging it (Agarwal & Ramaswami, 1992; Gatignon & Anderson, 1988; Gomes-Casseres, 1989; Hennart, 1991; Madhok, 1997; Stopford & Wells, 1972). Little has been done, however, to identify the factors that underlie success and failure in such ventures; this is a remarkable omission, given their high failure rate (Chowdhury, 1992; Gomes-Casseres, 1987; Hill & Hellriegel, 1994; Levine & Byrne, 1986). To the extent that international joint venture failure is studied, explanations have been confined to one area, namely, lack of the skills needed to manage affiliates dispersed in unfamiliar foreign environments (Buckley & Casson, 1988). To be successful in operating joint undertakings, however, firms also need to master sharing ownership with a partner whose interests only partially overlap with their own (Shenkar & Zeira, 1987).

We would like to thank the anonymous reviewers for their helpful comments and suggestions.

The present research examined the two sets of skills within an evolutionary perspective, to explain how firms learn to handle international joint ventures. Hypotheses were derived from organizational learning theory (Cohen & Levinthal, 1990; Cyert & March, 1963) to indicate learning stemming from experience with international wholly owned subsidiaries, with domestic joint ventures, and with previous international joint ventures. Data on 1,493 domestic and international expansions of 25 Dutch multinationals from 1966 to 1994 allowed for a longitudinal examination of learning paths and their implications for international joint venture longevity.

THEORY AND HYPOTHESES

According to organizational learning theory, prior learning facilitates the learning and application of new, related knowledge (Cohen & Levinthal, 1989, 1990, 1994). This idea can be extended to include the case in which the knowledge in question is itself a set of learning skills constituting a firm's absorptive capacity. This capacity increases incrementally as a function of the previous experience of the firm and its learning processes. In the foreign entry literature, advocates of the internationalization process school, or the Uppsala stage model (Johanson & Vahlne, 1977), have argued that firms expand slowly from their domestic bases into progressively distant areas. Experiential learning from previous entries is the driving force behind new investments (Barkema, Bell, & Pennings, 1996; Davidson, 1983; Denis & Depelteau, 1985; Johanson & Wiedersheim-Paul, 1975; Luostarinen, 1980). The internationalization process approach focuses, however, on the early steps in the internationalization process, ignoring the investment mode chosen (Kogut & Singh, 1988).

To successfully cross national boundaries, a firm must develop information processing and control capabilities so as to coordinate activities across diverse environments, and it must develop the skills of tuning into and interpreting strategic signals specific to a foreign environment. In this process, firms unlearn practices typical of their home countries (cf. Bettis & Prahalad, 1995; Hedberg, 1981; Lewin, 1947; McGill & Slocum, 1993; Prahalad & Bettis, 1986).

The complexities of working abroad are encountered not only in international joint ventures, but also in international wholly owned subsidiaries. Such subsidiaries offer firms the opportunity to learn to operate in a foreign environment incrementally, without having to simultaneously adapt to a foreign partner, thus facilitating an effective learning experience allowing for later success. Hence,

> *Hypothesis 1. The longevity of an international joint venture increases with the international wholly owned subsidiary experience of the firm investing abroad.*

One key challenge for firms operating abroad is bridging the distance to the host culture. Cultural distance has been defined as "the sum of factors creating, on the one hand, a need for knowledge, and on the other hand, barriers to knowledge flow and hence also for other flows between the home and the target countries" (Luostarinen, 1980: 131–132). It has often been cited as a factor in firms' choice of less committed entry modes (Root, 1987), specifically, their preference for joint ventures over wholly owned subsidiaries (e.g. Agarwal, 1994; Bell, 1996; Bell, Barkema, & Verbeke, 1997; Cho & Padmanabhan, 1995; Erramilli, 1991; Erramilli & Rao, 1993; Kogut & Singh, 1988; Larimo, 1993; Padmanabhan & Cho, 1996). Anderson and Gatignon (1986) noted that cultural distance caused foreign investors to avoid full ownership because distance increases information costs and difficulty in transferring management skills (Buckley & Casson, 1976; Vachani, 1991). Cultural distance adversely affects international joint ventures by eroding the applicability of the parent's competencies (Johanson & Vahlne, 1977; cf. Brown, Rugman, & Verbeke, 1989; Chowdhury, 1992; Gomes-Casseres, 1989; Harrigan, 1985, 1988; Hergert & Morris, 1988; Lorange & Roos, 1991; Parkhe, 1991). Woodcock and Geringer (1991) argued that cultural differences produce inefficient principal-agent contracts, and Li and Guisinger (1991) found that U.S. affiliates whose partners came from culturally dissimilar countries were more likely to fail. Thus,

> *Hypothesis 2. The longevity of an international joint venture decreases with the cultural distance between the country of the firm investing abroad and the host country.*

The need to select a partner and to cooperate and share control with the partner is a major source of complexity in joint ventures. Schaan and Beamish (1988) described the "subtle balancing act" that operating joint ventures requires. Officers at Otis, a company whose foreign venturing dates back to the 19th century, consider their firm's ability to quickly select partners and work effectively with them to be a key competitive advantage (Ingrassia, Naji, & Rosett, 1995). According to the chairman of Corning Glass, partnering skills include "the ability to cope with the constant compromise and give-and-take that successful joint ventures require" and the ability, when necessary, to "sit back and let someone else be in the driver's seat" (Mitchell, 1988). The capacity to work with others can be learned, however, not only from previous international joint ventures, but also from previous domestic joint ventures.

That knowledge relevant to the operation of international joint ventures can be gained from domestic joint ventures is a crucial yet neglected possibility. Since the international joint venture literature is largely a product of the broader domain of international business, such ventures have been juxtaposed with other forms of foreign direct investment but not with their domestic counterparts. Yet the two joint venture types have much in common in that both facilitate the learning of partnering skills. Furthermore, domestic venturing allows a firm to learn how to cooperate without simultaneously having to deal with the complexity of a foreign environment. Thus, domestic joint ventures, like international wholly owned subsidiaries, can be a stepping stone from which to launch international joint ventures. Hence,

Hypothesis 3. The longevity of an international joint venture increases with the previous domestic joint venture experience of the partner investing abroad.

That firms learn about international joint ventures from their previous experience with such ventures seems compelling—the experience entails exposure to both international and partnership activities. International joint venture experience has been found to increase firms' propensity to set up new ventures (Madhok, 1997), to improve their understanding of this vehicle (Lyles, 1987, 1988), and to enhance the performance of the investing firms (Mitchell, Shaver, & Yeung, 1994) and of the investment vehicles themselves (Li, 1995). An incremental approach implies, however, that learning both partnership and boundary-crossing skills at the same time may be a task that exceeds the absorptive capacity of naive entrants who lack both types of skills. Still, we offer the following hypothesis:

Hypothesis 4. The longevity of an international joint venture increases with the previous international joint venture experience of the firm investing abroad.

METHODS

Sample

Hypotheses were tested on data on all expansions reported in the annual reports of a sample of Dutch firms between 1966 and 1994. This sample comprised the 25 largest[1] Dutch companies but excluded the 4 largest (Royal Dutch, Unilever, Philips, and Akzo), which are a distinctive group in terms of their breadth of activities, international experience, scope, and size. Totals of national and international expansions during the period were 596 and 897, respectively. Of the international expansions, 244 were joint ventures.

Variables

Longevity. Following earlier research (Barkema et al., 1996; Carroll, Preisendorfer, Swaminathan, & Wiedermayer, 1993; Carroll & Swaminathan, 1991; Chowdhury, 1992; Li, 1995; Pennings, Barkema, & Douma, 1994), we used longevity as the independent variable. Although it is not a perfect performance measure, previous studies have shown that longevity provides the best estimate of managers' perceptions of the success of an expansion (Geringer & Hebert, 1991) and that it correlates with financial performance (Mitchell et al., 1994). Longevity was defined as the number of years a venture persisted.[2]

---

[1] In terms of firm value, these were the largest firms listed in 1994 on the Amsterdam Stock Exchange.

[2] Executives of a subset of 5 firms were asked to rate the success of the international joint ventures in our data set ($N = 31$) on a seven-point scale. Like Geringer and Hebert (1991), we calculated the Spearman correlation between the longevity of these international joint ventures and their success as perceived by the managers. The correlation coefficient was .55 ($p < .001$), a value comparable to that of the coefficient found by Geringer and Hebert (.46). In addition, we found that only one of the ventures was planned to be short-lived from the start.

Cultural distance. Cultural distance to the host country from the Netherlands was measured with Kogut and Singh's (1988) index. This index is an aggregate of the four dimensions of culture outlined in Hofstede (1980), and has been used often in studies of foreign entry (Agarwal & Ramaswami, 1992; Benito & Gripsrud, 1992; Cho & Padmanabhan, 1995).[3] Cultural difference scores unavailable from Hofstede's published work (1980, 1991) were obtained via personal communication with that author.

Experience. Experience with each of four types of affiliation— international joint venture, domestic joint venture, international wholly owned subsidiary, and domestic wholly owned subsidiary—was measured as the number of previous such affiliates a firm had had by the time of a new affiliate's founding.

Control variables. To mitigate potential omitted-variable problems, we controlled for experience with domestic wholly owned subsidiaries.[4] In addition, the following time-variant control variables were used: The logarithm of the assets of a firm in the year of an international joint venture's founding served as a proxy for firm size. The return on equity of the firm in that year was used as a proxy for firm profitability. We also controlled for the gross national product per capita of the host countries. Table 1 presents summary statistics on these and other variables.

Analysis

Analysis was done with LIFEREG, an event-history analysis method (SAS Institute, 1988). The model used is based on an assumed accelerated failure-time with a Weibull distribution. The analysis entailed the exploration of whether the hazard rate of ventures (the converse of the survival rate) varies with the amount and type of a firm's experience. For example, a negative coefficient associated with domestic joint venture experience implies that international joint ventures dissolve more slowly if the firm investing abroad has previous experience with domestic joint ventures.

RESULTS

Hypotheses 1 and 3 predict that international joint venture longevity increases with the experience of the firm that is investing abroad with international wholly owned subsidiaries and domestic joint ventures, respectively. Table 2 (model 1) shows that both effects are in the expected direction.

---

[3] The Kogut and Singh (1988) index of cultural distance is an arithmetic average of the deviations of each country from the index of the Netherlands along Hofstede's (1980) four cultural dimensions. Algebraically, it is calculated as $CD_j = \Sigma_{i=1,2,3,4} \, [(I_{ij} - I_{in})^2 / V_i]/4$, where CD_j = the cultural distance of the jth country from the Netherlands, I_{ij} = the index for the ith cultural dimension and jth country, n = the Netherlands, and V_i = the variance of the index of the ith dimension.

[4] Firms may also benefit from other sorts of experience when launching international joint ventures—from exporting, for example—but such data were not available. If firms learn from exporting, the effects measured in this study may overestimate the effects of learning from previous international expansions on the longevity of international joint ventures.

TABLE 1
Means, Standard Deviations, and Correlations[a]

Variable	Mean	s.d.	1	2	3	4	5	6	7
1. International joint venture experience	7.15	6.29							
2. Domestic joint venture experience	3.52	4.67	.25						
3. International wholly owned subsidiary experience	13.05	12.61	.50	.34					
4. Domestic wholly owned subsidiary experience	10.79	10.35	.23	.42	.60				
5. Cultural distance	3.04	1.25	.09	.06	.07	−.12			
6. Assets[b]	13.65	1.27	.50	.57	.15	.27	−.05		
7. Return on equity	0.11	0.12	−.20	−.17	.20	.28	−.01	−.23	
8. Gross national product	8.52	6.00	−.03	.21	.18	.37	−.27	.17	.14

[a] $N = 244$. Correlations with absolute values greater than .13 are significant at $p < .05$.
[b] Value is a logarithm.

The effects of both international wholly owned subsidiary experience and domestic joint venture experience are significant ($p < .05$ and $p < .10$, respectively). Since we predicted that experience with either international wholly owned subsidiaries or domestic joint ventures could be used as a stepping stone to success with international joint ventures, we also tested a version of the model that included the interaction between international wholly owned experience and domestic joint venture experience (see model 2). If either type of experience can be used as a stepping stone, a firm that already has experience with domestic joint ventures should benefit less from experience with international wholly owned subsidiaries, and vice versa. This observation implies that the interaction term (capturing firms' having both types of experience) and the two main effects should have opposite signs. The interaction term is indeed positive and significant ($p < .01$). The main effects of international wholly owned subsidiaries and domestic joint ventures become more significant in this model ($p < .001$) than they were in model 1. Support for the hypotheses strengthens when the incremental nature of learning (that either type of experience can serve as a stepping stone) is recognized in the model.

Hypothesis 2 predicts that international joint venture longevity decreases with the cultural distance between foreign investor and host country. The results contained in model 1 show that the effect of cultural distance is significant and in the expected direction ($p < .05$).

Hypothesis 4, predicting that firms benefit from previous international joint ventures when launching new ones, was not supported (see Table 2). Apparently, the firms in our sample did not learn from their previous international joint venture experience.

TABLE 2
Results of Event-History Analysis for Types of Experience[a]

Independent Variables	Model 1	Model 2
Intercept	0.87	0.59
	(1.15)	(1.22)
International joint venture experience	0.01	0.03
	(0.03)	(0.03)
Domestic joint venture experience	−0.05†	−0.19***
	(0.03)	(0.06)
International wholly owned subsidiary experience	−0.03*	−0.06***
	(0.02)	(0.02)
Domestic wholly owned subsidiary experience	0.01	−0.00
	(0.01)	(0.01)
Domestic joint venture × international wholly owned subsidiary		0.01**
experience		(0.00)
Cultural distance	0.12*	0.13*
	(0.07)	(0.07)
Assets[b]	0.14	0.18†
	(0.09)	(0.09)
Return on equity	1.55†	1.15
	(0.86)	(0.86)
Gross national product per capita	−0.01	−0.01
	(0.01)	(0.02)
Log likelihood	−195	−191

[a] Numbers in parentheses are standard deviations.
[b] Value is a logarithm.
† $p < .10$
* $p < .05$
** $p < .01$
*** $p < .001$

Product Diversification as a Moderator

A key notion underlying this research is that firms can only absorb experience if it relates to what they already know (Cohen & Levinthal, 1990). International expansion paths need to be incremental to allow firms to interpret new experience and to foster learning. This statement suggests that a firm learns from experience with international wholly owned subsidiaries and with domestic joint ventures if the experience is related to the firm's knowledge base—if it is acquired in the same line of business as the firm's principal business (constituting horizontal expansion), or in a related line of business (related expansion), or up or down the value chain (vertical expansion). In contrast, expansion into an unrelated line of business may trigger information overload and make it difficult for a firm's key managers to interpret the experience and benefit from it when entering international joint ventures later.

The sampled firms' expansion experience was thus separated into (1) horizontal, related, and vertical expansions (cf. Pennings et al., 1994) and

(2) unrelated expansions. Table 3 presents the estimation results, which show significant effects for both experience with international wholly owned subsidiaries and experience with domestic joint ventures in related businesses. The effects of previous experience in unrelated businesses are insignificant. The results are again consistent with an incremental learning approach.

Sensitivity Analysis

Firm-specific effects. In view of Hitt, Harrison, Ireland, and Best's (1995) findings for mergers and acquisitions, we also considered learning effects at

TABLE 3
Results of Event-History Analysis with Product Diversification as Moderator[a]

Independent Variables	Model 3
Intercept	0.46
	(1.37)
Unrelated international joint venture experience	0.02
	(0.09)
Related international joint venture experience	0.03
	(0.04)
Unrelated domestic joint venture experience	−0.13
	(0.13)
Related domestic joint venture experience	−0.20*
	(0.09)
Unrelated international wholly owned subsidiary experience	−0.07
	(0.12)
Related international wholly owned subsidiary experience	−0.05*
	(0.03)
Domestic wholly owned subsidiary experience	−0.00
	(0.01)
Unrelated domestic joint venture × international wholly owned subsidiary experience	−0.03
	(0.12)
Unrelated domestic joint venture × related international wholly owned subsidiary experience	0.00
	(0.01)
Related domestic joint venture × unrelated international wholly owned subsidiary experience	0.04
	(0.09)
Related domestic joint venture × related international wholly owned subsidiary experience	0.02*
	(0.01)
Cultural distance	0.13*
	(0.07)
Assets[b]	0.18
	(0.10)
Return on equity	1.77
	(1.07)
Gross national product per capita	−0.01
	(0.02)
Log likelihood	−188

[a] Numbers in parentheses are standard deviations.
[b] Value is a logarithm.
* $p < .05$

the individual firm level, using models with interactions between learning effects and dummy variables for firm. This procedure captured firm-specific learning gained from previous types of affiliation and applied to new international joint ventures. Not all 25 firms had engaged in all the affiliate types studied, so fewer than 25 interaction terms resulted for each type of learning effect. In addition, some interaction terms had to be removed from the models for reasons of multicollinearity. There remained 17 firm-specific effects of previous international wholly owned subsidiaries, 13 firm-specific effects of previous domestic joint ventures, and 16 firm-specific effects of previous international joint ventures. Of these effects, 11, 10, and 5, respectively, were significant and in the expected direction, mostly at the $p < .001$ level. The results suggest that most firms learned about international joint ventures from international wholly owned subsidiaries or domestic joint ventures and that some firms also learned from previous international joint ventures. A subsequent analysis suggested that firms did not learn from previous international joint ventures unless the latter experience was preceded by experience with either domestic joint ventures or with international wholly owned subsidiaries.[5] Finally, an exploratory analysis suggested that firms learned from failures rather than successes with international wholly owned subsidiaries, but this result was not obtained for domestic joint venture experience.

Shape of experience curves. To examine learning theory's assertion regarding decreasing marginal returns from experience (Yelle, 1979), we added quadratic terms of the experience variables to the linear effects. The quadratic effects were insignificant. We also estimated models that separated the experience with international wholly owned subsidiaries into two categories, experience with fewer than 10 international wholly owned subsidiaries, and experience with more than 10. We also estimated similar models for two categories of domestic joint venture experience and international joint venture experience, respectively. The analyses did not support the notion of decreasing returns to learning.[6] Learning about international joint ventures may be so complex that the experience curve had not leveled off yet for the firms studied, which were in their early decades of international expansion.

Hofstede's dimensions. Culture is a complex phenomenon that embodies a host of values, beliefs, and norms, many of which are subtle, intangible, and difficult to measure. Interpretation of culture as a unidimensional, aggregate phenomenon, although popular in the foreign entry literature (e.g., Agarwal & Ramaswami, 1992), oversimplifies a complex construct (Shenkar & Zeira, 1992) and may explain the mixed results studies have yielded regarding the

---

[5] We found no significant learning effects of previous international joint ventures that were not preceded by international wholly owned subsidiaries or domestic joint ventures. Exploratory analysis revealed a significant learning effect of international joint ventures preceded by at least 10 domestic joint ventures or 30 international wholly owned subsidiaries. The effect remained if firm dummies were added to the analysis.

[6] Similar conclusions were reached for other cut-off rates, for instance, for 5 and for 20 ventures.

impact of cultural distance on foreign expansion (Benito & Gripsrud, 1992; Kogut & Singh, 1988; Madhok, 1997; Padmanabhan & Cho, 1996).

To take account of this complexity, we did some further analysis regarding Hofstede's conjectures about the different impacts of gaps between two cultures along his four dimensions. Hofstede (1989) suggested that although some cultural gaps were not very disruptive or were even complementary, differences between two cultures in uncertainty avoidance were potentially very problematic for international cooperation because of correlated differences in tolerance toward risk, formalization, and the like. An uncertainty avoidance gap is likely to be detrimental to international joint venture operation because uncertainty is an inherent characteristic of operating in a foreign environment and because such a gap implies contrasting expectations regarding the predictability of partner behavior, also a key issue in international joint ventures. Indeed, the results show a significant effect for uncertainty avoidance (0.19, $p < .01$) but not for the other dimensions.[7]

Developed versus developing countries. Experience with international wholly owned subsidiaries in developed countries may be less useful when applied to joint ventures in developing countries, and vice versa. Hence, experience with international wholly owned subsidiaries was separated into experience in developed countries (Ronen and Shenkar's [1985] Nordic, Germanic, Anglo, and Latin European blocs) and in developing countries (the remaining Ronen and Shenkar blocs; see Table 4). The dummy variable "developed country" in Table 4 captures whether an international joint venture was in a developed country (or not), and the dummy variable "developing country" captures the opposite.

The results presented in Table 4 show that international joint ventures in developed countries benefit significantly from the experience of the firms investing abroad (the Dutch firms) with international wholly owned subsidiaries in developed countries, but not from such firms' previous ventures in developing countries. Similarly, international joint ventures in developing countries benefit significantly from investor's previous experience with international wholly owned subsidiaries in developing countries, but not from experience with such subsidiaries in developed countries.

Another interesting result given in Table 4 is that the effect of cultural distance is significant for international joint ventures in developing countries, but not for international joint ventures in developed countries. To get a sharper view of the effects of cultural differences between the foreign and host country on the longevity of international joint ventures in developed countries, we replaced the cultural distance variable (per Hofstede) for developed countries with dummy variables representing Ronen and Shenkar's blocs, making the Nordic bloc (to which the Netherlands belongs) the omitted

---

[7] No effects were found for the power distance and masculinity/femininity dimensions. The effect of individualism became significant if gross national product per capita was deleted from the model as a control variable.

TABLE 4
Results of Event-History Analysis for Developed/Developing Countries[a]

Independent Variables	Model 4
Intercept	1.71
	(1.31)
International joint venture experience	0.05
	(0.04)
Domestic joint venture experience	−0.15**
	(0.06)
Developed international wholly owned subsidiary experience × developed country	−0.07**
	(0.02)
Developed international wholly owned subsidiary experience × developing country	−0.01
	(0.03)
Developing international wholly owned subsidiary experience × developed country	−0.02
	(0.12)
Developing international wholly owned subsidiary experience × developing country	−0.11***
	(0.03)
Domestic wholly owned subsidiary experience	−0.01
	(0.01)
Domestic joint venture × international wholly owned subsidiary experience	0.01*
	(0.01)
Cultural distance × developed country	0.03
	(0.11)
Cultural distance × developing country	0.14*
	(0.07)
Assets[b]	0.08
	(0.10)
Return on equity	2.09*
	(1.05)
Gross national product per capita	0.01
	(0.02)
Log likelihood	−183

$* \ p < .05$
$** \ p < .01$
$*** \ p < .001$
[a] Numbers in parentheses are standard deviations.
[b] Value is a logarithm.

category.[8] The results showed significant effects for the Germanic, Anglo, and Latin European dummies (1.46, $p < .05$, 1.67, $p < .05$, and 1.55, $p < .05$, respectively), suggesting that joint ventures of Dutch companies with partners in the three latter blocks encountered more problems than Dutch ventures with partners from other Nordic block countries. Using any of the other three dummies (Germanic, Anglo, or Latin European) as the omitted

---

[8] The Ronen and Shenkar (1985) cultural blocs are based on a synthesis of eight clustering studies, including Hofstede (1980). The clustering represents the similarity of national cultures and transcends the explicit dimensions making up that complex construct.

category did not result in significant effects for the other two, suggesting that the magnitude of cultural problems did not vary significantly across these three cultural blocs.[9]

Further analyses. In further analyses, a number of control variables were added, including a time-variant measure of firm diversification (capturing the level of diversification for each firm for each year) and the level of diversification implied by the international joint venture (coded 1 for related, horizontal, or vertical diversification and 0 otherwise). These analyses did not lead to different conclusions. We also separated previous experience with international wholly owned subsidiaries into experience with start-ups and experience with acquisitions and obtained virtually identical results for both. Finally, we repeated all the analyses using distributions other than the Weibull distribution that underpins the above results, including gamma, logarithmic logistic, and logarithmic normal distributions. All the results were equally supportive.

DISCUSSION

The findings of the present study expand earlier findings illustrating the incremental nature of firms' learning of new technologies (Cohen & Levinthal, 1990), across industries (Chang, 1995; Pennings et al., 1994; Ramanujam & Varadarajan, 1989), and beyond national borders (Barkema et al., 1996; Johanson & Vahlne, 1977; Johanson & Wiedersheim-Paul, 1975). Specifically, this study identifies both experience with domestic joint ventures and experience with international wholly owned subsidiaries as stepping stones from which operation of international joint ventures can be successfully launched—as long as the experience is related to a firm's core business. Domestic joint ventures allow firms to learn about partnering without having to simultaneously handle the vagaries of foreign settings. International wholly owned subsidiaries allow firms to learn how to operate in foreign settings without the complexities of cooperating with a partner, provided the experience is accumulated in the same context—that is, in developed countries if the new expansion is into a developed country, and in developing countries if the new expansion is into a developing country. And, in line with previous conjectures (e.g., Hofstede, 1989), international joint venture longevity decreased with the cultural distance between a Dutch investor and a host country.

The significant role played by domestic joint ventures in preparing firms for cross-border joint ventures is especially noteworthy and represents a unique contribution of this research. In addition to pinpointing a crucial, yet neglected, way of learning to successfully operate international joint ventures,

---

[9] Not surprisingly, estimation results from the full model with dummies for all Ronen and Shenkar blocs (Germanic, Anglo, Latin European, Latin American, Far Eastern, African, etc., with Nordic as the omitted category) tested on the whole data set showed highly significant effects of the bloc dummies associated with non-European cultures.

this finding has implications for the learning process in international business. The finding confirms that an analysis of a multinational corporation's operations abroad should also include paths from its domestic activities, and that international business research should not be rigidly confined to nondomestic operations.

If one accepts the premise that the national culture of a multinational corporation can moderate its ability to learn to cooperate with others and to adapt to foreign settings (Hickson, 1996; Hofstede, 1983), the present study—which was limited to Dutch multinationals—should be replicated for firms rooted in other national settings. Given our confirmation of the importance of uncertainty avoidance (Hofstede, 1989), it would be interesting to compare the findings for the Netherlands, a country with low uncertainty avoidance, with results for a country with high uncertainty avoidance, such as Japan. Similarly, given the prominence of the Netherlands as a foreign investor, multinational corporations from developing and newly industrialized economies would make a valuable base for comparison.

The above strategies, combined with the broadening of potential learning paths to include trading activities as well as mergers and acquisitions, will go a long way toward enhancing scholars' understanding of the foreign investment learning process. This understanding will not be complete, however, without injecting the internal processes that are part and parcel of the learning process. The present findings suggest that most, but not all, firms benefit from their experience with domestic joint ventures and international wholly owned subsidiaries when entering international joint ventures. To understand why, researchers should examine the structural and process factors facilitating learning in alliances (cf. Hitt et al., 1995), as well as the customized channels allowing for the creation and transfer of knowledge within multinational corporations (cf. Bartlett & Ghoshal, 1989; Hedlund, 1994).

REFERENCES

Agarwal, S. 1994. Socio-cultural distance and the choice of joint ventures: A contingency perspective. *Journal of International Marketing*, 2: 63–80.

Agarwal, S., & Ramaswami, S. N. 1992. *Choice of organizational form in foreign markets: A transaction cost perspective.* Paper presented at the annual meeting of the Academy of International Business, Brussels.

Anderson, E., & Gatignon, H. 1986. Modes of foreign entry: A transaction cost analysis and propositions. *Journal of International Business Studies*, 17: 1–26.

Barkema, H. G., Bell, J. H. J., & Pennings, J. M. 1996. Foreign entry, cultural barriers, and learning. *Strategic Management Journal*, 17: 151–166.

Bartlett, C. A., & Ghoshal, S. 1989. *Managing across borders: The transnational solution.* London: Hutchinson Business Books.

Bell, J. H. J. 1996. *Single or joint venturing? A comprehensive approach to foreign entry mode choice.* Aldershot, England: Avebury.

Bell, J. H. J., Barkema, H. G., & Verbeke, A. 1997. An eclectic model of the choice between WOSs and JVs as modes of foreign entry. In P. W. Beamish & J. P. Killing (Eds.), *Cooperative strategies: European perspectives:* Forthcoming. San Francisco: New Lexington.

Benito, C. R. G., & Gripsrud, G. 1992. The expansion of foreign direct investments: Discrete rational location choices or a cultural learning process? *Journal of International Business Studies,* 23: 461–476.

Berg, S. V., Duncan, J. L., Jr., & Friedman, P. 1982. *Joint venture strategies and corporate innovation.* Cambridge, MA: Oelschlager, Gunn & Hain.

Bettis, R. A., & Prahalad, C. K. 1995. The dominant logic: Retrospective and extension. *Strategic Management Journal,* 16: 5–14.

Brown, L. T., Rugman, A. M., & Verbeke, A. 1989. Japanese joint ventures with western multinationals: Synthesising the economic and cultural explanations of failure. *Asia Pacific Journal of Management,* 6: 225–242.

Buckley, P. J., & Casson, M. 1976. *The future of the multinational enterprise.* London: MacMillan.

Buckley, P. J., & Casson, M. 1988. A theory of cooperation in international business. In F. J. Contractor & P. Lorange (Eds.), *Cooperative strategies in international business:* 31–55. Lexington, MA: Lexington Books.

Carroll, G. R., Preisendorfer, P., Swaminathan, A., & Wiedenmayer, G. 1993. Brewery and brauerei: The organizational ecology of brewing. *Organization Studies,* 14: 155–188.

Carroll, G. R., & Swaminathan, A. 1991. Density dependent organizational evolution in the American brewing industry from 1633 to 1988. *Acta Sociologica,* 34: 155–175.

Chang, S. J. 1995. International expansion strategy of Japanese firms: Capability building through sequential entry. *Academy of Management Journal,* 38: 383–407.

Cho, K. R., & Padmanabhan, P. 1995. Acquisition versus new venture: The choice of foreign establishment mode by Japanese firms. *Journal of International Management,* 1: 255–285.

Chowdhury, J. 1992. Performance of international joint ventures and wholly owned foreign subsidiaries: A comparative perspective. *Management International Review,* 32: 115–133.

Cohen, W. M., & Levinthal, D. A. 1989. Innovation and learning: The two faces of R&D. *Economic Journal,* 99: 569–596.

Cohen, W. M., & Levinthal, D. A. 1990. Absorptive capacity: A new perspective on learning and innovation. *Administrative Science Quarterly,* 35: 128–152.

Cohen, W. M., & Levinthal, D. A. 1994. Fortune favors the prepared firm. *Management Science,* 40: 227–251.

Contractor, F. J., & Lorange, P. 1988. Why should firms cooperate? The strategy and economics basis for cooperative ventures. In F. J. Contractor & P. Lorange (Eds.), *Cooperative strategies in international business:* 3–30. Lexington, MA: Lexington Books.

Cyert, R. M., & March J. G. 1963. *A behavioral theory of the firm.* Englewood Cliffs, NJ: Prentice-Hall.

Davidson, W. H. 1983. Market similarity and market selection: Implications of international marketing strategy. *Journal of Business Research,* 11: 439–456.

Denis, J. E., & Depelteau, D. 1985. Market knowledge, diversification and export expansion. *Journal of International Business Studies,* 16: 77–89.

Erramilli, M. K. 1991. The experience factor in foreign market entry behavior of service firms. *Journal of International Business Studies,* 22: 479–501.

Erramilli, M. K., & Rao, C. P. 1993. Service firms' international entry mode choice: A modified transaction-cost analysis approach. *Journal of Marketing,* 57(3): 19–38.

Gatignon, H., & Anderson, E. 1988. The multinational corporation's degree of control over foreign subsidiaries: An empirical test of a transaction cost explanation. *Journal of Law, Economics, and Organization,* 4: 305–336.

Geringer, J. M., & Hebert, L. 1991. Measuring performance of international joint ventures. *Journal of International Business Studies,* 22: 249–263.

Gomes-Casseres, B. 1987. Joint venture instability: Is it a problem? *Columbia Journal of World Business,* 22(2): 97–102.

Gomes-Casseres, B. 1989. Ownership structures of foreign subsidiaries: Theory and evidence. *Journal of Economic Behavior and Organization,* 11: 1–25.

Harrigan, K. R. 1985. *Strategies for joint ventures.* Lexington, MA: Lexington Books.

Harrigan, K. R. 1988. Strategic alliances and partner asymmetries. In F. J. Contractor & P. Lorange (Eds.), *Cooperative strategies in international business.* Lexington, MA: 205–226. Lexington Books.

Hedberg, B. 1981. How organizations learn and unlearn. In P. C. Nystrom & W. H. Starbuck (Eds.), *Handbook of organizational design:* 3–27. London: Oxford University Press.

Hedlund, G. 1994. A model of knowledge management and the N-form corporation. *Strategic Management Journal,* 15: 73–90.

Hennart, J-F. 1988. A transaction cost theory of equity joint ventures. *Strategic Management Journal,* 9: 361–374.

Hennart, J-F. 1991. The transaction costs theory of joint ventures: An empirical study of Japanese subsidiaries in the United States. *Management Science,* 37: 483–497.

Hergert, M., & Morris, D. 1988. Trends in international collaborative agreements. In F. J. Contractor & P. Lorange (Eds.), *Cooperative strategies in international business:* 99–110. Lexington, MA: Lexington Books.

Hickson, D. J. 1996. The ASQ years then and now through the eyes of a Euro-Brit. *Administrative Science Quarterly,* 41: 217–228.

Hill, R. C., & Hellriegel, D. 1994. Critical contingencies in joint venture management: Some lessons from managers. *Organization Science,* 5: 594–607.

Hitt, M. A., Harrison, J. S., Ireland, R. D., & Best, A. 1995. *Learning how to dance with the Tasmanian devil: Understanding acquisition success and failure.* Paper presented at the annual meeting of the Strategic Management Society, Mexico City.

Hofstede, G. 1980. *Culture's consequences: International differences in work-related values.* Beverly Hills, CA: Sage.

Hofstede, G. 1983. The cultural relativity of organizational practices and theories. *Journal of International Business Studies,* 2: 75–89.

Hofstede, G. 1989. Organising for cultural diversity. *European Management Journal,* 7: 390–397.

Hofstede, G. 1991. *Cultures and organizations: Software of the mind.* Berkshire, England: McGraw-Hill.

Ingrassia, L., Naji, A. K., & Rosett, C. 1995. Overseas, Otis and its parent get in on the ground floor. *Wall Street Journal,* April 21: A8.

Johanson, J., & Vahlne, J. E. 1977. The internationalization process of the firm: A model of knowledge development and increasing foreign market commitments. *Journal of International Business Studies,* 8: 23–32.

Johanson, J., & Wiedersheim-Paul, F. 1975. The internationalization of the firm: Four Swedish cases. *Journal of Management Studies,* 12: 305–322.

Kogut, B. 1988. Joint ventures: Theoretical and empirical perspectives. *Strategic Management Journal,* 9: 319–332.

Kogut, B., & Singh, H. 1988. The effect of national culture on the choice of entry mode. *Journal of International Business Studies,* 19: 411–432.

Larimo, J. 1993. *Foreign direct investment behaviour and performance: An analysis of Finnish direct manufacturing investments in OECD countries.* Acta Wasaensia, no. 32. Vaasa, Finland: University of Vaasa.

Levine, J. B., & Byrne, J. A. 1986. Corporate odd couples. *Business Week,* July 21: 100–105.

Lewin, K. 1947. Frontiers in group dynamics: Concepts, method, and reality in social science. *Human Relations,* 1: 5–41.

Li, J. T. 1995. Foreign entry and survival: Effects of strategic choices on performance in international markets. *Strategic Management Journal,* 16: 333–351.

Li, J. T., & Guisinger, S. 1991. Comparative business failures of foreign-controlled firms in the United States. *Journal of International Business Studies,* 22: 209–224.

Lorange, P., & Roos, J. 1991. Why some strategic alliances succeed and others fail. *Journal of Business Strategy,* 12(1): 25–30.

Luostarinen, R. 1980. *Internationalization of the firm.* Helsinki: Helsinki School of Economics.

Lyles, M. 1987. Common mistakes of joint venture experienced firms. *Columbia Journal of World Business,* 22(2): 79–85.

Lyles, M. A. 1988. Learning among joint venture-sophisticated firms. In F. J. Contractor & P. Lorange (Eds.), *Cooperative strategies in international business.* 301–316. Lexington, MA: Lexington Books.

Madhok, A. 1997: Cost, value and foreign market entry mode: The transaction and the firm. *Strategic Management Journal,* 18: 39–61.

McGill, M. E. & Slocum, J. W., Jr. 1993. Unlearning the organization. *Organizational Dynamics,* 22(2): 67–79.

Mitchell, C. 1988. Partnerships have become a way of life for Corning. *Wall Street Journal,* July 12.

Mitchell, W., Shaver, J. M., & Yeung, B. 1994. Foreign entrant survival and foreign market share: Canadian companies' experience in United States medical sector markets. *Strategic Management Journal,* 15: 555–567.

Padmanabhan, P., Cho, K. R. 1996. Ownership strategy for a foreign affiliate: An empirical investigation of Japanese firms. *Management International Review,* 36: 45–65.

Parkhe, A. 1991. Interfirm diversity, organizational learning, and longevity in global strategic alliances. *Journal of International Business Studies,* 22: 579–600.

Pennings, J. M., Barkema, H. G., & Douma, S. W. 1994. Organizational learning and diversification. *Academy of Management Journal,* 37: 608–640.

Prahalad, C. K., Bettis, R. A. 1986. The dominant logic: A new linkage between diversity and performance. *Strategic Management Journal,* 7: 485–501.

Ramanujam, V., & Varadarajan, P. 1989. Research on corporate diversification: A synthesis. *Strategic Management Journal,* 10: 523–551.

Ronen, S., & Shenkar, O. 1985. Clustering countries on attitudinal dimensions: A review and synthesis. *Academy of Management Review,* 10: 435–454.

Root, F. 1987. *Entry strategies for international markets.* Lexington, MA: Lexington.

SAS Institute. 1988. *SAS users guide: Statistics.* Durham, NC: SAS Institute.

Schaan, J. L., & Beamish, P. 1988. Joint venture general managers in LDCs. In F. J. Contractor & Lorange, P. (Eds.), *Cooperative strategies in international business:* 279–299. Lexington, MA: Lexington Books.

Shenkar, O., & Zeira, Y. 1987. Human resources management in international joint ventures: Directions for research. *Academy of Management Review,* 12: 546–557.

Shenkar, O., & Zeira, Y. 1992. Role conflict and role ambiguity of chief executive officers in international joint ventures. *Journal of International Business Studies,* 23: 55–75.

Stopford, J. M., & Wells, L. T., Jr. 1972. *Managing the multinational enterprise: Organisation of the firm and ownership of the subsidiaries.* New York: Basic Books.

Vachani, S. 1991. Distinguishing between related and unrelated international geographic diversification: A comprehensive measure of global diversification. *Journal of International Business Studies,* 22: 307–322.

Woodcock, C. P., & Geringer, M. J. 1991. An exploratory study of agency costs related to the control structure of multi-partner, international joint ventures. *Academy of Management Best Papers Proceedings:* 115–118.

Wysocki, B. 1990. Cross-border alliances become favorite way to crack new markets. *Wall Street Journal,* March 26: A1.

Yelle, L. E. 1979. The learning curve: Historical review and comprehensive survey. *Decision Sciences,* 10: 302–328.

Harry G. Barkema (Ph. D., Groningen University) is a professor of international management and the director of the Center for International Management Studies at Tilburg University. His current research focuses on organizational learning, foreign entry, and executive compensation.

Oded Shenkar (Ph.D., Columbia University) is a professor in and the director of the international business program at Tel-Aviv University and a professor of management at the University of Hawaii-Manoa. His current research focuses on international strategic alliances and Chinese managerial reforms.

Freek Vermeulen is a doctoral candidate in organization and strategy at Tilburg University. His research focuses on organizational learning and capabilities in foreign direct investment.

John H. J. Bell (Ph.D., Tilburg University) is an assistant professor of organization and strategy at Tilburg University. His research interests include entry modes, interfirm relationships (e.g., joint ventures, strategic alliances, networks), international management, and strategic decision making.

[23]

© Academy of Management Review
1998, Vol. 23, No. 4, 773-795.

MULTINATIONAL SUBSIDIARY EVOLUTION: CAPABILITY AND CHARTER CHANGE IN FOREIGN-OWNED SUBSIDIARY COMPANIES

JULIAN BIRKINSHAW
Stockholm School of Economics

NEIL HOOD
University of Strathclyde

In this article we develop a model of subsidiary evolution to shed light on the processes that drive changes in a subsidiary's activities and its underlying capabilities. We see subsidiary evolution as (1) the enhancement/depletion of capabilities in the subsidiary, coupled with (2) an explicit change in the subsidiary's charter. Building on this definition, we analyze the interaction between capability and charter change and identify five generic subsidiary evolution processes, developing propositions around the underlying drivers for each process.

There has been a profound evolution in thinking about multinational corporations (MNCs) during the past 10 years. Traditionally, in academic models researchers assumed that ownership-specific advantages were developed at the corporate headquarters and leveraged overseas through the transfer of technology to a network of foreign subsidiaries (Dunning; 1981; Vernon, 1966). As these overseas subsidiaries grew in size and developed their own unique resources, however, it became apparent to many researchers that corporate headquarters was no longer the sole source of competitive advantage for the MNC. Scholars developed models such as the heterarchy (Hedlund, 1986) and the transnational (Bartlett & Ghoshal, 1989) to reflect the critical role played by many subsidiaries in their corporations' competitiveness, and research attention began to shift toward understanding the new roles played by subsidiaries.

Implicit in this shift in research attention has been the concept of *subsidiary evolution*. We specify later in this article a precise definition of subsidiary evolution, but, for the moment, it can be understood broadly as the process of accumulation or depletion of resources/capabilities in the subsidiary over time. There is already widespread acknowledgment that subsidiaries evolve over time, typically through the accumulation of resources and through the development of specialized capabilities (Hedlund, 1986; Prahalad & Doz, 1981). There are also a number of

established typologies that suggest very different roles and responsibilities for the population of subsidiaries (e.g., Bartlett & Ghoshal, 1986; Jarillo & Martinez, 1990; White & Poynter, 1984). What is missing, we believe, is an understanding of *how* subsidiaries change roles. Is there a predictable evolution process toward, for example, greater specialization in terms of product, market, or technology? What are the factors promoting and/or suppressing such a shift? What are the underlying managerial processes that make such a shift possible?

These questions are made more complex by the enormous variety of multinational subsidiaries in existence. For example, subsidiary can refer to the totality of the MNC's holdings in a host country or to a single entity, such as a manufacturing or sales operation. Subsidiaries are established for a variety of motives (e.g., resource seeking, market seeking, or efficiency seeking) and through a variety of modes (e.g., greenfield, acquisition, or joint venture). The relationship of the subsidiary to the parent company can be anything from legal holding company to fully integrated. And recent shifts toward regional free trade have led to international divestments, rationalizations, mergers, and acquisitions—all of which lead to further changes in the make-up of the MNC's subsidiaries. The reality is that a single evolution process for subsidiaries cannot be readily identified. Subsidiaries contract or die out, as well as become larger or more specialized,[1] and there are many different factors that can influence the processes. In this article we therefore put forward a number of generic processes that are appropriate under certain conditions. We also draw extensively from the empirical literature to ensure that the ideas we present are grounded in the available evidence.

We organize this article into two parts. The first part is a systematic review of the literature on subsidiary evolution. This literature is fragmented, but we identify three broadly defined schools of thought on the processes underlying subsidiary evolution. The second part of the article is theoretical development. Building on foundations provided by the resource-based view of the firm, we define subsidiary evolution in terms of capability and charter change and then put forward five generic subsidiary evolution processes. For each one we develop propositions linking various antecedent conditions to subsidiary evolution.

We feel it is important to be clear on the boundaries of this study from the outset. We are concerned with those processes that occur once the MNC has made its initial foreign direct investment in the host country; hence, we do not consider issues of market entry (Johanson & Vahlne, 1977). We are concerned primarily with dominantly owned or wholly owned subsidiaries, because the literature addressing the phenomenon of subsidiary evolution has focused on such cases. Nonetheless, our expectation is that many of the processes we discuss in this article could be adapted to other forms of subsidiary, such as international joint ventures and alliances.

We define subsidiary as a value-adding entity in a host country. This definition reflects the reality that a given host country will sometimes have several subsidiaries (of the same parent) that are independent of one another and that, consequently, will have a separate evolutionary path. A subsidiary can perform a single activity (e.g., manufacturing) or an entire value chain of activities. Finally, subsidiary evolution refers to the enhancement or atrophy of subsidiary capabilities over time and the establishment or loss of the commensurate charter (Galunic & Eisen-

hardt, 1996). We elaborate on this definition later in the article, but, for the moment, it is important to recognize that changes to the subsidiary's stock of capabilities and its charter are closely tied to the subsidiary's ability to add value.

There is some danger, when considering subsidiary evolution, that one will develop a normative bias toward the *accumulation* of resources and specialized capabilities (i.e., subsidiary development), both because it is more commonly reported and because development is an intrinsically more attractive phenomenon to study than decline. We are careful in this article to avoid such a stance, partly because development is just one side of the story and partly because it is clearly possible that subsidiary development *is not always desirable* from the MNC's perspective. Host country laws or customer requirements may force the MNC to undertake activities in that country that it would rather do elsewhere, and subsidiary management may take certain actions to develop the subsidiary for the benefit of their country or for themselves (i.e. "empire building"). Our preference, then, is to model the generic processes of subsidiary evolution in positivist terms—that is, with regard to what the literature and experience tells us actually happens—and to ensure that our definition of subsidiary evolution accounts for the possible lack of alignment between subsidiary and parent company goals.

LITERATURE REVIEW

There exists a substantial body of literature concerned with various aspects of multinational subsidiary management (for reviews, see Birkinshaw & Morrison, 1995, and Jarillo & Martinez, 1989). In the past 10 years the focus of such research has been on the different roles taken by subsidiaries (e.g., Bartlett & Ghoshal, 1986; Gupta & Govindarajan, 1991, 1994; White & Poynter, 1984). Strangely, little explicit attention has been given to the question of how a particular subsidiary's role might shift over time (minor exceptions are Jarillo & Martinez, 1990; Papanasstasiou & Pearce, 1994; and White & Poynter, 1984). In part, this lack of attention reflects the cross-sectional nature of the research, but it also appears to emanate from an assumption that the subsidiary's role is "assigned" to it by the parent company according to such factors as the perceived capabilities of the subsidiary

---

[1] Hence lies our decision to focus on subsidiary evolution rather than subsidiary development.

and the strategic importance of the local market (Bartlett & Ghoshal, 1986).

Head-office assignment of roles is a critical determinant of subsidiary evolution, but in our reading of the literature, it is just one of three broad mechanisms that are responsible for driving the process. The second we refer to as *subsidiary choice*, which reflects the decisions taken by subsidiary management to define for themselves the role of their subsidiary. The third we refer to as *local environment determinism*, in that the role of the subsidiary can be understood as a function of the constraints and opportunities in the local market. Our basic understanding of subsidiary evolution is that the three mechanisms interact to determine the subsidiary's role at any given point in time. The subsidiary's role subsequently impacts the decisions made by head-office managers, the decisions made by subsidiary managers, and the standing of the subsidiary in the local environment. This creates a cyclical process through which the subsidiary's role changes over time. Figure 1 illustrates the process. We underscore, however, that this framework is simply a means of organizing the literature review that follows. In the second part of the article we provide a more detailed specification of the evolution process, as we see it.

Head-Office Assignment

Two theoretical perspectives shed light on the head-office-driven process of subsidiary evolution: (1) the product life cycle (PLC) model (Vernon, 1966) and (2) the internationalization process (Johanson & Vahlne, 1977). Both work on the assumption that the subsidiary is an instrument of the MNC and, consequently, that it acts solely with regard to head-office-determined imperatives. In Table 1 we summarize these two theoretical perspectives, along with the other three perspectives that we subsequently discuss.

Vernon's (1966) PLC model is well known. In the first stage the MNC manufactures and sells in its home market and also exports to certain foreign markets. As the product matures, low-cost production becomes important and foreign competition a threat, so the MNC establishes production overseas. This production is directed primarily toward the host country, but, as quality improves, it may also be exported back to the home country. Finally, once the host country advances to a stage where *its* costs are uncompetitive, production is shifted to a lower-cost host country (see also Mullor-Sebastian, 1983, and Norton & Rees, 1979).

FIGURE 1
Organizing Framework for Subsidiary Evolution

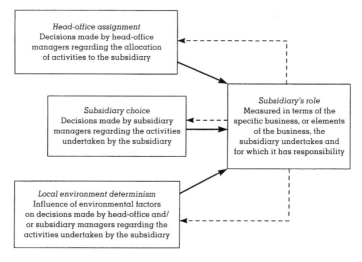

TABLE 1
Summary of Different Perspectives on Subsidiary Evolution

Perspective	Theoretical Roots	Drivers of Subsidiary Evolution	Role of Subsidiary in MNC	Role of Subsidiary in Host Country
Product life cycle	Economics; transaction cost theory	Economic development of host country; transfer of technology from parent to subsidiary	Subordinate entity; recipient of technology transfers	Manufactures and sells products in local market; exploitative role
Internationalization process	Cognitive and behavioral theory	Cognitive limitations of HQ management; incremental increase in commitment to foreign market	Subordinate entity; recipient of investment on basis of market experience	Learns about local market; builds experience and transfers it back to HQ
Network perspective	Sociology; resource dependency theory	Growth of resources through organic process; allocation of responsibilities on basis of relative power	Node in a network; potential source of ownership-specific advantages and equal partner with HQ	"Embedded" in local network, which can be a source of influence vis-à-vis HQ
Decision process	"Managerial" theory of the firm	Development of structural context that allows subsidiary management to develop organically	Role is function of subsidiary's structural context; may be subordinate or equal partner with HQ	Not discussed
Regional development	Economic geography; trade theory	Local environment growth and upgrading stimulates subsidiary development	Subsidiary provides access to local learning, which is disseminated through corporation	Participates in local industrial cluster; may be an active contributor to local economic development

The PLC model helps us to understand the development process as subsidiaries' roles shift toward high value-added activities—from servicing the local market to "adapting" the technology to local specifications, then exporting back to the home country, and, eventually, to contributing to product development (Harrigan, 1984; Vernon, 1979). However, it is limited in two ways: (1) the subsidiary is always subordinate to the center, and (2) the possibility of subsidiary decline is not considered. There are, however, a number of contributions from the same economic paradigm that begin to address both of these shortfalls. Some acknowledgment has been made of the greater role that the subsidiary can play in the MNC network (e.g. Dunning, 1993; Rugman & Verbeke, 1992) but still to a lesser degree than the subsidiary choice perspectives we discuss below. Also, the foreign *divestment* process has been modeled to understand the factors that precipitate the closure or sale of a foreign subsidiary (Boddewyn, 1979, 1983).

Building from a more micro perspective than the PLC model, authors of the *internationalization process* literature begin with assumptions about the cognitive limitations and behaviors of individual managers (Cyert & March, 1963) and seek to understand how firms move beyond their national borders (e.g., Agarwal & Ramaswami, 1992; Aharoni, 1966; Cavusgil, 1980; Johanson & Vahlne, 1977; Li, 1995). In their model, Johanson and Vahlne (1977) explain this process in terms of the reciprocal relationship between (1) levels of knowledge about, and existing commitment to, the foreign market and (2) decisions regarding further commitment to the market.

This model can be readily applied to the case of established subsidiaries. For example, the decision to enhance the manufacturing operation in a subsidiary represents a "commitment decision," based on an appreciation of the subsidiary's current strengths and weaknesses (i.e., *market knowledge*) and a desire to increase the quality of investment in that country (i.e., *market commitment*). That decision, thus, leads to increased commitment, greater understanding of the local business environment, and the possibility of a further investment in the future. Subsidiary development, then, is achieved through the cyclical interaction between investment and learning.[2] Again, though, there are limitations as to how applicable the theory is to the generic issue of subsidiary evolution—the most prominent being that it is more effective at modeling development than decline. Given that market knowledge and commitment *must* increase the longer the subsidiary is operating in its host market, the decision to reduce commitment or exit a country has to be interpreted as an exogenous input to the model. To be useful as a generic model, some modifications would appear to be necessary.

In terms of the empirical literature, there exists a large body of work in which scholars examine various aspects of subsidiary evolution from a headquarters assignment perspective. The most comprehensive evidence comes from researchers in the United Kingdom, who have, over a 30-year period, tracked the successive waves of U.S., European, and Japanese investment into the United Kingdom. This research shows that, in aggregate, there has been a clear development process—from "miniature replica" subsidiaries (White & Poynter, 1984) in the 1950s and 1960s to rationalized manufacturers and product specialists in the 1970s and 1980s (Hood & Young, 1983; Young, Hood, & Hamill, 1988)—in a manner that is consistent with both the PLC and internationalization models.

Evidence for the head-office assignment process also can be found in the case of foreign-owned subsidiaries in the United States, although not in the same detail as in the United Kingdom. Much has been written, for example, about the growth of Japanese manufacturing operations in the United States (e.g., Hamel & Prahalad, 1985; Lincoln, Olson, & Hanada, 1978; Sugiura, 1990), but the evidence simply indicates that these subsidiaries have grown and, to some extent, have adapted to the local environment. More fruitfully, research by Chang (1995, 1996) and Rosenzweig and Chang (1995a,b) ex-

plicitly models subsidiary growth as a sequential process of resource commitment and capability building. There have also been occasional studies from other parts of the world indicating the importance of head-office assignment as the driver of subsidiary development (e.g., Jarillo & Martinez, 1990; Malnight, 1995, 1996).

Researchers have also given subsidiary decline some attention. Boddewyn (1979, 1983) undertook a comprehensive review of foreign divestment and concluded that poor financial performance was the primary cause, followed by lack of strategic fit and various organizational problems, such as poor relationships between parent and subsidiary. More recently, research undertaken in the United Kingdom on the Europe-wide rationalization sparked by free trade has shown that the dynamics of *internal competition* between subsidiaries are a critical determinant of which subsidiaries survive (Almor & Hirsch, 1995; Sachdev, 1976; Young, McDermott, & Dunlop, 1991).

Three important implications can be drawn from this review. First, head-office assignment is not the sole determinant of subsidiary evolution. As the U.K. studies have shown, the changes in subsidiary roles were dictated by head office but motivated, in large part, by the changing economic conditions in the United Kingdom and Europe. They were also, to a large degree, driven by the *track record* of the subsidiary companies in question, especially during the recent phase of plant rationalization in Europe. Second, most of the evolution documented (development and decline) was at the low value-added end of the scale. Very few had "world mandates" (Roth & Morrison, 1992) or product development responsibilities. This leads to the observation that head-office assignment may be the driver of subsidiary evolution in the early stages of the process, when the level of resources and capabilities in the subsidiary is not too advanced. Third, theoretical perspectives have not been very helpful for understanding some of the higher-order value-adding activity that has emerged in subsidiaries, nor for understanding the process of subsidiary decline (however, see Boddewyn, 1979, for the one exception).

Subsidiary Choice

Two theoretical perspectives shed light on the subsidiary choice view of subsidiary develop-

---

[2] Madhok (1997) makes the point that the emphasis on knowledge accumulation in this model makes it essentially part of the *organizational capabilities* school that defines the firm on the basis of its proprietary capabilities rather than market failure considerations.

ment: (1) the network model of the MNC and (2) the decision process perspective. The network model of the MNC, in contrast to the PLC model discussed earlier, allows the subsidiary to move from a position of subordination (vis-à-vis head office) to one of equality, or even leadership. In terms of core assumptions, the network model recognizes that ownership-specific advantages do not have to be tied to the home country (Rugman & Verbeke, 1992) but can, instead, be acquired or developed by the subsidiary itself. In addition, the MNC is modeled as an "interorganizational network" (Ghoshal & Bartlett, 1991) of loosely coupled entities, rather than a hierarchical monolith. This loose coupling gives the subsidiary the necessary freedom to develop its own unique resource profile.

Much of the contemporary thinking on MNC organization conforms to these basic assumptions, without an explicit network conceptualization (e.g. Bartlett & Ghoshal, 1989; Hedlund, 1986; White & Poynter, 1984). More recently, scholars have attempted to model more formally the relationships between entities in the MNC according to their relative power (Forsgren, Holm, & Johanson, 1992; Forsgren & Pahlberg, 1992; Ghoshal & Bartlett, 1991). This latter stream of research has built on the concepts of network analysis developed in the fields of industrial marketing (Johanson & Mattson, 1988) and organizational theory (Emerson, 1962; Pfeffer & Salancik, 1978; Thompson, 1967). It is important to note that the resource-based view of the firm (Barney, 1991; Penrose, 1959; Wernerfelt, 1984) has a lot in common with the network model, once one recognizes that resource development can occur at the level of the subsidiary, rather than at the level of the MNC as a whole.

The network model provides a very valuable perspective on subsidiary evolution, because it reflects the reality that many subsidiaries have specialized capabilities on which the rest of the MNC is dependent. Evolution here is an organic process, built around the growth and decline of valuable and distinctive resources in the subsidiary. Subsidiary growth, in particular, is constrained by the natural rate of growth of resources (Penrose, 1958) and also by the actions of other entities (notably the parent company) who use their relative power to enforce their will on the subsidiary. As the subsidiary increases its stock of distinctive resources, it lessens its dependence on other entities and takes more complete control of its own destiny (Pfeffer & Salancik, 1978; Prahalad & Doz, 1981).

The second theoretical approach involves the decision process in large, complex organizations (Bower, 1970; Burgelman, 1983a, 1991, 1996; Noda & Bower, 1996; Prahalad, 1976). Like the internationalization process perspective, the body of literature on the decision process perspective begins with assumptions of bounded rationality on the part of individual managers. This literature has provided much of the foundations for the network model of the MNC, and various aspects of subsidiary management have also been studied from this perspective (Bartlett & Ghoshal, 1986; Prahalad & Doz, 1981). Surprisingly, though, subsidiary evolution has received only limited attention. Only Prahalad and Doz (1981) explicitly have considered subsidiary growth, and their concern was with how the head office could continue to exert control over its subsidiaries, rather than with the benefits of growth per se.

Of greater interest, in terms of this article, is the work of Burgelman (1983a,b), who studied internal corporate venturing using an extension of Bower's (1972) resource allocation model. His key contribution was a recognition that strategic behavior often occurs below top management levels and sometimes in ways that are not actively encouraged by top management. He termed this *autonomous behavior*. Regarding the MNC subsidiary, the concept of autonomous behavior is important, because it suggests a process of internal growth that is only loosely controlled by head-office directives. The idea that subsidiaries take the initiative to win world product mandates, for example, is very consistent with Burgelman's theory (Birkinshaw, 1995; Crookell, 1986).

In sum, both theoretical perspectives give us considerable potential for understanding subsidiary evolution. The network perspective provides important insights into the role of the underlying capabilities of the subsidiary and emphasizes that the subsidiary is part of a network—not just a dyadic relationship with a parent company. The decision process perspective provides us with a way of understanding autonomous action on the part of subsidiaries.

The empirical literature that draws on the subsidiary choice perspective is mostly from Canada, but smaller contributions come from Sweden, Ireland, and the United Kingdom. Canada appears to have been an attractive setting for research on subsidiary choice because of the consistently high levels of foreign ownership of industry (Safarian, 1966) and the deliberate policy of governments in the 1970s and 1980s to encourage foreign MNCs to grant their Canadian subsidiaries "world product mandates" (Hatch Report, 1979). A landmark study by the Science Council of Canada (1980) documented case studies of subsidiaries that had won such mandates, typically achieved through development of specialized capabilities and strong relationships with the parent company. Subsequent studies by Bishop and Crookell (1986) and Birkinshaw (1995) drew similar conclusions. Thus, while the macro changes in the Canadian business environment, and the strategic responses to those changes by parent company management, shaped the broad shift toward subsidiary specialization, there is strong evidence that specific subsidiaries' development paths were also swayed by the entrepreneurial actions of their managers.

Although Canadian researchers are alone in emphasizing subsidiary initiative as the driver of development, there has been some discussion of the concept for U.K. (Papanasstasiou & Pearce, 1994), Scottish (Young, Hood, & Peters, 1994), and Irish (Delaney, 1996) subsidiaries, and Gupta and Govindarajan (1994) have discussed it as well. In research on international R&D laboratories, scholars have offered similar conclusions (Behrman & Fischer, 1980; Håkanson & Zander, 1986; Pearce, 1989; Ronstadt, 1977)—namely, that over time R&D laboratories tend to evolve *through their own initiative* toward higher value-added R&D work. Finally, a number of Swedish researchers working from a head-office perspective have pursued the same themes in a rather different way. Their overall approach has been one of organizational development, but the evidence of subsidiaries building specialized resources and gaining recognition for their distinctive abilities is compelling (Forsgren et al., 1992, 1995; Forsgren & Pahlberg, 1992; Ghauri, 1992; Holm, Johanson, & Thilenius, 1995).

This evidence points to a number of implications for the subsidiary evolution process in general. First, autonomous subsidiary behavior (Burgelman, 1983b) appears to be a potent force for subsidiary development because it leads to the planned—rather than fortuitous—develop-

ment of resources and capabilities. Second, head-office support appears to be a necessary but not sufficient condition for subsidiary-driven development. Many of the failed cases of initiatives in the Canadian literature appear to have been the result of weak parent-subsidiary relationships or a somewhat *ethnocentric attitude* among parent managers (Birkinshaw, 1997; Perlmutter, 1969).[3] Third, subsidiary decline gets essentially no consideration in either the theoretical or the empirical literature. Clearly, it is meaningless to suggest that subsidiary managers might orchestrate their own demise, but we can certainly envision a process in which *inaction* by subsidiary managers leads to the atrophy and eventual demise of the subsidiary and its resources.

Local Environment Determinism

In much of the mainstream organization theory literature, scholars view organizational action as constrained or determined by the environment in which it occurs (Hannan & Freeman, 1977; Meyer & Rowan, 1977; Pfeffer & Salancik, 1978). MNC researchers have adapted this perspective by proposing that each subsidiary of the MNC operates in its own unique task environment, which constrains or determines the activities of that subsidiary (Ghoshal & Bartlett, 1991; Ghoshal & Nohria, 1989; Rosenzweig & Singh, 1991; Westney, 1994). The argument, in essence, is that each subsidiary operates under a unique set of conditions to which it has to adapt in order to be effective. The nature of the local environment, as defined by customers, competitors, suppliers, and government bodies, thus has an important influence on the activities undertaken by the subsidiary.

Although the static relationship between the subsidiary and its local environment has been studied (e.g., Andersson & Johanson, 1996; Ghoshal & Nohria, 1989; Rosenzweig & Nohria, 1995), there has been less consideration of the dynamic question—that is, the relationship between local/regional development and subsid-

---

[3] Note that there are cases of subsidiaries "assuming" charters (Hagström, 1994) without head-office support, but our argument is that these do not constitute part of the subsidiary development process. We return to this point in the theory development section.

iary evolution (Young et al., 1994).[4] In the literature that does exist, scholars have, for the most part, not explicitly considered the foreign-owned sector. One important line of thinking is the various "stages" models of economic growth that explicitly recognize the importance of foreign direct investment (FDI) by MNCs as a driver of the process. These include Ozawa's "dynamic paradigm of FDI-facilitated development" (1992) and Dunning's investment development cycle (1981, 1986). In both, the MNC subsidiary plays a critical role as a conduit for technology and skill development in the local economy.

Implicitly, the subsidiary itself also develops, in that it becomes capable of adopting and applying increasingly sophisticated levels of the MNC's technology. Porter (1990) proposes a stages model of growth based on his "diamond of competitive advantage," but he sees the role of the MNC subsidiary as primarily one of "selective tapping" (of ideas), rather than active development. The exception, he argues, is the few subsidiaries in leading-edge clusters that go on to become the MNC's home base for a particular business area.

We should briefly mention the theoretical rationale for linking regional development to subsidiary evolution. The heart of the issue is the argument that certain aspects of knowledge transfer occur more effectively between local firms (wholly owned or subsidiaries) than between parent and overseas subsidiary, because of geographical proximity and cultural similarity (Kogut & Zander, 1992; Krugman, 1991; Porter, 1990; Sölvell & Zander, 1998). Subsidiary evolution, thus, is driven by the dynamism of the local business environment (cf., Porter's diamond), as well as by the subsidiary's ability to access resources from the MNC.

The evidence for local environment-driven subsidiary evolution is rather limited. Both the U.K. and Canadian literature we discussed earlier make it clear that local environment characteristics factor into the decision to invest in or upgrade a subsidiary, but, typically, it is the subsidiary company or head-office managers who drive the process (e.g., Bishop & Crookell,

1986). There is, however, an increasing acknowledgment of the importance of inward investment agencies, such as Scottish Enterprise, whose role is not only to attract greenfield investments but also to help existing subsidiaries upgrade their activities (Hood, Young, & Lal, 1994).

In sum, there is strong evidence that the subsidiary development process is influenced by the local environment, through both (1) the broadly defined dynamism and attractiveness of the local business context and (2) the specific incentive programs offered by development agencies. But, as with many of the other perspectives, it is the early stages of subsidiary development that scholars best understand, while later-stage development and decline get little attention.

Integrating the Three Perspectives

In this review we took a broad approach in identifying any theoretical or empirical research that potentially shed light on the process of subsidiary evolution. In order to move forward, however, it is important to take a position and develop one line of thinking in detail. Our preference is to build upon the subsidiary choice perspective. We fully embrace the network conceptualizations of the MNC by modeling the subsidiary as a semiautonomous entity, capable of making its own decisions but constrained in its action by the demands of head-office managers and by the opportunities in the local environment. We also borrow heavily from the decision process perspective, notably the work of Burgelman (1983b) on autonomous behavior.

We draw on the other perspectives to a lesser degree. The PLC model offers important lessons in the early stages of subsidiary development, but it does not allow for autonomous action on the part of the subsidiary. The internationalization process, likewise, has implications for early-stage development but is rooted in a head-office perspective on MNC management. The local environment perspective has clear implications for subsidiary development, but in its pure form it is fundamentally opposed to the subsidiary choice perspective (Child, 1972). It is also less developed than the other perspectives.

The theory part of this article can be described as a "dynamic capabilities" approach to subsid-

---

[4] There is also a large body of literature originating from the field of economic geography, in which authors look at the spatial distribution of the MNC and its relationship with regional economic development (e.g., Clarke, 1985; Dicken, 1976; McNee, 1958).

iary evolution. We draw heavily on recent advances in thinking about organizational capabilities (Kogut & Zander, 1992; Madhok, 1997; Teece, Pisano, & Shuen, 1993), but we do so with an important distinction—namely, a focus on the subsidiary, rather than the entire firm, as the unit of analysis. Our approach is, of course, consistent with the network conceptualizations of the MNC, but it also raises a number of new challenges.

THEORETICAL DEVELOPMENT

Toward a Definition of Subsidiary Evolution

Following Amit and Schoemaker (1993), we define *resources* as the stock of available factors owned or controlled by the subsidiary and *capabilities* as a subsidiary's capacity to deploy resources, usually in combination, using organizational processes to effect a desired end. Subsidiary capabilities can be specific to a functional area—for example, flexible production, research into fiber optics, or logistics management—or they can be more broadly based—for example, total quality management, systems integration, innovation, or government relations.

Subsidiary evolution, we argue, is the result of an accumulation or depletion of capabilities over time.[5] In this respect, we are very close to the dynamic capabilities perspective of Nelson and Winter (1982), Dierickx and Cool (1989), Kogut and Zander (1992), and Teece et al. (1997), in that we are concerned with the "mechanisms by which firms accumulate and dissipate new skills and capabilities" (Teece et al., 1997: 19). To some extent, capabilities are accumulated and stored as organizational routines (Nelson & Winter, 1982) that have emerged over time, but the process also can be strongly influenced by various subsidiary, corporate, and local environment factors, many of which we discussed earlier.

An important point to underscore here is that the subsidiary's capabilities are, to some extent, distinct from the capabilities of the headquarters operation and its sister subsidiaries. In other words, the particular geographical setting and history of the subsidiary are responsible for defining a development path that is absolutely unique to that subsidiary, which, in turn, results in a profile of capabilities that is unique (Teece et al., 1997). There are also, of course, shared capabilities between subsidiaries, such as those codified in company manuals or blueprints. The evidence, however, indicates that the transfer of capabilities between units of the same firm is far from trivial and is a function of the codifiability of the capability in question (Zander, 1994), the motivations of the receiving units, and a host of contextual variables (Szulanski, 1996).[6] Capabilities, simply stated, are "sticky," and they cannot be easily transferred from one subsidiary to the next, even when the transfer is undertaken willingly.

Related to the stickiness of subsidiary capabilities is their path dependence.[7] Capabilities are not easily transferred and not readily dissipated. They develop over time as a result of past experiences and are subsequently applied to new or related areas of business. To some extent, new capabilities are always being developed, but they typically emerge at the margin of existing capabilities in response to competitive demands (see below). As a result, it is possible to think in terms of path-dependent trajectories of capabilities that gradually evolve over time. Large-scale grafting of new capabilities onto the subsidiary's existing stock of capabilities also can be achieved through merger or acquisition (Huber, 1991; Madhok, 1997), although such a process has been shown in the postacquisition integration literature to be far from trivial (Haspeslagh & Jemison, 1991).

---

[5] Note that the accumulation of capabilities is very different from the accumulation of resources. A resource-accumulating subsidiary may just be "fat," as a reviewer pointed out, whereas a capability-accumulating subsidiary is putting together new combinations of resources and deploying them in creative ways. This is an important departure from normal usage in the decision process and product life-cycle traditions, in which resource accumulation and capability accumulation are not distinguished.

[6] Of course, there is also a transaction cost argument here, in that there are costs associated with transacting with other units, even if they are part of the same firm. This reduces the likelihood of transfer, which adds to the stickiness of the capabilities in question.

[7] Barney (1991) and others have also elaborated on many other dimensions of capabilities, such as rarity, causal ambiguity, and tacitness. These characteristics have important implications when it comes to combining a subsidiary's capabilities with those of other subsidiaries and of protecting capabilities from competitor imitation, but we believe they are not central to a discussion of subsidiary evolution.

The visible manifestation of the subsidiary's role in the MNC is its *charter*, defined as the business—or elements of the business—in which the subsidiary participates and for which it is recognized to have responsibility within the MNC (Galunic & Eisenhardt, 1996). The term *charter* has implications for the organization's mission (Thompson, 1967) and for its institutional legitimacy (DiMaggio & Powell, 1983; Scott & Meyer, 1994), but our focus here, in keeping with Galunic and Eisenhardt (1996), is to focus on business activities and the underlying capabilities through which they are implemented.[8] Thus, we can define charter in terms of markets served, products manufactured, technologies held, functional areas covered, or any combination thereof. The charter is typically a shared understanding between the subsidiary and the headquarters regarding the subsidiary's scope of responsibilities.

The relationship between the subsidiary's charter and its underlying capabilities is not a simple one. In the case where the subsidiary's charter does not change for a long period of time, subsidiary managers are likely to steer resource deployment and capability accumulation efforts toward the fulfillment of that charter so that, eventually, the subsidiary's capability profile is a reflection of its charter. However, if there is a high level of change in the subsidiary's resource base (e.g., through merger and acquisition), in its charter, or in the markets that the charter is directed toward, then at any given point in time, there are likely to be mismatches between the subsidiary's capability profile and its official charter. The point here, which we elaborate on further in the next section, is simply that the *concept of subsidiary evolution must take into account both the charter of the subsidiary and its underlying capabilities.* It is dangerous to assume that the two simply move together.

One final line of reasoning regarding subsidiary charters and capabilities needs to be mentioned here—namely, that *in most corporations there is internal competition for charters.* The

internal competition is both for existing charters (where one subsidiary "steals" a charter from another) and for new charters (where two or more subsidiaries "bid" against one another). We find the best evidence for internal charter competition in the recent work of Galunic and Eisenhardt (1996) and Galunic (1996), who studied the processes through which divisions of Omni corporation gained and lost charters from one another. Charter competition is also mentioned in several studies of Canadian subsidiaries (Birkinshaw, 1996; Crookell, 1986).

The idea that charters might shift from one subsidiary to another appears strange at first, given that we have just argued that each subsidiary has a unique capability profile. However, in many cases subsidiaries will have similar, although not identical, capability profiles. Take, for example, the case of a large silicon chip manufacturer, which will typically have 10 or more fabrication plants in various sites around the world. These plants all have the basic capability to manufacture chips, but, at the same time, they do so with rather different technologies and different levels of quality control, cost, process enhancement, and so on. In all of these plants there is an ongoing process of internal benchmarking and capability upgrading,[9] because a new investment can potentially be made at any one of the existing plants.

Not all charters are "contestable" in this fashion. Some charters are country specific and so are linked inextricably to the local subsidiary operation; others are tied to large, immobile assets (e.g., an auto plant) so they cannot easily be shifted to another location. Many more, however, are readily contestable, especially when the underlying resources on which they are based are mobile. It is, we believe, the latent mobility of charters and the competition between subsidiary units for charters that is one of the fundamental drivers behind the subsidiary evolution process.

The importance of internal competition for charters can be shown in another way. Porter's (1980, 1990) thinking on competitive advantage suggests that it is exposure to demanding cus-

---

[8] It should be recognized that an institutional definition of the subsidiary's charter will not necessarily covary with the activity/capability-based definition. Thus, an interesting area for future research would be to examine divergences between institutional- and capability-based charter definitions in subsidiaries.

[9] An interesting side issue here is why competing manufacturing units choose to help one another to improve. The evidence suggests that they do, implying that managers are motivated more by their long-term allegiance to the corporation than by the short-term gain of a new charter.

tomers, leading-edge competitors, and high-quality suppliers that pressures firms to upgrade their capabilities. In the case of the subsidiary company, we can identify a competitive environment with both external and internal components. The external elements are customers, competitors, and suppliers in the local environment; the internal elements are other corporate units that buy from or sell to the focal[10] subsidiary and sister subsidiaries that are competing for new and existing charters. Our argument is that internal competitive forces—when they are released—are as critical to the capability enhancement process as external competitive forces. In some MNCs there is no internal competitive environment, because all sourcing relationships and charter allocations are centrally planned by head-office managers, but, increasingly, MNCs are making use of internal market mechanisms to foster the competitive dynamics we are describing here (Halal, 1994).

In summary, subsidiary evolution is defined in terms of (1) the enhancement/atrophy of capabilities in the subsidiary and (2) the establishment/loss of the commensurate charter. Subsidiary development consists of capability enhancement and charter establishment; subsidiary decline consists of capability atrophy and charter loss. Capability change may lead or lag the change in the commensurate charter, but, for evolution to have occurred, the charter must eventually reflect the underlying capabilities of the subsidiary. Note that this definition deliberately excludes cases of self-serving or empire-building behavior, in which the subsidiary develops capabilities that are *not* aligned with the strategic priorities of the MNC. Our argument is that the process of assigning a charter to the subsidiary is an explicit acknowledgment by corporate management that the underlying capabilities are valued. If the capabilities are not valued, there is no charter change, and evolution has not occurred.

Generic Subsidiary Evolution Processes

We now can reconsider the phenomenon of subsidiary evolution using the theoretical ideas

developed above. Our objective here is to put forward five generic processes of subsidiary evolution and to use the theoretical insights indicated above (and earlier in the article) to propose a series of causal relationships linking certain contextual factors to each of the five processes.

In Figure 2 we indicate the possible combinations of capability change and charter change in the subsidiary. As we noted earlier, it seems extremely unlikely that the subsidiary's charter will mirror exactly the subsidiary's capability profile. Instead, the capability change will either lead or lag the charter change.

In situation 1 the charter extension leads, subsequently, to an enhancement of the subsidiary's capability profile. Given that charter assignment is the parent company's responsibility and that the capabilities are not already in existence, we designate this process *parent-driven investment* (PDI). Although subsidiary managers may have some influence over the process (notably, through high performance), they are typically actively competing for the charter with other subsidiaries, so the development of the commensurate capabilities begins only once the charter has been assigned.

In situation 2 the capability enhancement leads, subsequently, to an extension to the sub-

FIGURE 2
Subsidiary Evolution As a Function of Capability and Charter Change

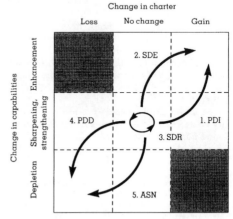

Note: Numbers refer to the five generic processes we discuss in the text.

---

[10] We use *focal subsidiary* to refer to the hypothetical subsidiary at the center of our analysis.

sidiary's charter. In essence, it represents a strategic move by subsidiary managers, who see the opportunity to gain a new or enhanced charter if they can demonstrate that they have the necessary capabilities. However, charter change in this case is not guaranteed—for example, if the capabilities in question are not deemed by corporate management to be valuable. We designate this process *subsidiary-driven charter extension* (SDE).

Situations 4 and 5 are the reverse of situations 1 and 2. The former is *parent-driven divestment* (PDD), where the subsidiary loses its charter for a certain product, technology, or market and then, gradually, the commensurate capabilities atrophy. The latter is *atrophy through subsidiary neglect* (ASN), where the subsidiary's capabilities gradually wither away over time, the subsidiary's performance (for that charter) suffers, and, eventually, the parent company takes away the charter.

Finally, situation 3 is *subsidiary-driven charter reinforcement* (SDR), which refers to the situation in which the subsidiary sharpens or strengthens its existing capabilities and maintains its charter. One could argue that this is not a pure case of subsidiary evolution, but we include it to account for the situation in which the subsidiary opts to deepen its capabilities in one specific area (i.e., its current charter), rather than seek out new charters. As part of a long-term strategy of subsidiary development, charter reinforcement is probably an important phase for the subsidiary to go through, because it ensures that the subsidiary has leading-edge capabilities vis-à-vis both internal and external competitors. Note, however, that in such a case it is harder (although not impossible) to identify when evolution has occurred, because the charter is maintained rather than enhanced.

Two further observations should be made at this stage. First, each process represents a discrete phase that, in our experience, may take anything from a few weeks to a few years to complete. Over a longer period of time, one would expect to see multiple phases of development, including positive and negative steps, as well as subsidiary- and parent-driven ones. The unit of analysis under investigation here, thus, is the single period of one charter change and a commensurate change in capabilities. Subsidiary evolution, broadly conceived, also can refer to aggregate changes over time, but, for the sake

of conceptual and operational clarity, we must work at the lower level of analysis. Second, we should be clear that we see the five processes as comprehensive and mutually exclusive so that every case of subsidiary evolution can be classified as belonging to one of the five. Whether this also means that the five generic processes constitute a type is more debatable, because the processes lack comparability in certain key dimensions. Moreover, some have argued that the term *typology* should be used in a very precise manner to retain its value for theory building (Doty & Glick, 1994: 232), so our preference here is to avoid claiming that a type exists, even though in certain respects it could probably be labeled as such.

Two questions follow from the categorization indicated in Figure 2. First, what do these five processes look like (in terms of action-outcome relationships)? Second, what contextual factors are responsible for promoting or suppressing them? In the remainder of the article, we address these two questions, using Table 2 as a framework. We consider each process in turn, with regard to the major actions undertaken by parent management, subsidiary management, and any other actors involved, and the anticipated outcomes. We then look at the contextual factors listed in Table 2 and consider the impact that each is predicted to have—if any—on the five generic processes. Note that we identified the contextual factors from the existing literature or during theoretical development.

Parent-driven investment (PDI). This process consists of one clearly defined event—that is, the decision to enhance the subsidiary's charter—preceded by a period of negotiation and deliberation by the parent and the subsidiary and followed by a period of capability enhancement by the subsidiary in order to deliver satisfactorily on the new charter. The action taken by parent management typically is an evaluation of the relative merits of various locations for the planned investment, followed by the decision to make the charter change (or not) in the focal subsidiary. The action taken by subsidiary management is typically lobbying parent managers to persuade them to decide in that subsidiary's favor. In most cases the process involves the commitment of considerable resources to the subsidiary—for example, through the establishment of a new factory or through creation of a research and development group. However, it is

TABLE 2
Five Generic Subsidiary Evolution Processes

Contextual Factors	Action	Outcome
Parent company factors • Competitive internal resource allocation • Decentralization of decision making • Ethnocentrism of parent management	**PDI** Parent: Decision to make investment; evaluation of various locations Subsidiary: Lobbying →	Establishment of new charter in subsidiary (CC); gradual development of commensurate capabilities (CB)
Subsidiary factors • Track record of subsidiary • Credibility of subsidiary management • Entrepreneurial orientation of subsidiary employees	**SCE** Subsidiary: Identification of new opportunities; building capabilities (CB); proposal to parent → Parent: Judgment on subsidiary proposal	Extension of charter in subsidiary (CC)
→	**SCR** Subsidiary: Competitiveness-driven search; upgrading of existing capabilities (CB) →	Reinforcement of existing charter in subsidiary
Host country factors • Strategic importance of country • Host government support • Relative cost of factor inputs • Dynamism of local business environment	**PDD** Parent: Decision to divest; evaluation of various locations → Subsidiary: Lobbying	Loss or diminution of charter (CC) in subsidiary; atrophy of existing capabilities (CD)
	ASN Subsidiary: Inaction; atrophy of capabilities (CD) → Parent: Judgment on subsidiary's lack of competitiveness	Loss or diminution of charter in subsidiary (CC)

Key: CC, charter change; CB, capability building; CD, capability depletion.

also possible that the decision will simply be one of charter change in the subsidiary—for example, the extension of market responsibility from the United Kingdom to Europe.

The process is driven by the parent company's desire to select, according to whatever criteria it deems appropriate, the optimum location for an investment. Some MNCs use a formalized request-for-proposal procedure in such cases, whereby proposed corporate-level investments are opened up to all interested subsidiary operations and allocated on the basis of the "bids" that are received. In other cases the process is less structured and may involve a variety of boundedly rational decision-making procedures (Cyert & March, 1963; Mintzberg, Raisinghani, & Theoret, 1976), such as localized search or politically motivated decision criteria. In both cases there is at least an implicit competition between locations for the new investment, which typically leads to active lobbying by various subsidiaries and host governments.

Subsidiary-driven charter extension (SDE). This involves a long and often slow process of capability building, followed by an extension to the subsidiary's charter. The process essentially is one of corporate entrepreneurship (Birkinshaw, 1997; Burgelman, 1983b) on the part of subsidiary management, in that it represents a conscious effort by the subsidiary to seek out and develop new business opportunities and then put them forward to parent company managers. On the assumption that parent company managers are inherently risk averse in their decisions about which subsidiaries should have responsibility for which charters, the logic here is that subsidiary management builds the required capabilities first and seeks the charter extension only once the subsidiary can demonstrate those capabilities.

The process involves three distinct steps by subsidiary managers: (1) an initiative-driven search for new market opportunities in both the subsidiary's local market and within the corporate system (Birkinshaw, 1997; Kirzner, 1973), (2) the pursuit of a specific market opportunity and the development of the appropriate capabilities to fulfill it, and (3) a proposal to the parent company that the subsidiary's charter be enhanced. For the parent company, the only action required is a judgment on whether to grant the subsidiary its requested charter enhancement. In many cases the parent company will be informed of the subsidiary's initiative throughout the process, whereas in other cases the subsidiary will have deliberately undertaken the process without the parent company's knowledge (Birkinshaw & Ridderstråle, in press). In all situations, however, we see the SDE process as fairly "political," in that it relies to a great degree on the subsidiary-level champion gaining support at the head office through his or her personal contacts. Our reasoning here is simply that parent company managers will naturally treat an initiative from a peripheral part of the corporation with suspicion, unless they know the individual promoting it.

Subsidiary-driven charter reinforcement (SDR). As with the previous process, this one is driven entirely by the actions of subsidiary managers. It is triggered by concerns about the subsidiary's competitiveness vis-à-vis both sister subsidiaries (Morrison & Crookell, 1990) and external competitors. The competitors provide specific cues to subsidiary management regarding their relative strengths and weaknesses, which leads to attempts to enhance the relevant set of capabilities. This process may or may not also involve external benchmarking and internal transfers of best practice (Szulanski, 1996). The net result, assuming the process has been effective, is lower costs and/or quality and service improvements and, thus, a reinforcement of the subsidiary's existing charter. There may be no head-office involvement in this process per se, given that no official change to the charter is being suggested, but the capability reinforcement process will lead to a stronger subsidiary performance and, hence, an enhanced level of credibility and visibility vis-à-vis head-office managers.

Parent-driven divestment (PDD). This is the mirror image of PDI. The typical scenario is that the parent company has made the decision to rationalize its international operations and/or to exit certain businesses but that the decision regarding *which* ones to divest has not been final-

ized. Such a scenario can be triggered by a need to cut costs or by the desire for greater strategic focus on core activities. The fate of the subsidiary, therefore, may be closure, sale to another company, or spinoff as a separate entity.

The evaluation process is influenced by a host of factors, including the existing capabilities of the subsidiary relative to others and the attractiveness of the host country market, according to a number of criteria. Subsidiary managers and host country governments will sometimes have the opportunity to lobby against closure, but more often the decision will be presented as a fait accompli by parent company management.

The final decision results in a charter loss for the focal subsidiary. This may include the sale or closure of all associated activities (e.g., when a plant is shut down). In such a case the subsidiary's capabilities are immediately lost at the same time. Equally likely is the case where a charter is lost but the subsidiary as a whole continues to exist (Galunic & Eisenhardt, 1996). In this case the capabilities that were associated with the old charter will gradually be lost as employees are reassigned to new roles and develop new skills. However, it is possible that the remaining capabilities are actually redeployed toward the development of a new charter (i.e., an SDE process as described above). This process has been labeled *charter renewal* (Birkinshaw, 1996).

Atrophy through subsidiary neglect (ASN). The final process is one in which the subsidiary's capabilities gradually atrophy while the charter is still retained. The argument here reverses that suggested in the SDE and SDR processes. Essentially, we see subsidiary management's *lack of attention* pushing this process along. The subsidiary becomes less and less competitive over time. This can be simply a case of poor management, but it is more likely to stem from a lack of competition. If, for example, the subsidiary has guaranteed internal contracts for its products and the corporation as a whole is making money, the pressure to reduce costs or improve service is likely to be low.

ASN occurs through two somewhat different processes. In the first, the subsidiary continues to fulfill its charter but on the basis of capabilities that are not leading edge and that gradually atrophy over time through lack of attention. Eventually, this situation comes to the attention of head-office managers, either because it is negatively impacting the competitiveness of the entire MNC or because internal performance measures indicate the sub-par performance of the focal subsidiary. Depending on the urgency of the change that is demanded of head-office managers, the subsidiary may be given the opportunity to turn things around itself, or it can lose its charter immediately.[11] The second scenario, given the discussion about SDR, is one in which the subsidiary is doing a satisfactory job of maintaining its capabilities, but, when faced with a global rationalization program, it becomes apparent that other subsidiaries have upgraded their capabilities more effectively. Charter loss follows simply because the focal subsidiary's capabilities are weaker than those of its sister subsidiaries. Atrophy, in this sense, refers to the level of the capabilities relative to other subsidiaries, rather than in an absolute sense.

Contextual Factors Impacting the Generic Processes

In the literature review and in the preceding description, we touched on a large number of factors at the corporate, subsidiary, and host country level, which, scholars have argued, have an impact on the presence of the five generic processes. In this section we take a much more systematic look at these factors (listed in Table 2) and put forward specific propositions relating the levels of the contextual factors to the extent to which the five processes occur. We make one point of clarification here—namely, that the factors identified are not a comprehensive list; they represent the main factors that previous researchers have identified, and, as such, there may well be other factors that also impact the occurrence of the five subsidiary evolution processes. We also acknowledge that our focus on three contexts (corporate, subsidiary, and host country) means that we have set aside several others, such as the parent company's industry environment or other subsidiaries within the corporation, that could potentially impact subsidiary evolution.

---

[11] Frequently, the charter loss process is rather more gradual than this, in that the subsidiary finds itself with increasingly unimportant charters.

Corporate-level factors. Central to our earlier discussion on capabilities was the notion of internal competition for charters among subsidiary units. Here, we develop the idea of *competitive internal resource allocation*, which means a corporate-wide system that promotes internal competition, either by allowing bids for new investments or by creating a system through which existing charters can be "challenged" by other units (Galunic & Eisenhardt, 1996; White & Poynter, 1984). A competitive internal resource allocation system has substantial implications for subsidiary evolution, because it legitimizes a process by which subsidiaries can both gain and lose charters. It also increases awareness of the relative capabilities among subsidiaries and provides a motivation for them to continually upgrade their capabilities. In contrast, in the absence of such a competitive system, resource allocation decisions are made by head-office decision makers through a central planning process, which typically means favoring investment locations with which the decision makers are familiar and maintaining charters over long periods of time. According to this logic, it will be the subsidiary-driven, rather than the parent-driven, processes that are favored by competitive internal resource allocation. Therefore, we argue that both PDI and PDD will be negatively impacted, and SDE, SDR, and ASN will be positively impacted.

ASN is a particularly interesting case. The core argument is that the number of cases of charters lost to internal competitors is likely to increase, because charters are more mobile and because sister subsidiaries are more proactively developing their own capabilities. However, there is also likely to be a mitigating factor—namely, that faced with such competitive pressure, the number of cases of *atrophying* capabilities should decrease. ASN, therefore, will occur through relative—not absolute—capability depletion. To summarize:

> *Proposition 1: A competitive internal resource allocation mechanism in the MNC will have a positive impact on the likelihood of SDE, SDR, and ASN and a negative impact on the likelihood of PDI and PDD.*

A second important corporate-level factor is the level of *decentralization of decision making* (i.e., the autonomy granted to subsidiaries).

MNC researchers have given a lot of attention to the issue of subsidiary autonomy, both as a cause and a consequence of certain behaviors and operational characteristics in subsidiaries (e.g., Gates & Egelhoff, 1986; Prahalad & Doz, 1981). Here, we argue that decentralized decision making will provide subsidiary managers with the degrees of freedom necessary to take autonomous action, as well as will empower them to take charge of the destiny of their own units, both of which should positively impact the likelihood of the three subsidiary-driven processes—SDE, SDR, and ASN—while having a corresponding negative impact on the parent-driven processes—PDI and PDD.

This point is, in some ways, very obvious, but it is worth further scrutiny. The idea is that for SDE, and to a lesser degree SDR, subsidiary managers need a critical amount of autonomy, below which they will be unable to put their development plans into action. Access to seed money, for example, is a critical precondition to building new capabilities, but it may not be available in centrally controlled subsidiaries. ASN is also likely to occur more often when decision making is decentralized, because the subsidiary can become isolated relatively easily from the rest of the corporation and thus be unaware of its competitive position vis-à-vis other subsidiaries. PDI and PDD, however, can probably be undertaken more effectively when the subsidiary is tightly integrated into the corporate system, because the level of knowledge of the subsidiary's capabilities by parent company managers is much higher. PDI and PDD, thus, do not require a significant level of subsidiary autonomy. Therefore, in summary:

> *Proposition 2: A decentralization of decision making in the MNC will have a positive impact on the likelihood of SCE, SCR, and ASN and a negative impact on the likelihood of PDI or PDD.*

Finally, as we noted in the literature review, the attitude of parent company managers toward foreign investment is very important in subsidiary evolution. Here, we use the well-established concept of *parent management ethnocentrism* (Perlmutter, 1969), which represents a preoccupation with their own national identity and a belief in its superiority over others (*Gage Canadian Dictionary*, 1983). Simply put, a high level of ethnocentrism will negatively impact the likelihood of significant investments being made outside the MNC's home country, thus limiting the prospects of subsidiary evolution. This we expect to be true not only for SCE but also for PDI, because many such investments can potentially be made in the home country. SCR, by contrast, is driven purely by the subsidiary and is therefore unlikely to be impacted one way or the other by parent management ethnocentrism. For the divestment cases (ASN and PDD), the situation is a little more complex. Some of the elements of ethnocentrism (e.g., uncertainty and ignorance about a foreign country) are likely to be ameliorated once the subsidiary investment is in place, but an ethnocentric parent company is still likely to be very receptive to signals, even weak ones, that suggest that the subsidiary really does not have the necessary capabilities to fulfill its charter. Thus, ASN and PDD will be positively impacted by the existence of parent management ethnocentrism. In summary:

> *Proposition 3: An ethnocentric attitude among parent company managers will have a positive impact on the likelihood of PDD and ASN, a negative impact on the likelihood of PDI and SDE, and no impact on SDR.*

Subsidiary-level factors. In terms of the attributes of the subsidiary itself, the most critical factor affecting subsidiary evolution is its *track record*—that is, the extent to which it has delivered, over the years, results at or above the expectations of the parent company. The importance of a strong track record is immediately apparent when one does fieldwork in this area, and it is consistently mentioned in the literature as a critical parameter (e.g., Delaney, 1996; Hood et al., 1994; Morrison & Crookell, 1990). The logic, from the parent company's perspective, is that any investment decision is uncertain. By deciding in favor of a subsidiary that has already been successful in the past, parent management is reducing the extent of that uncertainty, thereby providing a strong justification for its decision should it prove, in retrospect, to be poor. Both PDI and SCE are therefore likely to be positively impacted by a strong track record, whereas PDD and ASN are likely to be negatively impacted. In the case of SCR, the process is not actively controlled by parent management, but one can argue that the development of a track record in the subsidiary is *itself* part of the charter reinforcement process. The proposition is obvious:

> Proposition 4: A strong track record will have a positive impact on the likelihood of PDI, SCE, and SCR and a negative impact on the likelihood of PDD[12] and ASN.

Earlier, we also identified the *quality of parent-subsidiary relationships* as another important factor impacting the evolution process. This term refers to the informal ties between key decision makers in the parent company and senior managers in the subsidiary. Often, subsidiary managers will be expatriates or people who have spent a period at the head office and will therefore have built up a strong network of relationships at a personal level with parent company managers. Such networks represent a social control system that can be an effective means of holding the MNC together (Bartlett & Ghoshal, 1989; Ouchi, 1980).

The quality of parent-subsidiary relationships will have a very strong impact on SCE, because it is entrepreneurial in nature. As researchers consistently have shown, initiatives are evaluated more on the qualities of the individual putting them forward than on their technical merits (Bower, 1970; Day, 1994). Thus, where the individual is well known to parent company decision makers, it follows that the initiative he or she is championing will be far better received than one put forward by a relatively unknown manager. By the same logic, the quality of the parent-subsidiary relationship will also have a positive impact on PDI, although we should note that the magnitude of this effect is likely to be rather less than the impact of the subsidiary's track record on SCE.

The quality of parent-subsidiary relationships is likely to have a correspondingly strong negative impact on the two processes of subsidiary decline (PDD and ASN). Our reasoning here is that decisions to close or divest operations inevitably become politically charged, and during such periods the personal relationships between subsidiary management and decision makers in the parent company become critical. If the relationship is good, the subsidiary manager may convince the people at headquarters that he or she deserves another chance or that another subsidiary should take the hit. Finally, SCR will not be impacted because it does not involve the parent company.

> Proposition 5: A high-quality parent-subsidiary relationship will have a positive impact on the likelihood of PDI and SCE, a negative impact on the likelihood of PDD and ASN, and no impact on SCR.

The *entrepreneurial orientation of subsidiary employees* refers to the predisposition of employees throughout the subsidiary to be alert and responsive to new opportunities (Kirzner, 1973). Here, we argue that entrepreneurial subsidiary employees are on a constant lookout for new ways to add value and that their ideas will be brought forward, first to subsidiary management and then to corporate management, for active consideration (Birkinshaw, 1997). Entrepreneurial orientation, thus, becomes a necessary, although not sufficient, condition for the SCE and SCR processes, in that they cannot transpire unless the new ways of adding value are put forward. Using the reverse logic, we predict that the absence of an entrepreneurial orientation in subsidiary employees will breed an environment in which capabilities atrophy and, therefore, that an entrepreneurial orientation will have a negative impact on ASN. PDI and PDD, in contrast, we predict to be relatively unaffected by the entrepreneurial orientation of subsidiary employees, because they are initiated by the parent company.[13]

> Proposition 6: The entrepreneurial orientation of subsidiary employees will have a positive impact on the likelihood of SCE and SCR, a negative impact on the likelihood of ASN, and no impact on PDI and PDD.

Host-country-level factors. Propositions 7 through 10 involve the various characteristics of

---

[12] There is one mitigating factor here—namely, that a very poorly performing subsidiary cannot easily be sold, whereas a strong performer will fetch a high price. Thus, a very weak performer may actually be fixed rather than sold, depending on a host of other factors.

[13] Again, though, it is possible to suggest counterexamples, such as a parent company that invests in a subsidiary because it thinks subsidiary management will run with a high-risk/high-reward venture.

the host country market. The *dynamism of the local business environment* refers to the extent and quality of the interaction between competing and complementary firms in that environment. Using Porter's (1990) diamond framework, we define the dynamism of the local business environment in terms of demand conditions, the existence of related and supporting industries, strong factor endowments, and competition.[14] Our argument is that a dynamic local business environment provides the stimuli for upgrading the subsidiary's capabilities in much the same way that internal competition does, for the subsidiary reacts to competitive moves by other companies and sharpens its capabilities in line with the expectations of local customers and suppliers.

As a result, we see SCE and SCR positively impacted by local dynamism, whereas ASN is likely to occur through a *lack* of local dynamism. The parent-driven processes—PDI and PDD—are likely to be impacted rather less directly by the dynamism of the local business environment because such stimuli are, by their nature, local (Sölvell & Zander, 1998). However, it seems likely that there will be a small effect on the parent company that is transmitted *through* the subsidiary so that PDI will be positively impacted by the dynamism of the local business environment and PDD will be negatively impacted.

> Proposition 7: The dynamism of the local business environment will have a positive impact on the likelihood of PDI, SCE, and SCR and a negative impact on the likelihood of PDD and ASN.

The extent of *host government support* has a substantial impact on subsidiary evolution, as the literature review indicated. Even in today's almost free-trade world, host governments are still able to offer direct financial incentives for foreign investment, as well as a host of indirect incentives, such as soft loans, personnel training, and infrastructural support. In addition, host government agencies can help MNCs to identify and evaluate potential sites and introduce prospective partners.

---

[14] Porter (1990) was concerned primarily with leading-edge industry clusters, but we note that these four sets of factors can be used to assess the dynamism of any business environment.

We argue that host government support is likely to have a very strong impact in the case of PDI, primarily because most large, job-creating investments are of this type, and it is them that local politicians care most about. It will have an equally strong but negative impact in cases of subsidiary decline (PDD and ASN), in that government representatives will lobby hard with the MNC to reverse or ameliorate the decision to divest a subsidiary (even though, in our experience, such efforts rarely do more than delay the inevitable).

In the cases of SCE and SCR, we see host governments having a lesser, but not trivial, role. These processes are not contestable to the same extent that new investments are, but the increasing effort that many investment agencies are putting into after-care programs is evidence that many host governments believe they *can* influence SCE and SCR. Thus, we predict a small positive impact for SCE and SCR.

> Proposition 8: The support of the host government will have a positive impact on the likelihood of PDI, SCE, and SCR and a negative impact on the likelihood of PDD and ASN.

Finally, we consider together two further aspects of the host country: the *strategic importance of the country* to the MNC and the *relative cost of factor inputs*. In a global business environment MNCs weigh—at least implicitly—the relative pros and cons of a large number of possible locations for major investments and divestments. The above are two of the critical factors in any such decision. Strategic importance refers to the extent to which a competitive position in that country affects the MNC's worldwide competitive position. Relative cost of factor inputs is simply an assessment of all the major cost elements of the investment that are locally sourced.

In the case of PDI, then, strategic importance and relative cost of factor inputs are critical factors so that a new investment will tend to gravitate, ceteris paribus, toward the more strategically important country and the country with lower factor input costs. Equally, the case of PDD will likely include a consideration of the same set of factors. For SCE and ASN, however, the situation is more equivocal. One could argue that SCE and ASN will *not* be impacted substantially by these two sets of factors, in that they represent judgments on the subsidiary's management and their existing capabilities and not on the country per se, but, at the same time, it seems likely that such factors will inevitably find their way into the parent company managers' assessments and, hence, their decisions on whether to extend or reduce the subsidiary's charter.

Thus, we predict a positive impact for both on SCE and negative impact for both on ASN. SCR, however, because it does not involve parent company management in any significant way, is unlikely to be impacted one way or the other by the strategic importance of the country or the relative cost of factor inputs. To summarize:

> *Proposition 9: The strategic importance of the host country will have a positive impact on the likelihood of PDI and SCE, a negative impact on the likelihood of PDD and ASN, and no impact on SCR.*

> *Proposition 10: The relative cost of factor inputs in the host country will have a positive impact on the likelihood of PDD and SCE, a negative impact on the likelihood of PDI and ASN, and no impact on SCR.*

CONCLUDING COMMENTS

In this article we had three broad objectives. The first was simply to document and organize the rather fragmented body of literature on subsidiary evolution, the second to examine the phenomenon of subsidiary evolution using a dynamic capabilities perspective, and the third to put forward five generic processes of subsidiary evolution and identify those contextual factors expected to impact each one.

The dynamic capabilities perspective on subsidiary evolution raises two important theoretical issues that should be briefly addressed. First, it implies a much more fluid system than that suggested by traditional models of the MNC, in that charters are mobile and subsidiary companies are competing for them in an internal market system. This approach is consistent with the network perspective of Ghoshal and Bartlett (1991) and Hedlund (1986), but it also takes things further by specifying the processes through which charter changes occur. Second, it hints at one of the weaknesses of the resource-

based view of the firm—namely, its lack of consideration of the internal workings of the large firm. We are not suggesting that the resource-based view needs to be modified as such, because the subsidiary unit can be modeled readily in the same way that the firm is, but it seems clear that much more attention needs to be paid in future to the ways that capabilities are developed at a subfirm level and then disseminated or transferred within the firm, rather than just focusing on firm-level capabilities. Some researchers have already begun to address these issues (e.g., Kogut & Zander, 1992; Szulanski, 1996).

We see two principal limitations to our theoretical development. First, the model does not deal explicitly with merger and acquisition. If we take a case such as the Asea–Brown Boveri merger, it is clear that the assignment of charters within the merged company was a one-time, top-down process that was undertaken with regard to a host of strategic and political factors, as well as a consideration of where the appropriate capabilities were. This fits broadly within the head-office-driven investment process, but it represents an unusual case, because new capabilities are "appended" to the subsidiary rather than grown incrementally along an existing trajectory. Second, we have focused on wholly owned subsidiaries, rather than hybrid cases, such as joint ventures. The critical difference between the two cases, obviously, is that a joint venture has two parents, so it would be potentially quite easy to apply the same principles of capability development and charter change to joint venture companies. Indeed, from our reading of the literature, it is apparent that joint ventures go through parent-driven and subsidiary-driven phases of development that are typically part of an overall process of evolution toward higher-value-added activities (Doz, 1996; Ring & Van de Ven, 1994). It is also likely that the analytical approach adopted here could be applied to specific units or divisions within the firm, rather than thinking in terms of foreign subsidiaries as a special case.

What are the managerial implications of this study? At this stage of theory development, it is inappropriate to be too specific about the managerial consequences of our thinking, but a few issues can be highlighted nonetheless. For subsidiary managers, the primary message is that attention should be paid to the capabilities of the subsidiary. Capabilities need to be sharpened and upgraded in the face of competition from other subsidiaries as well as external firms, and new opportunities need to be proactively sought out in areas that are close to the existing strengths of the subsidiary and that are aligned with the priorities of the MNC as a whole. A second message is that the subsidiary appears to need a certain level of decision-making autonomy to be able to pursue charter-enhancing and -reinforcement initiatives. This autonomy has to be earned through a strong track record and relationships with parent company managers—not taken unilaterally. For head-office managers, the message is that competitive resource allocation procedures and the locus of decision making should be considered carefully as mechanisms for improving the MNC's ability to allocate charters to the appropriate subsidiaries. There are also interesting implications in terms of the mix of subsidiary managers (e.g., entrepreneurs versus risk-averse managers) that the parent company should select to keep the subsidiary's options open in the future. We are a long way from prescribing any particular courses of action, but this article highlights the questions that need to be asked.

In conclusion, we believe that the phenomenon of subsidiary evolution has considerable potential as an area for future research. There is a need for clinical studies of subsidiary evolution and more detailed examination of various aspects of the phenomenon, such as the interplay between parent and subsidiary management and the impact of host country policies on subsidiary evolution. Finally, there may also be important theoretical implications for the concepts developed here, both in terms of the role of the subsidiary in the MNC and for the theory of the MNC itself. Although it is too soon to predict how such extensions will transpire, our hope is that this article provides a grounding of theoretical perspectives and a framework of ideas around which subsequent studies can be built.

REFERENCES

Agarwal, S., & Ramaswami, S. 1992. Choice of foreign market entry mode: Impact of ownership, location and internalization factors. *Journal of International Business Studies,* 23: 1–28.

Aharoni, Y. 1966. *The foreign investment decision process.* Boston: Harvard Business School Press.

Almor, T., & Hirsch, S. 1995. Outsiders' response to Europe 1992: Theoretical considerations and empirical evidence. *Journal of International Business Studies,* 26: 223–239.

Amit, R., & Schoemaker, P. 1993. Strategic assets and organizational rent. *Strategic Management Journal,* 14: 33–46.

Andersson, U., & Johanson, J. 1996. Subsidiary embeddedness and its implications for integration in the MNC. *Proceedings of the European International Business Association:* 235–256.

Barney, J. 1991. Firm resources and sustained competitive advantage. *Journal of Management,* 17: 99–120.

Bartlett, C. A., & Ghoshal, S. 1986. Tap your subsidiaries for global reach. *Harvard Business Review,* 64(6): 87–94.

Bartlett, C. A., & Ghoshal, S. 1989. *Managing across borders: The transnational solution.* Boston: Harvard Business School Press.

Behrman, J. N., & Fisher, W. A. 1980. *Overseas R&D activities of transnational companies.* Cambridge, MA: Oelgeschlager, Gunn and Hain.

Birkinshaw, J. M. 1995. *Entrepreneurship in multinational corporations: The initiative process in Canadian subsidiaries.* Unpublished doctoral dissertation, Western Business School, University of Western Ontario, London, Ontario.

Birkinshaw, J. M. 1996. How subsidiary mandates are gained and lost. *Journal of International Business Studies,* 27: 467–496.

Birkinshaw, J. M. 1997. Entrepreneurship in multinational corporations: The characteristics of subsidiary initiatives. *Strategic Management Journal,* 18: 207–229.

Birkinshaw, J. M., & Morrison, A. 1995. Configurations of strategy and structure in subsidiaries of multinational corporations. *Journal of International Business Studies,* 26: 729–754.

Birkinshaw, J. M., & Ridderstråle, J. In press. Fighting the corporate immune system: Peripheral initiatives in large and complex organizations. *International Business Review.*

Bishop, P., & Crookell, H. H. 1986. Specialization in Canadian subsidiaries. In D. G. McFetridge (Ed.), *Canadian industry in transition:* 305–385. Toronto: University of Toronto Press.

Boddewyn, J. 1979. Foreign divestment: Magnitude and factors. *Journal of International Business Studies,* 10(3): 21–26.

Boddewyn, J. 1983. Foreign and domestic divestment and investment decisions: Like or unlike? *Journal of International Business Studies,* 14(3): 23–35.

Bower, J. L. 1970. *Managing the resource allocation process.* Homewood, IL: Irwin.

Burgelman, R. A. 1983a. A process model of internal corporate venturing in the diversified major firm. *Administrative Science Quarterly,* 28: 223–244.

Burgelman, R. A. 1983b. A model of the interaction of strategic behavior, corporate context and the concept of strategy. *Academy of Management Review,* 8: 61–70.

Burgelman, R. A. 1991. Intraorganizational ecology of strategy making and organizational adaptation: Theory and field research. *Organization Science,* 2: 239–262.

Burgelman, R. A. 1996. A process model of strategic business exit: Implications for an evolutionary perspective on strategy. *Strategic Management Journal,* 17: 193–214.

Cavusgil, S. T. 1980. On the internationalization process of the firm. *European Research,* 8: 273–281.

Chang, S.-J. 1995. International expansion strategy of Japanese firms: Capability building through sequential entry. *Academy of Management Journal,* 38: 383–407.

Chang, S.-J. 1996. An evolutionary perspective on diversification and corporate restructuring: Entry, exit and economic performance during 1981–1989. *Strategic Management Journal,* 17: 587–612.

Child, J. 1972. Organization structure, environment and performance: The role of strategic choice. *Sociology,* 6: 1–22.

Clarke, I. 1985. *The spatial organization of multinational corporations.* London: Croom Helm.

Crookell, H. H. 1986. Specialization and international competitiveness. In H. Etemad & L. S. Dulude (Eds.), *Managing the multinational subsidiary:* 102–111. London: Croom Helm.

Cyert, R., & March, J. G. 1963. *A behavioral theory of the firm.* Englewood Cliffs, NJ: Prentice-Hall.

Day, D. 1994. Raising radicals: Different processes for championing innovative corporate ventures. *Organization Science,* 5: 148–172.

Delaney, E. 1996. Strategic development of multinational subsidiaries in Ireland. In J. Birkinshaw & N. Hood (Eds.), *Multinational corporate evolution and subsidiary development:* 239–267. London: Macmillan.

Dicken, P. 1976. Geographical perspectives on United States investment in the United Kingdom. *Environment and Planning,* 8: 685–705.

Dierickx, I., & Cool, K. 1989. Asset stock accumulation and sustainability of competitive advantage. *Management Science,* 35: 1504–1513.

DiMaggio, P. J., & Powell, W. W. 1983. The iron cage revisited: Institutional isomorphism and collective rationality in organizational fields. *American Sociological Review,* 48: 147–160.

Doty, D. H., & Glick, W. H. 1994. Typologies as a unique form of theory building: Toward improved understanding and modeling. *Academy of Management Review,* 19: 230–251.

Doz, Y. L. 1996. The evolution of cooperation in strategic alliances: Initial conditions or learning processes? *Strategic Management Journal,* 17: 55–83.

Dunning, J. H. 1981. *International production and the multinational enterprise.* London: Allen & Unwin.

Dunning, J. H. 1986. The investment cycle revisited. *Weltwirtschaftliches Archiv,* 122: 667–677.

Dunning, J. H. 1993. *Multinational enterprises and the global economy.* Wokingham, England: Addison-Wesley.

Emerson, R. M. 1962. Power-dependence relations. *American Sociological Review,* 27: 31–41.

Forsgren, M., Holm, U., & Johanson, J. 1992. Internationalization of the second degree: The emergence of European-based centres in Swedish firms. In S. Young & J. Hamill (Eds.), *Europe and the multinationals:* 235–253. London: Edward Elgar.

Forsgren, M., Holm, U., & Johanson, J. 1995. Division headquarters go abroad—A step in the internationalization of the multinational corporation. *Journal of Management Studies,* 32: 475–491.

Forsgren, M., & Pahlberg, C. 1992. Subsidiary influence and autonomy in international firms. *International Business Review,* 1(3): 41–51.

Gage Canadian Dictionary. 1983. Toronto: Gage Educational Publishing Company.

Galunic, D. C. 1996. Recreating divisional domains: Intracorporate evolution and the multibusiness firm. In B. Keys & L. N. Dosier (Eds.), *Proceedings of the Academy of Management:* 219–224.

Galunic, D. C., & Eisenhardt, K. M. 1996. The evolution of intracorporate domains: Divisional charter losses in high-technology, multidivisional corporations. *Organization Science,* 7: 255–282.

Gates, S. R., & Egelhoff, W. G. 1986. Centralization in headquarters-subsidiary relationships. *Journal of International Business Studies,* 17: 71–92.

Ghauri, P. 1992. New structures in MNCs based in small countries: A network approach. *European Management Journal,* 10: 357–364.

Ghoshal, S., & Bartlett, C. A. 1991. The multinational corporation as an interorganizational network. *Academy of Management Review,* 15: 603–625.

Ghoshal, S., & Nohria, N. 1989. Internal differentiation within multinational corporations. *Strategic Management Journal,* 10: 323–337.

Gupta, A. K., & Govindarajan, V. 1991. Knowledge flows and the structure of control within multinational corporations. *Academy of Management Review,* 16: 768–792.

Gupta, A. K., & Govindarajan, V. 1994. Organizing for knowledge within MNCs. *International Business Review,* 3: 443–457.

Hagström, P. 1994. *The 'wired' MNC.* Stockholm: Institute of International Business.

Håkanson, L., & Zander, U. 1986. *Managing international research and development.* Stockholm: Sveriges Mekanförbund.

Halal, W. 1994. From hierarchy to enterprise: Internal markets are the new foundation of management. *Academy of Management Executive,* 8(4): 69–83.

Hamel, G., & Prahalad, C. K. 1985. Do you really have a global strategy? *Harvard Business Review,* 63(4): 139–145.

Hannan, M., & Freeman, J. 1977. The population ecology of

organizations. *American Journal of Sociology*, 82: 929–964.

Harrigan, K. R. 1984. Innovation within overseas subsidiaries. *Journal of Business Strategy*, 5: 47–53.

Haspeslagh, P. C., & Jemison, D. B. 1991. *Managing acquisitions: Creating value through corporate renewal*. New York: Free Press.

Hatch Report. 1979. *Strengthening Canada abroad. Industry, trade and commerce*. Ottawa, Ontario: Export Promotion Review Committee.

Hedlund, G. 1986. The hypermodern MNC: A heterarchy? *Human Resource Management*, 25: 9–36.

Holm, U., Johanson, J., & Thilenius, P. 1995. Headquarters' knowledge of subsidiary network contexts in the multinational corporation. *International Studies of Management and Organization*, 25(1–2): 97–120.

Hood, N., & Young, S. 1983. *Multinational investment strategies in the British Isles*. London: Her Majesty's Stationery Office (HMSO).

Hood, N., Young, S., & Lal, D. 1994. Strategic evolution within Japanese manufacturing plants in Europe. UK evidence. *International Business Review*, 3(2): 97–122.

Huber, G. 1991. Organizational learning: The contributing processes and the literatures. *Organization Science*, 2: 88–115.

Jarillo, J.-C., & Martinez, J. I. 1990. Different roles for subsidiaries: The case of multinational corporations. *Strategic Management Journal*, 11: 501–512.

Johanson, J., & Mattson, L. G. 1988. Internationalisation in industrial systems—A network approach. In N. Hood & J. E. Vahlne (Eds.), *Strategies in global competition*: 287–314. London: Croom Helm.

Johanson, J., & Vahlne, J.-E. 1977. The internationalization process of the firm—A model of knowledge development and increasing foreign market commitments. *Journal of International Business Studies*, 8: 23–32.

Kirzner, I. 1973. *Competition and entrepreneurship*, Chicago: University of Chicago Press.

Kogut, B., & Zander, U. 1992. Knowledge of the firm, combinative capabilities and the replication of technology. *Organization Science*, 3: 383–397.

Krugman, P. 1991. *Geography and trade*. Cambridge, MA: MIT Press.

Li, J. T. 1995. Foreign entry and survival: Effects of strategic choices on performance in international markets. *Strategic Management Journal*, 16: 637–655.

Lincoln, J. R., Olson, J., & Hanada, M. 1978. Cultural effects on organizational structure: The case of Japanese firms in the United States. *American Sociological Review*, 43: 829–847.

Madhok, A. 1997. Cost, value and foreign market entry mode: The transaction and the firm. *Strategic Management Journal*, 18: 39–61.

Malnight, T. 1995. Globalization of an ethnocentric firm: An evolutionary perspective. *Strategic Management Journal*, 16: 119–141.

Malnight, T. 1996. The transition from decentralized to network-based MNC structures: An evolutionary perspective. *Journal of International Business Studies*, 27: 43–66.

McNee, R. B. 1958. Functional geography of the firm with an illustrative case study from the petroleum industry. *Economic Geography*, 34: 321–337.

Meyer, J. W., & Rowan, B. 1997. Institutionalized organizations: Formal structure as myth and ceremony. *American Journal of Sociology*, 83: 340–363.

Mintzberg, H., Raisinghani, D., & Theoret, A. 1976. The structure of unstructured decision processes. *Administrative Science Quarterly*, 21: 246–274.

Morrison, A., & Crookell, H. 1990. Subsidiary strategy in a free-trade environment. *Business Quarterly*, 55(2): 33–39.

Mullor-Sebastian, A. 1983. The product life cycle theory: Empirical evidence. *Journal of International Business Studies*, 14(Winter): 95–105.

Nelson, R., & Winter, S. 1982. *An evolutionary theory of economic change*. Cambridge, MA: Harvard University Press.

Noda, T., & Bower, J. L. 1996. Strategy making as iterated processes of resource allocation. *Strategic Management Journal*, 17: 159–192.

Norton, R. D., & Rees, J. 1979. The product cycle and the spatial decentralization of American manufacturing. *Regional Studies*, 13: 141–151.

Ouchi, W. G. 1980. Market, bureaucracies and clans. *Administrative Science Quarterly*, 25: 124–141.

Ozawa, T. 1992. Foreign direct investment and economic development. *Transnational Corporations*, 1: 27–54.

Papanasstasiou, M., & Pearce, R. 1994. Determinants of the market strategies of US companies. *Journal of the Economics of Business*, 2: 199–217.

Pearce, R. D. 1989. *The internationalization of research and development by multinational enterprises*. New York: St Martin's Press.

Perlmutter, H. 1969. The tortuous evolution of the multinational corporation. *Columbia Journal of World Business*, 4: 9–18.

Penrose, E. T. 1959. *The theory of the growth of the firm*. Oxford, England: Basil Blackwell.

Pfeffer, J. R., & Salancik, G. R. 1978. *The external control of organizations*. New York: Harper & Row.

Porter, M. E. 1980. *Competitive strategy*. New York: Free Press.

Porter, M. E. 1990. *The competitive advantage of nations*. New York: Free Press.

Prahalad, C. K. 1976. *The strategic process in a multinational corporation*. Unpublished doctoral dissertation, Harvard University, Boston.

Prahalad, C. K., & Doz, Y. L. 1981. An approach to strategic control in MNCs. *Sloan Management Review*, 22(Summer): 5–13.

Ring, P. S., & Van de Ven, A. 1994. Development processes of cooperative interorganizational relationships. *Academy of Management Review,* 19: 90–118.

Ronstadt, R. C. 1977. *Research and development abroad by U.S. multinationals.* New York: Praeger.

Rosenzweig, P., & Chang, S.-J. 1995a. *An evolutionary model of the multinational corporation.* Paper presented at the annual meeting of the Academy of International Business, Seoul, Korea.

Rosenzweig, P., & Chang, S.-J. 1995b. *Sequential direct investment of European and Japanese firms in the U.S.* Paper presented at the annual meeting of the Academy of International Business, Seoul, Korea.

Rosenzweig, P., & Nohria, N. 1995. Influences on human resource management practices in multinational corporations. *Journal of International Business Studies,* 25: 229–252.

Rosenzweig, P., & Singh, J. 1991. Organizational environments and the multinational enterprise. *Academy of Management Review,* 16: 340–361.

Roth, K., & Morrison, A. 1992. Implementing global strategy: Characteristics of global subsidiary mandates. *Journal of International Business Studies,* 23: 715–736.

Rugman, A., & Verbeke, A. 1992. A note on the transnational solution and the transaction cost theory of multinational strategic management. *Journal of International Business Studies,* 23: 761–772.

Sachdev, J. C. 1976. *A framework for the planning of divestment policies for multinational companies.* Unpublished doctoral dissertation, University of Manchester, England.

Safarian, E. 1966. *Foreign ownership of Canadian industry.* Toronto: McGraw-Hill.

Science Council of Canada. 1980. *Multinationals and industrial strategy. The role of world product mandates.* Ottawa, Ontario: Science Council of Canada.

Scott, R., & Meyer, J. 1994. *Institutional environments and organizations: Structural complexity and individualism.* Beverly Hills, CA: Sage.

Sölvell, Ö., & Zander, I. 1998. International diffusion of knowledge: Isolating mechanisms and the role of the MNE. In A. D. Chandler, P. Hagström, & Ö. Sölvell (Eds.),

The dynamic firm: The role of technology, strategy, organization and regions: 402–416. Oxford, England: Oxford University Press.

Sugiura, H. 1990. How Honda localizes its global strategy. *Sloan Management Review,* 31(Fall): 77–82.

Szulanski, G. 1996. Exploring internal stickiness: Impediments to the transfer of best practices within the firm. *Strategic Management Journal,* 17(Special Issue): 27–44.

Teece, D. J., Pisano, G., & Shuen, A. 1997. Dynamic capabilities and strategic management. *Strategic Management Journal,* 18: 509–534.

Thompson, J. D. 1967. *Organizations in action.* New York: McGraw-Hill.

Vernon, R. 1966. International investments and international trade in the product cycle. *Quarterly Journal of Economics,* 80: 190–207.

Vernon, R. 1979. The product cycle in the new international environment. *The Oxford Bulletin of Economics and Statistics,* 41: 255–267.

Wernerfelt, B. 1984. A resource based view of the firm. *Strategic Management Journal,* 5: 171–180.

Westney, D. E. 1994. Institutionalization theory and the multinational corporation. In S. Ghoshal & D. E. Westney (Eds.), *Organization theory and the multinational corporation:* 53–76. New York: St Martin's Press.

White, R. E., & Poynter, T. A. 1984. Strategies for foreign-owned subsidiaries in Canada. *Business Quarterly,* 49(Summer): 59–69.

Young, S., Hood, N., & Hamill, J. 1988. *Foreign multinationals and the British economy.* London: Routledge.

Young, S., Hood, N., & Peters, E. 1994. Multinational enterprises and regional economic development. *Regional Studies,* 28: 657–677.

Young, S., McDermott, M., & Dunlop, S. 1991. The challenge of the single market. In B. Burgenmeir & J. L. Mucchelli (Eds.), *Multinationals and Europe:* 121–143. London: Routledge.

Zander, I. 1994. *The tortoise evolution of the multinational corporation.* Doctoral dissertation, Institute of International Business, Stockholm School of Economics.

Julian **Birkinshaw** is an assistant professor at the Institute of International Business, Stockholm School of Economics. He received his Ph.D. from the Richard Ivey School of Business, University of Western Ontario. His current research is concerned with the strategy and internal organization of large multinational firms.

Neil **Hood** is Professor of Business Policy and Director of the Strathclyde International Business Unit at the University of Strathclyde in Glasgow. His research concerns the strategy of multinational enterprises, globalization, and public policy issues surrounding inward investment.

[24]

Academy of Management Review
1999, Vol. 24, No. 1, 64-81.

ORGANIZATIONAL LEGITIMACY UNDER CONDITIONS OF COMPLEXITY: THE CASE OF THE MULTINATIONAL ENTERPRISE

TATIANA KOSTOVA
University of South Carolina, Columbia

SRILATA ZAHEER
University of Minnesota

We examine organizational legitimacy in the context of the multinational enterprise (MNE). After discussing three types of complexity (of the legitimating environment, the organization, and the process of legitimation) that MNEs typically face, we explore their effects on MNE legitimacy. In particular, we distinguish between the legitimacy of the MNE as a whole and that of its parts, and we develop propositions that include issues of internal versus external legitimacy and positive and negative legitimacy spillovers.

It has become a growing industry to critique Nike globally (Phil Knight, NBC Today Show, May 11, 1998).

One of the critical issues faced by multinational enterprises (MNEs) involves the establishment and maintenance of legitimacy in their multiple host environments. Instances of legitimacy problems in MNEs abound, ranging from censure of MNEs in the global media, such as that faced by Nike for its labor practices in Asia (Maitland, 1997; Marshall, 1997), to direct attacks on MNE operations, such as the destruction of Cargill's facilities in India (Dewan, 1994). In an even more extreme example, Shell was accused of conspiring with the Nigerian government to execute Ken Saro-Wiwa, who had led a campaign against its environmental practices (Newburry & Gladwin, 1997).

An examination of the MNE case suggests that not only is legitimacy a critical issue for MNEs but that current research leaves several questions on organizational legitimacy unaddressed. For instance, what exactly is the legitimacy of a complex organization such as an MNE, and where does it reside: at the level of the MNE as

We thank Eric Abrahamson, Jeff Arpan, Jean Boddewyn, Joe Galaskiewicz, Kendall Roth, Mike Russo, Aks Zaheer, the participants of the AMR theory development workshop, the participants of the Freeman International Economics Seminar at the Hubert Humphrey Institute of the University of Minnesota, and the reviewers of AMR for their comments and suggestions.

a whole or at its subunits? What constitutes the legitimating environment of an MNE operating in multiple institutional environments? What is the relationship between the overall legitimacy of the MNE and the legitimacy of its subunits? And, finally, why do MNEs find it so difficult to establish and maintain legitimacy and so often experience crises of legitimacy?

Research on organizational legitimacy (e.g., D'Aunno, Sutton, & Price, 1991; Dowling & Pfeffer, 1975; Meyer & Scott, 1983; Scott, 1987, 1995) provides us with a theoretical foundation on which to examine these questions. Scholars have defined organizational legitimacy as the acceptance of the organization by its environment and have proposed it to be vital for organizational survival and success (Dowling & Pfeffer, 1975; Hannan & Freeman, 1977; Meyer & Rowan, 1977). Institutional theorists have identified some of the determinants of organizational legitimacy and the characteristics of the legitimation process (Meyer & Rowan, 1977; Powell & DiMaggio, 1991; Scott, 1995; Selznick, 1957; Zucker, 1983), citing three sets of factors that shape organizational legitimacy: (1) the environment's institutional characteristics, (2) the organization's characteristics, and (3) the legitimation process by which the environment builds its perceptions of the organization (Hybels, 1995; Maurer, 1971).

In this article we suggest that examining the MNE case can potentially extend theories of organizational legitimacy since the MNE challenges some of the underlying assumptions behind these theories. The MNE is an organization that operates in two or more countries with multiple subunits linked through shared policies or strategy.[1] As such, MNEs introduce an element of complexity in all three factors that influence organizational legitimacy—in the legitimating environment, the organization, and the process of legitimation. We suggest that these complexities have significant implications for theories of organizational legitimacy, since they affect the nature of legitimacy, and the process of legitimation. Therefore, the MNE case can both advance our understanding of organizational legitimacy in general and shed light on the specific legitimacy-related difficulties experienced by MNEs.

Traditionally, researchers have examined legitimacy at two levels: (1) at the level of classes of organizations (Carroll & Hannan, 1989; Hannan & Freeman, 1977; Meyer & Rowan, 1977; Singh, Tucker, & House, 1986) and (2) at the organizational level (Ashforth & Gibbs, 1990; Covaleski & Dirsmith, 1988; Deephouse, 1996; Dowling & Pfeffer, 1975; Neilsen & Rao, 1987; Ritti & Silver, 1986; Suchman, 1995). Here, we adopt the latter approach and examine legitimacy at the level of the organization, which we call *organizational legitimacy*.

Organizational legitimacy can further be examined at the level of the MNE as a whole, as well as at the level of the subunit of the MNE in a particular country. The legitimacy of the MNE *as a whole* is the acceptance and/or approval of the MNE (not necessarily of any particular subunit) by its legitimating environment. For the MNE as a whole, the legitimating environment is the global "meta-environment" (Zaheer, 1995a), which consists of all of its home and host country institutional environments as well as supranational institutions, such as global me-

dia (e.g., *Financial Times* or CNN) and global activist groups (e.g., Greenpeace). The legitimacy of the MNE *subunit* is its acceptance by the specific host country institutional environment. In this article we examine both the legitimacy of the MNE as a whole and the legitimacy of the MNE subunit and discuss the relationships between them. We suggest that they are interrelated—that is, the legitimacy of the MNE as a whole is affected by the legitimacy of its subunits, and vice versa. However, MNE legitimacy may not be a simple average of the legitimacy of its subunits.

Several of our propositions are unique to the MNE because they are based on characteristics of the MNE that represent differences "in kind" from domestic organizations (Ghoshal & Westney, 1993). These propositions could be thought of as elements of *a theory of MNE legitimacy*. A few propositions, however, apply both to MNEs and to complex domestic organizations, for they are based on characteristics of the MNE that represent differences "in degree" (Ghoshal & Westney, 1993) from domestic organizations. These latter propositions are not unique to the MNE and serve, therefore, to expand our *theories of organizational legitimacy*.

We distinguish between the legitimacy of an MNE and two proximal concepts from the MNE literature: (1) overcoming entry barriers and (2) cultural adaptation. While a lack of legitimacy may act as a barrier to entry, legitimacy issues go beyond market entry and can become salient at any point in a company's history, as we have seen in such cases as Shell and Nike. Further, although cultural adaptation of an organization to a particular host country may contribute to its legitimacy, it is neither a necessary nor a sufficient condition for legitimacy because of the many other factors involved, including the nature of the product, and regulatory issues. In addition, legitimacy is socially constructed. Thus, there may not be a one-to-one correspondence between an organization's cultural adaptation and the way it is perceived by the environment. Therefore, it is possible for an MNE to be culturally adapted and still lack legitimacy in a particular environment.

In this article we also do not specifically examine the political processes or the negotiations between MNEs and host governments, as many scholars in international business have

---

[1] Currently, the most accepted definition of the MNE is that it is a specific organizational form that

comprises entities in two or more countries, regardless of legal form and fields of activity of those entities, which operates under a system of decision-making permitting coherent policies and a common strategy through one or more decision-making centers, in which the entities are so linked, by ownership or otherwise, that one or more of them may be able to exercise a significant influence over the activities of the others, and in particular, to share knowledge, resources, and responsibilities with others (Ghoshal & Westney, 1993: 4).

done (Behrman & Grosse, 1990; Doz, 1986; Doz & Prahalad, 1980; Dunning, 1993; Fagre & Wells, 1982; Kobrin, 1987; Lecraw, 1984; Murtha & Lenway, 1994; Vernon, 1971), which could affect the legitimacy of firms directly—in the regulatory domain—or indirectly—through the social construction engaged in by political interest groups. We focus, instead, on the background factors that could facilitate or hinder such firmstate negotiation processes.

In summary, we address the extent of the challenge encountered by MNEs in establishing and maintaining organizational legitimacy in the face of complexity in the environment, in the organization, and in the process of legitimation. As an illustration of the issues MNEs can face in their quest for legitimacy, we start with a brief description of Cargill's problems in India and use this case (and others) to discuss the criticality of legitimacy for MNEs, as well as the effects of complexity on legitimacy. We then develop propositions and conclude with a discussion of implications for theory and practice.

CARGILL IN INDIA

Cargill, Inc.,[2] is perhaps the world's largest private agricultural company, with 65,000 employees and annual sales of over $50 billion, as well as a presence in over 65 countries. Cargill entered the Indian market initially to create and distribute new high-quality hybrid seeds in Bangalore in South India, and subsequently to build a salt extraction and processing facility in western India. Its establishment in India has been marked by a series of crises that illustrate the critical importance of establishing and maintaining legitimacy for MNEs and their subunits.

Briefly, Cargill's seeds project in Bangalore experienced difficulties from the very beginning. This project was a response to the Indian government's new Seed Policy, introduced in September 1988, which sought "to upgrade seeds and provide the Indian farmer with the best planting material in the world so as to optimize his output" (Pania, 1992: 82). The company, at its inception, encountered substantial resistance from local farmers, encouraged by influential local politicians and intellectuals

who opposed the project on the grounds that it was the first step toward a "new colonization" of India by the West (Dewan, 1994). The farmers claimed that the seeds project would take away their traditional self-sufficiency in seed production, leave them dependent on multinational firms, and lead to their financial distress and economic exploitation—apart from destroying their traditional way of life. The tension increased to the point that some of Cargill's offices and warehouses in India were vandalized and burned down by angry farmers.

Meanwhile, Cargill had launched a project in Kandla, in western India, to build a 1-million-ton export-oriented salt extraction and processing facility. This project also experienced legitimacy problems. Various local groups vociferously opposed the project, ranging from environmentalists to local salt producers, who felt threatened by multinational competition, to politicians, who categorized this project as another step toward a neocolonization of India. For their arguments, these groups drew from history and from the symbolism of Mahatma Gandhi's protest march against the salt tax imposed by the British in 1942. The politicians attempted to suggest that foreign colonizers, once again, were threatening the country's economic freedom. "Salt, once the symbol of our freedom movement, is today a pointer to our economic serfdom" (V. P. Singh, Member of Parliament, quoted in Setalvad, 1993: 85). Although Cargill took several steps to moderate the criticism—for example, by moving toward more labor-intensive technology that would protect employment—it finally withdrew from this project. We believe that the legitimacy problems faced in India were not unrelated to Cargill's withdrawal.

THEORETICAL BACKGROUND AND PROPOSITIONS

Institutional theory suggests that organizational legitimacy is shaped by three sets of factors: (1) the characteristics of the institutional environment, (2) the organization's characteristics and actions, and (3) the legitimation process by which the environment builds its perceptions of the organization (e.g., Hybels, 1995, and Maurer, 1971). In this section we use the MNE to discuss how organizational legitimacy is affected when there is complexity in these three sets of factors. We suggest that a higher level of complexity in

---

[2] This section draws entirely on publicly available documentation and video material.

any of these factors—the institutional environment, the organization, and the process of legitimation—makes it more difficult for organizations to establish and maintain their legitimacy. We develop formal propositions on the relationship between complexity in these factors and the legitimacy challenges faced by MNEs and illustrate these propositions with examples from Cargill and other firms.

Organizational theorists long have recognized that *institutional environments* are complex and fragmented since they consist of multiple task environments (Galbraith, 1973; Lawrence & Lorsch, 1967; Thompson, 1967), multiple institutional "pillars" (Scott, 1995), multiple resource providers (Pfeffer & Salancik, 1978), and multiple stakeholders (Evan & Freeman, 1988). Drawing from this research and from the MNE case, we suggest that the complexity of the institutional environment is reflected in two major aspects. First, institutional environments are fragmented and composed of different *domains* reflecting different types of institutions: regulatory, cognitive, and normative (Scott, 1995). Second, MNEs conduct operations in *multiple countries* that may vary with respect to their institutional environments and, thus, are exposed to multiple sources of authority (Sundaram & Black, 1992).

Organizational researchers also have noted that *organizations* themselves can be complex and fragmented, for they may consist of multiple subunits with varying levels of interdependence and independence (Ghoshal & Bartlett, 1990; Lawrence & Lorsch, 1967). This type of complexity is particularly apparent in MNEs where the organization is fragmented not only by function or task but also by geographical region and location. As a result, each of the different subunits of the MNE faces its own host institutional environments, which vary across countries with respect to legitimacy requirements. In addition, organizations form their own internal institutional environments with their own legitimacy requirements over time (Selznick, 1957). Thus, each organizational subunit of the MNE is faced with the task of establishing and maintaining both *external* legitimacy in its host environment and *internal* legitimacy within the MNE (Rosenzweig & Singh, 1991; Westney, 1993).

Finally, research on the interaction between organizations and the environment from the social construction and symbolic interactionism perspectives (Berger & Luckman, 1967; Stryker & Statham, 1985) suggests that this interaction is a complex social and cognitive process, subject to bounded rationality. Therefore, the *process of legitimation*, which involves the continuous testing and redefinition of the legitimacy of the organization through ongoing interaction with the environment (Baum & Oliver, 1991), is likely to be a boundedly rational process. The implications of the complexity of this process for organizational legitimacy become particularly apparent in the MNE, since in this case both the organization and the legitimating environment may lack the information and the cognitive structures required to understand, interpret, and evaluate each other. Table 1 presents a summary of the types of complexities that emerge in the three factors that influence legitimacy when one examines the MNE case, and it briefly summarizes the consequences of these complexities for organizational legitimacy.

In the rest of this section we develop propositions that address the ease or difficulty of establishing and maintaining legitimacy at two levels of analysis: (1) the MNE as a whole and (2) the MNE subunit. We consider the establishment of legitimacy as particularly relevant for the MNE subunit when it enters a new country. Maintaining legitimacy, however, is relevant both for the MNE as a whole and for the MNE subunit. We also discuss the extent to which each of the propositions is unique to the MNE or is applicable to all organizations. A summary of the propositions is graphically presented in Figure 1.

Environmental Complexity and Legitimacy

The complexity of the MNE environment is reflected in the multiple domains of the institutional environment and in the multiplicity of institutional environments faced by MNEs.

Multiple domains of the institutional environment. Organizational theorists have suggested that institutional environments consist of a variety of institutions, including regulations, cultural norms, educational systems, and so on. Researchers have suggested that there are different types of legitimacy that reflect the different types of institutions operating in the environment, such as sociopolitical, cognitive, and pragmatic legitimacy, among others (Aldrich & Fiol, 1994; Boddewyn, 1995; Hannan & Carroll, 1992; Suchman, 1995). Although we acknowledge

TABLE 1
Legitimacy-Related Complexities Faced by MNEs

Factors Influencing Legitimacy	Types of Complexity	Description	Effects on Legitimacy
Institutional environment	Multiple domains of the institutional environment	Institutional environments consist of three types of domains—the regulatory, the cognitive, and the normative—all of which influence legitimacy.	The tacitness of the cognitive and normative domains presents a particular challenge to MNEs as they seek legitimacy.
	Many and varied country institutional environments	MNEs face at least as many different institutional environments as the number of countries in which they operate, since institutions tend to be country specific. Their number and variety pose specific challenges to MNE legitimacy.	The larger the number of countries, the larger the variance in the legitimacy requirements that MNEs have to deal with. However, the larger the number of countries, the more likely that the organization has developed competence in dealing with different institutional environments.
	Institutional distance between home and host environments	This is the difference or similarity between the regulatory, cognitive, and normative institutional environments of the home and the host countries of an MNE.	The greater the institutional distance, the more difficult it will be for the MNE to understand the host environment and its legitimacy requirements. Further, the greater the institutional distance, the higher the need will be to adapt organizational practices to meet host country legitimacy requirements.
Organization	MNE subunits face two institutional environments: (1) the external host country environment and (2) the internal environment of the MNE.	Legitimacy is required in both institutional environments since the survival of the MNE subunit is contingent on support from the parent company and from the host country.	Tension between internal and external legitimacy requirements can make achieving external legitimacy difficult for a subunit.
Process of legitimation	Bounded rationality and the liability of foreignness	Owing to the social and cognitive nature of the legitimation process, the acceptance of an MNE subunit is affected by the host environment's perception of and attitude toward foreign firms.	Foreignness presents challenges to legitimacy because of (1) the lack of information about the MNE on behalf of the host environment, (2) the use of stereotypes and different standards in judging foreign firms, and (3) the use of MNEs as targets for attacks by interest groups in the host country.
	Legitimacy spillovers from outside and within the organization	Owing to the bounded rationality of the legitimation process, the legitimacy of a particular unit is not independent of all other units to which it is cognitively related.	Under conditions of bounded rationality, the environment makes sense of the legitimacy of a given unit based on the legitimacy of other similar units—for example, other units of the same organization or classes of organizations to which the focal unit belongs.

FIGURE 1
Complexity and MNE Legitimacy: Summary of Propositions

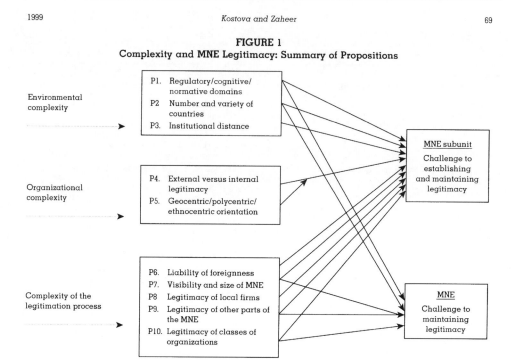

the existence of multiple domains of the institutional environment, in this article we treat the legitimacy of an organization or of an organizational subunit as holistic in nature (i.e., there is one overall legitimacy of an organizational unit), even though it may be affected by the different domains of the institutional environment in which the organization functions.

We draw from institutional theory (Meyer & Rowan, 1977; Scott, 1995; Zucker, 1983) to suggest a set of institutional domains based on the three pillars of institutional environments suggested by Scott (1995): the regulatory, the cognitive, and the normative. The *regulatory* pillar is composed of regulatory institutions—that is, the rules and laws that exist to ensure stability and order in societies (North, 1990; Streek & Schmitter, 1985; Williamson, 1975, 1991). Organizations have to comply with the explicitly stated requirements of the regulatory system to be legitimate, although they do have the ability, particularly in the long run, to influence the regulatory domain through interest intermediation (Murtha & Lenway, 1994).

The *cognitive* pillar draws from social psychology (Berger & Luckman, 1967) and the cognitive school of institutional theory (Meyer & Rowan, 1977; Zucker, 1983). Organizations have to conform to or be consistent with established cognitive structures in society to be legitimate. In other words, what is legitimate is what has a "taken for granted" status (Aldrich & Fiol, 1994; Suchman, 1995) in society.

The *normative* pillar goes beyond regulatory rules and cognitive structures to the domain of social values (Selznick, 1957). Organizational legitimacy, in this view, accrues from congruence between the values pursued by the organization and wider societal values (Parsons, 1960). It is "the degree of cultural support for an organization," which, presumably, will result from such congruence in values (Meyer & Scott, 1983: 201).

The three domains are not necessarily independent. Values, for instance, may drive cognitive categorization and, in turn, influence and be influenced by regulation. The cognitive and normative domains emerge through processes of education and socialization, and the regulatory domain, in particular, is influenced by governments and the interest intermediation process (Murtha & Lenway, 1994).

Cargill's problems with the salt project illustrate a variety of legitimacy issues associated with these domains, such as the cognitive issue of Cargill being a privately held multinational and the symbolic meaning of salt in India, the normative issue of protecting manual labor and traditional agricultural lifestyles, and the regulatory issue of whether Cargill could be given permission to operate on land owned by the Port Authority of Kandla. Inability to meet the minimum requirements for legitimacy on any of these dimensions could jeopardize the overall legitimacy of the project, and of the firm, in India.

The three domains of country institutional environments—the regulatory, cognitive, and normative—differ in their degree of formalization and tacitness—that is, the degree to which they are explicitly codified and the ease with which observers (especially outside observers such as a foreign company) can make sense of them. The regulatory domain is perhaps the easiest to observe, understand, and interpret correctly because it is formalized in laws, rules, and regulations. Compared to the regulatory domain, the normative domain is more tacit and part of the "deep structures" of a country (Gersick, 1990). It is, therefore, more difficult to sense and to interpret, particularly for an outsider. The cognitive domain perhaps lies between the regulatory and the normative domains, as to the degree to which it can be observed and interpreted correctly.

This suggests that legitimacy in the normative and cognitive domains, rather than in the regulatory domain, might pose a more difficult challenge for MNEs. After an MNE subunit has conducted operations in a host environment for some time, it may become easier for it to make sense of local cognitive and normative institutions. So will the hiring of "locals" to manage the operation (rather than posting expatriates), or working with a local partner. However, we believe that the cognitive and normative domains will always be relatively more challenging than the regulatory domain to MNE subunits trying to establish or maintain their legitimacy.

In both of Cargill's projects in India, for instance, there were many deeply embedded social values that played a role in the legitimating

process, which may not have been that transparent to an MNE coming into the country. These hidden values were reflected in such comments as "agriculture is not a market, it is a lifestyle" and "a self-sufficient community will become wage-laborers of the multinationals"—expressions by some of the groups opposing the seeds project (Dewan, 1994). Cargill was able to deal with the more explicit regulatory requirements (e.g., those related to environmental issues), but it appeared to have had much greater difficulty in understanding and dealing with the normative domain. We propose, therefore:

> *Proposition 1: The cognitive and normative domains of the institutional environment will present a greater challenge to MNE subunits in establishing their legitimacy, and to MNEs and MNE subunits in maintaining legitimacy, compared to the regulatory domain.*

Multiplicity of institutional environments. By definition, MNEs face multiple country institutional environments, each with its own set of regulatory, cognitive, and normative domains (Westney, 1993). The structure and the composition of these institutions, and their legitimacy requirements, typically vary across national environments (Kogut, 1991; Kostova, 1996). For example, most rules and regulations tend to be country specific, since they are created by governments and are often the outcome of local political processes. So are the cognitive and normative institutions (the shared social knowledge and the values, beliefs, and social norms), which are shaped through the educational system and through processes of social interaction, typically within national borders. Cargill, with operations in 65 countries, has faced 65 unique sets of regulatory, cognitive, and normative institutions that it has had to get to know, understand, and take into account in its operations. Such multiplicity and variety in the environments in which they operate clearly differentiate MNEs from domestic firms (Sundaram & Black, 1992).

In addition to the *number* of countries in which an MNE operates, its legitimacy is also likely to be affected by the extent of *variety* across these environments. The more similar the institutional profiles[3] (Kostova, 1997) of the multiple countries in which it operates, the easier it will be for the MNE to make sense of all of its environments and to respond appropriately to their legitimacy requirements. For example, MNEs operating in a set of countries in Asia alone will find it easier to establish their legitimacy in all of those countries than will MNEs operating in countries with different institutional profiles—say, in a set that includes Asian and European countries. In brief, the legitimacy of a given organization is "negatively affected by the number of different authorities sovereign over it and by the diversity or inconsistency of their accounts of how it is to function" (Meyer & Scott, 1983: 202).

As suggested by institutional theorists, organizations may achieve legitimacy by becoming "isomorphic" with the institutional environment—that is, by adopting organizational forms, structures, policies, and practices that are *similar* to the ones institutionalized in their environment (DiMaggio & Powell, 1983; Meyer & Rowan, 1977). In an MNE, given the multiplicity and variety of institutional environments and the cross-country differences between these environments, achieving legitimacy through isomorphism becomes a difficult, if not impossible, task (Westney, 1993). However, MNEs do manage to achieve legitimacy in seemingly conflicting multiple institutional environments; they do not necessarily adapt to the local environments in such cases but, rather, manage their legitimacy through negotiation with their multiple environments (Doz & Prahalad, 1980; Fagre & Wells, 1982; Lecraw, 1984; Oliver, 1991).

Operating in a large number of countries and a wide variety of environments suggests that a firm has extensive organizational experience in dealing with legitimacy issues and expertise in scanning different institutional environments, identifying important legitimating actors, making sense of their legitimacy requirements, and negotiating with them. It also suggests that the firm may have significant bargaining power with regard to the states and governments it deals with (Kobrin, 1987; Lecraw, 1984), particularly in the regulatory domain. Thus, large

MNEs with mature international operations facing dozens of institutional environments may find it easier to gain legitimacy compared to smaller or newer organizations that lack the organizational capability required for *establishing* legitimacy. However, operating in a multiplicity of environments may also present a challenge to *maintaining* legitimacy, because it makes it more likely that the firm faces legitimacy issues in one or the other of those environments, and this illegitimacy spills over to the rest of the MNE.

We suggest, therefore, that the effects on legitimacy of the number and variety of countries of operation will be different for *establishing* legitimacy from *maintaining* legitimacy. It will be easier for the "IBMs" (the more experienced international companies with many varied subunits) to enter a new environment and establish the legitimacy of their subunits there, because of their reputation, experience, and bargaining power. However, it might be more difficult for such MNEs and MNE subunits to maintain their legitimacy, because they will be more susceptible to problems caused by spillovers of illegitimacy from any of the other MNE subunits. Thus:

> *Proposition 2: The greater the number and variety of countries in which an MNE operates, the less of a challenge its subunits face in establishing their legitimacy in a particular host country, but the greater the challenge the MNE as a whole and its subunits face in maintaining their legitimacy.*

Another important effect of the variety of institutional environments that MNEs operate in is the *institutional distance* between the home and the host country. The institutional distance between two countries, defined as the difference/similarity between the regulatory, cognitive, and normative institutions of the two countries (Kostova, 1996), will affect both the difficulty of understanding and correctly interpreting local institutional requirements, as well as the extent of adjustment required. This is due to the fact that organizational structures, policies, and practices tend to reflect the institutional environment in which they have been developed and established (Kogut, 1993). Thus, it will be easier for an MNE to understand and adjust to the legitimacy requirements of a country that is institutionally similar to its home country than

---

[3] The institutional profile of a country is characterized by the set of regulatory, cognitive, and normative institutions established in the country.

of one that is institutionally distant from the home country (e.g., a U.S. MNE in Canada versus China). This effect of institutional distance on legitimacy operates at the level of the MNE subunit. Therefore, we propose the following:

> Proposition 3: The greater the institutional distance between the home country of an MNE and a particular host country, the greater the challenge an MNE subunit will face in establishing and maintaining its legitimacy in that host country.

Propositions 2 and 3 apply primarily to MNEs and not to purely domestic firms. Although some variance between local institutions is possible (especially in large and diverse countries like the United States), this within-country institutional variance is likely to be much smaller than between-country variances. Moreover, each country, regardless of how big and diverse it is internally, usually has country-wide institutions that supersede local institutions and can be used in case a conflict arises between local institutional requirements. For example, if a regulation in California is different from a regulation in Minnesota and a conflict occurs as a result of this, there probably exists an institutional mechanism at the federal level that will reconcile the differences. When national borders are crossed, however, as in the case of MNEs, the between-country differences in their multiple institutional environments might be substantial—and the institutional requirements of different countries contradictory. In addition, there are very few institutional mechanisms that have supranational jurisdiction to solve potential conflicts (Sundaram & Black, 1992).

Organizational Complexity and Legitimacy

By definition, complex organizations such as MNEs are not monolithic, unitary entities. They tend to be complex social systems consisting of different activities, product divisions, and locations, which are integrated and interdependent to various extents (Bartlett, 1986; Bartlett & Ghoshal, 1991; Prahalad & Doz, 1987; Rosenzweig & Singh, 1991). Organizational theorists have recognized the fragmentation of complex organizations (Fligstein, 1990; Lawrence &

Lorsch, 1967), but there has been relatively little discussion on the implications of this fragmentation for organizational legitimacy. For example, each subunit faces its own legitimacy issues, and, further, its legitimacy is both influenced by and influences the legitimacy of the whole organization. We discuss these effects in greater depth in the section on legitimacy spillovers.

Here, we focus on one particular issue related to organizational complexity and legitimacy: the need for organizational subunits to achieve internal legitimacy within the organization in addition to legitimacy with the external environment (Westney, 1993). We define internal legitimacy as the acceptance and approval of an organizational unit by the other units within the firm and, primarily, by the parent company. Similar to external legitimacy, internal legitimacy is important for the survival of an organizational subunit because of its dependence on other subunits and on the parent for continuing access to organizational resources such as capital and knowledge (Pfeffer & Salancik, 1978). We believe that the MNE case illustrates how considerations of internal legitimacy can constrain a subunit's efforts to achieve external legitimacy.

Internal legitimacy is likely to result from a unit's adoption of the organization structures, policies, and practices institutionalized within the MNE. These structures, policies, and practices tend to be imprinted by the external institutional environment in which the organization was founded (Kogut, 1993). Therefore, in purely domestic firms, internal legitimacy requirements are likely to be similar to or at least consistent with external legitimacy requirements. In MNEs, internal legitimacy requirements may differ substantially from the external legitimacy requirements in a host country, especially when there is high institutional distance between home and host countries (Kostova, 1997). In such cases adaptation to the external institutional requirements can result in internal inconsistency (Rosenzweig & Singh, 1991). For example, Cargill's willingness to move to labor-intensive technology for its salt operations in India presented a significant departure from its global strategy of using highly automated technologies. Thus:

Proposition 4: MNE subunits will face a greater challenge, compared to subunits of purely domestic firms, in establishing and maintaining legitimacy in their host environment because of the increased potential for conflict that they face between the requirements for internal versus external legitimacy.

However, the tradeoff between internal and external legitimacy may not necessarily cause illegitimacy, since certain characteristics of the MNE may, themselves, moderate the problem. Research in international management distinguishes between different types of MNEs, based on their *mindsets, mentalities,* and *strategies.* As suggested by Perlmutter (1969), some MNEs are "geocentric," in that they develop a global, cosmopolitan orientation that is not tied to any particular national identity. Others are "ethnocentric," in that their identity is strongly rooted in the home country. "Polycentric" MNEs develop a multiplicity of identities to reflect each of the countries they operate in.

The orientation of the MNE will affect the extent of tension between internal and external legitimacy. Geocentric MNEs will be able to respond successfully to the multiple institutional requirements in different countries by adopting supranational structures, policies, and practices that are legitimate worldwide. The adoption of such globally acceptable policies will also ensure internal consistency. Polycentric MNEs may also find it relatively easy to manage the tension between internal and external legitimacy, because they are used to internal inconsistency in their efforts to adapt to each local environment. Ethnocentric MNEs, however, will experience the greatest difficulty in managing this tension, for their practices and policies are not derived from universal principles, nor are they accustomed to internal variety. Formally:

Proposition 5: The extent of the challenge faced by MNE subunits in establishing and maintaining internal and external legitimacy will be moderated by the orientation of the parent company; it will be easier for subunits of geocentric and polycentric MNEs, compared to subunits of ethnocentric MNEs.

Complexity in the Legitimation Process

We now address the legitimacy issues that arise from complexity in the legitimation process. Legitimation—that is, the process through which legitimacy is achieved (Hybels, 1995; Maurer, 1971)—is largely sociopolitical and cognitive in nature. Both the organization and the environment are involved in the legitimation process, in which the organization's legitimacy is continuously tested and redefined. In this process the organization attempts to make sense of the legitimacy requirements of the institutional environment by observing, learning, interpreting, and even influencing those requirements (Doz & Prahalad, 1980; Weick, 1993). The legitimating environment also tries to make sense of the organization and to evaluate its acceptability.

Because of its social and cognitive nature, the process of legitimation is complex, imperfect, and boundedly rational (March & Simon, 1958), especially in the case of MNEs, where both the organization and the legitimating environment may lack the information necessary to correctly understand, interpret, and evaluate each other. We suggest that these characteristics of the legitimation process affect MNE legitimacy by influencing the environment's perceptions of the MNE, as captured in the "liability of foreignness," as well as in the phenomenon of "legitimacy spillovers."

Liability of foreignness. Firms doing business abroad face certain costs that purely domestic firms do not—that is, they face a liability of foreignness (Hymer, 1960; Zaheer, 1995b; Zaheer & Mosakowski, 1997), which can arise for a variety of reasons. Here, we focus on the cognitive aspects of the liability of foreignness, as reflected in the lack of information about the MNE on the part of the host country environment, the use of stereotypes and different standards in judging MNEs versus domestic firms, and the use of MNEs (especially large and visible MNEs) as targets for attack by host country interest groups.

The host country legitimating environment typically has *less information* with which to judge an MNE entrant. This could result in delays in legitimation, in continuing suspicion toward the MNE, and in scrutiny of the MNE to a much greater extent than that of domestic firms. In addition, the lack of information on a particular MNE may lead to the use of stereotypical judgments based on the legitimacy or illegitimacy of certain classes of organizations to which the MNE is perceived to belong. The *stereotypes* used to judge MNEs may arise from long-established, taken-for-granted assumptions in the host environment regarding MNEs in general, or of MNEs from a particular industry or a particular home country (say, for example, the suspicion that existed in the 1980s of Japanese real estate holdings in the United States). The case of Cargill also illustrates these points. Cargill's arrival in India was equated with the arrival of the British colonialists. "The metaphor really is colonization," "They have come like the British," and "Leave our seeds alone" were all comments made about Cargill by local interest groups (Dewan, 1994).

Another aspect of the liability of foreignness is the *different legitimacy standards* that some institutional environments hold for MNEs compared to domestic firms. MNEs are expected, in many countries, to do more than local companies in building their reputation and goodwill, in supporting local communities, in protecting the environment, and so on. Shell, for example, claims that it has contributed much more to the people of Nigeria and the local community of Ogoniland than any other company in the region, but it still has been subject to fierce criticism both in Nigeria and internationally (Newburry & Gladwin, 1997). Similarly, the standards against which Nike's labor practices are held in China are quite different from the standards that would be applied in judging a local shoe manufacturer. This leads us to the following:

> *Proposition 6: MNE subunits will find it a greater challenge to establish and maintain legitimacy in their host environments, compared to domestic firms, because of the stereotyping and different standards applied to foreign firms by the host environment.*

Further, MNEs can become the *target* of different interest groups in the host countries, which may attack the legitimacy of these companies for political reasons and not because of any evidence of wrongdoing (Maitland, 1997). Interest groups can campaign against MNEs simply to gain political clout or to gain publicity as a socially conscious political force. Under these conditions, the MNEs most likely to be targeted

are the larger, better-known MNEs, since they can provide the most publicity and visibility for the interest groups. The cases of Nike, Shell, and Cargill illustrate this *liability of being large and visible.*

Thus, although size may provide power in market activities, such as in obtaining a contract with a local supplier or the local government, it is perhaps a source of vulnerability in nonmarket activities[4] (Baron, 1994), such as the maintenance of legitimacy. While this would apply, to some extent, to all large firms— whether MNEs or purely domestic—we suggest that MNEs are more vulnerable to these types of attacks, for several reasons. First, MNEs operate in multiple institutional environments with varying regulatory, cognitive, and normative standards. This provides opportunities for interest groups to identify practices used by the firm in some country that may be unacceptable in another country and to use those as a rallying point. Further, such attacks are more difficult to counter because distance and language barriers make it difficult for the public to ascertain the facts. Thus, large and visible MNEs are particularly susceptible to legitimacy attacks from interest groups. Formally:

> *Proposition 7: Larger and more visible MNEs and their subunits will find it a greater challenge than will smaller and less visible MNEs and their subunits to maintain legitimacy, because they are more vulnerable to attacks from interest groups.*

Although, in general, multinational firms are subject to the liability of foreignness as reflected in Propositions 6 and 7, there could exist specific situations in which being an MNE brings with it an initial level of legitimacy, rather than illegitimacy. Such situations could arise in environments in which local firms have lost their legitimacy because of an economic, political, or social cataclysm (e.g., in Eastern

---

[4] Market activities include "those interactions between the firm and other parties that are intermediated by markets or private agreements. These interactions typically are voluntary and involve economic transactions and the exchange of property," whereas nonmarket activities are those that are "intermediated through public institutions," typically do not involve economic transactions or property exchange, and may be voluntary or involuntary (Baron, 1994: 1).

Europe or, more recently, in Indonesia). The resulting public awareness of local firms' misdeeds—whether it be links with organized crime or charges of nepotism and corruption—serves to legitimate nonlocal firms. The illegitimacy of local firms also could arise in countries that have protected local business to the point that the absence of competition has made them insensitive to their customers and the public, as well as in countries where there exists a longstanding sense of inferiority and xenophilia. In such cases it is possible that *all* local firms lack legitimacy and, as a result, almost *any* nonlocal firm is immediately perceived as more legitimate. Thus:

> Proposition 8: The less legitimate local firms are in a particular institutional environment, the less challenge MNE subunits will face in establishing and maintaining legitimacy in that host environment.

Legitimacy spillovers. We suggest that as a result of the complexity inherent in the social, cognitive, and boundedly rational nature of the legitimation process, the legitimacy of a given organizational unit in a particular environment is not independent of the legitimacy of other organizational entities with which the unit is cognitively related. As has been shown in cognitive psychology, people make sense of social events by categorizing them on the basis of such cognitive structures as schemas and stereotypes (e.g., Markus & Zajonc, 1985). Further, under conditions of bounded rationality, people's judgments about particular events are affected by their judgments about similar events that fall into the same cognitive category—a phenomenon often referred to as the "representativeness heuristic" (Tversky & Kahneman, 1974). Therefore, it is likely that when an institutional environment judges the legitimacy of a particular organizational unit, it will refer to the legitimacy of other organizational units that are similar to the focal unit, since they belong to the same cognitive category—for example, to the same class of organizations.

Thus, the legitimacy of a foreign subsidiary of an MNE may be judged based on the legitimacy of all subsidiaries of that MNE or of all subsidiaries of the same home country in that host country. For example, if a Brazilian shoe manufacturer were to open an operation in Indonesia,

it is likely that its legitimacy would be judged based on inferences drawn from such classes of organizations as "other Western firms in Indonesia," "other foreign shoe makers in Indonesia," and "Brazilian firms" in general. These judgments may also be influenced by the environment's knowledge about that firm's subunits in other countries.

We call this phenomenon a *legitimacy spill-over* and suggest that, although valid for all types of organizations, legitimacy spillovers are particularly salient for MNEs. Legitimacy spillovers can come from different sources and occur in different directions. There can be *positive* spillovers, which contribute to legitimacy, and *negative* spillovers, which hurt legitimacy. Positive and negative spillovers may not be completely symmetric in their effects, in that negative spillovers are likely to have a stronger effect on legitimacy than will positive spillovers. The fact that a particular subunit is legitimate does not necessarily add much to the legitimacy of other subunits or of the organization as a whole. However, the illegitimacy of any subunit is likely to hurt the legitimacy of other subunits and of the organization. The collapse of BCCI (Bank of Credit and Commerce International) worldwide, because of its problems in Britain and the United States, illustrates the potentially strong effects of negative spillovers.

We distinguish between *internal spillovers*, which occur within an organization, and *external spillovers*, which occur between organizations. Internal spillovers reflect the interdependence in legitimacy across subunits *within* an organization. They can happen vertically—that is, between the subunit and the MNE as a whole—or horizontally—that is, across subunits. Vertically, the parent firm's reputation could affect the legitimacy of its subunits (Fombrun, 1996), and vice versa. For example, with the Southeast Asian subsidiaries of Nike experiencing problems with the image of their labor practices, the legitimacy of Nike as a whole is being questioned. Horizontally, a firm's illegitimacy in one subunit (e.g., Cargill's seeds project in India) can have a negative impact on the legitimacy of its other subunits (Cargill's salt project in India). Thus, we offer the following:

> Proposition 9: MNE subunits will face a greater challenge in establishing and maintaining legitimacy when the

MNE as a whole or any of its other subunits experiences legitimacy problems; similarly, the MNE as a whole will also face a greater challenge in maintaining legitimacy if any of its subunits experiences legitimacy problems.

External spillovers reflect interdependence in legitimacy *between* organizations belonging to the same classes, such as those from the same home country or industry. For example, once there is a precedent for a Japanese auto maker to start operations in the United States, it becomes easier for other Japanese auto makers to do likewise. Historically shared perceptions about certain countries or regions in a particular host country can also influence the legitimacy of any firm from that country (e.g., Israeli firms in the Middle East or Russian firms in the former Eastern Bloc).

Spillover effects are likely to be particularly strong in the initial period of *establishing* the legitimacy of a new subsidiary (rather than while *maintaining* it), when both the subsidiary and the legitimating environment operate under conditions of bounded rationality. On the one hand, the subsidiary lacks knowledge about the institutional environment—its requirements and its legitimating actors—and, thus, is limited in its ability to achieve legitimacy by adapting to or negotiating with the institutional environment. On the other hand, the legitimating actors in the local environment lack knowledge about the particular subsidiary and may make initial judgments about its legitimacy based on inferences from other similar subsidiaries or from the parent MNE's reputation (Fombrun, 1996; Fombrun & Shanley, 1990). As time passes, the subsidiary is likely to learn about the institutional environment and how to deal with it, and the local environment is also likely to accrue information about the particular subsidiary and begin to judge it more correctly. As a result, the dependence on inferences from analogs may decrease. This proposition is congruent with the ideas of inertia and time dependence of legitimacy (Singh et al., 1986):

> Proposition 10: The extent of the challenge faced by an MNE or an MNE subunit in establishing and maintaining its legitimacy will be negatively (positively) related to the legitimacy

(illegitimacy) of other organizations belonging to the same organizational classes; these legitimacy spillover effects will be particularly strong for MNE subunits at the time of entry into a new host country.

DISCUSSION

In this article we have focused on MNEs because they provide a unique context in which to extend existing theories of organizational legitimacy, as well as to develop elements of a theory of MNE legitimacy. We have explored three types of complexity illustrated by the MNE case (in the legitimating environment, in the organization, and in the process of legitimation) and developed propositions on the extent of the challenge faced by MNEs and their subunits in establishing and maintaining legitimacy. Although some of these complexities (in particular, environmental complexity) have been recognized by scholars (e.g., Boddewyn, 1995; Evan & Freeman, 1988; Lawrence & Lorsch, 1967; Scott, 1995; Thompson, 1967), their implications for organizational legitimacy rarely have been explicitly examined.

With regard to the effects of environmental complexity, we have explored the influence of the normative and cognitive institutional domains and the greater challenge they present to MNE legitimacy than does the regulatory domain. As for organizational complexity, we have suggested that subunits of geocentric or polycentric MNEs will be better placed to manage the tension between internal and external legitimacy than will subunits of ethnocentric MNEs. Finally, exploring the boundedly rational nature of the legitimation process has led us to understand why, for instance, MNEs might suffer from a liability of foreignness in their acceptance by the environment, why large and visible organizations are particularly vulnerable to attack by political interests, and why complex organizations are vulnerable to legitimacy spillovers, both from within and outside.

This article contributes to theories of organizational legitimacy because the MNE presents an extreme example that pushes the boundaries of these theories in areas that have been overlooked in the past. For instance, the MNE example suggests *multiple levels* of organizational legitimacy: in complex organizations there are clearly issues of the legitimacy of the whole organization, as well as of its parts. The legitimacy of the whole organization is not necessarily simply the average legitimacy of its parts, although legitimacies at the two levels clearly are related. The tension between internal and external organizational legitimacy, while more apparent in the MNE case, also applies, to some extent, to all complex organizations. Finally, the case of the MNE reveals the social and cognitive nature of the legitimation process and its bounded rationality. For example, the MNE case pushes us to think about how positive and negative legitimacy spillovers may occur within an organization as well as between organizations.

This article also presents the first steps toward building a theory of MNE legitimacy. Although some aspects of MNE legitimacy can be accommodated by general theories of organizational legitimacy, there are certain characteristics of MNEs that are different enough to call for a distinct approach. To start with, the sheer number and, more important, the possibility of extreme variety across the multiple institutional environments that MNEs confront create legitimacy issues not faced by purely domestic firms. The overall legitimacy of an MNE may be affected to a greater extent by some host environments than by others. For instance, environments with the strictest legitimacy requirements may be most critical (e.g., BCCI lost its overall legitimacy from problems in Britain and the United States—not in its home countries of Abu-Dhabi and Luxembourg). In addition, the existence of multiple environments with varying legitimacy standards creates greater opportunities for interest groups to attack MNEs and MNE subunits and to question their legitimacy. Further, the tension between the MNE's internal legitimacy requirements, which are imprinted by the home country legitimating environment (Kogut, 1993), and the legitimacy requirements of its subunits' host countries is likely to create difficulties for the subunits—difficulties purely domestic firms will not have. However, these challenges to external legitimacy will be moderated by the parent MNE's international orientation—whether geocentric, polycentric, or ethnocentric. Finally, the boundedly rational nature of the legitimation process creates special problems for MNEs. For instance, the effects on legitimacy of insti-

tutional distance between home and host countries and the liability of foreignness, particularly at market entry, apply only to the MNE case.

When we speculate on the role of legitimacy in MNEs and other complex organizations, we must bear in mind some issues. Perhaps the most troubling question—one that becomes particularly salient as we consider the difficulties likely to be faced by MNEs in their quest for legitimacy in their multiple host environments—is why MNEs need to be legitimate at all in all of their different environments. While researchers traditionally have assumed that legitimacy is required for access to resources, and for survival, the answer may not be that simple. It is possible for organizations not to be wholly legitimate and still be profitable—even survive over the long term—especially if, as is often the case with MNEs, they have alternative sources of resources and organizational support. There is also the question of MNE legitimacy over time. Although over time MNEs may become more like domestic organizations in terms of their legitimacy (Zaheer & Mosakowski, 1997), the problem for MNEs is that they cannot afford to become complacent. MNEs are much more vulnerable to cross-border legitimacy spillovers than are purely domestic firms. Legitimacy, therefore, may take on a more "punctuated" quality in MNEs compared to the stable, inertial character of legitimacy in purely domestic firms. These issues would clearly benefit from empirical research.

With this article we hope to begin a conversation on aspects of organizational legitimacy that are brought to the surface when we examine complexity in the environment, in the organization, and in the process of legitimation. Clearly, this is just a beginning, for much more conceptual work is needed on exploring important issues that we have not addressed here. Some of the most interesting issues worth exploring further are the question of the contingencies that moderate the importance of a particular type of complexity and the question of the possible interactions between them that may have serious implications for the challenges organizations face in achieving organizational legitimacy. We believe that the ideas we introduce in this article can serve as a basis for such future theoretical developments.

The propositions we present here are testable, especially if one uses approaches to the measurement of organizational legitimacy that recently have begun to emerge in the literature. Deephouse (1996), for instance, codes public media reports to gauge the legitimacy of an organization, and this type of textual analysis could be used to establish legitimacy, as well as to identify the sources of legitimacy problems, such as in which institutional domain a problem had its origins. The propositions on the maintenance of legitimacy are particularly amenable to testing with these methods, since the loss of legitimacy is often a "critical incident" around which the textual analysis can be organized.

A downside of these methods, especially cross-nationally, arises from both language problems and from the fact that the media do not operate by the same norms across countries on what they report. A solution to this problem may be to examine a matched sample of foreign and domestic firms in the same country. Assessing the ease or difficulty of establishing and maintaining legitimacy, or the tension between internal and external legitimacy, is best done through surveys of international division managers and/or foreign subunit managers in large MNEs. Some of the propositions (e.g., Propositions 9 and 10 on legitimacy spillovers) may lend themselves more readily to traditional population ecology methods. Propositions regarding institutional distance can be operationalized by adapting constructs measuring the characteristics of different institutional environments (Kostova, 1997).

Our discussion of legitimacy issues in the MNE has significant practical implications. By identifying the factors that cause difficulty in establishing and maintaining legitimacy, we have given practitioners the basis for proactively managing the legitimacy of their organizations, instead of simply responding to legitimacy crises as they occur in a "trial and error" manner. Some specific practical recommendations include, but are not limited to, the following. MNEs need to continuously monitor legitimacy in all national environments and must not become complacent about legitimacy in any of them. They need to design strategies to respond to varied legitimacy requirements and, perhaps

even more important, have strategies in place to deal with legitimacy spillovers and crises. Further, managers of MNEs need to pay attention to all three domains of legitimacy—especially the more tacit normative and cognitive domains. They also need to recognize the tradeoff between internal and external legitimacy and the benefits of creating a geocentric or polycentric orientation within the MNE to reduce the tension between the two. Managers of MNEs need to be aware, too, of the stricter legitimacy standards to which MNEs are held, and of the legitimacy risks related to size and visibility.

As for legitimacy spillovers, MNEs can try to buffer themselves in the public eye from organizational classes that are likely to jeopardize their legitimacy, and they can deliberately identify with more legitimate organizations. Since positive and negative spillovers may also accumulate over time, a firm might build up a reputation for being legitimate and use this buffer to counter a potential loss of legitimacy in the future—akin to the notion of building a stock of "moral capital."[5] An example of an MNE subunit that has been successful in building moral capital to overcome the negative views of Japanese subsidiaries in the United States is Toyota's U.S. subunit. This subsidiary has taken pains to communicate to the American public—through corporate advertising—its espousal and support of quintessentially American causes. This example also illustrates the fact that MNEs need not only to build a good track record but also to clearly *communicate* that record to the legitimating environment because of the socially constructed nature of organizational legitimacy.

REFERENCES

Aldrich, H., & Fiol, C. M. 1994. Fools rush in? The institutional context of industry creation. *Academy of Management Review,* 19: 645–670.

Ashforth, B., & Gibbs, B. 1990. The double-edge of organizational legitimation. *Organization Science,* 1: 177–194.

Baron, D. 1994. *Integrated strategy: Market and nonmarket components.* Working paper, Graduate School of Business, Stanford University, Palo Alto, CA.

Bartlett, C. 1986. Building and managing the transnational: The new organizational challenge. In M. Porter (Ed.), *Competition in global industries:* 367–404. Boston: Harvard Business School Press.

---

[5] We are indebted to Joe Galaskiewicz for this idea.

Bartlett, C., & Ghoshal, S. 1991. Global strategic management: Impact on the new frontiers of strategy research. Guest Editor's comments, Special Issue on Global Strategy. *Strategic Management Journal,* 12: 5–16.

Baum, J., & Oliver, C. 1991. Institutional linkages and organizational mortality. *Administrative Science Quarterly,* 36: 187–218.

Behrman, J. N., & Grosse, R. 1990. *International business and governments: Issues and institutions.* Columbia, SC: University of South Carolina Press.

Berger, P., & Luckman, T. 1967. *The social construction of reality.* New York: Doubleday.

Boddewyn, J. 1995. The legitimacy of international-business political behavior. *International Trade Journal,* IX: 143–161.

Carroll, G., & Hannan, M. 1989. Density dependence in the evolution of populations of newspaper organizations. *American Sociological Review,* 54: 524–541.

Covaleski, M., & Dirsmith, M. 1988. An institutional perspective on the rise, social transformation, and fall of a university budget category. *Administrative Science Quarterly,* 33: 562–587.

D'Aunno, T., Sutton, R., & Price, R. 1991. Isomorphism and external support in conflicting institutional environments: A study of drug abuse treatment units. *Academy of Management Journal,* 34: 636–661.

Deephouse, D. 1996. Does isomorphism legitimate? *Academy of Management Journal,* 39: 1024–1039.

Dewan, M. 1994. *Patent pending: Indian farmers fight to retain freedom of their seeds.* Film, South View Productions.

DiMaggio, P., & Powell, W. 1983. The iron cage revisited: Institutional isomorphism and collective rationality in organizational fields. *American Sociological Review,* 48: 147–160.

Dowling, J., & Pfeffer, J. 1975. Organizational legitimacy: Social values and organizational behavior. *Pacific Sociological Review,* 18: 122–136.

Doz, Y. 1986. Government policies and global industries. In M. Porter (Ed.), *Competition in global industries:* 225–266. Boston: Harvard Business School Press.

Doz, Y., & Prahalad, C. K. 1980. How MNCs cope with host government intervention. *Harvard Business Review,* 58 (March–April): 149–157.

Dunning, J. H. 1993. *Multinational enterprises and the global economy.* Boston: Addison-Wesley.

Evan, W., & Freeman, E. 1988. A stakeholder theory of the modern corporation: Kantian capitalism. In T. Beauchamp & N. Bowie (Eds.), *Ethical theory and business:* 75–93. Englewood Cliffs, NJ: Prentice-Hall.

Fagre, N., & Wells, L. T. 1982. Bargaining power of multinationals and host governments. *Journal of International Business Studies,* 13(2): 9–23.

Fligstein, N. 1990. *The transformation of corporate control.* Cambridge, MA: Harvard University Press.

Fombrun, C. 1996. *Reputation: Realizing value from the corporate image.* Boston: Harvard Business School Press.

Fombrun, C., & Shanley, M. 1990. What's in a name: Reputation building and corporate strategy. *Academy of Management Journal,* 33: 233–258.

Galbraith, J. 1973. *Designing complex organizations.* Reading, MA: Addison-Wesley.

Gersick, C. 1990. Revolutionary change theories: A multilevel exploration of the punctuated equilibrium paradigm. *Academy of Management Review,* 31: 9–41.

Ghoshal, S., & Bartlett, C. 1990. The multinational corporation as an interorganizational network. *Academy of Management Review,* 15: 603–625.

Ghoshal, S., & Westney, E. 1993. Introduction. In S. Ghoshal & E. Westney (Eds.), *Organization theory and the multinational corporation:* 1–23. New York: St. Martin's Press.

Hannan, M., & Carroll, G. 1992. *Dynamics of organizational populations: Density, competition, and legitimation.* New York: Oxford University Press.

Hannan, M., & Freeman, J. 1977. The population ecology of organizations. *American Journal of Sociology,* 83: 929–984.

Hybels, R. C. 1995. On legitimacy, legitimation and organizations: A critical review and integrative theoretical model. *Best Paper Proceedings of the Academy of Management:* 241–245.

Hymer, S. 1960. *The international operations of national firms.* (Doctoral dissertation, published in 1976.) Cambridge, MA: MIT Press.

Kobrin, S. J. 1987. Testing the bargaining hypothesis in the manufacturing sector in developing countries. *International Organization,* 41: 609–638.

Kogut, B. 1991. Country capabilities and the permeability of borders. *Strategic Management Journal,* 12: 33–47.

Kogut, B. 1993. Learning, or the importance of being inert: Country imprinting and international competition. In S. Ghoshal & E. Westney (Eds.), *Organization theory and the multinational corporation:* 136–154. New York: St. Martin's Press.

Kostova, T. 1996. *Success of the transnational transfer of organizational practices within multinational companies.* Doctoral dissertation, University of Minnesota, Minneapolis.

Kostova, T. 1997. Country institutional profile: Concept and measurement. *Best Paper Proceedings of the Academy of Management:* 180–184.

Lawrence, P., & Lorsch, J. 1967. Differentiation and integration in complex organizations. *Administrative Science Quarterly,* 12: 1–47.

Lecraw, D. 1984. Bargaining power, ownership and profitability of transnational corporations in developing countries. *Journal of International Business Studies,* 15(1): 27–43.

Maitland, I. 1997. The great non-debate over international sweatshops. *Conference Proceedings of the British Academy of Management:* 240–265.

March, J., & Simon, H. 1958. *Organizations.* New York: Wiley.

Markus, H., & Zajonc, R. 1985. The cognitive perspective in social psychology. In G. Lindzey & E. Aronson (Eds.), *Handbook of social psychology* (3rd ed.), vol. 1: 137–230. New York: Random House.

Marshall, S. 1997. Nike Inc.'s golden image is tarnished as problems in Asia pose PR challenge. *Wall Street Journal,* September 26: 16.

Maurer, J. G. 1971. *Readings in organization theory: Open-system approaches.* New York: Random House.

Meyer, J., & Rowan, B. 1977. Institutionalized organizations: Formal structure as myth and ceremony. *American Journal of Sociology,* 83: 340–363.

Meyer, J., & Scott, R. 1983. Centralization and the legitimacy problems of local government. In J. Meyer & R. Scott (Eds.), *Organizational environments: Ritual and rationality:* 199–215. Beverly Hills, CA: Sage.

Murtha, T., & Lenway, S. 1994. Country capabilities and the strategic state: How national political institutions affect multinational corporations' strategies. *Strategic Management Journal,* 15: 113–129.

Neilsen, E., & Rao, M. 1987. The strategy-legitimacy nexus: A thick description. *Academy of Management Review,* 12: 523–533.

Newburry, W., & Gladwin, T. 1997. *Shell, environmental justice, and Nigerian oil.* Global Environment Program, Stern School of Business, New York University, New York.

North, D. 1990. *Institutions, institutional change and economic performance.* Cambridge, England: Cambridge University Press.

Oliver, C. 1991. Strategic responses to institutional pressures. *Academy of Management Review,* 16: 145–179.

Pania, T. 1992. Seeds: Awaiting the harvest. *Business India,* June 22–July 5: 82–84.

Parsons, T. 1960. *Structure and process in modern societies.* Glencoe, IL: Free Press.

Perlmutter, H. 1969. The tortuous evolution of the multinational corporation. *Columbia Journal of World Business,* 4: 9–18.

Pfeffer, J., & Salancik, G. 1978. *The external control of organizations.* New York: Harper & Row.

Powell, W., & DiMaggio, P. 1991. *The new institutionalism in organizational analysis.* Chicago: University of Chicago Press.

Prahalad, C. K., & Doz, Y. L. 1987. *The multinational mission: Balancing local demands and global vision.* New York: Free Press.

Ritti, R., & Silver, J. 1986. Early processes of institutionalization: The dramaturgy of exchange in interorganizational relations. *Administrative Science Quarterly,* 31: 25–42.

Rosenzweig, P. M., & Singh, J. V. 1991. Organizational environments and the multinational enterprise. *Academy of Management Review,* 16: 340–361.

Scott, R. 1987. The adolescence of institutional theory. *Administrative Science Quarterly,* 32: 493–511.

Scott, R. 1995. *Institutions and organizations.* Thousand Oaks, CA: Sage.

Selznick, P. 1957. *Leadership in administration.* New York: Harper & Row.

Setalvad, T. 1993. Cargill: Salt and protest. *Business India,* July 19–August 1: 85–87.

Singh, J., Tucker, D., & House, R. 1986. Organizational legitimacy and the liability of newness. *Administrative Science Quarterly,* 31: 171–193.

Streek, W., & Schmitter, P. 1985. Community, market, state— and associations? The prospective contribution of interest governance to social order. In W. Streek & P. Schmitter (Eds.), *Private interest government: Beyond market and state:* 1–29. Beverly Hills, CA: Sage.

Stryker, S., & Statham, A. 1985. Symbolic interaction and role theory. In G. Lindzay & E. Aronson (Eds.), *Handbook of social psychology* (3rd ed.), vol. 1: 311–378. New York: Random House.

Suchman, M. 1995. Managing legitimacy: Strategic and institutional approaches. *Academy of Management Review,* 20: 571–610.

Sundaram, A. K., & Black, J. S. 1992. The environment and internal organization of multinational enterprises. *Academy of Management Review,* 17: 729–757.

Thompson, J. 1967. *Organizations in action.* New York: McGraw-Hill.

Tversky, A., & Kahneman, D. 1974. Judgment under uncertainty: Heuristics and biases. *Science,* 185: 1124–1131.

Vernon, R. 1971. *Sovereignty at bay: The multinational spread of U.S. enterprises.* New York: Basic Books.

Weick, K. 1993. Sensemaking in organizations: Small structures with large consequences. In J. Murningham (Ed.), *Social psychology in organizations: Advances in theory and research.* Englewood Cliffs, NJ: Prentice-Hall.

Westney, E. 1993. Institutionalization theory and the MNE. In S. Ghoshal & E. Westney (Eds.), *Organization theory and the multinational corporation:* 53–76. New York: St. Martin's Press.

Williamson, O. 1975. *Markets and hierarchies: Analysis and antitrust implications.* New York: Free Press.

Williamson, O. 1991. Comparative economic organization: The analysis of discrete structural alternatives. *Administrative Science Quarterly,* 36: 269–296.

Zaheer, S. 1995a. Circadian rhythms: The effects of global market integration in the currency trading industry. *Journal of International Business Studies,* 26: 699–728.

Zaheer, S. 1995b. Overcoming the liability of foreignness. *Academy of Management Journal,* 38: 341–363.

Zaheer, S., & Mosakowski, E. 1997. The dynamics of the liability of foreignness: A global study of survival in financial services. *Strategic Management Journal,* 18: 439–464.

Zucker, L. 1983. Organizations as institutions. In S. Bacharach (Ed.), *Research in the sociology of organizations,* vol. 2: 1–47. Greenwich, CT: JAI Press.

Tatiana Kostova is an assistant professor of international business at the Darla Moore School of Business, University of South Carolina. She received her Ph.D. from the Carlson School of Management at the University of Minnesota. Her research interests include the transfer of organizational knowledge across borders, the social capital of the global firm, and psychological ownership and citizenship behavior in organizations.

Srilata Zaheer is an associate professor in the Carlson School of Management at the University of Minnesota. She received her Ph.D. from the Sloan School of Management, MIT. Her research interests include the dynamic capabilities and liabilities of international firms, the integration of management processes in multinational firms, especially in the financial services industry, and the transfer of knowledge across borders.

[25]

Strategic Management Journal
Strat. Mgmt. J., **21**: 473–496 (2000)

KNOWLEDGE FLOWS WITHIN MULTINATIONAL CORPORATIONS

ANIL K. GUPTA[1]* and VIJAY GOVINDARAJAN[2]
[1]*The Robert H. Smith School of Business, The University of Maryland, College Park, Maryland, U.S.A.*
[2]*The Amos Tuck School of Business, Dartmouth College, Hanover, New Hampshire, U.S.A.*

Pursuing a nodal (i.e., subsidiary) level of analysis, this paper advances and tests an overarching theoretical framework pertaining to intracorporate knowledge transfers within multinational corporations (MNCs). We predicted that (i) knowledge outflows from a subsidiary would be positively associated with value of the subsidiary's knowledge stock, its motivational disposition to share knowledge, and the richness of transmission channels; and (ii) knowledge inflows into a subsidiary would be positively associated with richness of transmission channels, motivational disposition to acquire knowledge, and the capacity to absorb the incoming knowledge. These predictions were tested empirically with data from 374 subsidiaries within 75 MNCs headquartered in the U.S., Europe, and Japan. Except for our predictions regarding the impact of source unit's motivational disposition on knowledge outflows, the data provide either full or partial support to all of the other elements of our theoretical framework. Copyright © 2000 John Wiley & Sons, Ltd.

In recent years, researchers in organization theory (Levitt and March, 1988), economics (Nelson and Winter, 1982), as well as strategic management (Prahalad and Hamel, 1994; Schendel, 1996) have identified organizational learning as one of the most important subjects for scholarly inquiry. Aimed at further deepening our understanding of a key topic within this broad area viz., intrafirm flows of organizational knowledge, this paper reports the results of a theoretical and empirical investigation into the determinants of internal knowledge transfers within multinational corporations. The following four observations underlie the motivations for this study.

First, every firm constitutes a bundle of knowledge. As a corollary of the "resource-based view of the firm" (Barney, 1991; Penrose, 1959; Wer-

nerfelt, 1984), this observation is now so widely accepted as to have become almost axiomatic (Grant, 1996; Huber, 1991; Kogut and Zander, 1992; Nelson and Winter, 1982; Nonaka, 1994). In the context of this paper, it is particularly important to note that, of all possible resources that a firm might possess, its knowledge base has perhaps the greatest ability to serve as a source of sustainable differentiation and hence competitive advantage (Dierickx and Cool, 1989; Lippman and Rumelt, 1982).

Second, the primary reason why MNCs exist is because of their ability to transfer and exploit knowledge more effectively and efficiently in the intra-corporate context than through external market mechanisms. This "internalization of intangible assets" argument, originally advanced by Hymer (1960), has been subjected to numerous confirmatory empirical tests and is now widely accepted as the "received theory" on why MNCs exist (Buckley and Casson, 1976; Caves, 1971, 1982; Ghoshal, 1987; Kindleberger, 1969; Porter, 1986; Teece, 1981). Of course, external markets

Key words: knowledge flows, multinational corporations, subsidiaries
*Correspondence to: Anil K. Gupta, The Robert H. Smith School of Business, The University of Maryland, College Park, MD 20742, U.S.A.

Received 27 August 1997
Final revision received 1 August 1999

474   *A. K. Gupta and V. Govindarajan*

continue to become more open, efficient, and global on an ongoing basis. Notwithstanding the increasing sophistication of external markets, they remain relatively ineffective mechanisms for knowledge transfer on at least two grounds: one, bulk of the specialized knowledge of any firm exists in a tacit and thereby non-tradeable form; two, market-based transfers of knowledge are often associated with negative externalities such as involuntary expropriation and the risk of creating a new competitor.

Third, the notion that MNCs exist primarily because of their superior ability (vis-a-vis markets) to engage in internal knowledge transfer does not in any way imply that such knowledge transfers actually take place effectively and efficiently on a routine basis. In perhaps the only study to date on the actual costs of cross-border knowledge transfers, Teece (1981: 84) examined a sample of 26 technology transfer cases and reported that "[T]he resource cost of international transfer is nontrivial. Transfer costs ranged from 2.25 percent to 59 percent of total project costs with a mean of 19.16 percent." The "tacitness" or "causal ambiguity" of knowledge is one of the most widely recognized barriers to its transfer and replication (Lippman and Rumelt, 1982; Polanyi, 1966; Zander and Kogut, 1995). Levinthal and March (1993), Simon (1991), Szulanski (1996) and others have suggested additional barriers to knowledge transfer e.g., barriers rooted in motivational dispositions and absorptive capacity.

Finally, notwithstanding the criticality of internal knowledge transfers within MNCs, with some notable exceptions (e.g., Ghoshal and Bartlett, 1988 and Zander and Kogut, 1995), very little systematic empirical investigation into the determinants of intra-MNC knowledge transfers has so far been attempted. As Ghoshal, Korine, and Szulanski (1994: 97) have observed, "A number of publications emphasize the importance of interunit communication for effective MNC management...but in none of them is the construct operationalized or measured, nor are the factors that influence such communication empirically explored."

Building on these observations, the primary objective of this paper is to advance the state of our theoretical as well as empirical understanding of the determinants of intra-MNC knowledge transfers. Data for this study were collected directly from the presidents of 374 subsidiaries belonging to 75 major MNCs headquartered in the U.S., Japan, and Europe. In order to ensure reliability, data on the most critical variables (pertaining to knowledge transfers) were collected also from the immediate HQ-level superiors of the presidents of a large subset of the sampled subsidiaries; further, the tests for the hypotheses were conducted after controlling for the possible effects of the parent corporation's country-of-origin, the resource characteristics of the parent corporation's industry, and the nature of the subsidiary's operations.

THE PHENOMENON OF INTEREST

Because MNCs are complex multi-dimensional entities, knowledge flows within such enterprises occur not only along multiple directions but also across multiple dimensions, e.g., the flow of information pertaining to the Brazilian subsidiary's financial performance over the last quarter to corporate headquarters, the transfer of packaging technology from a Swedish factory to one in India, or the transfer of customer service skills from a Japanese subsidiary to one in the U.S. In this study, we focus on the transfer of largely procedural types of knowledge (e.g., product designs, distribution know-how, etc.) but not on the transfer of largely declarative types of knowledge (e.g., monthly financial data). In other words, *this study focuses on the transfer of knowledge that exists in the form of "know-how" rather than on the transfer of knowledge that exists in the form of "operational information."*

As Ghoshal and Bartlett (1990), Gupta and Govindarajan (1991), and Hedlund (1994) have suggested, knowledge transfers within the MNC take place within the context of an interorganizational "network" of differentiated units. Thus, flows of knowledge through the network can be studied from at least three different levels of analysis: nodal (i.e., a focus on the behavior of individual units), dyadic (i.e., a focus on the joint behavior of unit pairs), and systemic (i.e., a focus on the behavior of the entire network). Given the highly complex nature of the phenomenon under investigation and the relative dearth of previous empirical work on it, in this study, we have chosen to limit our investigation to the "nodal" level. More specifically, we focus on *individual subsidiaries only* and examine the determinants of knowledge flows in each of the following four domains: (i) knowledge outflows to peer subsidiaries, (ii) knowledge outflows to the parent corporation, (iii) knowledge inflows from peer subsidiaries, and (iv) knowledge inflows from the parent corporation.

THEORY

An overarching theoretical framework

As Krone, Jablin, and Putnam (1987) have observed in their review of communication theory, even though different communication scholars have focused more (or less) heavily on different elements of the communication process, virtually all of them recognize the following as the basic elements of any two-person communication: a message, a sender, a coding scheme, a channel, transmission through the channel, a decoding scheme, a receiver, and the assignment of meaning to the decoded message. Consistent with these ideas from communication theory, we conceptualize knowledge flows (into or out of a subsidiary) to be a function of the following five factors: (i) value of the source unit's knowledge stock, (ii) motivational disposition of the source unit, (iii) existence and richness of transmission channels, (iv) motivational disposition of the target unit, and (v) absorptive capacity of the target unit. Barriers or facilitators to the transfer of knowledge can manifest themselves in any or all of these five factors:

(a) *Value of source unit's knowledge stock.* Knowledge flows across units are not cost free (Teece, 1981). We also know that different resources have different levels of value (Barney, 1991). Thus, the greater the value of a subsidiary's knowledge stock for the rest of the MNC, the greater would be its attractiveness for other units. This idea is broadly consistent with the concept of "relative advantage" in the literature dealing with diffusion of innovations which has argued that the adoption rate of an innovation is positively related to its relative advantage (Rogers, 1995). This idea has not yet been applied to the examination of interunit knowledge transfers within multinational corporations. Within such corporations, we visualize the knowledge stock of any subsidiary as com-

posed of both duplicative as well as non-duplicative knowledge. The presence of non-duplicative knowledge is a necessary, although not sufficient, condition for such knowledge to be of value to other units. Thus, we would anticipate that knowledge outflows from a subsidiary are likely to be high when the subsidiary's knowledge stock is non-duplicative as well as relevant for the rest of the global network.

(b) *Motivational disposition of the source unit.* As Cyert (1995) has suggested, an organizational unit with uniquely valuable know-how is likely to enjoy an "information monopoly" within the corporation. This reality coupled with the fact that power struggles are a ubiquitous phenomenon in any organization (Pfeffer, 1981) implies that at least some units will view uniquely valuable know-how as the currency through which they acquire and retain relative power within the corporation. Levitt and March (1988: 331) have observed similarly that "In many (but not all) situations...diffusion of experience has negative consequences for organizations that are copied." Therefore, we anticipate that factors which would enhance the motivational disposition of the source unit to share its knowledge with other units within the MNC are likely to counterbalance any "hoarding" tendencies and thereby to have a positive impact on the magnitude of knowledge outflows.

(c) *Existence and richness of transmission channels.* As would be expected, and as demonstrated empirically by Ghoshal and Bartlett (1988) in the domain of MNCs, knowledge flows cannot occur without the existence of transmission channels. Beyond mere existence, we would expect other properties of transmission channels to also affect the extent of knowledge flows – the most notable such property would be the richness/bandwidth of communication links, as captured in aspects such as informality, openness, and density of communications (Daft and Lengel, 1986; Gupta and Govindarajan, 1991; Jablin, 1979; Tushman, 1977).

(d) *Motivational disposition of the target unit.* The "Not-Invented-Here" (NIH) syndrome

476   *A. K. Gupta and V. Govindarajan*

is well-known and also has been the subject of scholarly inquiry (Katz and Allen, 1982). There are at least two drivers of the NIH syndrome: (i) ego-defense mechanisms (Allport, 1937; Sherif and Cantrill, 1947) which can lead some managers to block any information that might suggest that others are more competent than they are, and (ii) power struggles within organizations (Pfeffer, 1981) which can lead some managers to try to downgrade the potential power of peer units by pretending that the knowledge stock possessed by these peer units is not unique and valuable. In short, unless counterveiling forces are present, the NIH syndrome can act as a major barrier to the inflows of knowledge into any focal unit. These counterveiling forces can manifest themselves in several forms: the relative paucity of the focal unit's knowledge stock, incentives that increase subsidiary managers' eagerness to learn from peer units, or coercive pressures from corporate headquarters.

(e) *Absorptive capacity of the target unit.* Even when exposed to the same environment and even when there are insignificant differences in the desire to acquire new knowledge, individuals and organizations may differ in their "absorptive capacity" i.e., in their "ability to recognize the value of new information, assimilate it, and apply it to commercial ends" (Cohen and Levinthal, 1990: 128). There are at least two reasons why absorptive capacity may differ across organizations: (i) the extent of prior related knowledge, and (ii) the extent of inter-unit homophily of the receiving unit vis-à-vis the sending unit. Prior related knowledge is important because it shapes the filters through which the organization differentiates between more vs. less relevant signals and also because it determines the organization's ability to internalize and assimilate the more valued signals (Cohen and Levinthal, 1990). On the other hand, homophily – i.e., "the degree to which two or more individuals who interact are similar in certain attributes, such as beliefs, education, social status, and the like" (Rogers, 1995: 18–19) – is important because when the

interacting individuals "share common meanings, a mutual subcultural language, and are alike in personal and social characteristics, the communication of new ideas is likely to have greater effects in terms of knowledge gain, attitude formation, and overt behavior change" (Rogers, 1995: 19; see also Lazarsfeld and Merton, 1964).

Figure 1 presents a schematic diagram of the overarching framework developed in this section. From the perspective of the "nodal" level of analysis being pursued in this study, this framework can be translated into the following six propositions:

Proposition 1: Ceteris paribus, the value of a subsidiary's knowledge stock will be positively associated with outflows of knowledge from that subsidiary.

Proposition 2: Ceteris paribus, the motivational disposition of a subsidiary to share its knowledge with other units will be positively associated with outflows of knowledge from that subsidiary.

Proposition 3: Ceteris paribus, the existence and richness of transmission channels linking a subsidiary to other units within the MNC will be positively associated with outflows of knowledge from that subsidiary.

Proposition 4: Ceteris paribus, the existence and richness of transmission channels linking a subsidiary to other units within the MNC will be positively associated with inflows of knowledge into that subsidiary.

Proposition 5: Ceteris paribus, the motivational disposition of a subsidiary to seek/accept knowledge from other units will be positively associated with inflows of knowledge into that subsidiary.

Proposition 6: Ceteris paribus, the capacity of a subsidiary to absorb incoming knowledge from other units will be positively associated with inflows of knowledge into that subsidiary.

In the rest of this section, we operationalize the constructs underlying these propositions and

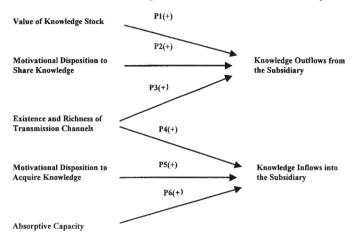

Figure 1. Determinants of intra-corporate knowledge outflows from and inflows to foreign subsidiaries: An overarching theoretical framework

develop more concrete and empirically testable hypotheses.

Value of source unit's knowledge stock

We argued earlier that, in order for a source unit's knowledge to be of value to other units, the source unit must (i) create non-duplicative knowledge on its own, and (ii) this non-duplicative knowledge must be of relevance for the rest of the global network. Based on this reasoning, we operationalize the construct of value of knowledge stock in terms of the following three variables: mode of entry, subsidiary size, and the economic level of the host country relative to that of the home country.

Mode of entry. As Caves (1982), Root (1987) and others have pointed out, an MNC may enter a foreign country through one of several modes – greenfield operations, strategic alliances, or acquisitions. Since our study focuses only on fully- or majority-owned subsidiaries, we examine here the impact of greenfield vs. acquisition modes only. At a general level, we can visualize every subsidiary to consist of three bundles of knowledge: duplicative knowledge, non-duplicative knowledge that is relevant only in the local environment, and non-duplicative knowledge that is relevant also for other units within the global network.

As the literature on foreign direct investment

has argued and demonstrated (Hennart and Park, 1993), the less the overlap between existing corporate know-how and the know-how required to succeed in a host market, the greater the probability of acquisition as the mode of entry. Thus, relative to greenfield subsidiaries, acquired subsidiaries on average can be expected to have a knowledge stock that is less duplicative vis-à-vis the knowledge stock of the rest of the corporation. It is true that only a subset of the non-duplicative knowledge would be of relevance for the global network. However, since the pool of non-duplicative knowledge would be higher for acquired subsidiaries as compared to greenfield subsidiaries, it is likely that acquired subsidiaries should have a larger pool of relevant knowledge to offer to the global network than greenfield subsidiaries. Based on these arguments, Proposition 1 can be operationalized in the form of the following two empirically testable hypotheses: *ceteris paribus, relative to greenfield operations, acquired subsidiaries will engage in greater knowledge outflows to peer subsidiaries (H1a) and to the parent corporation (H1a').*

Subsidiary size. We anticipate that the typical MNC would discourage investment of a subsidiary's resources in the reinvention of knowledge that exists elsewhere in the global network. Thus, we would expect that a subsidiary's own resources would generally be directed at the creation of non-duplicative knowledge. Since larger

478   *A. K. Gupta and V. Govindarajan*

subsidiaries will have a greater pool of resources dedicated to the creation of new knowledge, it follows that subsidiary size should have a positive impact on the ability of the subsidiary to offer non-duplicative knowledge to the rest of the corporation. Clearly, not all of the non-duplicative knowledge generated by a subsidiary would have global relevance; however, a subset of such knowledge will. These arguments yield the following additional operationalizations of Proposition 1: *ceteris paribus, the larger the size of a subsidiary, the greater will be the knowledge outflows from that subsidiary to peer subsidiaries (H1b) and to the parent corporation (H1b').*

Relative economic level. Countries differ in their levels of economic advancement. If we make the straightforward assumption that most, perhaps all, societies around the world strive to increase (rather than merely maintain or decrease) their levels of economic advancement, then it follows that, on average, more advanced countries are likely to serve as trend-setters and the sources of technological, marketing, as well as managerial know-how to a greater extent than less advanced countries. In other words, in the intracorporate context, on average, a focal unit is likely to view the knowledge stock of another unit located in an economically more advanced country relative to itself as more valuable than that of a unit located in a relatively less advanced country. These arguments also yield the following operationalization of Proposition 1: *ceteris paribus, the higher the level of the host country's economic development relative to the home country, the greater will be the knowledge outflows from that subsidiary to the parent corporation (H1c').* Since our empirical study was conducted at the nodal level of analysis, we did not collect any data regarding knowledge flows between *specific* inter-subsidiary dyads. Accordingly, in the above hypothesis, we have focused only on the relative economic level of the focal subsidiary vis-a-vis the parent corporation and not on that vis-a-vis other *specific* subsidiaries. Thus, we neither advance nor test any inter-subsidiary hypotheses pertaining to relative economic level.

Motivational disposition of the source unit

We posit that the extent to which the subsidiary president is rewarded for improvements in the performance of a network of subsidiaries (rather

than just the focal subsidiary) would be a major determinant of motivation to share knowledge with other subsidiaries. Based on this reasoning, we operationalized the construct of motivational disposition in terms of the subsidiary vs. corporate focus (i.e., nodal vs. network optimization focus) of the incentive system for the subsidiary president.

Incentive focus. As Salter (1973) suggested and as Gupta and Govindarajan (1986) and Pitts (1974) demonstrated, the incentive bonus for a division/subsidiary general manager may be linked solely to the performance of the focal unit, solely to the performance of several units, or to some combination of the two. As these authors have argued, the greater the need to motivate a unit general manager to focus on system-wide optimization as distinct from local optimization, the better it is to link the incentives to the performance of a cluster of units. These arguments result in the following operationalizations of Proposition 2: *ceteris paribus, the greater the extent to which a subsidiary president's bonus is network-focused rather than subsidiary-focused, the greater will be the knowledge outflows from that subsidiary to peer subsidiaries (H2a) and to the parent corporation (H2a').*

Existence and richness of transmission channels

As communications theory informs us (Daft and Lengel, 1986; Krone et al., 1987), transmission channels can be both formal and informal. Accordingly, we operationalize the construct of transmission channels in terms of two mechanisms: one formal (viz., formal integrative mechanisms) and one informal (viz., corporate socialization mechanisms).

Formal integrative mechanisms. Galbraith (1973) and Nadler and Tushman (1987) identified liaison positions, task forces, and permanent committees as some of the key formal structural mechanisms for integrating multiple units of an organization. It is easy to see that the greater the extent to which a subsidiary is linked to the rest of the global network through such integrative mechanisms, the greater would be the density of communication interface between the subsidiary and other units, thereby contributing positively to media richness (Daft and Lengel, 1986). Thus, focusing on knowledge *out*flows from the subsidiary, we can now operationalize Proposition 3 in terms of the following concrete hypotheses: *ceteris paribus, the greater the reliance on formal mechanisms (liaison personnel, task forces, permanent committees) to integrate a subsidiary with the rest of the MNC, the greater will be the knowledge outflows from that subsidiary to peer subsidiaries (H3a) and to the parent corporation (H3a')*. Similarly, focusing on knowledge *inflows* into the subsidiary, we can also operationalize Proposition 4 in terms of the following testable hypotheses: *ceteris paribus, the greater the reliance on formal mechanisms (liaison personnel, task forces, permanent committees) to integrate a subsidiary with the rest of the MNC, the greater will be the knowledge inflows into that subsidiary from peer subsidiaries (H4a) and from the parent corporation (H4a')*.

Corporate socialization mechanisms. Corporate socialization mechanisms refer to those organizational mechanisms which build interpersonal familiarity, personal affinity, and convergence in cognitive maps among personnel from different subsidiaries (Edstrom and Galbraith, 1977; Van Maanen and Schein, 1979). Greater interpersonal familiarity and personal affinity can be expected to increase the openness of communication between the interacting parties. Further, as Daft and Lengel (1986) have suggested, personal and more open communication increases the richness of communication channels. Thus, we would argue that greater participation in corporate socialization mechanisms would have a positive impact on the richness of transmission channels between the focal subsidiary and other units.

In this study, we separate "lateral" from "vertical" socialization mechanisms. Examples of the former would be: job transfers to peer subsidiaries and participation in multi-subsidiary executive programs; similarly, examples of the latter would be: job transfers to corporate headquarters and participation in corporate mentoring programs (Ghoshal and Bartlett, 1988). Focusing now on knowledge *outflows* from the focal subsidiary, we can advance the following additional operationalizations of Proposition 3: *ceteris paribus, the greater the lateral socialization of a subsidiary president, the greater will be the knowledge outflows from that subsidiary to peer subsidiaries (H3b); further, ceteris paribus, the greater the vertical socialization of a subsidiary president, the greater will be the knowledge outflows from*

that subsidiary to the parent corporation (H3b'). Similarly, focusing now on knowledge *inflows* into the focal subsidiary, we can advance the following additional operationalizations of Proposition 4: *ceteris paribus, the greater the lateral socialization of a subsidiary president, the greater will be the knowledge inflows into that subsidiary from peer subsidiaries (H4b); further, ceteris paribus, the greater the vertical socialization of a subsidiary president, the greater will be the knowledge inflows into that subsidiary from the parent corporation (H4b')*.

Motivational disposition of the target unit

We argued earlier that a subsidiary's motivational disposition to acquire/accept knowledge from other units within the enterprise would be a function of (i) incentives that increase subsidiary managers' eagerness to learn, (ii) the relative paucity of the subsidiary's knowledge stock, and/or (iii) coercive pressures from corporate headquarters. Based on this reasoning, we operationalized the construct of motivational disposition of the target unit in terms of three variables: subsidiary vs. corporate focus of the incentives for the subsidiary president (a determinant of eagerness to learn), relative economic level (a determinant of the paucity of local knowledge stock), and HQ-subsidiary decentralization (a determinant of coercive pressures).

Incentive focus. Unlike the case of knowledge outflows where the required motivational disposition can be characterized as "eagerness to help others," in the case of knowledge inflows, the required motivation would be characterized as "eagerness to learn and to help oneself." We would argue that, other things being equal, subsidiary personnel would be more eager to learn in those contexts where the linkage between incentives and the subsidiary's *own* capabilities is tighter rather than weaker i.e., in contexts where incentives are linked more tightly to the focal subsidiary's *own* performance than to the performance of a cluster of subsidiaries. This is so because, unlike cluster-based incentives, which can create free-rider problems, subsidiary-based incentives would create a stronger disposition to learn from any and all sources. These arguments yield the following operationalizations of Proposition 5: *ceteris paribus, the greater the extent to which a subsidiary president's bonus is subsidi-*

480   *A. K. Gupta and V. Govindarajan*

ary-focused rather than network-focused, the greater will be the knowledge inflows into that subsidiary from peer subsidiaries (H5a) and from the parent corporation (H5a').

Relative economic level. Paralleling our discussion on this variable in the context of knowledge outflows, we expect that, other things being equal, the lower the level of economic advancement of the "host" country (i.e., where the subsidiary is located) vis-a-vis the "home" country (i.e., where the parent is located), the more eager subsidiary personnel would be to learn from the parent corporation. They are likely to perceive the knowledge stock of the parent as relatively more valuable and, thus, are likely to regard knowledge inflows as a potential source of competitive advantage against other players in the local market. Knowledge inflows into such subsidiaries may also be facilitated by explicit public policy regimes that mandate technology inflows as the condition for allowing MNCs access to the local market; as an example, this is illustrated well by the recent decisions of the Chinese government (Smith and Hamilton, 1995: 2). These arguments suggest the following additional operationalization of Proposition 5: *ceteris paribus, the lower the level of the host country's economic development relative to the home country, the greater will be the knowledge inflows into the subsidiary from the parent corporation (H5b')*. As discussed in the context of knowledge outflows, given our nodal level of analysis, we neither advance nor test any hypotheses pertaining to the relative economic levels of subsidiary pairs.

Headquarters-subsidiary decentralization. The concept of decentralization (or its obverse i.e., centralization) has had a long history of research in organization theory (see Ford and Slocum, 1977 for an extensive review). Even in the domain of research on MNCs, scholars have argued that centralization is "one of the fundamental dimensions of organization design" (Egelhoff, 1988: 129). Our expectations of a linkage between decentralization and knowledge inflows into a subsidiary parallel the broader arguments of DiMaggio and Powell (1983), echoed also by Levitt and March (1988), that coercion is one of the major (but not the sole) drivers of inter-organizational isomorphism. In the MNC context also, similar arguments have been advanced by many scholars (e.g., Gates and Egelhoff, 1986; Ghoshal and Bartlett, 1988).

These arguments yield the following additional operationalization of Proposition 5: *ceteris paribus, the lower the decentralization of decision-making authority to a subsidiary, the greater will be the knowledge inflows into that subsidiary from the parent corporation (H5c')*. Since the construct of decentralization pertains to parent-subsidiary relationships only, we advance no hypotheses pertaining to the impact of decentralization on knowledge inflows from peer subsidiaries.

Absorptive capacity of the target unit

We argued earlier that the absorptive capacity of a subsidiary would be a function of (i) its familiarity with the incoming knowledge, and (ii) interunit homophily. Based on this reasoning, we operationalized the construct of absorptive capacity in terms of the following two variables: mode of entry (a determinant of the subsidiary's ex-ante familiarity with the corporate-wide knowledge base) and the proportion of local nationals vs. expatriates within the subsidiary's top management team (a measure of the interunit homophily of subsidiary managers).

Mode of entry. Literature on foreign direct investment (see e.g., Hennart and Park, 1993) has argued theoretically and demonstrated empirically that the less the overlap between existing corporate know-how and the know-how required to succeed in a host market, the greater the probability of acquisition as the mode of entry. Thus, as we discussed earlier, relative to greenfield operations, acquired subsidiaries are more likely to have a non-duplicative knowledge base vis-a-vis the parent corporation. Building on Cohen and Levinthal's (1990) arguments regarding the determinants of absorptive capacity, it follows that, on average, the novelty of acquired subsidiaries' knowledge base should also imply a lower absorptive capacity for intra-corporate knowledge relative to the case with greenfield subsidiaries. Based on these arguments, we can now operationalize Proposition 6 in terms of the following concrete hypotheses: *ceteris paribus, relative to greenfield operations, acquired subsidiaries will engage in less knowledge inflows from peer subsidiaries (H6a) and from the parent corporation (H6a')*.[1]

---

[1] An anonymous reviewer has pointed out that, at first glance, the two hypotheses under H6 might appear inconsistent with

Proportion of local nationals in the subsidiary's top management team. Several studies have indicated that national background accounts for significant differences in managerial perspectives (e.g., Tung, 1982; Zeira, 1986). Accordingly, the greater the proportion of local nationals (i.e., the lower the proportion of expatriates) within the subsidiary's top management team (TMT), the lower would be the homophily between the subsidiary and the rest of the corporation. Building on Rogers' arguments (1995), we would expect that inter-unit homophily is likely to be positively associated with absorptive capacity. This is so because greater homophily implies a greater commonality in language systems as well as in the meanings assigned to the artifacts of communication. Thus, on average, subsidiaries with a greater proportion of local nationals within the TMT can be expected to have lower absorptive capacity for incoming knowledge from the rest of the corporate network. These arguments yield the following operationalization of Proposition 6: *ceteris paribus, the greater the proportion of local nationals within the subsidiary's top management team, the less will be the knowledge inflows into that subsidiary from peer subsidiaries (H6b) and from the parent corporation (H6b').*[2]

---

the two hypotheses under H1. In H1, we predicted that, because of their large non-duplicative knowledge base, acquired subsidiaries would exhibit high knowledge outflows; an implicit assumption underlying this prediction was that such knowledge would be absorbed by the receiving units. However, H6 argues that unfamiliarity with incoming knowledge would reduce absorptive capacity among the receiving units. Thus, H1 could not be true unless mode of entry has a different effect on flows from the subsidiary to the MNC than it does on flows from the MNC to the subsidiary. We believe this to be the case. The roots of this differing effect lie in the following two observations: One, the typical acquisition represents a *voluntary* event for the acquiring MNC but an *involuntary* event for the acquired subsidiary; thus, the willingness of the acquiring MNC to integrate the new knowledge of the acquired unit should, on average, be greater than the willingness of the acquired unit to integrate the new knowledge of the acquiring MNC. Two, the typical MNC would have much greater experience at acquiring and integrating new units than the typical unit would have in being acquired and integrated; accordingly, on average, the acquirer's ability to digest new knowledge should be greater than that of the acquired unit.

[2]We should note that nationality structure of a subsidiary's TMT has the potential to affect knowledge inflows not only through its impact on absorptive capacity but also through its impact on richness of transmission channels between the local subsidiary and the rest of the global network. It does appear likely that, on average, relative to local nationals, expatriates should have stronger and longer-tenured social ties with man-

Control variables

Country of origin. There already exists a large body of both theoretical and empirical literature dealing with the fact that country of origin has a major impact on the propensities of MNCs vis-a-vis the choice of global strategies, organizational structures and control systems, as well as internal corporate cultures (e.g., Bartlett and Ghoshal, 1989; Egelhoff, 1984; Franko, 1976; Porter, 1994; Yip, Roos and Johansson, 1994). Accordingly, all of our hypotheses were tested after controlling for the effect of country-of-origin of the MNC.

Industry resource characteristics. As discussed earlier, economic theory posits that MNCs come to be primarily because external markets are less effective and efficient at knowledge transfer than intracorporate mechanisms (Caves, 1982; Hymer, 1960; Kindleberger, 1969). Empirical tests of this theory have consistently shown that industries characterized by greater degrees of knowledge intensities (industries with higher R&D-to-sales-ratios and/or higher advertising-to-sales ratios) tend to be more global than other industries (e.g., Goedde, 1978; Grueber, Mehta, and Vernon, 1967; Horst, 1972). Accordingly, we deemed it important that, in testing our hypotheses, we control also for the potential effects of three resource characteristics of the MNC's industry: R&D intensity, fixed asset intensity, and advertising intensity (Collis and Ghemawat, 1994).

Nature of subsidiary's operations. It is well accepted that foreign subsidiaries will often vary in the scope of value chain activities included within their operations (Porter, 1986). The pres-

---

agers at corporate HQ and in other subsidiaries. In fact, as the correlations in Table 1 indicate, there does exist a strong negative correlation (-0.59, $p < 0.001$) between proportion of local nationals in the subsidiary's TMT and vertical corporate socialization. Thus, as pointed out by an anonymous reviewer and the consulting editor, the question arises as to whether, in the context of our study, TMT nationality might be a better proxy for another factor (such as richness of transmission channels) rather than absorptive capacity. We believe that this would indeed be a serious concern if we did not have any direct measures of socialization mechanisms as one of the hypothesized antecedents of knowledge inflows. However, as captured in H3b, H3b', H4b, and H4b', we do test for the direct effect of socialization mechanisms on knowledge inflows. Thus, in a *multivariate* regression context, any remaining impact of TMT nationality on knowledge inflows is likely to be due primarily to absorptive capacity rather than transmission channel considerations.

ence or absence of any particular activity within the subsidiary's operations can be expected to shape the nature of the subsidiary's interactions with the rest of the corporation and, thus, the nature of knowledge inflows into and outflows from the subsidiary. Accordingly, all of our hypotheses were tested after controlling also for the potential effects of two dummy variables: presence of a primary upstream activity (i.e., R&D and/or manufacturing) and presence of a primary downstream activity (i.e., marketing and sales).

METHOD

Sample

Data for this study were collected through a combination of questionnaire surveys and secondary sources. The following steps guided the development of the questionnaire instrument: (i) interviews with subsidiary presidents and corporate-level executives in six MNCs to understand and clarify the phenomenon of interest, (ii) a review of previous research to locate, wherever possible, measures that would appropriately capture the constructs under study, and (iii) a pretesting of the questionnaire for clarity and relevance through face-to-face interviews with four subsidiary presidents (two American and two non-American).

The pre-tested questionnaires were mailed to the heads (variously titled as presidents, managing directors, or general managers) of 987 foreign subsidiaries of major MNCs headquartered in the U.S. (407 subsidiaries of 19 MNCs), Japan (270 subsidiaries of 41 MNCs), and Europe (310 subsidiaries of 15 MNCs). Subsidiary presidents within Japanese MNCs received both an English and a Japanese language questionnaire; initial interviews with the European companies indicated that only the English-language questionnaire would suffice. The U.S. sample was drawn from the list of the largest U.S.-based MNCs contained in the International Directory of Corporate Affiliations (National Register, 1991); this was also the approach used for developing a list of subsidiaries for 9 out of the 15 European MNCs. In the case of the other 6 European MNCs, the list of subsidiaries was drawn up in cooperation with the senior-most corporate executive in charge of strategic planning, an approach also used in the case of all of the Japanese MNCs. Given the constraints of time and funding and given the

need to obtain access, it was not possible to use a random sample either from the entire universe of MNCs or from the entire subset of MNCs headquartered in the U.S., Europe, and Japan. Nonetheless, given the diversity of industries in which the sampled firms operate (food products, industrial machinery, computers, telecommunications, pharmaceuticals, automobiles, chemical production, electronics, consumer durables, consumer nondurables, etc.), there is no *prima facie* reason to expect any systematic bias in the findings from subsidiaries within these firms.

A personalized cover letter accompanying each questionnaire explained the purpose of the study and provided assurances regarding the confidentiality of collected data. In order to minimize response bias, the participants were also provided with pre-addressed envelopes to enable them to return the completed questionnaires directly to the researchers without any risk of perusal by others in their firms. A total of 374 questionnaires (38 percent) were returned—a response rate that compares very favorably with past survey-based research studies in the strategic management area. The number of respondents for U.S., Japan, and European MNCs were 117 (28 percent), 112 (41 percent), and 145 (46 percent), respectively. To test for inter-rater reliability on the most critical variables in the study (knowledge outflows and inflows), we were also able to get responses on these knowledge flow variables from the immediate corporate-level direct-report superiors of 89 of the responding subsidiary presidents.

For the sample, median worldwide revenues and median number of total employees for the parent firms were \$5.8 billion and 32,100 respectively; at the subsidiary level, the median number of employees per subsidiary was 350. These figures pertain to 1991, the year in which the survey data were collected.

Measures

A summary of how the independent variables as well as the control variables were measured is contained in the Appendix. Wherever possible, we used standard well-established research instruments with minor changes in wording to adapt the instrument to the multinational context. Given below are details pertaining to how the four variables central to this study – knowledge outflows to peer subsidiaries (KO-S), knowledge outflows to the parent corporation (KO-P), knowledge inflows from peer subsidiaries (KI-S), and knowledge inflows from the parent corporation (KI-P) – were measured.

As stated earlier, in this study, we focus on the transfer of largely procedural types of knowledge (e.g., product designs, distribution know-how, etc.) but not on the transfer of largely declarative types of knowledge (e.g., monthly financial results). Knowledge flow data were collected on the following seven items: (1) marketing know-how, (2) distribution know-how, (3) packaging design/technology, (4) product designs, (5) process designs, (6) purchasing know-how, and (7) management systems and practices. For *each* of these seven items, the subsidiary president was asked to indicate on a 7-point scale (ranging from "not at all" to "a very great deal") the extent to which the subsidiary engaged in transfers of "knowledge and skills" in *each* of the following four directions: (1) "provides knowledge and skills to sister subsidiaries," (2) "provides knowledge and skills to parent corporation," (3) "receives knowledge and skills from sister subsidiaries," and (4) "receives knowledge and skills from the parent corporation." For *each* of these knowledge flow directions, responses across the seven items were averaged to yield composite measures of KO-S, KO-P, KI-S, and KI-P. For these four variables, the means, the standard deviations, and Chronbach alpha values respectively were as follows: KO-S (2.36, 1.25, 0.89), KO-P (2.39, 1.20, 0.87), KI-S (2.21, 1.27, 0.92), and KI-P (3.75, 1.59, 0.89).

Given the 1-to-7 range of the 7-point scale used to measure knowledge flows, the mean values of the four types of knowledge flows in our sample (2.36, 2.39, 2.21, and 3.75) may at first glance appear low. However, as clarified above, it should be noted that this study has focused on the transfers of largely procedural knowledge (i.e., know-how) rather than on the transfers of largely declarative knowledge (e.g., operational data). Given the tacit rather than codified nature of much procedural knowledge, we would expect the mean levels of knowledge transfers in this arena to be on the lower rather than higher side. It also should be noted that, as would be expected in the case of hierarchical organizations, pairwise t-tests revealed that knowledge inflows from the parent to focal subsidiaries (KI-P) were significantly greater (at

$p < 0.001$) than each of the other three types of knowledge flows.

Given the perceptual nature of these knowledge flow measures and given their centrality for our study, we deemed it critical that they be tested also for inter-rater reliability. Towards this goal, we were able to get responses on the same knowledge flow variables from the immediate corporate-level direct report superiors of 89 of the subsidiary presidents. Each superior completed a *separate* questionnaire containing the subsidiary's name for *each* of the sampled subsidiaries reporting to him/her. This questionnaire used exactly the same seven dimensions of knowledge. For each of these seven items, the superior was asked to indicate on a 7-point scale (ranging from "not at all" to "a very great deal") the extent to which he/she expected the named subsidiary to engage in transfers of "knowledge and skills" in each of the following two directions: (1) "provides knowledge and skills to the rest of the corporation," and (2) "receives knowledge and skills from the rest of the corporation." For *each* of these two knowledge flow directions, responses across the seven items were averaged to yield composite measures of expected "knowledge outflows from the subsidiary" (Chronbach alpha = 0.82) and expected "knowledge inflows into the subsidiary" (Chronbach alpha = 0.81) respectively. For these 89 subsidiaries, this corporate-level measure of expected knowledge outflows from the subsidiary correlates at 0.23 ($p < 0.05$) with the average of KO-S and KO-P; similarly, the corporate-level measure of expected knowledge inflows into the subsidiary correlates at 0.38 ($p < 0.001$) with the average of KI-S and KI-P. Given these positive correlations in the data from subsidiary presidents and their immediate superiors, in a context where they are typically separated by a geographic distance of thousands of miles, we believe that our measures of KO-S, KO-P, KI-S, and KI-P can be deemed as reliable.

Table 1 contains the matrix of zero-order correlations among these and all other variables utilized in this study. As this table indicates, the average correlation among the four knowledge flow variables is 0.32 implying that the four types of knowledge flows are distinct, albeit related, variables not only conceptually (Gupta and Govindarajan, 1991) but also empirically.

Table 1 Zero-order correlation coefficients among all variables under study

		X_1	X_2	X_3	X_4	X_5	X_6	X_7	X_8	X_9	X_{10}	X_{11}	X_{12}	X_{13}	X_{14}	X_{15}	X_{16}	X_{17}
X_1	KO-S	***																
X_2	KO-P	0.54***																
X_3	KI-S	0.58***	0.33***															
X_4	KI-P	0.00	0.19***	0.25**														
X_5	R&D Intensity	-0.12*	-0.07	-0.15**	0.15**													
X_6	Fixed Asset Intensity	-0.04	-0.03	0.02	-0.15	-0.28***												
X_7	Advertising Intensity	0.20***	0.14**	0.07	-0.02	-0.21***	-0.39***											
X_8	Upstream Activities[1]	0.14**	0.08***	0.05**	-0.08	-0.16	0.06	0.08	***									
X_9	Downstream Activities[2]	0.25***	0.22***	0.13	-0.06***	-0.05*	0.03	0.06	0.27***									
X_{10}	Mode of Entry[3]	0.09***	-0.03**	0.01	-0.32***	-0.12***	0.02	0.04	0.16***	0.04*								
X_{11}	Subsidiary Size	0.22	0.14**	0.01	0.06***	-0.20***	-0.00	-0.00*	0.37	0.09	0.03***							
X_{12}	Relative Economic Level	0.08	0.15	-0.05*	-0.36***	-0.22*	0.10	0.13	0.04	0.03	0.35*	0.06	***					
X_{13}	Incentive Focus[4]	0.08***	0.02	0.12	0.06	0.13	-0.05	-0.04	-0.01	0.01	-0.13*	-0.02	-0.18***					
X_{14}	Formal Integ Mechanisms	0.29***	0.24***	0.22***	0.21***	-0.06	-0.03	-0.01	0.01	-0.01	-0.12*	0.09***	-0.02	0.15**				
X_{15}	Lateral Socializn Mech.	0.25***	0.15**	0.21***	0.14**	-0.12*	-0.08***	0.11***	0.13**	0.20***	-0.08***	0.22	-0.11***	0.15***	0.21***			
X_{16}	Vertical Socializn Mech.	-0.22***	-0.14***	-0.25***	0.25*	0.21***	-0.19***	-0.20*	-0.09***	-0.08	-0.21*	0.06**	-0.18	0.15	0.21	0.03		
X_{17}	HQ-Sub Decentralization	0.06***	-0.06**	-0.04***	-0.13**	-0.17	0.06***	0.13***	0.25***	0.04***	0.11	0.16	0.03**	0.08*	0.00	0.08	-0.06***	
X_{18}	Local Nationals in TMT	0.19	0.14	0.22	-0.14	-0.14	0.18	0.23	0.22	0.22	0.08	0.02	0.12	0.10	0.01	0.06	-0.59***	0.12**

[1] 1 = Subsidiary has an upstream activity (R&D and/or manufacturing); 0 = Subsidiary has no upstream activity.
[2] 1 = Subsidiary has a downstream activity (marketing and sales); 0 = Subsidiary has no downstream activity.
[3] Mode of entry: 1 = Acquisition; 0 = Greenfield.
[4] Higher values signify that the incentive system is more network, rather than subsidiary, focused.
*one-tail $p < 0.05$; **one-tail $p < 0.01$; ***one-tail $p < 0.001$

RESULTS

We have four dependent variables (KO-S, KO-P, KI-S, or KI-P) and a set of hypotheses pertaining to each of these variables. Each set of these hypotheses was tested through a series of multivariate OLS regressions: first, we entered the four control variables pertaining to country-of-origin; second, we entered the three control variables pertaining to industry resource characteristics; third, we entered the two control variables pertaining to nature of subsidiary operations; finally, we entered the independent variables hypothesized as the determinants of that particular type of knowledge flows. Tables 2 through 5 contain the results of these regression analyses.

Knowledge outflows to peer subsidiaries

Table 2 presents the results of regression analyses to test our predictions regarding the impact of value of knowledge stock (P1), motivational disposition (P2), and transmission channels (P3) on knowledge outflows to peer subsidiaries.

Value of knowledge stock. In the context of knowledge outflows to peer subsidiaries, we operationalized this construct in terms of mode of entry and subsidiary size. The results in Table 2 (equation 4) support both of the resulting hypotheses. More specifically, knowledge outflows to peer subsidiaries are higher in the case of (i) subsidiaries that were acquired rather than set up as greenfield operations (beta for "mode of

Table 2. Determinants of knowledge outflows to peer subsidiaries
dependent variable = Knowledge outflows to peer subsidiaries (KO-S)

Independent Variables	Hypothesized Relationship	Standardized Beta Coefficients			
		Equation 1	Equation 2	Equation 3	Equation 4
Japan		−0.233***	−0.244***	−0.184**	−0.153**
U.K.		0.041	0.003	−0.003	−0.061
Sweden		−0.046	−0.031	−0.043	−0.080
Finland		0.065	−0.058	−0.045	−0.019
R&D Intensity			−0.069	−0.046	0.032
Fixed Asset Intensity			−0.086	−0.078	0.001
Advertising Intensity			0.128*	0.130*	0.155*
Upstream Activities[1]				0.070	0.005
Downstream Activities[2]				0.195***	0.187***
P1: Value of Knowledge Stock					
Mode of Entry[3]	H1a (+)				0.127**
Subsidiary Size	H1b (+)				0.169**
P2: Motivational Disposition					
Incentive Focus[4]	H2a (+)				−0.003
P3: Transmission Channels					
Formal Integrative Mechanisms	H3a (+)				0.256***
Lateral Socialization Mechanisms	H3b (+)				0.100*
R^2		0.072	0.095	0.139	0.256
d.f.		4,335	7,332	9,330	14,325
F		6.50***	4.99***	5.91***	8.00***
ΔR^2		0.072	0.023	0.043	0.117
d.f.		4,335	3,332	2,330	5,325
F		6.50***	2.84*	8.33***	10.27***

[1] 1 = Subsidiary has an upstream activity (R&D and/or manufacturing); 0 = Subsidiary has no upstream activity.
[2] 1 = Subsidiary has a downstream activity (marketing and sales); 0 = Subsidiary has no downstream activity.
[3] Mode of entry: 1 = Acquisition; 0 = Greenfield.
[4] Higher values signify that the incentive system is more network, rather than subsidiary, focused.
*$p < 0.05$
**$p < 0.01$
***$p < 0.001$ For t-tests, these are one-tail values.

486   A. K. Gupta and V. Govindarajan

Table 3.   Determinants of knowledge outflows to the parent corporation
Dependent variable = Knowledge outflows to the parent corporation (KO-P)

Independent Variables	Hypothesized Relationship	Standardized Beta Coefficients			
		Equation 5	Equation 6	Equation 7	Equation 8
Japan		−0.127*	−0.141*	−0.095	−0.088
U.K.		0.089	0.062	0.063	−0.038
Sweden		0.018	0.035	0.030	−0.021
Finland		0.020	−0.092	−0.079	−0.135
R&D Intensity			−0.043	−0.031	−0.002
Fixed Asset Intensity			−0.089	−0.081	−0.063
Advertising Intensity			0.120	0.120	0.129*
Upstream Activities[1]				−0.002	−0.033
Downstream Activities[2]				0.181***	0.174***
P1: Value of Knowledge Stock					
Mode of Entry[3]	H1a' (+)				−0.063
Subsidiary Size	H1b' (+)				0.121*
Relative Economic Level	H1c' (+)				0.169**
P2: Motivational Disposition					
Incentive Focus[4]	H2a' (+)				−0.018
P3: Transmission Channels					
Formal Integrative Mechanisms	H3a' (+)				0.208***
Lateral Socialization Mechanisms	H3b' (+)				−0.073
R^2		0.033	0.054	0.084	0.162
d.f.		4,322	7,319	9,317	15,311
F		2.75*	2.58**	3.23***	4.02***
ΔR^2		0.033	0.020	0.030	0.078
d.f.		4,322	3,319	2,317	6,311
F		2.75*	2.30	5.28**	4.84***

[1] 1 = Subsidiary has an upstream activity (R&D and/or manufacturing); 0 = Subsidiary has no upstream activity.
[2] 1 = Subsidiary has a downstream activity (marketing and sales); 0 = Subsidiary has no downstream activity.
[3] Mode of entry: 1 = Acquisition; 0 = Greenfield.
[4] Higher values signify that the incentive system is more network, rather than subsidiary, focused.
*$p < 0.05$
**$p < 0.01$
***$p < 0.001$ For t-tests, these are one-tail values.

entry" = 0.127, $p < 0.01$; thus, H1a is supported), and (ii) subsidiaries that are larger in size (beta for "subsidiary size" = 0.169, $p < 0.01$; thus, H1b is supported).

Motivational disposition. In the context of knowledge outflows to peer subsidiaries, we operationalized this construct in terms of the network vs. subsidiary focus of the incentive system for the subsidiary president. The results in Table 2 (Equation 4) do not support the resulting hypothesis (H2a).

Transmission channels. In the context of knowledge outflows to peer subsidiaries, we operationalized this construct in terms of formal integrative mechanisms and lateral socialization mechanisms. The results in Table 2 (Equation 4) support both of the resulting hypotheses. More

specifically, knowledge outflows to peer subsidiaries are higher in the case of (i) subsidiaries that are integrated more tightly with the rest of the corporation through formal mechanisms (beta for "formal integrative mechanisms" = 0.256, $p < 0.001$; thus, H3a is supported), and (ii) subsidiaries whose presidents have been involved in lateral socialization mechanisms with peer subsidiaries to a greater extent (beta for "lateral socialization mechanisms" = 0.100, $p < 0.05$; thus, H3b is supported).

Knowledge outflows to the parent corporation

Table 3 presents the results of regression analyses to test our predictions regarding the impact of

Table 4. Determinants of knowledge inflows from peer subsidiaries
dependent variable = Knowledge inflows from peer subsidiaries (KI-S)

Independent Variables	Hypothesized Relationship	Standardized Beta Coefficients			
		Equation 9	Equation 10	Equation 11	Equation 12
Japan		−0.333***	−0.362***	−0.349***	−0.231**
U.K.		−0.087	−0.166**	−0.164**	−0.169**
Sweden		−0.064	−0.084	−0.084	−0.087
Finland		−0.088	−0.216**	−0.212**	−0.195**
R&D Intensity			−0.202***	−0.200***	−0.164**
Fixed Asset Intensity			−0.098	−0.095	−0.062
Advertising Intensity			0.029	0.030	0.032
Upstream Activities[1]				−0.017	−0.026
Downstream Activities[2]				0.063	0.055
P4: Transmission Channels					
Formal Integrative Mechanisms	H4a (+)				0.167***
Lateral Socialization Mechanisms	H4b (+)				0.110*
P5: Motivational Disposition					
Incentive Focus[3]	H5a (−)				0.015
P6: Absorptive Capacity					
Mode of Entry[4]	H6a (−)				0.071
Local Nationals in TMT	H6b (−)				0.101
R^2		0.085	0.115	0.119	0.167
d.f.		4,341	7,338	9,336	14,331
F		7.90***	6.29***	5.04***	4.73***
ΔR^2		0.085	0.030	0.004	0.048
d.f.		4,341	3,338	2,336	5,331
F		7.90***	3.88**	0.69	3.80**

[1] 1 = Subsidiary has an upstream activity (R&D and/or manufacturing); 0 = Subsidiary has no upstream activity.
[2] 1 = Subsidiary has a downstream activity (marketing and sales); 0 = Subsidiary has no downstream activity.
[3] Higher values signify that the incentive system is more network, rather than subsidiary, focused.
[4] Mode of entry: 1 = Acquisition; 0 = Greenfield.
*$p < 0.05$
**$p < 0.01$
***$p < 0.001$ For t-tests, these are one-tail values.

value of knowledge stock (P1), motivational disposition (P2), and transmission channels (P3) on knowledge outflows to the parent corporation.

Value of knowledge stock. In the context of knowledge outflows to the parent corporation, we operationalized this construct in terms of mode of entry, subsidiary size, and relative economic level. The results in Table 3 (Equation 8) support two of the resulting three hypotheses. More specifically, knowledge outflows to the parent corporation are higher in the case of (i) subsidiaries that are larger in size (beta for "subsidiary size" = 0.121, $p < 0.05$; thus, H1b′ is supported), and (ii) subsidiaries that are located in countries with a higher level of economic advancement relative to the country of the parent corporation (beta for "relative economic level" = 0.169, $p < 0.01$; thus, H1c′ is supported). There was no

support for our prediction regarding the impact of mode of entry on KO-P (H1a′).

Motivational disposition. In the context of knowledge outflows to the parent corporation also, we operationalized this construct in terms of the network vs. subsidiary focus of the incentive system for the subsidiary president. The results in Table 3 (Equation 8) do not support the resulting hypothesis (H2a′).

Transmission channels. In the context of knowledge outflows to the parent corporation, we operationalized this construct in terms of formal integrative mechanisms and vertical socialization mechanisms. The results in Table 3 (Equation 8) support one of the two resulting hypotheses. More specifically, knowledge outflows to the parent corporation are higher in the case of subsidiaries that are integrated more tightly with the rest of

488   *A. K. Gupta and V. Govindarajan*

Table 5.   Determinants of knowledge inflows from the parent corporation
dependent variable = Knowledge inflows from the parent corporation (KI-P)

Independent Variables	Hypothesized Relationship	Standardized Beta Coefficients			
		Equation 13	Equation 14	Equation 15	Equation 16
Japan		−0.020	−0.042	−0.062	−0.073
U.K.		−0.245***	−0.278***	−0.276***	−0.086
Sweden		−0.077	−0.044	−0.040	0.011
Finland		−0.319***	−0.501***	−0.506***	−0.256***
R&D Intensity			−0.052	−0.063	0.014
Fixed Asset Intensity			−0.151**	−0.153**	−0.095
Advertising Intensity			0.205**	0.206**	0.168**
Upstream Activities[1]				−0.046	−0.009
Downstream Activities[2]				−0.039	−0.033
P4: Transmission Channels					
Formal Integrative Mechanisms	H4a′ (+)				0.182***
Vertical Socialization Mechanisms	H4b′ (+)				0.119*
P5: Motivational Disposition					
Incentive Focus[3]	H5a′ (−)				−0.097*
Relative Economic Level	H5b′ (−)				−0.209***
HQ-Subsidiary Decentralization	H5c′ (−)				−0.086*
P6: Absorptive Capacity					
Mode of Entry[4]	H6a′ (−)				−0.165***
Local Nationals in TMT	H6b′ (−)				−0.009
R^2		0.120	0.180	0.184	0.298
d.f.		4,325	7,322	9,320	16,313
F		11.11***	10.10***	8.01***	8.31***
ΔR^2		0.120	0.060	0.004	0.114
d.f.		4,325	3,322	2,320	7,313
F		11.11***	7.83***	0.74	7.28***

[1] 1 = Subsidiary has an upstream activity (R&D and/or manufacturing); 0 = Subsidiary has no upstream activity.
[2] 1 = Subsidiary has a downstream activity (marketing and sales); 0 = Subsidiary has no downstream activity.
[3] Higher values signify that the incentive system is more network, rather than subsidiary, focused.
[4] Mode of entry: 1 = Acquisition; 0 = Greenfield.
*p < 0.05
**p < 0.01
***p < 0.001 For t-tests, these are one-tail values.

the corporation through formal mechanisms (beta for "formal integrative mechanisms" = 0.208, p < 0.001; thus, H3a′ is supported). There was no support for our prediction regarding the impact of vertical socialization mechanisms on KO-P (H3b′).

Knowledge inflows from peer subsidiaries

Table 4 presents the results of regression analyses to test our predictions regarding the impact of transmission channels (P4), motivational disposition (P5), and absorptive capacity (P6) on knowledge inflows from peer subsidiaries.

Transmission channels. In the context of knowledge inflows from peer subsidiaries, we operationalized this construct in terms of formal

integrative mechanisms and lateral socialization mechanisms. The results in Table 4 (Equation 12) support both of the resulting hypotheses. More specifically, knowledge inflows from peer subsidiaries are higher in the case of (i) subsidiaries that are integrated more tightly with the rest of the corporation through formal mechanisms (beta for "formal integrative mechanisms" = 0.167, p < 0.001; thus, H4a is supported), and (ii) subsidiaries whose presidents have been involved in lateral socialization mechanisms with peer subsidiaries to a greater extent (beta for "lateral socialization mechanisms" = 0.110, p < 0.05; thus, H4b is supported).

Motivational disposition. In the context of knowledge inflows from peer subsidiaries, we operationalized this construct in terms of the network vs. subsidiary focus of the incentive system for the subsidiary president. The results in Table 4 (Equation 12) do not support the resulting hypothesis (H5a).

Absorptive capacity. In the context of knowledge inflows from peer subsidiaries, we operationalized this construct in terms of mode of entry and proportion of local nationals in the subsidiary's top management team. The results in Table 4 (Equation 12) do not support the resulting hypotheses (H6a and H6b).

Knowledge inflows from the parent corporation

Table 5 presents the results of regression analyses to test our predictions regarding the impact of transmission channels (P4), motivational disposition (P5), and absorptive capacity (P6) on knowledge inflows from the parent corporation.

Transmission channels. In the context of knowledge inflows from the parent corporation, we operationalized this construct in terms of formal integrative mechanisms and vertical socialization mechanisms. The results in Table 5 (Equation 16) support both of the resulting hypotheses. More specifically, knowledge inflows from the parent corporation are higher in the case of (i) subsidiaries that are integrated more tightly with the rest of the corporation through formal mechanisms (beta for "formal integrative mechanisms" = 0.182, $p < 0.001$; thus, H4a' is supported), and (ii) subsidiaries whose presidents have been involved in vertical socialization mechanisms with corporate HQ to a greater extent (beta for "vertical socialization mechanisms" = 0.119, $p < 0.05$; thus, H4b' is supported).

Motivational disposition. In the context of knowledge inflows from the parent corporation, we operationalized this construct in terms of the network vs. subsidiary focus of the incentive system for the subsidiary president, relative economic level, and HQ-subsidiary decentralization. The results in Table 5 (Equation 16) support all three of the resulting hypotheses. More specifically, knowledge inflows from the parent corporation are higher in the case of (i) subsidiaries whose presidents operate under more subsidiary-focused, rather than network-focused, incentives (beta for "incentive focus" = −0.097, $p < 0.05$; thus, H5a' is supported), (ii) subsidiaries that are located in countries with a lower level of eco-

nomic advancement relative to the country of the parent corporation (beta for "relative economic level" = −0.209, $p < 0.001$; thus, H5b' is supported), and (iii) subsidiaries that are given less decision-making autonomy by corporate headquarters (beta for "HQ-subsidiary decentralization" = −0.086, $p < 0.05$; thus, H5c' is supported).

Absorptive capacity. In the context of knowledge inflows from the parent corporation, we operationalized this construct in terms of mode of entry and proportion of local nationals in the subsidiary's top management team. The results in Table 5 (Equation 16) support only the first of the two resulting hypotheses. More specifically, knowledge inflows from the parent corporation are higher in the case of subsidiaries that were set up as greenfield operations rather than acquired (beta for "mode of entry" = −0.165, $p < 0.001$; thus, H6a' is supported).

DISCUSSION

Pursuing a nodal level of analysis, this study has investigated both theoretically and empirically the determinants of intra-MNC knowledge flow patterns. While previous studies have focused more narrowly on selected facets of intra-MNC knowledge transfer e.g., tacitness of know-how (Teece, 1977; Zander and Kogut, 1995), and normative integration and inter-subsidiary communication (Ghoshal and Bartlett, 1988), this study has advanced and adopted a more comprehensive theoretical approach. Building on communication theory, we have argued that a complete mapping of the knowledge transfer process requires attention to all of the following five major elements: (i) value of the knowledge possessed by the source unit, (ii) motivational disposition of the source unit regarding the sharing of its knowledge, (iii) the existence, quality, and cost of transmission channels, (iv) motivational disposition of the target unit regarding acceptance of incoming knowledge, and (v) the target unit's absorptive capacity for the incoming knowledge.

Further, unlike previous studies on intra-MNC knowledge transfers, we have conducted separate examinations of knowledge flows that occur *laterally* among peer subsidiaries and those which occur *hierarchically* between a subsidiary and the parent corporation. Given the ongoing devolution

490	A. K. Gupta and V. Govindarajan

of authority and responsibility from the center to the subsidiaries and the ability of information technology to enable direct communication among subsidiaries, we would agree with Bartlett and Ghoshal (1989), Hedlund (1994), Martinez and Jarillo (1989), and others that direct inter-subsidiary interactions are becoming increasingly important.

Utilizing the overarching theoretical framework and the broad propositions depicted in Figure 1, we advanced a set of hypotheses for each of the following four types of knowledge transfer contexts: (i) knowledge outflows to peer subsidiaries, (ii) knowledge outflows to the parent corporation, (iii) knowledge inflows from peer subsidiaries, and (iv) knowledge inflows from the parent corporation. These hypotheses were tested with data collected from the presidents of 374 subsidiaries of 75 MNCs headquartered in the U.S., Europe, and Japan. All hypotheses were tested after controlling for the effects of country-of-origin, the resource characteristics of the MNC's industry, and the nature of the subsidiary's operations.

Commentary on the results

As can be seen from Tables 2–5 (across-table comparisons of R^2 and ΔR^2 values as well as the number of significant beta coefficients), our data had the greatest success in uncovering the determinants of KI-P i.e., knowledge inflows to focal subsidiaries from the parent corporation. In this context, it may be useful to recall our earlier observation that, for the sample as a whole, of the four types of knowledge flows, the magnitude of KI-P was significantly greater than that of each of the other three types of flows. These two empirical observations lead us to draw the following conjectures: (i) Of the four types of knowledge flows examined in this study, the typical MNC has perhaps had the longest experience in undertaking knowledge outflows from the center to the units; (ii) Notwithstanding the fact that MNCs are indeed becoming "heterarchies" (Hedlund, 1994) i.e., integrated complex networks with significant devolution of authority and responsibility to the subsidiaries, the parent corporation continues to serve as the most active creator and diffuser of knowledge within the corporation; and (iii) MNCs' greater experience in managing knowledge outflows from the parent

to the subsidiaries has also made them more "systematic" (as distinct from "stochastic" or "experimental") in managing these particular types of knowledge flows.

Focusing now on the empirical validity of our overarching theoretical framework, we also note from Tables 2–5 that the results support our expectations regarding the importance of four of the five main constructs underlying this framework. More specifically, the results provide either complete or partial support to our predictions regarding the impact of value of knowledge stock and transmission channels on knowledge outflows; similarly, they also provide either complete or partial support to our predictions regarding the impact of transmission channels, motivational disposition to acquire knowledge, and absorptive capacity on knowledge inflows. However, they do not provide any support to our predictions regarding the impact of motivational disposition to share knowledge with other units on knowledge outflows. There are at least two possible explanations for this lack of support: (i) a subsidiary's motivational disposition to share knowledge may depend not only on the incentive system but also on other variables not examined in this study, and/or (ii) in the knowledge transfer process, the motivation of the target unit to acquire knowledge may be far more important than the motivation of the source unit to share its knowledge. An examination of the validity of any of these or other possible explanations must await future research.

At a more micro-level, a closer examination of the 8 hypotheses (out of the total of 23 hypotheses) that were not supported reveals that 3 pertained to "incentive focus," 2 to "mode of entry," 2 to "proportion of local nationals in subsidiary's TMT," and 1 to "vertical socialization mechanisms." Alternatively stated, results failed to support 3 out of the 4 hypotheses dealing with incentive focus, 2 out of the 4 dealing with mode of entry, 2 out of the 2 dealing with proportion of local nationals in subsidiary's TMT, and 1 out of the 2 dealing with vertical socialization mechanisms. There are at least three possible explanations for this lack of support: (i) logical errors in developing the hypotheses, and/or (ii) substitution effects among the independent variables, and/or (iii) irreducible noise in the data. Our conjecture at this stage would be that the last two explanations represent the more likely scenario. Nonetheless, any definitive explanations for the lack of support also must await future research.

Limitations of the study

We can identify three major limitations of this study. First, since every MNC is a network (Ghoshal and Bartlett, 1990), all intra-MNC knowledge transfers take place in the context of the network. As contrasted with "dyadic" or "systemic" approaches to the examination of network-related phenomena, we conducted our examination at the "nodal" level of analysis – the simplest level feasible. In the next subsection focusing on directions for future research, we identify some of the important questions that were not explored by us but which can be examined through future work that looks at knowledge transfers from a dyadic or a systemic perspective.

Second, despite the fact that, in this study, we focused on largely procedural types of knowledge which, on average, tends to be more tacit than declarative knowledge, we neither measured nor explored the impact of degrees of tacitness. Notwithstanding the pioneering studies of Teece (1977), Zander and Kogut (1995), and others, empirical research into how degrees of tacitness affect the knowledge transfer process is still in its infancy.

Finally, the third major limitation of this study has to do with the use of perceptual instruments to measure the extent of knowledge outflows and inflows. Barring the case of certain types of codifiable technology transfers (as in the case of technology licenses), this is a methodological challenge that researchers have yet to overcome. In our view, researchers face at least two hurdles in measuring the extent of knowledge transfers through objective data: (i) Unlike transfers of codified knowledge, the transfers of tacit knowledge leave at best partial objective traces that could be measured by an external researcher; and (ii) Because transfers of tacit knowledge tend to be slow, any real-time investigation of this phenomenon would often require the researcher to undertake a multi-year study of each transfer; by way of example, note that Zander and Kogut (1995) reported that, in their sample, the median time to transfer was five years and, without correcting for censored observations, the average was eight years. It is also instructive to note that,

notwithstanding their excellent access to the MNCs being studied, even Ghoshal and Bartlett (1988: 382) felt compelled to observe: "Collecting objective level measures for the relatively large number of variables for meaningful statistical analysis represented enormous and, for us, insurmountable practical problems."

Directions for future research

As we observed at the beginning of the paper, the creation, diffusion, and absorption of knowledge by organizations in general and, by MNCs in particular, constitutes one of the most important subjects for research in the fields of organization theory (Levitt and March, 1988: Huber, 1991), strategic management (Prahalad and Hamel, 1994), evolutionary economics (Nelson and Winter, 1982), and international business (Buckley and Casson, 1976; Ghoshal and Bartlett, 1988; Kogut and Zander, 1993; Teece, 1977). Conceptual work in this area is still in the early stages and empirical work is almost literally at the stage of infancy. Thus, although we view the contributions of this study as important, in light of future possibilities, we view them as at best modest. There are several promising directions for future research.

First, we believe that the payoffs from future investigations at the dyadic and/or systemic levels are likely to be high. At the *dyadic* level of analysis, at least two of the important issues to investigate would be: (i) the impact of bilateral homophily (Lazarsfeld and Merton, 1964) on dispositions to engage in outflows and inflows, and (ii) the importance of reciprocity i.e., is A's disposition to share its knowledge with B dependent on B's disposition to share its knowledge with A? At the *systemic* level of analysis, some of the important issues would be: (i) the impact of a unit's network centrality on the extent of knowledge outflows as well as knowledge inflows, (ii) the impact of network density on the overall magnitude of knowledge flows through the network, and (iii) the impact of global competitive intensity faced by the MNC on the magnitude and the directionality of knowledge flows.

A second line of productive inquiry would be to compare and contrast what we would term as "complementary" vs. "substitutive" knowledge transfer contexts. By complementary contexts, we refer to the transfer of knowledge along different

462

International and Global Strategy

492   A. K. Gupta and V. Govindarajan

stages in the company's value chain e.g., the transfer of technical knowledge from the development laboratories to the factories and the marketing units and the transfer of market knowledge from the field back to the facories and the laboratories; in these instances, knowledge transfers occur in contexts where the source and the target units possess complementary knowledge stocks. In contrast, substitutive knowledge transfer contexts can be said to exist when the source and the target units engage in identical or similar activities (e.g., two laboratories, or two factories, or two sales units) and the transfer involves the imposition of the source unit's superior knowhow over that of the target's allegedly inferior knowhow. We would expect that the motivational dispositions of both the source and the target units are likely to be radically different in the case of complementary vs. substitutive knowledge transfers.

A third line of productive inquiry would be a deeper application and examination of the overarching framework advanced in this paper. There are many other possible determinants of the value of a source unit's knowledge stock e.g., the resource base of the unit, the internal organization of the unit, and the competitive environment in the host country. Similarly, there are many other possible determinants of motivational dispositions to engage in inflows or outflows e.g., personal characteristics of subsidiary managers such as age or locus of control, their organizational commitment, and so forth. This is also true for the other elements in our model viz., transmission channels and absorptive capacity. In the case of transmission channels, the impact of communication mechanisms including the use of electronic media is an obvious topic for future research. Similarly, future investigations into how absorptive capacity of a receiving unit is affected not merely by its existing knowledge stock but also by its internal organization are likely to yield valuable insights. For example, building on Cohen and Levinthal (1990), it should be useful to examine the impact of intra-subsidiary communication as well as a subsidiary's activism at knowledge creation on its capacity to absorb incoming knowledge.

A fourth line of productive inquiry would be to go deeper into the question of tacitness. It seems to us that, while the conceptual literature on how the tacitness of knowledge affects its transfer is notable for its abundance, systematic

empirical investigations into how tacit knowledge gets tranferred and the extent to which its transfer does or does not require ex ante codification is all too rare. Thus, our advocacy would be to urge greater efforts towards empirical rather than conceptual studies on the topic of tacitness.

Finally, a productive line of inquiry would also be to examine the joint (i.e., interactive) effects of capability, motivation, and transmission channels on knowledge flow patterns. Given that research on knowledge flows within MNCs is still in its infancy, in this study, we focused exclusively on the main effects of these constructs. Nonetheless, since the results of this study lend support to the validity of our framework, a logical next step would be to develop and test more complex theoretical models.

ACKNOWLEDGEMENTS

Paritial funding support for this study was provided by the Center for International Business Education and Research (The University of Maryland at College Park), The Amos Tuck School of Business Administration (Dartmouth College), and The International Management Research Institute (Tokyo). The authors have benefited from comments on earlier versions of this paper from Robert Burgelman, Ranjay Gulati, Lee Preston, M. Susan Taylor, as well as participants at the 1997 Strategy Conference at Stanford University.

REFERENCES

Allport, G. W. (1937). *Personality: A Psychological Interpretation*. Holt, New York.
Barney, J. (1991). 'Firm resources and sustained competitive advantage', *Journal of Management*, **17**, pp. 99–120.
Bartlett, C. A. and S. Ghoshal (1989). *Managing across Borders: The Transnational Solution*. Harvard Business School Press, Boston, MA.
Buckley, P. J. and M. Casson (1976). *The Future of the Multinational Enterprise*: Holmes & Meier, New York, pp. 66–84.
Caves, R. E. (1971). 'International corporations: The industrial economics of foreign investment', *Economica*, **38**, pp. 1–27.
Caves, R. E. (1982). '*Multinational Enterprise and Economic Analysis*. Cambridge University Press, Cambridge, U.K.
Cohen, W. M. and D. A. Levinthal (1990). 'Absorptive

Copyright © 2000 John Wiley & Sons, Ltd.

Strat. Mgmt. J., **21**: 473–496 (2000)

capacity: A new perspective on learning and innovation', *Administrative Science Quarterly*, **35**, pp. 128–152.

Collis, D. and P. Ghemawat (1994). 'Industry analysis: Understanding industry structure and dynamics'. In L. Fahey and R. M. Randall (eds.), *The Portable MBA in Strategy*. John Wiley, New York, pp. 171–194.

Cyert, R. M. (1995). 'Management of knowledge'. Keynote address at the Carnegie Bosch Institute's 1995 International Conference on High Performance Global Corporations. Excerpted in *Global View*, Newsletter of the Carnegie Bosch Institute for Applied Studies in Management, The Carnegie-Mellon University.

Daft, R. L. and R. H. Lengel (1986). 'Organizational information requirements, media richness, and structural design', *Management Science*, **32**, pp. 554–571.

Dierickx, I. and K. Cool (1989). 'Asset stock accumulation and sustainability of competitive advantage', *Management Science*, **35**, pp. 1504–1514.

DiMaggio, P. J. and W. W. Powell (1983). 'The iron cage revisited: Institutional isomorphism and collective rationality in organizational fields', *American Sociological Review*, **48**, pp. 147–160.

Edstrom, A. and J. R. Galbraith (1977). 'Transfer of managers as a coordination and control strategy in multinational organizations', *Administrative Science Quarterly*, **22**, pp. 248–263.

Egelhoff, W. G. (1984). 'Patterns of control in U.S., U.K., and European multinational corporations', *Journal of International Business Studies*, **15**(3), pp. 73–83.

Egelhoff, W. G. (1988). *Organizing the Multinational Enterprise: An Information-processing Perspective*. Ballinger, Cambridge, MA.

Ford, J. D. and J. W. Slocum (1977). 'Size, technology, environment, and the structure of organizations', *Academy of Management Review*, **2**, pp. 561–575.

Franko, L. G. (1976). *The European Multinationals: A Renewed Challenge to American and British Big Business*. Greylock, Stamford, CT.

Galbraith, J. R. (1973). *Designing Complex Organizations*. Addison-Wesley, Reading, MA.

Gates, S. R. and W. G. Egelhoff (1986). 'Centralization in headquarters–subsidiary relationships', *Journal of International Business Studies*, **17**(2), pp. 71–92.

Ghoshal, S. (1987). 'Global strategy: An organizing framework', *Strategic Management Journal*, **8**(5), pp. 425–440.

Ghoshal, S. and C. A. Bartlett (1988). 'Creation, adoption, and diffusion of innovation by subsidiaries of multinational corporations', *Journal of International Business Studies*, **19**, pp. 365–388.

Ghoshal, S. and C. A. Bartlett (1990). 'The multinational corporation as an interorganizational network', *Academy of Management Review*, **15**, pp. 603–625.

Ghoshal, S., H. Korine and G. Szulanski (1994). 'Interunit communication in multinational corporations', *Management Science*, **40**(1), pp. 96–110.

Goedde, A. G. (1978). 'U.S. multinational manufacturing firms: The determinants and effects of foreign investment', Ph.D. dissertation, Duke University.

Grant, R. M. (1996). 'Toward a knowledge-based theory of the firm', *Strategic Management Journal*, Winter Special Issue, **17**, pp. 109–122.

Grueber, W., D. Mehta and R. Vernon (1967). 'The R&D factor in international trade and international investment of U.S. industries', *Journal of Political Economy*, **75**, pp. 20–37.

Gupta, A. K. and V. Govindarajan (1986). 'Resource sharing among SBUs: Strategic antecedents and administrative implications', *Academy of Management Journal*, **29**, pp. 695–714.

Gupta, A. K. and V. Govindarajan (1991). 'Knowledge flows and the structure of control within multinational corporations', *Academy of Management Review*, **16**(4), pp. 768–792.

Hedlund, G. (1994). 'A model of knowledge management and the N-form corporation', *Strategic Management Journal*, Summer Special Issue, **15**, pp. 73–90.

Hennart, J.-F. and Y.-R. Park (1993). 'Greenfield vs. acquisitions: The strategy of Japanese investors in the United States', *Management Science*, **39**, pp. 1054–1070.

Hofstede, G. H. (1967). *The Game of Budget Control*. van Gorcum, London.

Horst, T. (1972). 'Firm and industry determinants of the decision to invest abroad: An empirical study', *Review of Economics and Statistics*, **54**, pp. 258–266.

Huber, G. (1991). 'Organizational learning: The contributing processes and the literatures', *Organization Science*, **2**(1), pp. 88–115.

Hymer, S. H. (1960). 'The international operations of national firms: A study of direct foreign investment', Ph.D. dissertation, Massachusetts Institute of Technology.

Jablin, F. M. (1979). 'Superior-subordinate communication: The state of the art', *Psychological Bulletin*, **5**, pp. 1201–1222.

Katz, R. and T. J. Allen (1982). 'Investigating the Not Invented Here (NIH) syndrome: A look at the performance, tenure and communication patterns of 50 R&D project groups', *R&D Management*, **12**, pp. 7–19.

Kindleberger, C. P. (1969). *American Business Abroad: Six Lectures on Direct Investment*. Yale University Press, New Haven, CT.

Kogut, B. and U. Zander (1992). 'Knowledge of the firm, combinative capabilities, and the replication of technology', *Organization Science*, **3**(2). pp. 383–397.

Kogut, B. and U. Zander (1993). 'Knowledge of the firm and the evolutionary theory of the multinational corporation', *Journal of International Business Studies*, **24**, pp. 625–645.

Krone, K. J., F. M. Jablin and L. L. Putnam (1987). 'Communication theory and organizational communication'. In K. J. Krone, L. L. Putnam, K. H. Roberts, and L. M. Porter (eds.), *Handbook of Organizational Communication: An Interdisciplinary Perspective*. Sage, Newbury Park, CA, pp. 18–40.

Lazarsfeld, P. F. and R. K. Merton (1964). 'Friendship as social process: A substantive and methodological

494 A. K. Gupta and V. Govindarajan

analysis'. In M. Berger *et al.* (eds.) *Freedom and Control in Modern Society*. Octagon, New York, pp. 23–63.

Levinthal, D. A. and J. G. March (1993). 'The myopia of learning', *Strategic Management Journal*, Winter Special Issue, **14**, pp. 95–112.

Levitt, B. and J. G. March (1988). 'Organizational learning', *Annual Review of Sociology*, **14**, pp. 319–340.

Lippman, S. A. and R. P. Rumelt (1982). 'Uncertain imitability: An analysis of interfirm differences in efficiency under competition', *Bell Journal of Economics*, **13**, pp. 418–438.

Martinez, J. I. and J. C. Jarillo (1989). 'The evolution of research on coordination mechanisms in multinational corporations', *Journal of International Business Studies*, **20**, pp. 489–514.

Miller, D., M. F. R. Kets de Vries and J. M. Toulouse (1982). 'Top executive locus of control and its relationship to strategy-making, structure, and environment', *Academy of Management Journal*, **25**, pp. 237–253.

Nadler, D. A. and M. L. Tushman (1987). *Strategic Organization Design*. Scott, Foresman, New York.

National Register (1991). *International Directory of Corporate Affiliations: 1990–1991*. Wilmette, IL.

Nelson, R. R. and S. G. Winter (1982). *An Evolutionary Theory of Economic Change*. Belknap Press, Cambridge, MA.

Nonaka, I. (1994). 'A dynamic theory of organizational knowledge creation', *Organization Science*, **5**(1), pp. 14–37.

Penrose, E. T. (1959). *The Theory of the Growth of the Firm*. Basil Blackwell, Oxford.

Pfeffer, J. (1981). *Power in Organizations*. Pitman, Marshfield, MA.

Pitts, R. A. (1974). 'Incentive compensation and organization design', *Personnel Journal*, **53**, pp. 338–344.

Polanyi, M. (1966). *The Tacit Dimension*. Routledge & Kegan Paul, London.

Porter, M. E. (1986). 'Competition in global industries: A conceptual framework'. In M. E. Porter (ed.), *Competition in Global Industries*. Harvard Business School Press, Boston, MA, pp. 15–60.

Porter, M. E. (1994). 'Global strategy: Winning in the world-wide marketplace'. In L. Fahey and R. M. Randall (eds.), *The Portable MBA in Strategy*. John Wiley, New York, pp. 108–141.

Prahalad, C. K. and G. Hamel (1994). 'Strategy as a field of study: Why search for a new paradigm?', *Strategic Management Journal*, Summer Special Issue, **15**, pp. 5–16.

Rogers, E. M. (1995). *Diffusion of Innovations*. Free Press, New York.

Root, F. R. (1987). *Entry Strategies for International Markets*. Lexington Books, Lexington, MA.

Salter, M. S. (1973). 'Tailor incentive compensation to strategy', *Harvard Business Review*, **49**(2), pp. 94–102.

Schendel, D. (1996). 'Editor's introduction to the 1996 Winter Special Issue: Knowledge and the firm', *Strategic Management Journal*, Winter Special Issue, **17**, pp. 1–4.

Sherif, M and H. Cantrill (1947). *The Psychology of Ego Involvements, Social Attitudes and Identifications*. Wiley, New York.

Simon, H. A. (1991). 'Bounded rationality and organizational learning', *Organization Science*, **2**(1), pp. 125–134.

Smith, C. S. and D. P. Hamilton (18 December 1995). 'China's demands for technology sharing trouble American officials, executives', *The Asian Wall Street Journal*, p. 2.

Szulanski, G. (1996). Exploring internal stickiness: Impediments to the transfer of best practice within the firm, *Strategic Management Journal*, Winter Special Issue, **17**, pp. 27–44.

Teece, D. J. (1977). 'Technology transfer by multinational firms: The resource cost of transferring technological know-how', *The Economic Journal*, **87**, pp. 242–261.

Teece, D. J. (1981). 'The market for know-how and the efficient international transfer of technology', *Annals, AAPSS*, 458, pp. 81–96.

Tung, R. L. (1982). 'Selection and training procedures of U.S., European, and Japanese multinationals', *California Management Review*, **25**(1), pp. 57–71.

Tushman, M. L. (1977). 'Communications across organizational boundaries: Special boundary roles in the innovation process', *Administrative Science Quarterly*, **22**, pp. 587–605.

Van Maanen, J. and E. H. Schein (1979). 'Toward a theory of organizational socialization'. In B. M. Staw (ed.), *Research in Organizational Behavior*, Vol. 1. JAI Press, Greenwich, CT, pp. 209–264.

Vancil, R. F. (1980). *Decentralization: Managerial Ambiguity by Design*. Financial Executives Research Foundation, New York.

Wernerfelt, B. (1984). 'A resource-based view of the firm', *Strategic Management Journal*, **5**(2), pp. 171–180.

World Bank (1995). *World Development Report*. Oxford University Press, Oxford, UK.

Yip, G. S., J. Roos and J. K. Johansson (1994). 'Effects of nationality on global strategy in major American, European, and Japanese MNCs', CIBER working paper No. 94–02, Anderson Graduate School of Management, University of California at Los Angeles.

Zander, U. and B. Kogut (1995). 'Knowledge and the speed of the transfer and imitation of organizational capabilities', *Organization Science*, **6**(1), pp. 76–92.

Zeira, Y. (1986). 'Management development in ethnocentric multinational corporations', *California Management Review*, **18**(5), pp. 34–42.

APPENDIX

Measurement of variables
Independent variables

Mode of entry. Subsidiary presidents were asked to indicate whether their subsidiary became a part of this corporation as a result of an acquisition/merger (coded as 1) or whether the subsidiary was created as a greenfield operation (coded as 0). Summary statistics on this variable are: mean = 0.42, s.d. = 0.49).

Subsidiary size. This variable was measured in terms of the number of employees in the subsidiary (mean = 908, s.d. = 1552). In order to dampen the high variability in size and achieve a more normal distribution, the natural logarithm of the number of employees was used to indicate subsidiary size in our analyses.

Relative economic level. This variable was computed by dividing the per capita income for the "host" country (where the subsidiary is located) by that for the "home" country (the country-of-origin of the parent corporation). For each country, data on per capita income (i.e, gross national product per capita adjusted for purchasing power parity) were obtained from the World Development Report (World Bank, 1995). Summary statistics on this variable are: mean = 0.81, s.d. = 0.39.

Incentive focus. Based on Gupta and Govindarajan (1986) and Salter (1973), the following question was posed to the subsidiary presidents: "Your annual incentive bonus may depend solely on your subsidiary's performance or solely on the performance of a group of subsidiaries or some combination of both. Please indicate below how your incentive bonus was actually determined for the most recent year. Your answers should total 100%: (1) percentage of your incentive bonus that was based on your subsidiary's performance; (2) percentage of your incentive bonus that was based on the performance of a cluster of subsidiaries." Responses to the second item were used as a measure of the extent to which the incentive system was network-focused rather than subsidiary-focused (mean = 17.55, s.d. = 30.67).

Formal integrative mechanisms. Based on Galbraith (1973), Nadler and Tushman (1987), and Miller, Kets de Vries, and Toulouse (1982), this variable was measured through a 3-item Likert-type 7-point scale (ranging from "used rarely" to "used very frequently") that asked respondents to indicate the extent to which their subsidiary used liaison personnel, temporary task forces, and permanent teams to coordinate decisions and actions with sister subsidiaries. The final measure was a weighted average of

responses to the three items where the most complex mechanism (permanent teams) was given a weight of 3, the intermediately complex mechanism (temporary task forces) was given a weight of 2, and the least complex mechanism (liaison personnel) was given a weight of 1. Summary statistics on this variable are: mean = 2.92, s.d. = 1.53.

Lateral socialization mechanisms. This measure was adapted from Ghoshal and Bartlett (1988). Respondents were asked to provide "yes" or "no" answers to the following two questions: (1) "Have you worked for one or more years in other subsidiaries of this corporation?" and (2) "Have you participated in executive development programs involving participants from several subsidiaries?" For each respondent, the total count of "yes" responses was treated as a measure of participation in lateral socialization (mean = 1.08, s.d. = 0.77).

Vertical socialization mechanisms. This measure also was adapted from Ghoshal and Bartlett (1988). Respondents were asked to provide "yes" or "no" answers to the following two questions: (1) "Have you worked for one or more years at corporate headquarters in this corporation?" (2) "Do you have a mentor at corporate headquarters?" For each respondent, the total count of "yes" responses was treated as a measure of participation in vertical socialization mechanisms (mean = 0.95, s.d. = 0.84).

Headquarters-subsidiary decentralization. Following Vancil (1980), each respondent was provided with the following list of nine strategically relevant decisions: (i) formulation of your subsidiary's annual budget; (ii) discontinuing a major existing product or product line; (iii) investing in major plant and equipment to expand capacity for existing products; (iv) developing a major new product line; (v) increasing (beyond budget) the level of expenditure for advertising and promotion; (vi) changing the selling price on a major product or product line; (vii) increasing (beyond budget) the level of expenditure for research and development; (viii) buying from an outside vendor when the items required could be supplied by another unit of the country; and (ix) increasing (beyond budget) the number of personnel employed by your subsidiary. Using an approach similar to Hofstede (1967), for each of these decisions, each respondent was asked to indicate, on the following 5-point Likert scale,

496	*A. K. Gupta and V. Govindarajan*

the typical influence that they had in affecting the outcome of the decision: (1) your opinion not asked but decision is explained to you; (2) proposal by superior, your opinion is asked and it carries little weight; (3) proposal by superior, your opinion is asked and it carries a lot of weight; (4) proposal by you, decision made jointly by you and your superior; and (5) proposal by you, followed by consultation with superior, with your opinion prevailing. Responses on the 9 questions were averaged to create an index of headquarters-subsidiary decentralization (Chronbach alpha = 0.86). Higher values on this measure indicate higher decentralization (mean = 4.04, s.d. = 0.74).

Proportion of local nationals in the subsidiary's top management team. For managers heading each of seven positions, the subsidiary presidents were asked to indicate the nationality of each particular person on a four-point scale: "local national," "home country expatriate," "third country expatriate," and "not applicable" implying that there was nobody heading such a position. The instrument also explained the precise meanings of these terms. The seven positions were: "subsidiary president," "head of marketing," "head of manufacturing," "head of R&D," "head of finance," "controller," and "head of human resources." The percentage of *applicable* positions that were headed by local nationals was regarded as a measure of the extent to which the subsidiary top management team was localized (range = 0 to 100; mean = 63.87; s.d. = 38.48).

Control variables

Country-of-origin. Each MNC in this sample was headquartered in one of the following five countries: U.S., Japan, U.K., Sweden, and Finland. Treating the U.S. as the base case, dummy variables were created for each of the other four countries of origin. For example, in the case of Japanese MNCs, the variable "Japan" was given a value of 1; in the case of non-Japanese MNCs, this variable was given a value of 0. A similar approach was followed for U.K., Sweden, and Finland.

Industry resource characteristics. For each subsidiary, measures of industry resource characteristics were computed at the level of the parent corporation's dominant industry group along three dimensions: R&D intensity (i.e., R&D expenses to sales ratio), fixed asset intensity (i.e., net physical plant and equipment to sales ratio), and

advertising intensity (i.e., advertising expenses to sales ratio). All raw data were obtained from Standard & Poor's Compustat PC+ Database and were averaged for two years: 1990 and 1991. Utilizing these raw data, the three measures of industry resource characteristics were computed as follows. First, we identified the dominant industry group at the 2-digit SIC code level for the parent corporation. Second, utilizing industry-level data, for each 2-digit industry group, we computed the proportion of revenue contributed by each 4-digit industry segment within that industry group. Third, for each of these 4-digit industry segments, we computed measures of R&D intensity, fixed asset intensity, and advertising intensity. Finally, using the proportion of revenues contributed by each 4-digit industry segment to its 2-digit industry group as weights, we then computed weighted average measures of these three resource characteristics at the 2-digit industry group level. These measures, computed at the level of the parent MNC's dominant industry group, were then applied to all of the subsidiaries in our sample belonging to that particular MNC. For the sample, summary statistics on these three industry resource characteristics are: R&D intensity (mean = 0.03, s.d. = 0.02), fixed asset intensity (mean = 0.36, s.d. = 0.21), and advertising intensity (mean = 0.03, s.d. = 0.02).

Nature of subsidiary operations. We measured subsidiary operations through two dummy variables: "upstream activities" and "downstream activities." The variable "upstream activities" was coded as "1" if the subsidiary performed a primary upstream operation (R&D and/or manufacturing); otherwise, this variable was coded as "0." Similarly, the variable "downstream activities" was coded as "1" if the subsidiary performed a primary downstream operation (marketing and sales); otherwise this variable was coded as "0." The raw data for these two variables were obtained by asking each subsidiary president to provide "yes" or "no" answers to the following three questions: (i) "Does your subsidiary have one or more research and development facilities?", (ii) "Does your subsidiary have one or more manufacturing facilities?" and (iii) "Does your subsidiary have one or more marketing and sales facilities?" Summary statistics on the two dummy variables are: upstream activities (mean = 0.75, s.d. = 0.43) and downstream activities (mean = 0.84, s.d. = 0.37).

[26]
Managing Global Expansion: A Conceptual Framework

Anil K. Gupta and Vijay Govindarajan

There are at least five reasons why the need to become global has ceased to be a discretionary option and become a strategic imperative for virtually any medium-sized to large corporation.

1. *The Growth Imperative.* Companies have no choice but to persist in a neverending quest for growth if they wish to garner rewards from the capital markets and attract and retain top talent. For many industries, developed country markets are quite mature. Thus, the growth imperative generally requires companies to look to emerging markets for fresh opportunities.

Consider a supposedly mature industry such as paper. Per capita paper consumption in such developed markets as North America and Western Europe is around 600 pounds. In contrast, per capita consumption of paper in China and India is around 30 pounds. If you are a dominant European paper manufacturer such as UPM-Kymmene, can you really afford not to build market presence in places like China or India? If per capita paper consumption in both countries increased by just one pound over the next five years, demand would increase by 2.2 billion pounds, an amount that can keep five state-of-the-art paper mills running at peak capacity.

2. *The Efficiency Imperative.* Whenever the value chain sustains one or more activities in which the minimum efficient scale (of research facilities, production centers, and so on) exceeds the sales volume feasible within one country, a company with global presence will have the potential to create a cost advantage relative to a domestic player within that industry. The case of Mercedes-Benz, now a unit of DaimlerChrysler, illustrates this principle. Historically, Mercedes-Benz has concentrated its research and manufacturing operations in Germany and has derived around 20 percent of its revenues from the North American market. Given the highly scale-sensitive nature of the auto industry, it is easy to see that

Mercedes-Benz's ability to compete in Europe, or even Germany, hinges on its market position and revenues from the North American market.

3. *The Knowledge Imperative.* No two countries, even close neighbors such as Canada and the United States, are completely alike. So when a company expands its presence to more than one country, it must adapt at least some features of its products and/or processes to the local environment. This adaptation requires creating local know-how, some of which may be too idiosyncratic to be relevant outside the particular local market. However, in many cases, local product and/or process innovations are cutting-edge and have the potential to generate global advantage. GE India's innovations in making CT scanners simpler, transportable, and cheaper would appear to enjoy wide-ranging applicability, as would P&G Indonesia's innovations in reducing the cost structure for cough syrup.

4. *Globalization of Customers.* The term "globalization of customers" refers to customers that are worldwide corporations (such as the soft-drink companies served by advertising agencies) as well as those who are internationally mobile (such as the executives served by American Express or the globe-trotters serviced by Sheraton Hotels). When the customers of a domestic company start to globalize, the company must keep pace with them. Three reasons dictate such an alignment. First, the customer may strongly prefer worldwide consistency and coordination in the sourcing of products and services. Second, it may prefer to deal with a small number of supply

> Going international needs no grand design, but neither should a company wander aimlessly into the global jungle.

partners on a long-term basis. Third, allowing a customer to deal with different supplier(s) in other countries poses a serious risk that the customer may replace your firm with one of these suppliers even in the domestic market. Motivations such as these are driving GE Plastics to globalize. Historically, it supplied plastic pellets to largely U.S.-based telephone companies such as AT&T and GTE. As these firms globalized and set up manufacturing plants outside the U.S., GE Plastics had no choice but to follow them abroad.

5. *Globalization of Competitors.* If your competitors start to globalize and you do not, they can use their global stronghold to attack you in at least two ways. First, they can develop a first-mover advantage in capturing market growth, pursuing global scale efficiencies, profiting from knowledge arbitrage, and providing a coordinated source of supply to global customers. Second, they can use multi-market presence to cross-subsidize and wage a more intense attack in your own home markets. It is dangerous to underestimate the rate at which competition can accelerate the pace of globalization. Look at Fuji's inroads into the U.S. market, historically dominated by Kodak. The trend is happening in other industries as well, such as in white goods, personal computers, and financial services.

In the emerging era, every industry must be considered a global industry. Today, globalization is no longer an option but a strategic imperative for all but the smallest firms. The following framework and set of conceptual ideas can guide firms in approaching the strategic challenge of casting their business lines overseas and building global presence:

• *How should a multiproduct firm choose the product line to launch it into the global market?*

• *What factors make some markets more strategic than others?*
• *What should companies consider in determining the right mode of entry?*
• *How should the enterprise transplant the corporate DNA as it enters new markets?*
• *What approaches should the company use to win the local battle?*
• *How rapidly should a company expand globally?*

CHOICE OF PRODUCTS

When any multiproduct firm chooses to go abroad, it must ask itself whether it should globalize the entire portfolio simultaneously or use a subset of product lines. Firms can make this choice randomly and opportunistically or in a well thought out and systematic manner.

Consider the case of Marriott Corporation, which was essentially a domestic company in the late 1980s. It had two principal lines of business: lodging and contract services. Besides other activities, the lodging sector included four distinct product lines: full-service hotels and resorts ("Marriott" brand), midprice hotels ("Courtyard" brand), budget hotels ("Fairfield Inn" brand), and long-term stay hotels ("Residence Inn" brand). On the other hand, contract services included the following three product lines: Marriott Management Services, Host/Travel Plazas, and Marriott Senior Living Services (retirement communities). As the company embarked on globalization, it had to confront the question of which one or more of these product lines should serve as the starting point for its globalization efforts.

Global expansion forces companies to develop at least three types of capabilities: learning about foreign markets, learning how to manage people in foreign locations, and learning how to manage foreign subsidiaries. Until firms develop these capabilities, they cannot avoid remaining strangers in a strange land, with global expansion posing a high risk. Engaging in simultaneous globalization across the entire portfolio of products compounds these risks dramatically. So it is often wiser to choose one or a small number of product lines as the initial launch vehicles for globalization. The choice should adhere to the twin goals of maximizing the returns while minimizing the risks associated with early moves abroad. These initial moves represent experiments with high learning potential. It is important that these experiments succeed for the firm because success creates psychological confidence, political credibility, and cash flow to fuel further rapid globalization.

Figure 1 presents a conceptual framework to identify those products, business units, or lines of

Figure 1
A Framework for Choice of Products: Attractiveness of Product Lines as Launch Vehicles for Initial Globalization

		2 Moderately attractive	**1** Most attractive *(Marriott Full-Service Lodging)*
		4 Least attractive *(Marriott Senior Living Services)*	**3** Moderately attractive

Required Degree of Local Adaptation — Low / High; Expected Payoffs from Globalization — Low / High business that might be preferred candidates for early globalization. Underlying this framework are two essential dimensions by which to evaluate each line of business in the company's portfolio—one pertaining to potential returns (expected payoffs) and the other to potential risks (required degree of local adaptation).

The first dimension focuses on the magnitude of globalization's payoffs, which tend to be higher when the five imperatives (listed at the beginning of the article) are stronger. Looking at the case of Marriott, it is clear that such imperatives are much stronger for full-service lodging than they are for the retirement community business. The primary customers of full-service lodging are globe-trotting corporate executives. In such a business, worldwide presence can create significant value by using a centralized reservation system, developing and diffusing globally consistent service concepts, and leveraging a well-known brand name that assures customers of high quality and service. In contrast, none of these factors is of high salience in the retirement community business, thereby rendering the imperatives for globalization much less urgent.

The second dimension of our framework concerns the extent to which different lines of business require local adaptation to succeed in foreign markets. The greater the extent of such adaptation, the greater the degree to which new product and/or service features would need to be developed locally rather than cloned from proven and preexisting concepts and capabilities. Because any new development involves risk, the greater the degree of required local adaptation, the greater the risks of failure—particularly when such development entails the already significant "liability of foreignness." Marriott exemplifies these principles. Compared with full-service lodging, the retirement community business is a very local business and thus requires more local adaptation.

Combining both dimensions, as indicated in Figure 1, full-service lodging emerges as a particularly attractive candidate for early globalization. As the spearhead for globalization moves, it provides Marriott with a high return/low risk laboratory for developing the knowledge and skills needed for foreign market entry and managing foreign subsidiaries. Having thus overcome the "liability of foreignness," Marriott would be better positioned to exploit the globalization potential of its other lines of business.

To reiterate, hardly any line of business today is devoid of the potential for exploitation on a global scale. However, any multiproduct firm that is starting to globalize must remember that a logically sequenced rather than random approach is likely to serve as a higher-return, lower-risk path toward full-scale globalization.

CHOICE OF STRATEGIC MARKETS

Not all markets are of equal strategic importance. This is a central tenet of the conceptual framework presented in **Figure 2**. The following two dimensions determine the strategic importance of a market: (1) *market potential*, and (2) *learning potential.*

The concept of market potential encompasses both current market size and growth expectations for a particular line of business. For instance, one of the critical markets for AOL is Japan because 45 percent of the PCs sold in Asia are there. It is important to remember that, notwithstanding the importance of the size of a country's economy, market potential does not always go hand in hand with the country's GDP. A blindness to this reality has led some authors to conclude that companies are not global unless they are present in the triad of Europe, Japan, and North America. Such simplistic conclusions can often be dramatically fallacious. If you are managing ABB's power plant business, the bulk of your market for new power plants lies outside the triad.

There are two drivers of the learning potential of any market. The first is the presence of sophisticated and demanding customers for the particular product or service. Such customers (1) force a company to meet very tough standards for product and service quality, cost, cycle time, and a host of other attributes, (2) accelerate its learning regarding tomorrow's customer needs, and (3) force it to innovate constantly and continuously. France and Italy are leading-edge customer markets for the high fashion clothing industry—a fact of considerable importance to a company such as Du Pont, the manufacturer of Lycra and other textile fibers.

The second driver of a market's learning potential is the pace at which relevant technologies are evolving there. This technology evolution can emerge from one or more of several sources: leading-edge customers, innovative competitors, universities and other local research centers, and firms in related industries.

As indicated in Figure 2, the strategic importance of a market is a joint function of both market potential and learning potential. No firm is truly global unless it is present in all strategic markets. Nevertheless, despite their obvious importance, the timing of a firm's decision to enter strategic markets must also depend on its "ability to exploit" these markets. Going after a strategic market without

**Figure 2
Drivers of a Market's Strategic Importance**

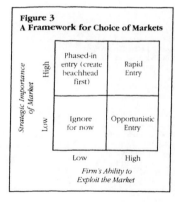

Figure 3
A Framework for Choice of Markets

		Low	High
Strategic Importance of Market	**High**	Phased-in entry (create beachhead first)	Rapid Entry
	Low	Ignore for now	Opportunistic Entry

Firm's Ability to Exploit the Market

such an ability is generally a fast track to disaster.

The ability to exploit a market is a function of two factors: (1) the height of entry barriers, and (2) the intensity of competition in the market. Entry barriers are likely to be lowest when there are no regulatory constraints on trade and investment (as in the case of regional economic blocks) and when new markets are geographically, culturally, and linguistically proximate to the domestic market. Even when there are low entry barriers, the intensity of competition can hinder a company's potential for exploiting a market. For example, the large U.S. market in the retailing industry has historically proven to be a graveyard for foreign entrants such as Marks & Spencer, precisely because of the intensity of local competition.

Figure 3 presents a conceptual framework that combines the two key dimensions—"strategic importance of market" and "ability to exploit"—to offer guidelines on how a firm can engage in directed opportunism in its choice of markets. The firm's stance toward markets that have high strategic importance and high ability to exploit ought to be to enter rapidly. By comparison, the firm can afford to be much more opportunistic and ad hoc with respect to markets that have low strategic importance but are easier to exploit. In the case of markets that have high strategic importance but are also very difficult to exploit, we recommend an incremental phased approach in which the development of needed capabilities precedes market entry. One attractive way for a company to develop such capabilities is to first enter a *beachhead market*: one that closely resembles the targeted strategic market but provides a safer opportunity to learn how to enter and succeed there. Some commonly used examples of beachhead markets are Switzerland and/or Austria for Germany, Canada for the U.S., and Hong Kong or Taiwan for China. Finally, the firm should stay away from those markets that are neither strategic nor easy to exploit.

MODE OF ENTRY

Once a company has selected the country or countries to enter and designated the product line(s) that will serve as the launch vehicles, it must determine the appropriate mode of entry. The entry mode issue rests on two fundamental questions. The first concerns the extent to which the firm will export or produce locally. Here, the firm has several choices. It can rely on 100 percent export of finished goods, export of components but localized assembly, 100 percent local production, and so on.

The second question deals with the extent of ownership control over activities that will be performed locally in the target market. Here also, the firm faces several choices: 0 percent ownership modes (licensing, franchising, and so on), partial ownership modes (joint ventures or affiliates), and 100 percent ownership modes (fully-owned greenfield operations or acquisitions). **Figure 4** uses these two dimensions to depict the array of choices regarding mode of entry that are open to any firm, and includes examples illustrating the variety of available options.

Choosing the right mode of entry is critical because the choice, once made, is often difficult and costly to alter. Inappropriate decisions can impose unwanted, unnecessary, and undesirable constraints on future development options.

Turning to the first question, greater reliance on local production would be appropriate under the following four conditions:

• *Size of local market is larger than minimum efficient scale of production.* The larger the size of the local market, the more completely local production will translate into scale economies for the firm while holding down tariff and transportation costs. One illustration of this argument is Bridgestone's entry into the U.S. market by acquiring the local production base of Firestone instead of exporting tires from Japan.

• *Shipping and tariff costs associated with exporting to the target market are so high* that they neutralize any cost advantages associated with producing in any country other than that market. This is why cement companies such as Cemex and Lafarge Coppee engage heavily in local production in every country they enter.

• *Need for local customization of product design is high.* Product customization requires two capabilities: a deep understanding of local market needs, and an ability to incorporate this understanding in the company's design and production decisions. Localizing production in the target market significantly enhances the firm's ability to respond to local market needs accurately and efficiently.

• *Local content requirements are strong.* This is one of the major reasons why foreign auto companies rely heavily on local production in markets such as the EU, China, and India.

Turning to the second question, given the differing costs and benefits of local market activities, neither alliances nor complete ownership are universally desirable in all situations. Unlike the complete ownership mode, alliance-based entry modes have the advantages of permitting the firm to share the costs and risks associated with market entry, allowing rapid access to local know-how, and giving managers the flexibility to respond more entrepreneurially and much more quickly to dynamic global competition than the conquer-the-world-by-yourself approach. However, a major downside of alliances is their potential for various types of conflict stemming from differences in corporate goals and cultures.

Taking into account the pros and cons, then, alliance-based entry modes are often more appropriate under the following conditions:

• *Physical, linguistic, and cultural distance between the home and host countries is high.* The more dissimilar and unfamiliar the target market, the greater the need for the firm to rely on a local partner to provide know-how and networks. Conceivably, the firm could obtain the requisite local knowledge and competencies through acquisition. However, in highly dissimilar and unfamiliar markets, its ability to manage an acquired subsidiary is often very limited. Ford's decision to enter the Indian market through the joint venture (JV) mode rested partly on the company's need to rely on an experienced and respected local partner, Mahindra & Mahindra.

• *The subsidiary would have low operational integration with the rest of the multinational operations.* By definition, tighter integration between a subsidiary and the rest of the global network increases the degree of mutual interdependence between the subsidiary and the network. In this context of high interdependence, it becomes crucial for the subsidiary and the network to pursue shared goals, and for the firm to be able to reshape the subsidiary according to the changing needs of the rest of the network. Shared ownership of the subsidiary puts major constraints on the firm's ability to achieve such congruence in goals and have the requisite freedom to reshape subsidiary operations as needed.

• *The risk of asymmetric learning by the partner is (or can be kept) low.* In a typical JV, two partners pool different but complementary know-how into an alliance. Ongoing interaction between their core operations and the alliance gives each an opportunity to learn from the other and appropriate the other's complementary know-how. In effect, this dynamic implies that the alliance often is not just a cooperative relationship but also a learning race. If Firm A has the ability to learn at a faster rate than Firm B, the outcome is likely to be asymmetric learning in favor of Firm A. Thus, over time, Firm A may seek to dissolve the alliance in favor of going it alone in competition with a still-disadvantaged Firm B.

• *The company is short of capital.* Lack of capital underlay Xerox's decision in the 1950s to

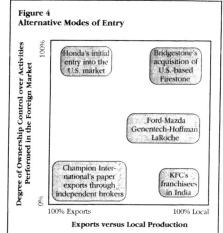

**Figure 4
Alternative Modes of Entry**

enter the European market through an alliance with the Rank Organization of the U.K.

• *Government regulations require local equity participation.* Historically, many countries with formidable market potentials, such as China and Brazil, have successfully imposed the JV option on foreign entrants, even when all other considerations might have favored the choice of a complete ownership mode.

A company that decides to enter the foreign market through local production rather than through exports faces a secondary decision. It must decide whether to set up greenfield operations or use an existing production base through a cross-border acquisition. A greenfield operation gives the company tremendous freedom to impose its own unique management policies, culture, and mode of operations on the new subsidiary. In contrast, a cross-border acquisition poses the much tougher challenge of cultural transformation and post-merger integration. However, setting up greenfield operations also has two potential liabilities: lower speed of entry, and more intense local competition caused by the addition of new production capacity as well as one more competitor. Taking into account both the pros and the cons, **Figure 5** provides a conceptual framework to determine when greenfield operations and/or cross-border acquisitions are likely to be the more appropriate entry modes.

This conceptual framework has two dimensions. The first pertains to the uniqueness of the globalizing company's culture. Nucor is a good example of a newly globalizing firm with a very

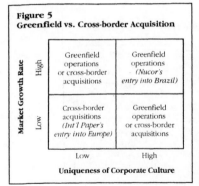

Figure 5
Greenfield vs. Cross-border Acquisition

		Low	High
Market Growth Rate	High	Greenfield operations or cross-border acquisitions	Greenfield operations *(Nucor's entry into Brazil)*
	Low	Cross-border acquisitions *(Int'l Paper's entry into Europe)*	Greenfield operations or cross-border acquisitions

Uniqueness of Corporate Culture

strong and unique culture. It is significantly different from other steel producers in its human resource policies, egalitarian work environment, performance-based incentives, teamwork, decentralization, and business processes. The more committed a company is to preserving its unique culture, the more necessary it becomes to set up greenfield operations when entering foreign markets. This is because building and nurturing a unique culture from scratch (as would be feasible in the case of greenfield operations) is almost always much easier than transforming an entrenched culture (as would be necessary in the case of a cross-border acquisition).

Aside from corporate culture considerations, the impact of entry mode on the resulting intensity of local competition must also carry considerable weight in a firm's decisions. If the local market is in the emerging or high growth phase (such as the auto industry in China and India), new capacity additions would have little downside effect on the intensity of competition. In contrast, when the local market is mature (such as the tire industry in the U.S.), new capacity additions will only intensify an already high degree of local competition. Within the forest products industry, Indonesia-based Asia Pulp & Paper has used the greenfield mode for expanding into other high-growth Asian markets. In the same industry, the U.S.-based International Paper has pursued a different path and relied on the acquisition mode for its expansion into the mature European market.

TRANSPLANTING THE CORPORATE DNA

Having decided on a mode of entry for a particular product line into a particular target market, the challenge of building global presence moves on to implementing actual entry. Among the first issues the globalizing company must address is how to transplant the core elements of its business model, its core practices, and its core beliefs—in short, its DNA—to the new subsidiary. The following example illustrates the challenge of transplanting the corporate DNA.

After acquiring 2,000 employees from Yamaichi Securities, Merrill Lynch & Co. counted on an American-style investment advisor approach to build a high-trust image in the securities brokerage industry in Japan. Historically, says Sugawara (1999), the industry has been

> tainted by unsavory practices....One well-known abuse...is "churning"—in which sales people persuade naïve investors to buy and sell a lot of securities so the sales people can boost their commissions. Merrill Lynch promised that there would be no churning. Instead, its sales people were instructed to try to get an overall picture of customers' finances, ascertain their needs and then suggest investments. Something got lost in the translation, however. Japanese customers have complained that Merrill Lynch sales people are too nosy, asking questions about their investments instead of just telling them what stocks to buy.

As this example illustrates, obstacles to transplanting the corporate DNA can emerge from any of several sources: local employees, local customers, local regulations, and so forth. Given such obstacles, every company needs to develop clarity regarding what exactly its "core" (as distinct from "peripheral") beliefs and practices are. Such clarity is essential for knowing where the company should stay committed to its own beliefs and practices and where it should be willing to adapt. Having achieved this clarity, the company needs to build mechanisms to transfer core beliefs and practices to the new subsidiary. Finally, and most important, it needs to embed these beliefs and practices in the new subsidiary.

Clarifying and Defining the Core Beliefs and Practices

Core beliefs and practices can be defined at any of varying levels of abstraction. Take Wal-Mart's practice of promoting "Made in America" goods in its U.S. stores. Assuming that promoting the origin-of-manufacture is a core practice for Wal-Mart, the company can define the practice in more or less abstract terms. A more abstract definition would be, "Wherever we operate, we believe in promoting locally manufactured products." On the other hand, a less abstract definition would be, "We promote products that are made in America." As this example points out, defining core beliefs and practices in more abstract terms permits a higher degree of local adaptation. At the same time, if the core beliefs and practices become too abstract, they could lose much of their meaning and value.

Notwithstanding its criticality, the definition of what constitutes a company's core beliefs and practices is and must always be the result of learning and experimentation over time. This is because the answers will almost certainly vary across industries, across firms within an industry, and, for the same firm, across time. As observed astutely by a senior executive of a major global retailer, "Cut your chains and you become free. Cut your roots and you die. Note, however, that differentiating between the two requires good judgment, something that you acquire only through experience and over time."

Transplanting Core Beliefs and Practices to the New Subsidiary

Transplanting core beliefs and practices to a new subsidiary, whether a greenfield operation or an acquisition, is always a transformational event—the challenge of transformation being greater in the case of an acquisition. The likelihood is very high that the transplanted beliefs and practices are likely to be at best partially understood and, in the case of an acquisition, will often be seen as alien and questionable. As such, transferring core beliefs and practices to a new subsidiary almost always requires transferring a select group of committed believers ("the DNA carriers") to the new operation. The size of this group would depend largely on the scale of the desired transformation effort. If the goal is to engage in a wholesale replacement of an entire set of preexisting beliefs and practices (as in the case of ABB's acquisitions in Eastern Europe), then it may be necessary to send in a virtual army of DNA carriers. On the other hand, if the goal is to create a new business model (as in the case of Mercedes-Benz's Alabama plant), then the transplants would need to be much fewer in number and would need to be very carefully selected.

Obloj and Thomas (1998) describe rather vividly how the invasion process worked in the case of ABB Poland:

> The transformation began with an influx and invasion of external and internal ABB consultants that signaled clearly the introductory stage of organizational change. Their behavior was guided by their perception of the stereotypical behavior of an inefficient state-owned firm typically managed by a cadre of administrators who do not understand how to manage a firm in a market economy. They did not initially perform any sophisticated diagnosis or analysis of local conditions or develop a strategic vision for the transformation process. Rather, they forcefully implemented market enterprise discipline in the acquired former state-owned firms by a series of high-

speed actions. They implemented massive training efforts aimed at exposing employees and managers of acquired firms to the principles of the market economy, modern management principles, and the ABB management system. This was adopted in all acquired firms following Percy Barnevik's dictum that the key to competitiveness is education and reeducation.

Embedding the Core Beliefs and Practices

While the process of transplanting the corporate DNA starts with transferring a select group of DNA carriers to the new subsidiary, it can be regarded as successful only when the new beliefs and practices have become internalized in the mindsets and routines of employees at the new subsidiary. Achieving such internalization requires (1) visibly explicit and credible commitment by the parent company to its core beliefs and practices, (2) deepening the process of education and reeducation within the new organization right down to middle managers and the local work force, and (3) concrete demonstration that the new beliefs and practices yield individual as well as corporate success.

The approach taken by the Ritz-Carlton chain at its new hotel in Shanghai, China illustrates how a company can go about successfully embedding its core beliefs and practices in a new subsidiary. Ritz-Carlton acquired the rights to manage this hotel, with a staff of about 1,000 people, under its own name as of January 1, 1998. The company believed that, consistent with its image and its corporate DNA, the entire operation required significant upgrading. As one would expect, the company brought in a sizable contingent of about 40 expatriates from other Ritz-Carlton units in Asia and around the world to transform and manage the new property. What is especially noteworthy, however, is the approach the managers took to embed the company's own standards of quality and service in the hearts, minds, and behavior of their local associates. Among its first actions in the very first week of operations under its own control, the company decided to start the renovation process from the employee's entrance and changing and wash rooms rather than from other starting points, such as the main lobby. As one executive explained, the logic was that, through this approach, every employee would see two radical changes in the very first week: one, that the new standards of quality and service would be dramatically higher, and two, that they, the employees, were among the most valued stakeholders in the company. This approach served as a very successful start to embedding the company's basic beliefs in every associate's mind: "We Are Ladies and Gentlemen Serving Ladies and Gentlemen."

WINNING THE LOCAL BATTLE

Winning the local battle requires the global enterprise to anticipate, shape, and respond to the needs and/or actions of three sets of host-country players: customers, competitors, and government.

Winning Host Country Customers

One of the ingredients in establishing local presence is to understand the uniqueness of the local market and decide which aspects of the firm's business model require little change, which require local adaptation, and which need to be reinvented. The global firm faces little need to adapt its business design if it targets a customer segment in a foreign market similar to the one it serves in its home market. However, if the firm wants to expand the customer base it serves in a foreign market, then adapting the business model to the unique demands of the local customers becomes mandatory.

Consider the case of FedEx when it entered China. As an element of its entry strategy, FedEx had to choose who its target customers should be: local Chinese companies or multinational corporations. The company chose to target multinational companies—a customer segment identical to the one it has historically served. Given the choice, FedEx was able to pretty much export the U.S. business model into China, including the use of its own aircraft, building a huge network of trucks and distribution centers, and adopting U.S.-style aggressive marketing and advertising. On the other hand, had FedEx selected local Chinese firms as its targeted customer segment, winning host country customers would have required a significantly greater degree of local adaptation of the business model.

Domino's Pizza is a good example of a company that has benefited from adapting its business model when it entered India. Unlike KFC, Domino's was successful in its initial entry into India, primarily because it tailored its approach to the Indian culture and lifestyle. Even though pepperoni pizza is one of the most popular items for Domino's in other markets, the company dropped it from the menu to show respect for the value Hindus place on the cow. Domino's also tailored other toppings, such as chicken, ginger, and lamb, to suit Indian taste buds.

Winning Against Host Country Competitors

Whenever a company enters a new country, it can expect retaliation from local competitors as well as from other multinationals already operating there. Successfully establishing local presence requires anticipating and responding to these competitive threats. Established local competitors enjoy several advantages: knowledge of the local market; working relationships with local customers; understanding of local distribution channels; and so on. In contrast, the new firm suffers from the "liability of newness." When a global firm enters a market, local competitors will feel threatened and will have a strong reason to retaliate and defend their positions. Such response constitutes entry barriers. In such a context, four possible options are available to the new invader:

1. Enter by acquiring a dominant local competitor.

2. Enter by acquiring a weak local competitor who can be quickly transformed and scaled up.

3. Enter a poorly defended niche.

4. Engage in a frontal attack on the dominant and entrenched incumbents.

Acquire a dominant local competitor. Acquiring a dominant local firm will prove to be successful if the following three conditions are met: (1) there is significant potential for synergies between the acquisition target and the global firm; (2) the global firm has the capability to create and capture such synergies; and (3) the global firm does not give away the synergies from a huge acquisition premium up-front.

A case of successful entry through acquisition of a dominant local competitor is Accor, the French hospitality company, which entered the U.S. market by acquiring Motel 6—the best managed market leader in the budget lodging category. On the other hand, Sony paid a huge premium to acquire Columbia Pictures; to date, however, it has had great difficulty in justifying this premium—despite the significant potential synergies between Sony's hardware competencies and the "content" expertise of Columbia Pictures.

Acquire a weak player. Acquiring a weak player in the foreign market is an attractive option under the following conditions:

1. The global firm possesses the capabilities that are required to transform the weak player into a dominant player; and

2. The global firm has the ability to transplant the corporate DNA in the acquired firm very quickly.

The sheer act of acquiring a weak player signals to other local competitors that they will soon be under attack. It is therefore to be expected that local competitors will retaliate. If the global firm is unable to transform the weak player within a very short time, the player could become even weaker under attack from local competitors.

Consider Whirlpool's entry into Europe in 1989 by acquiring the problem-ridden appliance division of Philips. Unfortunately, Whirlpool could not quickly embed the capabilities to turn around Philips's struggling appliance business. In the meantime, two European rivals—Sweden's Electrolux and Germany's Bosch-Siemens—got a wake-up call from Whirlpool's European entry. Quite naturally, the two invested very heavily in modernization, process improvements, new product introductions, and restructuring—all with a view to improving their competitiveness. The net result was a disappointment for Whirlpool in terms of its ambition to consolidate the white goods industry in Europe. By 1998, Whirlpool had 12 percent market share in Europe (half of its expected position) and was also underachieving in profitability. To quote Jeff Fettig, Whirlpool's head of European operations: "We underestimated the competition."

Enter a poorly defended niche. If acquisition candidates are either unavailable or too expensive, the global firm has no choice but to enter on its own. Under such circumstances, it should find a poorly defended niche for market entry under the following conditions:

1. Such a niche exists.
2. The global firm can use that niche as a platform for subsequent expansion into the mainstream segments of the local market. That is, the mobility barriers to move from the niche market to the mainstream segments are relatively low.

In the early 1970s, the Japanese car makers entered the U.S. market at the low end, a segment that was being ignored by the U.S. car companies and was thus a "loose brick" in their fortress. The Japanese companies used their dominance of the lower end segment to migrate to the middle and upper ends very effectively.

Frontal attack. The global company can choose a head-on attack on the dominant and entrenched incumbents provided it has a massive competitive advantage that can be leveraged outside its domestic market. If this were not true, taking on an 800-pound gorilla with all the liability of "newness" could prove suicidal. Lexus succeeded in its frontal attack on Mercedes and BMW in the U.S. market mainly because of a dominating competitive advantage in such areas as product quality and cost structure. For instance, Lexus enjoyed a 30 percent cost advantage. For Mercedes, given the high labor costs in Germany where it manufactured its automobiles, such a cost advantage could not be neutralized quickly.

Managing Relationships with the Host-Country Government

Local government can often be a key external stakeholder, particularly in emerging markets. Two points are worth noting in this context.

1. The global firm can ill afford to ignore non-market stakeholders such as the local government. For instance, the Chinese government recently banned direct selling. This action has an important bearing on such firms as Mary Kay Cosmetics and Avon, which depend on a highly personalized direct marketing approach.

2. Managing the non-market stakeholders should be seen as a dynamic process. Instead of simplistically reacting to existing government regulations, the firm should also anticipate likely future changes in the regulatory framework and even explore the possibility of helping shape the emerging framework. Instead of appeasement or confrontation, persistence and constructive dialogue with the local government are often critical elements of winning the local battle.

Enron's entry into India is a telling example of an active approach to transforming the entering firm's relationship with host governments. In 1995, mostly due to ideological and political reasons, the Maharashtra government put a sudden halt to Enron's partly built, $2.5 billion power plant. Yet by 1999, not only had Enron won back the original contract for the 826-megawatt unit, it even succeeded in getting a go-ahead to triple the capacity to 2,450 megawatts, representing India's largest foreign investment and Enron's biggest non-U.S. project. Instead of giving up, Enron persisted and helped shape evolving public policy. In the process, the company learned a lesson, but so did the Indian government.

SPEED OF GLOBAL EXPANSION

Having commenced the journey of globalization, a company must still address one major issue in building global presence: How fast should it expand globally? Microsoft's worldwide launch of Windows 95 *on the same day* epitomizes using globalization for aggressive growth. By moving quickly, a company can solidify its market position very rapidly.

However, rapid global expansion can also spread managerial, organizational, and financial resources too thin. The consequence can be to jeopardize the company's ability to defend and profit from the global presence thus created. Witness PepsiCo's helter-skelter rapid expansion in Latin America during the first part of the 1990s. In most cases, Pepsi's ambitious agenda resulted in market positions that have proven to be both indefensible and unprofitable.

Taking into account the pros and cons, an accelerated speed of global expansion is more appropriate under the following conditions:

• *It is easy for competitors to replicate your recipe for success.* This possibility is obvious for fast food and retailing companies such as KFC and Starbuck's, where it is easy for competitors to take a proven concept from one market and replicate it in another unoccupied market with a relatively small investment. However, this phenomenon is observable in other, very different types of industries as well, such as personal computers and software. The rapid globalization of companies like Compaq, Dell, and Microsoft reflects their determination to prevent replication and/or pirating of their product concepts in markets all around the world.

• *Scale economies are extremely important.* Very high economies of scale give the early and rapid globalizer massive first mover advantages and handicap the slower ones for long periods of time. This is precisely why rapid globalizers in the tire industry, such as Goodyear, Michelin, and Bridgestone, now hold considerable advantage over slower ones, such as Pirelli and Continental.

• *Management's capacity to manage (or learn how to manage) global operations is high.* Consider experienced global players like Coca-Cola, Citicorp, Unilever, and ABB. Should such a company successfully introduce a new product line in one country, it would be relatively easy and logical to globalize it rapidly to all potential markets around the world. Aside from the ability to manage global operations, the speed of globalization also depends on the company's ability to leverage its experience from one market to another. The faster the speed with which a firm can recycle its learning about market entry and market defense from one country to another, the lower the risk of spreading managerial and organizational capacity too thinly.

Becoming global is never exclusively the result of a grand design. At the same time, it would be naïve to view it as little more than a sequence of incremental, ad-hoc, opportunistic, and random moves. The wisest approach would be one of *directed opportunism*—an approach that maintains opportunism and flexibility within a broad direction set by a systematic framework. Our goal here has been to provide such a framework. ❑

References

D.A. Blackmon and D. Brady, "Just How Hard Should a U.S. Company Woo a Big Foreign Market?" *Wall Street Journal*, April 6, 1998. p. A1.

S. Ghoshal, "Global Strategy: An Organizing Framework," *Strategic Management Journal*, September-October 1987, pp. 425-440.

V. Govindarajan, "Note on the Global Paper Industry," case study, Dartmouth College, 1999.

G. Hamel and C.K. Prahalad, "Do You Really Have a Global Strategy?" *Harvard Business Review*, July-August 1985, pp. 139-148.

K. Iverson and T. Varian, *Plain Talk: Lessons from a Business Maverick* (New York: Wiley, 1997).

J.P. Jeannet and H.D. Hennessy, *Global Marketing Strategies* (Boston: Houghton Mifflin, 1998).

Jonathan Karp and Kathryn Kranhold, "Enron's Plant in India was Dead: This Month, It Will Go on Stream," *Wall Street Journal*, February 5, 1999, p. A1.

T. Khanna, R. Gulati, and N. Nohria, "Alliances as Learning Races," *Proceedings of the Academy of Management Annual Meetings*, 1994, pp. 42-46.

K. Obloj and H. Thomas, "Transforming Former State-owned Companies into Market Competitors in Poland: The ABB Experience," *European Management Journal*, August 1998, pp. 390-399.

G. Steinmetz and C.J. Chipello, "Local Presence Is Key to European Deals," *Wall Street Journal*, June 30, 1998, p. A15.

G. Steinmetz and C. Quintanilla, "Whirlpool Expected Easy Going in Europe, and It Got a Big Shock," *Wall Street Journal*, April 10, 1998, p. A1.

S. Sugawara, "Japanese Shaken by Business U.S.-Style," *Washington Post*, February 9, 1999, p. E1.

R. Tomkins, "Battered PepsiCo Licks Its Wounds," *Financial Times*, May 30, 1997, p. 26.

"Xerox and Fuji Xerox," Case No. 9-391-156, Harvard Business School.

Anil K. Gupta is a professor of strategy and international business at the University of Maryland, College Park, Maryland. **Vijay Govindarajan** is the Earl C. Daum 1924 Professor of International Business at Dartmouth College, Hanover, New Hampshire.

[27]

The Optimal Performance of the Global Firm: Formalizing and Extending the Integration-Responsiveness Framework

Timothy M. Devinney • David F. Midgley • Sunil Venaik

Australian Graduate School of Management, University of New South Wales, Sydney NSW 2052 Australia,
t.devinney@unsw.edu.au
INSEAD, Boulevard de Constance, 77305 Fontainebleau France, david.midgley@insead.fr
School of International Business, University of New South Wales,
Sydney NSW 2052 Australia, sunil@unsw.edu.au

Abstract

With the increasing globalization of business, there has been growing interest in how to create and manage a successful international enterprise. Although researchers and practitioners have grappled with the issue of globalization for some time, there is no one model that encompasses the range of phenomena we observe in the global economy, nor have those models that do exist been precisely formalized.

This paper provides an expanded approach to thinking about the organizational forms and linkages that exist in international business operations. Building on the popular integration-responsiveness framework of international strategic orientation, we develop a more expansive approach that is better able to account for the diversity of organizational forms and strategic choices open to managers. By adding a third set of environmental pressures, incorporating the beliefs of managers, and by employing the idea of efficient frontiers, we reformulate the integration-responsiveness framework, making it more consistent with modern economic models of the firm. Our integration-responsiveness-completeness (IRC) model argues that global firms can respond to these fundamental and competing pressures by configuring themselves in a variety of ways—rather than normatively prescribing that the transnational form is optimal. In addition, our model has methodological ramifications. Its formal structure suggests that empirical techniques that focus on the best rather than average performance are necessary to adequately investigate the performance differences among alternative organizational forms. This may explain the paradoxical lack of empirical support for a link between organizational form and performance.

(*Organization Structure; Multinational Management; Performance*)

1. Introduction

The global integration-local responsiveness framework has been one of the more enduring approaches to thinking about international business strategy and the organizational structure of global firms. Our goal is to build on this framework by incorporating a third set of pressures, namely the transactional pressures on the firm's value chain, while formalizing and extending the approach to encompass the differing organizational imperatives and efficient frontiers faced by firms. Our reshaping of the seminal work in international business and organizational economics allows for a more structured approach to thinking about multinational strategy and the impacts that the strategic choices of managers have on the performance of global firms.

1.1. Conceptual Background and Theoretical Perspective

Although economic and technological factors are driving industries to become global in competitive scope (Porter 1986), in many industries, "managers *can and do change the rules of the game*," (Prahalad and Doz 1987, p.30, italics original). Managers do so by altering the pattern of competition from local to global in character. Such change becomes a new source of competitive advantage for the firm—an advantage that derives not only from the accumulation of strategic resources, but from the intelligence with which managers distribute, configure, develop, and jointly use these resources across the globe. As the pressures on firms to internationalize increase, so, too, do the demands on companies to efficiently organize their value chains across diverse businesses and geographic markets. However, faced with a multiplicity of

1047-7039/00/1106/0674/$05.00
1526-5455 electronic ISSN

ORGANIZATION SCIENCE, © 2000 INFORMS
Vol. 11, No. 6, November–December 2000, pp. 674–695

organizational choices, even firms ostensibly classified as belonging to the same industry may organize their value chains in very different ways. Therefore, both environmental pressures and the strategic choices of managers are likely to have complex and significant influences on the performance of global firms.

In this paper, we extend the popular global integration-local responsiveness (hereinafter IR) framework by formalizing the approach and adding a third set of pressures we believe impact on global firms' choices of organization structure. In doing so, we provide an expanded and clarified approach to thinking about the organizational forms and linkages that exist in international business operations and the impact these forms have on firm performance. By accounting for the economic pressures that affect a firm's configuration of its value chain—which we call *transactional completeness*—as well as the tension between management's beliefs about the environmental pressures it faces and the constraints placed on them by existing organizational forms, systems, and resources— which we call *the organizational imperative*—we hope to show that the relationship between strategy and structure is richer and more complex than earlier thought. Yet our structure, because of its formality, captures this complexity in an internally consistent and empirically verifiable manner.

Our approach will be based on the idea of *efficient frontiers*. These frontiers represent the maximum performance of firms on a number of underlying dimensions, each of which in turn represent one of the sets of global competitive pressures facing firms. We postulate a three-dimensional model for these frontiers. The first two dimensions are familiar—*global integration* and *local responsiveness*. To these we add a third dimension describing the contractual nature of the value chain— *transactional completeness*. Put simply, transactional completeness describes the pressures to outsource or internalize steps in the value chain (e.g., purchase components, retain proprietary knowledge). By incorporating this third dimension we link the IR model to an extensive literature in organizational economics and contracting theory (e.g., Buckley and Casson 1976, Nelson and Winter 1982, Williamson 1991, Hennart 1991, 1993).

We also distinguish between the industry frontier of best practice and the frontier on which an individual firm can operate in the near-term future—which we call *the technologically feasible frontier of the firm*. Depending on the competitiveness of the firm's assets, structures, systems, and resources the technologically feasible frontier may or may not coincide with the best practice frontier. Stated simply, this frontier represents the strategic

and operational constraint of the firm at any moment in time.

However, despite its formality, our model does not neglect the important role that managerial decisions play in determining the firm's international strategies and structures. We define the concept of *managerial orientation* as the vision, philosophy and values of the management that taken together describe the strategic direction in which management wishes to take the firm. In other words, the firm's managerial orientation represents management's belief about where the best location for the firm lies within the three-dimensional space of global integration, local responsiveness and transactional completeness.

Thus, when we speak of the *organizational imperative* of the global firm we are talking about the tensions between what is possible for a firm given its technologically feasible frontier, and what its managers believe is best for the firm in the future. Stated succinctly, the strategic orientation of the firm is a complex interaction between the pressures in its environment, how well the firm's current structure matches with those pressures, and managers' beliefs about both these pressures and what is best for the firm in the future. Therefore, when a firm chooses a strategic orientation—that is, a location in the three-dimensional space—it is implicitly attempting to optimize its structure with the demands of the competitive environment. In that sense, we do not differ philosophically from prior writers (e.g., Prahalad and Doz 1987, Bartlett and Ghoshal 1989). Rather, the substantive difference between them and us is the formality we bring to the problem of goals, structure, and performance and the way in which we integrate the theory with extent thinking in economics and organization theory (particularly contingency theory).

1.2. General Structure and Contribution of the Proposed Model

The general structure of our thinking is presented in Figure 1. More detail will be given on this as we go through the model; however, a short overview is worthwhile here. The environmental and market conditions serve to determine the dimensional structure of the market—i.e., what determines global integration, transactional completeness, and local responsiveness. This further determines which strategic orientations are possible in any given market—e.g., driven by the nature of economies of scale, intermediate products, and the heterogeneity of customers. The existing structure of the firm, in conjunction with these forces, determines which orientations are possible for any particular company. Management's final decision about which strategic orientation to choose will be determined by its beliefs, which are affected by all of these

TIMOTHY M. DEVINNEY, DAVID F. MIDGLEY, AND SUNIL VENAIK *Optimal Performance of the Global Firm*

Figure 1   Overview of the Model of International Strategic Orientation

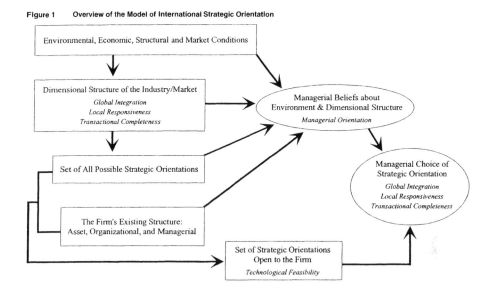

previously discussed factors, and what is feasible for the firm.

Our contribution is twofold. First, we overcome the limitations and underspecification of the IR framework by incorporating new and important concepts. We also clarify thinking in the area by assigning factors mentioned as important in the literature (e.g., scale economies, local demand conditions, transaction costs, the role of government, transportation, etc.) more precise roles in the model. Second, we both formalize the model and make it less deterministic—so that we can begin to ask questions about the optimal performance of the global firm. This formal model suggests not only a number of testable propositions but also that a new methodology is needed to measure the performance of multinational firms. Our most controversial proposition is that—because of the underspecification of the IR model—the typologies used in the literature (e.g., federal, transnational, etc.) may have no clear relationship to firm performance.

1.3. Outline of the Paper
Section 2 provides an overview of the literature on international strategy and gives a brief description of the integration-responsiveness framework. Section 3 discusses the limitations of this framework. Section 4 contains the main body of the paper and sets out our arguments as to how the IR model should be extended.

Section 4 also includes propositions arising from the extended model. Section 5 illustrates the potential merits of the extended model through case applications. In §6 we conclude by suggesting the implications of the model for strategy and research, and by discussing the unresolved issues arising from the model.

2. International Strategy Theories and Frameworks

2.1. Varying Perspectives on the Determinants of International Strategy
There is considerable variation in the perspectives and prescriptions of researchers in the arena of international strategy (Ghoshal 1987). For example, the key elements of a "global" strategy are variously considered to be standardization (Levitt 1983), delivering value to customers worldwide (Ohmae 1989), managing global cash flows (Hamel and Prahalad 1985), and achieving strategic flexibility (Kogut 1985). However, not all industries are "global" in character (Hout et al. 1982) and different structures will imply very different organizational and strategic imperatives. For example, "federal" or "multidomestic" firms are locally responsive with respect to their product lines and globally integrated with respect to

their production processes (Yetton et al. 1992). In spite of all of this theorizing, we are left with the disheartening fact that classifying businesses as either global or federal is not very useful because it hides variations among firms belonging to the same class (Prahalad and Doz 1987) and ignores similarities among firms belonging to different classes. Most authors agree that notwithstanding the opportunities existing in the global business environment, the key to securing opportunities and gaining competitive advantage lies in the multinational firm having the organizational systems, skills, and capabilities to coordinate strategies and activities throughout its complex multinational operations.

Dunning's (1981, 1995) "eclectic" OLI (ownership, location, and internalization) paradigm is one of the more comprehensive approaches, integrating both economic models of investment and organizational models of internationalization. Although Dunning's focus is on why firms engage in foreign direct investment (FDI), his approach has generally applicable insights and integrates a host of earlier literature in a comprehensive framework (Hymer 1960, Aharoni 1966, Kindleberger 1969, Caves 1971, Buckley and Casson 1976). A firm must satisfy three conditions in order to justify FDI. First, it must *own* (*O*) firm-specific assets (FSAs)—typically intangible assets such as brand name, marketing know-how, and other forms of intellectual property that provide a competitive advantage to the multinational firm against domestic firms and foreign multinationals. Second, it should be more advantageous to exploit these assets in combination with other immobile factors of production *located* (*L*) outside the home country. Third, the advantage accruing to the firm by exploiting these FSAs *internally* (*I*) should exceed those available by leasing, licensing or selling the FSAs. Dunning's paradigm clearly recognizes that the configuration of the value chain is a key decision for any globalizing firm.

Takeuchi and Porter's (1986) approach to internationalization, with its emphasis on the structure and organization of value chain activities, follows directly from Dunning's work. According to Takeuchi and Porter, the three key issues in international strategy are: (1) the *configuration* of activities; i.e., where the activities are performed—either centrally at the corporate or regional headquarters, or dispersed locally in the country subsidiaries; (2) the *coordination* of activities among country subsidiaries; i.e., whether the activities are standardized across all countries or adapted in each country; and, (3) the *linkage* of activities across firm functions, such as R&D, marketing, and manufacturing. However, in spite of their emphasis on the issues of coordination, linkage, and configuration of activities, Takeuchi and Porter have little to say about their contractual nature and how this affects the decision to source competencies internally or externally. Hennart (1982, 1991) addresses this weakness through the application of transaction cost economics to examine the roles of hierarchy, socialization, and price in controlling multinational enterprises. In his view, firms structure their international value chains using the mix of control mechanisms that minimize the costs of organization.

Most recent strategies of international organizations focus on the necessity of obtaining needed competencies externally through the development of an international network or transnational structure. According to Bartlett and Ghoshal (1987a,b), in the increasingly complex, diverse, and dynamic international business environment, many industries are becoming transnational in character because unidimensional strategies are inadequate for attaining competitive advantage. Success in transnational industries requires strategies that enable a multinational firm to simultaneously achieve the diverse and conflicting goals of efficiency, responsiveness, and learning on a worldwide basis. Strategies that are inherently multidimensional and complex require the firm to be capable of managing this multidimensionality in an effective manner. Bartlett and Ghoshal (1987a,b) see such a capability as necessary for survival in the new international business environment. However, the firm's administrative heritage—shaped by factors such as a strong leader, home country culture, decision-making processes, and internationalization history—becomes a critical constraint that limits the firm's ability to develop such a multidimensional capability. In these theories, the key constraint to more effective multinational management is limited organizational capability rather than a lack of analysis or insight among managers.

If we look for consistency in the work of Dunning, Takeuchi and Porter, Hennart, and Bartlett and Ghoshal, it is in the central importance they place on how firms organize and configure their value-adding activities around the globe.

2.2. The Integration-Responsiveness Framework
The most popular framework for studying international strategy in multinational firms is the IR framework (Figure 2). Originally developed from the differentiation and integration dimensions of Lawrence and Lorsch (1967), the use of the IR framework in global strategy was initially proposed by Prahalad (1975) and subsequently developed and applied by a number of authors, including Doz et al. (1981) and Bartlett and Ghoshal (1989).

According to Prahalad and Doz (1987, p.15), the managerial demands in a diversified multinational business

TIMOTHY M. DEVINNEY, DAVID F. MIDGLEY, AND SUNIL VENAIK *Optimal Performance of the Global Firm*

Figure 2 The Integration-Responsiveness Framework

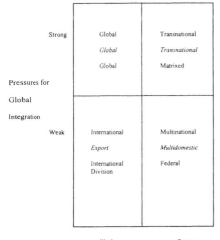

Industry environments—International, Multinational, Global, Transnational

Firm strategies—Export, Multidomestic, Global, Transnational

Organizational logic—International division, Federal, Global, Matrixed

Source: Adapted from Bartlett and Ghoshal (1987), Ghoshal and Nohria (1993), Porter (1986, p. 28), Prahalad and Doz (1987, p. 24).

fall into three categories—the need for global integration of ongoing activities, the need for global coordination of firm strategy, and the need for local responsiveness. Because the needs for integration and strategic coordination are often related, they "recognized two essential demands"—global integration (GI) and local responsiveness (LR)—and assumed "that the extent of strategic coordination is related to the need for integration" (1987, p.16). This focus on the two demands, together with their restatement of these demands as "pressures on a given business" (1987, p.18), resulted in the IR grid that is so popular today.

Integration pressures include the importance of multinational customers, the presence of multinational competitors, investment intensity, technology intensity, pressures for cost reduction, universal needs and access to raw materials and energy (1987, pp. 18–20). *Local respon-*

siveness pressures include differences in customer needs, differences in distribution channels, availability of substitutes and the need to adapt, market structure, and host government demands (1987, pp. 20–21).

Although the IR pressures on a given business represent the "center of gravity" of pressures across different functions, these requirements do vary considerably across functions. The example Prahalad and Doz use is the computer industry, where the R&D function is integrated and manufacturing is partly decentralized, whereas marketing is largely locally responsive (1987, p. 36). We would add to this that IR pressures might vary not only across functions, but also across different tasks and activities within each function. For example, the IR pressures may vary considerably across the marketing tasks of product, price, place, and promotion, as well as across the activities of setting advertising objectives, developing advertising copy, and selecting the media mix within the task of promotion. Thus, how the IR pressures impact on activities, tasks, functions, and businesses has profound implications for the ways in which multinational firms organize themselves.

Prahalad and Doz also sought to develop the concept of an ideal multinational organization—one that "can cope with the multitude of pressures that are the result of global competition" (1987, p. 9), in particular, by balancing the need for global uniformity with the requirements of different business units. Bartlett's and Ghoshal's (1988) "transnational solution" has similar aims. These normative prescriptions are echoed in the practitioner literature by the phrase "think global, act local."

3. Limitations of the Integration-Responsiveness Framework

The IR framework has proven useful in focusing attention on two of the major considerations of international strategic orientation: global integration and local responsiveness. However, we would make two criticisms of this approach. First, the IR framework does not adequately incorporate the transactional pressures on the firm's value chain. Second, there is a lack of clarity regarding the deterministic nature of the IR framework and the scope open to managerial creativity or organizational innovation. We will look at both of these issues before reviewing the empirical support for the framework.

3.1. Transactional Pressures on the Value Chain
Because the formal IR model is based on two drivers, global integration and local responsiveness, it does not elucidate effectively the transactional nature of interunit interactions. For example, one of the insights of Dunning's (1981, 1995) OLI model was his emphasis on the

importance of firm specific assets (FSAs) while Takeuchi and Porter (1986) concentrated on the need for coordination and linkage across business units and countries. As noted above, the basic IR approach to this problem is to aggregate these factors into the GI dimension. This would be satisfactory as long as there were no organizational implications associated with distinguishing between firms with different levels of firm-specific assets, coordination, etc. However, we know that this is not the case. For example, two firms could be facing exactly the same set of production conditions in each of its overseas plants and operating in identical markets. One may have complete property rights control over its operations (Firm A); the other may have no property rights control (Firm B). Given that Firm A can operate contractually and its interests remain protected, while Firm B cannot and must, hence, rely on some form of direct ownership to protect its position, we see that two identical sets of IR conditions lead to two different organizational outcomes. Furthermore, they would also lead to two different performance outcomes—given Firm B's need to invest in direct ownership.

Transaction cost theory (Williamson 1991) has shown us that the transferability and marketability of assets among economic agents is a critical determinant in the choice of organizational form. In the field of economics, this theory represents a major area of activity, whilst scholars such as Hennart (1982, 1991) have applied these ideas to international business with good results. Indeed, Hennart's analysis of control mechanisms demonstrates that the way the global value chain is coordinated is a major area of strategic choice for the multinational firm.

In much of their work Prahalad and Doz assume that there is a close relationship between global strategic coordination and global integration—albeit that they recognize that this may not always be the case (1987, p.15). However, where they do discuss coordination as a separate dimension (most notably in Chapter 6) their concern is with the interdependencies between diversified businesses rather than the value chains of those businesses. The markets for intermediate products, transaction costs, and price control mechanisms are not given prominence in their analysis, which focuses instead on hierarchy and socialization as the primary means to control multinational firms. We agree the latter are important, but argue that they are not the only means by which firms control their activities. Moreover, the existence of markets for intermediate products or the nature of transaction costs place different environmental pressures on firms to those of integration or responsiveness.

Therefore, by not accounting for transactional pressures on the value chain, the IR framework is inadequate

for dealing with all the relevant issues of interunit interaction and organizational form.

3.2. Determinism

The IR approach is unclear about whether GI and LR represent *exogenous* pressures or *endogenous* outcomes or managerial choices. In other words, how "deterministic" is the IR approach? Although this may appear to be a minor point, how we view the deterministic structure of the IR framework will dramatically affect any formal model we develop from it.

Let us take, for example, a situation of complete determinism and assume that the forces for global integration are weak and the need for local responsiveness is high. According to a deterministic reading of the IR framework, the only appropriate strategy in this situation would be to act as a federal organization. Thus all companies facing these pressures might be expected to pursue federal strategies—e.g., as in the case of food companies being driven by the diversity of country cultures and their impact on customer tastes for food. With complete determinism, competitive survival would imply the dominance of specific structural forms within specific industries. The empirical approach of Birkinshaw et al. (1995) explicitly assumes a deterministic model by concluding that some industries appear to be "under-globalized."

The opposite case is one of complete nondeterminism. In these circumstances, the choice of location in the IR matrix is unrelated to any set of pressures and simply relates to the beliefs of management. It should be clear that a completely nondeterministic approach to global structure could not be empirically falsified because there is no formal understanding about what drives the decisions of managers. Statistically speaking, we have an unidentified system because all its components are endogenous.

This lack of clarity about the deterministic nature of the IR framework has limited its applicability, even though there have been numerous attempts to derive broader organizational and strategic implications from the model. We can see this confusion by referring to Ghoshal's (1987) and Bartlett's and Ghoshal's (1987a,b) extension of Bartlett's (1986) original work. Although they correctly note the imperative facing managers of multinational firms to "optimize efficiency, responsiveness and learning" (Bartlett and Ghoshal 1987a, p.7) and emphasize the importance of the fit between a firm's "strategic posture and the dominant industry characteristics" (p.15), there is little to guide us as to the formal relationship between these industry characteristics and the firm's "optimal" solution.

The importance of determinism can be illustrated through a simple example. In Barlett's (1986) formulation each "function" is made up of "tasks", each firm's "strategy" is made up of "functions", and "industry configuration" is an accumulation of individual firm "strategies" for the market in question, in particular their relative positioning on the IR dimensions. Functionally, such an approach can be formalized as Equations 1 through 4 below:

$$Task_{j,i,M} = f(Customer\ Demand_M,$$
$$Production\ \&\ Cost_{Task,j,i} \mid \bullet) \qquad (1)$$

$$Function_{k,i,M}$$
$$= g(Task_{k,i,M}, Production\ \&\ Cost_{Task,k,i} \mid \bullet) \qquad (2)$$

$$Strategy_{l,i,M} = h(Function_{l,i,M},$$
$$Production\ \&\ Cost_{Function,l,i} \mid Strategy_{\forall -i}) \qquad (3)$$

$$Industry\ Configuration_M = p(Strategy_{\forall i,l,M}) \qquad (4)$$

Where subscript M is the market (e.g., *autos*), i is for firm i (e.g., *Ford*), and the first subscript, j, k, or l, indicates which task (j), function (k), or strategy (l) is being discussed (e.g., a *pricing* task in the case of a *marketing* function within the *Ford* strategy). $\forall i$ indicates "for all firms i". $\forall -i$ indicates "for all firms except i". Italicized items represent a vector of inputs; e.g., $Task_{k,i,M}$ represents the set of tasks making up function k in firm i in market M. Production & $Cost_{Function,l,i}$ is the representation of cost and production for the set of functions associated with strategy l in firm i. $(\ldots \mid \bullet)$ represents conditional factors such as government policies or intellectual property rights. The f, g, h, and p terms represent the functional forms that transform inputs into outputs.

The mathematical relationship flows from top (1) to bottom (4). For example, the industry configuration of the automobile industry is determined from an aggregation of the individual firm's strategies (e.g., global cars, cars with some degree of local adaptation, domestic cars).[1] These, in turn, are based on the mixture of "functions" used to develop those strategies. Furthermore, the mixture of tasks used within the functions determines the configurations of the functional areas. Therefore, the GI and LR mix of marketing tasks determines Ford's marketing function, and its overall strategy is based on the GI and LR distribution of its business functions, of which marketing is one.

The key to understanding this example is to recognize that if the customer/market drivers (Customer Demand$_M$)—normally associated with the LR dimension—and the production/cost drivers (Production &

Cost$_{Task,j,i}$)—normally associated with the GI dimension—are viewed as *exogenous*, then the firm's global strategy is fully determined and a singular strategy will dominate. In other words, there will be one "best" global orientation. Hence, assuming firms make "optimal" choices, Ford's orientation could only differ from Fiat's if the markets it serves differ from those served by Fiat. If they both served the same markets, either Fiat or Ford would dominate or both would be indistinguishable. Survival in such circumstances would require all firms to converge toward the dominant strategic orientation.

However, if we view the IR dimensions as structural choices made by the firm, we are left with the question of how exactly do the "dominant industry characteristics" find their way into the framework? If Toyota has chosen to take a global orientation and Fiat a federal one we are left with the question of why. Hence the conundrum. If the IR approach is to have structural validity (in other words, remain logically consistent), it must be deterministic. However, given that most authors (including us) would argue that the IR formulation is not completely deterministic, it must be underspecified. In other words, we are attempting to explain too many phenomena with too few determinants.

The underspecification of the IR typology can be seen in other areas as well. For example, Bartlett and Ghoshal (1987a) recognize the value of "organizational capabilities" as a key to success. However, it is one thing to note that a firm's capabilities are important but quite another to ensure that they are effectively integrated into the core of the model. Similarly, because the dimensional and deterministic nature of the framework is unclear, any attempt to integrate new factors into the framework becomes ad hoc. Are we to extend the framework by allocating the new factors to GI or LR? By allocating some elements of a factor to one dimension and some to the other (and thereby confounding the model)? Or by adding additional dimensions because the factors don't appear to fit into GI or LR? All of these are poor choices without a formal model.

Finally, although Bartlett and Ghoshal (1987a) emphasize that firms are attempting to optimize a number of factors in their choice of global structure, there is little argument that the IR approach is simply a descriptive typology and not any sort of true optimality-based model. Hence, unlike Dunning's OLI model, our ability to integrate the IR framework into existing economic and organizational models has been limited. For example, we have the four automobile companies (Ford, Toyota, Fiat, and Mercedes Benz) pursuing different strategies, no doubt due, at least in part, to the fact that the distribution of their tasks (and, hence, functions) is different. But what causes the distribution of tasks in the first place? Is this configuration of strategies sustainable? If they are sustainable, why are they so?

Therefore, although offering great insight, the IR framework's lack of formality makes validating and extending the model difficult. To progress we need a formal model incorporating a *partially deterministic* approach. That is, one that allows environmental pressures and managerial choices to interact simultaneously in a goal-driven manner.

3.3. Empirical Validation of the Integration-Responsiveness Framework

In addition to, or perhaps because of, its underlying theoretical confusions, empirical studies of the IR framework show no significant differences in performance according to firm strategy as defined by that framework (transnational, global, etc.). Both Roth and Morrison (1990) and Johnson (1995) found three distinct clusters of firms, (global, multidomestic, and multifocal), but no difference in the financial performance of the three groups. This further supports our contention that the framework is underspecified, as does Ghoshal and Nohria's (1993) finding that firms with better environment-structure fit perform better, and Martinez and Jarillo's (1991) evidence that firms in the three clusters use different coordination mechanisms, but show little difference in performance. All of this empirical evidence is consistent with a less deterministic formulation of the IR framework, as is the early work of Stopford and Wells (1972). Stopford and Wells advanced evidence that it was the *matching of form with strategy* that led to improved performance, namely, that within a specific *form* (international division, worldwide division) performance varied according to whether the firm had *matched* its product diversity or level of overseas sales to that *form* (1972, pp.81–82). In other words, firm performance is dependent on factors not accounted for in the IR framework (form, matching, and, by implication, managerial decisionmaking).

Prahalad and Doz (1987), Bartlett and Ghoshal (1989), and Johansson and Yip (1994) come closest to modeling the complete IR framework. Prahalad and Doz identify the economic, technological, political, and competitive factors that influence the varying need for GI and LR across businesses, functions, and activities in multinational firms. They omit considerations of managerial creativity or organizational form. Bartlett and Ghoshal, unwittingly perhaps, provide the strongest evidence that the IR model is, indeed, underspecified. Their study showed that the most successful firms were transnational organizations with multidimensional capabilities allowing them to simultaneously achieve the goals of GI, LR, *and* world-

wide learning—evidence that the two-dimensional IR framework is inadequate. We will defer discussion of organizational learning to §6 except to note that it too may be influenced by the nature of intellectual property rights and the organizational form within which this learning occurs.

Johansson and Yip (1994) show that, in addition to GI and LR pressures, the nationality of the parent company influences both the extent of interunit learning and firm performance. If parent nationality is viewed as a proxy for the orientation of senior management, then their work suggests the IR framework is underspecified in this area as well. Indeed, there is a literature documenting the influence of senior management on the direction and performance of international firms, including Aharoni (1966), Perlmutter (1969), Bartlett and Ghoshal (1989), and Kobrin (1994). More generally, Finkelstein and Hambrick (1996) have synthesized the substantial literature on strategic leadership. They conclude that top executives have significant effects on their companies through their exercise of strategic choice, but like all human decisionmakers are subject to cognitive biases and limitations. Note that while these phenomena are not included within the IR framework they are also not environmental pressures. Rather, they are related to the mental filters with which executives perceive environmental pressures, and the choices they favor in response to these pressures. Also, in making these choices, managerial creativity and organizational innovation can yield competitive advantage.

4. The Integration-Responsiveness-Completeness Model

We have identified two major limitations to the IR framework. The first is its failure to include an important set of environmental pressures on the value chains of firms. Second, its lack of formality and unclear stance on determinism make it hard to incorporate the choices of senior managers in an appropriate manner. Given our critique of the IR framework, two options are available. One option is to look to another model as a replacement. However, given the case-based support for the IR framework and its face validity, it is our contention that the lack of theoretical precision and underspecification can be resolved to yield a more formal model of the multinational enterprise. What, then, is the most appropriate alteration of the framework? Let us begin by assuming that a partially deterministic formulation as outlined in Figure 1 is indeed the more appropriate structure for a formal model.[2] In this section we incorporate the additional pressures and introduce efficient frontiers as the basis for a formal model. We use these frontiers to incorporate managerial choice. Finally, we list the theoretical contributions of the extended model.

4.1. The Pressures for Transactional Completeness

We have argued that the IR framework does not adequately account for organizational form, that it is important to do so if performance is to be explained, and that GI and LR in themselves do not describe all the environmental pressures that influence organizational form. How might we deal with these concerns? It is our belief that the most important dimension to add to the model if it is to adequately explain differences in international orientation and organizational form is *transactional completeness.* What do we mean by transactional completeness? Dunning (1981, 1995) and Takeuchi and Porter (1986) concentrated on FSAs, ownership, interunit linkages, and coordination. However, these are in essence descriptive concepts, and do not alone ensure that we can *explain* international orientation or organizational form. Williamson (1991) and others (e.g., Teece 1992, Amit and Schoemaker 1993) have shown that it is the desire to protect strategically valuable assets from competitors that drives organizational form. Therefore, it is not enough that a firm accounts for the diversity of its markets or the structure of its production and assets, the transactional nature of these factors must also be addressed. In other words, we are concerned about the transactional completeness of any set of interactions between economic agents as described by Grossman and Hart (1983).

Transactional completeness is best understood by referring back to the notion of complete markets in economics. A market is complete when all states of the world are priced. *In our terminology, an interaction between two agents is transactionally complete to the degree that all the characteristics of the transaction can be priced as if on an open market.*[3] Therefore, a firm selling a commodity where it could easily outsource distribution, advertising, and pricing would be operating in a more transactionally complete environment than a firm selling a specialized service that required an in-house sales force and individual pricing.

The interplay between intermediate products that are available on an open market and those that are produced within the firm can be argued to have a profound effect on organizational form. In industries where many intermediate products are available on an open market (e.g., personal computers), firms tend to focus on certain parts of the value chain (e.g., chip manufacturer, PC assembler, software firm). In industries where most intermediate products are produced within the firm (e.g., professional services) we see those firms owning much more of the value chain. More recently, we have also seen a trend for firms to concentrate on those activities where they have an advantage—through proprietary knowledge or strategic assets—and outsourcing those activities that are more efficiently provided by others and that are available to the firm through market and/or contractual mechanisms. This trend supports the argument that external markets have advantages over internal coordination (Hennart 1991) and that transactional pressures encourage firms to focus on that part of the value chain where they have the most to gain.

We should also note that the pressures for transactional completeness are not the same as transaction costs. Rather, they are all those pressures in the environment impacting on the firm's configuration of its value chain and its choice of an appropriate mix of control mechanisms (price, hierarchy, and socialization) with which to run its international operations. These pressures may include the relative costs of transactions versus management, but may also include other pressures such as the availability of intermediate products, nature of technology, proprietary knowledge, etc.

Our prior discussion noted that earlier theory put heavy emphasis on the issues of functional and interunit linkages and coordination, as well as the importance of economies of scale and scope. It should be emphasized that without accounting for the transactional completeness dimension, there is nothing to connect interunit linkages and economies of scale and scope with international orientation. The necessity of interunit linkages, coordination, and economies of scale and scope are necessary but not sufficient conditions for a specific international orientation. They specify that gains from trade will exist, but not how those gains will be realized or distributed across a particular organization. For example, an organization that can source components from open markets in a number of countries will be in a different position than one that has to make components in a single plant in one location and ship these to its subsidiaries. Knowing that one firm could potentially source components on the open market and one firm cannot (for proprietary or technological reasons) tells us a lot about the different ways in which each company will achieve economies of scale and scope, and how each will coordinate its activities.

Thus, we argue that transactional completeness is not only important, but represents a phenomena that is different from either global integration or local responsiveness. In the early literature "global integration" represents the pressures for economies of scale and scope and the integration of the strategic components that the firm needs to compete in its markets. Subsequently, Kobrin (1991) has argued that the increasing cost and complexity

TIMOTHY M. DEVINNEY, DAVID F. MIDGLEY, AND SUNIL VENAIK   *Optimal Performance of the Global Firm*

of technology is the "primary determinant of cross-border integration" and that manufacturing scale has become less important. Local responsiveness represents the pressures imposed by the diversity of conditions in these markets. Transactional completeness represents the competitive pressures in the markets for intermediate products and the organizational configurations that are necessary to procure and combine these intermediate products in an effective manner. Moreover, global integration represents truly market-spanning pressures, local responsiveness delineates pressures that differ from country to country, and transactional completeness represents pressures that traverse the countries and locations involved in the firm's value chain.

We have thus expanded the IR framework to encompass a third dimension, transactional completeness, leading to an IRC framework (Global *Integration*, Local *Responsiveness*, and Transactional *Completeness*). This leads to our first propositions.

PROPOSITION 1. *Transactional completeness represents a different set of phenomena from either global integration or local responsiveness—primarily the pressures on the configuration of the value chain and the "efficiency" in the transfer of intermediate products and services.*

PROPOSITION 2. *Ceteris paribus, the degree of transactional completeness in an industry will have significant impact on: a) value chain configurations, b) organizational structures, c) interunit co-ordination and d) intra- and interfirm networks.*

PROPOSITION 3. *The IRC framework will provide a better explanation of firm strategy, structure and performance than the IR framework.*

4.2. Dealing with the Determinism Dilemma: Efficient Frontiers

It should be clear that neither a deterministic or nondeterministic approach is quite satisfying as the basis of a model of international strategic orientation. We contend that any such model must be "partially deterministic" and optimality based. In other words, we would expect a find a number of possible firm configurations that would determine different mixtures of strategies with similar or different profit implications for any given market. Therefore, firms with distinctly different strategic configurations could compete for the same market (for example, Compaq versus Dell, Proctor & Gamble versus Nestle). Although this is not a profound statement in and of itself, the structure of our model is unique and greatly expands the IR approach to multinational structure and performance.

Figure 3 outlines the difference between the deterministic and partially deterministic approaches to the IR framework. The graph on the left-hand side (Figure 3(a)) shows the completely deterministic model. According to this model, given a specific mixture of markets and technologies, the efficient strategy (denoted λ in this case) would dominate all other strategies (denoted α, β, and γ), and we would expect that firms closer to the optimal strategy would have superior performance. For example, a firm with higher levels of both global integration and local responsiveness than λ would be viewed as inferior to strategy λ. The current imprecise expression of the IR framework in the literature puts forward this ideal (or gravity) point model, or, in the case of the practitioner literature, an ideal vector model in which firms must continue to increase both their local responsiveness and global integration in a 45-degree direction. The latter leads to normative prescriptions that all firms must improve global coordination and local responsiveness ("think global, act local" or the "transnational solution").

In contrast, the graph on the right-hand side (Figure 3(b)) shows an example based on a partially deterministic formulation. The *maximum isoprofit frontier* (or *efficient frontier*) for this particular market describes all the configurations that produce the maximum profit currently attainable (or in a multidimensional world, are maximally efficient).[4] Each strategy would have behind it a mixture of tasks and functional forms, where the latter transform tasks into functions, and functions into strategies. The choice of where to locate tasks would be the decision of management and would be sustainable based upon its survivorship characteristics; i.e., the ones that worked in the market would survive.

In the situation shown in Figure 3(b), there exists a set of strategies (represented by the efficient frontier, and with two examples denoted λ and Ψ) that are equally optimal and superior to those strategies on the interior of the isoprofit frontier.[5] Thus, firms can be operating with different strategies and still achieve the same performance outcomes (i.e., as long as they operate on a specific isoprofit frontier). For example, firm λ achieves the maximum profit by high global integration and low local responsiveness, while firm Ψ achieves the same profit by the opposite strategy. The isoprofit frontier is determined by the current limits of market opportunities and technological possibilities.

Note that Figure 3(b) is hypothetical. We might expect empirically determined frontiers to display a variety of topologies according to the nature of the market and industry we are examining. For example, in Figures 4(a) and 4(b) we show two different frontiers—one where the

TIMOTHY M. DEVINNEY, DAVID F. MIDGLEY, AND SUNIL VENAIK   *Optimal Performance of the Global Firm*

Figure 4   Alternative Industry Frontiers

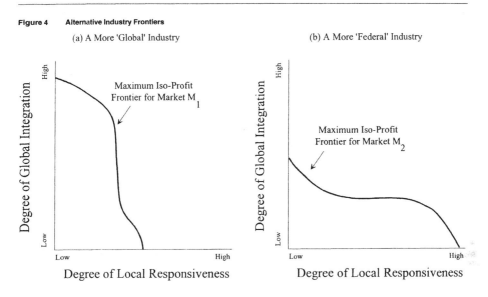

(a) A More 'Global' Industry

(b) A More 'Federal' Industry

Figure 3   Two Alternative Optimal Formulations Based on the IR Framework

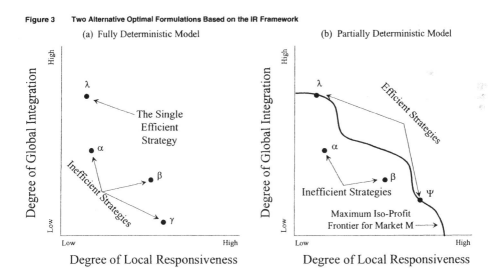

(a) Fully Deterministic Model

(b) Partially Deterministic Model

GI dimension has greater impact on the shape of the frontier (market M_1), and one where the LR dimension has greater impact on this shape (market M_2). Note, however, that in both cases there are a variety of strategies firms can follow to operate on the frontier. Thus the existence of a frontier—and not its specific shape—implies a number of viable strategies. For simplicity we have also chosen to present these figures as two dimensional—the extension to the three-dimensional space is straightforward. We might have contrasted more versus less transactionally complete variants of these industries for example.

Why do we consider that GI, LR, and TC generate the dimensionality of the frontier? If these three dimensions accurately reflect the environment of firms, then they describe all the possible strategic orientations that firms can adopt within the industry. Most of these orientations will be inefficient, and firms will either not adopt them or go out of business if they do. However, over time the forces of competition will lead to some firms defining the maximum performance available for a more limited set of orientations, and this becomes the current industry frontier.[6]

We can also extend the idea of a frontier from the industry to the firm. In Figure 5 we show one industry isoprofit frontier and two firm "technologically feasible" frontiers. These latter frontiers are not isoprofit frontiers because the level of profit changes as you move along them. Rather, they represent the maximum configurations of GI/LR possible for the firm at any given point in time. Referring back to Figure 1, these firm frontiers represent "the set of strategic orientations open to the firm" out of

the set of all possible strategic orientations. We will develop this idea of technologically feasible frontiers shortly.

Our use of frontiers has precedents in other literatures. They have a history of application in the areas of productivity and cost efficiency from both econometric and operations research perspectives (e.g., Aigner et al. 1977, Charnes et al. 1978). They have also been applied to strategic group theory (Day et al. 1995) and strategic alliances (Ali and Lerme 1997). As Day et al. (1995) note, frontiers involve an important conceptual shift from modeling average behavior to modeling extreme behavior (best, worst practice) and understanding the comparative advantage or disadvantage that derives from an organization being on or below the frontier (Ali and Lerme 1997). Both Day et al. and Aharoni (1993) argue that there are significant new insights and knowledge that can derive from this conceptual shift. Day et al. also suggest that frontiers may help separate industry-level effects from firm and strategic group-level effects. As we discuss later, this conceptual shift has methodological implications for strategy research; here we summarize the section with our next propositions.

PROPOSITION 4. *The performance of global firms is better measured by reference to an efficient frontier than in direct comparison using standard multivariate techniques. (Corollary: firms with different strategies and configurations can coexist with similar levels of performance.)*

PROPOSITION 5. *The regions of the frontier that represent feasible opportunities for an individual firm will be constrained by the firm's existing asset structure or technology.*

The concept of efficient frontiers provides us with a formal mechanism for allowing environmental pressures and managerial choices to interact in a partially deterministic but goal-driven manner. However, we still need to address how the firm chooses one strategic orientation out of the options available to it.

4.3. The Organizational Imperative: Technological Feasibility and Managerial Orientation

We noted earlier that there is little in the formal structure of the IR framework that accounts for the organizational and cultural orientation of the firm and its divisions. Admittedly, Bartlett and Ghoshal's notion of "administrative heritage" provides implicit recognition that historical organizational factors serve to determine a good deal of the production processes, location choices, and other factors that impact on the extent to which the firm is globally integrated or locally responsive. However, administrative

Figure 5   Feasible Technological Frontiers and Alternative Strategies

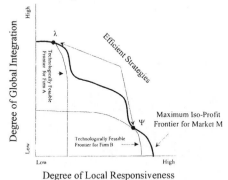

TIMOTHY M. DEVINNEY, DAVID F. MIDGLEY, AND SUNIL VENAIK *Optimal Performance of the Global Firm*

heritage blurs the distinction between what the firm is organizationally capable of doing (the frontier of feasible configurations for that firm), what managers believe is an appropriate orientation (the managerial orientation function), and what would succeed in the market (the market's efficient frontier).

4.3.1. Technological Feasibility. We must, therefore, come up with a mechanism that allows us to distinguish between these institutional and managerial factors whilst also helping us determine the choice of strategy from all those possible. One possibility is that firms are little more than profit maximizers and are simply attempting to get onto the highest profit frontier that is feasible for them. For example, as represented in Figure 5, Firm A has a history of centralization where the head office controls the actions of the local branches it set up around the globe. Firm B has a history of acquiring local companies as subsidiaries and then allowing these a reasonable degree of autonomy. Firm A, with its history of centralization, ends up at point λ while Firm B, with its history of local subsidiaries, ends up at point Ψ. Over the long run, and assuming no fundamental changes, the two points (λ, Ψ) are the only combination that allow these firms to operate with parity in the same market. Note that we have said nothing about the orientation of the management to this point, just the technologically feasible orientation of the firm. *Technological feasibility is defined as the set of possible strategies given the firm's existing structure, assets, and operating processes (independent of the current orientation of their management).* We thus define "technology" broadly—to include offices, products, information technology, reward systems, financial control systems and the like, as well as production processes. Technological feasibility is represented by a frontier of possibilities that is unique to each firm at any point in time.

We should also note that whilst we have shown both firms as being capable of operating on the efficient frontier, in reality firms may be constrained from reaching this frontier. For example, government labor policies might mandate inefficient working practices or a previous choice of production technology may not allow the firm to reach current levels of performance. The concept of "technological feasibility" allows us to incorporate a number of factors mentioned in the literature into our extended model as constraints.

4.3.2. Managerial Orientation. A second possibility is that a firm's senior managers have strong beliefs favoring certain types of managerial orientation—a "dominant logic" in the sense of Prahalad and Bettis (1986). This can be based on their history, cultural orientation, or managerial philosophy and several researchers have

shown how managerial philosophy affects strategic orientation (e.g., Kobrin 1994, Finkelstein and Hambrick 1996). Figure 6 shows one case where the addition of this facet to our organizational imperative adds richness to the model. The management of Firm A have a strong centralizing orientation with an increasing preference for control over responsiveness. This is represented on the diagram as the orientation function, O_A, which indicates the set of feasible paths given the management's orientation. Thus, O_A encloses paths that are generally in the direction of increased GI. In contrast, the management of Firm B believes in more responsiveness, and its orientation function, O_B, is skewed in this direction. The dotted lines show how this organizational imperative helps determine the evolutionary path of each firm's strategy. In the case of each firm, more GI and LR is better, but the firm is limited by its feasible technology to its current position on the frontier, and its forward path is partially constrained by its managerial orientation.[7]

Our approach explicitly defines the manager's orientation on the same dimensions as all the other components of the model. In the above example, global integration and local responsiveness. This allows for the explicit development of a constrained optimization approach to strategic development. Second, we explicitly distinguish between managerial orientation (soft constraints) and factors that limit the firm because of the "technology" it has available to it at any point in time (hard constraints).

Typically, we would expect technological feasibility and managerial orientation to be in tension but moving

Figure 6 **Strategic Orientation and Strategic Choice**

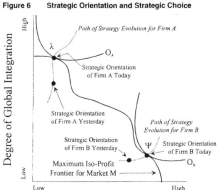

Degree of Global Integration (vertical axis, Low to High)

Path of Strategy Evolution for Firm A

λ

O_A

Strategic Orientation of Firm A Today

Strategic Orientation of Firm A Yesterday

Strategic Orientation of Firm B Yesterday

Maximum Iso-Profit Frontier for Market M

Path of Strategy Evolution for Firm B

Ψ Strategic Orientation of Firm B Today

O_B

Degree of Local Responsiveness (Low to High)

synchronously. That is, senior managers would be seeking incremental improvements from where they currently stood and in the general direction of the industry frontier. However, this need not be the case. The arrival of a new CEO from a different industry might result in a radical change of orientation and considerable tension between these new goals and current "technology." Whether this change succeeds depends on the topology of the frontiers and the degree of redirection sought.

The work of Murtha, et al. (1998) show that the sort of managerial orientation we are discussing not only exists but is both pervasive and measurable. Their measures of "the attitudes that underlie international strategy processes" include both "global mind-set" variables (expectations towards integration, responsiveness, etc.) and policy variables (career opportunities, global accountability, etc.). "Global mind-set" is analogous to "managerial orientation" in that both are concerned with the future direction in which management wishes to take the company. In the multinational studied, senior management sought greater coordination across the globe. Over the 30 months of the study, the mind-sets of senior and operating managers became more aligned and a "clear attachment of mind-set dimensions to policy variables" emerged. In other words, a new orientation began to influence the direction of the firm. This supports our contention that managerial orientation is an important component of an extended IR framework.

Our final propositions follow.

PROPOSITION 6. *It is possible to distinguish between the soft constraints of "managerial orientation" (senior management philosophy or direction) and the hard constraints of "technological feasibility" (current firm configuration).*

PROPOSITION 7. *The addition of managerial orientation and technological feasibility will add to the explanation of any gap between firm performance and the nearest region of the frontier.*

4.4. Theoretical Contribution of the Integration-Responsiveness-Completeness Model

Table 1 provides a summary of the components of the model. The four main components of the theory—global integration, local responsiveness, transactional completeness (sets of environmental pressures/dimensions), and managerial orientation (direction)—can be described based on:

• the source of the underlying forces determining differences between firms on these components;

• the objective that determines better performance on that component;

• the sources of competitive advantage associated with that component; and

• the observable strategic characteristics associated with that component.

Note that the frontiers are not separate constituents of the theory, rather they are surfaces defined on the three dimensions—one for the industry as a whole (the isoprofit frontier) and others describing the opportunities for each firm (technological feasibility).

The advantage of the IRC approach is that it:

• expands the IR framework—hence dealing with the issue of the underspecification of the typology while building on its fundamental logic;

• formalizes the concepts underlying the framework more clearly—hence dealing with the ill-defined nature of some of the components of earlier versions of the framework; and,

• redevelops the IR approach into an optimization-based model—hence providing for directly falsifiable propositions to be developed.

The IRC model is flexible because it puts few constraints on the structure of the components of the model. Rather, it concentrates on organizing them clearly and making sure that they are adequately defined, so as not to confuse one type of issue with another. By making the isoprofit frontier three-dimensional, we also ensure that all the major forces influencing the firm's decisions are accounted for. Although we view the model as one where the firm is optimizing the fit between its managerial orientation and its feasible technological opportunities while maximizing profit, the normative value of the model lies in what it says about how to move from a suboptimal to an optimal outcome. Furthermore, the model makes a strong distinction between what is feasible for the firm at any given point in time, what management thinks is a good or bad orientation, and what the industry environment is any given point in time.

It is also necessary to understand the process by which a firm changes its technological opportunities and its managerial beliefs. According to our theory, the key to achieving a more profitable fit is through the development of a joint solution where the opportunity set is the best that can be achieved while also being in line with the firm's organizational imperatives. Figure 7 shows two of the many paths to achieving strategic fit that are available in this three-dimensional space.

Figure 7(a) shows a situation in which the firm's management keeps its views consistent but alters the functioning of the firm to force the organization out onto the maximum iso-profit frontier. In this case, the functioning of the firm is altered on two of the three dimensions—global integration and transactional completeness. The

TIMOTHY M. DEVINNEY, DAVID F. MIDGLEY, AND SUNIL VENAIK *Optimal Performance of the Global Firm*

Table 1   Summary of the Components of the IRC Model

	Global Integration (GI)	Local Responsiveness (LR)	Transactional Completeness (TC)	Managerial Orientation (MO)
Forces	Economic/Technological	Market/Customer	Interactional	Psychological/Cultural
Objective	Efficiency	Customer satisfaction	Overcoming market inefficiencies	Organizational fit
Source of advantage	Cost and productivity	Differentiation & customer fit	Structure and organizational interaction	Matching of technology with philosophy
Observable strategic characteristics	Economies of scale; Internal trade	Autonomous local subsidiaries; Local marketing activities	Locus of decision making; Structure of local operations; Reliance on governance/contracts	Cultural orientation; Managerial hubris

firm's strategic orientation becomes more transnational as the firm moves from strategy ψ' to strategy ψ'' to strategy ψ''' as the firm alters its technologically feasible set of options from T_1 to T_2 to T_3. In doing so, the firm has become more globally integrated and subjects more of its value chain to market forces. Figure 7(b) shows a situation in which the firm alters its managerial orientation (either by replacing managers or changing beliefs) to accommodate the existing feasible options. Here the focus is on the dimensions of global integration and local responsiveness. In this situation, the changing beliefs alter the managerial orientation from O_B' to O_B'''' to O_B, and the firm's strategic orientation moves from ψ' to strategy ψ'''' to strategy ψ—becoming more federal as it does so. These two examples are, of course, stylized. In reality, a firm would change its strategic position through some combination of a change in managerial orientation and technologically feasible options. It might also simultaneously alter these in three rather than two dimensions as shown here. Firms might make mistakes in these strategic realignments, for example, attempting to orient the firm as a transnational when their feasible technology requires them to be more locally responsive, or restructuring to increase transactional completeness by outsourcing when internal knowledge is a vital ingredient of their success.

5.   Potential Merits of the Integration-Responsiveness-Completeness Model

The strength and longevity of our extended model will be based on its ability to explain the relevant phenomena better than its progenitor and to offer new insights about these phenomena. As our paper is purely conceptual, and we have yet to develop the methodologies to conduct an empirical test of the IRC model, in this next section we will simply illustrate its potential merits. We do so

through three illustrations. The first looks at how transactional completeness can affect the determination of organizational structure within the transnational quadrant of the IR grid, whilst the second uses real firms to illustrate the heterogeneity of firm structures within the global quadrant. The point of both is to illustrate how transactional completeness can add to our explanation of structure. The third reinterprets a well-known case to show how the components of the IRC model potentially offer new insights.

5.1.   The Determination of Organizational Structure

One of the normative results derived from the IR framework is the relationship between a firm's location on the IR grid and organizational structure. A complex issue, we will not be able to do the topic justice here. So let us concentrate on a simple question, are all transnational firms the same? Our intent is to show the importance of considering transactional completeness to explain organization form.

Within the transnational form there are many options open to firms. For example, what is the difference between an oil company owning a brand name but using contractual arrangements to explore for oil, extract it from the ground, refine it, market it, and franchise out retail locations, and one that does all these tasks in-house with a matrix structure? Similarly, how do we distinguish between a pharmaceutical company that relies on joint venture arrangements with small laboratories and one that employs its own scientists? What, too, of the company that outsources all marketing and distribution functions in Western countries but operates these functions in-house in Asia? Is one of these companies any less a transnational even though they all might have high degrees of global integration and local responsiveness? It is because of this dilemma that it is necessary to account for the need

Figure 7   Moving from Inefficient to Efficient Strategic Choice

(a) Altering Feasible Technology

(b) Altering Managerial Orientation

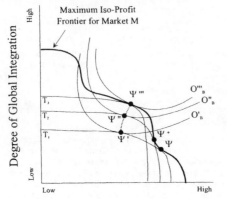
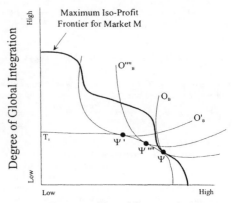

Degree of Transactional Completeness

Degree of Local Responsiveness

to own, operate and protect critical assets, tasks and functions when talking about the international strategic orientation of companies. We can illustrate how this need might vary by looking at the extremes of the transactional completeness dimension.

Low transactional completeness. At this extreme the desire to protect critical competencies and assets from competitors, along with the need to monitor and control the components of the value chain are the driving concern of management. These demands lead naturally to controlling tasks, functions and individuals through management and internalization. There is also a reliance on internal networks rather than interfirm networks. Formal matrix organizations represent the most obvious example of the internalization of multifunctional tasks and responsibilities.

High transactional completeness. At the other extreme, protection is achieved either through strong contractual bonds (such as patents or strong commercial codes), or because of the policing power of the marketplace (particularly in commodity markets). The concern of management in this case is not the management of specific tasks and skills but the coordination of a system and the protection of critical assets (such as brand names or the managerial skills associated with coordination). These contractual transnationals rely on interfirm networks of outsourced activities.

Because there is every reason to believe that the choice of organization structure will (ceteris paribus) affect firm performance, it is important to incorporate transactional completeness if we are to explain performance adequately. Transactional completeness has significant influence on the choice of structure within each of the four generic forms normally associated with the IR framework. Therefore, it is possible to repeat the exercise above for all the other standard international business forms. Our second example uses real companies to illustrate transactional completeness within the global form of organization.

5.2.   Alternative Organizational Forms in a Global Market: Ericsson, Motorola and Nokia

Our second example concerns Ericsson, Motorola, and Nokia—the global leaders in the mobile telephone market.[8] Mobile telephones are highly standardized, technologically intensive, scale-driven products that face strong forces for global integration. All three of these firms produce and sell large volumes of their products across the globe, and do so with coordinated strategies. Apart from transmission standards, an Ericsson, Motorola, or Nokia phone is similar when sold in Australia, China, or the United States. The standards themselves are country-specific conditions that all three firms face equally (e.g.,

TIMOTHY M. DEVINNEY, DAVID F. MIDGLEY, AND SUNIL VENAIK *Optimal Performance of the Global Firm*

GSM 1800 for Europe and GSM 1900 for North America). Other than standards, the forces for local responsiveness are relatively weak and largely confined to country pricing, distribution arrangements, and advertising copy. Thus, on the IR grid we would expect all three of these firms to be located in the global quadrant. *Yet the value chains and organizational structures of these three firms are significantly different.* Nokia has primarily grown to leadership by exporting from Finland. Both Ericsson and Motorola have much broader activities both in terms of products and in the depth and breadth of their value chains. Ericsson's strategy hinges on common technology across phone handsets and the cellular network systems themselves. Motorola builds on its own long-standing strength in the development and production of semiconductors whereas Ericsson partners with Texas Instruments to develop these strategic components. Nokia is involved in joint ventures in the United States and China, and to build scale also acts as an original equipment manufacturer (OEM) for other organizations (including Ericsson). These three firms therefore have different value chains. As to organizational structures, Nokia is the smallest of the three (primarily based in Finland), and has only changed from an exporting structure to a more global organizational form in the 1990s. In contrast, Ericsson and Motorola are much larger and longer-established global players and have major operating companies and manufacturing plants around the globe. Ericsson and Motorola also differ in organization structure. Ericsson has a matrix where the mobile phone business area interacts with local companies in each country. Motorola has autonomous business sectors where the mobile phone sector interacts with four regional organizations (e.g., Pan American, Greater China, etc.). We would argue that these differences in structure reflect the differences in their value chain strategies. However, the point of our example is to illustrate that three organizations classified identically by the integration-responsiveness framework differ significantly on a third important dimension—transactional completeness.

5.3. Reinterpreting the History of Philips and Matsushita Using the IRC Model

One important case discussed in the literature is that of Philips and Matsushita, two global competitors in the consumer electronics market (Bartlett and Ghoshal 1988, Bartlett 1994).[9] The older company, Philips, built its postwar success on "highly independent, fully integrated national organizations able to sense and respond to local needs," (Bartlett 1994, p.1). In terms of transactional completeness, Philips replicated a value chain in each country using local suppliers to source components and

services. Thus, Philips had a federal strategy—highly responsive to each market, but dependent on local supply and suffering from weak scale economies and problems of coordination across the whole organization. These problems led to a decrease in profits and a series of restructures from the 1970s to the 1990s.

In contrast, Matsushita succeeded by building scale economies in its larger home market, and even by 1982 had less than 10% of overseas sales manufactured outside Japan. In terms of transactional completeness, most value was added in Japan and dependent on supply conditions in the Japanese economy. Thus, Matsushita had an export strategy and, in contrast to the loose global coordination and highly autonomous national organizations of Philips, exerted strong central control through its product divisions, expatriate managers, and monitoring of results. However, in the mid-1980s the appreciating yen led to a fall in Matsushita's exports, which together with the company's reliance on VCR sales and lack of innovation in overseas subsidiaries also led to a series of restructurings continuing into the 1990s.

Philips' restructures had two objectives—increasing scale economies by plant consolidation and gaining greater control over manufacturing and R&D by central product divisions. Philips also sought to expose more of its value chain to market competition and to source more inputs from outside suppliers. Thus, Philips increased global integration and transactional completeness. However, none of this helped Philips' performance—in the decade ending 1996, Philips return on assets has averaged less than 5% and net income to sales less than 1%.

Matsushita's restructuring also focused on two objectives—reducing dependence on the VCR and increasing offshore production. Strong central control of the product divisions was also relaxed, ceding greater responsibility to local companies. Matsushita was thus attempting to increase local responsiveness and to move more of its value chain offshore—subjecting the latter to supply conditions in a variety of locations rather than just Japan. Matsushita has also succeeded in reducing its reliance on the VCR, but in moving from a focused exporter to a broader transnational, Matsushita has also not improved its performance. In 1996, Matsushita only made a net income to sales ratio of 1.6% and a return on assets of 3.3% (excluding extraordinary items). These figures are well below the peak achieved in 1985.

There are several observations we can make about this example. First, as Bartlett notes, these strategies are mirror images of each other and were undertaken with the goal of becoming more "transnational" (1994, p.8). Second, the example illustrates the concept of hard and soft constraints and their major impact on the strategy and

TIMOTHY M. DEVINNEY, DAVID F. MIDGLEY, AND SUNIL VENAIK *Optimal Performance of the Global Firm*

performance of organizations. The hard constraints are the many small-scale plants of Philips, the lack of overseas capacity of Matsushita, the control systems of Matsushita, etc. These we define as "technological feasibility," and they are clearly hard to change in the short-run. For example, Philips worked on concentrating production into larger plants for over a decade and Matsushita failed to achieve its overseas capacity goals throughout the 1980s.

These hard constraints are also distinct from the soft but equally important constraint of "managerial orientation." The vision of globalization via the transnational form had a powerful effect on the senior executives of both companies. Both have moved energetically to achieve this form, yet neither reached their espoused goals, and neither has achieved the performance they would have wished.

Indeed, in 1999 the question was still open as to whether both companies were wise to attempt to become more like each other. In the case of Philips, management is trying to radically remake the company as a transnational—yet its feasible technology (hard and soft) was initially very focused on being locally responsive and self-sufficient. It is therefore not surprising that the process has been arduous and not profitable. Matsushita too is trying to remake itself—this time from a highly integrated and focused exporter into a transnational. Again, hard and soft constraints have made this difficult. The question is whether alternative strategies would have been more profitable for both companies—in other words, the "path of efficient strategy" to an appropriate point on the frontier rather than the radical re-orientation that both embarked on. As the natural experiment has not been conducted we will never know the answer, but the IRC framework suggests it is a valid one to ask.

Whatever we think about the strategic choices made by these two firms, it is clear that we need to consider the nature of their value chains in any discussion. The transactional pressures facing Philips—with its numerous local operations—are likely to have been very different from those facing Matsushita with most of its manufacturing initially located in Japan. Moreover, we can see that despite competing for many of the same markets, and recording similar performance levels, Philips and Matsushita have different orientations on the three dimensions of global integration, local responsiveness, and transactional completeness, and these different orientations have coexisted for decades. Equally, whilst we do not know how their performance relates to any efficient frontiers, we can see that the new components of the IRC model potentially add insight to the interpretation of this case.

6. Conclusion

In this paper we have made a modest attempt to build on the seminal work of authors in the fields of organizational economics and international business. Although this earlier work has done much to explain the international strategies of firms, there are few frameworks that integrate what has been established in a compelling and rigorous manner. In particular, we focused on the IR framework as the best current approach for explaining international strategic orientation. Although this framework provides an excellent starting point for our endeavors, we believe it has important limitations. We try to overcome these limitations by formalizing and extending the IR framework into the IRC model described in §4. This model explains the transactional nature of interunit coordination and allows environmental pressures, organizational constraints, and managerial beliefs to interact in a goal-driven manner.

Whilst the IRC framework is less parsimonious than the IR framework on which it is built, it encompasses more completely the range of phenomena suggested by the literature. Any theory of international strategy needs, at the minimum, to encompass economies of scale and scope, local market conditions, organizational form, firm history, and managerial orientation. Any such theory needs to do so in a manner that explains firm performance—in particular why firms with quite different configurations in similar markets can have similar performance. By our three illustrations in §5—determination of organizational form; Ericsson, Motorola, and Nokia; and Philips and Matsushita—we showed that the IRC framework has the potential to shed light in areas that the IR framework cannot.

However, by no means do we regard the IRC framework as a finished work. First, the nature of the model raises important methodological issues that need to be addressed. Second, there are unresolved questions that suggest that further conceptual development may be required. We look at each in turn.

6.1. Methodological Issues

The first priority for any new theory should be validation through empirical analysis. The IRC model has two methodological implications that are important to highlight. The first is the distinction between formative and reflective indicators. The second is the form of empirical analysis implied by the model.

Formative and reflective indicators. Although many aspects of validating the theory appear straightforward—for example, defining the various facets of the three dimensions and managerial orientation and developing and validating measures of these constructs—special attention must be paid to which arrows in Figure 1 are formative and which are reflective. In particular, we would speculate that the three dimensions are best thought of as formative indicators. This is because their facets (subsets of pressures within a dimension) are not necessarily correlated in the same way as typical questionnaire scales. This is not a substantive issue as it is well understood by methodologists (Chin 1998).

Empirical frontier analysis. Perhaps the most important implication of the IRC model is that its use of an efficient frontier requires a de facto change in our analysis methodology. The three-dimensional topology of this frontier needs to be measured and the performance of the sample of firms related to this topology rather than to that of the average firm (Day et al. 1995). In a sample of firms we might expect to find some on the frontier and some not. Although economic theory might suggest that such inefficient firms would be driven out, in reality imperfections can exist for some time—particularly for complex organizations where cross-subsidies can exist between business units. We consider that an adaptation of either Data Envelopment Analysis (Charnes et al. 1978) or Stochastic Frontier Analysis (Bauer 1990) will provide the basic methodology for understanding the frontier. Both these methods match well with our model because they allow you to (1) measure the determinants of the frontier and (2) measure those firm-specific constraints responsible for less that optimal performance.

6.2. Unresolved Questions

There are three unresolved questions about the IRC model that we can identify at this time. In increasing order of importance they are (1) incorporating other factors mentioned in the literature, (2) integrating organizational knowledge and learning, and (3) creating a dynamic formulation of the model.

Integrating other factors. The logic of our modeling structure allows for the integration of other factors. For example, political influences can be directly related to one of the three dimensions (for example, government policies to encourage plant location to the global integration dimension) or integrated into the orientation of managers (e.g., focus of Chinese managers towards exports). Factors such as managerial competencies or internal mechanisms for marshalling resources and coordinating activities (such as teams or cross-business unit committees) can also be integrated into one of our three dimensions. For example, it is arguable that managers are hired or developed in accordance with the prevailing managerial orientation, and hence their competencies are likely to be

correlated with this construct. Similarly, we might speculate that organizational form heavily influences the efficacy of teams or committees, and hence these matters are secondary to transactional completeness.

Organizational knowledge and learning. A number of authors have proposed that organizational knowledge and learning need to be integrated into the theory of the global firm to make it more complete (e.g., Bartlett and Ghoshal 1989, Gupta and Govindarajan 1994, Roos et al. 1994). Although we agree that organizational learning is critical to the understanding of international business operations, we speculate that the nature of organizational learning, and the knowledge that results from it, is influenced by all three of the underlying dimensions.

Ceteris paribus, as the level of responsiveness to diverse local markets increases, there is the potential for the diversity of knowledge available to the firm to increase, as also will the diversity of applications to which the resultant learning might be applied (Nohria and Ghoshal 1997). The potential for learning may also increase as global integration increases due to the public good nature of information and the associated economies of scale. More globally integrated firms may be able to use and invest in more numerous sources of learning and, hence, be more efficient in the utilization of any one piece of knowledge. Finally, the nature of learning may be directly related to the transactional completeness of the market for knowledge. Proprietary and protectable knowledge will differ from nonproprietary and "public good" knowledge. It is generally recognized that the more important knowledge is to the competitive functioning of a firm, the more likely it is that the firm will attempt to internalize and protect this knowledge (Teece et al. 1997, Harvey and Lusch 1997).

For example, a firm that sources intermediate products on open markets (e.g., a personal computer manufacturer) will make a different set of strategic choices to one that is required to produce them internally (e.g., a professional services firm). These choices will in turn influence the nature and extent of any worldwide learning that occurs within each firm.

The difficulty that exists with integrating learning into the IRC model is the fact that it is a *meta-function*; that is, a function that may necessarily span other functions. Therefore, the management of organizational learning and knowledge is not neatly compartmentalized like the management of marketing or operations. Thus to us there is an issue as to whether organizational learning should be incorporated as an additional environmental dimension, as suggested by Bartlett and Ghoshal (1989), or as an endogenous outcome of managerial choice of strategy

TIMOTHY M. DEVINNEY, DAVID F. MIDGLEY, AND SUNIL VENAIK   *Optimal Performance of the Global Firm*

and structure. We prefer the latter for reasons that relate to our third and final unresolved question.

Toward a dynamic IRC model. The most critical limitation of the IRC model is that our analysis in this paper is essentially static. This static analysis is inadequate as firms continually learn and adapt to changing circumstances or they cease to exist. These circumstances include, *inter alia*, changes to their competitive environment and changes to their understanding of their own operations. We therefore need to incorporate a more dynamic perspective into the various components of the model. For example, the industry-efficient frontier can be redefined either because of the competitive actions of leading firms (e.g., technological innovation) or because of changes in underlying pressures (e.g., government regulations). The firm itself can also change its technological feasibility or managerial orientation in a variety of ways.

As Levinthal and March (1993) note, firm adaptations involve two types, exploitations and explorations. They argue that exploitations (incremental efficiency improvements, product extensions, etc.) tend to be favored by managers because they involve less risk, albeit also lower returns, than explorations (innovations, changing the rules of competition, etc.). Moreover, to be successful at exploration requires that the firm have the capabilities to create or absorb new knowledge from outside the firm, and to implement this knowledge effectively. Thus, we might speculate that exploration is related to redefining the industry frontier whilst exploitation is related to changing technological feasibility.

It is important to note that the IRC model is primarily about *why* managers make the choices they do. The model addresses the forces and influences that shape these managerial decisions and is not, as yet, a prescriptive one. That is, it does not identify, from all the possibilities, the one best trajectory that a specific firm should follow for achieving "best" performance. In order to do so, we need to incorporate additional forces and influences, and the preceding discussion suggests to us that the key is to incorporate the nature of competitive dynamics more formally into the model. These might include the degree of competitive pressure to change and the economic efficiency of the market. Both will be related directly to the level of the industry frontier (how much profit exists) and to the tolerance of inefficient performers (how far below the frontier a firm can be and still be viable). Competitive dynamics might also include the risks and returns of various courses of action, including both exploitation and exploration. Gaining a better understanding of competition pressures, risk and return would be an important step toward a more dynamic IRC model.

Acknowledgments
The authors would like to thank José de la Torre, Donald Lessard, Kendall Roth, John Stopford, Geoff Waring, the anonymous referees and editors of *Organization Science* and participants at seminars at Georgetown University, UCLA, Minnesota, the 1996 EIBA Meeting in Stockholm, the 1997 Marketing Science Conference at INSEAD and the 1998 AIB meeting in Vienna for comments on previous versions of this paper.

Endnotes

[1] For the sake of simplicity of exposition we assume the "market" and "industry" can be defined appropriately for any particular analysis. On many occasions this might be a strategic market segment (e.g., personal computers or prestige automobiles), or if there are production or marketing synergies between such segments we might analyze the larger industry (e.g., computers, automobiles).

[2] Which formulation is closer to reality is an empirical question. Our contention is that existing empirical research points toward a partially deterministic formulation. However, even if this were incorrect, although the form of the model would be different, the fundamental logic would remain the same.

[3] The "as if" in this sentence is important. It is possible that no external market exists, but that one could arise under different price and profit conditions. Under these circumstances the market would be transactionally complete even though it did not exist!

[4] We will use the term isoprofit and efficient frontier interchangeably. Our model is completely generalizable to situations in which firms are maximizing profit or a multidimensional measure of efficiency.

[5] The argument being made here is simply that a frontier of equally profitable and viable strategies exists. Mathematically, the only requirement made of the frontiers is monotonicity; i.e., the profits are strictly increasing or decreasing as one moves further and further from the origin.

[6] There are measurement issues concerning the operationalization of these dimensions in a manner consistent with the isoprofit frontier. As this is a conceptual paper, we have chosen not to discuss these.

[7] There is no reason to believe that the managerial orientation function is increasing continuously in either or both dimensions. One possibility is that managerial orientation is an "ideal point" where movement in any direction is viewed as bad by the management. This affects the normative conclusions derived from our framework and not the framework itself. We are grateful to José de la Torre for pointing this out to us.

[8] Our example is based on information from the websites of these companies. We chose mobile phones because they are significant revenue generators for these companies.

[9] Our example is based on material presented by these authors, together with press articles and annual reports.

REFERENCES

Aharoni, Y. 1966. *The Foreign Investment Decision Process.* Harvard University Press, Cambridge, MA.

——. 1993. In search for the unique: Can firm-specific advantages be evaluated. *J. Management Stud.* **1** (January) 31–49.

Aigner, D.J., C.A.K. Lovell, P. Schmidt. 1977. Formulation and estimation of stochastic production function models. *J. Econometrics* **6** 21–37.

TIMOTHY M. DEVINNEY, DAVID F. MIDGLEY, AND SUNIL VENAIK   *Optimal Performance of the Global Firm*

Ali, A.I., C.S. Lerme. 1997. Comparative advantage and disadvantage in DEA. *Ann. Oper. Res.* **73** 215–232.

Amit, R., P. Schoemaker. 1993. Strategic assets and organizational rents. *Strategic Management J.* **14**(1) 33–46.

Bartlett, C. 1986. Building and managing the transnational: The new organizational challenge. M.E. Porter, ed. *Competition in Global Industries.* Harvard Business School, Boston, MA. 367–401.

——. 1994. *Philips and Matsushita: A Portrait of Two Evolving Companies.* Harvard Business School, Boston, MA.

——, S. Ghoshal. 1987a. Managing across borders: New strategic requirements. *Sloan Management Rev.* **28**(4) 7–17.

——, ——. 1987b. Managing across borders: New organizational responses. *Sloan Management Rev.* **29**(1) 43–53.

——, ——. 1988. Organizing for worldwide effectiveness: The transnational solution. *California Management Rev.* **31**(1) 54–74.

——, ——. 1989. *Managing Across Borders: The Transnational Solution.* Harvard Business School, Boston, MA.

Bauer, P. 1990. Recent developments in the econometric estimation of frontiers. *J. Econometrics.* **46** (1/2) 39–56.

Birkinshaw, J, A. Morrison, J Hulland. 1995. Structural and competitive determinants of global integration strategy. *Strategic Management J.* **16**(8) 637–655.

Buckley, P.J., M. Casson. 1976. *The Future of the Multinational Enterprise,* Macmillan, London, UK.

Caves, R.E. 1971. International corporations: The industrial economics of foreign investment. *Economica* **38** 1–27.

Cavusgil, S. 1980. On the internationalisation process of firms. *European Res.* **8**(6) 273–281.

Charnes, A., W. Cooper, E. Rhodes. 1978. Measuring the efficiency of decision making units. *European J. Oper. Res.* **2**(6) 429–444.

Chin, W.W. 1998. The partial least squares approach to structural equation modeling. G.A. Marcoulides, ed. *Modern Methods for Business Research.* Erlbaum, Mahwah, NJ.

Day, D.L., A.Y. Lewin, H. Li. 1995. Strategic leaders or strategic groups: A longitudinal data envelopment analysis of the U.S. brewing industry. *European J. Oper. Res.* **80** 619–638.

Doz, Y., C. Bartlett, C. K. Prahalad. 1981. Global competitive pressures and host country demands: Managing tensions in MNCs. *California Management Rev.* **23**(3) 63–74.

Dunning, J. 1981. *International Production and the Multinational Enterprise.* Allen & Unwin, London, UK.

——. 1995. Reappraising the eclectic paradigm in an age of alliance capitalism. *J. Internat. Bus. Stud.* **3** 461–491.

Finkelstein, S., D. Hambrick. 1996. *Strategic Leadership: Top Executives and Their Effects on Organizations.* West Publishing, St. Paul, MN.

Ghoshal, S. 1987. Global strategy: An organizing framework. *Strategic Management J.* **8**(5) 425–440.

——, N. Nohria. 1993. Horses for courses: Organizational forms for multinational corporations. *Sloan Management Rev.* **34**(2) 23–35.

Grossman, S., O. Hart. 1983. An analysis of the principal-agent problem. *Econometrica* **51**(1) 7–45.

Gupta, A., V. Govindarajan. 1994. Organising for knowledge flows within MNCs. *Internat. Bus. Rev.* **3**(4) 443–457.

Hamel, G., C.K. Prahalad. 1985. Do you really have a global strategy? *Harvard Bus. Rev.* **63**(4) 139–148.

Harvey, M., R. Lusch. 1997. Protecting the core competencies of a company: Intangible asset security. *European Management J.* **15**(4) 370–380.

Hennart, J.F. 1982. *A Theory of Multinational Enterprise.* Lexington Books, Lexington, MA.

——. 1991. Control in multinational firms: The role of price and hierarchy. *Management Internat. Rev.* **31** 71–96.

——. 1993. Explaining the swollen middle: Why most transactions are a mix of market and hierarchy. *Organ. Sci.* **4**(4) 529–547.

Hout, T., M. Porter, E. Rudden. 1982. How global companies win out. *Harvard Bus. Rev.* **60**(5) 98–108.

Hymer, S. 1960. The international operations of international firms: A study of direct investment. Unpublished Ph.D. dissertation, Massachusetts Institute of Technology, Cambridge, MA.

Johanson, J., J–E. Vahlne. 1977. The internationalization process of the firm—a model of knowledge development and increasing foreign market commitments. *J. Internat. Bus. Stud.* **8**(1) 23–32.

——. F. Wiedersheim-Paul. 1975. The internationalisation of the firm—four Swedish cases. *J. Management Stud.* **12**(3) 305–322.

Johansson, J.K., G.S. Yip. 1994. Exploiting globalization potential: U.S. and Japanese strategies. *Strategic Management J.* **15**(8) 579–601.

Johnson, J., Jr. 1995. An empirical analysis of the integration-responsiveness framework: U.S. construction equipment industry firms in global competition. *J. Internat. Bus. Stud.* **26**(3) 621–635.

Kindleberger, C.P. 1969. *American Business Abroad.* Yale University Press, New Haven, CT.

Kobrin, S. 1991. An empirical analysis of the determinants of global integration. *Strategic Management J.* **12** (Summer) 17–31.

——. 1994. Is there a relationship between a geocentric mind-set and multinational strategy? *J. Internat. Bus. Stud.* **25**(3) 493–511.

Kogut, B. 1985. Designing global strategies: Profiting from operational flexibility. *Sloan Management Rev.* **27**(1) 27–38.

Lawrence, P., J. Lorsch. 1967. *Organization and Environment.* Harvard Business School, Boston, MA.

Levinthal, D.A., J.G. March. 1993. The myopia of learning. *Strategic Management J.* **14** 95–112.

Levitt, T. 1983. The globalization of markets. *Harvard Bus. Rev.* **61**(3) 92–102.

Martinez, J., J. Jarillo. 1991. Coordination demands of international strategies. *J. Internat. Bus. Stud.* **22**(3) 429–444.

Murtha, T., S. Lenway, R. Bagozzi. 1998. Global mind-sets and cognitive shift in complex multinational corporation. *Strategic Management J.* **19**(1) 97–114.

Nelson, R., S. Winter. 1982. *An Evolutionary Theory of Economic Change.* Belknap Press, Cambridge, MA.

Nohria, N., S. Ghoshal. 1997. *The Differentiated Network: Organizing Multinational Corporations for Value Creation.* Jossey-Bass, San Francisco, CA.

Ohmae, K. 1989. Planting for a global harvest. *Harvard Bus. Rev.* **67**(4) 136–145.

Perlmutter, H. 1969. The tortuous evolution of the multinational corporation. *Columbia J. World Bus.* **4** (January–February) 9–18.

Porter, M., ed. 1986. *Competition in Global Industries.* Harvard Business School, Boston, MA.

Prahalad, C.K. 1975. The strategic process in a multinational corporation. Unpublished Doctoral Dissertation, Graduate School of Business Administration, Harvard University, Cambridge, MA.

——, R.A. Bettis. 1986. The dominant logic: a new linkage between diversity and performance. *Strategic Management J.* **7**(6), 485–501.

——, Y. Doz. 1987. *The Multinational Mission: Balancing Local Demands and Global Vision.* Free Press, New York.

Roos, J., G. von Krogh, G. Yip. 1994. An epistemology of globalising firms. *Internat. Bus. Rev.* **3**(4) 395–410.

Roth, K., A. Morrison. 1990. An empirical analysis of the integration-responsiveness framework in global industries. *J. Internat. Bus. Stud.* **21**(4) 541–564.

Stopford, J., L. Wells. 1972. *Managing the Multinational Enterprise: Organization of the Firm and Ownership of the Subsidiaries.* Basic Books, New York.

Takeuchi, H., M. Porter. 1986. Three roles of international marketing in global strategy. M.E. Porter. *Competition in Global Industries.* Harvard Business School, Boston, MA. 111–146.

Teece, D. 1992. Competition, cooperation, and innovation: Organizational arrangements for regimes of rapid technological progress. *J. Econom. Behavior and Organ.* **18**(1) 1–25.

——, G. Pisano, A. Shuen. 1997. Dynamic capabilities and strategic management. *Strategic Management J.* **18**(7) 509–533.

Vernon, R. 1966. International investment and international trade in the product cycle. *Quart. J. Econom.* **80**(2) 190–207.

Williamson, O. 1991. Comparative economic organization: The analysis of discrete structural alternatives. *Admin. Sci. Quart.* **36**(2) 269–296.

Yetton, P., J. Davis, P. Swann. 1992. *Going International: Export Myths and Strategic Realities.* Australian Manufacturing Council, Melbourne, Australia.

Accepted by Arie Y. Lewin; received September 23, 1999.

[28]

Journal of International Business Studies (2003) 34, 586–599
© 2003 Palgrave Macmillan Ltd. All rights reserved 0047-2506 $25.00
www.jibs.net

MNC knowledge transfer, subsidiary absorptive capacity, and HRM

D Minbaeva[1], T Pedersen[1],
I Björkman[2,3], CF Fey[4,5],
HJ Park[6]

[1]Copenhagen Business School, Denmark;
[2]Swedish School of Economics, Helsinki, Finland;
[3]INSEAD Euro-Asia Centre, France; [4]Stockholm
School of Economics, Sweden; [5]Stockholm School
of Economics in Saint Petersburg, Russia;
[6]Cornell University, USA

Correspondence: Professor T Pedersen
Department of International Economics and
Management, Copenhagen Business
School, Howitzvej 60, 2th, Copenhagen
DK-2000 F, Denmark.
Tel: + 45 3815 2521;
Fax: + 45 3815 2500;
E-mail: tp.int@cbs.dk

Abstract
Based on a sample of 169 subsidiaries of multinational corporations (MNCs) operating in the USA, Russia, and Finland, this paper investigates the relationship between MNC subsidiary human resource management (HRM) practices, absorptive capacity, and knowledge transfer. First, we examine the relationship between the application of specific HRM practices and the level of the absorptive capacity. Second, we suggest that absorptive capacity should be conceptualized as being comprised of both employees' ability and motivation. Further, results indicate that both ability and motivation (absorptive capacity) are needed to facilitate the transfer of knowledge from other parts of the MNC.
Journal of International Business Studies (2003) 34, 586–599. doi:10.1057/palgrave.jibs.8400056

Keywords: knowledge transfer; absorptive capacity; HRM

Introduction

Research in the area of knowledge management indicates that the ability to create and transfer knowledge internally is one of the main competitive advantages of multinational corporations (MNCs). The MNC is considered to be a 'differentiated network', where knowledge is created in various parts of the MNC and transferred to several inter-related units (Hedlund, 1986; Bartlett and Ghoshal, 1989). Conceptualizing the MNC as a differentiated network has inspired a recent stream of research on the creation, assimilation, and diffusion of internal MNC knowledge emphasizing the role of subsidiaries in these processes (Holm and Pedersen, 2000).

It has been proposed in the knowledge transfer literature that the absorptive capacity of the receiving unit is the most significant determinant of internal knowledge transfer in MNCs (Gupta and Govindarajan, 2000). Subsidiaries differ in their absorptive capacity, and this affects the level of internal knowledge transfer from other MNC units. The literature, however, offers multiple methods to conceptualize and operationalize absorptive capacity, often not capturing the various facets of absorptive capacity. Moreover, little attention has been paid to the question of whether organizations can enhance the creation and development of absorptive capacity. Clearly, with a few exemptions, the characteristics of knowledge transfer and absorptive capacity have not been treated as endogenous to organizational processes and arrangements (Foss and Pedersen, 2002). This is true in spite of the commonly accepted idea that organizational learning is closely linked to how an

Received: 19 July 2001
Revised: 22 May 2002
Accepted: 20 December 2002
Online publication date: 16 October 2003

organization manages its human resources (e.g., Lado and Wilson, 1994). For instance, limited investments in training and development may result in low levels of employee knowledge and skills, thereby inhibiting learning. In their study of relative absorptive capacity and interorganizational learning, Lane and Lubatkin (1998) assert that both compensation practices and organizational structures are positively associated with absorptive capacity as well as interorganizational learning. However, our knowledge of how human resource management (HRM) influences the absorptive capacity of a subsidiary and internal MNC knowledge transfer is still very rudimentary.

The contribution of this paper is twofold. First, we contribute to the conceptualization of absorptive capacity by emphasizing employees' motivation as well as employees' ability as the important aspects of absorptive capacity. Second, while many other studies have focused on the importance of absorptive capacity for knowledge transfer (e.g., Lyles and Salk, 1996; Lane and Lubatkin, 1998; Lane et al., 2001), we extend these studies by exploring the types of organizational mechanisms that increase absorptive capacity. Our approach differs from the previously mentioned studies, as we do not just explore the impact of absorptive capacity on knowledge transfer. We go a step further by treating the development of absorptive capacity as an endogenous part of the model. The paper is structured as follows: in the next section, we review the literature on MNC knowledge transfer and absorptive capacity. Based on the literature review, we develop hypotheses on: (1) the relationship between different aspects of absorptive capacity – employees' ability and motivation – and the level of knowledge transfer and (2) HRM practices and employees' ability and motivation. Finally, we explain the methodology employed, followed by a discussion of the results and implications of the study.

Knowledge transfer within MNCs
The interest in knowledge within MNCs, its sources and transfer, has been expanding (e.g., Gupta and Govindarajan, 2000). MNCs are no longer seen as repositories of their national imprint but rather as instruments whereby knowledge is transferred across subsidiaries, contributing to knowledge development (Holm and Pedersen, 2000). A common theme in this line of research is that MNCs can develop knowledge in one location but exploit it in other locations, implying the internal transfer of

knowledge by MNCs. Thus, the competitive advantage that MNCs enjoy is contingent upon their ability to facilitate and manage intersubsidiary transfer of knowledge. Hedlund (1986) and Bartlett and Ghoshal (1989), for example, focused on how to organize and structure MNCs in order to facilitate the internal flow and transfer of knowledge in MNCs.

Szulanski (1996) emphasized that 'the movement of knowledge within the organization is a distinct experience, not a gradual process of dissemination' (p. 28). In his view, knowledge transfer is a process of dyadic exchanges of knowledge between the source and recipient units consisting of four stages: initiation, implementation, ramp-up and integration. While the first two stages comprise all events that lead to the decision to transfer and the actual flow of knowledge from the source to the recipient, the latter two stages begin when the recipient starts utilizing the transferred knowledge. Clearly, pure transmission of knowledge from the source to the recipient has no useful value if the recipient does not use the new knowledge. The key element in knowledge transfer is not the underlying (original) knowledge, but rather the extent to which the receiver acquires potentially useful knowledge and utilizes this knowledge in own operations. Knowledge transfer may lead to some change in the recipient's behavior or the development of some new idea that leads to new behavior (Davenport and Prusak, 1998). This is in line with the definition of organization learning often put forth in the literature, where organizational learning involves a change in organizational outcomes (see Fiol and Lyles (1985) for an overview of this literature). Accordingly, we define knowledge transfer between organizational units as a process that covers several stages starting from identifying the knowledge over the actual process of transferring the knowledge to its final utilization by the receiving unit. In the context of MNC, the other units are the headquarters and other subsidiaries in the corporation, while the receiving unit is the focal subsidiary.

Knowledge transfer is not a random process and organizations can institute various internal policies, structures, and processes to facilitate learning (Inkpen, 1998). More recently, much of the empirical research on intra-company knowledge transfer has been focusing on different factors that hinder or stimulate knowledge transfer (see Chapter 5 in Argote (1999) for a detailed review). Ghoshal and Bartlett (1988) concluded that communications between organizational units facilitate knowledge flows within MNC. Simonin (1999) suggested that knowledge ambiguity plays a critical role as mediator between explanatory variables (e.g., tacitness, prior experience, complexity, cultural distance, and organizational distance) and transfer outcomes. These effects were moderated by the capacity of the firm to support learning. Gupta and Govindarajan (2000) observed that the knowledge inflows into a subsidiary are positively associated with the richness of transmission channels, motivation to acquire knowledge, and capacity to absorb incoming knowledge.

Szulanski (1996) studied the impediments to the transfer using a slightly different approach. He applied all sets of factors together in an eclectic model to measure their relative impact on knowledge transfer (internal stickiness). His findings suggest that along with causal ambiguity and relationships between source and recipient units, the recipients' lack of absorptive capacity is the most important impediment to knowledge transfer within the firm. The role of absorptive capacity of the receiving unit also stands out as the most significant determinant of knowledge transfer in a number of other studies (e.g., Lane and Lubatkin, 1998; Gupta and Govindarajan, 2000).

Absorptive capacity

In their seminal work, Cohen and Levinthal (1990) defined *absorptive capacity* as the 'ability to recognize the value of new external information, assimilate it, and apply it to commercial ends' (p. 128). Cohen and Levinthal (1990) assumed that a firm's absorptive capacity tends to develop cumulatively, is path dependent and builds on existing knowledge: 'absorptive capacity is more likely to be developed and maintained as a byproduct of routine activity when the knowledge domain that the firm wishes to exploit is closely related to its current knowledge base' (p. 150).

Building on the concept of absorptive capacity, Lyles and Salk (1996) included international joint ventures' (IJV) capacity to learn as an independent variable to analyze knowledge acquisition from a foreign parent. Their results indicate that the 'capacity to learn, mainly the flexibility, and creativity' (p. 896), is a significant indicator of knowledge acquisition from the foreign partner. Taking Lyles and Salk's conclusion as a starting point, Lane *et al.* (2001) refined the absorptive capacity definition offered by Cohen and Levinthal. They propose that 'the first two components, the ability to understand external knowledge

and the ability to assimilate it, are interdependent yet distinct from the third component, the ability to apply the knowledge' (p. 1156).

Lane and Lubatkin (1998) further reconceptualized the concept and proposed that absorptive capacity is a dyad-level construct – denoted relative absorptive capacity – rather than a firm level construct. Lane and Lubatkin (1998) and later Lane *et al.* (2001) found support for the concept of relative absorptive capacity. In fact, Lane and Lubatkin (1998) tested the traditional measure of absorptive capacity of R&D as a share of sales (e.g., applied by Cohen and Levinthal, 1990) against their own measures of relative absorptive capacity (three bibliometric-based measures of knowledge and five knowledge-processing-similarity variables). They found that the traditional measure of R&D spending explained only 4% of the variance in interorganizational learning, while the knowledge similarity variables explained another 17% and the five knowledge-processing-similarity variables explained an additional 55%. A number of significant conclusions can be drawn from these studies. First, absorptive capacity should be understood in its context indicating that in some instances absorptive capacity should be treated as a dyad-level construct rather than as a firm-level construct. Second, traditional measures of absorptive capacity (e.g., R&D spending) may be inappropriate as they only partly capture the dyadic construct. Thus, relative absorptive capacity is 'more important to interorganizational learning than the commonly used measure of absolute absorptive capacity' (Lane and Lubatkin, 1998, 473) There is, however, a limitation to the generalizability of Lane and Lubatkin's conclusion. Both studies – Lane and Lubatkin (1998) and Lane *et al.* (2001) – were conducted within the context of IJVs where two independent companies were involved in the process of knowledge transfer. In this study, the knowledge transfer takes place between organizational units within the same firm, where the organizational structures, systems, practices, etc. are expected to be more similar than between independent companies. Thus, the relative absorptive capacity is of minor importance in the context of internal MNC knowledge transfer.

In a recent article, Zahra and George (2002) summarized representative empirical studies on absorptive capacity. According to Zahra and George (2002), absorptive capacity has four dimensions – acquisition, assimilation, transformation, and exploitation – where the first two dimensions form potential absorptive capacity, the latter two – realized absorptive capacity. They argue that more attention should be devoted to studying the realized absorptive capacity which emphasizes the firm's capacity to leverage the knowledge that has been previously absorbed (Zahra and George, 2002). As put forward by Zahra and George (2002) 'firms can acquire and assimilate knowledge but might not have the capability to transform and exploit the knowledge for profit generation' (p. 191). Zahra and George (2002) criticized the existing studies for applying measures (like R&D intensity, number of scientists working in R&D departments, etc.) that 'have been rudimentary and do not fully reflect the richness of the construct' (p. 199). Such an approach neglects the role of individuals in the organization, which is crucial for knowledge utilization and exploitation.

The aim of this paper is to add to the existing literature on absorptive capacity in two important directions: (1) *the concept*: in terms of the conceptualization and measurement of absorptive capacity, we follow the path of recent contributions (e.g., Zahra and George, 2002) and aim our efforts at studying the firm's capacity to utilize and exploit previously acquired knowledge. We identify employees' ability and motivation as the key aspects of the firm's absorptive capacity that in turn facilitates internal knowledge transfer; and (2) *the development*: we consider different organizational practices which may contribute to the development of absorptive capacity, thereby allowing us to examine the possible managerial influence on absorptive capacity that is not often examined in the literature. In particular, we identify specific HRM practices that managers might implement to develop the absorptive capacity of their organizations.

The concept

A firm's absorptive capacity is an organization-level construct that resides with its employees. The absorptive capacity has two elements: prior knowledge and intensity of effort (Cohen and Levinthal, 1990; Kim, 2001). 'Prior knowledge base refers to existing individual units of knowledge available within the organization' (Kim, 2001, 271). Thus, employees' ability, their educational background, and acquired job-related skills may represent the 'prior related knowledge' which the organization needs to assimilate and use (Cohen and Levinthal, 1990). However, in addition to the prior related knowledge, there should be a certain level of

'organizational aspiration' which is characterized by the organization's innovation efforts (Cohen and Levinthal, 1990). As proposed by Kim (2001), 'the intensity of effort refers to the amount of energy expended by organizational members to solve problems' (p. 271).

Employees' intensity of effort is well studied in the cognitive process theories such as the expectancy-valence theory of work motivation (see Vroom, 1964). Motivated employees want to contribute to organizational effectiveness. Even though the organization may consist of individuals with high abilities to learn, 'its ability to utilize the absorbed knowledge will be low if employees' motivation is low or absent' (Baldwin *et al.*, 1991, 52). The ability/can do factor usually denotes 'a potential for performing some task which may or may not be utilized' (Vroom, 1964, 198), while the motivation/will do factor reflects drive. The prior knowledge base (or employees' ability) and intensity of efforts made by the organization (or employees' motivation) is related to the concept of potential and realized absorptive capacity, since potential absorptive capacity is expected to have a high content of employees' ability while realized absorptive capacity is expected to have a high content of employees' motivation.

The behavioral science literature suggests that both employees' ability *and* motivation are of importance for organizational behavior. To achieve a high performance at any level, both the ability and motivation to perform effectively are needed (Baldwin, 1959). Empirical evidence supports an interactive, not additive, effect of ability and motivation on performance (e.g., French, 1957; Fleishman, 1958; Heider, 1958; O'Reilly and Chatman, 1994). Applying the concept of an interaction effect of ability and motivation on the issue of knowledge transfer, we expect that a higher rating in knowledge utilization will be achieved, if knowledge receivers have both the ability and motivation to absorb new external knowledge. Thus, we propose the following hypothesis:

Hypothesis 1. The interaction between employees' ability and motivation will increase the level of knowledge transfer to the subsidiary.

The development

Existing literature has paid little attention to how absorptive capacity is created and developed in the firm, rather taking for granted that this process does occur. To understand the sources of a firm's absorptive capacity, Cohen and Levinthal focused on 'the structure of communication between the external environment and the organization, as well as among the subunits of the organization, and also on the character and distribution of expertise within the organization' (p. 132). These factors emphasize environmental scanning and changes in R&D investments but pay very little attention to other internal organizational arrangements and their role in absorptive capacity creation and development. For example, little is known about how managerial practices may increase absorptive capacity and help diffuse knowledge inside the firm. The few studies that have included organizational characteristics (e.g., Lane and Lubatkin, 1998; Gupta and Govindarajan, 2000) call for further research on 'the learning capacities of organizational units,' 'organizational mechanisms to facilitate knowledge transfer,' etc. Based on our definition of absorptive capacity as being related to both employees' ability and motivation, we intend to treat the development of absorptive capacity endogenously by identifying the organizational mechanisms (HRM practices), which shape the organization's absorptive capacity.

HRM practices

In his influential study of the impact of '*high performance work practices*' on organizational turnover, productivity and corporate financial performance, Huselid (1995) factor-analyzed a number of HRM practices into two categories: those mainly influencing employees' abilities and those impacting employees' motivation. Huselid (1995) emphasized the interactive effect of HRM practices that influence ability and motivation. Similar results have been obtained by researchers who have clustered HRM practices into 'bundles' examining practices which influence the employees' ability and those that impact employees' motivation (e.g., Arthur, 1994; Ichniowski *et al.*, 1997; Delaney and Huselid, 1996).

As emphasized by Huselid (1995), HRM practices influence employees' skills and competencies through the acquisition and development of a firm's human capital. The competitive advantage of the firm is dependent on the existence of human resources with relevant competence profiles. An analysis of the competencies needed for different positions – together with an analysis of the firm's current pool of employee competencies – helps the organization hire people with the desired skills and

knowledge. In addition, performance appraisal (or performance management) systems provide employees with feedback on their performance and competencies and provide direction for enhancing their competencies to meet the needs of the firm. An integrated part of most performance appraisal systems is also the establishment of objectives and targets for the self-development and training of employees. There is also extensive evidence that investment in employees' training enhances the human capital of the firm, generally leading to a positive relationship between employee training and organizational performance (e.g., Delaney and Huselid, 1996; Koch and McGrath, 1996). Thus, we propose:

Hypothesis 2. Competence/performance appraisal and training are positively related to employee abilities.

'The effectiveness of even highly skilled employees will be limited if they are not motivated to perform' (Huselid, 1995, 637). In this context, several HRM practices may influence individual performance by providing incentives that elicit appropriate behaviors. Such incentive systems may include performance-based compensation and the use of internal promotion systems that focus on employee merit and help employees to overcome invisible barriers to their career growth (Huselid, 1995). Most studies have included performance-based compensation as a component of high performance HRM practices (e.g., Arthur, 1994; Huselid, 1995; MacDuffie, 1995; Delery and Doty, 1996).

While from an expectancy theory point of view it is the existence of a clear linkage between individual effort and reward that matters, from an equity theory (and organizational justice) perspective the main question is whether employees perceive that they receive the rewards that they are entitled to based on their contribution to the organization. Both perspectives would lead us to expect a positive relationship between performance-based compensation systems and employee effort. Promoting employees from within the firm is likely to provide a strong motivation for employees to work harder in order to be promoted (Pfeffer, 1994; Lepak and Snell, 1999). In addition, a philosophy of internal promotion indicates that a firm has decided to invest in its employees and is thus committed to them. Previous research has shown that employees are more motivated when they are informed about the firm. Sharing of information on, for example,

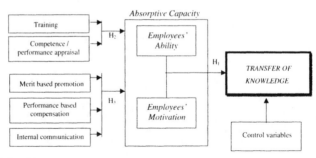

Figure 1 Conceptual model.

strategy and company performance conveys to the employees that they are trusted. Further, it is important that employees are informed so that they can use the knowledge that resides in the firm to its fullest potential (Pfeffer, 1998). As a result, extensive intra-organizational communication is also likely to contribute to employees' motivation. Based on the arguments presented above, we propose.

Hypothesis 3. Performance-based compensation, merit-based promotion and internal communication are positively related to employees' motivation.

The conceptual model is presented in Figure 1.

Data and method
This paper examines foreign-owned subsidiaries located in three host countries: Finland, Russia, and USA. These countries are different, for example, in terms of history, culture, and management style, making it a perfect sample for testing whether the proposed hypotheses on intra-organizational transfer of knowledge apply across the different contexts. The subsidiaries sampled have their MNC HQs located in five home countries: Sweden, Germany, Japan, USA, and Finland. We chose these countries because they were among the more active investors in Russia and Finland while still representing a reasonably diverse sample including countries from each of the triad regions of North America, Europe, and Asia.

Lists of subsidiaries of firms with headquarters in Japan, Germany, Sweden, and Finland operating in the USA were obtained from the foreign commercial sections of the respective embassies in the USA. In all, 320 subsidiaries were randomly selected from

the lists and HRM managers or General Managers of the subsidiaries were contacted via telephone and asked if they would participate in the study. Of these, 28 did not meet the age or size sampling criteria. This resulted in a base sampling of 292 firms in the USA. These 292 firms were sent a questionnaire and non-respondents were contacted up to three times at 2-week increments resulting in 79 responses or a 27% response rate. In Finland, 188 firms were contacted which met the size and age sampling requirements and a similar procedure to that employed in the USA to obtain 62 responses or a 33% response rate. In Russia, however, where there is little tradition of completing questionnaires and much worry about disclosing information, interviews were set up with the managers during which time managers were asked to complete the questionnaires. In a few cases, at the manager's request, the questionnaire was left with the manager and collected a few days later. In Russia 100 of the 357 contacted firms, which met the size and age sampling conditions, took part in the study (a 28% response rate).

The resulting data set consists of 62 subsidiaries operating in Finland, 100 subsidiaries operating in Russia, and 79 subsidiaries operating in the USA for a total of 241 participating subsidiaries. However, due to missing data, only 168 observations were used in our data analysis (55 subsidiaries in Finland, 81 in Russia, and 32 in USA). On average, the subsidiaries were existence for 15 years with 173 employees of which seven were expatriates. Further, on average, each MNC had subsidiaries in 40 different countries.

In all, 70% of our respondents were general managers or deputy general managers and 30% of our respondents were HR managers. No significant differences in responses were found between these subgroups and thus following Guest (1997) the questionnaires were combined into one data set for analysis. In total, 26% of the respondents were under 30 years old, 33% were between 30 and 39, 32% were between 40 and 49, and 9% over 50 years old.

A careful process was used to develop the questionnaire for this study. The items/scales used in the study drew on established research (Gardner *et al.*, 2001; Huselid, 1995; Wright *et al.*, 1998; Zander, 1991). In addition, five experts were asked to review the questionnaire and provide feedback. The questionnaire was then administered to 10 managers (not part of the sampling frame) to obtain their feedback before development of the final questionnaire. The questionnaire was administered in English in the USA and Finland and respondents in Russia had the option of using an English or Russian version. The Russian version was validated for accuracy using a translation back-translation procedure.

Following Podsakoff and Organ (1986), we used the Harman's one-factor test to examine the extent of common method bias in our data. A principal component factor analysis reveals there are 10 factors with an eigenvalue > 1, which together account for 69% of the total variance. The presence of several distinct factors combined with the relatively low amount of variance explained by the first factor and second factor (only 15 and 12%) indicates that the data do not suffer from common method variance (Podsakoff and Organ, 1986).

Measures
All data used in the analysis were from the administered questionnaire and all variables were standardized prior to the development of indices.

Transfer of knowledge
We define the level of knowledge transfer based on the level of knowledge utilization by the recipients assuming both acquisition and use of new knowledge. Accordingly, the subsidiaries were asked to what extent they utilize knowledge from the parent company and from other MNC units. The questions used a five-point Likert-type scale, where 1 indicates no use of knowledge and 5 indicates substantial use of knowledge (alpha=0.64).

Employees' ability
This construct captures employees' potential and ability. It is not a measure of an individual ability,

but a measure of the overall ability of subsidiary's employees. This construct was measured by asking respondents to assess the quality of the subsidiary's employees relative to that of its competitors in: overall ability, job-related skills, and educational level. Respondents indicated this on seven-point Likert-type scales ranging from 1='far below average' to 7='far above average' (alpha=0.77).

Employees' motivation
This construct consists of five items. In the same vein, this is a measure of the overall motivation of a subsidiary's employees and not the individual motivation. Two items asked respondents to assess the quality of the subsidiary's employees relative to those of its competitors on motivation and work effort using seven-point Likert-type scales (ranging from 1='far below average' to 7='far above average'). Three items were measured using a five-point scale (ranging from 1=strongly disagree to 5=strongly agree), where respondents were asked to indicate: (1) whether the employees behave in ways that help company performance; (2) whether employees contribute in a positive way to company performance; and (3) whether the subsidiary, compared with the parent company, has a highly motivated group of employees (alpha=0.75).

Training
The extent to which subsidiaries apply training is measured through two items capturing the number of days of formal training managerial and non-managerial employees, respectively, receive annually (alpha=0.83).

Competence/performance appraisal
An index examining the extent to which competence/performance appraisal is used in the subsidiary is used. One item measures the proportion of the workforce that regularly receives a formal evaluation of their performance (in per cent), another measures the proportion of jobs where a formal job analysis has been conducted (in percent), and the final item measures the proportion of new jobs for which a formal analysis of the desired personal skills/competencies/characteristics is carried out prior to making a selection decision (in percent) (alpha=0.66).

Merit-based promotion
The importance of internal promotion schemes is measured by an index comprised of three five-point Likert-type scale items. The first item measures

whether qualified employees have the opportunity to be promoted to positions of greater pay and/or responsibility within the subsidiary (1=no opportunities and 5=many opportunities), the second item measures whether the subsidiary places a great deal of importance on merit for promotion decisions (1=not at all and 5=to a large extent), and the third item measures the extent to which upper-level vacancies are filled from within (1=not at all and 5=to a large extent) (alpha=0.63).

Performance-based compensation

This three-item scale captures the extent to which compensation is performance-based. One item measures the proportion of employees who have the opportunity to earn individual, group or company-wide bonuses (percent), and two items ask the respondents to indicate whether the company uses performance-based compensation (1=not at all and 5=to a large extent) and whether the compensation systems are closely connected to the financial results of the subsidiary (1=not at all and 5=to a large extent) (alpha=0.61).

Internal communication

The extent to which exchange of information is promoted within the organization is measured through a scale comprised of three items (all on five-point scales). The items capture communication flows between: (1) employees in different departments, (2) non-managerial employees and managerial employees, and (3) the HR department and the top management team (1=not at all and 5=to a large extent) (alpha=0.72).

Control variables

Subsidiary age. Subsidiary age was included as a control variable since older subsidiaries tend to be more autonomous and thus more innovative (e.g., Foss and Pedersen, 2002). More innovative subsidiaries might be less dependent on knowledge from other parts of the MNC. On the other hand, more innovative subsidiaries may also be more interesting as knowledge exchange partners for other MNC units. Subsidiary age is measured as the number of years the subsidiary has operated in the host country.

Subsidiary size: Following the same logic as the subsidiary age variable, larger subsidiaries may acquire less knowledge from other MNC units than smaller subsidiaries because they are able to generate more knowledge themselves. Subsidiary size is

measured as the logarithm of the total number of employees in the subsidiary.

Relative size of subsidiary compared to the rest of the corporation: This variable measures the strategic importance of the subsidiary. Following Birkinshaw and Hood (1998) and Holm and Pedersen (2000), it is expected that the larger the relative size of the subsidiary compared to the rest of the corporation, the stronger strategic position the subsidiary will gain in the MNC. A stronger strategic position allows better access to knowledge and other resources in other parts of the MNC. Relative size is measured as the number of employees in the subsidiary divided by the total number of employees in the MNC.

Share of expatriates: Expatriates are used in MNCs as vehicles for knowledge transfer from other MNC units to the focal subsidiary where the higher number of expatriates in a subsidiary, the more knowledge may be transferred (Downes and Thomas, 2000; Bonache and Brewster, 2001). Therefore, we controlled for the relative number (in per cent) of expatriates in the subsidiary.

Strategic mission: As pointed out by Lyles and Salk (1996), a clear understanding and sharing of the mission statement facilitates knowledge transfer since employees understand what knowledge is important. In order to control for this variable, we asked the respondents to indicate to what extent the subsidiary has a clear strategic mission that is well communicated and understood at every level throughout the organization. The respondents indicated this on a 5-point Likert-type scale (1=not at all to 5=very much.).

Cultural relatedness: Lane and Lubatkin (1998) argue that absorptive capacity is a dyad-level construct dependent on the similarities/differences of both source and recipient firms in terms of knowledge bases, organizational structures and compensation practices, and dominant logic. We control for the cultural relatedness between the home country of the MNC and the host country of the subsidiary by applying the Kogut and Singh-index based on Hofstede's four dimensions of cultural difference (Kogut and Singh, 1988).

Home and host country: We expect that difference in local environments – economic, political, technological and socio-cultural – affect the process of knowledge transfer. Therefore, we control for the home country of the MNC (Finland, Germany, Japan, Sweden, and USA) as well as the host country of the subsidiary (Finland, Russia, and USA).

Industry: Following Gupta and Govindarajan (2000), we control for industry characteristics since some industries are more global and apply a higher level of knowledge transfer among MNC units. We group the subsidiaries into six industries: Metal & Electronics, Food, Pulp & Paper, Chemicals, Financial service, Wholesale & Retail, and Hotel & Transportation.

Results

The three hypotheses may be summarized in three basic equations:

1. Employees' ability=Competence/Performance appraisal + Training + Error
2. Employees' motivation=Merit-based Promotion + Performance-based compensation + Internal Communication + Error
3. Transfer of knowledge=Employees' ability + Employees' motivation + Employees' ability* Employees' motivation + Controls + Error

However, as the above equations represent decisions that are interdependent, the use of single equation models may yield biased results and obscure interesting theoretical possibilities. It is also possible that the joint optimization of all decisions involved may lead to the suboptimization of one or more individual decisions. Statistically, the interdependence is indicated by the high correlation between the error terms of the three equations. The appropriate model to estimate these decisions is a three-stage least square model that circumvents the problem of interdependence by using instrument variables (the exogenous variables) to obtain predicted values of the endogenous variables (in our case, knowledge transfer, employees' ability, and employees' motivation). As the scales of the variables varied considerably, all variables were standardized (mean=0 and standard deviation=1) before analysis.

Descriptive data (mean values, standard deviation, minimum and maximum values) on all exogenous variables are provided in Table 1. For all variables the descriptive data is given before transformation (e.g., standardization). The correlation coefficients are shown in Table 2. As expected, there is a relatively high correlation between the three host country dummies (−0.34, 0.28, and −0.67) and between the cultural relatedness variable and the country dummies (both host and home-country dummies). This can largely be explained by the way these measures are constructed. However, none of the other correlation

Table 1 Descriptive statistics for all independent variables before any transformation

	Means	Std. deviation	Min.	Max.
(1) Transfer of knowledge	3.51	0.83	1.5	5
(2) Employees' ability	5.19	0.8	3	7
(3) Employees' motivation	5.04	0.79	2.88	7
(4) Training	1.42	1.09	1	5
(5) Performance appraisal	3.32	1.44	1	5
(6) Promotion	3.8	0.62	1.67	5
(7) Performance-based compensation	3.62	0.96	1.05	5
(8) Communication	3.61	0.68	1	5
(9) Subsidiary age	14.5	17.2	1	110
(10) Subsidiary size	154	495	5	6000
(11) Expatriates	9.8	18	0	100
(12) Relative size of subsidiary	4.69	12.6	0.01	86.7
(13) Strategic mission	3.56	1.08	1	5
(14) Cultural relatedness	3.44	2.28	0.51	7.33
Home-country dummies				
(15) Germany	0.25	0.43	0	1
(16) Japan	0.32	0.47	0	1
(17) Finland	0.18	0.39	0	1
(18) Sweden	0.13	0.33	0	1
(19) USA	0.13	0.33	0	1
Host-country dummies				
(20) Russia	0.48	0.5	0	1
(21) Finland	0.33	0.47	0	1
(22) USA	0.2	0.4	0	1
Industry dummies				
(23) Metal and electronics	0.22	0.42	0	1
(24) Food, pulp and paper	0.1	0.3	0	1
(25) Chemicals	0.16	0.37	0	1
(26) Financial service	0.08	0.28	0	1
(27) Wholesale and retail	0.27	0.45	0	1
(28) Hotel and transportation	0.16	0.37	0	1

coefficients indicated the possibility of multicollinearity (i.e., $r > 0.5$), (Hair *et al.*, 1995). Moreover, running the models with some of the correlated variables omitted had no effect on the explanatory power of the main variables. Therefore, we concluded that the results are very stable in terms of the different specifications of the model (see Table 3).

Overall, the results indicate that the model including all three equations works well, explaining almost one third of the observed variation in the knowledge transfer (weighted $R^2 = 0.32$). This R^2

MNC knowledge transfer   D Minbaeva *et al*

595

Table 2 Correlation matrices including all independent variables

	1	2	3	4	5	6	7	8	9	10	11	12	13	14	15	16	17	18	19	20	21	22	23	24	25	26	27
(1)	1.00																										
(2)	0.12	1.00																									
(3)	0.36***	0.48***	1.00																								
(4)	0.37***	0.20*	0.22**	1.00																							
(5)	0.32**	0.19*	0.31***	0.27**	1.00																						
(6)	0.21**	0.27**	0.34***	0.17*	0.09	1.00																					
(7)	0.28**	0.20*	0.35***	0.25**	0.32***	0.34***	1.00																				
(8)	0.31**	0.19*	0.42***	0.29***	0.25**	0.41***	0.27***	1.00																			
(9)	-0.07	0.03	-0.03	-0.24**	-0.07	0.01	0.04	-0.16*	1.00																		
(10)	-0.15*	0.03	-0.07	-0.20**	-0.06	0.09	0.06	-0.13+	0.41***	1.00																	
(11)	0.16*	-0.09	0.05	0.07	0.05	-0.14+	-0.09	-0.07	-0.01	-0.35***	1.00																
(12)	-0.14+	-0.09	-0.08	0.05	0.04	-0.02	-0.17*	-0.04	-0.08	0.14+	-0.09	1.00															
(13)	0.21**	0.33***	0.43***	0.21**	0.18*	0.32***	0.23**	0.39***	-0.02	0.01	-0.18*	-0.03	1.00														
(14)	0.25**	0.02	0.11	0.32***	0.13	0.11	0.15*	0.14+	-0.36***	-0.32**	0.13+	-0.06	-0.03	1.00													
(15)	-0.05	0.005	0.02	0.07	0.02	-0.01	0.01	0.09	0.01	0.01	-0.23**	0.01	0.11	-0.41***	1.00												
(16)	0.21**	-0.34***	-0.05	-0.02	0.12	-0.16*	0.08	-0.08	-0.06	-0.25**	0.45***	-0.15*	-0.23**	0.32***	-0.39***	1.00											
(17)	-0.19*	-0.03	-0.03	-0.10	-0.09	-0.01	-0.01	-0.07	0.09	0.17*	-0.18*	0.01	0.17*	-0.44***	-0.28**	-0.32***	1.00										
(18)	0.01	0.15*	0.12	-0.05	-0.03	0.13+	-0.04	0.05	0.13	0.14+	-0.14+	0.01	0.02	0.09	-0.22**	-0.26**	-0.18*	1.00									
(19)	0.15+	-0.04	0.11	-0.06	0.03	0.03	-0.07	0.03	-0.16*	0.02	-0.13+	0.19*	-0.03	0.52***	-0.22**	-0.26**	-0.18*	-0.14+	1.00								
(20)	0.33***	0.07	0.14+	0.42***	0.24**	0.08	0.25**	0.23**	-0.39***	-0.37***	0.06	-0.01	0.12	0.75***	-0.17*	0.17*	-0.18*	-0.08	0.28**	1.00							
(21)	-0.21**	-0.06	-0.03	-0.36***	-0.31**	-0.09	-0.09	-0.07	-0.16+	0.23**	-0.27***	0.01	0.16*	-0.61***	0.30***	-0.28**	-0.16+	-0.11	0.15+	-0.67***	1.00						
(22)	-0.10	0.21**	-0.03	0.08	-0.17+	0.14	-0.09	-0.07	-0.16+	-0.01	0.21*	0.30**	0.02	0.67***	-0.19*	-0.36***	-0.16+	0.18+	N.A.	-0.28**	-0.34***	1.00					
(23)	0.03	0.03	0.09	0.09	0.03	-0.01	0.02	0.02	0.02	-0.07	0.05	-0.02	0.12	-0.04	0.06	0.07	-0.03	-0.11	-0.03	0.02	0.11	-0.09	1.00				
(24)	-0.03	0.13	-0.02	0.12	0.03	0.02	-0.01	0.12	0.12	-0.10	0.12	0.01	-0.05	-0.06	-0.14	0.15+	0.11	-0.01	0.03	0.02	0.01	0.18*	1.00				
(25)	-0.10	0.08	0.06	-0.03	-0.05	0.06	-0.04	0.01	-0.10	0.20*	-0.11	0.06	-0.03	-0.08	-0.03	-0.05	0.08	0.18*	-0.16*	-0.16*	-0.03	-0.19	-0.24**	-0.15+	1.00		
(26)	0.14+	0.17*	0.09	0.07	0.03	0.05	-0.02	0.06	-0.05	-0.09	0.19*	-0.09	-0.02	0.01	0.03	0.03	-0.03	0.02	-0.05	0.06	-0.12	-0.07	0.16*	-0.10	-0.13+	1.00	
(27)	-0.04	-0.20**	-0.05	-0.17*	0.11	-0.03	0.05	0.09	0.09	-0.08	-0.04	-0.09	-0.07	0.05	-0.02	0.22**	-0.09	-0.11	-0.07	-0.03	-0.03	-0.06	-0.33***	-0.20**	-0.27**	-0.18*	1.00
(28)	0.03	0.01	-0.15*	-0.03	-0.17*	0.07	-0.13+	0.02	-0.09	-0.07	0.04	0.03	-0.02	0.11	0.01	0.19*	-0.04	-0.02	0.32***	0.10	0.04	0.43***	-0.24*	-0.15+	-0.19*	0.13	-0.27*

Variable names corresponding to the numbers used above can be found in Table 1. ***, **, *, and +, significant at 0.1, 1, 5, and 10%, respectively

Table 3 The three-stage least squares estimation of a simultaneous equation model

	Employees' ability	Employees' motivation	Transfer of knowledge
Intercept	−0.1	−0.01	−0.01
	−(0.07)	(−0.07)	(−0.09)
Training	0.18		
	(0.07)***		
Performance appraisal	0.1		
	(0.06)+		
Promotion		0.08	
		(−0.07)	
Performance-based compensation		0.21	
		(0.07)***	
Communication		0.29	
		(0.07)***	
Ability			0.91
			(−0.73)
Motivation			0.31
			(−0.44)
Ability*motivation			0.33
			(0.12)***
Controls			
Age of subsidiary			0.03(0.12)
subsidiary size			0.07(0.12)
Share of expatriates			−0.11(0.12)
Relative size of subsidiary			−0.02(0.11)
Strategic mission			−0.11(0.14)
Cultural relatedness			0.02(0.29)
Home-country dummies (four)			yes[a]
Host-country dummies (two)			yes[a]
Industry dummies (five)			yes[a]
F-value	5.34***	18.00***	1.84*
R^2	0.06	0.25	0.22
N	167	167	167

***, **, * and +, significant at 0.1, 1, 5 and 10%, respectively.
[a]Indicate that dummies for home country (four) and host country (two) and industries (five) are included in the model, although, the 11 parameters is not shown in the table.

statistic has been corrected for the fact that the regression sum of squares and the error sum of squares do not sum to the total corrected sum of squares in methods using instrument variables where first-stage predicted values are substituted for endogenous regressors. Therefore, the overall R^2 value might be larger than the R^2 values for each of the three equations. The system weighted R^2 value

is the best measure of the overall goodness of fit of the model. We turn now to the tests of our explanatory hypotheses.

Hypothesis 2 posited a positive relationship between competence/performance appraisal and training (HR practices) and subsidiary employees' ability. This hypothesis is largely supported (see column 1; Table 3). Training has a significantly relationship with employees' ability ($P<0.01$). The effect of performance appraisal on employees' ability is marginally significant ($P<0.10$). This indicates that investments in HRM practices (e.g., training) directly aim at developing and upgrading the skills of the workforce have a stronger effect on employees' ability than the indirect (long-term) practice of competence and performance appraisal. Since the variables have been standardized, the two parameters 0.18 and 0.10, respectively, also indicate a substantial difference in the effects of these two variables on employees' ability.

Hypothesis 3 examined the relationship between merit-based promotion, performance-based compensation, and internal communication (HR practices) and employees' motivation. Only two variables had a significant positive relationship lending some support for the hypothesis (see column 2; Table 3). The two variables – performance-based compensation and internal communication – are highly significant ($P<0.001$) determinants of employees' motivation. An improvement in employees' motivation is more associated with the use of performance-based compensation and information sharing within the organization rather than with merit-based promotions.

Hypothesis 1 is concerned with two aspects of subsidiary absorptive capacity, ability and motivation, and their interaction effects as a facilitator of knowledge transfer in MNCs. While the main effects of both employees' ability and employees' motivation are positive but non-significant, the interaction effect between these two variables is highly significant ($P<0.001$; see column 3; Table 3). This indicates that neither employees' ability nor motivation by themselves is sufficient to facilitate knowledge transfer. The significant interaction of motivation and ability shows that in order to facilitate knowledge transfer both aspects of absorptive capacity – ability and motivation of employees' – are needed. It turns out that none of the control variables in the model are significant.

Concluding comments

This paper addresses the relationship between MNC subsidiary HRM practices, absorptive capacity, and knowledge transfer. We found overall support for the argument that the absorptive capacity of the subsidiary facilitates transfer of knowledge from other parts of the MNC. The greater the absorptive capacity, the higher the level of knowledge transfer. Moreover, and perhaps the most important finding of this study, we find that both aspects of absorptive capacity (ability and motivation) need to be present in order to optimally facilitate the absorption of knowledge from other parts of the MNC. Employee ability or motivation alone does not lead to knowledge transfer. These results fall in line with recent contributions like Zahra and George (2002) who distinguish between potential absorptive capacity (with an expected high content of employees' ability) and realized absorptive capacity (with an expected high content of employees' motivation). While much prior research on absorptive capacity has only focused on the ability aspect of absorptive capacity, our results indicate that ability is necessary but not sufficient.

There exists a large and growing body of research on the relationship between HRM and organizational performance (see Becker and Gerhart, 1996; Guest, 1997; Becker and Huselid, 1998). In particular, previous research has bundled different HRM practices into two main categories: those determining employees' ability and those determining employees' motivation. However, we diverge from previous work on HRM and firm performance by integrating the research on knowledge transfer within the MNC. The results of our study indicate that investments in employees' ability and motivation through the extensive use of HRM practices contribute to MNC knowledge transfer. Employees' ability and motivation constitutes the firm's absorptive capacity, which is seldom treated as an endogenous variable in the literature. While pre-vious studies have paid little attention to how absorptive capacity is created and developed in the firm, the implication of our results is that managers can improve the absorptive capacity of their organizations by applying specific HRM practices oriented towards employees' ability (training and performance appraisal) and employees' motivation (performance-based compensation and internal communication).

Future research should collect data from multiple respondents to minimize the risk of common method bias. The validity of the current data on employees' ability and motivation was limited due to the use of only one respondent per subsidiary, a weakness in most international research. Future research should also examine the possibility of a lagged effect of investments in HRM on employees' competencies and motivation, and knowledge transfer. Finally, examining other factors of knowledge transfer such as the relationship between the parties involved, the sender's characteristics, and the characteristics of the knowledge transferred can extend the present model. While this study makes important contributions to our understanding of the relationship between HRM, employees' ability and motivation, and knowledge transfer in the MNC, clearly, additional research is needed to further develop the field of knowledge management.

Acknowledgements

We thank editor Catherine Langlois, three reviewers, participants at the Nordic-IB Workshop, the AIB Meeting in San Juan, and the AOM-meeting in Denver for comments on an earlier version of this paper, as well as the Academy of Finland and the Swedish Research Council for financial support of this study.

References

Argote, L. (1999) *Organizational Learning: Creating, Retaining and Transferring Knowledge*, Kluwer Academic Publisher: Boston.

Arthur, J.B. (1994) 'Effects of human resource systems on manufacturing performance and turnover', *Academy of Management Journal* 37(3): 670–687.

Baldwin, A.L. (1959) 'The Role of an 'Ability' Construct in a Theory of Behavior', in D.C. McClelland, A.L. Baldwin, U. Bronfenbrenner and F.L. Strodtbeck (eds.) *Talent and Society*, Van Nostrand: Princeton.

Baldwin, T., Magjuka, R.J. and Loher, B.T. 1991 'The perils of participation: effects of choice of training on trainee motivation and learning', *Personnel Psychology* 44: 51–65.

Bartlett, C. and Ghoshal, S. (1989) *Managing Across Borders*, Harvard Business School Press: Boston.

Becker, B. and Gerhart, B. (1996) 'The impact of human resource management on organizational performance: progress and prospects', *Academy of Management Journal* 39(4): 779–801.

Becker, B. and Huselid, M. (1998) 'High performance work systems and firm performance: a synthesis of research and managerial implications', *Research in Personnel and Human Resource Management* 16: 53–101.

Birkinshaw, J. and Hood, N. (1998) 'Multinational subsidiary development: capability evolution and charter change in foreign-owned subsidiary companies', *Academy of Management Review* 23(4): 773–795.

Bonache, J. and Brewster, C. (2001) 'Knowledge transfer and the management of expatriation', *Thunderbird International Business Review* 43(1): 145–168.

Cohen, W.M. and Levinthal, D.A. (1990) 'Absorptive capacity: a new perspective on learning and innovation', *Administrative Science Quarterly* 35: 128–152.

Davenport, T. and Prusak, L. (1998) *Working Knowledge: How Organizations Manage What They Know*, Harvard Business School: Boston.

Delaney, J.T. and Huselid, M. (1996) 'The impact of human resource management practices on perceptions of organizational performance', *Academy of Management Journal* 39(4): 949–969.

Delery, J.E. and Doty, H. (1996) 'Models of theorizing in strategic human resource management: tests of universalistic, contingency, and configurational performance predictions', *Academy of Management Journal* 39(4): 802–835.

Downes, M. and Thomas, AS. (2000) 'Knowledge transfer through expatriation: the U-curve approach to overseas staffing', *Journal of Management Issues* 12(2): 131–149.

Fiol, M.C. and Lyles, M.A. 1985 'Organizational learning', *Academy of Management Review* 10(4): 803–813.

Fleishman, E.A. (1958) 'A relationship between incentive motivation and ability level in psychomotor performance', *Journal of Experiential Psychology* 56: 78–81.

Foss, N. and Pedersen, T. (2002) 'Transferring knowledge in MNCs: the roles of sources of subsidiary knowledge and organizational context', *Journal of International Management*, 8: 49–67.

French, E. (1957) 'Effects of interaction of achievement, motivation, and intelligence on problem solving success', *American Psychologist* 12: 399–400.

Gardner, T.M., Moynihan, L.M., Park, H.J. and Wright, P.M. (2001) 'Beginning to unlock the black box in the HR firm performance relationship: the impact of HR practices on employee attitudes and employee outcomes', in *Working Paper for The Center for Advanced Human Resource Studies*, Cornell University: Ithaca, NY.

Ghoshal, S. and Bartlett, C. (1988) 'Creation, adoption, and diffusion of innovations by subsidiaries', *Journal of International Business Studies* 19(3): 365–388.

Guest, D. (1997) 'Human resource management and performance: a review and research agenda', *The International Journal of Human Resource Management* 8: 263–276.

Gupta, A. and Govindarajan, V. (2000) 'Knowledge flows within MNCs', *Strategic Management Journal* 21: 473–496.

Hair, J.F., Anderson, R.E., Tatham, R.L. and Black, W.C. (1995) *Multivariate Data Analysis*, Prentice-Hall: New Jersey.

Hedlund, G. (1986) 'The hypermodern MNC – a heterarchy?', *Human Resource Management* 25(1): 9–35.

Heider, F. (1958) *The Psychology of Interpersonal Relations*, Wiley: New York.

Holm, U.I.F. and Pedersen, T. (2000) *The Emergence and Impact of MNC Centres of Excellence*, Macmillan Press: London.

Huselid, M. (1995) 'The impact of human resource management practices on turnover, productivity, and corporate financial performance', *Academy of Management Journal* 38: 635–672.

Ichniowski, C., Shaw, K. and Prennushi, G. (1997) 'The effects of human resource management practices on productivity: a study of steel finishing lines', *The American Economic Review* 87(3): 291–313.

Inkpen, A.C. (1998) 'Learning and knowledge acquisition through international strategic alliances', *Academy of Management Executive* 12(4): 69–80.

Kim, L. (2001) 'Absorptive Capacity, Co-operation, and Knowledge Creation: Samsung's Leapfrogging in Semiconducters', in I. Nonaka and T. Nishiguchi (eds.) *Knowledge Emergence – Social, Technical, and Evolutionary Dimensions of Knowledge Creation*, Oxford University Press: Oxford, pp: 270–286.

Koch, M.J. and McGrath, R.G. (1996) 'Improving labor productivity: human resource management policies do matter', *Strategic Management Journal* 17(5): 335–354.

Kogut, B. and Singh, H. (1988) 'The effect of national culture on the choice of entry mode', *Journal of International Business Studies* 19(3): 411–432.

Lado, A. and Wilson, M.C. (1994) 'Human resource systems and sustained competitive advantage: a competency-based perspective', *Academy of Management Review* 19(4): 699–727.

Lane, P. and Lubatkin, M. (1998) 'Relative absorptive capacity and interorganizational learning', *Strategic Management Journal* 19(5): 461–477.

Lane, P., Salk, J.E. and Lyles, M.A. (2001) 'Absorptive capacity, learning and performance in international joint ventures', *Strategic Management Journal* 22(12): 1139–1161.

Lepak, D.P. and Snell, S.A. (1999) 'The human resource architecture: towards a theory of human capital allocation and development', *Academy of Management Review* 24(1): 31–48.

Lyles, M.A. and Salk, J.E. (1996) 'Knowledge acquisition from foreign partners in international joint ventures', *Journal of International Business Studies* 27(5): 877–904.

MacDuffie, J.P. (1995) 'Human resource bundles and manufacturing performance: flexible production systems in the world auto industry', *Industrial & Labor Relations Review* 48(2): 197–221.

O'Reilly, C.A. and Chatman, J.A. (1994) 'Working smarter and harder: a longitudinal study of managerial success', *Administrative Science Quarterly* 39: 603–627.

Pfeffer, J. (1994) *Competitive Advantage through People: Unleashing the Power of the Work Force*, Harvard Business Press: Boston.

Pfeffer, J. (1998) *The Human Equation: Building Profits by Putting People First*, Harvard Business Press: Boston.

Podsakoff, P.M. and Organ, D. (1986) 'Self-reports in organizational research: problems and prospects', *Journal of Management* 12(4): 531–544.

Simonin, B.L. (1999) 'Transfer of marketing know-how in international strategic alliances: an empirical investigation of the role and antecedents of knowledge ambiguity', *Journal of International Business Studies* 30(3): 463–490.

Szulanski, G. (1996) 'Exploring internal stickiness: impediments to the transfer of best practice within the firm', *Strategic Management Journal* 17: 27–43.

Vroom, V. (1964) *Work and Motivation*, John Wiley and Sons, Inc: New York, London and Sydney.

Wright, P.M., McMahan, G.C., Snell, S.A. and Gerhart, B. (1998) 'Comparing line and HR executives' perceptions of HR effectiveness: services, roles, and contributions', in *Working Paper for The Center for Advanced Human Resource Studies*, Cornell University: Ithaca, NY.

Zahra, S.A. and George, G. (2002) 'Absorptive capacity: a review, reconceptualization, and extension', *Academy of Management Review* 27(2): 185–203.

Zander, U. (1991) *Exploiting a technological edge: voluntary and involuntary dissemination of technology*, Doctoral dissertation Institute of International Business: Stockholm.

About the authors

Ingmar Björkman is a professor of management and organization at the Swedish School of Economics in Helsinki, Finland. During 2003–04, he is visiting professor at INSEAD. His work appears in, among others, *Journal of International Business Studies*, *Journal of Management Inquiry*, *International Journal of Human Resource Management*, *Organizational Studies*, and *Scandinavian Journal of Management*. Björkman's current research interests focus on international human resource management. He is also involved in research on knowledge management in multinational corporations and the integration of international mergers and acquisitions.

Carl F Fey is an Assistant Professor at the Institute of International Business at Stockholm School of Economics in Sweden. He has also been helping Stockholm School of Economics to develop a branch campus for executive development work and research in St. Petersburg, Russia, where he serves as Associate Dean. His work focuses on international aspects of strategic HRM, organizational culture and effectiveness, and knowledge transfer. He has published over 25 articles in various journals including the *Journal of International Business Studies* and *Organization Science*.

Dana Minbaeva is a research assistant at the Department of International Economics and Management, Copenhagen Business School. She is completing her doctoral dissertation on the role of Human Resource Management practices in the

process of knowledge transfer in multinational corporations.

Hyeon Jeong Park is a doctoral student in the Department of Human Resource Studies at Cornell University. Her research interests focus broadly on the relationship of human capital and social networks on organizational performance. Her current research in the area of strategic human resource management explores the mediating factors through which human resource practices lead to firm performance in multinational corporations.

Torben Pedersen is a professor of International Business at the Department of International Economics and Management at Copenhagen Business School. He has published over 40 articles and books concerning the managerial and strategic aspects of multinational corporations. His research has appeared in journals such as *Strategic Management Journal, Journal of International Business Studies, Management International Review*, and *International Review of Law and Economics*.

Accepted by Thomas Brewer; outgoing Editor, 20 December 2002.

[29]

Strategic Management Journal
Strat. Mgmt. J., **25**: 801–822 (2004)
Published online in Wiley InterScience (www.interscience.wiley.com). DOI: 10.1002/smj.413

HOW DO MULTINATIONAL COMPANIES LEVERAGE TECHNOLOGICAL COMPETENCIES? MOVING FROM SINGLE TO INTERDEPENDENT EXPLANATIONS

MORTEN T. HANSEN[1]* and BJØRN LØVÅS[2]
[1] *INSEAD, Fontainebleau, France*
[2] *London Business School, London, U.K.*

This paper explores the relationships among four fundamental determinants of intrafirm competence transfers that have hitherto been analyzed only separately: formal organization structure, informal relations, geographical distance, and relatedness of competencies across subsidiaries. Using a data set consisting of 4840 dyads between new product development teams and subsidiaries that were potential targets for competence transfers in a high-technology multinational company, we find that these determinants interact in surprising ways to explain different patterns of transfers. Results revealed that teams preferred to approach people they knew rather than people who knew related technologies well. They also showed that teams steered away from spatially distant subsidiaries that had related competencies and that the negative effect of large spatial distances could be overcome through established informal relations. These findings indicate that studying one of the determinants separately can yield biased results, as their net effect may change when the moderating effects of the other determinants are considered. Research on synergies, integration, technology transfers, and geographical and cultural differentiation in multinational enterprises therefore needs to be broadened by analyzing multiple determinants of competence transfers. Copyright © 2004 John Wiley & Sons, Ltd.

As competition in a number of global industries is becoming more knowledge- and technology-intensive, the ability of multinational companies to leverage their competencies across dispersed subsidiaries is an increasingly important source of competitive performance (Doz, Santos, and Williamson, 2001). To understand why and how competence transfers occur in multinational companies, much strategic management research has focused on the determinants of such transfers. While one line of research has emphasized that formal organization structure is a fundamental determinant in achieving integration across dispersed

Keywords: international management; synergy; technology transfers; social networks; organizational capabilities
* Correspondence to: Morten T. Hansen, INSEAD, Boulevard de Constance, 77305 Fontainebleau Cedex, France.
E-mail: morten.hansen@insead.edu

subsidiaries (e.g., Galbraith, 1973; Stopford and Wells, 1972), another body of research has stressed the benefits of informal lateral linkages in facilitating competence transfers (e.g., Hedlund, 1986; Bartlett and Ghoshal, 1989; Nohria and Ghoshal, 1997). Research on geography has also found that geographical distance—in the form of spatial, cultural, and national differentiation among employees—can make it difficult to work together and may deter competence transfers (e.g., Kogut and Singh, 1988; Zaheer, 1995). In yet another line of research, scholars have shown that the degree of relatedness in competencies among subsidiaries in a multinational firm may lead to interunit transfers and synergy benefits (e.g., Markides and Williamson, 1994; Rumelt, 1974).

Although these research streams have advanced our understanding significantly, they have remained largely disconnected, yielding three shortcomings in existing research. First, while there has been a large body of research analyzing whether relatedness in competencies among subsidiaries in a firm leads to synergy benefits, this research has largely ignored the roles of geographical distance and informal linkages (Farjoun, 1998; Hansen, 2002; Ramanujam and Varadarajan, 1989). It is quite possible, however, that these factors moderate the effect of related competencies. In particular, do large spatial distances between subsidiaries deter employees from leveraging related competencies? And do established informal relations steer employees to others whom they know as opposed to others who possess related competencies? If so, these factors may explain why employees do not leverage related competencies across subsidiaries, even if such competencies exist.

Second, although existing research has shown that cultural and national differences may create problems in the acquisition of competencies and cooperation (e.g., Barkema and Vermeulen, 1997; Zaheer, 1995), this line of research has not focused on the extent to which informal and formal mechanisms mitigate this problem in multinational companies. In contrast, existing research on the role of informal and formal organizational mechanisms in enabling knowledge transfers has remained agnostic with respect to geographical distance (e.g., Gupta and Govindarajan, 2000; Nobel and Birkinshaw, 1998). This disconnect between research streams has left an important unanswered question: Does geographical distance, such as spatial distance and cultural differences, prevent a multinational firm from leveraging its competencies across dispersed subsidiaries, or can informal linkages and formal coordination among subsidiaries overcome this problem? If the answer is that spatial distance is an insurmountable obstacle, then one may conclude that multinational companies do not have a unique advantage based on their competencies, because they cannot leverage these across geographically distant subsidiaries.

Third, while some recent research has found that informal lateral linkages appear to be more effective than formal organization mechanisms in leveraging competencies across subsidiaries (e.g., Kim, Park, and Prescott, 2003; Tsai, 2002), there is an incomplete understanding of the potentially dissimilar roles of informal and formal integrative mechanisms in predicting the occurrence of competence transfers. In particular, are informal and formal mechanisms equally effective in leveraging competencies across geographically distant subsidiaries? And are employees more likely to rely on established informal relations or formal organization reporting lines when contacting others to leverage competencies? Answering these questions necessitates analyzing the relationships between informal linkages, formal mechanisms, and geographical distance.

The aim of this paper is to address these shortcomings by analyzing the relationships between formal organization mechanisms, informal relations, geographical distance, and relatedness in competencies. Our overall research question is therefore whether there are important interaction effects between these four fundamental determinants in predicting the occurrence of competence transfers in a multinational firm. We limit our discussion to the global research and development (R&D) function and focus on technological competence transfers between new product development teams situated in a focal subsidiary and other subsidiaries in a multinational firm (cf. Kuemmerle, 1998; Malnight, 1995). While product development teams are likely to differ in the extent to which they need to seek competencies from outside the focal subsidiary, our primary concern in this paper is not whether they decide to acquire competencies but, to the extent that they do, *where* they are likely to go within the company for technological competence transfers, which include the transfer of technical advice and technologies embodied in existing artifacts, such as software or hardware. Our unit of analysis is therefore a *dyad* involving a *focal team* situated in a focal subsidiary and a different subsidiary from which a focal team could potentially acquire technological competencies (i.e., a *target subsidiary*).

THEORY AND HYPOTHESES

Consistent with recent research on multinational and multiunit companies, we conceive of a multinational company as comprising a set of geographically dispersed subsidiaries that are combinations of heterogeneous technological competencies and product-market responsibilities (cf. Galunic and Eisenhardt, 2001; Nohria and Ghoshal, 1997). For a focal product development team that is located in one of the subsidiaries, this heterogeneity in competencies across subsidiaries presents an opportunity to improve work by leveraging competencies (cf. Ancona and Caldwell, 1992; Clark and Fujimoto, 1991; Eisenhardt and Santos, 2002; Katz and Tushman, 1979), but a team's tendency to engage in intersubsidiary competence transfers may depend on the existence of related competencies, geographical distance, and the presence of informal and formal mechanisms.

Four determinants of technological competence transfers

The relatedness of technological competencies is an important determinant of where in the company a focal project team will search for and acquire competencies (Ramanujam and Varadarajan, 1989). A target subsidiary possesses a related technological competence to the extent that its technologies and technical expertise fall in the same areas as those required by a focal new product development team (cf. Farjoun, 1998; Markides and Williamson, 1994; Rumelt, 1974). For example, a subsidiary that has an expertise in the area of robotics possesses a related competence for a focal team developing a new product that requires robotics technologies.[1] When obtaining competencies, new product development teams should want to match the needs of their project with the type of technological competencies possessed by a target subsidiary. Thus, product development teams should be more likely to engage in a transfer event with a target subsidiary that possesses a related technological competence for a focal project than with a target subsidiary that does not.

Geography also explains why product developers from different subsidiaries in a firm interact to acquire competencies while others do not. By geography, we refer to three dimensions: spatial distance (i.e., miles) between subsidiaries, the extent to which the national cultures of the countries in which subsidiaries are located differ (i.e., cultural distance), and whether interactions take place across national borders. A focal team and a subsidiary may be less likely to interact to the extent that the spatial distance between them is large. The tendency of actors to interact less with increasing spatial distance has been demonstrated in previous research, including studies of intraoffice distances among engineers (Allen, 1977)

and partnering patterns among venture capitalists located in different cities (Sorenson and Stuart, 2001). The explanation for this tendency is the accuracy and richness of information transfer, which declines with increasing spatial distance, as well as increasing communication costs with increasing spatial distance, such as travel time and burdensome meetings (cf. Krugman, 1991).

Working relations involving a focal team and target subsidiaries may also become more difficult when they involve employees located in different countries and when there is a large cultural distance, which includes differences in power distance, uncertainty avoidance, masculinity, individualism, and long-term orientation between national cultures (Hofstede, 2001; Kogut and Singh, 1988). With increasing cultural distance and national differences between a focal team and a target subsidiary, the level of comfort and trust is likely to decrease, making it more difficult to work together (Barkema and Vermeulen, 1997). Such differences may act as a deterrent to engaging in transfers (Kedia and Bhagat, 1988) and increase the tendency to interact with others from the same culture and country (cf. Earley and Mosakowski, 2000). A focal team and a subsidiary should therefore be less likely to interact and exchange technological competencies to the extent that they represent different national cultures and countries.

The formal organization structure is another determinant of competence transfers (e.g., Stopford and Wells, 1972; Galbraith, 1973). At the dyadic level, the formal organization links two subsidiaries to the extent that they are formally grouped together and report to the same superior in the organizational hierarchy (cf. Williamson, 1975). Formal groups that comprise two or more subsidiaries thus confer formal proximity that may lead to competence transfers. A formal group may have cooperative rules that direct members to acquire competencies from others in a group (Eisenhardt and Galunic, 2000). There may also be group-based incentives, such as bonuses based on common group performance, that encourage individuals to cooperate across subsidiaries in a formal group (cf. Milgrom and Roberts, 1992). In addition, subsidiaries that belong to the same formal group may have a common identity that leads members within a group to naturally think about leveraging competencies from one another (cf. Brewer, 1979; Katz and Allen,

---

[1] This relatedness does not guarantee that a subsidiary's competencies will in fact be useful for the focal team but only that they are likely to be so *ex ante*.

1988; Tajfel and Turner, 1986). Extensive within-group communication channels may also make product developers more aware of opportunities for leveraging competencies (Hansen, Nohria, and Tierney, 1999; Katz and Tushman, 1979). All these factors may motivate and enable product development teams to cooperate with others that are part of the same formal group.

Finally, informal cross-subsidiary relations, which we define as continuous work-related informal relations between individuals from two subsidiaries, affect cross-subsidiary competence transfers in a multinational company (Nohria and Ghoshal, 1997; Hansen, 1999). Informal relations are distinct from formal coordinating mechanisms in that they are grounded in norms, habits, and personal reciprocity rather than authority based on a formal hierarchy (cf. Emerson, 1962). These relations imply that the two subsidiaries are embedded in the same social structure and therefore exhibit a higher degree of trust and a higher capacity for information sharing and mutual problem solving than two subsidiaries with no informal relation between them (Granovetter, 1985; Gupta and Govindarajan, 2000; Uzzi, 1997). Because of these benefits, product development team members are more likely to seek technological competencies from other subsidiaries with which they have an established informal relation than from others with whom they do not have established informal relations.

In short, these four determinants affect the tendency for a focal product development team in a subsidiary to transfer technological competencies from a target subsidiary. Stated as a baseline hypothesis:

Hypothesis 1: A focal team is more likely to transfer from a target subsidiary (a) that has related competencies than from one that has not, (b) that is geographically close than from one that is distant, (c) if they are formally proximate than if they are not, and (d) if there is an established informal relation between them than if there is not.

The moderating effect of geographical distance on related competencies

If a team's only concern were to locate subsidiaries that had related competencies, the variable indicating whether a subsidiary possessed related technological competencies for a focal team should predict a transfer event irrespective of geographical distance. Geographical distance, however, may moderate the main effect of related competencies, in two situations. First, if a set of subsidiaries all possess related competencies for a focal team, the team is more likely to transfer from a subsidiary that is located in a facility nearby than from one that is located far away because of the increased search and transfer costs associated with greater spatial distance. Search costs in the form of actual hours spent searching and elapsed days before a useful competence is identified are likely to be higher over greater spatial distance (cf. Sorenson and Stuart, 2001). Although engineers can communicate via e-mail and phone messages, search may also involve phone conversations, which may be difficult to organize if engineers work in different time zones, and long-distance traveling to meet and discuss possible useful technological competencies. Once the team has identified a useful source of technological competencies, the transfer process may involve back-and-forth traveling to adequately absorb the competencies (Leonard-Barton and Sinha, 1993; Teece, 1977). In addition, team members may view the crossing of a national border as an impediment, especially if border crossing involves cumbersome checks upon entering a new country. The focal team may also be deterred to the extent that there is a large cultural distance between the focal team and a subsidiary, as the levels of comfort and trust between the two parties are likely to decrease with increasing cultural distance, making the working relationship more difficult (Kogut and Singh, 1988). These potential burdens associated with increased geographical distance may deter a focal team from interacting with subsidiaries that are geographically distant when other subsidiaries that have related technological competencies are geographically close:

Hypothesis 2a: A focal team is more likely to transfer from a target subsidiary with related competencies that is geographically close than from one with related competencies that is geographically distant.

The second situation in which geographical distance may moderate the main effect of related competencies involves transfer from subsidiaries that have related competencies vs. those that do not. Teams that engage in localized search may first approach subsidiaries that are geographically close and then broaden their search to more distant subsidiaries (cf. Cyert and March, 1992; Fleming and Sorenson, 2004). As geographical distance increases, however, a focal team's search and transfer costs are likely to increase because of the higher probability of longer travel distances and interactions taking place across different time zones, national borders, and national cultures. When the geographical distance is very large, the perceived search and transfer costs may be sufficiently high to offset the perceived benefits that can be derived from acquiring technological competencies from that subsidiary, deterring the team from attempting to engage in search and transfer over great geographical distance. In such a situation, teams may instead choose to interact with subsidiaries 'close to home' that do not have related competencies but nevertheless may have some useful analogous advice to provide (cf. Hargadon and Sutton, 1997):

Hypothesis 2b: A focal team is more likely to transfer from a target subsidiary without related competencies that is geographically close than from one with related competencies that is geographically distant.

The moderating effects of informal and formal determinants on geographical distance

While greater geographical distance is likely to reduce the chances of a transfer event, an established informal linkage between a focal team and a subsidiary may reduce the search and transfer costs associated with geographical distance.[2] As research on R&D functions in multinational companies has demonstrated, personal relations spanning subsidiaries are effective in integrating R&D personnel who are widely dispersed across country subsidiaries (De Meyer, 1992; Kim *et al.*, 2003). Team members may find it easier to contact people who work in a subsidiary many miles away to the extent that they know them or at least know their colleagues. Likewise, the engineers in the target subsidiary may respond favorably to an incoming request from a spatially distant person to the extent that they know the person making the request. In addition, the level of trust and comfort associated

with an established informal relation may mitigate the lack of trust and comfort that may result from cross-border interaction and increased cultural distance. Social proximity in the form of established informal relations thus reduces the effect of spatial, national, and cultural differentiation. Thus we predict:

Hypothesis 3: An established informal relation between a focal team and a target subsidiary mitigates the negative effect of geographical distance on the chances of a transfer event between them.

Formal proximity may also integrate subsidiaries that are geographically distant from one another. To the extent that rules, incentives, a common identity, and communication channels that foster cooperation are in place within a formal group, a focal team may feel more motivated and able to connect with subsidiaries that belong to the same formal group, even though they may be located many miles away, in a different country, or are dissimilar culturally. Stated in a hypothesis:

Hypothesis 4: A focal team's location in the same formal group as a target subsidiary mitigates the negative effect of geographical distance on the chances of a transfer event between them.

The moderating effects of informal relations and formal proximity on related competencies

So far we have argued that both informal relations and formal proximity mitigate the main negative effect of geographical distance. These arguments raise the issue of whether the same informal and formal organization mechanisms might moderate the effect of related competencies. There are two situations in which this may occur. In the first and most straightforward situation, two subsidiaries both have related competencies for the team, but only one has an established informal relation with the focal team. In this situation, it is more likely that the team will try to acquire competencies from the subsidiary with which it has an established informal relation than from the one with which no such relation exists. As discussed earlier, established informal relations are associated with trust and a capacity for information sharing and mutual problem solving that should prompt a team to rely

---

[2] Although spatial distance may reduce the likelihood that a relationship is established in the first place, we are not concerned with the establishment of relations but with how relations interact with spatial distance once they exist.

806   *M. T. Hansen and B. Løvås*

on them when there is no other difference with respect to related competencies.

The second situation is more complicated: one subsidiary has related competencies but no established relation with the focal team, while another subsidiary has no related competencies, but an established relation exists. There are three reasons why the focal team may choose the subsidiary with an established relation but no related competencies, even though this may appear to be irrational. First, although the subsidiary does not have related competencies for a focal team, an established relation may lead team members, out of habit, to contact the engineers in the subsidiary. They may not know *a priori* that the subsidiary does not possess such competencies, or, if they do know, they may believe that the subsidiary has analogous experiences that can be brought to bear on the project (cf. Hargadon and Sutton, 1997). Established relations thus become taken-for-granted channels through which competencies can be accessed, leading teams to direct their search to subsidiaries they know, regardless of whether they possess particular competencies for the focal project (cf. Ahuja and Katila, 2004; Eisenhardt and Galunic, 2000; Gulati, 1995).

A second reason is that, to save face, team members may feel safer exposing their ignorance and asking for help from others with whom they have an established relation than asking for help from strangers, who may think less of the focal team members as a result. In this way, as research on impression management has shown (Wayne and Liden, 1995), teams seek to manage their impressions on peers in different subsidiaries, an activity that is especially important among employees with a strong professional identity, such as engineers.

Finally, team members may also perceive that established informal relations make the search and transfer processes easier than they would be without such relations. In established relations, they may know the engineers in the subsidiary from past exchanges and thus should know their particular areas of expertise, lowering search costs, and feel comfortable working with them, lowering transfer costs. Thus, although team members choose to acquire competencies from a subsidiary that does not possess related competencies, they may still be behaving rationally, because they believe that the established relation reduces search and transfer costs. Taken together, these three explanations

suggest why teams may contact someone they know rather than someone who knows:

Hypothesis 5: A focal team is more likely to transfer from a target subsidiary that does not have related competencies but with which it has an established relation than from one that has related competencies but with which it has no established relation.

Formal proximity may also moderate the main effect of related competencies, in two situations. The most straightforward situation involves possible transfer from two subsidiaries that both possess related competencies for the team, but only one belongs to the same formal group as the focal team. In this situation, a focal team is more likely to transfer from the subsidiary in the same formal group than from the one outside the group, because of coordination, communication activities, and cooperative rules that likely operate within formal groups.

The more complicated situation, however, involves possible transfer from two subsidiaries, one of which has related competencies but is not in the same formal group as the team and one of which does not have related competencies but is in the same formal group as the focal team. The chances of a transfer event occurring within the formal group depend on the intensity of coordination efforts within it. Strict rules and incentive systems stipulating that product developers within the formal group ought to cooperate, a strong common identity among employees within the group, and extensive group-based communication activities may lead to greater motivations and abilities to exchange competencies within the formal group. To the extent that these coordination efforts are intense, the focal team is more likely to transfer from a subsidiary within its formal group than with a subsidiary in another formal group, even though the former subsidiary does not have related competencies but the latter does:

Hypothesis 6: A focal team is more likely to transfer from a target subsidiary in its formal group that does not have related competencies than from one that is not in its formal group but has related competencies.

METHODS AND DATA

Setting and data collection procedures

We tested the hypotheses with data from a large, multinational high-technology company that had sales of more than $5 billion at the time of the study. The company, which is based in the United States, was involved in developing, manufacturing and selling a range of electronics and computing products and systems. At the time of the study, the company was structured into 41 operating subsidiaries that were responsible for product development, manufacturing, and sales. After having negotiated access to the company through three senior corporate R&D managers, we conducted more than 30 preliminary open-ended interviews with R&D managers, engineers, and project managers to better understand the context.

We collected both archival and survey data. There were two surveys: a survey administered to the most senior R&D manager in each of the 41 subsidiaries (with a 100% response rate), asking about intersubsidiary relations and competencies of the subsidiary, and a survey for the project managers of the product development projects included in this study. We developed pilot designs of the two survey instruments and pretested them in 1-hour face-to-face interviews with two R&D managers and five project managers.[3]

To select product development projects to be included in the analysis, we first used the company's databases of projects to identify a list of all projects that the 41 subsidiaries had undertaken in the previous 3 years. We excluded very small projects (i.e., those with fewer than two project engineers) and proposals that had not yet moved from the investigation to the development phase, as these projects were difficult to track. We ended up with a list of 147 projects, and the project managers of 121 of these projects returned their survey, yielding a response rate of 82 percent. We analyzed the response rates but found no significant differences between the final sample and the others in terms of the number of engineers, budget, and age of the projects (as listed in the databases).

Table 1. Country locations of the 41 subsidiaries and the 121 project teams

	Subsidiaries		Project teams	
	Number	%	Number	%
U.S.	28	68.3	91	75.2
Canada	2	4.9	1	0.8
Germany	3	7.3	9	7.4
U.K.	3	7.3	9	7.4
France	1	2.4	0	0
South Korea	1	2.4	0	0
Japan	2	4.9	8	6.6
Australia	1	2.4	3	2.5
Total	41	100%	121	100%

The 121 projects took place in 27 of the 41 subsidiaries in the data set.[4] Table 1 depicts the distribution of subsidiaries and projects by country. As the table reveals, the subsidiaries and projects were concentrated in the home country, with 28 of the 41 subsidiaries and 91 of the 121 projects spread across the United States. While the list does not include a large number of countries, the data set allows for a large variance in spatial distance and some variance in cultural distance.

A dyadic approach

Because our hypotheses concern the potential for a transfer event between a focal project team and a target subsidiary, we treated the dyad of a focal team and a target subsidiary as the unit of observation. All our independent variables and the dependent variable pertain to the relational property of the dyads (i.e., using information about both the focal team and the target subsidiary) and not the properties of the individual project team or the target subsidiary.[5] Using this dyadic approach, we created a matrix comprising 4840 observations (i.e., 121 projects times 40 subsidiaries, excluding the focal subsidiary for each project).

This dyadic approach raises an issue of possible non-independence among the observations

---

[3] During pretests, we determined that project managers could reasonably answer the questions on behalf of the team, although relying on a single respondent for each project team is a limitation in our data.

[4] Because subsidiaries varied in the extent of their new product development efforts, some of the subsidiaries did not have any product development efforts that met our criteria for inclusion in the study. In addition, project managers in three subsidiaries did not respond to the survey.

[5] Although some product developers did not reside at their subsidiary's main location, most of them, including team members, were located at the main location of a subsidiary, facilitating the computation of dyadic variables.

Strat. Mgmt. J., **25**: 801–822 (2004)

808   *M. T. Hansen and B. Løvås*

(Greene, 1993; King and Zeng, 2001). While this issue is not salient in our data set, as we include dyadic variables that incorporate relational properties, we nevertheless wanted to address this potential problem in our model specifications. Guided by prior research analyzing dyads, we approached this issue in two ways (cf. Gulati, 1995; Sorenson and Stuart, 2001). First, as our primary approach, we used a conditional fixed-effects logistic regression analysis as implemented in STATA in which we specified the fixed effect for the focal subsidiary. This procedure conditions on the total number of events and groups together subsidiaries with the same number of events (e.g., it assumes that two subsidiaries that each received two transfers have the same baseline probability of receiving competencies). Because of the conditional effect, this approach excludes from the analysis five subsidiaries in our data set that did not receive any transfers, reducing the number of observations to 4360.

As a second approach, to verify the first, we also implemented a matched-pair sample approach that has been used by prior researchers studying dyads (e.g., Sorenson and Stuart, 2001). In this approach, we matched the observations with a transfer event (i.e., 87) with a randomly generated set of observations drawn from the set of non-event observations. Following the guidelines set by King and Zeng (2001), we chose a conservative number of matched dyads, which we set to twice the amount of events (i.e., 174 observations). Thus, this data set of 261 dyads does not rely on the full data set, thereby reducing the number of observations that are potentially non-independent. We used this model specification to verify the results from our conditional fixed-effect logit model.[6] Because both approaches produced similar results for the main independent variables, we report only the results from our primary approach.

Dependent and independent variables

Dyadic transfer event

The dependent variable is whether a transfer event occurred between a focal project team located in

the focal subsidiary and one of the other 40 subsidiaries (i.e., the target subsidiaries). To construct a measure of the transfer of technological competencies, the project manager was asked to indicate the percentages of a project's total hardware and software and the percentage of the project's total technical know-how and information that came from other subsidiaries. He or she was also prompted to indicate which subsidiary the transfer involved, using a list of 40 subsidiaries (the focal subsidiary was excluded from the list, as we were only interested in cross-subsidiary transfers).

Project managers frequently maintained log files tracking the sources of the code and hardware components and were thus in a position to readily answer this question. While it was more difficult for them to track the sources of technical advice, they were most likely aware of significant transfers, as they had to approve any travel costs involved and any compensation given for time spent by engineers in other subsidiaries. Thus, while project managers would not necessarily notice very brief *ad hoc* informal exchanges of advice (e.g., a phone call between an engineer on the project and another engineer in a target subsidiary), they would be aware of substantial transfers. Because we were interested in analyzing whether a transfer event occurred in a dyad, we dichotomized the dependent variable, which was set to '1' if the project manager reported a transfer from another specified subsidiary, and '0' otherwise. In all, 54 of the 121 project teams experienced between one or three transfer events, with a total of 87 such events.

Spatial distance in a dyad

We measured spatial distance as the number of direct air miles between the city where the office of the project team was located and the city of the target subsidiary in the dyad (*Miles (log)*). We logged this measure, as individuals most likely do not perceive that the burdens of travel increase linearly with air miles. For example, a 5000-mile air flight to a target subsidiary is most likely not perceived as five times more burdensome than a 1000-mile air flight, because some of the time-consuming activities of air travel, such as waiting time at airports, do not vary by the length of travel. The shortest dyadic distance was 0 (i.e., located on the same site), and the longest was 10,512 miles (between Edinburgh, Scotland, and

---

[6] Because this approach may produce underestimates of variables that predict a transfer event, we implemented a relogit procedure in STATA that corrects for this bias by adjusting the coefficient estimates, as recommended by King and Zeng (2001) and implemented by Sorenson and Stuart (2001).

Melbourne, Australia), with a median value of 1072 miles.

Different countries in a dyad

We recorded whether the office of the focal project team and the location of the target subsidiary were located in different countries (*International*). Of all the dyads, 48.3 percent crossed national borders.

Cultural distance in a dyad

We constructed a cultural distance measure based on the cultural indices developed by Hofstede (2001), who conceptualized differences among national cultures in terms of five national attributes: power distance between individuals in the society, tendency toward uncertainty avoidance, emphasis on masculinity, focus on individualism, and emphasis on long-term orientation. We followed prior measures developed by Kogut and Singh (1988) and Barkema and Vermeulen (1997), and computed the differences in these attributes between pairs of relevant countries. We then calculated the Euclidean distance, as follows (*Cultural distance*):

$$CD_j = \sqrt{\Sigma_{i=1,2,3,4,5} \left((I_{ij} - I_{in})^2 / V_i \right)}$$

where CD_j is the cultural distance between the focal team and a target subsidiary, I_{ij} is the index for the ith cultural dimension for the jth country in which the target subsidiary is located, n is the country of the focal team and subsidiary, and V_i is the variance of the index of the ith cultural dimension across all countries in our sample. This measure essentially assigns to a subsidiary the national cultural characteristics of the country in which it is located and then computes the distance between the focal and target subsidiaries in a dyad. We set both measures to zero if the dyad did not cross national borders. Among the international dyads, the smallest cultural distance was between subsidiaries and teams from Australia and the United States (i.e., a score of 0.4), while the largest distance was between subsidiaries and teams from Korea and Scotland (i.e., a score of 4.9), with a mean value of 0.95.

Existence of related competencies in a dyad

To measure whether a target subsidiary possessed technological competencies that were related to the focal project team, our first step involved working with the three senior corporate R&D managers to generate a list of 22 technological competencies in which one or more subsidiaries had developed a particular competence. Examples of competencies include digital signal processing, quartz/cesium resonance, fault diagnostics, and device physics. As a second step, we submitted a questionnaire to the R&D managers of each of the 41 subsidiaries, asking them to indicate their particular technological competencies on the list. The three senior corporate R&D managers then verified whether the responses made sense. In the third step, we asked the project managers of the 121 projects to indicate, from the same list, which technological competencies the project required. Thus, through this procedure, we obtained information on the competencies that existed in the subsidiaries and what competencies the project required. As a final step, we then constructed a dyadic variable that took a value of 1 if there was a match between at least one competence listed by the target subsidiary and the focal team, and zero otherwise (*Related competencies*). For example, this variable would take a value of 1 if the project required expertise in digital signal processing and the target subsidiary had reported that it possessed a particular competence in digital signal processing. Of the 4840 dyads, 42 percent were coded as having related competencies. To analyze interaction effects, we interacted this variable by multiplying it with the international variable (*International * Competence*), miles (*Miles * Competence*), cultural distance (*Cultural distance * Competence*), and the informal relation and formal proximity variables.

Established informal relation in a dyad

During the preliminary interviews, several engineers and managers explained how a relationship between two subsidiaries functioned: A group of engineers in a subsidiary typically maintained an informal regular contact with a group of engineers in a target subsidiary, and a project team would use such contacts to obtain technological competencies. Several times, people described these relations in terms such as 'we normally work with those units over there.' These types of contacts had been institutionalized in that they were regularly occurring patterns of activities between groups of people from different subsidiaries. They were common knowledge in that most product developers

810   *M. T. Hansen and B. Løvås*

seemed to know about their existence and how to use them, and we were told that a main responsibility of a subsidiary's managers was to provide these contacts for their project teams, should the need arise. Because of the saliency of these relations in the company, we decided to focus exclusively on them, although it may be more appropriate to study other types of lateral linkages in different settings.

We obtained information on these regularly occurring intersubsidiary contacts through the network survey to the R&D managers, who were asked: 'Over the past 2 years, are there any units [subsidiaries] from whom your unit [subsidiary] regularly sought technical and/or market-related input?' The question was followed by a list of the 41 subsidiaries included in the study, and the manager indicated on the list the relevant subsidiaries. We then merged the project data with the subsidiary network data by assigning a subsidiary's network relations to its projects that were included in this study.

It was important to verify that an informal relation existed *prior* to the start of a project because our theoretical arguments assume that a project team uses *established* pre-existing intersubsidiary relations to acquire competencies. Following established procedures in network research (e.g., Podolny and Baron, 1997), we asked the R&D manager how many years each of these reported relations had been in existence and then only included relations that had existed *prior* to the start of a focal product development project (*Informal relation*). Of all the dyads, 12 percent had an informal relation. To test the interaction effects, we interacted this variable with the international variable (*International * Informal relation*), miles (*Miles * Informal relation*), cultural distance (*Cultural distance * Informal relation*) and related competencies (*Competence * Informal relation*).

Finally, because prior research has shown that the strength of informal cross-unit relations matters for knowledge transfers (e.g., Hansen, 1999), we also included a control variable that indicates the strength of each intersubsidiary relation. Using 7-point scales, we asked the R&D managers how frequently the engineers from the two subsidiaries interacted (with anchors of 'once a day' to 'once every 3 months') and how close the working relationships had been (with anchors of 'very close, practically like being in the same work group' to 'distant, like an arm's length delivery of the input'). We reverse-scored the items and took the

average of the two items, which have a correlation of 0.83 (*Strength of relation*).

Formal proximity in a dyad

We used the two hierarchical levels in the company to construct a measure of formal proximity. First, the 41 subsidiaries had been structured into five broad *business groups*, each of which had a vice president and a small staff that coordinated the efforts across the subsidiaries within the business group. Second, several subsidiaries were grouped into *divisions* with between two and four subsidiaries in them. Sixteen out of the 41 subsidiaries were grouped into a division, while the remaining 25 were not. A subsidiary manager could therefore report directly to a division manager, who in turn reported directly to a business group vice president (see Figure 1 for a partial diagram of this organization structure). Thus, two subsidiaries could have a common hierarchical point of integration at one of three possible levels: by reporting to the President's office at the very top of the organization (i.e., the least proximate formal integrative point), as exemplified by subsidiaries A and E in Figure 1; by belonging to the same business group, as illustrated by subsidiaries A and C in Figure 1; and by reporting to the same divisional manager (i.e., the most proximate formal group), as exemplified by subsidiaries A and B in Figure 1. We constructed a three-level measure of formal proximity: 0, only integrated at the top; 1, integrated at the business group level; and 2, integrated at the division level (*Formal proximity*). Of all the dyads, 72 percent were at level 0, 25 percent at level 1, and the remaining 3 percent at level 2. We also used an alternative measure denoting whether the focal team and the target subsidiary were in the same business group (with a score of 1) or not (a score of 0). To test the hypothesized effects, we interacted the formal proximity variable with the international dimension (*International * Formal proximity*), miles (*Miles * Formal proximity*), cultural distance (*Cultural distance * Formal proximity*), and related competencies (*Competence * Formal proximity*).

Project control variables

While our theory focuses on *where* a project team would acquire competencies, we nevertheless wanted to control for a project's propensity to

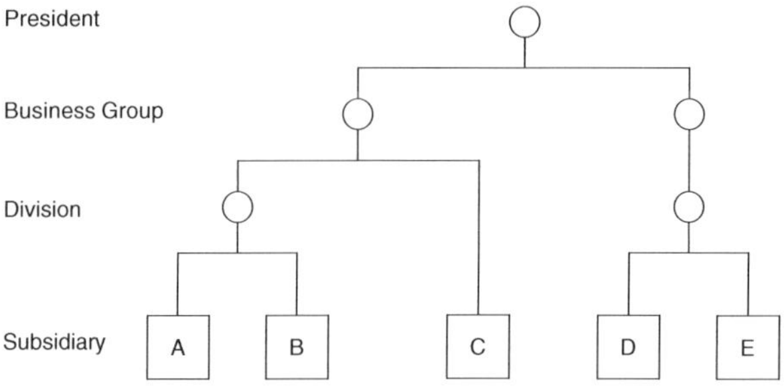

Figure 1. Diagram of levels in the formal organization

seek competencies from other subsidiaries in the first place. We used three project-level variables to control for this propensity. First, we constructed a variable by asking the project manager to indicate the percentage of the project's total software and hardware that came from the focal subsidiary (*Existing ware*). Assuming that a team would first use what its own subsidiary had already developed, this measure indicates the need to acquire new competencies from elsewhere: if projects could reuse their own technologies, they should have less need to seek technological competencies elsewhere. Second, we also entered a control variable measuring the size of the project. Larger projects may have had a higher propensity to seek competencies from other places, as they may have had higher needs or more personnel available to seek competencies. We used the initial budget (in $000) as an indicator of the project's size and logged this measure (*Budget*). Third, we controlled for a project's overall opportunities for acquiring competencies from other subsidiaries. We measured the number of the competencies on the pre-developed list of 22 competencies that the project manager reported that the project required (*No. competencies required*). The higher the number of competencies required on this list, the more likely that other subsidiaries could provide opportunities for competence transfers to the focal team, increasing the propensity for the project to seek competencies from other subsidiaries in the first place.

RESULTS

The descriptive statistics are reported in Table 2. We subtracted the mean from the independent

variables to avoid high correlations with the interactions terms.[7]

Main effects

The variables testing the main effects of the four determinants are entered sequentially in Models 2–5 in Table 3. First, as shown in Model 2, the related competencies variable is positive and significant, indicating that the probability of a transfer increases substantially when the target subsidiary possesses related competencies. Second, as seen in Model 3, the coefficient estimate for the log of miles is significant and negative, while the results pertaining to the country effect and cultural distance are not significant (and these results hold in models in which each distance variable is entered separately). That is, as the spatial distance increases between a project team and a target subsidiary, the probability of a transfer between them decreases.

Third, the effect for formal proximity is shown in Model 4 and is positive and significant, implying that teams and subsidiaries that are formally proximate are more likely to engage in a transfer than dyads that do not have such formal integration. Fourth, the effects for informal relations are entered in Model 5. Both the presence of a relation in a dyad and the strength of that relation are positive and significant.

In short, when viewed separately, there is support for the main effects of related competencies,

---

[7] We computed variance inflation factors to assess if our models had any multicollinearity problems. No variable had a VIF factor higher than 5, which is well below the recommended threshold of 10, indicating that there are no major multicollinearity concerns (Neter, Wasserman, and Kutner, 1990).

Table 2. Descriptive statistics (n = 4840)

Variables	Mean	s.d.	Min	Max	1	2	3	4	5	6	7	8	9	10	11	12	13	14	15	16	17	18	19	20
1. Existing ware	0.45	0.31	0.00	1.00																				
2. Budget	6.75	1.07	4.50	10.72	-0.26																			
3. No. competencies required	3.06	1.40	0.00	9.00	-0.09	0.26																		
4. Related competencies[1]	0.00	0.49	-0.42	0.58	-0.03	0.08	0.30																	
5. International[1]	0.00	0.50	-0.48	0.52	0.00	0.03	0.10	0.06																
6. Miles (log)[1]	0.00	2.34	-6.88	2.38	0.02	0.01	0.03	-0.05	0.61															
7. Cultural distance[1]	0.00	1.43	-0.95	3.95	-0.03	0.09	0.04	0.02	0.69	0.45														
8. Formal proximity[1]	0.00	0.53	-0.31	1.69	0.01	-0.01	0.01	0.10	-0.08	-0.29	-0.06													
9. Informal relation[1]	0.00	0.33	-0.12	0.88	-0.02	0.06	0.06	0.12	-0.02	-0.22	0.02	0.36												
10. Strength of relation	0.55	1.56	0.00	7.00	-0.01	0.05	0.06	0.15	-0.04	-0.27	-0.01	0.49	0.81											
11. International * Competence	0.01	0.25	-0.28	0.30	0.00	-0.01	-0.05	0.02	0.00	0.09	-0.02	-0.03	-0.05	-0.05										
12. Miles * Competence	-0.06	1.20	-3.99	2.89	-0.01	0.01	-0.03	-0.02	0.09	0.24	0.05	-0.12	-0.09	-0.13	0.62									
13. Cultural distance * Competence	0.01	0.70	-1.66	2.08	0.00	-0.02	-0.03	0.01	-0.02	0.05	-0.02	-0.03	-0.04	-0.03	0.68	0.45								
14. International * Informal relation	-0.00	0.16	-0.42	0.45	0.00	-0.01	-0.03	-0.05	-0.00	0.18	0.03	-0.21	-0.05	-0.16	0.11	0.14	0.07							
15. Miles * Informal relation	-0.16	1.17	-6.05	2.09	0.01	-0.03	-0.04	-0.06	0.12	0.39	0.10	-0.36	-0.33	-0.47	0.10	0.22	0.07	0.67						
16. Cultural distance * Informal relation	0.01	0.50	-0.83	3.15	0.01	0.02	-0.02	-0.03	0.03	0.14	0.07	-0.17	0.04	-0.13	0.07	0.09	0.07	0.71	0.48					
17. International * Formal proximity	-0.02	0.26	-0.81	0.87	0.01	-0.03	-0.05	-0.03	-0.01	0.23	-0.01	-0.14	-0.21	-0.25	0.10	0.15	0.06	0.35	0.40	0.19				
18. Miles * Formal proximity	-0.36	1.94	-11.60	4.01	0.04	-0.04	-0.06	-0.08	0.14	0.49	0.10	-0.36	-0.35	-0.49	0.11	0.25	0.07	0.40	0.71	0.25	0.67			
19. Cultural distance * Formal proximity	-0.04	0.67	-1.60	2.46	-0.01	-0.04	-0.02	-0.04	-0.01	0.17	-0.10	-0.17	-0.21	-0.22	0.06	0.11	0.08	0.22	0.30	0.18	0.70	0.51		
20. Competence * Informal relation	0.02	0.17	-0.37	0.51	-0.01	0.02	0.02	0.04	-0.05	-0.09	-0.03	0.18	0.26	0.29	-0.04	-0.22	0.01	-0.05	-0.15	-0.06	-0.02	-0.14	-0.03	
21. Competence * Formal Proximity	0.03	0.27	-0.71	0.98	-0.02	0.04	0.05	0.03	-0.03	-0.12	-0.03	0.18	0.18	0.23	-0.09	-0.31	-0.07	-0.03	-0.15	-0.03	-0.00	-0.19	-0.07	0.39

[1] Mean value subtracted.

Table 3. Results from Conditional Fixed-effects Logistic Regression Analysis of Dyadic Transfer Events

	Model 1	Model 2	Model 3	Model 4	Model 5	Model 6	Model 7	Model 8
Existing ware	-1.74(0.52)***	-1.79(0.53)***	-1.75(0.53)***	-1.77(0.54)***	-1.86(0.55)***	-1.82(0.56)***	-1.84(0.56)***	-1.83(0.56)***
Budget	0.12(0.13)	0.11(0.13)	0.12(0.13)	0.13(0.13)	0.17(0.14)	0.19(0.14)	0.19(0.14)	0.19(0.14)
No. competencies required	0.07(0.09)	-0.11(0.10)	-0.11(0.10)	-0.10(0.10)	-0.06(0.10)	-0.07(0.11)	-0.07(0.11)	-0.07(0.11)
Related competencies		1.66(0.27)***	1.60(0.28)***	1.50(0.28)***	1.36(0.29)***	1.18(0.30)***	1.10(0.32)***	1.01(0.33)***
International			0.49(0.47)	0.23(0.48)	-0.30(0.51)	-0.40(0.55)	0.97(0.84)	0.99(0.85)
Miles (log)			-0.19(0.05)***	-0.07(0.06)	0.03(0.06)	0.13(0.09)	-0.21(0.12)*	-0.25(0.18)*
Cultural distance			-0.08(0.16)	-0.08(0.16)	0.04(0.16)	-0.02(0.17)	0.10(0.20)	0.10(0.20)
Formal proximity				0.94(0.19)***	-0.13(0.24)	-0.11(0.24)	-0.12(0.24)	0.03(0.26)
Informal relation					2.10(0.45)***	2.14(0.45)***	2.52(0.50)***	2.46(0.50)***
Strength of relation					0.21(0.09)**	0.20(0.09)**	0.24(0.09)***	0.27(0.09)***
International * Competence						0.44(0.90)	0.48(0.94)	0.49(0.97)
Miles * Competence						-0.27(0.14)*	-0.27(0.14)*	-0.31(0.15)**
Cultural distance * Competence						0.25(0.24)	0.24(0.24)	0.30(0.25)
International * Informal relation							-2.26(1.01)**	-2.15(1.08)**
Miles * Informal relation							0.57(0.13)***	0.46(0.14)***
Cultural distance * Informal relation							-0.29(0.23)	-0.25(0.24)
International * Formal proximity								-0.09(0.70)
Miles * Formal proximity								0.16(0.09)*
Cultural distance * Formal proximity								-0.05(0.20)
Chi-square (d.f.)†		44.6(1)***	61.6(4)***	84.6(5)***	196.6(7)***	201.8(10)***	224.0(13)***	230.2(16)***

* $p < 0.1$; ** $p < 0.05$; *** $p < 0.01$. N = 4360. No. of groups = 22. Two-tailed tests for variables; standard errors are in parentheses. †Compared with Model 1.

814   *M. T. Hansen and B. Løvås*

spatial distance, formal proximity, and informal relations, confirming much prior research on these dimensions and lending support to Hypothesis 1. Model 5 in Table 3, however, reveals two interesting changes in the main effects. First, the main effect for spatial distance is no longer significant, suggesting that when the formal and informal mechanisms are controlled for, there is no overall negative effect of spatial distance. As revealed in subsequent models, however, spatial distance interacts with other variables to explain competence transfers. Second, when the informal relation variable is entered in Model 5, the effect of formal proximity is no longer significant. As the subsequent analysis of interaction variables reveals, however, formal proximity interacts with other determinants to predict transfer events.

Geographical distance and related competencies

Models 6–8 in Table 3 include the three interaction effects combining geographical distance and the existence of related competencies in a subsidiary. The interaction effect including related competencies and whether the dyad crosses national borders is insignificant, as is the interaction effect including related competencies and cultural distance. In contrast, the interaction term involving miles and related competencies (*Miles * Competence*) is negative and significant throughout the models. That is, the probability of a transfer event *decreases* as the spatial distance increases between

the focal team and a target subsidiary that has related competencies. To evaluate the combined effect of these results, we plotted the estimates for the interaction term and the main effects of miles and related competencies, as shown in Figure 2.[8] When the target subsidiary has related competencies (i.e., the upper line in Figure 2), the probability of a transfer event between a focal project and a subsidiary that has related competencies decreases as the number of miles between them increases. This result supports Hypothesis 2a.

Figure 2 also plots the effects when the target subsidiary has no related competencies (lower line in the figure). The probabilities in this situation are considerably lower than the other line in Figure 2 for all values of spatial distance, but some probabilities are higher in the lower line than in the upper line. Specifically, when the focal project team and the target subsidiary are located on the *same* site (i.e., mean-deviated miles is −6.88), the probability of a transfer event occurring between them is 0.60 when the target subsidiary does not possess related competencies (as seen from the lower line). In contrast, as seen from the upper line, when the subsidiary does possess related competencies but is located farthest away (i.e., mean-deviated miles is 2.37 or 10,512 miles), the

[8] Using estimates from Model 8 in Table 3 and holding other variables constant at their mean value, the equation for the plots is: Prob. $= 1/(1 + e^{-[\text{miles}*(-0.25-0.31*\text{competence})+1.01*\text{related competencies}]})$. Because the dummy variable for related competencies is mean-deviated, it takes on negative (-0.42) and positive (0.58) values instead of 0 and 1.

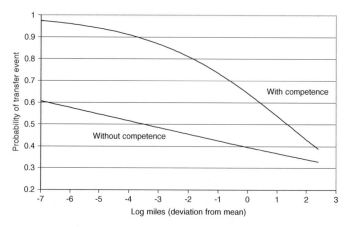

Figure 2.   Plot of the interaction effects of related competencies and miles on probability of a transfer event in a dyad

probability of a transfer event is 0.39, which is considerably lower than a probability of 0.60. The turning point occurs when mean-deviated miles is 0.40 (i.e., the distance between the focal team and the subsidiary is 1450 miles), beyond which the focal team is more likely to transfer from a target subsidiary that is close but has no related competencies than from a subsidiary that is very far away but has related competencies. In our data set, 47.8 percent of all dyad observations had a spatial distance of more than 1450 miles, including distances between Europe and the United States, Europe and Asia, and the West and East Coasts in the United States. In short, these results support Hypothesis 2b.

Geographical distance, informal relations, and formal proximity

Model 7 in Table 3 depicts the results involving the interaction effects for geographical distance and informal relations. The interaction effect including the presence of an informal relation and cultural distance is not significant, but the effect for international and informal relation is significant and negative, which is in the opposite direction from what we had predicted. We investigated this result further by partitioning the variables into four dummy variables but found no significant effect for the dummy variables involving the international dimension.[9] The interaction effect involving spatial distance and informal relations (*Miles ∗ Informal relation*) is positive and significant in Model 7, indicating that, with an increase in spatial distance in the dyad, the presence of an informal relation increases the likelihood of a transfer event in the dyad. Thus, informal relations mitigate the main negative effect of spatial distance, confirming Hypothesis 3.

Model 8 in Table 3 adds the moderating effects of formal proximity on geographical distance.

While the interaction effects involving an international dyad or cultural distance are not significant, the interaction effect involving spatial distance and formal proximity (*Miles ∗ Formal proximity*) is positive and significant. That is, with increasing spatial distance between the focal team and a target subsidiary, an increase in formal proximity between them enhances the probability of a transfer event between them, lending support to Hypothesis 4.

Figure 3 shows the moderating effects of informal relations and formal proximity on spatial distance, using the effects obtained in Model 8 in Table 3.[10] The line indicated as 'none' plots the effect of having no formal or informal integrative mechanisms, revealing a negative effect on the probability of a transfer in a dyad as the spatial distance increases between a focal team and a subsidiary. The two lines 'Formal 1' and 'Formal 2' indicate the presence of a common business group (i.e., the least proximate form of hierarchical integration) and a common division (i.e., the most proximate form of hierarchical integration), respectively. As revealed by the plots in Figure 3, the negative effect of miles is mitigated (but not overcome) by these two levels of formal proximity, but an informal relation is sufficient to turn the main negative effect of miles into a positive effect. In short, these results confirm Hypotheses 3 and 4.

Related competencies, informal relations, and formal proximity

Model 1 in Table 4 depicts the results for the interaction term involving related competencies and informal relations. This effect is significant and negative. The combined coefficient estimate for the two main effects (*Related competencies* and *Informal relation*) and the interaction effect (*Competence ∗ Informal relation*) is 0.84 when there were related competencies but no informal relation in the dyad. This coefficient estimate increases to 2.26, however, when there were no related competencies but an informal relation in

---

[9] Specifically, we created three dummy variables to test the movement from a baseline of 'national with no relation' to any other combination: one in which 1 indicates the existence of an informal relation in a national dyad (showing a significant and positive effect), another dummy variable in which 1 indicates the existence of an informal relation in an international dyad (a significant and positive effect), and a third dummy variable in which 1 indicates an international dyad with no relation (no significant effect). Thus, regardless of whether the dyad is national or international, moving to any state that has an informal relation has a positive and significant effect. This suggests that there is no overwhelming effect for the international variable in our data.

[10] The equation for plotting the lines is: Prob. $= 1/(1 + e^{-[\text{miles}∗(-0.25+0.16∗\text{formal}+0.46∗\text{informal})+0.03∗\text{formal}+2.46∗\text{informal}]})$. Because the variables are mean-deviated, we have used the mean-deviated variable scales to plot the results. For informal relations, those are -0.12 (no) and 0.88 (yes), while for formal proximity they are -0.31 (i.e., only organization president is common integration point), 0.685 (formal 1, i.e., same business group in dyad), and 1.69 (formal 2, i.e., same division in the dyad).

816   *M. T. Hansen and B. Løvås*

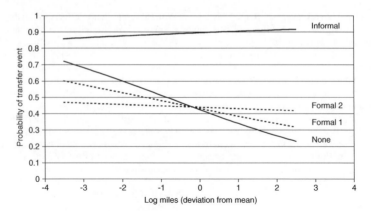

Figure 3.   Plot of the interaction effects of informal relations, formal groups and miles on probability of a transfer event in a dyad. Note: 'None' refers to a dyad with no established relation and a formal proximity value of 0; 'Formal 1' denotes the same business group in a dyad; 'Formal 2' denotes the same division in a dyad (the most proximate form); and 'Informal' refers to the presence of an established informal relation in a dyad

the dyad, suggesting that teams were *more likely* to transfer in a situation with no related competencies but an informal relation than in a situation with related competences but no informal relation.[11]

To investigate this result further, we created an alternative specification that categorizes the dyads according to the four possible combinations: 'no relation but related competence' (as the omitted baseline specification), 'both relation and competence,' 'relation but no competence,' and 'neither relation nor competence.' As shown in Model 2 in Table 4 and depicted in Figure 4(a), moving from the baseline combination of 'no relation but competence' to 'both relation and competence' substantially increased the probability of a transfer event (i.e., coefficient = 2.51). Also, moving to a situation in which there was neither a relation nor a related competence significantly reduced the probability of a transfer (−2.46). However, the results reveal a positive effect of moving from the baseline of 'no relation but related competence' to a situation in which there was a relation but the subsidiary had no related competencies

for the project (1.54). It appears that the teams went to those with whom they had relations, irrespective of whether they had related competencies for the project. This result lends support to Hypothesis 5.

Model 3 in Table 4 reports the result for the moderating effect of formal proximity as stated in Hypothesis 6. The interaction effect is not significant, but breaking out the interaction effect into four possible combinations produces some interesting results. Model 4 in Table 4 includes the effects from this alternative specification, using three dummy variables based on one dimension of the formal proximity variable—whether the team and the subsidiary in the dyad belonged to the same business group.[12] As shown in Model 4 in Table 4 and depicted in Figure 4(b), there is a *negative* effect of −0.93 of moving from a situation of 'not the same business group but related competence in the dyad' (i.e., the omitted baseline specification) to a situation in which there is a common business group but the target subsidiary has *no* related competencies (i.e., the 'same group but no competence' variable). This result indicates that teams are less likely to transfer competencies from a subsidiary that is in the same business group but has no related competencies than it is from a

---

[11] Because the two variables are mean-deviated, the two equations for the estimates are computed as follows:

Coefficient estimate (related competencies, no informal relation)
= $1.88 * 0.58 + 2.87 * -0.12 - 1.42 * 0.58 * -0.12 = 0.84$;
Coefficient estimate (no related competencies, informal relation)
= $1.88 * -0.42 + 2.87 * 0.88 - 1.42 * -0.42 * 0.88 = 2.26$.

[12] We used this variable because it is dichotomous and correlates 0.92 with the continuous formal proximity variable, which does not lend itself to this dichotomization of the variables.

Table 4. Results from Conditional Fixed-effects Logistic Regression Analysis of Transfer Events

	Model 1	Model 2	Model 3	Model 4
Existing ware	−1.82 (0.56)***	−1.85 (0.55)***	−1.82 (0.56)***	−1.85 (0.55)***
Budget	0.19 (0.14)	0.16 (0.14)	0.19 (0.14)	0.18 (0.14)
No. competencies required	−0.07 (0.11)	−0.07 (0.10)	−0.07 (0.11)	−0.07 (0.10)
Related competencies	1.88 (0.59)***		1.87 (0.59)***	
International	0.93 (0.90)	−0.29 (0.50)	0.92 (0.90)	−0.38 (0.51)
Miles (log)	−0.21 (0.12)*	0.02 (0.06)	−0.22 (0.13)*	0.06 (0.06)
Cultural distance	0.08 (0.21)	0.04 (0.16)	0.08 (0.21)	0.05 (0.16)
Formal proximity	0.05 (0.26)	0.13 (0.21)	0.01 (0.29)	
Informal relation	2.87 (0.57)***		2.86 (0.57)***	2.12 (0.44)***
Strength of relation	0.27 (0.09)***		0.27 (0.09)***	0.16 (0.08)*
International * Competence	0.26 (1.00)		0.28 (1.00)	
Miles * Competence	−0.30 (0.15)**		−0.29 (0.15)*	
Cultural distance * Competence	0.27 (0.26)		0.27 (0.26)	
International * Informal relation	−1.96 (1.10)*		−1.94 (1.10)*	
Miles * Informal relation	0.39 (0.14)***		0.39 (0.14)***	
Cultural distance * Informal relation	−0.22 (0.25)		−0.22 (0.25)	
International * Formal proximity	0.02 (0.70)		−0.03 (0.73)	
Miles * Formal proximity	0.16 (0.09)*		0.16 (0.10)*	
Cultural distance * Formal proximity	−0.06 (0.20)		−0.06 (0.20)	
Competence * Informal relation	−1.42 (0.70)**		−1.45 (0.74)**	
Competence * Formal proximity			0.12 (0.47)	
Alternative specifications:				
Relation and competence		2.51 (0.32)***		
Relation but no competence		1.54 (0.37)***		
Neither relation nor competence		−2.46 (0.63)***		
Same group and competence				0.56 (0.32)*
Same group but no competence				−0.93 (0.47)**
Neither same group nor competence				−1.20 (0.37)***
Chi-square (d.f.)†	234.4(17)***	197.0(7)***	234.5(18)***	199.4(8)***

* $p < 0.1$; ** $p < 0.05$; *** $p < 0.01$. N = 4360. No. of groups = 22. Two-tailed tests for variables; standard errors are in parentheses.
†Compared with Model 1 in Table 3.

subsidiary that is not in the same business group but has related competencies. This result contradicts Hypothesis 6 and is the opposite of what the results revealed for informal relations: while informal relations led teams to engage in transfers with subsidiaries without related competencies, formal proximity did not reveal this effect.[13] This is a highly unexpected result.

In addition to the lack of support for Hypothesis 6, there was no support for the posited cultural distance and country effects in our data set. Two issues pertaining to our context could explain this lack of results. First, only a relatively small number of countries were represented in our data, reducing the variance in cultural distance and the possibility that this variable would explain transfer events. Second, we studied transfers between engineers in a company that had a strong R&D culture. It is possible that this organizational culture was more salient than national differences and thus 'overrode' a possible national cultural effect. Data sets with larger variances in these two variables may therefore yield different results.

---

[13] To investigate the relationship between informal relations and formal proximity further, we performed an additional analysis not reported here. We created four dummy variables for various combinations of these two variables and used a baseline that denotes a common business group between the focal team and the subsidiary but no relation between them (i.e., formal only). Results showed that moving from the baseline to a situation of 'neither formal nor informal' has a significant negative effect on the probability of a transfer, indicating that formal proximity has a significant effect on the probability of a transfer when there are no informal relations. This result clarifies the result found in Model 5 in Table 3, where the main effect for formal proximity

turned insignificant once the informal relation variables were added.

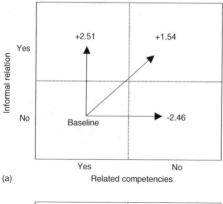

(a)

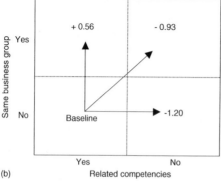

(b)

Figure 4. Coefficient estimate effects for various combinations of informal relations, formal business groupings, and related competencies. Note: Figure 4(a) is based on Model 2 in Table 4; Figure 4(b) is based on Model 4 in Table 4

DISCUSSION

In summary, all hypotheses except one were supported. As predicted in Hypothesis 1, the main effects of the four determinants of technological competence transfers were positive and significant when viewed separately: a focal team was more likely to transfer from a target subsidiary to the extent that the subsidiary had related competencies, was spatially close, had a prior relationship with the focal team, and belonged to the same formal subgroup as the team. These results confirm much prior research that has analyzed one of the determinants of transfers separately from the others. However, the results also revealed

several significant interaction effects that altered the net effects of these determinants. As predicted in Hypothesis 2, large spatial distances between subsidiaries deterred employees from leveraging related competencies. The negative main effect of spatial distance on the occurrence of a transfer event was, in turn, mitigated if the focal team and a target subsidiary belonged to the same formal group and overcome if they had a prior informal relation, confirming Hypotheses 3 and 4. Interestingly, the informal and formal organizational mechanisms revealed different moderating effects on the existence of related competencies: while informal relations led teams to engage in transfers with subsidiaries *without* related competencies, formal proximity did not. These results confirmed Hypothesis 5 but not Hypothesis 6.

These findings address the three shortcomings in existing research that we noted in the introduction to the paper: the tendency in the literature on synergies in diversified firms to ignore the roles of spatial distance and informal relations; the lack of research that examines how informal and formal integrative mechanisms may overcome a negative effect of geographical distance; and the largely unexplored comparison between formal and informal mechanisms in facilitating competence transfers. Our results suggest several important implications for research in these areas.

Challenging the construct of related competencies

The literature on synergy benefits based on relatedness in competencies has largely ignored two important explanations for why the relatedness construct does not explain synergy benefits better (Ramanujam and Varadarajan, 1989). First, studies have not considered the moderating effect of spatial distance between subsidiaries in a multiunit firm, but our results showed that large spatial distances reduced the tendency for focal teams to transfer from subsidiaries that had related competencies, to the point that large spatial distances overrode the effect of related competencies. When spatial distances are large, the notion of relatedness may simply fade as an explanatory factor.

Second, synergy studies have also ignored the possibility that units in a firm are more likely to connect with other units whose employees they know than with units that possess related competencies. This behavior may not be surprising, as product development teams are often encouraged to develop strong cross-functional and cross-unit relations (e.g., Clark and Fujimoto, 1991; Eisenhardt and Tabrizi, 1995), but these established patterns of interactions can become cemented and constrain search for related competencies elsewhere (cf. Ahuja and Katila, 2004; Henderson and Clark, 1990). If such behavior is prevalent in a firm, the relatedness construct may only partially explain the flow of competencies.

One implication of our findings is therefore that the explanatory power of the construct of related competencies is not as powerful as first envisioned (e.g., Rumelt, 1974). Perhaps the problem with the notion of related competencies does not concern the noted empirical imprecision of relatedness measures (Farjoun, 1998; Ramanujam and Varadarajan, 1989), but the limited explanatory power of this construct in explaining technological competence transfers in multinational firms that are characterized by large spatial distances and many horizontal informal relationships between subsidiaries. While we only studied one multinational firm and thus cannot easily generalize across firms, our findings suggest that research on synergies in diversified firms need to be broadened beyond the relatedness construct to consider other reasons why competencies are leveraged in a firm. Subsequent research can readily use a large sample of firms to test the hypothesis that the constructs of spatial distance and network relations among subsidiaries overwhelm the effect of relatedness in competencies in explaining the occurrence of transfers and the resultant firm-level performance.

Are large geographical distances an insurmountable obstacle?

Our results pertaining to geographical distance have implications not only for research on synergy but also for research on the use of informal and formal integrative mechanisms and for the notion of firm-wide learning as a source of competitive advantage in multinational firms (Doz *et al.*, 2001; Nohria and Ghoshal, 1997). In the introduction, we raised the issue of whether geographical distances in the form of spatial, cultural, and national differentiation present an insurmountable obstacle to leveraging widely dispersed competencies in a multinational enterprise. Our results suggest that this is not the case: the presence of informal relations among subsidiaries offset the

negative main effect of spatial distance on the leveraging of technological competencies, whereas formal proximity nearly offset the negative effect of spatial distance (as shown in Figure 3). These findings indicate that problems associated with leveraging competencies across large spatial distances can be managed through the use of informal and formal organizational mechanisms. To our knowledge, ours is the first study that empirically demonstrates this effect.

The finding that spatial distance problems can be overcome or mitigated by formal and informal integrative mechanisms has implications for research into whether multinational firms that participate in regional technology clusters around the world can benefit from spillovers from such clusters and thereby gain a firm-wide competitive advantage (Almeida and Kogut, 1999; Jaffe, Trajtenberg, and Henderson, 1993). Our results suggest that such firm-wide learning benefits are not automatic: without formal and informal integrative mechanisms, task units such as new product development teams are unlikely to leverage competencies from subsidiaries that are situated in spatially distant technology clusters, thereby preventing the firm from taking full advantage of its participation in regional technology clusters (cf. Feinberg and Gupta, 2004; Florida, 1997; Serapio, Dalton, and Yoshida, 2000). An emerging hypothesis that can be tested with a large sample of firms is therefore that increased firm-level performance requires both the participation of a firm in local technology clusters *and* the presence of internal formal and informal integrative mechanisms. Cluster participation without internal mechanisms, or internal mechanisms without cluster participation, is unlikely to lead to substantial firm-level performance.

Different effects of formal and informal integrative mechanisms

In the introduction to the paper, we posed the question of whether informal and formal mechanisms had different effects on the occurrence of competence transfers in multinational firms. Our results suggest that they do. Consistent with recent research on this topic in multinationals, we found that informal relations were a more potent integrator than formal proximity (e.g., Kim *et al.*, 2003; Nohria and Ghoshal, 1997; Tsai, 2002). One indication is that the positive main effect of formal proximity on the probability of a transfer event

820   M. T. Hansen and B. Løvås

became insignificant once the informal relationship variable was added to the model (see Models 4 and 5 in Table 3). Also, as noted above, informal relations were more effective than formal proximity in overcoming the negative effect of large spatial distances. The pervasive effects of informal relations stand out in our results. In fact, there were only a few contrasting situations when the presence of established informal relations did not lead to a higher probability of transfer.[14]

Moreover, our results also revealed another interesting contrast between informal and formal integrative mechanisms that have not been explicated by existing research: while informal relationships steered teams to subsidiaries without related competencies, a team was not more likely to contact a subsidiary without related competencies just because they belonged to the same formal subgroup. These different results suggest an unintended consequence of informal relations that is not associated with formal proximity.

However, whether the tendency of relying on informal relationships as opposed to relying on subsidiaries with related competencies lead to poor performance is unclear. On one hand, informal relations that lead task units to subsidiaries that do not possess related technological competencies may reduce task unit performance to the extent that task units obtain inferior knowledge (cf. Gargiulo and Benassi, 2000). This possibility suggests a potential 'dark-side' effect of established informal relations that provides an alternative explanation to the positive role of informal relations that is often noted by research on lateral informal linkages in multinational companies (e.g., Bartlett and Ghoshal, 1989; Birkinshaw, Nobel, and Ridderstrale, 2002; Nohria and Ghoshal, 1997).

On the other hand, connections to subsidiaries that do not possess related competencies may offer unexpected benefits. While such subsidiaries may not possess the most directly relevant knowledge for a project team, working with them may lead to the discovery of unexpected benefits such as novel combinations of existing technologies (Graebner, 2004). Thus, it is quite possible that a seemingly

irrational behavior of relying on informal relations as opposed to relying on subsidiaries with related competencies may in fact lead to innovative and high-performing teams. Because we did not study the performance implications of relying on informal relations, however, we could not disentangle whether it was detrimental or beneficial for teams to rely on those they knew as opposed to those with related competencies. While our study is one of the first to study the relationships among the four main determinants of competence transfers, subsequent research needs to study the associated performance implications of these findings.

CONCLUSION

This study was motivated by the observation that various lines of research that focus on the determinants of technological competence transfers in multinational enterprises have remained largely disconnected and have thus yielded incomplete and potentially biased results. To address this shortcoming, we posed the research question of whether there are important interaction effects between four fundamental determinants of technological competence transfers—i.e., between related competencies, geographical distance, formal proximity, and informal relations. The main finding of this study is that the effect of each of these four fundamental determinants of technological competence transfers depends to a large extent on the state of each of the other determinants. In particular, our results revealed that informal relations and large spatial distances between subsidiaries were relatively more important than the presence of related competencies in explaining the occurrence of technological competence transfers. While large spatial distances deterred competence transfers, however, both formal and informal integrative mechanisms mitigated this tendency. These findings challenge the premise that different determinants of technological competence transfers operate independently of one another and indicate the need for approaches that examine interdependencies among them. To advance research on this topic, studies need to shed the past tendency of analyzing one determinant to the exclusion of others and pursue approaches that integrate the various literatures on synergies, geography, informal relations, and formal structure.

---

[14] For example, the probability of a transfer was *higher* when there was *no* informal relation but related competencies and small spatial distance in the dyad, than when there was an informal relation but no related competencies and large spatial distance in the dyad.

ACKNOWLEDGEMENTS

We thank the guest editors of the special issue on the Global Acquisition, Leverage and Protection of Technological Competencies, two anonymous reviewers, Olav Sorenson, William Simpson, and the seminar participants at London Business School, INSEAD, and the *Strategic Management Journal* conference in Pittsburgh for helpful comments. Research support from the Division of Research at Harvard Business School is greatly acknowledged.

REFERENCES

Ahuja G, Katila R. 2004. Where do resources come from? The role of idiosyncratic situations. *Strategic Management Journal*, Special Issue **25**(8–9): 887–907.

Allen TJ. 1977. *Managing the Flow of Technology: Technology Transfer and the Dissemination of Technological Information Within the R&D Organization*. MIT Press: Cambridge, MA.

Almeida P, Kogut B. 1999. Localization of knowledge and the mobility of engineers in regional networks. *Management Science* **45**: 905–917.

Ancona DG, Caldwell DF. 1992. Bridging the boundary: external activity and performance in organizational teams. *Administrative Science Quarterly* **37**: 634–665.

Barkema HG, Vermeulen F. 1997. What differences in the cultural backgrounds of partners are detrimental for international joint ventures? *Journal of International Business Studies* **28**: 845–865.

Bartlett CA, Ghoshal S. 1989. *Managing Across Borders: The Transnational Solution*. Harvard Business School Press: Boston, MA.

Birkinshaw J, Nobel R, Ridderstrale J. 2002. Knowledge as a contingency variable: do the characteristics of knowledge predict organization structure? *Organization Science* **13**: 274–290.

Brewer MB. 1979. Ingroup bias in the minimal intergroup situation: a cognitive motivational analysis. *Psychological Bulletin* **86**: 307–324.

Clark KB, Fujimoto T. 1991. *Product Development Performance: Strategy, Organization, and Management in the World Auto Industry*. Harvard Business School Press: Boston, MA.

Cyert RM, March JG. 1992. *A Behavioral Theory of the Firm* (2nd edn). Blackwell Business: Cambridge, MA.

De Meyer A. 1992. Management of international R&D operations. In *Technology Management and International Business*, Granstrand O, Hakanson L, Sjolander S (eds). Wiley: New York; 163–179.

Doz Y, Santos J, Williamson P. 2001. *From Global to Metanational: How Companies Win in the Knowledge Economy*. Harvard Business School Press: Boston, MA.

Earley PC, Mosakowski E. 2000. Creating hybrid team cultures: an empirical test of transnational team functioning. *Academy of Management Journal* **43**: 26–50.

Eisenhardt KM, Galunic CD. 2000. Coevolving: at last, a way to make synergies work. *Harvard Business Review* **78**(1): 91–101.

Eisenhardt KM, Santos FM. 2002. Knowledge-based view: a new theory of strategy? In *Handbook of Strategy and Management*, Pettigrew A, Thomas H, Whittington R (eds). Sage: London; 139–164.

Eisenhardt KM, Tabrizi BN. 1995. Accelerating adaptive processes: product innovation in the global computer industry. *Administrative Science Quarterly* **40**: 84–111.

Emerson RM. 1962. Power–dependence relations. *American Sociological Review* **27**: 31–41.

Farjoun M. 1998. The independent and joint effects of the skills and spatial bases of relatedness in diversification. *Strategic Management Journal* **19**(7): 611–630.

Feinberg SE, Gupta AK. 2004. Knowledge spillovers and the assignment of R&D responsibilities to foreign subsidiaries. *Strategic Management Journal*, Special Issue **25**(8–9): 823–845.

Fleming L, Sorenson O. 2004. Science as a map in technological search. *Strategic Management Journal* **25**(8–9): 909–928.

Florida R. 1997. The globalization of R&D: results of a survey of foreign-affiliated R&D laboratories in the USA. *Research Policy* **26**: 85–103.

Galbraith JR. 1973. *Designing Complex Organizations*. Addison-Wesley: Reading, MA.

Galunic CD, Eisenhardt KM. 2001. Architectural innovation and modular corporate forms. *Academy of Management Journal* **44**: 1229–1249.

Gargiulo M, Benassi M. 2000. Trapped in your own net? Network cohesion, structural holes, and the adaptations of social capital. *Organization Science* **11**: 183–201.

Graebner M. 2004. Momentum and serendipity: how acquired leaders create value in the integration of technology firms. *Strategic Management Journal*, Special Issue **25**(8–9): 751–777.

Granovetter M. 1985. Economic action and social structure: the problem of embeddedness. *American Journal of Sociology* **91**: 481–510.

Greene WH. 1993. *Econometric Analysis*. (2nd edn). Macmillan: New York.

Gulati R. 1995. Social structure and alliance formation patterns: a longitudinal analysis. *Administrative Science Quarterly* **40**: 619–652.

Gupta AK, Govindarajan V. 2000. Knowledge flows within multinational corporations. *Strategic Management Journal* **21**(14): 473–496.

Hansen MT. 1999. The search-transfer problem: the role of weak ties in sharing knowledge across organization subunits. *Administrative Science Quarterly* **44**: 82–111.

Hansen MT. 2002. Knowledge networks: explaining effective knowledge sharing in multiunit companies. *Organization Science* **13**: 232–249.

Hansen MT, Nohria N, Tierney T. 1999. What's your strategy for managing knowledge? *Harvard Business Review* **77**(2): 106–116.

822 *M. T. Hansen and B. Løvås*

Hargadon A, Sutton RI. 1997. Technology brokering and innovation in a product development firm. *Administrative Science Quarterly* **42**: 716–749.

Hedlund G. 1986. The hypermodern MNC: a heterarchy? *Human Resource Management* **25**(1): 9–35.

Henderson RM, Clark KB. 1990. Architectural innovation: the reconfiguration of existing product technologies and the failure of established firms. *Administrative Science Quarterly* **35**: 9–30.

Hofstede G. 2001. *Culture's Consequences: Comparing Values, Behaviors, Institutions and Organizations Across Nations*, 2nd edn. Sage: Thousand Oaks, CA.

Jaffe AB, Trajtenberg M, Henderson R. 1993. Geographical localization of knowledge spillovers from patent citations. *Quarterly Journal of Economics* **108**: 577–598.

Katz R, Allen TJ. 1988. Investigating the not invented here (NIH) syndrome: a look at the performance, tenure, and communication patterns of 50 R&D project groups. In *Readings in the Management of Innovation* (2nd edn), Tushman ML, Moore WL (eds). Ballinger/Harper & Row: New York; 293–309.

Katz R, Tushman M. 1979. Communication patterns, project performance, and task characteristics: an empirical evaluation and integration in an R&D setting. *Management Science* **23**: 139–162.

Kedia BL, Bhagat RS. 1988. Cultural constraints on transfer of technology across nations: implications for research in international and comparative management. *Academy of Management Review* **13**: 559–571.

Kim K, Park JH, Prescott J. 2003. The global integration of business functions: a study of multinational businesses in integrated global industries. *Journal of International Business Studies* **34**: 327–344.

King G, Zeng L. 2001. Logistic regression in rare events data. *Political Analysis* **9**: 137–163.

Kogut B, Singh H. 1988. The effect of national culture on the choice of entry mode. *Journal of International Business Studies* **19**: 411–433.

Kuemmerle W. 1998. Optimal scale for research and development in foreign environments: an investigation into size and performance of research and development laboratories abroad. *Research Policy* **27**: 111–126.

Krugman P. 1991. Increasing returns and economic geography. *Journal of Political Economy* **99**: 483–499.

Leonard-Barton D, Sinha DK. 1993. Developer–user interaction and user satisfaction in internal technology transfer. *Academy of Management Journal* **36**: 1125–1139.

Malnight T. 1995. Globalization of an ethnocentric firm: an evolutionary perspective. *Strategic Management Journal* **16**(2): 119–141.

Markides C, Williamson P. 1994. Related diversification, core competencies and corporate performance. *Strategic Management Journal*, Summer Special Issue **15**: 149–167.

Milgrom PR, Roberts J. 1992. *Economics, Organization, and Management*. Prentice-Hall: Englewood Cliffs, NJ.

Neter J, Wasserman W, Kutner MH. 1990. *Applied Linear Statistical Models* (3rd edn). Irwin: Homewood, IL.

Nobel R, Birkinshaw J. 1998. Innovation in multinational corporations: control and communication patterns in international R&D. *Strategic Management Journal* **19**(5): 479–497.

Nohria N, Ghoshal S. 1997. *The Differentiated Network: Organizing Multinational Corporations for Value Creation*. Jossey-Bass: San Francisco, CA.

Podolny J, Baron J. 1997. Resources and relationships: social networks and mobility in the workplace. *American Sociological Review* **62**: 673–693.

Ramanujam V, Varadarajan P. 1989. Research on corporate diversification: a synthesis. *Strategic Management Journal* **10**(6): 523–551.

Rumelt R. 1974. *Strategy, Structure, and Economic Performance*. Harvard University Press: Boston, MA.

Serapio M, Dalton D, Yoshida PG. 2000. Globalization of R&D enters new stage as firms learn to integrate technology operations on world scale. *Research Technology Management* **43**: 2–5.

Sorenson O, Stuart TE. 2001. Syndication networks and the spatial distribution of venture capital investments. *American Journal of Sociology* **106**: 1546–1588.

Stopford J, Wells LT. 1972. *Managing Multinational Enterprise: Organization of the Firm and Ownership of the Subsidiaries*. Basic Books: New York.

Tajfel H, Turner JC. 1986. The social identity theory of intergroup behavior. In *Psychology of Intergroup Relations* (2nd edn), Worchel S, Austin WG (eds). Nelson Hall: Chicago, IL; 7–24.

Teece DJ. 1977. Technology transfer by multinational firms: the resource cost of transferring technological know-how. *Economic Journal* **87**: 242–261.

Tsai W. 2002. Social structure of 'coopetition' within a multiunit organization: coordination, competition, and intraorganizational knowledge sharing. *Organization Science* **13**: 179–190.

Uzzi B. 1997. Social structure and competition in interfirm networks: the paradox of embeddedness. *Administrative Science Quarterly* **42**: 35–67.

Wayne SJ, Liden RC. 1995. Effects of impression management on performance ratings: a longitudinal study. *Academy of Management Journal* **38**: 232–260.

Williamson OE. 1975. *Markets and Hierarchies: Analysis and Antitrust Implications: A Study in the Economics of Internal Organization*. Free Press: New York.

Zaheer S. 1995. Overcoming the liability of foreignness. *Academy of Management Journal* **38**: 341–364.

[30]

Strategic Management Journal
Strat. Mgmt. J., **26**: 1109–1128 (2005)
Published online in Wiley InterScience (www.interscience.wiley.com). DOI: 10.1002/smj.497

MNE COMPETENCE-CREATING SUBSIDIARY MANDATES

JOHN CANTWELL[1] and RAM MUDAMBI[2]*
[1] *Rutgers Business School-Newark and New Brunswick, Rutgers University, Newark, New Jersey, U.S.A.*
[2] *Fox School of Business and Management, Temple University, Philadelphia, Pennsylvania, U.S.A.*

The determinants of R&D intensity differ between subsidiaries in a multinational enterprise (MNE). Previous literature suggests that whether a subsidiary achieves a competence-creating output mandate depends on the qualities of its location. R&D strategies in competence-creating subsidiaries are supply-driven while those in purely competence-exploiting subsidiaries are demand-driven. Using data on U.K. subsidiaries of non-U.K. MNEs, we find that the level of subsidiary R&D depends on MNE group-level and subsidiary-level characteristics as well as locational factors. The R&D of mandated subsidiaries rises with acquisition, but for non-mandated subsidiaries R&D falls upon acquisition. MNEs that grow through acquisition have more inter-subsidiary R&D diversity. Copyright © 2005 John Wiley & Sons, Ltd.

Historically, multinational enterprises (MNEs) located R&D in their subsidiaries abroad mainly for the purposes of the adaptation of products developed in their home countries to local tastes or customer needs, and the adaptation of processes to local resource availabilities and production conditions. Subsidiaries depended on the competence of their parent companies, and so their role was essentially just competence exploiting, or in the terminology of Kuemmerle (1999) their local R&D was 'home-base exploiting.' In recent years instead, linked to the closer integration of subsidiaries into international networks within the MNE, some subsidiary R&D has gained a more creative role, to generate new technology in accordance with the comparative advantage in innovation of the country in which the subsidiary is located (Cantwell, 1989, 1995; Papanastassiou and Pearce, 1997; Cantwell and Janne, 1999; Pearce, 1999; Zander, 1999a). This transformation has led to an increase in the level of R&D undertaken in at least those subsidiaries that have acquired this kind of competence-creating mandate, and in these subsidiaries there has been a change in the motives for and thus in the drivers of local R&D.

The shift toward internationally integrated strategies within MNEs is partly grounded on a 'life cycle' effect within what have become mature MNEs. Longer-established MNEs have now created a sufficient international spread in their operations that they have the facility to establish an internal network of specialized subsidiaries. Selected subsidiaries in such a network may evolve a specific regional or global contribution to the MNE beyond the concerns of their own most immediate market (Birkinshaw, Hood, and Jonsson, 1998; Cantwell and Piscitello, 1999). Thus, subsidiaries that began as local market-oriented (import-substituting) units are gradually transformed into more export-oriented and internationally

Keywords: MNEs; competence; R&D; subsidiary entrepreneurship; mandates; acquisition
*Correspondence to: Ram Mudambi, Department of General and Strategic Management, Fox School of Business and Management, Temple University, Speakman Hall (006-00), Philadelphia, PA 19122, U.S.A. E-mail: ram.mudambi@temple.edu

Received 30 July 2001
Final revision received 23 May 2005

1110   *J. Cantwell and R. Mudambi*

integrated operations. While some of the sub-sidiaries within such a network may have essentially just a competence-exploiting or an 'assembly' role, others take on a more technologically creative function and the level and complexity of their R&D rise accordingly (Cantwell, 1987). The distinction between purely competence-exploiting and competence-creating activities is analogous to the distinction between exploitation and exploration in organizational learning theory (March, 1991; Danneels, 2002). Competitively stronger MNEs are more likely to locate R&D abroad, and to evolve toward a greater variance in the levels of R&D across their subsidiaries, with R&D becoming concentrated in sites where local conditions are most conducive to technology creation (Cantwell and Kosmopoulou, 2002).

While March (1991) focused upon the role of diversity across individuals within an organization as a means of facilitating exploration, the same principle applies with respect to the emergence of a greater diversity across subsidiary units within the organization of the MNE. The evolution of some subsidiaries towards a competence-creating role within the MNE implies a greater degree of organizational diversity at a corporate group level. This might be understood as a desirable adjustment by MNEs since it has the effect of promoting a better balance between exploitation and exploration in learning in the organization as a whole. In other words the benefits come not just from the direct contribution to their MNE group of competence-creating subsidiaries considered individually, but also because the organization as a whole gains in its collective capacity for exploration (with long-run performance advantages) owing to the greater degree of cross-subsidiary diversity and experimentation. Of course, the benefits from increased exploration in the learning of MNEs are subject to the costs of managing a more complex international network.

In this paper our central research question is how the Marchian distinction between exploration and exploitation in organizational learning (in our case, within the MNE) affects the level of R&D in each type of subsidiary (those that are competence-creating, vs. those that are purely competence-exploiting). This dichotomy of subsidiary types is not new, and is closely related to earlier such subsidiary typologies. Table 1 summarizes the relationship of our distinction between competence-creating and competence-exploiting subsidiaries with the other related typologies that can be found in the international corporate strategy literature. However, most of these previous conceptual schemes have focused on the location as the source of differentiation between subsidiaries, that is, on the potential for innovation in each subsidiary's own external environment. Thus the first contribution of our paper is to allow (in the R&D context) for the fact that subsidiary evolution may to some extent gain a logic of its own, such that managerial initiative and discretion affect how well a subsidiary takes advantage of its location.

Most of the earlier discussions focused upon the emergence of more complex organizational strategies required in more internationally integrated MNEs at a group level (Doz, 1986; Hedlund, 1986; Porter, 1986; Bartlett and Ghoshal, 1989), or the growing significance of asset-seeking motives at an MNE group level, as opposed to the better-established market-seeking and resource-seeking

Table 1. Alternative views of the competence-creating vs. competence-exploiting subsidiary mandate decision in the contemporary international business literature

Competence-creating subsidiary mandate	Competence-exploiting subsidiary mandate
Research-related production (Cantwell 1987)	Assembly-type production
Strategic asset-seeking investment (Dunning 1995, 1996)	Market-servicing investment
Element of internationally integrated MNE innovation network (Porter 1986, Doz 1986, Bartlett and Ghoshal 1989, Cantwell 1994)	Either element of multi-domestic strategy or non-innovating part of an internationally integrated network
Home-base augmenting investment (Kuemmerle 1999)	Home-base exploiting investment
Higher-order contributor to organizational heterarchy (Hedlund 1986)	Lower-order contributor to organizational hierarchy
Center of excellence subsidiary mandate (Birkinshaw,1998; Holm and Pedersen, 2000; Simões and Nevado, 2000; Frost, Birkinshaw, and Ensign, 2002)	Location in a site that is not a major center of excellence or a key hub

activities (Dunning, 1995, 1996). Against this backdrop, Pearce (1999) and Kuemmerle (1999) developed a typology for subsidiary-level R&D in which the drivers of R&D diverge between subsidiary types, but the role of each subsidiary is governed essentially by the characteristics of the location in which it is sited. Internationally integrated strategies at the MNE group level led to a search of locations for their supply-side (innovative and skill-related) potential, in addition to their conventional demand-side potential (as markets). Hence, R&D strategies in competence-creating subsidiaries are supply-driven, while those in purely competence-exploiting subsidiaries are demand-driven.

A more recent strand of literature has instead begun to examine strategy at the level of the subsidiary rather than the level of the corporate group as a whole. It has emphasized the analysis of subsidiary-level organizational strategies when subsidiaries are based in, and can themselves become for their corporate group, foreign centers of excellence (Birkinshaw, 1998; Taggart, 1998; Andersson and Forsgren, 2000; Ensign, Birkinshaw, and Frost, 2000; Holm and Pedersen, 2000; Simões and Nevado, 2000; Frost, Birkinshaw, and Ensign 2002). So following in the spirit of this newer literature, we allow here that the drivers of subsidiary R&D depend on subsidiary-level determinants as well as MNE group-level and location-specific influences.

The second contribution of our paper is that the earlier literature has examined the qualitative difference in the types of R&D conducted in different types of subsidiary (Pearce, 1999; Kuemmerle, 1999), while here we assess the implications of these differences for the quantitative level of subsidiary R&D. Building on the insights of March (1991), the knowledge generation associated with R&D is a bi-dimensional and not a uni-dimensional process. R&D may be high (or low) in both competence-creating and competence-exploiting subsidiaries, but for different reasons. Exploration activities tend to be costly, while exploitation activities are less expensive but tend to require a more extensive and continuous succession of development efforts.

The third contribution of this paper is that the previous literature on subsidiary R&D typology has implicitly focused on internal MNE growth and restructuring in response to external environmental stimuli (at the level of subsidiary locations, as

mentioned already). Here, instead, we also pay attention to the effect of the acquisition strategies of MNEs on the divergence in the quantitative determinants of R&D in each type of subsidiary. Thus, it matters not only whether a subsidiary has evolved toward a competence-creating status or remains purely competence-exploiting, but also whether that subsidiary has been acquired by its current MNE group. This is a vital issue, since survey evidence has often suggested that most foreign-located R&D in MNEs is the result of acquisitions.

In this paper we follow in the tradition of supposing that some subsidiaries evolve toward the attainment of a competence-creating mandate (while others do not), to examine empirically the factors that determine the likelihood of subsidiaries acquiring a competence-creating mandate. This competence-creating mandate is defined by the output responsibilities of the subsidiary, and so the mandate is measured independently of the R&D function. We then check whether the level of R&D tends to be higher on average in competence-creating subsidiaries, as might be anticipated, although we can also expect that the range of R&D levels found in each type of subsidiary will overlap extensively. Beyond this, and more substantively, we examine whether the two types of subsidiary have some common underlying process of determination of their R&D level, or whether instead their R&D levels are governed by two distinct processes. In the latter case, in particular, we are especially interested in any effects that run in directly opposite directions in the R&D process in the two kinds of subsidiaries.

THEORETICAL FRAMEWORK

The subsidiary mandates that we observe are the outcome of a process of subsidiary evolution. While this process is not the direct concern of this paper, linking our model to the prior evolutionary process is helpful, since the factors that influence this process are also those that regulate both the subsidiary mandate and the subsequent R&D behavior of each type of subsidiary. A useful organizing framework for subsidiary evolution is provided by Birkinshaw and Hood (1998), who identify local environmental factors, subsidiary choice, and headquarters assignment as the three key drivers of the subsidiary's role (formally defined

1112   *J. Cantwell and R. Mudambi*

by its charter or mandate), with dynamic feedback effects. Within this dynamic framework, subsidiaries can both advance and decline in terms of their roles within the firm. In a similar vein, Frost *et al.* (2002) propose that the three sets of influences on the ability of a subsidiary to develop a center of excellence for its group are the dynamism of the location, subsidiary-level autonomy and the degree of integration of competence-creating activities between the subsidiary and other parts of its group, and the extent of support from the parent company.

Subsidiaries with competence-creating mandates can arise either through parent-driven or subsidiary-driven processes (Birkinshaw and Hood, 1998). However, in each case the acquisition of a competence-creating mandate requires a gradual subsidiary-specific evolution. A subsidiary's capacity to evolve to the point at which a competence-creating mandate becomes viable depends upon the ability of its own managers to develop and exercise a 'voice' in the wider corporate group. Beyond the earliest stages of subsidiary evolution continued development requires some combination of local initiative and head office support. Thus, parent-driven investment strategies respond to subsidiary lobbying, while subsidiary-driven charter extension relies on a subsidiary-level champion gaining support at head office (Birkinshaw and Hood, 1998).

In turn, the ability of a subsidiary's managers to attain an effective voice within their corporate group depends upon the three sets of factors just mentioned. Namely, (i) the characteristics and development potential of the location in which the subsidiary is sited; (ii) the internal state of subsidiary-level capabilities and the scope for undertaking independent initiatives; and (iii) the

strategic practices and origins of the parent group with respect to their potential to encourage network formation across parts of the group and at a local level with external partners.

R&D will tend to be higher in subsidiaries that acquire competence-creating mandates as opposed to those that do not, and the award of such a mandate is more likely when the subsidiary is located in a regional center of technological excellence, when it has built up a higher degree of subsidiary-level capabilities for independent initiatives, and when the parent group encourages network formation. However, our central argument here is not merely that more R&D is now likely to gravitate to subsidiaries with a competence-creating mandate once the MNE's objective is to establish an internationally integrated network for innovation, in place of an independent collection of multi-domestic operations with diffused adaptation. Rather, we contend that this new kind of R&D undertaken in competence-creating subsidiaries will be differently motivated than the locally adaptive kind of R&D that still predominates in purely competence-exploiting subsidiaries, and so it is qualitatively distinct in its determinants. Our empirical approach aims to examine the nature of this qualitative difference in motivations in terms of the factors that influence investments in subsidiary-level R&D.

The framework of the relationships we are proposing is summarized in Table 2. In a suitably favorable combination of locational, subsidiary-level and MNE group-level conditions, subsidiaries will evolve to acquire competence-creating mandates (stage 1), and their local R&D will come to be driven mainly by the requirements of technological creativity (stage 2). A qualification here is that when subsidiaries are acquired, from the

Table 2.   The evolution of subsidiary mandates, and the varying determinants of localized R&D

		Process of subsidiary evolution		
		Stage 0	Stage 1	Stage 2
Locational, subsidiary-level and MNE group-level conditions	Highly favorable	Competence-exploiting mandate	Competence-creating mandate	Local R&D driven mainly by needs of technological creativity
	Less favorable	Competence-exploiting mandate	Competence-exploiting mandate	Local R&D continues to be driven mainly by needs of technological adaptation

Time →

perspective of the acquiring group they may even begin with competence-creating mandates (stage 0)—we address this issue in our discussion of MNE group-level determinants below. Conversely, in less favorable conditions subsidiaries retain purely competence-exploiting mandates (stage 1), and their local R&D continues to be driven mainly by the needs of technological adaptation (stage 2).

HYPOTHESIS DEVELOPMENT

Locational determinants

The first influence on the likelihood of a subsidiary gaining a competence-creating mandate is the characteristics of the location in which it is situated. In a region with a good local infrastructure, a science base and a more skilled workforce, subsidiaries are likelier to acquire competence-creating mandates on behalf of their corporate group, and, once they have such a mandate, to use it to be able to attract more of the mobile R&D facilities of their MNE (Cantwell and Iammarino, 2000; Cantwell and Piscitello, 2002). Owing to the complexity of technological learning, and the significance of maintaining face-to-face contacts, the accessing of technological resources tends to occur at a regional level within host countries (Jaffe, Trajtenberg, and Henderson, 1993; Almeida, 1996; Cantwell and Iammarino, 1998). Thus, subsidiaries with competence-creating mandates tap into the munificence of their specific location (Pearce, 1999; Andersson and Forsgren, 2000; Ensign *et al.*, 2000; Håkanson and Nobel, 2000). Hence, we expect that better-quality locations will see a higher R&D intensity in mandated subsidiaries. Non-mandated subsidiaries, on the other hand, are simply trying to adapt products to local markets and resource conditions. We expect the supply side quality of the location to have no effect on the R&D intensity of such subsidiaries.

In the United Kingdom, government investment incentive programs provide an inverse measure of overall locational quality, since they are made available to firms locating in areas with a combination of low labor skills and high unemployment, poor infrastructure, and many other drawbacks (Mudambi, 1998). These government incentives are provided under Regional Selective Assistance (RSA) in areas known as Assisted Areas (either

Development Areas or Intermediate Areas), and these incentives include capital subsidies, loans, tax allowances, training support, and R&D support. There is evidence that even lucrative investment incentives are insufficient to attract high-quality R&D investment by MNEs (Cantwell and Mudambi, 2000). Thus, locations designated as Assisted Areas have poorer qualities, while all other areas ineligible for such incentives enjoy higher locational qualities.

Hypothesis 1a: Location in an area covered by government investment incentives lowers the probability of a subsidiary achieving a competence-creating mandate.

Hypothesis 1b: Location in an area covered by government investment incentives lowers the R&D intensity of subsidiaries with competence-creating mandates, but has no effect on the R&D intensity of subsidiaries without competence-creating mandates.

Some locations offer high levels of local demand. The primary function of subsidiaries without competence-creating mandates is to serve the local market. Their role is predominantly demand-driven. Hence, the higher the level of local sales (demand) in a location, the more the incentive to undertake process improvements, as well as to differentiate output to bolster margins. Both these activities lead to increased R&D intensity in the adaptation of the firm's output to local conditions. However, the primary function of subsidiaries with competence-creating mandates is to tap into the local knowledge and resource base to augment the MNE group's overall strengths. This role is predominantly locally supply-driven. For such subsidiaries, higher or lower output (demand) in their location should not affect R&D intensity.

Hypothesis 2: Higher local output (demand) leads to a higher R&D intensity in subsidiaries without competence-creating mandates. The level of local demand does not affect the R&D intensity of subsidiaries with competence-creating mandates.

Some locations tend to experience more systematic fluctuations in demand, and so present a greater demand-side financial risk to the MNE. Reasoning as above suggests that substantial fluctuations

1114   *J. Cantwell and R. Mudambi*

in demand in a location (associated with higher variance in a subsidiary's rate of return) should reduce the commitment to undertake R&D activities in demand-driven subsidiaries with purely competence-exploiting mandates. However, such uncertainties over the state of local demand should have much less effect on the R&D activities of subsidiaries with competence-creating mandates, given again their supply-driven orientation.

> *Hypothesis 3: Greater variability in local demand leads to a lower R&D intensity in subsidiaries without competence-creating mandates. Such variability does not affect the R&D-intensity of subsidiaries with competence-creating mandates.*

Subsidiary-level determinants

Apart from the locational environment in which it operates, a recent subsidiary-level literature has suggested that the greater the extent of subsidiary autonomy, the better the ability of the subsidiary to form favorable external network linkages with other companies and institutions in its own local environment (Birkinshaw *et al.*, 1998; Andersson and Forsgren, 2000). In its turn, the greater the local embeddedness of the subsidiary, the higher the likelihood that it will acquire a competence-creating mandate. It has been shown that, compared to adaptive subsidiary R&D facilities, the creative subsidiary R&D establishments have adequate independence to have developed stronger external and internal network relationships that foster innovation (Nobel and Birkinshaw, 1998).

We should qualify this argument by noting that it is not strategic independence per se that is important, but the manner in which strategic independence is used by the subsidiary in the context of competence-creating mandates. If strategic independence becomes a substitute rather than a complement for close communication with the rest of the MNE, the subsidiary can drop 'out of the loop' and weaken its intra-firm position. Thus, although it is possible that at any point in time there may be subsidiaries that use their independence in pursuit of objectives that are tangential to those of the rest of the group (e.g., Mudambi and Navarra, 2004), such subsidiaries tend to lose influence within their group, and taken to the limit this may lead to the erosion of their independence (and their ability

to acquire and then retain a competence-creating mandate). Thus it is reasonable to suppose that *most* strategically independent subsidiaries cooperate with other MNE units, and so utilize strategic independence as a means of leveraging local assets and embeddedness to enhance the competitive advantages of their MNE group as a whole (Andersson, Forsgren, and Holm, 2002).

Once a subsidiary has a competence-creating mandate, it is probable that strategic independence will cumulatively reinforce the mandate. Strategic independence provides such a subsidiary an increased ability to build its local competence, and tends to increase its creative contribution to the MNE (Birkinshaw *et al.*, 1998). Thus, strategic independence leads to a higher level of R&D intensity. However, strategic independence in a subsidiary without a competence-creating mandate is unlikely to lead it to increase its R&D intensity, since its objectives are generally to exploit the existing competencies of the MNE. Increasing strategic independence may lead it instead to increase the level of other functions like local marketing.

> *Hypothesis 4a: A higher degree of subsidiary strategic independence increases the likelihood that the subsidiary achieves a competence-creating mandate.*

> *Hypothesis 4b: An increasing degree of strategic independence increases the R&D intensity of subsidiaries with competence-creating mandates. Increasing strategic independence does not affect the R&D intensity of subsidiaries without competence-creating mandates.*

MNE group-level determinants

The most notable group-level determinants of differences in R&D behavior in competence-creating as opposed to competence-exploiting subsidiaries may be with respect to the effect on local R&D intensity of whether a subsidiary was part of an acquired group. A number of studies have shown that a substantial proportion of internationalized R&D facilities in MNEs result from acquisition (e.g., Håkanson, 1981, 1995). When one group acquires another that has R&D facilities, some of the newly acquired facilities will tend to duplicate what is already done elsewhere in the acquiring group. In this case, duplication may well be eliminated in the post-acquisition integration process, and subsidiaries that were part of the acquired group are likelier to suffer the brunt of any cutbacks.

Acquired subsidiaries that are conducting only standard competence-exploiting R&D tasks that are replicated in the acquiring group are in a more vulnerable position in this respect. The ability of subsidiary managers to exercise a voice within their new head office will tend to be weaker than those in established subsidiaries whose ties and identification with the parent group go back longer. The managers that were part of an acquired group tend to be associated with a different corporate culture (Sambharya, 1996). Thus, R&D intensity is likely to fall as duplication in the merged group is eliminated following the acquisition. Since there are still many more purely competence-exploiting subsidiaries than there are competence-creating, this is consistent with the finding of Hitt *et al.* (1991) that on average acquisitions tend to reduce R&D intensity within the firm.

Conversely, acquired subsidiaries that have competence-creating mandates are likelier to make some novel contribution from the standpoint of the acquiring group. Local managers in this type of acquired subsidiary are in a more attractive position, and if the subsidiary is engaged in distinct competence-creating R&D tasks that are not found anywhere else in the acquiring group they are more likely to have the authority to exercise influence in their new head office. Therefore in this case they are likelier to be able to retain the resources needed to increase local R&D intensity.

At the level of the individual MNE group, the motivation for acquisition will influence which of these outcomes matters more. If the motives are mainly financial, or if they relate to other parts of the acquired business than to those subsidiaries that bring with them local R&D facilities, the elimination of R&D duplication in competence-exploiting subsidiaries is likely to be the dominant effect. However, when one of the motives for acquisition is the asset-seeking objective of incorporating the complementary R&D facilities of competence-creating subsidiaries, their competence-creating efforts are likely to be reinforced (Zander, 1999b; Simões and Nevado, 2000).

Hypothesis 5: Being part of an acquired group reduces R&D intensity for subsidiaries without competence-creating mandates, but increases it for subsidiaries with competence-creating mandates.

A further MNE group-level influence on the R&D of subsidiaries with competence-creating mandates, as opposed to those without, is the degree of product or business diversification required of the subsidiary. Hitt, Hoskisson, and Kim (1997) found that, although in general the degree of internationalization of the firm has a positive effect on R&D intensity, the interaction effects of internationalization with product diversification are negative. When they have competence-creating mandates, subsidiaries that are engaged in diversification away from the main lines of business activity of their MNE find themselves more tightly resource-constrained in the sense of Penrose (1959), which will tend to lower the extent of their local R&D. Subsidiaries with competence-creating mandates are all heavily committed to their creative tasks. Those that have to contend with a new line of business (LOB) must expend resources on other new functions associated with developing it and have fewer resources available for the R&D function. What is more, in running a new LOB it becomes more difficult for them to integrate their competence creation with the wider group of which they are part, so they are likelier to become isolated and to be seen as strategically marginal, and they get correspondingly less investment. In contrast, subsidiaries without competence-creating mandates have less responsibility and fewer binding resource constraints, and they may need more R&D for the purposes of new product adaptation of a kind that by definition is not carried out elsewhere in their group. For such subsidiaries, the impact of entering a new LOB is likely to have a smaller effect on R&D intensity.

Hypothesis 6: Operating outside of the parent MNE's main LOB leads to lower R&D intensity for subsidiaries with competence-creating mandates. Such diversification has no effect on the R&D intensity of subsidiaries without competence-creating mandates.

In addition, the proportion of subsidiaries that are able to earn a competence-creating mandate in any

MNE is regulated by the priority accorded to the technology sourcing motive in the group's international investment strategy. This will depend on the nationality of ownership of the group, since groups originating from countries whose outward investment is mainly of more recent vintage (like Japan, as opposed to the United States) are likelier to assign a higher priority to technology sourcing in their investment strategies. This is partly because they are generally trying to draw on their international operations to help them to catch up with more mature MNEs from countries of origin of longer standing, and partly because, while long-established MNEs have evolved towards cross-border networks, newer MNEs may attempt to put in place networked structures from the outset. Distinguishing U.S.-owned and Japanese-owned subsidiaries in the United Kingdom from those that were European-owned is also useful when considering further the effects on R&D among subsidiaries that have acquired a competence-creating mandate. Subsidiaries that acquire a competence-creating mandate may be likelier to attract more R&D resources if the group of which they are part does not have its competence-creating headquarters located close by in another European country.

Other controls

Besides the above factors, we introduce a number of other control variables. Although the sample is restricted to a single industry (engineering and engineering-related activities) to make the R&D activities comparable across firms, we nonetheless control for intra-industry variation by introducing sub-industry dummies. We expect the quantitative level of R&D intensity to be sensitive to a number of other factors. In addition to the above, we control for differences in relative parent–subsidiary risk by introducing a relative home country/host country risk measure. Differences in R&D intensity can stem from differences in subsidiary performance relative to other subsidiaries. We attempt to capture this by introducing the difference between the subsidiary's rate of return and the overall rate of return of the parent. Further, there may be duration effects over and above those captured in the strategic independence measure. We capture these by introducing the duration of the subsidiary's operations in the host country. Finally, the extent to which the subsidiary is externally focused, e.g., focused on exports from

the host country, may influence its R&D intensity. We control for this effect by introducing a measure of external focus.

METHODOLOGY AND DATA

The estimating procedure

Once a firm determines whether to locate technologically advanced (competence-creating) or assembly-based (competence-exploiting) production at a site, it must then decide the extent of R&D activity it will undertake at the host location. Our empirical measurement of whether or not a subsidiary has achieved a competence-creating mandate is closest to the output-based distinction of Cantwell (1987) in the typologies of Table 1. This is because we distinguished on a 5-point scale subsidiaries that reported the functional scope of their output mandate as being limited to sales and service, assembly, or manufacturing (a lack of any local competence-creating mandate) from those whose scope included either product development or international market development (the presence of a competence-creating mandate). The strategy choice presented here is that of a firm that has already decided on an internationally integrated strategy of competence development through technologically advanced production in selected foreign locations, and is next considering how wide a range of subsidiaries across which this function is to be implemented, and in which particular subsidiaries.

We set up this initial stage as a binary process under which the local subsidiary (with the support of the parent MNE) either achieves a competence-creating mandate (*subsidiary mandate* = 1) or not (*subsidiary mandate* = 0). If it does, the subsidiary's development function in production will be of a higher grade, which necessitates a more exploratory type of local R&D facility. The decision regarding the level and kind of R&D to site locally is therefore conditioned on whether or not a competence-creating mandate has been achieved by the subsidiary. This conditional approach is fairly standard in the modal choice literature on FDI (Czinkota, Ronkainen, and Moffett, 1996; Devereux and Griffith, 1998; Grant, 1995; Mudambi and Ricketts, 1998).

The level of R&D expenditure (and hence the R&D/sales ratio) is also determined by locational, subsidiary-level, and MNE group-level character- istics, with the binary *subsidiary mandate* vari- able providing an additive difference. Certain vari- ables affecting the *strategic* outcome regarding the competence-creating mandate also affect the *operational* choice of level of R&D spending (see Hypotheses 1 and 4 above). Thus, some variables affect both the quality as well as the quantity of R&D undertaken by the subsidiary. We esti- mate the *subsidiary mandate* and its *R&D intensity* as simultaneously determined variables (see the Appendix for more details).

Data

R&D is a very industry-specific activity. The dif- ferences in strategies and R&D intensities between firms are highly industry-specific. These industry effects might wipe out any more subtle strategic choice effects in a diverse dataset. With this in mind, we restrict our focus to a single industry group, so that the strategies and expenditures are generally comparable. We focus on firms in engi- neering and engineering-related industries.

The current study uses three levels of data: industry-level data, location-specific data and sub- sidiary-level data. Industry-level data are used mainly for classification purposes and were drawn from Dun & Bradstreet indexes (Dun & Bradstreet, 1994, 1995). The engineering and engineering- related industry group roughly corresponds to sub- sections 24(1 & 2), 26–32 and 34–35 under the 1992 U.K. Standard Industrial Classification code (Office of National Statistics, 1992). Location- specific data relate to the classification of the local area in terms of Regional Selective Assis- tance (RSA) program and are based on the relevant Department of Trade and Industry (DTI) assisted areas map (August, 1993). Data comparing loca- tion risk characteristics of the host country (the United Kingdom) with those in the companies' home countries were drawn from the financial mar- kets publication *Euromoney*. The subsidiary-level data were derived from a large 1995 postal sur- vey of foreign-owned firms in the United King- dom, supported by telephone and field interviews. Table 3 includes definitions all the variables used in the estimation, along with the source of the data. Descriptive statistics related to all these variables are presented in Table 4(a).

The target population for this survey was con- structed from Dun & Bradstreet indexes (Dun

& Bradstreet, 1994, 1995), supplemented by the London Business School company annual report library. The target population yielded a preliminary list of 601 subsidiaries with personal contact names. Subsidiaries for which separate data for the parent firm were unavailable were deleted. The final usable population consisted of 568 sub- sidiaries. The survey was mailed out in two waves of 224 and 344 in March and April 1995.

The first (pilot) wave focused on entries into the Midlands region (the most successful region in the United Kingdom in terms of attracting FDI), while the second wave targeted entries into the rest of the country. In order to improve the response rate, the questionnaire had to be short, concise, and of current interest or salient to the respondent (Heberlein and Baumgartner, 1978). Two reminders were faxed to the companies that had not yet responded 10 and 21 days after the survey was mailed out.

Overall, 244 responses were received to the mail survey (42.96%). Of these, seven were found to be U.K.-owned firms mistakenly identified as non-U.K.-owned firms, and 12 were unusable for various other reasons, leaving 225 (39.61%) valid responses for evaluation. The response rate is well within the range expected for an unsolicited mail survey.

Non-response bias was investigated with the widely used method suggested by Armstrong and Overton (1977). This involved comparing early and late respondents. Two sets of late respon- dents were defined corresponding to those who responded after receiving the first reminder and those who responded after receiving the second faxed reminder (the first set includes the second). Each set of late respondents was compared to the early respondents on the basis of six sample mea- sures. The comparisons were carried out using a χ^2 test of independence. In both cases, the responses from early and late respondents were virtually identical.

Survey responses were tested for veracity by comparing postal responses to responses obtained from field interviews. A total of 28 field inter- views were carried out. Using a χ^2 test of inde- pendence, responses from field interviews were found to be virtually identical to those obtained from the postal survey on the basis of four sample measures. Finally, 20 respondents were randomly selected and interviewed by telephone to confirm their survey responses.

Table 3. Variable definitions

Variable	Definition	Source
Dependent variables		
Subsidiary mandate	1, the U.K. subsidiary has achieved a competence-creating mandate[a] 0, otherwise	Survey, supplemented by company annual reports
R&D intensity	U.K. subsidiary's R&D/sales ratio, 1994	Survey, supplemented by company annual reports
Locational determinants of R&D		
RSA-1	1, if U.K. subsidiary is in a Development Area under the Regional Selective Assistance (RSA) Program[b] 0, otherwise	Department of Trade and Industry (DTI)
RSA-2	1, if the U.K. subsidiary is in an Intermediate Area under the Regional Selective Assistance (RSA) Program[b] 0, otherwise	Department of Trade and Industry (DTI)
Sales	U.K. subsidiary sales, 1994 (£million)	Survey, supplemented by company annual reports
Variability of demand	Variance of U.K. subsidiary's rate of return on capital, 1986–94	Survey, supplemented by company annual reports
Subsidiary-level determinants of R&D		
Subsidiary strategic independence: First principal component factor score generated from the variables below. The following variables load on this factor: *supplier decisions, hiring decisions, marketing decisions,* and *top management team*		
Supplier decisions	Extent to which decisions on suppliers are made in the U.K. (7-point Likert scale)	Survey
Hiring decisions	Extent to which U.K. subsidiary has responsibility for hiring management staff (7-point Likert scale)	Survey
Marketing decisions	Extent of responsibilities in the international marketing function (7-point Likert scale)	Survey
Top management team	Percentage of U.K. subsidiary top management (directors and above) from host country (U.K.)	Survey, supplemented by company annual reports
Export share	Exports as a percentage of U.K. subsidiary output	Survey, supplemented by company annual reports
Export duration	Years of exporting as a percentage of total duration of U.K. operations	Survey, supplemented by company annual reports
Geographic scope	Geographical scope of U.K. subsidiary's output mandate: (1) U.K. only; (2) U.K. and mainland Europe; (3) worldwide	Survey, supplemented by company annual reports
Process decisions	U.K. subsidiary's process engineering operational responsibilities (7-point Likert scale)	Survey
Training decisions	Extent to which U.K. subsidiary has responsibility for training in process engineering (7-point Likert scale)	Survey

MNE group-level determinants of R&D		
Acquired	1, if U.K. operations are the result of an acquisition	Survey, supplemented by DTI data
	0, otherwise	
Diversified	0, if operations in the U.K. are in parent's main line of business[c]	Survey, supplemented by company annual reports and DTI data
	1, otherwise	
U.S. parent	1, if parent firm HQ is in the U.S.	Survey, supplemented by company annual reports
	0, otherwise	
Japanese parent	1, if parent firm HQ is in Japan	Survey, supplemented by company annual reports
	0, otherwise	
Control variables		
External focus: Second principal component factor score generated from the subsidiary specific variables above. The following variables load on this factor: *export share, export duration,* and *geographic scope*		
Abnormal ROR	U.K. subsidiary's rate of return (ROR) on capital less parent firm's corporate ROR on capital, 1994	Survey, supplemented by company annual reports
Duration	Duration of U.K. subsidiary operations (years)	Survey, supplemented by company annual reports
Electrical Group	1, if U.K. subsidiary is in an electrical engineering and related industry	*Business Register*
	0, otherwise	
Mechanical Group	1, if U.K. subsidiary is in a mechanical engineering and related industry	*Business Register*
	0, otherwise	
Chemical Group	1, if U.K. subsidiary is in a chemical engineering and related industry	*Business Register*
	0, otherwise	
Location risk	Relative country risk, home country/host country (U.K.); average, 1993–94	*Euromoney*[d]

[a] *Subsidiary mandate* is generated on the basis of the functional scope of the U.K. subsidiary's output mandate. Output mandates were categorized as: (1) Sales and service; (2) Assembly; (3) Manufacturing; (4) Product development; (5) International strategy development. A competence-creating mandate is operationalized as a subsidiary whose output mandate is either (4) or (5).

[b] Department of Trade and Industry (DTI) Assisted Areas map (revised, August 1993).

[c] The parent firm's main line of business is defined to be its largest non-U.K. sales segments whose cumulative contribution to the entropy index of diversification just exceeds 60%. This definition is based on Hitt *et al*(1997).

[d] *Euromoney* risk index, which includes economic performance, political risk, debt indicators, debt default, credit ratings, access to bank, short-term and capital market finance, and the discount on forfaiting.

1120   *J. Cantwell and R. Mudambi*

Table 4(a).   Summary statistics

Variable	Mean	S.D.
Dependent variables		
Subsidiary mandate	0.2444	0.4307
R&D intensity	4.1822	2.7963
Locational determinants of R&D		
RSA-1	0.4089	0.4927
RSA-2	0.1200	0.3257
Sales	374.6445	327.7262
Variability of demand	3.6927	5.1599
Subsidiary-level determinants of R&D		
Strategic independence	0.0063	1.0403
MNE group-level determinants of R&D		
Acquired	0.6311	0.4836
Diversified	0.2089	0.4074
U.S. parent	0.2044	0.4042
Japanese parent	0.0711	0.2576
Control variables		
External focus	0.0280	0.9980
Abnormal ROR	−0.6821	3.9101
Duration	9.8889	5.5050
Electrical group	0.4267	0.4957
Mechanical group	0.4089	0.4709
Chemical group	0.1644	0.4307
Location risk	1.4808	1.0830

ESTIMATION AND RESULTS

Estimating R&D strategy and intensity

The simplest approach to comparing R&D intensity between competence-creating and competence-exploiting subsidiaries is presented using summary statistics in Table 4(b). The average level of *R&D intensity* is considerably higher for units with the *subsidiary mandate* = 1. The pattern of use of the competencies of the mandated subsidiaries appears here as well, with much higher levels of citations of their patents by other units within their corporate groups during the period 1995–2002. In contrast, the two types of subsidiary are much more similar in terms of the citations of their patents by other

firms in the host location (the U.K.). This serves to demonstrate that the knowledge generation strategies of competence-creating subsidiaries are more closely integrated with the needs of their MNE group, and suggests that their R&D may indeed be not just higher on average, but also differently motivated.

As discussed above, the subsidiary competence-creating mandate is specified to be endogenous to the firm (including the subsidiary). We assume that the decision process is sequential, so that the competence-creating strategy is selected first, and the level of R&D-intensity is selected conditional on the mandating decision. With this assumption, R&D intensity may be estimated using a single-equation (or limited information) approach. We estimate it using two alternative econometric models: a conventional instrumental variables (IV) model and a selection model using the Heckman procedure. Both models allow us to endogenize the *subsidiary mandate* choice variable.

The strategic decision model involved in granting a competence-creating mandate is estimated using binomial probit. Maximum likelihood estimates of this equation are reported in Table 5. Examining the estimates in Table 5, we find that the fit of the probit estimates to the data is very good, as measured by the likelihood ratio test. Location in a Development Area under the Regional Selective Assistance program (RSA-1) appears to exert a negative influence on the chance of achieving a competence-creating mandate. It would appear that the negative labor and infrastructural factors associated with a Development Area greatly reduce its probability of serving as a research-related hub for an MNE. Thus, we find evidence supporting Hypothesis 1a.

The subsidiary's strategic independence also appears to significantly increase the probability of gaining a competence-creating mandate. Thus,

Table 4(b).   R&D measures for subsidiaries with *subsidiary mandate* = 0 and *subsidiary mandate* = 1

	Subsidiary mandate = 0		Subsidiary mandate = 1	
	Mean	S.D.	Mean	S.D.
R&D intensity (%)	2.9118	2.5490	5.0182	2.9334
Forward citations by other patents assigned within the parent MNE group: 1995–2002[a]	1.6765	2.2735	3.0727	7.1666
Forward citations by other patents assigned within the host location (U.K.): 1995–2002[a]	2.4118	4.7768	2.8909	4.9488

[a] Source: U.S. Patent and Trademark Office.

Table 5. Estimating the probability of a subsidiary competence-creating mandate: maximum likelihood probit estimates
Regressand:
Binary variable: *Subsidiary mandate* $= 1$ (Subsidiary has competence-creating mandate); *Subsidiary mandate* $= 0$ (Subsidiary has no competence-creating mandate)

Regressor	Parameter estimate ('t' stat)
Constant	-0.4152 (1.49)
Locational determinants of mandate	
RSA-1	-0.5336 (2.53)*
RSA-2	-0.0780 (0.26)
Subsidiary-level determinants of mandate	
Strategic independence	0.2235 (2.39)*
MNE group-level determinants of mandate	
Acquired	0.1444 (0.65)
Diversified	-0.4666 (1.60)
U.S. parent	0.1664 (0.68)
Japanese parent	0.6988 (2.06)*
Control variables	
Electrical group	0.0007 (0.00)
Mechanical group	-0.0317 (0.12)
Diagnostics	
Log-likelihood	-114.9804
Restricted log-likelihood	-125.1335
Likelihood ratio test: $\chi^2(9)$	20.3063
p-value	0.0161
Iterations	5

t-statistics in parentheses
Estimate significant at the * 5% level; ** 1% level

the more strategically independent a subsidiary in terms of human resource management and marketing, the more likely it is to gain an independently creative research-related role as well. This evidence supports Hypothesis 4a.

Of the MNE group-level determinants, only Japanese parentage seems to increase the probability of gaining a competence-creating mandate. As outlined earlier, the home country dummy variables offer a means by which we can examine the effects on the likelihood of the emergence of competence-creating subsidiary mandates owing to the particular encouragement of the parent group. Thus, the greater observed likelihood of the acquisition of a competence-creating mandate in Japanese-owned subsidiaries may be attributable to the strategy of Japanese firms in the European Union as a whole and reflect their age as newer MNEs (than those that are U.S.-owned or

European-owned), which have accorded a higher priority to technology sourcing in their international investment strategies and attempted to put in place a networked organizational structure from the start. This is in line with our earlier expectations, and Cantwell and Mudambi (2000) report similar results.

We now turn to our estimates of subsidiary R&D intensity. Both IV and selection model estimates are reported in Table 6. The selection model enables us to explicitly estimate the selection parameter, λ. As the first stage estimates determining the probability of the strategy selection are probit estimates, the selection parameter is a hazard rate computed from the normal distribution. In the selection model, the direct effects of strategy selection (*subsidiary mandate*) are separated from the indirect effects (λ). While the IV model does not allow us to explicitly estimate the selection parameter, these linear estimates tend to be more robust than the non-linear Heckman selection estimates and serve as a useful robustness check. We will therefore focus on the results of the selection model.

When the selection model is applied to the entire sample (Table 6, column 3), the problem that arises is that the parameters of the regressors are restricted to be the same for subsidiaries that have competence-creating mandates (*subsidiary mandate* $= 1$) and those that do not (*subsidiary mandate* $= 0$). This restriction may well be questioned. Indeed, testing this restriction using a generalized 'F' test, we find that it is rejected. The way out is to estimate *R&D intensity* separately for subsidiaries that have competence-creating mandate (Table 6, column 5) and those that do not (Table 6, column 4). Greene (1993) suggests a procedure that may be used to generate such estimates and calls it the 'treatment' model. (See the Appendix for details; Shaver, 1998, makes similar use of the treatment model.)

The estimates of the treatment model are also presented in Table 6 and they provide us with the means of testing our remaining hypotheses. Locations in Development and Intermediate (*RSA-1* and *RSA-2*) areas have a very negative influence on R&D for subsidiaries that have competence-creating mandates. Local development characteristics play little role if such a mandate is lacking. This demonstrates that supply-related development characteristics are critical to the success of competence-creating subsidiaries, as their greater

1122   *J. Cantwell and R. Mudambi*

Table 6. Estimating R&D intensity: IV and selection estimates
Regressand: R&D intensity-(R&D/Sales ratio)

		Selection model		
		All subsidiaries	Treatment model	
			Subs mandate $= 0$	Subs mandate $= 1$
Regressor	IV estimates			
(1)	(2)	(3)	(4)	(5)
Constant	2.87 (2.58)**	1.70 (1.08)	1.27 (0.40)	-60.68 (1.94)@
Locational determinants of R&D				
RSA-1	0.4761 (0.63)	0.3116 (0.44)	0.6597 (0.52)	-24.58 (2.16)*
RSA-2	-0.4042 (0.56)	-0.5031 (0.97)	0.1478 (0.25)	-4.945 (2.67)*
Sales	0.114×10^{-5} (2.38)*	0.15×10^{-5} (2.71)**	0.21×10^{-5} (3.40)**	0.55×10^{-6} (0.44)
Variability of demand	-0.062 (2.04)*	-0.063 (2.02)*	-0.04 (2.99)**	-0.0607 (0.78)
Subsidiary-level determinants of R&D				
Strategic independence	0.2307 (0.79)	0.2229 (0.71)	-0.0056 (0.01)	10.066 (2.19)*
MNE group-level determinants of R&D				
Acquired	-1.63 (2.80)**	-1.50 (3.50)**	-1.53 (2.79)**	5.33 (1.79)†
Diversified	-1.50 (1.97)*	-1.54 (2.25)*	-1.589 (1.45)	-22.7 (3.28)**
U.S. parent	0.1148 (0.19)	-0.2478 (0.53)	-0.6573 (1.14)	8.4592 (2.33)*
Japanese parent	-1.1738 (1.54)	-1.7528 (1.53)	-2.5155 (1.19)	29.972 (2.12)*
Control variables				
External focus	0.1429 (0.64)	0.1018 (0.64)	0.094 (0.56)	-0.909 (1.67)†
Abnormal ROR	-0.0702 (1.19)	-0.0424 (1.08)	-0.0625 (1.44)	13.076 (1.25)
Duration	-1.0198 (1.19)	-0.10 (0.33)	-0.0696 (0.22)	-0.2583 (0.28)
Mechanical group	0.3925 (0.63)	0.2866 (0.64)	-0.1767 (0.35)	0.4333 (0.28)
Electrical group	0.4150 (0.76)	0.3361 (0.86)	0.1254 (0.29)	0.5503 (0.59)
Location risk	-0.0032 (1.06)	-0.0005 (0.31)	0.7×10^{-4} (0.05)	-0.0027 (0.32)
Subs. mandate	6.36 (3.86)**	4.464 (3.65)**	—	—
λ	—	-2.275 (2.13)*	-3.138 (0.55)	59.963 (2.12)*
Diagnostics				
Adj. R^2	0.2925	0.3397	0.4031	0.2150
Log-likelihood	-520.2024	-494.5561	-361.2707	-116.8958
Restricted log-likelihood	-550.1274		-413.5909	-133.2159
LR test: χ^2 (d.f.)	59.8500 (16)	111.1426 (17)	104.6404 (16)	32.6402 (16)
S.S.E.	2093.700	1068.790	697.962	225.927
Model stability: $F(17, 191)$; *p*-value	—		1.7621* (0.035)	
n	225		170	55

t-statistics in parentheses.
Estimate significant at the † 10% level; * 5% level; ** 1% level.

degree of research creativity requires a satisfactory educational and skill base locally, and the presence of other innovative enterprises with which to interact. This provides support for Hypothesis 1b.

It illustrates as well how Table 6 shows that the R&D behavior of subsidiaries with competence-creating mandates is not just quantitatively but also qualitatively different from that of other subsidiaries, in that the determinants of *R&D intensity* differ. Conversely, the positive influence of *Sales*, and the negative effect of *Variability of demand* for all firms considered together are seen to emanate

from subsidiaries that do not have a competence-creating mandate. They do not appear to influence *R&D intensity* for subsidiaries that have a mandate. For competence-creating subsidiaries the size or scale of local production and the variability of local demand matters less. We find support for both Hypotheses 2 and 3.

For all subsidiaries taken together, the degree of strategic independence of the subsidiary cannot be separately distinguished from the effect of the competence-creating mandate. However, once subsidiaries with or without the mandate are divided,

Strategic independence has a significant effect on R&D within the mandated group, but not for other subsidiaries. This might be thought of as a kind of cumulative effect. That is, once a subsidiary has achieved a competence-creating mandate, its capacity to fulfill that mandate will be strengthened by the extent to which the subsidiary is able to develop its own independent strategy, which will facilitate its own greater local creativity and warrant increased local R&D. Yet crucially this effect of subsidiary strategic independence is absent if the subsidiary itself is not mandated to be a constituent part of an internationally integrated network within its corporate group. Therefore the estimates provide support for Hypothesis 4b.

The negative influence of *Acquired* appears for subsidiaries that do not have a competence-creating mandate, in rather striking contrast to the positive influence of *Acquired* (which is significant at the 10% level) for subsidiaries that do. This is a very important result in the light of other recent research in the area of corporate mergers and acquisitions, and in view of the significance of acquisition for the overall internationalization of R&D. Cross-border acquisitions may, broadly speaking, be divided into those motivated mainly by financial considerations and those that are motivated by new asset acquisition and a synergy of complementary productive resources. Hence, as suggested by Table 6, in competence-creating subsidiaries the latter motives tend to dominate, subsidiary managers are able to use the distinctive contribution that their unit brings to the acquiring group to gain influence at their new head office, and acquired subsidiaries attract more research investment on average than do directly established subsidiaries. However, in the absence of such a mandate the tendency is for acquired subsidiaries to be obliged to eliminate R&D duplication since in this case the managers of an acquired subsidiary tend to have less influence at the head office than their counterparts in subsidiaries that were part of the acquiring group, and so acquired subsidiaries tend to become more reliant on R&D done elsewhere in the group to exploit their existing assets. The estimates of Table 6 therefore provide evidence in support of Hypothesis 5.

A similar but less striking contrast between R&D determinants in subsidiaries with or without competence-creating output mandates is observed in the significance of the negative impact of *Diversified* only in the competence-creating case. This is consistent with other evidence that has suggested that whereas at one time product diversification and technological diversification were complementary (or more precisely, they were different representations or ways of measuring of the same phenomenon), in more recent times they may be substitutes as a wider range of technologies is now needed to support a narrower range of products (Cantwell and Piscitello, 2000). This is indeed what our findings here suggest: that with a competence-creating mandate, a higher extent of product diversification tends to be a hindrance to investing in the creation of new technologies. It is not just that product diversification may now withdraw resources away from competence creation directly, but also that it makes it more difficult to integrate that competence creation with the needs of the wider group. In consequence subsidiary managers may lose influence within their group, and so attract less investment. However, this effect does not apply to the same extent to subsidiaries without this competence-creating function, for which the overwhelming goal in research is to adapt products (whether they are distinctive to that subsidiary or not) to the relevant markets. So our findings are supportive of Hypothesis 6.

There is one other especially notable difference in the two sets of estimates of Table 6, which (as with the MNE group-level effects on the mandate decision in Table 5) relates to influences that are captured through the use of home country dummy variables. Both Japanese and U.S. parentage seem to increase *R&D intensity* for subsidiaries with a mandate, but not for subsidiaries without one. While Japanese- and U.S.-owned MNEs have a smaller share of internationalized subsidiary R&D than European-owned MNEs, they are more likely to develop cross-border networks for innovation within Europe, since they do not have a home base on which to focus attention within the European area. Thus, when Japanese- and U.S.-owned subsidiaries gain competence-creating mandates, they tend to have greater opportunities for becoming sources of new knowledge within their respective European corporate groups.

Finally, following Shaver (1998), we ask: if subsidiaries in each category behaved like subsidiaries in the other, what would be their chosen R&D intensity? We address this question by computing the average R&D intensity for subsidiaries with competence-creating mandates using their average characteristics and their estimated coefficients

1124 *J. Cantwell and R. Mudambi*

Table 7. Estimated average R&D intensity
Subsidiaries with and without competence-creating mandates

Percent		Characteristics: average values	
		Subsidiary mandate $= 0$	*Subsidiary mandate* $= 1$
Estimated coefficients	*Subsidiary mandate* $= 0$	3.182	-4.093
	Subsidiary mandate $= 1$	-9.693	5.338

from Table 6. Then we pair the average characteristics of subsidiaries with mandates with the estimated coefficients for subsidiaries without mandates. We do the same, in reverse, for subsidiaries without mandates. These results are reported in Table 7. When subsidiaries behave to type, the estimated R&D intensity is a good fit to actual category average (compare the estimates on the diagonal in Table 7 with those reported in Table 4b). However, if mandated subsidiaries behaved like non-mandated subsidiaries, their estimated R&D intensity would become negative. The same occurs if non-mandated subsidiaries behaved like mandated subsidiaries. Clearly there is a qualitative difference in the way in which the two sets of subsidiaries conduct R&D.

What this demonstrates is that if non-mandated subsidiaries were to be asked to fulfill a competence-creating role, they would be unable to do so, and hence their R&D would tend to fall towards zero (the estimated R&D intensity appears to be negative). Conversely, the qualitative distinction in R&D types applies just as well the other way, i.e., if mandated subsidiaries were expected to play a mere competence-exploiting role, they would also be unable to do so effectively any longer. This reaffirms that the subsidiary-level strategy divergence we have identified is critical.

We recognize that the patterns of global technology strategy in multinational firms have evolved over the decade since we collected our data. There has been an increasing trend toward moving R&D on the basis of cost and not just capabilities to emerging market economies with highly skilled workforces. The recent location of many R&D establishments in Eastern Europe and South Asia fit this description. One weakness of our single-country focus is the inability to capture such global trends.

However, we argue that the current global R&D strategy of MNEs is characterized by the twin drivers of capabilities and cost. As MNEs implement such a strategy we should observe an increasing diversity in the R&D activities as some subsidiaries focus on cost and move toward competence exploitation, while others focus on capability development and move toward competence creation. From this perspective the age of our data provides us with a historical perspective, indicating that current R&D strategies in MNEs are the product of an evolutionary process that has been going on for a decade, if not longer. The suggestive results we present for the 1995–2002 period (Table 4b) support such an interpretation.

CONCLUDING REMARKS

Our findings are consistent with other studies that have pointed to the emergence of global networks for innovation within MNEs in recent years. In this literature, it has been proposed that a subsidiary can contribute more creatively to technology generation within such a network, the better is the local infrastructure in the location in which it is sited, which increases its potential skill base and local linkages with other innovative firms and research institutions; the wider is the functional scope of its mandate, which broadens its potential role within the MNE network; and the more mature it is, having had time to evolve away from a principally domestic orientation and towards more closely internationally integrated relationships.

We suggest that the decision regarding the achievement of a competence-creating mandate to an MNE subsidiary is an endogenous one. Thus, subsidiaries obtain or do not obtain such mandates depending upon subsidiary-, group-, and location-specific factors. We find that treating the mandating decision as endogenous rather than exogenous gives us a clearer picture of MNE R&D investment behavior. We show that the R&D investments of subsidiaries with competence-creating mandates are both qualitatively as well as quantitatively different from that of subsidiaries without such mandates.

In particular, supply-related local development potential and the degree to which subsidiaries are separately granted strategic independence both positively influence R&D in competence-creating subsidiaries, but not in other kinds of subsidiary. There is also a trade-off between technology-creating investments and product diversification in subsidiaries with competence-creating mandates, but not in other subsidiaries. However, while having been part of an acquired group positively affects R&D in subsidiaries with mandates, there is a negative impact of acquisition on local R&D in subsidiaries without mandates. This is an original finding, and one that carries very important implications in view of the sizeable proportion of foreign-located R&D that is the outcome of mergers and acquisitions. Likewise, there is no effect on R&D in mandated subsidiaries from the extent and variability of local demand, which clearly influence R&D in non-mandated subsidiaries since they conduct R&D primarily to adapt established products to local markets. These findings are very much in line with our expectations, but we believe they are novel results from our appropriate modeling of MNE R&D strategy decisions. The purposes and nature of R&D differ in these two types of subsidiary strategy, and so the determinants of R&D differ too. The tasks and the character of technology management diverge from their traditional pattern once subsidiaries achieve a competence-creating mandate.

In terms of the theoretical implications of the approach we have taken and our findings, we return to our earlier observation that the previous literature on the typology of subsidiary R&D has made the divergence of subsidiary roles (competence-creating vs. competence-exploiting) largely a function of the location in which the subsidiary is sited. Certainly, we find here further strong support for the influence of location on subsidiary mandates, as well as on the determination of R&D in each type of subsidiary. Yet it turns out that the Marchian distinction between competence-creating subsidiaries' focus on exploration, in contrast to the focus of competence-exploiting subsidiaries, has its starkest divergence of impact on R&D in the context of subsidiary acquisition. Following acquisition, R&D rises in competence-creating subsidiaries, but it falls in competence-exploiting subsidiaries.

Thus, the subsidiary typology matters most of all for the amount of localized R&D not with respect to locational characteristics (which earlier researchers have emphasized), but rather with respect to firm-specific MNE group-level acquisition strategies. This underscores the theoretical need to allow for the interaction between firm-specific corporate strategy and location-specific factors when examining the divergent determinants of subsidiary-level R&D. What is more, MNEs that grow through acquisition may have more inter-subsidiary diversity in the nature and level of localized R&D than those that rely on internal growth. As argued in our opening remarks, such intra-organizational diversity may well help to promote a better balance between exploration and exploitation in the technological learning of MNEs, but of course this potential benefit needs to be set against the costs of integrating and managing a more complex international network. While others have argued that acquisition strategies have particular advantages for laggard firms rather than leaders as a means of catching up by acquiring access to new capabilities in the context of specific host markets (e.g., Hennart and Park, 1993), our finding suggests that acquisitions may be useful for leader firms too in the wider context of the promotion of effective learning across international networks.

Our data show (from an historical vantage-point) that the bifurcation of subsidiary types we describe had already led to statistically significant differences in their paths by the early 1990s. Further research into these differences in subsidiary behavior would be welcome, but if subsidiary evolution has continued along alternative trajectories since that time then we might see a consolidation of this typological divide between subsidiaries.

ACKNOWLEDGEMENTS

We would like to thank Bruce Kogut, Steve Kobrin, discussants at the European International Business Academy meetings in Maastricht, as well as seminar participants at Wharton, Tsukuba, Kyoto and Paris, for helpful comments. Perceptive comments of two anonymous referees were extremely helpful. The usual disclaimer applies.

1126   *J. Cantwell and R. Mudambi*

REFERENCES

Almeida P. 1996. Knowledge sourcing by foreign multinationals: patent citation analysis in the U.S. semiconductor industry. *Strategic Management Journal*, Winter Special Issue **17**: 155–165.

Andersson U, Forsgren M. 2000. In search of centre of excellence: network embeddedness and subsidiary roles in multinational corporations. *Management International Review* **40**(4): 329–350.

Andersson U, Forsgren M, Holm U. 2002. The strategic impact of external networks: subsidiary performance and competence development in the multinational corporation. *Strategic Management Journal* **23**(11): 979–996.

Armstrong JS, Overton T. 1977. Estimating non-response bias in mail surveys. *Journal of Marketing Research* **14**(3): 396–402.

Bartlett CA, Ghoshal S. 1989. *Managing Across Borders: The Transnational Solution*. Harvard Business School Press: Boston, MA.

Birkinshaw JM. 1998. Foreign owned subsidiaries and regional development: the case of Sweden. In *Multinational Corporate Evolution and Subsidiary Development*, Birkinshaw J, Hood N (eds). Macmillan: London; 268–298.

Birkinshaw JM, Hood N. 1998. Multinational subsidiary evolution: capability and charter change in foreign-owned subsidiary companies. *Academy of Management Review* **23**(4): 773–795.

Birkinshaw JM, Hood N, Jonsson S. 1998. Building firm-specific advantages in multinational corporations: the role of subsidiary initiative. *Strategic Management Journal*, **19**(3): 221–241.

Cantwell JA. 1987. The reorganisation of European industries after integration: selected evidence on the role of transnational enterprise activities. *Journal of Common Market Studies* **26**(2): 127–151.

Cantwell JA. 1989. *Technological Innovation and Multinational Corporations*. Basil Blackwell: Oxford.

Cantwell JA. 1994. Introduction. In *Transnational Corporations and Innovatory Activities*, Cantwell JA (ed). Routledge: London; 1–32.

Cantwell JA. 1995. The globalisation of technology: what remains of the product cycle model? *Cambridge Journal of Economics* **19**(1): 155–174.

Cantwell JA, Iammarino S. 1998. MNCs, technological innovation and regional systems in the EU: some evidence in the Italian case. *International Journal of the Economics of Business* **5**(3): 383–408.

Cantwell JA, Iammarino S. 2000. Multinational corporations and the location of technological innovation in the UK regions. *Regional Studies* **34**(4): 317–332.

Cantwell JA, Janne OEM. 1999. Technological globalisation and innovative centres: the role of corporate technological leadership and locational hierarchy. *Research Policy* **28**(2–3): 119–144.

Cantwell JA, Kosmopoulou E. 2002. What determines the internationalisation of corporate technology? In *Critical Perspectives on Internationalisation*, Havila V, Forsgren M, Håkanson H (eds). Pergamon: Oxford; 305–334.

Cantwell JA, Mudambi R. 2000. The location of MNE R&D activity: the role of investment incentives, *Management International Review* **40** Special Issue (1): 127–148.

Cantwell JA, Piscitello L. 1999. The emergence of corporate international networks for the accumulation of dispersed technological competences. *Management International Review* **39** Special Issue (1): 123–147.

Cantwell JA, Piscitello L. 2000. Accumulating technological competence: its changing impact upon corporate diversification and internationalisation. *Industrial and Corporate Change* **9**(1): 21–51.

Cantwell JA, Piscitello L. 2002. The location of technological activities of MNCs in European regions: the role of spillovers and local competencies. *Journal of International Management* **8**(1): 69–96.

Czinkota MR, Ronkainen IA, Moffett MH. 1996. *International Business* (4th edn). Dryden Press: New York.

Danneels E. 2002. The dynamics of product innovation and firm competencies. *Strategic Management Journal* **23**(12): 1095–1124.

Devereux M, Griffith R. 1998. Taxes and the location of production: evidence from a panel of U.S. multinationals. *Journal of Public Economics* **68**(3): 335–367.

Doz Y. 1986. *Strategic Management in Multinational Companies*. Pergamon Press: Oxford.

Dun & Bradstreet. 1994. *Business Register*. Dun & Bradstreet: London.

Dun & Bradstreet. 1995. *Business Register*. Dun & Bradstreet: London.

Dunning JH. 1995. Reappraising the eclectic paradigm in an age of alliance capitalism. *Journal of International Business Studies* **26**(3): 461–491.

Dunning JH. 1996. The geographical sources of the competitiveness of firms: some results of a new survey. *Transnational Corporations* **5**: 1–29.

Ensign PC, Birkinshaw JM, Frost T. 2000. R&D centres of excellence in Canada. In *The Emergence and Impact of MNC Centres of Excellence: A Subsidiary Perspective*, Holm U, Pedersen T (eds). Macmillan: London; 131–153.

Frost TS, Birkinshaw JM, Ensign PC. 2002. Centers of excellence in multinational corporations. *Strategic Management Journal* **23**(11): 997–1018.

Grant RM. 1995. *Contemporary Strategy Analysis: Concepts, Techniques, Applications* (2nd edn). Blackwell: Oxford.

Greene WH. 1993. *Econometric Analysis* (2nd edn). Macmillan: New York.

Håkanson L. 1981. Organisation and evolution of foreign R&D in Swedish multinationals, *Geografiska Annaler*, Series B **63**: 47–56.

Håkanson L. 1995. Learning through acquisitions: management and integration of foreign R&D laboratories. *International Studies of Management and Organization* **25**(1–2): 121–157.

Håkanson L, Nobel R. 2000. Technology characteristics and reverse technology transfer. *Management International Review* **40** Special Issue (1): 29–48.

Heberlein TA, Baumgartner R. 1978. Factors affecting response rates to mailed questionnaires: a quantitative analysis of the published literature. *American Sociological Review* **43**(4): 447–462.

Heckman J. 1979. Sample selection bias as a specification error. *Econometrica* **47**(1): 153–161.

Hedlund G. 1986. The hypermodern MNC: a heterarchy? *Human Resource Management* **25**: 9–25.

Hennart J-F, Park YR. 1993. Greenfield vs. acquisition: the strategy of Japanese investors in the United States. *Management Science* **39**(9): 1054–1070.

Hitt MA, Hoskisson RE, Ireland RD, Harrison JS. 1991. Effects of acquisitions on R&D inputs and outputs. *Academy of Management Journal* **34**(3): 693–706.

Hitt MA, Hoskisson RE, Kim H. 1997. International diversification: effects on innovation and firm performance in product-diversified firms. *Academy of Management Journal* **40**(4): 767–798.

Holm U, Pedersen T. 2000. *The Emergence and Impact of MNC Centres of Excellence: A Subsidiary Perspective*. Macmillan: London.

Jaffe A, Trajtenberg M, Henderson R. 1993. Geographical localization of knowledge spillovers, as evidenced by patent citations. *Quarterly Journal of Economics* **58**: 577–598.

Kuemmerle W. 1999. The drivers of foreign direct investment into research and development: an empirical investigation. *Journal of International Business Studies* **30**(1): 1–24.

Maddala GS. 1983. *Limited-Dependent and Qualitative Variables in Econometrics*. Cambridge University Press: Cambridge, UK.

March JG. 1991. Exploration and exploitation in organizational learning. *Organization Science* **2**(1): 71–87.

Mudambi R. 1998. The role of duration in MNE investment strategies. *Journal of International Business Studies* **29**(2): 217–240.

Mudambi R, Navarra P. 2004. Is knowledge power? Knowledge flows, subsidiary power and rent-seeking within MNCs. *Journal of International Business Studies* **35**(5): 385–406.

Mudambi R, Ricketts MJ. 1998. Economic organisation and the multinational firm. in *The Organisation of the Firm: International Business Perspectives*, Mudambi R, Ricketts MJ (eds). Routledge: London; 1–18.

Nobel R, Birkinshaw JM. 1998. Innovation in multinational corporations: control and communication patterns in international R&D operations. *Strategic Management Journal* **19**(5): 479–496.

Office of National Statistics. 1992. *The UK Standard Industrial Classification of Economic Activities*. HMSO: London.

Papanastassiou M, Pearce RD. 1997. Technology sourcing and the strategic roles of manufacturing subsidiaries in the U.K.: local competences and global competitiveness. *Management International Review* **37**: 5–25.

Pearce RD. 1999. Decentralised R&D and strategic competitiveness: globalised approaches to generation and use of technology in MNEs. *Research Policy* **28**(2–3): 157–178.

Penrose ET. 1959. *The Theory of the Growth of the Firm*. Blackwell: Oxford.

Porter ME. 1986. Competition in global industries: a conceptual framework. In *Competition in Global Industries*, Porter ME (ed). Harvard Business School Press: Boston, MA; 15–60.

Sambharya R. 1996. Foreign experience of top management teams and international diversification strategies of U.S. multinational corporations. *Strategic Management Journal* **17**(9): 739–746.

Shaver JM. 1998. Accounting for endogeneity when assessing strategy performance: does entry mode choice affect FDI survival? *Management Science* **44**(4): 571–585.

Simões V, Nevado P. 2000. MNE centres of excellence and acquisitions: long evolutionary paths or capturing opportunities? Mimeo, Technical University of Lisbon.

Taggart JH. 1998. Strategy shifts in MNC subsidiaries. *Strategic Management Journal* **19**(7): 663–681.

Zander I. 1999a. How do you mean 'global'? An empirical investigation of innovation networks in the multinational corporation. *Research Policy* **28**(2–3): 195–213.

Zander I. 1999b. Whereto the multinational? The evolution of technological capabilities in the multinational network. *International Business Review* **8**: 261–291.

APPENDIX: COMPETENCE-CREATING MANDATES AND SELECTION BIAS

We are interested in the achievement of competence-creating mandates by subsidiaries. Subsidiaries obtain a mandate when the expected profitability of such a strategy is greater than that associated with a purely competence-exploiting strategy. This variable, which is defined as $MAND_i^*$, relates to the ith subsidiary and is driven by its resources and capabilities. These resources, capabilities, and environmental factors may be gathered together in a vector $\mathbf{Z}$, so that

$$MAND_i^* = \mu'\mathbf{Z}_i + e_i \qquad (1)$$

$MAND_i^*$, however, is a latent variable. The observed variable is the subsidiary mandate. It is denoted in this Appendix by $MAND_i$, where

$$MAND_i = 1 \; MAND_i^* > 0 (competence - creating$$
$$mandate \; obtained) \qquad (2)$$
$$MAND_i = 0 \; MAND_i^* \leq 0 (competence-$$
$$exploiting \; strategy \; undertaken)$$

This is a dichotomous choice model (Maddala, 1983). MAND is decided by the firm (including

1128   *J. Cantwell and R. Mudambi*

the subsidiary) and is therefore an endogenous variable.

The decision regarding R&D expenditure (and hence the R&D/sales ratio denoted by RD) is also determined by subsidiary, group, and location characteristics, with the binary $MAND_i$ variable providing an additive difference. The variables that affect R&D spending can be gathered together in a vector $\mathbf{X}$, which may share several variables with $\mathbf{Z}$. The estimation of RD may be specified as

$$RD_i = \beta'\mathbf{X}_i + \theta MAND_i + u_i \qquad (3)$$

Treating MAND as a normal exogenous variable in estimating the level of R&D intensity (RD) ignores its endogeneity—the common variables in $\mathbf{X}$ and $\mathbf{Z}$ mean that e_i and u_i are correlated. In other words, there is 'selectivity' correlation between MAND* and RD, which may be defined as ρ. The direct estimation of Equation 3 generates selectivity bias (Heckman, 1979). The effects of selection bias appear in both the mean and the variance of the estimator of θ in Equation 3. The estimate of θ is biased in the direction of the correlation between the errors u_i and e_i. The estimated standard error of θ is biased downwards, so the probability that it will appear significant is increased. For a more technical treatment of the problem of selection bias, see Greene (1993).

Assuming that the joint distribution of MAND* and RD is bivariate normal, we have what is called a 'selection' model. Defining the vector of location and firm factors affecting RD as $\mathbf{X}$ and the standard normal distribution and density functions as $\Phi(.)$ and $\phi(.)$, we have

$$E[RD_i] = \beta'\mathbf{X}_i + \theta MAND + E[u_i|MAND] \qquad (4)$$
$$= \beta'\mathbf{X}_i + \theta MAND + \beta_\lambda \lambda$$

where λ is the selection parameter, i.e., the adjustment for the effects of incidental truncation.

There are two problems with the standard selection model in the context of MNE mandating decisions. (a) The estimated parameter vector, β', is

restricted to be the same for both competence-creating and competence-exploiting strategies. (b) The coefficient on the selection parameter, β_λ, is difficult to interpret, since it is also restricted to be the same for both strategies.

One way around this is to estimate the R&D intensity equation separately for subsidiaries with competence-creating mandates and those without, while accounting for the incidental truncation created by the selection. Thus, λ is estimated from the strategy decision Equation 1 as

$$\lambda_i(MAND = 1) = \phi(\mu'\mathbf{Z}_i)/\Phi(\mu'\mathbf{Z}_i) \qquad (5)$$
$$\lambda_i(MAND = 0) = -\phi(\mu'\mathbf{Z}_i)/[1 - \Phi(\mu'\mathbf{Z}_i)]$$

Equation 4 can then be estimated separately for subsidiaries with and without competence-creating mandates. Explicitly, this amounts to estimating the following equations:

$$E[RD_i|MAND = 1] = \beta'\mathbf{X}_i + \theta$$
$$+ E[u_i|MAND = 1] \quad (6a)$$
$$= \beta'\mathbf{X}_i + \theta + \rho\sigma_u\lambda$$
$$\times (\mu'\mathbf{Z}_i|MAND = 1)$$
$$= \beta'\mathbf{X}_i + \theta + \rho\sigma_u$$
$$\times [\phi(\mu'\mathbf{Z}_i)/\Phi(\mu'\mathbf{Z}_i)]$$

and

$$E[RD_i|MAND = 0] = \beta'\mathbf{X}_i$$
$$+ E[u_i|MAND = 0] \quad (6b)$$
$$= \beta'\mathbf{X}_i + \rho\sigma_u\lambda$$
$$\times (\mu'\mathbf{Z}_i|MAND = 0)$$
$$= \beta'\mathbf{X}_i + \rho\sigma_u[-\phi(\mu'\mathbf{Z}_i)/$$
$$\{1 - \Phi(\mu'\mathbf{Z}_i)\}]$$

While these estimates are not efficient, they are consistent and therefore improve as the sample size is increased.

[31]

Journal of International Business Studies (2007) 38, 231–258
© 2007 Academy of International Business All rights reserved 0047-2506 $30.00
www.jibs.net

What we talk about when we talk about 'global mindset': Managerial cognition in multinational corporations

Orly Levy[1], Schon Beechler[2],
Sully Taylor[3] and
Nakiye A Boyacigiller[4]

[1]Culture Crossing Consulting, Tel Aviv, Israel;
[2]Duke Corporate Education, New York, NY, USA;
[3]School of Business Administration,
Portland State University, Portland, OR, USA;
[4]Faculty of Management, Sabanci University,
Istanbul, Turkey

Correspondence: Orly Levy,
Culture Crossing Consulting, 47 Mazze
Street, Tel Aviv 65788, Israel.
Tel: +972 54 337 517;
Fax: +972 3 566 9026;
E-mail: olevy43@netvision.net.il

Abstract
Recent developments in the global economy and in multinational corporations
have placed significant emphasis on the cognitive orientations of managers,
giving rise to a number of concepts such as 'global mindset' that are presumed
to be associated with the effective management of multinational corporations.
This paper reviews the literature on global mindset and clarifies some of the
conceptual confusion surrounding the construct. We identify common themes
across writers, suggesting that the majority of studies fall into one of three
research perspectives: cultural, strategic, and multidimensional. We also
identify two constructs from the social sciences – *cosmopolitanism* and *cognitive
complexity* – that underlie the perspectives found in the literature. We then use
these two constructs to develop an integrative theoretical framework of global
mindset. We then provide a critical assessment of the field of global mindset
and suggest directions for future theoretical and empirical research.
Journal of International Business Studies (2007) **38**, 231–258.
doi:10.1057/palgrave.jibs.8400265

Keywords: global mindset; managerial cognition; competitiveness

Introduction
As global competition continues to intensify, global mindset has
emerged as a key source of long-term competitive advantage in the
global marketplace. A growing number of academics and practitioners view global mindset, or the cognitive capabilities of key
decision-makers, as a critical success factor that affects a variety of
organizational outcomes (Murtha *et al.*, 1998; Harveston *et al.*,
2000; Jeannet, 2000; Gupta and Govindarajan, 2002; Levy, 2005).
This emerging consensus reflects a recognition that the present-day
competitive landscape requires a shift in focus from structural and
administrative mechanisms to mindset-based capabilities (Bartlett
and Ghoshal, 1990). As Govindarajan and Gupta (1998: 2) suggest:
'Success is all in the [global] mindset.'

The notion that global mindset, or the cognitive capabilities of
senior managers in multinational companies (MNCs), is important to
firm performance dates back to the early works on foreign direct
investment by Aharoni (1966) and Kindleberger (1969). However, it
was Perlmutter (1969) who focused attention on managerial cognition by offering a formal typology of MNCs that explicitly
incorporates the prevailing mindsets of senior executives. Over the

Received: 17 November 2003
Revised: 8 June 2006
Accepted: 11 July 2006

last decade, developments in the global economy have re-focused attention on the cognitive dimension of MNCs as business realities have given rise to tremendous managerial complexity (Prahalad, 1990; Doz and Prahalad, 1991). As globalization intensifies, MNCs are subjected to simultaneous and often conflicting pressures for global integration and local responsiveness (Prahalad and Doz, 1987; Bartlett and Ghoshal, 1990; Doz et al., 2001). As a result, senior managers need to integrate and coordinate geographically dispersed operations and a culturally diverse workforce (Bartlett and Ghoshal, 1990). In addition, managers must respond to local demands and manage inter-organizational relationships with diverse stakeholders, including host governments, strategic partners, customers, and suppliers (Rosenzweig and Singh, 1991). Senior managers in MNCs must find a balance between competing country, business, and functional concerns (Evans and Doz, 1993; Murtha et al., 1998). Researchers and practitioners alike suggest that managers who have developed a global mindset are better equipped to deal with the complexity wrought by multiple organizational environments, structural indeterminacy, and cultural heterogeneity – all of which characterize contemporary MNCs (Doz and Prahalad, 1991).

The growing recognition of the significance of the cognitive dimension of MNCs has led to the proliferation of different and often conflicting definitions and perspectives, as well as a limited number of empirical studies in this field. On the conceptual side, terms such as 'global mindset' (Rhinesmith, 1992), 'transnational mentality' (Bartlett and Ghoshal, 1989), and 'multinational mindset' (Caproni et al., 1992) have gained increasing cachet in both the academic and popular presses in recent years. At the same time, the properties of these constructs remain relatively opaque. Global mindset has come to stand for everything that is supposedly global or transnational, from individual attitudes, skills, competencies, and behaviors, through organizational orientations, structures, and strategies, to policies and practices. In short, the diversity of perspectives and the pervasive use of the concept 'global mindset' have resulted in conceptual ambiguities, as well as contradictory empirical findings.

In light of the significance of managerial cognition in MNCs, this paper analyzes and synthesizes the current thinking about global mindset. The following section reviews the research streams on global mindset, and identifies two primary dimensions that underlie the various perspectives on

global mindset. Next, we present a conceptual model of global mindset and develop some illustrative theoretical propositions. We then step back and present an overall assessment of the global mindset field. Finally, we summarize our key contributions and offer directions for further theoretical development and research.

Literature review

In this section we provide a thorough review of the theoretical and empirical studies of global mindset published in books and peer-reviewed journals, including those studies that use different terminology but substantively examine the same phenomenon. At the same time, we exclude studies that do not explicitly deal with global mindset but are focused on such topics as global leadership, expatriates, and expatriation, even though they may include some of the same underlying variables as the literature on global mindset. Cataloguing the literature and taking stock of what has been done thus far, both theoretically and empirically, is one goal of this review. At the same time, we believe that it is useful to trace the underlying themes in the global mindset literature to two important theoretical constructs from the social sciences – cosmopolitanism and cognitive complexity – and then to use these constructs to propose a new integrative approach to global mindset.

In our review of the literature we find that the majority of studies conceptualize global mindset in relation to two salient dimensions of the global environment, most notably in relation to (1) cultural and national diversity and/or (2) strategic complexity associated with globalization.

In the following section we first discuss the work of Perlmutter (1969), whose work on geocentrism (global mindset) spawned a stream of research focusing on the cultural dimension of the global environment. This first approach, which we label the *cultural perspective*, focuses on aspects of cultural diversity and cultural distance associated with worldwide operations and markets. It underscores the challenges of managing across cultural and national boundaries. We suggest that cosmopolitanism, and the attitudinal stance associated with cosmopolitanism, serves as an underlying theme of the cultural approach to global mindset.

Second, we introduce the theoretical approach of Bartlett and Ghoshal (1989) and the subsequent research stream in international management that focuses on strategic complexity. This stream of work, which we label the *strategic perspective*, springs out of work in international strategy and focuses on aspects of environmental complexity and strategic variety stemming from globalization. This approach highlights the challenge of managing complex operations and integrating geographically distant and strategically diverse businesses while simultaneously responding to local conditions (Prahalad and Doz, 1987). We propose that cognitive complexity and its associated cognitive capabilities serve as an underlying theme characterizing this stream of work in the literature on global mindset.

In the final section of our literature review we introduce a third approach, which we label the *multidimensional perspective*. This integrative stream of work, much of which draws on the foundational work of Rhinesmith (1992, 1993, 1996), conceptualizes global mindset using *both* cultural and strategic terms as well as a variety of additional characteristics.

To provide a reference for the reader, Table 1 summarizes the studies on global mindset reviewed in this paper. Table 2 provides a summary of the measures that have been used in empirical research of global mindset, and the Appendix lists scale items.

The cultural perspective
Studies within the cultural stream of research conceptualize global mindset in the context of the increased cultural diversity associated with globalization. According to this school of thought, as firms globalize, their senior managers face the challenges of overcoming domestic myopia and an ethnocentric mindset, crossing cultural boundaries, interacting with employees from many countries, and managing culturally diverse interorganizational relationships. The cultural perspective suggests that the answer to managing these challenges is to move away from an ethnocentric mindset and develop a global mindset – a mindset that involves cultural self-awareness, openness to and understanding of other cultures, and selective incorporation of foreign values and practices. Perlmutter's (1969) ground-breaking tripartite typology of managerial mindsets in MNCs serves as a conceptual anchor for the cultural perspective.

Breaking with previous work in international business, Perlmutter and his colleagues (Perlmutter, 1969; Heenan and Perlmutter, 1979; Chakravarthy and Perlmutter, 1985) offer a typology of MNCs that is explicitly based on the mindsets of senior executives. Perlmutter (1969) originally distin-

guished among three primary attitudes or states of mind toward managing a multinational enterprise: *ethnocentric* (home-country orientation), *polycentric* (host-country orientation), and *geocentric* (world-orientation). These orientations, Perlmutter proposed, influence and shape diverse aspects of the multinational enterprise, including structural design, strategy and resource allocation, and, most of all, management mindset and processes. An ethnocentric orientation is expressed in terms of headquarters and national superiority attitudes: 'We, the home nationals of X company, are superior to, more trustworthy and more reliable than any foreigner in headquarters or subsidiaries' (Perlmutter, 1969: 11). A polycentric orientation takes the form of a respectful disengagement from foreign cultures: 'Let the Romans do it their way. We really don't understand what is going on there, but we have to have confidence in them' (Perlmutter, 1969: 13). At their core, both of these attitudes represent beliefs regarding which persons and ideas are competent and trustworthy (foreigners *vs* compatriots) (Heenan and Perlmutter, 1979: 17). Managers with a geocentric orientation, or a global mindset, manifest universalistic, supra-national attitudes, downplaying the significance of nationality and cultural differences in determining who is competent or trustworthy: 'Within legal and political limits, they seek the best men [sic], regardless of nationality, to solve the company's problems anywhere in the world' (Perlmutter, 1969: 13). Superiority is not equated with nationality, as 'Good ideas come from any country and go to any country within the firm,' (Heenan and Perlmutter, 1979: 20–21). In their later work, Heenan and Perlmutter (1979) add a fourth attitude: the regiocentric attitude, meaning 'regionally oriented', which falls between the polycentric and geocentric attitudes.

Perlmutter's notion of geocentrism serves as an underlying construct for many of the contemporary conceptualizations of global mindset that focus on the challenge of overcoming ingrained ethnocentrism and transcending nationally entrenched perceptions (Adler and Bartholomew, 1992; Estienne, 1997; Doz *et al.*, 2001; Maznevski and Lane, 2004). For example, Maznevski and Lane (2004) view global mindset as a meta-capability characterized by two complementary aspects: a comprehensive cognitive structure that guides attention and interpretation of information, and a well-developed competence for changing and updating this cognitive structure with new experiences. They define

Table 1 Previous research on global mindset

Study	Definition	Level of analysis	Theoretical foundations	Key propositions/major findings
Cultural perspective Perlmutter (1969); Heenan and Perlmutter (1979)	Geocentrism is a global systems approach to decision-making where headquarters and subsidiaries see themselves as parts of an organic worldwide entity. Superiority is not equated with nationality. Good ideas come from any country and go to any country within the firm.	Individual and organization	Perlmutter (1969)	Geocentric approach influences and shapes diverse aspects of the multinational enterprise, including structural design, strategy and resource allocation, and management processes.
Adler and Bartholomew (1992)	Transnationals are defined by their knowledge and appreciation of many cultures and ability to effectively conduct business internationally.	Individual	Hambrick *et al.* (1989);Hamel *et al.* (1989); Bartlett and Ghoshal (1990)	To be effective, transnational managers need both the culturally specific knowledge and adaptation skills required in international firms, and the ability to acquire a worldwide perspective and to integrate the worldwide diversity required in multinational firms. The transnational manager must be discrete when choosing to be locally responsive and when to emphasize global integration.
Kobrin (1994)	A geocentric international human resource management system values ability over national origin.	Organization	Perlmutter (1969); Heenan and Perlmutter (1979)	In a sample of 68 American manufacturing firms, no significant relationship was found between geocentric mindset and firm size, length of international experience, organization structure, strategy, or globalization of the firm's industry. Geocentric mindset correlated significantly with geographic scope of the MNC and various aspects of IHRM policies and practices.
Estienne (1997)	International mindset is a 'willingness to learn' and an 'ability to adapt'.	Individual	Bartlett and Ghoshal (1989)	Developing global mindset allows companies to become truly transnational, and capable of using cultural diversity for competitive advantage.
Beechler *et al.* (2004)	Geocentrism is the extent to which nationality is unimportant when selecting individuals for managerial positions.	Organization	Perlmutter (1969); Heenan and Perlmutter (1979); Kobrin (1994)	In a sample of 521 employees working in two Japanese MNCs worldwide, perceptions of geocentrism were found to be positively related to employees' commitment, but not related to employees' excitement.

Table 1 Continued

Study	Definition	Level of analysis	Theoretical foundations	Key propositions/major findings
Maznevski and Lane (2004)	Global mindset is the ability to develop, interpret and implement criteria for personal and business performance that are independent from assumptions of a single country, culture, or context.	Individual	Cognitive schemas and systems thinking	Global mindset allows managers to make decisions in a way that increases the ability of their firms to compete internationally.
Strategic perspective				
Bartlett and Ghoshal (1989; 1990)	A transnational mindset is understanding the need for multiple strategic capabilities, viewing problems and opportunities from both local and global perspectives, and a willingness to interact well with others.	Individual and organization	Harvard Business School research in the 1970s	Based on their 5-year study of nine of the world's largest corporations, the transnational mindset is hypothesized to lead to superior long-term performance.
Tichy et al. (1992)	Global mindset is the ability to conceptualize complex geopolitical and cultural forces as they impact on business.	Individual		Global mindset leads to a heightened awareness of one's perceptions of other cultures and customs and fosters respect of these differences.
Murtha et al. (1998)	Global mindset is a cognitive process of balancing competing country, business, and functional concerns.	Individual	Porter (1986);Prahalad and Doz (1987); Bartlett and Ghoshal (1989).	In a sample of 305 managers working in a single MNC, global mindsets evolved over a three-year period as the change to a global strategy resulted in a cognitive shift toward a more global mindset across all managers in the organization.
Kefalas (1998)	Global mindset is a mental model characterized by high levels of both conceptualization and contextualization.	Individual	Rhinesmith (1992); Bartlett (1995); Redding et al. (1995).	People who are global thinkers and local actors possess the mindset that is the most appropriate for expanding an organization's activities globally.
Harveston et al. (2000)	Global mindset is the propensity of managers to engage in proactive and visionary behaviors to achieve strategic objectives in international markets.	Individual	Perlmutter (1969); Burpitt and Rondinelli (1998).	In a sample of 224 managers, managers of born global firms had more global mindsets, more international experience, and higher risk tolerance than managers of gradually globalizing firms.
Jeannet (2000)	Global mindset is a state of mind able to understand a business, an industry sector, or a particular market on a global basis.	Individual and organization	Levitt (1983).	Firms that implement a global mindset ahead of others will have a competitive advantage.
Govindarajan and Gupta (2001) and Gupta and Govindarajan (2002)	Global mindset combines an openness to and awareness of diversity across cultures and markets with a propensity and ability to synthesize across this diversity.	Individual and Organization	Cognitive psychology; Kobrin (1994); Murtha et al. (1998)	A deeply embedded global mindset is a prerequisite for global industry dominance. It enables the company to exploit emerging opportunities.
Harvey and Novicevic (2001)	Global mindset incorporates timescape dimensions into strategic decision-making processes.	Individual and organization	Rhinesmith (1992); Kedia and Mukherji (1999); Paul (2000)	The development of a time-oriented corporate mindset will become the primary driver of the firm's competitive posture in the marketplace.

(continued overleaf)

Table 1 Continued

Study	Definition	Level of analysis	Theoretical foundations	Key propositions/major findings
Begley and Boyd (2003)	Based on Maznevski and Lane's (2004) individual-level definition applied at the company level.	Organization	Doz and Prahalad (1987); Prahalad and Lieberthal (1998); Maznevski and Lane (2004)	Based on interviews with 39 HR executives in 32 high-technology MNCs headquartered in the United States, it was found that corporate global mindset emerges from policy development characterized by a high consistency/high responsiveness approach.
Arora *et al.* (2004)	Global mindset is the ability to analyze concepts in a broad global array and the flexibility to adapt to local environment and be sensitive to context.	Individual	Rhinesmith (1992); Kefalas and Weatherly (1998); Gupta and Govindarajan (2002)	In a sample of 65 US textile managers, managers were better in thinking globally than acting locally. Global mindset is related to several demographic and background characteristics.
Nummela *et al.* (2004)	Global mindset includes *proactiveness* on international markets, manager's *commitment* to internationalization, and an international *vision*.	Individual	Fletcher (2000); Kedia and Mukherji (1999); Gupta and Govindarajan (2002)	In a sample of 72 small and medium-size Finnish companies, a significant relationship was found between managerial international work experience, firm's market characteristics and global mindset, but no relationship between education and global mindset. Global mindset was found to be related to significantly more foreign partners and customers and larger percentage of revenues from foreign markets, but not related to manager's perception of international performance
Levy (2005)	Attention to the global environment is a primary manifestation of global mindset.	Top management team	Hambrick and Mason (1984); Bartlett and Ghoshal (1989); Ocasio (1997)	In a sample of 69 American firms, attention to the global/external environment and attention breadth were significantly positively related to global strategic posture of firms, whereas attention to the internal environment was negatively related.
Bouquet (2005)	Attention to global issues is a primary manifestation of global mindset.	Top management team	Prahalad and Doz (1987); Ocasio (1997)	In a sample of 136 MNCs, characteristics of the decision environment affected the attention structures established by the firm, which in turn affected TMT attention to global strategic issues. There was a concave relationship between TMT attention to global issues and firm performance

Table 1 Continued

Study	Definition	Level of analysis	Theoretical foundations	Key propositions/major findings
Multidimensional perspective				
Rhinesmith (1992, 1993, 1996)	A global mindset means that we scan the world from a broad perspective, always looking for unexpected trends and opportunities to achieve our personal, professional, or organizational objectives.	Individual		People with global mindsets drive for the bigger, broader picture, balance contradictions, trust process over structure, seek opportunities in surprises and uncertainties, value diversity, and continuously seek improvement.
Srinivas (1995)	Global mindset is characterized by eight components: curiosity and concern with context; acceptance of complexity; diversity consciousness; seeking opportunity; faith in organizational processes; focus on continuous improvement; extended time perspective; systems thinking.	Individual	Rhinesmith (1992); diverse sources	Global mindset leads to three strategic leadership thrusts: formulation and evocation of vision, crafting of a strategy to realize the vision, and focus on mobilization of human resources. These in turn result in business-goal outcomes and attitudinal outcomes.
Neff (1995)	Rhinesmith's (1993) characteristics of global mindset.	Individual	Rhinesmith (1993)	The combination of local leadership and global mindset enables the company to maintain that delicate balance between global efficiency and local responsiveness.
Ashkenas *et al.* (1995)	Rhinesmith's (1993) characteristics of global mindset.	Individual	Hedlund (1986); Rhinesmith (1993)	A successful global leader sees the larger worldview, focuses on process, and is willing and able to manage global complexities.
Kedia and Mukherji (1999)	Global mindset is characterized by openness, an ability to recognize complex interconnections, a unique time and space perspective, emotional connection, capacity for managing uncertainty, ability to balance tensions, and savvy.	Individual	Rhinesmith (1993); Kefalas and Neuland (1997); Gregersen *et al.* (1998).	To be globally competitive, managers need a global mindset and supportive knowledge and skills. Global mindset enables managers to understand the complexities of managing an interdependent and complex global network, and to play the required part within the network.
Paul (2000)	Global corporate mindset is the extent to which management encourages and values cultural diversity, while simultaneously maintaining a certain degree of strategic cohesion.	Organization	Porter (1980)	The more global the company's mindset, the easier it becomes to support a global business approach in existing markets, as well as to enter new markets and pursue a global strategy.

Table 2 Measures of global mindset

Study	Measured construct	Type of measure	Dimensionality
Individual level			
Murtha *et al.* (1998)	Global mindset	Expectation	Multidimensional • integration • responsiveness • coordination
Govindarajan and Gupta (2001) and Gupta and Govindarajan (2002)	Global mindset	Self-perception	Unidimensional
Harveston *et al.* (2000)[a]	Geocentric mindset	Self-perception	Unidimensional
Arora *et al.* (2004)[b]	Global mindset	Perception and self-perception	Multidimensional • conceptualization • contextualization
Nummela *et al.* (2004)	Global mindset	Perception	Multidimensional • proactiveness • commitment to internationalization • international vision
Group level			
Levy (2005)	TMT attention patterns	Content analysis	Multidimensional • attention to environmental elements • attention breadth

Bouquet (2005)	TMT attention patterns	Behavioral	Multidimensional
			• global scanning
			• CEO foreign travel
			• richness of communications
			  with overseas managers
			• discussions of globalization
			  decisions

Organization level			
Jeannet (2000)	Global mindset	Perception and quantitative organizational data	Multidimensional • business strategies • managerial talent pool • firm's organization
Govindarajan and Gupta (2001) and Gupta and Govindarajan (2002)	Global mindset	Perception	Multidimensional • Dimensions not specified
Begley and Boyd (2003)	Global mindset	Semi-structured interviews	Unidimensional
Kobrin (1994); Beechler *et al.* (2004)	Geocentrism	Perception	

[a]Items adapted from Burpitt and Rondinelli (1998).
[b]Measure developed by Kefalas and Neuland (1997).

global mindset as 'the ability to develop and interpret criteria for personal and business performance that are independent from the assumptions of a single country, culture, or context; and to implement those criteria appropriately in different countries, cultures, and contexts' (Maznevski and Lane, 2004: 172). The importance of transcending national borders and forming complex cultural understandings is also central in Adler and Bartholomew's (1992) discussion of the 'transnational manager'. They argue that the traditional interna-

tional manager approaches the world from a single-country perspective, whereas the transnational manager has a global perspective characterized by knowledge and appreciation of many foreign cultures.

Studies within the cultural stream often conceptualize global mindset in terms of cross-cultural skills and abilities.[1] Adler and Bartholomew (1992) suggest that the transnational manager is defined by his or her ability to tread smoothly and expertly within and between cultures and countries on a daily basis. Estienne (1997) also focuses on cultural adaptability, and notes that an international or global mindset can be thought of as a 'willingness to learn' and 'an ability to adapt'.

Kobrin (1994) conducted the first contemporary empirical study that specifically examined the construct of global mindset as defined by Heenan and Perlmutter (1979), and tested the oft-stated assumption that firms with a global, integrated strategy and/or global organizational structure will have a geocentric mindset. Kobrin (1994) measured geocentrism with a survey instrument that elicits the judgments, attitudes, and expectations of human resource managers about policies and managerial mindsets (see Appendix for scale items). Based on research results from data from 68 American manufacturing MNCs, Kobrin concludes that there is a relationship between a geocentric mindset and the geographic scope of the firm, although the direction of causality is not clear. He suggests that global mindset should be viewed as a multidimensional construct rather than as a single cognitive or attitudinal reflection of firm-level characteristics. Kobrin's measure was also used by Beechler *et al.* (2004), who found in a recent study of 521 employees in working in two Japanese MNCs that geocentrism is positively related to employees' level of commitment in these companies.

An underlying dimension of the cultural perspective: cosmopolitanism

Reviewing the literature on global mindset in the cultural stream, we observe that, although most writers do not mention the construct, cosmopolitanism and the attitudinal stance associated with it serve as an underlying theme of the cultural approach to global mindset. Therefore cosmopolitanism should be viewed as one of the major conceptual dimensions of global mindset represented in the literature.

The concept of cosmopolitanism has been part of the social sciences vocabulary for over 50 years (Gouldner, 1957),[2] and its meaning has evolved considerably over time. After falling out of favor, cosmopolitanism returned to the spotlight in the 1990s with the growth and proliferation of global systems and transnational cultures (see Hannerz, 1996; Beck, 2000; Breckenridge *et al.*, 2000; Harvey, 2000; Vertovec and Cohen, 2002a; Archibugi, 2003). As Harvey (2000: 529) asserts: 'Cosmopolitanism is back... Shaking off the negative connotations of its past...' Today it is embedded in a wider discourse on global order, world democracy, and

the cosmopolitan society (Held, 1995; Beck, 2000) and represents a complex and multilayered phenomenon (Harvey, 2000; Vertovec and Cohen, 2002b).[3] In their review of the recent conceptualization of cosmopolitanism, Vertovec and Cohen (2002b: 4) suggest that cosmopolitanism is something that simultaneously:

(1) transcends the nation-state model;
(2) mediates actions and ideals that are oriented both to the universal and the particular, the global and the local;
(3) is against cultural essentialism; and
(4) represents variously complex repertoires of allegiance, identity, and interest.

At the more personal or individual level, cosmopolitanism represents a 'perspective, a state of mind, or – to take a more process-oriented view – a mode of managing meaning' (Hannerz, 1996: 102). 'True' cosmopolitans are defined by their *'willingness to engage with the Other... openness* toward divergent cultural experiences, a search for contrasts rather than uniformity....' (Hannerz, 1996: 163; italics added). At the same time, however, cosmopolitanism has been described as 'a matter of competence... a personal ability to make one's way into other cultures, through listening, looking, intuiting, and reflecting' (Hannerz, 1996: 193). While cosmopolitans are usually footloose and often involved with global systems and transnational cultures, a number of writers suggest that 'it is not travel that defines cosmopolitans – some widely traveled people remain hopelessly parochial – it is mindset' (Kanter, 1995: 23).

It should be noted that, while cosmopolitans are celebrated by some as the new 'cultural heroes' of the global economy, they have frequently come under attack (Clifford, 1988; Robbins, 1992; Vertovec and Cohen, 2002a,b). As Robbins (1992: 171) expresses it: 'the word cosmopolitan immediately evokes the image of a privileged person: someone who can claim to be a "citizen of the world" by virtue of independent means, high-tech tastes, and globe-trotting mobility.' Beside the privilege of mobility, cosmopolitanism has been used to represent universalism, impartiality, and objectivity, as well as standing above cultural particularism and 'locals'. While considerable debate has focused on the value-laden aspects of cosmopolitanism, it is not necessary to overlay the construct with assumptions of superiority: 'Instead of renouncing cosmopolitanism as a false universal, one can embrace it as an impulse to knowledge that is shared with others, a striving to transcend partiality that is itself partial...' (Robbins, 1992: 181).

In our framework, cosmopolitanism does not denote an intrinsic value, but represents a state of mind that is manifested as an orientation toward the outside, the Other, and which seeks to reconcile the global with the local and mediate between the familiar and the foreign. A second key characteristic of cosmopolitanism is openness, a willingness to explore and learn from alternative systems of meaning held by others. Together, these two aspects encompass the key characteristics underlying the cultural approach in the literature to global mindset.

The strategic perspective

Whereas the studies reviewed above all emphasize the importance of understanding cultural diversity and transcending national borders, studies using the strategic perspective conceptualize global mindset in the context of the increased complexity generated by globalization. MNCs deal with the challenge of effectively managing environmental and strategic complexity and integrating geographically distant operations and markets, while simultaneously responding to local demands (Prahalad and Doz, 1987; Prahalad, 1990; Kim and Mauborgne, 1996; Sanders and Carpenter, 1998). In the past, environmental and organizational complexity could be mitigated by structural means and adequate administrative mechanisms (Chandler, 1962), but such solutions are insufficient for the present-day MNC (Prahalad and Bettis, 1986; Doz and Prahalad, 1991; Evans *et al.*, 2002). Moreover, complex structural solutions, such as the matrix form of organization, have proven all but unmanageable (Bartlett and Ghoshal, 1990; Pucik *et al.*, 1992; Ghoshal and Bartlett, 1995). In light of the limitations of structural and administrative solutions, the strategic perspective suggests that the critical determinant of the strategic capabilities of MNCs lies in developing a complex managerial mindset (Bartlett and Ghoshal, 1989; Caproni *et al.*, 1992).

The strategic perspective on global mindset has its foundations in international strategy research conducted at Harvard in the 1970s and 1980s, and most notably in the ground-breaking research of Bartlett and Ghoshal (1989, 1990, 1992). These authors address the importance of management's mentality in managing across borders, and identify the transnational organization as the ideal organization. The transnational organization is not a specific strategic posture or a particular organizational form but a new management mentality that 'recognize[s] that environmental demands and opportunities vary widely from country to country... [and] also recognize[s] that different parts of the company possess different capabilities' (Bartlett and Ghoshal, 1989: 64). Interestingly, the arguments of Bartlett and Ghoshal, writing in 1989, closely mirror the arguments proposed by Perlmutter and Heenan (Perlmutter, 1969; Heenan and Perlmutter, 1979) two decades earlier. The primary difference between them is their focus on the drivers of global mindset – cultural heterogeneity for Perlmutter and Heenan *vs* strategic complexity for Bartlett and Ghoshal.

The strategic stream of literature starts with the premise that the increased complexity, heterogeneity, and indeterminacy of MNCs (Doz and Prahalad, 1991) must be reflected in the cognitive abilities of its managers in order for companies to succeed (e.g., Murtha *et al.*, 1998; Paul, 2000). Accordingly, these studies describe the properties of global mindset in terms of high cognitive abilities and information-processing capabilities that help managers conceptualize complex global dynamics (e.g., Tichy *et al.*, 1992; Jeannet, 2000), balance between competing concerns and demands (e.g., Murtha *et al.*, 1998; Begley and Boyd, 2003), mediate the tension between the global and the local (e.g., Kefalas, 1998; Arora *et al.*, 2004), distinguish between and integrate across cultures and markets (e.g., Govindarajan and Gupta, 2001; Gupta and Govindarajan, 2002), and scan and pay attention to global issues (e.g., Rhinesmith, 1993; Bouquet, 2005; Levy, 2005).

For example, in defining global mindset, Jeannet (2000: 11) emphasizes the ability to integrate across domains: 'The executive with a global mindset has the ability to see across multiple territories and focuses on commonalities across many markets rather than emphasizing the differences among countries.' He identifies several critical elements of global mindset: assessing global markets, analyzing globalization pathways, and providing adequate strategic response. According to this approach, global mindset must encompass strategy formulation and global strategic thinking. Jeannet (2000) also applies the concept of a global mindset at the corporate level and suggests that it encompasses 'those cultural aspects of a company that define the extent to which the firm has learned to think, behave, and operate in global terms' (Jeannet,

2000: 199). He notes, however, that even if a company were populated with an adequate pool of managers, each possessing a global mindset, this would be insufficient if the company as a whole, expressed through its structure, processes, and behavior, did not also espouse the same principles.

While Jeannet (2000) and Tichy *et al.* (1992) define global mindset in terms of managers' abilities to understand, recognize, and integrate across complex global dynamics, a few studies within the strategic stream focus on balancing between global integration and local responsiveness (e.g., Murtha *et al.*, 1998; Begley and Boyd, 2003) or on mediating the tension between 'thinking globally' and 'acting locally', (e.g., Kefalas, 1998; Arora *et al.*, 2004). For example, Murtha *et al.* (1998) define global mindset as the 'cognitive processes that balance competing country, business, and functional concerns' and examine the relationship between global mindset and cognitive shift in a sample of 305 managers in a US-based diversified MNC. In their study, global mindset is operationalized in terms of individual expectations regarding the impact of globalization and strategic change along three dimensions: integration, responsiveness, and coordination. Using longitudinal data, these authors found that change in global strategy resulted in a cognitive shift toward a more global mindset across all managers in the organization.

Another study that focuses on mediating the tension between the global and the local was conducted by Begley and Boyd (2003), who examine global mindset at the corporate level in a sample of 39 human resource managers in 32 high-tech MNC headquartered in the United States. They state that global mindset or 'glocal' mentality is the skill 'to recognize when global consistency, local responsiveness, or a balance of global and local tensions is best' (Begley and Boyd, 2003: 30). These authors find that many respondents in their study consider a global mindset to be a desirable state, leading to competitive advantage. Begley and Boyd, like Jeannet (2000), argue that to embed global mindset in an organization, supporting policies and practices are needed to deal with tensions related to structural issue (global formalization *vs* local flexibility), processual issues (global standardization *vs* local customization), and power issues (global dictates *vs* local delegation).

Similarly, Kefalas (1998) and Arora *et al.* (2004) focus on the tension between 'thinking globally'

and 'acting locally'. Kefalas suggests that global mindset is characterized by high levels of both conceptualization and contextualization abilities. Conceptualization refers to articulation of main concepts that describe a phenomenon and identification of the main relationships among these concepts and to the whole. Contextualization, on the other hand, refers to adaptation of a conceptual framework to the local environment (Kefalas, 1998; Arora *et al.*, 2004). Using Kefalas and colleagues' approach to global mindset (e.g., Kefalas and Neuland, 1997; Kefalas, 1998; Kefalas and Weatherly, 1998), Arora *et al.* (2004) find in their empirical study of 65 managers in the textile industry that managers are better in thinking globally (conceptualization) than they are in acting locally (contextualization). Their research results also show that, among all demographic characteristics, training in international management, manager's age, foreign country living experience, family member from a foreign country, and job experience in a foreign country have statistically significant impacts on managers' global mindset. At the same time, they find no significant relationship between global mindset and tenure, job category, or managerial position. The authors conclude that global mindset is a trait that can be developed with training.

Govindarajan and Gupta (2001) and Gupta and Govindarajan (2002) also regard the ability to simultaneously consider local cultures and markets and global dynamics as the defining characteristic of global mindset. They conceptualize global mindset as a knowledge structure characterized by both high differentiation and high integration. At the corporate level, these authors define global mindset as the aggregated individual global mindset adjusted for the distribution of power and mutual influence among the group. Govindarajan and Gupta (2001) acknowledge that the highest returns to investment in cultivating a global mindset will come from focusing on the more senior level. Nevertheless, their advice is unequivocal: if a company's goal is to capture and sustain global market leadership in its industry, it has to regard the development of a global mindset as a goal that encompasses every unit and every employee. These authors go on to suggest several mechanisms that can be used to cultivate a global mindset such as formal education (e.g., language skills), cross-border teams and projects, utilizing diverse locations for meetings, cultural learning programs, and expatriation (Govindarajan and Gupta, 2001).

Three recent empirical studies (Harveston *et al.*, 2000; Nummela *et al.*, 2004; Bouquet, 2005) examine the relationship among firm strategic position, market characteristics, and global mindset. Harveston *et al.*, in their study of 224 managers in 'born global' firms (firms engaged in foreign activities accounting for 25% of sales within three years of founding), have more global mindsets, as well as more international experience and higher risk tolerance than managers of gradually globalizing firms. Nummela *et al.* (2004) examine the relationship among a firm's market characteristics, management international experience, and corporate global mindset in a sample of 72 small and medium Finnish companies. Their results show that market characteristics – globalness of the market in which the firm operates and the turbulence of the market – are positively related to global mindset. Management experience, measured as international work experience, is also positively related to global mindset, whereas international education is not. The research results also show a positive relationship between global mindset and financial indicators of the firm's international performance, whereas global mindset is not related to managers' subjective evaluations of international performance.

Bouquet (2005) also focuses on the relationship between a firm's decision environment and top management team (TMT) global mindset in his study of 136 MNCs. He defines global mindset as attention to global strategic issues, arguing that attention is the core element and a primary manifestation of global mindset. However, rather than hypothesizing a direct relationship between the firm's decision environment (i.e., firm's global strategic posture, firm's international interdependence, and global competition) and TMT attention to global strategic issues, he argues that global attention structures (i.e., structural positions related to globalization, global meetings, economic incentives for global efforts, and leadership development for globalization), which firms put in place to regulate allocation of attention, will partially mediate the relationship between firms' decision environments and TMT attention. Bouquet (2005) finds empirical support for the hypothesized relationships, suggesting that the firm's decision environment influences attention structures, which, in turn, affect TMT attention to global strategic issues. Furthermore, the results show a concave relationship between TMT attention to global issues and firm performance. Bouquet (2005) concludes that excessive as well as insufficient amounts of TMT attention to global strategic issues can have a negative effect on firm performance, which means that, contrary to accepted wisdom, more global mindset is not always better.

In contrast with the above studies that examine the relationship between a firm's characteristics and global mindset, Levy (2005) examines the relationship between TMT attention patterns, viewed as a primary manifestation of global mindset, and the global strategic posture of firms. She finds consistent support for the proposition linking TMT attention patterns, measured using content analysis of letters to shareholders of 69 American firms with the expansiveness of global strategic posture. The results suggest that firms are more likely to be highly global when their top management pays attention to the global environment and considers a diverse set of elements in this environment. On the other hand, firms led by top management teams that pay more attention to the internal environment are less likely to consider globalization as a viable strategic choice or to develop extensive global operations.

An underlying dimension of the strategic perspective: cognitive complexity

Although it is seldom mentioned explicitly, cognitive complexity and the cognitive capabilities associated with it serve as an underlying theme of the strategic perspective and therefore should be viewed as a second major conceptual dimension of global mindset. Work on cognitive complexity dates back more than 40 years (e.g., Bieri, 1955; Harvey *et al.*, 1961; Schroder *et al.*, 1967; Schroder and Suedfeld, 1971; Streufert and Streufert, 1978; Streufert *et al.*, 1988; Streufert and Swezey, 1986; Streufert and Nogami, 1989), and in the area of management the complexity of managerial cognition has long been recognized as a significant factor affecting decision-making, strategic choice, and organizational performance (Weick, 1979; Kiesler and Sproull, 1982; Bartunek *et al.*, 1983; Schwenk, 1984; Duhaime and Schwenk, 1985; Ginsberg, 1990; Miller, 1993). For example, Weick (1979: 261) advised managers to 'complicate yourself!', arguing that, for managers to be effective, they need to develop the capability to see events from multiple perspectives and to generate several competing interpretations of events and their interactive effects.[4]

Cognitive complexity represents the degree of differentiation, articulation, and integration within a cognitive structure (Bartunek *et al.*, 1983; Weick and Bougon, 1986). That is, a cognitive structure composed of a comparatively large number of finely articulated and well-integrated elements is regarded as relatively complex. While cognitive complexity usually represents the structural dimension of a cognitive structure (i.e., the internal organization of information units), when considering cognitive complexity in relation to a specific information domain, the structural and content (i.e., specific information units or knowledge) dimensions become entwined. That is, without adequate knowledge, an individual cannot form a complex representation of the information domain. Therefore our conceptualization of cognitive complexity encompasses both the structural and knowledge dimensions necessary to form complex representation and understanding.

Research on cognitive complexity has generally found that cognitively complex individuals have superior information-processing capabilities. Cognitively complex people search for more wide-ranging and novel information (Karlins and Lamm, 1967; Dollinger, 1984; Streufert and Swezey, 1986), spend more time interpreting it (Sieber and Lanzetta, 1964; Dollinger, 1984), perceive a larger number of dimensions, and simultaneously hold and apply several competing and complementary interpretations (Bartunek *et al.*, 1983). Cognitive complexity has also been associated with more well-rounded impressions (Streufert and Swezey, 1986), ability to redefine problems (Merron *et al.*, 1987; Lepsinger *et al.*, 1989), ability to balance contradictions, tolerance for ambiguity (Streufert *et al.*, 1968), and consideration of more alternative viewpoints (Chang and McDaniel, 1995). Taken together, these works attest to the significance of cognitive complexity or, alternatively, to the detrimental effects of cognitive simplicity in a rapidly changing, complex world. In the multinational context, cognitive complexity is needed to simultaneously balance the often contradictory demands of global integration with local responsiveness.

The multidimensional perspective

In addition to the two major streams in the global mindset literature identified above, there is a third stream of research in the global mindset literature that incorporates both the cultural and strategic dimensions, as well as several additional characteristics. This multidimensional research stream, increasingly evident in the literature beginning in 1994, is heavily influenced by the work of

Rhinesmith (1992, 1993, 1996), whose definition of global mindset (see Table 1) combines elements from both the cultural and strategic perspectives.

Rhinesmith (1992: 64) argues that people with global mindsets tend to drive for the bigger, broader picture, accept life as a balance of contradictory forces, trust organizational processes rather than structure, value diversity, are comfortable with surprises and ambiguity, and seek to be open to themselves and others. Thus, according to Rhinesmith, global mindset entails high levels of cognitive capabilities, especially scanning and information-processing capabilities, as well as the ability to balance competing realities and demands and to appreciate cultural diversity. Rhinesmith's approach represents a multidimensional perspective to global mindset, incorporating not only the cultural and the strategic dimensions but also individual characteristics drawn from the literature on global leadership.

Most work in the multidimensional stream builds directly on Rhinesmith's approach (e.g., Neff, 1995; Srinivas, 1995; Ashkenas *et al.*, 1995; Kedia and Mukherji, 1999; Paul, 2000). Authors writing in this stream, in addition to characterizing global mindset in terms of the abilities to recognize and understand complex and often unexpected business, cultural, and geopolitical dynamics, list a variety of attributes when describing global mindset. Kedia and Mukherji (1999), for example, state that global mindset is characterized by openness and an ability to recognize complex interconnections. Building on Rhinesmith (1993) and Kefalas and Neuland (1997), Kedia and Mukherji (1999) assert that three main characteristics of a global mindset that distinguish it from a non-global mindset are a unique time perspective, a unique space perspective, and a general predisposition. A unique time perspective means having a long-term view of international business activities, and a unique space perspective is defined as extending personal space well beyond immediate surroundings. Managers who have the general disposition required for global mindset are 'more tolerant of other peoples and cultures, consider cultural diversity an asset, thrive on ambiguity, balance contradictory forces, and rethink boundaries' (Kedia and Mukherji, 1999: 236). Kedia and Mukherji also draw on work in the global leadership literature and note that global mindset includes an emotional connection, capacity for managing uncertainty, ability to balance tensions, and savvy (Gregersen *et al.*, 1998). Moreover, they argue that, in order to be globally effective, managers need not only a global mindset, but also a certain set of supportive knowledge and skills.

Global mindset, information processing, and managerial performance: an integrative framework

In the following section, we propose an approach to global mindset that integrates across the literature reviewed above, drawing on the underlying constructs of cosmopolitanism and cognitive complexity. We purposefully restrict our discussion to the individual level of analysis and define global mindset at this level, while proposing that future work should also incorporate top management team and organizational level phenomena. In addition, while we acknowledge that others have included a variety of traits and skills in characterizing global mindset, we focus primarily on the cognitive properties of global mindset, as we view them as the most fundamental building blocks of the construct.

Defining global mindset

We view global mindset as an individual-level construct that captures and represents a unique multidimensional cognition. Thus global mindset is an individual-level cognitive structure or, more generally, a knowledge structure. We define global mindset as *a highly complex cognitive structure characterized by an openness to and articulation of multiple cultural and strategic realities on both global* *and local levels, and the cognitive ability to mediate and integrate across this multiplicity.* Elaborating on this definition, global mindset is characterized by three complementary aspects:

(1) an openness to and awareness of multiple spheres of meaning and action;
(2) complex representation and articulation of cultural and strategic dynamics; and
(3) mediation and integration of ideals and actions oriented both to the global and the local.

These three elements create a multidimensional continuum along which global mindset can be evaluated and measured. Thus individuals with the highest levels of global mindset are simultaneously aware of and open to multiple spheres of meaning and action, and are able to bridge and synthesize across these spheres.

Global mindset and information processing

The importance of global mindset rests on the proposition that cognitive structures not only represent and order an information domain, but also significantly affect information processing. We explore this link by examining how global mindset affects the cognitive capabilities of individuals and their decision-making patterns, thereby exerting significant influence on the strategic capabilities of firms. Figure 1 presents our integrated model of global mindset and information processing.

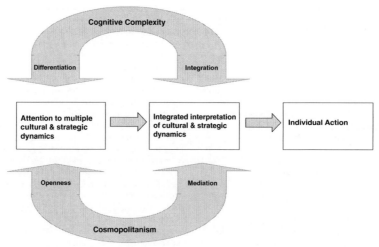

Figure 1   Information-processing model of global mindset.

Our framework is grounded in the information-processing theory.[5] Analytically, we begin with a basic information-processing model that involves three phases: attention (or information acquisition), interpretation, and action (Daft and Weick, 1984).[6] Cognitive structures, global mindset included, affect the processes of attention and interpretation, subsequently influencing future action. Moreover, the effects of individual cognitive structures are particularly pronounced in dynamic and complex environments that are characterized by information over-abundance, ambiguity, and uncertainty. Under such conditions, where the environment does not provide clear cognitive cues, attention and interpretation patterns tend to reflect individual propensities rather than environmental constraints (Abrahamson and Hambrick, 1997).

Drawing on the literature on cosmopolitanism and cognitive complexity we can explicate the effect of global mindset on the processes of 'noticing and constructing meaning' (Kiesler and Sproull, 1982) under conditions of rapid change, uncertainty, and complexity that characterize the environment facing managers in most global organizations. First, at the attentional or information-gathering stage, cognitive structures shape attention patterns by directing attention toward certain aspects of the environment while 'blocking' others. In this respect, cognitive structures act as a lens through which individuals perceive the environment. Thus global mindset affects information-processing patterns by directing attention to multiple and diverse sources of information about both the global and local environments. Cosmopolitanism brings an open, non-judgmental stance to the perception of information, thus enabling individuals to be open to and acquire information from a variety of sources and arenas without regard to its national or cultural origin. At the same time, cognitive complexity enables individuals to perceive and finely articulate more information elements and to integrate them into more complex schemas.

The effect of cognitive structures, however, goes beyond shaping attention and information acquisition to affect interpretative patterns. At the interpretation stage, cognitive structures affect the process of 'sense making' or how information is perceived, interpreted, assimilated, and understood (Daft and Weick, 1984). As mentioned above, global mindset is characterized by openness and high levels of differentiation and integrative capacity. Thus information is not only perceived, but also

evaluated without regard to its national or cultural origin. Moreover, individuals with high integrative abilities can synthesize information from varied and unlikely sources and incorporate diverse interpretative frameworks into the decision-making process. Finally, reflexive interpretative processes can potentially lead to the construction of a new and more complex understanding of the environment (Barr *et al.*, 1992). Thus global mindset shapes interpretative processes by promoting a non-prejudicial and non-judgmental perception and evaluation of information, integration of information from diverse sources, and reflection both on the interpretative process itself and on existing mental models. Individuals who have a global mindset are more likely to arrive at complex, innovative, and non-conventional interpretations that do not simplify global realities, but rather represent them in all their complexity, ambiguity, and indeterminacy.

The impact of an individual's global mindset does not stop with that person. Indeed, the processes of 'noticing and constructing meaning' that are associated with global mindset may have significant implications for the strategic capabilities of the firm. While strategic behavior is shaped by a multitude of factors, both the managerial cognition and the upper echelon perspectives suggest that information-processing capabilities of employees, particularly those in senior positions, significantly affect strategic response (e.g., Hambrick and Mason, 1984; Nystrom and Starbuck, 1984; Ford, 1985; Stubbart, 1989; Egelhoff, 1991; Thomas *et al.*, 1993; Finkelstein and Hambrick, 1996; Barkema and Vermeulen, 1998). Senior managers interpret issues relevant to strategic decision-making, and possess the power necessary for implementing choices derived from those interpretations (Hambrick and Mason, 1984). Moreover, information-processing capabilities of senior managers are especially important under conditions of rapid change, uncertainty, and complexity where strategic response involves interpreting and 'enacting' the business environment (Daft and Weick, 1984; Smircich and Stubbart, 1985; Carpenter and Fredrickson, 2001). Thus we propose that firms whose senior executives possess a global mindset will enact more effective global strategies.

At the same time, some recent evidence suggests that global mindset may not always lead to effectiveness. For example, Bouquet (2005) finds a curvilinear relationship between TMT global mindset and firm performance. It may be, as Bouquet (2005) asserts, that 'too much global mindset' may indicate or cause a fragmentation of attention across too many countries, that depth of understanding may suffer, and that there is a limit as to how much global mindset is effective. However, Bouquet (2005) takes a behavioral rather than cognitive approach to global mindset, measuring the behaviors rather than the cognitive capabilities of the TMT. Therefore it is not unrealistic to propose that the managers in his study may have been simply overwhelmed by the amount of information-processing requirements posed by the global context, thus leading to the fall in performance at higher levels of 'global mindset'.

Although empirical work has not yet examined this issue, we propose that there is an optimal fit between global mindset and organizational effectiveness. Under conditions of rapid change and high levels of complexity, key decision-makers must have a global mindset to understand and respond to their environment. However, a global mindset also entails high levels of information-processing demands, which could either overwhelm decision-makers or slow down decision-making to unacceptable levels in the face of rapid environmental change. Thus it is possible that higher levels of global mindset among key decision-makers will have a positive impact on a firm's effectiveness, but only when it is accompanied by support structures and processes within the firm, such as modular networks, communities of practice, distributed management and centers of excellence (Begley and Boyd, 2003). While an extensive discussion of these relationships is beyond the scope of this paper, we will explore a number of these ideas in the section below devoted to future research directions. Before doing so, however, we first provide a critical assessment of the field and discuss the implications of our integrative approach to global mindset.

Discussion

As the literature review indicates, the current thinking on global mindset can be categorized into three research streams: cultural, strategic, and multidimensional. Beyond these common themes, however, there is diversity both within and across research streams, as well as conceptual ambiguity in the field. Studies vary widely in their conceptualization and definition of the construct, level of analysis, and operationalization of global mindset. In addition, empirical studies report inconsistent and contradictory findings. Because of this diversity of perspectives and results, we offer here a critical

reading of the literature as a first step toward building a more theoretically grounded and rigorous research agenda.

The core properties of global mindset

The most fundamental inconsistency in the current literature concerns the core properties of global mindset. The above review indicates that studies provide diverse answers to the question 'What is a global mindset?' Its core properties are described in three, relatively distinct, sets of terms. The first set of terms is *cognitive*, where studies explicate the core properties of global mindset using cognitive and information-processing terms such as 'knowledge structure', 'cognitive structure', 'ability to develop and interpret', 'attention', 'sensemaking', and 'conceptualization and contextualization abilities'. The second set of terms used by authors to describe global mindset can be called *existentialist*, as studies define global mindset using terms such as a 'way of being', 'state of mind', 'orientation', 'openness', and 'awareness', although a careful reading of these definitions also reveals a strong cognitive underpinning. The third set of descriptors is *behavioral*, where studies define global mindset in behavioral, dispositional, and competency-related terms such as 'propensity to engage', 'ability to adapt', 'curiosity', and 'seeking opportunities', among others. Obviously, this diversity of terms and perspectives on global mindset, which draw on different and distinct theoretical and research perspectives, presents a considerable challenge for theoretical integration across the field.

Dimensionality of global mindset

As the literature review indicates, global mindset has been conceptualized and measured both as a unidimensional and as a multidimensional construct. The unidimensional conceptualizations focus primarily on the cross-cultural aspects of global mindset (Kobrin, 1994; Gupta and Govindarajan, 2002). On the other hand, the multidimensional approaches, which often draw on the international strategy literature, conceptualize global mindset in terms of integration and localization challenges faced by MNCs.[7] We have argued in this paper that there are two primary dimensions – cultural and strategic – that should be reflected in the conceptualization and measures of global mindset. Moreover, the level of complexity and multidimensionality of the global environment suggests that global mindset is likely to be a multidimensional construct.

Level of analysis

As Table 1 indicates, research on global mindset has been conducted at multiple levels of analysis (i.e., individual, group, and organization). Thus, in the current literature, global mindset can tentatively be considered as a multilevel construct, involving conceptual and methodological issues specific to multilevel research (see Rousseau, 1985, for an excellent discussion of methodological issues that arise from multilevel research). Because of the diversity of perspectives yet lack of debate on this issue, one of the most basic questions highlighted by our literature review is whether global mindset can indeed be considered an attribute of individuals, groups, and organizations. A related question concerns the theoretical relationships among the global mindset constructs at different theoretical levels.[8] For example, while researchers often speak of individual *and* organizational global mindsets (Bartlett and Ghoshal, 1989; Govindarajan and Gupta, 1998), the question of whether these constructs are identical across levels remains unanswered.

Operationalization of global mindset

Another source of methodological concern is the operationalization of global mindset. Global mindset has been operationalized using diverse measures and data sources both within and across theoretical levels – in some cases as a unidimensional construct (Kobrin, 1994; Gupta and Govindarajan, 2002) and in others as a multidimensional construct. As Table 2 indicates, measures at the individual level use two primary measures: self-report questionnaires measuring individual attitudes and preferences (Gupta and Govindarajan, 2002; Arora *et al.*, 2004) and expectations regarding the MNC's global strategy (Murtha *et al.*, 1998). At the team level, studies use behavioral and textual measures of top management team global mindset (Bouquet, 2005; Levy, 2005), and at the organizational level, studies utilize perceptual data of globalization-related organizational policies and practices (Kobrin, 1994; Gupta and Govindarajan, 2002).

This diversity of measures, which reflects the conceptual heterogeneity and ambiguity discussed above, calls for critical assessment of the content and construct validity of the various measures at different levels of analysis (level-specific validity). In general, establishing content validity would involve specifying the relevant content domain of global mindset at each level of analysis. Establishing construct validity would involve explicating a

theoretical network of constructs – antecedents and/or outcomes – that relate to global mindset in a consistent theoretically predicted way (Carmines and Zeller, 1979).[9] These specifications, which are theoretical in nature, may prove to be exceptionally difficult to identify for an abstract construct such as global mindset. Nevertheless, a first step toward ensuring an adequate level-specific operationalization of global mindset would be to map out the relevant universe of content that defines global mindset at each theoretical level, and explicate the theoretical relationships between global mindset and its antecedents and/or outcomes.

Empirical research

Although there have been very few empirical studies of global mindset to date, the above review indicates the diversity of perspectives taken by researchers. In fact, because of this diversity and results that are often inconsistent and conflicting, very few conclusions can be drawn about the empirical relationships between global mindset and other individual- or organizational-level variables. For example, one of the most significant questions is whether global mindset follows strategy and structure or vice versa. For example, Levy (2005) finds a significant relationship between global mindset and global strategy, suggesting that TMT global mindset drives globalization. On the other hand, Murtha *et al.* (1998), Harveston *et al.* (2000), and Nummela *et al.* (2004) suggest that managerial global mindset follows strategy, rather than the other way around. Yet another study, by Bouquet (2005), suggests that the relationship between TMT global mindset and firm characteristics is mediated by firms' attention structures, and that the link between these characteristics and global mindset is not straightforward. Finally, and contrary to the above findings, Kobrin (1994) and Arora *et al.* (2004) conclude that global mindset is not related to firm characteristics.

Another important question at the organizational level concerns the effect of global mindset on firm performance. Here the evidence is slim and again inconsistent. Nummela *et al.* (2004) find a positive relationship between global mindset and financial indicators of the international performance of firms, and no significant relationship between global mindset and managers' subjective evaluations of performance. Bouquet (2005), on the other hand, finds a curvilinear relationship between TMT attention to global issues and firm performance.

Finally, surprisingly little is known about the empirical relationship between global mindset and individual characteristics. While a few writers in the field of global leadership explore these issues (e.g., McCall and Hollenbeck, 2002; Maznevski and Lane, 2004), Arora *et al.* (2004) provide the only direct evidence that individual characteristics such as international management training, foreign country living experience, and foreign country job are related to managers' global mindset. Nummela *et al.* (2004) offer tangential evidence on this relationship with their finding that TMT international work experience is positively related to global mindset, whereas TMT international education is not related to global mindset.

Summary and implications

There are a number of important contributions to our understanding of the conceptual and empirical relationships involving global mindset that reflect the interest in global mindset as a way to cope with increasing cultural diversity and environmental complexity of the global arena. The capabilities associated with global mindset have been singled out as *the* critical building blocks of present-day MNCs, significantly affecting the global competitiveness of firms, yet researchers are faced with the challenge of explicating the complex construct of global mindset. To help move the field forward we have proposed a framework that specifies the core properties of global mindset and establishes a link between global mindset and global competitiveness of firms. In summary, we discuss the implications of our integrative framework and offer directions for future research.

Implications of the integrative framework

As our review and critique of the literature indicate, there are still fundamental unresolved issues regarding global mindset. The integrative framework we put forward offers a parsimonious conceptualization of global mindset and addresses the following major questions:

(1) What are the core properties of global mindset?
(2) At what level(s) of analysis should global mindset be studied?
(3) Is global mindset a unidimensional or a multidimensional construct?
(4) How should global mindset be operationalized and measured at each level of analysis?
(5) What are the possible links between global mindset and effective global management?

First, we conceptualize global mindset as a highly complex individual-level cognitive structure characterized by openness, differentiated articulation of cultural and strategic dynamics on both local and global scales, and integration across these multiple domains. Thus we define the core properties of global mindset in cognitive terms rather than provide an exhaustive list of attitudes, dispositions, and skills. At the same time, developing a clear model linking cognitions with traits, skills, and behaviors, while beyond the scope of this paper, represents a critical avenue for future work on global mindset.

Second, we define global mindset as an individual-level construct. By providing an explicit description of the target level of analysis, this definition enhances theory development and empirical work on global mindset (Rousseau, 1985; Klein *et al.*, 1994). However, while we define global mindset at the individual level, as a cognitive construct it is robust and can also be considered an attribute of groups and organizations and examined across multiple levels (Schneider and Angelmar, 1993; Walsh, 1995). In addition, a cognitive approach can help underpin the causal determinants of global mindset at different levels of analysis, and explicate the relationships between global mindset across levels.

Third, our approach clearly points out that global mindset is a multidimensional construct, incorporating both cultural and strategic dimensions, as well as local and global levels. These dimensions offer a preliminary mapping of the relevant content domain of global mindset. However, from a cognitive perspective, content is only one aspect of cognitive structures. Conceptually, cognitive structures can be analyzed in terms of their content and/or structure (Walsh, 1995). Thus, in addition to delineating the relevant content domain of global mindset, our definition of global mindset also explicates its structural properties by suggesting that it is a complex cognitive structure characterized by high differentiation, articulation, and integration.

Fourth, by defining global mindset using a cognitive framework, and by specifying both its structural and content dimensions, we provide an approach that is conducive to operationalization. While it is beyond the scope of this article to provide a systematic review of methods to assess cognition, the managerial cognition literature offers several approaches to assessing both the content and the structure of cognitive structures (see Walsh, 1995, for detailed review; see also Huff, 1990; Barr *et al.*, 1992; Lant *et al.*, 1992; Calori *et al.*,

1994). For example, Calori *et al.* used the cognitive mapping technique to measure the complexity of managerial mindset, and Barr *et al.* used textual analysis of organizational documents to measure the mental models of executives.

Finally, we explore the information-processing consequences of global mindset, thus proposing a clear, theoretically based link between global mindset and effective global management. We suggest that a global mindset has significant effects on information-processing patterns that may translate into superior managerial capabilities of firms operating in the global arena. Thus grounding global mindset in the cognitive and information-processing literature allows for the testing of the oft-stated but rarely tested assumption that a global mindset is necessary for the effective management of global firms (Ohmae, 1989; Doz and Prahalad, 1991; Bartlett and Ghoshal, 1992). If a global mindset is indeed found to be related to the organizational effectiveness of MNCs, this will have profound implications for research and practice in international management in general and international human resource management in particular.

As the literature reviewed in this article reveals, scholars from a number of disciplines have attempted to define global mindset, resulting in a myriad of definitions, which is the mark of a relatively young field. Moreover, the large number of dimensions often used to define global mindset makes it difficult to measure and test propositions involving global mindset. By defining global mindset using a cognitive framework, we provide an approach that is easier to both understand and operationalize in future research efforts. We also draw attention to managerial cognitive capabilities in MNCs in the hope of engendering a 'cognitive revolution' in international management research. In our call for a renewed focus on cognition, we follow the lead of Doz and Prahalad (1991), who argued that the newly emerging MNC mandates nothing less than a paradigmatic shift where the mindsets or cognitive orientations of managers constitute the basic unit of analysis.

Directions for future research
There are still numerous research areas that need to be addressed on global mindset, its antecedents, and its impact on the management and performance of MNCs. While the questions we have regarding global mindset are virtually limitless, our literature review and model suggest the following research agenda.[10]

How does global mindset develop over time?
The notion that global mindset is a capability that can be developed over time resonates in the recent work of Lane *et al.* (2004) and the earlier work of Srinivas (1995). In particular, Bird and Osland (2004), taking a developmental approach, make an important distinction between novice and expert global managers. Previous research suggests that international experience (cf. Black *et al.*, 1999a,b; Aycan, 2001; Arora *et al.*, 2004), as well as international management development and cross-cultural training programs (cf. Selmer *et al.*, 1998; Stahl, 2001) can play a role in the development of global managers and, by implication, their global mindsets (McCall and Hollenbeck, 2002).

At the same time it has also been argued that international experience may not lead to the development of a global mindset if an individual does not have a requisite level of inquisitiveness and openness (Bird and Osland, 2004; Black *et al.*, 1999a,b). Global mindset, like other cognitive capabilities, may require certain innate qualities:

> An individual's thinking style develops with *genetic* influence, modeling of others, and a process of formal education. In other words, one's ability to think critically is to a certain extent *genetically* predetermined but is strongly influenced by formal and informal learning experiences (Redding, 2001: 58, emphasis added).

This leads us to examine the role of nature *vs* nurture in developing a global mindset, and its implications regarding the selection and development of managers. An obvious next step would be to conduct longitudinal research on employees sent on international assignments to see whether global mindset does indeed grow with international exposure. Research is also needed to determine how international assignments may be designed and managed to ensure that they result in an increase in this important capability.

For example, what types of human resource management policy are more likely to foster the development of a global mindset within the TMT and throughout the organization? (Boyacigiller *et al.*, 2004). Can geocentric HR policies and greater opportunities for international assignments increase the development of a global mindset? Can company-wide, multicultural training programs foster the development of global mindset within employees? Stahl's work on intercultural assessment centers posits that characteristics that are important determinants of success in international assignments may be 'teachable' in management development programs (Stahl, 2001), and our own work suggests that selecting individuals with higher levels of cognitive complexity and cosmopolitanism is an important prerequisite to the success of such programs.

How is global mindset at the individual level related to global mindset at the TMT and organizational levels?

One question that has not been posed, but which we find crucial, is the relationship between global mindset at the individual level and the impact of global mindset at the organizational level. Who in an organization needs a global mindset? Is there a tipping point, or a critical mass of individuals within an MNC that needs to possess a global mindset in order for it to have an impact on organizational performance? Moreover, what is the influence of diversity within the TMT on this crucial managerial characteristic? The organizational literature presents somewhat conflicting results regarding the impact of diversity on team performance (Williams and O'Reilly, 1998), suggesting that perhaps the international management literature may be a bit too optimistic regarding the positive impact of organizational diversity on the development of global mindset.

What role does organizational culture play in developing and sustaining a global mindset? Will, for example, organizational cultural values of adaptability, fostering risk-taking and flexibility facilitate the experimentation that is conducive to the development of a global mindset? What role is played by organizational boundary-spanning processes and structure? Do organizations with formal mechanisms in place to transfer learning across national boundaries foster the development of a higher level of global mindset?

What is the relationship between global mindset and effective managerial action?

Having a global mindset is necessary but not sufficient to become an effective global manager. As Bird and Osland (2004: 60) note, global mindset must be combined with the ability to define the appropriate actions to take and the ability to actually execute those actions. These observations lead us to the question of what specific behavioral attributes are necessary for global mindset to result in actions that impact organizational performance.

What is the relationship between global mindset and organizational performance?

Is having a TMT with a global mindset a competitive advantage in all MNCs regardless of strategic focus? The prevailing literature generally supports the notion that, when it comes to global mindset, more is better, but Bouquet (2005) cautions that there may be limits to the effectiveness of global mindset. Is the relationship between global mindset and organizational performance strongest in those firms pursuing a transnational strategy, as suggested by Murtha *et al.* (1998), or may it be even more important in the meta-national organizations championed by Doz *et al.* (2001), who argue that 'learning from the world' is critical in today's global knowledge economy?

How does global mindset differ from other related constructs such as cultural intelligence, global leadership and expatriate success?

For example, how are global mindset and cultural intelligence (CQ) related (Earley and Mosakowski, 2004; Thomas and Inkson, 2004)? Earley and Mosakowski (2004) define CQ as 'the ability to make sense of unfamiliar contexts and then blend in'. This definition makes CQ quite distinctive from global mindset, yet one could argue that having a higher level of CQ could facilitate the development of a global mindset.

As a final note, we suggest that further theory-building and empirical work on global mindset should draw on broader theoretical perspectives beyond its current basis in international management, and should be conducted in diverse settings. It would be ironic if the construct of global mindset were to continue to be developed from a largely Western perspective and ignore the increasing number of voices calling for the testing of management theories in contexts that explicitly test their universality (Hofstede, 1980b; Boyacigiller and Adler, 1991).

Acknowledgements

This paper contains material based upon work supported by the National Science Foundation under Grant No. 0080703. Any opinions, findings, and conclusions or recommendations expressed in this material are those of the authors and do not necessarily reflect the views of the National Science Foundation. The authors would also like to thank Columbia University, Duke Corporate Education, Portland State University, Sabanci University, San Jose

State University, and the International Consortium for Executive Development Research for their support of this research. We also thank Professor Tom Murtha, colleagues at ION, C4, anonymous reviewers at the Academy of Management, the Academy of International Business, and *JIBS* for their helpful comments on earlier versions of this paper. The authors also gratefully acknowledge the research assistance of Elif Cicekli and Pinar Imer and the helpful guidance of *JIBS* Departmental Editor, Professor Mary Ann Von Glinow.

Notes

[1]Although outside the scope of this paper, a similar theme can be found in the literature on global leadership (e.g., McCall and Hollenbeck, 2002).

[2]Merton (1957) conceptualized cosmopolitans as individuals who are oriented toward the outside world, and locals as those who are narrowly concerned with the affairs of the community to the exclusion of world affairs. Extending this concept to university faculty, Gouldner (1957: 290) characterized cosmopolitans as 'those lower on loyalty to the employing organization, higher in commitment to their specialized role skills, and more likely to use outer reference group orientation'. While the cosmopolitan-local distinction was parsimonious, subsequent research (e.g., Gouldner, 1958; Glaser, 1963; Goldberg *et al.*, 1965; Flango and Brumbaugh, 1974; Goldberg 1976) found the construct to be more complex and multidimensional. For example, Gouldner (1958) divided cosmopolitans into two groups: outsiders and empire builders. Locals were split into four groups: dedicated, true bureaucrats, home-guards, and elders. Goldberg *et al.* (1965) expanded the cosmopolitan-local classification system to include four categories. In addition to the cosmopolitan and local categories, a third category, termed 'complex', described those employees who are simultaneously loyal to both their employing organization and their profession. The fourth category, termed 'indifferent', described those employees who were loyal to neither.

[3]Within the past 5 years, a host of initiatives and publications concerning cosmopolitanism have appeared (see Hollinger (2002) for a review of these developments). While we draw on this literature, a comprehensive discussion of the concept of cosmopolitanism is beyond the scope of this brief overview.

[4]The underlying logic behind this advice lies in the 'law of requisite variety' that maintains that, if a system is to survive, its internal complexity should match the complexity of its environment (Ashby, 1956).

[5]While information-processing theory has been applied at the individual (e.g., Wang and Chan, 1995; Hult and Ferrell, 1997; Leonard *et al.*, 1999), top management team (e.g., Sweet *et al.*, 2003), and organizational levels of analysis (e.g., Egelhoff, 1991; Wang, 2003), consistent with our approach to global mindset as an individual-level construct, our primary focus in this discussion is at the individual level. At the same time, there is an obvious and important overlap between the levels of analysis, as the more macro strategy literature views the top management team of MNCs as the location where a large portion of the strategic information-processing capacity of the organization lies (Egelhoff, 1991: 197).

[6]In general, the information-processing model is based on three fundamental tenets. First, individuals have limited information-processing capacity and therefore attend to only certain facets of the environment while ignoring others (Sproull, 1984). Second, environmental information undergoes interpretation that gives structure and meaning to the data (Daft and Weick, 1984). Third, these interpretations influence action (Kiesler and Sproull, 1982; Daft and Weick, 1984; Dutton and Duncan, 1987).

[7]The most explicit example of a multidimensional measure is used by Murtha *et al.* (1998), who draw on the integration–responsiveness framework (Prahalad and Doz, 1987). They measure global mindset in terms of managers' expectations regarding integration, responsiveness, and coordination. Similarly, Arora *et al.* (2004) use a self-report instrument that reflects two drivers of global value (local competencies and global coordination) suggested by Govindarajan and Gupta (2001).

[8]Put differently, the issue is whether the global mindset constructs theorized and measured at different levels are isomorphic, partially identical, or only weakly related (Rousseau, 1985). According to Rousseau (1985: 8): 'Isomorphism exists when the same functional relationship can be used to represent constructs at more than one level. isomorphism implies that constructs mean the same thing across levels...' Partial identity implies that constructs, although similar, 'behave' somewhat differently across levels. In addition, the same constructs used at different levels may be only weakly related.

[9]Arora *et al.* (2004), for example, established the construct validity of their global mindset measure by testing the relationships between global mindset and a set of individual background characteristics (training in international management, foreign country living experience and job experience, family member of foreign origin), often considered to be antecedents

of global mindset. They found that global mindset was significantly positively related to these characteristics. These theoretically predicted relationships tentatively support Arora's *et al.* (2004) global mindset measure.

[10]Some of the future research we are suggesting has already been conducted on related constructs (e.g., how to increase success on international assignments; global leadership development), but not on global mindset *per se.*

References

Abrahamson, E. and Hambrick, D.C. (1997) 'Attentional homogeneity in industries: the effect of discretion', *Journal of Organizational Behavior* **18**(Special Issue): 513–532.

Adler, N.J. and Bartholomew, S. (1992) 'Globalization and Human Resource Management', in A.M. Rugman and A. Verbeke (eds.) *Research in Global Strategic Management: Corporate Response to Change*, JAI Press: Greenwich, CT, pp: 179–201.

Aharoni, Y. (1966) *The Foreign Investment Decision Process*, Division of Research, Graduate School of Business, Harvard University: Boston.

Archibugi, D. (ed.) (2003) *Debating Cosmopolitics*, Verso: London.

Arora, A., Jaju, A., Kefalas, A.G. and Perenich, T. (2004) 'An exploratory analysis of global managerial mindsets: a case of US textile and apparel industry', *Journal of International Management* **10**(3): 393–411.

Ashby, W.R. (1956) *An Introduction to Cybernetics*, Wiley: New York.

Ashkenas, R., Ulrich, D., Jick, T. and Kerr, S. (1995) *The Boundaryless Organization: Breaking the Chains of Organizational Structure*, Jossey-Bass: San Francisco.

Aycan, Z. (2001) 'Expatriation: A Critical Step Toward Developing Global Leaders', in M.E. Mendenhall, T.M. Kuhlmann and G.K. Stahl (eds.) *Developing Global Business Leaders*, Quorum Books: Westport, CT, pp: 119–136.

Barkema, H.G. and Vermeulen, F. (1998) 'International expansion through start-up or acquisition: a learning perspective', *Academy of Management Journal* **41**(1): 7–26.

Barr, P.S., Stimpert, J.L. and Huff, A.S. (1992) 'Cognitive change, strategic action, and organizational renewal', *Strategic Management Journal* **13**(5): 15–36.

Bartlett, C.A. (1995) 'The New Global Challenge: Implementing Third-Generation Strategy through Second-Generation Organizations with First-Generation Management', in D.A. Ready (ed.) *In Charge of Change*, Lexington, MA: International Consortium for Executive Development Research, pp: 19–34.

Bartlett, C.A. and Ghoshal, S. (1989) *Managing Across Borders: The Transnational Solution*, Harvard Business School Press: Boston.

Bartlett, C.A. and Ghoshal, S. (1990) 'Matrix management: not a structure, a frame of mind', *Harvard Business Review* **68**(4): 138–145.

Bartlett, C.A. and Ghoshal, S. (1992) 'What is a global manager?', *Harvard Business Review* **70**(5): 124–132.

Bartunek, J.M., Gordon, J.R. and Weathersby, R.P. (1983) 'Developing "complicated" understanding in administrators', *Academy of Management Review* **8**(2): 273–284.

Beck, U. (2000) 'The cosmopolitan perspective: sociology and the second age of modernity', *British Journal of Sociology* **51**(1): 79–105.

Beechler, S., Levy, O., Taylor, S. and Boyacigiller, N. (2004) 'Does It Really Matter If Japanese MNCs Think Globally?', in A. Bird and T. Roehl (eds.) *Japanese Firms in Transition: Responding to the Globalization Challenge*, JAI Press: Greenwich, CT, pp: 265–292.

Begley, T.M. and Boyd, D.P. (2003) 'The need for a corporate global mind-set', *MIT Sloan Management Review* **44**(2): 25–32.

Bieri, J. (1955) 'Cognitive complexity–simplicity and predictive behavior', *Journal of Abnormal and Social Psychology* **51**(2): 261–268.

Bird, A. and Osland, J. (2004) 'Global Competencies: An Introduction', in H. Lane, M. Mendenhall, M. Maznevski, and J. McNett (eds.) *Handbook of Global Management: A Guide to Managing Complexity*, Blackwell: Oxford, pp: 57–80.

Black, J.S., Gregersen, H.B., Mendenhall, M.E. and Stroh, K. (1999a) *Globalizing People through International Assignments*, Addison-Wesley: Reading, MA.

Black, J.S., Morrison, A.J. and Gregersen, H.B. (1999b) *Global Explorers: The Next Generations of Leaders*, Routledge: New York.

Bouquet, C.A. (2005) *Building Global Mindsets: An Attention-Based Perspective*, Palgrave Macmillan: New York.

Boyacigiller, N.A. and Adler, N.J. (1991) 'The parochial dinosaur: organizational science in a global context', *Academy of Management Review* **16**(2): 262–291.

Boyacigiller, N., Beechler, S., Taylor, S. and Levy, O. (2004) 'The Crucial Yet Illusive Global Mindset', in H. Lane, M. Mendenhall, M. Maznevski and J. McNett (eds.) *Handbook of Global Management: A Guide to Managing Complexity*, Blackwell: Oxford, pp: 81–93.

Breckenridge, C.A., Pollock, S., Bhabha, H.K. and Chakrabarty, D. (eds.) (2000) *Cosmopolitanism*, Duke University Press: London.

Burpitt, W. and Rondinelli, D.A. (1998) 'Export decision-making in small firms: the role of organizational learning', *Journal of World Business* **33**(1): 51–68.

Calori, R., Johnson, G. and Sarnin, P. (1994) 'CEO's Cognitive Maps and the Scope of the Organization', *Strategic Management Journal* **15**(6): 437–457.

Caproni, P.J., Lenway, S.A. and Murtha, T.P. (1992) 'Multinational mindsets: sense making capabilities as strategic resources in multinational firms', Division of Research, School of Business Administration, The University of Michigan.

Carmines, E.G. and Zeller, R.A. (1979) *Reliability and Validity Assessment*, Sage Publications: Newbury Park, CA.

Carpenter, M.A. and Fredrickson, J.W. (2001) 'Top management teams, global strategic posture, and the moderating role of uncertainty', *Academy of Management Journal* **44**(3): 533–545.

Chakravarthy, A. and Perlmutter, H. (1985) 'Strategic planning for a global economy', *Columbia Journal of World Business* **20**(2): 3–10.

Chandler, A.D. (1962) *Strategy and Structure*, Cambridge, MA: MIT Press, pp 255–276.

Chang, C.K. and McDaniel, E.D. (1995) 'Information search strategies in loosely structured settings', *Journal of Educational Computing Research* **12**(1): 95–107.

Clifford, J. (1988) 'On orientalism', *The Predicament of Culture*, Harvard University Press: Cambridge, MA, pp: 255–276.

Daft, R.L. and Weick, K.E. (1984) 'Toward a model of organizations as interpretation systems', *Academy of Management Review* **9**(2): 284–295.

Dollinger, M.J. (1984) 'Environmental boundary spanning and information processing effects on organizational performance', *Academy of Management Journal* **27**(2): 351–368.

Doz, Y.L. and Prahalad, C.K. (1987) *The Multinational Mission: Balancing Local Demands and Global Vision*, New York: Free Press.

Doz, Y.L. and Prahalad, C.K. (1991) 'Managing DMNCs: a search for a new paradigm', *Strategic Management Journal* **12**: 145–164.

Doz, Y., Santos, J. and Williamson, P. (2001) *From Global to Metanational: How Companies Win in the Knowledge Economy*, Harvard Business School Press: Boston.

Duhaime, I.M. and Schwenk, C.R. (1985) 'Conjectures on cognitive simplification in acquisition and divestment decision making', *Academy of Management Review* **10**(2): 287–295.

Dutton, J.E. and Duncan, R.B. (1987) 'The influence of the strategic planning process on strategic chance', *Strategic Management Journal* **8**(2): 103–116.

Earley, P.C. and Mosakowski, E. (2004) 'Cultural intelligence', *Harvard Business Review* **82**(10): 139–146.

Egelhoff, W.G. (1991) 'Information-processing theory and the multinational enterprise', *Journal of International Business Studies* **22**(3): 341–368.

Estienne, M. (1997) 'The art of cross-cultural management: 'an alternative approach to training and development'', *Journal of European Industrial Training* **21**(1): 14–18.

Evans, P. and Doz, Y. (1993) 'Dualities: a Paradigm for Human Resource and Organizational Development in Complex Multinationals', in V. Pucik, N. Tichy and C. Barnett (eds) *Globalizing Management: Creating and Leading the Competitive Organization*, John Wiley & Sons: New York, pp: 85–106.

Evans, P., Pucik, V. and Barsoux, J.-L. (2002) *The Global Challenge: Frameworks for International Human Resource Management*, McGraw-Hill Irwin: Boston, MA.

Finkelstein, S. and Hambrick, D.C. (1996) *Strategic Leadership: Top Executives and Their Effects on Organizations*, West Publishing Company: St Paul, MN.

Flango, V.E. and Brumbaugh, R.B. (1974) 'The dimensionality of the cosmopolitan-local construct', *Administrative Science Quarterly* **19**(2): 198–210.

Fletcher, D. (2000) 'Learning to "think global and act local": Experiences from the small business sector', *Education & Training* **42**(4–5): 211–219.

Ford, J.D. (1985) 'The effects of causal attributions on decision makers', *Responses to Performance Downturns'*, *Academy of Management Review* **10**(4): 770–786.

Ghoshal, S. and Bartlett, C.A. (1995) 'Changing the role of top management: beyond structure to processes', *Harvard Business Review* **73**(1): 86–96.

Ginsberg, A. (1990) 'Connecting diversification to performance: a sociocognitive approach', *Academy of Management Review* **15**(3): 514–535.

Glaser, B.G. (1963) 'The local-cosmopolitan scientist', *American Journal of Sociology* **69**(3): 249–259.

Goldberg, A.I. (1976) 'The relevance of cosmopolitan/local orientations to professional values and behavior', *Sociology of Work and Occupation* **3**(3): 331–356.

Goldberg, L.C., Baker, F. and Rubenstein, A.H. (1965) 'Local-cosmopolitan: unidimensional or multidimensional?' *American Journal of Sociology* **70**(6): 704–710.

Gouldner, A.W. (1957) 'Cosmopolitans and locals: toward an analysis of latent social roles – I', *Administrative Science Quarterly* **2**(3): 281–306.

Gouldner, A.W. (1958) 'Cosmopolitans and locals: toward an analysis of latent social roles – II', *Administrative Science Quarterly* **2**(4): 444–480.

Govindarajan, V. and Gupta, A.K. (1998) 'Success is all in the mindset', *Financial Times*, February 27, p. 2.

Govindarajan, V. and Gupta, A.K. (2001) *The Quest for Global Dominance: Transforming Global Presence into Global competitive Advantage*, Jossey-Bass: San Francisco.

Gregersen, H.B., Morrison, A.J. and Black, J.S. (1998) 'Developing leaders for the global frontier', *Sloan Management Review* **40**(1): 21–32.

Gupta, A.K. and Govindarajan, V. (2002) 'Cultivating a global mindset', *Academy of Management Executive* **16**(1): 116–126.

Hambrick, D.C. and Mason, P. (1984) 'Upper echelons: the organization as a reflection of its top managers', *Academy of Management Review* **9**(2): 193–206.

Hambrick, D.C., Korn, L.B., Frederickson, J.W. and Ferry, R.M. (1989) *21st century report: re-inventing the CEO*, New York: Korn/Ferry and Columbia University's Graduate School of Business, pp: 1–9.

Hamel, G., Doz, Y.L. and Prahalad, C.K. (1989) 'Collaborate with your competitors – and win', *Harvard Business Review* **89**(1): 133–139.

Hannerz, U. (1996) 'Cosmopolitans and Locals in World Culture', in U. Hannerz (ed.) *Transnational Connections: Culture, People, Places*, London: Routledge, pp: 102–111.

Harveston, P.D., Kedia, B.L. and Davis, P.S. (2000) 'Internationalization of born global and gradual globalizing firms: the impact of the manager', *Advances in Competitiveness Research* **8**(1): 92–99.

Harvey, D. (2000) 'Cosmopolitanism and the banality of geographical evils', *Public Culture* **12**(2): 529–564.

Harvey, M. and Novicevic, M.M. (2001) 'The impact of hypercompetitive "timescapes" on the development of a global mindset', *Management Decision* **39**(5/6): 448–460.

Harvey, O.J., Hunt, D. and Schroder, H.M. (1961) *Conceptual Systems and Personality Organization*, Wiley: New York.

Hedlund, G. (1986) 'The Hypermodern MNC – A Heterarchy?' *Human Resource Management* **25**(1): 9–35.

Heenan, D. and Perlmutter, H. (1979) *Multinational Organizational Development: A Social Architecture Perspective*, Addison-Wesley: Reading, MA.

Held, D. (1995) *Democracy and the Global Order: From the Modern State to Cosmopolitan Governance*, Stanford University Press, Stanford, CA.

Hofstede, G. (1980) 'Motivation, leadership and organization: do American theories apply abroad?', *Organizational Dynamics* **9**(1): 42–63.

Hollinger, D.A. (2002) 'Not Universalists, Not Pluralists: The New Cosmopolitans Find Their Own Way', in S. Vertovec and R. Cohen (eds.) *Conceiving Cosmopolitanism: Theory, Context, and Practice*, Oxford University Press: Oxford, pp: 227–239.

Huff, A.S. (1990) 'Mapping Strategic Thought', in A.S. Huff (ed.) *Mapping Strategic Thought*, John Wiley & Sons: New York, pp: 11–49.

Hult, G.T.M. and Ferrell, O.C. (1997) 'A global learning organization structure and market information processing', *Journal of Business Research* **40**(2): 155–166.

Jeannet, J.-P. (2000) *Managing with a Global Mindset*, Financial Times/Prentice Hall: London.

Kanter, R.M. (1995) *World Class: Thriving Locally in the Global Economy*, Simon & Schuster: New York.

Karlins, M. and Lamm, H. (1967) 'Information search as a function of conceptual structure in a complex problem-solving task', *Journal of Personality and Social Psychology* **5**(4): 456–459.

Kedia, B.L. and Mukherji, A. (1999) 'Global managers: developing a mindset for global competitiveness', *Journal of World Business* **34**(3): 230–251.

Kefalas, A. (1998) 'Think globally, act locally', *Thunderbird International Business Review* **40**(6): 547–562.

Kefalas, A.G. and Neuland, E.W. (1997) 'Global mindsets: an exploratory study', Proceedings of Annual Conference of the Academy of International Business, Monterrey, Mexico, pp: 5–9.

Kefalas, A.G. and Weatherly, E.W. (1998) 'Global mindsets among college students in the United States and elsewhere: are we growing a globally minded workforce? Unpublished manuscript.

Kiesler, S. and Sproull, L. (1982) 'Managerial response to changing environments: perspectives on problem sensing from social cognition', *Administrative Science Quarterly* **27**(4): 548–570.

Kim, W.C. and Mauborgne, R.A. (1996) 'Procedural justice and managers', *In-Role and Extra-Role Behavior: The Case of the Multinational*, *Management Science* **42**(4): 499–515.

Kindleberger, C.P. (1969) *American Business Abroad: Six Lectures on Direct Investment*, Yale University Press: New Haven, CT.

Klein, K.J., Dansereau, F. and Hall, R.J. (1994) 'Levels issues in theory development, data collection, and analysis', *Academy of Management Review* **19**(2): 195–220.

Kobrin, S.J. (1994) 'Is there a relationship between a geocentric mind-set and multinational strategy?', *Journal of International Business Studies* 25(3): 493–511.

Lane, H.W., Maznevski, M.L., Mendenhall, M.E. and McNett, J. (eds.) (2004) *Handbook of Global Management: A Guide to Managing Complexity*, Blackwell: London.

Lant, K.T., Milliken, F.J. and Batra, B. (1992) 'The role of managerial learning and interpretation in strategic persistence and reorientation: an empirical exploration', *Strategic Management Journal* 13(8): 585–608.

Leonard, N.H., Scholl, R.W. and Kowalski, K.B. (1999) 'Information processing style and decision making', *Journal of Organizational Behavior* 20(3): 407–420.

Lepsinger, R., Mullen, T.P., Stumpf, S.A. and Wall, S.A. (1989) *Large Scale Management Simulations: A Training Technology for Assessing and Developing Strategic Management Skills. Advances in Management Development*, Praeger: New York.

Levitt, T. (1983) 'The globalization of markets', *Harvard Business Review* 61(3): 92–102.

Levy, O. (2005) 'The influence of top management team attentional patterns on global strategic posture of firms', *Journal of Organizational Behavior* 26(7): 797–819.

Maznevski, M.L. and Lane, H.W. (2004) 'Shaping the Global Mindset: Designing Educational Experiences for Effective Global Thinking and Action', in N. Boyacigiller, R.M. Goodman, and M. Phillips (eds.) *Crossing Cultures: Insights from Master Teachers*, Routledge: London, pp: 171–184.

McCall, M. and Hollenbeck, G. (2002) *Development Experiences of Global Executives*, Harvard Business School: Cambridge, MA.

Merron, K., Fisher, D. and Torbert, W.R. (1987) 'Meaning making and management action', *Group and Organizational Studies* 12(3): 274–286.

Merton, R.K. (1957) 'Patterns of influence: local and cosmopolitan influentials', in Merton, R.K. (ed.) *Social Theory and Social Structure*, Glencoe, IL: The Free Press, pp: 387–420.

Miller, D. (1993) 'The architecture of simplicity', *Academy of Management Review* 18(1): 116–138.

Murtha, T.P., Lenway, S.A. and Bagozzi, R.P. (1998) 'Global mind-sets and cognitive shift in a complex multinational corporation', *Strategic Management Journal* 19(2): 97–114.

Neff, P.J. (1995) 'Cross-cultural research teams in a global enterprise', *Research Technology Management* 38(3): 15–19.

Nummela, N., Saarenketo, S. and Puumalainen, K. (2004) 'A global mindset: a prerequisite for successful internationalization?', *Canadian Journal of Administrative Sciences* 21(1): 51–64.

Nystrom, P.C. and Starbuck, W.H. (1984) 'To avoid organizational crises, unlearn', *Organizational Dynamics* 12(4): 53–65.

Ocasio, W. (1997) 'Toward an Attention-Based View of the Firm', *Strategic Management Journal* 18(Summer, Special Issue): 187–206.

Ohmae, K. (1989) 'Managing in a borderless world', *Harvard Business Review* 67(3): 152–161.

Paul, H. (2000) 'Creating a mindset', *Thunderbird International Business Review* 42(2): 187–200.

Perlmutter, H. (1969) 'The tortuous evolution of the multinational corporation', *Columbia Journal of World Business* 4(1): 9–18.

Porter, M.E. (1980) *Competitive Strategy: Techniques for Analyzing Industries and Competitors*, New York: The Free Press.

Porter, M.E. (1986) 'Competition in global industries: A conceptual framework', In M.E. Porter (ed.) *Competition in Global Industries*, Boston, MA: Harvard Business School Press, pp: 15–60.

Prahalad, C.K. (1990) 'Globalization: the intellectual and managerial challenges', *Human Resource Management* 29(1): 27–37.

Prahalad, C.K. and Bettis, R.A. (1986) 'The dominant logic: a new linkage between diversity and performance', *Strategic Management Journal* 7(6): 485–501.

Prahalad, C.K. and Doz, Y.L. (1987) *The Multinational Mission: Balancing Local Demands and Global Vision*, The Free Press: New York.

Prahalad, C.K. and Lieberthal, K. (1998) 'The End of Corporate Imperialism', *Harvard Business Review* 76(4): 68–79.

Pucik, V., Tichy, N.M. and Barnett, C. (1992) *Globalizing Management: Creating and Leading the Competitive Organization*, John Wiley & Sons: New York.

Redding, D.A. (2001) 'The development of critical thinking among students in baccalaureate nursing education', *Holistic Nursing Practice* 15(4): 57–64.

Redding, G.S., Porter, L.W. and Crow, C. (1995) 'The Worldwide Movement of Human Resources and the Asia Pacific Challenge', in D.A. Ready (ed.) *In Charge of Change*, Lexington, MA: International Consortium for Executive Development Research, pp: 35–50.

Rhinesmith, S.H. (1992) 'Global mindsets for global managers', *Training & Development* 46(10): 63–69.

Rhinesmith, S.H. (1993) *Globalization: Six Keys to Success in a Changing World*, The American Society For Training and Development: Alexandria, VA.

Rhinesmith, S.H. (1996) *A Manager's Guide to Globalization: Six Skills for Success in a Changing World*, 2nd edn, McGraw-Hill: New York.

Robbins, B. (1992) 'Comparative cosmopolitanism', *Social Text*, No. 31/32, Third World and Post-Colonial Issues: 169–186.

Rosenzweig, P.M. and Singh, J.V. (1991) 'Organizational environments and the multinational enterprise', *Academy of Management Review* 16(2): 340–361.

Rousseau, D.M. (1985) 'Issues of level in organizational research: multi-level and cross-level perspectives', *Research in Organizational Behavior* 7: 1–37.

Sanders, W.G. and Carpenter, M.A. (1998) 'Internationalization and firm governance: the roles of CEO compensation, top team composition, and board structure', *Academy of Management Journal* 42(2): 158–178.

Schneider, S.C. and Angelmar, R. (1993) 'Cognition in organizational analysis: who's Minding the Store?' *Organization Studies* 14(3): 347–374.

Schroder, H., Driver, M. and Streufert, S. (1967) *Human Information Processing: Individuals and Groups Functioning in Complex Social Situations*, Holt, Rinehart & Winston: New York.

Schroder, H.M. and Suedfeld, P. (eds.) (1971) *Personality Theory and Information Processing*, Ronald Press: New York.

Schwenk, C.R. (1984) 'Cognitive simplification processes in strategic decision-making', *Strategic Management Journal* 5(2): 111–128.

Selmer, J., Torbiorn, I. and de Leon, C.T. (1998) 'Sequential cross-cultural training for expatriate business managers: predeparture and post-arrival', *International Journal of Human Resource Management* 9(5): 831–840.

Sieber, J.E. and Lanzetta, J.T. (1964) 'Conflict and conceptual structure as determinants of decision making behavior', *Journal of Personality and Social Psychology* 32(4): 622–641.

Smircich, L. and Stubbart, C. (1985) 'Strategic management in an enacted world', *Academy of Management Review* 10(4): 724–736.

Sproull, L.S. (1984) 'The nature of managerial attention', *Advances in Information Processing in Organizations* 1: 9–27.

Srinivas, K.M. (1995) 'Globalization of business and the third world: challenge of expanding the mindsets', *Journal of Management Development* 14(3): 26–49.

Stahl, G. (2001) 'Using Assessment Centers as Tools for Global Leadership Development: An Exploratory Study', in M.E. Mendenhall, T.M. Kuhlmann and G.K. Stahl (eds.) *Developing Global Business Leaders*, Quorum Books: Westport, CT, pp: 197–210.

Streufert, S. and Nogami, G. (1989) 'Cognitive Style and Complexity: Implications for I/O Psychology, in C.L. Cooper and I. Robertson (eds.) *International Review of Industrial and Organizational Psychology*, Wiley: Chichester, UK, pp: 93–143.

Streufert, S., Pogash, R.M. and Piasecki, M.T. (1988) 'Simulation based assessment of managerial competence: reliability and validity', *Personnel Psychology* 41(3): 537–555.

Streufert, S. and Streufert, S.C. (1978) *Behavior in the Complex Environment*, Winston: Washington, DC.

Streufert, S., Streufert, S.C. and Castore, C.H. (1968) 'Leadership in negotiations and the complexity of conceptual structure', *Journal of Applied Psychology* **52**(3): 218–223.

Streufert, S. and Swezey, R.W. (1986) *Complexity, Managers, and Organizations*, Academic Press: Orlando, FL.

Stubbart, C.I. (1989) 'Managerial cognition: a missing link in strategic management research', *Journal of Management Studies* **26**(4): 325–347.

Sweet, S., Roome, N. and Sweet, P. (2003) 'Corporate environmental management and sustainable enterprise: the influence of information processing and decision styles', *Business Strategy and the Environment* **12**(4): 265–277.

Thomas, D.C. and Inkson, K. (2004) *Cultural Intelligence: People Skills for Global Business*, Berrett-Koehler: San Francisco.

Thomas, J.B., Clark, S.M. and Gioia, D.A. (1993) 'Strategic sensemaking and organizational performance: linkages among scanning, interpretation, action, and outcomes', *Academy of Management Journal* **36**(2): 239–270.

Tichy, N.M., Brimm, M., Charan, R. and Takeuchi, H. (1992) 'Leadership Development as a Lever for Global Transformation', in V. Pucik, N.M. Tichy and C. Barnett (eds.) *Globalizing Management: Creating and Leading the Competitive Organization*, John Wiley & Sons: New York, pp: 47–60.

Vertovec, S. and Cohen, R. (eds.) (2002a) *Conceiving Cosmopolitanism: Theory, Context, and Practice*, Oxford University Press: Oxford.

Vertovec, S. and Cohen, R. (2002b) 'Introduction: Conceiving Cosmopolitanism', in S. Vertovec and R. Cohen (eds.) *Conceiving Cosmopolitanism: Theory, Context, and Practice*, Oxford University Press: Oxford, pp: 1–22.

Walsh, J.P. (1995) 'Managerial and organizational cognition: notes from a trip down memory lane', *Organization Science* **6**(3): 280–321.

Wang, E.T.G. (2003) 'Effect of the fit between information processing requirements and capacity on organizational performance', *International Journal of Information Management* **23**(3): 239–247.

Wang, P. and Chan, P.S. (1995) 'Top management perception of strategic information processing in a turbulent environment', *Leadership and Organization Development Journal* **16**(7): 33–43.

Weick, K.E. (1979) 'Cognitive Processes in Organizations', in B. Staw (ed.) *Research in Organizational Behavior*, JAI Press: Greenwich, CT, pp: 41–74.

Weick, K.E. and Bougon, M.G. (1986) 'Organizations as Cognitive Maps: Charting Ways to Success and Failure', in H.P. Sims and D.A. Gioia (eds.) *The Thinking Organization: Dynamics of Organizational Social Cognition*, Jossey-Bass: San Francisco, pp: 102–135.

Williams, K.Y. and O'Reilly, C.A. (1998) 'Demography and Diversity in Organizations', in B.M. Staw and R.M. Sutton (eds.) *Research in Organizational Behavior*, JAI Press: Stamford, CT, pp: 77–140.

Appendix: Global mindset scales

Individual level

Murtha *et al.* (1998)
Scale: seven-point Likert scale (ranging from 'extremely unlikely' to 'extremely likely').

Integration expectations
As the company globalizes, I believe that the country operations most familiar to me will:

(1) Have global marketing responsibility for one or more products.
(2) Produce one or more products for global markets.
(3) Go global with locally developed products.
(4) Lead global product development processes.

Responsiveness expectations
As the company globalizes, I believe that the country operations most familiar to me will:

(1) Demonstrate clear benefits to the local economy.
(2) Have flexibility to respond to local conditions.
(3) Harmonize the company's activities and products with national government policies.
(4) Adapt existing products to local markets.

Country coordination expectations
As the company globalizes, I believe that the country operations most familiar to me will:

(1) Provide early warning of global competitive threats.
(2) Put global objectives ahead of country bottom line.
(3) Identify local business opportunities with global potential.
(4) Learn from the company's operations in many other countries.

Divisional coordination expectations
As the company globalizes, I believe that the country operations most familiar to me will:

(1) Coordinate strategy on a global basis.
(2) Take product development input from more countries.
(3) Coordinate among countries to rationalize production.
(4) Anticipate countries' needs.
(5) Balance price and market share objectives.
(6) Respond quickly to countries' requests and needs.

Govindarajan and Gupta (2001) and Gupta and Govindarajan (2002)
Scale: five-point Likert scale (ranging from 'strongly disagree' to 'strongly agree').

(1) In interacting with others, does national origin have an impact on whether or not you assign equal status to them?
(2) Do you consider yourself as equally open to ideas from other countries and cultures as you are to ideas from your own country and culture of origin?

(3) Does finding yourself in a new cultural setting cause excitement or fear and anxiety?
(4) When visiting or living in another culture, are you sensitive to the cultural differences without becoming a prisoner of these differences?
(5) When you interact with people from other cultures, what do you regard as more important: understanding them as individuals or viewing them as representatives of their national cultures?
(6) Do you regard your values to be a hybrid of values acquired from multiple cultures as opposed to just one culture?

Arora *et al*. (2004)
Scale: five-point Likert scale (ranging from 'strongly disagree' to 'strongly agree').

Conceptualization

(1) In my job, the best one can do is to plan ahead for at the most one year.
(2) Doing business with former enemies is not patriotic.
(3) I think it is necessary today to develop strategic alliances with organizations around the globe.
(4) Projects that involve international dealings are long term.
(5) I take pride in belonging to an international organization.
(6) I believe that in the next 10 years the world will be the same as it is today.
(7) In this interlinked world of ours, national boundaries are meaningless.
(8) Almost everybody agrees that international projects must have a shorter payback period than domestic ones.
(9) We really live in a global village.
(10) In discussions, I always drive for bigger, broader picture.
(11) I believe life is a balance of contradictory forces that are to be appreciated, pondered, and managed.
(12) I consider it to be a disgrace when foreigners buy our land and buildings.
(13) I really believe that 5–10 years is the best planning horizon in our line of business.
(14) I find it easy to rethink boundaries, and change direction and behavior.
(15) I feel comfortable with change, surprise, and ambiguity.
(16) I get frustrated when someone is constantly looking for context.

(17) Contradictors are time wasters that must be eliminated.
(18) I have no time for somebody trying to paint a broader, bigger picture.
(19) I believe I can live a fulfilling life in another culture.
(20) Five years is too long a planning horizon.

Contextualization

(1) I enjoy trying food from other countries.
(2) I find people from other countries to be boring.
(3) I enjoy working on world community projects.
(4) I get anxious around people from other cultures.
(5) I mostly watch and/or read the local news.
(6) Most of my social affiliations are local.
(7) I am at my best when I travel to worlds that I do not understand.
(8) I get very curious when I meet somebody from another country.
(9) I enjoy reading foreign books or watching foreign movies.
(10) I find the idea of working with a person from another culture unappealing.
(11) When I meet someone from another culture I get very nervous.
(12) Traveling in lands where I can't read the street names gives me anxiety.
(13) Most of my professional affiliations are international.
(14) I get irritated when we don't accomplish on time what we set out to do.
(15) I become impatient when people from other cultures seem to take a long time to do something.
(16) I have a lot of empathy for people who struggle to speak my own language.
(17) I prefer to act in my local environment (community or organization).
(18) When something unexpected happens, it is easier to change the process than the structure.
(19) In trying to accomplish my objectives, I find, diversity, multicultural teams play valuable role.
(20) I have close friends from other cultural backgrounds (Arora *et al*., 2004: 409–410).

Nummela *et al*. (2004)
Scale: five-point Likert scale (ranging from 'disagree totally' to 'agree totally').

Proactiveness on international markets

(1) It is important for our company to internationalize rapidly.
(2) Internationalization is the only way to achieve our growth objectives.
(3) We will have to internationalize in order to succeed in the future.
(4) The growth we are aiming at can be achieved mainly through internationalization.

Commitment to internationalization

(1) The founder/owner/manager of the company is willing to take the company to the international markets.
(2) The company's management uses a lot of time in planning international operations.

International vision

(1) The company's management sees the whole world as one big marketplace.

Group level
Levy (2005)
Attention to the external and internal environment
Top management team attention was measured as attention paid to specific element of the environment in the letter to shareholders. External environment elements included: competitors, customers, dealers, strategic partners, and foreign-related aspects of the environment. Internal environment elements included: board of directors, employees, owners, and top management.

Attention breadth
Attention breadth was measured as dispersion across 10 environment element: : competitors, customers, dealers, strategic partners, Africa, Asia-Pacific, Europe, the Middle East, Latin America, and North America.

Bouquet (2005)
Scale: additive of the following four (A–D) indicators
(A) Global scanning
Scale: five-point Likert scale (ranging from signifies 'very rarely' to 'very frequently')

(1) Top executives collect strategic information (such as market share and competitor data from around the world) in a consistent format on a regular basis.
(2) The data your company collects from around the world is pre-filtered by information analysts before being disseminated.

(3) Your top executives use business intelligence software to analyze global market developments.
(4) Your top executives use benchmarking systems that routinely compare the company against key competitors worldwide.

(B) CEO foreign travel

(1) Indicate how much time (in percentage) the CEO spends working at the company headquarters, traveling throughout the domestic market, and traveling outside the domestic market.

(C) Communications with overseas managers

(1) Indicate how often they use email, letters and memo, telephone, videoconference, and/or face-to-face meetings to discuss non-routine decisions with overseas managers.

(D) Discussions pertaining to major globalization decisions
Scale: five-point Likert scale (ranging from signifies 'very rarely' to 'very frequently').

(1) Indicate the extent to which major globalization decisions are made after intensive discussions between top managers

Organization level
Jeannet (2000)
Scale: not provided
Looking at the business strategies pursued by the firm

(1) What number of businesses should actually compete on a global scale?
(2) Are there businesses with explicit global mandates?
(3) How large is the corporate volume generated by businesses operating under expressed global mandates?
(4) How many businesses operate under a formal global strategy?

Looking at a firm's managerial talent pool

(1) How many managers understand their business in global terms?
(2) How many managers in upper management pool operate under global mandates?

Looking at a firm's organization

(1) At which level does the first geographic split in organization occur?

(2) How many functional managerial positions operate under global mandates?
(3) How many teams or task forces have global mandates?
(4) Extent of global IT structure.

Govindarajan and Gupta (2001) and Gupta and Govindarajan (2002)
Scale: five-point Likert scale (ranging from 'strongly disagree' to 'strongly agree').

(1) Is your company a leader (rather than a laggard) in your industry in discovering and pursuing emerging market opportunities in all corners of the world?
(2) Do you regard each and every customer, wherever they live in the world, as being as important as a customer in your own domestic market?
(3) Do you draw your employees from the worldwide talent pool?
(4) Do employees of every nationality have the same opportunity to move up the career ladder all the way to the top?
(5) In scanning the horizon for potential competitors, do you examine all economic regions of the world?
(6) In selecting a location for any activity, do you seek to optimize the choice on a truly global basis?
(7) Do you view the global arena not just as a playground (that is, a market to exploit) but also as a school (that is, a source of new ideas and technology)?
(8) Do you perceive your company as having a universal identity and as a company with many homes or do you instead perceive your company as having a strong national identify?

Kobrin (1994)
Scale: five- or seven-point Likert scale (ranging from 'strongly agree' to 'strongly disagree').

(1) A manager who began his or her career in any country has an equal chance to become CEO of my company.
(2) In the next decade, I expect to see a non-US CEO in my firm.
(3) In the next decade, I expect to see one or more non-US nationals serving as a senior corporate officer on a routine basis.

(4) In my company, nationality is unimportant in selecting individuals for managerial positions.
(5) My company believes that it is important that the majority of top corporate officers remain American (reverse-coded).

About the authors

Orly Levy received her PhD in sociology from the University of Wisconsin-Madison. She is a consultant based in Tel Aviv, Israel. In her research and consulting practice she specializes in leading and managing cultural change in multinational corporations, managerial global mindset development, and cross-cultural team effectiveness.

Schon Beechler (PhD in sociology and business administration, University of Michigan) is Executive Director, Duke Corporate Education. Her research interests are in the management of multinational corporations, international HRM, Japanese management, and global mindset and global leadership. She is past chair of the International Management Division of the Academy of Management.

Sully Taylor (PhD University of Washington) is Associate Dean of the School of Business Administration, Portland State University, and Professor of International Management. Her research interests include the design of IHRM systems in MNCs and how the human organization helps create social capital, enhances organizational learning, and supports a sustainability strategy.

Nakiye Boyacigiller (PhD, University of California, Berkeley) is Dean of the Faculty of Management at Sabanci University in Istanbul, Turkey. Her research and teaching interests are in cross-cultural management. Her published work includes *Crossing Cultures: Insights from Master Teachers* (with R Goodman and M Phillips).

Accepted by Mary Ann Von Glinow, 7 November 2006. This paper has been with the author for two revisions.